Blackwell Handbook of Social Psychology:
Intraindividual Processes

Blackwell Handbook of Social Psychology

Series editors: Miles Hewstone and Marilynn Brewer

The four volumes of this authoritative handbook each draw together 25–30 newly commissioned chapters to provide a comprehensive overview of specific topics in the field of social psychology. Designed to have considerable depth as well as breadth, the volumes encompass theory and research at the intraindividual, interpersonal, intergroup, and group levels. Editors have been chosen for their expertise and knowledge of the subject, making *The Blackwell Handbook of Social Psychology* an invaluable companion for any serious social psychology scholar.

Intraindividual Processes, edited by Abraham Tesser and Norbert Schwarz

Interpersonal Processes, edited by Garth Fletcher and Margaret Clark

Intergroup Processes, edited by Rupert Brown and Samuel Gaertner

Group Processes, edited by Michael A. Hogg and Scott Tindale

Blackwell Handbook of Social Psychology: Intraindividual Processes

Edited by

Abraham Tesser and Norbert Schwarz

350 Main Street, Malden, MA 02148-5018, USA
108 Cowley Road, Oxford OX4 1JF, UK
550 Swanston Street, Carlton South, Melbourne, Victoria 3053, Australia
Kurfürstendamm 57, 10707 Berlin, Germany

First published 2001 by Blackwell Publishers Ltd
First published in paperback 2003

Library of Congress Cataloging-in-Publication Data

Handbook of intraindividual processes / edited by Abraham Tesser and Norbert
   Schwarz.
     p. cm.— (Blackwell handbook of social psychology)
   Includes bibliographical references and index.
   ISBN 0-631-21033-4 (alk. paper) —ISBN 0-631-21034-2 (pbk. alk. paper)
    1. Cognition—Social aspects. 2. Motivation (Psychology) —Social aspects.
   I. Tesser, Abraham. II. Schwarz, Norbert, Dr. phil. III. Series.

BF311 .H36 2000
302—dc21   00-34325

A catalogue record for this title is available from the British Library.

Set in 10.5 on 12.5pt Adobe Garamond
by Ace Filmsetting Ltd, Frome, Somerset
Printed and bound in the United Kingdom
by T. J. International Ltd, Padstow, Cornwall

For further information on
Blackwell Publishing, visit our website:
http://www.blackwellpublishing.com

Contents

Series Editors' Preface

The idea for a new international handbook series for social psychology was conceived in July 1996 during the triannual meeting of the European Association of Experimental Social Psychology in the idyllic setting of Gmunden, Austria. Over a glass of wine and pleasant breezes from the Traunsee, Alison Mudditt (then Psychology Editor for Blackwell Publishers) engaged the two of us in a "hypothetical" discussion of what a multi-volume handbook of social psychology at the start of the twenty-first century might look like. By the second glass of wine we were hooked, and the project that has culminated in the publication of this four-volume *Blackwell Handbook of Social Psychology* was commissioned.

The EAESP meeting provided a fitting setting for the origin of a project that was intended to be an international collaborative effort. The idea was to produce a set of volumes that would provide a rich picture of social psychology at the start of the new millennium: a cross-section of the field that would be both comprehensive and forward-looking. In conceiving an organizational framework for such a venture, we sought to go beyond a simple topical structure for the content of the volumes in order to reflect more closely the complex pattern of cross-cutting theoretical perspectives and research agendas that comprise social psychology as a dynamic enterprise. Rather than lengthy review papers covering a large domain of social psychological research, we felt that a larger number of shorter and more focused chapters would better reflect the diversity and the synergies representative of the field at this point in time.

The idea we developed was to represent the discipline in a kind of matrix structure, crossing levels of analysis with topics, processes, and functions that recur at all of these levels in social psychological theory and research. Taking inspiration from Willem Doise's 1986 book *Levels of Explanation in Social Psychology*, four levels of analysis – intrapersonal, interpersonal, intragroup, and intergroup – provided the basis for organizing the handbook series into four volumes. The content of each volume would be selected on the basis of cross-cutting themes represented by basic processes of social cognition, attribution, social motivation, affect and emotion, social influence, social comparison, self and identity, as they operate at each level. In addition, each volume would include methodological issues and areas of applied or policy-relevant research related to social psychological research at that level of analysis.

Armed with this rough organizational framework as our vision for the series, our role was to commission editors for the individual volumes who would take on the challenging task of turning this vision into reality. The plan was to recruit two experts for each volume, who would bring different but complementary perspectives and experience to the subject matter to work together to plan, commission, and edit 25–30 papers that would be representative of current and exciting work within their broad domain. Once selected, co-editors were encouraged to use the matrix framework as a heuristic device to plan the coverage of their volume, but were free to select from and embellish upon that structure to fit their own vision of the field and its current directions.

We have been extremely fortunate in having persuaded eight exceptionally qualified and dedicated scholars of social psychology to join us in this enterprise and take on the real work of making this Handbook happen. Once they came on board, our role became an easy one: just relax and observe as the project was brought to fruition in capable hands. We are deeply endebted and grateful to Abraham Tesser and Norbert Schwarz, Margaret Clark and Garth Fletcher, Michael Hogg and Scott Tinsdale, Rupert Brown, and Samuel Gaertner for their creative leadership in producing the four volumes of this series. Through their efforts, a rough outline has become a richly textured portrait of social psychology at the threshold of the twenty-first century.

In addition to the efforts of our volume editors and contributors, we are grateful to the editorial staff at Blackwell Publishers who have seen this project through from its inception. The project owes a great deal to Alison Mudditt who first inspired it. When Alison went on to new ventures in the publishing world, Martin Davies took over as our capable and dedicated Commissioning Editor who provided guidance and oversight throughout the operational phases. Our thanks to everyone who has been a part of this exciting collaborative venture.

Miles Hewstone
Marilynn Brewer

Preface

Why in the world would two grown people who are fully employed put a huge chunk of time into helping to edit yet another *Handbook of Social Psychology*? There are at least three scientific disciplinary reasons for this project. First, the discipline of social psychology is currently very broad and the amount of work that is appearing is prodigious, particularly in the intrapersonal processes area. Comprehensive coverage is not possible in one- or two-volume compendiums. Rather than a few chapters, the current volume is devoted entirely to intrapersonal process research. Indeed, we believe that this volume includes coverage of areas that is not available in handbook form elsewhere. Second, there is a very different array of chapter authors. Both of us have been consumers of research in this area for a long time and we had some well-developed ideas about the researchers who might be in a good position to describe particular areas of work. Many of these scientists have not contributed to other handbooks. Thus, they provide a fresh slant even in areas treated in other handbooks. Moreover, there has been a lag in recognizing the changing demography of the field of social psychology. Modern social psychology became viable and began to grow, almost exponentially, since World War II. The discipline was near exclusively North American. However, the decade of the 1990s brought a dramatic change. Social psychology has continued to increase in importance but it has become a *worldwide* enterprise. In this, as in the other volumes of this Handbook, we have made a self-conscious attempt to include authors from among productive scientists not only in the United States but in Europe and Australia as well. Third, the field of social psychology is developing and changing rapidly. A major handbook of social psychology was published in 1996 (edited by Tory Higgins and Arie Kruglanski) and another in 1998 (edited by Dan Gilbert, Susan Fiske, and Gardner Lindzey). However, because of changes in the field and inevitable publication lags some of the material is now dated. Why a new handbook? To provide more comprehensive coverage, to better reflect the international nature of the discipline and to bring the reportage up to date.

The Organization of this Volume

The *Blackwell Handbook of Social Psychology* comprises four volumes reflecting different levels of focus in social psychology. They range from a focus on intraindividual processes to interpersonal processes, group processes, and intergroup relations. This particular volume, "Intraindividual Processes," focuses on the individual as the unit of analysis. We attempt to present the state of the science regarding cognition, affect, and motivation. We also attempt to put this work into broad substantive and methodological perspective. Finally, there is a sampling of applications of the cognitive and motivational principles spelled out in the chapters devoted to basic research on these issues.

At the outset, we have attempted to provide the reader with a set of integrative perspectives. The evolutionary and cultural perspectives are very broad and are currently enjoying a renaissance of interest. However, as Burnstein and Branigan, and Miller point out, the potential of neither perspective has been close to fully exploited in our attempts to understand intrapersonal processes. The developmental perspective continues to lurk on the fringes of social psychology. Greater attention to the developmental perspective will certainly provide deeper insight into changes associated with age. According to Durkin, it will also force a renewed appreciation for the role of *social* variables in the unfolding of cognitive and affective processes. If we are to understand the results of studies involving emotion and cognition, we need to have an understanding of the methods used. Winkielman, Berntson, and Cacioppo review the progress we have made in being able to infer psychological events from psychophysiological responses and remind us of the importance of studying the same cognitive and affective processes across a variety of levels. Bassili prepares us by reviewing the three major dependent variables used in studies intended to illuminate cognitive processes, i.e. memory, response time, and the output of judgmental processes.

In the interest of making this compendium of chapters more manageable, and in line with current usage, we have divided the primary research chapters into two broad groupings: Cognition and Social Motivation. In some instances, the assignment of a chapter to a particular grouping is somewhat arbitrary. For example, from the Cognition grouping, chapter 7 on the social unconscious (Banaji, Lemm, and Carpenter) deals not only with nonconscious cognitive effects but also with the impact of nonconscious goals and affect as well; chapter 12 on standards, expectancies, and social comparison (Biernat and Billings) clearly implicates motivational as well as cognitive principles. From the Social Motivation grouping, chapter 19 on construction of attitudes (Bohner and Schwarz) and chapter 24 on constructing personal pasts and futures (Ross and Buehler) have strong cognitive themes running through them. Nevertheless, we believe that the assignment is not totally arbitrary and perhaps helps to put intellectual neighbors into proximity with one another.

Within each of the groupings the usual suspects emerge, but there are some new leads as well. Part II on Cognition has chapters on memory and judgment. However, chapter 6 (Smith and Queller) brings the memory work up to date in a highly readable overview. In addition, the work on judgment has been particularly well articulated in this volume: chapter 10 (Griffin, Gonzalez, and Varey) is about heuristics and biases, chapter 11 (Martin, Strack, and Stapel) is about the exquisite flexibility in assimilation and contrast effects, and chapter 12 (Biernat and Billings) discusses the broad impact of standards, expectancies, and social comparison. Compendiums in social psychology often slight the psychology of language. In this volume we explore the role of language in social cognition (chapter 8 by Semin) as well as the role of language pragmatics (chapter 9 by Hilton and Slugoski). Cross-cutting all this, chapter 7 (Banaji, Lemm, and Carpenter) documents the pervasiveness of nonconscious processes in each of the areas mentioned above . Finally, an area that is sometimes slighted in social cognition work is individual differences. Chapter 13 (Suedfeld and Tetlock) provides a nice overview of the individual difference constructs of need for cognition, conceptual/integrative complexity, and the need for closure.

Under the broad umbrella of Social Motivation (Part III) reside chapters on self-regulation and motivation, emotion and affect, attitudes and values, and self-related issues. Concerns with self-regulation have been with us for some time but there has been a recent upsurge of research attention to this area. Chapter 14 (Carver) provides an integrated account of how a feedback model can account for affect, behavior, and goal persistence, and behavior in the face of adversity. Chapter 15 (Oettingen and Gollwitzer) looks at fantasy and ruminative processes along with other variables that affect goal setting; it also describes the qualities of set goals that facilitate or interfere with goal striving. Chapter 16 (Dunning) uses a computer metaphor of the executive function to frame the recent research on social cognitive motivation. Within this frame, it examines motives concerned with the acquisition of knowledge, self-affirmation, and coherence or consistency. Closely related to motivation is the psychology of emotion and mood. Chapter 17 (Parrott) provides a highly readable, comprehensive, broad-brush description of current theoretical and empirical work in emotion. The last decade has seen an explosion of work on mood and judgment. Chapter 18 (Bless) summarizes and takes us to the cutting edge of that work.

Gordon Allport once suggested that "attitude" was the most important concept in social psychology. Although the popularity of attitude research has had peaks and valleys, it is difficult to disagree with him. In this volume, chapter 19 (Bohner and Schwarz) review mainstream work on attitudes, including attitude change and the relationship between attitudes and behavior. In chapter 20, Schwarz and Bohner make a persuasive argument for attitude as a construction and they carefully review the implications of taking this perspective seriously. Many of us believe that values and ideologies play an important role in understanding attitudes and behavior, yet discussions of values and ideologies are often neglected. Chapter 21 (Rohan and Zanna) provides working definitions of these constructs. It suggests that values play a particularly influential role in determining attitudes and behavior; ideology often serves as a rationalization for value-driven attitudes and behaviors.

The psychology of self has long had a prominent role in social psychological research and has enjoyed heightened research interest over the last fifteen or twenty years. Chapter 22 (Tesser) provides a broad overview of processes related to the maintenance of self-esteem. Chapter 23 (Oyserman) gives us a nuanced and subtle view of the role of culture in the construction of the self. Chapter 24 (Ross and Buehler) creatively reviews the processes involved in constructing personal pasts and futures.

Can research on social cognition and social motivation be put to use in applied settings? Indeed it can. Space constraints allow us to feature only a few examples of applications (Part IV). In the political realm, chapter 28 (Ottati) shows us how social cognition research has been helpful in understanding political judgment. In chapter 25 (Köhnken, Fiedler, and Möhlenbeck) we see how social cognition and social motivational principles can provide insights for (a) applications *in* law, e.g. how to improve witness memory; (b) for psychology *and* law, e.g. jury decision making; and (c) for psychology *of* law, e.g. why people obey the law. Chapter 26 (Shavitt and Wänke) on consumer behavior and chapter 27 (Aspinwall) on adversity nicely highlight the value of primary research for understanding consumer behavior and coping. What is particularly interesting about both of these chapters is the presence of a case for a more evenhanded view of the relationship between basic and applied research. The usual view is that basic research informs applied research. Both chapters present very persuasive arguments for the idea that applied research can usefully inform the agenda for basic research.

The authors of this volume are experts in their various areas and are busy, sought-after people. They spent a lot of time and energy writing their chapters. They had to endure our requests for revision and our persistent nagging that they get their chapters in on time and within our length limits. This could not have been pleasant for them and only on rare occasion was the nagging fun for us. In the end, however, we believe that the time and energy were well spent. The chapters provide an authoritative, comprehensive, up to date, and readable description of the field. We say, thank you, thank you, *thank you* to all the authors. And, we invite you, the reader, to sample the contents of this volume. We hope that you will find it informative, useful, and perhaps even enjoyable to read.

Abraham Tesser
Norbert Schwarz

PART I

Perspectives and Methods

Chapter One

Evolutionary Analyses in Social Psychology

Eugene Burnstein and Christine Branigan

The Concept of Adaptation

Early in the history of the field social psychologists such as William James and William McDougall viewed minds as biological systems, like the heart or lungs, designed to perform particular functions. How well a mind did this depended on the *fit* between what its design allowed it to do and what the environment required: we will often say a psychological mechanism increases or decreases fitness, meaning it causes individuals to be more or less adapted, to be better or worse suited to their environment. James and McDougall believed the invisible hand guiding the mind's design was natural selection or differential reproduction as a function of individual fitness. Good design, in short, drives out bad. At the biological level, natural selection is about genetic continuation: certain genotypes or, if you prefer, individuals with a specific genetic constitution, are more successful at reproducing than other genotypes (or individuals with different genetic constitutions). The evolution of the mind, therefore, is the result of changes in the human gene pool with one allele replacing another, the surviving alleles being those that give rise to a psychological system (and its underlying biology) that succeeds more than alternative systems in causing the replication of its underlying allele(s).

James and McDougall decomposed the mind into distinct psychological adaptations or, in the spirit of the times, instincts. James's *Principles of Psychology* had a long list of these devices (e.g. walking, climbing, hunting, acquisition, construction, pugnacity, anger, fear, and jealousy). McDougall added to James's list (e.g. gregariousness, parenting) and described them as "an inherited or innate psycho-physical disposition which determines its possessor to perceive, and to pay attention to, objects of a certain class, to experience an emotional excitement of a particular quality upon perceiving such an object, and to act in regard to it in a particular manner, or at least, to experience an impulse to such action" (McDougall, 1909, p. 30). Few say "instinct" today. We know evolved mechanisms are sensitive to context and we want to avoid implying something fixed and inevitable ("which determines its possessor"). Instead, terms like adaptation, strategy, heuristic, module, or, when stressing a mechanism's computational prowess, algorithm are used, often interchangeably. Generally they refer to a configuration of feelings, thoughts, and actions (plus supporting physiology) designed so as to advantage an individual's fitness relative to others in the population. Hence, a trait or strategy is adaptive if, compared to alternatives, it gives individuals a better chance to mature and acquire resources to perform *the* task essential to evolution, i.e. to reproduce, raise, and, finally, to provision others (kin) in aid of their reproduction. In a word, it insures genetic continuation.

In some respects, however, adaptations are like James's and McDougall's instincts. They do involve biological structures sensitive to ("perceive, and to pay attention to") a limited set of stimuli ("objects of a certain class"). And both must assume, of course, heritability: that intelligence (Bouchard and McGue, 1981), schizophrenia (Gottesman, 1991), manic depression (Tsuang and Faraone, 1990), alcoholism (Cloninger, 1987), neuroticism and extraversion (Loehlin, 1992) are known to be moderately heritable and that there is growing evidence of heritability for social attitudes (Tesser, 1993), religiosity (Waller, Kojetin, Bouchard, & Lykken, 1990), divorce (McGue and Lykken, 1992), and, yes, watching television (Plomin, Corley, DeFries, and Fulker, 1990) suggest how complex is the link between genotype and phenotype.

Analyzing Social Transactions: The Forms of Cooperation

In this section we discuss the cooperative transactions directly contributing to genetic continuation: kin altruism, mating effort, and parental investment. Later sections examine status negotiations and non-kin cooperation, transactions whose contributions to fitness are indirect but no less powerful since they determine what resources individuals have to invest in kin, mates, and offspring.

Generally, altruism denotes a form of cooperation whereby individuals assist another at significant expense to themselves and without reference to repayment. It is not an uncommon strategy. In most societies sharing goods and services without concern for balancing accounts is typical among friends and relatives. A second type of cooperation is one in which all parties benefit. It is called reciprocal altruism by evolutionary theorists, direct reciprocity, balanced reciprocity, or simply reciprocity by anthropologists, and cooperation by everybody else (Hawkes, 1992). What they are talking about are cases where individuals provide goods or services to one another, thereby incurring a short-term cost, with the expectation of receiving benefits in return. It characterizes mating, parental care, and other collaborations such as hunting, harvesting, building, playing games, providing mutual protection, or any activity in which return for one's effort comes directly from individuals who benefited. All the cases just cited may also involve indirect reciprocity where repayment is made by third parties not involved in the initial transaction and, thus, not directly benefiting therefrom. It might come from individuals who were assisted by still another person in a roundabout exchange of goods and services typical in the division of labor, or from the collective, as when it rewards its members by raising their status or providing them with extra resources and assistance.

Kin altruism

In traditional Darwinian theory fitness is measured by number of offspring. Hamilton (1964) reminded us, however, that reproductive success is significant for natural selection because it indicates the likelihood of one's genotype being replicated in future generations: reproductive success means genetic continuation and reproductive failure means genetic termination. But having offspring is not the only means of replicating a genotype, nor is it necessarily the most important one. Since we share genes identical by descent with kin, to get a true estimate of a strategy's impact on fitness, you have to factor in its effect on the strategist's relatives' fitness as well. Why? Because a heritable strategy that decreases the actor's own (Darwinian) fitness can still be adaptive and increase in frequency, if it improves the reproductive success of kin who have the genes for the same strategy. Hamilton's idea of assessing the adaptive value of a strategy in terms of its costs and benefits to kin as well as its costs and benefits to the actors themselves is called, in contrast with traditional Darwinian fitness, inclusive fitness or kin selection.

Kin selection theory is a good example of evolutionary models that predicts when a strategy, in this case altruism, is relatively beneficial or costly and, hence, when it prevails or is replaced by some alternative (non-altruistic) course of action. Assume C equals the cost to altruists of giving help and B the benefit to recipients of being helped, and, of course, that altruism is heritable. According to traditional Darwinian analysis a heritable strategy that causes reproductive harm is selected against. Hamilton's insight was that the opposite can happen when altruists and recipients are kin because they then probably share the genes underlying altruism. If so, the likelihood of their replication increases given that the cost of helping is less than the benefit to the recipient weighted by the degree of relatedness, r, or $Br > C$, Hamilton's well-known inequality. Less formally, Hamilton says that we are inclined to discriminate according to kinship, assisting close relatives over distant relatives or unrelated individuals; and that this inclination waxes when the costs and benefits of assisting are large (e.g. in dangerous, life-threatening emergencies) and wanes when they are small (e.g. simple everyday favors). Both the animal and human literature offer strong support for these hypotheses (e.g. Burnstein, Crandall, and Kitayama, 1994; Trivers, 1985; Sober and Wilson, 1998).

The starkest test of kin altruism in humans are studies comparing the cooperativeness of monozygotic (MZ) and dizygotic (DZ) twins. Findings from studies on reactions to separation, efforts to remain in close proximity as children and adults, and even in usage of the pronouns "I" versus "we" indicate MZ twins share a more intimate relationship than DZ twins. Over 60 years ago researchers found MZ twins tried to maintain equality of performance on mathematical and lexical tasks to the point that one twin would slow down to enable the co-twin to catch up, whereas DZ twins tried to outdo their co-twin. Similarly, the most recent research shows MZ twins avoid free-riding, work harder for their co-twin, and thereby complete their joint task more quickly than DZ twins (see review in Segal, 1999). Perhaps assisting another is intrinsically rewarding, the magnitude depending on the relationship between the individuals. Two sorts of finding support this. Research on autonomic functioning and empathy suggests potentially friendly people elicit positive affect in an observer when they succeed and negative affect when they fail, and potentially unfriendly people, negative affect when successful and positive affect when failing (e.g.

Lanzetta and Englis, 1989). In addition, operant conditioning research (Weiss, Buchanan, Alstatt, and Lombardo, 1971) demonstrates that when a response is instrumental in assisting another, assistance functions as a reward just as conventional reinforcers, namely, assistance occurring after every response (continuous reinforcement) or with minimal delay, produces a higher level of responding and shorter latency than intermittent assistance or assistance that occurs after an appreciable delay.

Kinship is not the only cue to how much someone contributes to one's fitness. Often other features assume greater significance and cause us to discount kinship. Sometimes, for instance, recipients are of an inappropriate age. In Hamilton's model kinship becomes increasingly unimportant when the recipients are too young to reproduce (and might not survive to reach this point) or are too old to do so. Comparable discounting is predicted to occur as a function of relatives' viability and resources, since sickness and impoverishment reduce their reproductive value. Studies using hypothetical decisions show if kin are in dire need and assisting them is risky, altruists discriminate in favor of the healthier, wealthier, and younger, but *against* the very young as infant mortality increases (Burnstein, Crandall, and Kitayama, 1994). Kin altruism can also pose stunning problems of choice. Wang (in press) finds decisions about which relatives should survive and which perish produce such intense conflict that individuals abandon their normal strategy, one they followed in deciding the fate of non-kin. Instead, in effect they refuse to choose. Wang used the Tversky-Kahneman framing task to create a paradigmatic "Sophie's Choice" dilemma. In the standard version, where life or death decisions are made about groups of strangers, individuals are risk-avoiding, preferring a certain outcome over a risky or probabilistic one if the alternatives are framed in terms of benefits, or lives saved (e.g. a choice between two medical procedures where one will save 60 percent of the people for sure and the other has a 60 percent chance of saving everyone); but they are risk-seeking, preferring the risky over the certain outcome, if the alternatives are framed in terms of costs, or number of deaths (e.g. 40 percent of the people would die for sure versus a 40 percent chance of everyone dying). One general finding of interest is that framing effects hold for large groups – about 600 or more members, the group size in the standard Tversky-Kahneman procedure – but vanish for smaller groups of around 60 members or less. Wang suggests that as group size approaches that of ancestral bands, people are averse to deciding who lives or dies and an "either we all live together or die together" rationality dominates. This refusal to choose is even more poignant when individuals must make life or death decisions regarding groups explicitly composed of close kin (e.g. siblings and parents). Then, for example, when problems are framed in terms of number of lives saved, over 70 percent chose the risky or probabilistic course, which is the reverse of what they do when group members are strangers (see Chagnon and Bugos, 1979, and Sime, 1983 for kin altruism in actual life or death situations).

Mating and parental investment

Darwin thought it useful to distinguish between two forms of selection, "natural" and "sexual". Not because their ultimate impact on reproduction differed but because natural selection, being concerned with adaptation to the physical world, could not account for the evolution of extravagance and imprudence: luxuriant plumage, cumbersome antlers, Armani suits, body piercing, bungee jumping and other remarkably profligate or risky displays. Nor was it evident to him why men put such great weight on women's looks, whereas women are most concerned with a man's character. Obviously, notions of beauty and personality in part reflect cultural norms and personal experience. However, research since Darwin also demonstrates that in important respects the aesthetics of mate preferences are universal and appear quite early in life. Buss's (1989; 1999) review of studies in over 30 countries finds in every case males are more concerned than females with a mate's appearance. Similar findings from pre-modern cultures are summarized by Ford and Beach (1951), who conclude a male's attractiveness depends much less on his handsomeness than on his skill and prowess. Finally, several experiments (e.g. Langlois, Ritter, Roggman, and Vaughn, 1991) indicate two- and three-month-old infants prefer attractive adult female faces more than unattractive ones and the effect holds independent of race of observer or target.

Darwin (1871/1981) reasoned that extravagant displays evolved because they increase mate value and give a reproductive edge at the expense of others of the sex. In humans this would imply physical appearance is more diagnostic in respect to female mate value than to that of males. Jones (1995) explains this using the adaptationist assumption: individuals have relatively fixed or "hard-wired" reactions to a stimulus pattern if the consequences to fitness have been constant over evolutionary time. "Given that learning entails costs, in terms of trial and error, organisms are expected to adapt to selectively important invariants in their environment with corresponding behavioral, cognitive, or motivational invariances" (Jones, 1995, p. 726). For example, aesthetic reactions to fatness in females – not obesity, which is rare in ancestral groups – varies over cultures. Fatness is advantageous and valued when the food supply is unreliable, average temperatures are low, early pregnancies are desirable (the likelihood of ovulation and lactation is positively related to percentage body fat, especially around the time of menarche), females enjoy low status or have little control over timing of their pregnancies, and pregnancy and childcare do not interfere with the work females perform or the work is not highly valued (Anderson, Crawford, Nadeau, and Lindberg, 1991). This implies that aesthetic reactions to fatness are not invariant but instead depend on its contribution to fitness in particular environments. Hence, when the opposite conditions obtain, when food is plentiful, climate temperate, early pregnancy discouraged, and females have relatively high status – specifically, among American college students – males rate fat females as less attractive (but more fecund) than slim females (Tassinary and Hansen, 1998); and middle-class American parents invest less in educating fat daughters than slim daughters but do not discriminate between fat and slim sons (Crandall, 1995).

Compared to that between fatness and fecundity, the relationship between age and fecundity is relatively invariant. In virtually any population, fertility rates decline much more precipitously for females than for males. Jones argues, therefore, that coding for attractiveness reflects an evolved mechanism for assessing age-related changes in a key component of female mate value, fecundity. As a result, signs of aging elicit an invariant reaction having more impact on males' estimates of females' attractiveness than on females' evaluation of males' attractiveness. The research results are largely consistent with this analysis. Neotenous or babyface features (large eyes, small nose, and full lips) are the markers of youthfulness

and female faces displaying them in exaggerated or supernormal form are perceived universally as particularly attractive and overly youthful by males (Jones, 1995). It is no accident
female models not only have more neotenous facial proportions and are considered more
attractive than, say, female undergraduates, but also their age is vastly underestimated.
Finally, a critical quality like fecundity may have multiple markers. Singh, for instance,
hypothesizes that the waist-to-hip ratio (WHR) is also a cue to a female's reproductive
potential and presents considerable evidence that females with a WHR of .7 are perceived
by males as more attractive than those with greater or smaller WHR values (Singh, 1993;
but see Tassinary and Hansen, 1998).

It is equally plausible that physical attractiveness signals fitness in the sense of heritable
viability or good genes instead of (or in addition to) age and, by extension, fecundity. This
assumes individuals and infectious pathogens have waged war over evolutionary time so
that natural selection has designed males to be attracted to females who "look" free of
parasites and, hence, are likely to have resistance to infectious diseases (Hamilton and Zuk,
1982). Obviously, choosing a mate of this sort enhances an offspring's viability. When it
comes to modern humans, however, recent research does not bode well for the hypothesis
that attractive individuals are relatively free of infections and generally healthy. Kalick,
Zebrowitz, Langlois, and Johnson (1998) found adolescent facial attractiveness was unrelated to health either at adolescence, middle adulthood, or late adulthood. Furthermore, in
attempting to estimate the target's health individuals mistakenly judged attractive targets
as healthier than unattractive targets. In fact, correlations between perceived health and
true (medically assessed) health increase only when attractiveness was statistically controlled, demonstrating attractiveness can mislead and actually suppress accurate detection of
good genes. This suggests that attractiveness, while perhaps a reliable cue to heritable viability in ancestral environments, can nowadays be employed in a deceptive manner to
influence others' choice. Again, keep in mind that displaying traits like physical attractiveness strategically does not imply a conscious intention to deceive; people could equally well
believe they are conforming to norms about personal beautification and ornamentation.
As Dawkins and Krebs (1978) cautioned, individuals may have evolved signals whose function is to manipulate another's action to their benefit without awareness on the part of the
sender or receiver. Certainly for senders, to be unaware is to be incapable of leaking the
scam (e.g. Alexander, 1987).

A different explanation of the evolution of physical attractiveness as a good genes marker
is offered by Gangestad and Thornhill (1997). They reasoned that universally attractive
features, whether having prominent cheekbones or being ambitious, are sufficiently costly
that only relatively fit individuals can afford to display them. Hence, they advertise individual fitness and do so honestly. This argument stems from Zahavi's (1975) strategic
handicap principle, according to which phenotypic prodigality signals latent resources in
senders that can assist receivers who, upon recognizing this, benefit the senders (e.g. chooses
him or her for a mate). Of course, senders gain by convincing a receiver they have more
resources than they actually possess, whereas receivers gain by detecting the dishonesty and
gauging others' hidden talents accurately. The handicap principle describes how in light of
this conflict honest advertising is positively selected: extravagant displays of beauty, strength,
courage, wealth, or power are costly because they waste resources or expose actors to risk.
They may still be adaptive, however, if the returns are sufficiently large. This occurs when

a display allows the receiver to size up senders accurately enough to discriminate in favor of the more endowed. In essence, Zahavi's model argues honest advertising is insured since high-quality individuals suffer lower marginal cost for each extra unit of display: resources expended in advertising are unavailable to deal with more immediate threats to fitness (e.g. pathogen resistance, parental investment). Hence, in aesthetic or behavioral contests, those with minimal resources have less left over per unit expended, and must break off signaling at a lower cost level than those with large resources. The upshot is that displays costly enough to constitute a real handicap signal the sender can afford it.

Gangestad and Thornhill argue physical appearance signals heritable viability, in particular a capacity to express ontogeny, one's developmental design, in the face of environmental and genetic insults. Their viability marker is fluctuating asymmetry (FA), a deviation from symmetry in bilateral morphological traits that are typically symmetrical (e.g. ears, legs, arms, etc.). Because the same genes control development of the trait on both sides of the body, asymmetries presumably reflect imperfect development, developmental instabilities due to toxins, pathogens, defective childcare, bullying, mutations, inbreeding, and the like. If so, at least two things follow. First, males evidencing developmental stability or minimal FA have more of whatever resources it takes – heritable viability – to resist these insults than males with maximal FA. And second, according to Zahavian honest advertising, males with minimal FA have more well developed expression of costly sexually selected handicap attributes and greater mating success than those evidencing development instability or maximal FA.

Gangestad and Thornhill measure FA by comparing bilateral widths or lengths of feet, ankles, hands, wrists, elbows, ears and pinky fingers – differences virtually undetectable without calipers. Based on these indices they found males' FA was negatively related to number of sexual partners, and number of extra-pair matings (among those in long-term romantic relations). Consistent with the principle that females benefit less than males from more matings, there was only a weak relationship at best between FA and the number of partners or extra-pair sex in females. Finally, facial attractiveness is negatively related to FA and, hence, may mediate the impact of FA on sexual experience, especially when FA is based on features that are difficult to detect. It is not the only factor influencing the impact of FA, however. An appreciable number of other handicapping attributes that typically play a role in male–male competition as well as in female choice, including energetically costly physical features (e.g. body mass, muscularity, robustness, and vigor) and risky behavioral traits (e.g. social dominance, heterosexual assertiveness, and narcissism) were discovered to have considerable impact as mediating processes. Again, this held only for men. Women's FA was unrelated to sexual experience or to any of the mediators; their social dominance predicts the number of partners but is uncorrelated with FA and, hence, does not mediate the relationship between FA and number of sexual partners.

These male–female differences in mate preferences correspond nicely to the different recurrent problems in reproduction each sex had to adapt to in the ancestral environment. Consider obligatory parental investment, the unavoidable somatic and psychic costs of reproduction. For a woman, the minimum is nine months of internal fertilization, gestation, and placentation, plus breast feeding, which among hunter-gatherers may last several years. In comparison, obligatory parental investment by men, i.e. performance of the sexual act, is derisory. The implication is that women, by investing more than men, suffer greater costs from a neglectful, incompetent mate and derive greater benefits from an attentive, resourceful one than men do. Needless to say, over evolutionary time such differences select for differences in mating strategies. Accordingly, Trivers (1985) assumes women are designed to accurately assess mate quality and maintain high standards, especially if male investment is problematic (e.g. short-term relationships). Whereas men's default strategy, unless constrained by female choice, is to mate promiscuously and claim high quality regardless of its truth. Note that Zahavi argues differently in respect to males. He predicts low-resource individuals cannot long continue building Potemkin villages to entice females or may not even attempt to, recognizing they will eventually be outspent by high-resource competitors. Perhaps both are right. In cheap, low-intensity competitions men can claim having large resources whether they do or not; but in expensive, high-intensity contests, they are constrained to advertise honestly and are no more prodigal than they can afford.

While evolutionary theory says the risks in mating are different for men and women, what they want in mates is often similar. Cross-national comparisons of thirteen characteristics commonly sought in a mate reveal that while males rank physical attractiveness third and females sixth for desirability in a mate, both sexes ranked kindness and intelligence as one and two, and good housekeeper and religious orientation as twelve and thirteen, respectively. Good heredity fell near the middle – heritable viability may not be a conscious priority and, perhaps, may be expressed only indirectly via markers such as good health and adaptability which are ranked high (Buss, 1989). Preferences do diverge in domains where theory says the sexes have confronted different adaptive problems. Take provisioning or ability to invest. Findings from a variety of cultures show women typically believe good financial prospects are nearly indispensable in a mate while men consider them relatively unimportant; and, when evaluating the standard marker for fecundity, age, men everywhere prefer a younger mate; whereas women want a mate older than they (Buss, 1999).

As to the actual adaptive value of mate preferences, although the number of studies is small the common finding is they do enhance fitness. Both among modern Kipsigis (Borgerhoff Mulder, 1988) and eighteenth-century Germans (Voland and Engel, 1990) a bride's youthfulness or physical attractiveness and a groom's wealth is positively related to lifetime reproductive success. The only study we know of in a modern society (Bereczkei and Csanaky, 1996) found that Hungarian men who choose younger mates and Hungarian women who choose higher status mates have more surviving offspring than those who pursue the opposite mating strategy; and that couples in which wives are younger than husbands and husbands more educated than wives stay together longer than other couples. This indicates that the relationship between mate preferences and reproductive success is mediated by the durability of the marriage. In other words, by strengthening pair-bonds, mate preference mechanisms establish a necessary condition for reproductive success in humans, extended parental investment.

The central problem of parental investment stems from the males' tendency to defect and divert resources elsewhere rather than assist his spouse in childrearing. Trivers's explanation that, *ceteris paribus*, promiscuity produces greater return to fitness for males, was discussed earlier. A second and perhaps more significant reason, certainly for father–child conflicts, is that paternity is inherently uncertain, although not if DNA testing of the newborn becomes standard practice. In any event, as paternal uncertainty increases – the coefficient of relatedness in Hamilton's inequality is weighted by a probability of less than one – at some point investing in his spouse's children detracts from the husband's fitness. It is no accident, therefore, that groups with high paternal uncertainty develop institutions relieving men of responsibility for assisting spouses' children and sanctioning investment in the latter by men whose kinship with the child is undisputed (e.g. the avunculate, an arrangement in which the mother's brother is responsible for provisioning his sister's children). Nonetheless, throughout the world mothers and fathers are prematurely widowed, and women are abandoned with dependent children. An evolutionary analysis predicts that since assisting step-children decreases the step-parent's fitness, if widowed or abandoned parents enter into a new marital relationship, the children's fate becomes insecure. Much cross-cultural evidence suggests pressures to invest in unrelated children commonly elicit meanness (Betzig, Mulder, and Turke, 1988). The most striking evidence, however, comes from modern societies. Children in North America living with a step-parent are more likely to suffer abuse than those living with their biological parents. In Ontario, Canada during 1983 the rate per capita child abuse for young children residing with one biological and one step-parent was over 13 per 1,000; whereas the rate for children residing with both biological parents was less than 1 per 1,000 (Daly and Wilson, 1988). And of young children whose mistreatment was fatal, 43 percent resided with step-parents. This means North American children living with a step-parent are about 100 times more likely to die due to abuse than those living with both biological parents.

A common device hypothesized to reduce paternal uncertainty and encourage parental investment is namesaking, a process of social categorization serving to identify the newborn as belonging to the family. If the function of namesaking is to elicit investment by establishing in the minds of kin and third parties a newborn's claim on kin resources, it should increase as investment becomes problematic (e.g. when children are adopted or parents are unmarried). In support, among unmarried teenage mothers infants named for a relative are almost always named for the presumed father; almost half even take the father's last name despite the parents never marrying. Similarly, analyses of namesaking in communities where wealth is transferred through the father's lineage found special efforts to assuage the patriline's worries and establish a claim to its resources: first children are twice as likely to be named after paternal grandparents than after maternal grandparents. A corollary is that as confidence in being accepted as a family member increases, the need to assert a claim to its resources decreases. In a sample of biological and adoptive parents slightly less than 50 percent of biological parents and slightly more than 75 percent of adoptive parents named their child for a relative; and because paternal uncertainty is an issue for biological parents but never for adoptive parents, it is unsurprising that biological parents favor patrilineal namesakes but adoptive parents don't (Johnson, McAndrew, and Harris, 1991).

Status Negotiations

Theoretically, hierarchization can be viewed as an n-person mixed-motive game where high status individuals gain greater access to resources and exert greater control over distribution as long as a sufficient number of low status members accept their dominance. High status members, therefore, should seek to legitimize the system by insuring returns to those not so advantaged sufficient to elicit cooperation. In short, the stability of a hierarchy depends on its costs and benefits relative to that of other arrangements (e.g. leaving and joining another group). Of course, owing to their control over distribution, dominant individuals are tempted to defect and monopolize resources. As a result most bands and tribes with stable hierarchies have institutions to punish those taking unfair advantage of rank, say, to bully or humiliate other members (Boone, 1992; Boehm, 1997). There also may be psychological mechanisms that encourage fair-sharing by dominant members and reinforce acceptance of hierarchy. For instance, it has been hypothesized that achieving dominance produces elation in people and elation is a mood known to increase generosity (Buss, 1999).

In any event, that hierarchy is universal and emerges quickly indicates a readiness to code the qualities in others signaling dominance. Moreover, a considerable experimental literature supports the hypothesis of a status computation mechanism (McGrath, 1984). To begin with, members are sensitive to individual differences in the capacity to contribute to group problem solving (task status) and willingness to do so amicably (social–emotional status). Even in short-lived groups of strangers, those signaling that they have resources and will share them are speedily differentiated from members who do not, within the first few minutes under laboratory conditions, despite minimal incentives to do so. This together with evidence of individuals ranking others when it is irrelevant to their task suggests status computation is automatic (Cummins, 1998; see review in Burnstein, Crandall, and Kitayama, 1994). And the mechanism is not peculiar to adult humans. Cheney and Seyfarth (1985) report young primates as well as children can infer another's position in a group after watching a small number of interactions between members.

Stratified groups offer members occasions to display their resources by doing things that consume energy or wealth, put somatic integrity at risk, and decrease reproductive success: "Consider the astounding wastage embodied in the gladiatorial displays and circuses underwritten by Roman elites, . . . or the elaborate, costly, and often risky recreational activities undertaken by contemporary Americans on their respective vision quests . . . all of these behaviors involve investments of time and energy . . . [that] go beyond what is required for the fulfillment of basic survival, maintenance, and reproductive goals" (Boone, 1998, p. 2; also see Veblen (1973) on conspicuous consumption). Adaptive problems arise in hierarchies when individuals engage in deceptive displays, claiming a status incommensurate with their resources. Since hierarchy has been a persistent feature of group life, mechanisms for detecting and punishing such deceptions are likely to have evolved. Certainly humans are sensitive to features they think signal important latent qualities. In fact, we take advantage of this sensitivity to reduce another's status by using these features as targets of derogation in partner selection contests. Women, for example, pan rivals for looks or promiscuity, whereas men, presumably, focus on their lack of intelligence or earning capacity (Buss, 1999).

Perhaps because facial expressions are more easily observed and less easily controlled than other features, we regularly use them to judge whether people measure up, to understand the emotion they are experiencing at a particular moment, or to estimate more stable qualities like kindness or dominance. Strong jaws and broad cheekbones, for example, increase others' perceived dominance probably by suggesting both physical strength and will power. Conversely, babyfaced individuals are described, even by themselves, as relatively submissive and friendly (Berry, 1991). Moreover, correlations between individual differences in facial dominance and testosterone level suggest the strong jaws–broad cheekbones versus babyfaced distinction may predict how likely individuals are to attempt to dominate (Gangestad and Thornhill, 1997). In any event, according to the strategic handicap argument facial features that enable receivers to accurately estimate senders' hidden qualities will evolve provided the marginal cost of signaling them is greater for low-quality senders. The set of features most identified with status, called facial dominance, is usually assessed by having judges rate portraits for the degree to which the person appears to be the sort that is respected, influential, assertive, a leader, gives direction, and the like. Using this procedure facial dominance has been found to be perceived in similar fashion over a variety of cultures and to be reasonably stable from early adulthood to middle age (see review in Mueller and Mazur, 1997). Moreover, it predicts mating success for males, which is expected since most evolutionary models assume that when males compete for mates the outcome is largely determined by relative status (Buss, 1999; Kenrick and Keefe, 1992).

Transactions between individuals of different statuses are successful to the extent that claims to superiority are accepted by others. The major threat to success is the likelihood that the person who looks or acts dominant is engaging in dishonest advertising. Hence, members negotiating their respective statuses are guarded in their transactions. On occasion those signaling dominance slip and reveal they do not merit it (e.g. they behave assertively when it is inappropriate). Once this is detected they may be rejected as arrogant or oafish and suffer the cost of the display with no return benefit. Mueller and Mazur (1997) studied this phenomenon in a well-defined hierarchy, the military, where status is distinctly marked by formal rank. They found that among West Point cadets facial dominance predicts cadet rank as well as army rank twenty or more years after graduating from West Point (cadet rank is unrelated to later army rank and, hence, does not mediate the impact of facial dominance), speed of promotion, and number of children. What is particularly interesting, and consistent with Zahavi, is that in negotiating status dominant looks serve to disadvantage men with inadequate resources: among individuals low in professional competence, as measured by academic standing, sociability, and participation in team sports, facial dominance is negatively correlated with final rank; whereas among those high in professional competence, facial dominance is positively correlated with final rank. Comparable differences in social outcomes are found for babyface individuals who advertise dishonestly and behave aggressively instead of complaisantly (Zebrowitz and Lee, 1999).

Cooperation in the Absence of Kinship

Given the possibility of free-riding why is cooperation so common, fluent, and stable? At least since Axelrod's (1984) TIT-FOR-TAT (TFT) simulation, a favorite evolutionary hypothesis is that general trust is the default code for social transactions. The same argument was made earlier by social psychologists such as Asch (1952; see his theory of mutually shared fields), albeit in different language, that a cooperative strategy is adaptive in iterated Prisoner's Dilemma Game-like situations because, absent information to the contrary, individuals perceive themselves as having interdependent costs and benefits, evaluate alternative strategies in this light, and are aware their partners are doing just as they are. Good evidence for this sort of coding mechanism comes from research comparing strategies under low and high social uncertainty. In the former, players know their own and others' costs and benefits, recognize the knowledge is shared, and, hence, believe they can predict each others' actions; in the latter, players are unclear about how their partners represent the transaction and, thus, cannot predict what the latter will do. For example, those who believe their unseen partner is a person tend to adopt a cooperative strategy, which depends on assuming both have a common understanding of each other's intentions (and, by default, judge them benign) and both know this. Whereas those supposedly playing against a computer are no doubt perplexed about its "intentions". As a result, they think defensively, adopting a competitive strategy to protect against the worst the partner can inflict (see review in Burnstein, 1969). Finally, it is worth noting that in these experiments both computer-partner and person-partner play a nice, forgiving strategy like TFT which typically evokes cooperation.

As you may know, TFT is called nice because it cooperates from the start and never defects as long as the partner cooperates (hence it never initiates a vicious cycle of mutual defections); and forgiving because it immediately begins cooperating again whenever the partner does. After Axelrod (1984) demonstrated that TFT contributed more to fitness than any alternative strategy game theory experts could devise, many thought being nice and forgiving were necessary and sufficient for the evolution of cooperation (but see Boyd and Lorberbaum, 1987). These early analyses, however, only compared *transaction strategies*, rules for when to behave cooperatively or competitively toward a partner. For parsimony, the option of rejecting a partner was not allowed. On its face, however, *partner selection strategies*, rules for deciding whether to have any dealings at all with someone, are prior to and, on its face, seem no less important than rules for deciding whether to cooperate or compete with him or her. But be this as it may, do these two sorts of strategies contribute differently to fitness? To answer this question comparisons were made between different partner selection strategies simply in conjunction with a single transaction strategy, usually TFT (see below). But sociality in essence is more complicated. All people have occasion to size-up strangers or members of other groups. In the nature of things, transactions with these individuals sometimes enhance fitness more than those with tried-and-true ingroup members. Consequently, individuals who deal only with those they know and trust suffer opportunity costs. On the other hand, ingroup members are less likely to cheat than strangers. Seeking to reduce opportunity costs by doing business with strangers, therefore, risks transaction costs or a sucker's payoff. The adaptive problem is how to achieve a good enough tradeoff between transaction costs and opportunity costs. This difficulty is inherent to any multi-group environment and must have been so throughout evolutionary history (for an empirical demonstration in modern business, see Uzzi, 1996). A solution that is likely to have evolved is suggested by Hayashi and Yamagishi (1998). Their research followed from Hayashi's earlier simulation comparing the contribution to fitness of various partner selection strategies *vis-à-vis* TFT. Opportunity costs, therefore, were nil. Under these conditions he demonstrated that reciprocating defection by quitting the relationship, finding a new, trustworthy partner and cooperating until the latter defects, called OUT-FOR-TAT (OFT), is optimal. However, when opportunity costs were significant OFT performed poorly. Too often sticking with trusted partners reduced returns below whatever the individual saved by avoiding being cheated. In the circumstances the best strategy by far turned out to be DOG, the Chinese characters of the name of the program's author (Jin). Hayashi and Yamagishi describe DOG as nice and cool; nice, because once a partner is selected it is unconditionally cooperative, which is nicer than Axelrodian niceness (i.e. TFT); and cool, because when selecting partners, players compare the expected benefits of alternative transactions, not whether partners are likely to cooperate or defect, and never accept a partner if the outcome anticipated is negative. However, what really distinguishes DOG from lesser strategies is that it displays general trust toward total strangers: in deciding to offer strangers the opportunity to be partners (or to accept such offers) DOG computes the expected benefits by averaging the *positive* outcomes with past partners, ignoring any negative outcomes. The implication is that if both transaction costs and opportunity costs have to be considered, general trust, expecting good of others even though you don't know them, is adaptive. Note also that DOG's triumph is unexpected in light of theories of intergroup relations postulating a social identity enhancement mechanism whereby members conspire to raise the ingroup's standing and lower that of the outgroup. This implies a partner selection strategy of ingroup cooperation and avoidance of dealings with strangers unless they are cooperators and can be betrayed with impunity (Tajfel and Turner, 1979).

In testing the psychological assumptions built into these simulations Yamagishi (1988) compared the strategies of Japanese and American players. Conventional wisdom is that Japanese trust ingroup members more than outgroup members or strangers and, hence, weigh transaction costs more heavily than opportunity costs; whereas Americans neither distinguish as much between ingroup and outgroup nor weigh one cost much more than the other (Markus and Kitayama, 1991). As Yamagishi predicted, in social dilemmas where transaction costs are a distinct possibility (i.e. decisions are anonymous so anyone can free-ride without fear of detection) Japanese reject strangers as partners, Americans don't. Yamagishi's results make the point that how partner selection strategies balance transaction costs and opportunity costs depends on how a culture weighs ingroup and outgroup ties. If ingroup ties are valued over outgroup ties, individuals worry more about being cheated than missing out on a bargain and, as a result, are averse to cooperating with strangers, even when the expected benefits are relatively large.

General Trust and the Collective Good

By demonstrating that optimal returns to fitness require dealings with strangers, simulations like DOG imply we are designed to display general trust. Do humans give priority to or even use this sort of partner selection strategy? Many years ago researchers had people estimate the likelihood of various dyadic and triadic social relations, some positive (e.g. What is the probability Mr A trusts Mr B?) and some negative (e.g. What is the probability Mr A distrusts Mr B?). Sometimes the person making the estimate knew nothing at all about the targets; other times they learned about another relationship involving one or more of the targets and, in effect, had to make estimates of reciprocity (e.g. Given Mr B trusts Mr A, what is the probability Mr A trusts Mr B?) and transitivity (Given Mr A trusts Mr B and Mr B trusts Mr C, what is the probability Mr A trusts Mr C?). The findings suggest people believe strangers are more inclined to like or trust than to dislike or distrust each other; and positive feelings are transitive, whereas negative feelings are not. Additional evidence of a default expectation corresponding to general trust is found in research on learning social structures demonstrating that relationships of trust and liking are encoded and remembered more easily than distrust and disliking (see Burnstein, 1969; Fiske and Taylor, 1991).

In sum, simulations make a plausible argument that general trust is adaptive and empirical research indicates that it is a likely default belief about social transactions. However, unless there is past experience with the individuals themselves or those similar to them, the expectation that people are cooperative is probably a false consensus effect, the projection onto others of one's own tendencies (Marks and Miller, 1987). The belief that one's own choice is diagnostic is not necessarily a foolish way of predicting another's behavior, however. Using one's own tendency to cooperate (or defect) as a base rate sample of size 1 when no other data is available increases accuracy in estimating others' strategy if it is not a *false* consensus effect and the tendency is common in the population. Which it usually is since, by definition, most people make majority choices. Two researchers who have carried out many studies with the *n*-person PDG report "Throughout fifteen years of experimentation, we have repeatedly observed positive correlations between one's own choice and estimates of the proportion of others in one's group who will cooperate . . . [hence,] the tendency to believe that a majority of other subjects will 'do as I do' is correct for cooperators, who constitute a majority of our subjects" (Dawes and Orbell, 1995, p. 67). Of course, this correlation between own choice and expected choice of others is not rational. To the contrary, since defection is tempting (and a dominant strategy), expectations that others will cooperate defy rationality, certainly in short-term transactions (e.g. one-shot games). Nonetheless, it is adaptive because it gives rise to an optimal partner selection strategy: cooperators who project their strategy onto a potential partner benefit more than defectors who do. The reason is that by projecting, cooperators accept another's offer more frequently and, hence, have more transactions than defectors. Moreover, partners who are cooperators will, by projecting, accept one's offer more frequently than competitors.

The most convincing evidence of a general trust mechanism comes from experiments on various social dilemmas. In a version called the public-goods dilemma a cooperative strategy obliges individuals to behave generously and benefit the group even though they could free-ride (e.g. donating blood). Typically the players are strangers who make a single decision, have absolutely no contact with each other either before, during, or afterward (except in a few studies where there is discussion prior to choosing), and, since choices are anonymous, are unaccountable. One of the more extensive research programs on social dilemmas (summarized in Caporael, Dawes, Orbell, and Van de Kragt, 1989) used a step-level public-goods problem in which a specified number of members have to contribute their own resources in order for the group to be awarded additional resources, typically money (e.g. when at least five members of a nine-person group contributed $5, all nine would get another $10, so contributors either lose $5 if the five-member quota is not met, or gain $10 if it is met; whereas non-contributors gain $5 if the quota is not met, or

$15 if it is met). Although free-riding is clearly a dominant strategy, slightly over 50 percent of the subjects contribute. When contributors no longer fear a loss regardless of others' intentions – a group norm was imposed whereby they got the $5 back if the quota was not met – cooperation increases to nearly 60 percent. And when they believe others' have no intention to free-ride since the incentives for it have vanished – the group norm insured non-contributors would wind up with no more than contributors, namely $10, if the quota was met – almost 90 percent contributes. This is a neat demonstration that confidence about the intentions of other group members is critical in deciding to cooperate compared, say, to confidence about losses, knowing suckers will be made whole whatever others intend to do.

An interesting discovery resulted when Caporael et al. (1989) lowered transaction costs relative to opportunity costs which, according to Yamagishi (1988), increases general trust. To do so they introduced a little normal sociality into the social dilemma paradigm. Before members decided whether to contribute, anonymity was suspended briefly and they discussed the matter. This simple change is important since absent social interaction the representation of "groupness" or entitativity may be too attenuated to activate general trust or other adaptations relevant to group living. How does social interaction do this? First and foremost, it reduces social uncertainty. Individuals learn about others' beliefs and feel less risk of mistaking how they will decide. In addition, discussion can also reduce expected transaction costs by increasing familiarity and liking (Berschied, 1985) as well as by making the membership concrete, vivid, and identifiable. As a result, individuals are more likely to categorize themselves as a member of the group and develop feelings of interdependence or common fate. That these effects actually occur when social dilemmas involve discussion has not been determined. However, Caporael et al. (1989) report an eleven-fold decrease in the variance of expected contributions following discussion, indicating a goodly decline in social uncertainty. In any event, although there is no further contact and choices remain anonymous, marked increases in cooperation appeared following discussion, with nearly 85 percent of members contributing and 100 percent of the groups providing the public good compared to about a 50 percent contribution rate and 60 percent provisioning rate in groups without discussion. Might these effects be due to conscience or social norms rather than general trust? Probably not; there is no evidence that discussion stirs the superego or a need to act in a socially approved fashion. Were it a matter of doing what conscience or society says is right then individuals would as likely assist strangers as ingroup members. Absent discussion, however, members assisted the ingroup slightly less than 40 percent of the time and strangers 20 percent; however, following discussion, assistance to the ingroup nearly doubled while assistance to strangers went up only by a third.

Conclusions

Evolutionary analyses describe the differential contribution of alternative phenotypes to individual fitness. The phenotypes of interest to us are heritable social strategies. In asking whether a strategy of this sort is adaptive, biologists refer to its impact on viability and reproduction; whereas social psychologists who ask the question mean its influence on thought, feeling, and action. The value of the evolutionary approach, besides reminding that theories of human sociality should have some relationship to explanations of group life in other species, is that it requires us to connect these two levels: we must evaluate the ultimate significance of psychological processes in terms of their influence on genetic continuation. At the same time evolutionary models give guidance by outlining the costs and benefits in classes of social transactions relevant to fitness, namely, kin altruism, mating, parental investment, status negotiations, and non-kin cooperation. The upshot is social psychological theorizing at last coming to grips with questions about functions of the mind that are shared by all humans and constitute our peculiar psychological adaptedness.

Substantively, the assumptions of an evolutionary analysis frequently cause a shock of recognition. This is never more vivid than upon looking into Darwinian explanations of a master problem in social psychology: why groups in similar environments develop dissimilar patterns of beliefs. The most fully developed model analyzing the evolution of group differences in terms of psychological adaptations was proposed by Boyd and Richerson (1985; Henrich and Boyd, 1998). They show that a social learning strategy called *conformist transmission* is sufficient to maintain uniformities within groups and differences between groups, meaning that this strategy produces optimal returns to fitness in a variety of circumstances. Conformist transmission is a coding bias whereby individuals send and receive ideas without processing all the information available in the environment. More to the point, it is a predisposition to adopt locally favored beliefs, those associated with familiar, liked, or trusted others over beliefs that are not locally favored. Therefore, once slight variations in initial positions on fitness landscapes begin to push similar groups toward more and more divergent adaptive peaks or solutions, as reflected in the beliefs peculiar to each, conformist transmission is the evolved mechanism that causes these beliefs to further increase in frequency and to endure. As in many other cases, what is striking about this evolutionary analysis is that the psychological assumptions are just the sort that would have been made by social psychological models generally considered to be untouched by Darwinism. We have in mind in this instance the classic theories of cognitive consistency. It is remarkable that the pattern of positive and negative relationships among senders, receivers, third-parties, and beliefs making for cultural variations in the Boyd–Richerson formulation are formally identical to those required to achieve structural balance, consonance, or congruity. *Mirabile dictu*, unbeknownst to us, social psychology may long have analyzed human sociality in terms of adaptations.

References

Alexander, R. D. (1987). *The biology of moral systems*. Hawthorne, NY: de Gruyter.

Anderson, J. L., Crawford, C. B., Nadeau, J., & Lindberg, T. (1992). Was the duchess of Windsor right? A cross-cultural review of the socioecology of ideas of female body shape. *Ethology and Sociobiology, 13*, 197–1240.

Asch, S. E. (1952). *Social psychology*. Englewood Cliffs, NJ: Prentice Hall.

Axelrod, R. M. (1984). *The evolution of cooperation*. New York: Basic Books.

Bereczkei, T. & Csanaky, A. (1996). Mate choice, marital success, and reproduction in a modern society. *Ethology and Sociobiology, 17*, 17–35.

Berry, D. S. (1991). Attractive faces are not all created equal: Joint effects of facial babishness and attractiveness on social perception. *Journal of Personality and Social Psychology, 17*, 523–531.

Berscheid, E. (1985). Interpersonal attraction. In G. Lindzey & A. Aronson (Eds.), *The handbook of social psychology*, 3rd. edn., vol. 2 (pp. 413–484). Reading, MA: Addison-Wesley.

Berscheid, E. (1994). Interpersonal relationships. *Annual Review of Psychology, 45,* 79–129.

Betzig, L., Mulder, M. B., & Turke, P. (1988). *Human reproductive behaviour: A Darwinian perspective*. Cambridge, UK: Cambridge University Press.

Boehm, C. (1997). Egalitarian behaviour and the evolution of political intelligence. In W. Andrew (Ed.), *Machiavellian intelligence II: Extensions and evaluations* (pp. 341–364). Cambridge, UK: Cambridge University Press.

Boone, J. L. (1992). Competition, conflict, and the development of social hierarchies. In E. A. Smith (Ed.), *Evolutionary ecology and human behavior* (pp. 301–337). Hawthorne, NY: de Gruyter.

Boone, J. L. (1998). The evolution of magnanimity: When is it better to give than to receive? *Human Nature, 9,* 1–21.

Borgerhoff Mulder, M. (1988). Reproductive success in three Kipsigis cohorts. In T. H. Clutton-Brock (Ed.), *Reproductive success: Studies of individual variation in contrasting breeding systems* (pp. 419–435). Chicago: University of Chicago Press.

Bouchard, T. J., & McGue, M. (1981). Familial studies of intelligence: A review. *Science, 212,* 1055–1059.

Boyd, R., & Lorberbaum, J. P. (1987). No pure strategy is evolutionarily stable in the repeated Prisoner's Dilemma game. *Nature, 327,* 58–59.

Boyd, R., & Richerson, P. J. (1985). *Culture and the evolutionary process*. Chicago: University of Chicago Press.

Burnstein, E. (1969). Interdependence in groups. In J. Mills (Ed.), *Experimental social psychology* (pp. 309–408). New York: Macmillan.

Burnstein, E., Crandall, C., & Kitayama, S. (1994). Some neo-Darwinian decision rules for altruism: Weighing cues for inclusive fitness as a function of the biological importance of the decision. *Journal of Social and Personality Psychology, 67,* 773–789.

Buss, D. M. (1989). Sex differences in human mate selection: evolutionary hypotheses tested in 37 cultures. *Behavioral and Brain Sciences, 12,* 1–49.

Buss, D. M. (1999). *Evolutionary psychology: The new science of the mind*. Boston: Allyn & Bacon.

Caporael, L. R., Dawes, R. M., Orbell, J. M., & Van de Kragt, A. J. C. (1989). Selfishness examined: cooperation in the absence of egoistic incentives. *Behavioral and Brain Sciences, 12,* 683–739.

Chagnon, N. A., & Bugos, P. E. Jr (1979). Kin selection and conflict: An analysis of a Yanomano ax fight. In N. A. Chagnon & W. Irons (Eds.), *Evolutionary biology and human social behavior: An anthropological perspective* (pp. 213–238). North Scituate, CA: Duxbury Press.

Cheney, D. L., & Seyfarth, R. M. (1985). Social and non-social knowledge in vervet monkeys. *Philosophical Transactions of the Royal Society of London, 308,* 187–201.

Cloninger, R. C. (1987). Neurogenetic adaptive mechanisms in alcoholism. *Science, 236,* 410–416.

Crandall, C. (1995). Do parents discriminate against their heavyweight daughters? *Personality and Social Psychology Bulletin, 21,* 724–735.

Cummins, D. D. (1998). *The evolution of mind*. New York: Oxford University Press.

Daly, M., & Wilson, M. (1988). *Homicide*. Hawthorne, NY: de Gruyter.

Darwin, C. (1871/1981). *The descent of man and selection in relation to sex*. London: John Murray.

Dawes, R. M., & Orbell, J. M. (1995). The benefit of optional play in anonymous one-shot prisoner's dilemma games. In K. J. Arrow, R. H. Mnookin, A. Tversky, L. Ross, & R. B. Wilson (Eds.), *Barriers to conflict resolution* (pp. 62–85). New York: Norton.

Dawkins, R., & Krebs, J. R. (1978). Animal signals: Information or manipulation? In J. R. Krebs & N. B. Davies (Eds.), *Behavioral ecology: An evolutionary approach* (pp. 282–309). Sunderland, MA: Sinauer.

Fiske, S., & Taylor, S. (1994). *Social cognition*. 2nd. edn. Reading, MA: Addison-Wesley.

Ford, C. S., & Beach, F. A. (1951). *Patterns of sexual behavior*. 1st edn. New York: Harper.

Gangestad, S. W., & Thornhill, R. (1997). Human sexual selection and developmental stability. In J. A. Simpson & D. T. Kenrick (Eds.), *Evolutionary social psychology* (pp. 169–196). Mahwah, NJ: Erlbaum.

Gottesman, I. I. (1991). *Schizophrenia genesis: The origins of madness.* New York: Freeman.

Hamilton, W. D. (1964). The genetical evolution of social behavior. Part I and II. *Journal of Theoretical Biology, 7,* 1–52.

Hamilton, W. D., & Zuk, M. (1982). Heritable true fitness and bright birds: A role for parasites? *Science, 218,* 384–387.

Hawkes, K. (1992). Sharing and collective action. In E. A. Smith & B. Winterhalder (Eds.), *Evolutionary ecology and human behavior* (pp. 269–300). New York: de Gruyter.

Hayashi, N., & Yamagishi, T. (1998). Selective play: Choosing partners in an uncertain world. *Personality and Social Psychology Review, 2,* 296–289.

Henrich, J., & Boyd, R. (1998). The evolution of conformist transmission and emergence of between-group differences. *Evolution and Human Behavior, 19,* 215–241.

James, W. (1890). *The principles of psychology.* New York: Holt.

Johnson, J. L., McAndrew, F. T., & Harris, P. B. (1991). Sociobiology and the naming of adopted and natural children. *Ethology and Sociobiology, 12,* 365–375.

Jones, D. (1995). Sexual selection, physical attractiveness and facial neoteny. *Current Anthropology, 36,* 723–748.

Kalick, S. M., Zebrowitz, L. A., Langlois, J. H., & Johnson, R. M. (1998). Does human facial attractiveness honestly advertise health? Longitudinal data on an evolutionary question. *Psychological Science, 9,* 8–13.

Kenrick, D. T., & Keefe, R. C. (1992). Age preferences in mates reflect sex differences in human reproductive strategies. *Behavioral and Brain Sciences, 15,* 75–133.

Komorita, S. S., & Parks, C. D. (1995). Interpersonal relations: Mixed-motives interaction. *Annual Review of Psychology, 46,* 183–207.

Langlois, J. H., Ritter, J. M., Roggman, L. A., & Vaughn, L. S. (1991). Facial diversity and infant preferences for attractive faces. *Developmental Psychology, 27,* 70–84.

Lanzetta, J. T., & Englis, B. G. (1989). Expectations of cooperation and competition and their effects on observers' vicarious emotional responses. *Journal of Personality and Social Psychology, 56,* 534–554.

Loehlin, J. C. (1992). *Genes and environment in personality development.* Thousand Oaks, CA: Sage.

McDougall, J. (1909). *An introduction to social psychology.* 2nd edn. Boston: H. W. Luce.

McGrath, J. E. (1984). *Groups: interaction and performance.* Englewood Cliffs, NJ: Prentice-Hall.

McGue, M., & Lykken, D. T. (1992). Genetic influence on risk of divorce. *Psychological Science, 3,* 368–373.

Marks, G., & Miller, N. (1987). Ten years of research on the false-consensus effect: An empirical and theoretical review. *Psychological Bulletin, 102,* 72–90.

Markus, H. R., & Kitayama, S. (1991). Culture and the self: Implications for cognition, emotion, and motivation. *Psychological Review, 98,* 224–253.

Mueller, U., & Mazur, A. (1997). Facial dominance in *Homo sapiens* as honest signalling of male quality. *Behavioral Ecology, 8,* 569–579.

Plomin, R., Corley, R., DeFries, J. C., & Fulker, D. W. (1990). Individual differences in television viewing in early childhood: Nature as well as nurture. *Psychological Science, 1,* 371–377.

Segal, N. L. (1999). *Entwined lives.* New York: Dutton.

Sime, J. D. (1983). Affiliative behavior during escape to building exits. *Journal of Environmental Psychology, 3,* 21–41.

Singh, D. (1993). Adaptive significance of female physical attractiveness: Role of waist-to-hip ratio. *Journal of Personality and Social Psychology, 65,* 293–307.

Sober, E., & Wilson, D. L. (1998). *Unto others.* Cambridge, MA: Harvard University Press.

Tajfel, H., & Turner, J. C. (1979). An integrative theory of intergroup conflict. In W. G. Austin & S. Worchel (Eds.), *The social psychology of intergroup relations* (pp. 33–47). Monterey, CA: Brooks/Cole.

Tassinary, L. G., & Hansen, K. A. (1998). A critical test of the waist-to-hip ratio hypothesis of female physical attractiveness. *Psychological Science, 9,* 150–155.

Tesser, A. (1993). The importance of heritability in psychological research: The case of attitudes. *Psychological Review, 100,* 129–142.

Trivers, R. (1985). *Social evolution*. Menlo Park, CA: Benjamin Cummings.

Tsuang, M. T., & Faraone, S. V. (1990). *The genetics of mood disorders*. Baltimore: Johns Hopkins University Press.

Uzzi, B. (1996). The sources and consequences of embeddedness for the economic performance of organizations: The network effect. *American Sociological Review, 61*, 764–796.

Veblen, T. (1973). *The theory of the leisure class*. Boston: Houghton Mifflin.

Voland, E., & Engel, C. (1990). Female choice in humans: A conditional mate selection strategy of the Krummerhorn women (Germany 1720–1874). *Ethology, 84*, 144–154.

Waller, N. G., Kojetin, B. A., Bouchard, T. J., & Lykken, D. T. (1990). Genetic and environmental influences on religious interests, attitudes, and values: A study of twins reared apart and together. *Psychological Science, 1*, 138–142.

Wang, X. T. (in press). A kith-and-kin rationality in risky choices: Empirical examinations and theoretical modeling. In F. Shorter (Ed.), *Risky transactions: Trust, kinship, and ethnicity*. Oxford, UK: Berghahn.

Weiss, R. F., Buchanan, W., Alstatt, L., & Lombardo, J. P. (1971). Altruism is rewarding. *Science, 171*, 1262–1263.

Yamagishi, T. (1988). Exit from the group as an individualistic solution to the free rider problem in the United States and Japan. *Journal of Experimental Social Psychology, 24*, 530–542.

Zahavi, A. (1975). Mate selection – a selection for handicap. *Journal of Theoretical Biology, 53*, 205–214.

Zebrowitz, L. A., & Lee, S. Y. (1999). Appearance, stereotype-incongruent behavior, and social relationships. *Personality and Social Psychology Bulletin, 25*, 569–584.

Chapter Two

The Cultural Grounding of Social Psychological Theory

Joan G. Miller

Interest in culture within social psychology has grown markedly in recent years. This change is evident not only in the sampling of populations in research that are more culturally diverse, but in the efforts by a growing number of investigators to integrate cultural considerations within basic psychological theory (e.g. Cole, 1996; Fiske, Kitayama, Markus, & Nisbett, 1998; Markus, Kitayama, & Heiman, 1996; Miller, 1997a, 1999; Shweder, 1990; Shweder & Sullivan, 1993; Shweder, Goodnow, Hatano, LeVine, Markus, & Miller, 1998). Notably, this turn to culture is occurring in the context of other important shifts in the field, such as an increased interest in evolutionary theory and in other biologically based approaches, and moves to ground psychological theory at the level of concepts whose functioning is not assumed to depend fundamentally on cultural considerations. Key questions arise in understanding the bases for this recent increased interest in culture within social psychology and the relationship of this cultural turn to these other important developments in the field.

Providing an overview of research in the newly reemerging tradition of cultural psychology, the present chapter seeks to identify potential contributions of this work for social psychology as well as challenges that must be addressed to fully realize these goals. The argument is made that a cultural perspective has the potential to provide new process understandings of psychological phenomena that both complete and broaden existing theoretical approaches. It can also contribute to efforts to reclaim the "social" in social psychology, through its power to make explicit the frequently ignored contributions of cultural

Appreciation is expressed to Meredith Bachman, Phoebe Ellsworth, Steve Heine, and Lynne Schaberg for their helpful comments on drafts of this chapter. This research was supported, in part, by Grant MH 42940-09 from the National Institute of Mental Health and by Grant SBR-9421218 from the Social Psychology and Cultural Anthropology Programs of the National Science Foundation.

beliefs and practices to the development and maintenance of individual subjectivity and behavior. The case will further be made, however, that in order to more fully realize these aims, increased effort needs to be made to insure the cultural as well as psychological sensitivity of the constructs, procedures, and theories that are adopted in psychological research.

The first section of the chapter examines reasons for the downplaying of cultural considerations within social psychology and developments that have contributed to the growing interest shown in culture by social psychologists in recent years. In turn, the second section provides a brief overview of recent cultural work in social psychology to highlight some of its empirical and theoretical contributions. Finally, in a brief concluding section, consideration is given to the relationship of work in cultural psychology to other recent theoretical and empirical developments in the field, as well as to challenges that must be met for cultural considerations to become integrated into social psychology in a way that qualitatively impacts on its central theoretical commitments.

Perspectives on Culture in Psychology

One of the enigmas of psychology as a discipline is its downplaying of the importance of culture in understanding human behavior, or, as Cole formulates the issue, "why . . . psychologists find it so difficult to keep culture in mind" (Cole, 1996, p. 1). Although recognizing that humans depend on culture, psychologists tend to accord cultural considerations only a superficial role in explaining individual psychological functioning. As Schwartz observes, "Psychologists accept that while everyone has culture, it is mainly relevant elsewhere where it produces certain exotic effects that anthropologists study. It is as if others have culture while we have human nature" (Schwartz, 1992, p. 329).

Addressing this issue, the discussion here will center on some of the reasons why cultural considerations have tended to be downplayed within social psychology. Attention will also be given to recent conceptual and empirical developments that are challenging this stance.

Downplaying of culture

At first blush, the concern of social psychologists with social aspects of psychological functioning and with situational influences on behavior may not appear to fit with a downplaying of cultural considerations. However, the neglect of culture by social psychologists may be seen to follow, at least in part, from the adoption within the field of explanatory frameworks that give little importance to cultural mediation, the limited challenges to social psychological theorizing posed by early cross-cultural research, and the field's embrace of disciplinary practices and of scientific ideals that tend to exclude culture.

Situationism without culture   The dominant, if not arguably the signature, explanatory framework developed within social psychology during the twentieth century has been situationism. From this perspective, behavior is understood to be affected by contextual factors that produce effects which not only may be highly counterintuitive but that may occur in ways that are outside of conscious awareness, such as through priming (e.g. Bargh, 1996). Supported by controlled laboratory experimentation, the dominant perspective has tended to be formulated in ways, however, that treat culture as having no independent explanatory force.

As approached within the dominant perspective, the situation is considered objective, in the sense that a given pattern of experience is assumed to present a determinate structure that is at least potentially knowable by an observer (e.g. Kelly, 1972). Importantly, it is also considered subjective in that it is assumed that the impact of the situation depends upon how it is construed. Thus, for example, observers with different information processing capacities may differ in the degree to which their attributions adequately take into account the information presented in a given situation (e.g. Nisbett & Ross, 1980). Equally, individuals with contrasting schematic understandings may give divergent weight to aspects of the same situation or interpret the meaning of the same situation in different ways (e.g. Markus, Smith, & Moreland, 1985). From the present perspective, individual difference approaches are seen as completing situational explanations in that they explain why the same situation may vary in its effects across individuals. Individual differences also account for regularities in behavior which persist across contexts, such as relatively enduring individual variation in attitudes, personality, motivation, cognitive style, etc.

The dominant perspective gives rise to dualistic modes of explanation, focused on both objective factors in the situation, such as the information available to individuals, and on subjective factors within the person, such as individuals' motivational status, cognitive capacities, attitudes, etc. From the dominant perspective, culture is assumed to be already taken into account in either the definition of the situation or of the person. Thus, for example, it is recognized that individuals in different cultural contexts vary in the everyday situations or experiences to which they are exposed. However, this is not viewed as calling into question the explanatory force of a focus on the objective situation, but merely suggests that the amount or type of information available to individuals differs in contrasting cultural environments. No consideration is given to divergent culturally shared meanings being given to the same objective information. Equally, evidence that individuals from different cultural backgrounds maintain contrasting systems of belief, value, or meaning is assimilated within the present type of model to an individual difference dimension. It is viewed as implying that individual differences in attitudes or understandings may relate to cultural group membership, but not as implying that there is a need to give any independent weight to cultural meanings and practices *per se* in explanation. This trend for basic theory in social psychology to be formulated in culture-free terms is reflected in the limited attention given to cultural considerations within major social psychology textbooks and review chapters. To give one example, in Higgins and Kruglanski's (1996) recent handbook on basic principles of social psychology, with only one exception, the only citations for "culture" in the index refer to pages within the single chapter on cultural psychology by Markus, Kitayama, and Heiman (1996), rather than to any of the other 27 chapters of the volume.[1] From the dominant perspective, taking culture into account is considered relevant in explaining diversity in psychological outcomes; however, it is not seen as making a necessary contribution in the formulation of basic psychological theory.

Universalistic emphasis of early work in cross-cultural psychology

Whereas culture has always had and continues to have a relatively marginal role in the discipline of psychology, it has remained a presence throughout its existence, as recent cultural histories of the field make clear (Cahan & White, 1992; Cole, 1996; Jahoda, 1993). Notably, much of this work has been in the tradition of cross-cultural psychology.[2] Research in the tradition of cross-cultural psychology has tended to employ the types of quantitative methodologies that are typical of mainstream social psychology. Generating a vast body of empirical research, it has given rise not only to the six-volume first edition of the *Handbook of Cross-Cultural Psychology* (Triandis, 1980), but to numerous other major handbooks, textbooks, and review chapters (e.g. Berry, Poortinga, Segall, & Dasen, 1992; Brislin, 1983). Its theoretical and methodological ties to social psychology, in fact, have been so close, that Tedeschi (1988, p. 17) once characterized cross-cultural psychologists simply as "social psychologists working in different cultures".

Despite its close affinity to social psychology, however, work in cross-cultural psychology has had little or no impact on basic social psychological theory. This has occurred, at least in part, as a result of the limited challenges which at least early work in this tradition posed to the mainstream discipline. Research in cross-cultural psychology has tended to assume an exclusively functional view of culture, in which naturally occurring ecological environments are viewed as presenting contrasting objective affordances and constraints to which individual behavior is adapted. Culture is portrayed as influencing the contexts in which psychological processes are displayed, and both the rate and endpoint of psychological development. However, culture is not considered to impact qualitatively on the form of psychological processes themselves.

These types of assumptions may be illustrated through consideration of the model of culture and personality developed by the Whitings and empirically tested in their landmark investigation of child development in six cultures (Whiting & Whiting, 1975). In this model, social institutions and childrearing practices are viewed as adapted to the divergent material constraints existing in different physical settings, and are seen as leading to the development of contrasting personality characteristics among individuals raised in these settings. Culture, in turn, is seen as evolving in ways to accommodate individuals' personalities. In one of its major correlational findings, for example, the Six Culture Study demonstrated that in societies that have rich natural ecologies, the social structure tends to be highly complex; children are socialized in ways that lead them to develop egoistic personality styles; and competitive cultural meaning systems and practices evolve to accommodate individuals' personalities. It is assumed that the processes underlying personality development are universal and can be explained within existing theoretical frameworks, such as psychoanalytic theory and social learning approaches. Culture is seen as affecting only the outcomes of personality development (e.g. whether individuals develop egoistic versus nurturing personalities), and not the basic processes of personality themselves.

The discussion in this section has identified reasons why the research tradition of cross-cultural psychology has not fundamentally challenged the view, maintained in mainstream social psychology, that culture gives rise only to relatively superficial content differences in psychological outcomes and can safely be ignored in the formulation of basic psychological theory. Like the dominant social psychological perspective, work in cross-cultural psychology has tended to treat culture and psychological processes as bearing the relationship of an independent to a dependent variable, rather than view them as mutually constitutive phenomena. The considerations raised here, it should be emphasized, however, do not detract from the groundbreaking contributions of investigations in the tradition of cross-cultural psychology in establishing a basis for much present work on cultural issues. They also do not call into question the substantial overlap in objectives between the current research traditions of cultural and cross-cultural psychology (Segall, Lonner, & Berry, 1998). However, the issues raised are relevant in helping to explain why much work in cross-cultural psychology has been viewed as primarily descriptive rather than theoretical in nature by investigators in mainstream social psychology, as well as why some cultural psychologists have given even classic work undertaken in this tradition a mixed appraisal as "not heretical enough, even as it raises its serious concerns" (Shweder, 1990, p. 12).

Embrace of physical science models of explanation   It may be noted that the models of explanation which have been embraced within social psychology have also contributed to the tendency of social psychologists to show little interest in cultural approaches. Whereas social psychology has always been multi-paradigmatic, it has tended historically to privilege an idealized physical science model of explanation. This type of model treats science as an enterprise that is engaged in the search for general laws. Higgins and Kruglanski (1996) have recently characterized this ideal as a vision for basic social psychological theory:

> A discovery of lawful principles governing a realm of phenomena is a fundamental objective of scientific research. . . . A useful scientific analysis needs to probe beneath the surface. In other words, it needs to get away from the "phenotypic" manifestations and strive to unearth the "genotypes" that may lurk beneath. . . . We believe in the scientific pursuit of the nonobvious. But less in the sense of uncovering new and surprising phenomena than in the sense of probing beneath surface similarities and differences to discover deep underlying structures. (Ibid., p. vii)

Entailed in this physical sciences model is a search for explanations that make it possible to account for a wide range of behavioral phenomena in terms of a relatively small set of principles.

From the present type of perspective, cultural variation in human behavior is considered as of limited interest. It is viewed as leading away from the search for underlying regularities to a focus on outward appearances, i.e. away from process and toward content and context: "Cultural differences are trivial because they are at the wrong level of abstraction, and stand as 'medium' rather than 'thing' in relation to the objects of study. The readily observable differences among cultural groups are probably superficial, and represent little if any differences at the level of psychological process" (Malpass, 1988, p. 31). To the extent that a cultural focus leads to the identification of local variation in fundamental psychological processes, it also is seen as threatening the achievement of the scientific goals of parsimony and predictive power.

The methodologies that are involved in culturally based research are also criticized as lacking adequate control (Messick, 1998). This concern has contributed to the recent historical trend for social psychology to privilege laboratory based approaches and to turn away from a consideration of difficult to measure constructs, such as culture, that require taking into account not only shared meanings but also everyday social practices and modes of life.

Renewed interest in culture and psychological theory   Although cultural work continues to have a marginal role in the discipline, interest in cultural research within social psychology nonetheless has increased dramatically in recent years. In a sociology of knowledge sense, this increased interest may be traced proximally to the emergence of a small but growing body of quantitatively based social psychological research that, going beyond early work in the tradition of cross-cultural psychology, is highlighting the need for greater attention to the cultural grounding of social psychological theories. Much of this work employs the same types of quantitative research designs as are common in social psychology, making it possible for its findings to be assimilated into the mainstream discipline more readily than could equally relevant ethnographic research. Without attempting to provide an indepth analysis of the foundations of cultural psychology, note will be made here of some of the key developments that, in combination, have contributed to its emergence. As may be seen, the conceptual and empirical advances that have given rise to cultural psychology did not arise specifically within social psychology, but rather developed over time in multiple research and disciplinary traditions.

Cognitive revolution   The insight of the Cognitive Revolution regarding the importance of meanings in mediating behavior represented an important foundation for cultural psychology. Through work on schemas, scripts, and other cognitive structures, it came to be understood that individuals go beyond the information given as they contribute meanings to experience, with these meanings, in turn, influencing individuals' affective, cognitive, and behavioral reactions. For many years the cultural implications of this cognitive shift were not appreciated within psychology, both because there was no recognition of the cultural bases of meanings and because of the assimilation of this insight into prevailing mechanistic explanatory frameworks. As Bruner (1990) notes, not only was there a tendency to emphasize the autonomous self-construction of meanings, independently of cultural influences, but the active interpretive nature of the meaning-making process tended to become lost as work turned to a focus on more passive information and information processing considerations. Still, the recognition that an act of interpretation may mediate between the stimulus and the response established a theoretical basis which could be drawn upon as investigators later increasingly began to appreciate the cultural aspects of meanings and their impact on thought and behavior.

Symbolic views of culture   A further key development that contributed to the emergence of cultural psychology was the advent within anthropology of symbolic views of culture (Geertz, 1973; Sahlins, 1976). Within symbolic perspectives, cultural systems are understood to do more than merely represent preexisting realities and regulate behavior. Rather, they are also seen as creating social realities, whose existence rests partly on these cultural definitions. It is recognized that not only social institutions (e.g. marriage, school) and roles (e.g. bride, student), but also key aspects of self (e.g. emotion, mind, etc.) depend, in part, for their existence on cultural distinctions embodied in natural language categories, discourse, and everyday social practices. Crucially, symbolic views of culture recognize the open and indeterminate relationship that exists between cultural meanings and practices and material forces. It is acknowledged that to assess the adaptive implications of particular ecological conditions requires taking into account not merely objective affordances and constraints but also nonrational systems of belief and value (LeVine, 1984).

In terms of the emergence of the perspective of cultural psychology, these assumptions of symbolic approaches have been important in underscoring the need to go beyond certain causal–functional views of culture as bearing a one-to-one relationship to ecological constraints. In calling attention to the role of culture in establishing criteria for objective knowledge, they also challenge the possibility of the self-construction of understandings proceeding independently of cultural input. In these ways, symbolic views of culture show cultural meanings and practices as contributing explanatory force to psychological explanations, beyond that accounted for by a focus on objective material constraints (e.g. the situation) or on individual information processing (e.g. the person).

Incompleteness thesis   Perhaps most critically, the move toward cultural psychology or toward a realization of culture as a necessary source of patterning of self emerged with the recognition of the necessary role of culture in completion of higher order psychological processes and of human activity in the creation of culture – an insight that has been termed the "incompleteness thesis" (Geertz, 1973; Schwartz, 1992). This stance does not assume a *tabula rasa* view of the individual, as having no inborn biological propensities, and does not deny biological influences as a source of patterning of individual psychological development. However, it calls attention to the pervasiveness of culture in human experience. Individuals are viewed not only as always acting in culturally specific environments and utilizing culturally specific tools, but also as carrying with them in their language and understanding systems, culturally grounded assumptions through which they interpret experience. This enculturative structure then, it is recognized, is not a feature that can be partialled out of human experience, through the controlled procedures of laboratory experimentation. Rather, it is understood to be something that is omnipresent and that invariably introduces a cultural-historical specificity to psychological functioning. As Wertsch (1995) articulates this point:

> Cultural, institutional, and historical forces are 'imported' into individuals' actions by virtue of using cultural tools, on the one hand, and sociocultural settings are created and recreated through individuals' use of mediational means, on the other. The resulting picture is one in which, because of the role cultural tools play in mediated action, it is virtually impossible for us to act in a way that is not socioculturally situated. . . . Nearly all human action is mediated action, the only exceptions being found perhaps at very early stages of ontogenesis and in natural responses such as reacting involuntarily to an unexpected loud noise.

This assumption of the interdependence of psychological and cultural processes represents the central idea of cultural psychology. Notably, the term "cultural psychology" was chosen by theorists to convey this insight that psychological processes need to be understood as always grounded in particular cultural-historical contexts that impact on their form and patterning, just as cultural communities depend for their existence on particular communities of intentional agents. Including diverse methodological approaches and inherently multi-disciplinary in nature, work within the framework of cultural psychology is focusing on bringing culture into process explanations of psychological phenomena.

The Cultural Grounding of Psychological Processes

Through consideration of some examples of empirical studies that embody these insights of cultural psychology, the discussion here will illustrate ways in which recent cultural work is challenging the completeness of many existing explanations of psychological processes as well as identifying qualitative variation in psychological forms. It is beyond the scope of this chapter to present an exhaustive or even a representative sample of the growing body of cultural research on social psychological topics. However, the present highly selective survey can serve to convey some of the types of contributions that cultural research is making to process understandings of psychological phenomena.

Self and cognition

Psychological theorists tend to treat the capacity for self-awareness as fundamental to psychological functioning. It is assumed that universally individuals maintain some awareness of their mental activity and of themselves as agents who exist in time and space and who act in the world. This type of view of the self underlies, for example, James's (1890) focus on a conscious selfhood or "I," Allport's (1937) identification of the self as that aspect of personality that allows one to realize that one is the same person when one awakes each day, as well as Neisser's (1988) conception of an "ecological self" that perceives itself as situated within a particular physical environment. Within these viewpoints, self-awareness is recognized to be necessary for the emergence of higher order psychological concepts as well as for social relations. As Hallowell argues:

> It seems necessary to assume self-awareness as one of the prerequisite psychological conditions for the functioning of any human social order, no matter what linguistic and culture patterns prevail. . . . The phenomena of self-awareness in our species is as integral a part of human sociocultural mode of adaptation as it is of a distinctive human level of psychological structuralization. (Hallowell, 1955, p. 75)

Interestingly, however, self-awareness not only gives rise to certain common experiences of the self, but makes it possible for humans, through symbolic means, to formulate and express culturally variable embodiments of the self. It is increasingly recognized that, whereas there exists universally "an empirical agent" (Dumont, 1970), the modern Western view of the self, with its associated cultural practices, represents a culturally specific form. As theorists have noted, this implies that certain self-related psychological processes are likely to be culturally variable as well (Baumeister, 1987; Oyserman, ch. 23, this volume).

In terms of empirical findings, in some of the earliest quantitative work on this topic, Shweder and Bourne (1984) documented that, when describing their peers, Indians place significantly greater emphasis on contextualized actions (e.g. "He is hesitant to give away money to his family") and significantly less emphasis on decontextualized personality traits (e.g. "He is selfish") than do Americans (for similar results in perception of the self, see Bond & Cheung, 1983; Cousins, 1989). This difference, their evidence suggested, could not be explained in terms of prevailing situational or cognitive explanations of cultural differences, focused on variation in individuals' schooling, literacy, socioeconomic status, linguistic resources, or capacities for abstract thought. Rather, the differences appeared to reflect the more sociocentric as compared with individualistic cultural conceptions of the person emphasized in traditional Hindu Indian as compared with secular European–American cultural contexts. It has also been shown that these contrasting cultural understanding systems and practices impact qualitatively on the course and endpoint of development. Reflecting their enculturation into highly individualistic cultural selfways, with increasing age, European–American children place greater weight on personality traits and describe others in increasingly impersonal terms (e.g. "She is kind") (Miller, 1987). In contrast, reflecting their enculturation into sociocentric cultural selfways, Hindu Indians show a contrasting pattern of developmental change. Unlike European–Americans, they show a significant age increase in their tendencies to describe persons in concrete terms and to use person descriptions that are self-involved (e.g. "She comes often with her sister to visit me").

In another major line of work in this area, research is focusing on cultural variability in attributional processes. Evidence, for example, suggests that Asian cultural populations may be less vulnerable than are North American populations to the fundamental attribution error, an assumed universal bias to overemphasize dispositional relative to situational explanations of behavior. Relative to North Americans, Asian populations tend to give greater weight to situational factors and less weight to dispositional factors in explanation (Lee, Hallanhan, & Herzog, 1996; Miller, 1984; Morris, Nisbett, & Peng, 1995; Morris & Peng, 1994). They also appear less prone to display the correspondence bias, involving ignoring relevant situational information to make the inference that behavior is reflective of individual dispositions (Choi & Nisbett, 1998) or to display cognitive dissonance biases (Heine & Lehman, 1997a; see also Kashima, Siegel, Tanaka, & Kashima, 1992).

In an emerging line of inquiry, research is focusing on cognitive differences that relate to the tendency in Western cultural traditions to emphasize an analytic epistemological orientation as contrasted with the tendency in Eastern cultural traditions to favor a more dialectical approach (Lloyd, 1990; Nakamura, 1985). The former perspective privileges a deductive logic, which emphasizes breaking up objects into their component elements, whereas the latter privileges a holistic stance, which stresses viewing objects in relational terms. Evidence suggests that these differences are associated with contrasting emphases in individual interpretation and processing of information (Choi, Nisbett, & Norenzayan, 1999). For example, it has been observed that Chinese perform less successfully than do Americans on a formal category learning procedure that requires the application of formal rules (Norenzayan, Nisbett, & Smith, 1998). In contrast, they perform more successfully than European–Americans in detection of covariation, a task that demands attending closely to the environment (Peng & Nisbett, 1997). Demonstrating that this type of cognitive variation depends on the content and context under consideration, work reveals the observed differences in this area to be a matter of cognitive style and not of basic cognitive capacity. Thus, for example, Koreans make less spontaneous use of categories for purposes of inductive inference than do Americans when reasoning about nonsocial categories (Choi, Nisbett, & Smith, 1997). However, they make greater use of categories for induction than do Americans when reasoning about people.

Summary   In summary, studies on cognition and the self are highlighting the need to take into account cultural meaning systems in understanding the form and developmental patterning of self-understandings, attributional biases, and spontaneous cognitive styles. Research in these areas challenges both the naive realism of certain social psychological approaches to attribution, with their exclusive focus on information and information processing considerations, as well as the pristine processor assumptions of certain developmental models, with their focus on the autonomous individual construction of knowledge. Broadening the normative models being brought to bear in understanding attribution and cognition, this work highlights the contextual dependence of cross-cultural differences in cognition.

Self-esteem and Well-being

A widely shared assumption in psychological theories of the self is that positive self-regard and high self-esteem are integral to psychological well-being. Recent cultural research is examining the implicit cultural underpinnings of these self processes, through identifying cultural influences on the determinants of positive self-regard and of psychological well-being, and through highlighting culturally specific assumptions that are implicit in present models of self-esteem.

   In a relatively short span of time, a growing body of research has emerged that establishes cultural variability in the tendency to enhance one's self-image. For example, it has been demonstrated that the mean and/or median self-esteem scores of Americans are higher than the midpoints of self-esteem scales (Baumeister, Tice, & Hutton, 1989), whereas those of Japanese approach the midpoint (Diener & Diener, 1995). Studies of open-ended descriptions have similarly shown that Americans typically describe themselves in more positive terms than do Japanese (Ip & Bond, 1995; Kanagawa, Cross, & Markus, 1999). For example, the self-descriptions of a representative sample of nearly 1,600 American adults were observed to include about four to five times as many positive attributes as negative ones (Herzog, Franks, Markus, & Holmberg, 1994). This contrasts markedly with the tendencies of Japanese college students to portray themselves primarily in terms either of weaknesses (e.g. "I'm somewhat selfish") or in terms of the absence of negative self-characteristics (e.g. "I'm not lazy") (Yeh, 1995). Similar types of cultural differences have been observed in attributions made for success and failure. Whereas European–Americans tend to attribute their successes to themselves and their failures to others, both Japanese and Chinese populations tend to attribute their successes to situational factors and their failures to lack of ability or effort (Kitayama, Takagi, & Matsumoto, 1995; Lee &

Seligman, 1997; Shikanai, 1978). Providing evidence that these types of cultural differences do not result merely from self-presentational processes, it has been shown that Japanese tend to maintain a self-effacing orientation even when their self-assessments are assessed by means of covert behavioral measures, rather than through overt questionnaire techniques (Heine, Takata, & Lehman, in press).

Cultural differences observed in the tendency to enhance the self, research suggests, are linked to the contrasting cultural views of the self and associated practices maintained in different cultural contexts. The emphasis in middle-class European–American culture on achieving independence, enhancing freedom, and on exercising choice, etc. appears to set up a cultural imperative to discover, confirm, and express positive attributes of the self. This contrasts markedly with the emphasis found in Chinese cultural populations on being members of and working through groups (Bond, 1996) or in Japanese cultural populations on developing self-discipline, restraint, balance, and perseverance (Kitayama, Markus, Matsumoto, & Norasakkunkit, 1997). Support for this enculturation interpretation may be seen in socialization research showing that whereas the self-esteem of Japanese visitors to the United States tends to increase over time, that of American visitors to Japan tends to decrease (Heine, Lehman, Markus, & Kitayama, in press). Self-report research has also demonstrated that both Americans and Japanese tend to interpret everyday cultural scripts within the United States as enhancing their sense of self, while tending to interpret everyday cultural scripts within Japan as leading them to adopt a more self-critical stance (Kitayama et al., 1997).

Recent evidence suggests that cross-cultural differences in self-enhancement cannot be explained merely in terms of Asian populations emphasizing contrasting aspects of the self than do North Americans. For example, it has been shown that Japanese do not enhance certain culturally salient aspects of the self, such as the valued interpersonal traits of perseverance, adaptability, etc. and tend to score lower than do Canadians on measures of collective self-esteem (Heine & Lehman, 1997b). Whereas Japanese enhance certain interpersonal aspects of the self, such as their close relationships (Endo, Heine, & Lehman, in press) and family names (Kitayama & Karasawa, 1997), this tendency is accompanied by other-enhancing stances which are not observed among North Americans. Such results suggest that enhancement of interpersonal aspects of the self by Japanese populations may result from a qualitatively distinct process than is observed among North Americans. In particular, self-enhancement for North Americans reflects concerns with fortifying the self to act autonomously, whereas enhancement of interpersonal aspects of the self for Japanese reflects concerns with strengthening interpersonal connections (Heine et al., in press).

Importantly, research is also uncovering cultural variability in sources of life satisfaction and is providing evidence that self-esteem, as assessed by existing psychological measures, does not play as central a role in adaptation in cultural populations that maintain more interdependent as compared with independent cultural selfways. It has been observed that self-esteem as well as the experience of positive emotions correlate more strongly with life satisfaction in individualistic as compared with collectivist cultural populations (Suh, Diener, Oishi, & Triandis, 1998). In contrast, relationship harmony as well as a concern with social norms show the reverse patterns of correlation (Kwan, Bond, & Singelis, 1997). Also, it has been found that whereas among Americans, the trait of self-esteem is positively related to the enhancing of ingroups and the derogation of outgroups in response to negative feedback, this protective role of self-esteem only occurs among Chinese who are relatively Westernized, as indicated by their maintaining independent rather than interdependent self-construals (Brockner & Chen, 1996).

Summary   In sum, cultural research implies that although universally individuals appear motivated to maintain positive feelings about the self, the tendency to achieve this through strategies of self-enhancement and defensive self-promotion is culturally variable, with Japanese populations emphasizing a culturally supported self-critical stance and Chinese populations emphasizing maintaining harmony within groups. This work implies that tendencies for self-esteem and life satisfaction to be higher among North American than among certain Asian cultural populations (Diener & Diener, 1995) cannot be interpreted at face value as an indicator of more successful patterns of adaptation being linked to individualism. Rather, they may be related, at least in part, to cultural differences in tendencies for self-enhancement. More generally, investigations in this area point to fundamental cultural variability existing in the determinations of life satisfaction and in the constituents of well-being. The results reveal that self-esteem embodies goals for the self that fit most closely individualistic cultural norms, practices, and self-definitions. It does not appear to capture as well central goals for the self in cultures which place greater emphasis on the fulfillment of interpersonal responsibilities and on interpersonal interdependence.

Emotions and Motivation

Emotions and motivation involve not merely perceptions but also behavioral action tendencies and somatic reactions, and thus entail a complexity beyond that observed in accounting for purely cognitive phenomena. Cultural work on emotions and motivation, it will be seen, is providing insight into respects in which these processes are constituted, in part, by cultural meanings and practices. More generally, it also highlights the open relationship that exists between biological and cultural systems.

Emotions

Cultural research is documenting variability in the types of emotions given cultural emphasis. It is recognized that cultures differ in the degree to which particular emotions are "hypercognized," in the sense that there are several, highly differentiated ways to characterize them and many culturally provided schemata in which they play a part, as compared with "hypocognized," in the sense that there is little cognitive or linguistic elaboration of them and few well developed cultural schemata which pertain to that domain of experience (Levy, 1984). Claims of this type are important not only in identifying commonalities in emotional experiences but in uncovering variability in the roles which particular emotions play in psychological functioning. For example, it has been demonstrated that social engagement/disengagement constitutes a universal dimension of emotional experience. However, among Americans, socially disengaged feelings (e.g. pride, feelings of superiority, etc.) are linked to general positive feelings, whereas among Japanese, only socially engaged feelings (e.g. friendliness, connection, etc.) show such positive links (Kitayama, Markus, & Kurokawa, 1998).

Recent cultural work is also highlighting variation in conceptions, if not also in experiences of emotions, that are revealed when emotions are examined in ways that give greater weight to culturally specific meanings (see also Parrott, ch. 17, this volume). This is being undertaken, for example, through attending to non-English language emotion concepts, utilizing open-ended response formats to characterize emotions, and assessing the social beliefs and practices that bear on the experience of emotions in particular cultural communities. Without denying the considerable commonality which exists in emotion categories cross-culturally, ethnographic work is providing evidence of cultural variation in many specific emotion concepts, including even such assumed basic emotions as anger and sadness, as well as in the concept of emotion itself (Russell, 1991, 1994). Cross-cultural differences have also been observed in appraisals of emotions, particularly in the case of dimensions of appraisal which relate to contrasting cultural views of the self, such as issues of control and responsibility (Mauro, Sato, & Tucker, 1992; Stipek, 1998) or in the case of culturally specific categories of emotion, such as the Japanese emotion of amae (Russell & Yik, 1996; Wierzbicka, 1992).

Perhaps most centrally, recent cultural work is highlighting the importance of approaching emotions in more process-oriented terms. The argument is made that it is arbitrary to privilege certain isolated components – such as physiological reactions or eliciting conditions – as the central features of emotions or to assume that the same components of emotion are invariably linked in the same temporal order (Ellsworth, 1994; Kitayama & Masuda, 1995; Russell, 1991; Shweder, 1994). Rather, it is maintained that emotions need to be understood as including a wide range of processes – such as physiological and somatic correlates, facial and vocal expressions, eliciting conditions, behavioral outcomes, etc. – that may bear contrasting temporal relations to each other and be instantiated in culturally variable ways.

This type of process-oriented view of emotions highlights the open relationship that exists between physiological and somatic reactions and emotional experiences. It has been observed that certain somatic experiences that tend to be given a psychological interpretation as emotions by Americans, are understood and reacted to purely as somatic or physical events within many other cultural communities (Russell & Yik, 1996; Shweder, 1994). In another example, research reveals that even in the presence of certain universal physiological reactions, the coding of experience in emotional terms depends on cultural meanings and practices (Levenson, Ekman, Heider, & Friesen, 1992). It has been demonstrated that although Minangkabau men and American men show the same patterns of autonomic nervous system arousal to voluntary facial posing of prototypical emotion expressions, the two groups differ in their emotional responses. Reflecting their culturally based assumption that social relations constitute a defining element in emotional experience, Minangkabau men, unlike American men, do not interpret their physiological arousal in this type of laboratory based situation in emotional terms.

Motivation   In regard to motivation, dominant social psychological theories stress the importance of voluntarism and choice, with agency assumed to be linked to self-determination, and socialization processes considered optimum to the extent that they balance interpersonal relatedness with autonomy (Deci & Ryan, 1985). Broadening existing normative models in this area, recent cultural work is pointing to the qualitatively distinct forms which agency assumes in cultures that emphasize a more social and interdependent view of self. At the same time, it is providing insight into culturally variable socialization practices that may give rise to adaptive motivational outcomes.

Cultural research is uncovering the culturally specific assumptions that have characterized a range of psychological theories pertaining to motivation. In the domain of morality, for example, work has shown that whereas European–Americans approach interpersonal commitments in terms of a voluntaristic stance, captured well by Gilligan's (1982) morality of caring framework, Hindu Indians maintain a qualitatively distinct "duty based" orientation that does not fit this existing psychological framework (Miller, 1994). Thus, for example, whereas both Americans and Indians value helping family and friends, Americans tend to approach this as a matter for discretionary personal decision making, while Hindu Indians tend to approach this as a relatively noncontingent role-related duty (Miller, Bersoff, & Harwood, 1990; Miller & Bersoff, 1998). In an example from the domain of relationships, research highlights the cultural boundedness of theories of romantic love (LeVine, Sata, Hashimoto, & Veerma, 1995). It has been shown that, within Hindu Indian communities, marital love entails emphases on duty, sacrifice, tolerance, and compromise, that are not central to North American conceptions (Dion & Dion, 1993), whereas, within Chinese cultural communities, romantic love tends even to be evaluated in negative terms, as hedonistic (Shaver, Wu, & Schwartz, 1992). In an example from the domain of achievement, it has been found that the focus on the individual in existing theories is not adequate to characterize achievement orientations emphasized in collectivist cultural communities (Spence, 1985). For example, it has been demonstrated that in certain Asian cultural groups as well as in certain ethnic minority subgroups within the United States, achievement tends to be experienced as family oriented rather than individually centered (Agarwal & Misra, 1986; Greenfield & Cocking, 1994).

A key motivational question arises in evaluating the relative adaptiveness of these types of duty based and familial motivational stances that tend to be emphasized within different collectivist cultural communities. In giving little weight to individual self-determination and freedom of choice – factors which existing motivational theories treat as highly important – such motivational stances are frequently assumed to be less personally satisfying, if not also less adaptive, than the motivational orientations emphasized within individualistic cultural communities. Reflecting this type of appraisal, Spence (1985), for example, has portrayed individualistic cultures as more agentic than collectivist cultures, and Hui and Triandis have characterized collectivism as, at its core, involving "the subordination of individual goals to the goals of collectives" (Hui & Triandis, 1986, pp. 244–5).

Recent cultural work on motivation, however, is increasingly challenging these types of assumptions that agency is linked only with individualism and is highlighting the qualitatively different ways that agency is experienced in contrasting cultural communities. The argument is forwarded that in cultural groups in which the self tends to be conceptualized as inherently social rather than as inherently autonomous, individuals are more prone to experience their true selves as expressed in the realization of social expectations rather than in acting autonomously (Miller, 1997b) . Consonant with this assertion, it has been demonstrated that whereas Americans interpret helping as more endogenously motivated and satisfying when individuals are acting autonomously rather than in response to social expectations, Indians regard helping as just as endogenously motivated and satisfying in the two types of cases (Miller & Bersoff, 1994). In a behavioral investigation of this issue, it has been shown that European–American children show less intrinsic motivation when choices on anagram and game tasks are made for them either by their mothers or by their peer group, as compared with when they make these choices for themselves (Iyengar & Lepper, 1999). In striking contrast, Asian–American children display highest levels of intrinsic motivation when acting to fulfill the expectations of these trusted others.

Extending this type of cultural perspective to issues of socialization, cultural work is demonstrating that not only the meaning but also the adaptive consequences of particular modes of socialization are culturally dependent. Whereas in European–American cultural communities authoritarian modes of parenting tend to be associated with more maladaptive outcomes than are less controlling authoritative modes of parenting (Baumrind, 1971), this same relationship does not obtain in various Asian cultural communities. Unlike European–American adolescents, Korean adolescents, for example, associate greater perceived parental warmth with greater perceived parental control (Rohner & Pettengil, 1985). Such effects reflect the view of parents in Korean culture as having a responsibility to exercise authority over their children, with the failure to exercise this authority experienced as parental neglect and associated with maladaptive outcomes (see also Berndt, Cheung, Lau, & Hau, 1993). Equally, it has been demonstrated that socialization practices among Chinese–American mothers combine an emphasis on training and control that tends to be experienced in positive terms and to be associated with higher levels of school achievement than are less controlling parenting styles (Chao, 1994).

Summary   In sum, work on emotions and motivation is uncovering respects in which cultural meanings and practices impact on the form of psychological processes. Culture is shown to influence which emotions are emphasized as well as more centrally whether or not particular somatic and physiological experiences are even interpreted in emotional terms. Research is also uncovering certain assumptions in existing psychological theories of motivation that appear specific to cultures emphasizing individualistic cultural beliefs and practices. Importantly, cultural investigations are demonstrating that there is not one particular mode of socialization that is optimum under all circumstances, but rather that the adaptive significance of particular modes of socialization depends, in part, on the practices, goals, and views of the self given cultural emphasis.

Implications

The present arguments for the importance of a cultural perspective in social psychology underscore the integral role which culture plays in psychological processes. A cultural psychology perspective, it may be seen, is compatible with, if not integrally related to, other major thrusts in the field, at the same time that it forwards a new vision that promises to broaden existing social psychological theory. To fully realize this vision, however, requires a commitment by investigators to take culture into account in their research and to address key conceptual and methodological challenges.

As the work discussed in this chapter illustrates, investigators in cultural psychology acknowledge the importance of uncovering universals and of engaging in comparison. It is recognized not only that there are many important universals to be identified, but that establishing commonality is critical to any claim of difference and to any attempts at comparison – whether the explicit comparisons of cross-cultural research or the implicit comparisons of ethnographic case studies. In contrast to both mainstream psychology and the research tradition of cross-cultural psychology, however, work in cultural psychology does not privilege universals. Rather, it is maintained that to the extent that many psychological phenomena depend on socioculturally contingent processses, they are likely to assume culturally, if not also cohort-specific, forms. It is also recognized that in many cases the universals that have been identified in social psychological theory to date suffer either from being so general that they are relatively uninformative, or from being spurious, in that they describe processes which, in fact, are culturally specific.

The thrust of cultural psychology is compatible with much recent work in evolutionary theory and in other biological based approaches, as well as with many of the findings of research on automaticity. In fact, a key challenge is to work toward integrating the insights of these diverse perspectives. The perspective of cultural psychology has a critical role to play in explaining ways in which biologically given genotypes, such as innate aspects of the human cognitive architecture, give rise to variable phenotypes, such as culturally specific cognitive biases, as well as in highlighting respects in which cultural beliefs and practices may be nonrational in nature and thus not fully explicable in adaptive terms. It must be understood that cultural processes may, in certain cases, be patterned by biological constraints and affordances, while, in other cases, they may bear an open relationship to these biological propensities. In regard to automatic cognition, the assumption must be avoided that nonconscious situational influences, such as those captured by the "mere exposure" effect, do not depend on cultural mediation. Rather, it must be recognized that one of the most striking features of culture is the degree to which cultural processes operate outside of conscious awareness, with individuals experiencing many cultural beliefs and practices as part of the natural order and being unaware of their influences on their behavior.

Importantly, bringing a cultural perspective more centrally into the basic constructs and theories of social psychology will not occur inevitably, given the practices in the field that contribute to the relative invisibility of culture. It also will not follow merely as a consequence of sampling more culturally diverse populations in research, although such sampling is critically important. Rather, achieving this goal requires that investigators develop greater openness to and understanding of cultural work, as well as that they make increased efforts to insure the cultural as well as psychological sensitivity of the constructs, theories, and procedures that are adopted in psychological inquiry.

In this regard, there is a need to go beyond the stereotypical generalities associated with the individualism/collectivism dichotomy and the related distinction between interdependent/independent cultural views of the self. While powerful, these types of frameworks have resulted in cultures being portrayed in terms that are overly global, uniform, isolated, and unchanging, as well as in limited attention being given to contextual variation in behavior. Effort must also be made to avoid approaching culture merely as a cognitive schema, with the circularity entailed in such a conception. Rather, greater attention needs to be directed to respects in which cultural influences on psychological phenomena depend on individuals' participation in cultural practices and on their involvement with cultural artifacts and tools (Cole, 1996; Markus, Mullally, & Kitayama, 1997). Investigators also need to be more open to diverse methodological approaches, not only through making greater use of qualitative methods themselves, but also by taking into account the findings and insights of ethnographic work on psychological questions. Finally, if not most crucially, effort must be made to enhance the cultural sensitivity of the constructs that are brought to bear in psychological inquiry, and to insure that research methodologies are sensitive enough to tap culturally based variation in psychological outlooks. Just as much of the most innovative and important work in social psychology has stemmed from investigators drawing on their own culturally based experiences to formulate new research questions and identify new constructs, there is a need at this juncture to bring a broader base of cultural knowledge to bear in the creation of future psychological theory.

In conclusion, bringing culture more centrally into the constructs and procedures of the field constitutes a move that is both contributing insight into existing social psychological theory, at the same time that it is identifying new possibilities for human psychological functioning. A cultural psychology perspective promises to give greater weight to human agency, with its treatment of mind and psyche as, in part, social creations, rather than as the result of processes that are fully mechanistically or organismically determined. It also stands to increase the cultural inclusiveness of psychology, in its key insight that there is no single population that can serve as a normative baseline for human development (Shweder & Sullivan, 1993).

Notes

1   The only other citation for culture made in the volume refers to a single page in the chapter on social identification by Deaux (1996).
2   The major contrast between cross-cultural and cultural psychology is conceptual, not methodological. Work in cultural psychology views culture and psychology as mutually constitutive and treats basic psychological processes as culturally dependent, if not also, in certain cases, as culturally variable. In contrast, work in cross-cultural psychology treats psychological processes as formed independently of culture, with cultural impacting on their display but not on their basic form.

References

Agarwal, R., & Misra, G. (1986). A factor analytic study of achievement goals and means: An Indian view. *International Journal of Psychology, 21 (6)*, 717–731.
Allport, G. W. (1937). *Personality: A psychological interpretation.* New York: Holt.
Bargh, J. A. (1996). Automaticity in social psychology. In E. T. Higgins & A. W. Kruglanski (Eds.), *Social psychology: Handbook of basic principles* (pp. 169–183) New York: Guilford Press.
Baumeister, R. F. (1987). How the self became a problem: A psychological review of historical research. *Journal of Personality and Social Psychology, 52*, 163–176.
Baumeister, R. F., Tice, D. M., & Hutton, D. G. (1989). Self-presentational motivations and per-

sonality differences in self-esteem. *Journal of Personality, 57,* 547–579.

Baumrind, D. (1968). Authoritarian vs. authoritative parental control. *Adolescence, 3 (11),* 255–272.

Baumrind, D. (1971). Current patterns of parental authority. *Developmental Psychology Monographs, 4 (1 Part 2).*

Berndt, T. J., Cheung, P. C., Lau, S., & Hau, K. (1993). Perceptions of parenting in mainland China, Taiwan, and Hong Kong: Sex differences and societal differences. *Developmental Psychology, 29 (1),* 156–164.

Berry, J. W., Poortinga, Y. H., Segall, M. H., & Dasen, P. R. (1992). *Cross-cultural psychology: Research and applications.* Cambridge, UK: Cambridge University Press.

Bond, M. H. (Ed.) (1996). *The handbook of Chinese psychology.* New York: Oxford University Press.

Bond, M. H., & Cheung, T. S. (1983). College students' spontaneous self-concept: The effect of culture among respondents in Hong Kong, Japan, and the United States. *Journal of Cross-Cultural Psychology, 14,* 153–171.

Brockner, J., & Chen, Y. (1996). The moderating roles of self-esteem and self-construal in reaction to a threat to the self: Evidence from the People's Republic of China and the United States. *Journal of Personality and Social Psychology, 71 (3),* 603–615.

Brislin, R. W. (1983). Cross-cultural research in psychology. *Annual Review of Psychology, 34,* 363–400.

Bruner, J. (1990). *Acts of meaning.* Cambridge, MA: Harvard University Press.

Cahan, E. D., & White, S. H. (1992). Proposals for a second psychology. Special Issue: The history of American psychology. *American Psychologist, 47,* 224–235.

Chao, R. K. (1994). Beyond parental control and authoritarian parenting style: Understanding Chinese parenting through the cultural notions of training. *Child Development, 65,* 1111–1119.

Choi, I., & Nisbett, R. E. (1998). Situational salience and cultural differences in the correspondence bias and actor–observer bias. *Personality and Social Psychology Bulletin, 25 (9),* 949–960.

Choi, I., Nisbett, R. E., & Norenzayan, A. (1999). Causal attribution across cultures: Variation and universality, *Psychological Bulletin, 125 (1),* 47–63.

Choi, I., Nisbett, R. E., & Smith, E. E. (1997). Culture, category salience, and inductive reasoning. *Cognition, 65,* 15–32.

Cole, M. (1996). *Cultural Psychology: A once and future discipline.* Cambridge, MA: Harvard University Press.

Cousins, S. D. (1989). Culture and self-perception in Japan and the United States. *Journal of Personality and Social Psychology, 56,* 124–131.

Deaux K. (1996). Social identification. In E. T. Higgins & A. W. Kruglanski (Eds.), *Social psychology: Handbook of basic principles* (pp. 777–798) New York: Guilford Press.

Deci, E. L. & Ryan, R. M. (1985). *Intrinsic motivation and self-determination in human behavior.* New York: Plenum Press.

Diener, E. & Diener, M. (1995). Cross-cultural correlates of life satisfaction and self-esteem. *Journal of Personality and Social Psychology, 68,* 653–663.

Dion, K. K., & Dion, K. L. (1993). Individualistic and collectivistic perspectives on gender and the cultural context of love and intimacy. *Journal of Social Issues, 49 (3),* 53–69.

Dumont, L. (1970). *Homo hierarchius: An essay on the caste system.* Chicago: University of Chicago Press.

Ellsworth, P. C. (1994). William James and emotion: Is a century of fame worth a century of misunderstanding? *Psychological Review, 101 (2),* 222–229.

Endo, Y., Heine, S. J, & Lehman, D. R. (in press). Culture and positive illusions in relationships: How my friendship is better than yours. *Personality and Social Psychology Bulletin.*

Fiske, A. P., Kitayama, S., Markus, H. R., & Nisbett, R. (1998). The cultural matrix of social psychology. In D. Gilbert, S. Fiske, & G. Lindzey (Eds.), *The cultural matrix of social psychology.* 4th edn. (pp. 915–981). New York: Random House.

Geertz, C. (1973). *The interpretation of cultures.* New York: Basic Books.

Gilligan, C. (1982). *In a different voice: Psychological theory and women's development.* Hillsdale, NJ: Lawrence Erlbaum Associates.

Greenfield, P. M. & Cocking, R. R. (1994). *Cross-cultural roots of minority child development*. Hillsdale, NJ: Lawrence Erlbaum Associates.

Hallowell, A. I. (1955). The self and its behavioral environment. In A. I. Hallowell (Ed.), *Culture and experience* (pp. 75–110). Philadelphia: University of Pennsylvania Press.

Heine, S. J., & Lehman, D. R. (1997a). Culture, dissonance, and self-affirmation. *Personality and Social Psychology Bulletin, 23,* 389–400.

Heine, S. J. & Lehman, D. R. (1997b). The cultural construction of self-enhancement: An examination of group-serving biases. *Journal of Personality and Social Psychology, 72,* 1268–1283.

Heine, S. J., Takata, T., & Lehman, D. R. (in press). Beyond self-presentation: Evidence for self-criticism among Japanese. *Personality and Social Psychology Bulletin.*

Heine, S. J., Lehman D. R., Markus, H. R., & Kitayama, S. (in press). Is there a universal need for positive self-regard? *Psychological Review.*

Herzog, A. R., Franks, M., Markus, H., & Holmberg, D. (1994). Sociocultural variation in the American self. Paper presented at the meeting of Gerontological Society of America, Atlanta, GA.

Higgins, E. T., & Kruglanski, A. W. (1996). *Social psychology: Handbook of basic principles*. New York: Guilford Press.

Hui, C. H., & Triandis, H. C. (1986). Individualism–collectivism: A study of cross-cultural researchers. *Journal of Cross-Cultural Psychology, 17,* 222–48.

Ip, G. W. M., & Bond, M. H. (1995). Culture, values, and the spontaneous self-concept. *Asian Journal of Psychology, 1,* 29–35.

Iyengar, S. S., & Lepper, M. R. (1999). Rethinking the value of choice: A cultural perspective on intrinsic motivation. *Journal of Personality and Social Psychology, 76 (3),* 349–366.

Jahoda, G. (1993). *Crossroads between culture and mind: Continuities and change in theories of human nature*. Cambridge, MA: Harvard University Press.

James, W. (1890). *Principles of psychology*. New York: Holt.

Kanagawa, C., Cross, S., & Markus, H. R. (1999). "Who am I?": The cultural psychology of the conceptual self. Manuscript submitted for publication.

Kashima, Y., Siegal, M., Tanaka, K., & Kashima, E. S. (1992). Do people believe behaviors are consistent with attitudes? Towards a cultural psychology of attribution processes. *British Journal of Social Psychology, 31,* 111–124.

Kelly, H. H. (1972). Causal schemata and the attribution process. In E. E. Jones et al. (Eds.), *Attribution: Perceiving the causes of behavior*. Morristown, NJ: General Learning Press.

Kitayama, S. & Karasawa, M. (1997). Implicit self-esteem in Japan: Name letters and birthday numbers. *Personality and Social Psychology Bulletin, 23 (7),* 736–742.

Kitayama, S., & Masuda, T. (1995). Reappraising cognitive appraisal from a cultural perspective. *Psychological Inquiry, 6 (3),* 217–223.

Kitayama, S., Markus, H. R., & Kurokawa, M. (1998). Does the nature of good feelings depend on culture?: A Japan–United States comparison. Unpublished manuscript.

Kitayama, S. Takagi, H., & Matsumoto, H. (1995). Causal attribution of success and failure: Cultural psychology of the Japanese self. *Japanese Psychological Review, 38,* 247–280.

Kitayama, S., Markus, H. R., Matsumoto, H., & Norasakkunkit, V. (1997). Individual and collective processes of self-esteem management: Self-enhancement in the United States and self-depreciation in Japan. *Journal of Personality and Social Psychology, 72,* 1245–1267.

Kwan, V. S. Y., Bond, M. H., & Singelis, T. M. (1997). Pancultural explanations for life satisfaction: Adding relationship harmony to self-esteem. *Journal of Personality and Social Psychology, 73,* 1038–1051.

Lee, F., Hallanhan, M., & Herzog, T. (1996). Explaining real life events: How culture and domain shape attributions. *Personality and Social Psychology Bulletin, 22,* 732–741.

Lee, Y., & Seligman, M. E. P., (1997). Are Americans more optimistic than the Chinese? *Personality and Social Psychology Bulletin, 23 (1),* 32–40.

Levenson, R. W., Ekman, P., Heider, K., & Friesen, W. V. (1992). Emotion and autonomic nervous system activity in the Minangkabau of West Sumatra. *Journal of Personality and Social Psychology, 62,* 972–988.

LeVine, R. A. (1984). Properties of culture: An ethnographic view. In R. A. Shweder & R. A.

LeVine (Eds.), *Culture theory: Essays on mind, self, and emotion* (pp. 67–87). Cambridge: Cambridge University Press.

LeVine, R. A., Sato, S., Hashimoto, T., & Verma, J. (1995). Love and marriage in eleven cultures. *Journal of Cross-Cultural Psychology, 26,* 554–571.

Levy, R. I. (1984). Emotion, knowing, and culture. In R. A. Shweder & R. A. LeVine (Eds.), *Culture theory: Essays on mind, self, and emotion* (pp. 214–237). Cambridge: Cambridge University Press.

Lloyd, G. E. R. (1990). *Demystifying mentalities.* New York: Cambridge University Press.

Malpass, R. S. (1988). Why not cross-cultural psychology?: A characterization of some mainstream views. In M. H. Bond (Ed.), *The cross-cultural challenge to social psychology. Cross-cultural research and methodology series, Volume 11* (pp. 29–35). Beverly Hills: Sage Publications.

Markus, H. R., Kitayama, S., & Heiman, R. J. (1996). Culture and "basic" psychological principles. In E. T. Higgins & A. W. Kruglanski (Eds.), *Social Psychology: Handbook of basic principles* (pp. 857–913). New York: Guilford Press.

Markus, H. R., Mullally, P. R., & Kitayama, S. (1997). Selfways: Diversity in modes of cultural participation. In U. Neisser (Ed.), *The conceptual self in context: Culture, experience, self-understanding* (pp. 13–61). New York: Cambridge University Press.

Markus, H. R., Smith, J., & Moreland, R. L. (1985). Role of the self-concept in the perception of others. *Journal of Personality and Social Psychology, 49,* 6, 1494–1512.

Mauro, R., Sato, K., & Tucker, J. (1992). The role of appraisal in human emotions: A cross-cultural study. *Journal of Personality and Social Psychology, 62,* 301–317.

Messick, D. M. (1988). On the limitations of cross-cultural research in social psychology. In M. H. Bond (Ed.), *The cross-cultural challenge to social psychology. Cross-cultural research and methodology series, Volume 11* (pp. 41–47). Beverly Hills: Sage Publications.

Miller, J. G. (1984). Culture and the development of everyday social explanation. *Journal of Personality and Social Psychology, 46,* 961–978.

Miller, J. G. (1987). Cultural influences on the development of conceptual differentiation in person description. *British Journal of Developmental Psychology, 5,* 309–319.

Miller, J. G. (1994). Cultural diversity in the morality of caring: Individually oriented versus duty-based interpersonal moral codes. *Cross-Cultural Research, 28,* 3–39.

Miller, J. G. (1996). Theoretical issues in cultural psychology. In J. W. Berry, Y. H. Poortinga, & J. Pandey (Eds.), *Handbook of cross-cultural psychology, Vol. 1: Theory and Method* (pp.85–128). Boston: Allyn & Bacon.

Miller, J. G. (1997a). Theoretical issues in cultural psychology. In J. W. Berry, J. Poortinga, & J. Pandey (Eds.), *Handbook of cross-cultural psychology: Vol. 1. Theoretical and methodological perspectives.* Revd. edn. (pp. 85–128). Boston: Allyn & Bacon.

Miller, J. G. (1997b). Cultural conceptions of duty: Implications for motivation and morality. In D. Munro, J. E. Schumaker, & S. C. Carr (Eds.), *Motivation and culture* (pp. 178–193). New York: Routledge.

Miller, J. G. (1999). Cultural psychology: Implications for basic psychological theory. *Psychological Science, 10 (2),* 85–91.

Miller, J. G., & Bersoff, D. M. (1994). Cultural influences on the moral status of reciprocity and the discounting of endogenous motivation. *Personality and Social Psychology Bulletin, 20:* The self and the collective: Groups within individuals. Special issue.

Miller, J. G., & Bersoff, D. M. (1998). The role of liking in perceptions of the moral responsibility to help: A cultural perspective. *Journal of Experimental Social Psychology, 34,* 443–469.

Miller, J. G., Bersoff, D. M., & Harwood, R. (1990). Perceptions of social responsibilities in India and the United States: Moral imperatives or personal decisions? *Journal of Personality and Social Psychology, 58,* 33–47.

Morris, M. W., & Peng, K. (1994). Culture and cause: American and Chinese attributions for social and physical events. *Journal of Personality and Social Psychology, 67,* 949–971.

Morris, M. W., Nisbett, R. E., & Peng, K. (1995). Causal understanding across domains and cultures. In D. Sperber, D. Premack, and A. J. Premack (Eds.), *Causal cognition: A multidisciplinary debate* (pp. 577–612). Oxford: Oxford University Press.

Nakamura, H. (1985). *Ways of thinking of Eastern peoples*. Honolulu: University of Hawaii Press.

Neisser, U. (1988). Five kinds of self-knowledge. *Philosophical Psychology, 1*, 35–59.

Nisbett, R. E. (in press). Essence and accident: Back to the future with Ned Jones and the correspondence bias. In J. Cooper and J. Darley (Eds.), *Attribution processes, person perception, and social interaction: The legacy of Ned Jones*. Washington, DC: American Psychological Association.

Nisbett, R. E., & Ross, L. (1980). *Human inference: Strategies and shortcomings of social judgment*. Englewood Cliffs, NJ: Prentice-Hall.

Norenzayan, A., Nisbett, R. E., & Smith, E. E. (1998). Rule based vs. memory based category learning East and West. Unpublished manuscript, University of Michigan.

Peng, K., & Nisbett, R. E. (1997). Cross-cultural similarities and differences in the understanding of physical causality. In M. Shield (Ed.), *Proceedings of conference on culture and science*. Frankfort: Kentucky State University Press.

Rohner, R. P., & Pettengill, S. M. (1985). Perceived parental acceptance–rejection and parental control among Korean adolescents. *Child Development, 56*, 524–528.

Russell, J. A. (1991). Culture and the categorization of emotions. *Psychological Bulletin, 110*, 426–450.

Russell, J. A. (1994). Is there universal recognition of emotion from facial expression? A review of the cross-cultural studies. *Psychological Bulletin, 115 (1)*, 102–141.

Russell, J. A., & Yik, M. S. M. (1996). Emotion among the Chinese. In M. H. Bond (Ed.), *The handbook of Chinese psychology* (pp. 166–188). Hong Kong: Oxford University Press.

Sahlins, M. (1976). *Culture and practical reason*. Chicago: University of Chicago Press.

Schwartz, T. (1992). Anthropology and psychology: An unrequited relationship. In T. Schwartz, G. M. White, & C. Lutz (Eds.), *New directions in psychological anthropology* (pp.324–349). New York: Cambridge University Press.

Segall, M. H., Lonner, W. J., & Berry, J. W. (1988). Cross-cultural psychology as a scholarly discipline: On the flowering of culture in behavioral research. *American Psychologist, 53 (10)*, 1101–1110.

Shaver, P. R., Wu, S., & Schwartz, J. C. (1992). Cross-cultural similarities and differences in emotion and its representation. In M. S. Clark (Ed.), *Emotion: Review of Personality and Social Psychology, Number 13* (pp. 175–212). Newbury Park, CA: Sage Publications.

Shikanai, K. (1978). Effects of self-esteem on attribution of success and failure. *Japanese Journal of Experimental Social Psychology, 18 (1)*, 35–46.

Shweder, R. A. (1990). Cultural psychology – what is it? In J. W. Stigler, R. A. Shweder, & G. Herdt (Eds.), *Cultural psychology: Essays on comparative human development* (pp. 1–43). New York: Cambridge University Press.

Shweder, R. A. (1994). "You're not sick, you're just in love": Emotion as an interpretive system. In P. Ekman & R. J. Davidson (Eds.), *The nature of emotion: Fundamental questions*. New York: Oxford University Press.

Shweder, R. A., & Bourne, L. (1984). Does the concept of the person vary cross-culturally? In R. A. Shweder & R. A. LeVine (Eds.), *Culture theory: Essays on mind, self, and emotion* (pp. 158–199). New York: Cambridge University Press.

Shweder, R. A. & Sullivan, M. A. (1993). Cultural psychology: who needs it? *Annual Review of Psychology, 44*, 497–523.

Shweder, R. A., Goodnow, J., Hatano, G., LeVine, R. A., Markus, H., & Miller, P. (1998). The cultural psychology of development: One mind, many mentalities. In W. Damon (Series Ed.) & R. M. Lerner (Vol. Ed.), *Handbook of child psychology: Vol. 1: Theoretical models of human development*. 5th edn. (pp. 865–937). New York: John Wiley and Sons.

Spence, J. T. (1985). Achievement American style: The rewards and costs of individualism. *American Psychologist, 40 (12)*, 1285–1295.

Stipek, D. (1998). Differences between Americans and Chinese in the circumstances evoking pride, shame, and guilt. *Journal of Cross-Cultural Psychology, 29 (5)*, 616–629.

Suh, E., Diener, E., Oishi, S., & Triandis, H. (1998). The shifting basis of life satisfaction judgements across cultures: Emotions versus norms. *Journal of Personality and Social Psychology, 74 (2)*, 482–493.

Tedeschi, J. T. (1988). How does one describe a platypus?: An outsider's questions for cross-cultural psychology. In M. H. Bond (Ed.), *The cross-cultural challenge to social psychology. Cross-cultural research and methodology series, Volume 11* (pp.14–28). Beverly Hills: Sage Publications.

Triandis, H. C. (1980). Introduction. In H. C. Triandis & W. E. Lambert (Eds.), *Handbook of cross-cultural psychology, Vol. 1: Perspectives* (pp. 1–14). Boston: Allyn & Bacon.

Wertsch, J. V. (1995) Sociocultural research in the copyright age. *Culture and Psychology, 1,* 81–102.

Whiting, B. B., & Whiting J. W. (1975). *Children of six cultures: A psycho-cultural analysis.* Cambridge, MA: Harvard University Press.

Wierzbicka, A. (1992).Talking about emotions: Semantics, culture and cognition. *Cognition and Emotion, 6,* 285–319.

Yeh, C. (1995). The clinical grounding of self and morality in Japan and the US. Unpublished doctoral dissertation, Stanford University.

Chapter Three

A Lifespan Developmental Perspective

Kevin Durkin

How does early human experience affect later progress? How do cognitive developments affect interaction with the social world? What promotes progress in human cognition and action? How can we characterize development beyond childhood?

These are basic questions for developmental psychologists, but they are also questions which overlap with the interests of social psychologists. If we delete the developmental keywords, we have just flagged classic issues revolving around the interaction of person and situation, the relative influence of internal and external variables, and the causes of cognitive, attitudinal, and behavioral change. That is not to say that social psychology can provide answers to all the developmentalist's questions, but simply to note a convergence of interests. In earlier phases of the history of psychology, developmental and social themes were in fact regarded as closely interwoven (Lewin, 1952), but the massive expansion of the field during the second half of the twentieth century resulted in compartmentalization and an often only remote and stilted interchange of ideas.

Nevertheless, many recent advances in theory and research have followed from cross-fertilization of developmental and social psychology (see Durkin, 1995; Ruble & Goodnow, 1998, for reviews). This chapter examines just some of the issues that arise at the areas of intersection between these two fields. The primary emphasis will be on intrapsychological processes – the "mental mechanics" that are presumed to unfold within the individual (Tesser, 1995, p. 7) – though it will soon become clear that the intrapersonal cannot be cordoned off from the interpersonal; it will also be clear that each field can learn from the other in this respect. In particular, it will be argued that an initial preoccupation of developmentalists with the inner mechanisms of the developing mind has led to sometimes unexpected encounters with the social; meanwhile, a preoccupation of social psychologists with interpersonal influences and relationships has led not only to cognition but also to attention to the origins and prospects of human characteristics. Within the space available, it will not be attempted to review the entirety of the human lifespan and the potential grounds for collaboration between developmental and social psychologists at each age or stage or on every theme. Instead, some key current topics in developmental psychology will be discussed with an emphasis on the relationship between developing cognitive processes and social reasoning or behavior. The focus will be on topics arising initially from research into the earlier parts of the lifespan, but their implications for development through adulthood will be illustrated. We begin in infancy, considering recent work on perceptual development and attachment. Then we turn to cognitive development, examining reasons why this field is shifting from the study of isolated mini-scientists to active social participants.

Infancy: Perception, Communication, and Social Selectivity

Traditionally, infants have been viewed (by lay people and some psychologists) as helpless and malleable. Clearly, in some quite fundamental respects human beings at this stage of life are dependent upon others: they are unable to meet their own physical needs (feeding, cleansing, finding shelter) and are unable to move around or engage in discussion. Observations such as these led to a widespread belief that the child is shaped by experience. The strongest expressions of this assumption have been provided by behaviorist psychologists, who assert that the child is the product of its reinforcement history (Skinner, 1953; Watson, 1924) and whose theories and methods in turn influenced the early development of social learning theory (Bandura & Walters, 1963), itself one of the major prospective meeting grounds for social and developmental psychology. Although these manifestations of the empiricist tradition were very influential in American psychology in the first half of the twentieth century, there have been longstanding alternative perspectives, such as the normative, maturational account offered by Gesell and his collaborators (Gesell & Ilg, 1943) and the constructivist genetic epistemology of Piaget and his followers (Piaget, 1971; Inhelder & Piaget, 1958). With respect to infancy, for example, Piaget (1952) stressed the active role of the child in discovering and continually refining his or her own capacities in light of their impact on the environment.

Over the last couple of decades, research by developmentalists specializing in infancy has shifted the pendulum away from the "blank slate" empiricist assumptions and in many respects beyond the constructivist and even some of the maturationist positions. Evidence has been accumulating that human infants are more richly endowed than earlier biologically oriented scientists supposed. Much of this work has been focused on infants' perceptual abilities, and an overarching concern has been to gauge infants' intrapsychological processes, asking questions such as: how do they interpret sensory information? Do they discern patterns? Can they make predictions? Although these are matters of "mental mechanics," a brief review will illustrate that the implications for our understanding of social development have never been far from the surface.

Perceptual Development

The human infant's visual system provides a crucial means of exploring and reacting to the physical and social environment (Bremner, 1994; Mehler & Dupoux, 1994). Although newborns' visual acuity is less than perfect, they can certainly take in a great deal of visual information and they soon show signs of pursuing it actively (Wentworth & Haith, 1998; Maurer & Lewis, 1998; von Hofsten, 1998). Within the first couple of months, infants can switch visual attention from objects immediately in front of them to events (such as a light flashing) on the periphery of their visual field (Atkinson, Hood, Wattam-Bell, & Braddick, 1992; Maurer & Lewis, 1998). It has long been known that infants have visual preferences: they devote more attention to some shapes than others. Fantz (1961, 1963) measured one- to six-month-olds' visual attention to a variety of stimuli, ranging from plain colors to complex symmetrical and asymmetrical patterns. The results showed clearly that the babies preferred (fixated for longer on) the complex patterns, and especially the symmetrical ones. Subsequent research has confirmed that children in the first year can discern a great deal of information in visual stimuli. For example, by three or four months they are able to organize complex visual configurations, distinguishing between intersecting forms (Quinn, Brown, & Streppa, 1998) and exploiting illusory contours to perceive boundaries and depth (Johnson & Aslin, 1998).

Infants' hearing also enables them to process important aspects of the environment. Although hearing is not fully developed at birth, very young infants are able to discriminate among sounds that vary in volume, duration, and repetitiveness (Kellman & Arterberry, 1998) and to organize their perception of the spatial environment (Clifton, 1992). Some of the starkest evidence against the "empty vessel" theory of human nature comes from the infant's discrimination among tastes and smells (Mennella & Beauchamp, 1997). Babies are not passive when it comes to food and drink, and display clear preferences. For example, their sucking rate increases for sweet liquids, but decreases for salty or bitter liquids (Crook, 1987). They show by their facial or vocal expressions whether they like or dislike a particular taste, and will protest vigorously if offered something they find unpalatable (Blass, 1997; Blass & Ciaramitaro, 1994; Chiva, 1983). They react to smells in similar ways. Their facial expressions or head orientations reveal whether they find a smell pleasant or unpleasant (Soussignan, 1997).

These preferences are by no means arbitrary, and may well have survival value. For example, one of the forms that appears particularly to interest babies is that of the face. Faces are very informative features of the social environment, helping us to distinguish among conspecifics and to derive information about the significance of surrounding stimuli or events. It has long been known that faces hold infants' attention and elicit smiles (Ahrens, 1954; Fantz, 1961; Spitz & Wolf, 1946). Some evidence indicates that even neonates less than one hour old prefer illustrations of a human face to other patterns of similar complexity, and they prefer regularly organized representations to pictures which jumble the facial features (Johnson & Morton, 1991). Such early preferences raise the serious (if controversial) possibility that infants have innate "face detectors" which direct their attention to this important aspect of the social environment (de Schonen, Mancini, & Liegeois, 1998; Johnson, 1997; Slater and Butterworth, 1997). There is also evidence that quite young babies can exploit facial cues from others (such as eye movements or emotional displays) in guiding their own exploratory behavior (Butterworth, 1996; Hood, Willen, & Driver, 1998; Nelson, 1987; Papousek & Papousek, 1993).

Preferences among tastes may also have survival value. For example, alcohol is potentially harmful to infants, and research suggests that they would prefer not to drink it (it can be offered indirectly, via their usual supplier). Mennella and Beauchamp (1994) compared babies' consumption of breastmilk when their mothers had been drinking either alcoholic beer or non-alcoholic beer; in the alcohol condition, the babies drank significantly less milk. Similarly, there is evidence that infants are attracted to the smell of amniotic fluid and to milk (Marlier, Schall, & Soussignan, 1998; Mennella & Beauchamp, 1998), and that as early as one or two weeks they can discriminate the smell of their own mother's breasts from those of other breastfeeding women (Porter, Makin, Davis, & Christensen, 1992). An important theme following from much of this work on infant perception is that their abilities to perceive, interpret, and select are more than mental achievements: they provide critical access to other members of the species, and are responded to as such by caregivers. Communication between the infant and parent does not await the emergence of language but proceeds throughout the first year. Very young infants show responsiveness to voices: they orient their attention to speakers, and even their larger body movements indicate sensitivity to the rhythm of speech. Caregivers are usually very responsive to the infant's sounds, treating vocalizations – even the humble burp – as though they were contributions to a conversation (Kaye, 1982). Some researchers in this area argue that infants derive a sense of subjectivity from their perceptual actions upon the world, a rudimentary awareness of their own capacity to action (Trevarthen, 1977). Further, at a very early stage, they become aware of the interrelationships between their own behavior and that of others, thus attaining a sense of primary intersubjectivity (Aitken & Trevarthen, 1997; Trevarthen, 1977, 1993; Hundeide, 1993).

In short, rather than being on the receiving end of a booming, buzzing confusion of events and stimuli which will gradually shape it into the prevailing shared culture, the infant attends selectively from the outset and displays preferences and desires – sometimes very forcefully. But the responsiveness of others is nevertheless critical to the engagement of these abilities with the social world and variations in the opportunities available will affect their development.

Social Selectivity

Perceptual abilities are exploited extensively by the infant in dealing with other people. And other people provide exactly the kinds of stimuli and behavior that infants find interesting. Anyone with an interest in babies and a little patience could provide much of the stimulation (coos, cuddles, facial displays, gentle handling) that infants enjoy, and babies will generally respond to opportunities for interaction with others. However, quite early in life, they begin to show one of the distinguishing features of human social behavior: selectivity (Schaffer, 1996). Schaffer and Emerson (1964) followed a sample of Scottish infants during the first year, observing them in various social situations at home with primary caregivers (mother, father, grandparents, etc.) and female strangers. By monitoring the babies' nonverbal reactions, they found a gradual increase in preference for specific individuals from around age 5 months. It appears that by at least the middle of the first year, the child has formed an attachment (or attachments) to a specific person (or persons). At around the same time, the child begins to show a quite different reaction – anxiety – when approached by unfamiliar people. The development of the two aspects of social selectivity – attachment and wariness – are closely related in onset and developmental significance (Schaffer & Emerson, 1964; Schaffer, 1996).

Many social developmentalists maintain that the formation of attachments is a vital aspect of early relations. Through attachment, the infant maximizes opportunities for nurturance and protection, establishing a secure base from which to explore the rest of the world (Bowlby, 1988). According to Bowlby, through the course of the first attachment (to the principal caregiver) the infant also begins to formulate an internal working model (an intrapsychological representation) of what a relationship involves. Ainsworth and colleagues have proposed that there are three main types of attachment relationship formed by infants and their caregivers (Ainsworth, Blehar, Waters, & Wall, 1978). This typology was tested by observing infants' reactions to a laboratory test (the "Strange Situation") in which the baby is initially playing with his or her mother and then approached by a stranger; after a while the mother leaves, and later she returns (and this departure–return sequence may be repeated).

Based on a careful coding system, scoring details of the child's responses throughout the session, Ainsworth and colleagues identified the following three types of relationship:

Type A: Insecurely attached: Avoidant. This infant is relatively indifferent to the mother's presence, does not seem greatly disturbed by her departure and does not show enthusiasm for contact on her return.

Type B: Securely attached. Infant plays happily in the new environment, shows some distress when the mother departs (especially for a second time), but responds positively to her return.

Type C: Insecurely attached: Resistant. Infant tends to explore less, is greatly distressed by the mother's departure, but is difficult to console upon her return and may struggle to be released from her embrace.

Much subsequent research has supported this classification (see van Ijzendoorn & Kroonenberg, 1988) and it has been used in studies of early child development around the world. Ainsworth and colleagues (1978) found that approximately 70 percent of infants form Type B relationships, and about 20 percent fall into Type A, 10 percent into Type C relationships. If it is true that the primary attachment is the base from which the infant begins to tackle the rest of life's challenges, then it follows that the Type B child has an advantage. Feeling secure and supported, he or she is ready to explore and learn; if problems occur, the caregiver is there, but the child should feel confident to try things out. Furthermore, because the basic relationship is a positive and enjoyable one, the child expects (has an internal working model) that other relationships will be enjoyable, and hence responds favorably to opportunities for social interaction. Many studies show that Type B infants tend to demonstrate higher levels of cognitive and social skills (Suess, Grossmann, & Sroufe, 1992; Meins, Fernyhough, Russell, & Clark-Carter, 1998; Youngblade & Belsky, 1992). The topic is controversial (see Schaffer, 1996), but it does appear that the quality of the infant's initial relationship can predict aspects of subsequent development.

Infancy Research in a Lifespan Perspective

We have considered just two active areas of research focused on infancy and early childhood: perceptual development and attachment. Both topics remind us that early developments provide foundations for later – an unremarkable conclusion for the developmentalist but an often neglected consideration for the social psychologist. Recent research illustrates just how important these foundations are. Reflecting the balance of research relating these topics to social psychological issues, we will note perceptual issues briefly and concentrate chiefly on attachment.

Perceptual Abilities

Perceptual abilities, of course, remain important beyond infancy, as a rather large field of psychology amply demonstrates. Intersubjectivity, which it was noted above emerges within the first few weeks of life, is a distinctive, species-specific feature of human social organization henceforth (Aitken & Trevarthen, 1997; Haslam, 1997), though it is still surprisingly little studied by mainstream social psychologists. (Interestingly, it does come to the fore among colleagues concerned with problems in human social behavior and adjustment, such as clinical psychologists and psychoanalysts; cf. Harwood & Pines, 1998). Developments at the opposite end of the lifespan highlight what we take for granted in perceptual development along the way: there is a strong connection between sensory functioning and intelligence in old age (Baltes & Lindenberger, 1997; Lindenberger & Baltes, 1997). The reductions in perceptual acuity with old age are often associated with a reduced sense of competence (Whitbourne, 1996). Gradual deficits in hearing, for example, can affect older people's ability to process speech in the context of other noise (Schneider, 1997), which in turn affects their ease of interaction with other people. Other people also respond differently to older individuals' actual or imagined communicative difficulties (Kemper, 1994; Ryan, Bourhis, & Knops, 1991; Williams & Giles, 1998), thereby compromising the interaction by conveying a presumption of incompetence. In short, although research into perceptual change in adulthood has been oriented primarily around psychobiological and information processing dimensions, it has direct relevance to social psychologists studying communication, self-esteem, attitudes, and intergenerational relations.

Attachment in Adulthood

Bowlby (1988) saw the initial infant–caregiver attachment as providing the crucial foundation to much of later development: from the working model of the initial relationship the child develops expectancies which govern her or his approach to subsequent relationships. Clearly, as adults we do form attachments to other people and, just as in infancy, these relationships are intensely emotional. Just as in infancy, our adult attachments motivate us to seek proximity to the person we feel we need, to engage in extensive eye contact, to hold, and, just as in infancy, we tend to become distressed at separation (Hazan & Shaver, 1987). Shaver and colleagues (Hazan & Shaver, 1987; Shaver & Clark, 1996; Mickelson, Kessler, & Shaver, 1997) have gone further, to argue that the types of attachments we form as adults can be classified using a framework similar to that Ainsworth and others developed to account for infant attachments, namely secure, anxious/ambivalent, and avoidant.

Securely attached lovers find intimate relationships comfortable and rewarding; they trust their partner, and feel confident of his/her commitment. Anxious/ambivalent lovers experience uncertainty in their relationships; sometimes, they fret that their partner does not love them enough and might leave, and they may respond to this anxiety by putting pressure on the partner, running the risk that this will cause the very outcome they fear. Avoidant lovers find getting close to others uncomfortable, find it difficult to trust others, and are reluctant to commit themselves fully to a relationship. Shaver and colleagues found that the proportions of adults who fall into these types is very similar to those of infant attachments, with (approximately) 59 percent secure, 11–19 percent anxious/ambivalent, and 25 percent avoidant (Hazan & Shaver, 1987; Mickelson et al., 1997).

Other research supports the attachment theorist's expectation that adults who fall into these different types recall their childhood relationships with their parents in ways that are consistent with these patterns. That is, the secure types reported relaxed and loving parents, the anxious/ambivalent felt their parents were over-controlling, and the avoidant reported lower levels of communication and emotional support from their parents (Rothbard & Shaver, 1994).

A large body of research has now grown testing predictions derived from attachment theory about adult relationships and adjustment. In general, securely attached adults report more trusting and more enduring relationships (Feeney, Noller, & Patty, 1993; Fincham & Beach, 1999; Fuller & Fincham, 1995; Kirkpatrick & Shaver, 1992; Mikulincer, 1998), more positive orientations toward their family of origin (Diehl, Elnick, Bourbeau, & Labouvie-Vief, 1998), and higher scores on measures of psychological well-being and coping with life stresses (Fraley & Shaver, 1998; Diehl et al., 1998; Mikulincer, Horesh, Levy-Shiff, Manovich, & Shalev, 1998). There is also preliminary evidence that secure attachments contribute to successful adaptation to the challenges of later life (Antonucci, 1994).

However, it would be an exaggeration (not necessarily promoted by attachment theorists) to assume that all of these benefits flow from a particular intrapsychological representation achieved in infancy and serving to filter experience and govern behavior reliably thereafter. First, some developmentalists have pointed out that the initial relationship is typically an enduring one, extending through childhood and beyond; hence, continuity inheres in the interpersonal environment rather than exclusively within the child (Lamb, Thompson, Garner, & Charnov, 1985; Lewis, 1990). Second, there is indisputably a lot more to adult relationships than (even) the affective ties that echo initial infant–parent attachment (Clark & Pataki, 1995; Fincham & Beach, 1999; Tesser, 1988). Ongoing cognitive appraisals, themselves influenced by the closeness of the relationship and the self-relevance of a given event or performance, influence affect (Beach, Tesser, Fincham, Jones, Jonson, & Whitaker, 1998; Tesser & Beach, 1998). Tesser and Beach, for example, found complex patterns of shifts in judgments of close relationships as negative life events increased.

The extension of attachment theory to adult relationships provides a classic example of the developmentalist's – especially the child developmentalist's – natural focus on the prospective consequences of early experience and competencies. However, evidence from social psychology reminds us that human social reasoning and behavior are influenced not only by prior experience, and not only by current situation, but also by anticipation of future events. Elder, George, & Shanahan (1996, pp. 265ff.) point out that individuals respond to life events by interpreting them in relation to an "expectable life course": stressful events may be experienced as more stressful if they occur at times inconsistent with expectations (e.g. an early menopause, the death of a child versus the death of a very old person).

Many social psychologists would agree with the attachment theorists that survival is a pretty powerful and pervasive human motivation, and we have seen that several aspects of early perceptual and cognitive activity appear to be oriented around this goal. This continues as a concern throughout the lifespan, but its salience and explicitness may vary with developmental status. Pittman (1998, p. 576) points out that the young person "immersed in the joys and setbacks of life" is at some time confronted with the uncomfortable realization that eventually life ends. Drawing on terror management theory (Pyszczynski, Greenberg, & Solomon, 1997), Pittman notes that this cognitive attainment has long-term affective consequences which may promote efforts to maintain self-esteem as a symbolic anxiety buffer, and a need for ideational affiliation with those who share similar opinions. From a lifespan perspective, this would predict that self-esteem and preference for similar others should vary as a function of age, health, and consciousness of mortality. There is evidence that this is the case. Older adults also "shift their horizon," anticipating decline on measures of well-being while younger adults expect gains (Ryff, 1991). During adulthood, social comparisons with agemates show self-enhancement biases that become particularly pronounced in areas in which a participant is experiencing problems, and particularly so among older adults (Heckhausen & Brim, 1997; Heckhausen & Kreuger, 1993). In other words, while attachment theory provides a rich basis for studying aspects of adult social relations it should not be taken as a "child determinist" prescription that can be read independently of other intra- and interpersonal processes that operate differently at different stages of the lifespan.

Summary

Some of the concerns of developmentalists working on the earliest stages of the lifespan might at one time have seemed somewhat remote from social psychology. These include work on infant perceptual abilities and attachment. Much of the impetus to research on infant perception came from attempts to reject empiricist theories of human knowledge, and this led to an emphasis on the challenges of uncovering the intrapsychological processes of the very young. Yet studies of these processes led rapidly to the conclusion that they are engaged pervasively in the infant's interpersonal world. While there is abundant evidence of the importance of perceptual processes throughout life, and some important contributions by social psychologists investigating adjustment among older people, there is considerable scope for future theory and research combining both social psychological and lifespan perspectives. The topic of infant–caregiver attachments also seemed very much the preserve of child psychologists until researchers took note of analogous features in adult relationships. This prompted extensive and productive research which now opens questions about the intersection of attachment styles and internal working models with other social cognitive dimensions of relationships and adjustment to lifespan status.

Cognitive Development and Social Processes

Developmental psychology during the last thirty years or so has been dominated by cognitive developmental theories, predominantly Piagetian and several neo-Piagetian offshoots and, more recently, various information processing accounts (for a variety of discussions and positions, see Case, in press; Flavell, Miller, & Miller, 1993; Gardner, 1985; Halford, 1993; Keil, in press; Nelson, 1996). There is by no means unanimity among cognitive developmentalists as to what is entailed in development and how change comes about, but many have rested on an implicit metaphor of the child as an autonomous mini-scientist. That is, the focus has been on how the individual seeker after knowledge obtains and organizes information, develops and tests hypotheses, and progresses by revising his or her earlier schemas. This perspective (very broadly characterized here) has been enormously fruitful, partly as a corrective to earlier empiricist models which attributed little to intrapsychological processes but chiefly as a route to richer conceptions of children's intellectual capacities. Debate tends to revolve around the degree to which the processes are endogenously constrained, whether modes of representation are domain-specific or general, and whether change is continuous or discontinuous.

Cognitive developmental research is very much concerned with the intrapsychological. Yet progress in this field has led, through a variety of routes, to a current focus on social and interpersonal processes. Among the principal routes, one has been a shift in content (i.e. focusing on hitherto neglected areas of developing understanding) and one has been a shift in process (i.e. focusing on new conceptions of how cognition proceeds and develops). These will be considered in turn.

Shifts in Content: Cognition and Social Phenomena

Much mainstream cognitive developmental research has been concerned with the child's understanding of physical, temporal, spatial, and causal phenomena, with the development of logic and the nature of children's problem-solving strategies. But during the late 1970s and the 1980s, researchers became interested in extending cognitive developmental paradigms toward the investigation of social understanding. This possibility was not entirely new: some of Piaget's own seminal texts had set the scene decades earlier (Piaget,

1932; Piaget & Weil, 1951) and sympathizers such as Kohlberg and Selman had maintained a strong tradition of cognitive developmental research in social topics such as morality, sex role acquisition, and social perspective taking (Kohlberg, 1966, 1976; Selman, 1976). Nevertheless, the implications of a cognitive approach to aspects of the child's social world became more widely appreciated in the 1980s as researchers increasingly acknowledged that social behavior often reflected social understanding – the ways in which situations and people were interpreted (cf. Ruble & Goodnow, 1998, p. 749). Again, this coincided with a shift in mainstream social psychology towards a more cognitive framework (Fiske & Taylor, 1991) and at the same time social learning theory was undergoing a major development as it incorporated a greater emphasis on information processing aspects of observational learning (Bandura, 1986).

The outcomes included a proliferation of studies of developmental changes in processes dear to the hearts of social psychologists, such as person perception (Barenboim, 1981; Damon & Hart, 1988; Feldman & Ruble, 1981; Yuill, 1992), concepts of friendship (Berndt, 1981; Hartup & Stevens, 1997; Ladd, 1999; Youniss and Volpe, 1978), social comparison (DePaulo, Tang, Webb, Hoover, Marsh, & Litowtiz, 1989; France-Kaatrude & Smith, 1985; Monteil, 1988; Ruble, 1983), attribution theory (Fincham, 1981; Karniol & Ross, 1976; Lepper, Sagotsky, Dagoe, & Greene, 1982; Kassin & Ellis, 1988; Miller & Aloise, 1989), social stereotypes (Aboud, 1988; Martin, 1989; Martin, Wood, & Little, 1990), and understanding societal structures (Berti & Bombi, 1988; Furth, 1980). (This list notes only a selection of this very large and still growing field; see Durkin (1995) and Ruble & Goodnow (1998) for fuller reviews.)

Most of these studies report age-related changes in the relevant domain. For example, younger children's accounts of friends tend to focus on relatively observable properties such as appearance, possessions, and shared activities, and there is a shift towards awareness of psychological attributes, interdependence, and reciprocal obligations during middle childhood, with a greater grasp of individual variability and inner complexity during adolescence. Social comparisons become more salient, more systematic, and more selective (e.g. as children decide with whom it is pertinent to compare oneself) over the same age range. Knowledge of the social structure becomes not simply more detailed but more sophisticated as children progress from a relatively heteronomous assumption that adults are all-powerful to a grasp of the societal constraints on behavior and agreed mechanisms for conducting business.

Research into the development of ethnic attitudes provides a good illustration of the contributions of this kind of work. It is sometimes assumed that prejudice is socially transmitted (racist parents nurture racist children; Adorno, Frenkel-Brunswik, Levinson, & Sanford, 1950). However, social cognitive developmental research shows that the story is more complex. There is evidence that children sometimes express prejudicial beliefs that their parents find abhorrent; it has also been found that the extent to which children subscribe to these beliefs varies with age (Aboud, 1988). In particular, expressed prejudice against minority outgroups tends to peak in white children at around age six to seven, and decline thereafter.

Aboud (1988) explains developments in terms of a transition from affective through perceptual to cognitive processes. Young children, as noted above, are wary of strangers. Children become sensitive to criteria which distinguish others from the self, and ethnicity is a relatively accessible one. Gradually, children acquire the relevant intergroup labels and assimilate cultural information about differences among social categories. For example, Jewish children in Israel acquire the label and the concept "an Arab" very early in life, and although their knowledge base about Arab people may be quite slender, the term has negative connotations with violence and aggression (Bar-Tal, 1997).

During middle childhood, however, other social cognitive developments moderate initially simplistic and exaggerated social judgments. These include a developing understanding of individual differences among members of a social category, the ability to distinguish the inner qualities of a person from his or her appearance, recognition of the arbitrariness of ethnic affiliation, and appreciation that social perceptions can be reciprocated. The outcome is a reduction in ingroup bias and prejudice against outgroups during this period (see Aboud, 1988, for a review of empirical evidence).

But there are limitations to this account. Some have argued that the decline in overt prejudice often reported in developmental studies may actually reflect increasing skill in providing socially desirable responses (Brown, 1995; Katz & Kofkin, 1997; Nesdale, in press). Certainly, ethnic stereotyping and prejudice do not disappear by adulthood, and there are clearly individual differences in this respect (Brown, 1995; Devine, 1995). The less prejudiced attitudes or decisions of older children might be interpreted as precursors of the "modern racism" phenomenon (McConahay, 1986; Monteith, 1996; Schnake & Ruscher, 1998), whereby individuals overtly reject traditional racist beliefs but express hostility towards other races indirectly (e.g. by opposition to anti-racist policies).

There is also evidence that the developmental course of prejudice interacts with social context. For example, in an Australian study Black-Gutman and Hickson (1996) obtained age-related developments broadly consistent with Aboud's account but also found that European Australian children showed greater hostility to Aboriginal Australians than to Asian Australians – a differential which is consistent with broader prejudices in the adult society. Furthermore, while the pattern of early ingroup favoritism peaking around age six to seven appears well supported in studies of white children in white societies, minority children in the same societies follow more variable paths (Aboud, 1988; Brown, 1995). Several researchers have reported that black children show a prowhite bias (Asher & Allen, 1969; Clark & Clark, 1947; Katz & Kofkin, 1997; Vaughan, 1964). One possible explanation has been couched in terms of social comparison processes and Social Identity Theory (Brown, 1995; Vaughan, 1987): essentially, white children may derive positive self-esteem from evidence that their ethnic group has superior social status, while minority children may arrive at the opposing inference about their group and thus develop preferences against it. Another, complementary possibility arises from studies of the family contexts within which children learn about race: Katz and Kofkin (1997) report that, among American families, black parents were more likely to discuss racial identity than were white parents (48 percent vs. 12 percent). The African American parents explained their input in terms of the child's need to be aware of race differences and to be prepared for the reality of encounters with prejudice. As Katz and Kofkin remark, "Ignorance of the 'other' is a luxury that minority group members cannot afford" (ibid., p. 67).

These considerations do not contradict the assumption that there is an important intrapsychological component to the developmental course of ethnic prejudice, but they do show once again that cognition is not detached from context. Similarly, recent social psychological research indicates that modern racism among adults is sensitive to contextual factors, such as normative information about stereotypic beliefs (Monteith, Deneen, & Tooman, 1996; Wittenbrink & Henly, 1996).

Shifts in Process: Interpersonal Aspects of Cognition

Somewhat independent of these developments in social cognition, yet converging on similar concerns, has been the explosion of research into children's theories of mind (Astington, Harris, & Olson, 1989; Bartsch & Wellman, 1995; Flavell, 1999; Wimmer & Perner, 1983). "Theory of mind" (ToM), as used in this literature, denotes an awareness that people have an internal mental life that affects their behavior yet is not directly accessible to others. How and when children attain this awareness is of interest to developmentalists in light of traditional theories which presume cognitive development proceeds from the concrete to the abstract, and claims that children below the age of about six years are "realists" who cannot distinguish between a mental image and its object (Piaget, 1929).

Part of the initial stimulus to ToM research came from comparative psychological study of chimpanzee cognition (Premack & Woodruff, 1978) and epistemological debate about the nature of intentionality (Dennett, 1978). In brief, these kinds of concerns led researchers to ask whether the child can understand that behavior reflects perception, belief, and intention. So, although not born of the same parents as the contemporaneous subfield of developmental social cognition, ToM research has resulted in a complementary channel: an emphasis on uncovering the intrapsychological processes of the naive individual confronted with the complex phenomena of the peopled world.

Research in this area has shown that by about age three, normally developing children can distinguish between mental and physical realities, can understand that people cannot observe their thoughts and can distinguish psychological from physical or biological causation (Flavell, Miller, & Miller, 1993; Wellman, Hickling, & Schult, 1997; Watson, Gelman, & Wellman, 1998). However, there is also experimental evidence that preschool and even older children have difficulties with some aspects of theory of mind, including the relationship between belief and perceptually based knowledge, understanding deception (i.e. attempts to create a false belief in others), and distinguishing between another person's belief and their own (Chandler, Fritz, & Hala, 1989; Durkin & Howarth, 1997; Gopnik & Astington, 1988; Moses & Flavell, 1990; Wimmer & Perner, 1983; Taylor, 1988).

Importantly, though, as ToM research has progressed, it has moved increasingly beyond its initial focus on intrapsychological processes. One reason reflects disparities in findings produced by different research methods. Much of the early work highlighting limitations to the young child's ToM was experiment based. However, researchers studying preschoolers' allusions to mental processes in more naturalistic contexts, such as spontaneously occurring parent–child discourse, noted many examples of explicit, meaningful and context-appropriate references to mental states, emotions, desires, and intentions (Bartsch & Wellman, 1995; Dunn, 1988), and purposeful uses of deception (e.g. by three-year-olds motivated to convince a parent that they were innocent of domestic misdeeds; Dunn, 1988, in press). That is, children manifest a fuller understanding of mind in everyday life much earlier than some experimental studies might have suggested.

A second reason for the shift is still more pertinent from a social psychological perspective, and it relates to the question of where theory of mind comes from (Astington, 1999; Dunn, in press; Flavell, 1999; Nelson, Plesa, & Henseler, 1998). Several studies have pointed to the contributions of interpersonal and emotional experiences (Cole & Mitchell, 1998; Dunn, Brown, Slomkowski, Tesla, & Youngblade, 1991; Hughes & Dunn, 1977; Lewis, Freeman, Kyriakidou, Maridaki-Kassotaki, & Berridge, 1996; Peterson & Siegal, 1997). For example, preschoolers from larger families tend to perform better in standard ToM tasks, possibly because older siblings render mental states salient through play and language (Jenkins & Astington, 1996; Perner, Ruffman, & Leekham, 1994; Ruffman, Perner, Naito, Parkin, & Clements, 1998). There is also evidence of links between ToM and communicative competence and interaction (Sabbagh & Callanan, 1998; Ziatas, Durkin, & Pratt, 1998). That is, individual differences in children's understanding of mental states are associated with variations in opportunities to join in interpersonal exchanges about these topics and the intensity of affective engagement that they precipitate (Dunn, in press). The shift of ToM research towards social processes is interesting because it has occurred almost despite the field's origins in individualistic approaches to cognitive development.

Progress elsewhere within cognitive developmental research has increasingly exposed the limits of some of the longstanding premises of the field (Case, in press; Keil, in press). Keil depicts the most prominent of these as a "solipsistic" preoccupation with internal mental machinery – that is, with exclusively intrapsychological processes that operate independently of content and context. In contrast, he draws an analogy with Gibsonian theory of perception to emphasise that there is a relationship between mental structures and the structure of what is being cognized. Keil remarks: "cognitive development can no more study the acquisition of knowledge by merely looking at the machinery inside the head than visual neurophysiology can study the retina by merely looking at retinal anatomy and not considering the nature of light."

Other influential current frameworks with quite different origins also underscore the critical implication of interpersonal processes in social cognitive development. These include the sociocognitive conflict theory of Doise and Mugny and their co-workers (Doise, Mugny, & Perez, 1998; Doise & Mugny, 1984), the revival of Vygotskyan approaches (Rogoff, 1990; van der Veer & Valsiner, 1991; Wertsch, in press), and developmental applications of Moscovici's social representations theory (Carugati & Selleri, 1998; Duveen & Lloyd, 1990). Although there are important differences among these theories (see Azmitia, 1996; Durkin, 1995; Goodnow, 1998), they share an assumption (and provide a great deal of evidence) that the development of cognition is grounded in social interactions. Doise and Mugny emphasize the consequences of exposure to alternative perspectives or solutions: their research shows that children can achieve new levels of understanding through problem solving with peers. Vygotskyans point to the fact that, in development, most knowledge is encountered initially on the social plane and only subsequently transferred to the individual. Researchers in social representations maintain that knowledge depends on sharing the same symbolic system and that development depends on gaining access to collective representations.

Cognitive Developmental Research in Lifespan Perspective

Although there are vast literatures on cognition and social cognition in adults, most of the work is adevelopmental (see also Blank, 1982; Valsiner & Lawrence, 1997). Nevertheless, there has been strong interest in qualitative changes in adult cognition, inspired in part by Riegel's (1976) proposal that adult experiences expose us to a new level of cognitive challenge: the discovery of dialectical (opposing) forces. Riegel argued that achieving the intellectual ability to deal with the contradictions that confront us in the complexity of the social world requires progress to a higher stage of reasoning (than captured in developmental theory such as Piaget's). He called this the stage of dialectical operations, now more commonly labeled as "postformal thought." Research into postformal reasoning indicates that development continues well into adulthood (Blanchard-Fields, 1986; Kramer, 1989; Kitchener & King, 1989; Labouvie-Vief, 1989; Sinnott, 1998).

Some researchers in social cognition have also pointed to developmental changes in the areas mentioned earlier, such as social comparison (Ruble & Frey, 1991), attribution processes (Blank, 1982; Rankin & Allen, 1991), and impression formation (Hess, 1994; Hess, McGee, Woodburn, & Bolstad, 1998). Ruble and Frey, for example, show that as people move through the lifespan their needs and reference points for social comparisons alter, depending on how skilled they are in a given domain, how important the attainment in the domain is to them and their peers, and the implications of different comparisons for self-esteem. Pratt and Norris (1994) show that although there are declines in some areas of social reasoning in later life, there are also gains (see also Baltes & Staudinger, 1996; Schwarz, Park, Knaueper, & Sudman, 1999).

This small but growing body of literature makes it clear that development in this respect is certainly not complete by early adulthood; indeed, even more than other areas of human development, there are good reasons for assuming that the experiences and shifting statuses of adult life promote and affect the course of social cognitive development. But if we are to progress in our study of it, then perhaps we should take heed of the lesson arising from the more extensive efforts of child developmentalists in this area: namely, that even the approaches most focused initially on the intrapsychological facets of social cognition have emerged with strong emphases on the interpsychological context (see also Schwarz et al., 1999).

Summary

Developmental psychologists have in recent years devoted increasing attention to the child's understanding of social and mental phenomena. Much of this work arose within individualistic traditions where the child is seen as a mini-scientist learning about the world. However, as the work has progressed, it has been driven increasingly to take note of aspects of the social context, either as influences on the content which is made salient or as factors in the very process of achieving understanding. In short, cognitive developmentalists have reached the point where, rather than assuming that inherent processes provide the foundation for engagement with all aspects of the world, the world is part of the processes all along. Although there is a large related body of research into social cognition in adults, this literature has not always accorded developmental features a prominent place. Yet there are irrefutable arguments that we continue to develop throughout life, and growing evidence that developmental status interacts with social cognition in complex ways. It has been suggested here that social psychologists could profit from the developmentalists' discovery that these processes may be social.

Conclusions

From a social psychological perspective, it would be very convenient if developmental psychologists could offer a compact set of clearly demarcated stages in which we knew reliably what individuals of a given age can and cannot do. Social psychologists interested in a given topic could take note of the developmental antecedents of adult behavior, and perhaps admit the possibility of further changes with aging, but then could get on with the job of studying the phenomena of interest within a particular age group (say, college students). Unfortunately, not only is developmental psychology unable to provide a ready-made framework, but the more the subdiscipline has to do with its neighbor, the more elusive such a packaging becomes. Similarly, from a developmental perspective, it would be very welcome if social psychologists could explain the conjunction of intrapersonal and interpersonal dimensions of cognition, affect, and behavior. Unfortunately, social psychologists have often settled for studying one or the other (intra- or inter-) and to some extent it could even be said that "social" has become associated with the presumed objects of human reasoning rather than with the mental processes through which it is enacted.

It has been argued here that recent work in developmental psychology directed to uncovering intrapsychological processes and their unfolding has led repeatedly to encounters with interpersonal processes. Infants' inherent perceptual abilities are more remarkable than was once thought, but their uses are closely linked to their engagements with other people. Infants' social relations (attachments) implicate cognitive representations (working models) but no one would claim that these are dissociable from emotional and interactive experiences. Most models of cognitive development presume internal activity, yet even paradigms which began with a commitment to uncovering these in the solitary mini-scientist have been driven to incorporate the child's interactions with others.

The point is not that intrapsychological processes do not occur or are not worthy of study, but rather that they are not the full story (Wertsch, in press) and, still more importantly, they may not be adequately understood if we attempt to investigate them in artificially arranged isolation from interpsychological processes. Two simple messages emerge for social psychology, which would be embarrassing to mention except for the fact that they have been so widely neglected. One is that cognition is socially situated (see also Schwarz, 1998), and the second is that social situations and their participants change through the lifespan (see also Elder, George, & Shanahan, 1996).

References

Aboud, F. E. (1988). *Children and prejudice*. Oxford: Blackwell Publishers.

Adorno, T. W., Frenkel-Brunswik, E., Levinson, D. J., & Sanford, R. N. (1950). *The authoritarian personality*. New York: Harper.

Ahrens, R. (1954). Beitrag zuer Entwiklung der Physiognomie und Mimikerkennens. *Zietschrift fur Experimentelle und Angewandte Psychologie, 2*, 414–514.

Ainsworth, M. D. S., Blehar, M., Waters, E., & Wall, E. (1978). *Patterns of attachment*. Hillsdale, NJ: Erlbaum.

Aitken, K. J., & Trevarthen, C. (1997). Self/other organization in human psychological development. *Development and Psychopathology, 9*, 653–677.

Antonucci, T. C. (1994). Attachment in adulthood and aging. In M. B. Sperling & W. H. Berman (Eds.), *Attachment in adults: Clinical and developmental perspectives* (pp. 256 –272). New York: Guilford.

Asher, S. R., & Allen, V. L. (1969). Racial preference and social comparison processes. *Journal of Social Issues, 25*, 157–167.

Astington, J. (1999). What is theoretical about the child's theory of mind? A Vygotskian view of its development. In P. Lloyd & C. Fernyhough (Eds.), *Lev Vygotsky: Critical assessments, future directions* Vol. IV (pp. 401–418). New York: Routledge.

Astington, J. W., Harris, P. L., & Olson, D. R. (Eds.) (1988). *Developing theories of mind*. New York: Cambridge University Press.

Atkinson, J. W., Hood, B., Wattam-Bell, J., & Braddick, O. (1992). Changes in infants' ability to switch visual attention in the first three months of life. *Perception, 21*, 643–653.

Azmitia, M. (1996). Peer interactive minds: Developmental, theoretical, and methodological issues. In P. B. Baltes & U. M. Staudlinger (Eds.), *Interactive minds: Life-span perspectives on the social foundations of cognition* (pp. 133–162). Cambridge, UK: Cambridge University Press.

Baltes, P. B., & Lindenberger, U. (1997). Emergence of a powerful connection between sensory and cognitive functions across the adult life span: A new window to the study of cognitive aging? *Psychology and Aging, 12*, 12–21.

Baltes, P. B., & Staudinger, U. M. (Eds.) (1996). *Interactive minds: Life-span perspectives on the social foundation of cognition*. New York: Cambridge University Press.

Baltes, P. B., Staudinger, U. M., & Lindenberger, U. (1999). Lifespan psychology: Theory and application to intellectual functioning. *Annual Review of Psychology, 50*, 471–507.

Bandura, A. (1986). *Social foundations of thought and action: A social cognitive theory*. Englewood Cliffs, NJ: Prentice-Hall.

Bandura, A., & Walters, R. H. (1963). *Social learning and personality development*. New York: Holt.

Barenboim, C. (1981). The development of person perception in childhood and adolescence: From behavioral comparisons to psychological constructs to psychological comparisons. *Child Development, 52*, 129–144.

Bar-Tal, D. (1997). Development of social categories and stereotypes in early childhood: The case of "the Arab" concept formation, stereotype and attitudes by Jewish children in Israel. *International Journal of Intercultural Relations, 20*, 341–370.

Bartsch, K., & Wellman, H. M. (1995). *Children talk about the mind*. Oxford: Oxford University Press.

Beach, S. R. H., Tesser, A., Fincham, F. D., Jones, D. J., Jonson, D., & Whitaker, D. J. (1998). Pleasure and pain in doing well together: An investigation of performance-related affect in close relationships. *Journal of Personality and Social Psychology, 74*, 923–938.

Berndt, T. J. (1981). Relations between social cognition, nonsocial cognition, and social behavior: The case of friendship. In J. H. Flavell & L. Ross (Eds.), *Social cognitive development: Frontiers and possible futures* (pp. 121–148). Cambridge, UK: Cambridge University Press.

Berti, A. E., & Bombi, A. S. (1988). *The child's construction of economics*. Cambridge, UK: Cambridge University Press.

Black-Gutman, D., & Hickson, F. (1996). The relationship between racial attitudes and social-cognitive development in children: An Australian study. *Developmental Psychology, 32,* 448–456.

Blanchard-Fields, F. (1986). Reasoning on social dilemmas varying in emotional saliency: An adult developmental perspective. *Psychology and Aging, 1,* 325–333.

Blank, T. O. (1982). *A social psychology of developing adults.* New York: Wiley.

Blass, E. M. (1997). Infant formula quiets crying human newborns. *Journal of Developmental and Behavioral Pediatrics, 18,* 162–165.

Blass, E. M., & Ciaramitaro, V. (1994). A new look at some old mechanisms in human newborns: Taste and tactile determinants of state, affect, and action. *Monographs of the Society for Research in Child Development, 59,* v–81.

Bowlby, J. (1988) *A secure base: Parent–child attachment and healthy human development.* New York: Basic Books.

Bremner, J. G. (1994). *Infancy.* 2nd. edn. Oxford: Blackwell Publishers.

Brown, R. (1995). *Prejudice: Its social psychology.* Oxford: Blackwell Publishers.

Butterworth, G. (1996). Pointing, joint visual attention and referential communication. In J. Georgas, M. Manthovli, E. Besevegis, & A. Koffevi (Eds.), *Contemporary psychology in Europe* (pp. 144–154). Seattle: Hodgrefe & Huber.

Carugati, F. F., & Selleri, P. (1998). Social representations and development: Experts' and parents' discourses about a puzzling issue. In U. Flick (Ed.), *The psychology of the social* (pp. 170–185). Cambridge, UK: Cambridge University Press.

Case, R. (in press). Cognitive development. In M. Bennett (Ed.), *Developmental psychology: Achievements and prospects.* London: Psychology Press.

Chandler, M., Fritz, A. S., & Hala, S. (1989). Small-scale deceit: Deception as a marker of two-, three-, and four-year-olds' early theories of mind. *Child Development, 60,* 1263–1277.

Chi, M., Hutchinson, J. E., & Robin, A. E. (1989). How inferences about novel domain-related concepts can be constrained by structured knowledge. *Merrill-Palmer Quarterly, 35,* 27–62.

Chiva, M. (1983). Gout et communication non verbale chez le jeune enfant. *Enfance, 1–2,* 53–64.

Clark, K. B., & Clark, M. P. (1947). Racial identification and preference in negro children. In E. E. Maccoby, T. M. Newcomb, & E. L. Hartley (Eds.), *Readings in social psychology.* London: Methuen.

Clark, M. S., & Pataki, S. P. (1995). Interpersonal processes influencing attraction and relationships. In A. Tesser (Ed.), *Advanced social psychology* (pp. 283–331). New York: McGraw-Hill.

Clifton, R. (1992). The development of spatial hearing in human infants. In L. A. Werner & E. W. Rubel (Eds.), *Developmental psychoacoustics* (pp. 135–157). Washington, DC: American Psychological Association.

Cole, K., & Mitchell, P. (1998). Family background in relation to deceptive ability and the understanding of the mind. *Social Development, 7,* 181–197.

Crook, C. (1987). Taste and olfaction. In P. Salapatek & L. Cohen (Eds.), *Handbook of infant perception* Vol. 1. Orlando, FL: Academic Press.

Damon, W., & Hart, D. (1988). *Self-understanding in childhood and adolescence.* Cambridge, UK: Cambridge University Press.

de Schonen, S., Mancini, J., & Liegeois, F. (1998). About functional cortical specialization: The development of face recognition. In F. Simion & G. E. Butterworth (Eds.), *The development of sensory, motor and cognitive capacities in early infancy: From perception to cognition.* (pp. 103–120). Hove, UK: Psychology Press.

Dennett, D. C. (1978). Beliefs about beliefs. *Behavioral and Brain Sciences, 1,* 568–570.

DePaulo, B. M., Tang, J., Webb, W., Hoover, C., Marsh, K., & Litowitz, C. (1989). Age differences in reactions to help in a peer tutoring context. *Child Development, 60,* 423–439.

Dessureau, B. K., Kurowski, C. O., & Thompson, N. S. (1998). A reassessment of the role of pitch and duration in adults' responses to infant crying. *Infant Behavior and Development, 21,* 367–371.

Devine, P. G. (1995). Prejudice and out-group perception. In A. Tesser (Ed.), *Advanced social psychology* (pp. 467–524). New York: McGraw-Hill.

Diehl, M., Elnick, A. B., Bourbeau, L. S., & Labouvie-Vief, G. (1998). Adult attachment styles: Their relations to family context and personality. *Journal of Personality and Social Psychology, 74,* 1656–1669.

Doise, W., & Mugny, G. (1984). *The social development of the intellect*. Oxford: Pergamon.

Doise, W., Mugny, G., & Perez, J. A. (1998). The social construction of knowledge: social marking and socio-cognitive conflict. In U. Flick (Ed.), *The psychology of the social* (pp. 77–90). Cambridge, UK: Cambridge University Press.

Dunn, J. (1988). The beginnings of social understanding. 1st edn. Cambridge, MA: Harvard University Press.

Dunn, J. (in press). Mindreading and social relationships. In M. Bennett (Ed.), *Developmental psychology: Achievements and prospects*. London: Psychology Press.

Dunn, J., Brown, J., Slomkowski, C., Tesla, C., & Youngblade, L. (1991). Young children's understanding of other people's feelings and beliefs: Individual differences and their antecedents. *Child Development, 62* (6), 1352–1366.

Durkin, K. (1995). *Developmental social psychology: From infancy to old age*. Oxford: Blackwell Publishers.

Durkin, K., & Howarth, N. (1997). Mugged by the facts? Children's ability to distinguish their own and witnesses' perspectives on televised crime events. *Journal of Applied Developmental Psychology, 18*, 245–256.

Duveen, G., & Lloyd, B. (Eds.) (1990). Social representations and the development of knowledge. Cambridge, UK: Cambridge University Press.

Elder, G. H., Jr, George, L. K., & Shanahan, M. J. (1996). Psychosocial stress over the life course. In H. B. Kaplan (Ed.), *Psychosocial stress: Perspectives on structure, theory, life course, and method* (pp. 247–292). Orlando, FL: Academic Press.

Fantz, R. L. (1961). The origin of form perception. *Scientific American, 204*, 66–72.

Fantz, R. L. (1963). Pattern and vision in newborn infants. *Science, 140*, 296–297.

Feeney, J. A., Noller, P., & Patty, J. (1993). Adolescents' interactions with the opposite sex: Influence of attachment style and gender. *Journal of Adolescence, 16*, 169–189.

Feldman, N. S., & Ruble, D. N. (1981) The development of person perception: cognitive and social factors. In S. S. Brehm, S. M. Kassin, & F. X. Gibbons (Eds.), *Developmental social psychology: Theory and research*. New York: Oxford University Press.

Fincham, F. D. (1981). Developmental dimensions of attribution theory. In J. Jaspars, F. Fincham, & M. Hewstone (Eds.), *Attribution theory and research*, Vol. 1 (pp. 45–73). London: Academic Press.

Fincham, F. D., & Beach, S. R. H. (1999). Conflict in marriage: Implications for working with couples. *Annual Review of Psychology, 50*, 47–77.

Fiske, S., & Taylor, S. (1994). *Social cognition*. 2nd. edn. Reading, MA: Addison-Wesley.

Flavell, J. H. (1999). Cognitive development: Children's knowledge about the mind. *Annual Review of Psychology, 50*, 21–45.

Flavell, J. H., Miller, P. H., & Miller, S. A. (1993). *Cognitive development*. 3rd. edn. Englewood Cliffs, NJ: Prentice-Hall.

Fraley, R. C., & Shaver, P. R. (1998). Airport separations: A naturalistic study of adult attachment dynamics in separating couples. *Journal of Personality and Social Psychology, 75*, 1198–1212.

France-Kaatrude, A.-C., & Smith, W. P. (1985) Social comparison, task motivation, and the development of self-evaluative standards in children. *Developmental Psychology, 6*, 1080–1089.

Fuller, T. L., & Fincham, F. D. (1995). Attachment style in married couples: Relation to current marital functioning, stability over time, and method of assessment. *Personal Relationships, 2*, 17–34.

Furth, H. G. (1980). *The world of grown-ups: Children's conceptions of society*. New York: Elsevier.

Gardner, H. (1985). *The mind's new science: A history of the cognitive revolution*. New York: Basicbooks.

Geen, J. A., Gustafson, G. E., & McGhie, A. C. (1998). Changes in infants' cries as a function of time in a cry bout. *Child Development, 69*, 271–279.

Gesell, A., & Ilg, F. L. (1943). *Infant and child in the culture of today: the guidance of development in home and nursery school*. London: Hamish Hamilton.

Goodnow, J. J. (in press). Families and development. In M. Bennett (Ed.), *Developmental psychology: Achievements and prospects*. London: Psychology Press.

Gopnik, A., & Astington, J. W. (1988). Children's understanding of representational change and its relation to the understanding of false belief and the appearance–reality distinction. *Child Development, 59*, 26–37.

Halford, G. S. (1993). *Children's understanding: The development of mental models*. Hillsdale, NJ: Erlbaum.

Hartup, W. W., & Stevens, N. (1997). Friendships and adaptation in the life course. *Psychological Bulletin, 121*, 355–370.

Harwood, I. N. H., & Pines, M. (Eds.) (1998). *Self experiences in group: Intersubjective and self psychological pathways to human understanding*. London: Jessica Kingsley Publishers.

Haslam, N. (1997). Four grammars for primate social relations. In J. A. Simpson & D. T. Kenrick (Eds.), *Evolutionary social psychology* (pp. 297–316). Mahwah, NJ: Lawrence Erlbaum.

Hazan, C., & Shaver, P. (1987) Romantic love conceptualized as an attachment process. *Journal of Personality and Social Psychology, 52*, 511–524.

Heckhausen, J., & Brim, O. (1997). Perceived problems for self and others: Self-protection by social downgrading throughout adulthood. *Psychology and Aging, 12*, 610–619.

Heckhausen, J., & Krueger, J. (1993). Developmental expectations for the self and most other people: Age grading in three functions of social comparison. *Developmental Psychology, 29*, 539–548.

Hess, T. M. (1994). Social cognition in adulthood: Aging-related changes in knowledge and processing mechanisms. *Developmental Review, 14*, 373–412.

Hess, T. M., McGee, K. A., Woodburn, S. M., & Bolstad, C. A. (1998). Age-related priming effects in social judgments. *Psychology and Aging, 13*, 127–137.

Hood, B. M., Willen, J. D., & Driver, J. (1998). Adult's eyes trigger shifts of visual attention in human infants. *Psychological Science, 9*, 131–134.

Hughes, C., & Dunn, J. (1997). "Pretend you didn't know": Preschoolers' talk about mental states in pretend play. *Cognitive Development, 12*, 477–499.

Hundeide, K. (1993). Intersubjectivity and interpretive background in children's development and interaction. *European Journal of Psychology of Education, 8*, 439–450.

Inhelder, B., & Piaget, J. (1958). *The growth of logical thinking: From childhood to adolescence: An essay on the construction of formal operational structures*. London: Routledge & Kegan Paul.

Jenkins, J. M., & Astington, J. W. (1996). Cognitive factors and family structure associated with theory of mind development in young children. *Developmental Psychology, 32*, 70–78.

Johnson, M. H. (1997). *Developmental cognitive neuroscience*. Oxford: Blackwell Publishers.

Johnson, M. H., & Morton, J. (1991). *Biology and cognitive development: the case of face recognition*. Oxford: Blackwell Publishers.

Johnson, S. P., & Aslin, R. N. (1998). Young infants' perception of illusory contours in dynamic displays. *Perception, 27*, 341–353.

Karniol, R., & Ross, M. (1976). The development of causal attributions in social perception. *Journal of Personality and Social Psychology, 34*, 455–464.

Kassin, S. M., & Ellis, S. A. (1988). On the acquisition of the discounting principle: An experimental test of a social-developmental model. *Child Development, 59*, 950–960.

Katz, P. A., & Kofkin, J. A. (1997). Race, gender, and young children. In S. S. Luthar, J. A. Burack, D. Cicchetti, & J. R. Weisz (Eds.), *Developmental psychopathology: Perspectives on adjustment, risk, and disorder* (pp. 51–74). Cambridge, UK: Cambridge University Press.

Kaye, K. (1982). *The mental and social life of babies*. Chicago: Chicago University Press.

Keil, F. C. (in press). Cognition, content and development. In M. Bennett (Ed.), *Developmental psychology: Achievements and prospects*. London: Psychology Press.

Kellman, P. J., & Arterberry, M. (1998). *The cradle of knowledge: Development of perception in infancy*. Cambridge, MA: Bradford Books.

Kemper, S. (1994). Elderspeak: Speech accommodation to older adults. *Aging Neuropsychology and Cognition, 1*, 17–28.

Kirkpatrick, L. A., & Davis, K. E. (1994). Attachment style, gender, and relationship stability: A longitudinal analysis. *Journal of Personality and Social Psychology, 66*, 502–512.

Kirkpatrick, L. A., & Shaver, P. R. (1992). An attachment-theoretical approach to romantic love and religious belief. *Personality & Social Psychology Bulletin, 18*, 266–275.

Kitchener, K. S., & King, P. M. (1989). The Reflective Judgment Model: Ten years of research. In M. L. Commons, C. Armon, L. Kohlberg, F. A . Richards,, T. A. Grotzer, & J. D. Sinnott (Eds.), *Adult development*, Vol. 2: *Models and methods in the study of adolescent and adult thought* (pp. 63–78). New York: Praeger.

Kohlberg, L. (1966). A cognitive–developmental analysis of children's sex-role concepts and attitudes. In E. E. Maccoby (Ed.), *The development of sex differences* (pp. 82–173). Stanford, CA: Stanford University Press.

Kohlberg, L. (1976). Moral stages and moralization: The cognitive–developmental approach. In T. Lickona (Ed.), *Moral development and behavior: Theory, research, and social issues*. New York: Holt.

Kramer, D. A. (1989). Development of an awareness of contradiction across the life span and the question of postformal operations. In M. L. Commons, J. D. Sinnott, F. A. Richards, & C. Armon (Eds.), *Adult development*, Vol. 1: *Comparisons and applications of developmental models* (pp. 133–159). New York: Praeger.

Labouvie-Vief, G. (1989). Modes of knowledge and the organization of development. In M. L. Commons, C. Armon, L. Kohlberg, F. A . Richards, T. A. Grotzer, & J. D. Sinnott (Eds.), *Adult development*, Vol. 2: *Models and methods in the study of adolescent and adult thought* (pp. 43–62). New York: Praeger.

Ladd, G. W. (1999). Peer relationships and social competence during early and middle childhood. *Annual Review of Psychology, 50*, 333–359.

Lamb, M. E., Thompson, R. A., Garner, W., & Charnov, E. L. (1985) *Infant–mother attachment: The origins and significance of individual differences in Strange Situation behavior*. Hillsdale, NJ: Erlbaum.

Lepper, M. R., Sagotsky, G., Dagoe, J., & Greene, D. (1982). Undermining children's intrinsic interest with extrinsic rewards: A test of the "overjustification" hypothesis. *Journal of Personality and Social Psychology, 28*, 129–137.

Lerner, R. M., & Galambos, N. L. (1998). Adolescent development: challenges and opportunities for research, programs, and policies. *Annual Review of Psychology, 49*, 413–446.

Lewin, K. (1952). *Field theory in social science*. London: Tavistock.

Lewis, C., Freeman, N. H., Kyriakidou, C., Maridaki-Kassotaki, K., & Berridge, D. M. (1996). Social influences on false belief access: Specific sibling influences or general apprenticeship? *Child Development, 67*, 2930–2947.

Lewis, M. (1990) Social knowledge and social development. *Merrill-Palmer Quarterly, 36*, 93–116.

Lindenberger, U., & Baltes, P. B. (1997). Intellectual functioning in old and very old age: Cross-sectional results from the Berlin Aging Study. *Psychology and Aging, 12*, 410–432.

Lumma, V., Vuorisalo, T., Barr, R. G., & Lehtonen, L. (1998). Why cry? Adaptive significance of intensive crying in human infants. *Evolution & Human Behavior, 19*, 193–202.

McConahay, J. B. (1986). Modern racism, ambivalence, and the Modern Racism Scale. In J. F. Dovidio & S. L. Gaertner (Eds.), *Prejudice, discrimination, and racism* (pp. 91–125). San Diego, CA: Academic Press.

Marlier, L., Schaal, B., & Soussignan, R. (1998). Neonatal responsiveness to the odor of amniotic and lacteal fluids: A test of perinatal chemosensory continuity. *Child Development, 69*, 611–623.

Marsiske, M., Klumb, P., & Baltes, M. (1997). Everyday activity patterns and sensory functioning in old age. *Psychology and Aging, 12*, 444–457.

Martin, C. L. (1989). Children's use of gender-related information in making social judgments. *Developmental Psychology, 25*, 80–88.

Martin, C. L., Wood, C. H., & Little, J. K. (1990). The relations of gender understanding to children's sex-typed preferences and gender stereotypes. *Child Development, 61*, 1427–1439.

Maurer, D., & Lewis, T. (1998). Overt orienting toward peripheral stimuli: Normal development and underlying mechanisms. In J. E. Richards (Ed.), *Cognitive neuroscience of attention: A developmental perspective* (pp. 51–102). Mahwah, NJ: Lawrence Erlbaum Associates.

Mehler, J., & Dupoux, E. (1994). *What infants know: The new cognitive science of early development*. Oxford: Blackwell Publishers.

Meins, E., Fernyhough, C., Russell, J., & Clark-Carter, D. (1998). Security of attachment as a predictor of symbolic and mentalising abilities: A longitudinal study. *Social Development, 7* (1), 1–24.

Mennella, J. A., & Beauchamp, G. K. (1994). Beer, breast feeding, and folklore. *Developmental Psychobiology, 26,* 459–466.

Mennella, J. A., & Beauchamp, G. K. (1998). The ontogeny of human flavor perception. In G. K. Beauchamp & L. Bartoshuk (Eds.), *Tasting and smelling: Handbook of perception and cognition,* 2nd. edn. (pp. 199–221). San Diego, CA: Academic Press.

Mikulincer, M. (1998). Attachment working models and the sense of trust: An exploration of interaction goals and affect regulation. *Journal of Personality and Social Psychology, 74,* 1209–1224.

Mikulincer, M., Horseh, N., Levy-Shiff, R., Manovich, R., & Shalev, J. (1998). The contribution of adult attachment style to the adjustment to infertility. *British Journal of Medical Psychology, 71,* 265–280.

Miller, P. H., & Aloise, P. A. (1989). Young children's understanding of the psychological causes of behavior: A review. *Child Development, 60,* 257–285.

Monteil, J.-M. (1988). Comparaison sociale. Strategies individuelles et mediations socio-cognitives. Un effet de differenciations comportementales dans le champ scolaire. *European Journal of Psychology of Education, 3,* 3–18.

Monteith, M. J. (1996). Contemporary forms of prejudice-related conflict: In search of a nutshell. *Personality and Social Psychology Bulletin, 22,* 461–473.

Monteith, M. J., Deneen, N. E., & Tooman, G. D. (1996). The effect of social norm activation on the expression of opinions concerning gay men and Blacks. *Basic & Applied Social Psychology, 18,* 267–288.

Moses, L. J., & Flavell, J. H. (1990). Inferring false beliefs from actions and reactions. *Child Development, 61,* 929–945.

Nelson, C. A. (1987). The recognition of facial expressions in the first two years of life: Mechanisms of development. *Child Development, 58,* 889–909.

Nelson, K. (1996). *Language in cognitive development: The emergence of the mediated mind.* Cambridge, UK: Cambridge University Press.

Nelson, K., Plesa, D., & Henseler, S. (1998). Children's theory of mind: An experiential interpretation. *Human Development, 41,* 7–29.

Nesdale, D. (in press). Development of prejudice in children. In M. Augoustinos & K. Reynolds (Eds.), *The psychology of prejudice and racism.* London: Sage.

Papousek, H., & Papousek, M. (1993). Early interactional signalling: The role of facial movements. In A. F. Kalverboer & B. Hopkins (Eds.), *Motor development in early and later childhood: Longitudinal approaches.* European Network on Longitudinal Studies on Individual Development (ENLS) (pp. 136–152). Cambridge, UK: Cambridge University Press.

Papousek, M. (1993). Early interactional signalling: The role of facial movements. In A. F. Kalverboer, A. Fedde, & B. Hopkins (Eds.), *Motor development in early and later childhood: Longitudinal approaches* (pp. 136–152). Cambridge, UK: Cambridge University Press.

Papousek, M., & von Hofacker, N. (1998). Persistent crying in early infancy: A non-trivial condition of risk for the developing mother–infant relationship. *Child: Care, Health & Development, 24,* 395–424.

Perner, J., Ruffman, T., & Leekham, S. R. (1994). Theory of mind is contagious: You catch it from your sibs. *Child Development, 65,* 1228–1238.

Peterson, C. C., & Siegal, M. (1997). Domain specificity and everyday biological, physical, and psychological thinking in normal, autistic, and deaf children. In H. M. Wellman & K. Inagaki (Eds.), *The emergence of core domains of thought: Children's reasoning about physical, psychological, and biological phenomena. New directions for child development,* No. 75. (pp. 55–70). San Francisco: Jossey-Bass.

Piaget, J. (1926). *The language and thought of the child.* London: Kegan Paul.

Piaget, J. (1928). *Judgement and reasoning in the child.* London: Kegan Paul.

Piaget, J. (1929). *The child's conception of the world.* London: Kegan Paul.

Piaget, J. (1932) *The moral judgment of the child.* Harmondsworth: Penguin Books.

Piaget, J. (1952). *The origins of intelligence in children.* Harmondsworth: Penguin Books.

Piaget, J. (1971). *Biology and knowledge: An essay on the relations between organic regulations and cognitive processes*. Chicago: University of Chicago Press.

Piaget, J., & Weil, A. (1951). The development in children of the idea of their homeland and of relations with other countries. *International Social Science Bulletin, 3*, 561–576.

Pittman, T. S. (1998). Motivation. In D. T. Gilbert, S. T. Fiske, & G. Lindzey (Eds.), *The Handbook of Social Psychology*, Vol. 1 4th. edn. (pp. 549–590). Boston: McGraw-Hill.

Porter, R. J., Makin, J. W., Davis, L. B., & Christensen, K. M. (1992). Breast-fed infants respond to olfactory cues from their own mother and unfamiliar lactating females. *Infant Behavior and Development, 15*, 85–93.

Pratt, M. W., & Norris, J. E. (1994). *The social psychology of aging*. Oxford: Blackwell Publishers.

Premack, D., & Woodruff, G. (1978). Does the chimpanzee have a theory of mind? *Behavioral and Brain Sciences, 1*, 515–526.

Pyszczynski, T. A., Greenberg, J., & Solomon, S. (1997). Why do we need what we need? A terror management perspective on the roots of human social motivation. *Psychological Inquiry, 8*, 1–20.

Quinn, P. C., Brown, C. R., & Streppa, M. L. (1997). Perceptual organization of complex visual configurations by young infants. *Infant Behavior & Development, 20*, 35–46.

Rankin, J. L., & Allen, J. L. (1991). Investigating the relationship between cognition and social thinking in adulthood: Stereotyping and attributional processes. In J. D. Sinnott & J. C. Cavanaugh (Eds.), *Bridging paradigms: Positive development in adulthood and cognitive aging* (pp. 131–151). New York: Praeger.

Riegel, K. (1976). The dialectics of human development. *American Psychologist, 31*, 689–700.

Rogoff, B. (1990). *Apprenticeship in thinking: Cognitive development in a social context*. New York: Oxford University Press.

Rothbard, J. C., & Shaver, P. R. (1994). Continuity of attachment across the life span. In M. B. Sperling, & W. H. Berman (Eds.), *Attachment in adults: Clinical and developmental perspectives* (pp. 31–71). New York: Guilford Press.

Ruble, D. N. (1983). The development of social-comparison processes and their role in achievement-related self-socialization. In E. T. Higgins, D. Ruble, & W. Hartup (Eds.), *Social cognition and social development: A socio-cultural perspective*. Cambridge, UK: Cambridge University Press.

Ruble, D. N., & Frey, K. S. (1991). Changing patterns of comparative behavior as skills are acquired: A functional model of self-evaluation. In J. Suls & T. A. Wills (Eds.), *Social comparison: Contemporary theory and research* (pp. 79–113). Hillsdale, NJ: Erlbaum.

Ruble, D. N., & Goodnow, J. J. (1998). Social development in childhood and adulthood. In D. T. Gilbert, S. T. Fiske, & G. Lindzey (Eds.), *The Handbook of Social Psychology*, Vol. 1, 4th. edn. (pp. 741–787). Boston: McGraw-Hill.

Ruffman, T., Perner, J., Naito, M., Parkin, L., & Clements, W. A. (1998). Older (but not younger) siblings facilitate false belief understanding. *Developmental Psychology, 34*, 161–174.

Ryan, E. B., Bourhis, R. Y., & Knops, U. (1991). Evaluative perceptions of patronizing speech addressed to elders. *Psychology and Aging, 6*, 442–450.

Ryff, C. D. (1991). Possible selves in adulthood and old age: A tale of shifting horizons. *Psychology and Aging, 6*, 286–295.

Sabbagh, M. A., & Callanan, M. A. (1998). Metarepresentation in action: 3-, 4-, and 5-year-olds' developing theories of mind in parent–child conversations. *Developmental Psychology, 34*, 491–502.

Schaffer, H. R. (1996). *Social development*. Oxford: Blackwell Publishers.

Schaffer, H. R., & Emerson, P. E. (1964) The development of social attachments in infancy. *Monographs of the Society for Research on Child Development, 29*, 3, Whole no. 94.

Schnake, S. B., & Ruscher, J. B. (1998). Modern racism as a predictor of the linguistic intergroup bias. *Journal of Language and Social Psychology, 17*, 484–491.

Schneider, B. (1997). Psychoacoustics and aging: Implications for everyday listening. *Journal of Speech–Language Pathology and Audiology, 21*, 111–124.

Schwarz, N. (1998). Warmer and more social: Recent developments in cognitive social psychology. *Annual Review of Sociology, 24*, 239–264.

Schwarz, N., Park, D. C., Knaueper, B., & Sudman, S. (Eds.) (1999). *Cognition, aging, and self-*

reports. Hove, UK: Psychology Press.

Selman, R. L. (1976). Social-cognitive understanding: A guide to educational and clinical practice. In T. Lickona (Ed.), *Moral development and behavior: Theory, research and social issues*. New York: Holt.

Shaver, P. R., & Clark, C. L. (1996). Forms of adult romantic attachment and their cognitive and emotional underpinnings. In G. G. Noam & K. W. Fischer (Eds.), Development and vulnerability in close relationships (pp. 29–58). Mahwah, NJ: Erlbaum.

Sinnott, J. D. (1998). *The development of logic in adulthood: Postformal thought and its applications*. New York: Plenum.

Skinner, B. F. (1953). *Science and human behavior*. New York: Macmillan.

Slater, A., & Butterworth, G. (1997). Perception of social stimuli: Face perception and imitation. In G. Bremner & A. Slater (Eds.), *Infant development: Recent advances* (pp. 223–245). Hove, UK: Psychology Press.

Soussignan, R. (1997). Olfaction, hedonic reactions, and facial expressiveness in infants and young children. *Enfance, 1*, 65–83.

Spitz, R. A., & Wolf, K. M. (1946). The smiling response: A contribution to the ontogenesis of social relations. *Genetic Psychology Monographs, 34*, 57–125.

Suess, G. J., Grossmann, K. E., & Sroufe, L. A. (1992). Effects of infant attachment to mother and father on quality of adaptation in preschool: From dyadic to individual organization of self. *International Journal of Behavioral Development, 15*, 43–65.

Taylor, M. (1988). Conceptual perspective taking: Children's ability to distinguish what they know from what they see. *Child Development, 59*, 703–718.

Tesser, A. (1988). Toward a self-evaluation maintenance model of social behavior. In L. Berkowitz (Ed.), *Advances in experimental social psychology*, Vol. 21 (pp. 181–227). San Diego, CA: Academic Press.

Tesser, A. (1995). Introduction. In A. Tesser (Ed.), *Advanced social psychology* (pp. 3–15). New York: McGraw–Hill.

Tesser, A., & Beach, S. R. H. (1998). Life events, relationship quality, and depression: An investigation of judgment discontinuity in vivo. *Journal of Personality and Social Psychology, 74*, 36–52.

Trevarthen, C. (1977). Descriptive analyses of infant communicative behaviour. In H. R. Schaffer (Ed.), *Studies in mother–infant interaction* (pp. 111–139). London: Academic Press.

Trevarthen, C. (1993). The self born in intersubjectivity: The psychology of an infant communicating. In U. Neisser (Ed.), *The perceived self: Ecological and interpersonal sources of self-knowledge*. Emory symposia in cognition, 5. (pp. 121–173). New York: Cambridge University Press.

Valsiner, J., & Lawrence, J. A. (1997). Human development in culture across the life span. In J. W. Berry, P. R. Dasen, & R. Pierre (Eds.), *Handbook of cross-cultural psychology*, Vol. 2: *Basic processes and human development* 2nd. edn. (pp. 69–106). Boston: Allyn & Bacon.

Van der Veer, R., & Valsiner, J. (1991). *Understanding Vygotsky: A quest for synthesis*. Oxford: Blackwell Publishers.

Van Ijzendoorn, M. H., & Kroonenberg, P. M. (1988). Cross-cultural patterns of attachment: A meta-analysis of the Strange Situation. *Child Development, 59*, 147–156.

Vaughan, G. M. (1964). Ethnic awareness in relation to minority group membership. *Journal of Genetic Psychology, 105*, 119–130.

Vaughan, G. M. (1987). A social psychological model of ethnic identity development. In J. S. Phinney & M. J. Rotheram (Eds.), *Children's ethnic socialization: Pluralism and development*. Newbury Park, CA: Sage.

Von Hofsten, C. (1998). The early development of visual perception and its relation to action and cognition. In M. Sabourin & F. Craik (Eds.), *Advances in psychological science*, Vol. 2: *Biological and cognitive aspects* (pp. 483–501). Hove, UK: Psychology Press.

Watson, J. B. (1924). *Behaviorism*. New York: Norton.

Watson, J. K., Gelman, S. A., & Wellman, H. M. (1998). Young children's understanding of the non-physical nature of thoughts and the physical nature of the brain. *British Journal of Developmental Psychology, 16*, 321–335.

Wellman, H. M., Hickling, A. K., & Schult, C. A. (1997). Young children's psychological, physical, and biological explanations. In H. M. Wellman & K. Inagaki (Eds.), *The emergence of core domains of thought: Children's reasoning about physical, psychological, and biological phenomena. New Directions for Child Development, 75,* 7–25. San Francisco: Jossey-Bass.

Wentworth, N., & Haith, M. M. (1998). Infants' acquisition of spatiotemporal expectations. *Developmental Psychology, 34,* 247–257.

Wertsch, J. (in press). Cognitive development. In M. Bennett (Ed.), *Developmental psychology: Achievements and prospects.* London: Psychology Press.

Whitbourne, S. K. (1996). *The aging individual: Physical and psychological perspectives.* New York: Springer.

Williams, A., & Giles, H. (1998). Communication of ageism. In M. L. Hecht (Ed.), *Communicating prejudice* (pp. 136–160). Thousand Oaks, CA: Sage.

Wimmer, H., & Perner, J. (1983). Beliefs about beliefs: Representations and constraining function of wrong beliefs in young children's understanding of deception. *Cognition, 13,* 103–128.

Wittenbrink, B., & Henly, J. R. (1996). Creating social reality: Informational social influence and the content of stereotypic beliefs. *Personality & Social Psychology Bulletin, 22,* 598–610.

Youngblade, L. M., & Belsky, J. (1992). Parent–child antecedents of 5-year-olds' close friendships: A longitudinal analysis. *Developmental Psychology, 28,* 700–713.

Youniss, J., & Volpe, J. (1978). A relational analysis of children's friendships. In W. Damon (Ed.), *New directions for child development,* Vol. 1. San Francisco: Jossey-Bass.

Yuill, N. (1992). Children's production and comprehension of trait terms. *British Journal of Developmental Psychology, 10,* 131–142.

Zeskind, P. S., Parker-Price, S., & Barr, R. G. (1993). Rhythmic organization of the sound of infant crying. *Developmental Psychobiology, 26,* 321–333.

Ziatas, K., Durkin, K., & Pratt, C. (1998). Belief term development in children with autism, Asperger syndrome, specific language impairment, and normal development: Links to theory of mind development. *Journal of Child Psychology & Psychiatry & Allied Disciplines, 39,* 755–763.

Chapter Four

Cognitive Indices of Social Information Processing

John N. Bassili

In one of the first reviews of methodologies for social cognition research, Taylor and Fiske (1981) suggested that these methodologies are for "getting inside the head." This evocative notion remains as apt today as it was in the fledgling days of social cognition. Psychology, of course, is inherently a science of what goes on inside the head, and it would be unfair to presume that paradigms predating social cognition were powerless against the barricade of the cranium. What made cognitive methodologies so attractive when they were added to the arsenal of social psychology is that they provided a vantage point on social information processing that is closer to the source of the processing than were those that had been available earlier. For example, rather than having to fathom the structure of how people organize their impressions of others by analyzing their verbal descriptions, as Asch (1946) did in his classic research on impression formation, one can get a more direct sense of that organization by looking at how information about others clusters when it is recalled from memory (Hamilton, Katz, & Leirer, 1980). Examples of this sort abound, many of which we will encounter in this survey of cognitive indices of social information processing.

Social cognitive methodologies are essentially methodologies for studying the representation of social information in memory and the mechanisms that are responsible for processing information from these representations and from the social world. The methodologies are, to a large extent, constrained by the measures, or dependent variables, that are available for the study of cognitive processes. Although the past two decades have witnessed the maturing of research on social cognition, it is still the case that relevant dependent variables fall into just three broad classes: measures of memory, measures of response time, and

The writing of this chapter was facilitated by Social Sciences and Humanities Research Council of Canada grant #410-97-1507. The author wishes to thank Colin M. MacLeod for helpful comments on an earlier version of the chapter and Rick Brown for his assistance with the subject index.

measures of the output of judgmental processes. Together, measures of memory, response time, and judgment can tap into just about any social psychological process with their methodological burden usually shared by a number of independent variables that enrich the insights that they yield.

As we set out to review dependent and independent variables in the study of social cognition, it is useful to remain cognizant of a distinction that has played an important role in cognitive psychology in the past fifteen years and that has now entered our field. The distinction is between explicit and implicit processes, and is usually premised on measures that either require conscious awareness on the part of the subject (e.g. in the context of self-reports) or that tap unobtrusively into tacit forms of knowledge or processing.

Another trend that is beyond the scope of this review is computerized simulations of social cognitive processes. Though simulations are not new to social psychology (e.g. Abelson, 1968), an approach commonly known as "connectionism" is just beginning to make inroads into social psychology. Whether this approach will have the near revolutionary effect that it has had in cognitive psychology, or will be a passing fashion that appeals primarily to technically inclined social psychologists, remains to be seen. The sophistication of connectionism, however, with its fine-grained analysis of processing at a quasi-neural level, is most provocative at this juncture. For a detailed discussion of this approach, see chapter 6, this volume.

Memory Measures

Free recall

Some of the earliest and most intriguing developments in social cognition were based on simple comparisons of the amount of information recalled under different study conditions or across different types of information. In a very rough sense, the amount of information recalled can serve as an index of how extensively the information was processed when it was first encountered. Much more can often be made of recall performance, however. In their classic extension of Asch's (1946) research on impression formation, Hamilton et al. (1980) presented participants with a series of sentence predicates (e.g. played ball with his dog in the park). Half of the subjects were told that their task was to form an impression of the person described in the sentences, whereas the other half were told that their task was to try to remember as many sentences as they could. After a brief filler task, participants were given a blank piece of paper and were asked to write down as many of the sentences as they could remember. Participants who studied the sentence predicates to form an impression recalled more of them than did participants who studied them with the expressed intent of remembering them as well as possible!

Hamilton et al.'s approach encompasses all of the essential elements of a free recall study. Participants are given a study task (to form an impression of a hypothetical person or to simply memorize the sentences), are presented with a study list (the sentence predicates), are asked to complete a filler task (often to count backwards by threes from an arbitrary number to flush the contents of working memory), and are finally asked to recall as much of the information from the study list as possible. Recalled information is then coded so as to quantify memory performance. In social cognition research, a loose gist criterion is typically used to index accurate recall without giving undue weight to surface features of the stimulus information.

Another classic example of research using a free recall methodology is Hastie and Kumar's (1979) study of expectancy congruent and expectancy incongruent information. Participants who were led to expect that a hypothetical person was very intelligent were then given a study list containing descriptions of behaviors of the person that included expectancy congruent behaviors (won the chess tournament), expectancy incongruent behaviors (made the same mistake three times), and expectancy neutral behaviors (took the elevator to the third floor). Free recall for incongruent behaviors was better than for congruent behaviors, with neutral behaviors being recalled least well (but see Stangor & McMillan (1992) for a review of the limits of this finding). This finding strongly suggests that person information is better organized in memory when it is learned with the intent to form an impression than when it is learned "by rote." Similarly, Hastie and Kumar's (1979) research strongly suggests that expectancy incongruent information receives more attention and is encoded more richly than expectancy congruent or neutral information.

Organization in free recall

The suggestiveness of the preceding results is not sufficient to uniquely support a particular theoretical account of the data. To supplement evidence based on free recall performance, it is often useful to look at the organization of recalled information. This is usually done by looking at sequential properties of recall output with an eye toward assessing the extent to which items are recalled in clusters that do not match the order of information in the study list. For example, the sentence predicates in one of Hamilton et al.'s (1980) studies contained items that belonged to each of four categories: interpersonal characteristics (had a party for some friends last week), intellectual characteristics (wrote an articulate letter to his congressman), athletic characteristics (jogs every morning before going to work), and religious characteristics (volunteered to teach a Sunday school class at his church). These items were presented in the study list in a scrambled order so that items from the same category did not occur in adjacent positions in the stimulus sequence.

As we saw earlier, those who studied a stimulus list to form an impression of a person recalled more information from that list than did those who simply tried to memorize it. This difference in performance suggests that the former group organized information better in memory. If this is the case, subjects trying to form an impression of a person and who studied category-relevant items in a scrambled order, should be more likely to recall that information in category-relevant clusters than subjects who studied the items to memorize them. Hamilton and his colleagues explored clustering by using a number of well-known formulas. For example, the Bousfield and Bousfield (1966) measure is a ratio of observed category repetitions to the number of repetitions expected by chance. Another measure known as the adjusted-ratio-of-clustering (ARC) index corrects for the number of categories presented and recalled and is easily interpreted because 0 always represents chance level clustering and 1 represents complete clustering (see Srull (1984) for more details on clustering measures). The clustering measures computed by Hamilton and his colleagues were highly intercorrelated and in all cases showed more clustering for subjects in the impression formation than in the memory condition, thus providing further direct evidence concerning impression formation processes.

The clustering measures just discussed require that the researcher delineate particular categories *a priori* in the study list. Organization in recall is only revealed if output clustering matches *a priori* categories. Social information processing, however, is often idiosyncratic, and low clustering scores can be difficult to interpret because they may simply fail to pick up on subjective organization (Tulving, 1964) that does not match the conceptual categories defined by the researcher. The bidirectional "pair frequency" (PF) measure recommended by Sternberg and Tulving (1977) provides a means of assessing idiosyncratic information organization in memory. The procedure involves the presentation of a series of stimulus items several times in a different order on each trial. Subjects are asked to recall as many items as possible following each presentation of the series. One then determines for each pair of successive recall protocols the frequency with which two stimulus items occur in adjacent positions. To the extent that items are recalled together time after time despite changes in their order in the study list, the organization must be imposed by the subject. Hamilton and his colleagues used the PF procedure in their person memory research and found that subjective organization increased over trials for subjects in both the impression formation and in the memory conditions. Thus, the superior recall performance of subjects in the impression formation condition is apparently linked to the organization of information along the social categories built into the study list. Subjects in the memory condition also organized information subjectively (in a way that is not knowable from the PF procedure), but this subjective organization did not appear to be as effective in aiding recall as the category based organization used by subjects in the impression formation condition.

On the assumption that retrieval proceeds by "traversing" links between information nodes, Srull (1981) reasoned that the recall of an incongruent behavior should be followed by either another incongruent behavior or by a congruent behavior (because the initial incongruent behavior is linked with both congruent and incongruent behaviors), whereas the recall of a congruent behavior should be followed primarily by the recall of an incongruent behavior (because congruent behaviors are not linked with each other). Srull (1981) calculated these conditional probabilities of recall. As hypothesized, after recalling a congruent behavior, subjects were much more likely to recall an incongruent one than a congruent one, whereas after recalling an incongruent behavior, subjects were about equally likely to recall a congruent or an incongruent one.

A few years later Srull, Lichtenstein, and Rothbart (1985) provided further evidence for the Hastie–Srull model by measuring the length of time separating the recall of congruent and incongruent behaviors. The logic for studying interresponse time is that the lapse of time separating the recall of items that are directly linked in memory should be shorter than that separating the recall of items that are not directly linked. Indeed, Srull and his colleagues found that whenever an incongruent behavior was recalled, the subsequent recall of an incongruent or congruent behavior was relatively quick. By contrast, whenever a congruent behavior was recalled, the subsequent recall of an incongruent behavior was quick, but the subsequent recall of a congruent behavior was slow. David Hamilton's and

Thomas Srull's studies offer examples of how sequential properties of the recall protocol can be used to reveal memory representations as well as the processes responsible for retrieving information from these representations.

Cued recall

Cued recall tasks are situations where the subject is provided with cues that may help the recall of memorized information. A clever application of a cued recall methodology in social psychology involves research on the spontaneity of trait inferences.

In the first experiment to use this approach in social psychology, Winter and Uleman (1984) presented subjects with a study list comprising sentences such as "The secretary solves the mystery halfway through the book." Pilot testing demonstrated that this sentence implies to most people that the secretary is "clever." How were Winter and Uleman to know, however, whether subjects infer spontaneously (without any probing from the experimenter) that the secretary is clever upon reading the sentence describing her? To look unobtrusively "inside the head" Winter and Uleman relied on the encoding specificity principle postulated by Tulving (e.g. Tulving & Thomson, 1973). According to this principle, contextual events at input determine the structure of a memory representation and, therefore, its later retrievability.

A critical element of the principle is that the effectiveness of a cue for retrieving information from memory depends on whether the cue was encoded with the information at the time of presentation. Thus, if subjects infer that the mystery-solving secretary is clever, the trait "clever" should be encoded with information from the stimulus sentence, and the cue "clever" should be particularly effective in retrieving that information from memory. To test this, Winter and Uleman (1984) created a study list made up of sentences that implied traits and then cued the recall of these sentences with either dispositional cues (like "clever"), semantic associates of the actor described in the sentence (like "typewriter"), or no cue. Dispositional cues were more effective at retrieving most sentence parts than were semantic associates of the actor, with recall being poorest when no cue was provided, a finding that suggested that dispositional inferences were made spontaneously when the stimulus sentences were encoded (but see Bassili & Smith (1986) for a cautionary note about this effect).

Some conditions of the preceding experiment led Uleman and his colleagues to suggest that trait inferences actually occur automatically during the comprehension process. They noted, in particular, that the superiority of dispositional cues over semantic cues in their experiments manifested itself under conditions where (a) subjects had no awareness of having inferred traits, (b) subjects had little reason to intend to infer traits, and (c) concurrent cognitive activities did not interfere with the effectiveness of trait cues. Because lack of awareness, intentionality, and interference have all been invoked as criteria for automatic processing in the cognitive literature (e.g. Shiffrin & Schneider, 1977), Winter, Uleman, and Cunniff (1985) decided to test whether trait inferences qualify as automatic processes. They did so by using a cognitive load manipulation where half of the subjects received trait-implying sentences while having to remember a relatively simple string of five digits, whereas the rest of the subjects received the trait-implying sentences while having to remember a longer and more difficult-to-recall string of digits. Disposition-cued recall was unaffected by digit recall difficulty, supporting the notion that trait inferences are made automatically without using cognitive capacity (but see Uleman, Newman, & Winter (1987) for a reversal of this conclusion, and Bargh (1989) for a more differentiated view of automaticity).

Recognition

The main difference between recall and recognition tasks is that recall requires that the subject reproduce learned information, whereas recognition requires no reproduction. Instead, recognition tasks involve information that may or may not have been part of learned material, and requires that the subject indicate whether the information had previously been presented. Specifically, the recognition test contains some items from the study list (for which the appropriate response would be "old" during the recognition task) and a number of unstudied distracters (for which the appropriate response would be "new" on the recognition task). The distracters are ordinarily selected from the same pool as the study items so as not to differ from them on any dimension; ideally, the two sets should be counter-balanced. It is typical for recognition lists to contain an equal proportion of study items and of distracters.

Guessing strategies can play an important role in recognition tasks. For example, a subject who said "old" to every item on the recognition list would have a perfect score for identifying old items without actually showing a hint of discrimination between old and new items. For this reason, principles of signal detection theory are usually applied to recognition responses to keep track of hits (saying old when the item is old) in conjunction with false alarms (saying old when the item is new). The measure usually computed to reflect recognition memory free of guessing is called d'.

Recognition tasks have not enjoyed as much popularity as recall tasks in social cognition research. Still, there are two characteristics of recognition tasks that make them attractive. First, recognition tasks are very sensitive. Generally speaking, recognition tasks are always more sensitive than recall tasks. This is consistent with the generate–recognize model (Kintsch, 1968), in which recall is viewed as requiring two phases of processing: a retrieval phase (generation) and a decision phase (recognition). According to this prevalent view, recognition tasks bypass the retrieval stage, and are therefore dependent only on discriminating old information from new. Second, when testing a claim about encoding processes (such as the notion that trait inferences are made spontaneously at encoding) recognition tasks put the emphasis where it needs to be by minimizing the potential role of retrieval processes, which can be under strategic direction.

As we saw earlier, Winter and Uleman's claims about the spontaneity of trait inferences generated some controversy. One element of the controversy was whether recall tests are sensitive enough to pick up the presence of inferences in memory. To test this, D'Agostino (1991) presented subjects with the same sentences as those used by Winter and Uleman with one important variation: half the sentences were identical to those used by Winter and Uleman, whereas the other half were altered so that the personality trait implied by the sentence was explicitly stated (e.g. "The clever secretary solves the mystery halfway through the book"). The recognition list contained traits that were explicitly stated in sentences (for which the correct response is "old"), as well as traits that were implied by the sentences without being explicitly stated (for which the correct response is "new"). D'Agostino reasoned that if subjects spontaneously encode dispositional inferences, then the recognition performance of subjects instructed to memorize the sentences should parallel the memory performance of subjects instructed to form impressions of the actors described by the sentences. This was not the case. This adds to the evidence that traits are not routinely inferred during the encoding of behavioral descriptions. As we will soon see, however, other methodologies insured that this was not the last word on this controversy.

Implicit memory tasks

Recall and recognition require the deliberate recollection of previously learned material. For this reason, these ubiquitous procedures have been called explicit memory tasks. About two decades ago, cognitive psychologists developed a keen interest in implicit memory tasks. These tasks differ from explicit memory tasks because subjects are not made aware of any connection between the test items and previously learned material (cf. Schacter & Graf, 1986). A good example of an implicit memory task is the word-fragment completion task. Consider the following words from which letters are missing: "g– – er – u –" and "c – – v – r." Research has shown that the probability of correctly completing a particular string increases substantially when the word on which the string is based has been read earlier. If you had an easier time completing the second word (clever) than the first (generous), it is probably because you have read the word clever earlier in this chapter. In fact, one of the very first studies to use an implicit memory task in social psychology did so to study the spontaneity of trait inferences and used word-fragments of dispositional traits like the ones shown here (Bassili & Smith, 1986).

One particularly interesting feature of implicit memory tasks such as word-fragment completion is that performance on these tasks remains high even when subjects are unable to recall or recognize the corresponding items (Tulving, Schacter, & Stark, 1982). This fact, along with the discovery that amnesic patients often show good memory retention on implicit tasks but not on explicit ones, has led some (e.g. Tulving, 1983) to posit separate underlying systems for explicit and implicit memory.

The word-fragment completion procedure is only one of the tasks that index implicit memory. Other tasks include word stem completion, where subjects are given the stem of a word such as "cle – – –" and attempt to complete it (e.g. Bassili, Smith, & MacLeod, 1989); word identification, where subjects are given a very brief exposure of a stimulus and attempt to identify it (e.g. Jacoby & Dallas, 1981); and savings in relearning, where improved performance in relearning material serves as an index of tacit retention of information (e.g. Carlston & Skowronski, 1994; Nelson, Fehling, & Moore-Glascock, 1979).

Response Time Measures

Pachella (1974) states that "The only property of mental events that can be studied directly, in the intact organism, while the events are taking place, is their duration." Although this assertion needs to be amended in light of sophisticated modern neural imaging methodologies such as function Magnetic Resonance Imaging (fMRI) and Positron Emission Tomography (PET), it helps to explain the immense popularity of response time methodologies ever since F. C. Donders (1868), a Dutch physiologist, introduced the approach.

Response time, which is best defined as the interval between the presentation of a stimulus to a subject and the subject's response, has been used in a number of ways in psychology. The Subtraction Method, which was originally developed by Donders (1868), is based on the logic that a researcher can create tasks that share a number of subcomponents, but where one task involves a single additional component not shared by the others. A less specific but more successful decomposition method developed by Sternberg (1969) is called the Additive Factors Method. Rather than attempting to measure precisely the duration of various steps of information processing, this method aims to identify qualitatively distinct subsystems by exploring the pattern of effects on response time produced by a set of independent variables.

The cognitive processes studied by social psychologists are usually too rich and complex to be amenable to strict decomposition by the Subtraction or Additive Factors methods. At the extreme, for example, one can treat the length of time a subject examines information as a general index of how diligently the information has been processed (Taylor, 1975). Although response time can be used at finer levels of analysis in social psychology, molar indexes often yield valuable information. The examples that follow demonstrate this in a variety of contexts.

Response time as a clue to mediation

As we saw earlier, questions about mediation are often at the core of theorizing about information processing. Attribution research that preceded the advent of social cognition examined a number of inferences that people make about others (whether an action is caused by something about the actor or about the situation, whether the action is intended, whether the action corresponds to a trait, etc.). Although this research generally implied that some inferences mediate others (for example, that the perceiver first decides whether it is something about the actor or the situation that caused the action, and if it is something about the actor, then decides whether the action reflects an actor's trait), very little evidence was available to substantiate these assumptions.

Smith & Miller (1983) used a simple response time procedure to study mediational relations in judgments about others. Subjects were presented with sentences such as "Andy slips an extra $50 into his wife's purse" and had to answer one of seven questions (e.g. Did Andy intend to perform the action? Did something about Andy cause the action? Does the adjective "generous" describe Andy?). Smith and Miller reasoned that "judgments that take longer to arrive at cannot plausibly mediate or come prior to judgments that take a shorter time" (ibid., p. 493). As it turned out, the answer to questions such as "Did something about Andy cause the action?" took on average 3.42 seconds, whereas those to questions such as "Does the adjective 'generous' describe Andy?" took 2.48 seconds. Following Smith and Miller's logic, causal judgments take longer than trait judgments and cannot, therefore, plausibly mediate them.

Compelling as Smith and Miller's assumption about judgment duration and mediation is, it is subject to an important caveat. The logic assumes that subjects apply equally strict decision criteria to all judgments. A decision criterion is the level of confidence that the subject considers sufficient for making a judgment. In the present example, it is possible (although not necessarily likely) that subjects made trait judgments more freely than causal judgments. Because decision criteria are not effectively controlled in simple response time methodologies, it is often difficult to compare response times across judgments.

Response time as an index of processing efficiency

In a more recent series of experiments investigating a different phenomenon, Eliot Smith and his colleagues (e.g. Smith 1989; Smith, Branscombe, & Bormann, 1988) presented subjects with a large number of trials (for example, 4 blocks of 50 trials) requiring yes/no judgments to whether a particular trait (e.g. friendly) was implied by each of a number of behaviors (e.g. hitting, smiling, etc.). These studies showed that judgments become faster with practice and that the speed-up follows a consistent progression. Although this finding is not particularly surprising, some experimental manipulations helped Smith to theorize about the basis of the speed up. For example, switching to a new trait in the last block of 50 trials did not result in much of a slow down for the highly practiced subjects. This led Smith to surmise that increased processing efficiency in his experimental situation was not caused by heightened accessibility of a specific trait such as "friendly" but by a more general form of procedural strengthening.

Response time as an index of attitude accessibility

Russel Fazio and his colleagues have used response time to attitude questions to index the accessibility of feelings about attitude objects. For example, Fazio and Williams (1986) asked respondents prior to the 1984 American presidential election if they felt that Ronald Regan and Walter Mondale would be good presidents for the next four years. On average, subjects took about two seconds to express their feelings towards each of the two candidates. What is interesting, however, is that when respondents were divided into a "high accessibility" (fast) and a "low accessibility" (slow) group by a median split of their response times, subjects in the high accessibility group were more likely to vote consistently with their attitudes toward the candidates than were subjects in the low accessibility group.

Fazio has used results such as these to develop a theory based on the notion that response time to attitude questions reflects the strength of the association in memory between the attitude object and a summary evaluation of the object. The stronger this association, the more likely it is that the evaluation will be activated when information about the attitude object is encountered. What is important here, according to Fazio, is that when summary evaluations are activated upon exposure to the attitude object, the evaluations are more likely to guide behavior towards the object. This is one of the important ideas that have helped resolve the conundrum about low attitude–behavior consistency in social psychology by demonstrating that only accessible attitudes are likely to play a guiding role in behavior.

Response time in opinion surveys

The marriage of telephones and computers has had an immense impact on the field of survey research, where the preponderance of data are now obtained using what is known as Computer Assisted Telephone Interviewing (CATI). In the typical CATI survey, the interviewer sits in front of a computer and administers the questionnaire over the telephone. The numbers that are called are usually generated by a procedure known as random digit dialing to insure that every phone number in the target population has a probability of being in the sample equal to that of every other number. Because CATI surveys offer a means for reaching large representative samples and because computers are an integral part of the methodology, the approach offers a remarkable opportunity to reach out of the laboratory.

One interesting adaptation of CATI surveys for social psychological research involves the measurement of response latency during telephone interviews (see Bassili (1996a) for a detailed discussion of this methodology). One application of this approach is to measure attitude strength. Although it is customary in survey research to probe attitude strength by asking respondents questions such as "How strongly do you feel about that?" or "How important is this issue to you personally?", these questions require that respondents report their impressions of their attitudes. For this reason, I have called them questions about "meta-attitudes." By contrast, response latency is based on the cognitive processes that underlie attitudes and requires no self-reflection. For this reason, I have called the measure and others like it "operative," a property that shares many elements of implicit cognitive processes. Tests comparing the predictive power of meta-attitudinal and operative measures of strength against criteria of attitude pliability and stability have shown operative measures to be more predictive than meta-attitudinal measures (Bassili, 1996b).

Another interesting application of response time to survey questions is as a measure of experienced conflict (Bassili, 1995). Response latencies to a voting intention question were measured prior to the 1993 Canadian Federal Election among three groups of respondents: unconflicted partisans, who identified with a party and intended to vote for that party; conflicted partisans, who identified with a party but intended to vote for a different party; and nonpartisans. Unconflicted partisans and nonpartisans expressed their voting intentions faster as the election approached, whereas conflicted partisans expressed them more slowly. This slow-down is probably linked to the heightened accessibility of the conflicting evaluations held by conflicted partisans.

Collecting and analyzing response time data

Response time data usually have a number of characteristics that require special precautions during collection and analysis (see Fazio (1990) for a detailed discussion). A number of sources, for example, can contribute to noise in response time data. These include variations in speed across trials caused by momentary waning of attention, fatigue, or confusion, as well as individual differences in response rates. One common way to reduce noise is to provide subjects with speed–accuracy instructions. Because it is well established that subjects make more errors the faster they try to respond, and because trials that contain errors do not reflect the successful application of the processes under study, subjects in response time experiments are usually instructed to respond as fast as possible while maintaining accuracy. Providing subjects with a number of practice trials prior to the test phase, as well as including a large number of trials in the test phase, also contribute to reducing noise in the data.

One common approach to controlling for noise created by atypical response times is by truncation. Suppose that a subject who takes 2 seconds to do a task on most trials takes 8 seconds on a particular trial. What is to be made of the atypically long "outlier" on that trial? Researchers often reason that such trials reflect momentary lapses in attention and should either be treated as missing data or set to a fixed maximum value. A common practice is to either eliminate data points that fall beyond two standard deviations above or below the mean, or to set these points to a particular maximum value.

Noise caused by individual differences in speed of responding can be controlled by calculating a baseline for each subject based on filler items. For example, an attitude questionnaire will contain a subset of questions that are only there for the purpose of determining how quickly each subject tends to respond to attitude questions. This baseline can then be subtracted from the subject's response time to the focal question to provide a purer index of speed of responding.

Response time data are usually highly positively skewed, with most latencies clumping around the mean, but with many others forming a long tail of slow latencies. The truncation method described above will take care of some of the skewness, but it does so at the risk of eliminating or capping some meaningfully long latencies. Another common method for reducing skewness involves mathematical transformations of the raw latencies. Logarithmic or reciprocal transformations are commonly employed for the purpose of reducing skewness and better approximating a normal distribution of response times (see Fazio, 1990).

Quick-sequence Priming: The Case of Higher Order Response Time

In the preceding examples, response time is an index of the duration of a process, with little consideration given to the effect of immediate concomitant events on that duration. For this reason, I like to think of measures of this type as first order response time measures. As we just saw, first order response time measures can yield interesting data on such things as the efficiency of a process, the accessibility of a construct, or even the amount of conflict experienced during the decision process. What first order response time measures are not very good at, however, is revealing relations between processes. For example, whereas response time to an attitude question may reveal the accessibility of the attitude, it does not reveal much about the relationship between one attitude judgment and other attitude judgments. For this, one needs to use what I will call higher order response time measures where the duration of a process when it is preceded by a particular prime is compared to the duration of the process when it is preceded by a different type of prime. A prime, in this context, is any item that precedes the target item in close temporal sequence. The approach is based on the well established finding that a process will take less time when information relevant to it has been rendered more accessible by the prior processing of the prime (Collins & Quillian, 1970; Meyer & Schvaneveldt, 1976). This type of priming, which is usually attributed to the spreading of activation from one knowledge structure to another, usually lasts mere fractions of seconds. The presentation of the prime and of the target stimulus in quick succession, however, can detect the effect quite readily.

To illustrate, consider research by Tourangeau, Rasinski, and D'Andrade (1991) that examined the structure of beliefs about abortion and welfare. In a preliminary study, subjects sorted statements about the two issues into groups based on their similarity. A statistical procedure was used to identify a number of topical clusters revealed by the sorts. For example, the statement "Women who have abortions always experience lingering guilt" belonged to a "Stigma and guilt" cluster for abortion, whereas the statement "Everyone in America is entitled to a comfortable life" belonged to a "Responsibility to the poor" cluster for welfare. In the main study, these items were presented to subjects one at a time with a two-second interval between successive responses so that each item served as a prime for the item immediately following it. Subjects were timed as they expressed their agreement or disagreement with each item. The results revealed that responses were fastest when an item was preceded by another item from the same topical cluster (e.g. a "Responsibility to the poor" item preceded by another "Responsibility to the poor" item) and slowest when an item was preceded by an item from an unrelated issue and cluster (e.g. a "Responsibility to the poor" welfare item preceded by a "Stigma and guilt" abortion item). This priming procedure, therefore, illustrates how quick-sequence priming can disclose relations between psychological constructs.

The task facilitation paradigm

From a methodological standpoint, the preceding example is somewhat anticlimactic because the quick-sequence priming methodology is used to confirm a structure that was already identified by a straightforward sorting procedure. The value of cognitive methodologies, of course, comes from their ability to reveal psychological processes that are not easily exposed by other methodologies. This is indeed often the case. Consider a line of research by Klein and his colleagues (Klein & Loftus, 1993) that focused on whether knowledge of traits is inseparable from specific autobiographical memories, or whether trait knowledge is represented in summary form and can be retrieved independently of autobiographical memories. For example, suppose you are asked if you are an impulsive person. One way you can answer this question is by reviewing instances of your past behavior that are relevant to impulsivity, and then making a judgment on that basis. Another possibility is that you already know whether you are impulsive and that this abstracted summary knowledge is retrieved directly from memory to answer the question.

These two views were tested using a task facilitation paradigm that required that participants do two tasks in quick succession. One task required that subjects judge whether a trait applied to them; another task required that they retrieve from memory a specific incident in which they manifested the trait. A third task, one that is important to this methodology because it served as a control, required that subjects simply generate a definition for the trait. The logic of the approach is that if, in the course of performing a task, information relevant to another task is made accessible, then the time required to perform the second task should be less than if the information is not primed by the first task.

Klein and Loftus found that under most circumstances subjects were no faster at verifying that a trait applied to them when they had just retrieved from memory a specific incident in which they manifested the trait than when they first performed an irrelevant control task. This lack of facilitation suggests that the trait judgment was made by accessing a summary representation of the trait rather than by considering specific autobiographical information pertinent to it. Only under circumstances where participants had little self-relevant experience in a context (how first-year students saw their traits since entering college) was facilitation observed.

The task-facilitation paradigm can reveal mediational properties of judgmental processes that would be very hard to explore using other methodologies. The paradigm also has the advantage of being applicable to any situation where the relations between processes relevant to judgments is explored. For example, my colleagues and I have used this paradigm to explore the relations between person and situation judgments in attribution (Bassili & Racine, 1990), and the relations between opinion and consequence judgments in policy attitudes (Bassili & Roy, in press).

Priming, associative strength, and automatic attitude activation

On each trial of a procedure developed by Russ Fazio and his colleagues (Fazio, Sanbonmatsu, Powell, & Kardes, 1986; Fazio, Jackson, Dunton, & Williams, 1995), subjects are presented with a prime consisting of an attitude object. In the case of racial attitudes, the attitude object consists of the face of a black person or that of a white person. The prime is followed by a positive (e.g. likable, wonderful) or negative (e.g. annoying, disgusting) adjective and the subject's task is to press a key labeled "good" or a key labeled "bad" as quickly as possible to indicate his or her judgment of the adjective.

Notice that the evaluative connotation of each adjective is quite clear. What Fazio and his colleagues are interested in is the extent to which the prime (say a black face) automatically activates a positive or negative evaluation in the subject's mind. To the extent that a positive evaluation is strongly associated with the prime and is therefore activated by it, subjects should be able to indicate the connotation of a positive adjective relatively quickly (a case of facilitation) and the connotation of a negative adjective relatively slowly (a case of interference).

The notion of associative strength, and of the automatic activation it leads to, are central to Fazio's approach and are of obvious social psychological importance, especially for racial attitudes. An important question, therefore, is how can one be sure that any facilitation or inhibition revealed by this paradigm is automatic? The answer is linked to a temporal parameter of the procedure known as stimulus onset asynchrony (SOA), or the interval between the onset of the prime and the onset of the target adjective. In Fazio's research on racial attitudes, the prime (black or white face) was presented for 315 milliseconds followed by a 135 millisecond interval before the onset of the adjective. The SOA, therefore, was 450 milliseconds. Research by Neely (1977) has demonstrated that this SOA is too brief to allow subjects to actively think about the relation between the prime and the target of judgment. Any effect of the prime on response time to the target is, therefore, taken as an indication of automatic processes.

Fazio and his colleagues tested white and black subjects in their research on racial attitudes, and their results revealed a clear picture of prejudice. Specifically, white subjects were quicker at indicating that a negative adjective was bad, and slower at indicating that a positive adjective was good, when the prime was a black face than when it was a white face. Black subjects showed the reverse pattern.

An important aspect of this priming procedure is that it measures prejudice completely unobtrusively, and therefore bypasses any defences that the subject may consciously put up to hide his or her feelings. In fact, the procedure, like most quick-sequence priming procedures, can be thought of as an implicit measure akin to word-fragment completion in memory research and has the advantage of measuring prejudice "operatively" (Bassili, 1996b) by focusing directly on the processing of racial stimuli rather than by means of self-reports of racial attitudes. Fazio and his colleagues were specifically interested in this issue and compared the racism measure derived from their priming procedure with a measure based on the Modern Racism Scale. The Modern Racism Scale was designed by McConahay (1986) specifically as a nonreactive measure of anti-Black feelings and has been widely used in research.

Note that the racism results just described are aggregated over subjects because they compare priming among white and black subjects as groups. Fazio and his colleagues were also able to compute an individual index of racism based on the pattern of facilitation for each subject. The effectiveness of this measure at predicting actual racist behavior (how friendly the subject was when interacting with a black experimenter) was compared to that of scores on the Modern Racism Scale. As it turns out, scores on the Modern Racism Scale did not predict friendliness towards the black experimenter whereas the pattern of facilitation did.

The Implicit Association Test: A New Methodology for Measuring Associative Strength

Anthony Greenwald and his colleagues (Greenwald, McGhee, & Schwartz, 1998) have recently developed what appears to be a powerful methodology for assessing implicit associations. The procedure is similar in intent to the quick-sequence priming procedure just discussed, in that it is also designed to resist self-presentational forces in socially sensitive tasks.

The implicit association test (IAT) involves two discrimination tasks that are combined in specific ways across a number of experimental phases. In a typical experiment, for example, the first discrimination task involves first names that are recognized in the United States (where the research was conducted) as White or European American (e.g. Meredith, Heather) and names that are recognized as Black or African American (e.g. Latonya, Tashika). Subjects are instructed to press a key with their left hand for white names, and a key with their right hand for black names. The second discrimination task involves pleasant (e.g. lucky, honor) and unpleasant (e.g. poison, grief) words and respondents are to press the left key if the word is pleasant and the right key if it is unpleasant. In the third phase of the experiment these two discrimination tasks are superimposed so that the subject is presented with names and words and has to press the left key for white names and pleasant words and the right key for black names and unpleasant words. The logic of the IAT is that the combined task will be easier when highly associated categories share a response key (say white names and positive evaluations in the case of white subjects) than when less associated categories share a key (white names and negative evaluations).

To gauge the strength of associations between names and evaluations, the experiment comprises two more phases. In the fourth phase, the subject learns a reversal of response assignments for the name discrimination task so that the left key is pressed for black names and the right key for white names. Finally, in the fifth phase the two discrimination tasks are superimposed again so that the left key is pressed for black names and pleasant words while the right key is pressed for white names and unpleasant words.

The critical comparison in the IAT is between response latencies in the superimposed discrimination tasks of phase three and phase five. To the extent that a subject is faster in phase three (when pressing the same key for white names and pleasant words and for black names and unpleasant words) than in phase five (when pressing the same key for white names and unpleasant words and for black names and pleasant words) positive evaluations are shown to be more strongly associated with white names than with black names. If the subject is faster in phase five than phase three, then the reverse is shown. An experiment using the procedures just described revealed that white subjects were about 200 milliseconds faster on average in phase three than in phase five (Greenwald, McGhee & Schwartz, 1998, Experiment 3), showing an aggregate white evaluative bias. As in Fazio et al.'s (1995) quick-sequence priming research, individual IAT indices were computed and correlated with scores on the Modern Racism Scale. Here, too, the correlations were not significant, suggesting that the IAT may be sensitive to consciously disavowed attitudinal effects. What is not yet clear about the IAT is whether it can predict behavior in the way Fazio et al.'s (1995) quick-sequence priming procedure does, and whether it measures substantially the same implicit associations as that priming procedure.

Category Priming and Its Effect on Judgment Processes

One of the most enduring concepts in modern social cognition research has to do with the effect of category accessibility on judgment. The approach, which is based on ideas originally formulated by Bruner (1957), was re-popularized by Tory Higgins and his colleagues in research on person perception (Higgins, Rholes, & Jones, 1977; Higgins, King, & Mavin, 1982). The basic notion is that stimuli can often be interpreted in a number of different ways. For example, Srull and Wyer (1979) give the example of someone who tells his girlfriend that her new hair style is unattractive. An observer could interpret this behavior as either "honest" or "unkind." Which of the two interpretations is given depends on the relative accessibility of the two conceptual categories at the time the information is encoded. Because much of social behavior is ambiguous or vague, this idea is of immense practical and theoretical importance.

The preceding theoretical insight begs a question about the determinants of category accessibility. In a nutshell, the accessibility of a category is determined by the recency and frequency of its activation as a result of its prior use. This prior use is called priming, just like the quick-sequence priming we discussed earlier. Category priming, however, tends to be much longer lasting than quick-sequence priming, often lasting several hours, and in cases of highly repetitive practice (as in Eliot Smith's proceduralization work described earlier) even lasting months.

The most common approach to testing the effects of category accessibility on judgment processes in social psychological research involves two phases that are presented to subjects as two totally unrelated experiments. This precaution is taken to prevent subjects from becoming aware of the relation between the priming procedure and the subsequent interpretation task. In the first phase, a category is primed by presenting subjects with information from it. For example, in the first phase of Srull and Wyer's (1979) study, subjects performed a scrambled sentence task in which they constructed sentences by underlining three words from a set of four supplied by the experimenter. For example, the four words "leg break arm his" could be used to form the sentence "break his arm" or "break his leg." Subjects in this experiment completed a total of either 30 or 60 sentences, either 20 percent or 80 percent of which were related to hostility. The hypothesis was that the sheer number of repetitions as well as the proportion of items relevant to the primed concept (hostility) would have an impact on subsequent judgments.

At the end of the priming procedure, subjects were turned over to another experimenter or were asked to return for the second experiment 1 hour or 24 hours later. The second, and ostensibly separate, experiment involved an impression formation task in which subjects were asked to read a brief vignette about a person called Donald. The Donald vignette contained five behaviors that were ambiguous with respect to the primed construct (for example, Donald's refusal to pay his rent until the landlord repainted his apartment). After reading the vignette, subjects were asked to form an impression of Donald and then to rate him on a series of dimensions relevant to hostility. The five ambiguous behaviors were also rated for hostility.

Subjects who were primed with 60 hostile sentences rated Donald and his behaviors as more hostile than did subjects primed with 20 hostile sentences. Similarly, subjects for whom 80 percent of the priming sentences were hostile rated Donald and his behaviors as more hostile than did subjects for whom 20 percent of the priming sentences were hostile. The preceding effects weakened with time, so that subjects who rated Donald immediately after the priming task showed stronger priming effects than did subjects who rated him an hour later or 24 hours later. Interestingly, despite the priming effects being weakest after a 24-hour delay, they were still significant.

Srull and Wyer's findings, and many others like them, have had a profound effect on social cognition research and the priming of conceptual categories is now entrenched as a basic cognitive methodology that is continuing to yield fascinating results. For example, Bargh, Chen, & Burrows (1996) primed subjects with scrambled sentences containing words relevant to the elderly stereotype and found that these subjects walked more slowly down a hallway as they left the experiment than subjects who were exposed to neutral primes!

Subliminal Priming

The influence of subliminal stimuli on judgment and behavior has been a subject of fascination in psychology. Claims that movie goers rushed to purchase refreshments when the messages "Hungry? Eat Popcorn" and "Drink Coca-Cola" were flashed imperceptibly during the projection of the film were greeted with outrage in the public and by skepticism among psychologists (Packard, 1957). Although skepticism about the wild claims made by commercial practitioners of subliminal advertising is well placed, recent developments in controlled research suggest that stimuli that are presented below the threshold of awareness can indeed have an effect on information processing.

One of the first demonstrations of the effect of subliminal stimuli on social cognition comes from research by John Bargh and his colleagues (e.g. Bargh & Pietromonaco, 1982; Bargh, Bond, Lombardi, & Tota, 1986). The research shares many of the features of Srull and Wyer's (1979) category priming study and was motivated in part by the desire to demonstrate that category priming operates automatically (that is, without conscious processing).

What is distinctive about these studies is that subliminal priming is effected by presenting subjects with stimulus words below the threshold of awareness. For example, "hostility" was primed in Bargh and Pietromonaco's (1982) first study with a list of 100 words that contained 0, 20, or 80 hostile words (actually 15 words such as hostile, inconsiderate, and thoughtless, were repeated a set number of times). Subjects sat in front of a computer screen and were instructed to fixate three Xs that appeared at its center. On each of the 100 trials, a word appeared for 100 milliseconds at one of four locations equidistant from the fixation point, falling in the parafoveal visual field (the region surrounding the foveal area). To control precisely the duration of the word, a backward masking procedure was used whereby the word was followed immediately by a 100 millisecond mask consisting of a string of 16 Xs. Although 100 millisecond stimulus duration is relatively long for subliminal presentations (other research by Bargh and his group used durations about half this long), the use of a mask as well as other factors such as the level of illumination of the screen probably contributed to the fact that subjects were not able to guess the words that were presented before the mask.

The effect of this subliminal priming was tested using the familiar Donald paragraph. The results showed that the higher the proportion of hostile words in the stimulus list, the more negative the subject's impression of Donald. This was taken by Bargh and his colleagues as evidence of the automatic and passive nature of category priming effects. This notion is reinforced by research on stereotypes (Devine, 1989) that shows that white subjects rate Donald as more hostile following subliminal exposure to primes associated with the social category Blacks (e.g. Blacks, Negroes) or stereotypic associates of this social category (e.g. athletic, poor, lazy)!

Research using subliminal stimuli is not limited to priming influences on Donald paragraphs. For example, Zajonc's (1968) mere exposure hypothesis (the notion that mere exposure to a stimulus enhances one's attitude towards it) as well as his (Zajonc, 1980) affective primacy hypothesis (the notion that the extraction of affective information from stimulation proceeds independently from and more swiftly than the extraction of cognitive information) have both been tested with subliminal stimuli. The effect of mere exposure has been detected even when the stimuli (octagons of various shapes) were presented on several occasions for only 1 millisecond (Kunst-Wilson & Zajonc, 1980). Similarly, the affective primacy hypothesis was supported by the finding that ratings of Chinese ideographs were influenced more by affective primes consisting of happy or angry faces when the primes were flashed for 4 milliseconds than when they were shown for 1 second (Murphy & Zajonc, 1993).

Conclusion

Cognition forms the basis of many social psychological phenomena. This is why behavioral indices of cognitive processes are essential for understanding social behavior. This chapter reported on methods for studying social cognition in a manner that recognizes the growing maturity of this approach. Twenty years ago a chapter such as this one would have dwelled more on what cognitive psychologists were doing (better to borrow their methodologies) than on what social psychologists had actually done with these methodologies. The borrowing has not ended, and creative contributions to research in social cognition still often rely on it. What has changed is the gradual realization that some indices of cognitive processes having to do with memory organization, response time, quick-sequence priming, and judgmental effects of category and subliminal priming (some of which operate at an explicit level and others at an implicit level) have become ordinary tools of the social psychological trade. These tools provide an excellent vantage point on core processes of social cognitive processes. We need no longer stand in awe of methods that allow us to "look inside the head." We have now taken more than one look with these methods and the job of mapping what goes on there is well under way.

References

Abelson, R. P. (1968). Simulation of social behavior. In G. Lindzey and E. Aronson (Eds.), *The handbook of social psychology* 2nd. edn. (pp. 274–356). Reading, MA: Addison-Wesley.

Asch, S. E. (1946). Forming impressions of personality. *Journal of Abnormal and Social Psychology, 41*, 258–290.

Bargh, J. A. (1989). Conditional automaticity: Varieties of automatic influence in social perception and cognition. In J. S. Uleman and J. A. Bargh (Eds.), *Unintended thought* (pp. 3–51). New York: Guilford Press.

Bargh, J. A., & Pietromonaco, P. (1982). Automatic information processing and social perception: The influence of trait information presented outside of conscious awareness on impression formation. *Journal of Personality and Social Psychology, 43*, 437–449.

Bargh, J. A., Chen, M., & Burrows, L. (1996). Automaticity of social behavior: Direct effects of trait construct and stereotype activation on action. *Journal of Personality and Social Psychology, 71*, 230–244.

Bargh, J. A., Bond, R. N., Lombardi, W. J., & Tota, M. E. (1986). The additive nature of chronic and temporary sources of construct accessibility. *Journal of Personality and Social Psychology, 50*, 869–878.

Bassili, J. N. (1995). On the psychological reality of party identification: Evidence from the accessibility of voting intentions and of partisan feelings. *Political Behavior, 17,* 339–358.

Bassili, J. N. (1996a). The "how" and "why" of response latency measurement in survey research. In N. Schwarz & S. Sudman (Eds.), *Cognitive processes in surveys* (pp. 319–346). New York: Josey-Bass.

Bassili, J. N. (1996b). Meta-judgmental versus operative indexes of psychological attributes: The case of measures of attitude strength. *Journal of Personality and Social Psychology, 71*, 637–653.

Bassili, J. N., & Racine, J. P. (1990). On the process relationship between person and situation judgments in attribution. *Journal of Personality and Social Psychology, 59*, 881–890.

Bassili, J. N., & Roy, J. P. (in press). On the representation of strong and weak attitudes about policy in memory. *Political Psychology.*

Bassili, J. N., & Smith, M. C. (1986). On the spontaneity of trait attributions: Converging evidence for the role of cognitive strategy. *Journal of Personality and Social Psychology, 50*, 239–245.

Bassili, J. N., Smith, M. C., & MacLeod, C. M. (1989). Auditory and visual word-stem completion: Separating data-driven and conceptually driven processes. *The Quarterly Journal of Experimental Psychology, 41*, 439–453.

Bousfield, A. K., & Bousfield, W. A. (1966). Measurement of clustering and of sequential constancies in repeated free recall. *Psychological Reports, 19,* 935–942.

Bruner, J. S. (1957). On perceptual readiness. *Psychological Review, 64*, 123–152.

Carlston, D. E., & Skowronski, J. J. (1994). Savings in the relearning of trait information as evidence for spontaneous inference generation. *Journal of Personality and Social Psychology, 66,* 840–856.

Collins, A. M., & Quillian, M. R. (1970). Facilitation of retrieval from semantic memory: The effect of repeating part of an inference. *Acta Psychologica, 33*, 304–314.

D'Agostino, P. R. (1991). Spontaneous trait inferences: Effects of recognition instructions and subliminal priming on recognition performance. *Personality and Social Psychology Bulletin, 17*, 70–77.

Devine, P. G. (1989). Stereotypes and prejudice: Their automatic and controlled components. *Journal of Personality and Social Psychology, 56*, 5–18.

Donders, F. C. (1868). Over de snelheid van psychischeprocessen. Onderzoekingen gedaan in het PhysiologishLaboratorium der Utrechsche Hoogeschool, 1868–1869, Tweede reeks, II, 92–120. Translated by W. G. Koster, in *Acta Psychologica, 30*, 1969, 412–431.

Fazio, R. H. (1990). A practical guide to the use of response latency in social psychological research. In C. Hendrick and M. S. Clark (Eds.), *Research methods in personality and social psychology*, Vol. 11 (pp. 74–97). Newbury Park, CA: Sage.

Fazio, R. H. & Williams, C. J. (1986). Attitude accessibility as a moderator of the attitude–perception and attitude–behavior relations: An investigation of the 1984 presidential election. *Journal of Personality and Social Psychology, 51*, 505–514.

Fazio, R. H., Jackson, J. R., Dunton, B. C., & Williams, C. J. (1995). Variability in automatic activation as an unobtrusive measure of racial attitudes: A bona fide pipeline? *Journal of Personality and Social Psychology, 69*, 1013–1027.

Fazio, R. H., Sanbonmatsu, D. M., Powell, M. C., & Kardes, F. R. (1986). On the automatic activation of attitudes. *Journal of Personality and Social Psychology, 50*, 229–238.

Greenwald, A. G., McGhee, D. E., & Schwartz, J. L. K. (1998). Measuring individual differences in implicit cognition: The implicit association test. *Journal of Personality and Social Psychology, 74*, 1464–1480.

Hamilton, D. L., Katz, L. B., & Leirer, V. O. (1980). Organizational processes in impression formation. In R. Hastie, T. M. Ostrom, E. B. Ebbesen, R. S. Wyer, D. L. Hamilton, & D. E. Carlston (Eds.), *Person memory: The cognitive basis of social perception* (pp.121–153). Hillsdale, NJ: Lawrence Erlbaum Associates.

Hastie, R. (1980). Memory for information which confirms or contradicts a general impression. In R. Hastie, T. M. Ostrom, E. B. Ebbesen, R. S. Wyer, D. L. Hamilton, & D. E. Carlston (Eds.), *Person memory: The cognitive basis of social perception* (pp. 155–177). Hillsdale, NJ: Lawrence Erlbaum Associates.

Hastie, R., & Kumar, P. A. (1979). Person memory: Personality traits as organizing principles in memory for behavior. *Journal of Personality and Social Psychology, 37*, 25–38.

Higgins, E. T., King, G. A., & Mavin, G. H. (1982). Individual construct accessibility and subjective impressions and recall. *Journal of Personality and Social Psychology, 43*, 35–47.

Higgins, E. T., Rholes, W. S., & Jones, C. R. (1977). Category accessibility and impression formation. *Journal of Experimental Social Psychology, 13*, 141–154.

Jacoby, L. L., & Dallas, M. (1981). On the relationship between autobiographical memory and perceptual learning. *Journal of Experimental Psychology: General, 110*, 306–340.

Kintsch, W. (1968). Recognition and free recall of organized lists. *Science, 78*, 481–487.

Klein, S. B., & Loftus, J. (1993). The mental representation of trait and autobiographical knowledge about the self. In T. K. Srull and R. S. Wyer (Eds.), *Advances in social cognition*, Vol. 5 (pp. 1–49). Hillsdale, NJ: Lawrence Erlbaum Associates.

Kunst-Wilson, W. R., & Zajonc, R. B. (1980). Affective discrimination of stimuli that cannot be recognized. *Science, 207*, 557–558.

McConahay, J. B. (1986). Modern racism, ambivalence, and the modern racism scale. In J. F. Dovidio and S. L. Gaertner (Eds.), *Prejudice, discrimination, and racism* (pp. 91–125). Orlando, FL: Academic Press.

Meyer, D. E., & Schvaneveldt, R. W. (1976). Meaning, memory structure and mental processes. *Science, 192*, 27–33.

Murphy, S. T., & Zajonc, R. B. (1993). Affect, cognition, and awareness: Affective priming with optimal and suboptimal stimulus exposures. *Journal of Personality and Social Psychology, 64*, 723–739.

Neely, J. H. (1977). Semantic priming and retrieval from lexical memory: Roles of inhibitionless spreading activation and limited-capacity attention. *Journal of Experimental Psychology: General, 106*, 225–254.

Nelson, T. O., Fehling, M. R., & Moore-Glascock, J. (1979). The nature of semantic savings for items forgotten from long-term memory. *Journal of Experimental Psychology: General, 108*, 225–250.

Pachella, R. G. (1974). The interpretation of reaction time in information-processing research. In B. H. Kantowitz (Ed.), *Human information processing: Tutorials in performance and cognition* (pp. 41–82). Hillsdale, NJ: Lawrence Erlbaum Associates.

Packard, V. (1957). *The hidden persuaders*. New York: McKay.

Read, S. J., & Marcus-Newhall, A. (1993). Explanatory coherence in social explanations: A parallel distributed processing account. *Journal of Personality and Social Psychology, 65*, 429–447.

Schacter, D. L., & Graf, P. (1986). Effects of elaborative processing on implicit and explicit memory for new associations. *Journal of Experimental Psychology: Learning, Memory and Cognition, 12,* 432–444.

Shiffrin, R. M., & Schneider, W. (1977). Controlled and automatic human information processing: II. Perceptual learning, automatic attending, and a general theory. *Psychological Review, 84,* 127–190.

Smith, E. R. (1989). Procedural efficiency and on-line social judgments. In J. N. Bassili (Ed.), *On-line cognition in person perception* (pp. 19–37). Hillsdale, NJ: Lawrence Erlbaum Associates.

Smith, E. R., & Miller, F. D. (1983). Mediation among attributional inferences and comprehension processes: Initial findings and a general method. *Journal of Personality and Social Psychology, 44,* 492–505.

Smith, E. R., Branscombe, N. R., & Bormann, C. (1988). Generality of the effects of practice on social judgment tasks. *Journal of Personality and Social Psychology, 54,* 385–395.

Srull, T. K. (1981). Person memory: Some tests of associative storage and retrieval models. *Journal of Experimental Psychology: Human Learning and Memory, 7,* 440–463.

Srull, T. K. (1984). Methodological techniques for the study of person memory and social cognition. In R. S. Wyer and T. K. Srull (Eds.), *Handbook of social cognition* (pp.1–72). Hillsdale, NJ: Lawrence Erlbaum Associates.

Srull, T. K., & Wyer, R. S. (1979). The role of category accessibility in the interpretation of information about persons: Some determinants and implications. *Journal of Personality and Social Psychology, 37,* 1660–1672.

Srull, T. K., Lichtenstein, M., & Rothbart, M. (1985). Associative storage and retrieval processes in person memory. *Journal of Experimental Psychology: Learning, Memory and Cognition, 11,* 316–345.

Stangor, C., & McMillan, D. (1992). Memory for expectancy-congruent and expectancy-incongruent information: A review of the social and social developmental literatures. *Psychological Bulletin, 111,* 42–61.

Sternberg, R. J., & Tulving, E. (1977). The measurement of subjective organization in free recall. *Psychological Bulletin, 84,* 539–556.

Sternberg, S. (1969) The discovery of processing stages: Extensions of Donders' method. *Acta Psychologica, 30,* 276–315.

Taylor, S. E. (1975). On inferring one's own attitudes from one's behavior: Some delimiting conditions. *Journal of Personality and Social Psychology, 31,* 126–131.

Taylor, S. E., & Fiske, S. T. (1981). Getting inside the head: Methodologies for process analysis in attribution and social cognition. In J. H. Harvey, W. Ickes, and R. F. Kidds (Eds.), *New directions in attribution research,* Vol. 3 (pp.459–524). Hillsdale, NJ: Lawrence Erlbaum Associates.

Tourangeau, R., Rasinski, K. A., & D'Andrade, R. (1991). Attitude structure and belief accessibility. *Journal of Experimental Social Psychology, 27,* 48–75.

Tulving, E. (1964). Intratrial and intertrial retention: Notes towards a theory of free recall verbal learning. *Psychological Review, 71,* 219–237.

Tulving, E. (1983). *Elements of episodic memory.* Oxford, UK: Clarendon Press.

Tulving, E., & Thomson, D. M. (1973). Encoding specificity and retrieval processes in episodic memory. *Psychological Review, 80,* 352–373.

Tulving, E., Schacter, D. L., & Stark, H. A. (1982). Priming effects in word-fragment completion are independent of recognition memory. *Journal of Experimental Psychology: Learning, Memory, and Cognition, 8,* 336–342.

Uleman, J. S., Newman, L., & Winter, L. (1987). Making spontaneous trait inferences uses some cognitive capacity at encoding. Unpublished manuscript.

Winter, L., & Uleman, J. S. (1984). When are social judgments made? Evidence for the spontaneousness of trait inferences. *Journal of Personality and Social Psychology, 47,* 237–252.

Winter, L., Uleman, J. S., & Cunniff, C. (1985). How automatic are social judgments? *Journal of Personality and Social Psychology, 49,* 904–917.

Zajonc, R. B. (1968). Attitudinal effects of mere exposure. *Journal of Personality and Social Psychology, 9,* 1–27.

Zajonc, R. B. (1980). Feeling and thinking: Preferences need no inferences. *American Psychologist, 35,* 151–175.

Chapter Five

The Psychophysiological Perspective on the Social Mind

Piotr Winkielman, Gary G. Berntson, and John T. Cacioppo

Introduction

In 1888, Fere reported that it is possible to measure bodily concomitants of mental activities by attaching two electrodes to a person's hand and measuring changes in electrical resistance. A century later, technological advances have made it possible to track the activity of the autonomic nervous system while people pursue their regular daily activities. We can peer into the waking brain of healthy individuals using functional imaging and measure activity of small groups of neurons with intracranial recording while patients undergo surgery. We have several techniques that can selectively modify activity of neural circuits and influence the levels of specific neurotransmitters. We can identify the location of neural circuits within millimeters and trace changes in electrical brain activity with millisecond precision. Equally breathtaking is the evolution of the ease and quality of data processing. Computers with huge storage capacity and fast processors have become as much a staple in this research as the electrode. Sophisticated analytic tools allow for accurate representation and analysis of even the most complex psychophysiological signals.

Clearly, modern psychophysiology offers an exciting set of tools for probing the relationship between psychological and physiological processes in humans. But how do we use these tools to our best advantage? How do we properly make the inference from a change in skin conductance or a blot of color on a brain scan to a psychological process? More important, are these tools really useful for a social psychologist? Can they reveal something that cannot be captured with other means? Can they help us advance social psychological

Work on this chapter was supported by the Ohio State University Postdoctoral Fellowship to Piotr Winkielman and by Grants from the National Institute of Mental Health (P50MH52384-01A1-3307560-12) and the John D. and Catherine T. MacArthur Foundation to John T. Cacioppo. We would like to thank Gwen Dewar, Danny McIntosh, Valerie Stone, Julie Wilbarger, and the book editors for their help with this manuscript.

theory? The goal of this chapter is to answer these questions, and show that when these tools are used with caution and understanding, they can reveal new phenomena, spur theoretical advances, and contribute to the continuing development of social psychology.

We start with a brief review of the history of the psychophysiological approaches to social psychology. We suggest that many problems plaguing early research were due to technical limitations, insufficient knowledge about the body, and incorrect assumptions about the relationships between social psychological constructs and physiological signals. We discuss improvements in these areas, focusing on the key issue of inferring the psychological significance from physiological signals. We point out that while modern psychophysiology makes no pretense to be able to describe social behavior as a list of physiological correlates of psychological events, it is nevertheless possible to draw strong inferences from psychophysiological data. Next, we focus on the question of the utility of a psychophysiological approach for social psychology. We argue that many important empirical organizations are obscured by a restricted focus on a social or a biological level of analysis alone, but are apparent through a multi-level analysis that considers a joint operation of social and biological factors. Finally, we discuss several examples of psychophysiology findings that shed light on theoretical debates in social psychology.

Before we start, let us acknowledge a few limitations and add a few clarifications. The psychophysiological approach to social psychology represents a vast literature. As a result, in the limited space of this chapter we are unable to cover such key topics as arousal, facial expression, emotional regulation, health, interpersonal processes, psychosomatics, stress, and many others. We also do not discuss many important moderating variables such as age, gender, and individual differences. Fortunately, there are many excellent recent reviews of these topics (see Adler & Matthews, 1994; Blascovich & Tomaka, 1996; Davison & Pennebaker, 1996; Gardner, Gabriel, & Diekman, in press; Levenson & Ruef, 1997; Uchino, Cacioppo, & Kiecolt-Glaser, 1996). Similarly, we do not discuss many important types of psychophysiological measures such as cardiovascular responses, electroencephalography, and many others. Again, we refer the reader to recent reviews (Blascovich, in press; Cacioppo, Tassinary, & Berntson, in press). The psychophysiological approach to social psychology has been used to investigate the physiological consequences of social variables as well as a way to make inferences about mental processes underlying social behavior. The focus of our chapter is biased somewhat toward the latter approach. Finally, we would like to clarify that we use the word "psychophysiology" to refer to investigations focusing on both the autonomic and central nervous system, although the latter focus has earned a separate term of "neuroscience."

Inferring the Psychological Significance of Physiological Signals: From Early Enthusiasm to Cautious Optimism

Early observations

The notion that social psychological processes can be inferred from physiological responses dates at least as far back as the third century BC, when the Greek physician Erasistratos used his observation of an irregular heartbeat in a young man when his attractive stepmother visited to infer that lovesickness, not a physical illness, was the cause of the young man's malady (Mesulam & Perry, 1972). Two millennia later, the potential value of the psycho-physiological data was recognized by McDougall (1908/1928) in the first social psychology textbook, who discussed the importance of biological influences (primarily instincts) on interpersonal interaction.

Empirical investigations of social psychological questions using psychophysiological data were not systematically pursued until the 1920s. Understandably, the initial studies were concerned primarily with establishing physiological correlates. For example, Riddle (1925) examined the correlation between deception and respiratory rhythms of people bluffing during a poker game. Smith (1936) investigated the usefulness of skin resistance for study-ing social influence by monitoring response of individuals confronted with the informa-tion that their peers' attitudes were discrepant from their own. Rankin and Campbell (1955) showed that Caucasian subjects showed a larger electrodermal response when an African American, rather than Caucasian, experimenter adjusted electrodes on their arms, a response that was interpreted as indication of prejudice.

After these modest beginnings, social psychophysiology grew in ambition, scope, and popularity. Books and chapters devoted to psychophysiological approaches to social behavior were published (Leiderman & Shapiro, 1964; Shapiro & Crider, 1969) and researchers began to hail the alleged objectivity and bias-free nature of psychophysiological measures.

But the enthusiasm was never universal. As a field, social psychology was always ambiva-lent toward biological measures and levels of analysis. Initially, biological factors were equated with innate causes such as instincts – an anathema to those who believed social psychology should focus on situational determinants. Thus, in 1924, Floyd Allport, author of an in-fluential social psychology textbook, argued that it is more important to study how people construe events than to reduce social processes to physiological variables. Gordon Allport (1947) agreed, emphasizing verbal reports as a primary way to study social psychological processes. Other critics dismissed psychophysiological measures as limited to crude ener-getic aspects of behavior or relegated them to an inferior status of "last resort" measures – useful only if one has to investigate responses over which subjects have no control (Dawes & Smith, 1985). In an ironic reversal of physiological reductionism, some argued that bodily manifestations are "epiphenomena" of social processes (McGuire, 1985). The criti-cal attitudes were bolstered in the late 1960s and early 1970s, when many psychophysi-ological studies of social processes proved disappointing. Among the findings were weak associations between self-reports and autonomic measurements, low correlations among various autonomic measures, and poor replicability across laboratories. In retrospect what these studies showed was that the mappings between social psychological processes and physiological events were less straightforward than initially believed (Cacioppo & Petty, 1983). Nevertheless, a number of investigators surmised that physiological approaches were irrelevant or unreliable indices (e.g. Barlow, 1988) and all chapters on social processes and biology were dropped from the *Handbook of Social Psychology*.

Contemporary perspectives

The criticisms did not stop the growth of the psychophysiological approach. Indeed, since 1986 more than 200 studies incorporating physiological variables have appeared in mainstream social psychological journals, and chapters discussing the interplay of biological and social processes can now be found in various handbooks in the field (e.g. Blascovich, in press; Cacioppo, Berntson, & Crites, 1996; Davison & Pennebaker, 1996). Two important reasons are behind this growth. First, researchers realized that the problem with the early research was not the biological level of analysis, but the assumptions and inferences drawn when formulating hypotheses, designing experiments, or interpreting psychophysiological data. This led to refinements in measurements and inference. Second, advances in neuroscientific techniques made increasingly possible investigations of the neural basis of social phenomena in normal populations, leading to the emergence of the field of social neuroscience. In the next few paragraphs we will discuss these developments.

Methodological and conceptual refinements   A number of early problems were attributable to technical or methodological limitations and have fallen as the field progressed. For example, the replicability of psychophysiological measurements was fostered by the establishment of standards by the Society for Psychophysiological Research (see Cacioppo, Tassinary, & Berntson, in press). Other early problems were linked to insufficient physiological knowledge or simplistic assumptions about the operation of physiological processes. For example, many early studies treated arousal as a generalized nonspecific activation that equally affects autonomic, muscular, and central activity. Hence, depending on the paradigm, arousal was assessed with a wide array of physiological measures, some designed to reflect central activation (electroencephalography) and others designed to reflect various aspects of peripheral activation (heart rate, skin conductance, etc.). This, of course, led to conflicting findings and conceptual confusion. With additional research and theoretical development, however, sturdier, more intricate bridges were built spanning activational and behavioral processes (see Berntson, Cacioppo, & Quigley, 1991; Cacioppo, Berntson, & Crites, 1996).

Other important developments occurred in psychophysiological inference. Early psychophysiology was guided by the assumption of isomorphism between the psychological and physiological domain (Sarter, Berntson, & Cacioppo, 1996). Thus, it was believed that most psychological phenomena have a straightforward one-to-one correspondence to physiological systems and processes. This assumption led to two problems. First, researchers rarely tested if such an assumption is empirically true. Second, researchers believed that isomorphism is necessary for a psychophysiological measure to be useful.

Initially, once a physiological response that differentiated the presence versus absence of a psychological operation was identified, it was then assumed to be an invariant index of the presence or absence of a psychological event across various situations and paradigms. However, without testing the assumption of invariance, interpreting physiological data in this manner risks the error of affirming the consequent (Cacioppo & Tassinary, 1990). For example, the observation that lying is associated with a cardiovascular and skin conductance response (SCR) was initially thought to justify using these measures as an indicator of lying. Others who found that anxiety increased skin conductance response (SCR), then used SCR as an indicator of anxiety across individuals, situations, and paradigms. The same form of interpretation was evident in neuropsychology, where the observation that damage to a brain area leads to a deficit in a psychological function was interpreted as evidence that the brain area is uniquely identified with the function.[1]

Today, researchers are more likely to perform multiple tests before declaring an isomorphic relationship between a psychological and a physiological element. For example, before researchers in neuroscience attribute a psychological function to a brain circuit, they look for convergence of evidence from a variety of top-down and bottom-up approaches. As Sarter et al. (1996) have argued, evidence that a change in the psychological domain leads to a change in the physiological domain (e.g. performance of a psychological function leads to an activation of a circuit) is especially convincing when accompanied by evidence that a change in the physiological domain leads to a change in the psychological domain (e.g. lesion of a circuit results in a psychological deficit).[2]

Similarly, today, researchers are more likely to carefully delineate conditions under which a psychophysiological relationship holds and consider other reasons why a physiological response may occur (i.e. the base rate problem) before declaring that a physiological response can be used to "index" a psychological function (Cacioppo, Tassinary, & Berntson, in press). This can be illustrated with an example from research on the relationship between the facial EMG activity and emotion. Several research studies demonstrated that unpleasant imagery and stimuli lead to enhanced EMG activity over the brow region (e.g. Cacioppo, Petty, Losch, & Kim, 1986). Such a relationship allows facial EMG to be used to test specific experimental hypotheses using hypothetico-deductive logic, as discussed below. Note, however, that by itself such research does not demonstrate that EMG activity over the brow region *indexes* emotion. This is because increases in EMG activity over the brow region can occur for other reasons as well. The base rate problem, however, can be addressed empirically. To do that, Cacioppo, Martzke, & Petty (1988) first defined different forms of EMG responses over the brow region, and then examined the relation of these forms to the psychological state of their participants. Specifically, in their study, participants were interviewed about themselves while recordings of EMG activity were made. Afterwards, the participants watched a videotape of specific segments of the interview and were asked to describe what they had been thinking and feeling during each. Results indicated that specific forms of EMG responses over the brow region were predictive of the valence of participants' feelings during the interview, suggesting that inferential limitations attributable to high base rates can be lessened if the responses of interest are well defined. It is important to note, however, that even when such relations are established, it is not clear whether they generalize to other experimental contexts. Said more generally, the experimental context is as important to consider when interpreting the psychological significance of a physiological signal as it is when interpreting the psychological meaning of verbal responses or reaction time data.

In the preceding section we argued that contemporary researchers realize that the existence of isomorphic psychophysiological relationships cannot be assumed, but rather needs to be empirically verified. As we suggested at the end of that section, the correspondence between most psychological and physiological elements is context dependent. That is, depending on the context, the same neural circuit may participate in a different function and the same autonomic response may be elicited by a different psychological state. Similarly, depending on the context, the same psychological function may be performed by different circuits and affect a variety of psychological responses (see Farah, 1994; Sarter et al., 1996 for discussion of these issues). This observation raises a critical question. Do we need to test the nature of psychophysiological correspondence in every imaginable context before we are able to interpret a physiological measure? The answer, of course, is no. What this observation points out, however, is the critical role of theory in relating psychological and physiological events. As noted above, if different predictions can be derived from two psychological theories, the hypothetico-deductive logic of the experimental design allows strong inferences to be drawn even when the physiological measure is context dependent (Cacioppo & Tassinary, 1990; Platt, 1964).

As long as the researcher is sensitive to these limitations, and considers the base rate of the physiological event of interest, mapping the relationship between psychological and physiological events even within a single paradigm can offer valuable insights. This point can be illustrated with the following study that used skin conductance responses (SCR) to examine the question of knowledge without awareness. Tranel, Fowles, and Damasio (1985) were interested in whether patients who, as result of injury or disease, lost the ability to recognize faces, somehow retained an implicit ability to perform this discrimination. To test this hypothesis, the authors needed an implicit measure that varied as a function of facial recognition. However, the authors were aware that skin conductance responses can occur spontaneously and that – like reaction time measures – the psychological interpretation of skin conductance responses depends on the experimental context in which it was observed. Thus, they first ran a study demonstrating that in normal subjects the presentation of familiar faces evoked larger skin conductance responses than did the presentation of unfamiliar faces. The authors then used the same stimuli and procedures to study patients with prosopagnosia (inability to recognize faces). The results showed that prosopagnosic patients showed larger skin conductance responses to familiar faces than to unfamiliar faces, despite the absence of any conscious awareness of this distinction. That is, the psychophysiological measure provided early evidence of knowledge without awareness. Note that the importance of this work does not depend on skin conductance response being an invariant index of the recognition – it certainly is not. For example, studies on the orienting reaction have found enhanced SCR to novel stimuli (Lynn, 1966).

In conclusion, the time when biological levels of analyses were seen as dealing with innate or invariant characteristics has long passed. Accordingly, psychophysiology should not be thought of as providing a list of physiological invariants with which to index psychological constructs, but rather as a field of knowledge rich in theory and methods that may help innovative scholars test social psychological hypotheses.[3] Importantly, the issues raised in this section are not unique to psychophysiological measures. In fact, self-report and chronometric measures would all have to be abandoned if they were held to the requirement that they must map psychological operations in a one-to-one manner across individuals and contexts. The power of traditional social and cognitive measures comes from our knowledge of their strengths and limitations and from our understanding of their meaning within our paradigms. It behooves one to think of psychophysiological measures similarly.

Neuroscience tools enter social psychology Another reason for the current excitement about the psychophysiological approach to social psychology are the advances in neuroscience. For decades, studies of the neural basis of behavior were limited primarily to animal models, postmortem examinations, and observations of patients with brain damage. Recent years, however, brought enormous advances in brain imaging, electrophysiological recording, and neurochemical techniques. These tools are now regularly used to explore elementary cognitive processes in normal populations (Gazzaniga, 1994). These advances were not missed by social psychologists and increasingly subtle social phenomena also began to succumb to neuroscientific inquiry. Such interdisciplinary research led to the emergence of social neuroscience, a discipline that explicitly concerns itself with the study of the relationship between neural and social processes (Cacioppo & Berntson, 1992).

Towards a Multi-level Analysis of Social Phenomena

In the preceding section we discussed the advances in psychophysiological measurement and inference as well as the emergence of new tools for studying the neural basis of social behavior. But the excitement behind the psychophysiological approach to social psychology extends beyond methodological refinements or the addition of a brain scanner and neurochemistry lab to the psychophysiologist's toolbox. Perhaps the most important reason behind this excitement is the growing realization that a comprehensive account of social behavior calls for going beyond the single level of analysis and requires joint attention to factors from both the biological and social levels.[4] This point might be easier to appreciate after considering three general principles from Cacioppo and Berntson's (1992) doctrine of multi-level analysis.

The principle of multiple determinism specifies that a target event at one level of organization may have multiple antecedents within or across levels of organization. For example, consider the multiple factors that contribute to drug abuse. On the micro-level, researchers identified the contribution of individual differences in the susceptibility of the endogenous opiod receptor system, while on the macro-level researchers point to the role of social variables such as socialization and peer pressure. Our understanding of drug abuse is incomplete if either perspective is excluded.[5]

The principle of nonadditive determinism specifies that properties of the collective whole are not always predictable from the properties of the parts. Said differently, some empirical regularities will not be detectable until one looks at the data across levels of organization. Consider an illustrative study by Haber and Barchas (1983). These investigators were interested in the effects of amphetamine on primate behavior. The behavior of nonhuman primates was examined following the administration of amphetamine or placebo. No clear differences emerged between these conditions until each primate's position in the social hierarchy was considered. When this social factor was taken into account, amphetamines were found to increase dominant behavior in primates high in the social hierarchy and to increase submissive behavior in primates low in the social hierarchy. The import-ance of this study derives from its demonstration of how the effects of physiological changes on social behavior can appear unreliable until the analysis is extended across levels of organization.

A strictly physiological (or social) analysis, regardless of the sophistication of the measurement technology, may not have unraveled the orderly relationship that existed.

Finally, the principle of reciprocal determinism specifies that there can be mutual influences between microscopic (e.g. biological) and macroscopic (e.g. social) factors. For example, as is well known, the level of testosterone in nonhuman male primates can promote sexual behavior. Less well known, however, is the fact that the availability of receptive females influences the level of testosterone in nonhuman primates (Bernstien, Gordon, & Rose, 1983). Within social psychology, research has demonstrated that exposure to violent and erotic materials influences the level of physiological arousal in males, and that the level of physiological arousal has a reciprocal influence on perceptions of and tendencies toward sex and aggression (Zillman, 1989). A comprehensive account of these phenomena cannot be achieved by social psychologists if biological levels of organization are considered irrelevant or outside their purview.

Considering multiple levels of analysis not only can ensure more comprehensive explanations of existing social phenomena, but can also reveal new empirical domains previously thought not to be subject to social influences. It can challenge existing theories in the neurosciences and physiology, resulting in inclusion of social variables. It can even lead to theoretical revolutions. For instance, immune functions were once considered only to reflect physiological responses to pathogens and tissue damage. It is now clear that social psychological variables are among the most powerful determinants of the expression of immune reactions (for reviews see Kennedy, Glaser, & Kiecolt-Glaser, 1990; Uchino, Cacioppo, & Kiecolt-Glaser, 1996).

Changing notions of the mind

The previous section emphasized a growing recognition of the value of looking at both the body and the mind in advancing psychological research. These developments, of course, did not happen in a theoretical vacuum. The notion of multi-level analysis fits the present *Zeitgeist* and coincides with the fading of two important assumptions about the mind.

The first fading notion is the traditional computer metaphor representing the mind as a "hardware-independent" software that can "run" on anything – neurons, silicon chips, or even wooden parts (Block, 1995). While the computer metaphor nicely clarified the benefits of analyzing psychological processes on a level of function, it misleadingly suggested a complete independence of the hardware and software levels. This meant that nothing useful about the organization of the mind can be learned from studying the organization of the brain, and, conversely, that nothing useful about the brain can be learned from the mind.

Another fading notion is the conception of the mind as a "general-purpose" mechanism that is limitlessly shapeable by environmental conditions and able to process all mental content with equal ease. The assumption of no biological constraints clashes with animal and human research showing the effects of preparedness and specialization for many psychological processes (Hirshfeld & Gelman, 1994; Seligman, 1970). It also conflicts with what we know about the powerful role of natural selection that shaped the design of the brain for millions of years (Cosmides & Tooby, 1995; Rozin & Schull, 1988).

How Can Psychophysiology Contribute to Social Psychology?

In the preceding sections we have suggested that, when used properly, the theory and methods of psychophysiology allow strong inferences about psychological processes. We have also argued that psychophysiological inquiry can foster comprehensive accounts of cognition, emotion, and behavior. In this section, we illustrate how social psychological theories can benefit from a psychophysiological approach. Specifically, we show that the psychophysiological research can (a) contribute to discovery of new phenomena and (b) help us decide between competing theories of existing phenomena. We draw our examples from two popular domains of research: social cognition and emotion. First, focusing on social cognition, we show how psychophysiology played a crucial role in discovery of implicit memory and then discuss how recent psychophysiological findings could contribute to the debate about differences between social and non-social cognition. We then turn to the topic of emotion and show how psychophysiology has contributed to the debate about the relation between affect and cognition, inspired a change in our understanding of the relation between positive and negative affect, and offered a new look at the role of emotions in reasoning.[6]

Social cognition

Implicit and explicit memory   A classic example of the influence of psychophysiology on theories in cognitive and social psychology comes from neuropsychological research on implicit memory. Until the mid 1950s, psychologists thought of long-term memory as a single, general mechanism responsible for storage of all types of information. This started to change with the now-famous neurological patient H.M.. In an attempt to treat epilepsy, H.M. underwent a bilateral resection of the medial portion of the temporal lobes, including the hippocampus and mammiliary bodies (Scoville & Milner, 1957). Although the surgery reduced H.M.'s epileptic seizures, the patient also appeared to have lost the ability to remember new information. Interestingly, further investigations determined that H.M.'s anterograde amnesia was not as complete as originally thought. In fact, H.M. showed a surprising ability to acquire new skills in the absence of any explicit recollection of learning those skills. This finding spurred research in cognitive psychology resulting in development of multi-memory models. These models distinguish between episodic memory, which enables people to retrieve specific events from the past, and semantic memory, which enables people to act on a knowledge without requiring a recollection of a specific event. Further refinements led to the concepts of explicit memory and implicit memory (see Squire, 1992 for a review). The theoretical changes sparked by H.M. and other neurological cases soon found their way into social psychology, inspiring a wave of research on implicit memory for social information and contributing to the current interest in automaticity (e.g. Bargh, 1996; Greenwald & Banaji, 1995).

What is social about social cognition?   Psychophysiological findings can also bear directly on existing theoretical controversies in social psychology. Consider the debate on whether mental processes dealing with social objects are different from mental processes dealing with non-social objects.

According to Ostrom (1984) social psychologists take three positions on the question "what is social about social cognition." The *fundamentalists* claim that the same cognitive capacities and processing mechanisms are available regardless of whether the stimuli involve social or non-social objects. The proponents of the *building-block* view say that the processes involved in dealing with social events build upon simpler and conceptually more fundamental processes involved in dealing with non-social events. For example, principles of non-social cognition such as classical conditioning and categorization need to be supplemented with variables such as self-relevance or personal goals. Finally, the *realists* oppose the building-block view, arguing that mental processes involved in dealing with non-social objects derive from processes designed to deal with social objects. Thus, social cognition represents the general case in the study of cognitive processes, whereas research with non-social objects represents a special case in which the parameters on the social dimension are set to zero.

Interestingly, Ostrom (1984, p. 23) noted that although "the question of social versus non-social cognition has implications for many different research areas, not enough data are yet available to determine whether different processes are involved in the two." We suggest that recent psychophysiological research on face perception and mental state inference offers relevant evidence.

A successful social interaction requires an ability to remember new faces, recognize familiar faces, and correctly interpret facial expressions.[7] Are faces processed just like other complex objects? Evidence suggests that at least some aspect of face perception involves unique processes. Such a conclusion is suggested by findings suggesting the existence of face-specific neurons in the temporal lobe (Perrett, Rolls, & Caan, 1982) and findings on dissociations between face and object recognition (Bruce & Young, 1986). As mentioned above, prosopagnosic patients lose the ability to recognize people based on their faces, yet they are able to recognize comparably complex non-facial stimuli.

The possibility that processing of some kinds of social information may be unique extends beyond perceptual stimuli like faces to reasoning about mental states such as intentions, beliefs, and desires – an ability that is long considered to be a marker of social cognition (Heider, 1958; Ostrom, 1984). In recent years researchers began noticing that some brain injuries compromise people's ability to make inferences about others' mental states. For example, patients with damage to the orbitofrontal cortex show selective deficits on advanced theory of mind tests (Stone, Baron-Cohen, & Knight, 1998). Neuroimaging data with normal populations provide complementary findings. For instance, Baron-Cohen, Ring, Moriarty, Schmitz, Costa, & Plaisted (1994) found that answering questions about mental state terms led to increased activation in orbitofrontal regions compared to answering questions about terms related to body parts. Interestingly, some developmental disorders are characterized by a selective impairment or selective sparing in the ability to make mental state inferences. A case in point are children with autism who have difficulty with false belief tasks and tasks requiring understanding of social interaction, but who perform well on tasks requiring understanding of non-mental representations and interactions with physical objects (Baron-Cohen, Leslie, & Firth, 1985). In contrast, individuals with Williams or Down Syndrome perform relatively well on theory-of-mind tasks but are impaired on other, less social tasks (Karmiloff-Smith, Klima, Bellugi, Grant, & Baron-Cohen, 1995).

What do these data tell about the relation between social and non-social cognition? They do not fit predictions from the realist or the fundamentalist model, emphasizing the generality of social or non-social cognition, respectively. According to these positions, we should not observe a relative impairment or advantage, or differences in the pattern of neural activation, while processing social versus non-social information (assuming task demands have been equated). The alternative "building-block" model assumes that social cognition derives from non-social cognition. The model is certainly correct when we consider basic perceptual and conceptual processes. However, the strong form of the model has trouble accounting for observations that the processing of social information can be relatively spared compared to processing of non-social information. In other words, it seems that processing of at least certain kinds of social information is not derivative from mechanisms involved in processing of complex non-social information. We hasten to clarify that the above data do *not* imply the existence of a physically separate, dedicated circuit for dealing with "social" information in general, or all face-related or mental-state related information in particular. We simply suggest that processing of certain kinds of social information may represent a unique combination of patterns across neural substrates.[8]

Human emotions

Another topic in social psychology that has benefited from progress in psychophysiology is emotion. The dialogue between psychological and physiological investigators began with James (1894) and continues to this day (e.g. Damasio, 1994; LeDoux, 1995; Panksepp, 1998). In this section, we limit discussion to three issues that have received quite a bit of attention in the social psychological community: the relation between affect and cognition, the relation between positive and negative affect, and the role of emotions in decision making.

Relation between cognition and emotion   In 1980 Zajonc argued for primacy and independence of affective processing. His argument has been criticized on conceptual grounds by researchers suggesting that regular cognitive mechanisms are fully sufficient to explain processing of affective stimuli (e.g. Lazarus, 1984). The empirical basis of Zajonc's argument was also criticized. For example, as evidence that some affective responses involve minimal cognitive participation, Zajonc cited the increase in positive affect as a result of repeated, unreinforced exposures to stimuli (the mere-exposure effect). Some researchers argued that the mere-exposure effect can be explained without any reference to affective change (e.g. Mandler, Nakamura, & Van Zandt, 1987).

In the years since 1980, psychophysiological evidence has shed new light on the emotion–cognition debate. Consistent with the assumptions of affective primacy, animal studies suggest the existence of a pathway that projects a coarse representation of a stimulus from the visual thalamus directly to the amygdala. When necessary, this pathway allows for a generation of a quick affective response based on an analysis of primitive stimulus features, before a more complex analysis is completed (LeDoux, 1995).

Consistent with the assumption of affect independence, recent animal and human studies suggest that emotional and cognitive processing rely on the integrity of partially different neural mechanisms. For example, in monkeys, damage to the amygdala affects emotional behavior but not memory, while damage to the hippocampal formation affects memory but not emotional behavior (Zola-Morgan, Squire, Alvarez-Royo, & Clower, 1991). In human studies, patients with damaged amygdala show impairments in emotional conditioning, but are able to acquire declarative knowledge about reinforcement contingencies, while patients with damaged hippocampus show impairments in declarative learning, but are able to acquire emotionally conditioned responses (Bechara, Tranel, Damasio, & Adolphs, 1995). The human findings are not limited to cases where researchers had to rely on naturally occurring damages to neural circuits. For example, neuroimaging studies with normal populations show selective activation of the amygdala during acquisition of conditioned responses (e.g. Morris, Oehman, & Dolan, 1998). Finally, the existence of a unique evaluative mechanism is consistent with the recent studies using event-related potentials. For instance, Crites and Cacioppo (1996) reported that affective categorizations were characterized by a right-lateralized late positive event-related brain potential, whereas non-affective categorizations were more symmetrical – a finding consistent with the importance of the right hemisphere in emotion (Tucker & Frederick, 1989).

Psychophysiological data also shed light on the mechanisms underlying the effects of mere-exposure. As noted above, some researchers argue that the mere-exposure effect can be fully explained by cognitive mechanisms. According to such an account, repeated exposure first leads to an increase in perceptual fluency (processing ease) of the stimulus. Participants then (mis)attribute the enhanced fluency to liking, or any other salient dimension, just like they have been shown to (mis)attribute fluency to features like fame, loudness, or clarity (Bornstein & D'Agostino, 1994; Klinger & Greenwald, 1994; see also Mandler et al., 1987 for a related account based on the notion of "non-specific" activation). Thus, according to these accounts, liking for the mere-exposed stimulus is not genuine, but an artifact of the judgment task. However, Winkielman and Cacioppo (1998) argued that the involvement of perceptual fluency mechanisms does not necessarily imply the absence of genuine affect. If so, these authors reasoned, increasing perceptual fluency should not only lead to increases in liking judgment, but also to increases in electromyographic (EMG) activity over the cheek region – an indicator of positive affect. In a series of studies using various manipulations of processing ease (e.g. stimulus degradation, presentation duration) Winkielman & Cacioppo found that easy-to-process stimuli generated stronger responses over the cheek region than hard-to-process ones, consistent with the posited increase in positive affect. The above findings are consistent with demonstrations that mere-exposed stimuli generate stronger EMG responses over the cheek region than novel stimuli (Harmon-Jones and Allen, 1996).[9] Interestingly, both Winkielman and Cacioppo (1998) and Harmon-Jones and Allen (1996) studies observed the growth of positive responses to initially neutral stimuli, not a decrease in negative responses, thus suggesting that the mere-exposure effect cannot be fully explained by the extinction of neophobia (Panksepp, 1998; Zajonc, 1998).

Relation between positive and negative affect   Psychophysiological evidence has also contributed to our understanding of affect organization. Past research has traditionally been guided by the notion that the qualitative features of affect could be represented along a single evaluative (pleasant/unpleasant) continuum (e.g. Osgood, Suci, & Tannenbaum, 1957; Thrustone, 1931). Such a conception considers approach–avoidance behavior, positive–negative mood, and favorable–unfavorable feelings as bipolar opposites, analogous to the physical construct of hot and cold temperatures. Although overt affective expressions may indeed tend toward bipolarity, Cacioppo, Gardner, & Berntson (1997) proposed in their bivariate model of evaluative space that the mechanisms underlying the experience and processing of positive and negative affect are partially independent and asymmetrical. Important to the emergence of the bivariate model were psychophysiological data suggesting the existence of partially separate systems involved in the processing of appetitive and defensive information (see review by Cacioppo, Gardner, & Berntson, in press). Another important foundation for this model was research on conflict behavior in rodents (Miller, 1959). This research provided one of the earliest demonstrations of positive/negative asymmetry by noting that the slope for the avoidance gradient was steeper than the slope for the approach gradient (see Cacioppo & Berntson, 1994 for discussion).

The bivariate model of evaluative space helps understand a variety of sociopsychological findings. It sheds new light on attitudinal ambivalence by specifying mechanisms subserving the coactivation of positive and negative affect toward the same stimulus (e.g. Katz, Wackenhut, & Hass, 1986; Gardner & Cacioppo, 1995), and also by predicting an asymmetry in the topography of attitude ambivalence (Cacioppo, Gardner, & Berntson, 1997). The model also helps explain the independence of positive and negative mood in daily ratings by allowing for a differential dynamic of systems responsible for regulation of positive and negative moods (e.g. Diener & Emmons, 1984). Finally, the model accounts for observations that processing of positive and negative information are not mirror images of each other, but are characterized by different activation functions. Specifically, when dealing with neutral stimuli, the organism shows a default tendency for positive behaviors – an operating characteristic referred to as "positivity offset." For example, given little information people expect happy events across a variety of life domains (Taylor, 1991) and tend to form positive impressions of unknown others (Peeters & Czapinski, 1990). However, as the amount of external information increases, the effects of the positivity offset give way to the effects of a second operating characteristic posited in the bivariate model of evaluative space – the negativity bias. The negativity bias refers to the organism's tendency to respond more strongly to the increase in the amount of negative information than to the comparable increase in the amount of positive information. For example, in impression formation, negative features weigh more heavily on the overall impression than do positive features (Skowronski & Carlston, 1989). Recent findings suggest that this negativity bias emerges at relatively early stages of evaluative processing. For instance, Ito, Larsen, Smith, & Cacioppo (1998) presented positive, negative, and neutral pictures embedded within sequences of other neutral pictures and recorded event-related potentials (ERPs) in response to these pictures. In prior research, the late positive potential of the ERP has been shown to be sensitive to evaluative categorizations. Ito et al. (1998) showed that the presentation of negative pictures was associated with larger ERPs than the presentation of equally probable, equally extreme, and equally arousing positive pictures, suggesting that the negativity bias emerges even before responses to the stimuli are selected or executed.[10]

The role of emotions in reasoning   Finally, recent psychophysiological evidence may suggest a revision in the traditional view that emotion is an impairment to reason – a view as old as the notion of "animal passions." Consider, for example, patients with damage to the prefrontal cortex. These individuals show only limited deficits in their ability to analyze the pros and cons of a situation, yet are reported to experience great difficulties in making everyday decisions. The decisions of these patients are often poor. For example, one patient repeatedly lost money on "promising" business deals. Moreover, these patients have problems with making decisions in a timely way. For example, one patient spent many hours deciding between two different days for his next doctor visit (Damasio, 1994).

To account for these observations, researchers suggest that one of the functions of the prefrontal cortex is to link the cognitive representations of various options with representations of the anticipated affective consequences of these options (Damasio, 1994; Tucker, Luu, & Pribram, 1995). Such a link gives the decision maker access to somatic representations of affective consequences of past decisions, thus accounting for the differences in rejection/acceptance of alternatives that past experience would deem wise or unwise. Moreover, such a link affectively prioritizes certain options, which allows the decision maker to sort more effectively through the decision tree, thus accounting for the differences in speed of decision making between normals and prefrontal patients.

In an interesting demonstration of the role of affective feedback in reasoning, Bechara, Damasio, Tranel, & Damasio (1997) asked prefrontal patients and normals to make money in a gambling game that required them to select cards from different decks. Some cards were associated with a payment while others were associated with a substantial loss. The rules of the game were complex enough to prevent the players from easily figuring out payoffs associated with each deck. Interestingly, after playing the game for a while, normals started to show anticipatory skin-conductance response to decks associated with a loss and began to avoid taking cards from these decks. The prefrontal patients, however, showed no anticipatory SCR responses to these decks and continued to take cards from them. Interestingly, these autonomic and behavioral differences emerged even though at this point of the game normals and prefrontal patients did not differ in their explicit understanding of the payoff rules. Bechara et al. (1997) interpreted these results to mean that the ability to make good decisions is at least partly dependent on intact mechanisms of affective feedback.

Conclusion

Biological approaches to social psychology have progressed enormously in recent years. Traditional tools have been improved and exciting new ones developed. Researchers have also learned to use these tools with more caution and understanding, thus advancing our ability to make strong inferences from psychophysiological data. Along with these methodological developments, social psychologists have increased their appreciation for the various biological (evolutionary, neural, hormonal) aspects of social phenomena. Today, social psychologists are more likely to realize that it is the social psychological phenomenon, not the particular measurement strategy or level of analysis, that is important in guiding research and theory in social psychology. They also realize that multi-level research can foster comprehensive accounts of existing phenomena, contribute to the discovery of important new phenomena, and inspire theoretical advances.

Obviously, not all investigators will decide to include a biological level of analysis in their research. However, many will discover that consideration of biological factors not only enriches their understanding of basic social psychological processes, but also allows them to better understand the implications of their research for problems of mental and physical health. It would be a shame if social psychologists did not use the best tools available to do that.

Notes

1 Such errors can be seen even today in popular interpretations of neuroscience findings. Once a brain area is found to be activated during the performance of a psychological function, it is then uniquely identified with the function (see Sarter, Berntson, & Cacioppo, 1996). The legacy of phrenology is long-lived and unfortunate as evidenced by the occasional dismissals of entire modern cognitive neuroscience as the "new phrenology."

2 Fortunately, modern neuroscience offers several bottom-up approaches that complement top-down approaches. Researchers can capitalize on naturally occurring disorders and traumas and can manipulate specific neural circuitry by means of selective lesions, activation by electrical stimulation or inactivation by cooling, pharmacological stimulations and blockades, etc.

3 Similarly, it is not a problem that concepts in the physiological domain do not correspond neatly to concepts in the psychological domain (Fodor, 1975). It is still possible to interpret psychophysiological measures in well-constructed psychological designs (Cacioppo & Berntson, 1992).

4 We wish to emphasize the difference between multi-level analysis and reductionism. Multi-level analysis is grounded in the belief that each level provides a unique way of looking at a phenomenon and reveals organizations obscured on other levels. Reductionism implies that one level of analysis is ultimately superior and all phenomena should be explained in its terms (Fodor, 1975).

5 A corollary to the principle of multiple determinism is that the mapping between elements across levels of organization becomes more complex as the number of intervening levels of organization increases. The implication is that the likelihood of erroneous mappings increases as one jumps over levels of organizations.

6 For additional examples and arguments see Klein and Kihlstrom (1998).

7 Recent research underscores the importance of the ability to interpret facial expressions in social interaction. Adolphs, Tranel, and Damasio (1998) asked normal subjects and subjects with amygdala damage for judgments of trustworthiness and approachability of several target individuals. The targets were presented in verbal descriptions and in facial portraits. When relying on the descriptions, participants with amygdala damage rated the targets similarly to controls. However, when relying on portraits, the subjects with amygdala damage rated the untrustworthy and unapproachable targets much less negatively than controls.

8 Recent evidence suggests that uniqueness of social cognition might be partly anchored in a "living versus non-living" distinction. For example, some patients selectively lose ability to recognize animals and plants while preserving the ability to recognize inanimate objects, such as tools (e.g. Caramazzo & Shelton, 1998). Interestingly, Heider (1958) anticipated this possibility by emphasizing the fundamental difference between perception of self-initiated action, and action driven by external forces. Additional research is obviously needed.

9   It is also relevant that in self-report studies subjects rate the perceptually fluent stimuli and the mere-exposed stimuli as more likable, but not as more dislikable, regardless of a question focus (Reber, Winkielman, & Schwarz, 1998; Seamon, McKenna, & Binder, 1998).

10   Such asymmetries in evaluative processing make evolutionary sense. Positivity-offset guarantees that an organism facing neutral or unfamiliar stimuli would be weakly motivated to approach and explore – after, of course, an initial neophobic response is habituated. On the other hand, a negativity bias guarantees that an organism shows caution when dealing with threatening stimuli. Such tendencies make good survival sense, since it is usually more difficult to reverse the consequence of an assault than an opportunity not pursued (Cacioppo, Gardner, & Berntson, in press). Incidentally, humans are not the only species to exhibit behavioral asymmetries in the domain of gains and losses (Stephens & Krebs, 1986).

References

Adler, N., & Matthews, K. (1994). Health psychology: Why do some people get sick and some stay well? *Annual Review of Psychology, 45*, 229–259.

Adolphs, R., Tranel, D., & Damasio, A. R. (1998). The human amygdala in social judgment. *Nature, 393*, 470–474.

Allport, F. H. (1924). *Social Psychology*. Boston: Houghton Mifflin.

Allport, G. W. (1947). Scientific models and human morals. *Psychological Review, 54*, 182–192.

Bargh, J. A. (1996). Automaticity in social psychology. In E. T. Higgins & A. W. Kruglanski (Eds.), *Social psychology: Handbook of basic principles* (pp. 169–183). New York: Guilford Press.

Barlow, D. H. (1988). *Anxiety disorders: the nature and treatment of anxiety and panic*. New York: Guilford Press.

Baron-Cohen, S., Leslie, A., & Frith, U. (1985). Does the autistic child have a "theory of mind"? *Cognition, 21*, 37–46.

Baron-Cohen, S., Ring, H., Moriarty, J., Schmitz, B., Costa, D., & Plaisted, K. (1994). Recognition of mental state terms: Clinical findings in children with autism and functional neuroimaging study of normal adults. *British Journal of Psychiatry, 165*, 640–649.

Bechara, A., Damasio, H., Tranel, D., & Damasio, A. R. (1997). Deciding advantageously before knowing the advantageous strategy. *Science, 275*, 1293–1295.

Bechara, A., Tranel, D., Damasio, H., & Adolphs, R. (1995). Double dissociation of conditioning and declarative knowledge relative to the amygdala and hippocampus in humans. *Science, 269*, 115–118.

Bernstien, I. S., Gordon, T. P., & Rose, R. M. (1983). The interaction of hormones, behavior, and social context in non-human primates. In B. B. Svare (Ed.), *Hormones and aggressive behavior* (pp. 535–561). New York: Plenum Press.

Berntson, G. G., Cacioppo, J. T., & Quigley, K. S. (1991). Autonomic determinism: The modes of autonomic control, the doctrine of autonomic space, and the laws of autonomic constraint. *Psychological Review, 98*, 459–487.

Blascovich, J. (in press). Social psychophysiological methods. In C. M. Judd & H. Reis (Eds.), *Advanced research methods in social psychology*. Cambridge, UK: Cambridge University Press.

Blascovich, J., & Tomaka, J. (1996). The biopsychosocial model of arousal regulation. In M. Zanna (Ed.), *Advances in experimental social psychology* Vol. 28 (pp. 1–51). New York: Academic Press.

Block, N. (1995). The mind as the software of the brain. In E. E. Smith, & D. N. Osherson (Eds.), *Thinking*. 2nd. edn., Vol. 3 (pp. 377–425). Cambridge, MA: MIT Press.

Bornstein, R. F., & D'Agostino, P. R. (1994). The attribution and discounting of perceptual fluency: Preliminary tests of a perceptual fluency/attributional model of the mere exposure effect. *Social Cognition, 12,* 103–128.

Bruce, V., & Young, A. (1986). Understanding face recognition. *British Journal of Psychology, 77*, 305–327.

Cacioppo, J. T., & Berntson, G. G. (1992). Social psychological contributions to the decade of the brain: Doctrine of multilevel analysis. *American Psychologist, 47*, 1019–1028.

Cacioppo, J. T., & Berntson, G. G. (1994). Relationship between attitudes and evaluative space: A critical review, with emphasis on the separability of positive and negative substrates. *Psychological Bulletin, 115*, 401–423.

Cacioppo, J. T., & Petty, R. (1983). *Social psychophysiology.* New York: Guilford Press.

Cacioppo, J. T., & Tassinary, L. G. (1990). Inferring psychological significance from physiological signals. *American Psychologist, 45*, 16–18.

Cacioppo, J. T., Berntson, G. G., & Crites, S. L. (1996). Social neuroscience: Principles of psychophysiological arousal and response. In E. T. Higgins & A. W. Kruglanski (Eds.), *Social psychology: Handbook of basic principles* (pp. 72–101). New York: Guilford Press.

Cacioppo, J. T., Crites, S. L., & Gardner, W. L. (1996). Attitudes to the right: Evaluative processing is associated with lateralized late positive event-related brain potential. *Personality and Social Psychology Bulletin, 22*, 1205–1219.

Cacioppo, J. T., Gardner, W., & Berntson, G. G. (1997). Beyond bipolar conceptualizations and measures: The case of attitudes and evaluative space. *Personality and Social Psychology Review, 1*, 3–25.

Cacioppo, J. T., Gardner, W. L., & Berntson, G. G. (in press). The affect system: Form follows function. *Journal of Personality and Social Psychology.*

Cacioppo, J. T., Martzke, J. S., & Petty, R. E. (1988). Specific forms of facial EMG response index emotions during an interview: From Darwin to the continuous flow hypothesis of affect-laden information processing. *Journal of Social and Personality Psychology, 54*, 592–604.

Cacioppo, J. T., Tassinary, L. G., & Berntson, G. G. (in press). Psychophysiological sciences. In J. T. Cacioppo, L. G. Tassinary, & G. G. Berntson (Eds.), *Handbook of psychophysiology.* New York: Cambridge University Press.

Cacioppo, J. T., Petty, R. E., Losch, M. E., & Kim, H. S. (1986). Electromyographic activity over facial muscle regions can differentiate the valence and intensity of affective reactions. *Journal of Personality and Social Psychology, 50*, 260–268.

Caramazzo, A., & Shelton, J. R. (1998). Domain-specific knowledge systems in the brain: The animate–inanimate distinction. *Journal of Cognitive Neuroscience, 10*, 1–34.

Cosmides, L., & Tooby, J. (1995). From function to structure: The role of evolutionary biology and computational theories in cognitive neuroscience. In M. S. Gazzaniga (Ed.), *The cognitive neurosciences* (pp. 1199–1210). Cambridge, MA: MIT Press.

Crites, S. L., & Cacioppo, J. T. (1996). Electrocortical differentiation of evaluative and non-evaluative categorizations. *Psychological Science, 7*, 318–321.

Crites, S. L., Cacioppo, J. T., Gardner, W. L., & Berntson, G. G. (1995). Bioelectrical echoes from evaluative categorization: II. A late positive brain potential that varies as a function of attitude registration rather than attitude report. *Journal of Personality and Social Psychology, 68*, 997–1013.

Damasio, A. R. (1994). *Descartes' error: Emotion, reason and the human brain.* New York: Grosset/Putnam.

Davison, K., & Pennebaker, J. W. (1996). Social psychosomatics. In E. T. Higgins & A. Kruglansky (Eds.), *Social psychology: Handbook of basic principles* (pp. 102–130). New York: Guilford Press.

Dawes, R. M., & Smith, T. L. (1985). Attitude and opinion measurement. In G. A. Lindzey (Ed.), *Handbook of social psychology.* 3rd. edn., Vol. 1 (pp. 509–566). New York: Random House.

Diener, E., & Emmons, R. A. (1984). The independence of positive and negative affect. *Journal of Personality and Social Psychology, 47*, 1105–1117.

Farah, M. J. (1994). Neuropsychological inference with an interactive brain: A critique of the "locality" assumption. *Brain and Behavioral Sciences, 17*, 43–104.

Fere, C. (1888/1976). Notes on change in electrical resistance under the effect of sensory stimulation and emotion. *Comptes rendues des seances de al societe de biologie, 5*, 217–219.

Fodor, J. A. (1975). *The language of thought.* New York: Crowell.

Gardner, W. L., & Cacioppo, J. T. (1995). Multi-gallon blood donors: Why do they give? *Transfusion, 35*, 795–798.

Gardner, W. L., Gabriel, S., & Diekman, A. B. (in press). Interpersonal Processes. In J. T. Cacioppo, L. G. Tassinary, & G. G. Berntson (Eds.), *Handbook of psychophysiology*. New York: Cambridge University Press.

Gazzaniga, M. S. (Ed.) (1994). *The cognitive neurosciences*. Cambridge, MA: MIT Press.

Greenwald, A. G., & Banaji, M. R. (1995). Implicit social cognition: Attitudes, self-esteem, and stereotypes. *Psychological Review, 102*, 4–27.

Haber, S. N., & Barchas, P. R. (1983). The regulatory effect of social rank on behavior after amphetamine administration. In P. R. Barchas (Ed.), *Social hierarchies: Essays toward a sociophysiological perspective* (pp. 119–132). Westport, CT: Greenwood Press.

Harmon-Jones, E., & Allen, J. J. B. (1996). Anterior EEG asymmetry and facial EMG as evidence that affect is involved in the mere exposure effect. *Psychophysiology, 33*, 544 (abstract).

Heider, F. (1958). *The psychology of interpersonal relations*. New York: Wiley.

Hirschfeld, L. A., & Gelman, S. A. (Eds.) (1994). *Mapping the mind: Domain specificity in cognition and culture*. New York: Cambridge University Press.

Ito, T. A., Larsen, J. T., Smith, N. K., & Cacioppo, J. T. (1998). Negative information weighs more heavily on the brain: The negativity bias in evaluative categorizations. *Journal of Personality and Social Psychology, 75*, 887–900.

James, W. (1894). The physical basis of emotion. *Psychological Review, 1*, 516–529.

Karmiloff-Smith, A., Klima, E., Bellugi, U., Grant, J., & Baron-Cohen, S. (1995). Is there a social module? Language, face processing and theory of mind in individuals with William's syndrome. *Journal of Cognitive Neuroscience, 7*, 196–208.

Katz, I., Wackenhut, J., & Hass, R. G. (1986). Racial ambivalence, value duality and behavior. In J. F. Dovidio & S. L. Gaetner (Eds.), *Prejudice, discrimination, and racism* (pp. 35–59). New York: Academic Press.

Kennedy, S., Glaser, R., & Kiecolt-Glaser, J. K. (1990). Psychoneuroimmunology. In J. T. Cacioppo & L. G. Tassinary (Eds.), *Principles of psychophysiology: Physical, social and inferential elements* (pp. 177–192). New York: Cambridge University Press.

Klein, S. B. & Kihlstrom, J. F. (1998). On bridging the gap between social-personality psychology and neuropsychology. *Personality and Social Psychology Review, 2*, 228–242.

Klinger, M. R., & Greenwald, A. G. (1994). Preferences need no inferences?: The cognitive basis of unconscious mere exposure effects. In P. M. Niedenthal & S. Kitayama (Eds.), *The heart's eye* (pp. 67–85). San Diego: Academic Press.

Lazarus, R. S. (1984). On primacy of cognition. *American Psychologist, 39*, 124–129.

LeDoux, J. E. (1995). Emotions: Clues from the brain. *Annual Review of Psychology, 46*, 209–235.

Leiderman, P. H. & Shapiro, D. (Eds.) (1964). *Psychobiological approaches to social behavior*. Stanford, CA: Stanford University Press.

Levenson, R. W., & Ruef, A. M. (1997). Physiological aspects of emotional knowledge and rapport. In W. J. Ickes (Ed.), *Emphatic accuracy* (pp. 44–72). New York: Guilford Press.

Lynn, R. (1966). *Attention, arousal and the orienting reaction*. Oxford, UK: Pergamon Press.

McDougall, W. (1908/1928). *An introduction to social psychology*. Boston: John W. Luce.

McGuire, W. J. (1985). Attitudes and attitude change. In G. Lindzey & E. Aronson (Eds.), *The handbook of social psychology* 3rd edn. (pp. 000–000). Reading, MA: Addison-Wesley.

Mandler, G., Nakamura, Y., & Van Zandt, B. J. (1987). Nonspecific effects of exposure on stimuli that cannot be recognized. *Journal of Experimental Psychology Learning, Memory, and Cognition, 13*, 646–648.

Mesulam, M. M., & Perry, J. (1972). The diagnosis of lovesickness: Experimental psychophysiology without polygraph. *Psychophysiology, 9*, 546–551.

Miller, N. E. (1959). Liberalization of basic S–R concepts: Extensions to conflict behavior, motivation and social learning. In S. Koch (Ed.), *Psychology: A study of a science, study 1* (pp. 198–292). New York: McGraw Hill.

Morris, J. S., Oehman, A., & Dolan, R. J. (1998). Conscious and unconscious emotional learning in the human amygdala. *Nature, 393*, 467–470.

Osgood, C. E., Suci, G. J., & Tannenbaum, P. H. (1957). *The measurement of meaning*. Urbana, IL: University of Illinois Press.

Ostrom, T. M. (1984). The sovereignty of social cognition. In R. S. Wyer & T. K. Srull (Eds.), *Handbook of social cognition* Vol. 1 (pp. 1–38). Hillsdale, NJ: Lawrence Erlbaum Associates.

Panksepp, J. (1998). *Affective neuroscience: The foundations of human and animal emotions.* New York: Oxford University Press.

Peeters, G., & Czapinski, J. (1990). Positive–negative asymmetry in evaluations: The distinction between affective and informational negativity effects. In W. Stroebe & M. Hewstone (Eds.), *European review of social psychology* Vol. 1 (pp. 33–60). New York: Wiley.

Perrett, D. I., Rolls, E. T., & Caan, W. (1982). Visual neurons responsive to faces in the monkey temporal cortex. *Experimental Brain Research, 47,* 329–342.

Platt, J. R. (1964). Strong inference. *Science, 146,* 347–353.

Rankin, R. E., & Campbell, D. T. (1955). Galvanic skin response to negro and white experimenters. *Journal of Abnormal and Social Psychology, 51,* 30–33.

Reber, R., Winkielman, P., & Schwarz, N. (1998). Effects of perceptual fluency of affective judgments. *Psychological Science, 9,* 45–48.

Riddle, E. M. (1925). Aggressive behavior in a small social group. *Archives of Psychology, 78.*

Rozin, P., & Schull, J. (1988). The adaptive–evolutionary point of view in experimental psychology. In R. C. Atkinson, R. J. Herrnstein, G. Lindzey, & R. D. Luce (Eds.), *Stevens' handbook of experimental psychology,* Vol. 1: *Perception and motivation;* Vol 2: *Learning and cognition* (pp. 503–546). New York: Wiley.

Sarter, M., Berntson, G. G., & Cacioppo, J. T. (1996). Brain imaging and cognitive neuroscience: Toward strong inference in attributing function to structure. *American Psychologist, 51,* 13–21.

Scoville, W. B., & Milner, B. (1957). Loss of recent memory after bilateral hippocampal lesions. *Journal of Neurology, Neurosurgery, & Psychiatry, 20,* 11–21.

Seamon, J., McKenna, P. A., & Binder, N. (1998). The mere exposure effect is differentially sensitive to different judgment tasks. *Consciousness and Cognition: An International Journal, 7,* 85–102.

Seligman, M. E. P. (1970). On the generality of the laws of learning. *Psychological Review, 74,* 406–418.

Shapiro, D., & Crider, A. (1969). Psychophysiological approaches to social psychology. In G. A. Lindzey (Ed.), *Handbook of social psychology.* 2nd. edn., Vol. 3 (pp. 1–49). Reading, MA: Addison-Wesley.

Skowronski, J. J., & Carlston, D. E. (1989). Negativity and extremity biases in impression formation: A review of explanations. *Psychological Bulletin, 105,* 131–142.

Smith, C. E. (1936). A study of autonomic excitation resulting from the interaction of individual opinion and group opinion. *Journal of Abnormal Psychology, 30,* 138–164.

Squire, L. R. (1992). Memory and the hippocampus: A synthesis from findings with rats, monkeys, and humans. *Psychological Review, 99,* 195–231.

Stephens, D. W., & Krebs, J. R. (1986). *Foraging theory.* Princeton, NJ: Princeton University Press.

Stone, V. E., Baron-Cohen, S., & Knight, R. T. (1998). Frontal lobe contributions to theory of mind. *Journal of Cognitive Neuroscience, 10,* 640–656.

Taylor, S. E. (1991). Asymmetrical effects of positive and negative events: The mobilization–minimization hypothesis. *Psychological Bulletin, 110,* 67–85.

Thrustone, L. L. (1931). The measurement of attitudes. *Journal of Abnormal Psychology, 26,* 249–269.

Tranel, D., Fowles, D.C., & Damasio, A. R. (1985). Electrodermal discrimination of familiar and unfamiliar faces: A methodology. *Psychophysiology, 22,* 403–408.

Tucker, D. M., & Fredrick, S. L. (1989). Emotion and brain lateralization. In H. Wagner & A. Manstead (Eds.), *Handbook of social psychophysiology* (pp. 27–70). Chichester, UK: Wiley & Sons.

Tucker, D. M., Luu, P. , & Pribram, K. H. (1995). Social and emotional self-regulation. In J. Grafman & K. J. Holyoak (Eds.), *Structure and function of the human prefrontal cortex* Vol. 769 (pp. 213–239). New York: New York Academy of Sciences.

Uchino, B. N., Cacioppo, J. T., & Kiecolt-Glaser, J. K. (1996). The relationship between social support and health: A review with emphasis on underlying psychophysiological processes. *Psychological Bulletin, 119,* 488–531.

Winkielman, P., & Cacioppo, J. T. (1998). Affective consequences of perceptual fluency: Evidence from facial EMG. Unpublished manuscript, Ohio State University.

Zajonc, R. B. (1980). Feeling and thinking: Preferences need no inferences. *American Psychologist, 35*, 117–123.

Zajonc, R. B. (1998). Emotions. In D. T. Gilbert, S. T. Fiske, & G. Lindzey (Eds.), *The handbook of social psychology*. 4th. edn. (pp. 591–632). Boston: McGraw-Hill.

Zillman, D. (1989). Aggression and sex: Independent and joint operations. In H. Wagner & A. Manstead (Eds.), *Handbook of social psychophysiology* (pp. 229–260). New York: Wiley.

Zola-Morgan, S., Squire, L.R., Alvarez-Royo, P., & Clower, R. P. (1991). Independence of memory functions and emotional behavior: Separate contributions of the hippocampal formation and the amygdala. *Hippocampus, 1*, 207–220.

PART II

Cognition

Chapter Six

Mental Representations

Eliot R. Smith and Sarah Queller

Introduction

Many of the core concepts of social psychology, including attitudes, the self-concept, stereotypes, and impressions of other persons, are mental representations. Thus, most theories in social psychology, because they deal with these concepts, implicitly or explicitly make assumptions about how mental representations are constructed, stored in memory, changed, and used to make judgments or plan actions. This chapter aims to explicate and clarify the most popular general conceptions of mental representation and their respective assumptions, which in many theories remain implicit and unelaborated. We review four types of representation: associative networks, schemas, exemplars, and distributed representations. The review focuses on types of representations rather than on "theories," for a single theory often incorporates several types of representation for distinct purposes. For example, Wyer and Srull's (1989) well-known theory includes both associative networks and schemas.

For each of the four types of representation, the chapter will first review basic assumptions regarding representation formation and use. Next, a number of key empirical effects will be described and each mechanism's ability to account for these effects will be discussed. We will discuss explicit, intentional forms of memory as well as the more implicit, unintended effects of mental representations that occur when past experiences influence current perceptions or judgments. Through this discussion, cases where several mechanisms can equally account for existing data will become apparent. The chapter ends with some more general comments on the relations between the different types of representation.

Psychologists generally define a representation as an encoding of information in memory.

Preparation of this chapter was facilitated by a research grant (R01 MH48640) and a Research Scientist Development Award (K02 MH01178) to the first author and an NRSA postdoctoral fellowship to the second author, from the National Institute of Mental Health.

An individual can create, retain, and access representations. Once accessed, the individual can then use the representation in various ways. For example, your impression of your neighbor is a mental representation that describes your feelings about her and your beliefs about what she is like. You might draw on your impression of your neighbor to describe her to a friend, evaluate her as a potential dog-sitter, or decide how to behave when she says something offensive.

Effects of a representation can be explicit in that a previously stored representation is intentionally retrieved from memory, or implicit in that a previously stored representation affects current perceptions or judgments without intention, and perhaps even without conscious awareness (Schacter, 1987, 1994). We typically say "I remember" to denote explicit recall. In contrast, phrases like "I know" or "I believe" are common when implicit memory effects are at work. We rely on explicit memory when remembering a friend's phone number, for example. Explicit memory is often conceptualized using metaphors involving search and retrieval, as if memory was a warehouse filled with different objects. It is implicit memory, on the other hand, that causes us to avoid approaching a person who looks like our childhood tormentor, even if the resemblance is not consciously recognized. Implicit memory fits less well with the notion of search, and instead evokes metaphors like "resonance" to describe the way a stored representation subconsciously influences the way the individual processes new information and makes judgments.

The explicit/implicit memory distinction is one between tasks or ways in which memory has effects rather than between "memory systems" such as semantic versus episodic memory (Tulving, 1972). It is tempting to assume that semantic memory (general knowledge about the world) shows itself in implicit tasks whereas episodic memory (autobiographical memory for specific events located in time and place) affects explicit tasks. But this is misguided. A specific episode can have implicit memory effects. For example, in the phenomenon of repetition priming, reading "elephant" can improve a person's ability to complete the word fragment E – E – – A – T even when the person does not consciously remember reading the word (Tulving, Schacter, & Stark, 1982). In addition, general knowledge can influence explicit memories through reconstructive processes (Ross & Conway, 1986). Thus, the explicit/implicit distinction refers to *uses* of memory – the consciously recollective use of memory versus its use in performing some other task without conscious awareness of memory *per se* (Jacoby & Kelley, 1987).

We now turn to descriptions of the four types of representation, and then discuss how each type accounts for a number of explicit and implicit memory effects.

Associative Networks

Influential theories of associative network representation in non-social cognition can be found in Collins and Quillian (1969), Collins and Loftus (1975), and Anderson and Bower (1973). Within social psychology, the assumptions of associative networks have been described in a number of reviews (Carlston & Smith, 1996; Ostrom, Skowronski, & Nowak, 1994; Fiske & Taylor, 1991; Wyer & Carlston, 1994). The assumptions are as follows:

1   *Fundamental representational assumption*: Representations are constructed from discrete nodes connected by links.

2   *Interpretation of nodes*: Each node stands for a concept. Part of the meaning of each concept is derived from the pattern of linkages to other nodes.

3   *Formation of links through contiguity*: Links are formed between nodes when the concepts the nodes represent are experienced or thought about together.

4   *Link strength*: Existing links are strengthened to the extent the objects they link are experienced or thought about together. Strength changes only slowly with time.

5   *Activation and its spread*: Nodes have a property termed activation, which can vary rapidly over time. A node can become activated if it is perceptually present or actively thought about. An activated node spreads activation to connected nodes via the intervening links, increasing activation of the connected nodes. This process is called "spreading activation" (for a quantitative model, see Anderson, 1983).

6   *Activation in long-term memory*: Long-term memory is a single, large, interconnected associative structure. Short-term memory is the currently activated subset of this structure. Memory retrieval amounts to raising a node's activation level above some threshold.

7   *Links as pathways for retrieval in free recall*: Activating one node may result in the spread of enough activation to a neighboring node to elicit its retrieval. As a direct implication, the more links connected to a particular node, the greater its probability of retrieval.

Though they tend to share the above assumptions in some form, associative network models in social psychology also have some points of variation. First, activation on a node decays with time, but estimates of the rate of decay vary widely (Anderson, 1983; Higgins, 1996; Ostrom et al., 1994, p. 225). Second, some conceptualize retrieval as resulting from the parallel spread of activation across all links connected to currently activated nodes (Anderson, 1983, ch. 3), and others as sequential traversal of links where activation spreads along only one of several possible links at a time (Hastie, 1988). Third, theorists disagree regarding the conceptual level of nodes (see Wyer & Carlston, 1994, p. 7). A node could be a feature, a concept, or a whole body of knowledge ("schema"). And finally, theorists disagree as to whether the links are labeled (e.g. Fiske & Taylor, 1991, p. 297) or unlabeled (Wyer & Srull, 1989, ch. 7). Unlabeled links limit the representational power of associative structures (Carlston & Smith, 1996). For example, if links for subjects versus objects are not distinguished, the representation of the proposition "Sean killed the tiger" would be the same as that of "The tiger killed Sean."

Schemas

Influential works on schematic representation in non-social cognition include Bartlett (1932), Bruner (1957), Bransford & Franks (1971), Anderson & Pichert (1978), and Schank & Abelson (1977). Schematic mechanisms in social psychology, as reviewed by Markus & Zajonc (1985), Carlston & Smith (1996), Fiske & Taylor (1991), and Wyer & Carlston (1994), generally share the following assumptions:

1   *Fundamental representational assumption*: A schema is a structured unit of knowledge about some object or concept. Schemas represent abstract or generalized knowledge as opposed to detailed knowledge about episodes tied to a specific time or context (Fiske & Taylor, 1991; Markus & Zajonc, 1985).

2   *Activation*: A schema can be activated by explicit thought about its topic or by an encounter with relevant information. Making the schema active renders readily accessible all the structured knowledge contained therein.

3   *Level of accessibility*: A schema is likely to become activated and used to the extent that it is accessible. Accessibility is increased by recent or frequent use.

4   *Independence of units*: Schemas are independent entities. Thus, if one schema becomes active this has no necessary implications for other, related schemas.

5   *Interpretive effect of schemas*: Schemas affect the interpretation of perceptual stimuli. That is, the way ambiguous information is construed and the default values that are assumed for unavailable information are influenced by active schemas. The schema-consistent interpretation of a stimulus may be encoded in memory as if it were perceptually present in the stimulus.

6   *Attentional effect of schemas*: Activated schemas direct attention, sometimes to schema-consistent information and sometimes to unexpected or inconsistent information, depending on the circumstances.

7   *Retrieval cueing/reconstructive function of schemas*: Schemas can also influence memory retrieval and judgment. A schema can serve as a source of cues, generally facilitating retrieval of schema-consistent information. It can also serve as a guide for guessing and reconstruction when retrieval attempts fail or produce ambiguous results.

Different theorists' assumptions about schematic mechanisms differ in some respects. First, schemas are typically assumed to represent information about the typical characteristics of particular concepts, such as restaurant dining or doctors. However, in some cases, schemas are assumed to represent general rules of inference independent of any particular content domain (e.g. Heiderian balance can be viewed as a schema.) Second, theorists have modeled schema accessibility in various ways, including Storage Bins, battery, and synapse models (Wyer & Srull, 1989; Higgins, 1996).

Exemplars

Exemplar representations trace directly back to exemplar models of categorization, such as the seminal work by Medin and Schaffer (1978). These models downplay the role of abstractions (such as summaries of the average characteristics of categories) and emphasize instead the role of specific experiences. In non-social cognition, influential works include Brooks (1978), Jacoby & Brooks (1984), and Whittlesea (1987), and in social psychology see Lewicki (1985), Smith (1988, 1990), and Linville, Fischer, & Salovey (1989). Exemplar mechanisms share the following core ideas:

1   *Fundamental representational assumption*: Representations record information about specific stimuli or experiences, rather than abstracted summaries or generalizations.

Such a representation may be constructed on the basis of veridical perception of a stimulus object, misperception of it, inference about it, imagination of it, second-hand communication about it, etc.

2   *Representations record feature co-occurrences*: Representations of specific stimuli record patterns of feature co-occurrences. Such representations support people's observed sensitivity to the correlation of features within categories (e.g. they know that small birds are more likely to sing than large ones; Malt & Smith, 1984). In contrast, a schema would contain only information about the typical values of features (i.e. that birds are typically small and that they typically sing), not about feature co-occurrences.

3   *Activation of exemplars by retrieval cues*: Retrieval cues (whether self-generated or external in origin) activate all stored exemplars in parallel. Each exemplar is activated to the extent that it is similar to the retrieval cue. Activation is not synonymous with retrieval, but instead makes the activated exemplars available to influence judgments or impressions (Hintzman, 1986).

4   *Parallel on-line computation*: When a new stimulus is to be evaluated, judged, or categorized, it is compared in parallel to many activated exemplar traces. Similarly, when generalizations about a type of stimulus are required they can be computed by activating all exemplars of that type and summarizing them.

5   *Effects on interpretation, attention, and judgment*: The effects of an activated mass of exemplars are assumed to be the same as those attributed to schemas. That is, the activated exemplars influence interpretation, attention, retrieval, and reconstruction at a preconscious level.

Exemplar theories differ regarding whether only exemplars are stored or, alternately, whether both abstractions and exemplars are stored.

Distributed or PDP representations

Detailed introductions to the newest category of models of mental representation, which have been termed distributed memory, connectionist, or parallel distributed processing (PDP) models, can be found in Churchland & Sejnowski (1992), Smolensky (1988), Rumelhart, McClelland, et al. (1986), as well as McClelland, Rumelhart, et al. (1986). Smith (1996) provides a brief overview oriented toward social psychologists. Distributed representation generally embodies these assumptions:

1   *Fundamental representational assumption*: A concept or object is represented by a distributed representation, where each representation is a different pattern of activation across a common set of simple nodes or units within a network. A useful analogy is a TV screen. No individual pixel has any specific meaning but different patterns of illumination over the entire array of pixels can produce a large number of different meaningful images. This assumption contrasts with associative representations, where individual nodes are semantically meaningful.

2   *Unity of representation and process*: A connectionist network is responsible for both

processing and storing information. In contrast, other types of representation require additional assumptions about processes that operate on static representations.

3   *Computing with distributed representations*: Units are interconnected and send activation to each other across weighted connections. A given unit's activation level at a particular time is a function of its previous activation level as well as the total activation flowing to it from other units across the weighted connections. Thus, the pattern of activation taken on by a given set of units is determined by the initial inputs to the network of units and the weights on the inter-unit connections.

4   *Positive or negative activation*: In most models, both the weights on inter-unit connections and the activation that flows between units can be either positive or negative. Negative activation decreases the activity level of the unit to which it flows (i.e. it has an inhibitory effect). This assumption contrasts with most associative-network models, in which "spreading activation" is always positive.

5   *Learning*: Connection weights are initially assigned random values, which are then shaped by a learning procedure that incrementally changes the weights as the network processes many stimuli.

6   *Connection weights as long-term memory*: The weights on the connections are assumed to change only slowly, in contrast to the quickly changing activation values. Thus, the connection weights are the repository of the network's long-term memory.

7   *Pattern transformation*: Networks with a feed-forward architecture (in which all connections run in one direction from inputs to outputs) can transform representations from one domain into another (Anderson, 1995). Examples are the transformation of input patterns representing behaviors into output patterns representing trait concepts, or inputs of letter sequences into output patterns representing a word's meaning or pronunciation. When the input pattern is presented to input units, activation flows over the connections and eventually produces a new pattern of activation on the network's output units.

8   *Pattern completion or memory*: Networks using a different type of architecture (recurrent connections that link units bidirectionally) can do pattern completion. After the network learns a set of patterns, when the inputs constitute a subset or an approximation of one of those patterns, flows of activation cause the network to reconstruct the entire pattern as output. Pattern completion can be viewed as a form of memory. However, the potential patterns are not explicitly "stored" anywhere. Instead, the network stores connection strengths that allow many patterns to be reproduced given the right cues.

9   *Reconstruction, not retrieval*: When a network must encode several patterns, the connection strengths are a compromise. Hence, reproduction of any given pattern from input cues will be imperfect and will be influenced by the other patterns encoded in the network. As new patterns are learned by the network, the representation of previously learned patterns may change. Thus, distributed representations are *evoked* or *reconstructed* rather than *searched for* or *retrieved* in invariant form (McClelland, Rumelhart, & Hinton, 1986, p. 31).

10   *Parallel constraint satisfaction*: In a network in which bidirectional flows of activation between units are possible, the network can be thought of as converging on a final pattern of activation that simultaneously satisfies the constraints represented

by the current inputs (representing external stimuli) and the network weights (representing learned constraints) (Barnden, 1995). Constraint satisfaction is "soft"; learned constraints and current inputs may conflict and each can only be satisfied as well as possible.

There are also points on which various models differ. Some related models accept most of these assumptions but use localist representational schemes in which single nodes have meaningful interpretations (Thorpe, 1995). A node may be interpreted as a feature, an object or concept, or a whole proposition. A connection between nodes is interpreted as encoding past experiences of covariation between the nodes (if nodes represent features or objects) or logical constraints such as consistency or inconsistency between propositions (if nodes represent propositions). Such networks perform parallel satisfaction of multiple constraints (Read & Marcus-Newhall, 1993; Kunda & Thagard, 1996). However, they lack other properties that stem from distributed representation, such as the ability to learn to represent new concepts (new concepts require the explicit addition of new nodes).

Within the class of distributed representation models, literally hundreds of competing models have been proposed with various architectures (numbers and interconnection patterns of nodes), activation equations, and learning rules (see Hertz, Krogh, & Palmer, 1991). In contrast, in each of the three types of representation considered to this point – exemplar, schematic, and associative network - there are perhaps a handful of serious, well-specified competing models. The properties of these diverse distributed models are being actively explored in ongoing theoretical and simulation studies.

Key Memory Effects in Social Psychology

With a basic understanding of the four memory mechanisms in hand, we now turn to describing how each of these mechanisms might account for a number of established effects of mental representations.

Related concepts or contextual factors as retrieval cues

One aspect of memory involves how information that has been learned in the past is retrieved at a later date. Suppose you are introduced to Arturo at a party. How can you recall Arturo's name when you meet him again? This amounts to retrieval of some information (name) from associated information (his appearance). Or how can you recall that he was among the people who attended that particular party? This is retrieval based on contextual cues (the party). These types of memory retrieval are central in most explicit memory tests including paired-associate and list-learning paradigms.

Associative representation   Nodes representing concepts that are perceived together or thought about together become linked. When one of the concepts is experienced later, its node becomes active. Activation then spreads across the link to the associated node, potentially raising the activation of this node above the threshold required for retrieval. In this manner, spreading activation explains how related concepts or contextual factors can act as retrieval cues.

The counter-intuitive finding that people recall more behaviors that are inconsistent with their impression of a person than behaviors that are consistent with their impression (Hastie & Kumar, 1979) has been explained in terms of associative representations. When an impression-inconsistent behavior is encountered, the perceiver may try to resolve or explain away the inconsistency. In doing so, the perceiver thinks about the relation of the impression-inconsistent behavior to previously stored impression-consistent and inconsistent behaviors. This process establishes additional links between the inconsistent behavior and other behaviors. These additional links provide more paths along which activation can spread, thus increasing the probability of retrieval of an impression-inconsistent behavior relative to that of recalling an impression-consistent behavior (Hastie, 1980; Srull, 1981).

Recognition of expectation-inconsistent items is also enhanced relative to expectation-consistent items, but only when recognition sensitivity measures are used (measures that correct for a guessing bias; Stangor & McMillan, 1992). Perceivers will guess they have seen consistent items before even when they do not actually recall having seen them, leading to a recognition advantage for consistent items when this bias is not taken into account. While associative representations deal nicely with the finding that expectation-inconsistent items are better *recalled*, the associative representation does not offer an explanation for why *recognition* of expectation-inconsistent behaviors is also enhanced. In recall, a cue is activated and activation spreads across links until an item reaches sufficient activation for retrieval. However, in recognition, an item is presented and the perceiver is asked if he or she previously studied the item. Inter-item associative links are not required as retrieval pathways when the item is directly thought about, so the inconsistency effect for recognition does not seem to be well explained by associative memory mechanisms.

Schematic representation   Schematic representations can easily account for the retrieval of items of information that are meaningfully related – that is, are part of the same schema – such as "bread" and "butter." Encountering one of these items activates the schema, which includes the other item. However, schematic models have more difficulty in accounting for a newly learned association (formed by meeting someone for the first time). One could assume that a new schema representing the person is created, but accounts of schema construction (as opposed to retrieval and use) are underdeveloped or entirely absent in most schema theories. In any case, one could argue that forming a new schema to represent a specific occurrence violates the definition of a schema as a representation of abstract, generic knowledge. The definition of schemas as abstract and generic also leads to the conclusion that schema representations do not account well for contextual cueing of retrieval.

Exemplar representation   An exemplar representation may preserve information about the specific context in which a stimulus was encountered as well as information about the stimulus characteristics. Therefore an exemplar representation (e.g. incorporating a person's appearance, name, and context) could account for these types of explicit memory retrieval. However, exemplars have more often been invoked to account for implicit rather than explicit memory effects.

Distributed representation   When a cue consisting of a partial pattern is presented as input to the network, retrieval occurs via reconstruction of the complete pattern that best satisfies the constraints of the cues provided as input (e.g. Chappell & Humphreys, 1994). In this explanation, a number of stimulus attributes and contextual details are all components of one large pattern, so any of these can act as retrieval cues for the entire pattern.

Accessibility

One important property of memory is that all mental constructs are not equally likely to be used. One determinant of whether a construct is applied is its fit to a current stimulus (Bruner, 1957; Higgins, 1996). Beyond that, mental representations vary in *accessibility*, affecting how readily a perceiver can apply them to the processing of an input. Thus, for example, a professor might tend to evaluate all new acquaintances in terms of intelligence. Intelligence would be an accessible construct for this person.

Associative representation   In associative representations, increased accessibility in response to recent use is explained as residual activation on a recently used node. This residual activation puts the node closer to the threshold activation for conscious recall and thus facilitates retrieval of the recently used concept. Increased accessibility in response to frequent use of a concept is explained in terms of link strength. The more a concept is thought about in relation to other concepts, the stronger the links between the corresponding nodes become. Since activation flows more readily over stronger links, retrieval via spreading activation is more likely for frequently used concepts.

Applying these principles, Fazio (1986) suggests that attitudes are represented by an attitude object node linked to an evaluative node. If the attitude is expressed frequently, the link can get strong enough that simply perceiving the object can result in automatic activation of the evaluation. This in turn can lead to evaluative priming effects where a prime facilitates processing of same-valence target items relative to opposite-valence targets (Fazio, Sanbonmatsu, Powell, & Kardes, 1986).

Schema representation   Higgins, Rholes, & Jones (1977) showed that recently used traits are more accessible and thus more likely to impact judgments. This finding can be interpreted in terms of increased accessibility of a trait schema due to recent use. In contrast to the short-lived effects of priming, chronic accessibility of a schema is assumed to result from frequent use of a schema over a long period of time (Higgins, King, & Mavin, 1982). For example, some people habitually interpret new information in terms of its implications for gender (Frable & Bem, 1985).

Effects of recency and frequency of use on schema accessibility do not follow directly from the basic assumptions of schema representation. Instead, schema theories have incorporated additional assumptions to account for accessibility. Wyer & Srull (1980) account for accessibility using a "Storage Bin" metaphor. Schemas are thought of as stacked in a

Storage Bin and a search for a schema that is applicable to the current stimulus occurs in a top-down fashion. A schema that is nearer the top of the Storage Bin is more accessible. They accounted for the effects of recent use by assuming that a schema was replaced at the top of the Storage Bin after each use, increasing the schema's probability of future use. To account for effects of frequent use, a copying function was later added (Wyer & Srull, 1989), such that when a schema is used, one copy stays in the original location in the Storage Bin and another copy is placed at the top. For frequency effects to be observed, the copies below the top must contribute to accessibility so the probability of using an applicable schema in the top-down search was restricted to p<1 in the revised model.

A "synapse" metaphor was suggested by Higgins, Bargh, & Lombardi (1985) that likened the activation of a schema to a charge that decays with time. Use of a schema fully charges it with activation. The activation subsequently decays. More recently used concepts have more residual activation and are thus more accessible. In order to account for the effect of frequent use on accessibility, the "synapse" model proposes that frequency of use decreases the rate of decay of activation. Note that these authors proposed two distinct mechanisms to deal with recency and frequency effects.

Exemplar representation   Frequent or recent use of a concept adds additional exemplar representations to the store in memory. This means that when these exemplars are activated (when a new judgment concerning the concept is required) their summed impact on judgment or memory retrieval is greater. Smith (1988) showed that Hintzman's (1986) MINERVA exemplar model could account for accessibility effects through this mechanism.

Distributed representation   Recall that distributed representations are formed through incremental changes in the common set of weights in a connectionist network. If a particular stimulus is presented frequently, the weights will be repeatedly adjusted, becoming better able to reconstruct the pattern corresponding to that stimulus. Consequently, the network will more accurately process frequently encountered patterns compared to less frequently encountered patterns. Recent exposure will also facilitate pattern recognition. In this case, the advantage in accessibility derives from a lessened opportunity for subsequent weight changes that would move the weight values away from those that best process the recent stimulus. Smith and DeCoster (1998) showed that typical effects of recency and frequency on accessibility can be modeled in a connectionist network through this mechanism.

Semantic priming

Semantic priming occurs when perceiving or thinking about one concept makes it easier to process related concepts. Thus, for example, the target word "nurse" is more quickly identified following the prime word "doctor" than following "tree" (Meyer & Schvaneveldt, 1971). The priming effect only lasts a brief period of time (Anderson, 1983; Ostrom et al., 1994, p. 225; Higgins, 1996) and it can be wiped out through the presentation of a single word intervening between prime and target (Masson, 1991; Ratcliff & McKoon, 1988). We know this is an implicit process because it occurs when the prime to target interval is too short for strategic generation of expectations about what is coming next (Neely, 1977) and because it occurs even when the prime is presented subliminally (Wittenbrink, Judd, & Park, 1997).

Associative representation   If two nodes are connected with a link then activation from one node can spread across the link to the associated node. When the prime node is activated, the linked target node increases in activation but, unlike the case of explicit recall, the node does not reach the threshold necessary for retrieval. Instead, the target becomes more retrievable in a subsequent task. (Although similar, the explanation of semantic priming should not be confused with that of recency. With recency, the target concept is directly activated and becomes more accessible at a later time. With semantic priming, a concept related to the target concept is directly activated and activation is spread to produce the sub-threshold activation of the target concept.)

Associative representations typically have been relied upon in explaining priming phenomena within social psychology. For example, white subjects responded more quickly to positive trait words following the prime word "white" than following the prime word "black" (Dovidio, Evans, & Tyler, 1986). The associative explanation is that "white" is semantically linked to positive concepts to a greater extent than is "black." This finding and the related suppositions about representation have relevance for racial stereotyping. Another effect that has been explained in associative terms is evaluative priming (Fazio et al., 1986). Processing of an evaluatively laden prime ("cockroach") results in facilitated processing of evaluatively similar targets ("death") and inhibited processing of evaluatively dissimilar targets ("beautiful"). This finding is robust, although there is debate regarding whether it holds only for objects about which the perceiver holds fairly strong attitudes (Bargh, Chaiken, Raymond, & Hymes, 1996; Fazio, 1993).

Schema representation   Semantic priming in schema representations occurs because a schema-relevant stimulus can activate the whole schema. Thus, for example, if the word "doctor" activates the schema for hospital or medical care, processing of the word "nurse" might be facilitated since it would be activated as part of that schema. In contrast, the word "tree" would not activate a hospital schema so "tree" would not facilitate processing of "nurse."

Exemplar representation   A mass of similar exemplars can function like a schematic general knowledge structure, since the respects in which they are similar reinforce each other while contextual or nonessential differences cancel out (Hintzman, 1986). Therefore numerous exemplars of medical care or hospital situations, most of which included both doctors and nurses, might account for semantic priming in the same way as a "medical care" schema.

Distributed representation   Semantically related concepts tend to share features and, thus, semantically related prime/target pairs will have overlapping patterns of activation in a distributed network. To the extent that the target's pattern of activation overlaps with the previously processed prime's pattern of activation, the network will more quickly and accurately process the target pattern. As activation is a short-lived property, the distributed mechanism accurately predicts that the priming effect should be wiped out by presentation of an unrelated stimulus between prime and target (Masson, 1991).

Repetition priming

Processing of a stimulus is facilitated when the same stimulus has been processed in the same way on a previous occasion. This phenomenon is long lasting (as long as months: Sloman, Hayman, Ohta, Law, & Tulving, 1988), in contrast with short-lived semantic priming effects. The previous exposure does not have to be consciously remembered for repetition priming to occur (Schacter, 1987; Smith, Stewart, & Buttram, 1992). For example, Smith, Stewart, & Buttram (1992) had subjects quickly decide if each of hundreds of behaviors were friendly or intelligent. Some of the behaviors were repeated and some were not. Repetition of behaviors resulted in faster judgment times, even when the delay following the initial exposure was a week. Faster judgment times occurred even when subjects could not recall the previous exposure to the behavior. Because repetition priming is so long lasting, it cannot be explained in terms of residual activation because in all four types of representation, activation is relatively short lived.

Associative representation   Repetition priming can be explained by assuming that a new association is formed linking the specific stimulus being judged or processed to the results of that processing. For example, attributes of a particular behavior would become associated with a trait like "friendly." When the same behavior is encountered again, activation would spread to the trait concept, facilitating a repetition of the same judgment.

Schema representation   The basic assumptions of schema representation do not readily lead to an explanation for repetition priming. Activation of a trait schema might occur when the trait judgments are made in the Smith, Stewart, & Buttram (1992) study, but the effect would be to speed *all* later judgments using that trait, rather than only judgments about specific repeated behaviors (which is what is empirically observed).

Exemplar representation   When an exemplar is judged in a particular way (say a behavior is judged on a trait) that judgment becomes part of the exemplar representation that is stored in memory (e.g. the trait implications become part of the behavior representation). This illustrates the general principle that exemplar representations are always stored *as processed* or interpreted by the perceiver, not in veridical form (Whittlesea & Dorken, 1993). When the same behavior is presented again at a later time, if the exemplar can be retrieved from memory the judgment is already available. Consequently, a second judgment is performed faster than an identical first judgment (Logan, 1988; Smith, 1990).

Distributed representation   Weight changes after exposure to a specific pattern will facilitate later processing of the same pattern. However, as additional patterns are presented to the network, they cause further weight changes, overwriting those that provide an advantage to the repeated stimulus. This argument is similar to that for accessibility of a pattern due to recent use. (See Wiles & Humphreys, 1993, pp. 157-163 for a quantitative analysis.)

Filling in default values and resolving ambiguity

Theorists have long understood that perceivers do not process new information in a strictly unbiased manner but, instead, rely on prior knowledge to help make sense of new information (Arbib, 1995; Bartlett, 1932; Bruner, 1957; Markus & Zajonc, 1985; Minsky, 1975; Neisser, 1976). Prior knowledge is helpful in resolving ambiguities in incoming information or filling in default values for unobserved characteristics. These effects of prior experience are implicit: we don't "remember," for example, that the bird we saw standing in the tall grass had feet, we just "know" it. As an example, imagine observing a car that does not slow down as a pedestrian crosses in front of it. The pedestrian raises his hand and a moment later, the driver extends his arm out the window. They might be waving at each other or they might be exchanging rude gestures.

Associative representation   Spreading activation across links makes linked nodes available for use in resolving ambiguity. In an associative framework, the way you interpret a situation and make assumptions about unknown aspects would depend on the concepts you have strongly linked together based on past experience (Anderson, 1983). If you thought the driver had been careless, links from that concept to the concept of anger might lead you to interpret the hand gestures as insults. You might also think that the driver shouted a curse, even though you could not hear the driver.

Schema representation   Schemas are activated in an all or none fashion and the content of an activated schema is applied to incoming information in an implicit manner. The ready explanation of the resolution of ambiguous information and the use of default values to fill in missing information have led to the popularity of schema models within social psychology. Stereotypes are often conceived of as schemas that allow us to generate expectations about types of people. For example, a girl who turned in a mixed performance on a test was rated as more academically talented by subjects who believed she came from an upper-middle-class background than by subjects who thought she was working class (Darley & Gross, 1983). Similarly, scripts are schemas that store generalized knowledge about a type of event, such as going to a birthday party or dining at a restaurant (Schank & Abelson, 1977). If a script for "road rage" is activated by the driver-pedestrian encounter, it may lead to interpretations and inferences that are consistent with an angry interchange.

Exemplar representation   The common characteristics of the mass of exemplars called to mind when making a judgment may be applied to the novel stimulus (Hintzman, 1986; Smith & Zarate, 1992). The effect is similar to that of a schema and the difference is only that a set of exemplars serve as the prior knowledge instead of a schema that contains generalized knowledge.

Distributed representation   The filling in of default values and resolution of ambiguities occurs in distributed representations through the flow of activation in a connectionist network whose weights have been tuned by past experiences (Rumelhart, Smolensky,

McClelland, & Hinton, 1986). The input to the network may be a partial pattern with only a few characteristics filled in. But as activation flows through the connection weights, the network outputs a complete pattern that best satisfies the constraints of the input and the knowledge currently stored in the connection weights (Smith & DeCoster, 1998). Thus, default values are automatically generated and ambiguities are resolved through constraint satisfaction in distributed networks.

Flexibility and context sensitivity

Recent thinking in social psychology has emphasized flexibility and context sensitivity in the areas of the self-concept (Markus & Wurf, 1987; Linville & Carlston, 1994; Higgins, Van Hook, & Dorfman, 1988; Turner, Oakes, Haslam, & McGarty, 1994), attitudes (Wilson & Hodges, 1992; Tourangeau & Rasinski, 1988; Strack & Martin, 1987; Schwarz & Clore, 1983; Wilson, 1990), and even stereotypes (Bodenhausen, Schwarz, Bless, & Wanke, 1995). Not only the accessibility of a representation, but the content of the representation can be altered by contextual information. That is, particular features are emphasized or de-emphasized in different contexts. In addition, Barsalou (1987) has shown that ad hoc concepts such as "things that might fall on your head" are structured in the same way as concepts with which one has had a great deal of experience and prior learning. Extending this finding to the social domain, people may easily generate stereotypes (summaries of and feelings about a group's typical characteristics) for previously unconsidered groups such as "people who fly only at night" or "adopted Latinos."

Associative representation   Associative representations are flexible to the extent that distinct sets of cues may activate different sets of associates. Thus, for example, the cue "bird" plus the cue "barnyard" might activate the concept "chicken," whereas the cue "bird" plus the cue "suburban backyard" may activate the concept "robin" (see Barsalou, 1987). This is consistent with research showing that although people rate "robin" as a better exemplar of the bird category than "chicken" without context, they rate "chicken" higher in a barnyard context. Interestingly, however, if the cue "bird" alone activates the concept "robin," in associative terms it seems that the compound cue "bird" plus "barnyard" should activate "robin" in addition to "chicken." (The same activation should spread from the "bird" node regardless of whether the "barnyard" node is also active.) Only if assumptions about spreading inhibition as well as activation are added might the "chicken" concept be retrieved without also retrieving the "robin" concept. Classic models using associative representations and spreading activation did not invoke inhibition (e.g. Anderson, 1983). However, recent associative formulations within social psychology have assumed that associative links can be inhibitory as well as facilitative (e.g. Carlston, 1994).

Schema representation   Schematic representations have difficulty accounting for context sensitivity. One would have to postulate, for instance, that distinct "bird-in-suburbs" and "bird-in-barnyard" schemas exist instead of a single "bird" schema. However, this leads to an explosion of the number of concepts that must be represented. Alternatively one could assume that general "bird" and "barnyard" schemas are combined on-line in some fashion to yield the new context-specific concept representation, but models of schema combination have received little attention (Wisniewski, 1997), and none in social psychology.

Exemplar representation   Exemplar representations can accommodate flexible use of prior knowledge (Smith, 1990). Different sets of exemplars may be activated when making different judgments, depending on context or other details of the specific set of cues provided. Judgments are then based on the activated set of exemplars.

Distributed representation   Distributed representations also allow fluid use of prior knowledge. The set of cues provided can include incidentally activated goals (e.g. enhancing self-esteem), context, mood, perceptually present objects, and/or objects of current thought. All of these cues are represented in the common set of weight values so retrieval is influenced by all of them (Rumelhart, Smolensky, McClelland, & Hinton, 1986; Clark, 1993).

Dissociations between recall, recognition, and judgment

If different memory tasks such as recall, recognition, and judgment all access the same underlying representational structure, one would expect dependence between the different tasks. For example, if a specific representation can be demonstrated to influence judgment, such as through a priming effect, the representation would be expected also to be available to explicit retrieval. However, this is not always the case. For example, priming manipulations often have similar or even greater effects on judgment when they cannot be consciously remembered as when they are explicitly retrievable (Lombardi, Higgins, & Bargh, 1987; Martin, Seta, & Crelia, 1990). And although a person might be judged to be honest, recall of the person's behaviors might include a large number of dishonest behaviors (Hastie & Kumar, 1979).

These and other dissociations have been shown to be a function of how the information was processed at learning (Carlston & Smith, 1996; Hastie & Park, 1986; Jacoby, 1983). For example, whether a target is processed perceptually (read the word "honest") or conceptually (read several honest behaviors and generate the relevant trait) will affect performance on different memory tasks. Fragment completion (complete the word "H – N – – T") is more strongly enhanced following a perceptual task, whereas recall (recall the trait words from the previous task) and category accessibility (read an ambiguous behavior and pick a trait that fits) show greater effects of a previous conceptual task (Smith & Branscombe, 1988). For a review of dissociations among implicit and explicit memory measures in non-social cognition, see Richardson-Klavehn & Bjork (1988) and Hintzman (1990).

Associative representation   With associative representations, dissociations occur when different cognitive structures are drawn on for different tasks. As Hastie and Park (1986) suggest, perceivers create different types of representations in memory depending on whether they initially process the incoming information in a "memory-based" fashion or in an "on-line" fashion. "Memory-based" processing initially stores representations of the input stimuli. When a judgment is called for, the stimulus details are recalled and summarized at the time of retrieval. In this case, recall of the details and the judgment should correspond, since the judgment is based directly on what can be recalled. With "on-line" processing, abstraction or summarization of the stimuli occurs as the stimuli are encountered, resulting in a summary representation as well as stimulus-specific details being stored in memory. When a judgment is required, the summary representation is accessed. When recall is performed, the detailed representations are accessed. Dissociation is explained by the use of these two distinct representations that may not contain exactly the same content. Similarly, Wyer and Gordon (1984) suggested that people store a target's behaviors in both trait-based associative clusters and an evaluative summary, stored independently in the "Storage Bin." An evaluative judgment task accesses the evaluative summary, whereas explicit recall of behaviors accesses the trait based clusters. Because the two tasks access different cognitive representations, there may be little relationship between the judgment and the behaviors recalled.

Schema representation   As noted earlier, models of schema formation are typically weak or underdeveloped, making schema models poor candidates for explaining phenomena that involve the creation of new representations. Leaving this issue aside, one could explain dissociations by suggesting that people form multiple schemas organized along different lines (as in the Wyer & Gordon model just described) as they process stimulus inputs.

Exemplar representation   Dissociations are assumed to be due to the distinct subsets of exemplars that are activated by the different cues provided by different tasks (such as implicit versus explicit memory tasks; Roediger & McDermott, 1993). Thus the exemplar representations that can be explicitly retrieved (e.g. the members of a category that one can recall or recognize) may not be the same as those that implicitly influence categorization judgments.

Distributed representation   Dissociations among different memory tasks may be due to differences in tasks that cause the perceiver to draw on distinct network representations. For example, Wiles and Humphreys (1993) suggest that explicit recall and semantic priming draw on pattern completion networks that reconstruct the features of past stimuli when partial cues are presented. In contrast, they suggest that repetition priming is due to changes in weights in pattern transformation networks that translate from perceptual (e.g. visual) to internal (e.g. semantic) types of representations. This proposal explains why repetition priming is specific to a given perceptual modality such as visual or auditory, while semantic priming is not modality specific. Another explanation for dissociations in distributed representations is that different cues might be presented in different types of memory tasks and this may give rise to independence between tasks (Humphreys, Bain, & Pike, 1989).

Summary and Conclusions

The two types of representation most frequently invoked in social psychology are associative and schema representations. Comparison of these two is informative. First, although associative representations focus on the acquisition of new knowledge as well as its use, schema models emphasize the use of existing general knowledge. Loosely, we might say that the construction of new associative representations accounts for episodic memory for particular events or stimuli, whereas schematic representations seem better aligned with semantic or generic memory. In other words, these different types of representation may be complementary rather than competing. Indeed, a number of theorists (McClelland, McNaughton, & O'Reilly, 1995; Humphreys, Bain, & Pike, 1989; Hirst, 1989; Masson, 1989; Macleod & Bassili, 1989; Squire, 1994; Schacter, 1994; Moscovitch, 1994) have recently posited two functionally independent memory systems. One system handles one-shot learning by constructing new representational structures (akin to social psychological assumptions regarding associative representations). The other system learns slowly, gradually building representations of the general characteristics of objects or events. These dual memory theories are supported by a number of psychological and neuropsychological studies of different types. For example, evidence suggests that rapid, episodic learning is mediated by the hippocampus and related structures whereas slow, semantic learning relies on cortical structures (Squire, 1994).

Comparison between associative and schematic representations also suggests that associative representations can mimic schema representations. A schema can be conceptualized in associative terms as a set of units that are so strongly interlinked that activating any one of them necessarily activates them all (Ostrom et al., 1994, p. 221; Anderson, 1983). As discussed above, exemplar and distributed representations can also mimic the effects of schemas that are typically emphasized in social psychology, such as using prior knowledge to interpret new inputs. Thus, we suggest that in social psychology, a schema is more a description of a *function* that can be performed by a learned knowledge representation, rather than a description of an actual entity inside our heads.

In fact, associative and exemplar representations as well as schemas may be more descriptions of memory function than they are accounts of actual underlying representations and processes. This consideration raises a distinction between associative, schema, and exemplar representations on the one hand and distributed representations on the other. The former three have all been formulated based on specific empirical phenomena. That is, a function was observed (e.g. accessibility) and a mechanism of memory was proposed to account for that function (e.g. position in a Storage Bin). This leads to a one-to-one correspondence between empirical evidence and theoretical mechanisms that makes theories relatively clear and understandable. Distributed representations tend to proceed in the opposite direction. Instead of starting from psychological findings, theorists who use distributed representations begin with a theoretical vocabulary (computationally simple units and interconnections, modeled very loosely on the properties of biological neurons). They then use this vocabulary to build specific models and see whether they can replicate known memory findings. It is possible that distributed representations may turn out to more often predict novel empirical effects, precisely because they are not originally formulated to provide a one-to-one correspondence with known phenomena.

This distinction between empirical observations and theoretical vocabulary as starting points for modeling may be regarded as a distinction between levels of theory (Smith, 1998; Smolensky, 1988). If a higher level of theory is sufficient to explain social psychological phenomena of interest, it might be argued that we need not consider the lower-level details of mental representations. However, there are several counterarguments. First, the details of how mental representations are formed and used necessarily constrain higher level theories. As an analogy, a theory about the chemical reactions between molecules will not stand if it is inconsistent with known properties of atoms. Second, new mechanisms display new properties. Distributed representations are certainly new to social psychology but have already been shown to generate novel predictions regarding social psychological issues such as accessibility (DeCoster & Smith, 1998) and stereotype learning and change (Queller & Smith, 1998). Third, distributed representations provide a dynamic approach that emphasizes learning. Many of the most interesting social psychological questions – about attitude change and stereotype change, for example – involve *changes* in representation. Finally, modeling at a lower level can lead to greater integration and parsimony. Traditionally within social psychology, theories have been developed and refined to account for the specifics of a relatively small domain. Taken to extremes, this approach can lead to a profusion of fragmentary mini-theories that have unclear relations with one another and no common basis of assumptions. Connectionist models offer the possibility of a broad integration not only within social psychology, but beyond, including areas of cognition, perception, development, and neuroscience (Elman, Bates, Johnson, Karmiloff-Smith, Parisi, & Plunkett, 1995; McClelland, McNaughton, & O'Reilly, 1995).

References

Anderson, J. A. (1995). Associative networks. In M. A. Arbib (Ed.), *Handbook of brain theory and neural networks* (pp. 102–107). Cambridge, MA: MIT Press.

Anderson, J. R. (1983). *The architecture of cognition.* Cambridge, MA: Harvard University Press.

Anderson, J. R., & Bower, G. H. (1973). *Human associative memory.* Washington, DC: Winston & Sons.

Anderson, R. C., & Pichert, J. W. (1978). Recall of previously unrecallable information following a shift in perspective. *Journal of Verbal Learning and Verbal Behavior, 17,* 1–12.

Arbib, M. A. (1995). Schema theory. In M. A. Arbib (Ed.), *Handbook of brain theory and neural networks* (pp. 830–834). Cambridge, MA: MIT Press.

Bargh, J. A., & Thein, R. D. (1985). Individual construct accessibility, person memory, and the recall–judgment link: The case of information overload. *Journal of Personality and Social Psychology, 49,* 1129–1146.

Bargh, J. A., Lombardi, W. J., & Higgins, E. T. (1988). Automaticity of chronically accessible constructs in person X situation effects on person perception: It's just a matter of time. *Journal of Personality and Social Psychology, 55,* 599–605.

Bargh, J. A., Lombardi, W. J., & Tota, M. E. (1986). The additive nature of chronic and temporary sources of construct accessibility. *Journal of Personality and Social Psychology, 50,* 869–879.

Bargh, J. A., Chaiken, S., Raymond, P., & Hymes, C. (1996). The automatic evaluation effect: Unconditional automatic attitude activation with a pronunciation task. *Journal of Experimental Social Psychology, 22,* 104–128.

Barnden, J. A. (1995). Artificial intelligence and neural networks. In M. A. Arbib (Ed.), *Handbook of brain theory and neural networks* (pp. 98–102). Cambridge, MA: MIT Press.

Barsalou, L. (1987). The instability of graded structure: Implications for the nature of concepts. In U. Neisser (Ed.), *Concepts and conceptual development* (pp. 101–140). Cambridge, UK: Cambridge University Press.

Bartlett, F. C. (1932). *Remembering.* Cambridge, UK: Cambridge University Press.

Bodenhausen, G. V., Schwarz, N., Bless, H., & Wanke, M. (1995). Effects of atypical exemplars on racial beliefs: Enlightened racism or generalized appraisals? *Journal of Experimental Social Psychology, 31*, 48–63.

Bransford, J. D., & Franks, J. J. (1971). The abstraction of linguistic ideas. *Cognitive Psychology, 2*, 331–350.

Brooks, L. (1978). Nonanalytic concept formation and memory for instances. In E. Rosch & B. B. Lloyd (Eds.), *Cognition and categorization* (pp. 169–211). Hillsdale, NJ: Lawrence Erlbaum Associates.

Bruner, J. S. (1957). Going beyond the information given. In H. Gruber, G. Terrell, & M. Wertheimer (Eds.), *Contemporary approaches to cognition*. Cambridge, MA: Harvard University Press.

Carlston, D. E. (1994). Associated systems theory: A systematic approach to cognitive representations of persons. In T. K. Srull & R. S. Wyer (Eds.), *Advances in social cognition: A dual process model of impression formation* Vol. 7 (pp. 1–78). Hillsdale, NJ: Lawrence Erlbaum Associates.

Carlston, D. E., & Smith, E. R. (1996). Principles of mental representation. In E. T. Higgins & A. Kruglanski (Eds.), *Social psychology: Handbook of basic principles* (pp. 184–210). New York: Guilford Press.

Chappell, M., & Humphreys, M. S. (1994). An auto-associative neural network for sparse representations: Analysis and application to models of recognition and cued recall. *Psychological Review, 101*, 103–128.

Churchland, P. S., & Sejnowski, T. J. (1992). *The computational brain*. Cambridge, MA: MIT Press.

Clark, A. (1993). *Associative engines: Connectionism, concepts, and representational change*. Cambridge, MA: MIT Press.

Collins, A., & Loftus, E. F. (1975). A spreading activation theory of semantic memory. *Journal of Verbal Learning and Verbal Behavior, 8*, 240–247.

Collins, A. M., & Quillian, M. R. (1969). Retrieval time from semantic memory. *Journal of Verbal Learning and Verbal Behavior, 8*, 240–247.

Darley, J. M., & Gross, P. H. (1983). A hypothesis-confirming bias in labelling effects. *Journal of Personality and Social Psychology, 44*, 20–33.

DeCoster, J., & Smith, E. R. (1998). Rapid recovery of accessibility: Empirical tests of a novel prediction of a connectionist memory. Unpublished paper, Purdue University.

Dovidio, J. F., Evans, N., & Tyler, R. B. (1986). Racial stereotypes: The content of their cognitive representations. *Journal of Experimental Social Psychology, 22*, 22–37.

Elman, J. L., Bates, E. A., Johnson, M. H., Karmiloff-Smith, A., Parisi, D., & Plunkett, K. (1995). *Rethinking innateness: A connectionist perspective on development*. Cambridge, MA: MIT Press.

Fazio, R. H. (1986). How do attitudes guide behavior? In R. M. Sorrentino & E. T. Higgins (Eds.), *Handbook of motivation and cognition* (pp. 204–243). New York: Guilford Press.

Fazio, R. H. (1993). Variability in the likelihood of automatic attitude activation: Data reanalysis and commentary on Bargh, Chaiken, Govender, and Pratto (1992). *Journal of Personality and Social Psychology, 64*, 753–758.

Fazio, R. H., Sanbonmatsu, D. M., Powell, M. C., & Kardes, F. R. (1986). On the automatic activation of attitudes. *Journal of Personality and Social Psychology, 50*, 229–238.

Fiske, S., & Taylor, S. (1994). *Social cognition*. 2nd. edn. Reading, MA: Addison-Wesley.

Frable, D. E. S., & Bem, S. L. (1985). If you are gender schematic, all members of the opposite sex look alike. *Journal of Personality and Social Psychology, 49*, 459–468.

Hastie, R. (1980). Memory for information which confirms or contradicts a general impression. In R. Hastie, T. M. Ostrom, E. B. Ebbesen, R. S. Wyer, D. Hamilton, & D. E. Carlston (Eds.), *Person memory* (pp. 155–177). Hillsdale, NJ: Lawrence Erlbaum Associates.

Hastie, R. (1988). A computer simulation model of person memory. *Journal of Experimental Social Psychology, 24*, 423–447.

Hastie, R., & Kumar, P. A. (1979). Person memory: Personality traits as organizing principles in memory for behaviors. *Journal of Personality and Social Psychology, 37*, 25–38.

Hastie, R., & Park, B. (1986). The relationship between memory and judgment depends on whether the judgment task is memory-based or on-line. *Psychological Review, 93*, 258–268.

Hertz, J., Krogh, A., & Palmer, R. G. (1991). *Introduction to the theory of neural computation*. Redwood City, CA: Addison-Wesley.

Higgins, E. T. (1996). Knowledge activation: Accessibility, applicability, and salience. In E. T. Higgins & A. W. Kruglanski (Eds.), *Social psychology: Handbook of basic principles* (pp. 133–168). New York: Guilford Press.

Higgins, E. T., Bargh, J. A., & Lombardi, W. (1985). Nature of priming effect on categorization. *Journal of Experimental Psychology: Learning, Memory and Cognition, 11,* 59–69.

Higgins, E. T., King, G. A., & Mavin, G. H. (1982). Individual construct accessibility and subjective impressions and recall. *Journal of Personality and Social Psychology, 43,* 35–47.

Higgins, E. T., Rholes, W. S., & Jones, C. R. (1977). Category accessibility and impression formation. *Journal of Experimental Social Psychology, 13,* 141–154.

Higgins, E. T., Van Hook, E., & Dorfman, D. (1988). Do self-attributes form a cognitive structure? *Social Cognition, 6,* 177–207.

Hintzman, D. L. (1986). "Schema abstraction" in a multiple-trace memory model. *Psychological Review, 93,* 411–428.

Hintzman, D. L. (1990). Human learning and memory: Connections and dissociations. *Annual Review of Psychology, 41,* 109–140.

Hirst, W. (1989). On consciousness, recall, recognition, and the architecture of memory. In S. Lewandowsky, J. C. Dunn, & K. Kirsner (Eds.), *Implicit memory: Theoretical issues* (pp. 33–46). Hillsdale, NJ: Lawrence Erlbaum Associates.

Humphreys, M. S., Bain, J. D., & Pike, R. (1989). Different ways to cue a coherent memory system: A theory for episodic, semantic, and procedural tasks. *Psychological Review, 96,* 208–233.

Jacoby, L. L. (1983). Perceptual enhancement: Persistent effects of an experience. *Journal of Experimental Psychology: Learning, Memory, and Cognition, 9,* 21–38.

Jacoby, L. L., & Brooks, L. R. (1984). Nonanalytic cognition: Memory, perception and concept learning. In G. Bower (Ed.), *The psychology of learning and motivation: Advances in research and theory* Vol. 18. New York: Academic Press.

Jacoby, L. L., & Kelley, C. M. (1987). Unconscious influences of memory for a prior event. *Personality and Social Psychology Bulletin, 13,* 314-336.

Kunda, Z., & Thagard, P. (1996). Integrating stereotypes with individuating information: A parallel constraint satisfaction model of impression formation. *Psychological Review, 103,* 284–308.

Lewicki, P. (1985). Nonconscious biasing effects of single instances of subsequent judgments. *Journal of Personality and Social Psychology, 48,* 563–574.

Linville, P. W., & Carlston, D. E. (1994). Social cognition of the self. In P. G. Devine, T. M. Ostrom, & D. L. Hamilton (Eds.), *Social cognition: Impact on social psychology* (pp. 143–193). Orlando, FL: Academic Press.

Linville, P. W., Fischer, G. W., & Salovey, P. (1989). Perceived distributions of the characteristics of in-group and out-group members: Empirical evidence and a computer simulation. *Journal of Personality and Social Psychology, 57,* 165–188.

Logan, G. D. (1988). Toward an instance theory of automatization. *Psychological Review, 95,* 492–527.

Lombardi, W. J., Higgins, E. T., & Bargh, J. A. (1987). The role of consciousness in priming effects on categorization: Assimilation versus contrast as a function of awareness of the priming task. *Personality and Social Psychology Bulletin, 13,* 411–429.

McClelland, J. L., McNaughton, B. L., & O'Reilly, R. C. (1995). Why there are complementary learning systems in the hippocampus and neocortex: Insights from the successes and failures of connectionist models of learning and memory. *Psychological Review, 102,* 419–457.

McClelland, J. L., Rumelhart, D. E., & Hinton, G. E. (1986). The appeal of parallel distributed processing. In D. E. Rumelhart, J. L. McClelland, et al. (Eds.), *Parallel distributed processing* Vol. 1 (pp. 3–44). Cambridge, MA: MIT Press.

McClelland, J. L., Rumelhart, D. E., et al. (Eds.) (1986). *Parallel distributed processing* Vol. 2. Cambridge, MA: MIT Press.

MacLeod, C. M., & Bassili, J. N. (1989). Are implicit and explicit tests differentially sensitive to item-specific vs. relational information? In S. Lewandowsky, J. C. Dunn, & K. Kirsner (Eds.),

Implicit memory: Theoretical issues (pp. 159–172). Hillsdale, NJ: Lawrence Erlbaum Associates.

Malt, B. C., & Smith, E. E. (1984). Correlated properties in natural categories. *Journal of Verbal Learning and Verbal Behavior, 23*, 250–269.

Markus, H., & Wurf, E. (1987). The dynamic self-concept: A social psychological perspective. *Annual Review of Psychology, 38*, 299–337.

Markus, H., & Zajonc, R. B. (1985). The cognitive perspective in social psychology. In G. Lindzey & E. Aronson (Eds.), *Handbook of social psychology*. 3rd. edn., Vol. 1 (pp. 137–230). New York: Random House.

Martin, L. L., Seta, J. J., & Crelia, R. A. (1990). Assimilation and contrast as a function of people's willingness and ability to expend effort in forming an impression. *Journal of Personality and Social Psychology, 59*, 38–49.

Masson, M. E. J. (1989). Fluent reprocessing as an implicit expression of memory for experience. In S. Lewandowsky, J. C. Dunn, & K. Kirsner (Eds.), *Implicit memory: Theoretical issues* (pp. 123–138). Hillsdale, NJ: Lawrence Erlbaum Associates.

Masson, M. E. J. (1991). A distributed memory model of context effects in word identification. In D. Besner & G. W. Humphreys (Eds.), *Basic processes in reading: Visual word recognition* (pp. 233–263). Hillsdale, NJ: Lawrence Erlbaum Associates.

Medin, D. L., & Schaffer, M. M. (1978). Context theory of classification learning. *Psychological Review, 85*, 207–238.

Meyer, D. E., & Schvaneveldt, R. W. (1971). Facilitation in recognizing pairs of words: Evidence of a dependence between retrieval operations. *Journal of Experimental Psychology, 90*, 227–234.

Minsky, M. (1975). A framework for representing knowledge. In P. H. Winston (Ed.), *The psychology of computer vision*. New York: McGraw-Hill.

Moscovitch, M. (1994). Memory and working with memory: Evaluation of a component process model and comparisons with other models. In D. L. Schacter & E. Tulving (Eds.), *Memory systems 1994* (pp. 269–310). Cambridge, MA: MIT Press.

Neely, J. H. (1977). Semantic priming and retrieval from lexical memory: Roles of inhibitionless spreading activation and limited-capacity attention. *Journal of Experimental Psychology: General, 1*, 226–254.

Neisser, U. (1976). *Cognition and reality*. San Francisco: Freeman.

Ostrom, T. M., Skowronski, J. J., & Nowak, A. (1994). The cognitive foundation of attitudes: It's a wonderful construct. In P. G. Devine, T. M. Ostrom, & D. L. Hamilton (Eds.), *Social cognition: Impact on social psychology* (pp. 195–257). Orlando, FL: Academic Press.

Queller, S., & Smith, E. R. (1998). Stereotype change from dispersed and concentrated disconfirming information: New insights from connectionist models. Unpublished paper, Purdue University.

Ratcliff, R., & McKoon, G. (1988). A retrieval theory of priming in memory. *Psychological Review, 95*, 385–408.

Read, S. J., & Marcus-Newhall, A. (1993). Explanatory coherence in social explanations: A parallel distributed processing account. *Journal of Personality and Social Psychology, 65*, 429–447.

Richardson-Klavehn, A., & Bjork, R. A. (1988). Measures of memory. *Annual Review of Psychology, 39*, 475–544.

Roediger, H. L., & McDermott, K. B. (1993). Implicit memory in normal human subjects. In F. Boller & J. Erafman (Eds.), *Handbook of neuropsychology* Vol. 8 (pp. 63–131). Amsterdam: Elsevier.

Ross, M., & Conway, M. (1986). Remembering one's own past: The construction of personal histories. In R. M. Sorrentino & E. T. Higgins (Eds.), *Handbook of motivation and cognition* (pp. 122–144). New York: Guilford Press.

Rumelhart, D. E., McClelland, J. L., et al. (Eds.). (1986). *Parallel distributed processing* Vol. 1. Cambridge, MA: MIT Press.

Rumelhart, D. E., Smolensky, P., McClelland, J. L., & Hinton, G. E. (1986). Schemata and sequential thought processes in PDP models. In J. L. McClelland & D. E. Rumelhart (Eds.), *Parallel distributed processing: Explorations in the microstructure of cognition* Vol. 2 (pp. 7–57). Cambridge, MA: MIT Press.

Schacter, D. L. (1987). Implicit memory: History and current status. *Journal of Experimental Psychology: Learning, Memory, and Cognition, 13*, 501–518.

Schacter, D. L. (1994). Priming and multiple memory systems: Perceptual mechanisms of implicit memory. In D. L. Schacter & E. Tulving (Eds.), *Memory systems 1994* (pp. 233–268). Cambridge, MA: MIT Press.

Schank, R., & Abelson, R. P. (1977). *Scripts, plans, goals, and understanding*. Hillsdale, NJ: Lawrence Erlbaum Associates.

Schwarz, N., & Clore, G. L. (1983). Mood, misattribution, and judgments of well-being: Informative and directive functions of affective states. *Journal of Personality and Social Psychology, 45,* 513–523.

Sloman, S. A., Hayman, C. A. G., Ohta, N., Law, J., & Tulving, E. (1988). Forgetting in primed fragment completion. *Journal of Experimental Psychology: Learning, Memory, and Cognition, 14,* 223–239.

Smith, E. R. (1988). Category accessibility effects in a simulated exemplar-only memory. *Journal of Experimental Social Psychology, 24,* 448–463.

Smith, E. R. (1990). Content and process specificity in the effects of prior experiences. Target Article in T. K. Srull & R. S. Wyer (Eds.), *Advances in social cognition* Vol. 3 (pp. 1–60). Hillsdale, NJ: Lawrence Erlbaum Associates.

Smith, E. R. (1996). What do connectionism and social psychology offer each other? *Journal of Personality and Social Psychology, 70,* 893–912.

Smith, E. R. (1998). Mental representation and memory. In D. Gilbert, S. Fiske, & G. Lindzey (Eds.), *Handbook of social psychology.* 4th. edn., Vol. 1 (pp. 391–445). New York: McGraw-Hill.

Smith, E. R., & Branscombe, N. R. (1988). Category accessibility as implicit memory. *Journal of Experimental Social Psychology, 24,* 490–504.

Smith, E. R., & DeCoster, J. (1998). Knowledge acquisition, accessibility, and use in person perception and stereotyping: Simulation with a recurrent connectionist network. *Journal of Personality and Social Psychology, 74,* 21–35.

Smith, E. R., & Zárate, M. A. (1992). Exemplar-based model of social judgment. *Psychological Review, 99,* 3–21.

Smith, E. R., Stewart, T. L., & Buttram, R. T. (1992). Inferring a trait from a behavior has long-term, highly specific effects. *Journal of Personality and Social Psychology, 62,* 753–759.

Smolensky, P. (1988). On the proper treatment of connectionism. *Behavioral and Brain Sciences, 11,* 1–74.

Squire, L. R. (1994). Declarative and nondeclarative memory: Multiple brain systems supporting learning and memory. In D. L. Schacter & E. Tulving (Eds.), *Memory systems 1994* (pp. 203–232). Cambridge, MA: MIT Press.

Srull, T. K. (1981). Person memory: Some tests of associative storage and retrieval models. *Journal of Experimental Psychology: Human Learning and Memory, 7,* 440–463.

Stangor, C., & McMillan, D. (1992). Memory for expectancy-congruent and expectancy-incongruent information: A review of the social and social developmental literatures. *Psychological Bulletin, 111,* 42–61.

Strack, F., & Martin, L. L. (1987). Thinking, judging, and communicating: A process account of context effects in attitude surveys. In H.-J. Hippler, N. Schwarz, & S. Sudman (Eds.), *Social information processing and survey methodology* (pp. 123–148). New York: Springer-Verlag.

Thorpe, S. (1995). Localized and distributed representations. In M. A. Arbib (Ed.), *Handbook of brain theory and neural networks* (pp. 549-552). Cambridge, MA: MIT Press.

Tourangeau, R., & Rasinski, K. A. (1988). Cognitive processes underlying context effects in attitude measurement. *Psychological Bulletin, 103,* 299–314.

Tulving, E. (1972). Episodic and semantic memory. In E. Tulving & W. Donaldson (Eds.), *Organization of memory.* New York: Academic.

Tulving, E., Schacter, D. L., & Stark, H. (1982). Priming effects in word-fragment completion are independent of recognition memory. *Journal of Experimental Psychology: Learning, Memory, and Cognition, 8,* 336–342.

Turner, J. C., Oakes, P. J., Haslam, S. A., & McGarty, C. (1994). Self and collective: Cognition and social context. *Personality and Social Psychology Bulletin, 20,* 454–463.

Whittlesea, B. W. A. (1987) Preservation of specific experiences in the representation of general knowledge. *Journal of Experimental Psychology: Learning, Memory, and Cognition, 13*, 3–17.

Whittlesea, B. W. A., & Dorken, M. D. (1993). Incidentally, things in general are particularly determined: An episodic-processing account of implicit learning. *Journal of Experimental Psychology: General, 122*, 227–248.

Wiles, J., & Humphreys, M. S. (1993). Using artificial neural nets to model implicit and explicit memory test performance. In P. Graf & M. E. J. Masson (Eds.), *Implicit memory: New directions in cognition, development, and neuropsychology* (pp. 141–165). Hillsdale, NJ: Lawrence Erlbaum Associates.

Wilson, T. D. (1990). Self-persuasion via self-reflection. In J. M. Olson & M. P. Zanna (Eds.), *Self-inference processes: The Ontario Symposium* Vol. 6 (pp. 43–68). Hillsdale, NJ: Lawrence Erlbaum Associates.

Wilson, T. D., & Hodges, S. D. (1992). Attitudes as temporary constructions. In L. L. Martin & A. Tesser (Eds.), *The construction of social judgments* (pp. 37–65). Hillsdale, NJ: Lawrence Erlbaum Associates.

Wisniewski, E. J. (1997). When concepts combine. *Psychonomic Bulletin and Review, 4*, 167–183.

Wittenbrink, B., Judd, C. M., & Park, B. (1997). Evidence for racial prejudice at the implicit level and its relationship with questionnaire measures. *Journal of Personality and Social Psychology, 72*, 262–274.

Wyer, R. S., & Carlston, D. E. (1994). The cognitive representation of persons and events. In R. S. Wyer & T. K. Srull (Eds.), *Handbook of Social Cognition.* 2nd. edn. (pp. 41–98). Hillsdale, NJ: Lawrence Erlbaum Associates.

Wyer, R. S., & Gordon, S. E. (1984). The cognitive representation of social information. In R. S. Wyer & T. K. Srull (Eds.), *Handbook of social cognition* Vol. 2 (pp. 73–150). Hillsdale, NJ: Lawrence Erlbaum Associates.

Wyer, R. S., & Srull, T. K. (1980). The processing of social stimulus information: A conceptual integration. In R. Hastie, T. M. Ostrom, E. B. Ebbesen, R. S. Wyer, D. Hamilton, & D. E. Carlston (Eds.), *Person memory* (pp. 227–300). Hillsdale, NJ: Lawrence Erlbaum Associates.

Wyer, R. S., & Srull, T. K. (1989). *Memory and cognition in its social context.* Hillsdale, NJ: Lawrence Erlbaum Associates.

Chapter Seven

The Social Unconscious

Mahzarin R. Banaji, Kristi M. Lemm, and Siri J. Carpenter

Contemporary social psychologists are aware that long before concepts of cognitive mediation were admissible in scientific psychology, their predecessors had been sufficiently entranced with matters of mind to study them even at risk of marginalization by the then dominant antimentalists. The first social psychologists were bold not so much in their recognition that thinking, feeling, and motivation were fundamental mental systems – for hundreds of years, thinkers even in the western world, had known the same. The unique audacity of these psychologists was in the belief that thought, feeling, and motive could be scrutinized, manipulated, and subjected to experimentation in a manner not unlike the treatment accorded to particles, ions, and bacteria. It should be of little surprise then, that a field so confident a century ago that processes of conscious mental life could indeed be measured is now equally confident about measuring mental life that lies beyond consciousness.

Johnson-Laird's (1983) question "What should a theory of consciousness explain?" produced four components, *awareness, control, intention*, and *self-reflection*, that a tractable theory of consciousness must explain. The focus of this chapter is on the hidden side of consciousness, which leads us to focus on the inverse of these components: thoughts, feelings, and actions performed outside conscious awareness, without conscious control, or without intention. At this stage, research on unconscious processes reflects a basic attempt to demonstrate that particular unconscious processes occur at all, to trace the boundary conditions of their operation, to document the full richness of the systems that are engaged (cognition, affect, motivation) and the levels of social objects they include (e.g. self, other, social group). With a strong emphasis on developing robust and replicable methods for investigation, researchers have asked: can knowledge that resides outside conscious awareness influence social thinking, feeling, and action? Is unawareness actually a precondition for observing particular effects? How should we characterize attitudes that are fully within

This research was supported by grant number SBR 9709924 from the National Science Foundation. We thank Richard Hackman and Aiden Gregg for their helpful comments and suggestions.

awareness but relatively outside conscious control? Is it possible to consider the unconscious activation of goals and motives as we have come to accept unconscious cognition and affect? What do these investigations imply regarding the notion of free-will, particularly as it concerns assumptions about the freedom or constraints to think, feel, and act toward one's self and others? These are among the questions that have mattered to contemporary psychologists interested in the analysis of the social unconscious.

Research on unconscious processes does not, unfortunately, reflect a sensible observance of terminology of constructs and processes. Terms like *automatic, implicit, unconscious,* and *indirect* are often used interchangeably, and sometimes to refer to divergent underlying processes (e.g. awareness versus control). In recognition of our own complicity in creating this confusion, we attempt to restore some order for future discussions by using the term *unconscious* to refer to the family of processes that occur outside conscious awareness, without conscious control, or without intention to perform. The use of the term *unconscious* reflects a deliberate attempt to capture its usage from still largely psychodynamic meaning. In addition, we use the term *implicit* to refer to those processes that operate without the actor's conscious awareness, and the term *automatic* to refer to processes that operate without the actor's conscious control. In time, these issues and concerns about predictive validity and relationships among families of measures will be resolved. However, progress will be greatly speeded-up by charting a clear research agenda and encouraging greater collaboration across laboratories with divergent perspectives and methodological allegiances.

Much social psychological research can be said to be, in essence, the study of processes that operate outside conscious awareness and intention. After all, experiments must routinely create circumstances in which the behavior that is observed and measured is free of the concerns of social desirability and demand characteristics, and in that sense unawareness about the source of influence on behavior is the norm. Yet, it is only more recently that unconscious processes in social behavior have been examined in their own right, rather than as a methodological by-product of social psychological experimentation. This review revolves around those experiments that bring a deliberate focus to unconscious processes because of a genuine interest in the limits on introspection, in understanding the extent and nature of the social unconscious, and in using the study of unconscious processes as the basis to challenge commonplace notions of individual responsibility on the part of social actors, and assumptions of justice in interpersonal treatment of social targets.

Over two hundred years ago, Immanuel Kant wrote:

> We can reduce all the powers of the human mind, without exception, to these three: the *cognitive power,* the *feeling of pleasure and displeasure,* and the *power of desire.* It is true that philosophers who otherwise deserve unlimited praise for the thoroughness in their way of thinking have asserted that this distinction is only illusory, and have tried to bring all powers under nothing but the cognitive power. Yet it is quite easy to establish, and has in fact been realized for some time, that this attempt to bring unity into that diversity of powers, though otherwise undertaken in the genuine philosophic spirit, is futile. (Kant, 1790/1987, p. 394; italics in original)

Two centuries later, we find it worthwhile to retain this triumvirate, and are bemused by the similar dominance of the "cognitive power" then, as it is now. We include research on unconscious forms of affect, and note that research on unconscious motives is at such an early stage of development that it would be hard to provide a responsible review of such work at this time.

This chapter brings together selected samples of research on unconscious processes as they inform cognition and affect (for reviews see Bargh, 1997; Bornstein & Pittman, 1992; Greenwald, 1992; Kihlstrom, 1990; Kihlstrom, Mulvaney, Tobias, & Tobis, in press; Uleman & Bargh, 1989; Wegener & Bargh, 1998). By necessity, the treatment here is not historical, and the attention to any single area is superficial. Should the review reflect a sense of the potential pervasiveness and emerging lawfulness of unconscious processes as they are revealed in social life, it will have succeeded.

Unconscious Cognition

By far the most research attention has been devoted to the study of unconscious social cognition. This is not surprising because of disproportionate attention given to the study of social perception, attention, memory, categorization, and judgment more generally. In this section, we devote our attention to three aspects of unconscious social cognition: the study of self, other, and social group. Admittedly, the demarcation is somewhat arbitrary, but it will allow us to build the case that a wide bandwidth of learning has become possible within a relatively short time on how humans think about themselves, others individuals, and the social groups of their species.

Self

Proposals to study the self as a cognitive structure have appeared since the 1970s (see Banaji & Prentice, 1994; Markus, 1977; Greenwald & Pratkanis, 1984; Kihlstrom, Cantor, Albright, Chew, Klein, & Niedenthal, 1988; Klein & Loftus, 1990; Linville & Carlston, 1994) and these set the stage for contemporary research on unconscious processes involving the self. These position papers and experimental accounts placed the study of self firmly in cognitive space, often using the dominant language of models that allowed a connection to established constructs such as memory (e.g. Greenwald & Banaji, 1989; Klein, Loftus, & Kihlstrom, 1996). The language of these models and the demystification of self that emerged out of these accounts permitted unconscious self processes to also be measured. The research may roughly be separated into analyses of the unconscious manner by which shifts in self-related processes such as self-presentation and self-evaluation occur, and the role of unconscious self-related processes in guiding an understanding of the social world.

The most illustrative findings that show that unconscious activation of significant others can have implications for self-evaluation come from studies in which the priming procedure uses subliminal presentation. Baldwin (1994) used subliminal primes to activate representations of a significant other (one's adviser) who is critical or accepting in orientation and showed parallel shifts in views of self; also, that approval or disapproval from unconsciously activated others can influence one's evaluation of one's own work (Baldwin, Carrell, & Lopez, 1990). Besides the role accorded to significant others, the idea that membership in social groups has repercussions for individual psychological functioning has been of perennial interest to social scientists (see Walsh & Banaji, 1997, for a review). In its most recent form, this idea has led to research suggesting a potential link between activated knowledge of beliefs about one's group and performance on ability tests. Steele and Aronson (1995, p. 808) point out that "the existence of a negative stereotype about a group to which one belongs . . . means that in situations where the stereotype is applicable, one is at risk of confirming it as a self-characterization, both to one's self and to others who know the stereotype. That is what is meant by stereotype threat." In their experiments, Black Americans underperformed on tests of intellectual ability, and women underperformed on tests of mathematical ability (Steele, 1997) when subtly made aware of their group membership or the link between the group and the negative attribute. Several additional demonstrations of this finding now exist. For example, Levy (1996) showed that subliminally activated negative stereotypes about old age creates decrements in memory performance among elderly subjects; Croizet & Claire (1998) showed that eliciting information about parents' level of education led to a decrement in verbal ability among low SES students; Shih, Pittinsky, & Ambady (1999) showed that activating gender identity or ethnic identity among Asian women shifted performance to be respectively inferior or superior on a math test. Evidence about the robustness and ease of replication of these effects is only just beginning to be determined, and the mechanisms by which such effects are produced are not yet identified. Yet their implications for the ease with which equality and fairness in treatment can be compromised by group membership are sufficiently shocking to require particularly intensive study by investigators with varying theoretical perspectives.

In other research we learn that who one is and how one assesses oneself can implicitly influence views of others, just as we observed previously that significant others and social groups can influence judgments of self. Spencer, Fein, Wolfe, Fong, and Dunn (1998) showed that threat to self-image can automatically activate stereotypes of social groups even under conditions that otherwise do not produce such activation. And Sedikides & Skowronski (1993) showed the role of self in forming impressions of others more generally, by demonstrating that central dimensions of the self-concept were influential in judgments of others. Perhaps the most impressive corpus of research showing the role of one's significant others in shaping social perception has been obtained by Andersen and her colleagues (Andersen & Glassman, 1996). In providing the first experimental evidence for transference, they show that activation of information pertaining to significant others implicitly lead to inferences about new individuals that mimic representations of significant others and self. Moreover, such activation can also elicit facial affect that captures the evaluation of the significant other and produces behavioral confirmation in interpersonal interaction.

To demonstrate the role of unconscious processes in short-cuts to self-evaluation, Swann, Hixon, Stein-Seroussi, & Gilbert (1990) demonstrated that under conditions of limited cognitive capacity, participants showed a simpler preference for self-enhancing social agents, whereas the availability of resources led to more informative self-verifying strategies. It also appears that processes of social comparison occur with minimal cognitive resources or intention to compare, and even when the source of comparison is nondiagnostic for self-assessment. Social comparison can lead to decrements in self-evaluation in such cases when resources are unavailable to adjust for the inappropriate comparison (Gilbert, Giesler, & Morris, 1995).

Studies showing the involvement of unconscious self-related processes are numerous, and these examples are selected to show that lack of both awareness and control play a role in assessments of self, and that self-knowledge and personal relationships can unconsciously influence assessments of the surrounding social world. The breakdown of simple distinctions between thinking and feeling are quite obvious in many analyses of self, and examining the role of unconscious processes shows such interrelations among mental systems to be fundamental, and defying of our imposed separation of these systems for expository purposes.

Other

Few topics in social psychology can be regarded as more central to the field's mission of understanding the stuff of human relations than the processes involved in one person observing, understanding, and assessing another. Although Katz and Braly (1933) and Icheiser (1949) explicitly recognized the role of unconscious processes in person and group perception, it was a later generation of experimenters who with their newfangled technologies studied the unconscious operation of person perception: to what degree and in what manner, they asked, are awareness, control, and intention components of the pervasive act of judging others? It is now clear that spontaneous, fluid, and effortless acts of person perception, when brought under scientific scrutiny, reveal the operation of a vastly intricate thought system, able to perform social gymnastics of incredible speed and elegance. The social gymnast, however, does not always land on the balance beam. The research we review shows also a more clumsy side of person perception: susceptibility to situational intrusions, the constraints of routinized thought patterns, of errors in computation and application that create costs of varying magnitude.

Implicit perception of others stems from the constructs in the perceiver's mind   Among the highlights of this research literature are experiments conducted by Higgins, Rholes, & Jones (1977) which appeared without heralding the study of unconscious processes in person perception. Yet it ushered in a wave of research that has produced what some regard to be a law of social perception: constructs that are active in a perceiver's mind implicitly shape perception and judgment of others (Sedikides & Skowronski, 1990). Participants read material that served to activate knowledge about personality qualities such as "stubborn" or "persistent." Later, in a test of reading comprehension ostensibly unrelated to the previous session, participants judged an ambiguously described target to be more in line with the previously activated knowledge; those who had been primed with "stubborn" were inclined to find the target to be relatively stubborn, and others who had been primed with "persistent" judged the identical target to be more persistent. Participants in such experiments were not *aware* of the influence of previous experience in shaping their judgment, and in the absence of such awareness, there was no opportunity to *control* judgment. Certainly, we assume that participants *intended* to provide an unbiased judgment, on the basis of the actions of the target. Yet, as this experiment and the countless others using variations of this procedure suggest, person perception can be guided by factors that may emanate elsewhere, outside consciously accessible cognition (see Higgins, 1996, and Sedikides & Skowronski, 1990, for reviews).

The many experiments that followed on the heels of Higgins, Rholes, & Jones (1977) served as more than just the clean-up crew. These experiments, continuing up to the present, reveal a rich understanding of unconscious person perception. Additionally, theoretical frameworks of various levels of specificity have been proposed that offer working explanations, suggest useful metaphors, and specify mechanisms (Higgins, Bargh, & Lombardi, 1985; Higgins, 1989; Herr, Sherman, & Fazio, 1983; Martin, 1986; Wyer & Srull, 1980). While we cannot review the theoretical models here, it is clearly the case that the experimental findings and theoretical attempts to understand unconscious person perception (e.g. recency, frequency, awareness, specificity, chronicity, contrast) have allowed hidden aspects of unconscious processes themselves to be revealed. Together, they have created a view of person perception that is altogether more complex and complete, and more troubling in its implications: perceivers believe that their judgments of others reflect properties of the target, and not of the thoughts that are implicitly active in their mind. That such influences on judgment occur without the intention to create bias in the judgment process, and without awareness that such bias may even exist, starkly raises the question of the extent to which "mental due process" (Banaji & Bhaskar, in press) in interpersonal interaction can be assumed.

The robustness of a theoretical construct is evident when a diversity of applications provide supporting evidence for the principle. The activation of constructs, either temporary or chronic, have been shown to influence behavior in a variety of domains: desire to work with a gay person (Johnson, Bryant, Jackson, Gatto, Nowak, & MacVittie, 1994); reducing risk of pregnancy (Norris & Devine, 1992); increasing the assessment of "alcoholic" (Southwick, Steele, & Lindell, 1986); explaining the cognitive states of depressives (Gotlib & McCann, 1984); priming aggression by sports (Wann & Branscombe, 1989); explaining individual differences in aggression (Graham & Hudley, 1994); increasing judgments of women as sexual objects (Rudman & Borgida, 1995); implicating television viewing as a vehicle of priming (Shrum & O'Guinn, 1993); the role of chronic accessibility in electoral choice (Lau, 1989); and the role of priming self-interest in political reasoning (Young, Thomsen, Borgida, Sullivan, & Aldrich, 1991).

Implicit perception of others follows from spontaneous trait inferences   The construct accessibility literature shows that our judgments of others are influenced by the concepts that are active in our own minds at the time of perception. But what exactly is perceived when we observe others' behavior? Knowing that there may be multiple causes for behavior, to what do we attribute a particular action? Following decades of research in person perception beginning with Lewin and Heider, we know that the most common inference made is a trait attribution – we encounter a behavior, and infer that some trait about the actor must be associated with its occurrence.

Uleman and colleagues (Newman & Uleman, 1989) kicked off a controversy in the field of person perception by suggesting that traits are inferred spontaneously, or possibly automatically, upon encountering a behavior. In an early demonstration, Winter and Uleman (1984) had participants study descriptions of people performing behaviors that implied traits, such as "the sailor leaves his wife with 20 pounds of laundry." Later, participants were asked to recall the sentences they had previously read, given recall cues that were either traits that had been implied by the sentences (e.g. inconsiderate), non-trait semantic associates of the sentences (e.g. sea or wash), or no cue. Trait cues facilitated sentence recall better than no cue, and as well as or better than strong semantic associates, suggesting that participants had automatically made trait inferences at the time of learning about the behavior.

The original STI effect has been replicated in many iterations, providing convincing evidence that traits are inferred outside of conscious awareness (Moskowitz & Roman, 1992) and without conscious impression-formation goals (e.g. Skowronski, Carlston, Mae, & Crawford; 1998; Uleman, Newman, & Winter, 1992; Whitney, Waring, & Zingmark, 1992). Although the trait-cued recall paradigm has been challenged methodologically (D'Agostino & Beegle, 1996), evidence that traits are inferred spontaneously at encoding has been provided by research using methods other than cued recall, including probe recognition (Uleman, Hon, Roman, and Moskowitz, 1996), savings in a relearning task (Carlston & Skowronski, 1994), and using blatant or subtle priming at encoding to inhibit or facilitate STI (Newman & Uleman, 1990).

Spontaneous trait inferences may provide input to dispositional inference processes   The bulk of the evidence suggests that most trait inferences made without intention are inferences about *behavior*, not dispositional inferences directly linked to the actor (e.g. Carlston, Skowronski, & Sparks, 1995; Moskowitz, 1993; Uleman, Moskowitz, Roman, & Rhee, 1993; Whitney, Davis, & Waring, 1994). However, STI may play an essential role in the formation of personality inferences. Several models of person perception have proposed that dispositional inference proceeds in multiple stages, the first of which requires minimal cognitive resources or control, and may thus be considered spontaneous or automatic (e.g. Burnstein & Schul, 1982; Brewer, 1988; Higgins, Strauman, & Klein, 1986; Ross & Olson, 1981).

Trope's two-stage inference model (Trope, 1986; Trope & Liberman, 1993) and Gilbert's three-stage model (Gilbert, Pelham, & Krull, 1988; Gilbert & Krull, 1988; Gilbert & Osborne, 1989) propose that observed behavior, the situation in which it occurs, and prior information about the actor are automatically identified in terms of underlying traits (e.g. "this is a friendly behavior"). The output of this automatic identification stage in turn becomes the input for the dispositional inference, in which behavioral, situational, and prior information that has been identified in terms of traits is combined to form a trait attribution about the actor. Experimental evidence shows that people make behavioral identifications even under conditions of diminished cognitive resources, whereas conscious correction for situational contributions to behavior may be inadequate if perceivers do not have adequate cognitive resources (Trope & Alfieri, 1997; Gilbert, Pelham, & Krull, 1988). The implications about human nature and nurture from these models are also troubling: because people are so often engaged in concurrent activities, behavior characterizations are often not appropriately adjusted for situational contributions to behavior. This can tilt toward trait- (rather than situation-) correspondent inferences, a phenomenon also termed the fundamental attribution error (Ross, 1977).

What early attribution theorists had predicted, research over the last twenty years has confirmed about the swift and remarkably sophisticated inferences that are made about individual others in one's social world. The methods that are used are reliable, and this has allowed a healthy exporting of methods outside the laboratories in which they were developed. The theories of human inference processes in social context that have emerged are creative and continuously generative of research. All in all, research on unconscious processes in perceiving, understanding, and judging others shows how intelligent but fallible systems operate within the constraints of the cognitive architecture that evolution and learning allows and the demands of daily social life.

Social group

Perhaps the most distinguishing mark of social psychological research on unconscious processes is its interest in the social group as a legitimate unit of analysis. In the previous sections, we discussed how judgments about individual personality qualities can arise from unconsciously perceived sources. In this section, we discuss research on the unconscious activation of stereotypes and their application in judgments of individuals and groups. In the next section on unconscious affect, we will review related research on attitudes of prejudice that reside outside of conscious control or awareness.

As has often been argued, stereotypes about social groups are heuristics that simplify and organize perception of the social world. In so doing, beliefs about social groups and their use in individual judgment merely reveal ordinary processes of learning and generalization. Our discussion of these particular short-cuts will show the various ways in which unconscious processes reveal their presence. Our discussion will also point out the moral question that emerges from this rather ordinary discovery about category learning, generalization, and inferences. Stereotypes exact a toll by subsuming individuals into the larger social categories and by giving to individuals privileges and punishments that are not their due. We noted previously that social judgment may not reflect the actions of the target but of unconsciously applied constructs in the perceiver's mind. It is unsettling, at least in societies that consciously affirm that judgments ought to be based on the "content of one's character," to discover the extent to which judgments of individuals may reflect beliefs about their social group.

Unconscious stereotypes are rooted in social categorization　A rich literature on social categorization processes indicates that such processes are automatically prompted by the mere presence of a stimulus target (Banaji & Hardin, 1996; Blair & Banaji, 1996; Blascovich, Wyer, Swart, & Kibler, 1997; Brewer, 1988; Eckes, 1994; Fiske & Neuberg, 1990; Ford, Stangor, & Duan, 1994; Hamilton & Sherman, 1994; Perdue, Dovidio, Gurtman, & Tyler, 1990; Pendry & Macrae, 1996; Stangor & Lange, 1994; Stroessner, 1996; Zárate, Bonilla, & Luévano, 1995). And in the mind of the social perceiver, stereotypes that accompany a particular category automatically accrue to its members.

Unconscious stereotyping is ubiquitous　In an influential demonstration of unconscious race stereotyping, Devine (1989) found that subliminally presenting race information influenced how participants subsequently judged the ambiguous behavior of a race-unspecified target. Both high- and low-prejudiced participants rated the target as more hostile when they had been presented with a list containing 80 percent stereotypically black words (e.g. jazz, basketball, Africa) than when the list contained only 20 percent stereotypically black words. Devine's evidence that stereotypes could be automatically activated by presenting cues about a stereotyped group inspired research on how stereotypes operate without conscious awareness, control, and intention (see Fiske, 1998, and Greenwald & Banaji, 1995, for reviews). This body of research provides strong evidence that beliefs about social groups are readily activated, and influence perception of the target. What's more, the research suggests that unconscious processes not only facilitate stereotyped responding but also inhibit counterstereotypical associations, perhaps making stereotypes additionally resistant to changing in the face of atypical group exemplars (Trope & Thompson, 1997; Van Knippenberg & Dijksterhuis, 1996).

Gender, as a category, has received much attention, in part because of its fundamental nature and presence in all human societies and in part for its convenience in not attracting attention to social category as the focus of the experiment (Banaji & Greenwald, 1995; Banaji & Hardin, 1996; Blair & Banaji, 1996; Dunning & Sherman, 1997; Lambert, 1995; Macrae, Bodenhausen, Milne, & Thorn, 1997; Nelson, Acker, & Manis, 1996; Pratto & Bargh, 1991). This research has shown that information about one's gender, whether conveyed through names, pictures, or gender stereotypical words, exerts an unconscious influence on judgment. For example, Banaji and Greenwald (1995) found that more male names than female names were identified as famous under conditions of memory uncertainty, suggesting that stereotypical beliefs about fame were implicitly applied in assigning fame to people. In other research, using traditional semantic priming procedures, participants were found to more quickly identify male and female target names (Blair & Banaji, 1996) or pronouns (Banaji & Hardin, 1996) when the names matched the gender stereotypicality of the primes than when they were incongruent with the primes.

Support is also found for the unconscious operation of race stereotypes (Bodenhausen, Schwarz, Bless, & Wänke, 1995; Dovidio, Evans, & Tyler, 1986; Gilbert and Hixon, 1991; Glaser & Banaji, 1998; Kawakami, Dion, & Dovidio, 1998; Lepore & Brown, 1997; Spencer, Fein, Wolfe, Fong, & Dunn, 1998; Von Hippel, Sekaquaptewa, & Vargas, 1997; Wittenbrink, Judd, & Park, 1997). These studies show, for example, that race stereotypes are easily activated upon encountering members of stereotyped groups (e.g. Gilbert & Hixon, 1991; Gaertner & McLaughlin, 1983; Lepore & Brown, 1997). Other research has indicated that activating unconscious stereotypes can influence not only individuals' judgments of others but also their overt behavior (Bargh, Chen, & Burrows, 1996). Such experiments starkly reveal that perceivers may have less control over the knowledge they use in social interaction than they or even the scientists who study them may have assumed. When knowledge about the social groups to which one belongs enters into the equation of social judgment early and with force, it can shape the cumulative record of social interaction without the hindrance of awareness or hence responsibility.

Is unconscious stereotyping unavoidable?   Despite the preponderance of evidence that unconscious stereotypes hold a tight grasp over everyday thinking, the extent to which they are related to explicit beliefs and attitudes, the circumstances under which they are activated, and the degree to which unconscious stereotypes can be brought under deliberate control remain less certain. The question of the relationship between conscious and unconscious measures emerged early. Are those who hold weaker forms of conscious stereotypes also likely to evidence weaker forms of unconscious stereotypes? Early attempts to address this question suggested that unconscious stereotypes, assessed indirectly by examining nonverbal behavior, social perception, memory, and speeded reactions to social stimuli, are often unrelated or only slightly related to explicitly expressed stereotypes assessed by self-report measures (Banaji & Greenwald, 1995; Banaji & Hardin, 1996; Devine, 1989; Dunning & Sherman, 1997; Gaertner & McLaughlin, 1983; Hense, Penner, & Nelson, 1995; Von Hippel, Sekaquaptewa, & Vargas, 1997; Wittenbrink, Judd, & Park, 1997). However, there is also a body of recent evidence that suggests the contrary (Augoustinos, Innes, & Ahrens, 1994; Dovidio, Brigham, Johnson, & Gaertner, 1996; Hense, Penner, & Nelson, 1995; Kawakami, Dion, & Dovidio, 1998; Lepore & Brown, 1997; Locke, MacLeod, & Walker, 1994; Wittenbrink, Judd, & Park, 1997).

Lepore and Brown (1997, 1999) argued that individual differences in consciously expressed prejudice should predict unconscious stereotyping. Using a procedure similar to that used by Devine (1989), Lepore and Brown subliminally primed high- and low-prejudiced participants either with evaluatively neutral words that connoted the social category Blacks (without connoting particular stereotypes), or with nonsense syllables. Then, participants read behavioral descriptions of a race-unspecified target person and rated the target on a number of traits stereotypic of Blacks. Participants who had scored high in prejudice against Blacks employed more negative stereotypes and fewer positive stereotypes in the prime condition than in the no-prime condition. In contrast, low-prejudiced participants used more positive stereotypes in the prime condition than in the no-prime condition, but showed no difference on the negative scales. Lepore and Brown concluded that when race *category* information is primed but race *stereotypes* are not, unconscious race stereotyping is contingent upon how much one explicitly endorses prejudice.

Recently, Kawakami, Dion, & Dovidio (1998) proposed an additional explanation for the murky relationship between implicit and explicit beliefs. They noted that even in research in which implicit and explicit measures are associated, the association is relatively weak, and proposed that highly sensitive procedures may be necessary to pick up relationships between implicit stereotyping and explicit beliefs and attitudes. In addition, Cunningham, Nezlak, & Banaji (1999) have shown that a general ethnocentric personality disposition is related to specific unconscious prejudices (toward foreigners, Black Americans, the poor, Jews, and gays). Such efforts represent initial strides in identifying the conditions under which implicit and explicit beliefs converge and diverge, by identifying methodological, statistical, and theoretical hurdles that need to be set aside before a more complete picture regarding the relationship between conscious and unconscious stereotypes or prejudice may be observed.

Can unconscious stereotypes be controlled?   The controllability of unconscious stereotypes has sparked considerable theoretical debate and empirical research. There is abundant evidence that stereotypes that operate unconsciously defend their territory fiercely, influencing social interactions even when perceivers are consciously vigilant and motivated to defeat them (Banaji & Greenwald, 1995; Bargh, in press; Blair & Banaji, 1996; see Greenwald & Banaji, 1995). Indeed, conscious attempts to purge stereotypic thoughts can easily backfire, bringing stereotypes to the fore with redoubled force (Macrae, Bodenhausen, Milne,

& Ford, 1997; Nelson, Acker, & Manis, 1996; Nelson, Biernat, & Manis, 1990; Sherman, Stroessner, Loftus, & Deguzman, 1997). Bargh (in press) has proposed a metaphor to characterize unconscious stereotyping, comparing it to a monster whose influence cannot be restrained once it is set into motion. The solution may lie in motivated individuals' ability to develop, over time, chronically accessible *egalitarian* beliefs that can counter the effects of unconscious stereotypes.

Our assessment of the issue of controlling automatic processes is in line with Bargh (in press). When a process operates unconsciously, there is little, if anything, that can be done to retract, revoke, or rescind. If this message from basic research on unconscious stereotypes is to make contact with the world it seeks to improve, the responsible suggestion at the present time is not the simplistic one to "just say no." Automatic stereotypes can and will influence perception, memory, and judgment. If the goal of judging individuals by the content of their character is one that this and other societies wish to take seriously, this body of social psychological research suggests two radical strategies. First, create the social conditions that allow new associations and new learning about social groups that blur the bright line that demarcates social groups. Second, generate individual and group-based strategies for compensation in conscious recognition of the stark and pervasive unconscious biases that operate in social judgment.

Unconscious Affect

Whereas no uncertainty is expressed about the existence of an unconscious form of cognition and whether it can be reliably assessed, there is still active debate regarding the existence of unconscious affect (Clore, 1994; Clore & Ketelaar, 1997; Kihlstrom, Mulvaney, Tobias, & Tobis, in press; LeDoux, 1994, 1996; Zajonc, 1994, 1998). Research on unconscious affect (and related concepts better recognized by the labels emotion, evaluation, attitude, and prejudice) has acquired increased prominence in social psychology in part from the desire to provide more complete models of social behavior, and in part from the availability of tractable methods to measure these warm and wet constructs. Perhaps a rigorous analysis of unconscious affect is naturally located in social psychology because of the field's long-standing interest in constructs that tap feeling, most obviously that of attitude and esteem (see Greenwald & Banaji, 1995). Research on unconscious evaluation, attitudes, and affect has its origins in a multitude of experimental traditions necessitating tough choices regarding selection for review. However, no attempt is made here to distinguish between the various terms that are used to refer to slightly differing aspects of the basic construct. For additional coverage and differing emphases see Kihlstrom, et al. (in press) and Zajonc (1998).

Physiological measures of evaluation and attitude

Among the reasons to probe evaluation and attitudes in their physiological form, Cacioppo, Crites, Gardner, & Berntson (1994, p. 121) offer the following rationale: "Unfortunately, the attitudes that individuals are least willing to report are often those that are most impor-

tant to measure accurately, as they may differentiate individuals along theoretically important dimensions." Autonomic measures of unconscious evaluation were initially viewed
with hope, but such assessments failed to separate intensity and valence of attitude (see
Petty and Cacioppo, 1983; Zanna, Detweiler, & Olson, 1984). Facial EMG responses
have also been obtained (Cacioppo, Martzke, Petty, & Tassinary, 1988) but again, their
disadvantages have been noted, including the inability of such measures to protect against
masking and distortion (see Cacioppo, Petty, Losch, & Kim, 1986). Recently, experiments in which a late positive potential (LPP) of the event-related brain potential (ERP)
was related to evaluative categorization have been reported (Cacioppo, Crites, Berntson, &
Coles, 1993). Further, the amplitude of LPP increases as a function of the mismatch between evaluative categorization and expectation of evaluative significance through salient
contextual cues (Cacioppo et al., 1994). The amplitude of LPP is larger when a negative
(rather than positive) attitude stimulus is presented within a sequence of positive stimuli,
and such measures also appear to show sensitivity to intensity of negative stimuli. The
obvious utility of such a measure to provide a marker of individual differences (e.g. fear
responses to social situations implicated in phobia or negative responses to members of
social groups as revealed in prejudice) will be realized in future experiments to test the
construct and predictive validity of the measure.

Sensory-motor processes in evaluation and attitude

Evidence suggesting the involvement of motor processes and their sensory consequences in
attitude formation merits attention here, because it points to yet another path that can
reveal the role of unconscious evaluative processes in social cognition. Wells and Petty
(1980) showed that the motor action of shaking versus nodding one's head while listening
to persuasive messages resulted in lesser or greater agreement with the message. Likewise,
Strack, Martin, & Stepper (1988) showed that motor activity that facilitated smiling increased ratings of the humor of cartoons compared with slightly differing motor activity
that inhibited smiling. Such effects emerged in spite of subjects' being unaware of the
meaning of the contractions of the zygomaticus muscle. Other research supports these
findings that manipulations of facial expressions create affective states or influence attitudinal
responses outside conscious awareness (Martin, Harlow, & Strack, 1992; Zajonc, Murphy,
& Inglehart, 1989). Stepper & Strack (1993) have shown that proprioceptive cues from
body posture (upright versus slumped) can influence the affective experience of pride, just
as it can influence nonaffective judgments of effort, and Förster and Strack (1996) have
shown that head nodding versus shaking increases memory for valence-consistent words.
A distinction has been proposed between *experiential* knowledge, in which "feelings are
'immediately given' to the individual and have a distinct phenomenal quality" (Stepper &
Strack, 1993, p. 218) versus *noetic* representations which reflect inferred, indirect knowledge, with the former being implicated in the information that is obtained from bodily
posture or facial expression without conscious awareness. Finally, there is suggestive
evidence that somatic manipulations involved in arm flexion versus arm extension can
have small but reliable effects on the evaluation of attitudinally neutral stimuli such as
ideographs, leading the authors to conclude that "attitudinal effects involve active motor

processes and that a person does not need to know the evaluative or motivational significance of the motor process for it to have attitudinal effects" (Cacioppo, Priester, & Berntson, 1993, p. 16). This intriguing research needs to be nurtured and developed further, for it has the potential to inform about the role of unconscious processes in a most fundamental association of body and mind, and the potential for the products of such unconscious operation to influence feeling and social behavior.

Perception and memory reveal unconscious forms of affect

With the increased usage of indirect measures of *perception* and *memory*, a welcome blurring of the sharp distinction between these two processes has occurred. Viewing unconscious processes of memory and perception as they inform about the nature of affective experience and expression has contributed to a broadening of our understanding of consciousness.

Mere exposure   Among the most influential ideas linking perception and affect comes from the discovery that exposure to a stimulus leads to enhanced liking for it (Zajonc, 1968). There have been over two hundred published experiments testing this hypothesis (Bornstein, 1989; Bornstein & D'Agostino, 1994) that verify the reliability and robustness of the basic effect across a wide variety of stimulus forms, dependent variable formats, methods of exposure, and experimental settings. The finding that mere exposure produces liking has also been extended to research on interpersonal interaction (Bornstein, Leone, & Galley, 1987). The literature on category accessibility (see previous section on unconscious cognition) showed the peculiar effect of awareness on unconscious thought and social judgment (i.e. the influence of the priming event is most visible when that event is least available to conscious recollection). Research on the mere exposure effect has pointed up a parallel finding regarding unconscious affect: the magnitude of the effect is greater under conditions of subliminal rather than supraliminal exposure (Bornstein, 1989, 1992; Bornstein & D'Agostino, 1992). Theoretically, the mere exposure effect has shifted from being considered a phenomenon unique to the expression of affect to one that most parsimoniously fits into the broader landscape of familiarity and its effect on judgment more generally (Bornstein & D'Agostino, 1994; Jacoby & Kelley, 1987; Jacoby, Toth, Lindsay, & Debner, 1992; Mandler, Nakamura, and Van Zandt, 1987). Whatever the interpretational leaning, the mere exposure effect will remain among the most important discoveries of twentieth-century psychology. Here, its importance is in having identified a dissociation between what is consciously known and what is unconsciously felt.

Automatic evaluation In the early 1970s the discovery was made that meaning is automatically activated upon the mere presentation of a word (Meyer & Schevaneveldt, 1971; Posner & Snyder, 1975). Efforts to resist activation of default meaning are moot when conditions do not permit the exerting of conscious control (Neely, 1977). The evidence to be reviewed here pertains to the finding that just as semantic meaning is extracted automatically upon presentation of a word, the evaluative meaning of information is also grasped without conscious control. Fazio, Sanbonmatsu, Powell, & Kardes (1986) showed that judgments of a target were facilitated when its valence was congruent rather than incongruent with that of the prime. Bargh, Chaiken, Govender, & Pratto (1992; Bargh, Chaiken, Raymond, & Hymes, 1996) replicated and extended this finding, additionally proposing that automatic evaluation occurs regardless of the strength (extremity) of prime valence, a claim about which there is debate (Chaiken & Bargh, 1993; Fazio, 1993), and even in the absence of a focus on the evaluative properties of information in judgment. Glaser & Banaji (1998) have reported a series of studies in which contrast effects in automatic evaluation appear when primes are of extreme valence, and they interpret this finding as an automatic correction for the implicitly perceived biasing influence of the prime.

In an effort to test the reliability, robustness, and boundary conditions of automatic evaluation, Greenwald, Draine, & Abrams (1996) and Greenwald, Klinger, & Liu (1989) effectively showed that the evaluative meaning of words is automatically registered by presenting the prime subliminally. In their most recent research they did this by inventing a variation of the technique called the "response window" that reliably produces the effect. As this research reveals, experiments have relied on time (measured in milliseconds) to respond to the target as an indicator of automatic evaluation. A second procedure has also been used in which evaluative primes, usually in the form of evaluative facial expressions, are briefly flashed (on the order of 4 milliseconds to prevent conscious registration) following which a neutral target (e.g. a Chinese ideograph) is to be rapidly judged. The replicated finding is that judgments of the neutral stimuli shift in the direction of the evaluative position of the prime (Murphy & Zajonc, 1993; Niedenthal, Setterlund, & Jones, 1994). Pratto & John (1991) used a Stroop color-naming task with evaluative stimuli in place of color names to extend the generality of automatic evaluation, showing that automatic evaluation can interfere with a conscious cognitive task.

Together, these experiments on automatic evaluation have changed our thinking about the existence and tractability of unconscious affect. First, they demonstrate that the affective quality of information registers without conscious awareness of the stimulus (as in the subliminal presentation studies) and without conscious control over the response (Murphy, Monahan, & Zajonc, 1995). Second, it appears that automatic evaluations are sensitive only to gross distinctions of polarity and not to anything that can be considered to be a more fine-grained evaluative assessment (see Pratto, 1994; Zajonc, 1994). Finally, although the experiments have examined unconscious perception and memory for evaluative material, they have been interpreted as revealing an attitude. This is a noteworthy shift in social psychology's understanding of the concept of attitude. In commenting on research on unconsciously activated attitudes, Cacioppo, et al. (1993, p. 16) which one? note that "Indeed, the day may come when we regard attitudes as being 'evaluative perceptions' . . . aroused by stimuli." Because conceptions of attitudes as necessarily accessible to conscious awareness and control are difficult to shake off, the research summarized here will come to be viewed as historically important – as the first robust and reliable demonstrations that permitted a sufficient breakthrough to allow us to conceptualize attitudes as automatic evaluations.

Attitudes of prejudice

Experts who study attitudes and beliefs toward social groups have emphasized the need to treat attitude (prejudice) with the same importance as has been accorded to belief (stereotype), and have resisted the merging of these two constructs both in theory and in experimental practice. In part, this desire has stemmed from the conviction that attitudes of prejudice represent a unique and separable component from stereotypic beliefs. The organization of this chapter allows that distinction to continue even at the expense of separating research on unconscious prejudice from its cousin, unconscious stereotypes (see previous section). Just as the study of unconscious cognition has received greater attention than the study of unconscious affect, the parallel constructs of unconscious stereotype and unconscious prejudice have received similarly differential treatment. For evidence of this, see the greater coverage allowed to research on unconscious stereotypes compared with unconscious prejudice in a recent review (Fiske, 1998). Even since that review, however, attention to the study of unconscious prejudice has increased, largely from straightforward extensions of techniques to study automatic attitudes more generally. As with the study of stereotypes, such research is already challenging accepted notions of what prejudice means and raising troubling questions regarding the implications for how to regard human nature and human nurture (see Banaji & Bhaskar, 1999).

Indirect measures of prejudice have been of interest for over two decades (Crosby, Bromley, & Saxe, 1980), with continuing interest in related issues such as physiological indicators of prejudice (Vanman, Paul, Ito, & Miller, 1997; Vrana & Rollock, 1998), the relationship between public and private expressions of prejudice (Lambert, Cronen, Chasteen, & Lickel, 1996), and the impact of single direct or indirect exposure to negative behavior on judgments of groups and members of groups (Henderson-King & Nisbett, 1996). Yet a rigorous analysis of the role of consciousness and the disjunction between the unconscious roots of prejudice and its conscious manifestations has only just become possible. With methods to measure automatic evaluation and automatic stereotypes in place, it was only a matter of time before such techniques were used to study applications to prejudice. In fact, research to show that priming of race stereotypes produced evidence of linking evaluatively positive information with White compared with Black has been available for some time (Dovidio, Evans, & Tyler, 1986), in addition to evidence of a more general liking for one's own group. Associating neutral syllables with "we," "us," "ours' versus "they," "them," "theirs" produced greater liking for syllables attached to ingroup compared with outgroup primes (Perdue, Dovidio, Gurtman, & Tyler 1990).

With the first publication in 1998, the Implicit Association Test (IAT; Greenwald, McGhee, & Schwartz, 1998) has already attracted attention as a measure of automatic association, most notably in the investigation of automatic *evaluative* associations toward social groups and self. The attraction of the method lies in two of its most salient properties: (a) the ability to obtain large effects compared with priming methods of automatic evaluation, and (b) the ability to compellingly reveal a lack of control over automatic evaluative associations. Like related measures of automatic association (e.g. semantic priming) the technique is based on the assumption that if two concepts have come to be associated in memory, they will be associated more quickly when they are encountered. The IAT procedure operationalizes this assumption by requiring participants to swiftly associate exemplars of categories such as "old" and "young" along with exemplars of the evaluative category "bad" or "unpleasant." The speed with which old–good and young–bad are classified compared to the speed with which old–bad and young–good are classified produces a robust measure of the relative automatic evaluation of young and old. The original research demonstrated that the method is capable of detecting robust positive automatic associations toward flowers compared with insects, toward White compared with Black Americans (among non-Black subjects), and automatic ingroup positivity among Korean and Japanese Americans. (Reports of ongoing explorations with the technique are available at <www.yale.edu/implicit> or <depts.washington.edu/iat>, showing the wide application of the technique to investigate the attitudinal basis of depression or smoking, and attitudes toward a variety of social groups, e.g. Turks/Germans, Jews/Christians, East/West Germans, old/young, omnivore/vegetarian, male/female, overweight/thin.)

Research with the technique has explored attitudes toward self and social groups: female/male, feminine/masculine, or female leader/male leader, and the relationship between self-identity and gender attitude (Carpenter & Banaji, 1998; Lemm & Banaji, 1998; Mitchell, Nosek, & Banaji, 1998; Rudman & Glick, 1998; Rudman & Kilianski, 1998; Rudman, Greenwald, & McGhee, 1998); attitudes toward math/science versus arts and the relationship among automatic gender identity, gender stereotypes about math/science, self-math identity, and performance (Nosek, Banaji, & Greenwald, 1998); race identity, group-esteem, and self-esteem (Rosier, Banaji, & Greenwald, 1998); dissociated attitudes toward multiply categorizable objects (Mitchell, Nosek, & Banaji, 1998); attitudes regarding age, nationality, and religion (Rudman, Greenwald, Mellot, & Schwartz, 1998); and the role of personality in automatic prejudice (Cunningham, Nezlak, & Banaji, 1999). New designs for research have been suggested, based on a unified view of social cognition that draws on consistency theories (especially the Heiderian notion of balance) and associationist networks (Greenwald, et al., in press). However, several questions regarding its construct validity are only beginning to be addressed. The theoretical questions of utmost interest concern the predictive validity of this and other measures of automatic association (see Fazio, Jackson, Dunton, & Williams, 1995; Bessenoff & Sherman, 1998), developing measures of motivation to control prejudice (Dunton & Fazio, 1997; Plant & Devine, 1998), the relationship between automatic and controlled prejudice (Dovidio, Kawakami, Johnson, Johnson, & Howard, 1997; Kawakami, Dion, & Dovidio, 1998; Lepore & Brown, 1997; Von Hippel, Sekaquaptewa, & Vargas, 1997; Wittenbrink, Judd, & Park, 1997), and the malleability of automatic evaluative associations (Carpenter & Banaji, 1999; Dasgupta & Greenwald, 1999). Research on unconscious forms of prejudice elicits attention, in part because it speaks to a problem of great social significance. Because of this, and because of the potential to challenge many assumptions about the propensity to create harm without intention and awareness, this research requires the attention of a diversity of methodological and theoretical perspectives.

Conclusion

Beings with consciousness have the luxury to speculate that their own mind and behavior may also operate in a strikingly different mode, detached from consciousness. For hundreds of years, lay people and experts have believed that not only is there a mental world that remains hidden from consciousness, but that the workings of this world have important and far-reaching consequences for understanding who we are and who we aspire to be.

Yet it is only in the last hundred years, beginning with experiments on humans and other animals, that a science of the unconscious was attempted and succeeded. In this chapter, we attended to the work of those who grounded their investigations firmly in the social world, the ether in which mental life operates.

The assumption that human social behavior can only be understood by asking those capable of language to say, preferably in grammatical English, what they think, feel, and intend to do about themselves and others in their world is a limiting one. In the last two decades, social psychology has shown the advances that are possible when such an assumption is momentarily set aside. In another context, we made the point that it is not difficult to imagine why it is that social perceivers and social psychologists have trouble imagining and investigating those processes that lie outside conscious awareness (Banaji, Blair, & Glaser, 1997). We argued that when the source of an action emanates in time and space unconnected to the observed action, it is difficult to grasp the connection between the source and target of influence. It took Newton's genius to discover that light, a source unattached to physical objects, was responsible for producing the subjective experience of color. Likewise, sources of influence on thoughts, affect, and motives are not likely to be discerned easily because their causes lie in places that are unreachable by conscious awareness. In addition, as we observed, even under conditions that permit awareness, the ability to control thoughts, feelings, and motives may be weaker than assumed. The problem here is more complex than contemplating an understanding of the physical world, for unlike the physical world, the object of inquiry (unconscious mind) is a part of the thinking system that must conduct the inquiry. The limits on being able to look inward are serious, and here the social world offers a solution for theory and praxis: a rich array of events, situations, and opportunities to explore the manner in which unconscious processes operate, in contexts in which they have significant impact on happiness, liberty, and justice. It is perhaps the case that as we discover the extent to which unconscious processes control social thought, feeling, and behavior, we will arrive at a fuller appreciation of the unique role played by consciousness in a species with the capability to evaluate the nature of the social unconscious.

References

Andersen, S. M., & Glassman, N. S. (1996). Responding to significant others when they are not there: Effects on interpersonal interference, motivation, and affect. In R. M. Sorrentino & E. T. Higgins (Eds.), *Handbook of motivation and cognition* Vol. 3 (pp. 262–321). New York: Guilford Press.

Augoustinos, M., Innes, J. M., & Ahrens, C. (1994). Stereotypes and prejudice: The Australian experience. *British Journal of Social Psychology, 33,* 125–141.

Baldwin, M. W. (1994). Primed relational schemas as a source of self-evaluative reactions. *Journal of Social and Clinical Psychology, 13,* 380–403.

Baldwin, M. W., Carrell, S. E., & Lopez, D. F. (1990). Priming relationship schemas: My advisor and the Pope are watching me from the back of my mind. *Journal of Experimental Social Psychology, 26,* 435–454.

Banaji, M. R., & Bhaskar, R. (1999). Implicit stereotypes and memory: The bounded rationality of social beliefs. In D. L. Schacter and E. Scarry (Eds.), *Belief and memory.* Cambridge, MA: Harvard University Press.

Banaji, M. R., & Greenwald, A. G. (1995). Implicit gender stereotyping in judgments of fame. *Journal of Personality and Social Psychology, 68,* 181–198.

Banaji, M. R., & Hardin, C. (1996). Automatic stereotyping. *Psychological Science, 7* (3), 136–141.

Banaji, M. R., & Prentice, D. A. (1994). The self in social contexts. *Annual Review of Psychology, 45,* 297–332.

Banaji, M. R., Blair, I. V., & Glaser, J. (1997). Environments and unconscious processes. In R. S. Wyer (Ed.), *The automaticity of everyday life: Advances in social cognition,* vol. 10 (pp. 63–74). Mahwah, NJ: Erlbaum.

Banaji, M. R., Hardin, C., & Rothman, A. J. (1993). Implicit stereotyping in person judgment. *Journal of Personality and Social Psychology, 65,* 272–281.

Bargh, J. A. (1997). The automaticity of everyday life. In R. S. Wyer, Jr. (Ed.), *The automaticity of everyday life: Advances in social cognition* Vol. 10 (pp. 1–61). Mahwah, NJ: Lawrence Erlbaum Associates.

Bargh, J. A. (1999). The cognitive monster: The case against the controllability of automatic stereotype effects. In S. Chaiken & Y. Trope (Eds.), *Dual process theories in social psychology.* New York: Guilford Press.

Bargh, J. A., Chen, M., & Burrows, L. (1996). Automaticity of social behavior: Direct effects of trait construct and stereotype activation on action. *Journal of Personality and Social Psychology, 71,* 230–244.

Bargh, J. A., Chaiken, S., Govender, R., & Pratto, F. (1992). The generality of the automatic attitude activation effect. *Journal of Personality and Social Psychology, 62,* 893–912.

Bargh, J. A., Chaiken, S., Raymond, P., & Hymes, C. (1996). The automatic evaluation effect: Unconditional automatic attitude activation with a pronunciation task. *Journal of Experimental Social Psychology, 32,* 104–128.

Beck, A. T. (1976). *Cognitive therapy and the emotional disorders.* New York: Penguin Books/Meridian.

Bessenoff, G. R., & Sherman, J. W. (1998). Automatic and controlled components of prejudice toward the overweight: Evaluation versus stereotype activation. Unpublished manuscript, Northwestern University.

Blair, I. V., & Banaji, M. R. (1996). Automatic and controlled processes in stereotype priming. *Journal of Personality and Social Psychology, 70,* 1142–1163.

Blascovich, J., Wyer, N. A., Swart, L. A., & Kibler, J. L. (1997). Racism and racial categorization. *Journal of Personality and Social Psychology, 72,* 1364–1372.

Bodenhausen, G. V., Schwarz, N., Bless, H., & Wänke, M. (1995). Effects of atypical exemplars on racial beliefs: Enlightened racism or generalized appraisals? *Journal of Experimental Social Psychology, 31,* 48–63.

Bornstein, R. F. (1989). Exposure and affect: Overview and meta-analysis of research, 1968–1987. *Psychological Bulletin, 106,* 265–289.

Bornstein, R. F. & D'Agostino, P. R. (1992). Stimulus recognition and the mere exposure effect. *Journal of Personality and Social Psychology, 63,* 545–552.

Bornstein, R. F., & D'Agostino, P. R. (1994). The attribution and discounting of perceptual fluency: Preliminary tests of a perceptual fluency/attributional model of the mere exposure effect. *Social Cognition, 12,* 103–128.

Bornstein, R. F., & Pittman, T. S. (1992). *Perception without awareness: Cognitive, clinical, and social perspectives.* New York: Guilford Press.

Bornstein, R. F., Leone, D. R., & Galley, D. J. (1987). The generalizability of subliminal mere exposure effects: Influence of stimuli perceived without awareness on social behavior. *Journal of Personality and Social Psychology, 53,* 1070–1079.

Brewer, M. B. (1988). A dual process model of impression formation. In T. K. Srull & R. S. Wyer (Eds.), *Advances in social cognition* Vol. 1 (pp. 1–36). Hillsdale, NJ: Erlbaum.

Burnstein, E., & Schul, Y. (1982). The informational basis of social judgments: Operations in forming an impression of another person. *Journal of Experimental Social Psychology, 18,* 217–234.

Cacioppo, J. T., Priester, J. R., & Berntson, G. G. (1993). Rudimentary determinants of attitudes:

II. Arm flexion and extension have differential effects on attitudes. *Journal of Personality and Social Psychology, 65,* 5–17.

Cacioppo, J. T., Crites, S. L., Berntson, G. G., & Coles, M. G. (1993). If attitudes affect how stimuli are processed, should they not affect the event-related brain potential? *Psychological Science, 4,* 108–112.

Cacioppo, J. T., Crites, S. L., Gardner, W. L., & Berntson, G. G. (1994). Bioelectrical echoes from evaluative categorizations: I. A late positive brain potential that varies as a function of trait negativity and extremity. *Journal of Personality and Social Psychology, 67,* 115–125.

Cacioppo, J. T., Martzke, J. S., Petty, R. E., & Tassinary, L. G. (1988). Specific forms of facial EMG response index emotions during an interview: From Darwin to the continuous flow hypothesis of affect-laden information processing. *Journal of Personality and Social Psychology, 54,* 592–604.

Cacioppo, J. T., Petty, R. E., Losch, M. E., & Kim, H. S. (1986). Electromyographic activity over facial muscle regions can differentiate the valence and intensity of affective reactions. *Journal of Personality and Social Psychology, 50,* 260–268.

Carlston, D. E., & Skowronski, J. J. (1994). Savings in the relearning of trait information as evidence for spontaneous inference generation. *Journal of Personality and Social Psychology, 66,* 840–856.

Carlston, D. E., Skowronski, J. J., & Sparks, C. (1995). Savings in relearning: II. On the formation of behavior-based trait associations and inferences. *Journal of Personality and Social Psychology, 69,* 420–436.

Carpenter, S. J., & Banaji, M. R. (1998). Implicit attitudes and behavior toward female leaders. Paper presented at Midwestern Psychological Association meeting, Chicago.

Chaiken, S., & Bargh, J. A. (1996). Occurrence versus moderation of the automatic attitude activation effect: Reply to Fazio. *Journal of Personality and Social Psychology, 64,* 759–765.

Clore, G. L. (1994). Why emotions are never unconscious. In P. Ekman & R. J. Davidson (Eds.), *The nature of emotion: Fundamental questions* (pp. 285–190). New York: Oxford University Press.

Clore, G. L., & Ketelaar, T. (1997). Minding our emotions: On the role of automatic, unconscious affect. In R. S. Wyer (Ed.), *The automaticity of everyday life: Advances in social cognition* Vol. 10 (pp. 105–120). Mahwah, NJ: Lawrence Erlbaum Associates.

Croizet, J., & Claire, T. (1998). Extending the concept of stereotype threat to social class: The intellectual underperformance of students from low socioeconomic backgrounds. *Personality and Social Psychology Bulletin, 24,* 588–594.

Crosby, F., Bromley, S., & Saxe, L. (1980). Recent unobtrusive studies of Black and White discrimination and prejudice: A literature review. *Psychological Bulletin, 87,* 546–563.

Cunningham, W. A., Nezlak, J. B., & Banaji, M. R. (1999). The roots of prejudice. Unpublished manuscript, Yale University.

D'Agostino, P. R., & Beegle, W. (1996). A reevaluation of the evidence for spontaneous trait inferences. *Journal of Experimental Social Psychology, 32,* 153–164.

Dasgupta, N., & Greenwald, A. G. (1999). Exposure to admired group members reduces implicit prejudice. Paper presented at the annual meetings of the American Psychological Society, Denver, CO.

Devine, P. G. (1989). Stereotypes and prejudice: Their automatic and controlled components. *Journal of Personality and Social Psychology, 56,* 5–18.

Dovidio, J. F., Evans, N., & Tyler, R. B. (1986). Racial stereotypes: The contents of their cognitive representations. *Journal of Experimental Social Psychology, 22,* 22–37.

Dovidio, J. F., Brigham, J., Johnson, B., & Gaertner, S. (1996). Stereotyping, prejudice, and discrimination: Another look. In N. Macrae, C. Stangor, & M. Hewstone (Eds.), *Stereotypes and stereotyping* (pp. 1276–1319). New York: Guilford Press.

Dovidio, J. F., Kawakami, K., Johnson, C., Johnson, B., & Howard, A. (1997). On the nature of prejudice: Automatic and controlled processes. *Journal of Experimental Social Psychology, 33,* 510–540.

Dunning, D., & Sherman, D. A. (1997). Stereotypes and tacit inference. *Journal of Personality and Social Psychology, 73,* 459–471.

Dunton, B. C., & Fazio, R. H. (1997). An individual difference measure of motivation to control prejudiced reactions. *Personality and Social Psychology Bulletin, 23,* 316–326.

Eckes, T. (1994). Explorations in gender cognition: Content and structure of female and male subtypes. *Social Cognition, 12* (1), 37–60.

Fazio, R. H. (1993). Variability in the likelihood of automatic attitude activation: Data reanalysis and commentary on Bargh, Chaiken, Govender & Pratto (1992). *Journal of Personality and Social Psychology, 64,* 753–758.

Fazio, R. H., Jackson, J. R., Dunton, B. C., & Williams, C. J. (1995). Variability in automatic activation as an unobtrusive measure of racial attitudes: A bona fide pipeline? *Journal of Personality and Social Psychology, 69,* 1013–1027.

Fazio, R. H. Sanbonmatsu, D. M., Powell, M. C., & Kardes, F. R. (1986). On the automatic activation of attitudes. *Journal of Personality and Social Psychology, 50,* 229–238.

Fiske, S. T. (1998). Stereotyping, prejudice, and discrimination. In D. T. Gilbert, S. T. Fiske, & G. Lindzey (Eds.), *The handbook of social psychology* Vol. 2 (pp. 357–411). Boston: Mcgraw-Hill.

Fiske, S. T., & Neuberg, S. L. (1990). A continuum of impression formation, from category-based to individuating processes: Influences of information and motivation on attention and interpretation. In M. P. Zanna (Ed.), *Advances in experimental social psychology* Vol. 23 (pp. 1–74). New York: Academic Press.

Ford, T. E., Stangor, C., & Duan, C. (1994). Influence of social category accessibility and category-associated trait accessibility on judgments of individuals. *Social Cognition, 12* (2), 149–168.

Förster, J., & Strack, F. (1996). Influence of overt head movements on memory for valenced words: A case of conceptual–motor compatibility. *Journal of Personality and Social Psychology, 71,* 421–430.

Gaertner, S. L., & McLaughlin, J. P. (1983). Racial stereotypes: Associations and ascriptions of positive and negative characteristics. *Social Psychology Quarterly, 46,* 23–30.

Gilbert, D. T., & Hixon, J. G. (1991). The trouble of thinking: Activation and application of stereotypic beliefs. *Journal of Personality and Social Psychology, 60,* 509–517.

Gilbert, D. T., & Krull, D. S. (1988). Seeing less and knowing more: The benefits of perceptual ignorance. *Journal of Personality and Social Psychology, 54,* 93–102.

Gilbert, D. T., & Osborne, R. E. (1989). Thinking backward: The curable and incurable consequences of cognitive busyness. *Journal of Personality and Social Psychology, 57,* 940–949.

Gilbert, D. T., Giesler, R. B., & Morris, K. A. (1995). When comparisons arise. *Journal of Personality and Social Psychology, 69,* 227–236.

Gilbert, D. T., Pelham, B. W., & Krull, D. S. (1988). On cognitive busyness: When person perceivers meet persons perceived. *Journal of Personality and Social Psychology, 54,* 733–740.

Glaser, J., & Banaji, M. R. (1998). Assimilation and contrast in automatic evaluation and prejudice. Paper presented at the annual meeting of the Society for the Psychological Study of Social Issues, Ann Arbor, MI.

Gotlib, I. H., & McCann, C. D. (1984). Construct accessibility and depression: An examination of cognitive and affective factors. *Journal of Personality and Social Psychology, 93,* 19–30.

Graham, S., & Hudley, C. (1994). Attributions of aggressive and nonaggressive African–American male early adolescents: A study of construct accessibility. *Developmental Psychology, 30,* 365–373.

Greenwald, A. G. (1992). New look 3: Unconscious cognition reclaimed. *American Psychologist, 47,* 766–779.

Greenwald, A. G., & Banaji, M. R. (1989). The self as a memory system: Powerful, but ordinary. *Journal of Personality and Social Psychology, 57,* 41–54.

Greenwald, A. G., & Banaji, M. R. (1995). Implicit social cognition: Attitudes, self-esteem, and stereotypes. *Psychological Review, 102* (1), 4–27.

Greenwald, A. G., & Pratkanis, A. R. (1984). The self. In R. S. Wyer & T. K. Srull (Eds.), *Handbook of social cognition* Vol. 3 (pp. 129–178). Hillsdale, NJ: Erlbaum.

Greenwald, A. G., Banaji, M. R., Rudman, L. A., Farnham, S. D., Nosek, B. A., & Rosier, M. (in press). Prologue to a unified theory of attitudes, stereotypes, and self-concept. In J. P. Forges (Ed.), *Feeling and thinking: The role of affect in social cognition and behavior.* New York: Cambridge University Press.

Greenwald, A. G., Draine, S. C., & Abrams, R. L. (1996). Three cognitive markers of unconscious semantic activation. *Science, 283,* 1699–1702.

Greenwald, A. G., Klinger, M. R., & Liu, T. J. (1989). Unconscious processing of dichoptically masked words. *Memory & Cognition, 17,* 35–47.

Greenwald, A. G., McGhee, D. E., & Schwartz, J. K. (1998). Measuring individual difference in implicit cognition: The Implicit Association Test. *Journal of Personality and Social Psychology.*

Hamilton, D. L., & Sherman, J. W. (1994). Stereotypes. In R. S. Wyer, Jr., & T. K. Srull (Eds.), *Handbook of social cognition* Vol. 2 (pp. 1–68). Hillsdale, NJ: Erlbaum.

Henderson-King, E. I., & Nisbett, R. E. (1996). Anti-black prejudice as a function of exposure to the negative behavior of a single black person. *Journal of Personality and Social Psychology, 71,* 654–664.

Hense, R. L., Penner, L. A., & Nelson, D. L. (1995). Implicit memory for age stereotypes. *Social Cognition, 13* (4), 399–415.

Herr, P. M., Sherman, S. J., & Fazio, R. H. (1983). On the consequences of priming: Assimilation and contrast efforts. *Journal of Experimental Social Psychology, 19,* 323–340.

Higgins, E. T. (1989b). Knowledge accessibility and activation: Subjectivity and suffering from unconscious sources. In J. S. Uleman & J. A. Bargh (Eds.), *Unintended thought* (pp. 75–123). New York: Guilford Press.

Higgins, E. T. (1996). Knowledge activation: Accessibility, applicability, and salience. In E. T. Higgins & A. W. Kruglanski (Eds.), *Social psychology: Handbook of basic principles* (pp. 133–168). New York: Guilford Press.

Higgins, E. T., Bargh, J. A., & Lombardi, W. (1985). The nature of priming effects on categorization. *Journal of Experimental Psychology: Learning, Memory, and Cognition, 11,* 59–69.

Higgins, E. T, Rholes, W. S., & Jones, C. R. (1977). Category accessibility and impression formation. *Journal of Experimental Social Psychology, 13,* 141–154.

Higgins, E. T., Strauman, T., & Klein, R. (1986). Standards and the process of self-evaluation. In R. M. Sorrentino & E. T. Higgins (Eds.), *Handbook of motivation and cognition: Foundation of social behavior* Vol. 1 (pp. 23–63). New York: Guilford Press.

Icheiser, G. (1949). Misunderstandings in human relations: A study in false social perception. *American Journal of Sociology, 55,* Part 2.

Jacoby, L. L. & Kelley, C. M. (1987). Unconscious influences of memory for a prior event. *Personality and Social Psychology Bulletin, 13,* 314–336.

Jacoby, L. L., Toth, J. P., Lindsay, D. S., & Debner, J. A. (1992). Lectures for a layperson: Methods for revealing unconscious processes. In R. F. Bornstein and T. S. Pittman (Eds.), *Perception without awareness: Cognitive, clinical, and social perspectives* (pp. 81–120). New York: Guilford Press.

Johnson, J., Bryant, M., Jackson, L. A., Gatto, L., Nowak, A., & MacVittie, T. (1994). Construct accessibility, AIDS, and judgment. *Journal of Social Behavior and Personality, 9,* 191–198.

Johnson-Laird, P. N. (1983). A computational analysis of consciousness. *Cognition and Brain Theory, 6,* 499–508.

Kant, I. (1790/1987). *Critique of judgment.* Trans. W. S. Pluhar. Indianapolis, IN: Hackett Publishing.

Katz, D., & Braly, K. (1933). Racial stereotypes of one hundred college students. *Journal of Abnormal and Social Psychology, 28,* 280–290.

Kawakami, K., Dion, K. L., & Dovidio, J. F. (1998). Racial prejudice and stereotype activation. *Personality and Social Psychology Bulletin, 24* (4), 407–416.

Kihlstrom, J. F. (1990). The psychological unconscious. In L. A. Pervin (Ed.), *Handbook of personality: Theory and research* (pp. 445–464). New York: Guilford Press.

Kihlstrom, J. F., Mulvaney, S., Tobias, B. A., & Tobis, I. P. (in press). The emotional unconscious.

Kihlstrom, J. F., Cantor, N., Albright, J. S., Chew, B. R., Klein, S. B., & Niedenthal, P. M. (1988). Information processing and the study of the self. In. L. Berkowitz, et al. (Eds.), *Advances in experimental social psychology* Vol. 21 (pp. 145–178). San Diego: Academic Press.

Klein, S. B., & Loftus, J. (1990). The role of abstract and exemplar-based knowledge in self-judgments: Implications for a cognitive model of the self. In T. K. Srull & R. S. Wyer (Eds.), *Content and process specificity in the effects of prior experiences: Advances in social cognition* Vol. 3 (pp. 131–139). Hillsdale, NJ: Lawrence Erlbaum Associates.

Klein, S. B., Loftus, J., & Kihlstrom, J. F. (1996). Self-knowledge of an amnesic patient: Toward a neuropsychology of personality and social psychology. *Journal of Experimental Psychology: General, 125,* 250–260.

Lambert, A. (1995). Stereotypes and social judgment: The consequences of group variability. *Journal of Personality and Social Psychology, 68,* 388–403.

Lambert, A. J., Cronen, S., Chasteen, A. L., & Lickel, B. (1996). Private vs. public expressions of racial prejudice. *Journal of Experimental Social Psychology, 32,* 437–459.

Lau, R. R. (1989). Construct accessibility and electoral choice. *Political Behavior, 11,* 5–32.

LeDoux, J. E. (1994). Emotional processing, but not emotions, can occur unconsciously. In P. Ekman & R. J. Davidson (Eds.), *The nature of emotion: Fundamental questions* (pp. 291–292). New York: Oxford University Press.

LeDoux, J. E. (1996). *The emotional brain.* New York: Simon & Schuster.

Lemm, K., & Banaji, M. R. (1998). Implicit and explicit gender identity and attitudes toward gender. Paper presented at the Midwestern Psychological Association meeting, Chicago.

Lepore, L., & Brown, R. (1997). Category and stereotype activation: Is prejudice inevitable? *Journal of Personality and Social Psychology, 72,* 275–287.

Lepore, L., & Brown, R. (1999). Exploring automatic stereotype activation: A challenge to the inevitability of prejudice. In D. Abrams & M. A. Hogg (Eds.), *Social identity and social cognition* (pp. 141–163). Oxford: Blackwell Publishers.

Levy, B. (1996). Improving memory in old age through implicit self-stereotyping. *Journal of Personality and Social Psychology, 71,* 1092–1107.

Linville, P. W., & Carlston, D. E. (1994). Social cognition of the self. In P. G. Devine, D. C. Hamilton, & T. M. Ostrom (Eds.), *Social cognition: Impact on social psychology* (pp. 143–193). New York: Academic Press.

Locke, V., MacLeod, C., & Walker, I. (1994). Automatic and controlled activation of stereotypes: Individual differences associated with prejudice. *British Journal of Social Psychology, 33,* 29–46.

Macrae, C. N., Bodenhausen, G. V., Milne, A. B., & Ford, R. L. (1997). On the regulation of recollection: The intentional forgetting of stereotypical memories. *Journal of Personality and Social Psychology, 72,* 709–719.

Macrae, C. N., Bodenhausen, G. V., Milne, A. B., Thorn, T. M. J., & Castelli, L. (1997). On the activation of social stereotypes: The moderating role of processing objectives. *Journal of Experimental Social Psychology, 33,* 471–489.

Mandler, G., Nakamura, Y., & Van Zandt, B. J. S. (1987). Nonspecific effects of exposure on stimuli that cannot be recognized. *Journal of Experimental Psychology: Learning, Memory, & Cognition, 13,* 646–648.

Markus, H. (1977). Self-schemata and processing information about the self. *Journal of Personality and Social Psychology, 3,* 445–450.

Martin, L. L. (1986). Set/reset: Use and disuse of concepts in impression formation. *Journal of Personality and Social Psychology, 51,* 493–504.

Martin, L. L., Harlow, T. F., & Strack, F. (1992). The role of bodily sensations in the evaluation of social events. *Personality & Social Psychology Bulletin, 18,* 412–419.

Meyer, D. E., & Schevaneveldt, R. W. (1971). Facilitation in recognizing pairs of words: Evidence of a dependence between retrieval operations. *Journal of Experimental Psychology, 90,* 227–234.

Mitchell, J., Nosek, B., & Banaji, M. R. (1998). A rose by any other name? Dissociated attitudes toward social group members. Paper presented at the American Psychological Society meeting, Washington, DC.

Moskowitz, G. B. (1993). Person organization with a memory set: Are spontaneous trait inferences personality characteristics or behaviour labels? *European Journal of Personality, 7,* 195–208.

Moskowitz, G. B., & Roman, R. J. (1992). Spontaneous trait inferences as self-generated primes: Implications for conscious social judgment. *Journal of Personality and Social Psychology, 62,* 728–738.

Murphy, S. T., & Zajonc, R. B. (1993). Affect, cognition, and awareness: Affective priming with suboptimal and optimal stimulus. *Journal of Personality and Social Psychology, 64,* 723–739.

Murphy, S. T., Monahan, J. L., & Zajonc, R. B. (1995). Additivity of nonconscious affect: Combined effects of priming and exposure. *Journal of Personality and Social Psychology, 69,* 589–602.

Neely, J. H. (1977). Semantic priming and retrieval from lexical memory: Roles of inhibitionless spreading activation and limited-capacity attention. *Journal of Experimental Social Psychology, 26,* 505–527.

Nelson, T. E., Acker, M., & Manis, M. (1996). Irrepressible stereotypes. *Journal of Experimental Social Psychology, 32,* 13–38.

Nelson, T. E., Biernat, M. B., & Manis, M. (1990). Everyday base rates (sex stereotypes): Potent and resilient. *Journal of Personality and Social Psychology, 59,* 664–675.

Newman, S. L., & Uleman, J. S. (1989). Spontaneous trait inference. In J. Uleman & J. A. Bargh (Eds.), Unintended thought (pp. 155–188). New York: Guilford Press.

Newman, L. S., & Uleman, J. S. (1990). Assimilation and contrast effects in spontaneous trait inference. *Personality and Social Psychology Bulletin, 16,* 224–240.

Niedenthal, P. M., Setterlund, M. B., & Jones, D. E. (1994). Emotional organization of perceptual memory. In P. M. Niedenthal & S. Kitayama (Eds.), *The heart's eye: Emotional influences in perception and attention* (pp. 87–113). San Diego: Academic Press.

Norris, A. E., & Devine, P. G. (1992). Linking pregnancy concerns to pregnancy risk avoidant action: The role of construct accessibility. *Personality and Social Psychology Bulletin, 18,* 118–127.

Nosek, B., Banaji, M. R., & Greenwald, A. G. (1998). Math = Bad + Male, Me = Good + Female, therefore Math π Me. Paper presented at the American Psychological Society meeting, Washington, DC.

Pendry, L. F., & Macrae, C. N. (1996). What the disinterested perceiver overlooks: Goal-directed social categorization. *Personality and Social Psychology Bulletin, 22,* 249–256.

Perdue, C. W., Dovidio, J. F., Gurtman, M. B., & Tyler, R. B. (1990). "Us" and "Them": Social categorization and the process of intergroup bias. *Journal of Personality and Social Psychology, 59,* 475–486.

Petty, R. E., & Cacioppo, J. T. (1983). The role of bodily responses in attitude measurement and change. In J. T. Cacioppo and R. E. Petty (Eds.), *Social psychophysiology: A sourcebook* (pp. 51–101). New York: Guilford Press.

Plant, E. A., & Devine, P. A. (1998). Internal and external motivation to respond without prejudice. *Journal of Personality and Social Psychology, 75,* 811–832.

Posner, M. I., & Snyder, C. R. R. (1975). Attention and cognitive control. In R. L. Solso (Ed.), *Information processing and cognition: The Loyola Symposium* (pp. 55–85). Hillsdale, NJ: Lawrence Erlbaum Associates.

Pratto, F. (1994). Consciousness and automatic evaluation. In P. M. Niedenthal and S. Kitayama (Eds.), *The heart's eye: Emotional influences in perception and attention* (pp. 115–143). San Diego: Academic Press.

Pratto, F., & Bargh, J. A. (1991). Stereotyping based on apparently individuating information: Trait and global components of sex stereotypes under attention overload. *Journal of Experimental Social Psychology, 27,* 26–47.

Pratto, F., & John, O. P. (1991). Automatic vigilance: The attention-grabbing power of negative social information. *Journal of Personality and Social Psychology, 61,* 380–391.

Rosier, M., Banaji, M. R., & Greenwald, A. G. (1998). Implicit and explicit self-esteem & group membership. Paper presented at the Midwestern Psychological Association meetings, Chicago.

Ross, L. (1977). The intuitive psychologist and his shortcomings. In L. Berkowitz (Ed.), *Advances in experimental social psychology* Vol. 10 (pp. 173–220). New York: Academic Press.

Ross, M., & Olson, J. M. (1981). An expectancy-attribution model of the effects of placebos. *Psychological Review, 88,* 408–437.

Rudman, L. A., & Borgida, E. (1995). The afterglow of construct accessibility: The behavioral consequences of priming men to view women as sexual objects. *Journal of Experimental Social Psychology, 31,* 493–517.

Rudman, L. A., & Glick, P. (1998). Implicit gender stereotypes and backlash toward agentic women: The hidden costs to women of a kinder, gentler image of managers. Unpublished manuscript, Rutgers University.

Rudman, L. A., & Kilianski, S. (1998). Implicit and explicit attitudes toward female authority. Unpublished manuscript, Rutgers University.

Rudman, L. A., Greenwald, A. G., & McGhee, D. E. (1998). Sex differences in gender stereotypes revealed by the Implicit Association Test. Unpublished manuscript, Rutgers University.

Rudman, L. A., Greenwald, A. G., Mellot, D. S., & Schwartz, J. L. K. (1998). Automatic prejudices: Flexibility and generality of the Implicit Association Test. Unpublished manuscript, Rutgers University.

Sedikides, C., & Skowronski, J. J. (1990). Towards reconciling personality and social psychology: A construct accessibility approach. *Journal of Social Behavior and Personality, 5,* 531–546.

Sedikides, C., & Skowronski, J. J. (1993). The self in impression formation: Trait centrality and social perception. *Journal of Experimental Social Psychology, 29,* 347–357.

Sherman, J. W., Stroessner, S. J., Loftus, S. T., & Deguzman, G. (1997). Stereotype suppression and recognition memory for stereotypical and nonstereotypical information. *Social Cognition, 15* (3), 205–215.

Shih, M., Pittinsky, T. L., & Ambady, N. (1999). Stereotype susceptibility: Identity salience and shifts in quantitative performance. *Psychological Science, 10,* 81–84.

Shrum, L. J., & O'Guinn, T. C. (1993). Processes and effects in the construction of social reality: Construct accessibility as an explanatory variable. *Communications Research, 20,* 436–471.

Skowronski, J. J., Carlston, D. E., Mae, L., & Crawford, M. T. (1998). Spontaneous trait transference: Communicators take on the qualities they describe in others. *Journal of Personality and Social Psychology, 74,* 837–848.

Southwick, L., Steele, C., Lindell, M. (1986). The roles of historical experience and construct accessibility in judgments about alcoholism. *Cognitive Therapy and Research, 10,* 167–186.

Spencer, S. J., Fein, S., Wolfe, C. T., Fong, C., & Dunn, M. A. (1998). Automatic activation of stereotypes: The role of self-image threat. *Personality and Social Psychology Bulletin, 24* (11), 1139–1152.

Stangor, C., & Lange, J. E. (1994). Mental representations of social groups: Advances in understanding stereotypes and stereotyping. *Advances in Experimental Social Psychology, 26,* 357–416.

Steele, C. M. (1997). A threat in the air: How stereotypes shape the intellectual identities and performance of women and African Americans. *American Psychologist, 52,* 613–629.

Steele, C. M., & Aronson, J. (1995). Stereotype threat and the intellectual test performance of African Americans. *Journal of Personality and Social Psychology, 69,* 797–811.

Stepper, S., & Strack, F. (1993). Proprioceptive determinants of emotional and nonemotional feelings. *Journal of Personality and Social Psychology, 64,* 211–220.

Strack, F., Martin, L. L., & Stepper, S. (1988). Inhibiting and facilitating conditions of the human smile: Unobtrusive test of the facial feedback hypothesis. *Journal of Personality and Social Psychology, 54,* 768–777.

Stroessner, S. J. (1996). Social categorization by race or sex: Effects of perceived non-normalcy on response times. *Social Cognition, 14* (3), 247–276.

Swann, W. B., Hixon, J. G., Stein-Seroussi, A., & Gilbert, D. T. (1990). The fleeting gleam of praise: Cognitive processes underlying behavioral reactions to self-relevant feedback. *Journal of Personality and Social Psychology, 59,* 17–26.

Trope, Y. (1986). Identification and inferential processes in dispositional attribution. *Psychological Review, 93,* 237–257.

Trope, Y., & Alfieri, T. (1997). Effortfulness and flexibility of dispositional judgment processes. *Journal of Personality and Social Psychology, 73,* 662–674.

Trope, Y., & Liberman, A. (1993). The use of trait conceptions to identify other people's behavior and draw inferences about their personalities. *Personality and Social Psychology Bulletin,* 553–562.

Trope, Y., & Thompson, E. P. (1997). Looking for truth in all the wrong places? Asymmetric search of individuating information about stereotyped group members. *Journal of Personality and Social Psychology, 73,* 229–241.

Uleman, J. S., & Bargh, J. A. (Eds.) (1989). *Unintended thought.* New York: Guilford Press.

Uleman, J. S., Newman, L., & Winter L. (1992). Can personality traits be inferred automatically? Spontaneous inferences require cognitive capacity at encoding. *Consciousness and Cognition, 1,* 77–90.

Uleman, J. S., Hon, A., Roman, R. J., & Moskowitz, G. B. (1996). On line evidence for spontaneous trait inferences at encoding. *Personality and Social Psychology Bulletin, 22,* 377–394.

Uleman, J. S., Moskowitz, G. B., Roman, R. J., & Rhee, E. (1993) Tacit, manifest, and intentional reference: How spontaneous trait inferences refer to persons. *Social Cognition, 11,* 321–351.

Van Knippenberg, A., & Dijksterhuis, A. (1996). A posteriori stereotype activation: The preservation of stereotypes through memory distortion. *Social Cognition, 14* (1), 21–53.

Vanman, E. J., Paul, B. Y., Ito, T. A., & Miller N. (1997). The modern face of prejudice and structural features that moderate the effect of cooperation on affect. *Journal of Personality and Social Psychology, 73,* 941–959.

Von Hippel, W., Sekaquaptewa, D., & Vargas, P. (1997). The linguistic intergroup bias as an implicit indicator of prejudice. *Journal of Experimental Social Psychology, 33,* 490–509.

Vrana, S. R., & Rollock, D. (1998). Physiological response to a minimal social encounter: Effects of gender, ethnicity, and social context. *Psychophysiology, 35,* 462–469.

Walsh, W. A., & Banaji, M. R. (1997). The collective self. In J. G. Snodgrass & R. L. Thompson (Eds.), *The self across psychology: Self-recognition, self-awareness, and the self concept. Annals of the New York Academy of Sciences* Vol. 818 (pp. 193–214). New York: New York Academy of Sciences.

Wann, D. L., & Branscombe, N. R. (1990). Person perception when aggressive or nonaggressive sports are primed. *Aggressive Behavior, 16,* 27–32.

Wegner, D. M., & Bargh, J. A. (1998) Control and automaticity in social life. In D. T. Gilbert, S. T. Fiske, & G. Lindzey (Eds.), *The handbook of social psychology* Vol. 2 (pp. 446–496). Boston: McGraw-Hill.

Wells, G. L., & Petty, R. E. (1980). The effects of overt head movement on persuasion: Compatibility and incompatibility responses. *Basic and Applied Social Psychology, 1,* 219–230.

Whitney, P., Davis, P. A., & Waring, D. A. (1994). Task effects on trait inference: Distinguishing categorization from characterization. *Social Cognition, 12,* 19–35.

Whitney, P., Waring, D. A., & Zingmark, B. (1992). Task effects on the spontaneous activation of trait concepts. *Social Cognition, 10,* 377–396.

Winter, L., & Uleman, J. S. (1984). When are social judgments made? Evidence for the spontaneousness of trait inferences. *Journal of Personality and Social Psychology, 47,* 237–252.

Wittenbrink, B., Judd, C. M., & Park, B. (1997). Evidence for racial prejudice at the implicit level and its relationship with questionnaire measures. *Journal of Personality and Social Psychology, 72,* 262–274.

Wyer, R. S., Jr., & Srull, T. K. (1980). The processing of social stimulus information: A conceptual integration. In R. Hastie, E. B. Ebbesen, T. M. Ostrom, R. S. Wyer, D. L. Hamilton, & D. E. Carlton (Eds.), *Person memory: The cognitive basis of social perception* (pp. 227–300). Hillsdale, NJ: Erlbaum.

Young, J., Thomsen, C. J., Borgida, E., Sullivan, J. L., & Aldrich, J. A. (1991). When self-interest makes a difference: The role of construct accessibility in political reasoning. *Journal of Experimental Social Psychology, 27,* 271–296.

Zajonc, R. B. (1968). The attitudinal effects of mere exposure. *Journal of Personality and Social Psychology,* Monograph Supplement, 9, (2, Pt. 2).

Zajonc, R. B. (1994). Evidence for nonconscious emotions. In P. Ekman and R. J. Davidson (Eds.), *The nature of emotion: Fundamental questions* (pp. 293–297). New York: Oxford University Press.

Zajonc, R. B. (1998). Emotions. In D. T. Gilbert and S. T. Fiske (Eds.), *The handbook of social psychology* Vol. 2, 4th. edn. (pp. 591–632). Boston: McGraw-Hill.

Zajonc, R. B., Murphy, S. T., & Inglehart, M. (1989). Feeling and facial efference: Implications of the vascular theory of emotions. *Psychological Review, 96,* 395–416.

Zanna, M. P., Detweiler, R. A., & Olson, J. M. (1984). Physiological mediation of attitude maintenance, formation, and change. In W. M. Waid (Ed.), *Sociophysiology* (pp. 163–196). New York: Springer-Verlag.

Zárate, M. A., Bonilla, S., & Luévano, M. (1995). Ethnic influences on exemplar retrieval and stereotyping. *Social Cognition, 13* (2), 145–162.

Chapter Eight

Language and Social Cognition

Gün R. Semin

Introduction

The mutual influence of language and social cognition is a classic problem not only in social psychology but also in human intellectual history. The theme is this: does language influence, shape, or perhaps even determine human cognitive activities, or alternatively, do cognitive processes affect language? A closer inspection of this research field suggests that some of the unspoken, meta-theoretical assumptions, by which our notions of language and cognition are shaped, constitute the key for a systematic understanding of the domain. Let us briefly review these assumptions that will be elaborated upon in the main body of this chapter.

The most commonly shared assumption by both scientists and lay persons alike is that cognition and language should be viewed from an *individual* perspective. In this approach, language is a tool for thinking, representation, and computation. Similarly, social cognition refers to individual processes: encoding, representing, thinking, retrieving, etc. For instance, if two cultures linguistically code the color spectrum differently, do they then perceive and represent colors incommensurably or not? Not surprisingly, thinking of language and cognition in this way leads to the fascinating and classic issues that have occupied many minds about the relationship between language and cognition and their mutual influence. Do linguistic tools influence cognitive processes, or vice versa?

However, language and cognition are not merely for representation, processing, and computation. Both are essential(ly) for action. Language is also a tool for doing. While it is true that language is a tool to construct and represent meaning, it is also true that language is a tool to transform reality by conveying meaning. All acts of communication entail a

The writing of this chapter was facilitated by the Netherlands Organization for Scientific Research, No. PGS56–381 Pionier Grant and Aandachstsgebied No. 575–12.020. I would like to express my thanks to Tony Manstead for his careful and constructive comments on an earlier version of this chapter.

transformation of some reality. To bring about transformation is an essential feature of language use, like being able to invite somebody for a first dinner, a first dance, to get somebody to agree with your view or opinion, to get a body to approve a grant, a piece of legislation, or a donation. Such transformation is only possible when language is used as a structuration device by which we strategically present aspects of reality or an idea in communication in order to *influence or shape the social cognitive processes of the recipient* to a message. The language–cognition relationship and their mutual influence acquire an entirely different complexion when considered in this way. In this view, assumptions about language and cognition originate within a transformational communicative context. Language refers to a tool that aids the strategic structuring of the representation of some reality or notion in communication. This strategic use is designed by the transmitter to effect a transformation in its recipient. In such a transformational context cognitive processes refer not only to the processes by which the transmitter gives strategic shape to the communicative act, but also to those processes that determine how the communicative act (the linguistic representation) is received by the recipient.

A third set of assumptions introduces an entirely different level of analysis. There are numerous cognitive tasks that exceed the capabilities of a single individual. These types of tasks, such as navigating a large ship (Hutchins, 1996), rely on knowledge that is distributed among members of the task group. This type of distributed knowledge and its communication is socially organized. In this particular instance, we have assumptions about both cognition and language that are defined in terms of task characteristics. Such tasks are often encountered in human society, and facilitate the coordination of socially distributed and socially constituted cognition. In other words, it is shared knowledge that is critical in terms of facilitating the achievement of the group's goal. An instance is successfully navigating a large vessel to its destination. Similarly, the transmission and reproduction of culture is an achievement that requires cooperative activities to facilitate the acquisition of capabilities that go beyond those of an individual. The developmental take on this is the Vygotskian notion of "zone of proximal development." This refers to the finely tuned interaction between caregivers and children where language is used as a tool for structuring and controlling action in order to produce interpsychological events critical for the child to succeed at a task beyond its capabilities.

Two distinctive features distinguish the three sets of assumptions about language and cognition. The first is the levels of analysis that are tacitly assumed, and which are respectively the *individual, inter-individual,* and *group* levels. Each level of analysis has a dramatic impact on the definition of the language–cognition interface. Equally, if not more importantly, the second distinctive feature of these three sets of assumptions is how action is conceptualized in relation to language and cognition. Whereas the first set of assumptions entails a disembodied individual, the second set involves a transformational context of influence and focuses upon language as a tool for action – namely a tool to effect transformation. The third set goes beyond individual actors and focuses upon communicative action as the primary objective to examine how socially distributed cognition is effectively maintained, as in the attainment of supra-individual goals or the transmission of task mastery and knowledge.

The main body of this chapter consists of an overview of the work on the relationship between language and social cognition from these three different types and levels of analysis. This is prefaced with a brief analysis of language and language use. This analysis furnishes an explanation of why each of the three levels of analysis has emerged and appears plausible, as well as how they relate to each other.

The Different Faces of the Language–Social Cognition Interface

Language and language use

The peculiar relationship between language and language use is best introduced by drawing upon the related metaphor of tool and tool-use. The use of this metaphor in the context of language is in itself not new (see, for example, Clark, 1997; Gauker, 1990; Semin, 1995, 1998; Vygotsky, 1981; Wertsch, 1991). My purpose in using this metaphor is to explicate the language–language use relationship, which I will then use to highlight how the different levels of analyses in investigations of the language–social cognition interface have arisen.

Tools have *structural properties* that have been engineered to optimize their use. For instance, hammers have a shaft and a peen, a hard solid head at a right angle to the handle, sometimes a claw, etc. Such structural properties are distinct from the variety of things that one can do with it, or its uses. Thus, while any tool has a finite set of structural properties that can in principle be identified, its uses are *indeterminate*. The same tools in the hand of one person may create a hut, in the hands of another a chalet, or a Chinese pagoda, etc. What is noteworthy is that the use of the very same tools can yield a great variety of unique outcomes. One can refer to the variety of uses that one can put tools to as their *affordances*, to use Gibsonian terminology (Gibson, 1979). Such affordances are possible only to the extent that human beings have the *capacity* to use them. Hence, "usability as a hammer" as an "affordance" is relational and manifested pragmatically only in the interface between tool and tool-user.

Where the tool and tool-use analogy falls short is in the following. While literal tools have a real existence independent of their use, linguistic tools do not have an existence independent of communication. Linguistic tools are *reproduced in communication*. In terms of social behavior, the fact that I utter a sentence in English contributes to the reproduction of English as a language. This is an unintended consequence (Giddens, 1979) of uttering that sentence. Let me elaborate. The use of language has two fundamental aspects (Bakthin, 1979; Giddens, 1976; Ricoeur, 1955). One is the communication of meaning and the other is a structure that carries this meaning. What is being proposed is that human verbal communication has two interrelated fundamental features, namely (a) the reproduction of a structure, without which (b) meaning, could not be conveyed.

Any speech act presupposes a structured system of signs that is understood by everybody. Language use displays traceable consistencies that are repeated and reproduced in every speech act. These reiterative and reproducible properties of language constitute the *structural properties of language* (syntactical and semantic) that simultaneously carry unique and situated meanings. Whereas "meaning" is subjective, the structural properties of language are intersubjective. For example, word meanings, syntactic rules, and the like must be shared in order to be able to convey meaning that is initially unshared or subjective. Language use then amounts to drawing on shared structure in order to convey a potentially novel and unique meaning. The same structure can convey a wide range of meanings to a great variety of actors. While structure is determinate in terms of its properties (specified by semantic and syntactic rules), its affordances and potential uses are indeterminate (Semin, 1998). Language use not only transmits meaning, but also reproduces and reinforces the structure (syntax and semantics).

Implications of the language and language use distinction

We can now take a new look at the three different levels of analysis adopted in examinations of the language–cognition interface in the light of the distinction between the structural properties of language and language use. This distinction is instrumental in understanding how these different and practically independent levels of analyses have emerged, namely the individual centered, transformational, and socially distributed approaches to language and social cognition.

   The first level of analysis – the individualistic – relies on the treatment of language in terms of a structure that is disembodied, by attending to only those aspects of language that are repeated, reiterative, and reproducible, and not its non-reiterative, unique, and individual aspects. Language is regarded as an abstract set of "rules" that are "virtual and outside of time" (Ricoeur, 1955). This is treating language "without a subject," namely not as the property or production of any one particular speaker. The focus is upon language as an extra-individual and systematic set of abstract properties. Regarding language in this way makes it "subjectless" and "timeless" and presents the ideal assumption for examining the relationship between specific linguistic properties (e.g. lexical semantics, grammatical categories) and cognitive processes that are also conceptualized in a disembodied, timeless, and subjectless manner. The classic discussion of the mutual influence between language and thought (Whorf, 1957) and related work in the social cognition–language tradition is cast at this level (see section 1 below). The distinctive feature of all these "modern" versions of the language–social cognition relationship is their focus upon the individual as a unit of analysis for both language and cognition. This is a version that is also characteristic of more recent analyses (e.g. Hardin & Banaji, 1993; Hoffman, Lau, & Johnson, 1986; Hunt & Agnoli, 1991). In a sense, this has been the mainstream approach not only to understanding social cognition but also language: what are the human capacities that are responsible for the production and interpretation of language and what are the properties of language that can influence cognitive processes. This is the first part of the research reviewed here.

   The second level of analysis relies on the assumption that language is a "medium for practical activity" (Ricoeur, 1955). The focus now is upon language use in terms of the situated doings of subjects in terms of the types of transformations that they intend in communicative contexts. This level of analysis requires both an understanding of the structural properties of language and the situated purposes that they serve. Language use presupposes a subject, acknowledges the presence of the "other," and is dialogical. Cognition in this context becomes intended activity and language the tool for the implementation of such action. Additionally at this level, extralinguistic factors such as conversational rules (Grice, 1975) become significant to understand transmission of meaning. This research is reviewed in section 2 below.

The third level of analysis has a similar focus upon language, namely as practical activity, except that it is not concerned with the production of language at any level. Rather, the focus is upon how language as practical activity is deployed in contexts that require the reproduction of new structures (navigation) as well as their situated realization (navigating a large vessel into the harbor). At this level, the focus is the role played by language as a medium by which cultural artifacts are reproduced and transmitted. Verbal communication is seen as a means by which joint solutions are achieved. Thought in this context refers to socially distributed cognition that is embodied – as is the coordination of social action through communication. This constitutes the third part of the overview.

1   Language and Social Cognition: Individual Centered Approaches

Linguistic relativity

An obligatory reference in any discussion of the language–social cognition relationship is to the influential but problematic issue of linguistic relativity and determinism. The most influential formulation of the relationship between language, thought, and culture is the one advanced by Benjamin Lee Whorf (1957), whose contribution derives from a long intellectual heritage. Whorf argued for a correspondence between the structural properties of language to represent aspects of the world and the implications of such structural properties upon thinking about the world. His classic observation was that "the world is presented in a kaleidoscopic flux of impressions which has to be organized by our minds – and this means largely by the linguistic systems of our minds" (ibid., p. 213). This argument is based on the following reasoning. If one notes differences in the formal meaning structure of two languages then this is also likely to be manifested in the "habitual thought" of the speakers of these languages. The observation at the heart of Whorf's "linguistic relativity hypothesis" is the following: "Users of markedly different grammars are pointed by their grammars toward different types of observations and different evaluations of external similar acts of observation, and hence are not equivalent as observers, but must arrive at somewhat different views of the world" (ibid., p. 221). The classic example is the often-cited difference in the encoding of time in the Hopi and English languages. In English, time is encoded in nouns (years, days, and hours), a *grammatical form* that is used for objects. Putting what is essentially cyclical and continuous into a discrete grammatical form means that we can do things with time, like measure it or count it. For the Hopi, time is represented as a recurrent event. Although they have words that we can recognize as years, days, etc., their grammar does not have a tense system like English and does not permit the emergence of an abstract notion of time as is the case in English. Whorf concluded that the experience of time is very different for Hopi and English-speakers.

The general linguistic relativism argument is that differences in linguistic categories (grammatical and lexical) across languages influence individuals' "habitual thought" patterns. Thus, *linguistic determinism* refers to the argument derived from linguistic relativity that there is a causal influence of semantic patterns on cognition. Language determines the very way we think about the social and physical world. There is a strong and a weak version of this hypothesis. The argument of the strong version, which is mostly regarded as a "straw man" (e.g. Gumpertz & Levinson, 1996, p. 24; Lucy, 1992, p. 3) suggests that concepts that are not coded linguistically are unattainable. The more widely accepted weaker version suggests that linguistically coded concepts are facilitated, thus more accessible, easier to remember, etc.

Hoffman, Lau, & Johnson (1986) illustrate how the presence or absence of a *lexical category* facilitates the activation of knowledge or information structures. These authors selected a number of personality descriptions in Chinese and English which were presented to Chinese and English native speakers. For some of these descriptions (e.g. attributes such as progressive, left-wing, tolerance, open-mindedness, Bohemian) English has an economic lexical category (i.e. liberal), but Chinese does not. For others (e.g. strong family orientation, socially skilled, experienced), Chinese has an economic lexical category (i.e. *shi-gu*), but English does not. A recognition memory test showed that accuracy of recognition was influenced by the availability of lexical category. Both Chinese and English subjects showed less recognition accuracy for items that were consistent with "their" economic category. When subjects were given previously presented items that were congruent with the category of their language, they were less confident in recognizing these. Moreover, they had greater difficulty in rejecting category-congruent new items. Recognition memory was superior overall in the case of items for which the language did not have a category.

The above two examples are instances of how grammatical and lexical categories are related to thought. Whorf's position on this relation was primarily in terms of language influencing "unconscious habitual thought" rather than the potential to think. The precise nature of this relationship was however not further specified. There exists a variety of attempts to paint a clearer picture of this relation. It is to the credit of Lenneberg and his colleagues (e.g. Brown & Lenneberg, 1954) that the research agenda of how color lexically is coded and how it influences cognitive processes was set. This is a domain that has occupied center stage in the discussion of linguistic relativity and determinism in psychology. Also, the agenda defined more clearly what was to be understood by the term "cognitive processes." "Does the structure of a given language affect the thoughts (or thought potential), the memory, the perception, the learning ability of those who speak that language?" (Lenneberg, 1953, p. 463). Do linguistic structures influence non-linguistic categorization, memory, perception, thinking, etc.?

The lexical domain of color became a major one in debating whether or not the Whorfian hypothesis had any merit. Color was interesting because it constituted a domain for which there were objectifiable external referents. Earlier research suggested that if color is distinctively differentiated in the lexicon then it is more likely to be memorable. For instance, Brown and Lenneberg's (1954) classic study showed that colors that were more codable in English (had shorter names, and elicited more agreement in naming) tended to be the ones that were recognized and remembered more readily.

The early support for linguistic relativity came to an end with Berlin and Kay's (1969) seminal work. They showed that basic colors had a salience that was independent of language. This work provided the stepping-stone for E. Rosch's well-known studies that set a new landmark in color perception and memory. She showed that when the Dani (who only had two basic color terms) were asked to learn eight arbitrary names for eight focal color terms and a different eight arbitrary names for non-focal color terms, they learned the names for the focal colors better (Rosch, 1973). This and other research by Rosch was regarded as the critical turning-point for the linguistic relativity argument because it suggested that primary color categories had real psychological significance for the Dani, although they did not have any linguistic categories for them.

Currently, different views prevail about how to interpret the overall evidence. The weight of the recent work (e.g. Kay & Kempton, 1984; Lucy, 1992) suggests that under specific task conditions the availability of lexical categories leads to non-linguistic cognitive effects in classification and categorization tasks. This overview of the color domain is brief in view of the fact that there exist extensive reviews of the field (e.g. Brown, 1976; Lucy, 1992; Hardin & Maffi, 1997).

Language, memory, cognitive processes, and behavior

It is possible to conceptualize and examine linguistic relativity (with more experimental control) in terms of a single language that provides its speakers with different ways of talking and/or representing the same thing. This perspective opens the door to a very broad range of relevant research in social psychology. Below, indications are given of relevant literature in social cognition that has implications for how linguistic cues influence cognitive processes.

Probably the best-known studies on the effects of language upon memory come from eyewitness testimony research (Loftus, 1979). For instance, having been misleadingly asked about a blue car that was green in the video that they had seen, participants were more likely to remember it as blue than a control group that was given no color. Modifying verbal references to a car-collision implying differences in velocity (e.g. "smash" vs. "hit") has been shown to lead participants to remember that the cars were traveling at a higher speed in the "smash" condition than the "hit" condition. These participants were also more likely to erroneously report broken glass at the incident.

Another body of research addresses the influence of verbalization on visual memory. For instance, it has been shown that describing a previously seen face impairs recognition of this face, a phenomenon termed "the verbal shadowing effect" (e.g. Dodson, Johnson, & Schooler, 1997; Schooler & Engsler-Schooler, 1990). The explanation is based on a confusion between previously encoded visual and verbal encoding, because verbalization creates or activates a corresponding verbal representation that is in conflict with other representations in memory (Chiu, Krauss, & Lau, 1998). Earlier studies with visual forms have shown that verbalization interferes with visual recognition (e.g. Bahrick & Boucher, 1968; Ranken, 1963; Santa & Ranken, 1968).

A substantial body of research shows that verbal-framing influences problem representation and judgments (e.g. Kahnemann & Tversky, 1984; Levin, Schnijttjer, & Thee, 1988). The effects of verbalization on memory and judgment are also underlined in studies by Higgins and his colleagues (e.g. Higgins & Rholes, 1977). They found that when participants read an ambiguous narrative about a person containing positive, negative, and neu-

tral information and were asked to summarize this ambiguous information, having a negative attitude (like vs. dislike) influenced not only what participants wrote, but also their
subsequent memory and judgments. The written summaries were congruent with recipients' attitudes as were participants' subsequent memory and judgments of the target person, which became more exaggerated over time. These effects were not found for a control
group who did not write down a summary of the target (see also Higgins & McCann,
1984; Higgins, McCann, & Fondacaro, 1982).

Further, research on semantic priming (Neely, 1977; Meyer & Schvanefeldt, 1971)
suggests that priming with lexical categories has cognitive and behavioral consequences. A
typical example is the research by Dovidio, Evans, & Tyler (1986), who showed that priming with the label of a group activates group-related trait terms. The use of subliminal
primes (us, we vs. they, them) has been shown to influence reaction times to traits in
ingroup and outgroup related valence classification tasks (Perdue, Dovidio, Gurtman, &
Tyler, 1990). In a related context, Devine (1989) showed that stereotypes of African Americans become activated even when verbal stimuli (related to African Americans) were presented subliminally. This suggests that verbal stimuli can have an effect upon the activation
of knowledge structures in the absence of a participant's awareness along with some individual differences in the strength of the activated knowledge . The subliminal presentation
of trait terms has been shown to influence recognition and judgment processes (e.g. Bargh
& Pietromonaco, 1982). Indeed, it has also been found that verbal priming can influence
behavioral responses, as in the case of performance on "Trivial Pursuit." Participants score
higher when primed with the word "professor" than with the word "hooligan" (Dijksterhuis
& Van Knippenberg, 1998). More recently, Dijksterhuis, Aarts, Bargh, & Van Knippenberg
(in press) have shown that priming participants subliminally with words associated with
"the elderly" (old, walking stick, bingo) can influence their memory performance (forget-
fulness) as a function of their experience with the elderly. Even the subliminal priming of
letters appears to have an effect on estimates of the number of words beginning with that
letter (Gabrielcik & Fazio, 1984), which would suggest that the activation of knowledge
structures in the most minimal sense can have judgmental consequences.

The more recent work sketched in this section has to do with the activation of knowledge by supraliminal or subliminal stimuli. One of the significant advances of this type of
work – which was not directly conducted to examine the linguistic relativity hypothesis –
is that it is concerned with the detailed examination of the processes that lead to the cognitive consequences of using, for instance, a prime to activate a stereotype. In that sense,
despite the fact that this research is not conducted across different linguistic communities,
it is more sophisticated in terms of uncovering process aspects of the cognitive and behavioral
consequences of language.

Cognitive inferences mediated by interpersonal verbs

There is one domain in social psychology where the language–social cognition interface
has been explicitly researched. This has been on the types of inferences that are mediated
by interpersonal verbs. Interpersonal verbs (to help, to dislike, to cheat, to amaze, etc.) are
the linguistic tools that do the hardcore work when it comes to describing interpersonal

events and relationships. Broadly speaking, there are two general classes of interpersonal verbs, namely verbs of action (e.g. help, kick, and talk) and verbs of state (e.g. like, hate, and respect). Whereas the former refers to *observable* acts, the latter refers to *unobservable psychological* states.

Interpersonal verbs as implicit qualifiers: the logic of generalization   The very first systematic treatment of interpersonal verbs is to be found in a series of studies by Abelson (e.g. Abelson & Kanouse, 1966; Kanouse, 1971). This research examined the contribution of linguistic factors to how individuals form inductive and deductive generalizations from a given event or relation.

The conclusion across these diverse studies is that interpersonal verbs influence generalizations systematically. Action verbs are found to lead to stronger inductive generalizations than do state verbs (action verb example: Jack buys *Newsweek*. Does Jack buy magazines? vs. state verb example: Jack likes *Newsweek*. Does Jack like magazines?). For deductive generalizations (e.g. Jack reads magazines. Does Jack like *Newsweek*? vs. Jack likes magazines. Does Jack like *Newsweek*?) the pattern they uncover is the reverse. Sentences with action verbs are found to give rise to much weaker deductive generalizations when compared to their role in contributing to inductive generalizations. Sentences with verbs of state produce a somewhat ambiguous pattern, although the overall pattern suggests that they produce a tendency to yield stronger deductive generalizations than inductive ones. An explanation advanced by Abelson and Kanouse is whether action and state verbs imply different types of quantifiers for sentence subject and object. For instance, does the sentence "Jack likes (buys) magazines" imply "all," "most," "many," "some," or just "a few" magazines? For this type example, Kanouse (1972) has shown that state verbs such as "like" imply a higher quantity than action verbs such as "read."

Interpersonal verbs as mediators of person attributions: the causal schema hypothesis   This research by the Yale group anticipated and foreshadowed what was to be termed "the causality implicit in interpersonal verbs" by Brown and Fish (1983). Brown and Fish's contribution had a major influence on further research development in this field. This was in part due to the fact that they introduced a way in which it was possible to systematically differentiate between different verb classes by examining the semantic roles that are associated with the sentence subject and object (noun predicates). For a group of verbs that have to do with overt and observable *actions* such as help, disagree, cheat, the relevant semantic roles are that of *agent* and *patient*. The agent role refers to somebody who causes or instigates an action. The patient role refers to somebody who is undergoing change. In the case of verbs of *state* (like, hate, trust) the relevant roles are those of *stimulus* and *experiencer*. The stimulus role refers to the originator of the experience and the latter role to the person who has a specific experience. Furthermore, Brown and Fish showed that sentences with action verbs lead to stronger causal attributions to the sentence subject, and sentences with state verbs lead to stronger causal attributions to the sentence object. For instance, when participants are given the sentence "John helped David, because *he* is a kind person" and asked to disambiguate the "he," then the predominant response is "John." Replacing the action verb "helped" in the example with the state verb "likes" leads to the reverse. Now the predominant disambiguation is to David.

According to Brown's (e.g. Brown & Fish, 1983) "causal schema" hypothesis a sentence with an action verb (e.g. "John helps David") activates an agent–patient schema, whereas a state verb sentence (e.g. "John likes David") elicits an experiencer–stimulus schema. These schemata are further coupled to the attribution theoretical principles of consensus and distinctiveness, whereby the agent-patient schema is associated with a low consensus–low distinctiveness schema and the experiencer–stimulus schema is associated with a high consensus–high distinctiveness schema (Rudolph & Försterling, 1997). Therefore, sentences with action verbs are easily generalized to other objects or patients, whereas sentences with state verbs are more easily generalized across subjects or experiencers.

Alternative explanations   Brown and Fish advanced and rejected the possibility of a morphological explanation. According to this hypothesis adjectives derived from interpersonal verbs mediate the causal choices people make. In a stimulus sentence such as "John likes David" the morphologically related adjective is "likable" and refers to David, the sentence object to whom the causal attribution is made. Similarly, "helpful" refers to John in a sentence such as "John helps David," again the source to whom causality is attributed in the depicted event. An examination of the lexicon reveals that most adjectives derived from action verbs are subject referent and those derived from state verbs are mostly object referent. Brown and Fish reject this morphological hypothesis.

Hoffman and Tchir (1990) have pointed out that this hypothesis has not been directly tested and that the verb selection in Brown and Fish has methodological problems. They attempted to rectify this by a careful selection of action and state verbs that have only subject referent (action: help–helpful; state: resent–resentful) and object referent adjectives (action: tickle–ticklish; state: like–likable). Their first experiment provided ambiguous evidence for the morphological hypothesis. Ascription of causality does not seem to be clearly predictable from the attributive reference of the derived adjectives. In fact, only in the case of action verbs did they get a verb-type based causal inference pattern. Their second experiment indicated that "the relation between causal asymmetry embodied in interactive verbs and the attributive reference derived from those verbs was not fully explained by the third variable of role generality (i.e. distinctiveness and consensus)" (ibid., p. 772). In a later study, Semin and Marsman (1994), controlling in a completely balanced design for verb-derived adjectives, showed that the availability of derived adjectives does not influence the causal inferences that subjects make.

One of the alternative explanations is Fiedler and Semin's (1988) "antecedent-consequent event structure" account of implicit causality. When participants are given a stimulus sentence (John helped David) and asked "why," then they imagine the stimulus sentence context which consists of what happened before and after the stimulus sentence. The argument is that for action verbs the event preceding the stimulus sentence (antecedent) shows more frequent references to the stimulus sentence subject (John). In the case of state verbs the antecedent sentence has stronger references to the stimulus sentence object (David). The sentences that subjects generate about what happened after the event in the stimulus sentence had occurred (consequent) reverses this pattern. In this case, sentences with action verbs elicit more frequent references to the stimulus object (David). In the case of sentences with state verbs, the more frequent consequent response is to the sentence subject (John). The correlational data provide reasonable but not entirely convincing evidence, particularly for the consequences of action verbs and for the antecedents of state verbs.

Gilovitch and Regan (1986) propose a "volitional model" to explain implicit causality. They draw attention to the asymmetries in volition inherent in the semantic roles of agent-patient versus stimulus-experiencer. Whereas actions are under the volitional control of agents, experiences are under the control of stimuli. According to them this volitional asymmetry contributes to the differential elicitation of the semantic role schemata proposed by Brown and Fish (1983).

Kasoff and Lee (1993) advance an "implicit salience" argument to explain how causal inferences are mediated by interpersonal verbs. According to this view, "sentences that describe interpersonal events evoke mental representations in which subjects and objects differ in salience" (ibid., p. 878). The idea is then that people are more likely to attribute causality to the more salient object rather than the less salient one. In two studies they find evidence for this. In a secondary analysis of data from a variety of sources, they show that the correlations between salience and causality ratings vary between .26 and .94 for action verbs and $-.04$ and .61 for state verbs.

Conclusions   There is a remarkable paradox when one views this research in its entirety. All the studies that have been conducted with interpersonal verbs rely on correlational evidence. Mostly, they rely on the simultaneous measurement of implicit causality and some other dependent variable (DV). Such DVs include the dispositionality of the agent, the temporal duration of an event, the salience of an agent. Despite the fact that a variety of different inferences are made apart from event agency inferences, implicit causality is taken as the epistemically privileged anchor for explanations. However, there is no particular *a priori* theoretical or empirical reason to privilege implicit causality over any of the other properties of interpersonal verbs (e.g. sentence context, salience, event recurrence, etc.). It is also logically incoherent to suggest that *all* of these inferences be made at once when a participant is given a simple subject–verb–object sentence. The paradox is largely due to the fact that the diverse inferences are interpreted from an individual centered point of view and not considered in terms of what the main function of language is: it is not merely a tool for representational purposes but a device for communication purposes.

2   Language and Social Cognition: Language as a Transformational Device

The emphasis in this section is upon language as a medium for practical activity, or a medium to achieve particular ends (Chiu, Krauss, & Lau, 1998; Krauss & Fussell, 1996; Higgins, 1981). Language is not merely a tool for representing the world but a device by which changes in one's social world can be implemented. This is a conception of language in terms of a tool by which we can affect each other's behavior (Clark, 1997; Gauker, 1990). Such activity consists of the situated doings of subjects in order to achieve some transformation of social reality in communicative contexts. Cognition in this perspective becomes intended action with language as the tool to implement such action. A speaker, in trying to give public shape to a subjective goal, has to construct a linguistic representation. To this end, different linguistic tools have to be accessed to shape the desired or optimal representation of some aspect of reality. This way of looking at language means that we now have to consider how different lexical and grammatical categories are used as structuring resources that give shape to the representational space between a speaker and a listener. This contrasts strongly with the individual centered view of language, above. While linguistic relativity addresses lexical and grammatical categories as constraints on variation, the language use framework treats them as resources that facilitate variations in linguistic representations of the same event. Language is treated in this framework as a structuring resource for communication purposes. There are different ways in which a speaker can structure the public shape of a query in order to form a representation that will influence a listener's response.

The twin objectives are (1) to describe a model analyzing dimensions or properties of interpersonal language, and (2) to review two research domains showing how properties can be used as a structuring resource in formulating messages. The domain of language that is of particular relevance as structuring resources are interpersonal predicates, namely transitive verbs that refer to actions (to confide, to help, to cheat), to states (to like, to abhor, to respect) or feelings, and adjectives (friendly, trustworthy, unreliable) (Semin, 1998).

The linguistic category model (LCM)

The linguistic category model (Semin & Fiedler, 1988, 1991) was developed to identify properties or dimensions of interpersonal language that transcend specific semantic fields or word meanings. The model is based on a distinction between (a) systematic properties of language as a tool, and (b) psychological processes that entail using specific tools with differing properties to maximize some goal. The LCM is *not* a model of psychological processes. It therefore also involved a shift in methodological commitment, namely from one that privileges individual processes and properties to one that emphasizes the properties of "tools" by which communication is enabled (see Semin, 1998, p. 250ff.).

The LCM is a taxonomy of interpersonal predicates developed on the basis of a number of independent but converging linguistic criteria (see Semin & Fiedler, 1991) to differentiate between different verb categories and adjectives. A distinction is made between the following five categories. *Descriptive action verbs* refer to an invariant feature of the action (kick, push, talk). *Interpretative action verbs* provide a frame for a variety of actions (to help – an old lady cross a street, a friend in financial difficulty, etc.). *State action verbs* refer to the psychological consequences of an action (to bore, to thrill, to disgust). *State verbs* (to love, to abhor, to respect) refer to invisible psychological conditions. As a final category, *adjectives* (friendly, aggressive) refer to properties of individuals. Importantly, it has been shown that these categories have a number of inferential properties that vary systematically. Chief among these are (1) the degree to which a dispositional inference can be made; (2) the ease and difficulty of confirming and disconfirming statements constructed with these predicates; (3) the temporal duration of an interpersonal event depicted by these terms; (4) the likelihood of an event recurring at a future point in time (see Semin &

Fiedler, 1991, 1992). These variables have been shown to form a concrete–abstract dimension in which the five categories are ordered systematically. That is, the first category mentioned above (descriptive action verbs) constitutes the most concrete one and adjectives the most abstract one, with categories two to four occupying – in that same sequence – intermediate positions in this dimension. Additionally, a second dimension is constituted by event agency, salience, and induced emotionality implied by interpersonal verbs (Semin & Fiedler, 1991).

What is central to understanding this model and its use is the distinction between semantic or meaning fields (e.g. the domain of economic transactions) and general properties such as event agency or the specific properties that are bundled in the abstraction–concreteness dimension. These constitute grammatically coded properties of the predicates represented by the LCM. It is by means of these dimensions that a number of different social phenomena have been analyzed by systematically examining situated messages that people generated in experimentally controlled or natural settings with regard to the types of predicates used. Instead of giving a comprehensive overview of all the diverse studies conducted with this model, I shall review just two domains that have attracted substantial research interest. The first is the so-called linguistic intergroup bias introduced by Maass and her colleagues (Maass, Salvi, Arcuri, & Semin, 1989) and the other is the question–answer paradigm (Semin, Rubini, & Fiedler, 1995).

The linguistic transmission of stereotypes GRS

The linguistic intergroup bias (LIB) refers to a differentiated use of predicates in descriptions of ingroup and outgroup behaviors that contribute to the transmission and maintenance of stereotypes (e.g. Maass, Salvi, Arcuri, & Semin, 1989). Typically, this means that behaviors or events showing the ingroup in a favorable way and outgroups in an unfavorable way are represented with abstract language. In contrast, behaviors that depict the ingroup in undesirable ways and outgroup in desirable ways are communicated with concrete language. The use of abstract language conveys the suggestion that the properties in question are enduring, and likely to recur in the future. In contrast, concrete language suggests that the behavior in question is contextually determined and therefore transitory, and of no enduring significance. This is precisely what Maass, et al. (1989) found. The phenomenon is a stable one. It has been repeatedly demonstrated using different dependent variables (i.e. forced choice response formats for predicate choice and open-ended narratives). It has also been demonstrated in analyses of newspapers and television (Maass, Corvino, & Arcuri, 1994).

Systematic variations in predicate use in messages can serve a two-fold diagnostic function. On the one hand, the message structure can be an indicator of the psychological processes (motivational or cognitive) that have led to particular message structure. On the other hand, the message structure is important in order to examine its impact on recipients' inferences. Thus, message structure can be seen as both a dependent and an independent variable. If the aim is to investigate the psychological processes that lead to a particular message composition then message structure is a dependent variable. Message structure can also be an independent variable when the aim is to assess its impact upon recipients' inferences, judgments, and actions.

The work on the psychological processes responsible for linguistic intergroup bias is an instance for the dependent variable case. Two distinctive processes have been held responsible for the LIB. One is based on ingroup protective motives and social identity (Tajfel & Turner, 1979). In this analysis, the LIB serves to maintain a positive ingroup image (Maass, Ceccarelli, & Rudin, 1996). The other process is assumed to be a cognitive one based on expectations (Maass, Milesi, Zabbini, & Stahlberg, 1995). The argument is that positive outgroup and negative ingroup behaviors are unexpected and behavior that is inconsistent with expectancies is described more concretely. In contrast, expectancy-consistent behavior is described more abstractly. The evidence is equivocal (Maass, et al., 1995, 1996) and suggests that the motivational and cognitive processes may be complementary.

When these types of messages become independent variables in a design that examines the impact of their structure upon recipient inferences, then we have the more typical question "How does language influence thought?" (Semin & De Poot, 1997a). Wigboldus, Semin, & Spears (in press) showed that when recipients were presented with messages produced by transmitters, messages that were expectancy-consistent were attributed more strongly to dispositional factors. In contrast, recipients found that events described in expectancy-inconsistent stories were due to situational factors. These effects were shown to be mediated by the level of abstraction in the stories.

The question–answer paradigm

The research done within the question–answer paradigm (Semin, Rubini, & Fiedler, 1995) is an instance of how strategic language use can contribute to the shaping of targets' answers and third parties' perceptions. This research dissects the continuous feedback loop in an interview exchange into separate stages in order to examine the distinct features of each step in the sequence. This gives rise to three interdependent questions. The first is whether specific expectations shape preferences regarding how a question is structured. Second, do particular question structures contribute to the shape of a target's answer? Third, how does a target's answer influence the perception and expectations of the respondent or a third party?

The first part of this research is based on how one can vary event agency in question formulation. The following four questions give a flavor of the possibilities:

1   "Did you dance with Stephen?"
2   "Did Stephen dance with you?"
3   "Why did Ed confide in Jeremy?"
4   "Why does Ed trust Jeremy?"

Changing the sentence subject or object positions in the question modifies implied event agency (in sentence 1 *you* and in sentence 2 *Stephen*). Implied agency is modified in sentences 3 (*Ed*) and 4 (*Jeremy*) by verb choice (action verb vs. state verb). Semin & De Poot (1997b) used a simulated rape victim interview scenario in which participants were given no expectation (control) or were led to expect that the victim was either trustworthy or untrustworthy. Participants selected questions that implied the agency of the perpetrator for the event if they expected the victim to be trustworthy. Participants who expected the victim to be untrustworthy chose predominantly questions implying victim agency. The control group was in between. The issue of how question formulation influences the message structure of answers was addressed by Semin & De Poot (1997a). When they analyzed the message structure in terms of abstraction–concreteness and implied agency, they found, as predicted, that questions formulated with action verbs gave rise to message structures that implied the agency of the respondent to the recalled autobiographical event. Furthermore, these narratives had a relatively concrete message structure. In contrast, autobiographical events prompted with state verbs were found to have a more abstract message structure and to imply the agency of "others" in the event (see also, De Poot & Semin, 1995; Semin, Rubini, & Fiedler, 1995; Rubini & Kruglanski, 1997). In a second step, Semin & De Poot (1997a) asked the respondents who generated these messages to judge implied agency, the likelihood of the event recurring at a future date, implied dispositionality, and perceived stability of the relationship between the persons described in the event. All these variables were known to measure inferences that are systematically mediated by the abstractness–concreteness of a message. There were no systematic effects on respondents' judgments with respect to these variables. These results suggest that respondents are not aware that the question structure influences the structure of the answers they give. However, when third parties were given the same task with the same narratives, by assigning a third party participant to each respondent–narrative, all the expected differences were shown to obtain. Events generated by state verb questions and which had an abstract message structure were perceived to be caused by others, more likely to recur at a future date, be less situationally determined, and to be indicative of a stable relationship, compared to the more concrete action verb generated narratives. Furthermore, it was shown that these inferences were directly mediated by the linguistic abstraction of the narratives. More significantly, these results suggest that the underlying properties tapped by the abstractness–concreteness dimension are insensitive to the specific narrative content or semantics, since each narrative was unique. More recent research in another domain confirms this general conclusion (Wigboldus, Semin, & Spears, in press).

Conclusions

An approach that regards language as a transformational device and investigates the tacit dimensions of language is in this sense a very significant development, in that it highlights not only message properties, but also message comprehension. The grammatical relationships induced by interpersonal verbs convey systematic information about dimensions such as time, causation, dispositionality, and distance of interpersonal relationship. These are significant in communicating and interpreting events, as we have seen. Dimensions that are coded in language and cut across lexical fields are critical in text construction and comprehension and are valuable features in how language shapes comprehension.

Furthermore, by focusing upon properties of language as properties of a tool, the transformational approach also introduces a perspective on how specific ways of structuring a "conversational opening" are likely to influence a response to such an opening. Thus, if you say "Thank you" after an event, then the most likely response is "You're welcome," although the recipient to the "Thank you" may not feel like making you welcome at all. What's more, an uninvolved outsider listening to this conversation may think that you *are* actually welcome. The difference between this example and the research on inferences mediated by interpersonal predicates is that the person saying "welcome" is well aware that she does not mean what she says. The predicate mediated research suggests that the person answering questions is neither aware that their response is being structured by the question and nor are they aware of its impact on listeners. One of the implications of viewing language as a structuring device is that it can be seen as a device that induces a powerful and tacit mindlessness (cf. Langer, 1989) into conversations, a mindlessness that we do not at all register as performers, but which is certainly recorded by an audience that judges us (Semin & De Poot, 1997a, 1997b).

3   Language and Social Cognition: Socially Distributed Knowledge

The focus here is on language and social cognition at the group level. Cognition in this context refers to knowledge that is socially shared and language use as communication plays a central role in achieving goals that exceed the capabilities of any single individual. As Hutchins (1996) notes, "Shifting attention from the cognitive properties of an individual to those of a system of socially distributed cognition casts language in a new light. The properties of language itself interact with the properties of the communications technology in ways that affect the computational properties of the larger cognitive system" (ibid., pp. 231–232). The type of cognitive activities that Hutchins is referring to is distributed across social space. In such situations, the kind of language that is used is critical in affecting the cognitive properties of the group. Thus, language or language use is a structuring device that will influence the group even if it does not affect the cognitive properties of the individuals. The general point raised by such a perspective is that there is a multitude of tasks in all human societies that cannot be achieved by individuals on their own. These kinds of tasks necessitate a social organization of distributed cognition. Such organization may or may not be appropriate to the task. Language becomes a very important factor as a tool for structuring and controlling action. Hutchin's empirical research focuses upon navigation, a group-task situation in which all members share a joint superordinate goal. He provides a great number of ethnographic instances of how language influences the cognitive properties of the group. For instance, in one illustration he shows how the structure of the lexicon constrains the cognitive process of the group, when the Marine commander phones the charthouse to find out the phase of the moon. The reply he gets is "gibbous waning." When receiving the answer there is confusion and the commander then wants to know whether it is "new," "first," "full," or "last." The answer then is "last," which is the nearest match to "gibbous waning" – with the following private comment of the commander in the chartroom after the phone exchange: "Rock is a great guy with a brain about this big [making a circle with the tip of his index finger matching the first joint of his thumb]. He must never have taken an amphib mission onto a beach at night. He might get by on a crescent moon, but on a gibbous waning he'll be dead" (ibid., p. 231). This example illustrates the limitations introduced by lexical capabilities, which are important determinants of the computations that have to be accomplished, the signifi-cance of such input for action. In other connectionist simulations, Hutchins (1996) inves-tigated the implications of different communication constraints by creating the behavior of communities of networks.

In social psychology there is currently no work that investigates the link between so-cially distributed knowledge and language as a structuring device. It is likely that this domain will prove of considerable significance in the not-so-distant future.

The revival of attention on the social bases of cognition is seen in diverse approaches. For instance, Clark (1996) refers to the information that is shared between participants as "common ground." Similarly, Krauss and his colleagues (e.g. Krauss & Fussell, 1991) have examined the construction of common frameworks. The socially shared cognition "devel-opment" (Ostrom, 1984) is in fact a reassessment of the social bases of cognition. This development has a different emphasis from "socially distributed cognition" and the role that language and communication play in the social distribution of knowledge. The work that comes closest to this type of analysis comes from Vygotski's sociocultural approach. It is in particular the notion of the "zone of proximal development" that has commanded a considerable amount of attention in recent years. This is defined "as the distance between a child's actual developmental level as determined by independent problem solving" and the higher level of "potential development as determined through problem solving under adult guidance or in collaboration with more capable peers (Vygotsky, 1978, p. 86)" (Wertsch, 1991, p. 90). Clark (1997) refers to this type of action as "scaffolded action" in that it relies on some kind of external support. "Such support could come from the use of tools or from exploitation of the knowledge and skills of others; that is to say scaffolding . . . denotes a broad class of physical, cognitive, and social augmentations – augmentations that allow us to achieve some goal that would otherwise be beyond us" (Clark, 1997, pp. 194–195). In the context of the zone of proximal development, the primary caregiver walks the child through a difficult problem, by engaging in an exchange including verbal instructions. In tackling the same problem at a later point in time, the child conducts a dialogue but on her own. Language in this case also functions as a structuring device in that it shapes and controls the child's actions.

This closing perspective on the language–social cognition interface is intended to hint at a possible window for social psychological research. Such research could have considerable implications for an improved understanding of the social nature of social cognition. Moreo-ver, this type of analysis is very likely to contribute to a clearer picture of the relationship between individual based approaches to socially shared cognition and socially distributed aspects of cognition as defined here.

Conclusions and Future Directions

An assessment of the interface between language and social cognition is simultaneously an invitation to consider and reassess a number of issues and assumptions that are in the heart of social psychology. One is undoubtedly what *is* social and what *is* psychological. The original linguistic relativity debate revolved around the question: what are the non-linguistic cognitive consequences of lexical or grammatical categories? Crudely put, this is a question about how the "social" influences the psychological, to the extent that language is a socially and not an individually constituted institution. The recent work on semantic priming, stereotyping, and automatic processes is precisely about how the social (linguistic primes) influences and shapes cognitive processes.

The work reviewed in sections 1 and 2 above on the properties of interpersonal predicates suggests that there are systematic ways in which interpersonal predicates vary with regard to the types of inferences they mediate. One potential implication of this conclusion is that in studies that use verbal stimuli about persons or social events we will have to be more careful about the nature of the stimuli we use. A majority of studies in social cognition proceed by using verbal stimuli and sometimes these stimuli may have some consistent "biases" that may contribute to the phenomenon under investigation. For instance, take the research on spontaneous trait inferences (Winter & Uleman, 1984; Winter, Uleman, & Cunniff, 1985). Here, all the critical stimulus sentences are constructed with action verbs. Would one get the same results if one were able to change the action verbs to state verbs and retain the same sentence otherwise? The answer is no, as Semin & Marsman (in press) have shown. The point is that the linguistic properties of stimuli require more attention than they have received to date.

Equally importantly, spoken and written language have qualitative differences that may systematically affect cognitive processes. Most of our research is based on written stimuli, although most of our interest is to extrapolate from that to phenomena that occur by other means of communication. For instance, the ease or difficulty of decoding written material may prove to be an important factor that has to be taken into account. This is illustrated by the observation that the algebraic development of the Greeks was stunted by their failure to develop an arithmetic notation based on symbols and their reliance on ordinary language, and an algebra that utilized letter symbols to represent unknown quantities (cf. Seanger, 1997, p. 132). One of the main arguments underlying this is that "Effective mathematical notation allows a maximum amount of information to be unambiguously displayed in foveal and parafoveal vision" (ibid.). Similar arguments have been raised in connection with the emergence of music notation (Levin & Addis, 1979, pp. 71–76).

There are a number of ways in which new directions are likely to evolve, but a significant and difficult avenue is the one that attempts to integrate the three views on the language–social cognition interface outlined in the three main sections of this chapter. In general, considering language and language use seriously in social cognition is likely to yield innovative syntheses. This can be achieved by systematic investigation of the constraints that are introduced by language and language use. In other words, a detailed examination of language furnishes the possibility of taming a significant source of variance, which if unattended can run wild.

References

Abelson, R. P., & Kanouse, D. E. (1966). Subjective acceptance of verbal generalizations. In S. Feldman (Ed.), *Cognitive consistency: motivational antecedents and behavioral consequences* (pp. 171–197). New York: Academic Press.

Bahrick, H. P., & Boucher, B. (1968). Retention of verbal and visual codes of the same stimuli.

Journal of Experimental Psychology, 78, 417–422.

Bakthin, M. M. (1979). *The esthetics of verbal creativity.* Moscow: Iskusstvo. Quoted in Wertsch (1994).

Bargh, J. A., & Pietromonaco, P. (1982). Automatic information processing and social perception: The influence of trait information presented outside of conscious awareness on impression formation. *Journal of Personality and Social Psychology, 43,* 437–49.

Berlin, B., & Kay, P. (1969). *Basic color terms: their universality and evolution.* Berkeley: University of California Press.

Brown, R. (1976). Reference: In memorial tribute to Eric Lenneberg. *Cognition, 4,* 125–153.

Brown, R., & Fish, D. (1983). The psychological causality implicit in language. *Cognition, 14,* 237–273.

Brown, R., & Lenneberg, E. H. (1954). A study in language and cognition. *Journal of Abnormal and Social Psychology, 49,* 454–462.

Chiu, C., Krauss, R. M., & Lau, I. Y.-M. (1998). Some cognitive consequences of communication. In S. R. Fussell & R. J. Kreuz (Eds.), *Social and cognitive approaches to interpersonal communication* (pp. 259–279). Hillsdale, NJ: Lawrence Erlbaum Associates.

Clark, A. (1997). *Being there: Putting brain, body, and world together.* Cambridge, MA: MIT Press.

Clark, H. H. (1996). *Using language.* Cambridge: Cambridge University Press.

De Poot, C. J, & Semin, G. R. (1995). Pick your verbs with care when you formulate a question! *Journal of Language & Social Psychology, 14,* 351–368.

Devine, P. G. (1989). Stereotypes and prejudice: Their automatic and controlled processes. *Journal of Personality and Social Psychology, 45,* 1096–1103.

Dijksterhuis, A. & Van Knippenberg, A. (1998). The relation between perception and behavior or how to win a game of Trivial Pursuit. *Journal of Personality and Social Psychology, 74,* 865–877.

Dijksterhuis, A., Aarts, H., Bargh, J. A., & Van Knippenberg, A. (in press). Unintentional forgetting: Direct experience as a trailblazer of automatic behavior. *Journal of Personality and Social Psychology.*

Dodson, C. S., Johnson, M. K., & Schooler, J. W. (1997). The verbal overshadowing effect: Why descriptions impair face recognition. *Memory & Cognition, 25,* 129–139.

Dovidio, J. F., Evans, N., & Tyler, R. B. (1986). Racial stereotypes: The content of their cognitive representations. *Journal of Experimental Social Psychology, 22,* 22–37.

Fiedler, K., & Semin, G. R. (1988). On the causal information conveyed by different interpersonal verbs: The role of implicit sentence context. *Social Cognition, 6,* 21–39.

Gabrielcik, A., & Fazio, R. (1984). Priming and frequency estimation: A strict test of the availability heuristic. *Personality and Social Psychology Bulletin, 10,* 85–90.

Gauker, C. (1990). How to learn language like a chimpanzee. *Philosophical Psychology, 3,* 31–53.

Gibson, J. J. (1979). *The ecological approach to visual perception.* Boston: Mifflin.

Giddens, A. (1976). *New rules of sociological method.* London: Hutchinson.

Giddens, A. (1979). *Critical problems in social theory.* London: McMillan Press.

Gilovich, T., & Regan, D. (1986). The actor and the experiencer: Divergent patterns of causal attribution. *Social Cognition, 4,* 342–352.

Grice, H. P. (1975). Logic and conversation. In P. Cole & J. Morgan (Eds.), *Syntax and semantics* (pp. 41-58). New York: Academic Press.

Gumpertz, J. J., & Levinson, S. C. (1996). Introduction to part 1. In J. J. Gumpertz & S. C. Levinson (Eds.), *Rethinking linguistic relativity* (pp. 21–37). Cambridge: Cambridge University Press.

Hardin, C. L., & Banaji, M. R. (1993). The influence of language on thought. *Social Cognition, 11,* 277–308.

Hardin, C. L., & Maffi, L. (1997). *Color categories in thought and language.* Cambridge, UK: Cambridge University Press.

Higgins, E. T. (1981). The "communication game": implications for social cognition and persuasion. In E. T. Higgins, M. P. Zanna, and C. P. Hermans (Eds.), *Social cognition: The Ontario symposium*, Vol. 1 (pp. 343–392). Hillsdale, NJ: Erlbaum.

Higgins, E. T., & McCann, C. D. (1984). Social encoding and subsequent attitudes, impressions, and memory: "Context-driven" and motivational aspects of processing. *Journal of Personality and Social Psychology, 47,* 26–39.

Higgins, E. T., & Rholes, W. S. (1977). "Saying is believing": Effects of message modification on memory and linking of the person described. *Journal of Experimental Social Psychology, 14,* 363–378.

Higgins, E. T., McCann, C. D., & Fondacaro, R. A. (1982). The "communication game": Goal-directed encoding and cognitive consequences. *Social Cognition, 1,* 21–37.

Hoffman, C., & Tchir, M. A. (1990). Interpersonal verbs and dispositional adjectives: The psychology of causality embodied in language. *Journal of Personality and Social Psychology, 58,* 765–778.

Hoffman, C., Lau, I. J., & Johnson, D. R. (1986). The linguistic relativity of person cognition: An English-Chinese comparison. *Journal of Personality and Social Psychology, 51,* 1097–1105.

Hunt, E., & Agnoli, F. (1991). The Whorfian hypothesis: A cognitive psychology perspective. *Psychological Review, 98,* 377–389.

Hutchins, E. (1996). *Cognition in the wild.* Cambridge, MA: MIT Press.

Kahneman, D., & Tversky, A. (1984). Choices, values, and frames. *American Psychologist, 39,* 341–350.

Kanouse, D. E. (1971). Language, labelling, and attribution. In E. E. Jones, D. E. Kanouse, H. H. Kelley, R. E. Nisbett, S. Valins, & B. Weiner (Eds.), *Attribution: Perceiving the causes of behavior* (pp. 121–134). New York: General Learning Press.

Kanouse, E. E. (1972). Verbs as implicit quantifiers. *Journal of Verbal Learning and Verbal Behavior, 11,* 141–147.

Kasoff, J., & Lee, J. Y. (1993). Implicit causality as implicit salience. *Journal of Personality and Social Psychology, 65,* 877–891.

Kay, P., & Kempton, W. (1984). What is the Sapir–Whorf hypothesis? *American Anthropologist, 86,* 65–79.

Krauss, R. M., & Fussell, S. R. (1991). Constructing shared communicative environments. In L. B. Resnick, J. M. Levine, & S. D. Teasley (Eds.), *Perspectives on socially shared cognition* (pp. 172–200). Washington, DC: American Psychological Association.

Krauss, R. M., & Fussell, S. R. (1996). Social psychological models of interpersonal communication. In E. T. Higgins & A. W. Kruglanski (Eds.), *Social psychology: Handbook of basic principles* (pp. 655–701). New York: Guilford Press.

Langer, E. J. (1989) Minding matters. In L. Berkowitz (Ed.), *Advances in experimental social psychology* Vol. 22 (pp. 137–173). NY: Academic Press.

Lenneberg, E. H. (1953). Cognition in ethnolinguistics. *Language, 29,* 463–471.

Lepore, L., & Brown, R. (1997). Category and stereotype activation: Is prejudice inevitable? *Journal of Personality and Social Psychology, 72,* 275–287.

Levin, H., & Addis, A. B. (1979). *The eye–voice span.* Cambridge, MA: MIT Press.

Levin, I. P., Schnijttjer, S. K., & Thee, S. L. (1988). Information framing effects in social and personal decisions. *Journal of Experimental Social Psychology, 24,* 520–529.

Levinson, S. C. (1996) Introduction to part 2. In J. J. Gumpertz & S. C. Levinson (Eds.), *Rethinking linguistic relativity* (pp. 133–144). Cambridge: Cambridge University Press.

Loftus, E. F. (1979). *Eyewitness testimony.* Cambridge, MA: Harvard University Press.

Lucy, J. A. (1992) *Language, diversity and thought: A reformulation of the linguisitic relativity hypothesis.* Cambridge: Cambridge University Press.

Maass, A., Ceccarelli, R., & Rudin, S. (1996). Linguistic intergroup bias: Evidence for in-group-protective motivation. *Journal of Personality and Social Psychology, 71,* 512–526.

Maass, A., Corvino, P., & Arcuri, L. (1994). Linguistic intergroup bias and the mass media. *Revue de psychologie social, 1,* 31–43.

Maass, A., Milesi, A., Zabbini, S., & Stahlberg, D. (1995). The linguistic intergroup bias: Differential expectancies or in-group-protection? *Journal of Personality and Social Psychology, 68,* 116–126.

Maass, A., Salvi, D., Arcuri, L., & Semin, G. R. (1989). Language-use in intergroup contexts: The linguistic intergroup bias. *Journal of Personality and Social Psychology, 57,* 981–993.

McCann, D. C., & Higgins, E. T. (1992). Personal and contextual factors in communication: A review of the "communication game." In G. R. Semin & K. Fiedler (Eds.), *Language, interaction and social cognition* (pp. 144–172). Newbury, CA: Sage.

Meyer, D. E., & Schvaneveldt, R. W. (1971). Facilitation in the recognition of word pairs: Evidence of a dependence between retrieval operations. *Journal of Experimental Psychology, 90,* 227–234.

Neely, J. H. (1977). Semantic priming and retrieval from lexical memory: Roles of inhibitionless spreading activation and limited-capacity attention. *Journal of Experimental Psychology: General, 1,* 226–254.

Ostrom, T. M. (1984). The sovereignty of social cognition. In R. S. Wyer & T. K. Srull (Eds.), *Handbook of social cognition* Vol. 1 (pp. 12-27). Hillsdale, NJ: Erlbaum.

Perdue, C. W., Dovidio, J. F., Gurtman, M. B., & Tyler, R. B. (1990). Us and them: Social categorization and the process of intergroup bias. *Journal of Personality and Social Psychology, 59,* 475–486.

Polanyi, M. (1967). *The tacit dimension.* London: Routledge.

Ranken, H. B. (1963). Language and thinking: Positive and negative effects of naming. *Science, 141,* 48–50.

Ricoeur, P. (1955). The model of the text: meaningful action considered as text. *Social Research, 38,* 530–547.

Rosch, E. (1973) On the internal structure of perceptual and semantic categories. In T. E. Moore (Ed.), *Cognitive development and the acquisition of language* (pp. 111–157). New York: Academic Press.

Rubini, M., & Kruglanski, A. W. (1997). Brief encounters ending in estrangement: Motivated language use and interpersonal rapport in the question–answer paradigm. *Journal of Personality and Social Psychology. 72,* 1047–1060.

Rudolph, U., & Försterling, F. (1997). The psychological causality implicit in verbs: A review. *Psychological Bulletin, 121,* 192–218.

Santa, J. L., & Ranken, H. B. (1968). Language and memory: reintegrative memory for shapes facilitated by naming. *Psychonomic Science, 13,* 109–110.

Schooler, J. W., & Engsler-Schooler, T. Y. (1990). Verbal overshadowing of visual memories: Some things are better left unsaid. *Cognitive Psychology, 22,* 36–71.

Seanger, P. (1997). *Space between words.* Stanford, CA: Stanford University Press.

Semin, G. R. (1998). Cognition, language, and communication. In S. R. Fussell and R. J. Kreuz (Eds.), *Social and cognitive psychological approaches to interpersonal communication* (pp. 229–257). Hillsdale, NJ: Lawrence Erlbaum Associates.

Semin, G. R., & De Poot, C. J. (1997a). The question–answer paradigm: You might regret not noticing how a question is worded. *Journal of Personality and Social Psychology, 73,* 472–480.

Semin, G. R., & De Poot, C. J. (1997b). Bringing partiality to light: Question wording and choice as indicators of bias. *Social Cognition, 15,* 91–106.

Semin, G. R., & Fiedler, K. (1988). The cognitive functions of linguistic categories in describing persons: Social cognition and language. *Journal of Personality and Social Psychology, 54,* 558–568.

Semin G. R., & Fiedler, K. (1992). The inferential properties of interpersonal verbs. In G. R. Semin & K. Fiedler (Eds.), *Language, interaction and social cognition* (pp. 58–78). Newbury Park, CA: Sage Publications.

Semin, G. R., & Greenslade, L. (1985). Differential contributions of linguistic factors to memory based ratings: Systematizing the systematic distortion hypothesis. *Journal of Personality and Social Psychology, 49,* 1713–1723.

Semin, G. R., & Marsman, G. J. (1994). "Multiple inference inviting properties" of interpersonal verbs: Event instigation, dispositional inference, and implicit causality. *Journal of Personality and Social Psychology, 67,* 836–849.

Semin, G. R. & Marsman, G. J. (in press). The mnemonic functions of interpersonal verbs: Spontaneous trait inferences. *Social Cognition.*

Semin, G. R., Rubini, M., & Fiedler, K. (1995). The answer is in the question: The effect of verb causality on locus of explanation. *Personality and Social Psychology Bulletin, 21,* 834–842.

Tajfel, H., & Turner, J. C. (1979). An integrative theory of intergroup conflict. In W. S. Austin &

S. Worchel (Eds.), *The social psychology of intergroup relations* (pp. 33–47). Monterey, CA: Brooks/ Cole.

Vygotsky, L. S. (1981) The instrumental method in psychology. In J. V. Wertsch (Ed.), *The concept of activity in Soviet psychology* (pp. 196–227). Armonk, NY: M. E. Sharpe.

Wertsch, J. V. (1991). *Voices of the mind: A sociocultural approach to mediated action.* Cambridge, MA: Harvard University Press.

Wertsch, J. V. (1994). The primacy of mediated action in socio-cultural studies. *Mind, Culture, and Activity, 1*, 202–208.

Whorf, B. L. (1957). *Language, Thought, and Reality.* Cambridge, MA: MIT Press.

Wigboldus, D. H. J., Semin, G. R., & Spears, R. (in press). How do we communicate stereotypes? Linguistic bases and inferential consequences. *Journal of Personality and Social Psychology, 78.*

Chapter Nine

Conversational Processes in Reasoning and Explanation

Denis J. Hilton and Ben R. Slugoski

Many psychologists conceive of judgment and reasoning as cognitive processes which go on "in the head" and involve intrapsychic information processing. Although it is incontestable that processes of attention, memory, and inference underpin judgment and reasoning, psychologists have perhaps overlooked the extent to which the operation of these higher mental processes is constrained by higher level assumptions about the social context of the information to be processed (Bless, Strack, & Schwarz, 1993; Hilton, 1990, 1991, 1995; Hilton & Slugoski, in press; Schwarz, 1994, 1996; Turnbull, 1986; Turnbull & Slugoski, 1988). On the other hand, philosophers have in recent years drawn attention to the way in which reasoning from ordinary language is shaped by the nature of social interaction and conversation (e.g. Austin, 1962; Grice, 1975; Mackie, 1980; Strawson, 1952). These higher level assumptions can determine how we formulate messages, what we attend to in them, which relevant memories we search, and what kinds of inference we draw. An awareness of how the social context can shape explanation, reasoning, and judgment can lead to a better understanding of why people formulate explanations and reason in the way they do, and prevent theorists from misunderstanding why people make the judgments they do. In particular, this perspective can help psychologists better understand when an "error" of judgment is really due to faulty cognitive processes, such as memory failures or failure to process certain kinds of information, or is simply due to skilled deployment of socially shared rules of message interpretation (cf. Kahneman & Tversky, 1982).

A New Look at Rationality: The Logic of Conversation

Our view of the rationality of responses to questions can be changed radically by taking the conversational context into account. Consider how seemingly inconsistent responses to the same question can be explained using Grice's (1975) logic of conversation, which entitles hearers to assume that speakers are generally cooperative, and follow several maxims of conversation in trying to say what they believe to be true (maxim of quality), not to say too much or too little (maxim of quantity), to say what is relevant (maxim of relation), and to say it clearly and succinctly (maxim of manner). This can be illustrated by imagining the following question–answer exchange between a man and his colleague at work (cf. Strack, Martin, & Schwarz, 1988):

> Q: How is your family?
> A: Fairly well, thank you.

The man might answer that way if he reflects that his wife has been saddened by the recent loss of a close friend, but that his two children are in fine form. The respondent interprets family to mean the wife and kids. Suppose, however, that the colleague had first asked the man about his wife and then about his family. The question–answer exchange might then have run like this:

> Q: How is your wife?
> A: Not too good, I'm afraid.
> Q: And how is your family?
> A: Extremely well, thank you!

In this case, the man would normally feel bound to interpret family as just the kids because he already gave information about his wife and did not wish to burden the questioner with redundant information she already has. So he gives an answer which is apparently inconsistent with his answer to the same question posed in the earlier context.

Saying one thing on a topic one minute, and then something quite different the next, is often taken as a sign of irrationality and folly (Strawson, 1952), unless, perhaps, the speaker is a politician. But most people would not feel that the man in the example above is being silly, mad, or ingratiating. Rather, we would tacitly assume that he is following Grice's rules of conversation. Being a cooperative fellow, he wants to answer honestly (following the maxim of quality), but does not want to burden his interlocutor with information she already knows (following the maxim of quantity). Therefore, if he has already given her information about his wife, he assumes that she is interested in just the children's well-being and answers according to the reinterpreted focus of the question (following the maxim of relation). He does so using clear, simple, and concise language (following the sub-maxims of manner). There is no need to assume that his answer varies from one context to the other because of cognitive deficiencies, such as memory, comprehension, or reasoning failures.

Nevertheless, many psychologists may have neglected the interactional context of question–answer exchanges and misattributed seemingly inconsistent responses observed in their experiments to cognitive deficiencies rather than the skilled application of socially shared rules of message interpretation. As an example, we consider the influential work of Jean Piaget (e.g. Inhelder & Piaget, 1958), who made inferences about children's logical abilities on the basis of "experimental conversations" in which children were interrogated about their mastery of concepts such as mass and number.

In one typical experiment examining the child's concept of number, children sat across a table from an experimenter, who laid two rows of sweets in parallel lines in front of her/ him. The lines each had an equal number of sweets and were of the same length. The experimenter then asked the child whether the lines had the same number of sweets or whether one line had more sweets than the other. The children usually judged that the lines had the same number of sweets. The experimenter then transformed the arrays by lengthening one of the lines by spacing out the sweets at wider intervals without, however, adding to the number of sweets in the line. However, when asked the same question about number again, most children under seven years of age altered their responses and stated that the longer line had "more" sweets. Piaget concluded from this research that younger children were unable to "conserve" the concept of number across the visual transformation of the array, arguing that they were "perceptually dominated." His conclusions were widely accepted from the 1960s onward, and had an enormous impact on psychological theorizing and educational practice in America and Europe.

However, subsequent research has suggested that the younger children's non-conserving responses may have been due to their expectations about the nature of conversation (Donaldson, 1978, 1982). If an adult repeats a question after transforming the array, the child may suppose that there must have been a reason, especially if that adult is a very wise-looking gentleman from the University of Geneva. She/he therefore judges that the number of sweets has for some reason changed. Older children who have been in school for a while may, however, have become used to "exam questions" designed to test their knowledge rather than to give new information to their interlocutor and thus not change their response. In an ingenious experiment, McGarrigle & Donaldson (1974) showed how effecting the transformation "accidentally" (rather than intentionally) caused younger children correctly to hold on to their original answers. After the first phase of the experiment, when the adult had set the rows of sweets out on the table and the child had judged the rows to have the same number of sweets, they arranged for a "naughty teddy" to come along and try to "spoil the game" by scattering the sweets all over the table. After the naughty teddy's intervention, the experimenter rearranged the sweets as in the second phase in the experiment. Now that the child had a good reason for the transformation, the number of correct conserving responses in 4–6-year-old children increased from 16 percent to 62 percent.

This general result has been replicated with similar experiments on concepts of mass and spatial reasoning, supporting the view that younger children have a better grasp of logical and spatial concepts than Inhelder & Piaget (1958) originally supposed. Indeed, Winer, Hemphill, & Craig (1988) have since shown how to get adults to give non-conserving responses as well, through the use of trick questions, such as "When do you weigh more, when you are standing up or crouching?" Adult respondents tended to rationalize their answers by such explanations as that they are more likely to sweat when standing up, and therefore to weigh less. Thus, like the younger children in Piaget's experiments, adults can also be shown to be susceptible to such leading question effects (unless they are led to doubt the credibility of the experimenter by being asked flagrantly bizarre questions beforehand such as "Why is this a car?" when being shown a picture of a couch).

Results such as these demonstrate that psychology experiments and survey questionnaires do not take place in a social vacuum. Changes to the context of interaction have substantial effects on both children's and adults' responses. Below, we present a framework which addresses these issues explicitly, and show how it illuminates widely studied phenomena in judgment, reasoning, and explanation.

An Attributional Model of Conversational Inference: Rationality in Interpretation and Reasoning

Conversational inference is itself a form of judgment under uncertainty. Hearers need to form hypotheses about the speaker's intended meaning on the basis of what is explicitly said. For example, most hearers routinely go beyond the information given in the utterance "I went to the cinema last night" to infer that the speaker saw a film last night. The additional information conveyed in this way is termed a *conversational implicature* (Grice, 1975). Grice thus argued that to understand a speaker's full meaning, the listener must both understand the meaning of the sentence itself ("what is said") and what it conveys in a given case ("what is implicated").

Conversational inference thus shares some important properties with inductive inference (Levinson, 1983). First, it is *ampliative*, i.e. the conclusion contains more information than the premises. The inference that the speaker went to the cinema and saw a film contains more information than the assertion that she just went to the cinema. Consequently, the consequences of both conversational and inductive inference are both *defeasible*, i.e. they can be cancelled by the addition of new information. The speaker may cancel the implicature that he or she saw a film at the cinema last night by saying "I went to the cinema last night, but couldn't get in."

As with inductive inference, a major issue for conversational inference is to select the hypothesis about the speaker's intended meaning that is most likely in the circumstances. We argue that the interpretations that hearers choose may in large part depend on attributions that they have made about the speaker's knowledge about and interests in the topic under discussion. For example, consider the statement:

1   "Some of the policemen beat up the protester"

This statement could convey one of two different implicatures, either:

2   "Some of the policemen beat up the protester" (but the speaker knows that not all of them did)

or

3   "Some of the policemen beat up the protester" (but the speaker does not know whether all of them did)

Levinson (1983) characterizes the first implicature as a K-implicature (because the speaker *knows* that the stronger assertion is not the case), and the second a P-implicature (because the stronger assertion is *possible*, due to the speaker's lack of relevant knowledge). One may reasonably surmise that the hearer is more likely to draw the K-implicature if he or she considers the speaker to be very knowledgable about the topic (e.g. an eyewitness who was present) than not (e.g. a person reporting the incident at second or third hand).

However, one can imagine circumstances in which the hearer would not draw the K-implicature even if she or he assumed that the speaker is indeed knowledgeable about the event. Such would be the case if the speaker were a police spokesperson who wished to limit perceptions of police brutality. The spokesperson may not want to tell lies, thus observing the maxim of quality, but may only want to commit her/himself to the weakest possible statement about police aggression that is consistent with evidence known to the public. If the hearer were to attribute such non-cooperative intent to the speaker, then she or he may assume that the spokesperson may be seeking to avoid committing himself to stronger statements that would be relevant, but damaging to the public's image of the police.

It is not difficult to think of other factors that might affect the interpretation of such statements. For example, if the hearer knows that the speaker is a foreigner with a limited control of English who did not know words such as *a few* or *many* which the speaker might

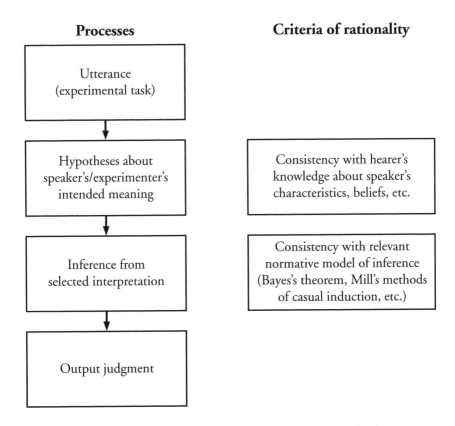

Figure 1   Two-stage resolution of uncertainty: utterance interpretation and judgment.

reasonably have used to specify the proportion of policemen involved, then the hearer might treat *some* as being vague, and consistent with either a low or a high proportion of policemen (see Moxey & Sanford (1987) and Politzer (1993) for further discussions of the pragmatic interpretation of quantifiers).

We have therefore argued (Hilton, 1995; Hilton & Slugoski, in press) that theories of judgment and reasoning need to add a front-end component that determines how an incoming message should be interpreted in its context. In the first stage the participant chooses the most rational interpretation using the criterion of consistency with higher-order assumptions about conversation and knowledge about the discourse context, and specifically attributions about the speaker. The second stage involves applying a normative model of reasoning to the representation thus formed, e.g. by applying Bayes's theorem to a belief updating problem, Mill's method of difference to a causal inference problem, etc. A schematic diagram of this two-stage process is given in figure 1.

We argue that this scheme may help psychologists determine whether an "error" is due to faulty reasoning about the information given, or to the application of correct reasoning procedures to "incorrect" or "irrelevant" information that a respondent has incorporated into her representation of the reasoning problem (Henle, 1962; Johnson-Laird, 1983).

Most research on reasoning, judgment, and explanation has focused on the rational inference stage. As will be seen below, anomalies found in experiments have often been attributed to inadequate use of normative models of inference such as *modus tollens* in reasoning, Bayes's rule in probability judgment, or Mill's method of difference in causal attribution. However, apparently irrational judgment may in fact be due to interpretations made at the conversational inference stage. Manipulating participants' perceptions of cooperativeness, intentionality, authority, knowledge, and interests should affect the interpretations of the questions that are posed, and hence the judgments and explanations that are given. Below, we review some well-known judgmental phenomena which illustrate the utility of taking the conversational perspective into account.

Leading questions and memory: The importance of attributions about speaker intention

An example of the importance of taking the conversational context into account comes from a classic experiment by Loftus & Palmer (1974) that was conducted to illustrate leading question effects on eyewitness reports. They showed that presuppositions loaded into questions about an automobile accident affected participants' judgments about that accident. Participants were shown a film of a car crashing into a truck. They were then asked either to say how fast the car was going when it *smashed* into the truck, or how fast it was going when it *hit* the truck. Their important finding was that participants gave substantially higher speed estimates when the question was worded with *smash* rather than *hit*, which they attributed to *smash*'s stronger memory associations with speed.

However, Dodd & Bradshaw (1980) showed how the "priming" effect observed by Loftus and Palmer seems to be specific to only certain social situations, such as conventional psychology experiments. They replicated Loftus and Palmer's results when the leading question was posed by the experimenter, as in the original study. However, when presented in the context of a court setting, they found that when the question was attributed to a prosecution lawyer trying to secure the conviction of the defendant, no priming effects occurred. Clearly, the priming effect only seems to occur when the question is asked by a presumably cooperative source (the experimenter), but not when it is asked by a presumably hostile source (the prosecution lawyer in the scenario created by Dodd and Bradshaw). Nevertheless, the power of suggestion of these leading questions, when asked by supposedly neutral sources, such as experimental psychologists and police officers, seems clear.

Intentional and "random" presentations of information in base-rate experiments

A further illustration of how well-known judgmental biases may be affected by conversational context comes from Tversky & Kahneman's (1974) research program on errors in adult judgment and reasoning. Their research has been used to argue that people make systematically and predictably irrational judgments even when there is no time pressure to make a decision or emotional involvement in it. For example, in one of their best-known judgment tasks (Kahneman & Tversky, 1973), participants are told that psychologists have constructed personality profiles of 100 engineers and lawyers. In one experimental condition, participants are told that there are 30 engineers and 70 lawyers, and in another that there are 70 engineers and 30 lawyers. Participants are then informed that a panel of psychologists has interviewed the members of this sample, and has summarized their impressions of these individuals in a series of brief descriptions. For example, in one condition they are told that one of the interviewees "shows no interest in political and social issues and spends most of his free time on his many hobbies which include home carpentry, sailing and mathematical puzzles." This description clearly matches culturally held stereotypes about the characteristics of engineers, and indeed most participants judge that the person is much more likely to be an engineer, regardless of how many engineers and lawyers there are in the sample.

Kahneman & Tversky (1973) use this result to argue that people's judgments are irrational because they fail to recognize the relevance of the *a priori* distribution (base-rate information) in making their judgments. The difference in the distribution of engineers and lawyers in the sample will clearly change the *a priori* probability that a given personality profile comes from an engineer or a lawyer. This can be shown mathematically, using Bayes's theorem for calculating *a posteriori* probabilities from *a priori* probabilities combined with the diagnosticity of a given observation (in this case the probability that someone with a certain personality profile will be an engineer rather than a lawyer, all other things being equal). However, Kahneman and Tversky propose that people do not use Bayes's theorem (or some psychological equivalent) in reasoning, but rather base their judgments of probability on the perceived similarity of the target's profile to their stereotype of engineers. This process of similarity matching, which they term the representativeness heuristic, does not take account of information about *a priori* statistical distributions, and thus frequently leads to error in judgments.

However, once again, recent research has shown that the underuse of base-rate information is very sensitive to the conversational context. For example, Schwarz, Strack, Hilton,

& Naderer (1991) noted that the experimental materials were written in such a way that participants suppose that the personality information is meant by the experimenter to be particularly relevant to the judgment task. Thus, the experimenter is himself a psychologist, and has taken the trouble to mention that a panel of expert psychologists has made the effort to interview all the members of the sample and produce personality profiles. We therefore rewrote the task to undermine the assumption that some information is more relevant than other information by suggesting that the personality descriptions had been drawn at random from the psychologists' file by a computer. In this condition, we found that participants' average estimate of the probability that the target is an engineer was 40 percent, in line with the normative use of base-rate information. This compares with our control condition, where we used Kahneman and Tversky's original procedure, and obtained an average estimate of 76 percent, in line with their original results.

Our research fits well with the findings of some related studies. For example, the order in which information is presented can also cue participants as to which information is most relevant. In Kahneman and Tversky's procedure, base-rate information was always presented first and personality information second. If participants assume that the information mentioned first was more relevant and weighted it accordingly, this alone would explain the underuse of base-rate information. Consistent with this reasoning, Krosnick, Li, & Lehman (1990) found that base-rate information was used more when the page on which it was printed was presented second and the page containing personality information was presented first. However, they found that presentation order did not affect the relative weighting of base-rate and personality information when they were explicitly told that the order of the pages had been decided "at random." Krosnick, et al. (1990) took memory measures to assess whether the effects of presentation order on information use were due to differential recall of information given, but found no evidence for the operation of such a mediating cognitive mechanism.

These results again suggest that if the assumption that aspects of the "experimental conversation" have been constructed intentionally is undermined, then the judgments that participants give change radically. In line with this thinking, we would expect that variations in the credibility of the source of information in the engineers and lawyers problem would affect use of information. Consistent with this analysis, Ginossar & Trope (1987, Expt. 5) found that participants rated the personality information as having the highest probability of being true when the source was a trained psychologist ($M = .78$), lowest when the source was a palm reader ($M = .31$), and intermediate when the source was a beginning interviewer ($M = .59$).

The assumed relevance of nondiagnostic information: Accountability and the activation of conversational norms

Although Grice's (1975) maxim of relation prescribes that speakers should only convey relevant information, experimenters routinely violate this assumption by deliberately including information that is quite irrelevant to the task in hand. A clear example of this is the "dilution" effect studied by Nisbett, Zukier, & Lemley (1981). They found that participants rationally used information about a target person such as I.Q. or effort that is diagnostic of that person's grade point average. However, when the description included irrelevant information (age, hair color, etc.), participants made less use of the diagnostic information. From the point of view of probability theory, there is no rational reason for this, as the diagnostic information is still as predictive when presented with nondiagnostic information as when presented alone. Nisbett, et al. (1981) posited an intrapsychic explanation in terms of the representativeness heuristic; that is, the irrelevant nondiagnostic information reduced the perceived similarity of the target person to the target category, hence "diluting" the predictive value of the diagnostic information.

However, as Tetlock, Lerner, & Boettger (1996) pointed out, the effect is also consistent with an explanation in terms of rational processes of conversational inference (see also Kahneman & Tversky, 1982). Participants may assume that all the information they are given, whether diagnostic or nondiagnostic, is mentioned because it is relevant. They may therefore weight all the information as diagnostic. On the assumption that the nondiagnostic information is weighted negatively, the dilution effect would be observed. On this account, it should be possible to eliminate the effect if the participants believed that the information had been presented without conscious design.

Tetlock, et al. (1996) therefore presented the information to participants as either having been screened for its relevance (thus activating conversational norms), or randomly sampled from a computer database (deactivation of conversational norms), or with no information about the conversational relevance of the information (normal context). Half of the participants were subjected to an accountability manipulation, being told that they would have to explain their decision to others when the experiment was over. This manipulation has been extremely successful in attenuating biases in judgment usually attributed to heuristic processing, due to its presumed effect in inducing more cognitive effort (Tetlock, 1992).

Tetlock, et al. (1996) found that the accountability manipulation led to more use of the diagnostic information in the conditions where conversational norms had been activated and in the normal context, where no information either way had been given. This is consistent with participants' belief that the nondiagnostic information must be relevant (otherwise it would not have been mentioned), and that accountable participants desire to perform well in the judgment task by making maximal use of information which they presume has been guaranteed by the maxim of relation. These results replicate the findings of Tetlock & Boettger (1989), and suggest that participants' default assumption is that conversational rules are operative in the experiment. Most importantly, when conversational norms had been deactivated, participants were less likely to use the nondiagnostic information, and thus less likely to produce the dilution effect. The finding reinforces the view that the occurrence of dilution effect in the normal context (as in the condition of explicitly activated conversational norms) is due to the unreciprocated respect that participants have for conversational norms in this particular experimental paradigm.

Conversational inference and part–whole contrasts

Earlier we suggested that asking a man the question *How is your wife?* before asking the question *How is your family?* leads the question to be reinterpreted as *How are the kids?* This is a case of a general process of inference in ordinary conversation, where such part–whole contrasts usually prompt rational listeners to "subtract" an earlier-mentioned part (e.g. the wife) from a subsequently mentioned whole (e.g. the family). As we shall see below, this process gives an alternative explanation of other judgment patterns that might otherwise seem irrational.

For example, survey researchers often worry about the accuracy of their data when respondents answer the same question differently in different surveys. However, some of this variation may be due to variations in the context in which the same question may get asked, due to variations in which questions preceded the target question. Thus Strack, Martin, & Schwarz (1988) showed that American college students questioned in a survey about happiness did seem to "subtract" an earlier-mentioned part (e.g. "Are you satisfied with your dating life?") from a later-mentioned whole (e.g. "Are you satisfied with your life in general?") if the two questions appeared to belong together (they were printed together on the same page as part of the same group of questions).

However, when the specific question was asked at the end of one page and the general question was asked at the beginning of the next page (as part of an apparently different set of questions), Strack, et al. (1988) reasoned that there would be no subtraction effect. As predicted, when the questions appeared together there was a low correlation (.26) between the ratings of happiness on a 7-point scale given to both questions, consistent with the operation of a subtraction effect leading to use of different information in each answer. However, when the questions were separated the correlation between the ratings of happiness was much higher (.55), consistent with the hypothesis that overlapping information would be used in this case.

Another example of how part–whole contrasts may give rise to apparently "irrational" responses comes from an experimental procedure used by Tversky & Kahneman (1983). In one version of this task, participants are given the following description:

> Linda is 31 years old, single, outspoken, and very bright. She majored in philosophy. As a student, she was deeply concerned with issues of discrimination and social justice and also participated in antinuclear demonstrations.

Participants were then asked which of the following two alternatives was more probable:

> Linda is a bank teller (T)
> Linda is a bank teller and active in the feminist movement (T&F).

Tversky and Kahneman reported that 85 percent of their subjects considered that the conjunction (T&F) was more probable than the conjunct (T). As Tversky and Kahneman point out, this appears to violate one of the most fundamental laws of probability, the conjunction rule, which states that a conjunction cannot be more probable than one of its conjuncts. For example, just as tossing two heads cannot be more probable than tossing one head, so the set of bank tellers who are feminists is included in the set of bank tellers. However, in the Linda example, Tversky and Kahneman argue that participants are once again victims of using the representativeness heuristic. Because Linda resembles the stereotypical image of a bank teller more than she resembles the image we might have of a bank teller who is also a feminist, people assume that the conjunction is more probable than the conjunct. They labeled this effect the conjunction fallacy.

However, Tversky and Kahneman's argument holds true only if we interpret *bank teller* in this context to mean *bank teller whether or not she is a feminist*, which they call the extensional interpretation, rather than use the logic of part–whole contrasts to interpret it as *bank teller and not a feminist*, or something like it, which is an implicit conjunct. Rating the implicit conjunct as being more probable than the explicit conjunct would not be a violation of the conjunction rule. Dulany & Hilton (1991) therefore presented the Linda problem to participants and assessed their interpretations explicitly by asking them to check descriptions of the alternatives they might have used. They found that only 55 percent of their participants reported interpreting the conjunct extensionally in the manner presupposed by Tversky and Kahneman. Of these, only a half (26 percent) also judged the conjunction to be more probable than the conjunct, thus committing the conjunction fallacy.

The conversational analysis also allowed us to make some more specific predictions about how participants interpreted the information given to them in this task. Following Levinson (1983), Dulany & Hilton (1991) reasoned that participants are more likely to use the extensional interpretation (P-implicatures) when they have no grounds for inferring that the speaker, this case the experimenter, knows much about Linda, and thus simply leaves open the logical possibility as to whether she is a bank teller or not. This would be the case in Tversky and Kahneman's "no-model" condition, where participants were given only the information that "Linda is 31 years old." Tversky and Kahneman had already found that this condition leads to hardly any conjunction fallacies, suggesting that people do have a basic grasp of the conjunction rule. However, it is also in this condition that, as predicted, more subjects (74 percent) used the extensional interpretation.

Grice (1975) considered that there may be *clashes* between two or more of the maxims, such that it may be impossible fully to meet one maxim without breaching the other(s). For example, when required to make judgments under uncertainty, respondents often will find themselves unable both to be completely certain (maxim of quality) as well as maximally informative (maxim of quantity), and will resolve the conflict by finding a principled balance between the two. Tversky & Kahneman (1983) had in fact considered the possibility that the conjunction error results from participants' tendency to assign probabilities to the alternatives in terms of their highest expected value, that is, some product of truthfulness *and* informativeness. Although Tversky and Kahneman rejected this interpretation of their results, Mosconi & Macchi (1996) recently showed that in a realistic context such as the courtroom, a person who provides the more inclusive class as an answer (e.g. "the accused is blond") is perceived as being evasive or "reticent" relative to the one that provides the included class (e.g. "the accused is blond and has a moustache"), and indeed the latter answer was judged "more probable" than the former. This undoubtedly reflects the expectation for felicitous responses to be both true and informative (for related pragmatic interpretations of the conjunction fallacy, see also Fiedler, 1988; Politzer & Noveck, 1991; Hertwig & Gigerenzer, in press; Macdonald & Gilhooly, 1990; Wolford, Taylor, & Beck, 1991; but see Agnoli, 1991; Donovan & Epstein, 1997, for opposing views).

A final example of how the conversational perspective can aid understanding of part–whole relationships is shown through Macchi's (1995) reanalysis of Tversky & Kahneman's (1982) suicide problem. In one version of this problem, participants were informed that

80 percent of a population of young adults were married, whereas 20 percent were single. They were also told that the percentage of deaths by suicide is "three times higher" among single rather than married individuals. In this problem, Tversky and Kahneman observed that participants do not take the base-rate into account when making their judgments, citing this as another example of base-rate neglect. However, as Macchi observed, the phrasing "three times higher" is ambiguous between the percentage of all suicides (implying that 75 percent of deaths are singles whereas 25 percent are marrieds) and the percentage among singles as opposed to the percentage among marrieds. When the problem was rephrased more perspicuously as required by Grice's maxim of manner, as "30 percent of single individuals and 10 percent of married individuals commit suicide," thus clarifying the superset–subset relations involved, participants used the base-rate information appropriately. Macchi's finding that clear writing about probabilities can enhance statistical reasoning has clear implications for how probabilities should be described by the media.

Category relevance and illusory correlations

Illusory correlation, defined as the erroneous judgment of a contingency between two variables when none in fact exists (Chapman, 1967), has been a prominent topic in social cognition for over two decades. Hamilton & Gifford (1976) first related the phenomenon to the development and maintenance of negative group stereotypes. In their experiments, participants read, in random order, 26 statements that described the behaviors of individuals who belonged to a hypothetical group A, and 13 statements describing behaviors of individuals from a second group B. For both groups, 69 percent of the behaviors were positive in nature and 31 percent were negative. Subsequently, participants were found to attribute more negative behaviors to group B than had actually been presented, recalled that group B members had performed more negative behaviors than they actually did, and rated group B members more negatively than group A members on a number of evaluative dimensions. That is, they had apparently formed a negative stereotype of the minority group B despite no difference between the two groups in the conditional probabilities of engaging in negative behaviors in the original stimulus set. A recent meta-analysis confirmed the robust nature of the phenomenon (Mullen & Johnson, 1990), which is of obvious importance to those interested in eradicating prejudicial attitudes and discriminatory behavior.

Dominant explanations stress the purely cognitive underpinnings of the phenomenon. The original, "shared distinctiveness" explanation (Hamilton & Gifford, 1976; and see Hamilton & Sherman, 1989) postulates that because the two classes of events, being a member of group B and performing a negative behavior, are both statistically infrequent, their co-occurrence will be highly distinctive to the perceiver. This distinctiveness is assumed to lead to greater attention to, deeper encoding of, and hence enhanced availability of the distinctive events in memory (Tversky & Kahneman, 1973). It is this enhanced availability in memory that then drives biased attributions, recall, and evaluation of group B members. A second, cognitive account views illusory correlations as resulting from information loss from memory. According to Fiedler (1991), because group A contains twice the number of exemplars as does group B, information about that group is more reliably encoded; that is, it is less subject to a regression effect as forgetting takes place and judgments are made.

However, recently McGarty, Haslam, Turner, & Oakes (1993) showed that familiar illusory correlation effects could be obtained in the absence of explicitly provided stimulus information. All that was required was that participants initially be given (a) expectations as to relative group sizes or behavior valence (Study 1), or (b) behavioral statements unaccompanied by group designation (Study 2). Finding that participants still associated the minority group with negative behaviors even under such minimal conditions, these researchers explained their results in terms of self-categorization theory; that is, the motivation for participants to make sense of the task by maximizing the comparative fit between group membership and behavior valence.

The self-categorization account implies a two-stage model of the process of forming illusory correlations. In the first stage, participants infer on the basis of an essentially Gricean logic that the group labels provided by the experimenter are informative or diagnostic of underlying group differences (i.e. "why would the experimenter provide this information if it wasn't relevant to the task?"); in the second, inductive inference processes are recruited to determine the group–behavior relationship. Of critical importance, it would seem to follow that *unless the assumption of underlying group differences is first made there is no reason for people to engage in the inductive reasoning phase.* If this is correct, then it should be possible to eliminate stereotype formation by cueing participants to the arbitrary nature of the group/behavior pairings; that is, by in effect removing their motivation to identify some purpose for, and impose some meaning on, the display of stimulus sentences. Haslam, McGarty, & Brown (1996) did just this by telling participants that the A and B groups corresponded to right and left handers, handedness having been pretested to ensure that it was nondiagnostic of behavior desirability. In this case, there was no evidence of illusory correlations having been formed on any of the dependent measures. Moreover, compared to the standard condition, participants were relatively unlikely to report having actively sought to discriminate between the groups. It should be clear that our conversational model would also predict attenuation of the effect if participants were to be led to believe that the allocation of behaviors to groups was accomplished by some non-intentional means, for example, via computer lottery in the manner of Schwarz, Strack, Hilton, & Naderer (1991) or Tetlock, Lerner, & Boettger (1996) previously described.

Elsewhere we have shown how the Gricean analysis of part–whole contrasts can be used to reinterpret "errors" in children's reasoning about categories, and survey respondents' answers to paired specific and general questions (Hilton, 1995; see also Schwarz, 1994, 1996). The Gricean approach can also be extended to explain direction of comparison asymmetry effects in relational judgments (Roese, Sherman, & Hur, 1998), and the confirmatory response bias in Wason's (1968) selection task (Sperber, Cara, & Girotto, 1995; and see Slugoski & Wilson, 1998; Hilton & Slugoski, in press). The interested reader is referred to these sources for further details. Below, we address the question of how the conversational approach can illuminate causal attribution and explanation processes, before we return to the question of whether thought itself can be conceptualized as a form of internalized conversation.

Conversational Processes and Causal Explanation

We begin our analysis by noting that causal explanation is a form of conversation. Explanation is a three-place predicate: someone explains something to someone. This renders causal explanation different from causal attribution and causal induction, with the consequence that causal explanation, being a form of conversation, must follow the rules of conversation. Good explanations must therefore follow Grice's (1975) maxims, balancing truth, informativeness, relevance, and clarity (Hilton, 1990, 1991; Turnbull, 1986; Turnbull & Slugoski, 1988).

From this it follows that speakers will alter their explanations as a function of what their hearers need to know. Slugoski, Lalljee, Lamb, & Ginsburg (1993) demonstrated this in an experiment where participants were asked to explain a young delinquent's behavior to interlocutors who had varying background knowledge (personal or situational) concerning a juvenile delinquent who had committed a criminal act. Slugoski, et al. (1993) hypothesized that participants would try to be informative, and provide their interlocutors with information that they did not already possess, thus satisfying Grice's (1975) maxim of quantity. Their results confirmed this hypothesis: when the interlocutor already had background information about the youth's personality, participants tended to refer to situational factors in order to explain the crime. On the other hand, when interlocutors already possessed relevant situational information, participants' explanations tended to refer to personal factors about the youth. These findings are striking because they suggest that people are quite aware that events are multidetermined, and can readily switch between internal and external factors in explanation as a function of the conversational context.

Slugoski, et al. (1993) note that their results fit in well with the notion of causality as an *abnormal condition* (Hart & Honoré, 1959), which Hilton & Slugoski (1986) advanced as an important criterion in commonsense causal ascription. Their results suggest that speakers give explanations that refer to conditions that are unusual or abnormal from the other's point of view. Hilton & Slugoski (1986) suggested that in causal attribution, people identify as causes conditions that are abnormal *from their own point of view*. They showed that participants' prior world knowledge about what was normal affected their causal judgments in the attribution task pioneered by McArthur (1972).

Explanatory relevance: Focusing on abnormal conditions

Hilton & Slugoski's (1986) abnormal conditions focus (ACF) model of causal attribution suggests that people tend to identify as a cause the condition that is abnormal in the circumstances. For any given event, there is a plethora of necessary conditions which could all count as causes, yet we typically mention only one or two factors when providing an explanation. As an example, consider the car accident in which Diana, Princess of Wales, died in 1997. As generally reported in the weeks following the accident, the circumstances of the crash were the following: Diana was the subject of great public interest, especially after her divorce from the Prince of Wales, her estrangement from the British royal family, and her involvement with the millionaire playboy Dodi El-Fayed. She left the Ritz Hotel in

Paris (owned by Dodi El-Fayed's father) after dinner with Dodi El-Fayed, and the hotel chauffeur was instructed to drive fast in order to escape from the waiting paparazzi who gave chase. He was drunk, and lost control in the tunnel under the Alma bridge. The car hit a concrete pillar at high speed, and the only survivor of the crash was Diana's bodyguard, the only one in the car to have fastened his safety belt.

All the above features of the accident could be said to be necessary conditions of the accident, in the sense that had they been otherwise, the accident would probably not have happened. Thus, in any counterfactual world where Diana was not of great public interest; she had not divorced the Prince of Wales, and so on down to fastening her seat belt, she would not have died. This fact poses a great problem for the covariational criterion of causal attribution as posed by Kelley (1967, p. 154), which argues that a cause "is that condition that is present when the effect is present, and that is absent when the effect is absent." Following this criterion, over a dozen factors could be identified as "causes" of Diana's death. Hence the problem of causal selection is posed: how do we select from the plethora of necessary conditions the one that we choose to dignify with the title of cause (Hesslow, 1988)?

Hilton & Slugoski (1986) argue that people tend to select that condition which they regard as abnormal in the circumstances. They argue that the traditional Kelleyan dimensions of consensus, distinctiveness, and consistency can be used to define what is abnormal in a given case. To return to the example of the car accident, many people find it unusual that a car should be traveling at such high speed through the tunnel (low consensus: most cars do not travel fast through the tunnel), leading this to be a popular candidate as cause. However, on the day after the accident, one of the Ritz chauffeurs observed that it was normal for them to drive at such high speed through the tunnel (high consensus: most Ritz cars drive at high speed through the tunnel without crashing), prompting him to suggest that it must have been something that the paparazzi did that caused the accident (high distinctiveness: most Ritz cars drive at high speed through the tunnel without being chased by these paparazzi).

Research has shown that people select the condition that is abnormal in the circumstances as the cause. For example, if people learn that a watch smashes after a hammer has hit it, they usually attribute the breaking of the glass to the hammer blow. However, if they then learn that this procedure occurs as part of a routine testing procedure in a watch factory, they tend to prefer the explanation that the watch broke because of a fault in the glass (Einhorn & Hogarth, 1986). Hilton & Erb (1996) showed that this change was not due to any change in the perceived probability of the explanation that the watch broke because the hammer hit it, but due to its decreased informativeness and relevance in the watch factory context. This finding supported the distinction that Hilton & Erb (1996) drew between causal *backgrounding*, where an explanation is still presupposed to be true but is relegated to the backgrounded "causal field" of necessary conditions (Mackie, 1980), and causal *discounting*, where the explanation is considered less likely to be true because another, more probable explanation has been offered (cf. Kelley, 1973; Morris & Larrick, 1995). In both cases, additional contextual information may lead to an explanation being discarded, but for quite different reasons (see McClure, 1998, for further discussion).

The explanatory relevance of goals and preconditions for actions

The conversational approach to explanation also explains why goals are generally (but not always) preferred to preconditions as explanations of simple actions (Schank & Abelson, 1977; Wilensky, 1983). Leddo, Abelson, & Gross (1984) showed that a goal-state (such as being hungry) would generally be preferred as an explanation for stopping in at a restaurant to eat than would relevant preconditions (such as having money in one's pocket, or the restaurant being open). They attributed this to a "pattern-matching" process, whereby events were fitted to an explanatory prototype for actions which contained slots for goals and preconditions. One problem for this perspective is that it was quite soon discovered that goals are not always perceived as better explanations for actions (McClure, Lalljee, Jaspars, & Abelson, 1989).

   Hilton & Knott (1998) suggested an alternative approach to the problem. They showed that the goals in the scenarios used by Leddo, Abelson, & Gross (1984) were generally perceived as being necessary and sufficient conditions for the occurrence of the action concerned, whereas the preconditions were more likely to be perceived as necessary but not sufficient conditions. Consequently, goals (e.g. being hungry) but not preconditions (e.g. having money, the restaurant being open) typically satisfied Mackie's (1980) criterion that conditions be "sufficient in the circumstances" for an action (e.g. stopping in to eat) to occur. In addition, Hilton and Knott showed that goals were more likely than preconditions to be perceived as informative about and relevant to the question as to why the action occurred, suggesting that they had greater explanatory relevance. Finally, they showed that the perceived quality of explanations based on goals and preconditions was based on their perceived relevance independently of their perceived probability, further underscoring the conversational aspect of explanations.

   McClure & Hilton (1997) took the conversational approach a step further, by showing how changes in the context could make preconditions preferred over goals as explanations. Consider the case of an Ethiopian refugee, who has not eaten for months, but who eats when food becomes available. Since in the normal case food is not available for a starving refugee, a good explanation would refer to the availability of food (a precondition) as the "abnormal condition" that makes the difference between the refugee eating and not eating (the normal case), rather than to the goal-state (being hungry), which does not make a difference to the refugee's eating. In a series of experiments which used the same scenarios as Hilton & Knott (1998), McClure and Hilton showed that preconditions were favoured as explanations when their existence was abnormal in the context. For example, when participants were informed that Joe was unemployed and did not normally have the money to pay for a meal in a restaurant, fulfilment of a precondition (e.g. Joe was invited for a meal by his brother) would be judged as a better explanation than the existence of the goal (Joe was hungry). Preconditions were perceived as more relevant explanations than goals in these cases, and relevance predicted explanatory quality independently of perceived probability. In addition, McClure & Hilton (1998) showed that subtle changes to the causal question made a difference to the favored explanation: thus people tend to furnish goal explanations in response to why-questions, but when simply asked to "explain" the event, they give as many preconditions as goals in their explanations. Again, these changes in explanation preferences were predicted by their perceived relevance to the kind of causal question asked. These results suggest that changes in preference for given explanations are due to changes in their perceived explanatory relevance, independent of changes in their perceived truth-value.

Verb effects in conversational context: Pragmatic vs. semantic aspects of explanation

We developed the ACF model to address attribution processes in social perception. Nevertheless, it is important to note that there are two major kinds of question involved in social perception. The first is quite similar to that facing the lawyer, where we are concerned with the question of why an individual behaved the way she or he did. Thus, in social psychological theories of causal attribution, the typical question posed concerns an individual's behavior: "Why did my friend enjoy the movie?" (Heider, 1958); "Why did Alice choose to go to Princeton rather than Yale?" (Jones & Davis, 1965); "Why did John laugh at the comedian?" (Kelley, 1967; McArthur, 1972), and so on. Most attribution experiments follow this form: participants are given descriptions of a particular named person performing a behavior on a specific occasion, and are asked to explain why the behavior happened. Sometimes no further information is provided (e.g. Brown & Fish, 1983; McArthur, 1972; Semin & Fiedler, 1988). In other cases, further background information is provided, often in the form of covariation information defined by Kelley's (1967) cube (e.g. Cheng & Novick, 1990; Försterling, 1989; Hilton & Slugoski, 1986; McArthur, 1972), and sometimes in a more naturalistic story-like form (e.g. Leddo, Abelson, & Gross, 1984; McClure & Hilton, 1997; Slugoski, Lalljee, Lamb, & Ginsburg, 1993).

However, causal explanation of particular events needs to be distinguished from *dispositional attribution* (Bassili, 1989; Hamilton, 1988; Hilton, Smith, & Kim, 1995), which involves learning about the propensity of an entity to produce a certain kind of effect. Dispositional attributions may be regarded as certain kinds of causal generalizations; thus "Tom is helpful" implies that "Tom helps many people" (Brown & Fish, 1983; Hilton, Smith, & Kim, 1995). Dispositional attributions may, of course, be *used* as causal explanations. Thus we may explain a particular event by saying "Tom gave money to charity because he is generous" (as opposed to "because he was in a good mood that day").

Our perspective predicts some interesting interactions between dispositional attribution and causal explanation. For example, work on "implicit causality" contained in verbs has shown that actions are typically explained with reference to some quality of the actor (Brown & Fish, 1983; Semin & Fiedler, 1988). Thus spontaneous completions of sentences such as *Ted helps Bill* because . . . tend to refer to something about the actor. Participants also are more likely to consider that Ted covaries with the helping behavior, agreeing that *Ted helps many other people* and *Few other people help Paul*, and to attribute the disposition of helpfulness to Ted by rating their agreement with the statement *Ted helps Paul because he is the kind of person who helps people* on a 7-point rating scale. These findings fit in with the idea that causality is determined by covariation (Rudolph & Försterling, 1997). On the other hand, we would note that low consensus, as well as suggesting covariation between the actor and the target event, also throws the actor into focus as abnormal (Hilton &

Slugoski, 1986), and therefore that the ACF model would make the same prediction here. However, note that these results have almost all been obtained with contextless sentences involving two named, but otherwise unspecified individuals.

First, consider what happens when the participant is given some relevant prior knowledge about one of the individuals concerned. Slugoski, Hilton, & Turnbull (1997) did this by manipulating role-expectancies about actors involved in the production of the event. Thus, participants would read a sentence such as *The fireman helps Kevin.* Here, it is part of our world knowledge that firemen help people. When asked to use rating scales, subjects judged that it was more likely that the fireman helped Kevin "because he is the kind of person who helps people" than "because Kevin was the kind of person that people help." This presumably reflects the fact that people consider helping behavior to covary more strongly with the actor when the actor was described as a fireman than simply referred by a male proper name (e.g. Ted).

This finding allowed us to pit the predictions of a simple-minded covariational model of causal explanation directly against those of the conversational model. If participants were just following a covariational rule in assigning causality, then spontaneous explanations should refer to something about the missionary. However, an explanation which refers to some quality of the missionary risks being uninformative if it were to refer to culturally presupposed knowledge about what firemen generally do (Grice, 1975). The attribution of a helpful disposition to firemen is just such a culturally shared belief. In line with our prediction, we found that in these cases (e.g. *The fireman helps Kevin*), explanations were significantly more likely to refer to something about the object (Kevin), than when the actor was some unspecified male (as in *Ted helps Paul*). This finding was consistent with our prediction that participants would identify something abnormal about Kevin, that distinguished him, say, from other people that the fireman might have helped. Note that participants follow the abnormality rule even though an unspecified actor is perceived as both covarying less with the target event than the missionary, and as having less of a disposition to help people.

In subsequent experiments, we took the conversational approach further by asking participants to imagine that they had been asked the same questions, but in a "realistic" social context. In line with the conversational model, we reasoned that recipients of causal questions would interpret the intended causal focus of a question differently as a function of their interlocutor's perceived knowledge and interests. Thus, participants were asked to imagine that they were preparing food in the kitchen while their interlocutor was watching television in the next room. If their interlocutor was an adult visitor who had been out of the country for 18 months, and thus could not be expected to be *au fait* about recent developments in television serials, then we reasoned that participants would answer questions of the type *Why did the fireman help Kevin?* as focusing on Kevin, because competent adults would already be assumed to know what firemen do. Our results confirmed this reasoning: participants tended to give explanations that identified characteristics about the individual who might be unfamiliar to the listener (i.e. Kevin).

However, the conversational model will make quite different predictions about perceived question focus if the interlocutor was a 4-year-old child or a visitor from outer space. Here, participants cannot presuppose that their interlocutor knows what firemen do. In this case, cooperative participants should focus on aspects of the role-defined figure (i.e. the missionary), whose characteristics would presumably be unknown to this kind of interlocutor. Again, our results indicated a very strong tendency for participants to give explanations in line with the conversational model.

These examples illustrate the point that although covariation and perceived abnormality often coincide, people seem to follow the abnormality principle where they diverge. This, of course, is not to argue that people attribute causes to factors that do not covary with effects. It is rather to say that where certain covariations are already known about because they are culturally shared, then they are presupposed rather than focused in the communicated explanation (see also McGill, 1989). It is thus the normality principle that determines which covariations get focused on and which are presupposed and hence "backgrounded" in spontaneous explanation. In interpersonal explanation, this normality principle is relativized to what covariations are likely to be already known by the interlocutor, and thus may be treated as mutual knowledge.

Finally, the latter experiment enabled us to assess the attributions made by participants *about* the speaker posing the question. Recall that the Gricean model presupposes that in normal conversation, speakers are fully cooperative and rational, and should have an acceptable reason for posing the question. When the interlocutor was someone who could not be assumed to have relevant world knowledge, such as a 4-year-old child or an alien, or an adult who had been out of the country for 18 months, participants could (and did) attribute rationality and cooperativeness to their interlocutors. However, when the questioner was a fellow adult member from the same Western culture who had been following the television serial in previous weeks, questions about normal events (e.g. *Why did the conman cheat Bill?*) led our respondents to attribute lack of intelligence, irrationality, and uncooperativeness to the questioner. This was consistent with our prediction that such questions would be perceived as "unGricean" when posed by a competent adult speaker. Interestingly, these adults were judged to be *less* cooperative, knowledgeable, reasonable, and intelligent than the 4-year-old children – a striking finding for any parent!

Closing the Circle: Thinking as Inner Speech

Plato conjectured that thinking is but "inward dialogue carried on by the mind within itself without spoken sound" (*The Sophist*). More recently, Vygotsky (1962) hypothesized that thought is inner speech, consequent on the child's internalization of the spoken speech used to regulate behavior. In this concluding section, we consider some empirical evidence to support the contention that reasoning and decision making can be viewed as internalized conversation.

Reason based decision making: The effects of accountability on judgment

Some recent research has examined the effect of requesting explanations on people's thinking processes. For example, Simonson (1989) found that when people were asked to explain their preferences, they were more likely to make certain choices rather than others.

One part of Simonson's research concerned consumer decisions about six-packs of beer, as below:

A   Quality rating: 50   Cost: $1.80
B   Quality rating: 70   Cost: $2.60
C   Quality rating: 40   Cost: $1.80

When asked to justify their choice, people were more likely to choose *A* than when they were asked to choose without giving a justification. This effect can be predicted if one assumes that when asked to justify their choice, people look for relevant contrasts in order to find reasons to prefer one option over the other (cf. Hilton, 1990). Option *A* offers the most possible reasons, since it is better than option *B* on price, better than *C* on quality, and no worse than *C* on price, though worse than *B* on quality, leading overall to two reasons pro- and one reason against. Option *B* offers two reasons for (being better than *A* and *C* on quality) and two against (being worse than both on price). People are more likely to choose *A* over *B* when *C* is present, and less likely to do so when *C* is absent, even though the "expected value" of *A* and *B* do not change.

This phenomenon is called the "attraction" effect, because the inclusion of an asymmetrically dominated item in the choice set (*C*) causes *A* to attract more choices, despite the fact that *C* is hardly ever chosen itself. Intriguingly, the attraction effect becomes even stronger when respondents are told that they will have to justify their choice to a peer group (Simonson, 1989), further supporting the view that the decision process is driven by conversational goals. Along with other findings, these results have prompted theorists to propose that decision making proceeds by the calculation of reasons for and against a choice, thus leading to predictable violations of rational choice theory (Hilton, 1997; Shafir, Simonson, & Tversky, 1993).

Giving explanations to others may force decision makers to articulate assumptions and explore options more fully. For example, Pilkington & Parker-Jones (1996) found that trainee doctors who were asked to explain their reasoning to a non-expert showed evidence of better learning and diagnostic performance. More generally, Tetlock (1992) has found that asking people to give explanations for their judgments improves decision making if the request is made before people start analyzing the relevant information. Tetlock attributes this effect to the increased motivation that people feel if they know that they are going to have to justify their decision to others. However, if the request for explanations is made after a decision has been made, it may lead to worse decision performance as people hold on to a defective decision even when they are given new information that would allow them to improve their initial decision. Tetlock attributes this to "face" concerns due to the motivation to appear consistent in one's choices. Like the conversational approach, Tetlock's (1985, 1992) work on accountability emphasizes the need to take the social context into account in order to fully understand human judgment and decision processes.

Conversational skill and judgmental bias

We have argued that human beings can easily be led "up the garden path" into error when socially shared rules of conversation about how information should be communicated are violated. Consistent with this position, we have shown that attention to and respect for socially shared rules of conversation can lead to impressive facilitation of human reasoning performance. This position would seem to imply that people who are skilled at conversational inference should be more susceptible to being "misled" in experiments on judgment and reasoning where the normal rules are exploited by "uncooperative" experimenters.

Consistent with this prediction, Levinson (1995) has argued that Tversky & Kahneman (1974) have identified heuristics such as representativeness which are very adaptive in conversation because they allow inferences to be made about what is presupposed or probably true, and which can easily be corrected if they are mistaken. This is because normal conversation takes place interactively, and we quickly notice and correct a mistaken interpretation by our conversational partner. However, in the modern world, we often have to deal with decontextualized information where such opportunities for quick repair do not exist, leading to persistent, and often tragic, errors in the management of complex systems such as nuclear power stations.

If thinking is indeed constrained by processes of conversational inference, then variations in skill at conversational inference should predict propensity to produce biases in reasoning and decision making. Slugoski & Wilson (1998) examined this proposition by constructing measures of conversational skill, and attempting to relate this to the propensity to produce bias on some well-known decision tasks. Their measure of conversational skill was derived using an adaptation of Clarke's (1975) method of reconstruction of conversations. They got 32 university students to divide into pairs and to converse for approximately ten minutes in a "getting to know you" session. These conversations were tape recorded and each conversational turn was typed on to a file card. Each participant then had to return to the laboratory and try to sort the file cards, which had been randomized, into their original order. This was done for all fifteen conversations not involving themselves, and enabled each participant to be scored on (a) how easily her conversation could be reconstructed by others, and (b) how well she could reconstruct others' conversations. These two scores were non-significantly correlated in a negative direction (– 0.23), suggesting that the tendency to pursue one's own theme in a conversation differs markedly from the ability to discern patterns in the conversations of others. These scores were combined into an overall measure of conversational skill, termed "pragmatic competence."

The results indicated that pragmatic competence predicted a greater tendency to produce some biases, but also a lesser tendency to produce others. Thus pragmatic competence predicted greater confirmation bias on the Wason selection task (Wason & Johnson-Laird, 1972), greater underuse of consensus information when making attributions about the person (McArthur, 1972), and greater underuse of base-rate information in the engineers-and-lawyers task (Kahneman & Tversky, 1973). However, pragmatically competent individuals exhibited less likelihood of a primacy effect when forming an impression of another person described by a series of traits (Asch, 1946), less likelihood of producing the conjunction effect (Tversky & Kahneman, 1983), and less likelihood of producing the dilution effect (Nisbett, Zukier, & Lemley, 1981). The finding that conversationally adept participants are more prone to certain "biases" and less prone to others has since been broadly replicated and extended on larger samples (McKay & Slugoski, 1997).

Previous research suggesting that measures of intelligence have had relatively little success in predicting performance on these reasoning tasks renders the ability of measures of conversational skill to predict superior performance on some tasks but inferior performance on others all the more striking. Whatever the final interpretation of this line of investigation, these results suggest that conversational skill and reasoning strategies are intricately linked, and pose intriguing questions for future research.

Conclusions

The studies we have reviewed have shown how important work in ordinary language philosophy and conversational pragmatics is for understanding human judgment and reasoning processes. No survey or experiment takes place in a social vacuum, and psychologists need to understand better how the interactional context shapes human reasoning processes. We have seen how understanding this conversational context can lead us to see why responses that seem to be errors can instead be understood as rational. This leads us to a less pessimistic view of human rationality than may have seemed justified by some recent research, since human beings may be better reasoners in natural contexts than was previously thought to be the case. Indeed, some of the research that we have reviewed suggests that the same processes that lead us into error in some contexts may be adaptive in others.

References

Adler, J. E. (1991). An optimist's pessimism: Conversation and conjunction. In E. Eells & T. Maruszewski (Eds.), *Probability and rationality: Poznan Studies in the Philosophy of the Sciences and the Humanities, 21*, (251–82).

Agnoli, F. (1991). Development of judgmental heuristics and logical reasoning: Training counteracts the representativeness heuristic. *Cognitive Development, 6*, 195–217.

Asch, S. (1946). Forming impressions of personality. *Journal of Abnormal and Social Psychology, 66*, 258–290.

Austin, J. L. (1962). *How to do things with words.* Oxford, UK: Clarendon Press.

Bassili, J. N. (1989). Trait encoding in behavior identification and dispositional inference. *Personality and Social Psychology Bulletin, 15*, 285–96.

Bless, H., Strack, F., & Schwarz, N. (1993). The informative functions of research procedures: Bias and the logic of conversation. *European Journal of Social Psychology, 23*, 149–165.

Brown, R., & Fish, D. (1983). The psychological causality implicit in language. *Cognition, 14*, 237–273.

Chapman, L. J. (1967). Illusory correlation in observational report. *Journal of Verbal Learning and Verbal Behavior, 6*, 151–155.

Cheng, P. W., & Novick, L. R. (1990). A probabilistic contrast model of causal induction. *Journal of Personality and Social Psychology, 58*, 545–567.

Clarke, D. D. (1975). The use and recognition of sequential structure in dialogue. *British Journal of Social and Clinical Psychology, 14*, 333–339.

Dodd, D. H., & Bradshaw, J. M. (1980). Leading questions and memory: Pragmatic constraints. *Journal of Verbal Learning and Memory, 19*, 695–704.

Donaldson, M. (1978). *Children's minds.* New York: W. W. Norton.

Donaldson, M. (1982). Conservation: What is the question? *British Journal of Psychology, 73*, 199–207.

Donovan, S., & Epstein, S. (1997). The difficulty of the Linda conjunction problem can be attributed to its simultaneous concrete and unnatural representation, and not to conversational implicature. *Journal of Experimental Social Psychology, 33*, 1–16.

Dulany, D. E., & Hilton, D. J. (1991). Conversational implicature, conscious representation, and the conjunction fallacy. *Social Cognition, 9 (1)*, 67–84.

Einhorn, H., & Hogarth, R. M. (1986). Judging probable cause. *Psychological Bulletin, 99*, 1–19.

Fiedler, K. (1988). The dependence of the conjunction fallacy on subtle linguistic cues. *Psychological Research, 5*, 123–125.

Fiedler, K. (1991). The tricky nature of skewed frequency tables: An information-loss account of distinctiveness-based illusory correlations. *Journal of Personality and Social Psychology, 60*, 24–36.

Försterling, F. (1989). Models of covariation and attribution: How do they relate to the analysis of variance? *Journal of Personality and Social Psychology, 57*, 615–625.

Ginossar, Z., & Trope, Y. (1987). Problem solving in judgment under uncertainty. *Journal of Personality and Social Psychology, 52*, 464–474.

Grice, H. P. (1975). Logic and conversation. In P. Cole & J. L. Morgan (Eds.), *Syntax and semantics*, Vol. 3: *Speech acts*. New York: Academic Press.

Hamilton, D. L. (1988). Causal attribution viewed from an information-processing perspective. In D. Bar-Tal & A. W. Kruglanski (Eds.), *The social psychology of knowledge* (pp. 359–385). Cambridge: Cambridge University Press.

Hamilton, D. L., & Gifford, R. K. (1976). Illusory correlation in interpersonal perception: A cognitive basis of stereotypic judgments. *Journal of Experimental Social Psychology, 48*, 5–17.

Hamilton, D. L., & Sherman, S. J. (1989). Illusory correlations: Implications for stereotype theory and research. In D. Bar-Tal, C. F. Graumann, A. W. Kruglanski, & W. Stroebe (Eds.), *Stereotypes and prejudice: Changing conceptions* (pp. 59–82). New York: Springer-Verlag.

Hart, H. L. A., & Honoré, A. M. (1959). *Causation in the law.* Oxford: Clarendon Press.

Haslam, S. A., McGarty, C., & Brown, P. M. (1996). The search for differentiated meaning is a precursor to illusory correlation. *Personality and Social Psychology Bulletin, 22*, 611–619.

Heider, F. (1958). *The psychology of interpersonal relations.* New York: Wiley.

Henle, M. (1962). On the relation between logic and thinking. *Psychological Review, 69*, 366–378.

Hertwig, R., & Gigerenzer, G. (in press). The "conjunction fallacy" revisited: How intelligent inferences look like reasoning errors. *Journal of Behavioral Decision Making.*

Hesslow, G. (1988). The problem of causal selection. In D. J. Hilton (Ed.), *Contemporary science and natural explanation: Commonsense conceptions of causality.* Brighton, UK: Harvester Press; New York: New York University Press.

Hilton, D. J. (1990). Conversational processes and causal explanation. *Psychological Bulletin, 107*, 65–81.

Hilton, D. J. (1991). A conversational model of causal explanation. In W. Stroebe and M. Hewstone (Eds.), *European Review of Social Psychology, 2*, 51–81.

Hilton, D. J. (1995). The social context of reasoning: Conversational inference and rational judgment. *Psychological Bulletin, 118*, 248–271.

Hilton, D. J. (1997). Constructive processes in judgment and decision making: Implications for psychology and marketing. *Swiss Journal of Psychology, 56*, 112–126.

Hilton, D. J., & Erb, H.-P. (1996). Mental models and causal explanation: Judgments of probable cause and explanatory relevance. *Thinking and Reasoning, 2*, 273–308.

Hilton, D. J., & Knott, I. C. (1998). Explanatory relevance: Pragmatic constraints on the selection of causes from conditions. Unpublished manuscript.

Hilton, D. J., & Slugoski, B. R. (1986). Knowledge-based causal attribution: The abnormal conditions focus model. *Psychological Review, 93*, 75–88.

Hilton, D. J., & Slugoski, B. R. (in press). Judgment and decision making in social context: Discourse processes and rational inference. In T. Connolly, K. Hammond, & H. Arkes (Eds.), *Judgment and decision making: An interdisciplinary reader.* 2nd. edn. Cambridge: Cambridge University Press.

Hilton, D. J., Smith, R. H., & Kim, S.-H. (1995). The processes of causal explanation and dispositional attribution. *Journal of Personality and Social Psychology, 68*, 377–387.

Inhelder, B., & Piaget, J. (1958). *The growth of logical thinking from childhood to adolescence.* New

York: Basic Books.

Johnson-Laird, P. N. (1983). *Mental models.* Cambridge: Cambridge University Press.

Jones, E. E., & Davis, K. E. (1965). From acts to dispositions: The attribution process in person perception. In L. Berkowitz (Ed.), *Advances in Experimental Social Psychology* Vol. 2 (pp. 219–226). New York: Academic Press.

Kahneman, D., & Tversky, A. (1973). On the psychology of prediction. *Psychological Review, 80,* 237–251.

Kahneman, D., & Tversky, A. (1982). On the study of statistical intuitions. *Cognition, 11,* 123–141.

Kahneman, D., Slovic, P., & Tversky, A. (Eds.) (1982). *Judgment under uncertainty: Heuristics and biases.* Cambridge, UK: Cambridge University Press.

Kelley, H. H. (1967). Attribution in social psychology. *Nebraska Symposium on Motivation 5,* 192–238.

Kelley, H. H. (1973). The process of causal attribution. *American Psychologist, 28,* 103–128.

Krosnick, J. A., Li, F., & Lehman, D. R. (1990). Conversational conventions, order of information acquisition, and the effect of base rates and individuating information on social judgments. *Journal of Personality and Social Psychology, 59,* 1140–1152.

Leddo, J., Abelson, R. P., & Gross, P. H. (1984). Conjunctive explanation: When two explanations are better than one. *Journal of Personality and Social Psychology, 47,* 933–944.

Levinson, S. C. (1983). *Pragmatics.* Cambridge, UK: Cambridge University Press.

Levinson, S. C. (1995). Interactional biases in human thinking. In E. Goody (Ed.), *Social intelligence and interaction.* Cambridge, UK: Cambridge University Press.

Loftus, E. F., & Palmer, J. C. (1974). Reconstruction of automobile destruction. *Journal of Verbal Learning and Verbal Behavior, 13,* 585–589.

McArthur, L. A. (1972). The how and the what of why: Some determinants and consequences of causal attribution. *Journal of Personality and Social Psychology, 22,* 171–193.

Macchi, L. (1995). Pragmatic aspects of the base-rate fallacy. *The Quarterly Journal of Experimental Psychology, 48 (1),* 188–206.

McClure, J. L. (1998). Discounting causes of behavior: Are two reasons better than one? *Journal of Personality and Social Psychology, 74,* 7–20.

McClure, J. L., & Hilton, D. J. (1997). For you can't always get what you want: When preconditions are better explanations than goals. *British Journal of Social Psychology, 36,* 223–240.

McClure, J. L., & Hilton, D. J. (1998). Are goals or preconditions better explanations? It depends on the question. *European Journal of Social Psychology, 28,* 897–911.

McLure, J. L., Lalljee, M., Jaspars, J., & Abelson, R. P. (1989). Conjunctive explanations of success and failure: The effect of different types of causes. *Journal of Personality and Social Psychology, 56,* 19–26.

Macdonald, R. R., & Gilhooly, K. J. (1990). More about Linda *or* conjunctions in context. *European Journal of Cognitive Psychology, 2,* 57–70.

McGarrigle, J. & Donaldson, M. (1974). Conservation accidents. *Cognition, 3,* 341–350.

McGarty, C., Haslam, S. A., Turner, J., & Oakes, P. J. (1993). Illusory correlation as accentuation of actual intercategory difference. *European Journal of Social Psychology, 23,* 391–410.

McGill, A. L. (1989). Context effects in causal judgment. *Journal of Personality and Social Psychology, 57,* 189–200.

McKay, K., & Slugoski, B. R. (1997). Pragmatic competence, perspective-taking, and susceptibility to judgmental biases. Paper presented at the Sixth International Conference on Language and Social Psychology, Ottawa, Canada.

Mackie, J. L. (1980). *The cement of the universe.* 2nd. edn. Oxford: Oxford University Press.

Strack, F., Martin, L. L., & Schwarz, N. (1988). Priming and communication: Social determinants of information use in judgments of life satisfaction. *European Journal of Social Psychology, 18,* 429–442.

Morris, M. W., & Larrick, R. P. (1995). When one cause casts doubt on another: A normative analysis of discounting in causal attribution. *Psychological Review, 102,* 331–365.

Mosconi, G., & Macchi, L. (1996). Pragmatic factors in the conjunction fallacy. Paper presented at the Third International Conference on Thinking, London, UK.

Moxey, L., & Sanford, A. J. (1987). Quantifiers and focus. *Journal of Semantics, 5,* 189–206.

Mullen, B., & Johnson, C. (1990). Distinctiveness-based illusory correlations and stereotyping: A meta-analytic integration. *British Journal of Social Psychology, 29,* 11–27.

Nisbett, R. E., Zukier, H., & Lemley, R. E. (1981). The dilution effect: Non-diagnostic information weakens the implications of diagnostic information. *Cognitive Psychology, 13,* 248–277.

Pilkington, R., & Parker-Jones, C. (1996). Interacting with computer-based simulation: The role of dialogue. *Computer Education, 27,* 1–14.

Politzer, G. (1993). La Psychologie du raisonnement: Lois de la pragmatique et logique formelle. (The psychology of reasoning: Laws of pragmatics and formal logic). Thesis for the Doctorat d'Etat ès Lettres et Sciences Humaines. University of Paris VIII.

Politzer, G., & Noveck, I. A. (1991). Are conjunction rule violations the result of conversational rule violations? *Journal of Psycholinguistic Research, 20,* 83–103.

Roese, N. J., Sherman, J. W., & Hur, T. (1998). Direction of comparison asymmetries in relational judgment: The role of linguistic norms. *Social Cognition, 16,* 353–362.

Rudolph, U., & Försterling, F. (1997). The psychological causality implicit in verbs: A review. *Psychological Bulletin, 121,* 192–212.

Schank, R. C., & Abelson, R. P. (1977). *Scripts, plans, goals and understanding: An enquiry into human knowledge structures.* Hillsdale, NJ: Erlbaum.

Schwarz, N. (1994). Judgment in a social context: Biases, shortcomings, and the logic of conversation. *Advances in Experimental Social Psychology, 26,* 123–162.

Schwarz, N. (1996). *Cognition and communication: Judgmental biases, research methods, and the logic of conversation.* Mahwah, NJ: Erlbaum.

Schwarz, N., Strack, F., Hilton, D. J., & Naderer, G. (1991). Base rates, representativeness, and the logic of conversation: The contextual relevance of "irrelevant" information. *Social Cognition, 9 (1),* 67–84.

Semin, G., & Fiedler, K. (1988). The cognitive functions of linguistic categories in describing persons: Social cognition and language. *Journal of Personality and Social Psychology, 54,* 558–568.

Semin, G., & Fiedler, K. (1991). The linguistic category model: Its bases, applications and range. In W. Stroebe & M. Hewstone (Eds.), *European Review of Social Psychology,* Vol. 2. Chichester, UK: Wiley.

Shafir, E., Simonson, I., & Tversky, A. (1993). Reason-based choice. *Cognition, 49,* 11–36.

Simonson, I. (1989). Choice based on reasons: The case of attraction and compromise effects. *Journal of Consumer Research, 16,* 158–174.

Slugoski, B. R., & Wilson, A. (1998). Contribution of conversation skills to the production of judgmental errors. *European Journal of Social Psychology, 28,* 575–601.

Slugoski, B. R., Hilton, D. J., & Turnbull, W. M. (1997). Implicit verb causality: Pragmatic versus semantic contributions. Unpublished manuscript.

Slugoski, B. R., Shields, H. A., & Dawson, K. L. (1993) Relation of conditional reasoning to heuristic processing. *Personality and Social Psychology Bulletin, 19,* 158–166.

Slugoski, B. R., Lalljee, M. G., Lamb, R., & Ginsburg, G. P. (1993). Attribution in conversational context: Effect of mutual knowledge on explanation-giving. *European Journal of Social Psychology, 23,* 219–238.

Sperber, D., Cara, F., & Girotto, V. (1995). Relevance theory explains the selection task. *Cognition, 57,* 31–95.

Strack, F. (1994). Response processes in social judgment. In R. S. Wyer & T. Srull (Eds.), *Handbook of social cognition,* Vol. 1: *Basic processes* (pp. 287–322). Hillsdale, NJ: Lawrence Erlbaum Associates.

Strawson, P. F. (1952). *Introduction to logical theory.* London: Methuen.

Tetlock, P. E. (1985). Accountability: The neglected social context of judgment and choice. *Research in Organisational Behavior, 7,* 297–332.

Tetlock, P. E. (1992). The impact of accountability on judgment and choice: Toward a social contingency model. In M. P. Zanna (Ed.), *Advances in experimental social psychology* Vol. 25. New York: Academic Press.

Tetlock, P. E., & Boettger, R. (1989). Accountability: A social magnifier of the dilution effect. *Journal of Personality and Social Psychology, 57,* 388–98.

Tetlock, P. E., Lerner, J., & Boettger, R. (1996). The dilution effect: Judgmental bias or conversational convention or a bit of both? *European Journal of Social Psychology, 26,* 914–934.

Turnbull, W. (1986). Everyday explanation: The pragmatics of puzzle resolution. *Journal for the Theory of Social Behaviour, 16,* 141–160.

Turnbull, W., & Slugoski, B. R. (1988). Conversational and linguistic processes in causal attribution. In D. J. Hilton (Ed.), *Contemporary science and natural explanation: Commonsense conceptions of causality.* Brighton, UK: Harvester Press; New York: New York University Press.

Tversky, A., & Kahneman, D. E. (1974). Judgment under uncertainty: Heuristics and biases. *Science, 185,* 124–131.

Tversky, A., & Kahneman, D. (1982). Causal schemas in judgments under uncertainty. In M. Fishbein (Ed.), *Progress in social psychology,* Vol. 1. Hillsdale, NJ: Lawrence Erlbaum Associates.

Tversky, A., & Kahneman, D. (1983). Extensional versus intuitive reasoning: The conjunction fallacy in probability judgment. *Psychological Review, 90 (4),* 293–315.

Vygotsky, L. S. (1962). *Thought and language.* Cambridge, MA: MIT Press.

Wason, P. C. (1968). Reasoning about a rule. *Quarterly Journal of Experimental Psychology, 20,* 273–281.

Wason, P. C., & Johnson-Laird, P. N. (1970). A conflict between selecting and evaluation of information in an inferential task. *British Journal of Psychology, 61,* 509–515.

Wason, P. C., & Johnson-Laird, P. N. (1972). *The psychology of reasoning: Structure and content.* London: Batsford.

Wilensky, R. (1983). *Planning and understanding: A computational approach to human reasoning.* Reading, MA: Addison-Wesley.

Winer, G. A., Hemphill, J., & Craig, R. K. (1988). The effect of misleading questions in promoting conservation questions in children and adults. *Developmental Psychology, 24,* 197–202.

Wolford, G., Taylor, H. A., & Beck, J. R. (1991). The conjunction fallacy? *Memory and Cognition, 18,* 47–53.

Chapter Ten

The Heuristics and Biases Approach to Judgment Under Uncertainty

Dale Griffin, Richard Gonzalez, and Carol Varey

Heuristics, Heuristics, and Heuristics

"Predictions are difficult to make, especially about the future." This statement, attributed by different sources to a United Nations official, Niels Bohr, and Yogi Berra, may be taken as self-excusing, self-mocking, or simply confused. Although most of us would agree that the world, both physical and social, is too complex to predict, we also have the experience of easily and effortlessly making many predictions. It is difficult to consider all relevant factors when evaluating the probability of a sports team winning, a stock increasing in value, or a relationship leading to marriage, but somehow when we consider such matters a feeling of certainty or uncertainty seems to "pop out" of the given situation. For example, on the day that we are writing this, a respected British politician was asked whether the current Kosovo peace talks would lead to a settlement; after a brief pause, he stated with confidence "the balance of probabilities are 40–60 against."

According to the "heuristics and biases" approach to human judgment, people typically use cognitive short-cuts that make probability assessments easy, but prone to error. Such short-cuts occur not only in predictions but in retrospective judgments of probability as well. Consider a recent article in a major British national newspaper. The article, titled the "20 million to 1 family," described how a couple had "broken all records by having eight children born in symmetrical girl–boy, girl–boy, girl–boy, girl–boy order." The heuristics explanation is that people incorrectly (but easily and effortlessly) judge that particular sequence to be extremely unlikely because the symmetrical pattern of births is extremely *unrepresentative* of a random series. Formal probability theory, in contrast, prescribes that any sequence of four boys and four girls is as likely as any other.

We thank Roger Buehler, Tom Gilovich, Peter Harris, Derek Koehler, Jason Riis, Norbert Schwarz, Winston Sieck, David Smith, and Frank Yates for helpful comments on a previous draft.

Based partly on their experience teaching statistics and on their observations of judgments and predictions in applied settings, Daniel Kahneman and Amos Tversky (Kahneman & Tversky, 1972; Tversky & Kahneman, 1973, 1974) proposed that intuitive judgments under uncertainty are typically controlled by judgmental "heuristics" rather than by the formal laws of probability. Kahneman and Tversky were not the first to suggest that classical "rational" models of statistical reasoning fail to describe actual human reasoning in many settings, but their program of research has been both more radical and more influential than most others. Their challenge to rational models influenced theory and research not only in cognitive psychology but also in social psychology, economics, political science, medical decision making, and legal studies. Some discussion of the three original heuristics, and a description of some of the classic example problems used by Kahneman and Tversky (summarized in Kahneman, Slovic, & Tversky, 1982), is a standard part of virtually all introductory textbooks in both social and cognitive psychology. Because of this ubiquity in the social psychological literature (see Sherman & Corty, 1984, for a review), we focus on the broader implications of the program and present a few selected examples in the Appendix.

There are at least three reasons why social psychologists should be interested in understanding the applications and implications of the heuristics and biases tradition. First, there is a fundamental tension in social psychology about whether to model human judgment as fundamentally rational or irrational (e.g. Asch, 1952; Nisbett & Ross, 1980), although the precise meaning of rationality is rarely defined. Second, models and explanations from the heuristics and biases program have been applied in social psychology to explain phenomena as diverse as causal attribution (Quattrone, 1982), self-perception (Schwarz, Bless, Strack, Klumpp, Rittenauer-Schatka, & Simons, 1991), egocentric biases (Ross & Sicoly, 1979), vividness effects (Moser, 1992), and risk perception (Sherman, Cialdini, Schwartzman, & Reynolds, 1985.). Third, many models currently in vogue in social psychology bear at least a superficial resemblance to the heuristics and biases approach, e.g. the cognitive miser metaphor (Fiske & Taylor, 1984); the heuristic–systematic model of persuasion (Chaiken, Liberman, & Eagly, 1989); the feelings-as-information model of Clore, Schwarz, and colleagues (e.g. Schwarz & Clore, 1988); and the stereotype-as-heuristic model (Bodenhausen, 1993), and a clarification of the overlap between models could be useful. The current review will address each of these three concerns. We first discuss the meaning of "rationality" that is most relevant to the heuristics and biases program, review the negative and positive messages of the original program, explore the chief criticisms of that program, and finally present a framework to organize the "second wave" of heuristics and biases research.

Heuristics in Historical Context

The rational model

The classical model of rational choice is central to the discipline of economics, and at its heart is the guiding principle of maximizing Subjective Expected Utility (SEU). According to this model, the "rational actor" assesses the attractiveness of a given option by evaluating the probability of achieving each possible outcome and combining that subjective probability with the subjective utility of each outcome. The rational economic actor then chooses the best option on the basis of the optimal combination of probability and utility. Economic theories that guide public policy in areas as diverse and important as taxation, environmental safety, and social security rely on the central assumption that individuals and organizations are rational in this sense. The behavioral work of Kahneman and Tversky (and many colleagues) questions the fundamental assumption of this model.

In a frequentistic definition, the laws of probability describe how to maximize the number of correct judgments over a large number of trials. The classical rational actor is expected to follow the basic rules of probability even for unique events, such as forecasting the probability of a recession in the year 2010 or the chance of peace talks succeeding. There are many events for which it is easy to calculate the "correct" probability (e.g. the chance of a given hand of cards). But in other cases, such as the prediction of peace in our time, the appropriateness of the probability judgment can only be tested by examining its *coherence* relative to other judgments (e.g. the probability of a subcategory must be smaller than or equal to its superordinate category) and by examining its *calibration* when aggregated together with several other judgments equated on probability (i.e. events predicted with .70 probability must occur 70 percent of the time). Note that coherence can be satisfied with regard to purely internal criteria, whereas calibration is specifically defined in regard to external criteria: how many things actually happened in the world. Violations of rationality in this model, then, do not imply anything about the relative importance of "hot" emotional versus "cool" cognitive factors, only about whether people follow the rules of subjective probability and evaluate their own preferences consistently.

To explain coherence, consider Bayes's Rule, which has been described as the "master rule" of categorical inference or categorical prediction (see Fischhoff & Beyth-Marom (1988) for a detailed and psychologically oriented discussion of Bayesian hypothesis-testing). Bayes's Rule defines how to use probability theory to update the probability for a hypothesis given some data. For example, when inferring the probability that a patient has heart disease (H1) on the basis of a positive diagnostic test (D), a rational physician would (implicitly or explicitly) calculate the following quantity, where H2 refers to the probability that the patient does not have heart disease.

$$\frac{P(H1|D)}{P(H2|D)} = \frac{P(D|H1)}{P(D|H2)} * \frac{P(H1)}{P(H2)}$$

The first quantity on the right-hand side is the likelihood ratio, which expresses the *relative* likelihood that a patient known to have heart disease would yield the test result D (for data) compared to a patient known not to have heart disease. The likelihood ratio thus expresses the *diagnosticity* of the given evidence D. In general, diagnosticity increases with increasing separability of the two competing hypotheses, increasing quality of the diagnostic data, and increasing sample size of the diagnostic data. For example, a given blood pressure reading would be more diagnostic in distinguishing between heart disease and a healthy heart than between heart disease and another vascular disease; it would be more diagnostic if it were taken by an experienced physician than by a beginning medical student; and it would be more diagnostic if it were based on the average of many readings than based on a single reading. The second quantity on the right-hand side is the odds ratio, or prior odds, which expresses the judge's belief about the relative prevalence of the two outcomes in the relevant population, that is, the relative probability of encountering a given member of each class (in the frequentist approach, the chance of encountering a given member from a random draw).

The strength of inference that can be drawn from a given set of evidence depends on the relative balance of the likelihood ratio and the prior odds ratio. If, for example, the diagnostic test has good validity such that the likelihood ratio is 9 : 1 in favor of heart disease, then a prior odds of 1 : 9 against heart disease leaves the rational physician with posterior odds of 1 : 1, or a .5 probability that the patient has heart disease. If, on the other hand, prior odds of 1 : 9 against are matched by a likelihood ratio of 1 : 9 against, then the posterior odds are 1 : 81 against, or a little over a .01 probability that the patient has heart disease.

Note that using Bayes's Rule to describe "ideal" probabilistic judgment in frequentistic settings, with repeated, exchangeable events such as drawing balls from an urn, is entirely uncontroversial. However, when Bayes's Rule is used to prescribe the updating of subjective probabilities about a unique event, some controversy entails (e.g. Savage, 1954). In particular, some statisticians argue that probability theory can only be applied to the frequentist case. However, as many applied researchers (including Keynes, 1921) have argued, if probabilistic statements about unique, real-world events are excluded from the domain of probability theory, nothing interesting is left. Wars, depressions, mergers, marriages, and divorces may happen with some regularity, but each is experienced as a unique event. Are probability judgments about such events without guidelines or standards? For now, it is enough that the classical economic model of rationality requires subjective probability judgments to follow Bayes's Rule.

Attacks on the rationality assumption

In the 1950s, inspired by the use of expert judgment in engineering systems developed during World War II, by the cognitive revolution that required human judgment to be modeled in terms of computer systems, and by the increasing contact between experimental psychology and economic decision making models, a number of research programs examined the issues of coherence and calibration in human probabilistic judgment. Herbert Simon (1957), early in his Nobel prize-winning research on economic models, argued that "full" rationality was an unrealistic assumption because of processing limitations in living systems (and, incidentally, in virtually all computers currently available). He proposed a limited form of rationality, termed "bounded rationality," that accepted the limited search and computational ability of human brains but nonetheless assumed that after a truncated search and after considering a limited subset of alternatives, people did act and reason rationally. For the moment, Subjective Expected Utility theory (and the underlying assumption of rationality) was safe, as long as it was modeled on a reduced set of stimuli.

Research by Ward Edwards (reviewed in Edwards, 1968) was designed to test the rationality assumptions more directly. From his research on how people revised, or "updated," their probabilities in the face of new evidence, Edwards concluded that people are not perfectly calibrated, but are generally coherent in their judgments. In particular, people do reason in accordance with the rules of probability (as summarized by Bayes's Rule) but they give new evidence too little weight and thus are "conservative." It is important to our later arguments to note that conservatism was only the most *common* finding in this research program. Systematic exceptions were found when participants were given new evidence of low probative weight; in this case, judgments were typically "radical," giving too much weight to the new evidence.

The work by Simon and by Edwards and colleagues is generally seen as the precursor of the heuristics and biases approach. However, there were several other flourishing research programs on subjective probability through the 1950s and 1960s, programs that cast further doubt on the rationality assumption. For example, Adams & Adams (1961) examined the calibration of subjects' probability judgments about their own knowledge, and found consistent "overconfidence:" for most probability levels, the actual percentage of correct answers was too low to justify the judged probability of success. Researchers using the Signal Detection model to study human perceptual judgments (e.g. Pollack & Decker, 1958) found that the correspondence between the rated probability of a "signal" being present and the actual probability of a signal depended on the difficulty of the recognition problem. When the stimulus was relatively difficult to recognize (e.g. because a tone was degraded with random noise or because a visual stimulus was very small), receivers' subjective probability judgments were too close to 1.0, that is, they were overconfident. When the stimulus was relatively easy to recognize, receivers' subjective probability judgments corresponded closely to the actual probability of receiving a signal and sometimes were even too low.

Throughout the 1950s, J. Cohen (e.g. Cohen & Hansel, 1956) studied intuitive conceptions of probability in children and adults, especially in terms of belief in "chance" and "luck" in gambling and risk-taking behavior. He concluded that intuitive conceptions of probability were qualitatively different than those described by the axioms of probability theory. Anomalies in conceptions of randomness noted by Cohen and others included two particularly robust phenomena: the gambler's fallacy and probability matching. The gambler's fallacy is the belief (implicit or explicit) that the "law of averages" requires that the probability of a given outcome of a chance device (e.g. tossing Tails on a coin) increases with a run of the alternate outcome (e.g. tossing Heads many times). Probability matching is the practice of predicting the more common event on a proportion of the trials corresponding to the base rate frequency of that event (e.g. if a roulette wheel was designed to end up "red" on 70 percent of spins, a probability-matching bettor would bet "red" on 70 percent of the trials, instead of betting "red" on each trial, which would maximize the probability of winning).

Also about the same time, Paul Meehl was describing two fundamental challenges to the optimality of clinical judgment. First, he noted that clinical prediction was almost entirely based on characteristics of the case being judged, with little or no concern for the relative prevalence or "base rates" of the possible outcomes (Meehl & Rosen, 1955). Second, he compiled a list of studies that compared the accuracy of clinical prediction with actuarial or formula-based prediction: formulas did better (Meehl, 1954). Some time afterwards, Oskamp (1965) demonstrated how trained clinical judges become increasingly miscalibrated (overconfident) as they gained more data about a case. Later, Mischel (1968) challenged the validity of clinical interviews to predict future behavior in very different situations. Most important for the present review, he pointed to the discrepancy between judges' beliefs and the empirical evidence of poor predictive validity.

These diverse findings and perspectives set the stage for Kahneman and Tversky's judgmental heuristics model of intuitive probability. The heuristics and biases program was not in any sense a deliberate attempt to account for the anomalies that littered the field of human judgment; it was simply an attempt to describe human judgment as experienced in the classroom and in the real world. Simon and Edwards had brought the potential conflict between normative rational models and descriptive human models into sharp focus, but had concluded that people were approximately or boundedly rational, within limits determined by their computational processes. However, there was considerable evidence that the assumption of calibration was generally untenable, and some evidence from Cohen's work that the axioms that predicted coherence were not consistent with intuitive judgments of probability. In this context, Kahneman and Tversky took a radical step: they proposed that the rules of probability, which define the rational "best guess" about outcomes, are not natural or intuitive methods of assessing degrees of belief or likelihood. Furthermore, they implied, simplifying the search set or restricting the number of computations was not enough to rescue the rationality assumptions. Instead, in many situations people naturally and spontaneously assess the likelihood of an outcome by processes that are qualitatively different from the rules of probability theory. In other words, "intuitive" judgment is not boundedly rational, but (at least in the classical sense) not rational at all.

Later critics have argued that the heuristics and biases program marked a sudden and arbitrary shift away from the past research on conservatism, which largely upheld the assumption of rationality (e.g. Lopes, 1991; Gigerenzer & Murray, 1987). This criticism is ill-founded, for, as we explain below, the heuristics and biases model is consistent with conservatism as well as with the other anomalies listed above. The heuristics and biases program accounted for the previous findings and also predicted many specific laboratory-based anomalies presented and tested in Kahneman and Tversky's early papers. We must emphasize that the laboratory-based demonstrations were never meant to be the phenomena to be explained – they were meant to illustrate the *processes* thought to underlie the phenomena of interest. The phenomena to be explained were judgments in the real world that seemed to be at odds with the dictates of probability theory.

Negative and Positive Aspects of the Heuristics Program: First Wave

From the first articles on heuristics and biases, Kahneman and Tversky noted that their program had two interrelated messages, one negative, about how intuitions do *not* work, and one positive, about how intuitions *do* work. In retrospect, it seems possible to identify two distinct stages of the program. In the first stage, the focus was on the surface structure of judgmental heuristics, and demonstrations were designed to show how case-specific information dominated intuitive judgment and led to the complete neglect of other normatively important information. The second stage (or as we describe it below, the "second wave") attempted to describe the deep psychological structure of judgmental heuristics, and the accompanying demonstrations were more likely to show how the (often conflicting) multiple sources of information were weighted.

A negative model of neglect

In the first stage, which dates from the original collaboration in 1969 to the 1974 summary paper, Kahneman and Tversky focused primarily on defining three judgmental heuristics (representativeness, availability, and anchoring-and-adjustment) by means of analogies with perceptual illusions. In simple, between-subject scenario experiments, Kahneman and Tversky demonstrated that people neglect prior odds ("base rates"), sample size, evidence quality, and diagnosticity, and instead rely on their immediate evaluation of the strength of the sample evidence to construct their subjective probability judgments. The experiments focused on everyday judgments and predictions about hospital births, school achievement, and professional membership, rather than abstract textbook probability questions about balls and urns, or dice and coins. Such a shift in context was neither irrelevant nor unplanned, as the authors noted that questions about chance devices were most likely to trigger the use of statistical rules rather than intuitive thinking. The authors acknowledged that almost any problem could be made "transparent" enough to allow participants to "see through" its purpose and therefore reason statistically, but argued that between-subject manipulations in non-chance settings were most informative about how people typically reasoned in everyday life.

The "negative" conclusion from this program of research – that intuitive judgments typically reflect only case-specific evidence, neglecting base rates and other features about the broader distribution – is enough to explain many of the anomalies in probability judgment listed earlier. If people focus only on the sample-specific evidence, then conservatism should be prevalent when base rates, sample sizes, evidence, and diagnosticity are high, and radical or overconfident judgments should prevail when they are low. This "psychology of evidential neglect" was implicit in the defining papers in the heuristics and biases program, and was later made explicit by Griffin and Tversky's (1992) "strength-weight" theory and then modeled by Brenner's (1995) random support theory. Koehler, Brenner, & Griffin (1999), using random support theory to model the neglect predictions, found substantial support for the basic neglect model in the everyday probabilistic judgments of physicians, economists, and lawyers working in real-world settings. Even weather forecasters, aided by computer projections and immediate outcome feedback, showed substantial neglect of base rate and validity considerations until they received specific feedback about their biases.

Criticisms of the "neglect" message began soon after the early laboratory studies were published. The initial focus of attention was the "lawyer–engineer" paradigm (Kahneman and Tversky, 1972), in which participants were given a personality description (see example 2 in the Appendix) and asked to judge the probability that the individual was an engineer rather than a lawyer. Although participants were also told the number of engineers and lawyers in the relevant population (70 vs. 30, or 30 vs. 70), the judgments reflected only the personality description; the base rates were neglected. Soon afterwards, one prominent critic claimed that he had "disproved the representativeness heuristic almost before it was published; and therewith . . . also disproved the base rate fallacy" (Anderson, 1996). In particular, Anderson had shown that base rates and case-specific information received about equal weight when manipulated across scenarios in a within-subject design. Kahneman and Tversky accepted that within-subject designs revealed the *capacity* for rule-based thinking whereas between-subject designs revealed the *actual* application of rules in practice. However, a later demonstration (Fishhoff & Beyth-Marom, 1984) cast doubt on the utility of within-subject designs to reveal much about reasoning capacity. When participants received a set of scenarios in which characteristics such as base rates were varied, such base rates were used whether or not they were normatively informative. It seemed that the participants were actively trying to make sense of the experimental game and felt that they should use what they were given, and especially that they should use what varied. Furthermore, when within-subject manipulations are examined more closely, it is found that participants combine the two types of information additively rather than multiplicatively, demonstrating that even when the base rates are made salient, they are not used in accord with Bayes's Rule (Kahneman, 1998; Novemsky & Kronzon, 1999).

Many economists, whose theories would suffer most if the heuristics challenge to classical rationality was widely accepted, wondered about whether the observed neglect biases would disappear with appropriate incentives or market conditions. In a series of studies, an economist (Grether, 1992) found that judgments consistent with the Bayesian model did increase very slightly, but significantly, with incentives for accuracy. More important, even in a chance set-up (balls sampled from bingo cages), with both sample evidence and base rates determined by drawing balls from a cage, there was still considerable evidence of heuristic thinking. The experimenter was puzzled to find that the direction of bias in the student economist subjects varied according to the size of the sample drawn and the discriminability of the two hypotheses under test. When the sample size was small and the two hypotheses were similar (so a sample of evidence had low diagnosticity), the data revealed apparent overconfidence which fit his definition of "representativeness effects." When the sample size was larger and the two hypotheses were very different (so a sample of evidence had high diagnosticity), the data revealed underconfidence or apparent "conservatism." However, as noted above, this pattern is consistent with the basic neglect model. Similarly, studies of business students in market games involving repeated plays and real incentives also revealed biased judgments in accord with the heuristic model (Camerer, 1987), but biases seemed to decline with repeated playing of the game.

Not to be outdone, social psychologists were quick to suggest a variety of ways to change the original scenarios demonstrating base rate neglect, from stressing the representativeness of the sampling procedure, to making the base rates more extreme, to making the target case less extreme, to changing the order in which the case and the base rate are received, to giving the case-specific information in a list rather than in an organized personality description, to varying the occupations of the people who put the personality descriptions together (see J. Koehler (1996) for a comprehensive list). Although none of these manipulations changed neglect into truly Bayesian judgment, they did demonstrate the familiar social psychological adage that people are active searchers for meaning (Griffin & L. Ross, 1991), and seemingly small changes in presentation and content can lead to marked changes in judgment (Tversky & Kahneman, 1982). It is important to note, however, that studies of social judgment in which people actively discovered the base rate for themselves (instead of deciding which of the experimenter's numbers was relevant to the task) also support a strong form of base rate neglect (e.g. Dawes, Mirels, Gold, & Donahue, 1993; Griffin & Buehler, 1999; Yates & Estin, 1999; Yates, Lee, Shinotsuka, Patalano, & Sieck, 1998).

The positive model: The original perceptual metaphor

Along with the negative message that people do not intuitively follow Bayes's Rule, Kahneman and Tversky developed a descriptive model of statistical intuitions. When people infer the likelihood of a hypothesis from evidence, they asserted, people intuitively compute a feeling of certainty based on a small number of basic operations that are fundamentally different from Bayes's Rule. In particular, these basic heuristic processes include computing the similarity between a sample case and the category prototype or generating mechanism (representativeness), computing how easily instances of the relevant category come to mind (availability), and adjusting an already existing impression or number to take into account additional factors (anchoring and adjustment). Thus, representativeness measures the fit between a case and a possible cause, or between a sample and a possible distribution. Availability measures the ease with which specific examples come into consciousness: a highly unlikely event is one that seems literally "unimaginable." Anchoring-and-adjustment is something quite different; it is not a measure, but a simplistic process of combination that fails to weight each component by its evidential value. These are heuristics because they are "short-cut" tools that bypass a more complicated and optimal algorithmic solution, where an algorithm is a step-by-step set of rules that guarantees a correct or optimal answer. Heuristics can be described in the language of "if–then" procedural rules. "*If* seeking the probability that a case is a member of a given category (or that a sample was generated by a given population), *then* compute the similarity between the case/sample and the category/population prototype." "*If* seeking the probability that an event will occur, *then* compute the ease with which examples of that event come to mind." "*If* a number is available for use and on the right scale, *then* adjust that number upwards or downwards according to knowledge that comes to mind." Whether such procedures were meant to be conscious strategies was not generally clear in the original papers.

Each of the operations described by Kahneman and Tversky yield a feeling or impression of certainty or uncertainty, but none of the heuristic operations are affected by some of the central features of the Bayesian algorithm, such as prior odds ratio, separability of the hypotheses, validity of the evidence, or sample size. Instead, these "direct assessments" of probability are fundamentally *non-extensional* and *non-statistical*, because they operate directly on the sample evidence without considering the relevant set-inclusion relations (the extensional rules), and without considering the degree of variability or uncertainty in sampling case information that is controlled by considerations of sample size and evidence quality (statistical rules).

In this approach, deviations from the normative model were not considered "failures of reasoning" but "cognitive illusions." This term emphasizes that the outputs of the judgmental heuristics, like the processes involved in vision and hearing, lead to compelling impressions that do not disappear even in the presence of relevant rule based knowledge. Furthermore, the heuristics do not represent a "strategy" chosen by the individual judge;

again like perceptual processes, the heuristics produced their output without guidance or active awareness of their constructive nature. This general notion was not novel; it had been introduced by J. Cohen (1960) in his study of "psychological probability:"

> Psychological probabilities which deviate from norms based on an abstract or "idealized" person are not errors, in a psychological sense, any more than optical "illusions" as such are errors. They can only be described as errors in terms of a non-psychological criterion. Knowledge of the objective lengths of the Muller–Lyler lines, for example, does not appreciably affect our subjective impressions of their magnitude. Precisely the same is true of the Monte Carlo fallacy [gambler's fallacy] . . . even mathematicians who are perfectly convinced of the independence of the outcomes of successive tosses of a coin are still inclined to predict a particular outcome just because it has not occurred for a relatively long time in a series of tosses. (Cohen, 1960, p. 29)

One of the novel aspects of the heuristics and biases approach was the deliberate strategy of creating "cognitive illusions" to demonstrate the heuristics at work; this naturally led to a focus on judgmental errors (as defined by the normative *non-psychological* model) in order to demonstrate the compelling nature of the heuristics.

The heuristic approach helped to explain existing anomalies in statistical intuition as well as predict new phenomena. In particular, the gambler's fallacy and probability matching can be seen as examples of representativeness at work. A long run is unrepresentative of a random chance process, and so we expect to see alternations to make the sequence seem more representative. In probability matching, the strategy of always predicting the most common outcome is completely unrepresentative of the kinds of patterns that seem likely to occur by chance, so predictions are made with the same kind of alternations that are representative of a random or chance process. Later, Gilovich, Vallone, & Tversky (1985) showed that people systematically misperceive random sequences because of the expectation that the sample sequence will "represent" the random nature of the causal distribution and contain many alternations and few long runs. When basketball fans were presented with a sequence of shots described as hits and misses, a majority perceived a sequence with a .5 probability of alternation as representing a "streak," because it included more long runs than they expected. An even larger majority perceived a sequence with a .8 probability of alternation as representing a "chance" sequence, because there were few long runs, and so the observed pattern matched the defining characteristics of a "random" process. Not surprisingly, such fans perceived actual players to be streak shooters, even though none of the players studied had shooting patterns that deviated from a simple independence model based on the assumption that hits were no more likely to follow a hit than to follow a miss.

The often-observed difficulties people have in understanding and identifying regression artifacts (e.g. Campbell & Kenny, 1999) also follow from the application of representativeness: people expect an effect to be just as extreme as its cause, regardless of the strength of the predictive relationship. Thus, children are expected to be just as tall, short, or clever as their parents, and experimental replications are expected to be just as significant as the original (significant) studies (see "Replicating a study" in the Appendix). Kahneman and Tversky (1973) coined the term "prediction by evaluation" to describe the process of matching the size of the effect with the size of the cause; the extremity of the causal variable is *evaluated* and then an outcome is *predicted* that is equally as extreme.

Furthermore, when, by the statistical law of regression that operates whenever predictive relationships are not perfect, children are less clever than their parents or replications yield weaker results than their originals, people invariably seek out causal explanations. Such findings have profound implications beyond the rejection of an unrealistic model of rationality. If people see random sequences as systematic deviations from chance, and develop causal explanations for phenomena that represent simple regression artifacts, we can expect an intellectual culture that develops and maintains unfounded superstitions and useless home medical treatments, that sustains multiple competing explanations of social phenomena, and distrusts the quantitatively guided conservatism of science.

Each of the three original heuristics has both process data and application data to support it (Heath, et al., 1994). Probably the most direct demonstration of representativeness is the Tom W. problem (see Appendix), in which participants were asked to predict the graduate concentration of an individual based on a sketch derived from a projective test. The predictions for Tom W.'s college major (measured in ranks) were negatively correlated with the base rate likelihood of each major listed, but were almost perfectly correlated with ratings of the similarity of the personality description to the prototypical college major. Note that in this study, no numbers were given by the experimenters to the participants or by the participants to the experimenters. The input variables were the personality description and the list of majors, and the output variables were three sets of rankings: base rate likelihood of majors, rated similarity between the description and the prototypes, and likelihood that Tom W. majored in each subject. More recently, Bar-Hillel & Neter (1993) showed that people not only rank the probability of category membership in order of the similarity of a description to its category prototype (i.e. by representativeness), but also are willing to bet according to representativeness, even when this violates the most basic rules of class-inclusion. Evidence consistent with prediction by representativeness has been observed in several applied domains, including foreign policy decisions and predictions of clinical psychologists and accountants (see Gilovich & Savitsky (1999) for a review).

The availability heuristic has been used to explain why people overestimate the probability of highly memorable risks, e.g. murder, and underestimate the probability of less memorable risks, e.g. suicide (Slovic, Fischhoff, & Lichtenstein, 1982). Although some critics questioned whether the ease of retrieving instances actually mediated the link between vividness and higher probability judgments (e.g. Shedler & Manis, 1986), Moser (1992) showed that ease of retrieval was a mediator, but needed to be measured appropriately using a self-generated measure of memory. In a series of studies, Schwarz and colleagues demonstrated that ease of retrieval – and not amount or content of retrieval – was, as Kahneman and Tversky surmised, the key determinant of availability effects (see Schwarz, Bless, et al., 1991).

The anchoring and adjustment heuristic also received close scrutiny in both laboratory environments (e.g. Cervone, 1989; Quattrone, 1984; Strack & Mussweiler, 1997; Wilson, Houston, Etling, & Brekke, 1996) and applied settings (e.g. Northcraft & Neale, 1987). These demonstrations confirmed that both explicitly random values and irrelevant values can serve as anchors and influence the final judgment of probability (as well as many other quantities). In one memorable applied demonstration, Northcraft & Neale (1987) suggested that even experienced real estate agents who should have ignored the asking price of a house anchored on this value when making evaluation estimates.

Critical perspectives on the heuristics and biases program

The prominence of the heuristics and biases program has made it a salient target for critics who object to its "negative" view of human rationality. The rather hot-blooded nature of the anti-heuristics backlash can be seen in the following quote, which is by no means the most extreme: "Are heuristics-and-biases experiments cases of cognitive misers' underachieving, or of their receiving a Bayesian hazing by statistical sophisticates?" (Barone, Maddux, & Snyder, 1997). Below we review and evaluate the major criticisms of the heuristic approach (see also Kahneman & Tversky, 1996).

Some of the criticisms have been aimed at the insular culture of the heuristics and biases tradition. These criticisms include: the approach is an abrupt and arbitrary departure from the boundedly rational conservatism model that preceded it (Gigerenzer & Murray, 1987; Lopes, 1991); the explanations are merely restatements of the phenomena (Gigerenzer & Murray, 1987; Gigerenzer, 1996); concerns about the generalizability of the heuristic and biases attack on human rationality (Lopes, 1991); and puzzlement over why only three heuristics were identified (Wallsten, 1980).

As described in the historical overview above, the heuristics and biases approach helps organize anomalies already observed, and can account for both conservative and overly extreme judgments. Ironically, given critiques about the atheoretical nature of the heuristics and biases approach, the perspective has more in common with modern conceptions of the mind such as connectionist models (Sloman, 1996; Smith, 1996) than it does with the modified humans-as-rule-based Bayesian models that came before it. Early citation analyses asserting that reports of poor judgment were over-cited in the literature (Christensen-Szalanski & Beach, 1984) have been overturned with more recent and comprehensive analyses indicating no "bias for bias" (e.g. Robins & Craik, 1993). The restriction to three basic heuristics made for a simple and elegant framework for thinking about judgment, which may have contributed to the immense impact of the original research paradigm. As understanding about judgment processes progressed, more heuristics have been added to the original list (e.g. causal simulation, Kahneman & Tversky, 1982a). We will return to the expanding scope of the program in our final section.

More recently, alternative frameworks have been proposed. Gigerenzer (1996) has criticized the lack of clear computational models underlying the heuristics and biases approach, and has developed his own set of judgmental heuristics based on computer simulations. These "optimal heuristics" (our term) are based on a satisficing model of judgment that goes back to Simon. Essentially, the two modern programs of heuristics differ in their guiding assumption: "fast and frugal" heuristics are based on the assumption that human judgment is optimal within processing limits, whereas heuristics and biases are based on the guiding assumption that unobservable heuristics should be no more optimal than the observed judgments used to explain them. Other frameworks, such as the problem-solving model of Ginossar & Trope (1987) and the adaptive decision making model of Payne, Bettman, & Johnson (1993), emphasize the flexible and goal-driven nature of judgment processes. Like dual process models of persuasion (e.g. Chaiken, Liberman, & Eagly, 1989; Petty & Cacioppo, 1986), the flexible or adaptive approach proposes that people strategically choose whether to save effort and use heuristic methods of judgment or to invest time and effort in using more complex, rule-guided processes. These dual process models differ from the heuristics and biases approach primarily in terms of emphasis. Even though the heuristics and biases approach explicitly acknowledges that people can represent and use abstract rules, its essential claim is that heuristic thinking is widespread even under the ideal conditions of high motivation, high ability, and high effort. It is possible to create a more inclusive model of heuristic thinking, as we attempt below (see also Fiedler, 1996; Dougherty, Gettys, & Ogden, 1999), but the message of the heuristics and biases program is that heuristic thinking is the standard and rule based thinking is the exception.

We next turn to two critiques that have attracted much research attention and raise questions about the fundamental underpinnings of heuristics and biases research. First, the claim that findings of the program are merely artifacts of the conversational rules between subject and experimenter, and second, the criticism that workers in this program have confused different definitions of probability. We take these two criticisms in turn.

Critics have claimed that many of the apparently "irrational" judgments observed in such studies were actually caused by rules of conversational implicature. There are two versions of this claim. The first is that people actively make sense of their environment, actively search for the appropriate meaning of questions, statements, conversations, and questionnaires, and that the same objective information can mean something different in different social or conversational contexts. This perspective is part of a *constructivist* approach to judgment (Griffin & Ross, 1991) that is consistent with the second wave of heuristics and biases research discussed below (e.g. Kahneman & Miller, 1986). Kahneman and Tversky (1982c) themselves discussed the problems with using what they called the "conversational paradigm" and noted that participants were actively involved in figuring out what the experimenters wanted to convey, just as if they were engaged in a face-to-face conversation. They further noted the relevance of Grice's maxims of communication to their problems (see chapter 9, this volume) and explicitly attempted to overcome the common-language ambiguity of terms such as "and" and "or" (Tversky & Kahneman, 1983).

However, this acknowledgment did not prevent a second and more critical version of the conversational perspective. The claim is that results of the scenario studies lacked external validity because changes in wording and context could reduce the rate of biased responses to questionnaire scenarios. For example, Macchi (1995) argued that base rate neglect may arise from textual ambiguity such that the verbal expression of $P(D|H1)$ is interpreted as $P(H1|D)$. Thus, the text "The percentage of deaths by suicide is three times higher among single individuals . . ." may be interpreted to mean "within the suicide group the percentage of single individuals who died by suicide is three times higher" (ibid., p. 198). To test this hypothesis, Macchi changed the key phrase to read "1 percent of married individuals and 3 percent of single individuals commit suicide" and found that this dramatically increased the number of participants who used both the base rate and the specific information. Of course, it is possible to re-apply a conversational analysis to the revised question, and it is difficult to know when the cycle should end. That is why it is so useful to have a real-world phenomenon to guide the evaluation of laboratory studies that otherwise can get lost in a perpetual cycle of "experiments about experiments."

The conversational perspective has also focused on the lawyer–engineer paradigm. Some follow-up studies challenged the explanation that the base rate neglect observed in the original paradigm was due to judgment by representativeness, and have been widely cited as evidence that heuristic thinking is eliminated in familiar, real-world social settings (e.g. Barone, Maddux, & Snyder, 1997). For example, Zukier & Pepitone (1984) found greater attention to base rate information when participants were instructed to think like scientists than when participants were instructed to understand the person's personality. A related study (Schwarz, Strack, Hilton, & Naderer, 1991) found greater attention to base rate information when participants were told that the personality sketch was written by a psychologist than when it was assembled by a computer. Thus, one might be tempted to conclude (despite the many other demonstrations of representativeness in the laboratory and the real world) that the use of statistical logic depends largely on social roles and contextual implications. However, a closer look at these studies leads to an interpretation more in line with a "constructive" perspective more congenial to the heuristics and biases approach. In both studies participants were presented only with a *low* base rate of engineers; inferences about base rate use were based on a paradigm that did not manipulate base rate. When, as part of our preparation for this chapter, we replicated each of these studies, crossing a base rate manipulation with the role/context manipulations, we found that within each base rate condition, the social context mattered, but across base rate conditions, the pattern of results was identical. In other words, even though people are sensitive to the role and context information, and use such information to shape their reaction to the personality description, they are still not sensitive to the statistical structure of the problem. Thus, these studies suggest not that judgment by representativeness is an artifact of a specifically contrived experimental situation, but rather that heuristics operate upon information that is actively constructed by the perceiver.

The second major critique is the claim that the heuristics and biases program is built solely on observations of probability judgments for unique events. Many defenders of the "objective" or "frequentist" school of probability have denied any role for the rules of probability in describing events that cannot be replicated for an infinite series. Nonetheless, it is undeniable that physicians, judges, and stockbrokers, along with virtually everyone else, use terms such as "probability" and "chance" to describe their beliefs about unique events. One of the greatest statisticians of the twentieth century has described the logical foundation of the subjective probability viewpoint as follows: "The formal rules normally used in probability calculations are also valid, as conditions of consistency for subjective probabilities. You must obey them, not because of any logical, empirical or metaphysical meaning of probability, but simply to avoid throwing money away" (De Finetti, 1970). We note that this point can also be made with respect to throwing lives away, or even throwing happiness away.

The frequentist critics of the heuristics and biases approach claim that when the classic demonstrations of heuristics are reframed in terms of aggregate frequency, the biases decline substantially or even disappear (e.g. Gigerenzer, 1994, 1998; Cosmides & Tooby, 1996; Jones, Jones, & Frisch, 1995). However, proponents of the heuristics and biases approach have explored this possibility for some time. For example, Kahneman and Tversky (1979) proposed that when making aggregate frequency judgments, people were more likely to recruit statistical rules of reasoning, especially rules of set-inclusion relationships, than when making individual probability judgments. Tversky and Kahneman (1983) proposed that set-inclusion relations were more compelling arguments when framed in frequentistic "counting" contexts. Griffin and Tversky (1992) proposed that aggregate frequency judgments led to greater attention to "background" information such as past performance (i.e. base rates). And Tversky and Koehler (1994) proposed that the violations of set-inclusion relations observed when compound hypotheses were explicitly "unpacked" into elementary hypotheses would be smaller for frequency than probability judgments. Thus, the dispute between critics and proponents of the heuristics and biases tradition arises not about whether probability and frequency judgments are psychologically distinct, or that frequency presentations are intrinsically simpler than probability interpretations, or even that the magnitude of biases are typically smaller in frequentistic formulations. The dispute is about the *causes* of the discrepancy and its implication for understanding the classic demonstrations of judgmental heuristics and heuristic thinking in real-world applications.

According to the heuristics and biases approach, the discrepancy between single-event probability and aggregate frequency judgments occurs because aggregate frequency judgments are less amenable to natural assessments that operate "holistically" on unique cases and are more sensitive to statistical or logical rules because the application of such rules is more transparent. Further, comparisons of the two tasks are difficult to interpret because different experimental artifacts affect each format (Griffin & Buehler, 1999). According to the frequentist advocates, a "frequency format" is consistent with the evolved software of the mind, and single-event "subjective" probability judgments are inherently unnatural (Gigerenzer, 1994, 1998). Supporting this perspective is evidence that people are extremely efficient, and seemingly unbiased, at encoding and storing the frequencies of letters and words they have been exposed to. On the other hand, this perspective cannot account for the observation that virtually all uses of the concept "chance" (meaning likelihood) in early English literature are consistent with a subjective, single-event judgment (Bellhouse & Franklin, 1997), nor that people untutored in Bayesian statistics regularly use expressions of subjective probability to describe their beliefs about the word.

The power of the frequentist critique rests on empirical demonstrations that judgmental biases "disappear" when aggregate frequency replaces single-event probability as the scale of judgment (e.g. May, 1986). Ironically, one of the first demonstrations of frequency effects on probability judgment was by Tversky and Kahneman (1983). They proposed that when a within-subject design was combined with a frequentistic presentation format, the conjunction rule of probability would be decisive over a heuristic answer. They created a conjunction scenario (the number of men over the age of 55 who have heart attacks) that could naturally be described in frequency terms: as predicted, when presented within-subjects the frequentistic version (but not the probability version) led participants to follow the conjunction rule (see "heart attack" in the Appendix). Gigerenzer (1991; see also Fiedler, 1988) replicated this finding, and concluded that frequency made the conjunction fallacy disappear. However, Kahneman and Tversky (1996) showed that conjunction effects consistent with judgment by representativeness were robust even with frequency judgments when manipulations occurred in between-subjects designs, reiterating that the combination of frequency and within-subject designs were necessary to create an "easy" or "transparent" version of the problem.

The frequency versus single event debate continues to generate new research questions, especially on the problems of base rate neglect and overconfidence (Brenner, Koehler, Liberman, & Tversky, 1996; Gigerenzer, 1994; Griffin & Buehler, 1999; Griffin & Varey, 1999). More importantly, the high volume of research activity, both by proponents and critics, suggests that the heuristic and biases approach is "healthy" and is still guiding research. These research problems have not "remained in the laboratory" but have branched out, with great influence, to applied areas (see Heath, et al. (1994) for a review of real-world applications). One reason why the area has remained fertile is because of a second wave of research that refocused the direction of the original work.

The Second Wave of Research: Heuristics Unbound

The original set of heuristics and biases demonstrations had a tremendous impact, both in terms of challenging existing theories and stimulating criticism. But as with any initial statement of a theory, there were some empirical anomalies left to be explained. Most prominent was the problem of "causal base rates" (Ajzen, 1977): when base rates could be given a causal interpretation (e.g. a high proportion of failures on an exam implied that a difficult exam *caused* the failure rate) they received substantial weight in judgment. This forced Tversky & Kahneman (1982) to include the computation of causality as a basic heuristic operation (see below), and to acknowledge that the distinction between case-specific and population based information was less sharp than originally proposed. This latter conclusion was reinforced by the finding that people were sometimes most responsive to the size of a sample *relative* to the size of a population (Bar-Hillel, 1979). Such a "matching" approach to sample size implied a broader kind of representativeness calculation, or as Bar-Hillel termed it, a second-order representativeness. The sharp distinction between heuristics that operated on cases, and rules that operated on abstract statistical quantities, it appeared, was not always so sharp, and seemed better captured by a more flexible distinction between "holistic" and "analytic" thinking. Furthermore, the initial statements of the heuristics and biases approach contained some ambiguity with regard to whether judgmental heuristics were deliberate strategies to avoid mental effort, or largely automatic processes that were uncontrolled and uncontrollable. These issues were addressed by a second generation of papers on judgmental heuristics by Kahneman and Tversky.

The second wave of heuristics research began with an analysis of the "planning fallacy," the tendency for people to make optimistic predictions even when aware that similar projects have run well over schedule (Kahneman & Tversky, 1979). This paper introduced a new form of the perceptual metaphor, contrasting an "inside" and an "outside" perspective on prediction. Using an inside or internal perspective, a judge focuses on the specific details of the current case; using an outside perspective, a judge "sees" the specific case as one instance of a broader set of instances. Shortly afterwards, a paper on causal reasoning (Tversky & Kahneman, 1982) demonstrated how intuitive or heuristic processes could be applied to both case-specific and distributional information as long as both types of information were in a form amenable to "natural assessments." For example, base rates that have causal implications (e.g. a sports team has won nine of its last ten games) may induce a computation of a "causal disposition" (Kahneman and Varey (1990); e.g. see "Blue cab/green cab" in the Appendix). These two approaches blur the sharp distinction between case-specific and statistical information and instead distinguish between information that can be directly evaluated by natural assessments in a holistic manner and information that requires logical inference before it can be used.

Two key papers in this second wave of research included the exploration of the "conjunction fallacy" (Tversky & Kahneman, 1983), which introduced the notion of low-level natural assessments, and the statement of "support theory" (Tversky & Koehler, 1994), which described how assessments of evidential support are translated into probability judgments. Although cited primarily for the memorable "Linda problem" (see Appendix), the 1983 paper further developed the perceptual model of judgmental heuristics and clarified the role of abstract rules in intuitive statistical judgment. In this and related papers (e.g. Kahneman & Tversky, 1982a; Kahneman & Miller, 1986), Kahneman, Tversky, and colleagues distinguished low-level "natural" or "routine assessments" that are relatively automatic and spontaneously evoked by the environment, from higher-level judgmental heuristics, which are typically evoked by an attempt to answer a question. The clearest candidates for natural assessments are computations of similarity, causal potency, and counterfactual surprise.

Tversky & Kahneman (1983) chose the conjunction rule of probability as a case study in the conflict between heuristic thinking and rule based reasoning. They argued that the conjunction rule of probability (no conjunction of events can be more probable than either constituent event alone) is the most basic and compelling rule of probability and is understood, in some form, by virtually every adult. Thus, in a wide variety of contexts, they examined when the conjunction rule would overcome the "conjunction fallacy," the tendency to judge a conjunction as more probable than its least likely constituent. They made conjunctions seem likely by using representativeness (the combination of events or descriptions were more similar to the target description than one or both of the constituents), availability (the combination of events or descriptions were better search cues than one or both of the constituents), and causal relatedness (the combination of events created a causal link that seemed plausible, easy to imagine, and therefore more likely than one or both of the constituent events). The real-world phenomenon that is reflected in the conjunction fallacy studies is that as predictive scenarios become more detailed, they become objectively more unlikely, yet "feel" more likely. The authors noted that many participants reported being simultaneously aware of the relevance of the conjunction rule and the feeling that the conjunction was more likely than the constituent categories. Conjunction fallacies were extremely common in between-subject designs, quite common in non-transparent within-subject designs, and only reduced by a combination of a within-subject design and a frequentistic design in which participants could see that the *number* of people with *A&B* must be less than the number of people with *A*. Except in special circumstances, then, heuristic thinking overwhelms the rules of probability, even when those rules are known and endorsed by the intuitive judges.

Note how this model is fundamentally different from the "cognitive miser" model that dominates current social cognition. Heuristic judgments are not explained as the result of too little thought due to cognitive laziness or reduced motivation, but as the result of "thinking too much" in quick and natural ways. This model of spendthrift automatic processes was termed "mental contamination" by Kahneman & Varey (1991), who related the basic processes of heuristic thinking to a wide range of perceptual, cognitive, and social examples, including the Stroop effect and motor effects on persuasion (Varey, 1991). Wilson and colleagues have also used the same term, but more narrowly, to describe the process of contamination by prior information (Wilson & Brekke, 1994).

Whereas the original heuristics and biases program focused on situations where only heuristics were evoked, and the conjunction fallacy paper examined how heuristics and rules might compete, Griffin & Tversky (1992) described how strength of impression and the statistical weight of evidence might combine. Using the anchoring and adjustment process as the "master heuristic," they suggested that people typically anchor on the strength of their impressions and then adjust (insufficiently) according to rule based arguments about sample sizes or evidential validity. In "support theory," Tversky and his colleagues (e.g. Tversky & Koehler, 1994; Rottenstreich & Tversky, 1997) further developed the notion that even when relatively high-level controlled processes are used to combine and evaluate evidence, intuitive probability judgments are heuristic rather than statistical. In this model, intuitive probability corresponds to an assessment of the relative balance of support for and against a hypothesis. The support may come from direct heuristic assessments or the combination of heuristic assessments and logical arguments. But the use of support as probability is fundamentally non-statistical in two ways. First, the combination of evidence used to derive support need not follow Bayesian rules. Both judgmental heuristics and abstract rules can be used as arguments and summarized by a simple evidence operator, rather than combined according to a Bayesian-type algorithm. Consistent with this, rated balance of support for a hypothesis (an assessment of what is available in the judge's *mind*) is virtually a perfect predictor of the judged probability of the event (the outcome in the *world*), even though the evidence available to the judge cannot be exhaustive (Koehler, 1996; Brenner, 1995). Second, because the relative support is derived according to a *specific hypothesis*, it will change when the objectively identical event is specified in different ways. For example, the judged probability of death due to homicide increases when it is "unpacked" into homicide by an acquaintance or homicide by a stranger (Rottenstreich & Tversky, 1997). Thus, from the high-level evaluation of evidence to the low-level natural assessments, the message from the heuristics and biases program is that intuitive probability judgment is based on "heuristics all the way down."

Heuristic Models and Models of Heuristics

In this section we briefly sketch a framework that we are in the process of developing to model the view of judgmental heuristics as developed in the "second wave." We distinguish five roughly sequential types of variables that progress from features of the environment, to automatic assessments, to basic heuristics, to analytic arguments, to combination heuristics (see Figure 1). Note that not all judgments will entail a mental journey through all levels; processing will stop at the basic heuristics if there is nothing available to combine with the heuristic output.

As Figure 1 shows, we distinguish between three types of automatic assessments that underlie the basic judgmental heuristics: *object based computations* such as similarity or

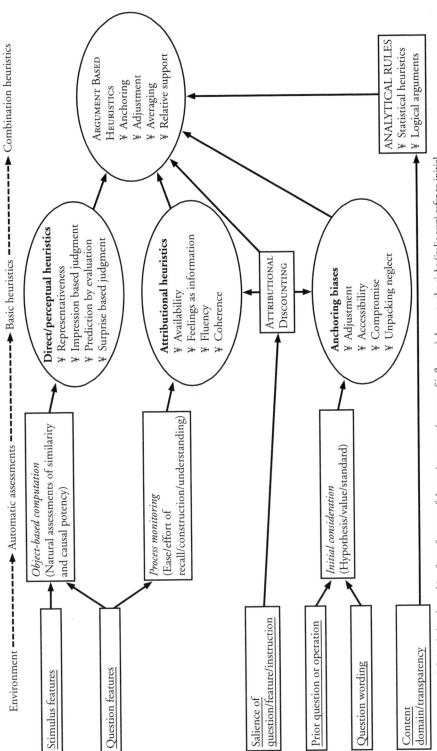

Figure 1   A sketch of a model of judgmental heuristics

Note: Boxes on left (underlined words) refer to features of the environment (sources of influence); boxes to the right (italic text) refer to initial low-level automatic processes prompted by stimulus and question; ovals (bold text) refer to semi-automatic heuristic operations that are activated to answer questions; boxes to the farther right (capital text) refer to analytic conscious processes that require cognitive effort.

causal relatedness, *process monitoring operations* that assess qualities such as mental ease versus effort, and *biased consideration* of information due to prior questions and comparisons. Object based computations tend to fire automatically in response to the stimulus field and are directly translated onto the judgment scale by "direct heuristics" such as representativeness. Process monitoring operations are triggered by specific questions, and their outputs are used by "attributional heuristics" unless discounting cues are present (e.g. Schwarz & Clore, 1988; Strack, 1992). Notable examples of attributional heuristics include the "fluency heuristic" (e.g. Kelley & Jacoby, 1998), in which people use the ease with which items are read or recognized to infer familiarity; using "feelings as information" (Schwarz & Clore, 1988) to infer general well-being from momentary mood state; and recent work on question based availability effects (Schwarz, 1998). These are all instances of attributional heuristics because the use of process monitoring can be blocked or modified if the information is attributed to the environment (i.e. familiarity due to a prior exposure, feelings due to a situational influence, and ease due to the demand to generate a certain number of examples).

A prior question or the presence of a salient value can trigger the third type of automatic assessment, the intentional or unintentional consideration of a hypothesis. In many circumstances merely considering a hypothesis leads to anchoring biases, such that the answer to a following question is contaminated by the initial question or suggestion (Wilson, Houston, Etling, & Brekke, 1996). Note that modern conceptions of anchoring (e.g. Kahneman, 1992) describe it as a bias rather than a heuristic because the initial consideration of a value or hypothesis is rarely *chosen* to serve as an aid in answering the following question. Anchoring effects can be discounted using external cues, but only under very special circumstances (Mussweiler & Strack, 1999).

The final set of heuristics, those involved in evidence combination and evaluation, receives holistic impression based input from the direct heuristics and attributional heuristics, and combines them with whatever rule based or analytic information is salient. These "higher" level heuristic processes operate on consciously represented propositions, combining impressions and rule based arguments, and operate through "inferential" or "argument based" heuristics such as anchoring and adjustment and averaging. Notable rule based arguments include the "statistical heuristics" identified by Nisbett and colleagues (e.g. Nisbett, Krantz, Jepson, & Kunda, 1983); these are simple but abstract rules of thumb such as "you can't learn much from a single experience – it may have been a fluke." Statistical heuristics are most likely to be used in contexts (such as gambling or sports) where statistical or sampling considerations are most salient. The term "inferential heuristics" indicates that even statistical principles are treated as arguments rather than as computational guidelines, except when statistical theory is formally invoked to force the judge to follow optimal algorithmic rules.

According to this model, heuristic processes can be arranged along a continuum ranging from purely impression-based (and the result of purely automatic processes) to purely argument-based (and the result of purely controlled processes). A rough ordering of heuristic processes runs from direct evaluation of impression strength (where the impression *is* the judgment, as in the Tom W. problem), to prediction by evaluation (where the impression is translated into an output scale of judgment, as in non-regressive prediction based on an interview), to anchoring and adjustment via biased accessibility (where a preliminary comparison primes a biased set of evidence that gives rise to a biased judgment: see chapter 11, this volume), to anchoring and adjustment via biased combination (where an existing, perhaps irrelevant, value is adjusted according to an impression), to attributional discounting (where the impression is "checked" for relevance and unbiasedness: Strack, 1992), to argument evaluation (where specific rules or arguments are consciously considered). The extent to which impressions versus arguments are used depends primarily on the transparency of the problem and secondarily on the resources and motivation of the judge. That is, for highly opaque problems such as the "social judgment" problems favored by Kahneman and Tversky, only impression based (perceptual) heuristic processes will be used, regardless of whether cognitive effort and motivation are high or low.

Although our model of heuristics includes automatic processes (natural assessments), conditionally automatic processes (process monitoring that is triggered by attention to particular questions), and controlled processes (attributional inferences and rules of reasoning), it provides a very different perspective than current dual-processing models of social cognition. Dual-process models build on the cognitive miser metaphor by postulating that people typically use low-effort strategies to process information and make decisions, especially when their cognitive resources are strained, but when highly motivated and/or involved, people are capable of using qualitatively different high-effort strategies. In the heuristic–systematic model of persuasion (e.g. Chaiken, Liberman, & Eagly, 1989), for example, depending on motivation, involvement, and cognitive resources, people respond to persuasive messages either with heuristic processing or with systematic processing. Heuristic processing consists of using "if . . . then" rules that operate only on the "shallow" surface structure of the information presented, such as "If it's a credible source, accept the message"; systematic processing consists of deeper processing of the actual meaning of the message. The "stereotypes as heuristics" model (Bodenhausen, 1993) is similar, with variables such as time pressure and mood determining whether stereotypic beliefs are used to guide judgment or whether the available information is deeply processed. Note that depth of processing is simply not *relevant* to the standard heuristics and biases model; in general, the heuristics and biases model describes judgment in high motivation and high capacity contexts, where heuristic processing is dominant simply because of its direct, perceptual nature. However, we would expect the contribution of statistical rules and attributional discounting to be reduced under conditions of high cognitive load, time pressure, or low motivation (e.g. Schwarz, 1998).

According to this view, direct heuristics are not strategically employed to avoid the use of more deliberate rules of reasoning, but are unavoidable aspects of human thought. Rule-based reasoning requires that the heuristic output is "overruled" by deliberate strategies at the level of heuristic evaluation of evidence, and both the recruitment and power of rules will vary according to the context. In this account, motivation and incentives should be less effective in producing rule based thinking than content domain (e.g. strict chance set-ups versus social judgments) and problem structure. This is supported by a recent study (Stephan, 1998) on advanced business students and stock-market professionals. He found that neither incentives, nor domain specific expertise, nor need for cognition (Petty & Cacioppo, 1986) substantially weakened the effects of anchoring, the gambler's fallacy, or the conjunction fallacy. Similarly, Lerner & Tetlock (1999) concluded that the extra effort and motivation induced by accountability serve to increase bias as commonly as to diminish bias. Note that violations of rationality due to ideological and emotional influences are not inconsistent with the heuristics and biases approach, but are simply treated as additional sources of bias (or in some cases, as additional sources of rule based thinking).

Conclusion

In this chapter we have telescoped thirty years of ground-breaking and controversial research into only a few pages. We have been able to highlight only a small selection of the vast literature in this area, and because we have only been able to include a few research examples in the Appendix, much of the richness has been lost. Nonetheless, there is value in the sweeping historical panorama, despite the details and subtleties of the landscape that are lost to sight. The heuristics and biases approach has enriched social psychological theory and research, and in turn, social psychologists have helped enrich the heuristics and biases perspective.

Appendix: A Few Classic Demonstrations of Heuristics and Biases

1   *"Tom W.:" Representativeness, non-regressive predictability, and base rate neglect*

Tom W. is of high intelligence, although lacking in true creativity. He has a need for order and clarity, and for neat and tidy systems in which every detail finds its appropriate place. His writing is rather dull and mechanical, occasionally enlivened by somewhat corny puns and by flashes of imagination of the sci-fi type. He has a strong drive for competence. He seems to have little feel and little sympathy for other people and does not enjoy interacting with others. Self-centered, he nonetheless has a deep moral sense.

A *similarity* group ranked nine areas of graduate study in terms of "how similar is Tom W. to the typical graduate student." A *prediction* group was informed that the description was written by a high school psychologist on the basis of projective tests, and then ranked the nine areas of graduate study in terms of "the likelihood that Tom W. is now a graduate student in each of these fields. " A *base-rate* group estimated the percentage of graduate students in each field without reading the description.

Results: across the nine graduate fields (e.g. engineering, social sciences, business administration), the judged likelihood correlated .97 with ranked similarity, but − .65 with estimated base rate (Kahneman & Tversky, 1973).

2   *"Jack:" Representativeness and base rate neglect*

A panel of psychologists have interviewed and administered personality tests to 30 (70) engineers and 70 (30) lawyers. . . . You will find on your forms five descriptions, chosen at random from the 100 available descriptions. For each description, please indicate your probability that the person described is an engineer, on a scale from 0 to 100.

Jack is a 45-year-old man. He is married and has four children. He is generally conservative, careful, and ambitious. He shows no interest in political and social issues and spends most of his free time on his many hobbies which include home carpentry, sailing, and mathematical puzzles.

Results: when given no information about the individual, respondents predicted the base rate likelihood (either 30 percent or 70 percent depending on condition). Respondents typically gave a 80–90 percent probability that Jack was an engineer, regardless of whether they were presented with the 30 percent base rate or 70 percent base rate conditions (Kahneman & Tversky, 1973). This holds true even when respondents sample the description from an urn, and estimate the base rates for themselves (Griffin & Buehler, 1999).

3 *"Replicating a study:" Representativeness and sample size neglect*

Suppose you have run an experiment on 20 Ss, and have obtained a significant result which confirms your theory (z = 2.23, p < .05, two-tailed). You now have cause to run an additional group of 10 Ss. What do you think the probability is that the results will be significant, by a one-tailed test, separately for this group?

Results: expert mathematical psychologists estimated a median probability of .85 that the replication would be "significantly" successful. In fact, the normative value is slightly less than .50 (Tversky & Kahneman, 1971). This is presumably because people expect a sample to be overly "representative" of the population, and so underestimate sampling variability.

4 *"Blue cab–green cab:" Causal vs. incidental base rates*

A cab was involved in a hit and run accident at night. Two cab companies, the Green and the Blue, operate in the city. You are given the following data:

(a)   85 percent of the cabs in the city are Green and 15 percent are Blue (or)
(a′)   Although the two companies are roughly equal in size, 85 percent of cab accidents in the city involve Green cabs and 15 percent involve Blue cabs.
(b)   A witness identified the cab as Blue. The court tested the reliability of the witness under the same circumstances that existed on the night of the accident and concluded that the witness correctly identified each one of the two colors 80 percent of the time and failed 20 percent of the time.

What is the probability that the cab involved in the accident was Blue rather than Green?

Results: when the "incidental" base rates are presented, as in (a), the median and modal answers are .80, demonstrating base rate neglect. When the "causal" version is presented, as in (a′), the median answer was .60, demonstrating an effect of the base rates (Tversky & Kahneman, 1982). This difference presumably occurred because the causal base rate, implying a certain level of carelessness or accident proneness, provided the Green (but not the Blue) cab company with a "causal disposition" to have accidents (Kahneman & Varey, 1991).

5   *"Linda:" Representativeness, the conjunction fallacy and the neglect of set inclusion (extensionality)*

Linda is 31 years old, single, outspoken, and very bright. She majored in philosophy. As a student, she was deeply concerned with issues of discrimination and social justice, and also participated in an antinuclear demonstration.
    Please rank the following statements by their probability.

    Linda is a bank teller.
    Linda is a bank teller and is active in the feminist movement.

    Results: when only two alternatives were presented, making the problem "transparent" to those who knew the conjunction rule of probability, only statistically naive students rated the conjunction as more probable than the simple event. However, when the two key phrases are embedded in a set of eight targets, even statistically sophisticated students showed a massive conjunction effect (85 percent rated the conjunction more probable; Tversky & Kahneman, 1982, 1983).

6   *"Invasion:" Causality, the conjunction fallacy, and scenario-based prediction*

Please evaluate the probability of (either):

    A complete suspension of diplomatic relations between the USA and the Soviet Union, sometime in 1983. (or)
    A Russian invasion of Poland, and a complete suspension of diplomatic relations between the USA and the Soviet Union, sometime in 1983.

    Results: professional analysts at a forecasting conference rated the second (conjunctive) version as significantly more probable (0.47 percent) than the first (simple event) version (0.14 percent) (Tversky & Kahneman, 1983).

7   *"Heart attacks:" Frequency, representativeness, and the conjunction fallacy*

A health survey was conducted in a sample of 100 adult males in British Columbia, of all ages and occupations. Please give us your best estimate of the following values:

    How many of the 100 participants have had one or more heart attacks?
    How many of the 100 participants both are over 55 years old and have had one or more heart attacks?

Results: only 25 percent of the students surveyed in this frequentist version judged that the second (conjunctive) category was more numerous compared to about 65 percent surveyed in a percentage version. Asking participants to estimate the number of men over 55 years old in the sample further reduced the incidence of the conjunction fallacy to 11 percent (Tversky & Kahneman, 1983).

References

Adams, J. K., & Adams P. A. (1961). Realism in confidence judgments. *Psychological Review, 68*, 33–45.

Ajzen, I. (1977). Intuitive theories of events and the effects of base-rate information on prediction. *Journal of Personality and Social Psychology, 35*, 303–314.

Anderson, N. H. (1996). Cognitive algebra versus representativeness heuristic. *Behavioral and Brain Sciences, 19*, 17.

Asch, S. E. (1952). *Social psychology*. New York: Prentice-Hall.

Bar-Hillel, M. (1979). The role of sample size in sample evaluation. *Organizational Behavior and Human Decision Processes, 24*, 245–257.

Bar-Hillel, M., & Neter, E. (1993). How alike is it versus how likely is it: A disjunction fallacy in probability judgments. *Journal of Personality and Social Psychology, 65*, 1119–1131.

Barone, D. F., Maddux, J. E., & Snyder, C. E. (1997). *Social cognitive psychology*. New York: Plenum Press.

Bellhouse, D. R., & Franklin, J. (1997). The language of chance. *International Statistical Review, 65*, 73–85.

Bodenhausen, G.V. (1993). Emotions, arousal, and stereotypic judgments: A heuristic model of affect and stereotyping. In D. M. Mackie & D. L. Hamilton (Eds.), *Affect, cognition, and stereotyping*. San Diego: Academic Press.

Brenner, L. A. (1995). A stochastic model of the calibration of subjective probabilities. Unpublished doctoral dissertation, Stanford University.

Brenner, L. A., Koehler, D. J., Liberman, V., & Tversky, A. (1996). Overconfidence in probability and frequency judgments: A critical examination. *Organizational Behavior and Human Decision Processes, 65*, 212–219.

Camerer, C. (1987). Do biases in probability judgment matter in markets? Experimental evidence. *The American Economic Review, 77*, 981–998.

Campbell, D. T., & Kenny, D. A. (1999). Primer on regression artifacts. New York: Guilford.

Chaiken, S., Liberman, A., & Eagly, A. H. (1989). Heuristic and systematic processing within and beyond the persuasion context. In J. S. Uleman & J. A. Bargh (Eds.), *Unintended thought* (pp. 215–252). New York: Guilford Press.

Christensen-Szalanski, J. J. J., & Beach, L. R. (1984). The citation bias: Fad and fashion in the judgment and decision literature. *American Psychologist, 39*, 75–78.

Cohen, J. (1960). *Chance, skill, and luck*. Baltimore: Penguin Books.

Cohen, J. (1972). *Psychological probability*. London: George Allen.

Cohen, J., & Hansel, C. E. M. (1956). *Risk and gambling*. New York: Philosophical Library.

Cohen, L. J. (1981). Can human irrationality be experimentally demonstrated? *Behavioral and Brain Sciences, 4*, 317–370.

Cohen, M. S. (1993). The naturalistic basis of decision biases. In G. A. Klein, J. Orasanu, R. Calderwood, & C. E. Zsambok (Eds.), *Decision making in action: Models and methods* (pp. 51–102). Norwood, NJ: Ablex.

Cosmides, L., & Tooby, J. (1996). Are humans good intuitive statisticians after all? Rethinking some conclusions from the literature on judgment and uncertainty. *Cognition, 58*, 1–73.

Dawes, R. M., Mirels, H. L., Gold, E., & Doahue, E. (1993). Equating inverse probabilities in implicit personality judgments. *Psychological Science, 4*, 396–400.

De Finetti, B. (1970). Logical foundations and measurement of subjective probability. *Acta Psychologica, 34,* 129–145.

Dougherty, M., Gettys, C., & Ogden, E. (1999). MINERVA–DM: A memory processes model for judgments of likelihood. *Psychological Review, 106,* 180–209.

Edwards, W. (1968). Conservatism in human information processing. In B. Kleinmuntz (Ed.), *Formal representation of human judgment* (pp. 17–52). New York: Wiley.

Fiedler, K. (1996). Explaining and simulating judgment biases as an aggregation phenomenon in probabilistic, multiple-cue environments. *Psychological Review, 103,* 193–214.

Fischoff, B., & Bar-Hillel, M. (1984). Focusing techniques: a shortcut to improving probability judgments? *Organizational Behavior and Human Decision Processes, 34,* 175–194.

Fischoff, B., & Beyth-Marom, R. (1988). Hypothesis evaluation from a Bayesian perspective. *Psychological Review, 90,* 239–260.

Gigerenzer, G. (1991). How to make cognitive illusions disappear: Beyond heuristics and biases. *European Review of Social Psychology, 2,* 83–115.

Gigerenzer, G. (1994). Why the distinction between single-event probabilities and frequencies is important for psychology (and vice versa). In G. Wright & P. Ayton (Eds.), *Subjective probability* (pp. 129–161). New York, Wiley.

Gigerenzer, G. (1996). On narrow norms and vague heuristics: A reply to Kahneman and Tversky. *Psychological Review, 103,* 592–596.

Gigerenzer, G. (1998). Ecological intelligence: An adaptation for frequencies. In D. Dellarosa Cummins & C. Allen (Eds.), *The evolution of mind.* New York: Oxford University Press.

Gigerenzer, G., & Murray, D. J. (1987). *Cognition as intuitive statistics.* Hillsdale, NJ: Lawrence Erlbaum.

Gigerenzer, G., Hell, W., & Blank, H. (1988). Presentation and content: The use of base rates as a continuous variable. *Journal of Experimental Psychology: Human Perception and Performance, 14,* 513–525.

Gigerenzer, G., Hoffrage, U., & Kleinbölting, H. (1991). Probabilistic mental models: A Brunswikian theory of confidence. *Psychological Review, 98,* 506–528.

Gilovich, T., & Savitsky, K. (1999). Like goes with like: The role of representativeness in everyday beliefs. In T. Gilovich, D. Griffin, & D. Kahneman (Eds.), *The psychology of judgment: Heuristics and biases.* New York: Cambridge University Press.

Grether, D. M. (1992). Testing Bayes rule and the representativeness heuristic: Some experimental evidence. *Journal of Economic Behavior and Organizations, 17,* 31–57.

Griffin, D. W., & Buehler, R. (1999). Frequency, probability, and prediction: Easy solutions to cognitive illusions? *Cognitive Psychology, 38,* 48–78.

Griffin, D. W., & Ross, L. (1991). Subjective construal, social inference and human misunderstanding. In M. P. Zanna (Ed.), *Advances in experimental social psychology* Vol. 21. New York: Academic Press.

Griffin, D., & Tversky, A. (1992). The weighing of evidence and the determinants of confidence. *Cognitive Psychology, 24,* 411–435.

Griffin, D. W., & Varey, C. A. (1999). *Frequency, probability, and aggregation.* Unpublished manuscript, University of Sussex.

Heath, L., Bryant, F. B., Edwar, J., Fugres-Bakazar, J., Henderson-King, E., Posavacs, E., & Tinsdale, R. S. (Eds.) (1994) *Social psychological applications to social issues, III: Applications of heuristics and biases to social issues.* Chicago: Loyola University Press

Jones, S. K., Jones, K. T., & Frisch, D. (1995). Biases of probability assessment: A comparison of frequency and single-case judgments. *Organizational Behavior and Human Decision Processes 61,* 109–122.

Kahneman, D. (1992). Reference points, anchors, norms, and mixed feelings. *Organizational Behavior and Human Decision Processes, 51,* 296–312.

Kahneman, D. (1998). Rationality, utility, and the mind. Lionel Robbins Memorial Lecture, London School of Economics.

Kahneman, D., & Miller, D. T. (1986). Norm theory: Comparing reality to its alternatives. *Psychological Review, 93,* 136–153.

Kahneman, D., & Tversky, A. (1972). Subjective probability: a judgement of representativeness. *Cognitive Psychology, 3*, 430–454.

Kahneman, D., & Tversky, A. (1973). On the psychology of prediction. *Psychological Review, 80*, 237–251.

Kahneman, D., & Tversky, A. (1979). Intuitive prediction: Biases and corrective procedures. *TIMS Studies in Management Science, 12*, 313–327.

Kahneman, D., & Tversky, A. (1982a). The simulation heuristic. In D. Kahneman, P. Slovic, & A. Tversky (Eds.), *Judgment under uncertainty: Heuristics and biases* (pp. 201–210). Cambridge, UK: Cambridge University Press.

Kahneman, D., & Tversky, A. (1982b). Variants of uncertainty. In D. Kahneman, P. Slovic, & A. Tversky (Eds.), *Judgment under uncertainty: Heuristics and biases* (pp. 509–520). Cambridge, UK: Cambridge University Press.

Kahneman, D., & Tversky, A. (1982c). On the study of statistical intuitions. *Cognition, 11*, 123–141.

Kahneman, D., & Tversky, A. (1996). On the reality of cognitive illusions. *Psychological Review, 103*, 582–591.

Kahneman, D., & Varey, C. A. (1990). Propensities and counterfactuals: The loser that almost won. *Journal of Personality and Social Psychology, 59*, 1101–1110.

Kahneman, D., & Varey, C. A. (1991). Mental contamination. Paper presented at the annual meeting of the Society for Experimental Social Psychology, Buffalo.

Kahneman, D., Slovic, P., & Tversky, A. (Eds.), *Judgment under uncertainty: Heuristics and biases.* New York: Cambridge University Press.

Kelley, C. M., & Jacoby, L. L. (1998). Subjective reports and process dissociation: Fluency, knowing, and feeling. *Acta Psychologica, 98*, 127–140.

Keynes, J. M. (1921). *A treatise on probability.* London: MacMillan.

Kleiter, G. D., Krebs, M., Doherty, M. E., Garavan, H., Chadwick, R., & Brake, G. (1997). Do subjects understand base rates? *Organizational Behavior and Human Decision Processes, 72*, 25–61.

Koehler, D. J. (1996). A strength model of probability judgments for tournaments. *Organizational Behavior and Human Decision Processes, 66*, 16–21.

Koehler, D. J., Brenner, L., & Griffin, D. (1999). The calibration of probabilities in theory and practice. Unpublished manuscript, University of Waterloo, Waterloo, Ontario.

Koehler, J. J. (1996). The base rate fallacy reconsidered: Descriptive, normative, and methodological challenges. *Behavioral and Brain Sciences, 19*, 1–53.

Lerner, J. S., & Tetlock, P. E. (1999). Accounting for the effects of accountability. *Psychological Bulletin, 125*, 255–275.

Lichtenstein, S., Fischhoff, B., & Phillips, L. (1982). Calibration of probabilities: The state of the art to 1980. In D. Kahneman & A. Tversky (Eds.), *Judgment under uncertainty: Heuristics and biases* (pp. 306–334). Cambridge, UK: Cambridge University Press.

Macchi, L. (1995). Pragmatic aspects of the base-rate fallacy. *Quarterly Journal of Experimental Psychology, 48A*, 188–207.

May, R. M. (1986). Inferences, subjective probability, and frequency of correct answers: A cognitive approach to the overconfidence phenomenon. In B. Brehmer, H. Jungermann, P. Lourens, & A. Sevoaan (Eds.), *New directions in research on decision making* (pp. 175–189). Amsterdam: North-Holland.

Meehl, P. E. (1954). *Clinical versus statistical prediction.* Minneapolis: University of Minnesota Press.

Meehl, P. E., & Rosen, A. (1955). Antecedent probability and the efficacy of psychometric signs, patterns or cutting scores. *Psychological Bulletin, 52*, 194–216.

Moser, D. V. (1992). Does memory affect judgment? Self-generated versus recall memory measures. *Journal of Personality and Social Psychology, 62*, 555–563.

Mussweiler, T., & Strack, F. (1999). Hypothesis-consistent testing and semantic priming in the anchoring paradigm: A selective accessibility model. *Journal of Experimental Social Psychology, 35*, 136–164.

Nisbett, R. E., & Ross, L. (1980). *Human inference: Strategies and shortcomings of social judgment.* Englewood Cliffs, NJ: Prentice-Hall.

Nisbett, R. E., Krantz, D. H., Jepson, C., & Kunda, Z. (1983) The use of statistical heuristics in everyday inductive reasoning. *Psychological Review, 90,* 339–363.

Northcraft, G. B., & Neale, M. A. (1987). Experts, amateurs, and real estate. An anchoring-and-adjustment perspective on property pricing decisions. *Organizational Behavior and Human Decision Processes, 39,* 84–97.

Novemsky, N., & Kronzon, S. (1999). How are base-rates used, when they are used: A comparison of additive and Bayesian models of base-rate use. *Journal of Behavioral Decision Making, 12,* 55–69.

Oskamp, S. (1965). Overconfidence in case-study judgments. *Journal of Clinical and Consulting Psychology, 29,* 261–265.

Payne, J. W., Bettman, J. R., & Johnson, E. J. (1993). *The adaptive decision maker.* New York: Cambridge University Press.

Pollack, I., & Decker, I. (1958). Confidence ratings, message reception, and the receiver operating characteristic. *Journal of the Acoustical Society of America, 30,* 286–292.

Quattrone, G. A. (1982). Overattribution and unit formation: When behavior engulfs the person. *Journal of Personality and Social Psychology, 42,* 593–607.

Quattrone, G. A. (1984). Anchors aweigh. Unpublished manuscript, Department of Psychology, Stanford University.

Reeves, T., & Lockhart, R. S. (1993). Distributional versus singular approaches to probability and errors in probabilistic reasoning. *Journal of Experimental Psychology: General, 122,* 207–226.

Robins, R. W., & Craik, K. H. (1993). Is there a citation bias in the judgment and decision making literature? *Organizational Behavior and Human Decision Processes, 54,* 225–244.

Ross, M., & Sicoly, F. (1979). Egocentric biases in availability and attribution. *Journal of Personality and Social Psychology, 37,* 322–336.

Rottenstreich, Y., & Tversky, A. (1997). Unpacking, repacking, and anchoring: Advances in support theory. *Psychological Review, 104,* 406–415.

Savage, L. J. (1954). *The foundations of statistics.* New York: Wiley.

Schwarz, N. (1998). Accessible content and accessibility experience: The interplay of declarative and experiential information in judgment. *Personality and Social Psychological Review, 2,* 87–99.

Schwarz, N., & Clore, G. L. (1988). How do I feel about it? Informative functions of affective states. In K. Fielder & J. Forgas (Eds.), *Affect, cognition, and social behavior* (pp. 44–62). Toronto: Hogrefe.

Schwarz, N., & Sudman, N. (1992). *Context effects in social and psychological research.* New York: Springer-Verlag.

Schwarz, N., Strack, F., Hilton, D., & Naderer, G. (1991). Base rates, representativeness, and the logic of conversation: The contextual relevance of "irrelevant" information. *Social Cognition, 9,* 67–84.

Schwarz, N., Bless, H., Strack, F., Klumpp, G., Rittenauer-Schatka, H., & Simons, A. (1991). Ease of retrieval as information: Another look at the availability heuristic. *Journal of Personality and Social Psychology, 61,* 195–202.

Shedler, J., & Manis, M. (1986). Can the availability heuristic explain vividness effects? *Journal of Personality and Social Psychology, 51,* 26–36.

Sherman, S. J., & Corty, E. (1984). Cognitive heuristics. In R. S. Wyer & T. Srull (Eds.), *Handbook of Social Cognition,* Vo. I. Hillsdale: Erlbaum.

Sherman, S. J., Cialdini, R. B., Schwartzman, D. F., & Reynolds, K. D. (1985). Imagining can heighten or lower the perceived likelihood of contracting a disease: The mediating effects of ease of imagery. *Personality and Social Psychology Bulletin, 11,* 118–127.

Simon, H. (1957). *Models of man: Social and rational.* New York: Wiley.

Sloman, S. A. (1996). The empirical case for two systems of reasoning. *Psychological Bulletin, 119,* 3–22.

Slovic, P., Fischhoff, B., & Lichtenstein, S. (1982). Facts versus fears: Understanding perceived risk. In D. Kahneman, P. Slovic, & A. Tversky (Eds.), *Judgment under uncertainty: Heuristics and biases* (pp. 463–489). Cambridge, New York: Cambridge University Press.

Smith, E. (1996). What do connectionism and social psychology have to offer each other? *Journal of Personality and Social Psychology, 70,* 893–912.

Stephan, S. (1998). Anchoring and adjustment in economic forecasts. Paper presented at the ESRC conference on Judgmental Inputs to the Forecasting Process, London.

Strack, F. (1992). The different routes to social judgments: Experiential versus informational strategies. In L. L. Martin & A. Tesser (Eds.), *The construction of social judgments* (pp. 249–276). Hillsdale, NJ: Erlbaum.

Strack, F., & Mussweiler, T. (1997). Explaining the enigmatic anchoring effect: Mechanisms of selective accessibility. *Journal of Personality and Social Psychology, 73*, 437–446.

Thomas, G., Vallone, R., & Tversky, A. (1985). The hot hand in basketball: On the misperception of random sequences. *Cognitive Psychology, 17*, 295–314.

Tversky, A., & Kahneman, D. (1971). The belief in the "law of small numbers." *Psychological Bulletin, 76*, 105–110.

Tversky, A., & Kahneman, D. (1973). Availability: A heuristic for judging frequency and probability. *Cognitive Psychology, 5*, 207–232.

Tversky, A., & Kahneman, D. (1982). Evidential impact of base rates. In D. Kahneman, P. Slovic, & A. Tversky (Eds.), *Judgment under uncertainty: Heuristics and biases*. New York: Cambridge University Press.

Tversky, A., & Kahneman, D. (1983). Extensional versus intuitive reasoning: The conjunction fallacy in probability judgment. *Psychological Review, 90*, 293–315.

Tversky, A., & Koehler, D. J. (1994). Support theory: A nonextensional representation of subjective probability. *Psychological Review, 101*, 547–567.

Varey, C. A. (1991). Crosstalk and contamination in cognitive processes. Unpublished dissertation, University of California, Berkeley.

Wilson, T. D., & Brekke, N. (1994). Mental contamination and mental correction: Unwanted influences on judgments and evaluations. *Psychological Bulletin, 116*, 117–142.

Wilson, T. D., Houston, C., Etling, K. M., and Brekke, N. (1996). A new look at anchoring effects: Basic anchoring and its antecedents. *Journal of Experimental Psychology: General, 4*, 387–402.

Yates, J. F., & Estin, P. A. (1999). Understanding and improving "people judgment." Manuscript submitted for publication. University of Michigan, Ann Arbor.

Yates, J. F., Lee, J., Shinotsuka, H., Patalano, A. L., & Sieck, W. R. (1998). Cross-cultural variations in probability judgment accuracy: Beyond general knowledge overconfidence? *Organizational Behavior & Human Decision Processes, 74*, 89–117.

Zukier, H., & Pepitone, A. (1984). Social roles and strategies in prediction: Some determinants of the use of base-rate information. *Journal of Personality and Social Psychology, 47*, 349–360.

Chapter Eleven

How the Mind Moves: Knowledge Accessibility and the Fine-tuning of the Cognitive System

Leonard L. Martin, Fritz Strack, and Diederik A. Stapel

Two monks were arguing about the temple flag as it waved in the wind. One monk believed that it was the wind that was moving. The other believed that it was the flag that was moving. Despite considerable debate, neither monk was able to convince the other of his point of view. Finally, the Master arrived, and the two monks broached the issue with him. The Master noted, "It is not the wind that moves. It is not the flag that moves. It is your mind that moves." At this, the two monks were enlightened.

Zen parable

This chapter is about the mind moving. More precisely, it explores the general proposition that social perception is not a neutral registration of objective reality, but an active construction that is influenced by concurrent processes of thought, memory, feeling, and motivation (cf. Bruner, 1992; Martin & Tesser, 1992). In elaborating upon this proposition, we discuss some of the early research (e.g. Bruner, 1957) that demonstrated the constructive nature of social perception. Then, we discuss the theoretical advancements made with regard to this issue in some of the early social cognition research (e.g. Higgins, Rholes, & Jones, 1977). Finally, we discuss some recent findings that have helped to refine our understanding of the constructive nature of social perception. The chapter ends by suggesting that the processes involved in social perception are more complex than was reflected in the earlier research. Individuals are not cognitive misers who use whatever information is on the top of their heads. Rather, they are cognitive optimizers. They have access to a variety of different types of information and they use these selectively in the service of a range of processing objectives and motivations.

A Classic Example of the Mind Moving

The 1951 football game between Princeton and Dartmouth was an especially rough one. A large number of penalties were called, and Princeton's star quarterback had to leave the game because of a broken nose and a concussion. Although students from both schools agreed that the game had been rough, they did not agree on exactly how rough it had been, and on which team had started the rough play. To gain a better understanding of this lack of agreement, Hastorf & Cantril (1954) conducted a study. First, they assessed the attitudes of some Princeton and Dartmouth students toward the game. Then, they showed these students a film of the game, and asked them some questions about the film they had just seen.

Not surprisingly, the attitudes of the students at the two schools differed. The Princeton students generally thought that the game was rough and dirty, and that the Dartmouth team had started the dirty play. The Dartmouth students also thought that the game was rough, but they were more likely than the Princeton students to see the game as fair and to see both sides as to blame for the rough play. More interestingly, though, for present purposes, was the way in which these differences in attitudes reflected themselves in the two groups' perceptions of the game film. Although students from the two schools watched the exact same film, the Princeton students saw the Dartmouth team make many more infractions than their own team, whereas the Dartmouth students saw both teams make about the same number of infractions, with their team making half the number of infractions attributed to it by the Princeton students.

In explaining these different perceptions in the face of the same objective information, Hastorf & Cantril (1954) proposed that "there is no such 'thing' as a 'game' existing 'out there' in its own right which people merely 'observe'" (ibid., p. 133). Rather, "an 'occurrence' on the football field or in any other social situation . . . becomes an 'event' only when the happening . . . reactivates learned significances already registered in what we have called a person's assumptive form-world" (ibid., p. 132). Stated differently, the objective reality of the game resulted in different subjective experiences because students from the two schools viewed the game using different previously stored knowledge structures, which, in turn, led them to attend selectively to different occurrences and to interpret the same occurrences in different ways.

This general conclusion has been supported in a variety of subsequent studies (for a review, see Martin & Tesser, 1992). What these studies have shown is that individuals do not make judgments (e.g. How much do I like my mother?) by retrieving a single invariant score from memory (e.g. my evaluation of my mother). Rather, individuals construct their judgments as needed, using previously stored information as well as information from the current context (e.g. my evaluation of my mother given that I am in a bad mood and that she just grounded me). Thus, judgment of the same stimulus by the same individual can differ depending on the context in which the judgment is rendered.

It should be noted, though, that from a constructivist perspective, these context dependent changes in judgment do not reflect an inability on the part of the perceiver to retrieve his or her *real* evaluation. Rather, context dependency is assumed to be a natural by-product of the processes by which evaluations are rendered. After all, a person who is home alone *should* have a different interpretation of the sound of a window breaking than a person who is home with children playing in the next room. The children provide a ready explanation for the window breaking, but who is breaking the window if the person is home alone? From a constructivist perspective, this example does not reflect different interpretations of the same stimulus. It reflects different interpretations of different stimuli. This is because, from a constructivist perspective, the stimulus is not "the sound of a window breaking." It is "the sound of a window breaking while I am home alone" or "the sound of a window breaking while children are playing in the next room." People respond contextually. By the same reasoning, an individual who has had a heart attack *should* interpret a chest pain differently than a person who has recently eaten a bowl of extra spicy jambalaya. The stimulus is not "a chest pain," but "a chest pain in the light of my memory of what has just happened" (i.e. heart attack versus jambalaya). The more general point is that individuals bring aspects of themselves (e.g. memories, motivations), as well as aspects of the current context, to bear in evaluating any given target stimulus. This is what is meant by saying that social judgments are constructed.

It is important to point out that in assuming that social judgments are constructed, one need not assume that such judgments are arbitrary or that there are no general rules. In fact, quite the opposite is true. There are general rules, and these rules are beginning to be understood. For example, research has shown that social judgments depend, in predictable ways, not only on the particular knowledge that individuals bring to the judgment, but also on factors such as the relation between this knowledge and the target stimulus, the timing of the activation of the knowledge, the method by which the knowledge was activated, and the perceiver's motivational state. These are the kinds of issues we examine in this chapter. We begin by briefly reviewing some of the early research that emphasized the constructive nature of perception.

The Role of Accessibility: Some Initial Considerations

The research that is most often cited as the prime influence on the study of knowledge accessibility in social psychology today is that of Bruner (1957). The goal of this early work was to show that individuals do not respond to a direct copy of the objective world, but to their categorization of the objective world (Bruner, 1992). This is the case, according to Bruner, because most information is relatively meaningless until it has been identified with a mental category. A dark tubular object, for example, would elicit little reaction in an individual until he or she had categorized the object as a snake or a stick. Perhaps the main contribution of Bruner's early work was highlighting some of the factors that make individuals more likely to interpret information in terms of one category as opposed to another.

According to Bruner, the central factor in determining which category individuals use to interpret information was the relative accessibility of the relevant categories (i.e. the ease with which the individual could retrieve the category). The greater the accessibility of a category the less the stimulus input needed for categorization to occur in terms of that category, the wider the range of input characteristics accepted as belonging in the category, and the more likely it was that categories that provide a better or equally good fit for the input would be masked. Category accessibility was assumed to be a function of the expectancies of the perceiver and the search requirements imposed by the perceiver's processing objectives. Thus, a dark tubular shape would be more likely to be categorized as a stick if the perceiver were walking through the snow looking for firewood than if he or she were wading through a jungle stream looking for zoo specimens.

In sum, Bruner proposed that stimulus information was generic until it had been interpreted in terms of a mental category. When individuals have more than one category they could use to interpret information, they use the one whose accessibility had been increased by their motivational state (e.g. hunger) and/or their expectancy (e.g. being in an orchard).

The Classic Social Cognition View: Accessibility X Applicability

Current interest in category accessibility in social psychology can be traced to a study by Higgins, Rholes, & Jones (1977). The initial interest of these investigators was in understanding the way in which the accessibility of trait concepts could influence a person's interpretation of behaviors as he or she attempted to form an impression of another person. The assumption was that the implications of any given behavior (e.g. skydiving) would depend on the concept (e.g. adventurous versus reckless) used to interpret that behavior. They also assumed, following Bruner, that when behavioral information was interpretable in terms of more than one concept, individuals would use the one that was most accessible. Unlike Bruner, however, Higgins, et al. did not emphasize the role of motivation and expectancy in heightening accessibility. Rather, they emphasized the role of previous activation, which they referred to as priming. They proposed that if a concept had been recently used for almost any processing whatsoever (i.e. if it had been primed), then this concept would be more accessible and thus be more likely to be used to interpret subsequently encountered target information – provided the concepts were applicable to that information. Applicability, in this case, referred to denotative similarity.

To test this passive priming X applicability hypothesis, Higgins, Rholes, & Jones (1977) had participants perform in what, ostensibly, were two unrelated experiments. In the first, participants had to name the color of ink in which various words were written. Then, in the second, participants were presented with a description of a person and were asked to form an impression of this person. This description contained behaviors that were open to several interpretations. For example, the target person was described as being "well aware of his ability to do things well." This behavior could be interpreted as either self-confident or conceited.

To prime different concepts, Higgins, et al. embedded different words in the color naming task. For some participants, these words were positive and were descriptively relevant to interpreting the target's behaviors (e.g. self-confident). For other participants, the words were negative yet descriptively relevant to interpreting the target's behaviors (e.g. conceited). Other participants were exposed to words that were either positive (e.g. neat) or negative (e.g. listless) but that were not relevant to interpreting the target's behaviors. Consistent with the passive priming X applicability hypothesis, participants rendered more favorable impressions of the target following activation of the positive compared to the negative concepts, but only when the concepts were denotatively related to the information in the target paragraph.

These results were consistent with Bruner's formulation in the sense that participants used the most accessible, relevant category to interpret target information. The results extended Bruner's formulation, however, by emphasizing the passive possibilities in priming. In the Higgins, Rholes, & Jones (1977) study, participants used the relevant primed concepts even though they were not motivated to do so, had no reason to expect the primed concepts more than their alternatives, and the primed concepts were relevant to the target information only by virtue of their denotative relatedness. It seemed that merely activating a trait concept was sufficient to increase the likelihood that the concept would be used to interpret information to which it was denotatively related.

This view of priming was fleshed out in a number of subsequent studies. Srull & Wyer (1980), for example, demonstrated that primed concepts are used to interpret target information at the time this information is initially encoded. Priming a concept after participants have interpreted the target information has no effect at all on the subsequently formed impression (see also Wyer & Martin, 1986). Higgins, Bargh, & Lombardi (1985) suggested that if a concept is primed frequently enough it can become chronically accessible. When this occurs, the concept is likely to be used in interpreting information even when the concept has not been recently primed by contextual stimuli. Moreover, mental operations performed on information related to a chronically accessible concept may be performed automatically (Bargh & Thein, 1985). Finally, priming effects are not restricted to mental operations or to pencil-and-paper measures. Priming can also affect overt behavior. Priming the concept *aggressive*, for example, can lead individuals to behave more aggressively (Berkowitz, 1993; Carver, Ganellen, Froming, & Chambers, 1983).

Taken together, these early studies painted a very clear and coherent picture of concept priming. The picture was so compelling in fact that a large number of researchers were motivated to use this conceptualization to help make sense of phenomena in a wide variety of areas. For example, researchers applied this passive priming X applicability view of accessibility to stereotypes (Devine, 1989), attitudes (Fazio, Sanbonmatsu, Powell, & Kardes, 1986), goals (Bargh, 1997), relationships (Baldwin, Carrell, & Lopez, 1990), death concerns (Greenberg, Simon, Pyszczynski, & Solomon, 1992), aggression (Berkowitz, 1993), the answering of questions on surveys (Sudman, Bradburn, & Schwarz, 1996), explanations (Wilson, Hodges, & LaFleur, 1995), and anchoring effects (Strack & Mussweiler, 1997).

The advantage of this explosion in research was that the field gained a great deal of knowledge about priming as well as about phenomena that seemed to have priming as one of its underlying components. The flip side of this explosion, of course, was that researchers also became aware of areas of incompleteness. As Smith, Steward, & Buttram (1992, p. 759) noted, "the familiar conceptualization that categorization is a function of Accessibility X Fit now appears to be inadequate." In the remainder of this chapter, we address these inadequacies. More specifically, we present research showing that (a) concept applicability involves more than the denotative fit between the concept and the target; (b) information can be accessible and applicable yet not used to interpret information; (c) increasing the accessibility of different types of knowledge structures (e.g. traits versus exemplars) produces different effects; and (d) priming can do more than increase the likelihood that a concept will be used to interpret information. We also examine the role of awareness, accuracy motivation, and correction processes in determining the use of primed information.

Non-motivational Qualifications of the Passive Accessibility X Fit View

When distilled to its essence, the passive accessibility X fit view can be seen to consist of five elements: *trait concepts* are used to *interpret* information to the extent that these concepts are *accessible* and *applicable* with applicability being defined in terms of the *denotative similarity* between the primed concept and the target information. In the following sections, we describe qualifications on each of these five elements.

Beyond denotative applicability

As just noted, the initial work on concept accessibility (e.g. Higgins, Rholes, & Jones, 1977) emphasized the denotative fit between the primed knowledge and the target information as a determinant of the likelihood that a primed concept would be used to categorize target information. Subsequent research has suggested, however, that denotative relatedness may not be the only determinant of concept applicability. Stapel & Koomen (1999), for example, had participants form an impression of an ambiguously described target person. As in Higgins, Rholes, & Jones (1977), some participants were primed with concepts that were either denotatively applicable or inapplicable to interpreting the subsequent target information, and that had moderate evaluative connotations (e.g. applicable: assured versus arrogant; inapplicable: unrealistic versus idealistic). With these primes, the results would presumably parallel those of Higgins, Rholes, & Jones (1977). Participants would assimilate their impressions of the target behavior toward the implications of the applicable concepts but not the inapplicable ones.

What would happen, though, if participants were primed with concepts that had no clear denotative implications but that had relatively broad and strong evaluative implications (good versus bad)? Similarly, what would happen if participants were primed with concepts that were denotatively inapplicable to the target information but that had relatively narrow but strong evaluative implications (aggressive versus sweet)? Stapel and Koomen hypothesized that in these cases participants might use the strong evaluative implications to help disambiguate the target information, even though the denotative applicability is low. If so, then participants should assimilate their impression of the target toward the implications of the primed information even though this information is not denotatively relevant to interpreting the target behaviors.

The results of Stapel & Koomen (1999) supported this reasoning. They found that participants' impressions were assimilated toward the implications of the primed concepts not only when these were denotatively applicable, but also when they were generally evaluative with no clear denotative implications and when they were denotatively inapplicable but possessing strong evaluative implications. It is only when the primed concepts were denotatively inapplicable and both relatively narrow and evaluatively weak that participants' impressions did not assimilate toward the implications of the primed concepts (e.g. Higgins, Rholes, & Jones, 1977). What these results suggest is that denotative applicability is not a necessary ingredient of concept applicability (see also Martin, 1986; Martin, Seta, & Crelia, 1990). In some cases, strong connotation may be sufficient to allow target information to be interpreted in a manner consistent with the implications of primed information, even when this information consists of denotatively inapplicable concepts.

Different types of representations produce different effects

Another feature of the passive priming X applicability view was its emphasis on the use of trait concepts to interpret target information. We know, however, that individuals possess knowledge structures other than trait concepts. These include exemplars, scripts, and procedural knowledge. Subsequent research has begun to explore the effects of priming these knowledge structures. The question is whether effects like those obtained with the priming of trait concepts would also be obtained if one of these other knowledge structures were activated. There is some reason to think not.

Consider, for example, that trait concepts represent diffuse semantic information that can be applicable to a wide range of behaviors. The trait "aggressive," for example, could be used to characterize behaviors as diverse as shoving, verbal abuse, and cutting someone off in traffic. An exemplar, on the other hand, reflects knowledge about a specific person (e.g. Hitler), and this may be less likely to generalize to thoughts about another specific person. An exemplar, however, might make a useful standard of comparison (e.g. Herr, Sherman, & Fazio, 1983). For example, almost anyone would appear less aggressive compared to Hitler. It is possible, therefore, that with the same degree of denotative applicability, priming a trait concept may give rise to assimilation, whereas priming an exemplar may give rise to contrast. These hypotheses were tested, and supported, by Stapel, Koomen, & Van der Pligt (1997). They found that participants primed with trait concepts assimilated their impressions of the target toward the implications of the primed concepts, whereas participants primed with exemplars contrasted their target impressions away from the implications of these exemplars.

If it is true that exemplar priming produces contrast because exemplars make good standards of comparison, then it should be possible to eliminate exemplar-induced contrast by undermining the comparison relevance of the exemplar. This hypothesis was tested by Stapel, Koomen, & Van der Pligt (1997). They primed participants with hostility-related but *non-person* exemplars such as "Shark" and "Tiger" or "Puppy" and "Bunny." These exemplars reflect distinct entities associated with varying degrees of hostility, making them, at least in principle, good candidates for standards of comparison. The exemplars also represent animals, however, and animals are generally not relevant standards of comparison when judging humans. As a result, priming of these non-person exemplars may not lead to contrast of the target person.

These exemplars, however, are associated with different levels of hostility. So, it is possible that when this hostility-related information is made accessible, the result may be assimilation. That is, participants primed with non-person exemplars may assimilate their impression of an ambiguously described hostile/friendly target person toward the implications of the primed (non-relevant) hostile or friendly exemplars. These were in fact the results obtained by Stapel, Koomen, & Van der Pligt (1997).

In sum, it appears that with the same degree of denotative applicability, priming a trait concept or a non-relevant exemplar is likely to give rise to assimilation, whereas priming a relevant exemplar is likely to give rise to contrast. The former two knowledge structures appear to influence participants' interpretations of the target information, whereas the latter one seems to facilitate a comparison process.

Different effects of primes at encoding versus output

If traits and exemplars play different roles in the impression formation process (i.e. interpretation versus comparison), then priming these different knowledge structures at different times should produce different effects. Recall Srull & Wyer's (1980) finding that priming trait concepts before participants had interpreted the target information resulted in assimilation, whereas priming these same concepts after participants had interpreted the target information had no effect on participants' judgments (see also Wyer & Martin, 1986). What these results suggest is that primed traits are used to disambiguate target information at the time participants first encode that information. When are exemplars used? According to Stapel, Koomen, & Van der Pligt (1997), exemplars may be used as a standard of comparison either at encoding or after individuals have formed an impression and are attempting to translate it into an overt response. What this means is that priming of a trait concept is likely to produce assimilation if the priming occurs before, but not after, participants have encoded the target information, whereas the priming of an exemplar is likely to produce contrast regardless of whether it is primed before or after participants have encoded the information.

To test these ideas, Stapel, Koomen, & Van der Pligt (1997) primed participants with either trait concepts or exemplars, and this occurred either before or after participants had read the target information. In replication of Srull & Wyer (1980), they found assimilation when a trait concept was primed before but not after participants had read the target information. With the priming of exemplars, however, they found contrast regardless of whether the priming occurred before or after participants had read the target information. This pattern of results suggests that trait concepts are generally used in interpreting or disambiguating information as individuals first encode it, whereas exemplars are used as standards of comparison either as individuals are interpreting information or after they have already formed their impression.

The role of procedural knowledge

Another feature common to most early priming research was the tendency to explain priming effects in terms of what might be called structural changes in semantic knowledge. The synapse model (Higgins, et al., 1985), for example, suggested that use of a concept increases its hypothetical charge, which, in turn, made the concept more likely to be used. The bin model (Wyer & Srull, 1989) suggested that use of a concept causes that concept to get placed, metaphorically, on the top of a semantic bin in memory. Because of this placement, the concept would be encountered more quickly than a less recently used concept in any subsequent search of that bin. This, in turn, would make a recently activated concept more likely to be used. As can be seen, despite their differences, both models assumed that priming effects were the result of a change in the status of semantic information. Smith & Branscombe (1987) suggested an alternative. They proposed that at least some category accessibility effects might reflect the operation of procedural knowledge.

Procedural knowledge can be thought of as cognitive structures that represent skills or "how to" knowledge. Such knowledge can be represented hypothetically as production systems or if–then statements. These systems are selected for execution when their conditions (i.e. the "if") match the current contents of working memory or the perceptual environment. The execution of the action part of a production system (i.e. the "then") can result automatically in the performance of cognitive tasks, such as generating inferences. For example, a person may have a production system that specifies something like the following:

IF you observe one *<person> <exert power over> <another>*,
THEN interpret that behavior as hostile.

The variables (i.e. *person, exert power, another*) within the production system become instantiated with the values in a given situation. So, if an individual has practiced the production system described above, and if this individual has just observed Donald giving orders to Jamal, then the individual is likely to interpret Donald's action as hostile even though the action might simply reflect Donald's attempt to be efficient. Production systems are assumed to develop out of practice. The basic assumption is that people typically get better at doing things they do frequently.

It is interesting in this context to note that in many priming studies, the priming tasks gave participants repeated practice at interpreting behaviors in terms of a trait. For example, it was not uncommon to prime participants by asking them to construct meaningful sentences out of scrambled words (e.g. "hit he the it"). In performing this task, participants may gain practice in generating trait based interpretations (e.g. hostile) of ambiguous behavior. Could it be that practice of this interpretation procedure (rather than a change in the activation status of concept in semantic memory) was responsible for the subsequent assimilation of the target information? In other words, when presented with a target who engaged in behavior that was relatively ambiguous with regard to its level of hostility, participants may have used the interpretational procedure they had just practiced in the priming task to interpret the target behavior in terms of a hostile concept.

How can we tell if any given priming effect is the result of procedural knowledge or changes in the accessibility of semantic knowledge? According to Smith and Branscombe, the effects of procedural knowledge are more specific and longer lasting than those of semantic priming. To test these hypotheses, Smith & Branscombe (1987, Experiment 2) had participants perform a task that either allowed them to practice the procedure of interpreting behavior in terms of a concept or that increased the accessibility of semantic knowledge. In the first case, participants were asked to construct meaningful sentences from a scrambled list of words. In the second case, participants were asked to judge pairs of words (e.g. hostile–crude) in terms of whether or not the words had the same meaning. Then, either immediately following these tasks or three minutes later, participants were presented with a behavioral description that was ambiguous with regard to the trait (or procedure) that had been primed in the earlier tasks.

Consistent with the hypothesis that procedurally mediated priming effects last longer than semantically mediated priming effects, Smith and Branscombe found that when the priming task consisted of unscrambling sentences, participants' impressions assimilated toward the implications of the primed concepts in both the short and the long delay. When the priming task consisted of judging the meaning of words, participants' impressions assimilated toward the implications of the primed concepts only in the short delay condition.

In a second study, Smith and Branscombe found some evidence consistent with their second proposed distinction between procedurally mediated and semantically mediated priming effects. They found that the effects of procedural priming are more specific than those of semantic trait priming. Taken together, the results of these two studies suggest that the activation of procedural knowledge can account for at least some priming effects, and that theoretical conceptualizations of priming that focus only on the activation of semantic concepts are incomplete.

Priming does more than facilitate categorization

We have seen that information other than traits (e.g. exemplars, procedures) can be primed and that effects other than interpretation (e.g. contrast) can occur. Such results suggest that priming does more than increase the probability that individuals will use primed trait concepts to interpret behaviors. It appears, instead, that priming increases the likelihood that the primed knowledge will be used in whatever processing occurs at the time, whether this be interpretational or otherwise. This more general view of priming may be best illustrated in research showing that priming can influence quantitative judgments that do not even involve interpretation. Strack & Mussweiler (1997), for example, used priming to explain the anchoring and adjustment effect.

In one demonstration of the anchoring and adjustment effect, Tversky & Kahneman (1974) asked participants whether the percentage of African nations in the United Nations was higher or lower than 80 percent (or 20 percent). Then, they asked these same participants to estimate the actual percentage of African nations in the United Nations. Tversky and Kahneman found that participants given the high standard (e.g. 80 percent) in the comparison task provided higher estimates on the absolute judgment task than did participants given the low standard (e.g. 20 percent).

Explanations of this effect have focused on the numerical value provided as a standard in the initial comparison task. More specifically, it has been suggested (e.g. Jacowitz & Kahneman, 1995) that participants start their estimation of the absolute value at the value presented in the comparison task. Then, they adjust upward or downward (depending on the condition) until they encounter the outer limits of their acceptable range of responses.

This results in higher estimates when participants are adjusting downward than when they are adjusting upward.

Strack & Mussweiler (1997) explored the possibility that performing the initial comparison task might do more than leave a numerical standard salient. It might also prime a more general mental representation relevant to rendering the subsequent absolute judgment. Specifically, Strack and Mussweiler proposed that in performing the comparison task, participants might create a representation of the target as possessing the standard. For example, if participants were asked whether the Mississippi River is longer or shorter than 3,000 miles, they might imagine the north–south extension of the United States and use their geographic knowledge to compute the answer. If they do this using a positive test strategy (Klayman & Ha, 1987), then they are likely to bring to mind information consistent with the target possessing the value supplied in the standard. This standard-consistent information may then be consulted when participants make the subsequent absolute judgment, and it is this information that leads to the anchoring and adjustment effect.

Note that this standard-consistent information would not be brought to mind if the standard provided by the comparison task were clearly implausible (e.g. "Is the Mississippi River longer or shorter than 1 mile?"). In this case, the standard would be so clearly wrong that participants could generate an answer to the comparison question without bringing a great deal of related information to mind. If this theoretical analysis is correct, then participants should take longer to make the initial comparison judgment when a plausible rather than implausible standard is provided.

The effects of standard plausibility should be different, however, on the time it takes participants to render the absolute judgment. Because participants presented with a plausible standard would already have brought related information to mind, they should perform the absolute judgment relatively quickly. Participants presented with an implausible standard, on the other hand, will not have brought such information to mind, so they must do so when they make the absolute judgment. This could take time. This reasoning implies a crossover interaction in response times. Relative to participants who have been primed with an implausible standard, those primed with a plausible standard will take more time to make the initial comparison judgment but less time to make the subsequent absolute judgment. This crossover pattern was in fact obtained by Strack and Mussweiler.

If, as these results suggest, informational priming plays a role in (at least some) anchoring and adjustment effects, then these effects might not be seen if the primed information were inapplicable to the absolute judgment. This is because primed information is applied only to the extent it is applicable (Higgins, Rholes, & Jones, 1977; Stapel & Koomen, 1999). To test this idea, Strack and Mussweiler asked participants to render a comparison judgment (e.g. "Is the Brandenburg Gate taller or shorter than 50 (or 150) meters?") followed by an absolute judgment. The absolute judgment was either related to the information primed in the comparison task (e.g. "How tall is the Brandenburg Gate?") or it was not (e.g. "How wide is the Brandenburg Gate?"). Consistent with the priming applicability hypothesis, an anchoring and adjustment effect was observed only when the information primed in the comparison task was applicable to the absolute judgment (e.g. both judgments involved height).

Taken together, these studies suggest that at least some anchoring and adjustment effects are not due simply to participants starting from a numerical standard and then adjusting upward or downward to an insufficient degree. Rather, priming of more general, judgment relevant information seems to be involved. This primed information is not a trait concept, however, and it is not used to interpret target information. It is a mental representation of the target possessing the value primed in the standard, and it can influence subsequent quantitative judgments to the extent that it is applicable to those judgments.

Content or Phenomenology?

The studies we have discussed so far were concerned primarily with the nature of the content that had been made accessible. These studies examined the effects of priming concepts, exemplars, or procedures that varied in their applicability to the target information. In each case, the general assumption was that target judgments are affected because of the implications of the content that has been brought to mind. Note, however, that priming not only brings information to mind, it also increases the ease with which this information comes to mind. Could the subjective experience of ease of retrieval also be informative? This possibility was first raised by Tversky & Kahneman (1974) in their discussion of the availability heuristic. They suggested that individuals sometimes assess the frequency of an occurrence (e.g. words beginning with the letter k) by assessing the ease with which they can retrieve instances of that occurrence.

Schwarz, Bless, Strack, & Klumpp (1991) examined the effects of priming in a condition in which the implications of the primed content were at odds with the implications of subjective ease of retrieval. Specifically, they had participants recall either 6 or 12 instances of either assertive or submissive behaviors they had performed. Then, they had participants rate themselves in terms of how assertive–submissive they were. Participants who recalled 12 instances of the target behavior would have twice as much evidence that they possessed the target trait than participants who only recalled 6 instances. So, we might expect participants who recalled 12 instances to rate themselves higher in the direction of the recalled instances than participants who recalled only 6. This would reflect the impact of information accessibility.

On the other hand, it is more difficult to recall 12 instances than 6 instances. So, if participants used ease of retrieval to estimate frequency, then we might expect those who recalled 12 instances to rate themselves as possessing less of the trait than participants who recalled only 6 instances. If participants really were assertive (or submissive), then why would it be so hard for them to recall 12 instances in which they displayed this trait? Or so their thinking would go.

The results suggested that both accessibility and ease of retrieval were informative. When participants recalled only 6 instances, those who recalled the assertive behaviors rated themselves as more assertive than those who recalled the submissive behaviors. When participants recalled 12 instances, however, those who recalled the assertive behaviors rated themselves as less assertive than those who recalled the submissive behaviors. In short, individuals can gain information not only from what comes to mind but also from *how* that information comes to mind.

Motivated Limits on the Passive Priming X Fit View

What we have seen so far is that the familiar conceptualization of accessible, applicable trait concepts being used to interpret information can be qualified in each of its major components. Different knowledge structures activated at different times can have different effects. Note, however, that each of the qualifications we discussed were non-motivational. That is, they were based on the nature of the knowledge structure primed and/or the time at which the structures were primed. There is evidence, however, that motivational factors can also determine the nature of priming effects. We can take a trait concept with a given level of accessibility and applicability, for example, and influence the extent to which participants are likely to use that concept to interpret information by manipulating variables such as accuracy motivation (Thompson , Roman, Moskowitz, Chaiken, & Bargh, 1994) and cognitive effort (Martin, Seta, & Crelia, 1990). One implication of such findings is that a distinction needs to be maintained between a concept's accessibility and its use in interpreting information (Martin, 1986).

To the extent that a concept's accessibility and its use are distinct, it should be possible to manipulate the two orthogonally. This was accomplished by Stapel & Koomen (under review). They hypothesized that priming a concept would lead to different judgments among participants who approached the judgment task with an interpretational mindset compared to participants who approached the task with a comparison mindset. To induce an interpretational set, Stapel and Koomen presented participants with a list of different behaviors and asked the participants to describe each behavior with a single word. To induce a comparison mindset, participants were asked to compare the persons performing the behaviors to different standards (e.g. the average woman, the average student). Following this task, participants were primed with either a positive or a negative concept and asked to form an impression of a target whose behavior was relatively ambiguous with regard to the primed traits.

Consistent with the idea that priming of the same trait can have different effects on judgments of the same behavior depending on one's mindset, participants who had completed the interpretation task assimilated their impressions toward the implications of the primed concepts, whereas participants who had completed the comparison task contrasted their impressions with the implications of the primed concepts. Thus, motivational variables can influence priming effects even when the structural properties of the situation (e.g. the applicability and accessibility of the primed concepts) are held constant.

Epistemic motivation

Within social psychology, motivation has often been identified with the irrational, such as dissonance or ego-defensive biases, and it has typically been contrasted with cold, analytical, logical thinking such as that typified in attribution theory. From a general information processing perspective, however, there can also be motivations toward accuracy and analytic thinking. Moreover, these kinds of motivations can moderate the effects of concept priming.

Ford & Kruglanski (1995) and Thompson, et al. (1994), for example, found that participants with no particular incentive to be accurate while forming an impression assimilated their impression of an ambiguous target person toward the implications of the primed traits. The impressions of participants who were highly motivated to form an accurate impression, on the other hand, showed no influence of the primed concepts. Apparently, the motivation to be accurate can, at least in some cases, inoculate participants from the assimilative effects of concept priming.

In a conceptually related study, Sedikides (1990) found that the more specific motivation of communicating a particular impression can also attenuate the assimilative effects of concept priming. Participants who thought they were to communicate their impression of an ambiguously described target person to an audience that liked the target rendered more favorable impressions of the target than participants who thought they had to convey their impression to an audience that disliked the target. More importantly, for present purposes, these differences in judgment occurred even when participants were primed with concepts that were opposite in valence to the presumed attitudes of the audience. In other words, participants communicating an impression to an unfavorable audience formed a negative impression despite being primed with a positive, applicable concept. Taken together, these studies suggest that certain processing objectives (e.g. be accurate, communicate a specific impression) can override the effects of passive contextual priming.

Not all priming effects are susceptible to moderation by accuracy motivations, however. Stapel, Koomen, & Zeelenberg (1998) found that accuracy motives were less likely to overcome contrastive influences than assimilative influences. These investigators induced assimilation or contrast by priming a trait concept or an exemplar, respectively (cf. Stapel, Koomen, & Van der Pligt, 1997). Following this, they had participants form an impression of an ambiguously described target person. To manipulate accuracy motivation, half of the participants were told that the tasks they were performing were merely part of a pilot study and might possibly be used in some future study. The remaining participants were told that they should try to be as accurate as possible in their judgments. In replication of earlier work, trait priming led to assimilation among low accuracy participants, but had no effect among the high accuracy participants. Unlike earlier studies, however, exemplar priming led to contrast in both the low accuracy and the high accuracy participants. Taken together, the studies discussed in this section suggest that different motivations have different consequences for different types of knowledge accessibility effects.

Awareness of a bias

Another type of motivation that has been studied is more specific, namely, removing perceived bias from the target judgment. Note that the initial priming research (e.g. Higgins, Rholes, & Jones, 1977) emphasized the passive nature of priming. This was true, in part, because the initial studies used disguised priming tasks in the so-called "two-experiment" paradigm. These steps were taken to rule out the possibility that the results were due to demand characteristics. They were successful in doing this, but they may also have ruled out the possibility that participants would engage in other theoretically important psychological processes. As Martin (1986, p. 494) noted:

When a concept is primed very subtly, individuals may not even be aware that it has been activated in them (Bargh & Pietromonaco, 1982). Consequently, when this concept comes to mind in the subsequent impression formation task they have no reason to believe that it is anything other than their own spontaneous reaction to the target. This means that they have no reason not to use the primed concept in interpreting the target information, provided that it is consistent with the implications of that information.

The same may not hold true, however, when a concept is primed more blatantly. Under these conditions, individuals may associate the activation of the concept with their exposure to the priming stimuli rather than with the target stimulus. As a result, they may actually avoid using the primed concept to interpret the target information, as its use would appear to bias their independent evaluation of the target.

In short, a quite different set of processes may come into play when concepts are primed more blatantly, and these processes may produce quite different effects than those found in the initial priming studies. Evidence for this possibility has been obtained in a variety of studies. Strack, Schwarz, Bless, Kübler, & Wänke (1993), for example, had participants perform what they thought were a series of cognitive and perceptual tasks. In one of these tasks, participants heard a series of tones paired with words. Participants were asked to classify the tones as high or low and to write down the words. For half of the participants, the words were positive (e.g. friendship), whereas for the other half, the words were negative (e.g. dishonest). Following the tone–word task, participants were asked to form an impression of a person whose actions (e.g. stole exam questions for a desperate friend) were interpretable in terms of either the positive or the negative primed concepts.

To manipulate the blatancy of the priming stimuli, Strack, et al. (1993) had some participants perform the tone–word task and then form their impression. Other participants were asked to answer some questions about the tone–word task (e.g. how well they were able to discriminate the tones) prior to forming their impressions. The point of this questioning was to remind participants of the priming stimuli (i.e. the positive or negative words used in the tone–word task).

In replication of earlier priming studies (e.g. Higgins, Rholes, & Jones, 1997), Strack, et al. (1993) found that impressions of the target assimilated toward the primed concepts when participants were not reminded of the priming task. When participants were reminded, however, their impressions were contrasted with the implications of the primed concepts. What these results suggest is that a concept may be highly accessible and applicable to interpreting information, but if participants are aware that this concept has been primed by a non-target event (i.e. the priming stimuli), then they may not use this concept in interpreting the target information (see also Lombardi, Higgins, & Bargh, 1987). The next question, of course, is why. Why do participants avoid the use of blatantly primed concepts?

Several explanations have been offered (Lombardi, Higgins, & Bargh, 1987; Martin, 1986; Strack & Hannover, 1996; Wegener & Petty, 1995; Wilson & Brekke, 1994). Despite their differences, these explanations generally agree that, in some way or another, participants sense a threat to the genuineness of their evaluation of the target and (in some form or another) they take steps to remove the perceived bias from their evaluation of the target. So, now we can ask, what is the nature of the bias that is sensed? How do people correct for this bias? One possible answer to both questions entails naive theories, that is, beliefs about the effects of a context on a target.

Theory Based Correction

According to Wilson & Brekke (1994), individuals generally have weak introspective abilities (see also Nisbett & Wilson, 1977). One implication of this weakness is that individuals may generally fail to appreciate the influence of contextual factors on their judgments. In other words, individuals may not be able to discriminate reliably between biased and unbiased judgments merely by turning inward. So, if they are to remove the bias from their judgments, then they must look elsewhere for guidance.

One source of guidance may be naive theories. Consider, for example, a person who is asked to rate a moderately attractive face after having just rated some extremely attractive faces. In this context, the moderately attractive face may appear to the person to be unattractive (i.e. a contrast effect). Although this is a biased judgment, the person may not realize it. The assessment of the face as unattractive may feel like the person's genuine assessment of the target. Suppose, however, that the person retrieved a theory that suggested that ratings of moderately attractive faces could be lowered by previously rating more attractive faces. Armed with this knowledge, the person would be in a position to correct for the biasing influence of the context. In this way, individuals' naive theories could potentially alert them to biases that they might miss if they relied solely on introspection.

It appears, further, that naive theories may help people to remove the perceived bias from their judgments. Specifically, it has been suggested (Strack, 1992; Strack & Hannover, 1996; Wegener & Petty, 1995; Wilson & Brekke, 1994) that when people believe that their judgments are being biased, they consult their naive theories to determine the extent and direction of the bias. Then, they adjust their target ratings in a direction that is opposite to the theorized bias and to an extent that is commensurate with the theorized amount of bias. As Strack (1992, p. 269) put it, "People can apply norms, rules, or theories to adjust their response for the effect of the pernicious influence. . . . It is important, however, that judges have such rules at the ready; otherwise, they would not know how to alter their responses."

Evidence suggestive of a role for naive theories in the correction of contextual bias has been obtained in a series of studies by Wegener and Petty (for a review, see Wegener & Petty, 1997). They began by providing participants with a series of context–target configurations and asking participants to indicate what effect the context might have on ratings of the target. In this way, Wegener and Petty were able to find sets of stimuli for which participants held theories of either assimilation or contrast. For example, most participants believed that their ratings of a product would be biased toward desirability if the product were endorsed by attractive as compared to unattractive women (i.e. an assimilation effect). Most also believed that ratings of moderately attractive women would be biased away from ratings of extremely attractive or extremely unattractive women (i.e. a contrast effect).

After establishing that there were sets of stimuli for which participants held theories of either assimilation or contrast, Wegener & Petty (1995) had participants actually make their ratings of these stimuli. Half of the participants were asked without further elaboration to rate the context and target items, whereas half were given an explicit warning not to let their judgments of the context influence their judgments of the target. This warning informed participants of a possible bias, but it did not specify the direction or magnitude of that bias. It was assumed that this information would be gleaned by participants from their naive theories. The results were consistent with this hypothesis.

When participants simply rated the context and target stimuli, their target judgments reflected assimilation when participants rated stimuli they had earlier theorized would lead to assimilation, but reflected contrast when they rated stimuli they had earlier theorized would lead to contrast. When participants had been instructed to remove the contextual bias, however, their judgments showed the opposite pattern. There was assimilation when participants rated stimuli they had earlier theorized would lead to contrast, but contrast when they had rated stimuli they had earlier theorized would lead to assimilation. This pattern is consistent with the hypothesis that when individuals are alerted to a potential bias in their judgments, they consult their naive theories in order to understand the nature of the contextual influence, and then they adjust their judgments in a direction opposite to the theorized influence.

Target Based Correction

According to the theory based models of correction, individuals cannot correct for a contextual influence without having some sort of understanding of the nature of that influence. Although this assumption is plausible, it is not entirely clear that the knowledge individuals need to correct their judgments has to come from a theory that specifies the context–target relation. As Stapel, Martin, & Schwarz (1998) noted, the blatant warning used in the Wegener and Petty studies may have allowed participants to by-pass their use of theories. The warning (i.e. "Please don't let your ratings of the target be influenced by your rating of the context") essentially told participants that the contextual stimuli were likely to be biasing their target judgments. As a result, participants did not have to consult their theories to determine if the context were biasing their judgments. They already had reason to believe it was. So, a blatant warning may allow participants to by-pass the first step of theory-guided correction (i.e. use theory to detect bias).

Of course, even if participants do not use their theories to detect the contextual bias, then they may still consult their theories when correcting for the bias. After all, participants still need to know the direction and extent of the influence if they are to correct for it. Stapel, Martin, & Schwarz (1998) hypothesized, however, that participants may even be able to correct without recourse to a theory that specifies the relation between the context and the target. If participants experience an inclination to evaluate the target favorably and are told that there may be a bias in their judgments, then participants may infer that an unbiased judgment would be one that was less favorable. Conversely, if they experience an inclination to evaluate the target unfavorably and are told that there may be a bias in their judgments, then participants may infer that an unbiased judgment would be one that was more favorable. In this way, participants' evaluative inclinations in the context of a blatant warning may allow participants to adjust their judgments without consulting theories to assess bias or guide correction.

Stapel, Martin, & Schwarz (1998) addressed this issue by examining the nature of correction induced by blatant and subtle warnings. All participants were asked to rate some target stimuli in a context that typically produced contrast (e.g. they rated the desirability of the weather in Midwestern US cities after having rated the desirability of the weather in vacation spots). One group of participants was asked merely to rate the context and target stimuli. Two other groups rated these same stimuli, but received a warning between their ratings of the context and the targets. For some participants, this warning was the blatant one used by Wegener and Petty. Specifically, these participants were instructed to "Make sure that your perceptions of the weather in the vacation spots above do not influence your ratings of the following places." The remaining participants received a conditional warning. They read "When you feel there is something that may have an unwanted influence on your ratings, please try to adjust for that influence." The first warning implies that there is a bias; the second allows participants to determine on their own whether or not there is a bias.

The next step was to manipulate the amount of bias participants perceived to be coming from the context. This was accomplished by having half of the participants rate the context and target stimuli on the same dimension, but having half rate the context on one dimension and the targets on another dimension (e.g. job satisfaction verus desirability of weather). The potential biasing influence of the context should be more obvious when the stimuli are considered on the same dimension than when they are considered on different dimensions (cf. Brown, 1953). So, if participants correct only when they perceive a bias, then they are likely to correct only when they rate the context and target on the same dimension.

The results indicated a clear difference between the effects of the subtle and blatant warnings. When participants received no warning, their judgments reflected contrast regardless of whether they rated the targets on the same dimension as the contextual stimuli or on different dimensions. This suggests that the uncorrected effect of this context was contrast. What this also means is that if the warned participants correct for the contextual influence, then their judgments will shift toward assimilation. When participants were given the conditional warning, such a shift toward assimilation was seen, but only when the perceived influence of the context was obvious.

Judgments of participants who had been blatantly warned, on the other hand, reflected a correction toward assimilation regardless of the dimension on which the contextual stimuli had been judged. In other words, the blatantly warned participants adjusted their responses regardless of whether the level of bias coming from the contextual stimuli was salient or non-salient. More importantly, the blatantly warned participants adjusted their target evaluations even in a condition in which the conditionally warned participants did not perceive any bias. If the conditionally warned participants did not detect a bias coming from this context, then what were the blatantly warned participants correcting for?

These data raise the possibility that correction may take place without reference to a theory that specifies the context–target influence. Participants may simply consider their target judgment in the context of a blatant warning. If they experience an inclination to render a favorable judgment, then they might make their judgments less positive. If they experience an inclination to render an unfavorable judgment, then they might make their judgments more positive.

Summary and Conclusions

The early priming research depicted the processes involved in priming as rather simple. It was generally assumed that individuals used whatever concepts were accessible and applicable with applicability being defined in terms of denotative similarity. Subsequent research, however, has qualified this view. In fact, it appears that this view of priming holds only under the conditions used in the initial studies. When changes, even relatively small ones, are made to the procedures used in the early studies, quite different results are obtained. The recent studies highlight the sophisticated and conditional nature of priming effects. These effects depend on the type of knowledge structure activated, the timing of the activation, and the motivation level and mental set of the participants.

Although social judgments that have been influenced by priming are not always accurate in an objective sense, this should not take away from the function of priming, which is to fine-tune individuals' processing to the specific judgment task at hand. It is in the nature of judgment that individuals bring aspects of themselves (memories, processing objectives) to bear and these aspects influence the individuals' judgments in predictable ways. We should continue to explore the regularities governing the construction of social judgments and we should give the social perceiver his or her due as sophisticated processors of social information.

References

Baldwin, M. W., Carrell, S. E., & Lopez, D. F. (1990). Priming relationship schemas: My advisor and the pope are watching me from the back of my mind. *Journal of Experimental Social Psychology, 26*, 435–454.

Bargh, J. A. (1997). The automaticity of everyday life. In R. S. Wyer, Jr. (Ed.), *Advances in social cognition* Vol. 10 (pp. 1–61). Mahwah, NJ: Lawrence Erlbaum Associates.

Bargh, J. A., & Pietromonaco, P. (1982). Automatic information processing and social perception: The influence of trait information presented outside of conscious awareness on impression formation. *Journal of Personality and Social Psychology, 43*, 437–449.

Bargh, J. A., & Thein, R. D. (1985). Individual construct accessibility, person memory, and the recall–judgment link: The case of information overload. *Journal of Personality and Social Psychology, 49*, 1129–1146.

Berkowitz, L. (1993). Towards a general theory of anger and emotional aggression: Implications of the cognitive–neoassociationistic perspective for the analysis of anger and other emotions. In R. S. Wyer, Jr., & T. K. Srull (Eds.), *Advances in social cognition* Vol. 6 (pp. 1–46). Hillsdale, NJ: Lawrence Erlbaum Associates.

Brown, D. R. (1953). Stimulus–similarity and the anchoring of subjective scales. *American Journal of Psychology, 66*, 199–214.

Bruner, J. S. (1957). On perceptual readiness. *Psychological Review*.

Bruner, J. S. (1992). Another look at New Look 1. *American Psychologist, 47*, 780–783.

Carver, C. S., Ganellen, R. J., Froming, W. J., & Chambers, W. (1983). Modelling: An analysis in terms of category accessibility. *Journal of Experimental Social Psychology, 16*, 779–804.

Devine, P. G. (1989). Stereotypes and prejudice: Their automatic and controlled components. *Journal of Personality and Social Psychology, 56*, 5–18.

Fazio, R. H., Sanbonmatsu, D. M., Powell, M. C., & Kardes, F. R. (1986). On the automatic activation of attitudes. *Journal of Personality and Social Psychology, 50*, 229–238.

Ford, T. E., & Kruglanski, A. W. (1995). Effects of epistemic motivations on the use of accessible constructs in social judgment. *Personality and Social Psychology Bulletin, 21,* 950–962.

Greenberg, J., Simon, L., Pyszczynski, T., & Solomon, S. (1992). Terror management and tolerance: Does mortality salience always intensify negative reactions to others who threaten one's worldview? *Journal of Personality and Social Psychology, 63,* 212–220.

Hastorf, A. H., & Cantril, H. (1954). They saw a game: A case study. *Journal of Abnormal and Social Psychology, 49,* 129–14.

Herr, P. M., Sherman, S. J., & Fazio, R. H. (1983). On the consequences of priming: Assimilation and contrast effects. *Journal of Experimental Social Psychology, 19,* 323–340.

Higgins, E. T., Bargh, J. A., & Lombardi, W. (1985). Nature of priming effects on categorization. *Journal of Experimental Psychology: Learning, Memory, and Cognition, 11,* 59–69.

Higgins, E. T., Rholes, W. S., & Jones, C. R. (1977). Category accessibility and impression formation. *Journal of Experimental Social Psychology, 13,* 141–154.

Jacowitz, K. E., & Kahneman, D. (1995). Measures of anchoring in estimation tasks. *Personality and Social Psychology Bulletin, 21,* 1161–1166.

Klayman, J., & Ha, Y. W. (1987). Confirmation, disconfirmation, and information in hypotheses testing. *Psychological Review, 94,* 211–228.

Lombardi, W. J., Higgins, E. T., & Bargh, J. A. (1987). The role of consciousness in priming effects on categorization: Assimilation versus contrast as a function of awareness of the priming task. *Personality and Social Psychology Bulletin, 13,* 411–429.

Martin, L. L. (1986). Set/reset: The use and disuse of concepts in impression formation. *Journal of Personality and Social Psychology, 51,* 493–504.

Martin, L. L., & Achee, J. W. (1992). Beyond accessibility: The role of processing objectives in judgment. In L. L. Martin & A. Tesser (Eds.), *The construction of social judgments* (pp. 195–216). Hillsdale, NJ: Erlbaum.

Martin, L. L., & Tesser, A. (1992). *The construction of social judgment.* Hillsdale, NJ: Lawrence Erlbaum Associates.

Martin, L. L., Seta, J. J., & Crelia, R. (1990). Assimilation and contrast as a function of people's willingness and ability to expend effort in forming an impression. *Journal of Personality and Social Psychology, 59,* 27–37.

Nisbett, R. E., & Wilson, T. D. (1977). Telling more than we can know: Verbal reports on mental processes. *Psychological Review, 84,* 231–259.

Schwarz, N., Bless, H., Strack, F., & Klumpp. G. (1991). Ease of retrieval as information: Another look at the availability heuristic. *Journal of Personality and Social Psychology, 61,* 195–202.

Sedikides, C. (1990). Effects of fortuitously activated constructs versus activated communication goals on person impressions. *Journal of Personality and Social Psychology, 58,* 397–408.

Smith, E. R., & Branscombe, N. R. (1987). Procedurally mediated social inferences: The case of category accessibility effects. *Journal of Experimental Social Psychology, 23,* 361–382.

Smith, E. R., Steward, T. L., & Buttram, R. T. (1992). Inferring a trait from a behavior has long-term, highly specific effects. *Journal of Personality and Social Psychology, 62,* 753–759.

Srull, T. K., & Wyer, R. S. (1979). The role of category accessibility in the interpretation of information about persons: Some determinants and implications. *Journal of Personality and Social Psychology, 37,* 1660–1672.

Srull, T. K., & Wyer, R. S. (1980). Category accessibility and social perception: Some implications for the study of person memory and interpersonal judgments. *Journal of Personality and Social Psychology, 38,* 842–856.

Stapel, D. A., & Koomen, W. (1997). Using primed exemplars during impression formation: Interpretation or comparison? *European Journal of Social Psychology, 27,* 357–367.

Stapel, D. A., & Koomen, W. (in press). How far do we go beyond the information given? The impact of knowledge activation on interpretation and inferences. *Journal of Personality and Social Psychology.*

Stapel, D. A., & Koomen, W. (under review). The impact of interpretation versus comparison goals on knowledge accessibility effects. Manuscript under review.

Stapel, D. A., Koomen, W., & Van der Pligt, J. (1997). Categories of category accessibility: The impact of trait concept versus exemplar priming on person judgments. *Journal of Experimental Social Psychology, 33*, 47–76.

Stapel, D. A., Koomen, W., & Zeelenberg, M.. (1998). The impact of accuracy motivation in interpretation, comparison, and correction processes: Accuracy X knowledge accessibility effects. *Journal of Personality and Social Psychology, 74*, 878–898.

Stapel, D. A., Martin, L. L., & Schwarz, N. (1998). The smell of bias: What instigates correction processes in social judgments? *Personality and Social Psychology Bulletin, 24*, 797–806.

Strack, F. (1992). The different routes to social judgments: Experiential vs. informational strategies. In L. L. Martin & A. Tesser (Eds.), *The construction of social judgment* (pp. 249–275). Hillsdale: Erlbaum.

Strack, F., & Hannover, B. (1996). Awareness of influence as a precondition for implementing correctional goals. In P. M. Gollwitzer & J. A. Bargh (Eds.), *The psychology of action: Linking cognition and motivation to behavior* (pp. 579–596). New York: Guilford Press.

Strack, F., & Mussweiler, T. (1997). Explaining the enigmatic anchoring effect: Mechanisms of selective accessibility. *Journal of Personality and Social Psychology, 73*, 437–446.

Strack, F., Schwarz, N., Bless, H., Kübler, A., & Wänke, M. (1993). Awareness of the influence as a determinant of assimilation vs. contrast. *European Journal of Experimental Social Psychology, 23*, 53–62.

Sudman, S., Bradburn, N. M., & Schwarz, N. (1996). *Thinking about answers: The application of cognitive processes to survey methodology*. San Francisco: Jossey-Bass Publishers.

Thompson, E. P., Roman, R. J., Moskowitz, G. B., Chaiken, S., & Bargh, J. A. (1994). Accuracy motivation attenuates covert priming: The systematic reprocessing of social information. *Journal of Personality and Social Psychology, 66*, 474–489.

Tversky, A., & Kahneman, D. (1974). Judgment under uncertainty: Heuristics and biases. *Science, 185*, 1124–1131.

Wegener, D. T., & Petty, R. E. (1995). Flexible correction processes in social judgment: The role of naive theories in corrections for perceived bias. *Journal of Personality and Social Psychology, 68*, 36–51.

Wegener, D. T., & Petty, R. E. (1997). The flexible correction model: The role of naive theories of bias in bias correction. In M. P. Zanna (Ed.), *Advances in experimental social psychology* Vol. 29 (pp. 141–208). San Diego: Academic Press.

Wilson, T. D., & Brekke, N. (1994). Mental contamination and mental correction: Unwanted influences on judgments and evaluations. *Psychological Bulletin, 116*, 117–142.

Wilson, T. D., Hodges, S. D., & LaFleur, S. J. (1995). Effects of introspecting about reasons: Inferring attitudes from accessible thoughts. *Journal of Personality and Social Psychology, 69*, 16–28.

Wyer, R. S., Jr., & Martin, L. L. (1986). Person memory: The role of traits, group stereotypes, and specific behaviors in the cognitive representation of persons. *Journal of Personality and Social Psychology, 50*, 661–675.

Chapter Twelve

Standards, Expectancies, and Social Comparison

Monica Biernat and Laura S. Billings

Judgment and experience are relative phenomena; they occur against the backdrop of comparative frames of reference. When we say "I'm happy" or "she's very bright" or "that building is ugly," we mean happy, bright, or ugly relative to some standard of comparison. A number of researchers have introduced this theme and have described the wide variety of sources or types of standards that may be used to define and describe our everyday encounters with the world. Beginning with research on such diverse areas as psychophysics (Helson, 1947; Parducci, 1956; Stevens, 1957; Volkmann, 1951) and the self (James, 1890/1948), psychologists have long emphasized the relativity of all forms of intra- and interpersonal experience.

In this chapter, we will focus primarily on the role of judgment standards and expectations in evaluations of others and the self. Two key themes guide this work. One is the constructivist nature of comparisons and judgment – individuals pick and choose their reference points, drawing from a broad knowledge base as well as the specifics of a situation or context to subjectively define evaluative standards (Kahneman & Miller, 1986; Miller & Prentice, 1996). The second theme is that the outcome of a comparative process can be viewed in terms of the basic principles of assimilation and contrast – a target of evaluation (e.g. another person, a group, the self) is either pulled toward or differentiated from a comparative frame. For example, in impression formation, one might judge an individual consistently with primed trait adjectives (Higgins, Rholes, and Jones, 1977); in stereotyping, group perceptions may be contrasted from each other (accentuation effects; Tajfel, 1969, 1978); in self-evaluation, one may experience inspiration from (assimilation to) a "superstar" (Lockwood & Kunda, 1997), and self-relevant health behavior may also be affected by assimilative comparison to a favorably viewed "risky" health image (Gibbons & Gerrard, 1995, 1997).

Before going further, some clarification of the terms *standards* and *expectancies* is in order. Higgins (1990) provides a useful definition of the first construct: "a standard is a criterion or rule established by experience, desires, or authority for the measure of quantity and extent, or quality and value" (ibid., p. 302). Standards are assumed to take a variety of forms. For example, Higgins (1990; Higgins, Strauman, & Klein, 1986) describes three general types: (1) *factual standards* (beliefs about the attributes of others), (2) *guides* ("criteria of excellence or acceptability"; Higgins, Strauman, & Klein, 1986, p. 30), and (3) *possibilities* (standards regarding what will, could, or might exist).

Expectancies have also been broadly defined as "beliefs about a future state of affairs . . . subjective probabilities linking the future with an outcome at some level of probability ranging from merely possible to virtually certain" (Olson, Roese, & Zanna, 1996, p. 211). This definition incorporates the notion of anticipation more than evaluation or measurement, but expectancies are nonetheless similar to standards in that they are mental constructs, based on both memory and current experience, that provide the backdrop against which outcomes and events are experienced. Thus, a social stereotype can be viewed as an expectation about the likely attributes of a group of people (e.g. Hamilton & Sherman, 1994), or as a judgment standard against which individual group members are evaluated (Biernat, Manis, & Nelson, 1991; Biernat & Manis, 1994). Similarly, one's goals and aspirations can be conceptualized in terms of perceived probability or expectation of future success (e.g. Atkinson, 1957) or as future (possible) self-standards (Higgins, 1990; Markus & Nurius, 1986).

Furthermore, standards and expectancies can be either met or not met, confirmed or disconfirmed, with predictable consequences. For example, the violation of an expectation is likely to produce negative affect, deeper (more systematic) subsequent processing, attributional search, reduced certainty, and a more explicit knowledge or awareness of the expectation (Olson, Roese, & Zanna, 1996). Unmet standards are likely to produce at least some of the same effects (e.g. Stangor & McMillan, 1992; Bettencourt, Dill, Greathouse, Charlton, & Mulholland, 1997; Biernat, Vescio, & Billings, 1999, on stereotypes; Higgins, 1987, on self-evaluation). For these reasons, we will often use the terms "standards" and "expectancies" interchangeably. As will become apparent in our discussion, however, standards are often viewed as conducive to contrast effects (e.g. a target's differences from the standard are noted as a result of comparison), whereas expectations are typically viewed as conducive to assimilation (e.g. a target is perceived in line with an expectation). The similarity again lies in the fact that targets and events are perceived/judged/evaluated with reference to these constructs.

Coverage of the literature on standards and expectancies could fill this entire volume. For example, the role of these constructs can be seen in theories of achievement motivation, self-efficacy, and other expectancy–value models, as well as in the large literature on self-fulfilling prophecy. Even restricting focus to standards/expectancies that are used to judge *others*, one can identify at least four general sources: (1) contextual cues (e.g. priming), (2) the self, (3) specific individuals or exemplars, and (4) group stereotypes. Similarly, standards used to judge the *self* include both internal referents or guides (for purposes of evaluation and self-regulation), as well as other people. Because a number of these topics receive coverage elsewhere in this volume, we have chosen to focus our attention on just two areas in which standards and expectancies are relevant: social stereotyping (using category-defined expectations to judge others) and social comparison (using others as referents to judge the self). It may seem odd to include these apparently disparate research areas in a single chapter. However, both serve to illustrate the basic processes of intrapersonal construal and judgmental assimilation and contrast that are triggered by expectations and standards.

Judging Others: Stereotyping

Stereotypes fall most clearly under Higgins' (1990) category of "factual" standards, although they may also function as "guides." For example, they may not only represent our beliefs about what groups *are* like, but also our prescriptions regarding what group members *should* be like (e.g. Hogg & Abrams, 1988; Rabbie & Horwitz, 1988; Wilder & Shapiro, 1991). In this sense, stereotypes can be viewed as norms that include both descriptive and prescriptive components (Miller & Prentice, 1996).

The study of group stereotypes and their effects on judgments of individuals is a long-standing and still very active tradition. The main theme of this body of work is that to the extent that we possess stereotypes – sets of "beliefs about the personal attributes of a group of people" (Ashmore & Del Boca, 1981, p. 16) – we use them to structure our impressions of individual members of those groups. In fact, some evidence suggests that stereotypes may be activated automatically, upon merely encountering an individual who belongs to a relevant social category (e.g. Devine, 1989; Perdue & Gurtman, 1990; cf. Gilbert & Hixon, 1991; Lepore & Brown, 1997; Locke, MacLeod, & Walker, 1994). In this sense, they are highly available standards or expectations, ready for use in evaluating others. Stereotypes are generally assumed to function as expectations or interpretive frames toward which judgments of individual targets are drawn (assimilated). For example, we tend to perceive and judge individual women, Blacks, soccer hooligans, and hairdressers in accordance with our group stereotypes (see Brewer, 1996; Fiske, 1998; Hamilton & Sherman, 1994; Hilton & Von Hippel, 1996; Stangor & Lange, 1994; Von Hippel, Sekaquaptewa, & Vargas, 1995, for recent reviews), particularly when category information is available prior to encoding of other information about the target (e.g. Bodenhausen, 1988).

Stereotyping models

Several models of the stereotyping process have been offered, and the most prominent of these are Brewer's (1988) dual process model and Fiske & Neuberg's (1990) continuum model of impression formation. Both assume that upon encountering a stimulus person, an automatic identification or categorization process occurs (e.g. a target is identified as a Black, elderly female). Assuming at least some minimal relevance, this is followed by additional processing that generally takes the form of confirmatory categorization. At this categorization stage, the target is compared to the expectation or standard of the social category (e.g. to what extent does this individual match the features of the category "female?"). If fit is good – and it frequently will be, for "once a particular category has been activated, the threshold for identifying a match between the category prototype and incoming stimulus information is lowered" (Brewer, 1988, p. 18; see also Higgins & King, 1981) – perceptions and judgments of the target will be category based, or assimilated to the group stereotype.

However, if fit is not good, the person is recategorized (in Fiske and Neuberg's model) or individuated (in Brewer's model). Both processes involve seeking a better category or subtype with which to characterize the target (for Fiske & Neuberg (1990) an exemplar or even the self-concept can serve as a category at this stage). It is only after failure at the recategorization stage that perceivers turn to individuated or piecemeal processing of the target in Fiske & Neuberg's (1990) model; in this sense, "perceivers give priority to category-based processes" (ibid., p. 13).

More recently, Kunda & Thagard (1996) offered a parallel constraint satisfaction model of impression formation as an alternative to the serial models of Brewer (1988) and Fiske & Neuberg (1990). Kunda and Thagard's model suggests that category information and associated stereotypes comprise just one node in a connectionist network of information that perceivers may possess about a target person. Other nodes, for example, may include observed behavior or attributes of the target as well as myriad associations to those attributes. The nodes of the network are activated and adjusted in parallel, constraining each other's meaning, until the network settles, at which point an overall impression of the target emerges. Although this model gives no special status to stereotypes, it has been used to account for a number of findings supporting the notion that judgments are often assimilated to social stereotypes. For example, the fact that a construction worker who "hit someone" is judged to be more aggressive than a housewife who "hit someone" may derive from the fact that the construction worker node has stronger links to the trait "aggressive" and the behavior of "punching" than does the housewife node (which, in fact, may have inhibitory links to those other constructs; Krueger & Rothbart, 1988; Kunda & Sherman-Williams, 1993).

Discussion of the relative merits of these models is not our purpose here. We note, instead, their common utility in accounting for (1) the assimilative influence of stereotypes, particularly when little, ambiguous, or irrelevant individuating information is available about a target person (such that the fit of a target to the category is facilitated), and (2) the relatively lesser impact of stereotypes when unambiguous, diagnostic information is available (such that the target may not fit the category, or the clarity of the behavior gives it greater weight; see Kunda & Thagard (1996) for a review). Furthermore, these models highlight the fact that stereotypes, in their role as interpretive frameworks, can affect the *meaning* or construal of other information (behaviors, traits) about a target person. "Aggressiveness" may be construed as "arguing and complaining" if the target is a lawyer, but as "punching and yelling insults" if the target is a construction worker (Kunda, Sinclair, & Griffin, 1997). Similarly, the behavior of "terminating a few employees" is likely to be *remembered* as "firing a few people" if the actor heads a computer software company but as "killing a few people" if he is a drug dealer (Dunning & Sherman, 1997; see also Kobrynowicz & Biernat, 1997). We interpret findings such as these in assimilation terms: stereotypes serve as expectations toward which perceptions of others are drawn.

Stereotypes as standards

Another view suggests that in addition to serving as interpretive frameworks, stereotypes also function as comparison standards for judging individual group members on stereotype-relevant dimensions (Biernat, Manis, & Nelson, 1991; Biernat & Kobrynowicz, 1997; Biernat & Manis, 1994; Biernat, Vescio, & Manis, 1998; Billings, Vescio, & Biernat, in press; Manis, Paskewitz, & Cotler, 1986). For example, the stereotype that women are more verbally able than men may not only lead perceivers to expect that a given woman will have higher verbal skill than a given man, but it may prompt them to compare the woman's skill to the expected (high) skill level of women, and to compare the man's skill to the expected (lower) skill level of men. Because women are compared to women and men to men, standards can be thought of as "shifting" with category membership. The result in this example is that women are held to a higher standard than men, with the potentially paradoxical consequence that a given woman may be judged as *less* verbally skilled than a comparable man – a contrast effect (see Biernat & Manis, 1994; Biernat & Kobrynowicz, 1997).[1]

Biernat and colleagues have noted, however, that such contrastive patterns are more likely to result when judges use "subjective" evaluative language (labels such as "high" or "low," "good" or "bad") rather than "objective" assessments (e.g. estimates of verbal SAT scores). This is the case because subjective language is slippery – there is no inherent, stable, agreed-upon meaning of the label "good" – and therefore it can be used and interpreted in a within-category fashion. "Good verbal skill" for a woman may mean something quite different (objectively better) than "good verbal skill" for a man. By definition, objective units of evaluation cannot shift in meaning as one moves from one category to another – a SAT score retains the same meaning regardless of the category membership of the target to whom it is applied. In this example, objective estimates of verbal skill (SAT scores, grades) tend to reveal higher estimates for female than male targets, even when subjective evaluations for the sexes are identical (Biernat & Manis, 1994). Indeed, the signature finding of research on the "shifting standards model" is that stereotype-assimilative findings tend to emerge when target judgments are made in objective units, but reductions or reversals (contrast) appear when subjective evaluations are rendered (see Biernat, Vescio, & Manis, 1998, for a review).

This model shares some features with the impression formation models of Fiske & Neuberg (1990) and Brewer (1988). Specifically, all of these perspectives suggest that there is some assessment of fit (some comparison) between category expectations and target features, and that discrepancy from expectations will prompt different processes or outcomes. In the impression formation models, discrepancy leads to recategorization (called "individuation" in Brewer's model), until an appropriate relevant category is found. Even in Kunda & Thagard's (1996) parallel constraint satisfaction model (which does not incorporate comparative processes), counterstereotypic targets are assumed to activate subtypes of the broader category. The shifting standards model assumes that the global category remains activated in these cases, but that stereotype-discrepant targets are judgmentally contrasted from the group standard ("he has good verbal skills, for a man").

This contrastive judgment pattern is also described in the literature on "expectancy violation theory" (Bettencourt, et al., 1997; Biernat, Vescio, & Billings, 1999; Jackson, Sullivan, & Hodge, 1993; Jussim, Coleman, & Lerch, 1987). According to this perspective, when information about a target violates stereotype based expectations, evaluations are extremitized in the direction of that violation. Thus, Blacks with strong academic credentials may be judged as more competent than Whites with comparable credentials (Jackson, Sullivan, & Hodge, 1993; Linville & Jones, 1980), Whites who speak nonstandard English may be viewed more negatively than Blacks who do the same (Jussim, Coleman, & Lerch, 1987), and baby-faced children who commit serious misbehavior may receive harsher punishment than their mature-faced peers (Zebrowitz, Kendall-Tackett, & Fafel, 1991; see also Zebrowitz & Lee, 1999). An important distinguishing characteristic of the shifting standards model, however, is its contention that these contrastive patterns may be more apparent than real, in that they tend to diminish when targets are judged along a common continuum (i.e. in objective units).

For example, an employer may hold a stereotype that women are less competent than men in a particular position. Because of this relatively low expectation for women, any given female applicant will have a better chance than a male applicant of surpassing within-category standards. Thus, paradoxically, the employer may be more impressed with a strong female applicant than with a male applicant with comparable credentials. Biernat & Kobrynowicz (1997) found just such a pattern of low expectations and relatively high subjective evaluations of women in an applicant evaluation setting of this sort. However, the same study revealed that when other judgments and decisions were made about the applicants (e.g. objective performance estimates, decision rules to be certain of the applicant's ability) women were judged more negatively than men (lower "objective" performance appraisals were given; harsher decision rules for diagnosing ability were applied). In other words, assimilation to stereotypes persisted (see also Foschi, 1998).

A very similar pattern emerged in a study of expectations and stereotypes based on baby-facedness. Berry & Zebrowitz-McArthur (1988) found that baby-faced defendants who committed intentional (as opposed to negligent) offenses were sentenced more severely than comparable mature-faced defendants. However, this contrast effect appeared only on the subjective sentencing decision (rated from "minimum" to "maximum"). In more objective judgments of guilt (yes or no), baby-faced defendants received the benefits of the benign stereotype associated with their group – they were less likely than mature-faced defendants to be found guilty of intentional crimes.

Research on expectancy-violation nonetheless highlights the dual role that stereotypes and expectations may play in social judgment: They tell us what we are likely to see (and thereby influence our perceptions in the process), and they serve as benchmarks against which deviations from expectation can be noted. The outcomes of these processes seem to depend, in part, on the form that judgments take. An additional avenue that should be pursued in research on expectancy based judgment concerns the role of affect. The broader psychological literature suggests that met expectations generate positive affect (Mandler, 1975), and that violations of expectancies may lead to arousal, negative emotionality, and emotion intensification (Burgoon, 1993; Clary & Tesser, 1983; Clore, Schwarz, & Conway, 1994; Olson, Roese, & Zanna, 1996). This suggests that extremitized subjective judgments of expectancy-violating targets may be mediated by emotional response (Biernat, Vescio, & Billings, 1999). The more objective judgments we've described – verdicts, decision rules for diagnosing ability – may be less driven by the immediate emotional reaction to a perceived violation and subject instead to the assimilative influence of stereotypes/expectations.

Related issues

It's clear that perceptions and judgments of others may be either assimilated to or contrasted from social stereotypes, depending on features of the target person and the nature and form of the judgment. Abele & Petzold (1998) have offered an additional and intriguing perspective on this issue that focuses on perceivers' ability to use category information about target persons in "flexible and pragmatical" ways. These researchers compare the role of stereotypes as expectations (which can produce assimilation effects, in that assumptions about the "typical case" are integrated into judgments of the target; Anderson, 1981), and stereotypes as frames of reference or "perspectives" (which can produce contrast in that the target is judged relative to the category range or boundaries; Biernat, Manis, & Nelson, 1991; Eiser & Van der Pligt, 1982; Ostrom & Upshaw, 1968; Parducci, 1965; Upshaw, 1962).

The functional consequence of using stereotypes as expectations is that the distinction *between* categories is enhanced, and differentiation *within* categories is reduced. When stereotypes are used as frames of reference, however, greater within-category distinction relative to between-category differentiation results. Abele & Petzold (1998) argue that "if the differentiation within categories is more important than the differentiation between them, then the reliance on the category boundaries (frame of reference) . . . is the pragmatically adequate psychological mechanism" (ibid., p. 8). Thus, this perspective suggests that assimilative effects will be observed whenever conditions are present that emphasize the need for between-category differentiation. These may include motivational factors such as social identity concerns (Hogg & Abrams, 1988; Tajfel, 1957; Turner, Hogg, Oakes, Reicher, & Wetherell, 1987) or position in a high power role (Fiske, 1993), as well as explicitly stated task purposes or "metainformational cues" (Leyens, Yzerbyt, & Schadron, 1994). This work emphasizes that stereotypes can be applied to the judgment of individual group members in varied, flexible, and functional ways (for a related view in the social identity theory tradition, see Oakes, Haslam, & Turner, 1994).

Judging the Self: Social Comparison

In this section, we focus on one source of standards according to which we evaluate, appraise, and regulate the self: other people. We provide an overview of the literature on social comparison, focusing on comparison motives, choice of comparison target or direction of comparison, and consequences of comparison. For the reader's convenience, we have summarized these aspects of the comparison process in table 1, emphasizing the manner in which motives can be satisfied through choice of comparison target and construal of information. Although social comparison may seem inherently *inter*personal on the sur-

Table 1 Summary of comparison motives, choices, and associated outcomes

Motive	Choice	Consequences
Self-assessment	Lateral (similar others)	Self-knowledge Validation
Self-enhancement	Lateral (esp. ingroup members) Downward Upward	Self-esteem protection, especially if perceiver is member of stigmatized group Contrast of self from target → positive affect and self-evaluation; increased self-esteem Assimilation of self to target → positive affect and self-evaluation; increased self-esteem; inspiration
Self-improvement	Upward	If perceiver has chronic high self-esteem if target's success is perceived as attainable, if target is not a competitor, or if perceiver compares on a dimension that is unimportant to the self-concept: Inspiration, motivation, improvement If perceiver has chronic low self-esteem, if target's success is perceived as unattainable, if target is a competitor, or if perceiver compares to a close other on a dimension that is important to the self concept: Negative affect and self-evaluation
Self-verification	Lateral	Verify self-view by comparison and assimilation to similar others

face, we believe it can be understood as a result of *intra*personal processes that occur primarily within the perceptual system of the comparer (Orive, 1988).

Social comparison has been conceptualized in a variety of ways (see Wheeler, 1991, for a review). As early as the first half of the twentieth century, theorists began to recognize the importance of reference groups for defining the self. Sherif's (1936) classic paper on social influence in ambiguous situations provided a compelling demonstration of how one's perceptions of reality can be socially constructed. Relatedly, Hyman (1942) pointed out that one's status on different dimensions may be determined by an understanding of oneself within the context of one's reference group. Researchers have also conceptualized social comparison as affiliation, arguing specifically that fear-produced affiliation results from a desire to compare one's emotional reactions to those of others (Gerard, 1963; Schachter, 1959; see also Taylor & Lobel, 1989).

Without denying the significance of these pioneering contributions, it is Festinger who deserves credit for stimulating the vast amount of research in social comparison that has been produced over the past several decades. In his classic theory of social comparison, Festinger (1954) argued that (a) people have a drive to evaluate their opinions and abilities, and (b) "to the extent that objective, non-social means are not available, people evaluate their opinions and abilities by comparison respectively with the opinions and abilities of others" (ibid., p. 118). Relatedly, Festinger maintained that people will compare with others who are *similar* to themselves in ability or opinion, due to the fact that accuracy in self-assessment is more difficult to achieve through comparison with dissimilar others.

Many studies have generated support for the latter idea – that we compare with similar others (Miller, Turnbull, & McFarland, 1988; Nosanchuk & Erikson, 1985; Wheeler, 1966) – but a number of researchers have taken issue with Festinger on several counts. Goethals & Darley (1977), for instance, proposed a revised definition of "similar others," and more recently, Klein (1997) provided evidence that, contrary to Festinger's Corollary IIB, people will compare with others even when they have access to some objective standard for evaluation (see also Chaplin & Buckner, 1988; Goolsby & Chaplin, 1988; Marsh, 1993).

Perhaps the most pervasive disagreement has been with Festinger's contention that people are objective self-evaluators who seek accurate information (e.g. Kruglanski & Mayseless, 1990; Wood, 1989). Recent trends in social comparison research show quite clearly that people make comparisons for many reasons, only one of which is self-evaluation in the sense meant by Festinger (hereafter referred to as *self-assessment*). Further, evidence shows that the comparison process is anything but unbiased. Comparisons often depend on the subjective *construal* of information (e.g. perceiving oneself to be more similar to a superior other than is actually the case; see Collins, 1996, for a review) that results from a variety of motives, to be discussed shortly. In this way, social comparison is largely an intrapersonal process.

Motives of the comparer

In addition to self-assessment – the attempt to gain an accurate understanding of the self – researchers have focused primarily on two other motives for social comparison: self-enhancement and self-improvement. Additionally, we will consider self-verification, a motive that is much less discussed in the context of social comparison theory.[2]

Self-enhancement That people wish to be held in high esteem by both themselves and others constitutes one of the most fundamental assumptions in the field (e.g. Solomon, Greenberg, & Pyszczynski, 1991; Tajfel, 1982; Taylor, 1989; Taylor & Brown, 1988; Turner, 1975). Social comparison researchers have accommodated this assumption as well with an emphasis on *self-enhancement* as a motive of comparison (Armor & Taylor, 1998; Brown, Novick, Lord, & Richards, 1992; Buunk & Ybema, 1997; Collins, 1996; Goethals & Darley, 1977; Hakmiller, 1966; Tesser, 1988; Wills, 1981), which may involve either *attaining* or *maintaining* a positive self-concept (Taylor, Neter, & Wayment, 1995).

In a comparative study, Sedikides (1993) found self-enhancement to be the strongest of three motives in the general process of self-evaluation. Apparently, people will go to great lengths to maintain their positive self-views by making use of such strategies as comparing downward (to worse-off others), choosing the dimension(s) along which to compare (Crocker & Major, 1989; Wood, 1989), attending to only certain comparison others (Crocker & Major, 1989; Diener & Fujita, 1997; Major, 1994; Wood, 1989), fabricating comparison targets if no self-enhancing targets are immediately available (Taylor & Lobel, 1989; Taylor, Wood, & Lichtman, 1983), denying the meaningfulness of a particular comparison (Lockwood & Kunda, 1997), and sometimes simply avoiding comparison altogether (Brickman & Bulman, 1977; Buunk, Collins, Taylor, VanYperen, & Dakof, 1990; Wood, 1989).

Among those particularly concerned with self-enhancement should be members of stigmatized groups. According to Crocker & Major (1989), the stigmatized are often faced with the difficult task of protecting their self-esteem in the face of negative outcomes and will utilize several creative strategies in order to do so. One of these strategies is inherently comparative in nature; specifically, Crocker and Major proposed that stigmatized individuals will make within-group comparisons in order to avoid the potential loss of self-esteem that could result from comparisons with members of relatively advantaged groups (Major, 1994; see also Tajfel, 1982).

Self-improvement   Other research documents the existence of a *self-improvement* motive for social comparison, whereby the individual looks to others in the social environment for inspiration and/or uses comparisons to motivate the self to improve (Collins, 1996; Lockwood & Kunda, 1997). This motive is also reflected in the "unidirectional drive upward" described by Festinger (1954).

Comparison motivated by self-improvement may occur, however, only under certain conditions. For example, although Taylor & Lobel (1989) found that cancer patients may find a source of inspiration in other patients who are coping better than themselves, it is only affiliating with or seeking information from superior copers that patients have found inspiring; self-evaluation with such targets is arguably threatening and ego-deflating. Further, Lockwood & Kunda (1997) found that individuals will be inspired by upward comparison targets only to the extent that (1) such targets are relevant to the comparer's self-definition, and (2) the comparer believes that he or she can also attain the target's level of success. Finally, individual difference variables such as Type A behavior pattern and an achievement orientation may predispose one to use comparisons for self-improvement (Wood, 1989).

Self-assessment   Although research has placed increasing emphasis on a variety of comparison motives, Festinger's original hypothesis that we are motivated to self-assess has also stood up to empirical investigation (Gerard, 1963; Raynor & McFarlin, 1986; Scheier & Carver, 1983). Trope (1986), for example, found that, when given a choice of tasks to complete, participants selected tasks that diagnosed their abilities accurately, even if unfavorably. As with other motives, however, comparison motivated by self-assessment may be especially likely under certain conditions. First, certain individual difference variables, such as depression, may predispose a comparer to be more concerned with accuracy (self-assessment) than with other comparison goals (Weary, Marsh, & McCormick, 1994; Taylor, 1989). Relatedly, a sad mood may prompt self-assessment (Sedikides, 1993; cf. Buunk & Ybema, 1997; Wheeler & Miyake, 1992). Second, people may be motivated to accurately assess their skills on dimensions for which improvement is possible, as opposed to attitude-related dimensions, on which they may wish to see themselves more positively (Sedikides, 1993). Finally, people may be especially concerned with self-assessment when trying to determine whether or not they can actually perform a particular behavior (Wheeler, Martin, & Suls, 1997).

Self-verification Although it has not typically been considered under the rubric of social comparison, *self-verification* constitutes yet another goal that a comparer may seek to attain (see Taylor, Neter, & Wayment, 1995). According to self-verification theory (e.g. Swann, 1987), people are motivated by a desire to keep intact the self-views that they have developed, whether these views are positive or negative. Thus, when asked to choose to interact with one of two partners – one who views them negatively versus one who views them positively, about 75 percent of respondents prefer partners who confirm their self-views (positive or negative), and indicate that they do so for epistemic reasons (Swann, Stein-Seroussi, & Giesler, 1992). According to Swann (1987), a person may self-verify by selecting social environments that foster self-views as well as by cognitively distorting information so that it is consistent with self-views (e.g. by preferentially attending to self-confirmatory feedback or by endorsing the validity only of self-confirmatory feedback).

It is possible, then, that social comparison constitutes one avenue by which self-verification strivings may be satisfied. To verify a self-view, we may surround and compare ourselves to others with similar attributes; by a process of assimilation, we may come to see ourselves as even more like others in the environment (and therefore more consistent with the self-view) than was originally the case.

Choice of comparison target/direction of comparison

An issue closely tied to comparison motives concerns the particular targets that perceivers choose for comparison purposes. Much has been written on this point (Miller & Prentice, 1996; Suls, 1986; Suls & Wills, 1991; Taylor, Neter, & Wayment, 1995; Wilder & Allen, 1978; Wills & Suls, 1991). Kruglanski & Mayseless (1990) argued that one's choice of comparison target depends on three variables: (1) whether a comparison with the target will satisfy one's comparison motive, (2) whether the target is relevant, and (3) the accessibility of common heuristics (e.g. the rule "grown-ups know best" may prompt youngsters to compare with dissimilar others). Similarly, Levine & Moreland (1986) suggest that a perceiver will choose a given target to the extent that the target is salient and attractive, where attractiveness is defined as the degree to which the target is able to satisfy the perceiver's comparison motives. Most often, the issues regarding choice of comparison target have been those of similarity and direction; that is, whether people compare with similar others (lateral comparison) or dissimilar others (upward or downward comparison).

Lateral comparison Considerable research evidence suggests that we do in fact choose similar others with whom to compare (e.g. Kahneman & Miller, 1986; Mettee & Smith, 1977; Miller, Turnbull, & McFarland, 1988; Nosanchuk & Erickson, 1985; Taylor, Neter, & Wayment, 1995; Wheeler, 1966). For example, Wheeler (1966) found that participants who had taken a personality test chose to compare to others who had scores similar to their own. Furthermore, related evidence suggests that people may be unresponsive to comparison information when similarity is lacking. In a study examining outcomes of comparison rather than choice of comparison target (Cash, Cash, & Butters, 1983), female participants rated their own attractiveness lower when exposed to attractive as compared to unattractive targets, except when they believed the attractive targets to be professional models (i.e. dissimilar in an important way).

Comparison with similar others is not always the rule, however (Major, Testa, & Bylsma, 1991; Miller, 1982, 1984; Miller, Turnbull, & McFarland, 1988; Samuel, 1973; Suls, Gaes, & Gastorf, 1979). Rather, certain factors seem to make such comparisons more likely. First, similar others are more likely to be chosen when one is relatively certain about how to interpret one's standing on a dimension (Wood, 1989). Second, when people are called upon to make subjective judgments (i.e. judgments that follow from both the object's characteristics and the perceiver's attitudes or values), rather than objective judgments, they prefer to compare with similar others (Gorenflo & Crano, 1989).

Although we are using "similarity" to refer specifically to a perceiver's position relative to others on the comparison dimension itself, theorists have also offered broader definitions of "similarity." Goethals & Darley (1977), for instance, argued that similar others could include those who are similar to the comparer on attributes that are *related* to, not just specific to, the comparison dimension (cf. Major, Testa, & Bylsma, 1991). To illustrate, a young man may choose to compare his performance at the piano with the performance of others who have studied piano for approximately the same amount of time as himself, believing years of study, a related attribute, to be a good predictor of performance, the central comparison dimension.

Wood (1989) reviewed research that extends the definition of similarity even further, to include apparently unrelated attributes. Similarity may be defined by features as diffuse as shared group membership (e.g. gender category) and broad personality traits (Crocker & Major, 1989; Miller, Turnbull, & McFarland, 1988; Tesser, 1988). Among possible explanations advanced for such comparisons are that people may (1) perceive themselves to be closer to others who are similar in a broad sense (Miller, Turnbull, & McFarland, 1988; Tesser, 1988); (2) make ingroup comparisons to protect self-esteem (Crocker & Major, 1989); (3) believe that targets similar with respect to unrelated attributes are potential competitors, and thereby relevant to one's outcomes; (4) believe attributes such as gender to be related to performance across a wide variety of domains; and (5) view some attributes (such as gender) as self-defining, even if unrelated to a given comparison dimension (Miller, Turnbull, & McFarland, 1988; Wood, 1989).

Downward comparison   On the other hand, one may choose to compare with another who is dissimilar in that he or she is worse-off than the self. Downward comparison was demonstrated in early research by Hakmiller (1966), and according to Wills (1981) downward comparison serves a self-enhancing function, particularly under conditions of threat:

> People do not necessarily regard misfortune to others as a desirable occurrence or view comparison with less fortunate others as a wholly admirable process; yet the psychological benefit of doing so is substantial, thus the temptation is strong, and all of the evidence suggests that people yield frequently to this temptation. (Ibid., p. 265)

More recent research supports Wills's (1981) depiction of downward comparisons as highly tempting (see Affleck & Tennen, 1991; Gibbons & Gerrard, 1991; Wills, 1991). Buunk, et al., (1990), for example, examined comparisons relevant to health status and marital satisfaction. In two studies, self-enhancing downward comparisons that generated positive affect were made more frequently than any other type of comparison. Not only is positive affect a likely *result* of downward comparison, but there is also evidence to suggest that positive as opposed to negative affect may *lead* to downward comparisons (Wheeler & Miyake, 1992), and may make one more responsive to downward than to upward comparisons (Lyubomirsky & Ross, 1997).

Self-esteem, a variable that may be related to positive affect, plays a similar role. Consistent with Wills's theory, downward comparisons have been shown to improve an initially low level of self-esteem (Aspinwall & Taylor, 1993; Hakmiller, 1966). However, individuals with high self-esteem tend to engage in downward comparisons more often than individuals with low self-esteem (Buunk & Ybema, 1997; Wheeler & Miyake, 1992; but cf. Wills, 1991), and tend to emphasize the positive qualities that they have but that others do not (Schütz & Tice, 1997).[3]

Another variable that influences whether one chooses to compare downward or otherwise is the way in which social comparison is defined in a given situation – for example, as self-evaluation or as affiliation. If the comparer's goal is an evaluative one, he or she may reap the self-enhancing benefits associated with downward comparison. If, on the other hand, an individual is seeking out someone with whom to associate, a downward target may represent a threat (Buunk, et al., 1990; Buunk & Ybema, 1997; Taylor & Lobel, 1989), especially if the comparer believes the target's situation to be due to uncontrollable factors (Major, Testa, & Bylsma, 1991).

Upward comparison   Although there are obvious benefits of comparing downward, upward targets are especially likely to be useful in satisfying motives such as self-improvement, inspiration, and information-seeking (Lockwood & Kunda, 1997; Nosanchuk & Erickson, 1985; Taylor, Neter, & Wayment, 1995). Although superior others may initially evoke negative affect, they may be chosen as comparison targets to the degree that they motivate the comparer to improve (Wheeler & Miyake, 1992). Other research is consistent with this perspective as well (Major, Testa, & Bylsma, 1991; Taylor & Lobel, 1989). Surprisingly, upward targets may also be used to self-enhance; we will return to this issue in our treatment of comparison consequences.

The active comparer?   Research on choice of comparison others makes clear that people must be adept at controlling the comparison situations they are in such that they will be sure to have at their disposal comparison targets who satisfy relevant motives. If no satisfactory targets are available, people may employ creative strategies such as comparing themselves to social stereotypes (Brickman & Bulman, 1977; Gibbons, Gerrard, Lando, & McGovern, 1991; Perloff & Fetzer, 1986), inventing comparison targets (Taylor, Wood, & Lichtman, 1983), or avoiding comparison completely. A picture begins to emerge in which an active perceiver sorts through a variety of possible targets for comparison, and in which the final choice results primarily from an internal state (e.g. self-esteem) or motive (e.g. self-enhancement), rather than the "objective" constraints of the environment (Buunk, et al., 1990; Buunk & Ybema, 1997; Diener & Fujita, 1997; Kruglanski & Mayseless, 1990; Levine & Moreland, 1986; Taylor, Neter, & Wayment, 1995; Wheeler, 1966; Wheeler & Miyake, 1992; Wills, 1981).

However, one might also imagine a more active environment that forces comparisons on an unprepared or unwitting perceiver. For example, research on entitlement and relative deprivation has demonstrated that the availability of comparison targets detemines whether one feels satisfied or dissatisfied with outcomes in a given context (Crosby, 1976; Major, 1994; J. Martin, 1986; Masters & Smith, 1987; Olson, Herman, & Zanna, 1986; Tyler & Smith, 1998). Relatedly, research on the "frog-pond" effect (more positive self-evaluation if one is a "big frog in a small pond" rather than a "small frog in a big pond"), has documented the power of one's comparative context to affect subjective well-being and self-concept (Davis, 1966; Marsh & Parker, 1984; McFarland & Buehler, 1995; Smith & Tyler, 1997). Furthermore, proximal others are especially likely to serve as comparison targets and affect self-perceptions, given their greater availability (Levine & Moreland, 1987; Major, 1994), and threatening comparisons may be particularly difficult to escape as they are highly salient in the environment (Miller & Prentice, 1996). Indeed, social comparisons are often spontaneous, effortless, and unintentional; thus, comparison information present in the environment may affect one's self-evaluation without deliberate awareness (e.g. Baldwin & Holmes, 1987), and even though one may later "correct" for such comparisons (Gilbert, Giesler, & Morris, 1995).

Nonetheless, it seems reasonable to conclude that, *within* a given environment, people may still exercise considerable choice over the target with whom they compare. To quote Gilbert, Giesler, & Morris (1995, p. 233), "a lack of complete control is not a complete lack of control." Although comparisons may be automatic to some extent, the perceiver may still be able to control with whom he or she comes into contact and which comparisons to correct or revise (for related themes on the strategic selection of social environments, see Frank, 1985; Parducci, 1995). Further, within a comparison context, people will often engage in creative strategies to satisfy various motives (e.g. selectively choosing the dimension along which to compare; Crocker & Major, 1989). In short, there is much evidence to suggest that people will go to great lengths to "get what they want," so to speak, from the comparative process (Collins, 1996; Wood, 1989).

Consequences of social comparison

The final social comparison topic to which we turn concerns consequences of the comparison process. In general, the literature distinguishes between affective (including self-esteem), cognitive, and behavioral reactions to comparison (Levine & Moreland, 1986; Wheeler & Miyake, 1992). Although behavioral reactions are studied rarely, some research indicates that making upward comparisons not only generates feelings of inspiration but can sometimes lead to actual behavioral improvement (Major, Testa, & Bylsma, 1991; Seta, Seta, & Donaldson, 1991). Cognitive and affective consequences of comparison are highly interrelated, and indeed, individual studies often measure both. Perhaps the most frequently studied affective response is self-esteem. A classic study in this vein is Morse & Gergen's (1970) "Mr Clean/Mr Dirty" study, in which prospective job candidates' self-esteem was harmed by upward comparison to the well-dressed competitor, Mr Clean, but improved by downward comparison to the sloppy competitor, Mr Dirty.

More generally, how people react to comparisons often has more to do with their subjective construal of the comparison information than with its objective nature (DeVellis, et al., 1991; Diener & Fujita, 1997). In a study by DeVellis, et al. (1991), women with rheumatoid arthritis were asked to compare their coping ability with that of women who were portrayed as coping either better or worse than themselves. Although participants exposed to the superior coper rated her coping ability higher than their own on an indirect measure (separate ratings of self and other), they overwhelmingly denied the superior coping of the other when asked to make a direct comparison. Participants may have reconstructed their perceptions of either themselves or the stimulus woman so as to avoid a comparison that would reflect badly on the self. That construal and reconstruction are pervasive and robust is often captured in the very definition of comparative consequences: Levine & Moreland (1986) defined cognitive responses to comparison as the "source's *distortions* of his or her own outcomes or related attributes or those of the target" (p. 293, emphasis added).

The important role of construal in reactions to social comparison is illustrated quite nicely by considering a comparer's attempts to self-enhance through *upward* comparison. Although this topic has only recently received much attention (Collins, 1996), self-enhancement by assimilation to an upward target was demonstrated very early in the history of social comparison research (Wheeler, 1966). In reflecting on the paradox that people are often motivated to compare upward despite the negative affect and unfavorable evaluation that might result, Wheeler (1966) suggested that in such situations the comparer assumes similarity with the superior other and will experience negative comparison consequences only to the extent that he or she is not as similar to the target as expected. Wheeler's results were consistent with this interpretation: A majority (75 percent) of participants who compared upward perceived themselves as similar to the comparison target, but only a minority (36 percent) of those who compared downward assumed they were similar to the upward targets.

More recently, Collins (1996) directly invoked the processes of *assimilation* and *contrast* to explain the differing consequences of comparing upward. On the one hand, if one expects to be different from an upward target, particular attention is paid to these differences and contrast may occur; the comparer may see him- or herself as even more different from (worse than) the target than is actually the case. On the other hand, an expectation of similarity may result in the perceptual "blurring" of actual differences between self and target, leading the comparer to assimilate to the target. Wood (1989) also argued that upward comparisons will produce positive affect and self-evaluation, including feelings of inspiration, unless the upward target is perceived as a competitor (such that differences are enhanced), and Lockwood & Kunda (1997) found positive consequences of upward comparison so long as the target's success on a self-defining dimension was perceived as attainable (see also Buunk, et al., 1990). It is through the assimilative process that an upward comparison target may actually be used to self-enhance. This analysis suggests that individuals with chronic low self-esteem are unlikely to benefit from upward comparison because expectations of dissimilarity with superior others will lead to contrast effects in comparison (Collins, 1996).

Also relevant to the issue of consequences of upward comparison is Tesser's self-evaluation maintenance (SEM) theory (Tesser, 1988). The SEM proposes that two processes — reflection and comparison — affect self-evaluation when we are outperformed by close others (i.e. upward targets). If a close other performs well on a dimension that is irrelevant to one's self-definition, one benefits by being able to bask in the reflected glory of the other —

an assimilative response. However, if a close other performs well on a dimension that is central to the self, social comparison jealousy and depressed self-esteem result, perhaps by virtue of a contrastive process. Several other researchers also emphasize the processes of assimilation and contrast in comparison outcomes (Brewer & Weber, 1994; Brown, Novick, Lord, & Richards, 1992; Cash, Cash, & Butters, 1983; McFarland & Buehler, 1995; Mussweiler & Strack, in press; Pelham & Wachsmuth, 1995).

Just as upward comparison, traditionally considered detrimental, can have positive consequences, downward comparison, traditionally thought to be self-enhancing, can have adverse consequences for the comparer. Specifically, comparing with a worse-off other may be threatening to the extent that the target's outcome is perceived to be uncontrollable (Major, Testa, & Bylsma, 1991). In Taylor & Lobel's (1989) review of their work with cancer patients, they note that comparing downward may remind one of what the future might hold. Taken as a whole, the literature relevant to comparison consequences leads us to conclude, in the words of Buunk, et al. (1990), that either direction of comparison – upward or downward – "has its ups and downs." The impact of a comparison will ultimately be determined not by its direction but by the way in which it is perceived and interpreted by the comparer.

Conclusions

This chapter has described just a small segment of the wide range of theory and research on the roles of expectations and judgment standards in the evaluation of others and the self. Daily life compels us to make judgments such as whether we have what it takes to succeed in a chosen profession, whether the salesperson can be trusted, or whether a new acquaintance has an aggressive streak. It is in making these types of judgments that people often make reference to the types of standards that we have discussed – for example, stereotypes in the case of judging others, and specific comparison others or groups for judging the self. In such evaluative contexts, people may not necessarily desire to reach an accurate judgment but rather to support a pre-existing belief, such as a social stereotype or a positive view of the self (see Kruglanski & Webster, 1996). It is in pursuing such motives that perceivers may turn from objective information, if it is available, to those comparison standards that can be subjectively construed to support one's motives. Thus, a student whose positive academic self-concept has been threatened may decide that his performance is not so bad after all by comparing with students less accomplished than himself (Wills, 1981). Similarly, a perceiver who endorses racial stereotypes may be motivated to construe ambiguous information about a Black individual in a manner that confirms these pre-existing beliefs ("that behavior was a violent push," not a jovial shove; Duncan, 1976).

These examples highlight one central theme of this chapter: comparison processes and judgment outcomes are *intra*personal in that they are based largely on the subjective construal of information by the perceiver. Recent research on social comparison has demonstrated the substantial control individuals have over the comparisons they make and the interpretation of feedback from those comparisons, particularly in field settings (see Collins, 1996; Taylor & Lobel, 1989; Wood, 1989). Though not reviewed here, other research suggests that when the self is used as a referent to evaluate others, the perceiver has considerable license to define attributes such that they reflect favorably on the self, and to view others as either similar to or distinct from the self depending on dominant motives (Beauregard & Dunning, 1998; Hoorens & Buunk, 1993). Constructs such as personal stereotypes, representations of significant others, and internalized guides also affect the construal of newly encountered information in a manner unique to a given perceiver. This is not to deny the power of the situation to impose comparisons upon us and to dictate the outcomes of those comparisons. Still, individuals have substantial latitude in interpreting information (is my lower pay justified or not?; can this goal be attained?), and it is the subjective interpretation that determines behavioral response (protesting over low pay, exerting effort toward a goal).

A second theme that underlies this chapter is the conceptualization of experience and judgment outcomes in terms of the basic processes of assimilation and contrast. Expectations and standards function to either draw in (assimilate) or drive away (contrast) perception and judgment. By serving as interpretive frameworks, expectations may bias perception in that targets are viewed as more similar to the expected state than would be the case had no expectation been present. And by serving as points of comparison, targets may be seen as more discrepant from standards than they would be in the absence of those comparative standards.

Predicting which of these outcomes will occur has been the objective of much theorizing and research (Manis & Paskewitz, 1984; L. Martin, 1986; Schwarz & Bless, 1992; Stapel & Winkielman, 1998; Wegener & Petty, 1997). Although the specifics may vary slightly across domains, a few factors have been identified as central to this issue:

1   *Similarity (feature overlap) between the target and referent.* In general, assimilation toward the expectation or standard is enhanced to the extent that the target is seen as similar to, or included in the scope of, the referent. For example, (a) targets are assimilated to stereotypes to the extent that they "fit" the social category (Brewer, 1988; Fiske & Neuberg, 1990), and (b) upward social comparison results in positive self-views (assimilation to the status of the upward referent) only when the comparer assumes similarity between the self and the referent other (Collins, 1996).

2   *Ambiguity of the target's features or behavior.* Related to the similarity principle, the ambiguity of the judgment target also contributes to assimilation effects. As Stapel & Winkielman (1998, p. 635) put it, a construct "will be a guide to interpretation only when there is something to be interpreted, that is, when the target stimulus is ambiguous rather than unambiguous." For example, (a) assimilative stereotyping effects are strongest when perceivers know only little or ambiguous information about a target person (see Kunda & Thagard, 1996, for a review); *un*ambiguous stereotype-inconsistent information, however, may lead to contrast (Biernat, Vescio, & Manis, 1998; Jussim, Coleman, & Lerch, 1987), and (b) in the domain of social comparison, ambiguous self-standing can be construed in such a way that it is assimilated upward, toward a superior other (Collins, 1996; DeVellis, et al., 1991).

3   *Motives.* That perceivers' motives may affect their use of expectations or standards (and thereby the outcome of any comparative process) was an explicit theme in our discussion of social comparison. Motives to self-enhance may prompt downward

comparison and motives to self-improve may induce upward comparisons, and enhancement may also be attained by assimilation to an upward comparison if self–other similarity is assumed (Buunk, et al., 1990; Collins, 1996; Lockwood & Kunda, 1997). Though less explicitly highlighted, the influence of motivational states can also be seen in a variety of other judgment domains. For example, (a) assimilation to stereotypes is reduced when perceivers are motivated (e.g. by interdependence goals) to attend to individuating information about a target (Brewer, 1988; Fiske & Neuberg, 1990), and enhanced when perceivers are in powerful, high status, roles (Fiske, 1993), and (b) social identity needs (and self-categorization at the group level) contribute to stereotype-assimilative effects (Brewer & Weber, 1994; Hogg & Abrams, 1988; Tajfel, 1957; Turner, et al., 1987).

This set of factors is not meant to be exhaustive, but rather to highlight the fact that across a variety of judgment domains, some basic principles of assimilation and contrast can be identified. By focusing on these cross-cutting themes, research in areas as seemingly diverse as social stereotyping and social comparison may inform and enhance each other (in both methodology and insight), thereby contributing to the progress of our science as a whole (see Schaller, Rosell, & Asp, 1998).

Future themes and directions

The dual role of expectations and standards in judgment (as interpretive frameworks and as points of comparison) has also been emphasized throughout this chapter. Manis & Paskewitz (1984) have argued that these roles are played simultaneously. Expectations tell us that the future will be like the past, and therefore we may encode and interpret information in a manner consistent with these expectations (Von Hippel, Sekaquaptewa, & Vargas, 1995). At the same time, deviations from expectations are noted because we use expectations as referents against which new stimuli are compared and contrasted. This duality of function deserves further investigation. Whether these opposing roles are played out simultaneously or sequentially, whether one is more automatic and less effortful than the other, and how these functions are affected by aspects of the to-be-judged information, have not been fully answered. In general, we assume that daily life offers many opportunities for our expectations to be confirmed – much information we receive about both others and ourselves is ambiguous, allowing room for perception, interpretation, and construal that is consistent with expectations. It is when stimuli are disambiguated or unexpected that the effects of the more comparative function of expectations (standards) are likely to be seen (Olson, Roese, & Zanna, 1996).

Future work should also be geared toward addressing the fact that different judgmental patterns (assimilation, contrast, or no effect of expectations) often appear on different *measures* or types of assessment. In research on social comparison, for example, direct comparative measures may indicate that one perceives similarity to a superior other at the same time that separate ratings of self and other recognize the superiority of the other (DeVellis, et al., 1991; Miyake & Zuckerman, 1993). Relative deprivation effects tend to be strongest on direct comparative measures, and on indicators of affect, than they do on indirect or non-affective ratings (Smith & Pettigrew, 1998). Findings from the stereotyping literature suggest that White perceivers may recognize a competent Black target as intelligent, but at the same time continue to think of the self as even more so (Gaertner & Dovidio, 1986). Whether judgments are assessed on objective response scales or on subjective scales that allow for within-category meaning shifts, or whether participants are attuned to minimum judgment standards or ability standards, may also determine the pattern of results that emerges (Biernat & Kobrynowicz, 1997; Biernat, Manis, & Nelson, 1991).

We also recommend that *behavioral* outcomes of expectations and standards be more frequently assessed. Although there are some exceptions (e.g. Andersen, Reznik, & Manzella, 1996; Bargh, Chen, & Burrows, 1996; Dijksterhuis & Van Knippenberg, 1998; Monteith, 1993), few researchers have ascertained whether judgment effects translate into parallel behavioral outcomes. Informed by the literature on attitudes and attitude–behavior consistency, we assume that dissociations between judgment and behavior are not rare. We also recommend continued attention to the interplay of cognitive and motivational factors in the study of expectancy- and standard-based judgment. Expectations and standards play an important and ubiquitous role in our encounters with, perceptions of, judgments about, and behavior within the social environment. We hope that this review will trigger continued research into the basic principles that underlie these effects.

Notes

1   The idea that perceivers routinely make within-group comparisons also appears in McGill's (1993) research on causal explanation, based in part on Kahneman & Miller's (1986) norm theory. In McGill's (1993) research, participants were asked to explain the failure of a male or female actor on either a masculine (e.g. shooting pool) or feminine (e.g. sewing) task (Study 1). Men's failure was explained by comparison to males who succeeded, regardless of type of task. This suggests that "male failure mutates readily to male success" (ibid., p. 704). Women's failure on feminine tasks was explained by reference to women (another within-sex comparison), but failure at masculine tasks was explained by reference to men. This work suggests that the tendency to make within-category comparisons may be muted to the extent that the context cues a different referent – in this case, women's performance on a masculine task cued the gender category linked to the task as the comparison standard rather than the gender category of the actor.

2   Additional motives for social comparison have also been proposed, including the desire for a "common bond" or affiliation, altruism, and self-destruction (Helgeson & Mickelson, 1995). However, these have received relatively little research attention and will not be discussed here.

3   Some have suggested that self-esteem may have a larger effect on the motive for comparison rather than the direction of comparison. For example, Helgeson & Mickelson (1995) found that low self-esteem participants were more likely than those high in self-esteem to socially compare for reasons of "self-destruction" (e.g. "to confirm my belief that I am in trouble").

References

Abele, A. E., & Petzold, P. (1998). Pragmatical use of categorical information in impression formation. *Journal of Personality and Social Psychology, 75,* 347–358.

Affleck, G., & Tennen, H. (1991). Social comparison and coping with major medical problems. In J. Suls & T. A. Wills (Eds.), *Social comparison: Contemporary theory and research* (pp. 369–394). Hillsdale, NJ: Erlbaum.

Andersen, S. M., Reznik, I., & Manzella, L. M. (1996). Eliciting facial affect, motivation, and expectancies in transference: Significant-other representations in social relations. *Journal of Personality and Social Psychology, 71*, 1108–1129.

Anderson, N. H. (1981). *Foundations of information integration theory.* New York: Academic Press.

Armor, D. A., & Taylor, S. E. (1998). Situated optimism: Specific outcome expectancies and self-regulation. In M. P. Zanna (Ed.), *Advances in experimental social psychology* Vol. 30 (pp. 309–379). Orlando, FL: Academic Press.

Ashmore, R. D., & Del Boca, F. K. (1981). Conceptual approaches to stereotypes and stereotyping. In D. L. Hamilton (Ed.), *Cognitive processes in stereotyping and intergroup behavior* (pp. 1–35). Hillsdale, NJ: Erlbaum.

Aspinwall, L. G., & Taylor, S. E. (1993). Effects of social comparison direction, threat, and self-esteem on affect, self-evaluation, and expected success. *Journal of Personality and Social Psychology, 64*, 708–722.

Atkinson, J. W. (1957). Motivational determinants of risk-taking behavior. *Psychological Review, 64*, 359–372.

Baldwin, M. W., & Holmes, J. G. (1987). Salient private audiences and awareness of the self. *Journal of Personality and Social Psychology, 52*, 1087–1098.

Bargh, J. A., Chen, M., & Burrows, L. (1996). Automaticity of social behavior: Direct effects of trait construct and stereotype activation on action. *Journal of Personality and Social Psychology, 71*, 230–244.

Beauregard, K. S., & Dunning, D. (1998). Turning up the contrast: Self-enhancement motives prompt egocentric contrast effects in social judgment. *Journal of Personality and Social Psychology, 74*, 606–621.

Berry, D. S., & Zebrowitz-McArthur, L. (1988). What's in a face?: Facial maturity and the attribution of legal responsibility. *Personality and Social Psychology Bulletin, 14*, 23–33.

Bettencourt, B. A., Dill, K. E., Greathouse, S. A., Charlton, K., & Mulholland, A. (1997). Evaluations of ingroup and outgroup members: The role of category-based expectancy violation. *Journal of Experimental Social Psychology, 33*, 244–275.

Biernat, M., & Kobrynowicz, D. (1997). Gender- and race-based standards of competence: Lower minimum standards but higher ability standards for devalued groups. *Journal of Personality and Social Psychology, 72*, 544–557.

Biernat, M., & Manis, M. (1994). Shifting standards and stereotype-based judgments. *Journal of Personality and Social Psychology, 66*, 5–20.

Biernat, M., Manis, M., & Nelson, T. E. (1991). Stereotypes and standards of judgment. *Journal of Personality and Social Psychology, 60*, 485–499.

Biernat, M., Vescio, T. K., & Billings, L. S. (1999). Black sheep and expectancy violation: Integrating two models of social judgment. *European Journal of Social Psychology, 29*, 523–542.

Biernat, M., Vescio, T. K., & Manis, M. (1998). Judging and behaving toward members of stereotyped groups: A shifting standards perspective. In C. Sedikides, J. Schopler, & C. A. Insko (Eds.), *Intergroup cognition and intergroup behavior*, pp. 151–175. Hillsdale, NJ: Lawrence Erlbaum Associates.

Billings, L. S., Vescio, T. K., & Biernat, M. (in press). Race-based social judgment by minority perceivers. *Journal of Applied Social Psychology.*

Bodenhausen, G. V. (1988). Stereotypic biases in social decision making and memory: Testing process models for stereotype use. *Journal of Personality and Social Psychology, 55*, 726–737.

Brewer, M. B., (1988). A dual process model of impression formation. In T. K. Srull & R. S. Wyer (Eds.), *Advances in social cognition* Vol. 1 (pp. 1–36). Hillsdale, NJ: Erlbaum.

Brewer, M. B. (1996). When stereotypes lead to stereotyping: The use of stereotypes in person perception. In C. N. Macrae, C. Stangor, & M. Hewstone (Eds.), *Stereotypes and stereotyping* (pp. 254–275). New York: Guilford Press.

Brewer, M. B., & Weber, J. G. (1994). Self-evaluation effects of interpersonal versus intergroup social comparison. *Journal of Personality and Social Psychology, 66* (2), 268–275.

Brickman, P., & Bulman, R. J. (1977). Pleasure and pain in social comparison. In J. M. Suls & R. L. Miller (Eds.), *Social comparison processes: Theoretical and empirical perspectives* (pp. 149–186). Washington, DC: Hemisphere.

Brown, J. D., Novick, N. J., Lord, K. A., & Richards, J. M. (1992). When Gulliver travels: Social context, psychological closeness, and self-appraisals. *Journal of Personality and Social Psychology, 62* (5), 717–727.

Burgoon, J. (1993). Interpersonal expectations, expectancy violations, and emotional communication. *Journal of Language and Social Psychology, 12,* 30–48.

Buunk, B. P., & Ybema, J. F. (1997). Social comparisons and occupational stress: The identification-contrast model. In B. P. Buunk & F. X. Gibbons (Eds.), *Health, coping, and well-being: Perspectives from social comparison theory* (pp. 359–387). Mahwah, NJ: Lawrence Erlbaum Associates.

Buunk, B. P., Collins, R. L., Taylor, S. E., VanYperen, N. W., & Dakof, G. A. (1990). The affective consequences of social comparison: Either direction has its ups and downs. *Journal of Personality and Social Psychology, 59* (6), 1238–1249.

Cash, T. F., Cash, D. W., & Butters, J. W. (1983). "Mirror, mirror, on the wall . . .?": Contrast effects and self-evaluations of physical attractiveness. *Personality and Social Psychology Bulletin, 9,* 351–358.

Chaplin, W. F., & Buckner, K. E. (1988). Self-ratings of personality: A naturalistic comparison of normative, ipsative, and idiothetic standards. *Journal of Personality, 56,* 509–530.

Clary, E. G., & Tesser, A. (1983). Reaction to unexpected events: The naive scientist and interpretive activity. *Personality and Social Psychology Bulletin, 9,* 609–620.

Clore, G. L., Schwarz, N., & Conway, M. (1994). Affective causes and consequences of social information processing. In R. S. Wyer & T. K. Srull (Eds.), *Handbook of social cognition, Vol. 1: Basic Processes.* 2nd. edn. Hillsdale, NJ: Lawrence Erlbaum Associates.

Collins, R. L. (1996). For better or worse: The impact of upward social comparison on self-evaluation. *Psychological Bulletin, 119,* 51–69.

Crocker, J., & Major, B. (1989). Social stigma and self-esteem: The self-protective properties of stigma. *Psychological Review, 96* (4), 608–630.

Crosby, F. (1976). A model of egoistical relative deprivation. *Psychological Review, 83,* 85–113.

Davis, J. A. (1966). The campus as a frog pond: An application of the theory of relative deprivation to career decisions of college men. *American Journal of Sociology, 72,* 17–31.

De Vellis, R. F., Blalock, S. J., Holt, K., Renner, B. R., Blanchard, L. W., & Klotz, M. L. (1991). Arthritis patients' reactions to unavoidable social comparisons. *Personality and Social Psychology Bulletin, 17* (4), 392–399.

Devine, P. G. (1989). Stereotypes and prejudice: Their automatic and controlled components. *Journal of Personality and Social Psychology, 56,* 5–18.

Diener, E., & Fujita, F. (1997). Social comparisons and subjective well-being. In B. P. Buunk & F. X. Gibbons (Eds.), *Health, coping, and well-being: Perspectives from social comparison theory* (pp. 329–357). Mahwah, NJ: Lawrence Erlbaum Associates.

Dijksterhuis, A., & Van Knippenberg, A. (1998). The relation between perception and behavior, or how to win a game of Trivial Pursuit. *Journal of Personality and Social Psychology, 74,* 865–877.

Duncan, B. L. (1976). Differential social perception and attribution of intergroup violence: Testing the lower limits of stereotyping of blacks. *Journal of Personality and Social Psychology, 34,* 590–598.

Dunning, D., & Sherman, D. A. (1997). Stereotypes and tacit inference. *Journal of Personality and Social Psychology, 73,* 459–471.

Eiser, J. R., & Van der Pligt, J. (1982). Accentuation and perspective in attitudinal judgment. *Journal of Personality and Social Psychology, 42,* 224–238.

Festinger, L. (1954). A theory of social comparison processes. *Human Relations, 7,* 117–140.

Fiske, S. T. (1993). Controlling other people: The impact of power on stereotyping. *American Psychologist, 48,* 621–628.

Fiske, S. T. (1998). Stereotyping, prejudice, and discrimination. In D. T. Gilbert, S. T. Fiske, & G. Lindzey (Eds.), *Handbook of social psychology* Vol. 2. 4th. edn. Boston, MA: McGraw-Hill.

Fiske, S. T., & Neuberg, S. L. (1990). A continuum of impression formation, from category-based to individuating processes: Influences of information and motivation on attention and interpretation. In M. Zanna (Ed.), *Advances in experimental social psychology* Vol. 23 (pp. 1–74). New York: Academic Press.

Foschi, M. (1998). Double standards: Types, conditions, and consequences. *Advances in group processes, 15*, 59–80.

Frank, R. H. (1985). *Choosing the right pond*. New York: Oxford University Press.

Gaertner, S. L., & Dovidio, J. F. (1986). The aversive form of racism. In J. F. Dovidio & S. L. Gaertner (Eds.), *Prejudice, discrimination, and racism* (pp. 61–89). Orlando, FL: Academic Press.

Gerard, H. B. (1963). Emotional uncertainty and social comparison. *Journal of Abnormal and Social Psychology, 66* (6), 568–573.

Gibbons, F. X., & Gerrard, M. (1991). Downward comparison and coping with threat. In J. Suls & T. A. Wills (Eds.), *Social comparison: Contemporary theory and research* (pp. 317–346). Hillsdale, NJ: Erlbaum.

Gibbons, F. X., & Gerrard, M. (1995). Predicting young adults' health-risk behavior. *Journal of Personality and Social Psychology, 69*, 505–517.

Gibbons, F. X., & Gerrard, M. (1997). Health images and their effects on health behavior. In B. P. Buunk & F. X. Gibbons (Eds.), *Health, coping, and well-being: Perspectives from social comparison theory* (pp. 63–94). Mahwah, NJ: Erlbaum.

Gibbons, F. X., Gerrard, M., Lando, H. A., & McGovern, P. G. (1991). Social comparison and smoking cessation: The role of the "typical smoker." *Journal of Experimental Social Psychology, 27*, 239–258.

Gilbert, D. T., Giesler, R. B., & Morris, K. A. (1995). When comparisons arise. *Journal of Personality and Social Psychology, 69* (2), 227–236.

Gilbert, D. T., & Hixon, J. G. (1991). The trouble of thinking: Activation and application of stereotypic beliefs. *Journal of Personality and Social Psychology, 60*, 509–517.

Goethals, G. R., & Darley, J. M. (1977). Social comparison theory: An attributional approach. In J. M. Suls & R. L. Miller (Eds.), *Social comparison processes: Theoretical and empirical perspectives* (pp. 259–278). Washington, DC: Hemisphere.

Goolsby, L. L., & Chaplin, W. F. (1988). The impact of normative, ipsative, and idiothetic information on feelings about academic performance. *Journal of Research in Personality, 22*, 445–464.

Gorenflo, D. W., & Crano, W. D. (1989). Judgmental subjectivity/objectivity and locus of choice in social comparison. *Journal of Personality and Social Psychology, 57*, 605–614.

Hakmiller, K. L. (1966). Threat as a determinant of downward comparison. *Journal of Experimental Social Psychology, 2* (Suppl. 1), 32–39.

Hamilton, D. L., & Sherman, J. W. (1994). Stereotypes. In R. S. Wyer & T. K. Srull (Eds.), *Handbook of social cognition* Vol. 2 (pp. 1–68). Hillsdale, NJ: Erlbaum.

Helgeson, V. S., & Mickelson, K. D. (1995). Motives for social comparison. *Personality and Social Psychology Bulletin, 21*, 1200–1209.

Helson, H. (1947). Adaptation-level as frame of reference for prediction of psychophysical data. *American Journal of Psychology, 60*, 1–29.

Higgins, E. T. (1987). Self-discrepancy: A theory relating self and affect. *Psychological Review, 94*, 319–340.

Higgins, E. T. (1990). Personality, social psychology, and person-situated relations: Standards and knowledge activation as a common language. In L. A. Pervin (Ed.), *Handbook of personality* (pp. 301–338). New York: Guilford Press.

Higgins, E. T., & King, G. (1981). Accessibility of social constructs: Information processing consequences of individual and contextual variability. In N. Cantor & J. Kihlstrom (Eds.), *Personality, cognition, and social interaction* (pp. 69–121). Hillsdale, NJ: Erlbaum.

Higgins, E. T., Rholes, W. S., & Jones, C. R. (1977). Category accessibility and impression formation. *Journal of Experimental Social Psychology, 13* (2), 141–154.

Higgins, E. T., Strauman, T., & Klein, R. (1986). Standards and the process of self-evaluation. In

R. M. Sorrentino & E. T. Higgins (Eds.), *Handbook of motivation and cognition* Vol. 1 (pp. 23–63). New York: Guilford Press.

Hilton, J. L., & Von Hippel, W. (1996). Stereotypes. *Annual Review of Psychology, 47*, 237–271.

Hogg, M. A., & Abrams, D. (1988). *Social identifications: A social psychology of intergroup relations and group processes.* London: Routledge.

Hoorens, V., & Buunk, B. P. (1993). Social comparison of health risks: Locus of control, the person positivity bias and unrealistic optimism. *Journal of Applied Social Psychology, 23*, 291–302.

Hyman, H. (1942). The psychology of subjective status. *Psychological Bulletin, 39*, 473–474.

Jackson, L. A., Sullivan, L. A., & Hodge, C. (1993). Stereotype effects on attributions, predictions, and evaluations: No two social judgments are quite alike. *Journal of Personality and Social Psychology, 65*, 69–84.

James, W. (1890/1948). *Principles of psychology.* New York: Holt.

Jussim, L., Coleman, L. M., & Lerch, L. (1987). The nature of stereotypes: A comparison and integration of three theories. *Journal of Personality and Social Psychology, 52*, 536–546.

Kahneman, D., & Miller, D. T. (1986). Norm theory: Comparing reality to its alternatives. *Psychological Review, 93* (2), 136–153.

Klein, W. M. (1997). Objective standards are not enough: Affective, self–evaluative, and behavioral responses to social comparison information. *Journal of Personality and Social Psychology, 72* (4), 763–774.

Kobrynowicz, D., & Biernat, M. (1997). Decoding subjective evaluations: How stereotypes provide shifting standards. *Journal of Experimental Social Psychology, 33*, 579–601.

Krueger, J., & Rothbart, M. (1988). The use of categorical and individuating information in making inferences about personality. *Journal of Personality and Social Psychology, 55*, 187–195.

Kruglanski, A. W., & Mayseless, O. (1990). Classic and current social comparison research: Expanding the perspective. *Psychological Bulletin, 108* (2), 195–208.

Kruglanski, A. W., & Webster, D. M. (1996). Motivated closing of the mind: "Seizing" and "freezing." *Psychological Review, 103*, 263–283.

Kunda, Z., & Sherman-Williams, B. (1993). Stereotypes and the construal of individuating information. *Personality and Social Psychology Bulletin, 19*, 90–99.

Kunda, Z., & Thagard, P. (1996). Forming impressions from stereotypes, traits, and behaviors: A parallel–constraint–satisfaction theory. *Psychological Review, 103*, 284–308.

Kunda, Z., Sinclair, L., & Griffin, D. (1997). Equal ratings but separate meanings: Stereotypes and the construal of traits. *Journal of Personality and Social Psychology, 72*, 720–734.

Lepore, L., & Brown, R. (1997). Category and stereotype activation: Is prejudice inevitable? *Journal of Personality and Social Psychology, 72*, 275–287.

Levine, J. M., & Moreland, R. L. (1986). Outcome comparisons in group contexts: Consequences for the self and others. In R. Schwarzer (Ed.), *Self-related cognitions in anxiety and motivation* (pp. 285–303). Hillsdale, NJ: Erlbaum.

Levine, J. M., & Moreland, R. L. (1987). Social comparison and outcome evaluation in group contexts. In J. C. Masters & W. P. Smith (Eds.), *Social comparison, social justice and relative deprivation: Theoretical, empirical and policy perspectives* (pp. 105–127). Hillsdale, NJ: Lawrence Erlbaum Associates.

Leyens, J. P., Yzerbyt, V., & Schadron, G. (1994). *Stereotypes and social cognition.* London: Sage.

Linville, P. W., & Jones, E. E. (1980). Polarized appraisals of out-group members. *Journal of Personality and Social Psychology, 38*, 689–703.

Locke, V., MacLeod, C., & Walker, I. (1994). Automatic and controlled activation of stereotypes: Individual differences associated with prejudice. *British Journal of Social Psychology, 33*, 29–46.

Lockwood, P., & Kunda, Z. (1997). Superstars and me: Predicting the impact of role models on the self. *Journal of Personality and Social Psychology, 73* (1), 91–103.

Lyubomirsky, S., & Ross, L. (1997). Hedonic consequences of social comparison: A contrast of happy and unhappy people. *Journal of Personality and Social Psychology, 73*, 1141–1157.

McFarland, C., & Buehler, R. (1995). Collective self-esteem as a moderator of the frog-pond effect in reactions to performance feedback. *Journal of Personality and Social Psychology, 68* (6), 1055–1070.

McGill, A. L. (1993). Selection of a causal background: Role of expectation versus feature mutability. *Journal of Personality and Social Psychology, 64*, 701–707.

Major, B. (1994). From social inequality to personal entitlement: The role of social comparison, legitimacy appraisals, and group membership. In M. P. Zanna (Ed.), *Advances in experimental social psychology* Vol. 26 (pp. 293–355). Orlando, FL: Academic Press.

Major, B., Testa, M., & Bylsma, W. H. (1991). Responses to upward and downward social comparisons: The impact of esteem-relevance and perceived control. In J. Suls & T. A. Wills (Eds.), *Social comparison: Contemporary theory and research* (pp. 237–260). Hillsdale, NJ: Lawrence Erlbaum Associates.

Mandler, G. (1975). *Mind and emotions.* New York: Wiley.

Manis, M., & Paskewitz, J. R. (1984). Judging psychopathology: Expectation and contrast. *Journal of Experimental Social Psychology, 20*, 363–381.

Manis, M., Paskewitz, J. R., & Cotler, S. (1986). Stereotypes and social judgment. *Journal of Personality and Social Psychology, 50*, 461–473.

Markus, H., & Nurius, P. (1986). Possible selves. *American Psychologist, 41*, 954–969.

Marsh, H. W. (1993). Academic self-concept: Theory, measurement, and research. In J. Suls (Ed.), *Psychological perspectives on the self,* Vol. 4 (pp. 1–26).

Marsh, H. W., & Parker, J. W. (1984). Determinants of student self-concept: Is it better to be a relatively large fish in a small pond even if you don't learn to swim as well? *Journal of Personality and Social Psychology, 47* (1), 213–231.

Martin, J. (1986). The tolerance of injustice. In J. M. Olson, C. P. Herman, & M. P. Zanna (Eds.), *Relative deprivation and social comparison: The Ontario Symposium* Vol. 4 (pp. 217–240). Hillsdale, NJ: Erlbaum.

Martin, L. L. (1986). Set/reset: Use and disuse of concepts in impression formation. *Journal of Personality and Social Psychology, 51*, 493–504.

Masters, J. C., & Smith, W. P. (Eds.) (1987). *Social comparison, social justice, and relative deprivation: Theoretical, empirical, and policy perspectives.* Hillsdale, NJ: Erlbaum.

Mettee, D. R., & Smith, G. (1977). Social comparison and interpersonal attraction: The case for dissimilarity. In J. M. Suls & R. L. Miller (Eds.), *Social comparison processes: Theoretical and empirical perspectives* (pp. 69–101). Washington, DC: Hemisphere.

Miller, C. T. (1982). The role of performance-related similarity in social comparison of abilities: A test of the related attributes hypothesis. *Journal of Experimental Social Psychology, 18*, 513–523.

Miller, C. T. (1984). Self-schemas, gender, and social comparison: A clarification of the related attributes hypothesis. *Journal of Personality and Social Psychology, 46*, 1222–1229.

Miller, D. T., & Prentice, D. A. (1996). The construction of social norms and standards. In E. T. Higgins & A. W. Kruglanski (Eds.), *Social psychology: Handbook of basic principles* (pp.799–829). New York, NY: Guilford Press.

Miller, D. T., Turnbull, W., & McFarland, C. (1988). Particularistic and universalistic evaluation in the social comparison process. *Journal of Personality and Social Psychology, 55*, 908–917.

Miyake, K., & Zuckerman, M. (1993). Beyond personality impressions: Effects of physical and vocal attractiveness on false consensus, social comparison, affiliation, and assumed and perceived similarity. *Journal of Personality, 61*, 411–437.

Monteith, M. J. (1993). Self-regulation of prejudiced responses: Implications for progress in prejudice-reduction efforts. *Journal of Personality and Social Psychology, 65*, 469–485.

Morse, S., & Gergen, K. J. (1970). Social comparison, self-consistency, and the concept of self. *Journal of Personality and Social Psychology, 16*, 148–156.

Mussweiler, T., & Strack, F. (in press). Consequences of social comparison: Selective accessibility, assimilation and contrast. In J. Suls & L. Wheeler (Eds.), *Handbook of social comparison: Theory and research.* New York: Plenum.

Nosanchuk, T. A., & Erickson, B. H. (1985). How high is up? Calibrating social comparison in the real world. *Journal of Personality and Social Psychology, 48* (3), 624–634.

Oakes, P. J., Haslam, S. A., & Turner, J. C. (1994). *Stereotyping and social reality.* Oxford: Blackwell Publishers.

Olson, J., Herman, C. P., & Zanna, M. P. (Eds.) (1986). *Relative deprivation and social comparison:*

The Ontario Symposium on Social Cognition Vol. 4. Hillsdale, NJ: Erlbaum.

Olson, J. M., Roese, N. J., & Zanna, M. P. (1996). Expectancies. In E. T. Higgins & A. W. Kruglanski (Eds.), *Social psychology: Handbook of basic principles* (pp. 211–238). New York, NY: Guilford Press.

Orive, R. (1988). Social projection and social comparison of opinions. *Journal of Personality and Social Psychology, 54* (6), 953–964.

Ostrom, T. M., & Upshaw, H. S. (1968). Psychological perspective and attitude change. In A. G. Greenwald, T. C. Brock, & T. M. Ostrom (Eds.), *Psychological foundations of attitudes* (pp. 217–242). San Diego, CA: Academic Press.

Parducci, A. (1956). Direction of shift in the judgment of single stimuli. *Journal of Experimental Psychology, 51*, 169–178.

Parducci, A. (1965). Category judgment: A range frequency model. *Psychological Review, 72*, 407–418.

Parducci, A. (1995). *Happiness, pleasure, and judgment.* Mahwah, NJ: Erlbaum.

Pelham, B. W., & Wachsmuth, J. O. (1995). The waxing and waning of the social self: Assimilation and contrast in social comparison. *Journal of Personality and Social Psychology, 69* (5), 825–838.

Perdue, C. W., & Gurtman, M. B. (1990). Evidence for the automaticity of ageism. *Journal of Experimental Social Psychology, 26*, 199–216.

Perloff, L. S., & Fetzer, B. K. (1986). Self–other judgments and perceived vulnerability to victimization. *Journal of Personality and Social Psychology, 50*, 502–510.

Rabbie, J. M., & Horwitz, M. (1988). Categories versus groups as explanatory concepts in intergroup relations. *European Journal of Social Psychology, 18*, 117–123.

Raynor, J. O., & McFarlin, D. B. (1986). Motivation and the self-system. In R. M. Sorrentino & E. T. Higgins (Eds.), *Handbook of motivation and cognition: Foundations of social behavior* (pp. 315–349). New York: Guilford Press.

Samuel, W. (1973). On clarifying some interpretations of social comparison theory. *Journal of Experimental Social Psychology, 9*, 450–465.

Schachter, S. (1959). *The psychology of affiliation.* Stanford, CA: Stanford University Press.

Schaller, M., Rosell, M. C., & Asp, C. H. (1998). Parsimony and pluralism in the psychological study of intergroup processes. In C. Sedikides, J. Schopler, & C. Insko (Eds.), *Intergroup cognition and intergroup behavior* (pp. 3–25). Mahwah, NJ: Lawrence Erlbaum Associates

Scheier, M., & Carver, C. (1983). Self-directed attention and the comparison of self with standards. *Journal of Experimental Social Psychology, 19*, 205–222.

Schütz, A., & Tice, D. M. (1997). Associative and competitive indirect self-enhancement in close relationships moderated by trait self-esteem. *European Journal of Social Psychology, 27* (3), 257–273.

Schwarz, N., & Bless, H. (1992). Constructing reality and its alternatives: An inclusion/exclusion model of assimilation and contrast effects in social judgment. In L. Martin & A. Tesser (Eds.), *The construction of social judgment* (pp. 217–245). Hillsdale, NJ: Erlbaum.

Sedikides, C. (1993). Assessment, enhancement, and verification determinants of the self-evaluation process. *Journal of Personality and Social Psychology, 65*, 317–338.

Seta, J. J., Seta, C. E., & Donaldson, S. (1991). The impact of comparison processes on coactor's frustration and willingness to expend effort. *Personality and Social Psychology Bulletin, 17*, 560–568.

Sherif, M. A. (1936). *The psychology of social norms.* New York: Harper.

Smith, H. J., & Pettigrew, T. F. (1998). *Relative deprivation: A conceptual critique and meta-analysis.* Manuscript submitted for publication.

Smith, H. J., & Tyler, T. R. (1997). Choosing the right pond: The impact of group membership on self-esteem and group-oriented behavior. *Journal of Experimental Social Psychology, 33*, 146–170.

Solomon, S., Greenberg, J., & Pyszczynski, T. (1991). Terror management theory of self-esteem. In C. R. Snyder & D. Forsyth (Eds.), *Handbook of social and clinical psychology: The health perspective* (pp. 21–40). New York: Pergamon.

Stangor, C., & Lange, J. E. (1994). Mental representations of social groups: Advances in understanding stereotypes and stereotyping. *Advances in Experimental Social Psychology, 26*, 357–416.

Stangor, C., & McMillan, D. (1992). Memory for expectancy-congruent and expectancy-incongruent social information: A review of the social and social developmental literatures. *Psychological Bulletin, 111*, 42–61.

Stapel, D. A., & Winkielman, P. (1998). Assimilation and contrast as a function of context–target similarity, distinctness, and dimensional relevance. *Personality and Social Psychology Bulletin, 24*, 634–646.

Stevens, S. S. (1957). On the psychophysical law. *Psychological Review, 64*, 153–181.

Suls, J. (1986). Notes on the occasion of social comparison theory's thirtieth birthday. *Personality and Social Psychology Bulletin, 12* (3), 289–296.

Suls, J., & Wills, T. A. (Eds.) (1991). *Social comparison: Contemporary theory and research.* Hillsdale, NJ: Lawrence Erlbaum Associates.

Suls, J. M., Gaes, G. G., & Gastorf, J. W. (1979). Evaluating a sex-related ability: Comparison with same-, opposite-, and combined-sex norms. *Journal of Research in Personality, 13*, 294–304.

Swann, W. B., Jr. (1987). Identity negotiation: Where two roads meet. *Journal of Personality and Social Psychology, 53*, 1038–1051.

Swann, W. B., Jr., Stein-Seroussi, A., & Giesler, R. B. (1992). Why people self-verify. *Journal of Personality and Social Psychology, 62* (3), 392–401.

Tajfel, H. (1957). Value and the perceptual judgment of magnitude. *Psychological Review, 64*, 192–204.

Tajfel, H. (1969). Cognitive aspects of prejudice. *Journal of Social Issues, 25*, 79–97.

Tajfel, H. (1978). *Differentiation between social groups: Studies in the social psychology of intergroup relations.* New York: Academic Press.

Tajfel, H. (1982). Social psychology of intergroup relations. *Annual Review of Psychology, 33*, 1–39.

Taylor, S. E. (1989). *Positive illusions: Creative deception and the healthy mind.* USA: Basic Books.

Taylor, S. E., & Brown, J. D. (1988). Illusion and well-being: A social psychological perspective on mental health. *Psychological Bulletin, 103* (2), 193–210.

Taylor, S. E., & Lobel, M. (1989). Social comparison activity under threat: Downward evaluation and upward contacts. *Psychological Review, 96* (4), 569–575.

Taylor, S. E., Neter, E., & Wayment, H. A. (1995). Self-evaluation processes. *Personality and Social Psychology Bulletin, 21* (12), 1278–1287.

Taylor, S. E., Wood, J. V., & Lichtman, R. R. (1983). It could be worse: Selective evaluation as a response to victimization. *Journal of Social Issues, 39*, 19–40.

Tesser, A. (1988). Toward a self-evaluation maintenance model of social behavior. *Advances in Experimental Social Psychology, 21*, 181–226.

Trope, Y. (1986). Self-enhancement and self-assessment in achievement behavior. In R. M. Sorrentino & E. T. Higgins (Eds.), *Handbook of motivation and cognition: Foundations of social behavior* (pp. 350–378). New York: Guilford Press.

Turner, J. C. (1975). Social comparison and social identity: Some prospects for intergroup behaviour. *European Journal of Social Psychology, 5*, 5–34.

Turner, J. C., Hogg, M. A., Oakes, P. J., Reicher, S. D., & Wetherell, M. (1987). *Rediscovering the social group: A self-categorization theory.* Oxford: Blackwell Publishers.

Tyler, T. R., & Smith, H. J. (1998). Social justice and social movements. In D. T. Gilbert, S. T. Fiske, & G. Lindzey (Eds.), *Handbook of social psychology.* 4th edn. Vol. 2 (pp. 595–629). Boston, MA: McGraw-Hill.

Upshaw, H. S. (1962). Own attitude as an anchor in equal-appearing intervals. *Journal of Abnormal and Social Psychology, 64*, 85–96.

Volkmann, J. (1951). Scales of judgment and their implications for social psychology. In J. H. Rohrer & M. Sherif (Eds.), *Social psychology at the crossroads.* New York: Harper.

Von Hippel, W., Sekaquaptewa, D., & Vargas, P. (1995). On the role of encoding processes in stereotype maintenance. In M. P. Zanna (Ed.), *Advances in experimental social psychology* Vol. 27 (pp. 177–254). New York: Academic Press.

Weary, G., Marsh, K. L., & McCormick, L. (1994). Depression and social comparison motives. *European Journal of Social Psychology, 24*, 117–129.

Wegener, D. T., & Petty, R. E. (1997). The flexible correction model: The role of naive theories of bias in bias correction. In M. P. Zanna (Ed.), *Advances in experimental social psychology* Vol. 29 (pp. 141–208).

Wheeler, L. (1966). Motivation as a determinant of upward comparison. *Journal of Experimental Social Psychology, 2* (Suppl. 1), 27–31.

Wheeler, L. (1991). A brief history of social comparison theory. In J. Suls, & T. A. Wills (Eds.), *Social comparison: Contemporary theory and research* (pp. 3–21). Hillsdale, NJ: Lawrence Erlbaum Associates.

Wheeler, L., & Miyake, K. (1992). Social comparison in everyday life. *Journal of Personality and Social Psychology, 62* (5), 760–773.

Wheeler, L., Martin, R., & Suls, J. (1997). The proxy model of social comparison for self-assessment of ability. *Personality and Social Psychology Review, 1*, 54–61.

Wilder, D. A., & Allen, V. L. (1978). Group membership and preference for information about others. *Personality and Social Psychology Bulletin, 4*, 106–110.

Wilder, D. A., & Shapiro, P. (1991). Facilitation of outgroup stereotypes by enhanced ingroup identity. *Journal of Experimental Social Psychology, 27*, 431–452.

Wills, T. A. (1981). Downward comparison principles in social psychology. *Psychological Bulletin, 90* (2), 245–271.

Wills, T. A. (1991). Similarity and self-esteem in downward comparison. In J. M. Suls & T. A. Wills (Eds.), *Social comparison: Contemporary theory and research* (pp.51–78). Hillsdale, NJ: Erlbaum.

Wills, T. A., & Suls, J. (1991). Commentary: Neo-social comparison theory and beyond. In J. Suls & T. A. Wills (Eds.), *Social comparison: Contemporary theory and research* (pp. 395–411). Hillsdale, NJ: Lawrence Erlbaum Associates.

Wood, J. V. (1989). Theory and research concerning social comparisons of personal attributes. *Psychological Bulletin, 106* (2), 231–248.

Zebrowitz, L. A., & Lee, S. Y. (1999). Appearance, stereotype incongruent behavior, and social relationships. *Personality and Social Psychology Bulletin, 25*, 569–584.

Zebrowitz, L. A., Kendall-Tackett, K., & Fafel, J. (1991). The influence of children's facial maturity on parental expectations and punishment. *Journal of Experimental Child Psychology, 52*, 221–238.

Chapter Thirteen

Individual Differences in Information Processing

Peter Suedfeld and Philip E. Tetlock

Because cognition is integral to all of the processes that underlie social behavior, any meaningful investigation must separate it into manageable parts. One way to divide the field is by differentiating questions about *what* people think (content) from *how* people think (process). A thorough analysis of individual differences in thought content would have to deal with self-schemata and personality traits as well as variations in just about every topic in social psychology, from self-esteem through attitudes to helping behavior, about which any given person may think consistently over time and across situations.

Studying *how* people think, a somewhat less daunting enterprise, addresses fundamental consistencies that, at least theoretically, permeate the individual's thinking across domains. One major approach is to look at the *quality* of thought: intelligence, a largely unchanging and substantially heritable characteristic (Plomin & Rende, 1991). Intelligence strongly influences how well people process information about any issue. It is clearly an important aspect of all cognition, and a potent predictor of life outcomes. This notoriously controversial topic has been reviewed in many other publications.

Our topic will be a second aspect of how people think: the structure of thought, as opposed to either its content or its quality. This area is generally referred to as the study of cognitive styles. We shall start with a concise history of the field, and then – because here, too, a large literature has accumulated over the decades – examine in detail three representative constructs: need for cognition, conceptual/integrative complexity, and need for closure. We shall give a brief account of the origins and measurement of each, and then address three major topics: correlations with other cognitive style measures, relevant experimental research, and the implications of the findings for adaptive, rational thinking.

During the writing of this chapter, Peter Suedfeld was a Visiting Scholar at the Mershon Center of the Ohio State University. The support of the Center and of its Director, R. Ned Lebow, is gratefully acknowledged.

Origins of Cognitive Styles Research

Although there were precursors, systematic research on cognitive styles began with a study of what makes people differentially susceptible to the attractions of Fascist ideology (*The Authoritarian Personality*, Adorno, Frenkel-Brunswik, Levinson, & Sampson, 1950). The theory was that certain types of childrearing affect the development of attitudes and beliefs (e.g. submissiveness to authority, punitiveness against deviants, aversion to introspection, and propensity for dichotomous good–bad thinking) that in combination make for a potentially Fascistic personality orientation. One of many flaws in this work was that the researchers inadvertently confounded content with process: for example, a predisposition toward automatic obedience to authority may well include the demands of anti-Fascist authorities, or demands that are unrelated to Fascism or even to politics. The same criticism applies to other aspects of the scale. Recognition of such problems led to attempts to develop theories and measures that were relatively content-free, such as the concepts of dogmatism, rigidity, and tolerance of ambiguity (Budner, 1962; Rokeach, 1960).

The pioneering work of Adorno, et al., Rokeach, and their critics catapulted cognitive styles into a prominent place in psychology. In part, the issues attracted interest because of their topical relevance. Authoritarianism and dogmatism, and the controversy about whether authoritarian styles of thinking are confined to the political right or are also found in the political left, were topical during the Cold War.

Simultaneously, the cognitive revolution had arrived and was influencing new areas of psychology. During the 1950s and 1960s many cognitive style theories were developed, published, and assessed, each with its own measurement techniques for identifying individual differences. These included self-report instruments (Budner, 1962; Rokeach, 1960), semi-projective measures (Harvey, Hunt, & Schroder, 1961; Loevinger, 1976), statistical techniques such as multidimensional scaling and cluster analysis (Driver, 1965), and tests of perceptual and conceptual performance (Scott, Osgood, & Peterson, 1979; Witkin, Dyk, Faterson, Goodenough, & Karp, 1962).

Interest in cognitive styles has waxed, waned, and waxed again, somewhat independently of the importance or quality of the work (Sternberg & Grigorenko, 1997). Some studies failed to find expected relationships among methodologically dissimilar measures of theoretically related cognitive traits, casting doubt upon the robustness of the theorized dimensions. The resultant skepticism was exacerbated by Mischel's (1968) attack on the very existence of important stable individual differences, whether in cognition or other realms.

Many psychologists considered this to be an overstatement, so contrary to common sense that it could not be accepted holus-bolus. The idea that all human beings share a uniform approach to thinking – always seeking consistency, according to the theories of the 1960s and 1970s (Abelson, et al., 1968), or always minimizing cognitive effort, according to the theories of the next decade (Fiske & Taylor, 1991; Tversky & Kahneman, 1974) – made researchers uneasy. There was also widespread recognition that attention to individual differences could help us to understand variation that otherwise had to be consigned to the category of "noise."

The result was the recent resurgence of investigation into cognitive styles. The new theorists recognize the naivete of the assumption that traits are expressed uniformly, regardless of other factors. Accordingly, they tend to consider both endogenous predilections (cognitive styles) and situational influences on thinking, as well as interactions between the two. Although earlier measurement techniques (Schroder, 1971) remain popular, methodologists have added observer ratings (Tetlock, Peterson, & Berry, 1993), the thematic analysis of natural language (Suedfeld & Rank, 1976; Winter, 1973), and performance on realistic simulations (Streufert & Streufert, 1978).

Representative Theories

Constraints of space require us to limit our focus to three theories of cognitive styles (but see Suedfeld, in press, a). They deal with stable individual differences: in need for cognition, which we shall abbreviate as nCogn (the tendency to engage in and enjoy effortful cognitive endeavors), conceptual/integrative complexity (the tendency to process information in differentiated and integrated ways), and need for closure, nClos (the tendency to make judgments and decisions confidently in ways that minimize ambiguity and subjective uncertainty).

Overview

We selected these three theories because they are representative of the field in important ways. Each has stimulated considerable research, and illustrates a distinctive methodological approach to measurement and hypothesis derivation and testing. They also share the pervasive problem of value bias. From the beginning, at least among educated people in Western democracies, some cognitive styles were considered less effective and less morally acceptable than their opposite. Authoritarianism and dogmatism are associated with failure to consider new information, unwillingness to tolerate dissent, prejudice toward members of groups other than one's own, and self-righteous moralistic hostility. This is actually a trickily contextual issue: a Nazi social scientist (Jaensch, cited in Brown, 1965) argued that low authoritarianism reflects a decadent lack of clear and strong moral values. Need for cognition, need for closure, and integrative complexity also attract value judgments. Most scholars assume that effective, rational, and socially beneficial thinking is the end product of high need for cognition (enjoying thinking), high integrative complexity (recognizing the legitimacy of alternative perspectives and having the ability to find viable integrative solutions), and low need for closure (refraining from jumping to quick conclusions).

How does one judge whether a thought process is effective and socially beneficial? Some possibilities are:

1   Assess whether it adheres to the rules of probability and formal logic, avoiding cognitive shortcuts and emotional biases (Tversky & Kahneman, 1974). This option is available only for a narrow range of tasks, and even here there is controversy over the right answers.

2   Assess how successful the final decision proves to be in the real world or as compared to the judgment of experts (Kruglanski, 1989).
3   In the eyes of some, there is also moral or ethical superiority associated with the supposedly preferable ends of these cognitive style dimensions. Just as in the earlier theories, the "right" cognitive styles are seen as leading to good democratic citizenship: tolerance, openness, cooperativeness, and willingness to compromise (Sniderman, 1975).
4   See which cognitive style leads to mentally healthy, satisfying ways of interacting with the world (wanting the right things and living the right way).

Recent theorists are not unanimous on these questions. Most notably, some of the most prolific researchers have argued that high conceptual/integrative complexity does not necessarily lead to the most successful decisions nor to the most morally or ethically defensible ones.

These three (and all other) cognitive style constructs may not be completely independent of intellectual ability. Smarter people are more likely to enjoy cognitive challenges (high need for cognition), to prolong their engagement with such challenges (low need for closure), and to create solutions that incorporate and combine a variety of considerations and approaches (high complexity). Related to this issue is the question of how independent the three dimensions are of each other. Do they in fact represent facets of one cognitive style, perhaps generic open-mindedness (Tetlock, Peterson, & Berry, 1993)? There is significant shared variance among the three constructs, and also between them and intelligence. But the interrelationships are not of sufficient magnitude to conclude that the stylistic constructs should either be lumped together or equated with intellectual ability.

Finally, cognitive style theorists cannot avoid taking a stand on that hardy perennial: the trait–state issue. The two "need" constructs are broad, stable personality characteristics that apply to the individual's typical cognitive behavior across issues and situations. Complexity is somewhat different: although the original theory proposed a personality trait (conceptual complexity), more recent developments have emphasized the complexity of thought processes as determined by the interaction of personality and situational factors (integrative complexity). Thus, complexity theory combines trait and state components. Actual research programs on all three styles recognize that the expression of personality dispositions is affected by other influences; the research is sensitive to how judgments and social interaction are shaped by trait x situation interactions.

Need for cognition

Cacioppo & Petty (1982) proposed that there are stable individual differences in the tendency to engage in and enjoy cognitive effort, captured by a single factor that they labeled "need for cognition." People with high nCogn ("chronic cognizers") were hypothesized to seek and reflect on information to impose meaningful structure on events. By contrast, people with low nCogn ("cognitive misers") were hypothesized to rely on low-effort heuristics and the opinions of others to impose this structure.

Like all of the cognitive styles that have attracted attention in the late twentieth century, nCogn has obvious intellectual forebears in the mid-twentieth century. Cohen (1957) first used the label "need for cognition," but the Petty and Cacioppo variable is perhaps closer in spirit to Fiske's (1949) concept of the inquiring intellect: it focuses on process (positive orientation toward thoughtful effort) rather than outcome (finding a cognitive structure to interpret events).

Correlational studies   Need for cognition is generally measured using either the original 34-item scale or an 18-item short form that has been the product of extensive psychometric winnowing. Illustrative items include: "Thinking is not my idea of fun" (reverse scored) and "I find satisfaction in deliberating hard for long hours."

Petty and Cacioppo take pains to distinguish nCogn from intellectual ability. They concede that high nCogn individuals who are also highly intelligent are likely to receive more encouragement for engaging in cognitive activity than are less intelligent high nCogn individuals. Operant learning theory thus predicts a positive correlation between need for cognition and indices such as verbal intelligence. Petty and Cacioppo also argue that a certain level of intelligence is a necessary but not sufficient condition for significant variation in need for cognition to develop (a hypothesis that finds support in the integrative complexity literature). However, in their view, nCogn is a cognitive–motivational variable, not an intellectual ability. They point to correlations in the 0.2 to 0.3 range between nCogn and verbal intelligence – which also support the learning theory prediction – as evidence for the distinction. Curiously, though, similar correlations among other cognitive styles are often interpreted as showing convergent validity.

Is nCogn unidimensional? Much hinges on how one decides whether a single-factor as opposed to a multi-factor factor-analytic solution is more appropriate – an issue that has loomed large in the intelligence literature. There is evidence across studies for a general factor that explains between 25 percent and 40 percent of the variance among items in the Need for Cognition scale. But under some conditions it appears useful to break the scale up into subscales that include cognitive persistence, confidence, and complexity (Tanaka, Panter, & Winborne, 1988).

With respect to convergent and discriminant validity, the Need for Cognition scale again does reasonably well. Individual differences in nCogn are negatively correlated with measures of dogmatism, the tendency to rely heavily on social-comparison cues (the self-monitoring subscale), the tendency to ignore, avoid, or distort new information (the simplification scale: Venkatraman, Marlino, Kardes, & Skylar, 1990), and need for closure (nClos). As predicted, nCogn is negatively correlated with decisiveness, closed-mindedness, personal need for structure, and preference for order and predictability.

High nCogn scorers are more likely to make complex attributions, to base judgments on empirical observations or rational arguments (Leary, et al., 1986), to seek out, scrutinize, and use information when making decisions involving problems (Berzonsky & Sullivan, 1992), to be curious (Olson, Camp, & Fuller, 1984), to maximize information gain (uncertainty orientation: Sorrentino, et al., 1988), and to be open to new ideas. Finally, nCogn loads positively on Openness to Experience, one of the Big Five factors of personality, which emphasizes generic receptivity to new ideas, a preference for varied experiences, and willingness to consider alternative interpretations (Cacioppo, Petty, Feinstein, & Jarvis, 1996).

Construct-validational evidence from experiments   Beyond patterns of correlations with other individual difference constructs, there is considerable laboratory evidence that nCogn predicts engagement in effortful information processing. Not surprisingly, given that the inventors of the scale are also the authors of the elaboration-likelihood model of persuasion, the bulk of this evidence comes from attitude change experiments. Some relevant findings are:

1   High nCogn scorers have superior recall for persuasive arguments.
2   High scorers possess more information on a broad array of issues.
3   As predicted by the elaboration-likelihood model, high scorers are more influenced by well-crafted and probative arguments and less persuaded by illogical and tangential arguments than are low scorers.
4   Again as predicted by the elaboration-likelihood model, there is an interaction between nCogn and peripheral cues. Low nCogn individuals are more swayed by superficial, easy-to-process information such as the number of reasons the source claims to have in support of a position, characterizations of the source as possessing low or high credibility or as being attractive or unattractive, and the number of people who applaud the speaker.
5   In response to persuasive communications, high nCogn individuals generate more issue-relevant thoughts.
6   High scorers show stronger correlations between open-ended measures of thought and rating-scale measures of attitudes, suggesting that they possess more tightly integrated belief systems.
7   High scorers perform better on a wide range of intellectual tasks, including arithmetic problems, anagrams, and college coursework.

In research paradigms other than persuasion experiments, the moderator-variable role of nCogn is less clear. For example, there is mixed evidence on whether high nCogn individuals are more likely to display attitude polarization effects as a result of merely thinking about the issue (Tesser, 1978). Cacioppo, Petty, Feinstein, & Jarvis (1996) argue that when high nCogn respondents spontaneously engage in thought, their attitudes tend to polarize, consistent with Tesser's original discovery. But when respondents are specifically told to consider their attitudes, those high in nCogn may carefully consider all sides of the issue and thus show moderation instead of polarization. This is the preferred explanation for why both attitude polarization and attitude moderation have been found when high nCogn individuals devoted thought to a message (Smith, Haugtvedt, & Petty (1994) and Leone & Ensley (1986), respectively).

The inconsistent results underscore the importance of adopting a multivariate approach to cognitive styles. Perhaps high nCogn individuals think in complex ways about topics that activate genuinely mixed feelings, becoming more likely to move toward moderation, but simplify and polarize when all the relevant arguments point in one direction (as predicted by the models of Tetlock, 1986, and Liberman & Chaiken, 1991). There is also an obvious interaction prediction between nClos and nCogn. Individuals who are high in both should be especially likely to polarize, whereas high nCogn individuals with low nClos should be especially likely to moderate. The effects of thought on the attitudes of low nCogn individuals should, however, be relatively weak regardless of nClos.

Adaptiveness/rationality of need for cognition   Cacioppo, Petty, and their colleagues repeatedly caution against assuming that high nCogn individuals will always be less biased or more objective. For example, people in positive moods are more likely to recall positive memories and to overestimate the probability of positive events. Petty, Schumann, Richman, & Strathman (1993) found that mood effects were especially pronounced among high nCogn people who were asked to react to a persuasive message. Wegener, Petty, & Klein (1994) clarified the boundary conditions of this effect: high nCogn respondents who were in a good mood were more influenced by persuasive messages that stressed the benefits of adopting a policy, whereas high nCogn respondents who were in a bad mood were more persuaded by a message that stressed the costs of not adopting a policy. Mood had negligible effects on low nCogn respondents.

Petty & Jarvis (1996) argued that high nCogn subjects are more susceptible to priming effects than low nCogn subjects, for three distinct but usually mutually reinforcing reasons: (a) high scorers possess more accessible and more interconnected concept nodes in memory; (b) high scorers generate more thoughts, creating greater potential for the activated concept to bias thought; (c) the judgments of individuals high in nCogn are based more on the thoughts they themselves generate than are those of low nCogn individuals, so that biased thoughts would have greater impact on subsequent judgments of the former group. As predicted, high nCogn respondents who were primed as to the prospect of either winning or losing before placing roulette bets were indeed more influenced by the primes than were low nCogn respondents.

Cacioppo, Petty, Feinstein, & Jarvis (1996) proposed that priming effects should be especially strong among high nCogn respondents when the primes are subtle and the respondents are unaware of their influence. But if people are informed of a potential biasing effect on their judgments and they are motivated to be accurate, then high nCogn respondents should try especially hard to compensate for the anticipated effect of the biasing factor by adjusting their judgments. This prediction follows because corrections require mental effort that should be more acceptable to high nCogn respondents.

The elaboration-likelihood model predicts that individuals high in nCogn should be more susceptible to primacy effects, because they elaborate the initial arguments more, form stronger attitudes as a result, and are thus in a better position to resist or discount subsequent inconsistent information. One study did find the predicted result (Kassin, Reddy, & Tullock, 1990), but another found the opposite: stronger primacy among low nCogn individuals (Ahlering & Parker, 1989). Cacioppo, Petty, Feinstein, & Jarvis (1996) argue that low nCogn individuals should show greater primacy effects even when there are good reasons to suspend judgment until all the available evidence has been processed; high nCogn individuals should exhibit primacy effects only when they see no compelling reason to suspend judgment. This issue has not been resolved but there is, once again, a strong case to be made for a nCogn x nClos interaction. Individuals high on both measures should be especially prone to primacy effects, whereas those who are high in nCogn but low in nClos should be especially resistant to them. *Mutatis mutandis*, the same argument applies when one substitutes integrative complexity for nClos.

Conceptual/integrative complexity

Complexity theory is a successor to George Kelly's (1955) Theory of Personal Constructs, which measured people's perceptions of similarities and differences among objects of thought (other people, inanimate objects, concepts, etc.). Most versions of cognitive complexity theory (Goldstein & Blackman, 1978; Linville, 1985; Satish, 1997; Schroder & Suedfeld, 1971) concentrate on the degree to which people make distinctions among various aspects of a cognitive domain. We shall examine a theory that goes a step beyond this to consider also the perceived relationships among different aspects.

The first version of what became conceptual complexity theory considered how styles of cognition developed from different childrearing strategies (Harvey, Hunt, & Schroder, 1961). In this, it was similar to authoritarianism theory; and it similarly confounded structural with content variables. The next version (Schroder, Driver, & Streufert, 1967) presented the first truly structural theory. The processes that define conceptual complexity were described as discrimination (the ability to perceive gradations within a stimulus dimension, e.g. shades of color, or shades of opinion within a religious or political group), differentiation (the perception of different dimensions or different perspectives, e.g. different legitimate goals related to a political issue), and integration (the perception of relationships among differentiated dimensions, such as seeing how different strategies may interact or how different programs may be components of an overarching high-level strategy). The theory holds that stable individual differences exist in the levels of discrimination, differentiation, and integration that people achieve in processing information, regardless of the topic, task, or situation. Subsequently, only differentiation and integration have been studied in any detail.

The most frequently used measure of conceptual complexity has been the Paragraph Completion Test (PCT). Research subjects write paragraphs on the topics given in several stems until time expires (usually after 90–120 seconds, depending on the age, educational level, and verbal skills of the subjects). The stems tap three major areas of social cognition: relations to authority, social disapproval, and uncertainty. Completions are scored on a 1–7 scale, with 1 = undifferentiated response, 3 = differentiation but no integration, 5 = integration, and 7 = high-level integration within a superordinate conceptual schema. Scores of 2, 4, or 6 are assigned when a completion shows implicit signs of functioning at the next higher level but the signs are not clear-cut (Baker-Brown, et al., 1992). Table 1 presents examples of integrative complexity coding.

Correlational studies Because measures of complexity are not highly correlated with each other (Goldstein & Blackman, 1978; Vannoy, 1965), inter-study consistency is low when researchers use different tests. However, there are some well-established findings. We present a brief summary of the highlights, without identifying the source of each, as most of these studies have been described in primary as well as other secondary publications (e.g. Goldstein & Blackman, 1978; Streufert & Streufert, 1978; Suedfeld, Tetlock, & Streufert, 1992).

Conceptual complexity shows a positive correlation with Kohlberg's measure of moral development (De Vries & Walker, 1986) and negative correlations with authoritarianism and dogmatism. Persons operating at low levels of complexity are more certain of their

Table 1   Examples of integrative complexity from US senatorial speeches on abortion

Integrative complexity	Differentiation	Integration	Example	Rationale
Low	Low	Low	"Abortion is a basic right that should be available to all women. To limit a woman's access to an abortion is an intolerable infringement on her civil liberties. Such an infringement must not be tolerated. To do so would be to threaten the separation of church and state so fundamental to the American way of life."	This individual only sees a single perspective on this issue and does not acknowledge that other legitimate perspectives might exist
Medium	High	Low	"Many see abortion as a basic civil liberty that should be available to any woman who chooses to exercise this right. Others, however, see abortion as infanticide."	This individual acknowledges the legitimacy of different perspectives but perceives no relationships between perspectives
High	High	High	"Some view abortion as a civil liberties issue; others see abortion as tantamount to murder. One's opinion depends on a complicated mixture of legal, moral, and perhaps scientific judgments. Is there a constitutional right to abortion? What criteria should be used to determine when life begins? Who possesses the authority to resolve these issues?	This individual acknowledges the legitimacy of different viewpoints and develops complex rules to compare and contrast these perspectives

own judgments and less tolerant of ambiguity and inconsistency, especially when there is a lack of clarity on the evaluative (good–bad) dimension.

Observers judge highly complex individuals to be assertive, extroverted and gregarious, warm and nurturant in relationships, and socially adept. They are also seen as easily bored, self-centered, risk-seeking, open to novel experiences, narcissistic, and high in initiative.

Simpler individuals are seen as good team members, calm and confident in difficult situations, but too submissive to superiors and too domineering toward subordinates.

The measured relationship between complexity and intelligence parallels that between nCogn and intelligence. Positive mid-range correlations are the mode: the smarter the sample studied, the weaker the relationship. Predictably, complexity is unrelated to performance on multiple-choice examinations, but is positively related to marks on essay examinations. Complexity is most reliably associated with knowledge in such areas as problem-solving and language, verbal intelligence, and especially with the ability to think up novel solutions to problems (Suedfeld & Coren, 1992). Others perceive complex subjects as intelligent; they think of themselves as being creative, and have personality profiles resembling those of creative architects, writers, and scientists (Tetlock, Peterson, & Berry, 1993).

Experimental and archival studies   The research described by Schroder, Driver, & Streufert (1967) is fairly diverse, but many studies used either a tactical simulation game or a stock-market simulation. The major situational variables were information load and degree of success or failure.

Homogeneously complex groups consistently searched for more information, incorporated it in their decisions, and linked their decisions to previous decisions and to feedback. Both temporal and strategic connections among their moves were richer and more far-reaching. They were also more adaptive in functioning under stress: flexible in changing their plans in response to negative feedback, and less likely to ignore important information during periods of overload.

Other studies have found that less complex groups or individuals are less likely to change their attitudes or judgments in response to persuasive messages or a discrepant judgment by another person or a group. However, once their attitude does change, the change generalizes to related attitudes, to the source of the message, etc., more than it does among complex subjects. Conceptually simple individuals are also more likely to exhibit interpersonal rejection as a consequence of disagreement or failure, expressive (as opposed to instrumental) aggression, and less tolerance for cognitive dissonance, inconsistency, or imbalance. Higher conceptual complexity is consistently associated with more finely graded reactions to environmental conditions, and with more interconnected strategic planning and execution (Streufert & Streufert, 1978). Tetlock (in press) found that more conservative managers preferred simplifying heuristics and tolerated more cognitive biases (such as the fundamental attribution error and over-confidence) linked to the application of these heuristics.

There has also been considerable research dealing with integrative complexity, the level of differentiation and integration exhibited in a particular set of spoken or written material circumscribed in time or situation. The first study emphasizing this variable (Suedfeld & Rank, 1976) was also the first to apply the PCT scoring technique to archival material, which has made possible the scoring of an almost infinite variety of verbal communications. Theoretically, integrative (state) complexity is determined by the joint action of conceptual (trait) complexity and contextual factors. The effects are hypothesized to follow Selye's General Adaptation Syndrome: a challenging situation requiring a response or solution evokes the application of cognitive resources (i.e. higher complexity). However, if the challenge is too severe, too persistent, occurs simultaneously with too many other demands, or if cognitive resources are depleted through fatigue, illness, fear, or other adversities, complexity decreases ("disruptive stress"). The addition of integrative complexity to conceptual complexity theory integrates dispositional and processing variables (Mischel & Shoda, 1998).

Integrative complexity is sensitive to many situational variables. The cognitive manager model (Suedfeld, 1992) posits that the integrative complexity of thought is a positive function of the investment of cognitive effort and resources. Because such an investment has both opportunity costs and direct costs (in time, effort, attention, and material resources), decision makers judge (a) the importance of the problem compared to others requiring resolution during the same time frame; and (b) the cognitive resources available. They then tend to make decisions at the lowest practicable level of complexity. Apparent cognitive miserliness may in fact be good management. If one makes cost–benefit calculations (rather than using a probabilistic or logical criterion, or comparing the decision with some ideal outcome), a simple solution may be preferable for many problems.

Proposition (a) above predicts that higher complexity will emerge when people are experiencing important personal problems, a prediction that has been supported by many studies. The theoretical limit of this increase in complexity is an interactive effect of trait complexity and the onset of cognitive resource depletion (disruptive stress) – (b) above. Findings of decreased complexity during time pressure, the imminence of examinations, societal upheaval, the death of loved ones, and the approach of one's own death, support the hypothesis.

Among other influences on complexity are accountability demands and self-presentation goals. Both may raise, lower, or leave unchanged an individual's level of complexity depending on circumstances (e.g. Tetlock, 1992). Still another variable, value pluralism, can explain – across domains and without invoking personality differences – why extremists show lower complexity than moderates (e.g. Tetlock, Armor, & Peterson, 1994).

Adaptive/rational aspects of complexity   Social scientists have often assumed, explicitly or implicitly, that high complexity is more adaptive than low (Suedfeld & Tetlock, 1991). On the other hand, Tetlock, et al. (1993) had found that complex decision makers are likely to be perceived by personnel experts as indecisive, wishy-washy, and slow to act. Even if this is a misperception, it can have important adverse consequences for a leader's future support and effectiveness. In practical situations, "Complexities are fun to talk about, but, when it comes to action, simplicities are often more effective" (O'Rourke, 1998, p. 209).

Early researchers predicted and usually found that people high in conceptual complexity performed better on experimental tasks. However, "better" was sometimes defined as "in a more complex way," which may be somewhat tautological. In the Schroder, Driver, & Streufert (1967) simulations, complex groups (especially under stress) were more concerned with long-term strategies, more likely to take the other side's point of view into account, and more sensitive to information. In real situations, these characteristics would not necessarily translate into more successful outcomes or more favorable cost–benefit balances. Archival studies do not uniformly show superior outcomes for complex information processing. For example, Adolf Hitler's pronouncements at the Munich Conference were considerably less complex than Neville Chamberlain's, but most analysts would agree that Hitler came out ahead.

Flexibly adjusting one's integrative complexity may enhance the chances of success. In changes of government (whether a revolutionary victory or an election), opposition leaders operating at simple levels who increase their complexity after taking office do better than those who are consistently complex or simple. On the other hand, consistently high integrative complexity even during crises is associated with long, successful government careers. A complex person may not commit premature closure or become closely identified with any side of a controversial decision, and thus can never be unequivocally shown to have been wrong.

Excessive complexity can consume more resources than the problem is worth, cause fatal delays in making a decision, or lead to diversion from important points by trivial or irrelevant information (Tetlock & Boettger, 1989). Tetlock and Boettger (1994) have also shown that complex information processors are especially likely to pass the buck and procrastinate. Such findings support critics of the assumption that high complexity is an ideal general approach to information processing.

Cross-domain differences in complexity are related to a variety of influences. For example, religiously orthodox subjects wrote at a significantly lower level of complexity about a religious than about a non-religious controversial issue, while less orthodox subjects showed no difference (Pancer, Jackson, Hunsberger, Pratt, & Lea, 1995). Another possible factor is familiarity or information availability: new parents showed higher complexity in thinking about parenthood than they had before their baby was born (Pancer, Gallant, Pratt, & Hunsberger, 1994). This particular pattern may have also been affected by the greater immediacy of the issue once the baby had arrived, as the cognitive manager model would predict – an inference supported by the further finding that women who had experienced high prenatal stress and exhibited low complexity (disruptive stress) were more likely to suffer from postnatal depression than those who had also experienced high stress but maintained high complexity in thinking about the situation. Similarly, there is a higher level of complexity when politicians address issues that are close to their important interests than when they deal with issues of less personal interest but of high relevance to their campaign (Suedfeld, in press, b).

Most writers have agreed that complexity can be taught, and that changes can be induced (or evoked) both during child development and later in life. According to Harvey, Hunt, & Schroder (1961), training environments in which rules are handed down and conformity to them is rewarded, and training in which the learner develops his own rules and the environment provides positive feedback if information search and processing are appropriate, respectively define the lowest and highest likelihood of developing complex thinking. Streufert & Streufert (1978) add that being prompted to take another person's point of view, encountering information that is moderately incongruent, and not being consistently reinforced for operating at a low level of complexity, all lead to increases in conceptual complexity.

Attempts to change (mostly, to raise) complexity among adults have met with some success, using simple instructions (Hunsberger, Lea, Pancer, Pratt, & McKenzie, 1992) as well as Streufert, Nogami, Swezey, Pogash, & Piasecki's (1988) disaster-management simulation. There have been few follow-ups to establish how long such changes may last.

It is worth noting that when people who have not been educated in psychology or the social sciences read solutions at various levels of complexity, they are quite accurate at assigning still other hypothetical solutions to the correct level. They also have an intuitive understanding of how a long list of environmental, endogenous, and task-specific variables would affect complexity. They show a fairly consistent preference for decisions that reflect a level of complexity at, or slightly higher than, the levels at which they think they would operate to solve a problem (Suedfeld, et al., 1996). Thus, complexity is a construct whose reality exists beyond explicit psychological theory.

Need for closure

Need for closure (nClos), like need for cognition, spans cognitive and motivational characteristics. In fact, the originators of the theory emphasize its motivational basis and reject having it classified as a cognitive style. The theory defines need for closure as the desire to obtain definite knowledge on some issue (Kruglanski & Webster, 1996). The theory, like the cognitive manager model, argues that constructing knowledge – by integrating external information, memory, "inchoate sensations," and thinking – is an effortful activity, which requires the allocation of considerable resources. It is initiated by a need to find a desirable answer to a question ("specific closure") or the need to find an answer, regardless of its desirability ("nonspecific closure"). These needs are thought to affect behavior in the entire domain of judgment, including social perception, intergroup relations, attribution, attitude change, and group dynamics.

When closure is reached, two goals have been attained: the person can cease devoting resources to finding an answer to the problem, and has a knowledge base from which he can move ahead to make decisions and take action. When for any reason action seems important, there is high pressure toward reaching closure; the same is true when the task of information-processing is unpleasant or boring, and closure is a way to escape having to confront the problem. According to Kruglanski & Webster (1996) the need subsumes two tendencies: the desire to reach closure as soon as possible ("seizing") and the desire to maintain closure for as long as possible once it has been reached ("freezing"). The demarcation point between the two processes is the point of crystallization, when a belief "turns from hesitant conjecture to a subjectively firm "fact."

At the opposite end of the nClos dimension, there may be a need to avoid closure. This is activated in cases when the person is reluctant to begin the action that must follow closure; when closure may lead to a serious error; or when the cognitive tasks involved are inherently enjoyable. In the last of these situations, the person may prefer to derive positive reinforcement from engaging in the process to obtaining reinforcement from reaching the goal. Thus, just like the level of integrative complexity, the level of nClos is influenced by situational factors.

Webster & Kruglanski (1994) summarize research that confirms the roles of some of these factors. High nClos can be inferred when subjects make decisions on the basis of primacy effects (relying on the first information obtained and ignoring later, possibly discrepant, information), stereotypes (basing what should be specific decisions in an individual case on preexisting, global judgments), and anchoring heuristics (making small adjustments from one's original judgment when change is necessary, rather than rejecting early solutions and finding new ones). This pattern is evoked when solutions must be found under time pressure, and when the task is unattractive or demanding. Need for closure, and reliance on first impressions, can also be enhanced by instructions to form global, rather than differentiated, judgments (Freund, Kruglanski, & Schpitzajzen, 1985). When nClos is increased through either time pressure or the presence of a distracting stressor, people who delay closure by expressing disagreement with the group judgment are rejected more strongly and those who enhance closure by trying hard to obtain consensus are more valued.

On the other hand, nClos and related cognitive strategies can be dramatically reduced in situations where delaying closure is advantageous. For example, primacy effects are reduced when the cost of an incorrect decision is high; evaluation apprehension, the fear of being perceived as incapable or inefficient, increases the need to avoid closure.

Like many other cognitive style constructs, nClos can be traced back to the theories of Adorno, et al. (1950) and Rokeach (1960), which identify some individuals as closed-minded and as desiring certainty on all issues. Current nClos theory does not base itself on the defense mechanisms of the ego, as its predecessors did. Kruglanski and Webster accept a role for developmental anxieties and ego defenses, but also view the internalization of cultural norms and pragmatic goals as leading to need for closure. They reject the earlier assumption that certainty-orientation is pathological and/or maladaptive; in fact, there are situations in which rapid closure is highly functional (particularly when the first conclusion reached is in fact correct) and delayed closure is counterproductive (when it leads to missing a deadline, or to ignoring or diluting correct first judgments). The construct is related to intolerance for ambiguity or inconsistency (as is conceptual complexity, although in the opposite direction, cf. Schroder, Driver, & Streufert, 1967).

Need for closure has individual difference as well as situational components. Trait nClos is measured by the Need for Closure Scale (NFCS: Webster & Kruglanski, 1994), a 42-item Likert scale whose items can be classified within five subsets: preference for order and structure, discomfort when experiencing ambiguity, decisiveness, desire for predictability, and closed-mindedness. Illustrative items include: "I think that having clear rules and order at work is essential for success" and "I prefer interacting with people whose opinions are very different from my own" (reverse scored). People who score high on the NFCS are theorized to make decisions rapidly, impatiently, and impulsively; they are rigid in their thinking and unwilling to tolerate opinions different from their own. People who score low enjoy uncertainty and inconsistency, and are likely to come to definite conclusions slowly and only after considering all possible alternatives.

The measure is controversial. Neuberg & Newsom (1993) criticize its multidimensionality and redundancy with a self-report measure of need for structure (cf. Kruglanski, et al., 1997; Neuberg, Judice, & West, 1997). Researchers using the scale should check the factor structure for their sample and determine whether subscales have similar functional relations to criterion variables.

Correlational studies Webster & Kruglanski (1994) report the results of an extensive validation study, using the NFCS and a variety of measures that tap potentially related variables. They found significant positive correlations in the .20–.30 range with impulsivity, need for environmental structure, intolerance for ambiguity, dogmatism, and F-scale authoritarianism, and significant negative correlations with cognitive (not conceptual) complexity, fear of making errors, and nCogn. Correlations with specific NFCS subsets were sometimes higher than with the entire NFCS, and some correlations were inflated because of items common to both tests. In addition to the significant relationships, there were nonsignificant negative correlations with intelligence and social desirability. Tetlock (in press) reports that in a sample of historians and political scientists, the NFCS correlates between 0.3 and 0.4 with measures of integrative complexity derived from thought protocols.

Experimental studies   Several research paradigms have been used to explore the predictive power of nClos. For example, the primacy effect in social perception, the classic example of early closure and the ignoring of additional information, becomes more powerful under time pressure and less so under evaluation apprehension (accountability). Subjects high in trait nClos are more likely to exhibit the primacy effect. They also expect to need less time to make a judgment and are more confident about the correctness of the judgment they will make. High NFCS scorers also correctly predict that they will need less time to make a judgment, and report higher desire to make a quick decision. NFCS scores mediate the degree to which subjects perceive that a speaker was actually expressing his or her real opinion ("correspondence bias"). When the speaker is described as being able to choose what to say, differences in nClos do not affect the correspondence judgment; however, when told that the speaker did not have such a choice, high nClos subjects nevertheless attribute correspondence between the speaker's own attitude and the content of the speech. Subjects who score in the middle or low ranges on the scale exhibit less correspondence bias.

Kruglanski, Webster, & Klem (1993) varied the degree of information availability concerning a judgment that was to be made after discussion with another subject (actually a confederate of the experimenter who was trained to disagree with whatever decision the real subject made). When complete information was presented, high NFCS subjects showed more pre-discussion confidence than low scorers in the correctness of their eventual judgment. No such difference was found in an incomplete-information condition. More importantly, in the complete information situation high NFCS scorers were more resistant to persuasion and more argumentative than low scorers, while the opposite was the case when information was incomplete.

When one is sure of one's judgment, rapid closure can be attained by defending that position; otherwise, closure can best be attained by avoiding arguments and going along with the other person's conclusions. Webster, Kruglanski, & Pattison (1997) required subjects to make judgments concerning a target person who was presented as either agreeing or disagreeing with the subject on an important issue (abortion) and as having engaged in either an altruistic or a dishonest act. As usual, high nClos subjects were more confident about their impressions and considered the impression formation task to be easier and less time-consuming than did low scorers. Further, in describing the target's behavior, high scorers used a higher level of abstraction (referring to more generalized states or traits, rather than to a specific, concrete action) in describing the positive (altruistic) behavior of the target person when the latter was a member of their ingroup (defined as agreeing with them on abortion) or in describing the negative (dishonest) behavior of an outgroup target. High nClos was thus associated with more generalized attribution when this enhanced the valuation of the ingroup or the devaluation of the outgroup. Need for closure, therefore, may be implicated in the development of ingroup solidarity on the one hand and prejudice against outgroups on the other, as well as in the choice of attributional strategies.

Adaptiveness/rationality   The adaptiveness of rapid closure hinges on several factors. These include the adequacy of the judgments or decisions that can be made quickly; when the response that is highest in the person's hierarchy is the correct one – whether because of past experience, overlearning, intuition, or for that matter, fortuitously – both Kruglanski and Webster and the cognitive manager model would agree that seizing is desirable. Freezing may not be, though; reliance on the availability heuristic (the use of the most salient previous experience) in a future similar situation may not be as good a strategy as looking for a different solution.

In many ways, this question is really about the adaptiveness of cognitive shortcuts in general. We have already considered this issue in the discussion of integrative complexity. Recent thinking is moving away from the earlier bias in favor of exhaustive information processing as a panacea; if shortcuts lead to preferable cost–benefit balances, the same is true of rapid closure. Kruglanski and Webster formulate an interesting point concerning resource allocation and depletion. They see cognitive capacity and the motivation to engage in cognitive activity as acting together to determine cognitive activity or effort. Making judgments and decisions requires some degree of both. If the person is not motivated to think about an issue, the availability of cognitive resources becomes irrelevant; conversely, no matter how highly motivated one may be to engage with an issue, one cannot do so if cognitive resources have been completely depleted. If above-zero levels of both capacity and motivation exist, the relationship between the two may be independent or causal. If the latter is the case, the depletion of cognitive capacity increases the motivation to reduce cognitive effort, raising state nClos.

Given that the cognitive manager model proposes a similar hypothesis for the effects of resource depletion on complexity, it seems likely that complexity and nClos are closely related state, not trait, variables. Of course, it is also possible that there may be a compensatory pattern: as capacity decreases because of depletion, increased motivation may lead to increased cognitive effort and thus keep cognitive activity or complexity high, at least until the point where further depletion makes that impossible.

A recent set of studies of the cognitive styles of historians and social scientists underscores how controversial normative judgments of both the nClos and integrative complexity constructs can be. Tetlock (1998) found that a composite multi-method measure of the two constructs proved a potent predictor of experts' openness to scenarios implying that twentieth-century history could have been radically redirected by minor alterations in the historical record ("close-call counterfactuals"). Faced with such scenarios, which undercut accepted theories of world politics such as nuclear deterrence or balance-of-power theory, experts who were low in integrative complexity and high in nClos were the most prone to argue not only that theoretically dissonant outcomes did not occur, but that they never even came close to occurring. The normative question arises, whom should we applaud: the open-minded (confused) experts who were willing to consider dissonant counterfactuals, or the closed-minded (logically consistent) experts who categorically rejected such counterfactuals?

By contrast, in a study of prospective reasoning, Tetlock found the opposite relationship between cognitive style and receptivity to close-call counterfactuals. For example, high nClos/low complexity respondents who predicted in 1988 that five years later the Soviet Communist Party would still be firmly in control of the country deemed it most plausible that the coup plotters of August, 1991 could have succeeded had only certain highly contingent events unfolded slightly differently. Again, the normative question arises: were these respondents justified in invoking the "I-was-almost-right" defense? Was history truly a close call, or are those who invoke this defense falling prey to cognitive conservatism, and failing to adjust their beliefs in a proper Bayesian fashion?

Observations

Each of the three research programs has, in key respects, followed the classic logic of construct validation. We know a lot more than we once did about the individual difference correlates, situational determinants, and behavioral consequences of the needs for cognition and closure and of integrative complexity. As evidence accumulates, it becomes increasingly difficult to resist the conclusion that the operational measures of those hypothetical constructs are indeed assessing what they purport to be assessing.

There is indeed a tale of progress, of knowledge accumulation, to be told here. But a balanced appraisal requires sounding some cautionary notes. Consider a typical empirical study. Variation in the cognitive style measure is shown to predict variation in a social or cognitive dependent variable in one class of situations, but perhaps not in another class of situations – a prediction that follows from the logic of the cognitive style construct, assumptions about the validity of the measures in question, and assumptions about the logic of the situations.

Relatively few studies, however, incorporate controls for the role of cognitive ability in obtaining the observed effects. Even fewer studies assess the relative predictive power of potentially competing and statistically overlapping cognitive-style constructs. How many demonstrations of nClos effects (to single-out a construct) would hold up after controlling for variation in such conceptual kissing cousins as nCogn, integrative complexity, uncertainty orientation (Sorrentino, et al., 1988), tolerance for ambiguity (Budner, 1962), need for structure (Neuberg & Newsom, 1993), need to evaluate (Jarvis & Petty, 1996), dogmatism (Rokeach, 1960), right-wing authoritarianism (Altemeyer, 1981), attributional complexity (Fletcher, Danilovics, Fernandez, Peterson, & Reeder, 1988), wisdom (Baltes, Smith, & Staudinger, 1992), causal uncertainty (Weary & Jacobson, 1997), and perhaps half a dozen other fashionable contenders?

The pattern of systematic (albeit low to moderate) intercorrelations among measures suggests that there may be a generic open-mindedness factor underlying the cognitive-style constructs that have been introduced over the last fifty years. Such openness may stand in relation to specific cognitive style measures as Spearman's "g" stands in relation to measures of specific cognitive abilities. Given the blurriness of the conceptual boundaries, and the patterns of statistical overlap, between cognitive styles, the constructs examined here are best viewed as fuzzy overlapping sets in the spirit of natural-category models of personality traits.

Although isolating cognitive styles and their antecedents and consequences has proven a formidable challenge, our understanding of the conditions under which particular styles are likely to prove adaptive or maladaptive, praiseworthy or deplorable, has grown appreciably over the decades. The early psychodynamically inspired cognitive-style constructs of the 1950s offered individual-difference continua with well-defined good and bad ends. Who wants to be a mean-spirited, insecure authoritarian prone to status anxiety, prejudice toward outgroups, and Fascist ideological appeals? It would be an exaggeration to say that the *fin-de-siècle* family of cognitive styles is strictly value-neutral, but researchers have made good-faith efforts to explore the negative aspects of the consensually favored ends of their cognitive-style continua (enjoying thinking, resisting jumping to conclusions, and appreciating the legitimacy of competing viewpoints) and the positive aspects of the suspect ends (preference for low-effort shortcuts and for reaching firm conclusions quickly, and an unwillingness to concede legitimacy to alternative points of view). As a result, we move into the next stage of research with a much more nuanced (we are tempted to say, integratively complex) appreciation of when different styles of reasoning are likely to yield substantial payoffs and when they are likely to prove counterproductive. And that, to close with a value judgment of our own, is probably a good thing.

References

Abelson, R. P., Aronson, E., McGuire, W. J., Newcomb, T. M., Rosenberg, M. J., & Tannenbaum, P. (Eds.) (1968). *Theories of cognitive consistency: A source book*. Chicago: Rand McNally.

Adorno, T. W., Frenkel-Brunswik, E., Levinson, D. J., & Sampson, R. N. (1950). *The authoritarian personality*. New York: Harper & Row.

Ahlering, R. F. & Parker, L. D. (1989). Need for cognition as a moderator of the primacy effect. *Journal of Research in Personality, 23*, 313–317.

Altemeyer, R. A. (1981). *Right-wing authoritarianism*. Winnipeg: University of Manitoba Press.

Baker-Brown, G., Ballard, E. J., Bluck, S., DeVries, B., Suedfeld, P., & Tetlock, P. (1992). The integrative complexity coding manual. In C. P. Smith (Ed.), *Motivation and personality: Handbook of thematic analysis* (pp. 401–418). Cambridge, UK: Cambridge University Press.

Baltes, P. B., Smith, J., & Staudinger, U. M. (1992). Wisdom and successful aging. In T. B. Sonderegger (Ed.), *Nebraska symposium on motivation* Vol. 39 (pp. 23–167). Lincoln: University of Nebraska Press.

Berzonsky, M. D., & Sullivan, C. (1992). Social-cognitive aspects of identity style: Need for cognition, experiential openness, and introspection. *Journal of Adolescent Research, 7*, 140–155.

Brown, R. (1965). *Social psychology*. Glencoe, IL: Free Press.

Budner, S. (1962). Intolerance of ambiguity as a personality variable. *Journal of Personality, 30*, 29–50.

Cacioppo, J. T., & Petty, R. E. (1982). The need for cognition. *Journal of Personality and Social Psychology, 42*, 116–131.

Cacioppo, J. T., Petty, R. E., & Morris, K. J. (1983). Effects of need for cognition on message evaluation, recall and persuasion. *Journal of Personality and Social Psychology, 45*, 805–818.

Cacioppo J. T., Petty, R. E., Feinstein, J., & Jarvis, W. B. G. (1996). Dispositional differences in cognitive motivation: The life and times of individuals varying in need for cognition. *Psychological Bulletin, 119*, 197–253.

Cohen, A. R. (1957). Need for cognition and order of communication as determinants of opinion change. In C. I. Hovland (Ed.), *The order of presentation in persuasion* (pp. 79–97). New Haven,

CT: Yale University Press.

DeVries, B., & Walker, L. J. (1986). Moral reasoning and attitudes toward capital punishment. *Developmental Psychology, 22*, 509–513.

DeVries, B., & Walker, L. J. (1987). Conceptual/integrative complexity and attitudes toward capital punishment. *Personality and Social Psychology Bulletin, 13*, 448–457.

Driver, M. J. (1965). *A structural analysis of aggression, stress, and personality in an Inter–Nation simulation* (Institute Paper No. 97). Lafayette, IN: Purdue University.

Fiske, D. W. (1949). Consistency of the factorial structures of personality ratings from different sources. *Journal of Abnormal and Social Psychology, 44*, 329–344.

Fiske, S., & Taylor, S. (1991). *Social cognition*. New York: McGraw-Hill.

Fletcher, F. J. O., Danilovics, P., Fernandez, G., Peterson, D., & Reeder, G. D. (1988). Attributional complexity: An individual difference measure. *Journal of Personality and Social Psychology, 51*, 875–884.

Freund, T., Kruglanski, A. W., & Schpitzajzen, A. (1985). The freezing and unfreezing of impression primacy: Effects of need for structure and the fear of invalidity. *Personality and Social Psychology Bulletin, 11*, 479–487.

Goldstein, K. M., & Blackman, S. (1978). *Cognitive style: Five approaches and relevant research*. New York: Wiley.

Harvey, O. J., Hunt, D., & Schroder, H. M. (1961). *Conceptual systems and personality organization*. New York: Wiley.

Hunsberger, B., Lea, J., Pancer, S. M., Pratt, M. W., & McKenzie, B. (1992). Making life complicated: Prompting the use of integratively complex thinking. *Journal of Personality, 60*, 95–114.

Jarvis, B., & Petty, R. E. (1996). The need to evaluate. *Journal of Personality and Social Psychology, 70*, 172–194.

Kassin, S. M., Reddy, M. E., & Tullock, W. F. (1990). Juror interpretations of ambiguous evidence: The need for cognition, presentation order and persuasion. *Law and Human Behavior, 14*, 43–55.

Kelly, G. A. (1955). *The psychology of personal constructs, Vol. 1: A theory of personality*. New York: Norton.

Kruglanski, A. W. (1989). The psychology of being "right:" The problem of accuracy in social perception and cognition. *Psychological Bulletin, 106*, 395–409.

Kruglanski, A. W., & Webster, D. M. (1996). Motivated closing of the mind: "Seizing" and "freezing." *Psychological Review, 103*, 263–268.

Kruglanski, A. W., Webster, D. M., & Klem, A. (1993). Motivated resistance and openness to persuasion in the presence or absence of prior information. *Journal of Personality and Social Psychology, 65*, 861–876.

Kruglanski, A. W., Atash, M. N., DeGrada, E., Mannetti, L., Pierro, A., & Webster, D. M. (1997). Psychological theory testing versus psychometric nay-saying: Comment on Neuberg et al.'s (1997) critique of the Need for Closure Scale. *Journal of Personality and Social Psychology, 73*, 1005–1016.

Leary, M. R., Sheppard, J. A., McNeil, M. S., Jenkins, T. B., & Barnes, B. D. (1986). Objectivism in information utilization: Theory and measurement. *Journal of Personality Assessment, 50*, 32–43.

Leone, C., & Ensley, E. (1986). Self-generated attitude change: A person by situation analysis of attitude polarization and attenuation. *Journal of Research in Personality, 20*, 434–446.

Liberman, A., & Chaiken, S. (1991). Value conflict and thought-induced attitude change. *Journal of Experimental Social Psychology, 27*, 203–216.

Linville, P. W. (1985). Self-complexity and affective extremity: Don't put all your eggs in one cognitive basket. *Social Cognition, 3*, 94–120.

Loevinger, J. (1976). *Ego development: Conceptions and theories*. San Francisco: Jossey-Bass.

Mischel, W. (1968). *Personality and assessment*. New York: Wiley.

Mischel, W., & Shoda, Y. (1998). Reconciling processing dynamics and personality dispositions. In J. T. Spence, J. M. Darley, & D. J. Foss (Eds.), *Annual review of psychology*, Vol. 49 (pp. 229–258). Palo Alto, CA: Annual Reviews.

Neuberg, S. L., & Newsom, J. T. (1993). Personal need for structure: Individual differences in the desire fore simple structure. *Journal of Personality and Social Psychology, 65*, 113–131.

Neuberg, S. L., Judice, T. N., & West, S. G. (1997). What the Need for Closure Scale measures and what it does not: Toward differentiating among related epistemic motives. *Journal of Personality and Social Psychology, 72*, 1396–1412.

Olson, K., Camp, C., & Fuller, D. (1984). Curiosity and need for cognition. *Psychological Reports, 54*, 71–74.

O'Rourke, P. J. (1998). *Eat the rich: A treatise on economics.* New York: Atlantic Monthly Press.

Pancer, S. M., Gallant, M., Pratt, M., & Hunsberger, B. (1994). *Coping with baby: The relationship between prenatal expectations and postnatal adjustment.* Paper presented at the Waterloo Conference on Child Development, Waterloo, Ont., Canada.

Pancer, S. M., Jackson, L. M., Hunsberger, B., Pratt, M. W., & Lea, J. (1995). Religious orthodoxy and the complexity of thought about religious and nonreligious issues. *Journal of Personality, 63*, 213–232.

Petty, R. E., & Jarvis, W. B. (1996). The need to evaluate. *Journal of Personality and Social Psychology, 70*, 172–194.

Petty, R. E., Schumann, D. W., Richman, S. A., & Strathman, A. J. (1993). Positive mood and persuasion: Different roles for affect under high- and low-elaboration conditions. *Journal of Personality and Social Psychology, 64*, 5–20.

Plomin, R. & Rende, R. (1991). Human behavioral genetics. *Annual Review of Psychology, 42*, 161–190.

Rokeach, M. (1960). *The open and closed mind.* New York: Basic Books.

Satish, U. (1997). Behavioral complexity: A review. *Journal of Applied Social Psychology, 27*, 2047–2067.

Schroder, H. M., Driver, M. J., & Streufert, S. (1967). *Human information processing.* New York: Holt, Rinehart & Winston.

Schroder, H. M., & Suedfeld, P. (Eds.) (1971). *Personality theory and information processing.* New York: Ronald.

Scott, W. A., Osgood, D. W., & Peterson, C. (1979). *Cognitive structure: Theory and measurement of individual differences.* New York: Wiley.

Smith, S. M., Haugtvedt, C. P., & Petty, R. E. (1994). Need for cognition and the effects of repeated expression of attitude accessibility and extremity. *Advances in Consumer Research, 21*, 234–237.

Sniderman, P. (1975). *Personality and democratic politics.* Berkeley: University of California Press.

Sorrentino, R. M., Short, J. C., & Raynor, J. O. (1984). Uncertainty orientation: Implications for affective and cognitive views of achievement behavior. *Journal of Personality and Social Psychology, 46*, 189–206.

Sorrentino, R. M., Bobocel, D. R., Gitta, M. Z., Olson, J. M., & Hewitt, E. C. (1988). Uncertainty orientation and persuasion: Individual differences in the effects of personal relevance on social judgments. *Journal of Personality and Social Psychology, 55*, 357–371.

Sternberg, R. J., & Grigorenko, E. L. (1997). Are cognitive styles still in style? *American Psychologist, 52*, 700–712.

Streufert, S., & Streufert, S. C. (1978). *Behavior in a complex environment.* Washington, DC: Winston.

Streufert, S., Nogami, G. Y., Swezey, R. W., Pogash, R. M., & Piasecki, M. T. (1988). Computer assisted training of complex managerial performance. *Computers in Human Behavior, 4*, 77–88.

Suedfeld, P. (1992). Cognitive managers and their critics. *Political Psychology, 13*, 435–454.

Suedfeld, P. (in press, a). Cognitive styles. In A. L. Harris (Ed.), *Encyclopedia of psychology.* Washington: American Psychological Association.

Suedfeld, P. (in press, b). Domain-related variation in integrative complexity: A measure of political importance and responsiveness? In C. De Landtsheer, & O. Feldman (Eds.), *Beyond public speech and symbols: Explorations in the rhetoric of politicians and the media.* Westport, CT: Praeger.

Suedfeld, P., & Coren, S. (1992). Cognitive correlates of conceptual complexity. *Personality and Individual Differences, 13*, 1193–1199.

Suedfeld, P., & Rank, A. D. (1976). Revolutionary leaders: Long-term success as a function of changes in conceptual complexity. *Journal of Personality and Social Psychology, 34,* 169–178.

Suedfeld, P., & Tetlock, P. E. (Eds.) (1991). *Psychology and social policy.* Washington, DC: Hemisphere.

Suedfeld, P., Tetlock, P. E., & Streufert, S. (1992). Conceptual/integrative complexity. In C. P. Smith (Ed.), *Personality and motivation: Handbook of thematic content analysis* (pp. 401–418). New York: Cambridge University Press.

Suedfeld, P., De Vries, B., Bluck, S., Wallbaum, A. B. C., & Schmidt, P. W. (1996). Intuitive perceptions of decision-making strategy: Naive assessors' concepts of integrative complexity. *International Journal of Psychology, 31,* 177–190.

Tanaka, J. S., Panter, A., & Winborne, W. C. (1988). Dimensions of the need for cognition: Subscales and gender differences. *Multivariate Behavioral Research, 23,* 35–50.

Tesser, A. (1978). Self-generated attitude change. In L. Berkowitz (Ed.), *Advances in experimental social psychology* Vol. 11 (pp. 289–338). New York: Academic Press.

Tetlock, P. E. (1981). Pre- to post-election shifts in presidential rhetoric: Impression management or cognitive adjustment? *Journal of Personality and Social Psychology, 41,* 207–212.

Tetlock, P. E. (1986). A value pluralism model of ideological reasoning. *Journal of Personality and Social Psychology, 50,* 819–827.

Tetlock, P. E. (1992). The impact of accountability on judgment and choice: Toward a social contingency model. *Advances in Experimental Social Psychology, 25,* 331–376.

Tetlock, P. E. (1998). Close-call counterfactuals and belief system defenses: I was not almost wrong but I was almost right. *Journal of Personality and Social Psychology, 75,* 639–652.

Tetlock, P. E. (in press). Cognitive biases and organizational correctives: Do both disease and cure depend on the ideological beholder? *Administrative Science Quarterly.*

Tetlock, P. E., & Boettger, R. (1989). Accountability: A social magnifier of the dilution effect. *Journal of Personality and Social Psychology, 57,* 388–398.

Tetlock, P. E., & Boettger, R. (1994). Accountability amplifies the status quo effect when change creates victims. *Journal of Behavioral Decision Making, 7,* 1–23.

Tetlock, P. E., Armor, D., & Peterson, R. (1994). The slavery debate in antebellum America: Cognitive style, value conflict, and the limits of compromise. *Journal of Personality and Social Psychology, 66,* 115–126.

Tetlock, P. E., Peterson, R., & Berry, J. (1993). Flattering and unflattering personality portraits of integratively simple and complex managers. *Journal of Personality and Social Psychology, 64,* 500–511.

Tversky, A., & Kahneman, D. (1974). Judgment under uncertainty: Heuristics and biases. *Science, 185,* 1124–1131.

Vannoy, J. S. (1965). Generality of cognitive complexity–simplicity as a personality construct. *Journal of Personality and Social Psychology, 2,* 385–396.

Venkatraman, M. P., Marlino, D., Kardes, F. R., & Skylar, K. B. (1990). The interactive effects of message appeal and individual differences on information processing and persuasion. *Psychology and Marketing, 7,* 85–96.

Weary, G., & Jacobson, J. A. (1997). Causal uncertainty beliefs and diagnostic information seeking. *Journal of Personality and Social Psychology, 73,* 839–848.

Webster, D. M., & Kruglanski, A. W. (1994). Individual differences in need for cognitive closure. *Journal of Personality and Social Psychology, 67,* 1049–1062.

Webster, D. M., Kruglanski, A. W., & Pattison, D. A. (1997). Motivated language use in intergroup contexts: Need-for-closure effects on the linguistic intergroup bias. *Journal of Personality and Social Psychology, 72,* 1122–1131.

Wegener, D. T., Petty, R. E., & Klein, D. J. (1994). Effects of mood on high elaboration attitude change: The mediating role of likelihood judgments. *European Journal of Social Psychology, 24,* 25–43.

Winter, D. G. (1973). *The power motive.* New York: Free Press.

Witkin, H. A., Dyk, R. B., Faterson, H. F., Goodenough, D. R., & Karp, S. A. (1962). *Psychological differentiation.* New York: Wiley.

PART III

Social Motivation

Chapter Fourteen

Self-Regulation

Charles S. Carver

Social behavior is built in part on motivational processes. Traditionally, motivational constructs have been used to account for behavior's "direction" (the choice of one action from among many available possibilities) and its "intensity" (the speed, vigor, persistence, thoroughness, or force with which the action is carried out). Many motivational constructs have been proposed, which vary substantially in their elements and in their dynamics.

Some theories of motivation focus on how people differ in what concerns underlie the activities of their lives (e.g. Murray, 1938). For example, some people have strong motives toward social interaction, some don't. Some people have strong motives toward achievement, some don't. Even if everything else is the same, these people will be very different in how they act and react to many events in their lives. This individual-difference aspect of motivation is important, but it is not the focus of this chapter.

This chapter focuses on the dynamics behind the scenes. Most views on motivation include ideas about processes by which motives become action. For social motives, at least, the processes presumably are largely the same, regardless of the motive's "content." That is, the desire to interact with people probably becomes behavior by the same processes as does the desire to achieve. What is the nature of those processes? What is their structure, and how do they function? In this chapter I describe one approach to these questions.

The approach described here is identified with the word *self-regulation* (e.g. Carver & Scheier, 1981, 1990, 1998). This word means somewhat different things to different people and in different contexts. When I use it, I do so to convey several things. One is the sense that the processes are purposive. Another is the sense that self-corrective adjustments are taking place, as necessary, to stay on track for whatever purpose is under pursuit. Another is the sense that corrective adjustments originate from within the system. These ideas converge in the view that behavior is a continual process of moving toward (and away from) various goal representations, and that this movement involves processes of feedback control. Although this chapter makes additional points, these ideas lie at its heart.

Preparation of this chapter was facilitated by NCI grants CA64710 and CA78995.

I should also be explicit that I'm not claiming the processes described here are the *only* processes behind behavior. This isn't a complete picture of motivation, or even of self-regulation (cf. Ford, 1987; Kuhl, 1994). For example, chapter 15 of this volume covers an aspect of motivation that's very different from what I'm covering. Failing to address those ideas doesn't mean I think they're unimportant. I'm simply emphasizing another set of principles.

The view presented here is easily integrated with many ideas in personality–social psychology. It's a view of the structure of behavior that can accommodate diverse ways of thinking about what qualities of behavior matter and why. For this reason, I think it complements a wide variety of other ideas about what goes on inside humans.

Behavior as Goal Directed and Feedback Controlled

I begin with the goal concept. My use of goals as a starting point is consonant with a re-emergence of goal constructs in today's personality–social psychology (Austin & Vancouver, 1996; Elliott & Dweck, 1988; Read & Miller, 1989; Pervin, 1982, 1989). Writers use a variety of labels, reflecting differences in emphasis – for example, *current concern* (Klinger, 1975), *personal striving* (Emmons, 1986), *life task* (Cantor & Kihlstrom, 1987), *personal project* (Little, 1989). In all these constructs there are overall goals and subgoals. There's also room for individualization. That is, a goal can be reached in many ways, and people choose paths that are compatible with other aspects of their situations (since many concerns must be managed simultaneously) and aspects of their personality.

Two goal constructs somewhat broader than those just named are the *possible self* (Markus & Nurius, 1986) and the *self-guide* (Higgins, 1987, 1996). These constructs are intended to bring a dynamic quality to conceptualization of the self-concept. Consistent with other goal models (but contrasting with traditional views), possible selves are future-oriented. They concern how people think of their as-yet-unrealized potential, the kind of person they might become. Self-guides similarly reflect dynamic aspects of the self-concept.

Theorists who use these various terms – and others – have their own emphases (for broader discussions see Austin & Vancouver, 1996; Carver & Scheier, 1998; Pervin, 1989), but many points are the same. All include the idea that goals energize and direct activities (Pervin, 1982). All convey the sense that goals give meaning to people's lives. In each theory there's an emphasis on the idea that understanding the person means understanding the person's goals. Indeed, in such theories, it's often implicit that the self consists partly of the person's goals and the organization among them.

Feedback loops

How are goals used in acting? One answer to this question is to say that goals serve as reference values for feedback processes. A feedback loop, the basic unit of cybernetic control, is a system of four elements in a particular organization (cf. Miller, Galanter, & Pribram, 1960; MacKay, 1966; Powers, 1973; Wiener, 1948). These elements are an input func-

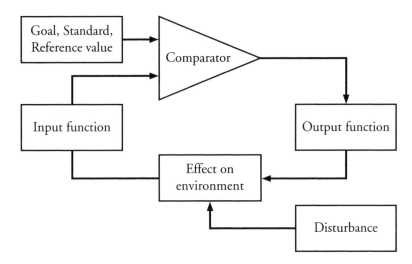

Figure 1   Schematic depiction of a feedback loop, the basic unit of cybernetic control. In such a loop a sensed value is compared to a reference value or standard, and adjustments are made in an output function (if necessary) to shift the sensed value in the direction of the standard.

tion, a reference value, a comparator, and an output function (figure 1). Together, they serve an important purpose.

An input function is a sensor. It brings information in. I'll treat this input function as equivalent to perception. A reference value is a second source of information (i.e. besides that coming from the input function). I'll treat the reference value in the loops discussed here as goals. A comparator is a device that makes comparisons between the input and the reference value. The comparison results in one of two outcomes: either the values being compared are discriminably different from one another, or they're not.

Following this comparison is an output function. I'll treat this as equivalent to behavior, though sometimes the behavior is internal. If the comparison yields a judgment of "no difference," the output function remains whatever it was. This may mean no output, or it may mean that the ongoing output continues. If the comparison yields a judgment of "discrepancy," however, the output function changes.

There are two different kinds of feedback loops, with two kinds of functions. In a negative, or discrepancy reducing loop, the output function aims at diminishing or eliminating any discrepancy noted between input and reference value. This sort of functioning is seen in human behavior in the attempt to approach or attain a valued goal, or to conform to a standard.

The second kind of feedback loop is a positive, or discrepancy enlarging loop. The value here isn't one to approach, but one to avoid. It may be simplest to think of this as an "anti-goal." One psychological example of an anti-goal is a feared or disliked possible self (Markus & Nurius, 1986; Ogilvie, 1987). More concrete examples would be traffic accidents, having your date make a scene in public, and being fired from your job. A positive loop senses present conditions, compares them to the anti-goal, and tries to enlarge the discrepancy between the two. As an example, consider the rebellious adolescent who wants to be different from his parents. He senses his behavior, compares it to his parents' behavior, and tries to make his own behavior as different from theirs as he can.

The action of discrepancy enlarging processes in living systems is typically constrained by discrepancy reducing processes. To put it differently, avoidance behaviors often lead into approach behaviors. An avoidance loop tries to increase distance from the anti-goal. The movement away occurs until the tendency to move away is joined by the influence of an approach loop. This then serves to pull the sensed input into its orbit. The rebellious adolescent, trying to be different from his parents, soon finds a group of other adolescents to conform to, all of whom are remaining different from their parents.

The use of the word "orbit" in the last paragraph suggests a metaphor that may be useful if these concepts don't feel very intuitive to you. You might think of these feedback loops as metaphorically equivalent to gravity and anti-gravity. The discrepancy reducing loop exerts a kind of gravitational pull on the input it's controlling, pulling that input closer to its ground zero. The positive loop has a kind of anti-gravitational push, moving sensed values ever farther away. Don't forget, though, that this is only a metaphor. More is involved here than a force field.[1]

Another issue (which gets a little complicated to think about) concerns the fact that feedback processes are not limited to creating and maintaining steady states. Some goals *are* static end states. But many are dynamic and evolving courses of activity (e.g. take a month's vacation in Europe, write a book chapter). In such cases, the goal at any given moment is fluid and changing, as the person traverses the path of activity. Other goals are recurrent (do the laundry), and are re-evoked for regulatory activity as the situation changes (running out of clean socks) across the passage of time and events. In short, feedback processes (and human behavior) can deal with a variety of moving targets.

Self-focus and feedback control

Some years ago Michael Scheier and I suggested that the comparator of a feedback loop managing conscious behavior is engaged by increases in self-focused attention (Carver & Scheier, 1981). Indeed, similarities between the literature of self-focus (Duval & Wicklund, 1972) and the processes in the feedback loop helped draw us to the feedback model in the first place. Self-focused attention leads to more comparisons with salient standards (Scheier & Carver, 1983), and enhances conformity to salient standards; self-focus also exaggerates some "anti-conformity" effects, such as rejection of attitudinal positions held by a disliked reference group (Carver & Scheier, 1981, 1998).

The literature of self-awareness isn't the only social psychological literature that fits the feedback loop picture. Social comparison processes can also be viewed in these terms (Carver & Scheier, 1998). Upward comparisons help people pull themselves toward desired reference points (discrepancy reduction). Downward comparisons help them force themselves farther away from people who are worse off than they are (discrepancy enlargement).

Feedback loops and affect

Thus far I've dealt only with behavior. Most believe that motivational experience requires more. It requires feelings – affect. Does the feedback-based self-regulation view have anything to say about affect? We think it does (Carver & Scheier, 1990, 1998). Again we use feedback control as an organizing principle, but now the control bears on a different quality.

What are feelings and what makes them exist? What's the internal mechanism by which feelings arise? We've suggested that feelings arise as a consequence of a feedback process that operates automatically, simultaneously with the behavior-guiding function, and in parallel to it. One way to describe what this process is doing is to say it's checking on how well the *behavior* loop is reducing *its* discrepancies. Thus, the input for this second loop is some representation of the *rate of discrepancy reduction in the action system over time.* (I'll discuss discrepancy reducing loops first, then turn to enlarging loops.)

An analogy may be useful here. Because action implies change between states, consider behavior analogous to distance. If the action loop deals with distance, and if the affect loop assesses the progress of the action loop, then the affect loop is dealing with the psychological equivalent of velocity, the first derivative of distance over time. To the extent this analogy is meaningful, the perceptual input to the affect loop should be the first derivative over time of the input used by the action loop.

This input can't create affect by itself, because a given rate of progress has different affective consequences in different circumstances. We believe that, as in any feedback system, this input is compared to a reference value (cf. Frijda, 1986, 1988). In this case, the reference is an acceptable or desired rate of behavioral discrepancy reduction. As in other feedback loops, the comparison checks for a deviation from the standard. If there is one, the output function changes.

Our position is that the result of the comparison process at the heart of this loop is manifest phenomenologically in two forms. One is a hazy and nonverbal sense of expectancy – confidence or doubt. The other is affect, feeling, a sense of positiveness or negativeness. This, we think, is the mechanism that generates affect. There isn't a lot of information bearing on this hypothesis. But what there is seems generally consistent with it (see Carver & Scheier, 1998, 1999a).

If the input function of the affect loop is a sensed rate of progress, the output function is a change in rate. Some changes are straightforward – go faster. Sometimes it's less straightforward. The rates of many "behaviors" aren't defined by the pace of physical action. Rather, they're defined in terms of choices among potential actions. For example, increasing your rate of progress on a work project may mean choosing to spend a weekend working rather than playing. Increasing your rate of being kind means choosing to do an action that reflects that value. Thus, adjustment in rate must often be translated into other terms, such as concentration, or reallocation of time and effort.

Here's another metaphor, to help this feel more intuitive: this is a kind of "cruise control" model of affect's origins and consequences. That is, the system I've just described functions much the same way as a car's cruise control. If you're going too slowly in your behavior, negative affect arises. You respond by increasing effort, trying to speed up. If you're going faster than you need to, positive affect arises, and you coast. A car's cruise control is very similar. Coming to a hill slows you down. The cruise control responds by feeding the engine's cylinders more gas, bringing the speed back up. If you come across the crest of a hill and roll downward too fast, the system cuts back the gas and drags the speed back down.

The analogy is intriguing in part because it incorporates a similar asymmetry in consequences of deviating from the set point. That is, both in a car and in behavior, going too slow requires adding effort and resources. Going too fast doesn't. It requires only pulling back on resources. That is, the cruise control doesn't apply the brakes, it just cuts back the gasoline. The car coasts back to the velocity set point. In the same fashion, people usually don't react to positive affect by actively trying to make themselves feel worse. We do think, though, that they ease off and coast.

Two kinds of behavioral loops, two dimensions of affect

Now consider discrepancy enlarging loops. The theory just outlined rests on the idea that positive feeling results when a behavioral system is making rapid progress in doing *what it's organized to do*. The systems considered thus far are organized to close discrepancies. There's no obvious reason, though, why the principle shouldn't apply just as well to systems with the opposite purpose. If the system is making rapid progress doing what it's organized to do, there should be positive affect. If the system is doing poorly, there should be negative affect.

That much would seem comparable across the two types of systems. In each case there's a positive pole and a negative pole. But the positives don't seem quite the same, nor do the negatives. Our view of this difference derives partly from insights of Higgins (1987, 1996) and his colleagues (to which I return a bit later). We've suggested that the dimension of affect relating to discrepancy reducing loops runs (in its purest form) from depression to elation (figure 2). The dimension of affect relating to discrepancy enlarging loops runs (in its purest form) from anxiety to relief or contentment. These two dimensions seem to capture the core qualities of affective experience.

Merging affect and action

Let's briefly consider the integration between affect and action. Affect theories tend to hold that affect both prompts action and arises from action, but the connection beyond that point is often vague. Does the feedback model add anything on this question? It may. The two layers of systems we've postulated both deal with aspects of behavior, but different aspects. It should be apparent, though, that the action system and affect system work in concert with one another. Both are always involved in the flow of behavior.

The notion of two feedback systems functioning in concert with one another is something we sort of stumbled into. Interestingly enough, however, there is precedent for such an arrangement in a very different application of feedback concepts. This other application is the literature of control engineering (e.g. Clark, 1996). It has long been recognized by

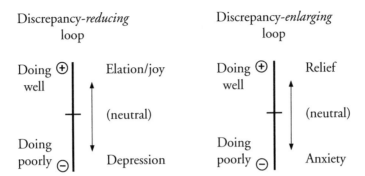

Figure 2   Two sorts of meta-level systems and the affective dimensions we believe arise from the functioning of each. Discrepancy reducing systems are presumed to yield affective qualities of sadness or depression when progress is below standard and happiness or elation when progress is above standard. Discrepancy enlarging systems are presumed to yield anxiety when progress is below standard and relief or contentment when progress is above standard.

engineers that having two feedback systems in concert – one controlling position, the other controlling velocity – permits responding that is both quick and stable (i.e. without overshoots and oscillations). Without the two systems, these qualities don't come together.

The combination of quickness and stability in responding is valuable in the kinds of electro-mechanical devices that engineers deal with, but its value surely is not limited to such devices. For biological entities, being able to respond quickly yet in a stable (accurate) way confers an adaptive advantage. We would argue that the creation of this combination of quick and stable responding is a consequence of our having a combination of behavior-managing and affect-managing control systems. Affect causes people's responses to be quicker (this control system is time sensitive), and as long as the affective system isn't hyper-responsive, the responses are also stable.

Related Motivation–Emotion Models

The description in the preceding section dealt with feedback processes, how they work, and how the structure of these processes might underlie behavior. This section turns to consider how these ideas connect to ideas from other areas of psychology. These latter ideas also bear on motivation and emotion, but they approach the concepts from very different directions.

Appetitive and aversive motivational–behavioral systems

In the past fifteen years or so, a family of motivational theories with roots in neuropsychology, psychopathology, animal conditioning, and psychopharmacology has received increasing attention. These theories all incorporate the idea that two systems are core determinants of behavior. One deals with appetitive motivation, approach behavior. It has been termed a behavioral activation system (Fowles, 1980; Cloninger, 1987), behavioral approach system (Gray, 1981, 1990, 1994), and behavioral facilitation system (Depue & Collins, in press). The other system deals with aversive motivation, withdrawal or avoidance behavior. It is usually called a behavioral inhibition system (Cloninger, 1987; Gray, 1981, 1990, 1994), though the term withdrawal system has also been used to label a comparable construct (Davidson, 1992, 1995).

The two systems are believed to have different neural substrates and distinct influences on action. Consider Gray's theory as an example (for a review see Gray, 1994). Gray holds that the behavioral activation system responds to incentives. Activity in this system causes the organism to begin (or increase) movement toward goals. He holds that the behavioral inhibition system responds to threats. Its activation inhibits ongoing behavior, thus stifling movement toward goals.

Most of the work stimulated by this theory has focused on the determinants of action. However, Gray has also argued that the two motivational systems also influence emotional experience (e.g. Gray, 1981, 1990). Activity in the behavioral activation system (BAS) leads to positive feelings such as eagerness, elation, and happiness. Activity in the behavioral inhibition system (BIS) leads to negative feelings such as fear, anxiety, frustration, and sadness. Following this line of thought, Carver & White (1994) created self-report measures to assess the sensitivity of people's BIS and BAS. Consistent with Gray's argument, BIS sensitivity (but not BAS) related to anxiety in response to anticipation of a punishment, and BAS sensitivity (but not BIS) related to happiness in response to anticipation of a reward (Carver & White, 1994).

Emotion–motivational systems and cortical activity

Gray's work, which rests heavily on animal models, is an effort to understand regulation of behavior in response to incentives and threats. His focus has been on action (and learning), with implications for affect being secondary. Another relevant body of work took the opposite path. It focused on humans; it focused on neural substrates of *emotional* experience; and it used emotions as a way to link the neural substrates to motivational–behavioral processes (see Davidson, 1995; Davidson & Sutton, 1995). Despite this different starting point, this work leads to a conceptual position not too different in many respects from that of Gray.

Most of this work examines EEG activity (though other physiological indicators have also been used). Much of it involves assessing activation in particular areas of the cerebral cortex in response to affect-inducing stimuli. Other studies involve assessing individual differences in patterns of cortical activation as they relate to individual differences in susceptibility to the experience of affect qualities.

Among the findings (reviewed by Davidson, 1992, 1995) are these: subjects exposed to unpleasant film clips or confronted with threat of punishment showed elevations in *right* frontal cortical activation. In contrast, subjects presented with incentives and with positive emotional adjectives showed higher levels of *left* frontal cortical activation. An elevation in left frontal activity has also been found in 10-month-olds viewing their mothers approaching.

Asymmetries in resting activity also seem to reflect differential susceptibility to affect. Higher left frontal activation at rest relates both to higher dispositional levels of positive affect and to more positive feelings in response to pleasant film clips. Higher resting levels of right frontal activation relates to stronger negative affect in response to unpleasant film clips. Self-reported BAS and BIS sensitivities have shown even stronger relations to relative left and right frontal resting activation, respectively (Harmon-Jones & Allen, 1997; Sutton & Davidson, 1997).

On the basis of these and other findings, Davidson (e.g. 1992, 1995) has concluded that specialized neural substrates for approach and withdrawal (and thus positive and negative affect) are lateralized in the left and right frontal regions of the cerebral cortex, respectively. The broad outlines of this view – approach and withdrawal, and their concomitant affects, being managed by separate neural systems – have much in common with Gray's view. Both also converge with the ideas described earlier in the chapter – that behavior is self-regulated by approach systems (as discrepancy reducing loops) and avoidance systems (as discrepancy enlarging loops). To blend the language used earlier with the language of theories such as those of Davidson and Gray, goals are incentives, and anti-goals are threats.

Self-discrepancies and emotion–motivational systems

From yet another theoretical path comes self-discrepancy theory (Higgins, 1987, 1996; Strauman, 1989), which holds that people relate perceptions of their actual selves to self-guides, particularly ideals and oughts. Ideals are qualities the person desires to embody – aspirations, hopes, positive wishes for the self. Living up to an ideal means attaining something desired. An ideal seems to be purely an approach goal.

Oughts are defined by a sense of duty, responsibility, or obligation. An ought is a self that one feels compelled to be, rather than intrinsically desires to be. The ought self is a positive value, in the sense that people try to conform to it. However, living up to an ought also implies acting to *avoid a punishment* – self-disapproval or the disapproval of others.

Thus oughts seem more complex structurally than ideals. Oughts seem intrinsically to imply both an avoidance process and an approach process. Their structure resembles what was described earlier as a discrepancy enlarging loop captured by a discrepancy reducing loop. Several kinds of evidence of the avoidance aspect of the dynamics behind the ought self have been reported (e.g. Carver, Lawrence, & Scheier, in press; Higgins & Tykocinski, 1992).

Consistent with this difference in regulation, Higgins (e.g. 1996, 1997) has begun to use the terms *promotion* focus and *prevention* focus. Promotion is approach, prevention is avoidance. In principle, either focus could apply to any kind of goal. In practice, however, promotion focus is more common with ideals, prevention focus with oughts.

This pairing of self-guide and motivational focus is also joined by particular affect qualities. Ought-based self-regulation relates to anxiety and guilt, and sometimes relief; ideal-based self-regulation relates to sadness, and sometimes happiness (Higgins, 1987, 1996; see also Carver, Lawrence, & Scheier, in press). Thus, this theory links an approach process to one dimension of affect, and it links avoidance to another dimension. The result is very similar to what appeared earlier in figure 2.

Several different theoretical starting points, then, have led to structural similarities, linking approach systems to certain affects, avoidance systems to other affects. Nor are these the only ones to share this structure (see, for example, Roseman, 1984).

Summary

The feedback model described in earlier sections depicts an internal guidance system that lets people move toward values that are desired and away from those that are undesired. The model is two-layered (in that it has both action and affect control), and it deals with both approach and withdrawal (or avoidance). This model converges with ideas that have been developed from studies of animal conditioning, from behavioral neuropsychology, and from other aspects of personality–social psychology. This convergence is both intriguing (because the origins are disparate) and heartening (because the convergence is so substantial).

In the foregoing I've left out parts of the complexity I usually bring to the discussion of these ideas. For example, it's obvious that goals vary in abstractness. You can have the goal of being a sensitive, caring person (or a financially successful person), but you can also have the goal of parking your car straight (which entails the even more concrete goal of turning the steering wheel with just the right pressure). Several have addressed this by asssuming that goals are organized hierarchically, with some at abstract levels and others at more concrete levels (Carver & Scheier, 1998, 1999a, 1999b; Powers, 1973; Vallacher & Wegner, 1987). Abstract goals are attained by attaining the more concrete goals that help define them.

Although this issue is very important in some contexts, it's not really critical to the themes of this chapter. Another set of issues is critical, however, to which I turn now.

Confronting Adversity

So far I've mostly assumed that when people want to do something, they do it. When they want to avoid something, they just avoid it. Sometimes that's not so easy, though. Sometimes people confront impediments. This issue arose by implication in the discussion of affect. That is, impediments often slow people down. As suggested earlier, this creates negative affect.

In discussing affect I said we've assumed that the mechanism that yields affect as a subjective readout also produces a hazy sense of confidence versus doubt about the immediate future. Let's now consider this second readout. Confidence and doubt can have important effects on behavior. However, an immediate sense of confidence or doubt usually is modified by other influences.

Specifically, when people experience adversity in trying to move toward their goals, they periodically interrupt their efforts to assess in a more deliberative way the likelihood of success (Carver & Scheier, 1981, 1990, 1998). In effect, people suspend the behavioral stream, step outside it, and evaluate their situation more thoroughly than while acting. In this assessment people depend heavily on memories of prior outcomes in similar situations, and consider such things as additional resources they might bring to bear or alternative approaches to the problem.[2]

Whether deriving mostly from real-time processing of the situation or from consolidated memories, the expectancies with which people return to action influence what they do. People who expect a successful outcome return to effort toward the goal. If doubts are strong enough, the result is an impetus to disengage from effort, and potentially to disengage from the goal itself (Carver & Scheier, 1981, 1998; Klinger, 1975; Kukla, 1972; Wortman & Brehm, 1975; Wright, 1996). Most responses seem ultimately to fall into these two categories: trying again and quitting.

Importance can impede disengagement

Presumably disengaging from many goals is easy. Indeed, disengagement from subgoals is quite common, even while continuing to pursue a broader activity's overall goal. For example, if you go to buy something and the store is closed for inventory, you're likely to leave this store and head for another one. Sometimes, though, disengagement is difficult, because of situational constraints or because of the goal's importance.

Concrete goals vary in how closely they're linked to values at a higher level (including the core values of the self), and thus how important they are. To disengage from concrete goals that are closely related to a central goal causes discrepancy enlargement for the central goal. One cannot disengage from goals that are central to one's life (or disregard them, or tolerate large discrepancies regarding them) without reorganizing one's value system (Kelly, 1955; McIntosh & Martin, 1992; Millar, Tesser, & Millar, 1988). In such a case, disengagement can be quite difficult.

Now recall the affective consequence of this situation. The desire to disengage was prompted by unfavorable expectancies. These expectancies are paralleled by negative affect. In this situation, then, the person has negative feelings (being unable to make progress toward the goal) and is unable to do anything about the feelings (being unable to give up). The person simply stews in the feelings (see also Martin & Tesser, 1996; Wyer & Srull, 1989, ch. 12). This situation – commitment to an unattainable goal – seems a sure prescription for distress, at least in the short term.

Is disengagement good or bad?

Is disengagement good or bad? The answer is both. Disengagement is a natural and indispensable part of self-regulation. If people are ever to turn away from unattainable goals, back out of blind alleys (literal or metaphorical), they must be able to disengage – to give up and start over somewhere else.

The importance of disengagement is most obvious for concrete goals. It's also important, though, regarding some higher-level goals. For example, it can be important to disengage and move on with life after the loss of close relationships (e.g. Cleiren, 1993; Stroebe, Stroebe, & Hansson, 1993). People sometimes must even be willing to give up values that are deeply embedded in the self, if those values create too much conflict and distress in their lives.

Sometimes, however, people give up too quickly. Situations exist where effort is never fully engaged, where the person could succeed but stopped trying and abandoned the goal too soon. One of the important lessons of life is the need to be persistent in pursuit of one's goals. Thus the value of disengagement in the face of adversity must be tempered by a realization that it is not always the right response.

Giving up tends to be a functional and adaptive response *when it leads to the taking up of other goals*, whether these are substitutes for the goal that's being abandoned or simply a new goal in a different domain. Giving up in that way can provide the person an opportunity to re-engage and move ahead again. In such cases, giving up occurs in service to the broader function of returning the person to an engagement with some goal and thereby an engagement with life.

What's happening when disengagement occurs?

The idea that effort may give way to disengagement as expectancies become more negative raises an issue. How does this idea mesh with the model presented in earlier sections? If behavior operates under the principle of feedback control, why shouldn't people try endlessly to reduce discrepancies, however ineffectively? Why should the distress and doubt not simply persist or intensify? What permits disengagement to happen?

One speculation on these questions begins with the realization that people always have many motives, desires, and goals competing for access to consciousness (e.g. Atkinson & Birch, 1970; Murray, 1938). There must be parallel paths of goal pursuit, some engaged more fully than others, some accorded greater importance (higher priority) than others. A mechanism presumably exists for "scheduling," allocating greater and lesser attention to those accorded different priorities (e.g. Shallice, 1978). It seems likely that many goals are partially active and engaged in people's minds most of the time (perhaps all the time), out of awareness but competing for access to attentional resources (Bargh, 1997; Wegner & Bargh, 1998).

The strength of each motive is subject to many influences. It may be that one influence is the person's confidence or doubt regarding the outcome. Perhaps (all other things being equal) the tendency to pursue the focal goal diminishes as confidence of success becomes lower. In this view, another behavior simply becomes prepotent at some point, and the person turns from the previous behavior to the newly focal one. Disengagement from one goal would be identical to the new goal's becoming focal.

Presumably there is a range of variability in degree of engagement (and thus in degree of access to consciousness). For a person actively struggling to overcome an impediment, that goal and self-regulatory attempt are fully conscious. For someone experiencing ruminative intrusions about a goal (Martin & Tesser, 1996), that goal is near the top of the queue but a bit below the level needed for active effort. For the person who's gone on to other things and no longer experiences intrusions, that goal has drifted yet lower. It may not be gone.

Some part of the mind may still be grinding away at resolving the blockage. But this process is at present no longer sufficiently potent to obtain access to attentional resources.

What conditions might increase access to attentional resources for a goal that's far down on the priority list? One final speculation: if the internal problem solver that's picking at the problem suddenly lurches forward, doubt decreases. If, as suggested above, doubt is one factor causing a goal to drop in priority, a decrease in doubt may increase its priority. Thus, an out-of-awareness partial resolution of the problem might cause the goal to rise in priority, even to pop into mind.

Scaling Back Aspirations and Recalibration of the Affect System

In the short term, being unable to move forward at an adequate pace toward a goal you are unable to disengage from creates distress. What happens *in the longer term*? In many cases the distress eventually subsides, even if the person remains behaviorally engaged in that domain with the same level of success. But how does this happen?

We have suggested that the system responsible for affect and the system responsible for behavior both can undergo changes in reference value over extended experience in a do-main of activity (Carver & Scheier, 1998). In the case of the affect system, the result of this would be that an experience that previously produced distress would become less likely to do so.

Let's consider the possibility of shifts in reference value, first with respect to the affect system, then the behavior system. Throughout, for clarity, I focus on approach loops. The same logic is applicable, however, to avoidance loops.

Shifts in velocity standards

We've suggested that the reference value used by the system that yields affect shifts as a function of recurrent experience (cf. Lord & Hanges, 1987). As people accumulate experi-ence in a domain, the pacing that's expected adjusts. This shifting of the reference value creates a kind of recentering of the system around the experience.

Sometimes the adjustment is downward, as in the cases that led to this discussion. For example, a researcher or a businessman experiencing difficulty in meeting his personal timetable for career development may gradually use less stringent standards of pacing. The lower pace will then begin to feel more satisfying. One consequence of such a shift is to increase the potential for positive affect and to decrease the potential for negative affect in that domain.

It should be clear, however, that the process can work in either direction. Sometimes the adjustment is upward. A person who gains work-related skills may undertake greater chal-lenges, requiring quicker handling of action units. Upward adjustment of a rate criterion means that the person will be satisfied only with faster progress in that domain. Such a shift has the side effect of decreasing the potential for positive affect and increasing the potential for negative affect, because there now is more room to fail to reach the rate standard.

These changes probably don't happen quickly or abruptly. As I said earlier, when people have trouble maintaining a demanding pace, lowering the reference value isn't their first response. First they try harder to keep up. Only more gradually, if this fails, does the standard of the affect loop shift to accommodate. Similarly, an upward shift in reference value isn't the immediate response when someone's rate exceeds the standard. The more typical response is to coast for a while. Only when the overshoot is frequent does the standard shift upward.

Such adjustments *themselves* appear to reflect a self-corrective feedback process, as the person reacts to insufficient challenge by taking on a more demanding pace, and reacts to too much challenge by scaling back (see figure 3). This secondary feedback process is slower than the ones addressed earlier, because it's weaker. Assume a signal to change the standard occurs every time there's a signal to change the output, but the former was much weaker than the latter. Given this, it would take a fairly long time for the standard to change. Indeed, as long as deviations from the standard occurred in both directions (under and over) with comparable frequency, the standard wouldn't change at all. It's only with repeated deviations in one direction or the other that there would be an appreciable effect on the standard.

It's of interest that these shifts in reference value (and the resultant effects on affect)

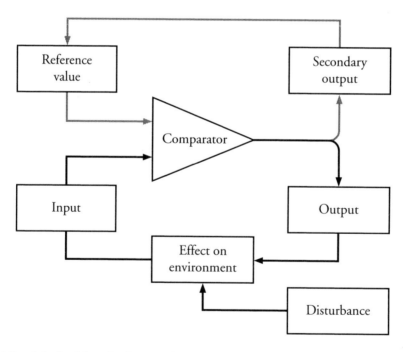

Figure 3   A feedback loop (in this case, the postulated meta loop) acts to create change in the input function, to shift it toward the reference value. Sometimes an additional process is in place as well (gray lines), which adjusts the reference value in the direction of the input. This additional process is presumed to be weaker or slower; thus, the reference value is stable, relative to the input value.

imply a mechanism that actively prevents the too-frequent occurrence of positive feeling, as well as the too-frequent occurrence of negative feeling. That is, the (bi-directional) shifting of the rate criterion over time would tend to control pacing such that affect continues to vary in both directions around neutral, roughly as it had before. Such an arrangement would provide continuous recalibration of the feeling system across changes in situation. The affective consequence would be that the person experiences roughly the same range of variation in affect over extended periods of time and circumstances (cf. Myers & Diener, 1995).

Scaling back on behavioral goals

The same principle can be seen to operate on behavioral goals. Sometimes progress toward a goal is impeded, expectancies of success are dim, and you want to quit. Rather than quit altogether, you trade this goal for a less demanding one. This is a kind of limited disengagement, in the sense that you've given up on the first goal at the same time as you're adopting the lesser one. This limited disengagement has the positive consequence of keeping you engaged in the general domain you'd wanted to quit. By scaling back the goal (giving up in a small way), you keep trying to move ahead. Thus you're *not* giving up, in a larger way.

As a concrete example, a student who wants an A in a course, but who's struggling ineffectually to attain high exam scores, may decide that an A is out of the question and lower his sights to a B or C. Given the change in goal, exam scores in the B or C range will represent better movement toward the goal than they would have been toward the initial goal. The result is that the student keeps plugging along, completes the course adequately, and may feel satisfied with a C.

Small-scale disengagement happens often in the context of moving forward in a broader way. Consider results of research on couples in which one partner is becoming ill and dying from AIDS (Moskowitz, Folkman, Collette, & Vittinghoff, 1996). Some healthy subjects initially have the goal of overcoming their partners' illness and continuing active lives together. As the illness progresses and it becomes apparent that this goal won't be met, it's not uncommon for the healthy partners to scale back their aspirations. Now the goal is to do more limited activities. Choosing a goal that's more limited and manageable ensures it will be possible to move successfully toward it. The result is that even in these difficult circumstances, the person experiences more positive feeling than would otherwise be the case and stays engaged behaviorally with efforts to move forward.

I think the scaling back of goals reflects the kind of process I described regarding affect. If the output function of the loop is inadequate at moving the input in the direction of the standard, a second (slower-acting) process may move the standard in the direction of the input (figure 3).

Affect and action

I treated the behavioral goal (and changes in it) as the relevant issue just above. But in many cases a change in the parameters of behavior also implies a change in the parameters of velocity. Attaining a C requires learning less than attaining an A. This implies different "amounts" of behavior. However, there's also a sense of velocity in this situation, because the task is time dependent. The student who's shifted to a lower goal will be happier about a B on the next exam than one who's held onto the higher goal. Why? Because the first student's velocity standard has dropped (he now has to master less material *in a given time* to reach his more limited action goal). He now perceives an actual velocity that exceeds his standard.

Earlier in the chapter I argued that the action loop and the affect loop work in concert with each other. They seem interconnected in influence and functioning. This example further illustrates this interdependence in operation.

Summary redux

The sections since the first summary have added several pieces to the self-regulation puzzle, mostly based on the need to ask how people deal with adversity. Part of the answer is that what people do depends on their confidence of success. Confidence leads to renewed effort; doubt leads to a tendency to disengage. Sometimes disengagement is easy, sometimes it's not. Disengagement is more difficult when the goal is more important. Sometimes goals are important enough that people don't give them up at all.

When a person wants to give up but can't, the short-term experience is enhanced distress. If the experience goes on long enough in some domain, however, the longer term result may be a *partial* giving up, a lowering of the standard of comparison. This idea seems applicable both with respect to action (lowering an aspiration) and with respect to affect (having less demanding pacing). Although the idea of changing reference values was broached in the context of the failure to reach desired goals, the mechanism of change also applies in the other direction, causing reference values to go up instead of down. The result is a system of floating recalibration, as an extended inability to keep up causes the standard to drop and an extended overattainment causes the standard to rise.

The cumulative picture is of a set of systems making a variety of adjustments – some quick, others slow. The systems are attaining intended goals, avoiding undesired events, and adjusting aspirations to be more or less consonant with previous experience.

Restraint and Conflict

One more issue to be considered concerns the fact that people sometimes try to override one tendency with another one. Sometimes the tendencies are mental, sometimes they are behavioral. Often the attempt to override works for a while (sometimes a long while), but sometimes it fails.

Ironic processes in mental control

One literature bearing on this theme was developed by Wegner (e.g. 1994) and his colleagues. The study that began this work was simple. Some people were told not to think of a white bear for five minutes. Then they were told to think about the bear. When the thought now was permitted, it came more frequently than for people who hadn't had to suppress the thought first. Something about trying not to think of the bear seemed to create pressure to think of it.

This study was followed by many more. Most of this research looked not at rebounds, but at what goes on during people's attempts to control their thoughts. Consistently the data indicate that an instruction to exert mental control yields better control if the person has no other demands. If something else is going on, however – for example, if the person is trying to remember a 9-digit number – the instruction backfires, and people tend to do the opposite of what they were trying to do.

Wegner (1994) interprets this as follows: trying to suppress a thought engages two processes. An intentional operating process tries to suppress. An ironic monitoring process looks for the occurrence of what's being suppressed. If it finds it, it increases the first mechanism's effort. The ironic monitor is sensitive, but it's automatic and doesn't require much mental resources. The intentional process requires more resources. Thus any reduction in mental resources (e.g. being distracted by a second thought or task) disrupts the intentional process more than the ironic monitor. The monitor, searching for lapses, in effect invites them to enter.

This theory also applies to the opposite pattern – attempts to concentrate. In this case, the intentional process concentrates, the ironic process looks for the occurrence of distractions. As in the first case, if mental resources are stretched thin, the ironic process seems to invite the undesired thought into consciousness. In this case, the thought is a distraction.

This research indicates that trying hard to do something (or suppress something) gets harder when your mental resources are stretched thin. Not only does it get harder, but you become prone to do the opposite of what you're trying to do.

Lapses in self-control

Another literature bearing on this theme concerns what Baumeister & Heatherton (1996) called self-regulatory failure and I will call lapse in self-control.[3] This occurs when someone has both the desire to do something (e.g. overindulge in food or drink) and also the desire to restrain that impulse. This is a conflict in which reaching one goal (restraint) involves overriding any attempt to reach the other one (overindulge). Self-control is often hard, and sometimes the restrained impulse breaks free.

Consider binge eating as an example. The binge eater wants to eat but also wants to restrain that desire. If self-control lapses, the person stops trying to restrain the desire to eat, lets himself or herself go, and binges.

In characterizing the decision to quit trying to restrain, Baumeister and Heatherton noted that restraint is hard work and mental fatigue plays a role, but quitting rarely requires total exhaustion. Rather, there's a point where the person says "Enough," and stops trying to control the impulse. We've suggested that confidence about resisting the impulse plays a role in whether the person stops trying (Carver & Scheier, 1998). The person who's confident continues the struggle to restrain. The person whose confidence has sagged is more likely to give up.

Muraven, Tice, & Baumeister (1998) have extended this line of thought to argue that self-control is a resource that not only is limited but also can become depleted by extended self-control efforts. When it's depleted, the person becomes vulnerable to a failure of self-control. This view also suggests that there's a shared pool of self-control resources, so that exhausting the resource with one kind of self-control (e.g. concentrating very hard for many hours on a writing assignment) can leave the person vulnerable to a lapse in a different domain (e.g. eating restraint).

It seems worthwhile to compare the cases considered here and those described just earlier. Both sections dealt with efforts at self-control. In many ways the situations are structurally quite similar. Each is an attempt to override one process by another, which falters under conditions of depletion of mental resources. Even the overdoing of the restrained behavior in Baumeister and Heatherton's cases resembles the rebound quality in Wegner's research.

One difference is that the cases emphasized by Baumeister and Heatherton explicitly involve desires that direct the person in opposing directions. In most cases studied by Wegner, there's no obvious reason why the suppressed thought (or the distractor) would be desirable. This difference between cases seems far from trivial, but the similarities in findings are striking enough to warrant further thought to the relation between these literatures in the future.

Concluding Comment

In this chapter I've presented a series of ideas I think are useful in thinking about the self-regulation of behavior. I believe the idea that behavior is goal-directed and feedback-controlled complements and supplements other ideas about approach and avoidance as core processes. I think these ideas also help us understand affect. How confidence and doubt influence persistence versus giving up is crucial to many different motivational models; these responses to adversity are clearly important in understanding self-regulation. Another part of self-regulation, slower and more subtle, is a continuing process of recalibration. It lets people be happy with less when things have gone poorly and find challenge even when they've gotten good at something. The final principle is a reminder that when we are stretched thin, trying to exert mental control and control over competing behaviors can have undesired consequences.

As I said at the chapter's outset, the ideas outlined here cover only parts of the puzzle. Potentially important ideas not included here come from dynamic systems theory and catastrophe theory (Carver & Scheier, 1998; Nowak & Vallacher, 1998). How important these ideas will be remains to be determined. Creating models of self-regulation, as is true of all of psychology, remains a work in progress.

Notes

1   The feedback model holds that a checking-and-comparison process is taking place, which is more complex than the action of a force field. But is there even more complexity? In outlining these processes I've made them sound as though they just happen. What about will? What about self-determination? In this chapter I've chosen to side-step such questions. Here I describe processes that do just seem to happen, and do so fairly automatically (indeed, sometimes fully automatically – Bargh, 1997). Readers interested in further discussion of the self-regulation model and issues such as will and self-determination will find discussions elsewhere (Carver & Scheier, 1998, 1999a, 1999b).

2   The fact that goals vary in specificity – from very concrete and specific, to those concerning a particular domain, to the very general – suggests that people have a comparable range of variations in consolidated expectancies. That is, you can be confident or doubtful about tying your shoes, about finding good food for dinner, about winning a particular tennis match, about performing well in socially evaluative circumstances, or about having good outcomes in life (Scheier & Carver, 1992). Each of these senses of confidence versus doubt may matter to behavior.

3   Baumeister & Heatherton (1996) used the term self-regulation to refer solely to instances in which the person acts to override or suppress another action tendency. The literature as a whole has used the term self-regulation more broadly, as I have done throughout this chapter. In my view, the cases discussed by Baumeister and Heatherton are more appropriately labeled self-control, a term that has a long history of referring to the restraint of impulses.

References

Atkinson, J. W., & Birch, D. (1970). *The dynamics of action*. New York: Wiley.

Austin, J. T., & Vancouver, J. B. (1996). Goal constructs in psychology: Structure, process, and content. *Psychological Bulletin, 120*, 338–375.

Bargh, J. A. (1997). The automaticity of everyday life. In R. S. Wyer, Jr. (Ed.), *Advances in social cognition* Vol. 10 (pp. 1–61). Mahwah, NJ: Erlbaum.

Baumeister, R. F. (1991). *Escaping the self*. New York: Basic Books.

Baumeister, R. F., & Heatherton, T. F. (1996). Self-regulation failure: An overview. *Psychological Inquiry, 7*, 1–15.

Cantor, N., & Kihlstrom, J. F. (1987). *Personality and social intelligence*. Englewood Cliffs, NJ: Prentice-Hall.

Carver, C. S., & Scheier, M. F. (1981). *Attention and self-regulation: A control-theory approach to human behavior*. New York: Springer-Verlag.

Carver, C. S., & Scheier, M. F. (1990). Origins and functions of positive and negative affect: A control-process view. *Psychological Review, 97*, 19–35.

Carver, C. S., & Scheier, M. F. (1998). *On the self-regulation of behavior*. New York: Cambridge University Press.

Carver, C. S., & Scheier, M. F. (1999a). Themes and issues in the self-regulation of behavior. In R. S. Wyer, Jr. (Ed.), *Advances in social cognition* Vol. 12 (pp. 1–105). Mahwah, NJ: Erlbaum.

Carver, C. S., & Scheier, M. F. (1999b). Several more themes, a lot more issues: Commentary on the commentaries. In R. S. Wyer, Jr. (Ed.), *Advances in social cognition* Vol. 12 (pp. 261–302). Mahwah, NJ: Erlbaum.

Carver, C. S., & White, T. L. (1994). Behavioral inhibition, behavioral activation, and affective responses to impending reward and punishment: The BIS/BAS scales. *Journal of Personality and Social Psychology, 67*, 319–333.

Carver, C. S., Lawrence, J. W., & Scheier, M. F. (in press). Self-discrepancies and affect: Incorporating the role of feared selves. *Personality and Social Psychology Bulletin.*

Clark, R. N. (1996). *Control system dynamics.* New York: Cambridge University Press.

Cleiren, M. (1993). *Bereavement and adaptation: A comparative study of the aftermath of death.* Washington, DC: Hemisphere.

Cloninger, C. R. (1987). A systematic method for clinical description and classification of personality variants. *Archives of General Psychiatry, 44,* 573–588.

Davidson, R. J. (1992). Anterior cerebral asymmetry and the nature of emotion. *Brain and Cognition, 20,* 125–151.

Davidson, R. J. (1995). Cerebral asymmetry, emotion, and affective style. In R. J. Davidson, & K. Hugdahl (Eds.), *Brain asymmetry* (pp. 361–387). Cambridge, MA: MIT Press.

Davidson, R. J., & Sutton, S. K. (1995). Affective neuroscience: The emergence of a discipline. *Current Opinion in Neurobiology, 5,* 217–224.

Depue, R. A., & Collins, P. F. (in press). Neurobiology of the structure of personality: Dopamine, facilitation of incentive motivation, and extraversion. *Behavioral and Brain Sciences.*

Duval, S., & Wicklund, R. A. (1972). *A theory of objective self-awareness.* New York: Academic Press.

Elliott, E. S., & Dweck, C. S. (1988). Goals: An approach to motivation and achievement. *Journal of Personality and Social Psychology, 54,* 5–12.

Emmons, R. A. (1986). Personal strivings: An approach to personality and subjective well being. *Journal of Personality and Social Psychology, 51,* 1058–1068.

Ford, D. H. (1987). *Humans as self-constructing living systems: A developmental perspective on behavior and personality.* Hillsdale, NJ: Erlbaum.

Fowles, D. C. (1980). The three arousal model: Implications of Gray's two-factor learning theory for heart rate, electrodermal activity, and psychopathy. *Psychophysiology, 17,* 87–104.

Frijda, N. H. (1986). *The emotions.* Cambridge: Cambridge University Press.

Frijda, N. H. (1988). The laws of emotion. *American Psychologist, 43,* 349–358.

Gray, J. A. (1981). A critique of Eysenck's theory of personality. In H. J. Eysenck (Ed.), *A model for personality* (pp. 246–276). Berlin: Springer-Verlag.

Gray, J. A. (1990). Brain systems that mediate both emotion and cognition. *Cognition and Emotion, 4,* 269–288.

Gray, J. A. (1994). Three fundamental emotion systems. In P. Ekman, & R. J. Davidson (Eds.), *The nature of emotion: Fundamental questions* (pp. 243–247). New York: Oxford University Press.

Harmon-Jones, E., & Allen, J. J. (1997). Behavioral activation sensitivity and resting frontal EEG asymmetry: Covariation of putative indicators related to risk for mood disorders. *Journal of Abnormal Psychology, 106,* 159–163.

Higgins, E. T. (1987). Self-discrepancy: A theory relating self and affect. *Psychological Review, 94,* 319–340.

Higgins, E. T. (1996). Ideals, oughts, and regulatory focus: Affect and motivation from distinct pains and pleasures. In P. M. Gollwitzer, & J. A. Bargh (Eds.), *The psychology of action: Linking cognition and motivation to behavior* (pp. 91–114). New York: Guilford Press.

Higgins, E. T. (1997). Beyond pleasure and pain. *American Psychologist, 52,* 1280–1300.

Higgins, E. T., & Tykocinski, O. (1992). Self-discrepancies and biographical memory: Personality and cognition at the level of psychological situation. *Personality and Social Psychology Bulletin, 18,* 527–535.

Kelly, G. A. (1955). *The psychology of personal constructs.* New York: W. W. Norton.

Klinger, E. (1975). Consequences of commitment to and disengagement from incentives. *Psychological Review, 82,* 1–25.

Kuhl, J. (1994). Motivation and volition. In G. d'Ydewalle, P. Eelen, & P. Bertelson (Eds.), *International perspectives on psychological science* Vol. 2 (pp. 311–340). Hove, UK: Erlbaum.

Kukla, A. (1972). Foundations of an attributional theory of performance. *Psychological Review, 79,* 454–470.

Little, B. R. (1989). Personal projects analysis: Trivial pursuits, magnificent obsessions, and the search for coherence. In D. M. Buss, & N. Cantor (Eds.), *Personality psychology: Recent trends and emerging directions* (pp. 15–31). New York: Springer-Verlag.

Lord, R. G., & Hanges, P. J. (1987). A control system model of organizational motivation: Theoretical development and applied implications. *Behavioral Science, 32,* 161–178.

McIntosh, W. D., & Martin, L. L. (1992). The cybernetics of happiness: The relation of goal attainment, rumination, and affect. In M. S. Clark (Ed.), *Review of personality and social psychology, Vol. 14: Emotion and social behavior* (pp. 222–246). Newbury Park, CA: Sage.

MacKay, D. M. (1966). Cerebral organization and the conscious control of action. In J. C. Eccles (Ed.), *Brain and conscious experience* (pp. 422–445). Berlin: Springer-Verlag.

Markus, H., & Nurius, P. (1986). Possible selves. *American Psychologist, 41,* 954–969.

Martin, L. L., & Tesser, A. (1996). Some ruminative thoughts. In R. S. Wyer, Jr. (Ed.), *Advances in social cognition* Vol. 9 (pp. 1–47). Mahwah, NJ: Erlbaum.

Millar, K. U., Tesser, A., & Millar, M. G. (1988). The effects of a threatening life event on behavior sequences and intrusive thought: A self-disruption explanation. *Cognitive Therapy and Research, 12,* 441–458.

Miller, G. A., Galanter, E., & Pribram, K. H. (1960). *Plans and the structure of behavior.* New York: Holt, Rinehart, & Winston.

Moskowitz, J. T., Folkman, S., Collette, L., & Vittinghoff, E. (1996). Coping and mood during AIDS-related caregiving and bereavement. *Annals of Behavioral Medicine, 18,* 49–57.

Muraven, M., Tice, D. M., & Baumeister, R. F. (1998). Self-control as a limited resource: Regulatory depletion patterns. *Journal of Personality and Social Psychology, 74,* 774–789.

Murray, H. A. (1938). *Explorations in personality.* New York: Oxford University Press.

Myers, D. G., & Diener, E. (1995). Who is happy? *Psychological Science, 6,* 10–19.

Nowak, A., & Vallacher, R. R. (1998). *Dynamical social psychology.* New York: Guilford Press.

Ogilvie, D. M. (1987). The undesired self: A neglected variable in personality research. *Journal of Personality and Social Psychology, 52,* 379–385.

Pervin, L. A. (1982). The stasis and flow of behavior: Toward a theory of goals. In M. M. Page, & R. Dienstbier (Eds.), *Nebraska symposium on motivation* Vol. 30 (pp. 1–53). Lincoln: University of Nebraska Press.

Pervin, L. A. (Ed.) (1989). *Goal concepts in personality and social psychology.* Hillsdale, NJ: Erlbaum.

Powers, W. T. (1973). *Behavior: The control of perception.* Chicago: Aldine.

Read, S. J., & Miller, L. C. (1989). Inter-personalism: Toward a goal-based theory of persons in relationships. In L. Pervin (Ed.), *Goal concepts in personality and social psychology* (pp. 413–472). Hillsdale, NJ: Erlbaum.

Roseman, I. J. (1984). Cognitive determinants of emotions: A structural theory. In P. Shaver (Ed.), *Review of personality and social psychology* Vol. 5 (pp. 11–36). Beverly Hills, CA: Sage.

Scheier, M. F., & Carver, C. S. (1983). Self-directed attention and the comparison of self with standards. *Journal of Experimental Social Psychology, 19,* 205–222.

Scheier, M. F., & Carver, C. S. (1992). Effects of optimism on psychological and physical well-being: Theoretical overview and empirical update. *Cognitive Therapy and Research, 16,* 201–228.

Shallice, T. (1978). The dominant action system: An information-processing approach to consciousness. In K. S. Pope & J. L. Singer (Eds.), *The stream of consciousness: Scientific investigations into the flow of human experience* (pp. 117–157). New York: Wiley.

Strauman, T. J. (1989). Self-discrepancies in clinical depression and social phobia: Cognitive structures that underlie emotional disorders? *Journal of Abnormal Psychology, 98,* 14–22.

Stroebe, M. S., Stroebe, W., & Hansson, R. O. (Eds.) (1993). *Handbook of bereavement: Theory, research, and intervention.* Cambridge, UK: Cambridge University Press.

Sutton, S. K., & Davidson, R. J. (1997). Prefrontal brain asymmetry: A biological substrate of the behavioral approach and inhibition systems. *Psychological Science, 8,* 204–210.

Vallacher, R. R., & Wegner, D. M. (1987). What do people think they're doing? Action identification and human behavior. *Psychological Review, 94,* 3–15.

Wegner, D. M. (1994). Ironic processes of mental control. *Psychological Review, 101,* 34–52.

Wegner, D. M., & Bargh, J. A. (1998). Control and automaticity in social life. In D. Gilbert, S. T. Fiske, & G. Lindzey (Eds.), *Handbook of social psychology* 4th. edn. (pp. 446–496). Boston, MA: McGraw-Hill.

Wiener, N. (1948). *Cybernetics: Control and communication in the animal and the machine.* Cambridge, MA: MIT Press.

Wortman, C. B., & Brehm, J. W. (1975). Responses to uncontrollable outcomes: An integration of reactance theory and the learned helplessness model. In L. Berkowitz (Ed.), *Advances in experimental social psychology* Vol. 8 (pp. 277–336). New York: Academic Press.

Wright, R. A. (1996). Brehm's theory of motivation as a model of effort and cardiovascular response. In P. M. Gollwitzer, & J. A. Bargh (Eds.), *The psychology of action: Linking cognition and motivation to behavior* (pp. 424–453). New York: Guilford Press.

Wyer, R. S., Jr., & Srull, T. K. (1989). *Memory and cognition in social context.* Hillsdale, NJ: Erlbaum.

Chapter Fifteen

Goal Setting and Goal Striving

Gabriele Oettingen and Peter M. Gollwitzer

In this chapter we focus on the determinants and processes of goal emergence and goal implementation. We first address personal and situational variables leading to the formation of behavioral goals and what kind of psychological processes help or hinder goal setting. In the second part of the chapter, we discuss how set goals of different qualities predict goal attainment and which self-regulatory strategies help successful goal striving. Goal effects on cognition are discussed as possible mediators of the goal–behavior link.

The History of the Goal Concept

Behaviorists recognize goal-directed behavior by its features. Goal-directed behavior is *persistent*. A hungry rat persists in searching a maze until the pellets are reached (Tolman, 1925). Goal-directed behavior is *appropriate*. When one path is blocked, another path to the same goal is taken, or if the goal moves, the organism readily follows it. Finally, goal-directed organisms start *searching* when exposed to stimuli associated with the goal.

A behaviorist's statement that a certain piece of food is a goal for the hungry organism means (1) that the food qualifies as an incentive for the organism, and (2) that the researcher has chosen to describe the behavior of the organism relative to the food stimulus rather than relative to any other object or event. Skinner (1953) referred to goal-directedness as a shorthand description of behavior resulting from some kind of operant conditioning. Thus in the behaviorist tradition, the reference point for goal-directed behavior is not the intention or the goal set by the organism itself.

In contrast, the reference point of modern goal theories is the internal subjective goal. Goal-directed behavior refers to goals held by the individual (e.g. a person's goal to stop smoking serves as the reference point for his or her efforts to achieve this goal). Research questions focus on how and in what form goals are set and how goal setting affects behavior.

The behaviorist distinctions between needs (motives), incentives, and goal-directed behavior are, however, still present in modern goal theories which consider needs (e.g. the need for approval) as forces that narrow down classes of incentives (e.g. being popular or accomplished), and see behavioral goals in the service of these incentives. For example, Geen (1995) defined an incentive as a desired outcome that subsumes several lower order goals. Incentives (e.g. being popular or accomplished) are considered to be a product of a person's need (i.e. the need for social approval) and the perceived situational opportunities (i.e. the person's friends or scientific community, respectively). Intentions to attain popularity or to accomplish outstanding scientific achievements are understood as higher order goals served by many lower order behavioral goals (e.g. intending to use the weekend to visit friends or to write an outstanding scientific article, respectively).

The modern perspective of analyzing goal-directed behaviors in relation to subjective goals has its own precursors: William James and William McDougall in America, and Narziß Ach and Kurt Lewin in Europe. In his *Principles of Psychology* (1890/1950) James held that behavior can be regulated by resolutions (i.e. intentions, subjective goals), even though this may be difficult at times. However, if certain preliminaries are fulfilled, behavior specified in resolutions comes true. McDougall (1908/1931) postulated that goals guide behavior through cognitive activity that pertains to the analysis of the present situation and the intended goal. Progress towards, and the attainment of, the goal are seen as pleasurable and thwarting and failing as painful.

In Europe, the scientific debate on goal striving was dominated by controversy between Ach and Lewin. Ach (1935) assumed that mental links between an anticipated situation and an intended behavior create what he called a determination, which urges the person to initiate the intended action when the specified situation is encountered. The strength of a determination should depend on how concretely the anticipated situation is specified and on the intensity of the intention. Determination was seen as directly eliciting the behavior without conscious intent. Lewin (1926) critically referred to Ach's ideas as a "linkage theory of intention" and proposed a need theory of intention. Goals (intentions), like needs, are assumed to assign a valence (*Aufforderungscharakter*) to objects and events in one's surroundings. Similar to basic needs (e.g. hunger) which can be satisfied by a variety of behaviors (e.g. eating fruit, vegetables, or bread), the quasi-needs associated with intentions (e.g. to be popular) may be satisfied by various behaviors (e.g. inviting one's friends for a party, buying birthday gifts). The tension associated with the quasi-need determines the intensity of goal striving. This tension depends on the strength of relevant real needs (i.e. superordinate drives or general life goals) and how strongly these are related to the quasi-need. Lewin's tension-state metaphor accounts for the flexibility of goal striving.

Many of the ideas on goal-directed behaviors as presented by James, McDougall, Ach, Lewin, and the behaviorists, have been absorbed into modern goal theories, whereby goal implementation has received much more theoretical and empirical attention than goal setting. Karoly (1993, p. 27) states that "the study of goals as dependent variables remains infrequent" and Carver & Scheier (1999) conclude that "the question of where goals come from and how they are synthesized is one that has not been well explored." We will start, then, with the question of what factors determine goal selection and which psychological processes promote goal setting.

Goal Setting

Determinants of goal setting

Assigned goals   Goals are often *assigned* by others (e.g. employers, teachers, parents). It matters who assigns goals to whom, and how the persuasive message is framed. Relevant variables may include attributes of the source, the recipient, and the message (McGuire, 1969). Locke & Latham (1990) report that source variables, such as legitimacy and trust-worthiness, play an important role in the transformation of an assigned goal into a personal goal. For recipients of such assignments, perception of the goal as desirable and feasible, personal redefinition of the goal, and integration with other existing goals are important (Cantor & Fleeson, 1994). Finally, relevant message variables may be the discrepancy between the suggested goal and the recipient's respective current goal (e.g. when a very low calorie diet is suggested to a person with a moderate dieting goal), and whether fear appeals are used (e.g. information on the dramatic medical consequences of health-damaging behavior is provided). Effective sellers of goals must also consider the processing ability and motivation of the recipient as a moderator of the effects of source, recipient, and message variables on accepting assigned goals as personal goals (Petty & Cacioppo, 1986; Chaiken, 1987).

Self-set goals   Goals do not need to be assigned, as people also set goals on their own. Self-set goals, however, are often influenced by others, for example, when goals are conjointly set (e.g. in participative decision making and employee involvement; Wilpert, 1994), or when goals are adopted from highly respected models (e.g. adopting standards for self-reward; Mischel & Liebert, 1966). Cantor & Fleeson (1994) point out that social context cues, such as normative expectations of the social community, also influence goal selection.

   The personal attributes that most strongly determine goal choice are perceived desirability and feasibility. People prefer to choose goals that are desirable and feasible (Ajzen, 1985; Heckhausen, 1991; Gollwitzer, 1990; Locke & Latham, 1990). Desirability is determined by the estimated attractiveness of likely short-term and long-term consequences of goal attainment. Such consequences may pertain to anticipated self-evaluations, evaluations by significant others, progress toward some higher order goal, external rewards of having attained the goal, and the joy/pain associated with moving towards the goal (Heckhausen, 1977). Feasibility depends upon people's judgments of their capabilities to perform relevant goal-directed behaviors (i.e. self-efficacy expectations; Bandura, 1997), their belief that these goal-directed behaviors will lead to the desired outcome (i.e. outcome expectations; Bandura, 1997), or the judged likelihood of attaining the desired outcome (i.e. generalized expectations; Oettingen, 1996) or desired events in general (general optimism; Scheier & Carver, 1985). The information source for efficacy expectations, outcome expectations, generalized expectations, and optimism is past experiences: one's own past performances, the observed performances of others, received relevant persuasive messages, and one's previous physiological responses to challenge (Bandura, 1997). Proper assessment of the feasibility and desirability of a potential goal also requires seeing the goal in relation to other potential goals. A goal associated with many attractive consequences may suddenly appear less desirable in light of a superordinate goal, or it might seem more feasible in connection with other, compatible goals (Cantor & Fleeson, 1994; Gollwitzer, 1990).

Estimated desirability and feasibility determine the choice of a goal's difficulty level. Festinger (1942), in his theory of resultant valence, argued that people choose goal difficulty levels where the resultant expected valence is the highest – this being a multiplicative function of the probability of success or failure and the valence of success or failure. Atkinson's (1957) risk taking model modified and extended Festinger's reasoning to make separate predictions for individuals with hope for success versus fear of failure. The latter prefer low and high difficulty levels, whereas the former choose goals of medium difficulty.

Set goals may also differ in other structural features (e.g. abstract vs. concrete) and in content (e.g. materialistic vs. social integrative). People generally prefer to set themselves abstract goals, and adopt concrete goals only when they run into problems attaining an abstract goal. According to act identification theory (Vallacher & Wegner, 1987), people conceive of their actions in rather abstract terms (e.g. cleaning the apartment) and only drop down to lower, concrete levels (e.g. vacuuming the carpet) when difficulties in carrying out the activity as construed at the higher level arise. Some people typically think of their actions in low-level terms, whereas others prefer high-level identifications (Vallacher & Wegner, 1989). This general preference for either an abstract or a concrete level of identifying actions should be reflected in the choice of abstract versus concrete goals.

Goals can be framed with a positive or negative outcome focus (i.e. goals that focus on establishing and keeping positive outcomes as compared to avoiding and ameliorating negative outcomes). Higgins (1997) argues that people construe their self either as an ideal self that they intrinsically desire to be, or as an ought self that they feel compelled to be. The former orientation focuses on promotion, whereas the latter focuses on prevention. Part of the promotion orientation is a predilection for setting goals with a positive outcome focus, whereas part of the prevention orientation is a predilection for setting goals with a negative outcome focus.

Goals can also be framed as performance versus learning goals (Dweck, 1996), also referred to as performance versus mastery goals (Ames & Archer, 1988), or ego involvement versus task involvement goals (Nicholls, 1979). Goals in the achievement domain, for example, can either focus on finding out how capable one is (performance goals) or on learning how to carry out the task (learning goals). Dweck (1996) reports that implicit theories on the nature of ability determine the preference for performance versus learning goals. If people believe that ability is fixed and cannot be easily changed (i.e. hold an entity theory of ability), they prefer performance goals. However, if people believe that ability can be improved by learning (i.e. hold an incremental theory of ability), they prefer learning goals. Similar implicit theories concerning the malleability of moral character affect the selection of punitive versus educational correctional goals.

The content of set goals is influenced by needs, wishes, and higher order goals. Ryan, Sheldon, Kasser, & Deci (1996) argue, for example, that the content of people's goals reflect their needs. Autonomy, competence, and social integration needs are expected to promote goal setting focused on self-realization rather than materialistic gains. Markus & Nurius (1986; Oyserman, chapter 23, this volume) argue that people conceive of themselves not only in terms of what they are (i.e. the self-concept), but also what they wish to become in the future (i.e. the possible self). These possible selves should give people ideas on what kind of personal goals they may strive for.

Once higher order goals are formed (e.g. to become a physician), they determine the contents of lower order goals. The contents of such "Be" goals determine the contents of respective "Do" goals which in turn determine the contents of respective "motor-control" goals (Carver & Scheier, 1998, p. 72; Carver, chapter 14, this volume). "Be" goals have been described by using terms such as current concerns (Klinger, 1977), self-defining goals (Wicklund & Gollwitzer, 1982), personal projects (Little, 1983), personal strivings (Emmons, 1996), and (individualized) life tasks (Cantor & Fleeson, 1994). Whereas choosing higher order "Be" goals should be determined by their perceived desirability and feasibility (Klinger, 1977), choosing the respective lower order "Do" goals also depends on the commitment to the respective "Be" goals (Gollwitzer, 1987).

Processes of goal setting

Reflective processes   So far we have discussed which variables determine the choice of goals with certain structural and thematic features. We now consider the question of what triggers goal setting. Bandura (1997) suggests that having successfully achieved a set goal stimulates the setting of ever more challenging goals, due to a person's heightened sense of efficacy which is based on having successfully attained the prior goal. Others have pointed out that the core processes of goal setting involve committing oneself to achieving a certain incentive (Klinger, 1977). Heckhausen & Kuhl (1985) argued that the lowest degree of commitment to an incentive is a mere wish to attain it. A wish that is tested for feasibility becomes a want which carries a higher degree of commitment. To develop a full goal commitment (i.e. to form the intention or goal to achieve the incentive), a further relevance check must be carried out relating to necessary means, opportunities, time, relative importance, and urgency.

In their Rubicon model of action phases Heckhausen & Gollwitzer (1987; Heckhausen, 1991; Gollwitzer, 1990) assume that people entertain more wishes than they have time or opportunities to realize. Therefore they must select between wishes in order to accomplish at least some of them. The criteria for selection are feasibility and desirability. Wishes with high feasibility and desirability have the best chance to become goals. The transformation of wishes into goals is a resolution, resulting in a feeling of determination to act. Through this resolution the desired end state specified by the wish becomes an end state that the individual feels committed to achieve. To catch the flavor of this transition from wishing to willing, the metaphor of crossing the Rubicon is used.

What are the preliminaries of crossing the Rubicon? The model of action phases (Gollwitzer, 1990; Heckhausen, 1991) states that the realization of a wish demands the completion of four successive tasks: deliberating between wishes to select appropriate ones (predecision phase), planning the implementation of chosen wishes (i.e. goals or intentions) to help get started with goal-directed behaviors (preaction phase), monitoring goal-directed behaviors to bring them to a successful ending (action phase), and evaluating what has been achieved as compared to what was desired to terminate goal pursuit or to restart it (evaluation phase). People decide to "cross the Rubicon" (i.e. move from the predecision phase to the preaction phase) when they sense that the feasibility and desirability of a wish is not only acceptably high, but has been exhaustively deliberated and correctly assessed. Gollwitzer, Heckhausen, & Ratajczak (1989) observed that undecided people more readily formed goals when they had been asked to judge the likelihood of wish fulfillment and to list likely positive and negative, short-term and long-term consequences. In addition, when undecided people were lured into planning the implementation of the wish by simply connecting anticipated opportunities with intended goal-directed behaviors, they also showed a greater readiness to cross the Rubicon. Apparently, when undecided people feel that the task of assessing the feasibility and desirability of a given wish is completed, they show a greater readiness to move on and set themselves the respective goal.

A recent theory on fantasy realization (Oettingen, 1996) analyzes goal setting by delineating different routes to goal formation. The theory distinguishes between two forms of thinking about the future, expectations and free fantasies. Expectations are judgments of the likelihood that a certain future behavior or outcome will occur. Free fantasies about the future, to the contrary, are thoughts and images of future behaviors or outcomes in the mind's eye, independent of the likelihoods that these events will actually occur. For example, despite perceiving low chances of successfully resolving a conflict with a partner, people can indulge in positive fantasies of harmony.

Fantasy realization theory specifies three routes to goal setting which result from how people deal with their fantasies about the future. One route is expectancy based, while the other two are independent of expectations. The expectancy based route rests on mentally contrasting positive fantasies about the future with negative aspects of impeding reality. This mental contrast ties free fantasies about the future to the here and now. Consequently, the desired future appears as something that must be achieved and the impeding reality as something that must be changed. The resulting necessity to act raises the question: can reality be altered to match fantasy? The answer is given by the subjective expectation of successfully attaining fantasy in reality. Accordingly, mental contrasting of positive fantasies about the future with negative aspects of the impeding reality causes expectations of success to become activated and used. If expectations of success are high, a person will commit herself to fantasy attainment; if expectations of success are low, a person will refrain.

The second route to goal setting stems from merely indulging in positive fantasies about the desired future, thereby disregarding impeding reality. This indulgence seduces one to consummate and consume the desired future envisioned in the mind's eye. Accordingly, no necessity to act is experienced and relevant expectations of success are not activated and used. Commitment to act towards fantasy fulfillment reflects solely the pull of the desired events imagined in one's fantasies. It is moderate and *in*dependent of a person's perceived chances of success (i.e. expectations). As a consequence, the level of goal commitment is either too high (when expectations are low) or too low (when expectations are high).

The third route is based on merely dwelling on the negative aspects of impeding reality, thereby disregarding positive fantasies about the future. Again, no necessity to act is experienced, this time because nothing points to a direction in which to act. Expectations of success are not activated and used. Commitment to act merely reflects the push of the negative aspects of impeding reality. Similar to indulgence in positive fantasies about the future, dwelling on the negative reality leads to a moderate, expectancy *in*dependent level of commitment, which is either too high (when expectations are low) or too low (when expectations are high).

Fantasy realization theory is supported by various experimental studies. In one study (Oettingen, in press-a, Study 1) participants were confronted with an interpersonal opportunity: getting to know an attractive person. Female participants first judged the probability of successfully getting to know an attractive male doctoral student, whose picture they saw. Participants then generated positive aspects of getting to know the attractive man (e.g. love, friendship) and negative aspects of impeding reality (e.g. being shy, his potential disinterest). They were then divided into three groups for elaboration of these aspects. In the fantasy–reality contrast group, participants mentally elaborated both positive aspects of getting to know the man and negative aspects of reality standing in the way; this was done in alternating order beginning with a positive aspect. In the positive fantasy group, participants mentally elaborated only positive aspects of getting to know the man; and in the negative reality group, participants mentally elaborated only negative aspects of impeding reality.

In the fantasy–reality contrast group, goal commitment (assessed as eagerness to get to know the person and anticipated frustration in case of failure) was strictly dependent on participants' expectations, while in the positive fantasy and the negative reality groups, expectations had no effects on goal commitment. Whether expectations were low or high, goal commitment was at a medium level. Apparently, mental contrasting makes people set themselves binding goals when expectations of success are high, and it makes people refrain from goal setting when expectations of success are low. Indulging in positive fantasies and ruminating about impeding reality, to the contrary, cause goal commitment to be weakly pulled by the positive future or pushed by the negative reality, respectively.

A further experiment (Oettingen, in press-a, Study 2) with childless female doctoral students dealt with the emergence of the goal to combine work and family life. Again, mental contrasting of positive fantasies about the future with negative aspects of impeding reality made expectations determine goal commitment (assessed as anticipated frustration in case of failure, intended effort expenditure, and planning goal implementation via process simulations; Taylor, Pham, Rivkin, & Armor, 1998). Goal commitment was mild and unaffected by expectations in participants who had indulged in positive fantasies or who had dwelled on the negative reality. In both experiments only contrasting participants behaved rationally in the sense that their expectations of success determined their level of commitment. Fantasizing and ruminating participants behaved irrationally. Their level of commitment was either too high (when expectations of success were low) or too low (when expectations of success were high). A series of further experiments (Oettingen, in press-b) using various fantasy themes related to personality development (e.g. academic achievement, conflict resolution, emotional and financial independence, occupational success) and different experimental paradigms to induce the three modes of self-regulatory thought (i.e. mental contrasting, indulging in positive fantasies about the future, dwelling on impeding reality) replicated this pattern of results. Taken together, the experimental findings suggest that whether people arrive at goal commitment in a rational (expectancy based) or irrational (expectancy *in*dependent) manner depends on how they mentally deal with a desired future.

Reflexive processes   So far we have discussed goal setting as a reflective process. People think about potential goals in different ways, and based on these reflections they either choose a goal or refrain from doing so. However, goals may become activated outside of awareness (Bargh, 1990). Bargh's automotive theory suggests that strong mental links develop between the cognitive representation of situations and the goals the individual chronically pursues within them. As a consequence of repeated and consistent pairing, these goals are activated automatically when the person enters the critical situation. The automatically activated goal then guides behavior within the situation without choice or intention. Reflective choice, originally crucial, is now by-passed.

Bargh, Gollwitzer, Lee Chai, and Barndollar (1999) tested the assumption of direct goal activation in several experiments by assessing whether directly activated goals lead to the same behavioral consequences as reflectively set goals. Indeed, nonconscious priming of an achievement goal caused participants to perform better on an intellectual task than a non-primed control group. Moreover, nonconsciously primed achievement goals led to increased persistence and a higher frequency of task resumption. By applying a dissociation paradigm it could be ruled out that these effects were based on the mere priming of the semantic concept of achievement.

The processes described by Bargh and colleagues are based on reflective goal setting at an earlier point in time. Automatization relates only to the activation of a set goal in a given situation. It seems possible, however, that goal-directed behavior can occur in the absence of previously or ad hoc set goals. As noted in the introduction, behaviorist research has shown that conscious goal setting or the nonconscious activation of the representation of a goal are not needed to produce behavior that carries features of goal-directedness. Such behavior can also be produced by applying principles of operant conditioning.

The idea that goal-directed behavior can be reflexively elicited is supported by recent work in the area of motor control that adheres to dynamic systems theorizing (Kelso, 1995). This work suggests that complex goal-directed behaviors can emerge without mental representations of goals. Moreover, robotics research (Brooks, 1991; Maes, 1994) finds that robots can be programmed to perform rather complex, goal-directed like behaviors without having to install goal concepts. Connectionist theorizing is also wary of the goal concept. Some connectionist theories completely abolish the goal concept, while others try to replace the reflective processes of goal choice by suggesting parallel constraint satisfaction models (Read, Vanman, & Miller, 1997).

Finally, Carver & Scheier (1999) point out that there might be two kinds of goal related automaticity. The first is described by Bargh (1990) in his automotive model and relates to automatization through repeated and consistent pairing of a goal with a situational context. The second relates to primitive built-in behavioral tendencies that are present also in nonhuman species. Carver and Scheier describe this type of automaticity as an intuitive, crudely differentiated "quick and dirty" way of responding to reality that provides a default response. One does not wait to form an intention, but acts immediately. This mode of responding reminds of what McClelland and his colleagues (McClelland, Koestner, & Weinberger, 1989) describe as behavior based on implicit motives. Implicit motives are believed to be biologically based, directly guiding behavior through natural incentives.

We have pointed to these reflexive origins of goal-directed behavior to make the reader aware that (as behaviorists have long asserted) behaviors carrying features of goal-directedness do not necessarily require subjective goal setting based on reflective thought or the activation of a mental representation of an existing goal. Although some theorists may question the existence and relevance of reflective goal setting or the mental representation of goals, a more challenging research question for the future is how the two (reflective and reflexive) systems interact.

Goal Striving

Determinants of goal striving

Goal contents vary in structural features. They may be challenging or modest, specific or vague, abstract or concrete, proximal or distal, framed with a negative or positive outcome focus, and so forth. As well, goals differ thematically. All of these differences affect the success of goal striving.

Locke & Latham (1990) demonstrated that challenging goals spelled out in specific terms are superior to modest specific goals, as well as to challenging but vague (i.e. "do your best") goals in facilitating goal attainment. This effect has a number of prerequisites: frequent performance feedback, a strong goal commitment, the goal should not be too complex, and limitations in talent or situational constraints should not make goal attainment impossible. What does not seem to matter is whether goal setting is determined from outside (assigned goals), freely chosen by individuals (self-set goals), or chosen in interaction with others (participative goals). As potential mediators of the goal specificity effect Locke & Latham (1990) point to heightened persistence, focusing attention on the execution of goal-directed behaviors, a greater readiness to plan the goal pursuit, and to feedback and self-monitoring advantages.

Further structural differences between goals include time frame, outcome focus, and learning versus performance orientation. Bandura & Schunk (1981) divide the time frame of goal attainment into proximal and distal goals. Proximal goals relate to what the individual does in the present or near future, while distal goals point far into the future. Children who were weak and uninterested in mathematics pursued a program of self-directed learning (a total of 42 pages of instruction) under conditions involving either a distal goal only (42 pages in 7 sessions), or the distal goal plus proximal subgoals (6 pages per session for 7 sessions). Additional proximal goals improved the children's arithmetic scores by providing more performance feedback, thus making it easier to monitor progress in goal pursuit. However, this feedback advantage may turn into a detriment when inhibitional goals (e.g. dieting goals) are concerned, as people more readily discover failures which may cause them to give up prematurely. Indeed, Cochran & Tesser (1996) observed that the goal proximity effect is reversed for goals framed in terms of preventing failures.

Higgins (1997) reports that goals framed with a positive outcome focus lead to task performance that is strongest when both expectations of success and the incentive value of success are high; when people hold goals with a negative outcome focus this effect is less pronounced. In other words, when highly desirable and feasible wishes are transferred into goals it seems wise to frame these goals with a positive outcome focus. Goals with a positive outcome focus construe achievement as accomplishment, whereas goals with a negative outcome focus construe achievement as providing security.

Finally, learning goals and performance goals have different effects on performance (Dweck, 1996). Learning goals lead to better achievements than performance goals because the former allow for a more effective coping with failure than the latter. For people with performance goals, failure signals a lack of ability and thus cause reactions of giving up. People with learning goals, on the other hand, view set-backs as cues to focus on new strategies. Accordingly, their behavior is oriented toward mastering the causes of the set-back, ultimately furthering goal attainment. Elliot & Church (1997) have recently found that performance goals are less detrimental when they are framed as approach goals (e.g. I want to get good grades) rather than avoidance goals (e.g. I do not want to get bad grades).

With respect to the thematic contents of goals, Ryan, Sheldon, Kasser, & Deci (1996) suggest that goals of autonomy, competence, and social integration lead to greater creativity, higher cognitive flexibility, greater depth of information processing, and more effective coping with failure. These effects are mediated by an intrinsic self-regulation, as the needs of autonomy, competence, and social integration are assumed to further intrinsic goal striving. This positive kind of goal striving is contrasted with being unreflectively controlled from outside (e.g. goal assignments from authorities) or from inside (e.g. goal setting based on feelings of obligation). Ryan, et al. (1996) also discuss side effects of goal-directed actions. Goals based on autonomy, competence, and social integration needs are associated with higher well-being and life satisfaction. Kasser & Ryan (1993) observed that people with goals such as making money, becoming famous, and acquiring high status, experience a worse subjective well-being as compared to those with goals such as cultivating friendship or becoming active in communal services. This is particularly true for individuals who feel highly efficacious, implying that people who successfully implement materialistic goals are particularly at risk for low well-being.

Well-being has been analyzed in other goal content approaches as well. Emmons (1996) reports that a strong predictor of a person's well-being is the proportion of intimacy goals to the total number of goals. The proportion of achievement and power goals, however, tends to be negatively related to well-being. Moreover, highly abstract goals (e.g. getting to know people) tends to be associated with psychological distress (particularly anxiety and depression), whereas low level strivings (e.g. speak friendly to strangers) are linked to greater levels of psychological well-being, but also to more physical illness. Finally, having a high proportion of avoidance strivings (e.g. avoid being lonely, avoid being upset) is associated with suppressed positive mood, reduced life satisfaction, heightened anxiety, and weaker physical health.

Recently, Brunstein, Schultheiss, & Maier (in press) pointed out that structural features also matter in predicting well-being on the basis of goal pursuit. For instance, high commitment to a personal goal furthers life satisfaction only when the person perceives the personal goal as feasible; when feasibility is low, goal commitment reduces life satisfaction. Moreover, the positive effects of intimacy goals strongly depend on social support from significant others. The effects of goals on emotional well-being are also influenced by how well people's goals match their needs or implicit motives (McClelland, 1985). People with strong achievement and power needs, and goals of the same theme – as well as people with strong affiliation and intimacy needs, and goals of the same theme – report higher emotional well-being than those whose needs and goals do not match.

Processes of goal striving

Experience tells us that it is often a long way from goal setting to goal attainment. Having set a goal is just a first step, usually followed by a host of implementational problems that must be successfully solved. In the section above, predictions about successful goal attainment were made on the basis of structural and thematic properties of the set goals. A process-related approach focuses on how the problems of goal pursuit are solved by the individual. To effectively solve these problems, which pertain to initiating goal-directed actions and bringing them to a successful ending, the person needs to seize opportunities to act, ward off distractions, flexibly step up efforts in the face of difficulties, by-pass barriers, compensate for failures and shortcomings, and negotiate conflicts between goals. Various theories address how the individual effectively solves these problems of goal implementation.

Implemental mindset   The model of action phases (Heckhausen & Gollwitzer, 1987; Gollwitzer, 1990; Heckhausen, 1991) sees successful goal pursuit as solving a series of successive tasks: deliberating wishes (potential goals) and choosing between them, planning goal-directed actions and getting started, bringing goal pursuit to a successful end, and evaluating its outcome. The task notion implies that people can promote goal pursuit by developing the respective mindsets which facilitate task completion (Gollwitzer, 1990). Studies conducted on the mindsets associated with either deliberating between wishes (i.e. deliberative mindset) or with planning goal-directed actions (i.e. implemental mindset) support this idea.

When participants are asked to plan the implementation of a set goal, an implemental mindset with the following attributes originates (Gollwitzer & Bayer, 1999): participants become closed-minded in that they are no longer distracted by irrelevant information, while processing information related to goal implementation very effectively (e.g. information on the sequencing of actions). Moreover, desirability-related information is processed in a partial manner favoring pros over cons, and feasibility-related information is analyzed in a manner that favors illusory optimism. This optimism extends to an illusion of control over uncontrollable outcomes, and even holds for depressed individuals. Self-perception of important personal attributes (e.g. cheerfulness, smartness, social sensitivity) is strengthened, while perceived vulnerability to both controllable and uncontrollable risks is lowered (e.g. developing an addiction to prescription drugs or losing a partner to an early death, respectively). The implemental mindset favors goal attainment by helping the individual to effectively cope with classic problems of goal striving, such as becoming distracted, doubting the attractiveness of the pursued goal, or being pessimistic about its feasibility.

Planning   Set goals commit an individual to attaining the specified desired future, but they do not commit the individual to when, where, and how she intends to act. Such additional commitments can be added by planning goal pursuit via implementation intentions with the format of "if I encounter situation x, then I will perform the goal-directed behavior y!" Gollwitzer (1993) argued that implementation intentions are a powerful self-regulatory strategy for overcoming problems of getting started with goal-directed actions (e.g. when people are tired, absorbed with some other activity, or lost in thoughts, and thus miss good opportunities to act). In support of this hypothesis, it was observed in numerous studies (for a summary, see Gollwitzer, 1999) that difficult to reach goals benefit greatly from being furnished with implementation intentions. This effect extends to projects such as resolving important interpersonal conflicts, performing a medical self-examination, regular intake of a vitamin supplement, eating healthy foods, and doing vigorous exercise. It also holds true for people who have problems turning goals into action, such as opiate addicts under withdrawal or schizophrenic patients.

Because implementation intentions spell out links between situational cues and goal-directed behavior, it is assumed (Gollwitzer, 1993) that by forming such intentions people delegate the control of behavior to the environment, thus facilitating the initiation of goal-directed actions. The mental representations of the specified situational cues become highly activated, making these cues more accessible. Various experiments (for a summary, see Gollwitzer, 1999) demonstrate that situational cues specified in implementation intentions are more easily detected and remembered, as well as more readily attended to than comparable non-intended situations. Moreover, implementation intentions create strong associative links between mental representations of situations and actions which otherwise are achieved only through consistent and repeated pairing. As a consequence, action initiation becomes automatized. Various experiments demonstrate that the goal-directed behavior specified in implementation intentions is initiated swiftly and effortlessly in the presence of the critical situation. Moreover, the subliminal presentation of the critical situation suffices to activate cognitive concepts and knowledge relevant to the efficient initiation of the intended behavior. Finally, patients with a frontal lobe injury, who have severe deficits in the conscious and effortful control of behavior, while remaining unaffected in performing automatized behaviors, benefit greatly from forming implementation intentions.

Implementation intentions ameliorate not only problems of the initiation of goal-directed behavior, but also other problems of goal striving (Gollwitzer & Schaal, 1998). In a series of studies, implementation intentions created resistance to tempting distractions while solving tedious arithmetic problems. Moreover, set goals to escape unwanted habitual responses (i.e. stereotypical beliefs and prejudicial feelings) are more successfully attained when furnished with implementation intentions. Finally, implementation intentions can protect people from the unwanted influences of goals directly activated by situational cues (Bargh, 1990). People need only prepare themselves by setting antagonistic behavioral goals and furnish them with implementation intentions (Gollwitzer, 1999).

In summary, implementation intentions create a type of behavioral automaticity that does not originate from laborious and effortful practice. Rather, people strategically delegate their control over goal-directed behavior to anticipated, critical situational cues. This easily accessible self-regulatory strategy of forming implementation intentions can be used to increase tenacity in initiating goal-directed action. At the same time it helps to increase flexibility in escaping unwanted habits of thinking, feeling, and behaving.

There are other effective types of planning besides forming implementation intentions. Planning can be approached in a more reflective way as in mental simulations exploring possible ways to achieving a goal. Taylor, Pham, Rivkin, & Armor, (1998) call such mental simulations process simulations. If applied repeatedly, they further goal attainment, such as achieving good grades in academic exams. Apparently, repeated mental simulations of how to achieve a goal also result in firm plans.

Action versus state orientation   Competing goal pursuits are paid particular attention in Kuhl's action control theory (for a summary, see Kuhl & Beckmann, 1994). For an ordered action sequence to occur, a current guiding goal must be shielded from competing goal intentions (e.g. the goal of making a phone call from the competing intention to tidy one's desk). Kuhl calls this shielding mechanism action control and differentiates a number of control strategies, such as attention control, emotion control, and environment control. Through environment control, for example, the individual prevents the derailing of an ongoing goal pursuit by removing competing temptations from the situation.

Whether and how effectively these strategies are used depends on the current control mode of the individual. An action-oriented person concentrates on planning and initiating of goal-directed action, responds flexibly to situational demands, and uses control strategies effectively. A state-oriented person, in contrast, cannot disengage from incomplete goals and is caught up in uncontrollable perseveration of thoughts related to aversive experiences or in dysfunctional thoughts about future successes. Action and state orientation may be induced by situational variables (e.g. a surprising event, persistent failure), but is founded in personal disposition.

Recent experimental research on state orientation has discovered a further volitional handicap. State-oriented individuals readily misperceive assigned goals as self-generated. These findings have stimulated a new theoretical perspective (Kuhl, in press) which sees the volitional control of action as a result of the cooperation of various mental subsystems (i.e. intention memory, extension memory, intuitive behavior control, and object recognition). Action versus state orientation is understood as a parameter that modulates the cooperation between these systems thus leading to different kinds of volitional control of action with different outcomes.

Resumption of disrupted goal pursuit   Higher order goals (e.g. to become popular) offer multiple routes to approach them. If one pathway is blocked, an individual can approach the goal another way. Self-completion theory (Wicklund & Gollwitzer, 1982) addresses this issue of compensation by analyzing self-defining goals. Such goals specify as the desired end state an identity, such as scientist, mother, or a political liberal. As many different things indicate the possession of such identities, the striving for an identity is a process of collecting these indicators (or self-defining symbols). These indicators extend from relevant material symbols (e.g. for a scientist, books and awards) to relevant self-descriptions (e.g. using titles) and performances (e.g. accomplishing important research). Whenever shortcomings in one type of symbol are encountered, an individual will experience self-definitional incompleteness, which leads to compensatory self-symbolizing efforts. These may take the form of pointing to the possession of alternative symbols or acquiring new symbols.

This compensation principle has been supported with various self-defining goals and different types of symbols (for a summary, see Gollwitzer & Kirchhof, 1998). Easily accessible symbols (e.g. self-descriptions) are powerful substitutes for symbols that are harder to come by (e.g. relevant performances). Newcomers to a field of interest (e.g. science) can thus symbolize the related identity without full command of the relevant performances. Further, elderly people do not have to leave the field when age related deficits hamper performance. Research on self-completion has discovered that effective self-symbolizing requires a social reality. Compensatory efforts are particularly effective when other people notice them. This, however, has costs. Compensating individuals see others only in terms of their capability to notice compensatory efforts and thus lack social sensitivity. Also, when people make public their intention to acquire a certain self-definitional indicator (e.g. studying hard), actual effort will be reduced, as the proclamation alone produces self-definitional completeness (Gollwitzer, Bayer, Scherer, & Seifert, in press).

Finally, self-completion theory may sound similar to Steele's (1988) self-affirmation theory, but self-completion is a goal theory, not a self-esteem theory (for a different view, see Tesser, Martin, & Cornell, 1996). According to Steele, anything that makes you feel good will reaffirm a weakened self-esteem. Self-completion theory, however, postulates that self-definitional incompleteness can only be substituted for by acquiring an alternative but related symbol. Recent research demonstrates that merely reaffirming self-esteem cannot produce self-definitional completeness (Gollwitzer, et al., in press).

Mobilization of effort   People may promote goal achievement by compensating for failures but they also try to avoid committing errors in the first place. Warding off failure becomes a pressing issue whenever difficulties mount. Brehm & Wright's (Brehm & Self, 1989; Wright, 1996) energization theory of motivation assumes that the readiness to exert effort is directly determined by the perceived difficulty of a task. As perceived difficulty increases, so does effort expenditure, unless the task is recognized to be unsolvable. There is, however, a second limit to the increase of effort in response to heightened task difficulty: potential motivation. Potential motivation is fed by need related variables (i.e. strength of the related need or higher order goal, the incentive value of the task, and the instrumentality of task completion for satisfaction or attainment). If potential motivation is low, people do not find it worthwhile to expend more effort when an easy task becomes more difficult. The upper limit of effort expenditure is low and quickly reached. If potential motivation is high, however, an increase in difficulty is matched by investment of effort up to high levels of difficulty. The upper limit of effort expenditure is high and is reached only after much effort expenditure has occurred.

Empirical tests of the theory have varied potential motivation either by offering high or low rewards for task completion or making a high reward more or less likely. Effort mobilization is usually assessed by cardiovascular responses (i.e. heart rate and systolic blood pressure). In general, low potential motivation curbs the linear relationship between task difficulty and effort. Recent research uses energization theory to understand the differences between men and women in effort on sex-typed tasks, and to explore the effects of private versus public performance conditions on effort (Wright, Tunstall, Williams, Goodwin, & Harmon-Jones, 1995; Wright, Murray, Storey, & Williams, 1997).

Discrepancy reduction   The goal striving theories discussed so far implicitly or explicitly view goals as something attractive that the individual wants to attain. Goals are not simply "cold" mental representations that specify standards or reference points, but are cognitively explicated and elaborated incentives. Such motivational goal theories are rivaled by a more cognitive view that sees goals as specifying performance standards. According to Bandura (1997), goals have no motivational consequences per se. They only specify the conditions that allow a positive or negative self-evaluation. If the set goal is attained, positive self-evaluation prevails, whereas staying below one's goal leads to negative self-evaluation. The individual is pushed by the negative self-evaluation associated with the discrepancy, and pulled by the anticipated positive self-evaluation linked to closing the gap between the status quo and the goal. Accordingly, goals stimulate effortful action only when people notice a discrepancy between the status quo and the set goal. Bandura proposes frequent feedback as a powerful measure to stimulate goal pursuit. However, people will try to reduce a discrepancy only when they feel self-efficacious with respect to goal-directed actions.

Carver & Scheier (1998) propose a different discrepancy reduction theory of goal pursuit. Based on cybernetic control theory, the central concept of their analysis is the negative feedback loop. Carver and Scheier highlight goal pursuits' hierarchical structure and assume a cascading loop structure. Goal-directed behavior is regulated at the middle level ("Do-goals") with actions at higher levels ("Be-goals") suspended until the individual becomes self-aware. Discovery of discrepancies on the "Be-level" or the "Do-level" triggers lower level goals or behaviors aimed at discrepancy reduction, respectively. An individual tries to close discrepancies only when outcome expectations are high. However, a positive affective response as a consequence of goal attainment is not assumed, nor is the detection of a discrepancy associated with negative affect. Rather, the source of positive or negative feelings in goal pursuit is the speed of discrepancy reduction. The intensity of these feelings is regulated again in a negative feedback loop. If the speed meets a set criterion, positive feelings result, whereas negative feelings are experienced with speeds that stay below this criterion.

The discrepancy notions discussed above construe goals as "cold" mental representations of performance standards with no links to needs or incentives. This conceptualization of goals makes it difficult to explain why motivation (see Brehm and Wright's notion of potential motivation) moderates the relation between task difficulty and effort. Moreover, according to discrepancy theory an increase in task difficulty should reduce efforts at task completion, because an experienced increase in task difficulty should lead to reduced self-efficacy and less positive outcome expectations. As Brehm and Wright have repeatedly demonstrated, however, high potential motivation makes it worthwhile for people to mobilize additional effort whenever heightened task difficulty threatens task completion. Finally, Carver and Scheier's construal of the regulation of the speed of discrepancy reduction assumes that positive discrepancies (i.e. moving towards the goal too fast) are reduced as readily as negative discrepancies (i.e. moving towards the goal too slowly). However, from the perspective that goals represent a desired outcome, a person should be less motivated to reduce positive discrepancies than negative discrepancies (Gollwitzer & Rohloff, 1999).

Prospects of Future Research on Goals

Although research on the determinants and processes of goal setting and goal striving has won momentum in recent years, there are goal related phenomena that have not yet received much theoretical and empirical attention. One is the issue of goal conflict. For instance, future research will have to discover how conflicting goals emerge. Answers may come from an analysis of when and how fantasies about a desired future originate. Such visions should be a product of a person's cultural context and the needs, values, attitudes, and interests the person has developed within it. Moreover, whether a person is willing to transfer these fantasies into binding goals should depend on whether the person is ready to contrast her fantasies with reality; again, this mode of self-regulatory thought about the future may have cultural underpinnings (Oettingen, 1997).

Once set goals are in conflict, these conflicts have to be resolved. Emmons (1996) points to the possibility of creative integrations, where new goals are formed which serve both of the conflicting goals (e.g. agentic and communal strivings are reconciled by taking on communal responsibilities). Moreover, Cantor & Fleeson (1994) argue that to meet higher order life tasks (e.g. graduating from college) people can strategically link behavioral goals that apparently conflict (e.g. the conflict between studying and being with other people is reconciled by studying in a group). But more often than not, conflicts can only be resolved by giving up one goal. This raises the question of when and how people most effectively disengage from goals. Although Klinger (1977) has offered a stage theory of disengagement from incentives, systematic research on disengagement from set goals is still missing. Simply ruminating about the impediments of attaining the goal should not suffice (Martin & Tesser, 1996; Oettingen, 1996). Rather, people's low expectations of success need to be activated and used to foster active disengagement, and this becomes more likely when the desired future is mentally contrasted with negative aspects of impeding reality.

References

Ach, N. (1935). Analyse des Willens. In E. Abderhalden (Ed.), *Handbuch der biologischen Arbeitsmethoden* Vol. 6. Berlin: Urban & Schwarzenberg.

Ajzen, I. (1985). From intentions to actions: A theory of planned behavior. In J. Kuhl & J. Beckmann (Eds.), *Action control: From cognition to behavior* (pp. 11–39). Heidelberg: Springer-Verlag.

Ames, C., & Archer, J. (1988). Achievement goals in the classroom: Students' learning strategies and motivation processes. *Journal of Educational Psychology, 80*, 260–267.

Atkinson, J. W. (1957). Motivational determinants of risk-taking behavior. *Psychological Review, 64*, 359–372.

Bandura, A. (1997). *Self-efficacy: The exercise of control.* New York: Freeman.

Bandura, A., & Schunk, D. H. (1981). Cultivating competence, self-efficacy and intrinsic interest through proximal self-motivation. *Journal of Personality and Social Psychology, 41*, 586–598.

Bargh, J. A. (1990). Auto-motives: Pre-conscious determinants of social interaction. In E. T. Higgins, & R. M. Sorrentino (Eds.), *Handbook of motivation and cognition* Vol. 2 (pp. 93–130). New York: Guilford Press.

Bargh, J. A., Gollwitzer, P. M., Lee Chai, A., & Barndollar, K. (1999). Bypassing the will: Nonconscious self-regulation through automatic goal pursuit. Manuscript submitted for publication.

Brehm, J. W., & Self, E. A. (1989). The intensity of motivation. *Annual Review of Psychology, 45*, 560–570.

Brooks, R. A. (1991). New approaches to robotics. *Science, 253*, 1227–1232.

Brunstein, J. C., Schultheiss, O. C., & Maier, G. W. (in press). The pursuit of personal goals: A motivational approach to well-being and life adjustment. In J. Brandtstädter, & R. M. Lerner (Eds.), *Action and self-development: Theory and research through the life span*. Thousand Oaks, CA: Sage.

Cantor, N., & Fleeson, W. (1994). Social intelligence and intelligent goal pursuit: A cognitive slice of motivation. In W. Spaulding (Ed.), *Nebraska symposium on motivation* Vol. 41 (pp. 125–180). Lincoln: University of Nebraska Press.

Carver, C. S., & Scheier, M. F. (1998). *On the self-regulation of behavior*. New York: Cambridge University Press.

Carver, C. S., & Scheier, M. F. (1999). Themes and issues in the self-regulation of behavior. In R. S. Wyer (Ed.), *Advances in social cognition*. Mahwah, NJ: Erlbaum .

Chaiken, S. (1987). The heuristic model of persuasion. In M. P. Zanna, J. M. Olson, & C. P. Herman (Eds.), *Social influence: The Ontario symposium* Vol. 5 (pp. 3–39). Hillsdale, NJ: Erlbaum.

Cochran, W., & Tesser, A. (1996). The "what the hell" effect: Some effects of goal proximity and goal framing on performance. In L. L. Martin, & A. Tesser (Eds.), *Striving and feeling* (pp. 99–120). Mahwah, NJ: Erlbaum.

Dweck, C. S. (1996). Implicit theories as organizers of goals and behavior. In P. M. Gollwitzer, & J. A. Bargh (Eds.), *The psychology of action: Linking cognition and motivation to behavior* (pp. 69–90). New York: Guilford Press.

Emmons, R. A. (1996). Striving and feeling: Personal goals and subjective well-being. In P. M. Gollwitzer, & J. A. Bargh (Eds.), *The psychology of action: Linking cognition and motivation to behavior* (pp. 313–337). New York: Guilford Press.

Festinger, L. (1942). A theoretical interpretation of shifts in level of aspiration. *Psychological Review, 49*, 235–250.

Geen, R. G. (1995). *Human motivation*. Pacific Grove, CA: Brooks/Cole Publishing.

Gollwitzer, P. M. (1987). The implementation of identity intentions. In F. Halisch, & J. Kuhl (Eds.), *Motivation, intention, and action*. Berlin: Springer.

Gollwitzer, P. M. (1990). Action phases and mind-sets. In E. T. Higgins, & R. M. Sorrentino (Eds.), *Handbook of motivation and cognition* Vol. 2 (pp. 53–92). New York: Guilford Press.

Gollwitzer, P. M. (1993). Goal achievement: The role of intentions. In W. Stroebe, & M. Hewstone (Eds.), *European review of social psychology* Vol. 4 (pp. 141–185). Chichester, UK: John Wiley.

Gollwitzer, P. M. (1999). Implementation intentions: The strategic preparation of automatic goal pursuit. *American Psychologist 54*, 493–503.

Gollwitzer, P. M., & Bayer, U. (1999). Deliberative versus implemental mindsets in the control of action. In S. Chaiken, & Y. Trope (Eds.), *Dual process theories in social psychology* (pp. 403–422). New York: Guilford Press.

Gollwitzer, P. M., & Kirchhof, O. (1998). The willful pursuit of identity. In J. Heckhausen, & C. S. Dweck (Eds.), *Motivation and self-regulation across the life-span* (pp. 389–423). New York: Cambridge University Press.

Gollwitzer, P. M., & Rohloff, U. (1999). The speed of goal pursuit. In R. S. Wyer (Ed.), *Advances in social cognition* Vol. 12 (pp. 147–159). Hillsdale, NJ: Erlbaum.

Gollwitzer, P. M., & Schaal, B. (1998). Metacognition in action: The importance of implementation intentions. *Personality and Social Psychology Review, 2*, 124–136.

Gollwitzer, P. M., Heckhausen, H., & Ratajczak, H. (1990). From weighing to willing: Approaching a change decision through pre- or postdecisional mentation. *Organizational Behavior and Human Decision Processes, 45*, 41–65.

Gollwitzer, P. M., Bayer, U., Scherer, M., & Seifert, A. E. (in press). A motivational–volitional perspective on identity development. In J. Brandtstädter, & R. M. Lerner (Eds.), *Action and self-development*. Thousand Oaks, CA: Sage.

Heckhausen, H. (1977). Achievement motivation and its constructs: A cognitive model. *Motivation and Emotion, 1*, 283–329.

Heckhausen, H. (1991). *Motivation and action.* Heidelberg: Springer-Verlag.

Heckhausen, H., & Gollwitzer, P. M. (1987). Thought contents and cognitive functioning in motivational versus volitional states of mind. *Motivation and Emotion, 11*, 101–120.

Heckhausen, H., & Kuhl, J. (1985). From wishes to action: The dead ends and short cuts on the long way to action. In M. Frese, & J. Sabini (Eds.), *Goal-directed behavior: The concept of action in psychology* (pp. 134–159). Hillsdale, NJ: Erlbaum.

Higgins, E. T. (1997). Beyond pleasure and pain. *American Psychologist, 52*, 1280–1300.

James, W. (1890/1950). *Principles of psychology.* 2 vols. New York: Dover.

Karoly, P. (1993). Mechanisms of self-regulation: A systems view. *Annual Review of Psychology, 44*, 23–52.

Kasser, T., & Ryan, R. M. (1993). A dark side of the American dream: Correlates of financial success as a central life aspiration. *Journal of Personality and Social Psychology, 65*, 410–422.

Kelso, J. A. S. (1995). *Dynamic patterns: The self-organization of brain and behavior.* Cambridge, MA: MIT Press.

Klinger, E. (1977). *Meaning and void.* Minneapolis: University of Minnesota Press.

Kuhl, J. (in press). A functional-design approach to motivation and self-regulation: The dynamics of personality systems interactions. In M. Boekaerts, P. R. Pintrich, & M. Zeidner (Eds.), *Self-regulation: Directions and challenges for future research.* New York: Academic Press.

Kuhl, J., & Beckmann, J. (1994). *Volition and personality.* Göttingen: Hogrefe.

Lewin, K. (1926). Vorsatz, Wille und Bedürfnis. *Psychologische Forschung, 7*, 330–385.

Little, B. R. (1983). Personal projects: A rationale and methods for investigation. *Environment and Behavior, 15*, 273–309.

Locke, E. A., & Latham, G. P. (1990). *A theory of goal setting and task performance.* Englewood Cliffs, NJ: Prentice-Hall.

McClelland, D. C. (1985). *Human motivation.* Glenview, Ill.: Scott, Foresman.

McClelland, D. C., Koestner, R., & Weinberger, J. (1989). How do self-attributed and implicit motives differ? *Psychological Review, 96*, 690–702.

McDougall, W. (1908/1931). *Social psychology.* London: Methuen.

McGuire, W. J. (1969). The nature of attitudes and attitude change. In G. Lindzey, & E. Aronson (Eds.), *Handbook of social psychology* Vol. 3, 2nd. edn. (pp. 136–314). Reading, MA: Addison-Wesley.

Maes, P. (1994). Modeling adaptive autonomous agents. *Artificial Life, 1*, 135–162.

Markus, H., & Nurius, P. (1986). Possible selves. *American Psychologist, 41*, 954–969.

Martin, L. L., & Tesser, A. (1996). Some ruminative thoughts. In R. S. Wyer (Ed.), *Advances in social cognition* Vol. 9 (pp. 1–47). Mahwah, NJ: Erlbaum.

Mischel, W., & Liebert, R. M. (1966). Effects of discrepancies between observed and imposed reward criteria on their acquisition and transmission. *Journal of Personality and Social Psychology, 3*, 45–53.

Nicholls, J. G. (1979). Quality and equality in intellectual development: The role of motivation in education. *American Psychologist, 34*, 1071–1084.

Oettingen, G. (1996). Positive fantasy and motivation. In P. M. Gollwitzer, & J. A. Bargh (Eds.), *The psychology of action: Linking cognition and motivation to behavior* (pp. 236–259). New York: Guilford Press.

Oettingen, G. (1997). Culture and future thought. *Culture and Psychology, 3*, 353–381.

Oettingen, G. (in press-a). Expectancy effects on behavior depend on self-regulatory thoughts. *Social Cognition.*

Oettingen, G. (in press-b). Free fantasies about the future and the emergence of developmental goals. In J. Brandtstädter, & R. M. Lerner (Eds.), *Action and self-development: Theory and research through the life span.* Thousand Oaks, CA: Sage.

Petty, R. E., & Cacioppo, J. T. (1986). *Communication and persuasion: Central and peripheral routes to attitude change.* New York: Springer-Verlag.

Read, S. J., Vanman, E. J., & Miller, L. C. (1997). Connectionism, parallel constraint satisfaction processes, and Gestalt principles: (Re)introducing cognitive dynamics to social psychology. *Review of Personality and Social Psychology, 1*, 26–53.

Ryan, R. M., Sheldon, K. M., Kasser, T., & Deci, E. L. (1996). All goals are not created equal: an organismic perspective on the nature of goals and their regulation. In P. M. Gollwitzer, & J. A. Bargh (Eds.), *The psychology of action: Linking cognition and motivation to behavior* (pp. 7–26). New York: Guilford Press.

Scheier, M. F., & Carver, C. S. (1985). Optimism, coping, and health: Assessment and implications of generalized outcome expectancies. *Health Psychology, 4,* 219–247.

Skinner, B. F. (1953). *Science and human behavior.* New York: Macmillan.

Steele, C. M. (1988). The psychology of self-affirmation: Sustaining the integrity of the self. In L. Berkowitz (Ed.), *Advances in experimental social psychology* Vol. 21 (pp. 261–302). New York: Academic Press.

Taylor, S. E., Pham, L. B., Rivkin, I. D., & Armor, D. A. (1998). Harnessing the imagination. *American Psychologist, 53,* 429–439.

Tesser, A., Martin, L. L., & Cornell, D. P. (1996). On the substitutability of self-protective mechanisms. In P. M. Gollwitzer, & J. A. Bargh (Eds.), *The psychology of action: Linking cognition and motivation to behavior* (pp. 48–67). New York: Guilford Press.

Tolman, E. C. (1925). Purpose and cognition: The determinants of animal learning. *Psychological Review, 32,* 285–297.

Vallacher, R. R., & Wegner, D. M. (1987). What do people think they're doing? Action identification and human behavior. *Psychological Review, 94,* 3–15.

Vallacher, R. R., & Wegner, D. M. (1989). Levels of personal agency: Individual variation in action identification. *Journal of Personality and Social Psychology, 57,* 660–671.

Wicklund, R. A., & Gollwitzer, P. M. (1982). *Symbolic self-completion.* Hillsdale, NJ: Erlbaum.

Wilpert, B. (1994). Participation research in organizational psychology. In G. d'Ydewalle, P. Eelen, & P. Bertelson (Eds.), *International perspectives on psychological science* Vol. 2 (pp. 293–310). Hove, UK: Erlbaum.

Wright, R. A. (1996). Brehm's theory of motivation as a model of effort and cardiovascular response. In P. M. Gollwitzer, & J. A. Bargh (Eds.), *The psychology of action: Linking cognition and motivation to behavior* (pp. 424–453). New York: Guilford Press.

Wright, R. A., Murray, J. B., Storey, P. L., & Williams, B. J. (1997). Ability analysis of gender relevance and sex differences in cardiovascular response to behavioral challenge. *Journal of Personality and Social Psychology, 73,* 405–417.

Wright, R. A., Tunstall, A. M., Williams, B. J., Goodwin, J. S., & Harmon-Jones, E. (1995). Social evaluation and cardiovascular response: An active coping approach. *Journal of Personality and Social Psychology, 69,* 530–543.

Chapter Sixteen

On the Motives Underlying Social Cognition

David Dunning

One of the most popular metaphors in social psychology over the past thirty years has been that of person as computer. Like a computer, people input information about others, process it, and then produce some judgmental output that can take the form of an evaluation, attribution, or prediction. The metaphor has proven to be a useful one, given the voluminous research it has generated about the sophisticated (albeit imperfect) "software" people use to reach judgments about themselves and their social worlds.

However, thirty years of research on social cognition has surprisingly ignored, although not completely, one important task that the mindful computer must complete: it must monitor when a judgment is called for, if at all, among all the myriad of opportunities it has for social judgment every day. This fact has been finessed for decades in social psychology, in that it has been the experimenter who acts as the instigator of social judgment, providing participants with a target to judge and a questionnaire that specifies what issues participants must address.

But who, or rather what, acts as an instigator of social judgment in everyday life? People clearly cannot mull over and analyze all the actions of all the people they meet on all personality dimensions ever identified. To do so would render the mindful computer as one sitting in an easy chair, lost in contemplation over a social world it is too preoccupied to join. The social computer requires a mechanism that tells it to run its arsenal of applications and software selectively, ignoring many circumstances that could potentially call for judgmental efforts. But that is not all. The social computer requires a mechanism that tells it when enough is enough, that sufficient information has been gathered or that enough processing has ensued. Finally, the social computer needs a mechanism that monitors the conclusions that it reaches, to make sure that these conclusions do not violate principles that it wishes to honor.

Preparation of this chapter was financially supported by National Institute of Mental Health Grant RO1-56072.

Some researchers, especially those on the more cognitive side, will wince at the way I am introducing these issues. To them, I suggest that the social computer requires a homunculus that peers into the social world, hitting the "execute" button when it is time to analyze the behavior of self and others, monitoring the social computer's programs as they proceed through their subroutines. It is often considered bad form, and appropriately so, to refer to cognitive mechanisms as a homunculus. The term conjures images of an unpredictable and incomprehensible apparatus, one even imbued with free will, that is invoked by psychological researchers when they cannot account for the phenomena they observe.

However, I submit that the discomfort of these researchers is misplaced, for two specific reasons. First, it is inescapable that the social computer requires the mechanism that handles the tasks of instigator, terminator, and monitor of social judgment. Indeed, such functions are often referred to in cognitive psychology as *executive functions*, and although they are often difficult to account for, an adequate portrayal of social cognitive processes requires some understanding of the executive mechanisms governing social thought.

Second, and most important, several decades of research in social psychology reveal that this executive or homunculus hardly operates as an unpredictable free agent. Several principles shape when the creature will start the social judgment process and control the conclusions it reaches. In particular, in this chapter I highlight the goals or motives that preoccupy the executive as it monitors the social judgmental process. If one scans the last fifty years of social psychological research, one finds three general goals that the executive "has in mind" as it carries out its duties. First, and most obvious, the executive has a *desire for knowledge* about its environment. It must reach conclusions about itself and other people in order to navigate its social world without too much pain and folly and hopefully with much success and reward. Second, the executive possesses a *desire for affirmation* of the competence of its owner, in that it acts to bolster favorable images of self. Finally, the executive possesses a *desire for coherence*, being interested in making sure that all new information is consistent with the beliefs it already has.

In this chapter, I discuss each desire and describe what social psychological research has to say about the executive's pursuit of it. I explain how each need shapes and molds social judgment. I also talk about controversies that research on these motives has prompted. I end the chapter with observations about current research on motivation.

Desire for Knowledge

The executive is curious. By that, I mean it possesses a strong motive to acquire information about its world. Indeed, many scholars have noted that curiosity is a motive that is surprisingly strong among humans. People like to know the answers to questions even when it provides no direct benefit to them, a situation that befuddles traditional economic analysis (Loewenstein, 1994). All of us have had the experience of sitting in front of the television watching some infotainment program, vowing to turn the set off at the next commercial break, only to have a television announcer tease us with a trivia question (such as, "Which city in the United States has the highest percentage of citizens holding college degrees?") that makes us stay with the program against our best wishes.

More formal documentation of the power of curiosity comes from work on behavioral economics, which shows that people will forego money in order to see a photograph of an individual after being shown pictures of that individual's body parts, even though seeing the entire person carries no personal consequences for them (Loewenstein, 1994). That the power of curiosity is counterintuitively strong comes from work showing that people mispredict how much of an appetite they have for trivia. When given a hypothetical choice between knowing the answer to trivia questions versus some candy bars to take home with them, people intuit that they would rather have the candy bars. However, when given an actual choice, people opt for feeding their curiosity and finding out the answers (Loewenstein, Prelec, & Shatto, 1997). (Do not worry, if you keep reading, you will find the answer to the college degree question.)

Conditions promoting curiosity

As such, one straightforward and prevalent motive that preoccupies the social cognitive executive is the simple need to know. However, that curiosity must be selective or the individual would be overwhelmed with puzzles to solve and answers to find. Clearly, people are more curious about some matters (e.g. what's my next door neighbor's annual income?) than they are about others (e.g. is income inequality rising in my country?), so what distinguishes the former situation from the latter?

Prior information   Surprisingly, people are more curious about issues to the extent that they are familiar and well-informed about them. Children are more interested in finding out the answers to questions posed about familiar animals than they are about unfamiliar ones (Berlyne, 1954). College students are more curious about answers for questions they are confident they know the answer already than they are questions they do not have a clue about (Crandall, 1971). The greater people rate their knowledge in a particular domain, the more they want to know the answers to questions in those domains (Jones, 1979). To be sure, when people are so knowledgeable that they feel they already *know* with certainty the answers to the questions posed, they are not all that curious about confirming that fact (Crandall, 1971) However, below absolute certainty people tend to desire the answers to questions they believe they are knowledgeable about.

Expectancy violation   People become curious when some new piece of information fails to conform to their expectations. When such expectancy violations occur, people expend great effort to find ways to dismiss or explain away the data, or reconcile those data with their preconceptions. Work on spontaneous attributional activity demonstrates this the best. It is when people are confronted with surprising information that they think the hardest about the causes of other persons' or their own behavior.

For example, Pyszczynski & Greenberg (1981) presented participants with another person that they were about to meet in a "get acquainted" conversation. While waiting for that conversation, they saw that person either agree or refuse to help out the experimenter with another task, with that task being either trivial or time-consuming. Participants subsequently wanted to see more information about the target when the target's behavior violated their expectancies about social norms (i.e. refused to do the trivial task or agreed to do the onerous one) than when the target's behaviors conformed to them. In a similar vein, Hastie (1984) discovered that people engage in spontaneous attributional activity when presented with another person's behavior (e.g. won a chess game) that violated their expectations of that person (e.g. he is rather unintelligent). In these situations, participants were more likely to list attributions for the behavior in their thoughts than they were when the target's behavior conformed to expectations (see also Clary & Tesser, 1983, for similar data). Evidence of such spontaneous cognition work is also apparent in real world contexts. Businesses take greater pains to explain the reasons for unexpected failures or successes in their annual reports than they do expected outcomes (Bettman & Weitz, 1983).

The role of hedonic consequences

The motive toward curiosity does serve a purpose. The ability to possess knowledge and an understanding of the social world gives people predictability and control over their social worlds. Such predictability and control allows people to adapt their behavior toward ways that provide the most pleasure and avoid the most pain. As such, the primary purpose of social cognition is to guide people in their actions (for discussions, see Heider, 1958; Trope, 1986).

Nowhere was that statement made so explicitly than by traditional attribution theorists, who stated that "The attributor is not simply a seeker after knowledge. His [or her] latent goal in gaining knowledge is that of effective management of himself [or herself] and his [or her] environment" (Kelley, 1972, p. 22). As such, it stands to reason that people are more curious about others when the actions of those others carry consequences for the social perceiver. Perhaps more important, this deeper curiosity often leads to more accurate conclusions about other people. Consider the following conditions.

Outcome dependency   People think more effortfully about other people when the outcomes they will experience depend on those other people. This fact was perhaps best demonstrated by Berscheid and colleagues in a study of dating relationships (Berscheid, Graziano, Monson, & Dermer, 1976). Berscheid and colleagues brought college student volunteers into the laboratory and coaxed them into dating for five weeks only those individuals that the researchers had specified. The volunteers then watched videotaped interviews of three study participants, all of the opposite sex. Some participants were told that one specific interview was of a person they would be dating (indeed, some participants were told that this was the *only* person they would be allowed to date, inside and outside of the study, for five weeks). Participants paid more attention to the interviews of their putative dating partners and remembered more about them. They also made more extreme and confident trait attributions about their designated dating partners than they did of the other targets, indicating that they had thought long and hard about those specific individuals who could bring joy or boredom to the next few weeks of their lives.

Beyond making people think more deeply, outcome dependency also makes people think more accurately. Monson, Keel, Stephens, & Genung (1982) showed that people made more appropriate attributions for the behavior of other people when they expected to interact with them in a Prisoner's Dilemma Game. Erber & Fiske (1984) discovered that people paid more attention to information that was inconsistent with their prior expectations about the competence of another person when their chance of winning a prize depended, in part, on that person's skill.

Indeed, Neuberg & Fiske (1987) demonstrated that outcome dependency can cause people to put aside their stereotypes and to pay more attention to specific information about the attributes and strengths of another person. They asked college students to play an interactive "creativity" game with an individual who had just been released from the hospital after his schizophrenia had gone into remission. Students who had to work with the former patient to win a prize in the game, relative to those who did not, spent more time looking over information about the patient before the game started. As a consequence, those participants tended to view the formerly mentally ill individual more positively, thus dismissing their stereotype of schizophrenic patients.

Self-improvement   People also desire knowledge, particularly about the self, when presented with situations that call for self-improvement. Usually, this means after confronting a failure. For example, when university students fail a test of "professional skills," they exhibit more causal reasoning than when they succeed, regardless of whether that failure was expected or unexpected (Bohner, Bless, Schwarz, & Strack (1988); see Weiner (1985) for similar findings, and chapter 18 of this volume about the role played by negative affect in information processing). In a survey asking people questions about themselves, people cite situations in which they have experienced a failure or a threat, as well as situations in which they are about to confront some future challenge (Taylor, Neter, & Wayment, 1995). No other type of situation comes close in prompting people to evaluate themselves (see chapter 12, this volume, for a discussion).

Accountability   Social reproach is an unpleasant prospect. As such, when people must justify their opinions and beliefs to others, that is, when they are *accountable*, they take more care and apply more effort toward the formation of those opinions (for a review, see Tetlock, 1992). In a wide-ranging series of studies, Tetlock showed that making people accountable for their judgments was a substantial palliative that prevented people from falling prey to many biases and errors. First, accountability made people consider many alternative interpretations of the facts they received. It also prompted them to spend more effort integrating the facts they confronted, finding causal or conceptual links between them. As a consequence, the judgments that people reached were of better quality than the judgments people reached with no accountability. In addition, when accountable, people were found to have more insight into the determinants of their judgments. They processed persuasive communications more thoughtfully, paying more attention to the quality of arguments presented. They failed to succumb to the *correspondence bias* (also known as the *fundamental attribution error*), which refers to the overweighing of personal characteristics of others and the underweighing of situational factors, when explaining the behavior of others. They made more accurate predictions about the responses of others, and more correctly gauged the likelihood that those predictions would later prove to be right.

However, three caveats must be mentioned about this impact of accountability on social thought. First, at times accountability can prompt people to give too much weight to information that is irrelevant to the judgmental task at hand, thus leading them to under-weight diagnostic information, a tendency known as the *dilution effect* (Tetlock, 1992). Second, people must not know the opinions and beliefs of the individuals they must justify their attitudes to. When they have such knowledge, they tend to bend their beliefs "lazily" in the direction of those individuals (Tetlock, 1983). Third, people must be told they are accountable *before* they begin to consider information and form their judgments. If they reach an opinion first, and then are told they are accountable for it, a very different motive with a very different outcome ensues.

Need for control

Central to any treatment of the desire for knowledge is the issue of control. People desire knowledge so that they can predict and control their worlds. Thus, it is not surprising that events that question an individual's control over his or her environment motivate the individual toward gathering information and thinking through their opinions. For example, after Swann, Stephenson, & Pittman (1981) gave participants failure feedback on an intellectual task, participants subsequently asked for more information about a person they were about to interview.

In addition, questioning people's control paradoxically makes them more competent in social cognitive tasks. In one such study, questioning participants' control made them more accurate in distinguishing information they had actually received about another person as opposed to information that could only be inferred (Pittman & D'Agostino, 1989). In another study, participants whose ability to control their fates was questioned made arguably more accurate attributions about another person's behavior, noticing whether the target had written an essay for pay or privately in his diary, inferring weaker attitudes in the former case than they did in the latter (Pittman & Pittman, 1980). This need for control may also explain another curious finding, namely, that depressives tend to think more analytically and carefully about social information, and with the consequence of falling prey to fewer biases in judgment. To the extent that depressed individuals are motivated to regain cognitive control over their lives, they would be inclined to think more carefully about the information they are given (see chapter 18, this volume, and Edwards & Weary, 1993).

Individual differences

Finally, there are stable individual differences in who is curious about their world and wishes to contemplate it (see also chapter 13, this volume). People, for example, differ in their level of *uncertainty orientation* (Roney & Sorrentino, 1995). Uncertainty-oriented individuals are motivated toward discovery, finding out facts about their worlds and particularly about themselves. Certainty-oriented individuals are more interested in avoiding ambiguity and bolstering previously held beliefs.

People also differ in their motivation to pursue effortful, deliberative, and thoughtful analysis. High *need for cognition* individuals seek out and mull over information they receive about their social worlds, and enjoy doing so, more than their low *n cog* peers (Cacioppo

& Petty, 1982). In several different empirical demonstrations, high *n cog* participants seek out more information about other people, generate more thoughts about the information they were given, pay more attention to the quality of the arguments they are presented when considering social issues, and, perhaps most telling, remember the information they were given more accurately than low *n cog* individuals (for a review, see Cacioppo, Petty, Feinstein, & Jarvis, 1996).

The need for closure

Curiosity and discovery are good things, but sometimes people need not only to think about an issue or to get to an answer, but they need to know an answer *now*. Kruglanski and colleagues (for a review, see Kruglanski & Webster, 1996) have delineated the important role played by this *motive toward closure*, that is, needing an answer to a question, any answer, immediately. They have heightened people's desire for immediate answers, for example, by putting people under time constraints or placing them in a room with a noisy and bothersome printer. When need for closure is increased, people consider fewer possible solutions to intellectual puzzles and express more confidence in the conclusions they reach. They are more likely to base their impressions of others on the first few pieces of information they obtain and are more likely to attribute the person's behavior to dispositional rather than to situational factors. They are also more likely to base their judgments of others on relevant stereotypes.

Other researchers have identified another motivation that attends people's curiosity about the world. People harbor the motivation to seek a simple and manageable cognitive representation of their world, although people differ in the degree of this *personal need for structure* (Neuberg & Newsom, 1993). People high on the need for personal structure, relative to their peers, are more likely to "organize social and nonsocial information in less complex ways" (Neuberg & Newsom, 1993, p. 113). Consistent with this assertion, people high on the need have been found to interpret ambiguous information to be more consistent with previously held stereotypes. A woman experiencing trouble in her college classes, for example, is imbued with more traditionally female attributes (e.g. irrationality). High need individuals are also more likely to simplify their world by forming stereotypes, even clearly erroneous ones, of novel groups (Schaller, Boyd, Yohannes, & O'Brien, 1995). (The answer to the college degree question is Los Alamos, New Mexico.)

Desire to Affirm

If there is any theme that emerges again and again in social psychology, it is that the executive of social cognition is a prideful one. In its observations about its owner and the owner's place in the social world, the executive is eager to affirm the belief that its owner is a competent, masterful, successful, and moral individual.

There is evidence everywhere that the executive is successful in its mission to affirm its owner. If one examines the self-esteem of the typical individual, one finds that the individual tends to hold overly positive views of self (for a provocative review, see Taylor & Brown, 1988). The typical person, on average, states that he or she is more capable and moral than his or her peers, a finding that defies the logic of statistics (Alicke, 1985; Dunning, Meyerowitz, & Holzberg, 1989). For example, in a survey of nearly one million American high school seniors, virtually all said they were above average in "getting along with others," with nearly 60 percent stating that they were in the top 10 percent in this ability (College Board, 1976–1977), a collection of self-views that defy objective analysis. People also tend to believe they have more control over events than they objectively do. For example, people overestimate their control over the throw of a pair of dice, a blatantly chance event (Langer, 1975). They also overestimate their ability to predict future events (Vallone, Griffin, Lin, & Ross, 1990), and to finish tasks before they are due (Buehler, Griffin, & Ross, 1994). They are also overly optimistic relative to objective criteria in their ability to bring about positive life events (such as a happy marriage and a well-paying job) while avoiding negative ones (divorce and crime victimization) (Weinstein, 1980).

The theme that people guide their judgments toward self-affirmation has emerged in so many ways in so many contexts that it has arguably reached the status of being a truism that produces both nods and yawns from those who hear it. However, it is just not that simple. Two complications have dogged this truism since social psychologists started to study it in earnest in the 1940s. First, it is often devilishly hard to show that any bias in social cognition, no matter how congenial it is to the social perceiver, is indisputably prompted by the motive to bolster self-worth. Second, the motive to self-affirm fails to show up in contexts where it should be playing a starring role. Let us consider each complication in turn.

Documenting self-affirmation biases

The cycle of research involving self-affirmation processes often involves three phases. In the first phase, researchers present evidence that the motive to affirm positive images of self leads to a judgmental bias. In the second phase, other researchers show how nonmotivational processes could produce the same bias. In the third phase, researchers struggle to construct clever experiments to decide which account is correct. Or they just give up. In social psychology, there are two instances in which supposed self-affirmational biases were documented, only to have the affirmational origin of those biases called into question.

The new look in perception   In the late 1940s, many experimental psychologists asserted that perceptions and representations of the social world were fundamentally shaped by needs, wants, and desires, in a movement that became known as the "New Look" (Erdelyi, 1974). For example, poor children guessed that coins were larger than did rich children, presumably because the need for money especially felt by poor children led them literally to see those coins as bigger (Bruner & Goodman, 1947). People had a more difficult time recognizing threatening words (e.g. *homicide*) when they were flashed on a T-scope than they did more common words (e.g. *flower*), indicating a filter that inhibited the recognition of ominous stimuli, a phenomenon known as *perceptual defense* (Bruner & Klein, 1960).

However, the basic findings of the New Look approach fell under both logical and empirical critiques, with the latter being most devastating. For example, the finding that people failed to recognize threatening words as efficiently as they did nondescript ones was finally attributed to the fact that threatening words were less frequent, and thus less familiar, than were their nonthreatening counterparts (Broadbent, 1967). The New Look never recovered from these critiques, and research in this tradition evaporated as the 1950s turned into the 1960s.

Self-serving attributions   In the 1970s, a similar cycle emerged for people's attributions for their successes and failures. The basic finding was that people attributed their successes to their own abilities, whereas they attributed their failures to mercurial external forces such as task difficulty or luck (for a review, see Zuckerman, 1979), an apparent motivational phenomenon. However, a number of scholars noted that this so-called self-serving attributional pattern was also logically warranted. In particular, given that people often have good reason to expect that they will succeed, it is only natural for them to attribute their successes to their own capacities and their failures to some exceptional or interfering circumstance in the environment, or to just bad luck (Miller & Ross, 1975).

Failures of the motive to appear

At times, the executive seems surprisingly disinterested in maintaining self-esteem. Nowhere is this surprising disinterest more apparent than in the gathering of social information. According to the tenets of a self-affirmation motive, people should selectively expose themselves to information that is congenial to treasured beliefs rather than information that is contradictory.

   However, early research on selective exposure failed to find any consistent results that would support the notion of a defensive executive. When people were given a chance to look over information that supported or threatened their recent purchase of a car, supported or denigrated the political candidate of their party, or suggested that cigarette smoking caused or did not cause cancer, some studies showed a preference for congenial information, some no preference, and others a preference for threatening information (Freedman & Sears, 1965).

   Another research program, coming several years after these studies, also showed a surprising absence of self-affirmational motives in situations where people evaluated their own abilities. For example, Trope (1980) examined when people wanted feedback about themselves. He found that people preferred to receive feedback about themselves equally in situations in which they could succeed or fail, and equally in situations in which success or failure carried decisive information about themselves. In short, people were just as willing to receive potentially self-damning information as they were self-glorifying data.

The knowledge versus the affirmation motive

It is worth pausing to reflect on these failures to find a selective exposure effect, for the counterintuitive nature of these findings does force one to consider when the need to know will drive people's cognition and when the need to self-affirm will. If one takes a long, hard look at how self-affirmational motives bias human judgment, one begins to see the situational factors that promote the need to know over the need to affirm, and vice versa.

Explicitness of informational choices   If one scrutinizes the methods of the studies reviewed above, one finds that they have one telling common element. These studies present participants with an explicit and rather transparent choice between receiving congenial versus uncongenial information (Freedman & Sears, 1965), or between diagnostic versus nondiagnostic tests (e.g. Trope, 1980). In short, the uncongenial option was an explicit option that the participant had to consider.

A different picture of selective exposure arises when the choice between congenial and uncongenial options is not so explicit. For example, Pyszczynski, Greenberg, & LaPrelle (1985) led participants to succeed or fail on a test of social sensitivity. They were then given the option of seeing how other participants had performed. After failure, participants asked to see the responses of a greater number of other participants when they were led to believe that those others had performed badly as opposed to well, a selective exposure effect that seems designed to affirm the self. Note, however, participants were not given an explicit choice between seeing bolstering or threatening information. Given the between-subject nature of this design, participants never had to choose explicitly between looking at people who had outperformed versus underperformed them.

Similar effects arise when people search their memories for information consistent with flattering conclusions. Sanitioso, Kunda, & Fong (1990) led participants to believe that either extraversion or introversion was related to success in life pursuits. Not surprisingly, participants in the former condition later described themselves as more extraverted than did their counterparts in the latter. In examining how people could revise their self-images in such flattering ways, Sanitioso, et al. found evidence for a selective exposure effect in memory search. Participants in the extraversion condition selectively searched their memories for data that they had acted in extraverted ways in the past; participants in the introversion condition selectively searched for memories of introverted behavior. Again, participants had not been presented with a transparent choice between favorable and unfavorable information. With that choice obscured, people roamed free in their search through memory for information flattering to their self-images.

Finally, people reveal self-affirmation impulses via their tendency to *self-handicap* under threat. Faced with the explicit acquisition of self-relevant information that they are not sure will reflect well on them, people will sabotage their own performance if that sabotage gives them an adequate excuse for inadequate performance (Berglas & Jones, 1978). For example, college students not sure that they will succeed at an intellectual task volunteer to drink alcohol before confronting the task (Tucker, Vuchinich, & Sobell, 1981). Again, in this situation, there is no explicit choice between self-affirming and non-affirming options, and given this cover participants choose to act in self-affirming or protecting ways.

Timing of the information search   Another circumstance that could determine whether people seek out unbiased versus congenial information depends on whether a conclusion or a decision has been made. For example, I recently traveled to an antique fair where I found a dining room table I was rather ambivalent about buying. Faced with my ambivalence, I pulled my traveling companion aside and began peppering her with questions. After a long while, exasperated, she asked me what I wanted her to tell me. I said that I only wanted her honest opinions, regardless of the decision I made (which was true). Finally, after a tortuous back and forth, I decided to buy the table. As we walked back to the antique dealer, I turned to her again and told her from now on I only wanted to hear (which was true) why I had made the right decision.

This example, as well as rigorous empirical research, suggests that the motive that dominates thought before a decision is reached can be quite different from the motive that governs thought afterward. According to Gollwitzer and colleagues (e.g. Gollwitzer & Kinney, 1989; chapter 15, this volume), pre-decision thought is governed by a *deliberative* mind-set in which the individual dispassionately seeks out impartial and accurate information. However, after a decision has been made, people enter an *implementational* mind-set where they are focused on how to attain the goal they wish to attain. Once that Rubicon of decision has been crossed, people favor information that flatters their decisions over information that threatens them. Consistent with this analysis, people choosing between two pieces of experimental machinery do not overestimate their ability to make the machinery function. However, once people have chosen a machine and have started to try to make it function, they hold inflated views of their ability to make it work. Buttressing this general analysis, making people accountable for their decisions *after* they have reached them makes them seek out information selectively in order to bolster their decisions (Tetlock, 1992).

This distinction between pre- and post-decision phases serves as a specific example of a more general distinction that separates circumstances that prompt the need for accuracy over the need for affirmation. People seek out unbiased and accurate information when they have some control over their state of affairs. When they do not have control, they move instead toward the psychic analgesic of self-affirmation. Supporting this notion, Dunning (1995) examined when people desired accurate information about their abilities, no matter how pleasant or unpleasant that information was, versus when people would want only the pleasant information. He found that when people thought they could control the development of the ability, they desired information no matter how unpleasant it might be. When they thought they could not control the development of the trait, they tended to censor unpleasant news and gravitate toward congenial data. In a similar vein, Frey (1986) provided evidence that people seek out unfriendly information if they felt they could control its implications, that is, they had ample ammunition to refute it if need be.

Biases in interpretation

In some respects, the failures to find a universal tendency toward selective exposure should not come as a surprise, for it is not in the exposure to information that the self-affirming executive reveals its genius. Rather, its expertise lies in its interpretation once that information is received. The social cognitive executive has a vast array of strategies and techniques to evaluate, organize, and make sense of the information it receives, both pleasant and unpleasant. Because of this, unpleasant information is often neutralized once the executive has a chance to mull it over. To be sure, the executive is often constrained in the conclusions that it can reach, for its conclusions must remain plausible and justifiable (see Kunda, 1990, for a discussion of the important role played by "reality constraints"), but within those bounds the executive is likely to make judgments of the self and the social world that are quite pleasant and bolstering.

For example, unpleasant information is sometimes given *more*, not less, attention and scrutiny, with an eye toward dismissing its implications. Ditto & Lopez (1992), for example, asked people to take a test for an enzyme deficiency. Relative to a group who received favorable news, those who received an unfavorable result spent more time scrutinizing that result. They took longer to decide that the test had been completed and were more likely to repeat it.

Often, this greater scrutiny "pays off," in that it allows the executive to unloose its interpretive machinery toward discounting the information (for reviews, see Baumeister & Newman, 1994; Kunda, 1990). First, the scrutiny given to unfriendly information allows people to find flaws in that information. For example, people find methodological problems in scientific studies that question their personal views on the death penalty (Lord, Ross, & Lepper, 1979). Second, increased scrutiny can allow people to develop alternative explanations, often reasonable, for unpleasant outcomes that spare self-esteem (Ditto & Lopez, 1992). For example, people receiving a bad medical diagnosis are more likely to pay (appropriate) attention to the probability that some alternative source caused the result, or to remember irregularities in their recent behavior that could have thrown the test off (Ditto, Scepansky, Munro, Apanovitch, & Lockhart, 1998).

The interpretative expertise of the self-affirming executive is revealed by many other techniques. For example, when assessing the ability of self or others, people use biased and self-flattering definitions of those traits. When defining such traits as "talent," people tend to emphasize the attributes they possess and de-emphasize the attributes they do not (Dunning & Cohen, 1992; Dunning, Meyerowitz, & Holzberg, 1989). Thus, the behavioral criteria that people use to judge self and others are tacitly stacked in favor of the self.

As well, the affirmational executive is facile at denigrating the importance of the self's failures. When people do poorly on a task, their subsequent reaction is often one of deriding the importance of the skill involved (Tesser & Paulhus, 1983). Indeed, when people rate both their skill level in a domain and their importance they attach to it, one sees strong positive correlations (Pelham, 1991). Finally, when a person is induced to act in a way that violates his or her personal attitudes, the individual often comes to hold the attitude as trivial "in the grand scheme of things" (Simon, Greenberg, & Brehm, 1995).

The executive also minimizes the implications of its owner's shortcomings by perceiving those shortcomings to be common among others (Mullen & Goethals, 1990). For example, people who hold hidden fears (e.g. of public speaking, of spiders) tend to overestimate the percentage of the population who also holds those fears. In doing so, they reduce the distinctiveness of these failings (Suls & Wan, 1987). In contrast, people do not tend to perceive their strengths and proficiencies as common. If anything, they tend to *underestimate* their prevalence of those skills in the relevant population (Mullen & Goethals, 1990).

Finally, if all else fails, the executive is adept at finding other individuals who are worse than its owner. People often engage in downward social comparison, finding an individual whose level of skill or desirability of circumstance is inferior to the self, with this comparison activity becoming more fervent after threats to self-esteem (chapter 12, this volume; Wills, 1981).

Implicit self-affirmation

Recent research suggests that the affirmational executive is not only adept but zealous in its guardianship of self-esteem. The evidence that people discount their own failings and extol their own virtues is not a surprise. However, what may be a surprise is that people not only make claims about themselves that directly bolster self-esteem, but also provide judgments of others that implicitly and indirectly enhance their own self-images. That is, even when it is another person who is to be judged and not the self, people make judgments that reflect favorably on the self.

For example, Dunning & Cohen (1992) examined the judgments made of others by "low" and "high" performers in a domain (e.g. athletics). Low performers judged virtually everybody, regardless of performance level, as pretty capable – thus allowing themselves by implication to see themselves as capable. In contrast, high performers denigrated the achievements of anyone whose performance was inferior to their own. In doing so, they could claim to be uniquely capable among their peers. Tellingly, these types of self-aggrandizing judgments were exacerbated by threats to self-esteem (Beauregard & Dunning, 1998; for similar data, see Dunning, Leuenberger, & Sherman, 1995).

Other researchers have shown that the need to bolster the self prompts people to revise their impressions of others in self-aggrandizing ways. When esteem is threatened, people are more likely to apply derogatory stereotypes in their judgments of other people (Fein & Spencer, 1997), and to denigrate the achievements of their peers in order to accentuate the superiority of their own achievements (Brown & Gallagher, 1992). When their personal mastery is questioned by asking them to think about their own death, they derogate people from other social groups or those who espouse opinions that differ from their own (Solomon, Greenberg, & Pyszczynski, 1991). People are also motivated to extol the skills of those who outperform them. By doing so, they give themselves more perceptual wiggle room to extol their own meager achievements (Alicke, LoSchiavo, Zerbst, & Zhang, 1997).

The most developed and researched model of this implicit self-affirmation is Tesser's (1988) *self-evaluation maintenance* (SEM) model. In the model, Tesser proposes two strategies that people pursue to bolster their self-esteem. First, people engage in *comparison* processes, in which they compare their abilities with those of their peers, particularly close peers. This comparison occurs for abilities that people consider important and ones in which they believe they outperform others. Second, people engage in *reflection* processes, in which they bask in the reflected glory of the proficiencies and achievements of close others. That basking, however, can occur only in domains that people consider unimportant for themselves, so that they are not threatened by the fact that close others outperform them.

In a number of ingenious studies, Tesser and colleagues have shown that the interplay of comparison and reflection processes has a number of implications for social life. People consider an ability as important to the extent that they believe they outperform people they are close to. People denigrate the performances of their peers in domains they consider self-defining, but not in domains they do not consider self-defining. People's choices of their friends are based, in part, on whether those others are inferior on self-defining abilities (better for the comparison process) yet superior in nonself-defining domains (better for the reflection process). People will even sabotage the performances of their friends in self-defining domains more than they will of strangers in order to maintain favorable comparisons (for a review, see Tesser, 1988; chapter 22, this volume).

Desire for Coherence

As much as nature abhors a vacuum, the executive despises incoherence in its beliefs about the world. As such, the executive is motivated to reduce the contradictions that it confronts in its social environment. As discussed above, inconsistencies between what people learn about their worlds and what they already believed is a prime instigator of curiosity. But in 1957, Leon Festinger raised the stakes. In his theory of cognitive dissonance, Festinger proposed that inconsistencies among beliefs, especially if one or both of those beliefs is important or relevant, cause negative psychological tension that must be relieved by any means necessary. There are many ways to resolve the inconsistency and thus reduce the tension. First, people can "add" cognitions that explain away the inconsistency. They can change one of the beliefs to be more compatible with the other belief. They can also trivialize the importance of either or both beliefs.

Researchers throughout the years have developed three distinct paradigms to study whether and how people resolved contradictory beliefs. In the *forced compliance* paradigm, people are asked to perform an action that goes against their beliefs and principles. In the classic first demonstration of dissonance principles, participants who were asked to lie about a dreadful experiment they had just completed, by saying that it was exciting and informative, later viewed the experiment as more enjoyable when they had little justification to lie (i.e. they were paid only $1) than when they had ample justification (i.e. they were paid $20) (Festinger & Carlsmith, 1959). In the *effort justification* paradigm, participants come to hold an object as more valuable to the extent that they had to work hard to get it, placing them in a position in which they had to justify all the effort expended. Finally, in the *free choice* paradigm, participants are given a choice between two items of similar desirability. After choosing one, participants tend to denigrate the value of the rejected item to resolve the dissonance caused by the choice (for reviews of these techniques, see Abelson, Aronson, McGuire, Newcomb, Rosenberg, & Tannenbaum, 1968; Aronson, 1969).

However, although dissonance theory has inspired the successful completion of thousands of empirical studies, it still is hardly a noncontroversial series of proposals. Almost from its inception, researchers enveloped the theory under a cloud of questions and concerns.

Controvery 1: does dissonance exist?

For example, Festinger's motivational theory generated alternative accounts based solely on cognitive or informational principles, much like had happened with research on the New Look and self-serving attributions. Bem (1972), for example, questioned whether dissonance as a "hot" and negative affective state existed at all. Instead, in his *self-perception* theory, he proposed that people add or alter cognitions in the face of inconsistency simply as a result of a dispassionate review of their actions and opinions. For example, why would people change their opinion of a dreadful experiment based on the fact that they had lied to another person about it for $1? That opinion change need not be to alleviate negative psychological tension, for just look at the facts: the participant had said the experiment was exciting, did it for only $1, and thus the study could not have been that noxious after all, QED. Hence, the so-called dissonance effect could be the logical outcome of dispassionate review of the events surrounding the "lie."

Perhaps the biggest dissonance reaction of them all was the upset and outrage expressed by dissonance researchers at Bem's (1966) reanalysis. The controversy between dissonance and self-perception perspectives prompted innumerable studies to resolve the contradiction between what dissonance researchers believed and what Bem proposed.

Over the years, those studies have produced two types of resolutions between Festinger's motivational proposal and Bem's purely cognitive alternative. First, researchers have taken great care to show that contradictions between beliefs, as produced in classic dissonance research paradigms, do indeed produce physiological arousal (Elkin & Leippe, 1986) and self-reports of negative affect (Elliot & Devine, 1994). Other evidence suggests this heightened emotion plays the role it has been proposed to play in dissonance processes. Giving people a way to explain away their arousal prompts them to be less interested in resolving inconsistencies (Zanna & Cooper, 1974). Preventing people from feeling dissonance, by letting them drink a few alcoholic beverages, also makes people disinclined to resolve dissonance (Steele, Southwick, & Critchlow, 1981). Most telling, allowing people to resolve dissonance by changing their attitudes reduces the arousal (Elkin & Leippe, 1986) and negative affect (Elliot & Devine, 1994) that they feel.

Second, researchers have taken pains to delineate conditions in which dissonance processes may govern people's reactions to contradictory events and those in which self-perception processes may prevail. Fazio, Zanna, & Cooper (1977) looked at the degree of discrepancy between the participant's attitude and the position they were asked to publicly espouse. Fazio, et al. proposed that when the discrepancy was great, so great that the position that participants were asked to support was not something they could agree with, participants should feel dissonance. However, when the discrepancy was trivial, that is, the participant did not necessarily disagree with the position they were asked to take, they should feel no dissonance, although they may change their attitudes due to self-perception processes. The experimental data agreed with this analysis. When participants wrote essays supporting a position greatly discrepant from their own, they changed their attitudes toward that position only when they did not have a chance to explain away the negative affect they were feeling. However, when the discrepancy was not so great, all participants changed their attitudes toward the position, regardless of what they were told about the "affect" they should be feeling, indicating that participants were feeling no dissonance when dealing with positions not that discrepant from their own.

Controversy 2: what causes dissonance?

The second controversy surrounding dissonance involves which specific inconsistencies, if any at all, cause the dissonant state. As Festinger (1957) originally noted, not all inconsistencies would provoke dissonance. The inconsistencies had to involve "important" cognitions and behaviors. But what made a cognition or behavior important?

There have been three major proposals to the question of which inconsistencies count. Cooper & Fazio (1984) suggested that it was not inconsistency *per se* that prompted dissonance. Instead, to provoke dissonance, a researcher had to induce participants to perform a behavior that (a) had been freely chosen and that (b) had adverse consequences that were (c) clearly foreseeable. Only then would people feel adverse emotions that they would quell via dissonance reduction. In support of this view, Sher & Cooper (1989) conducted a study showing that no inconsistent behavior need take place to arouse dissonance, but just a behavior that fulfilled the three conditions described above. They asked participants to give a speech that either favored or opposed the participant's own opinions, and independent of this varied whether the speech would result in negative consequences. Sher and Cooper found attitude change in line with the speech only in those situations in which negative outcomes would occur, regardless of whether the speech contradicted the participant's original views.

Aronson (1969) developed a completely different analysis of which inconsistencies and conditions led to dissonance. In his view, inconsistency again *per se* did not lead to dissonance but rather inconsistencies about the self. That is, people tended to possess views of themselves that they wished to maintain and bolster. When their behavior contradicted those beliefs, then they would experience dissonance and work to resolve it. Perhaps his clearest demonstration of this analysis was a series of studies conducted in the 1990s on *hypocrisy*, in which Aronson and colleagues showed that making discrepancies about the self salient led to changes in behavior.

In one such study, participants were asked to make a videotaped speech in which they attempted to persuade high school students to practice safe sex. Before beginning the speech, some participants completed a questionnaire about their own adherence to safe sex principles, which, of course, for virtually all participants turned out to be imperfect. According to Aronson and colleagues, having participants review their past failings should prompt them to see the hypocrisy between what they practiced and what they were about to preach. As such, participants in this condition should feel dissonance, and thus be motivated to reduce it. And they did, purchasing more condoms at the end of the experiment than did participants who merely gave the speech (Stone, Aronson, Crain, Winslow, & Fried, 1994). Key to this demonstration, and contradicting the proposals of Cooper & Fazio (1984), dissonance effects were obtained in situations involving no foreseeable aversive consequences (for, after all, the students' speeches could only steer their audiences toward taking more safe sex precautions).

Close to Aronson's analysis of dissonance arousal was the approach taken by Steele

(1988), who also emphasized the importance of beliefs about the self in dissonance arousal. According to Steele, it was not necessarily contradictions with self-beliefs that provoked dissonance but contradictions with the specific belief that the self was a moral and effective individual. Cast a person's morality or mastery into doubt, and dissonance would kick in. Supporting this *self-affirmational* view, Steele provided many demonstrations that reminding people that they were effective and ethical individuals tended to stop dissonance processes in their tracks. For example, in one such study, participants were asked to write essays opposing state funding for facilities for the handicapped. Participants showed dissonance effects, changing their own attitudes to be in line with the essay, unless they had been given a chance to volunteer to help a blind person. In this last situation, participants could affirm the notion that they were charitable individuals, thus making the essay less threatening (Steele & Liu, 1983).

The logical conclusion of consistency motives

At its logical conclusion, the motive toward epistemic coherence would lead people to seek out and remember only the information that confirms previously held beliefs. In the realm of beliefs about the self, that motive has been well-documented. In work on *self-verification* motives, Swann (1997) and colleagues have shown that people prefer to gather information that reaffirms views already held about the self. Of key import, people seek out this confirmatory information even when it supports negative self-beliefs.

For example, people with negative self-views pay more attention to information if they believe that information will portray them in an unfavorable light than they do information that promises to be favorable. They are also willing to pay money to receive such negative information. People also surround themselves with other individuals who verify views, even negative ones, about the self. For example, they feel more intimate with their marriage partners when those partners hold the same impression that people hold about themselves, even if those impressions are unfavorable ones. In short, people actively arrange their social environments to confirm views held of the self (for reviews, see Swann, 1990, 1997). Finally, people with low self-views distort their memory for feedback about their abilities in a self-denigrating direction, in contrast to high self-view individuals who distort in a positive direction (Story, 1998).

But why do people self-verify? At first blush, one might think that people with negative self-views simply are not as upset by negative information as are people with high self-views, and thus do not fear it. However, when people with low self-views are given negative information, they are just as unhappy and upset as are their high self-view peers (Swann, 1990). So why do low self-view individuals choose information that is emotionally punishing?

Two desires appear to underlie the motive toward self-verification. Swann, Stein-Serroussi, & Geisler (1992) asked people why they chose self-verifying information. In pouring over people's explanations, they found, first, that people desired to maintain the overarching belief that they knew themselves. By maintaining that belief, people also maintained some notion that the world was a coherent and predictable place. In people's explanations for the information they sought, these concerns over *epistemic* matters were the most frequent reason that people cited. But beyond epistemic concerns, people also expressed *pragmatic* concerns. When choosing people to interact with, participants opted for the person who was the likeliest to lead to a smooth and productive social interaction. That person was likeliest to be the individual who had an accurate impression of the information gatherer.

Current Thinking and Future Directions

Thus, scanning the social psychological literature over the decades, one sees ample empirical support for the three motives to seek out information, to make sure it is favorable, and to insure that it is consistent with prior beliefs. However, there is still much work to be done ascertaining how these motives influence human thought and action. Consider the following questions, all of which are currently receiving or deserve scientific attention.

Relation of the three motives to each other

The first question is how the motives toward knowledge, affirmation, and coherence interact with one another. Recent theorists have put forth only the simplest of conclusions about the interrelations of these motives, signaling the start of work that still has several years to go.

For example, some theorists have tackled the question of, if push ever came to shove, which motive would rank supreme over the others? Sedikides (1993) conducted a study on "self-reflection," that is, what information would people seek to find out about themselves when wrapped up in a moment of contemplation about the self. In asking people to design the questions they would ask about themselves, he found that self-enhancement ranked supreme. His participants tended to ask questions about their strong points, ones to which they already knew the answer. Other theorists have reached similar conclusions about the supremacy of the motive to affirm one's self (Baumeister, 1998; Heider, 1958).

However, there are two reasons to be cautious about making any claim about the supremacy of any motive over the others. First, which motive is supreme in any given situation likely depends on the specific circumstances surrounding that situation. Sedikides (1993), for example, found that the motive toward affirmation reigned supreme, but note that his self-reflection situation carried no concrete consequences for participants. What if college seniors had been asked about their chances to pass the course exam taking place next week? That situation carries immediate consequences for the question-asker and a very different set of motivations might have been invoked. After all, recall that people become more motivated to acquire accurate information when they are faced with decisions that carry obvious, real, and immediate consequences for them.

Second, the question of which motive is supreme presupposes that the motives are distinct. Any researcher who squints into the fact of any of these motives soon sees that they tend to morph into each other in the experiments reviewed above. For example, noticing an inconsistency in the environment may make one curious (the need to know), but if the inconsistency is relevant enough it can cause dissonance (the need for coherence).

Question a person's mastery over the world (that is, make them need to affirm themselves), and sometimes the result is more attributional activity and more accurate judgment (the need to know). Make a person confront an important inconsistency and they will strive to resolve it, unless you first buttress his or her positive self-views through an exercise in self-affirmation (Steele, 1988) or by reminding them of a way in which they compare favorably with people they know (Tesser & Cornell, 1991).

In short, the three motives tend to blend in together, so much so that it is difficult to know if they are distinct. At their heart, each motive involves the same issue: the person's sense of mastery over the world. By gathering knowledge, a person renders the world comprehensible, predictable, and controllable. By pursuing the motive for self-affirmation, a person establishes that he or she is competent enough to master happy fates and avoid fearful ones. By fulfilling the motive for coherence, one gains the mastery conferred by possessing a predictable world. Scratch beneath the surface, and each motive addresses the same basic issue, and thus it is difficult to know if they are distinct or rather different manifestations of the same underlying motive (see Aronson, 1992; Tesser & Cornell, 1991, for similar conclusions).

Individual differences

A curious feature of motivational approaches to social cognitive phenomena is that they make theorists think in terms of individual differences more than they do when those theorists adopt cognitive perspectives. Consider all the individual difference variables that have been evoked in analyses of epistemic motives, such as need for cognition, need for personal structure, and uncertainty orientation. Other theorists have explored the need to self-affirm through studies of self-esteem (Blaine & Crocker, 1993) and narcissism (John & Robins, 1994). Even cognitive dissonance has been approached via an individual difference perspective, for it has been found that people high in the *preference for consistency* display dissonance effects more strongly than do their peers who are low in this need (Cialdini, Trost, & Newsom, 1995). If one looks over the history of purely cognitive approaches to social judgment, one would be hard pressed to find such a proliferation of individual difference variables.

Thus, it would not be a surprise if a re-emergence of motivational approaches in social cognition prompted more interest in individual difference work. However, three notes are worth making about such individual difference work. First, it is an interesting research question in itself why it is so much easier to think of individual differences in terms of motivational differences as opposed to cognitive ones. (Could that say something important about how people make attributions about others in their everyday world?) Second, researchers should make sure to verify that the individual differences they observe are actually due to needs and motives as opposed to some other factor. Take, for example, the need for cognition. People do differ in the tendency to engage in effortful thought (Cacioppo, Petty, Feinstein, & Jarvis, 1996), but is that due to a motive? It could simply be a predisposition toward caution and analysis, or a product of familial training, or an indication of intellectual ability, for people will tend to think hard if they are often successful at it.

The third note to be made is more telling for theoretical work on human motives. The interesting story about motives may not be how they drive human judgment in general, but how they drive the thoughts and actions of important classes of people. Take the late lamented New Look in perception. While the New Look lies largely dormant in social psychology, this perspective has arisen independently, and forcefully, in the field of psychopathology. Evidence abounds that certain clinical populations show great evidence of perceptual defense that holds many similarities to the proposals promoted by New Look theorists.

For example, Amir, Foa, & Coles (1998) found evidence that people with generalized social phobias are vigilant toward but ultimately repress any material that evokes their phobia. Amir, et al. showed social phobics and nonphobics a number of sentences that ended with words that had double meanings, one of which was socially threatening (e.g. *She wrote down the mean.*). Participants were asked if a following target word was consistent with the material in the sentence (e.g. *unfriendly*). The target word was not consistent with the sentence – but it was consistent with a socially threatening interpretation of the last word in that sentence. When the target word closely followed the stimulus sentence, social phobics relative to their nonphobic peers took longer to state that the target word was inconsistent, indicating that they had activated the socially threatening meaning of the target word. However, when the target word followed the sentence after a pause of nearly a second, social phobics were faster at denying the consistency of the target word, indicating that they had begun to inhibit the socially threatening meaning of that word.

Culture

Perhaps the most intriguing set of individual differences in social cognitive processes are those that covary with geographic borders. At first blush, it would seem to be a human universal, one hardly worth mentioning, that people are motivated to find things out, to affirm their own worth, and to see a coherent world. However, these obvious motives may not survive a transfer off the shores of North America and Europe. An emerging body of work suggests that the denizens of many cultures fail to be influenced as much, if at all, by the motivational forces (see chapter 23, this volume, for a review of research on culture).

For example, take the motive to affirm the self. In some extant studies, people of Eastern cultures, such as China and Japan, fail to show any evidence of this motive. For example, Japanese respondents fail to show any self-serving biases in their impressions of themselves, quite unlike the usual positive biases demonstrated by North American respondents. In an illustrative study, Canadian and Japanese respondents were asked to rate their ability relative to their peers. Canadian respondents tended, on average, to say that they were above average in their abilities, replicating a typical but logically impossible set of self-views. Japanese participants showed no such "above average" bias, even in situations that should be the most threatening to self-image (Heine & Lehman, 1995). These findings suggest that Japanese individuals are not interested in enhancing the self *per se*, but rather focused on criticizing the self to find ways to improve themselves. In particular, they engage in self-analysis in order to find ways that they can fit themselves into collective interpersonal relations that are harmonious (Markus & Kitayama, 1991).

As well, the desire for coherence in the social world may be an obsession found more in the West than in the East, judging from recent experiments on dissonance effects. Heine & Lehman (1997) asked Canadian and Japanese participants to choose between equally valued compact discs. Whereas Canadian participants showed the usual dissonance effect, disparaging the nonchosen compact disc relative to the chosen one, Japanese participants showed no such pattern. Interestingly, receiving positive feedback (a self-affirmation exercise) prevented Canadian participants from displaying the usual dissonance effect and receiving negative feedback exacerbated it. Feedback had no effect on Japanese participants, showing once again a lack of concern for self-affirmation.

Further data on the need for coherence reveals more subtle, and perhaps deeper, differences between Eastern and Western cultures. In a study of preferences for consistency among American and Chinese respondents, Peng (1997) found that Westerners tended to prefer propositions, as embedded in proverbs, that were logically coherent (*as the twig is bent, so grows the tree*), whereas Chinese respondents found relatively more favor in propositions that contained logical contradictions (*too humble is half proud*).

Mechanisms of motivation

Future research could also focus on what "level" motivation influences social judgment. In particular, over the past twenty years in social psychology, a distinction has emerged between processes that occur on the *explicit* level, with conscious control and effort, and those that occur on the *implicit* level, without any awareness, control, or monitoring (chapter 7, this volume; Greenwald & Banaji, 1995). It would be useful to see the extent to which affirmational and coherence motives occur at either level. Such an investigation would be useful in answering the important question of whether the biases that these motives produce are correctable. To the extent that their influence is implicit, with their influence occurring outside of consciousness and control, correcting for motivational biases would be difficult, if not impossible. Thus, the distinction between implicit and explicit processing becomes more important as one stirs motivation into the mix of social cognition.

Parallel constraint satisfaction systems

Upon examining the style of research typically adopted to examine motivation in human judgment, one might be tempted to surmise that social psychology, if it is ever to take motivation seriously, will have to abandon its rigorous and computer based information processing methods and learn (or perhaps to relearn) how to conduct high impact psychodramas that provoke the psychic needs of participants. One would have to re-invent, for example, the style of the old dissonance experiments, which presented participants with vivid conflicts not easily resolved.

Although a return to high impact methodology might be called for, an emphasis on motivation should not cause psychological researchers to run from their personal computers. In fact, motivational perspectives on social cognition may call for an increased emphasis on computer based research tools. Consider parallel constraint satisfaction models, in which researchers set up computer simulations where they give an organism in the computer some *a priori* beliefs, and then revise some of those beliefs to see how the system alters the other beliefs it has been given. The key in such systems is that all changes must bring all beliefs in harmony, or at least in some steady state, with one another (chapter 6, this volume; Smith, 1998).

One can easily see how parallel constraint satisfaction models could be useful for expressing and exploring how motivations influence social judgment. Suppose we built a system that mimicked the human desire to think well of itself, a belief that could not be changed unless under tremendous fire. We could then feed the system with social information to see how interpretations of that information and other beliefs about the "self" were changed or shaped when constrained by the overarching belief that the self is good. In fact, such a system has already been built to model processes associated with cognitive dissonance, and has done a splendid job of accounting for classic dissonance findings (Shultz & Lepper, 1996).

Concluding Remarks

At the outset of this chapter, I raised the issue of executive functions in social judgment, raising questions about what factors instigate, monitor, shape, control, and terminate the processes of social judgment. In short, I asked how we could characterize the homunculus that carries out these functions. Several systematic principles turned out to shape the efforts of that creature. Work on curiosity and the desire for knowledge shows that the creature desires information the most under circumscribed situations. Work on the desire for affirmation and coherence shows the constraints that the creature is under as it works its way toward its conclusions about the social world. For the most part, those conclusions must affirm the self-esteem of its owner and be coherent with important beliefs already possessed.

As such, the time may be ripe for turning research attention more directly on the executive functions governing social judgment. However, to do so, researchers may have to adopt research strategies that may have to differ from the usual ones used in social psychology. In particular, to determine when people spontaneously decide to judge others, and on what dimensions, researchers will have to forego handing their participants questionnaires containing predefined questions. Instead, researchers will have to present participants with opportunities to make judgments that they may choose to pass on. As well, to determine the importance and prevalence of constraints, such as affirmation and coherence, on participants' judgments, researchers will have to lie back and let participants decide when they will make judgments and invoke those constraints themselves.

These types of research paradigms will call for some cleverness, but the results of pursuing them will be useful. Like the executive, scientists are curious and like to form coherent theories of the world (and have been shown not to mind the occasional self-affirmation). Thus, to satiate these needs, scientists will have to alter the methods they use to address more completely how social judgment is motivated.

References

Abelson, R. P., Aronson, E., McGuire, W. J., Newcomb, T. M., Rosenberg, M. J., & Tannenbaum, T. M. (1968). *Theories of cognitive consistency: A sourcebook*. Skokie, IL: Rand McNally.

Alicke, M. D. (1985). Global self-evaluation as determined by the desirability and controllability of trait adjectives. *Journal of Personality and Social Psychology, 59*, 1621–1630.

Alicke, M. D., LoSchiavo, F. M., Zerbst, J., & Zhang, S. (1997). The person who outperforms me is a genius: Maintaining perceived competence in upward social comparison. *Journal of Personality and Social Psychology, 72*, 781–789.

Amir, N., Foa, E. B., & Coles, M. E. (1998). Automatic activation and strategic avoidance of threat-relevant information in social phobia. *Journal of Abnormal Psychology, 107*, 285–290.

Aronson, E. (1969). The theory of cognitive dissonance: A current perspective. In L. Berkowitz (Ed.), *Advances in experimental social psychology* Vol. 4 (pp. 1–34). New York: Academic Press.

Aronson, E. (1992). The return of the repressed: Dissonance theory makes a comeback. *Psychological Inquiry, 3*, 303–311.

Baumeister, R. F. (1998). The self. In D. T. Gilbert, S. T. Fiske, & G. Lindzey (Eds.), *Handbook of social psychology* Vol. 1. 4th. edn. (pp. 680–740). New York: McGraw-Hill.

Baumeister, R. F., & Newman, L. S. (1994). Self-regulation of cognitive inference and decision processes. *Personality and Social Psychology Bulletin, 20*, 3–19.

Beauregard, K. S., & Dunning, D. (1998). Turning up the contrast: Self-enhancement motives prompt egocentric contrast effects in social judgments. *Journal of Personality and Social Psychology, 74*, 606–621.

Bem, D. J. (1966). Self-perception: An alternative interpretation of cognitive dissonance phenomena. *Psychological Review, 74*, 183–200.

Bem, D. J. (1972). Self-perception theory. In L. Berkowitz (Ed.), *Advances in experimental social psychology* Vol. 6 (pp. 1–63). New York: Academic Press.

Berglas, S., & Jones, E. E. (1978). Drug choice as a self-handicapping strategy in response to noncontingent success. *Journal of Personality and Social Psychology, 36*, 405–417.

Berlyne, D. E. (1954). An experimental study of human curiosity. *British Journal of Psychology, 45*, 256–265.

Berscheid, E., Graziano, W., Monson, T., & Dermer, M. (1976). Outcome dependency: Attention, attribution, and attraction. *Journal of Personality and Social Psychology, 34*, 978–989.

Bettmann, J. R., & Weitz, B. A. (1983). Attributions in the boardroom: Causal reasoning in corporate annual reports. *Administrative Science Quarterly, 28*, 165–183.

Blaine, B., & Crocker, J. (1993). Self-esteem and self-serving biases in reactions to positive and negative events: An integrative review. In R. F. Baumeister (Ed.), *Self-esteem: The puzzle of low self-regard* (pp. 55–85). New York: Plenum Press.

Bohner, G., Bless, H., Schwarz, N., & Strack, F. (1988). What triggers causal attributions? The impact of valence and subjective probability. *European Journal of Social Psychology, 18*, 335–345.

Broadbent, D. E. (1967). Word-frequency effect and response bias. *Psychological Review, 74*, 1–15.

Brown, J. D., & Gallagher, F. M. (1992). Coming to terms with failure: Private self-enhancement and public self-effacement. *Journal of Experimental Social Psychology, 28*, 3–22.

Bruner, J. S. (1957). On perceptual readiness. *Psychological Review, 64*, 123–152.

Bruner, J. S., & Goodman, C. C. (1947). Value and need as organizing factors in perception. *Journal of Abnormal and Social Psychology, 42*, 33–44.

Bruner, J. S., & Klein, G. S. (1960). The functions of perceiving: New Look retrospective. In S. Wapner & B. Kaplan (Eds.), *Perspectives on psychological theory: Essays in honor of Heinz Werner* (pp. 61–77). New York: International Universities Press.

Buehler, R., Griffin, D., & Ross, M. (1994). Exploring the "planning fallacy": Why people underestimate their task completion times. *Journal of Personality and Social Psychology, 67*, 366–381.

Caccioppo, J. T., & Petty, R. E. (1982). The need for cognition. *Journal of Personality and Social Psychology, 42*, 116–121.

Caccioppo, J. T., Petty, R. E., Feinstein, J. A., & Jarvis, W. B. G. (1996). Dispositional differences in cognitive motivation: The life and times of individuals varying in need for cognition. *Psychological Bulletin, 119*, 197–253.

Cialdini, R. B., Trost, M. R., & Newsom, J. T. (1995). Preference for consistency: The development of a valid measure and the discovery of surprising behavioral implications. *Journal of Personality and Social Psychology, 69*, 318–328.

Clary, E. G., & Tesser, A. (1983). Reactions to unexpected events: The naive scientist and interpretative activity. *Personality and Social Psychology Bulletin, 9*, 609–620.

College Board (1976–1977). *Student descriptive questionnaire.* Princeton, NJ: Educational Testing Service.

Cooper, J., & Fazio, R. H. (1984). A new look at dissonance theory. In L. Berkowitz (Ed.), *Advances in experimental social psychology* Vol. 17 (pp. 229–268). New York: Academic Press.

Crandall, J. E. (1971). Relation of epistemic curiosity to subjective uncertainty. *Journal of Experimental Psychology, 88*, 273–276.

Ditto, P. H., & Lopez, D. L. (1992). Motivated skepticism: Use of differential decision criteria for preferred and nonpreferred conclusions. *Journal of Personality and Social Psychology, 63*, 568–584.

Ditto, P. H., Scepansky, J. A., Munro, G. D., Apanovitch, A. M., & Lockhart, L. K. (1998). Motivated sensitivity to preference-inconsistent information. *Journal of Personality and Social Psychology, 75*, 53–69.

Dunning, D. (1995). Trait importance and modifiability as factors influencing self-assessment and self-enhancement motives. *Personality and Social Psychology Bulletin, 21*, 1297–1306.

Dunning, D., & Cohen, G. L. (1992). Egocentric definitions of traits and abilities in social judgment. *Journal of Personality and Social Psychology, 63*, 341–355.

Dunning, D., Leuenberger, A., & Sherman, D. A. (1995). A new look at motivated inference: Are self-serving theories of success a product of motivational forces? *Journal of Personality and Social Psychology, 69*, 58–68.

Dunning, D., Meyerowitz, J. A., & Holzberg, A. D. (1989). Ambiguity and self-evaluation: The role of idiosyncratic trait definitions in self-serving assessments of ability. *Journal of Personality and Social Psychology, 57*, 1082–1090.

Edwards, J. A., & Weary, G. (1993). Depression and the impression-formation continuum: Piecemeal processing despite the availability of category information. *Journal of Personality and Social Psychology, 64*, 636–645.

Elkin, R., & Leippe, M. (1986). Physiological arousal, dissonance, and attitude change: Evidence for a dissonance–arousal link and a "don't remind me" effect. *Journal of Personality and Social Psychology, 51*, 55–65.

Elliot, A. J., & Devine, P. G. (1994). On the motivational nature of cognitive dissonance: Dissonance as psychological discomfort. *Journal of Personality and Social Psychology, 67*, 382–394.

Erber, R., & Fiske, S. T. (1984). Outcome dependency and attention to inconsistent information. *Journal of Personality and Social Psychology, 47*, 709–726.

Erdelyi, M. H. (1974). A new look at the New Look: Perceptual defense and vigilance. *Psychological Review, 81*, 1–25.

Fazio, R. H., Zanna, M. P., & Cooper, J. (1977). Dissonance and self-perception: An integrative view of each theory's proper domain of application. *Journal of Experimental Social Psychology, 47*, 709–726.

Fein, S., & Spencer, S. J. (1997). Prejudice as self-image maintenance: Affirming the self through derogating others. *Journal of Personality and Social Psychology, 73*, 31–44.

Festinger, L. (1957). *A theory of cognitive dissonance.* Evanston, IL: Row, Peterson.

Freedman, J. L., & Sears, D. O. (1965). Selective exposure. In L. Berkowitz (Ed.), *Advances in experimental social psychology* Vol. 2 (pp. 58–98). San Diego, CA: Academic Press.

Frey, D. (1986). Recent research on selective exposure to information. In L. Berkowitz (Ed.), *Advances in experimental social psychology* Vol. 19 (pp. 41–80). New York: Academic Press.

Gollwitzer, P. M., & Kinney, R. F. (1989). Effects of deliberative and implemental mind-sets on illusion of control. *Journal of Personality and Social Psychology, 56*, 531–542.

Greenwald, A. G. (1980). The totalitarian ego: Fabrication and revision of personal history. *Ameri-*

can *Psychologist, 35,* 608–618.

Greenwald, A. G., & Banaji, M. R. (1995). Implicit social cognition: Attitudes, self-esteem, and stereotypes. *Psychological Review, 102,* 4–27.

Hastie, R. (1984). Causes and effects of causal attribution. *Journal of Personality and Social Psychology, 46,* 44–56.

Heider, F. (1958). *The psychology of interpersonal relations.* New York: Wiley.

Heine, S. J., & Lehman, D. R. (1995). Cultural variation in unrealistic optimism: Does the West feel more invulnerable than the East? *Journal of Personality and Social Psychology, 68,* 595–607.

Heine, S. J., & Lehman, D. R. (1997). Culture, dissonance, and self-affirmation. *Personality and Social Psychology Bulletin, 23,* 389–400.

John, O. P., & Robins, R. W. (1994). Accuracy and bias in self-perception: Individual differences in self-enhancement and the role of narcissism. *Journal of Personality and Social Psychology, 66,* 206–219.

Jones, S. (1979). Curiosity and knowledge. *Psychological Reports, 45,* 639–642.

Kelley, H. H. (1972). Attribution in social interaction. In E. E. Jones, D. E. Kanouse, H. H. Kelley, R. S. Nisbett, S. Valins, & B. Weiner (Eds.), *Attribution: Perceiving the causes of behavior* (pp. 1–26). Morristown, NJ: General Learning Press.

Kruglanski, A. W., & Webster, D. M. (1996). Motivated closing of the mind: "Seizing" and "freezing." *Psychological Review, 103,* 263–283.

Kunda, Z. (1987). Motivated inference: Self-serving generation and evaluation of causal theories. *Journal of Personality and Social Psychology, 53,* 37–54.

Kunda, Z. (1990). The case for motivated reasoning. *Psychological Bulletin, 108,* 480–498.

Langer, E. J. (1975). The illusion of control. *Journal of Personality and Social Psychology, 32,* 311–328.

Lau, R. R., & Russell, D. (1980). Attributions in the sports pages: A field test of some current hypotheses in attribution research. *Journal of Personality and Social Psychology, 39,* 29–38.

Loewenstein, G. (1994). The psychology of curiosity: A review and reinterpretation. *Psychological Bulletin, 116,* 73–98.

Loewenstein, G., Prelec, D., & Shatto, C. (1997). Hot/cold intrapersonal empathy gaps and the prediction of curiosity. Unpublished manuscript, Carnegie Mellon University.

Lord, C. G., Ross, L., & Lepper, M. (1979). Biased assimilation and attitude polarization: The effects of prior theories on subsequently considered evidence. *Journal of Personality and Social Psychology, 37,* 2098–2109.

Markus, H., & Kitayama, S. (1991). Culture and the self: Implications for cognition, emotion, and motivation. *Psychological Review, 98,* 224–253.

Miller, D. T., & Ross, M. (1975). Self-serving biases in the attribution of causality: Fact or fiction? *Psychological Bulletin, 82,* 213–225.

Monson, T. C., Keel, R., Stephens, D., & Genung, V. (1982). Trait attributions: Relative validity, covariation with behavior, and prospect of future interaction. *Journal of Personality and Social Psychology, 42,* 1014–1026.

Mullen, B., & Goethals, G. R. (1990). Social projection, actual consensus and valence. *British Journal of Social Psychology, 29,* 279–282.

Neuberg, S. L., & Fiske, S. T. (1987). Motivational influences on impression formation: Outcome dependency, accuracy-driven attention, and individuating processes. *Journal of Personality and Social Psychology, 53,* 431–444.

Neuberg, S. L., & Newsom, J. T. (1993). Personal need for structure: Individual differences in the desire for simple structure. *Journal of Personality and Social Psychology, 65,* 113–131.

Peng, K. (1997). Naive dialecticism and its effects on reasoning and judgment about contradiction. Unpublished doctoral dissertation, University of Michigan, Ann Arbor.

Pittman, T. S. (1998). Motivation. In D. T. Gilbert, S. T. Fiske, & G. Lindzey (Eds.), *Handbook of social psychology* Vol. 1. 4th. edn. (pp. 459–490). New York: McGraw-Hill.

Pittman, T. S., & D'Agostino, P. R. (1989). Motivation and cognition: Control deprivation and the nature of subsequent information processing. *Journal of Experimental Social Psychology, 25,* 465–480.

Pittman, T. S., & Pittman, N. L. (1980). Deprivation of control and the attribution process. *Journal of Personality and Social Psychology, 39*, 377–389.

Pyszczynski, T. A., & Greenberg, J. (1981). Role of disconfirmed expectancies in the instigation of attributional processing. *Journal of Personality and Social Psychology, 40*, 31–38.

Pyszczynski, T. A., Greenberg, J., & LaPrelle, J. (1985). Maintaining consistency between self-serving beliefs and available data: A bias in information processing. *Personality and Social Psychology Bulletin, 11*, 179–190.

Roney, C. J. R., & Sorrentino, R. M. (1995). Self-evaluation motives and uncertainty orientation: Asking the "who" question. *Personality and Social Psychology Bulletin, 21*, 1319–1329.

Sanitioso, R., Kunda, Z., & Fong, G. (1990). Motivated recruitment of autobiographical memory. *Journal of Personality and Social Psychology, 59*, 229–241.

Schaller, M., Boyd, C., Yohannes, J., & O'Brien, M. (1995). The prejudiced personality revisited: Personal need for structure and formation of erroneous group stereotypes. *Journal of Personality and Social Psychology, 68*, 544–555.

Sedikides, C. (1993). Assessment, enhancement, and verification determinants of the self-evaluation process. *Journal of Personality and Social Psychology, 65*, 317–338.

Sher, S. J., & Cooper, J. (1989). Motivational basis of dissonance: The singular role of behavioral consequences. *Journal of Personality and Social Psychology, 56*, 899–906.

Shultz, T. R., & Lepper, M. R. (1996). Cognitive dissonance as constraint satisfaction. *Psychological Review, 103*, 219–240.

Simon, L., Greenberg, J., & Brehm, J. (1995). Trivialization: The forgotten mode of dissonance reduction. *Journal of Personality and Social Psychology, 68*, 247–260.

Smith, E. R. (1998). Mental representations and memory. In D. T. Gilbert, S. T. Fiske, & G. Lindzey (Eds.), *Handbook of social psychology* Vol. 1. 4th. edn. (pp. 391–445). New York: McGraw-Hill.

Solomon, S., Greenberg, J., & Pyszczynski, T. (1991). A terror management theory of social behavior: The psychological function of self-esteem and cultural worldview. In M. P. Zanna (Ed.), *Advances in experimental social psychology* Vol. 24 (pp. 91–159). San Diego, CA: Academic Press.

Steele, C. M. (1988). The psychology of self-affirmation: Sustaining the integrity of the self. In L. Berkowitz (Ed.), *Advances in experimental social psychology* Vol. 21 (pp. 261–302). San Diego, CA: Academic Press.

Steele, C. M., & Liu, T. J. (1983). Dissonance processes as self-affirmation. *Journal of Personality and Social Psychology, 45*, 5–19.

Steele, C. M., Southwick, L., & Critchlow, B. (1981). Dissonance and alcohol: Drinking your troubles away. *Journal of Personality and Social Psychology, 41*, 831–846.

Stone, J., Aronson, E., Crain, A. L., Winslow, M. P., & Fried, C. B. (1994). Inducing hypocrisy as a means for encouraging young adults to use condoms. *Personality and Social Psychology Bulletin, 20*, 116–128.

Story, A. L. (1998). Self-esteem and memory for favorable and unfavorable personality feedback. *Personality and Social Psychology Bulletin, 24*, 51–64.

Suls, J., & Wan, C. K. (1987). In search of the false uniqueness phenomenon: Fear and estimates of social consensus. *Journal of Personality and Social Psychology, 52*, 211–217.

Swann, W. B., Jr. (1990). To be adored or to be known: The interplay of self-enhancement and self-verification. In R. M. Sorrentino & E. T. Higgins (Eds.), *Foundations of social behavior*, vol. 2 (pp. 408–448). New York: Guilford Press.

Swann, W. B., Jr. (1997). The trouble with change: Self-verification and allegiance to the self. *Psychological Science, 8*, 177–180.

Swann, W. B., Jr., Stein-Serroussi, A., & Geisler, R. B. (1992). Why people self-verify. *Journal of Personality and Social Psychology, 62*, 392–401.

Swann, W. B., Jr., Stephenson, B., & Pittman, T. S. (1981). Curiosity and control: On the determinants of the search for social knowledge. *Journal of Personality and Social Psychology, 40*, 635–642.

Taylor, S. E., & Brown, J. D. (1988). Illusions and well-being: A social psychological perspective on mental health. *Psychological Bulletin, 116*, 193–210.

Taylor, S. E., Neter, E., & Wayment, H. A. (1995). Self-evaluation processes. *Personality and Social*

Psychology Bulletin, 21, 1278–1287.

Tesser, A. (1988). Toward a self-evaluation maintenance model of social behavior. In L. Berkowitz (Ed.), *Advances in experimental social psychology* Vol. 21 (pp. 181–227). New York: Academic Press.

Tesser, A., & Cornell, D. P. (1991). On the confluence of self processes. *Journal of Experimental Social Psychology, 27*, 501–526.

Tesser, A., & Paulhus, D. (1983). The definition of self: Private and public self-evaluation management strategies. *Journal of Personality and Social Psychology, 44*, 672–682.

Tetlock, P. E. (1983). Accountability and complexity of thought. *Journal of Personality and Social Psychology, 45*, 74–83.

Tetlock, P. E. (1992). The impact of accountability on judgment and choice: Toward a social contingency model. In M. Zanna (Ed.), *Advances in experimental social psychology* Vol. 25 (pp. 331–376). San Diego, CA: Academic Press.

Trope, Y. (1980). Self-assessment, self-enhancement, and task performance. *Journal of Experimental Social Psychology, 16*, 116–129.

Trope, Y. (1986). Self-enhancement and self-assessment in achievement behavior. In R. M. Sorrentino, & E. T. Higgins (Eds.), *Handbook of motivation and cognition: Foundations of social behavior* (pp. 350–378). New York: Guilford Press.

Tucker, J. A., Vuchinich, R. E., & Sobell, M. B. (1981). Alcohol consumption as a self-handicapping strategy. *Journal of Abnormal Psychology, 20*, 220–230.

Vallone, R. P., Griffin, D. W., Lin, S., & Ross, L. (1990). Overconfident prediction of future actions and outcomes by self and others. *Journal of Personality and Social Psychology, 58*, 582–592.

Weiner, B. (1985). "Spontaneous" causal thinking. *Psychological Bulletin, 97*, 74–84.

Weinstein, N. D. (1980). Unrealistic optimism about future life events. *Journal of Personality and Social Psychology, 39*, 806–820.

Wills, T. A. (1981). Downward comparison principles in social psychology. *Psychological Bulletin, 90*, 245–271.

Zanna, M. P., & Cooper, J. (1974). Dissonance and the pill: An attribution approach to studying the arousal properties of dissonance. *Journal of Personality and Social Psychology, 29*, 703–709.

Zuckerman, M. L. (1979). Attribution of success and failure, or: The motivational bias is alive and well. *Journal of Personality, 47*, 245–287.

Chapter Seventeen

The Nature of Emotion

W. Gerrod Parrott

Most topics studied by social psychologists involve emotion in some way. Consider how cognitive dissonance is motivated by anxiety about self-esteem, or how conformity is influenced by the embarrassment of conspicuous deviation and the contentment of belonging. The list is impressively long: social comparisons generate envy, dejection, and pride; social anxiety underlies many group processes; romantic relationships have their love and jealousy, aggression its anger, altruism its sympathy, and persuasive communications almost any emotion one can name. Emotions, then, are at the heart of many social psychological phenomena.

This chapter presents an overview of perspectives on the nature of emotion. The first section discusses foundational issues in the study of emotion, including its definitions, the functions of emotion, and the general approaches that have been taken in studying it. The general thesis is that emotion spans all of the levels of analysis that psychologists apply to their subject matter: to reduce them to three, these are the social and cultural, the cognitive, and the physiological. The remainder of this chapter describes emotion at each of these three levels and presents some of the most important issues and findings that may be gleaned from each.

Definitions, Conceptions, and Basic Issues

Defining emotion

Although there is no single, agreed-upon definition of emotion, there is considerable consensus that emotional states are best thought of as processes that unfold in time, involving a variety of components. Whether these components are necessarily or only typically part of emotions is a matter of some debate. The beginning of an emotional episode typically includes an evaluative perception of the nature of the situation, known as an *appraisal*

(Lazarus, 1991). An emotional appraisal evaluates events or objects as significantly affecting a person's concerns, goals, or values in a positive or negative way. The presence of appraisals is one reason why many theorists have argued that emotions have a cognitive aspect (e.g. Solomon, 1976), although, as I will discuss later, not all theorists are persuaded that appraisals are necessary.

Emotional reactions can involve changes in thinking, behavior, physiology, and expression. The effects of these changes may influence readiness to think and act in certain ways, as well as signal this readiness to others, thereby affecting social interaction and relationships. The development of an emotion over time depends on how the situation is evaluated and coped with. In a narrow sense, an emotional state ends when attention is drawn to another issue, but, in a larger sense, the emotional episode may be said to continue until such point as the evaluation of the event changes significantly (Frijda, Mesquita, Sonnemans, & Van Goozen, 1991). In summary, then, an emotion can be loosely defined as a reaction to personally significant events, where "reaction" is taken to include biological, cognitive, and behavioral reactions, as well as subjective feelings of pleasure or displeasure. The issues surrounding the definition of emotion have been reviewed in several recent volumes (e.g. Ekman & Davidson, 1994; Russell, Fernández-Dols, Manstead, & Wellenkamp, 1995).

Even with such a loose definition it is important to realize that the meaning of "emotion" in academic psychology often differs somewhat from that in ordinary language. First of all, the general term "emotion" plus the terms for specific emotions such as "sadness" and "shame" are all words in the English language, and these words often have no precise equivalents in other languages (Wierzbicka, 1992). Whether psychologists can or should strive for definitions that span cultural and linguistic boundaries is unclear (Russell, et al., 1995). Second, the everyday connotation of "emotion" often includes the judgment that the response is in some way exceptional, such as by being excessive, inappropriate, dysfunctional, immoral, or praiseworthy. Emotion terms have developed for the purposes of everyday speakers of the language; these purposes often include judgments of the appropriateness of a person's actions, but social psychologists do not necessarily share those purposes. Finally, in everyday usage, the term "emotion" refers to a wide range of phenomena that have little in common. The concept of emotion is fuzzy around the edges. For example, there is little doubt that anger and sadness are emotions, but there is less agreement about whether to include moods (depression, irritability), long-term emotions (love that continues for years), dispositions (benevolence, cantankerousness), motivational feelings (hunger, sexual arousal), cognitive feelings (confusion, *deja vu*), and "calm" emotions (sympathy, satisfaction).

If the goals of research require fidelity to everyday usage, loose definitions of emotion appear to be the best that are possible. In order to be true to the everyday usage of the word "emotion," many investigators have proposed that its meaning be represented as a "fuzzy category" with no precise definition (Fehr & Russell, 1984). This representation is often proposed to have the structure of a script or narrative (Shaver, Schwartz, Kirson, & O'Connor, 1987). On the other hand, if the goals of research are to develop objective understanding of aspects of emotion independent of folk conceptions, the preferred strategy may be to develop more precise definitions independent of everyday usage (Clore & Ortony, 1991). For example, for purposes of research it may be helpful to postulate attributes that will be considered necessary and sufficient for a psychological event to be considered an emotion. Researchers seeking this latter goal must be careful to distinguish their concepts from everyday conceptions that may bear the same labels.

Relation of emotions to other aspects of mind

For centuries, philosophers and psychologists have found it convenient to distinguish between different aspects of the mind. Plato, in *The Republic*, has Socrates argue that the soul can be divided into three parts: an appetitive part that produces various irrational desires, a spirited part that produces anger and other feelings, and a reasoning part that permits reflection and rationality. This tricotomy shows similarity to one expressed in contemporary psychology between *conation*, the aspect of mind directed toward action, *affect*, the aspect of mind involving subjective feeling, and *cognition*, the aspect of mind involving thought.

It is certainly legitimate to observe that mental activity involves these aspects, and there is no doubt that a valid conceptual distinction can be made between them. Nevertheless, disagreement and confusion has resulted from these distinctions because some psychologists have treated these *aspects* of the mind as if they were *distinct parts* of the mind, whereas others have not. The rationale for separating these aspects of mind is usually based on the fact that people sometimes feel an emotion that they believe to be irrational, or fail to feel an emotion they believe to be warranted. Such conflicts can make it appear that motivation, emotion, and cognition can act as independent entities, and some theorists have been persuaded to adopt such a view, although it then becomes necessary to account for the many ways that these entities influence one another (see chapter 18, this volume). Other theorists, however, stress that emotions have both cognitive and motivational qualities, and therefore think of these elements as referring to different *aspects* of mental events, not as corresponding to actual separations within the mind (e.g. Peters, 1958).

Level of analysis

In any science, phenomena can be studied at any of several levels of analysis. For example, in the physical sciences water can be considered from the points of view of the elementary particles and forces of physics, or of the atoms and molecules of chemistry. In the biological sciences evolution can likewise be studied at a variety of levels, ranging from molecular genetics to ecology. The same is true in psychology, with emotion serving as a good example. Emotion can be studied in terms of biology, of thinking, and of the social context. The choice of level of analysis determines a number of important aspects of research, including the choice of measures. On the biological level, emotions are measured in terms of activity in the nervous system and in terms of changes in the periphery of the body (e.g. sweaty palms, muscle tension). On the cognitive level, measures might include people's ratings of their beliefs about the cause of a certain event, their expectations that a certain action will bring about a certain end, or their attention toward or away from certain classes of stimuli. On the social level, measures might include the amount of time people spend making eye contact, changes in how people are perceived, or changes in interpersonal relationships.

Other levels of analysis could be distinguished from these, but these three are sufficient to illustrate the basic point, which is that no one level of analysis is more central or more "scientific" than any other. Each addresses important aspects of emotion, and a complete understanding of emotional phenomena often requires that insights from all three be combined.

Function

What is the function of the emotions? Some have construed emotions as either dysfunctional or, at best, as lacking function. For example, the Stoics, such as Epictetus and Marcus Aurelius, believed that (most) emotions were the result of erroneous thought and should be avoided. More recently, Charles Darwin (1872/1955) understood emotional expressions as vestigial movements that formerly had functions in our evolutionary past but are now mostly useless, and philosopher Jean-Paul Sartre (1948) characterized emotions as ways of avoiding responsibility and truth. Arguments for the dysfunctionality of emotions thus encompass the biological, cognitive, and social levels of analysis.

Others, however, have maintained that emotions serve a variety of useful functions, and their functionalist approaches to emotions can be found at all levels of analysis, too. Ironically, the theory that has been most influential in this regard is that of Darwin, whose theory of natural selection, not his theory of vestigial emotional expression, has formed the basis of post-Darwinian evolutionary biology. Evolutionists use the theory of natural selection to understand emotions as adaptations that often serve useful functions. They argue that, although emotions can sometimes be maladaptive or inappropriate, anything as common and significant as emotions must have been subject to evolutionary pressures, so animals possessing emotions must have had some advantages over animals that did not. This argument, of course, leaves open the possibility that emotions were advantageous to our ancestors in their habitats but are no longer useful to us in ours. There are some emotions that seem to be of this latter type: some of our reactions to stress, such as increases of heart rate and of certain hormone levels, seem much more useful in fleeing from predators than in preparing for presentations, and these responses may be responsible for such stress-related illnesses as heart attacks and stomach ulcers (Selye, 1976). But, on the whole, it is generally thought that emotions serve useful roles of various sorts. At the biological level, they can be viewed as preparing the body for actions that are usually adaptive in the situations that produce the emotion (Frijda, 1986). Functionalism may be found at the cognitive level of analysis as well. The theory of Oatley & Johnson-Laird (1987) finds functionality in the way that emotions alter a person's priorities, thereby serving to allocate limited resources among multiple plans and goals. At the social level, emotions' functions have been examined in units as small as the interactive dyad (e.g. communication of social intentions: Fridlund, 1994) and as large as an entire culture (e.g. to express and fortify cultural values and social structures: Lutz, 1988). For a thorough review of functionalist perspectives see Gross & Keltner (in press).

This range of opinions about the functionality of emotions can be rather confusing. It may be that it results in part from confusions between the academic and everyday meanings of "emotion." Theorists using the everyday sense may be more likely than theorists using an academic definition to consider cases that are irrational, that result from ulterior motives such as the need for self-esteem, or that are otherwise especially likely to be maladaptive. Yet the disagreements are not only definitional. Another problem is that emotions do not have fixed effects; any given category of emotion, such as anger or happiness, can motivate a variety of expressions and actions, and socialization and choice of self-regulation strategies can have an enormous effect on whether a particular emotion is adaptive or maladaptive (Parrott, in press). Perhaps a reasonable compromise position is that emotions have the potential to be functional and adaptive, but only if socialized and regulated to be appropriate for the particular context in which they occur. Further research on the ways in which emotions may be functional or dysfunctional would be helpful in improving understanding of this issue.

Social and Cultural Approaches to Emotion

To take a social approach to emotion is to focus on how emotion pertains to social situations and relationships. Many emotions have to do with our appearance to others, our relationships with others, our duties toward others, and our expectations of others. Communication, culture, and the social functions of individual emotions thus form the main emphases of the social approach.

Communication

The social nature of emotion is apparent when considering how people communicate their emotions to others and how they recognize others' emotions. Considerable research has investigated the ways in which such communication takes place in humans and animals. Charles Darwin (1872/1955) is the person most responsible for directing attention to expressions of emotion. Research by Ekman (1973) and others has extended Darwin's work, suggesting that there exists a set of human facial expressions that are universally recognizable and innate. These facial expressions include those of sadness, fear, joy, anger, disgust, and surprise.

Certain limitations to the research paradigms employed to date have led some to question the validity of this conclusion. The use of still photographs of posed facial expressions and of forced-choice response formats, for example, might compromise the validity and ecological relevance of the findings (Russell, 1994). Moreover, controversy exists about how to interpret the meaning of facial expressions. According to Ekman, facial expressions of emotion automatically occur when emotions are experienced. To some extent, they may be suppressed, modified, or exaggerated to conform with social conventions, known as *display rules,* but there nevertheless exists an innate connection between facial expressions and emotional experience. This theory has been challenged by Fridlund (1994), who argues that facial expressions of emotion do not so much express an inner emotional state as they communicate intentions and wishes to others. At present there does not seem to be decisive evidence favoring either approach. The disagreement has spurred a new wave of theory and research on nonverbal expressions (see Russell & Fernández-Dols, 1997). Future theoretical developments may well involve a combination of current theories.

Social constructionism

The current debate about facial expressions addresses a second issue as well, the question of whether emotions are universal or differ across cultures. The position that emotions are universal is well represented by Ekman's approach, and is usually justified in terms of the genetic basis of human emotionality, which is approached at the biological level of analysis described later in this chapter. The position that human emotions are shaped by particular cultures is necessarily approached at the social and cultural level of analysis. *Social constructionism* is the thesis that, to some extent, emotions are the products of culture. (See Harré, 1986, and Harré & Parrott, 1996, for collections of articles reflecting this approach.)

   According to social constructionists, human cultures influence the emotions by influencing the beliefs, values, and social environment that members of the culture possess. The emotions may be understood as being enmeshed within an entire system of beliefs and values, so an emotion can hardly be said to exist independent of the culture of which it is a part. Consider, for example, an emotion that existed in Western cultures in medieval times but seems to have become extinct by the year 1400 or so: *accidie*. Accidie occurred when one was bored with one's religious duties and procrastinated in carrying them out; one felt both bored and also sad about one's religious failings and the loss of one's former enthusiasm for religious devotions. The cure for accidie was to resume one's religious duties and to feel joyful in doing so. The emotion was intimately tied to a set of moral values concerning one's religious duties; to feel it at all was a sin. The emotion faded from existence when values changed during the Renaissance. Now, when people in Western cultures are bored and procrastinate, they feel guilt, an emotion that is related to a culture based on individual responsibility, not one of spiritual duty (Harré & Finlay-Jones, 1986). The implication is that cultural beliefs and values make certain emotions possible, and that the same culture may permit a somewhat different set of emotions at one time than at another.

   A similar point can be made about two different cultures existing at the same time. The anthropologist Lutz (1988) argues that the emphasis on social relationships and sharing that exists in the South Pacific atoll of Ifaluk gives rise to emotions that are not equivalent to any Western emotion. *Fago*, for example, is something like our sadness, but it differs by being specific to a close relationship toward a less fortunate person – a person in need – to whom one feels compassion. This point has been made by studying a culture in depth, as Lutz did, and also by comparing multiple cultures. For example, Markus & Kitayama (1991) have argued that cultures may be plotted along a dimension of self-construal that ranges from being relatively independent with others at one extreme to being relatively interdependent of others at the other. They argue that "ego-focused" emotions such as anger, frustration, and pride will be experienced more by people with relatively independent selves, whereas "other-focused" emotions such as shame, belongingness, and sympathy will be experienced more by people with relatively interdependent selves. (For a review of cultural perspectives in social psychology, see chapter 2, this volume.)

Social functions of emotions

Regardless of whether emotions are considered to be universal or culturally relative, the social level of analysis is characterized by attention to the ways that emotions function in social situations. This attention is often best directed to particular emotions rather than to the broad category of emotion in general. For example, anger has been found to play important roles in the regulation of interpersonal behavior in many North American cultures. Anger is part of a system that enforces normative standards, arising when a person interprets another's actions as a voluntary, unjustified transgression, and often functioning to repair the relationship between the angry person and the target of the anger (Averill, 1982).

Studies of shame, guilt, and embarrassment have suggested that these emotions can function to motivate behavior that conforms to social and moral norms and that makes restitution for past misdeeds. Shame is generally found to focus on the adequacy of a person's self, or on the exposure of that self to public disapproval; guilt, in contrast, is generally found to focus more on particular misdeeds and to be more the result of a person's private conscience than of public exposure (for a comprehensive review, see Tangney & Fischer, 1995). Embarrassment is in some ways similar to shame, in that it is linked to public exposure, but may be distinguished from it in several ways: unlike shame, it does not require belief that one is immoral or defective, and it is not experienced in private. Embarrassment results from the perception that the present social situation is socially awkward, often (but not necessarily) because others perceive the self in some negative way. Embarrassment thus motivates people to mind how they are perceived by others, to behave in role-consistent ways, and generally to conform (for a review, see Miller, 1996).

Envy and jealousy may also be considered from the standpoint of their social functions. "Envy" refers to the painful or negative emotion experienced toward a person who has what oneself wants but lacks. It typically includes a mix of hostility and inferiority. The emotion can motivate achievement and innovation to catch up with the rival, or hostility to undercut the rival's advantage. There is wide variation in the extent to which expression of envy is tolerated in different cultures, and thus in the extent to which it is necessary for those with enviable qualities to fear the envy of others (Schoeck, 1969). Because of fear of envy, self-presentations often conceal or downplay a person's successes and advantages. The word "jealousy" can be used to refer to envy, but it can also be used to refer to a quite different type of emotional reaction, one that requires a more complex set of relationships among three people rather than just two. Jealousy, in this sense, is an emotion that occurs when one person perceives that his or her relationship with another person is threatened by a rival who could take the jealous person's place. Like envy, jealousy comes in a variety of forms, but these generally may be seen as motivating a person to protect and nurture the threatened relationship or, if it is too late for that, to cope with its loss. Salovey (1991) provides a good collection of articles on envy and jealousy.

There are, of course, many more emotions that can be studied at the social level of analysis, but this sample will serve to illustrate the approach.

Cognitive Approaches to Emotion

The way people think is clearly related to their emotions. This is not to say, of course, that the social or the biological approach is "wrong," only that it is often helpful to talk about emotions as a set of beliefs or a mode of information processing rather than as a social role or a set of events in the brain (even though the cognitions are socialized by culture and require brain activity). On the cognitive level of analysis certain truths about emotion are more readily apparent than at other levels of analysis.

One clear advantage of the cognitive level is that it facilitates discussion of a person's beliefs. Emotions usually occur because events have been interpreted in a certain way, and, once emotions occur, people often think in a somewhat altered manner. Thus, certain types of thinking characteristically precede emotion, and emotions themselves involve ways of thinking as well as social functions and bodily responses. Each of these cognitive aspects of emotion has been the topic of investigation by psychologists.

Appraisal

The thinking that leads to emotion is usually called the *appraisal*. It is characterized by an assessment of the current situation and its implications for the well-being of oneself and the things that one cares about. The classic experiments demonstrating the importance of appraisals in emotions were performed by Richard Lazarus, who asked people to watch movies showing extremely unpleasant scenes of people being mutilated in primitive rites or in woodworking accidents. Before viewing the films, some of the people were encouraged to interpret the filmed events as harmful and painful, whereas others were encouraged to deny the extent of the harm and interpret them as benign, and still others were encouraged to distance themselves from the victims and view the scenes in a more detached, intellectual manner. All of the people then viewed the same films, yet the first group experienced more stress and more intense, negative emotions than did the other two groups. After the film Lazarus asked the viewers to describe how they were feeling, and he also measured certain physiological symptoms of autonomic nervous system activity; the groups differed on both the self-report and the physiological measures. These experiments demonstrated how changes in cognitive appraisal could produce differences in the intensity of emotions that occur (Lazarus, 1966).

There is controversy over the type of judgments that should be included in the concept of "appraisal." Some appraisals are quite careful and deliberate, as when one thinks through a remark one heard and only gradually realizes that it was inconsiderate and derogatory to oneself – and then one becomes angry. Many times, however, it seems that appraisals, if they indeed play a role in producing emotions, must be very quick, outside conscious awareness, and independent of our rational faculties.

There are two ways to resolve this dilemma, and a lively debate over which alternative is better occurred in the pages of *American Psychologist* (Lazarus, 1982, 1984; Zajonc, 1980, 1984). One resolution was advocated by Robert Zajonc (1980), who proposed that cognition and emotion may be conceived as two independent systems, often working together, but capable of being at odds. Zajonc's theory can account for discrepancies between emotion and reason, but it does so in a manner that creates many problems. Why is it possible to call certain emotions "irrational" if emotions do not intrinsically entail beliefs? Why does emotional development seem to require cognitive development (e.g. children don't get embarrassed until they know about social roles and appearances)? Most emotions are "about" something, such as "not studying for the test," but it seems necessary to be cognitive to be "about" something. In short, there is a host of problems with proposing a separation between emotion and cognition (Lazarus, 1982; Solomon, 1976). The most important problem is the fact that the way in which a person thinks about a situation obviously affects how he or she feels. If one becomes angry when one discovers that one's friend has once again left a pile of dirty dishes in the sink, and then discovers that the friend had been about to do the dishes when he received news about the death of his father, one's anger goes away and different emotions (surprise at the news, feeling sorry for your friend) take its place. The dual system account appears to deal only awkwardly with such an ordinary case.

A different alternative to Zajonc's "dual system" solution is suggested by such theorists as Lazarus (1982) and Beck (1976), both of whom view emotion as always linked to cognition. The key to their solutions is a claim that is routinely made about non-emotional cognition as well, namely, that there are *different types* of cognition, and that not all cognition is conscious, deliberate, or verbal (Parrott & Sabini, 1989).

Recognizing that cognition can be difficult to control and that people can perseverate in beliefs that they recognize to be undesirable permits one to account for conflicts between emotion and reason in a manner that nevertheless conceives of emotion as involving cognition, and many psychologists prefer this solution for this reason. Other psychologists prefer Zajonc's dual systems solution. More recent criticisms of research on appraisal have focused on whether appraisals are necessary causes of emotion. Critics contend that appraisals are but one of many causes of emotions, some of which are best understood at the social or physiological levels of analysis (Parkinson, 1997). Continuing debate over this issue can be expected in years to come.

Regardless of the outcome of this debate, it is clear that in most cases there is a good deal of agreement between a person's way of thinking and the emotions that person feels, and much research has been directed at characterizing the types of assessment that are associated with different emotions. That is, what thoughts lead to what emotions? Logical and experimental analysis suggests that emotions can be classified according to the type of beliefs that underlie them (Ortony, Clore, & Collins, 1988). Many emotions have to do with reactions to events, and these emotions can be subcategorized according to whether the event is judged simply according to desirability (joy) or undesirability (distress), or whether further judgments are also involved. For example, if the event is desirable for *another* person, one may be pleased about this (happy-for) or displeased (resentment). And if one is anticipating a future event, one may have an emotion if this event would be desirable (hope) or undesirable (fear). And if one has pleasant anticipations, they may later be dashed (disappointment) or confirmed (satisfaction), and if one has unpleasant anticipations, they too may later go unrealized (relief), or be confirmed ("fear confirmed"). For other emotions the cognitive focus is less on the event itself than it is on the people who are *responsible* for the event. If other people are believed to be the agents responsible for the event, then one may find their actions praiseworthy (admiration) or blameworthy (contempt). If one believes oneself to be responsible for the event, then one may find one's own actions to be praiseworthy (pride) or blameworthy (shame). Some emotions seem to combine assessments of responsibility with assessments of the consequences of the events for oneself or for others; emotions such as anger, gratitude, remorse, and gratification are of this hybrid type. Anger, for example, combines distress over an undesired event with reproach of an agent responsible for producing it (Ortony, Clore, & Collins, 1988). Still other emotions seem related not to events or agents, but to our overall liking or disliking of a person or object: love and hate are common examples of this class. A variety of schemes for representing the appraisals associated with various emotions have been proposed, such as appraisal components or themes (for a review, see Smith & Pope, 1992).

Several conclusions may be drawn from these attempts at classification. First, not all emotion words correspond to a single, simple appraisal as do the ones mentioned above. Jealousy, for example, refers not so much to a single appraisal as to an entire syndrome of appraisals and emotions that are likely to occur in a certain situation, namely, when one faces the threat of losing a valued relationship to a rival. Envy (as used in modern English) similarly can refer to anything from longing or admiration of someone who has something desired by oneself to hatred of that person for being superior. It is therefore possible to distinguish single emotions from what might be called emotional *episodes* (Parrott, 1991).

It also becomes clear that the *concepts* of emotions that are being developed by researchers are not identical with the *emotion words* used in everyday language. For example, in the classification described above there is clearly a logical place for an emotion in which a person is pleased that an undesirable event has happened to another person – and, in fact, most people have experienced such pleasure at another's misfortune. The English language, however, does not have a good word for such an emotion. German does, though: they call it *schadenfreude*. This example illustrates that the correspondence between our language and our experience is imperfect.

Finally, analysis of emotional appraisals suggests the sort of things that determine what people get emotional about and thus, in a sense, what people care about. They care about their goals, plans, and values; they care about social relationships; they care about duties and responsibilities; they care about the good and evil in people's characters. It is assessments along these lines that define and distinguish the various emotions. There is no one perfect classification scheme for emotions. Which classification is best depends on one's purposes.

Emotion's effects on cognition

Given that cognition leads to emotion in these ways, what can be learned about how people think once they are emotional? Answers to this question tend to be of two types. Some accounts depict emotional thought as being biased by a person's *motivation*. Because it is often possible to construe events in more than one way, people may have a tendency to select interpretations that are most consistent with the way they wish the world to be. (See chapter 16, this volume, for a review of motivated biases.)

Not all accounts of emotional bias invoke motivation, however; some emotional biases can be explained as the result of normal judgmental or memory processes. Being in an emotional state, say, of anger, may provide information about one's present situation (Schwarz, 1990), or may tend to remind one of previous times when one has been angry and of beliefs that are consistent with being angry (Blaney, 1986). (See chapter 18, this volume, for more detail about the ways in which emotions affect people's thinking.)

Two-factor theory

One application of the cognitive approach to emotion has come from investigating people's understanding of the causes of their own emotional feelings. Studies conducted in 1924 by the Spanish physician Gregorio Marañon suggested that most people injected with adrenalin reported feeling no emotion at all, or felt "as if" they were emotional but only in a cold or empty way. A very few people felt a genuine emotion, and these appeared to be people who had been thinking about emotional situations in their present lives. These findings led Stanley Schachter to propose that emotions consist of two components: physiological arousal *plus* cognitive attributions linking the arousal with emotional circumstances believed to have caused it (Schachter & Singer, 1962). This theory gave rise to an enormous amount of research over the following two decades in which researchers investigated its implications.

The one implication that has received consistent experimental support is that arousal from one source can intensify an emotion unrelated to the true source of the arousal. For example, people who are aroused because they have recently gotten off an exercise bicycle may feel angrier and act more aggressively after being insulted than do people lacking arousal. The people apparently feel angrier because they attribute their arousal to having been insulted. Evidence supporting this claim comes from findings that there is no increase in anger immediately after getting off the bicycle – at this point people have plenty of arousal, but they are aware that exercise caused it so do not attribute it to anger. Six minutes after getting off the bicycle there again is no increase in anger – at this point there is no more arousal. Two minutes after getting off the bicycle, however, people do feel more anger, apparently because they no longer attribute their lingering arousal to bike riding and instead misattribute it to having been insulted (Zillmann, 1979). Such findings, plus the original Marañon experiment, support the idea that Schachter's two-factor theory describes a genuine phenomenon, but this theory cannot seriously be considered as a general account of emotions. As will be described later, arousal is not necessary for emotional experience. Furthermore, the support for most other predictions of the theory is lacking (Reisenzein, 1983).

Physiological Approaches to Emotion

Physiological approaches to emotion may be divided into two types. The first type emphasizes the bodily symptoms of emotions: the pounding heart, dry mouth, sweaty palms, and "butterflies in the stomach" that are characteristic of many powerful emotions. This approach emphasizes regions of the body that lie beyond the brain and spinal cord in the periphery of the nervous system, and for this reason it may be termed the *peripheral approach* to emotion. The second physiological approach to emotion has the opposite emphasis, on brain activities that appear to be responsible for emotions. It may be termed the *central approach* to emotion.

The peripheral approach

The most influential statement of the peripheral approach was made by William James (1884), who tried to account for why emotions have the feeling qualities that they do. James proposed what he intended to be a very counterintuitive theory, namely, that emotional feelings are simply the awareness of various bodily changes. If one encounters a ferocious bear, James said, one first perceives the bear, and then one's body responds to this perception with increased heart rate, greater blood flow to the leg muscles, deeper breathing, widening of the eyes, and so forth. Emotions, James claimed, are nothing other than the awareness of such bodily changes – there is no "emotion" that precedes such changes.

The strength of James's theory is that it attempts to account for the "feel" of emotions, a task that most psychologists have shied away from despite its centrality to many conceptions of emotion. But there are many problems with James's view, some factual and some conceptual. One central prediction of the theory must be recognized in order to understand its problems. If we allow that there can be more than one type of emotion, and if emotions are simply our awareness of bodily changes, then it follows that different emotions must be characterized by different patterns of bodily changes and that these changes are what distinguish the emotions for us. This prediction has not fared well.

The most famous of the many attacks on James's theory was made by Walter Cannon (1927), who was an expert on the autonomic nervous system. One of the two parts of the autonomic nervous system, the sympathetic nervous system (SNS), is closely associated with many of the bodily responses characteristic of powerful emotions: it produces the "arousal" that formed part of Schachter's two-factor theory. The SNS controls a variety of responses that may be easily understood in terms of a scheme invented by Cannon himself: the SNS produces changes in the body that are needed for the *fight-or-flight response*. That is, in many emergency situations it is adaptive for animals to be able to mobilize all of the energy they can muster for a relatively short, intense burst of life-saving activity – to fight for its life or to flee from a predator or to escape from some catastrophe. The SNS affects the body so that adrenalin is produced, oxygen is absorbed, blood is pumped, energy is burned, and muscles work at their peak capacity. Cannon's research led him to conclude that the fight-or-flight response is almost always the same for such intense but otherwise different-seeming emotions as rage and fear. He also knew that the full SNS response often takes a second or more to occur, whereas people seem to experience emotions without such a delay. Furthermore, such non-emotional causes as exercise and fevers produce SNS arousal without emotional experience, and injections of adrenalin do not cause most people to feel an emotion. These and other facts persuaded Cannon that emotion could not be equated with the awareness of emotion-like changes in the body.

Subsequent investigations have supported most of Cannon's criticisms of James. Consider recent research on people who have suffered spinal cord injuries. Some spinal cord injuries not only confine people to wheelchairs, but also prevent them from receiving sensations from much of their bodies. If emotional feeling were dependent on sensations from the body, one would expect such people to experience emotions less strongly, but this is not the case – they experience emotions as intensely as they did before their injuries, as intensely as do people without injuries, and as intensely as people who have spinal cord injuries that do not block feelings from the body (Chwalisz, Diener, & Gallagher, 1988).

A conceptual problem also exists for James's theory. His claim – that people first perceive an event and then their bodies respond – appears to beg a crucial question: how does the body know how to respond appropriately? Clearly, what James called "perception" must involve more than just that. The event must be interpreted and evaluated for significance to some extent before an appropriate response can be made. The need for such an evaluation – an appraisal – is one of the main reasons that the physiological approach to emotion can be usefully supplemented by cognitive and social approaches.

But just because SNS arousal is not necessary for our emotional feelings it does not mean that this activity cannot contribute to our emotional experience or that it is not an important part of an emotional response. There is some evidence that bodily feelings contribute somewhat to emotional experience – smiling does seem to make people feel a bit happier than they do when not smiling, for example – but the contribution to emotional intensity seems fairly small compared to other factors such as the significance of the event (Laird, 1984). Emotional bodily changes evolved because they prepare the body to function in adaptive ways. Powerful emotions are characterized by a preparedness for emergency activity, and bodily changes are part of this preparation. Not all emotions are like this, however – consider sadness. Autonomic changes can also function as signs that a person is emotional; sometimes people recognize emotion in themselves and in others by noting the presence of SNS arousal, and the detection of such activity is the basis of so-called "lie detector" testing. A review of the peripheral approach to emotion may be found in Cornelius (1996).

The central approach

In response to Cannon's critique of James in the 1920s, researchers taking a physiological approach to emotion increasingly began to adopt what may be termed the *central approach*. Other researchers joined Cannon in proposing that there exist structures in the brain that are responsible for controlling many aspects of emotions, including the SNS. Papez (1937) and MacLean (1970) proposed that an interconnected set of structures located near the middle of the brain – called the *limbic system* – produced emotional feelings and responses.

Evidence for this claim is of several types. It is possible to stimulate activity in nerves by applying small amounts of electrical current to them, and stimulation of parts of the limbic system can produce emotional behavior. Damage to parts of the limbic system alters emotional behavior. Humans with epilepsy that alters the activity of the limbic system can undergo dramatic changes in emotion. Drugs that alter moods are known to work on the nerves in the limbic system. Diseases that damage parts of the nervous system produce changes in mood and emotional behavior. For example, one part of the limbic system is a structure called the *amygdala*. Stimulation of regions of the amygdala can produce aggressive behavior, whereas damage to it can result in the reduction of aggression. Epileptic seizures focused on the amygdala can cause humans to go into a rage and violently attack others, and surgical removal of these regions (as last-resort treatment of epilepsy) can end these episodes of rage. Rabies is known to produce violent behavior, and it causes damage to the nervous system, particularly in the region around the amygdala. A few violent criminals have been found to have had brain tumors near the amygdala. Although there are good reasons to be cautious in interpreting these types of evidence, there does appear to be a general trend across many types of evidence linking structures in the limbic system to emotional thinking, feelings, and behavior (Frijda, 1986). A well-known synthesis of research in the centralist tradition would be that of LeDoux (1993).

Certain assumptions of the central approach do seem valid, then. It is possible to learn about emotions by studying the brain structures and processes that are associated with them. It is important to understand that the discovery of physiological processes linked with emotion does not mean that emotions are "just physiological," however. The functions of the limbic areas appear to be linked to the evaluations, judgments, and feelings that go into emotion and to a variety of social and sexual functions. Emotions' cognitive and social aspects require brain processes to occur and emotions can be studied on that level, but they cannot be understood completely without considering all three levels of explanation.

Conclusion

In this chapter we have seen how emotion has been studied in psychology at three different levels of analysis: the physiological, the cognitive, and the social and cultural. Insights have been gained from all three levels, and it should now be clear that the levels are complementary, not contradictory. The fact that different cultures can have somewhat different emotions in no way implies that these emotions do not have cognitive or physiological aspects as well, nor does the fact that modern antidepressant medications might have "cured" accidie imply that this emotion did not require a certain set of beliefs and institutions. One of the most important tasks of psychology is to understand the interrelations between these different aspects of emotion, and social psychologists are well-positioned to contribute to that understanding.

References

Averill, J. R. (1982). *Anger and aggression: An essay on emotion.* New York: Springer.
Beck, A. T. (1976). *Cognitive therapy and the emotional disorders.* New York: Meridian.
Blaney, P. H. (1986). Affect and memory: A review. *Psychological Bulletin, 99,* 229–246.
Cannon, W. B. (1927). The James–Lange theory of emotions: A critical examination and an alternative theory. *American Journal of Psychology, 39,* 106–124.

Chwalisz, K., Diener, E., & Gallagher, D. (1988). Autonomic arousal feedback and emotional experience: Evidence from the spinal cord injured. *Journal of Personality and Social Psychology, 54*, 820–828.

Clore, G. L., & Ortony, A. (1991). What more is there to emotion concepts than prototypes? *Journal of Personality and Social Psychology, 60*, 48–50.

Cornelius, R. R. (1996). *The science of emotion: Research and tradition in the psychology of emotions.* Upper Saddle River, NJ: Prentice Hall.

Darwin, C. (1872/1955). *The expression of the emotions in man and animals.* New York: Greenwood Press.

Ekman, P. (1973). Cross-cultural studies of facial expression. In P. Ekman (Ed.), *Darwin and facial expression: A century of research in review* (pp. 169–229). New York: Academic Press.

Ekman, P., & Davidson, R. J. (1994). *The nature of emotion: Fundamental questions.* New York: Oxford University Press.

Fehr, B., & Russell, J. A. (1984). Concept of emotion viewed from a prototype perspective. *Journal of Experimental Psychology: General, 113*, 474–486.

Fridlund, A. J. (1994). *Human facial expression: An evolutionary view.* San Diego, CA: Academic Press.

Frijda, N. H. (1986). *The emotions.* Cambridge, UK: Cambridge University Press.

Frijda, N. H., Mesquita, B., Sonnemans, J., & Van Goozen, S. (1991). The duration of affective phenomena or emotions, sentimenta and passions. In K. T. Strongman (Ed.), *International review of emotion* Vol. 1 (pp 187–255). Chichester, UK: Wiley.

Gross, J., & Keltner, D. (in press). *The functions of emotion: A special issue of Cognition and Emotion.* Hove, UK: Psychology Press.

Harré, R. (Ed.) (1986). *The social construction of emotions.* Oxford: Blackwell Publishers.

Harré, R., & Finlay-Jones, R. (1986). Emotion talk across times. In R. Harré (Ed.), *The social construction of emotions* (pp. 220–233). Oxford: Blackwell Publishers.

Harré, R., & Parrott, W. G. (1996). *The emotions: Social, cultural and biological dimensions.* London: Sage Publications.

James, W. (1884) What is an emotion? *Mind, 9*, 188–205.

Laird, J. D. (1984). The real role of facial response in the experience of emotion: A reply to Tourangeau and Ellsworth, and others. *Journal of Personality and Social Psychology, 47*, 909–917.

Lazarus, R. S. (1966). *Psychological stress and the coping process.* New York: McGraw-Hill.

Lazarus, R. S. (1982). Thoughts on the relations between emotion and cognition. *American Psychologist, 37*, 1019–1024.

Lazarus, R. S. (1984). On the primacy of cognition. *American Psychologist, 39*, 124–129.

Lazarus, R. S. (1991). *Emotion and adaptation.* New York: Oxford University Press.

LeDoux, J. E. (1993). Emotional networks in the brain. In M. Lewis, & J. M. Haviland (Eds.), *Handbook of emotions* (pp. 109–118). New York: Guilford Press.

Lutz, C. A. (1988). *Unnatural emotions: Everyday sentiments on a Micronesian atoll and their challenge to Western theory.* Chicago: University of Chicago Press.

MacLean, P. D. (1970). The triune brain, emotion, and scientific bias. In F. O. Schmitt (Ed.), *The neurosciences: Second study program* (pp. 336–349). New York: Rockefeller University Press.

Markus, H. R., & Kitayama, S. (1991). Culture and the self: Implications for cognition, emotion, and motivation. *Psychological Review, 98*, 224–253.

Miller, R. S. (1996). *Embarrassment: Poise and peril in everyday life.* New York: Guilford Press.

Oatley, K., & Johnson-Laird, P. N. (1987). Towards a cognitive theory of emotions. *Cognition and Emotion, 1*, 29–50.

Ortony, A., Clore, G. L., & Collins, A. (1988). *The cognitive structure of emotions.* New York: Cambridge University Press.

Papez, J. (1937). A proposed mechanism of emotion. *Archives of Neurology and Psychology, 38*, 725–744.

Parkinson, B. (1997). Untangling the appraisal–emotion connection. *Personality and Social Psychology Review, 1*, 62–79.

Parrott, W. G. (1991). The emotional experiences of envy and jealousy. In P. Salovey (Ed.), *The psychology of jealousy and envy* (pp. 3–30). New York: Guilford Press.

Parrott, W. G. (in press). Multiple goals, self-regulation, and functionalism. In A. Fischer (Ed.), *Proceedings of the Xth Conference of the International Society for Research on Emotions.* Amsterdam: ISRE Publications.

Parrott, W. G., & Sabini, J. (1989). On the "emotional" qualities of certain types of cognition: A reply to arguments for the independence of cognition and affect. *Cognitive Therapy and Research, 13,* 49–65.

Peters, R. S. (1958). *The concept of motivation.* London: Routledge & Kegan Paul.

Reisenzein, R. (1983). The Schachter theory of emotion: Two decades later. *Psychological Bulletin, 94,* 239–264.

Russell, J. A. (1994). Is there universal recognition of emotion from facial expression? A review of methods and studies. *Psychological Bulletin, 115,* 102–141.

Russell, J. A., & Fernández-Dols, J.-M. (Eds.) (1997). *The psychology of facial expression.* Cambridge, UK: Cambridge University Press.

Russell, J. A., Fernández-Dols, J.-M., Manstead, A. S. R., & Wellenkamp, J. (Eds.) (1995). *Everyday concepts of emotion.* NATO ASI series D, Vol. 81. Dordrecht: Kluwer.

Salovey, P. (1991). *The psychology of jealousy and envy.* New York: Guilford Press.

Sartre, J.-P. (1948). *The emotions: Outline of a theory.* New York: Philosophical Library.

Schachter, S., & Singer, J. E. (1962). Cognitive, social, and physiological determinants of emotional state. *Psychological Review, 69,* 379–399.

Schoeck, H. (1969). *Envy: A theory of social behaviour.* Indianapolis, IN: Liberty Press.

Schwarz, N. (1990). Feelings as information: Informational and motivational functions of affective states. In R. Sorrentino, & E. T. Higgins (Eds.), *Handbook of motivation and cognition* Vol. 2 (pp. 527–561). New York: Guilford Press.

Selye, H. (1976). *The stress of life.* 2nd edn. New York: McGraw-Hill

Shaver, P., Schwartz, J., Kirson, D., & O'Connor, C. (1987). Emotion knowledge: Further exploration of a prototype approach. *Journal of Personality and Social Psychology, 52,* 1061–1086.

Smith, C. A., & Pope, L. K. (1992). Appraisal and emotion: The interactional contributions of dispositional and situational factors. In M. S. Clark (Ed.), *Review of Personality and Social Psychology, Vol. 14: Emotion and social behavior* (pp. 32–62). Newbury Park, CA: Sage.

Solomon, R. C. (1976). *The passions.* Notre Dame: University of Notre Dame Press.

Tangney, J. P., & Fischer, K. W. (Eds.) (1995). *Self-conscious emotions: The psychology of shame, guilt, embarrassment, and pride.* New York: Guilford Press.

Wierzbicka, A. (1992). Talking about emotions: Semantics, culture and cognition. *Cognition and Emotion, 6,* 285–319.

Zajonc, R. B. (1980). Feeling and thinking: Preferences need no inferences. *American Psychologist, 35,* 151–175.

Zajonc, R. B. (1984). On the primacy of affect. *American Psychologist, 39,* 117–123.

Zillman, D. (1979). *Hostility and aggression.* Hillsdale, NJ: Erlbaum.

Chapter Eighteen

The Consequences of Mood on the Processing of Social Information

Herbert Bless

Introduction

Imagine yourself leaving the movie theater having just enjoyed an interesting film that put you in a happy mood. Perhaps you'll spend the rest of the evening with friends: conversing, reminiscing about the past, forming impressions about other people, or discussing the most recent developments in politics. Although you may no longer think of the enjoyable movie, your thinking about the social situation is presumably in many ways influenced by the mood the movie elicited.

The general notion that our judgments and behaviors are influenced by how we feel in a particular situation reflects more a common sense understanding than the latest scientific evidence. While the impact of affective states on social cognition and behavior may seem trivial on this general level, a closer look reveals a highly interesting and fascinating research domain. Scientific interest in that domain has manifested itself in a long tradition of philosophical speculation (e.g. Descartes, 1649/1961) and psychological thinking (e.g. Freud, 1940–1968; James, 1890).

In view of this long tradition, it is not surprising that psychologists' interest in how individuals' affective states influence their thinking has varied over time. With the advent of the information processing paradigm, in particular, emotional processes seemed to fall outside the main focus of most researchers. In a highly influential article published in 1980, Zajonc (1980; see also Hilgard, 1980) complained about this situation and argued that more attention should be paid to the role of affect. As Tomkins (1981) predicted, the situation soon changed, and psychologists' interest in emotional processes was revived.

The reported research was supported by grants Bl 289/5 from the Deutsche Forschungsgemeinschaft to H. Bless, N. Schwarz, and M. Wänke.

Over the last two decades, research has accumulated a large body of empirical and theoretical contributions, documenting the pervasive influences of affective states on cognitive processes in virtually every domain of social psychology (see Clore, Schwarz, & Conway, 1994; Forgas, 1991, in press-a; Fiedler & Forgas, 1988; Isen, 1987; Martin & Clore, in press). Affective states have been shown to influence encoding, storage, retrieval, and judgmental processes, as well as general strategies of information processing. These processes are, of course, highly intertwined. For reasons of presentation, however, memory, judgmental processes, and general style of information processing will be discussed in turn in the following sections. First, however, some points of terminology will be addressed in the remainder of this section.

Emotions and moods are often subsumed under the general term "affective states." While "states" refer to temporary conditions of an organism, "affect" refers to the positive or negative personal value of these states (Clore, et al., in press; Morris, 1989). Although moods and emotions share many aspects, a number of differences need to be examined separately. First, emotions usually have a specific referent, for example we are "happy about" something. In contrast, moods lack such a specific referent and are more diffuse in nature. Thus, our happiness about something may leave us in a diffusely positive mood once the happiness-inducing event is no longer the focus of our attention. Second, moods are less intense and usually do not attract the individual's attention. Third, very intense emotions are less frequent and are linked to more specific consequences (for a more detailed discussion, see Morris, 1989). Fourth, because of their diffuse nature, moods may function in the background of other cognitive processes. These processes are then likely candidates for the impact of mood. What makes moods so interesting to researchers in social cognition is presumably the fact that they do function in the background and that their consequences are evident in a wide spectrum of processes.

Mood and Memory

The revival of interest in emotional processes within the information processing paradigm was driven to a large degree by the assumption that affective states may influence the nature of the information that comes to a person's mind. For example, individuals are more likely to recall positive materials from memory when they are in a happy rather than a sad mood. Perhaps the most influential contribution addressing these processes was provided by Bower's (1981) associate network model of human memory (for related assumptions see Isen, Shalker, Clark, & Karp, 1978).

Based on assumptions derived from existing associative network models (for example, Anderson & Bower, 1973), researchers assume that mood states function as central nodes in an associative network. These mood nodes are linked to related ideas and events of correspondence valence, as well as to autonomic activity and muscular and expressive patterns. When new material is learned, it is associated with the nodes that are active at the time of learning. Material that is learned in a particular affective state is linked to the respective affective node. Conversely, when an affective node is stimulated, activation spreads along the pathways, increasing the activation of other nodes connected to it.

Two main hypotheses have been derived from this conceptualization. First, the state-dependency hypothesis, which focuses on the match of affective states at encoding and retrieval, holds that memory performance is improved when individuals are in the same affective state at the time of encoding and at the time of retrieval. Second, the mood-congruent recall hypothesis, which focuses on the match of mood at retrieval and the valence of the information, holds that material is more likely to be recalled if its affective tone matches the individuals' affective state at the time of retrieval (for a discussion of the conceptual and empirical issues, and the separability of state-dependency and mood-congruency, see Isen, 1987; Clore, Schwarz, & Conway, 1994).

Initially, the two hypotheses received considerable support. For example, when asked to recall personal life-events, happy participants recalled more positive than negative life-events, while sad participants recalled more negative than positive life-events (Bower, 1981; for reviews and additional evidence see Blaney, 1986; Bower, Montiero, & Gilligan, 1978; Forgas & Bower, 1987; Isen, 1987; Nasby & Yando, 1982; Morris, 1989). Converging evidence was reported in clinical psychology, indicating that depressed moods facilitate the recall of negative material from memory (for example, Teasdale, Taylor, & Forgarty, 1979; for a review see Ingram, 1990).

Subsequent research, however, revealed that the effects of mood-dependent memory were less reliable than initially assumed (see also Bower's own discussion of problems with replicating mood dependent memory effects, in Bower & Mayer, 1985). Accordingly, various reviewers of the topic concluded that mood dependent memory may be a rather fragile phenomenon whose occurrence may be dependent on a number of limiting conditions (Clore, et al., 1994; Kihlstrom, 1989; Ucros, 1989; for a review, see Eich & Macaulay, in press). In the remainder of this section, some of the empirical and conceptual complications that have emerged in the discussion about the reliability of mood dependent memory will be briefly addressed.

First, mood dependent memory has been shown to be asymmetrical, a pattern that already emerged in Bower's initial evidence (Bower, 1981). On the one hand, happy moods facilitate the recall of happy memories and inhibit the recall of sad memories. On the other hand, however, sad moods may inhibit the recall of happy memories, but rarely increase the recall of sad memories (Isen, Shalker, Clark, & Karp, 1978; see Isen, 1984). Isen (1984, 1987) explains this asymmetry by more controlled motivational processes that operate in addition to the automatically spreading activation suggested by Bower (1981). Specifically, individuals in negative affective states may be motivated to "repair" their mood by attempting "to stop the process of thinking about negative material that might be cued by sadness" (Isen, 1987, p. 217). These controlled processes may in turn override the automatic impact of sad moods on the accessibility of (sad) mood congruent material (see also Morris, 1989, for a critical review).

Second, it has been argued that mood congruent memory is based on meta-cognitions about the effects of being in a particular mood rather than the mood itself (Clore, et al., in press; Wyer & Srull, 1989). For example, Perrig & Perrig (1988; see also Parrott, 1993) instructed participants to act as if they were in a happy or sad mood. The recall of participants in these simulated moods showed a mood congruency. This again suggests that mood congruent memory may be mediated at least in part by individuals applying their meta-knowledge about how mood might affect their memory. The application of this knowledge is presumably elicited by directing individuals' attention to their moods. Supporting this assumption, Parrott & Sabini (1990) observed no mood congruent recall unless participants' attention was directed toward their mood either by explicitly asking them to label their moods, or by implicitly inducing mood rather blatantly.

Third, it has been demonstrated that mood congruent memory depends on various aspects of the learning and recall task. For example, mood congruency effects are less likely if the stimulus material is highly structured. In these cases the internal structure of the material presumably renders mood a rather ineffective retrieval cue (for related evidence see Eich, 1980; Fiedler, Pampe, & Scherf, 1986; Hasher, Rose, Zacks, Sanft, & Doren, 1985). Relatedly, mood congruency effects are usually more pronounced in free recall as compared to cue recall. Again, the efficiency of the retrieval cue by individuals' mood is reduced by the cue provided in the cued recall task (see Eich & Macaulay, in press). Additionally, the available evidence suggests that retrieval cues that are produced by participants themselves are more likely to elicit mood congruent recall than retrieval cues that are provided by the experimenter (for example, Eich & Metcalfe, 1989; for a general discussion of these aspects see Eich & Macaulay, in press; Fiedler, 1991, in press).

The research discussed so far pertains to the relationship between the valence of individuals' mood and the valence of the information recalled from memory. Other accounts assume that affective states may influence memory performance independent of the valence of the material to be retrieved. Ellis and colleagues (Ellis, 1991; Ellis & Ashbrook, 1988) have argued that negative affective states bring to mind self-referential thoughts that might restrict individuals' resources, and in turn interfere with other tasks. As a result, negative affective states impair individuals' memory performance (see, however, Hertel & Hardin, 1990, who attribute these effects to the lack of initiating strategies rather than to reduced resources). Research in social psychology, usually using more structured materials than Ellis and colleagues, has revealed rather little evidence in support of the reduced resource assumption (see Clore, Schwarz, & Conway, 1994, for a more extensive discussion). We will return to the possibility that mood might influence cognitive resources when discussing the impact of mood on style of processing.

Mood and Evaluative Judgments

The general finding that individuals' evaluative judgments tend to be congruent with their mood state has been reported in almost every judgmental domain. Independent of whether the judgmental target pertains to other persons, consumer products, the quality of life, performance appraisals, and so on, individuals in positive affective states have been found to report more positive evaluations than individuals in negative affective states (cf. Clore, Schwarz, & Conway, 1994; Forgas, 1992a, 1995a; Schwarz & Clore, 1996).

One possibility of accounting for these findings rests on Bower's (1981) memory model that was already discussed above. Here it is assumed that individuals form their judgments on the basis of the information they recall. As happy individuals selectively recall positive information, their judgments will be more favorable than judgments formed by sad individuals (see Bower, 1981; Forgas, 1992a, 1995a). This line of reasoning seemed straightforward, and mood congruent judgments have therefore been treated as evidence for mood congruent recall. However, various factors question this line of reasoning. First, in many cases judgments may not be based on the information that is retrieved from memory (Hastie & Park, 1986; Lichtenstein & Srull, 1987). Second, the reliable effects of mood on evaluative judgments seem at odds with the rather less reliable effects of mood on memory. Especially since it can be assumed that in many cases the information relevant for social judgments is often very structured or interconnected, a variable that has been demonstrated to reduce mood effects on memory (Eich, 1980; Fiedler, Pampe, & Scherf, 1986). Third, and perhaps most importantly, an alternative explanation suggests that mood congruent judgments need not to be mediated by mood dependent recall.

Schwarz and Clore (see Clore, et al., in press; Schwarz, 1990, in press; Schwarz & Clore, 1983, 1996) have suggested that affective states may themselves serve as relevant information in making a judgment. According to this mood-as-information assumption, individuals may simplify complex judgmental tasks by asking themselves, "How-do-I-feel-about-it?", turning to their apparent affective reaction to the target as a basis for judgment. In fact, some evaluative judgments refer, by definition, to one's affective reaction to the stimulus (e.g. judgments of liking), and the current affective state may indeed be elicited by the target. However, due to the unfocused character of mood states, it is often difficult to distinguish between one's affective reaction to the object of judgment and one's pre-existing mood state. Accordingly, individuals may misread their pre-existing feelings as a reaction to the target, which results in more favorable evaluations under happy than under sad moods.

Several predictions can be derived from the mood-as-information approach that are incompatible with the assumption that mood congruent judgments are mediated by mood congruent recall or retrieval. Perhaps most central in the debate over the two approaches, the mood-as-information hypothesis holds that individuals will only use their affective state as a basis of judgment if its informational value has not been called into question. In line with this prediction, the impact of mood on judgment was found to be eliminated if individuals attributed their moods (either correctly or incorrectly) to a source that rendered them irrelevant to the judgment at hand. For example, participants reported lower life-satisfaction when they were in a bad mood due to lousy weather rather than in a happy mood due to nice weather; but this effect was eliminated when their attention was drawn to the weather, thus rendering it uninformative with regard to the quality of their life in general (Schwarz & Clore, 1983). Such a discounting effect would not be expected if the impact of mood were mediated by mood congruent recall. According to this latter account, participants in a sad (happy) mood would report lower (higher) life-satisfaction because they recall negative (positive) information about their life from memory. The implications of this retrieved information, however, should not be called into question by drawing participants' attention to the weather. Thus, the discounting effect is hardly compatible with the assumption that mood dependent recall led to the mood congruent life-satisfaction judgments.

In sum, mood may influence evaluative judgments either directly, by serving as a basis of judgment, or indirectly, by influencing what information comes to mind. While presumably both processes may be operating under some conditions, the former process seems more likely than the latter, given the robustness of mood effects on evaluative judgments on the one hand, and the fragility of mood congruent recall on the other hand (for more extensive reviews see Clore, Wyer, et al., in press; Clore, Schwarz, & Conway, 1994; Schwarz, 1990, in press; Schwarz & Clore, 1996).

Although the general conclusion that individuals may use their own mood state as a basis for evaluative judgments is widely accepted, there are still a number of issues that are controversially debated. Three of these issues will be addressed in the remainder of this section: (a) the role of consciousness of the attributional processes, (b) the role of the amount of processing, and (c) the question whether relying on mood as information necessarily results in mood congruent judgments.

(a) First, it has been debated whether the mood-as-information assumption implies that when individuals use their mood as information for evaluating a specific target, a conscious attribution of the mood to the target is required (e.g. see Forgas, 1995a). Schwarz (in press; Schwarz & Clore, 1988) argues that a conscious attribution is not necessary when individuals use their affective state as a source of information. It is assumed that information that comes to mind, in this case one's current mood, is considered relevant by default (cf. Schwarz & Bless, 1992), unless the relevance is questioned by other aspects of the situation. In contrast, discounting the relevance or diagnosticity of information usually requires additional and presumably more conscious attributional processing (see Martin & Achee, 1992; Schwarz & Bless, 1992). In combination, this suggests that different levels of attributional processes may mediate the use versus non-use of mood as a source of information. Interestingly, the valence of the mood state itself has been shown to influence the amount of attributional processes. Presumably because of their differential frequency, negative affective states are more likely to trigger attributional processes than positive affective states (Bohner, Bless, Schwarz, & Strack, 1988). In line with this conclusion, the effects of misattributing individuals' mood have often been more pronounced for sad rather than for happy individuals (Schwarz & Clore, 1983).

(b) Second, in many situations the reliance on a "How-do-I-feel-about-it?" heuristic can be considered a quick and efficient strategy that allows for a simplification of evaluative judgments. In line with this assumption, mood congruency effects have been reported to increase when judgments were formed under time pressure (Siemer & Reisenzein, in press). In addition, more global judgments that presumably were more complex and required a simplification of the judgmental task (cf. Bodenhausen & Lichtenstein, 1987) were more likely to reflect the respondents' mood than more specific judgments (Levine, Wyer, & Schwarz, 1994; Schwarz, Strack, Kommer, & Wagner, 1988).

According to the "How-do-I-feel-about-it?" heuristic, mood congruent judgments should be more pronounced under conditions that elicit a simplified, heuristic processing. Seemingly taking a different position, Forgas (1995a, in press-b) proposes that affect infusion and, in turn, mood congruent judgments are more likely under conditions of substantive, elaborative processing. In accordance with Bower's network model, Forgas assumes that individuals' mood state may serve as a prime, increasing the accessibility of evaluatively consistent constructs. The more extensive the individuals' processing when forming a judgment, the more likely it is that the judgment will reflect the impact of these constructs and thus also the individuals' mood state. In work that supports these assumptions, Forgas and colleagues have reported considerable converging evidence pertaining to the direction of judgment, judgmental latencies, and the recall of information (e.g. Forgas, 1992b, 1995b; for overviews, see Forgas, 1992a, 1995a).

At the moment, these seemingly conflicting sets of data still need to be reconciled, and various aspects need to be clarified. It will be important to disentangle judgments that are primarily based on recall of information, and judgments that are primarily based on the "How-do-I-feel-about-it?" heuristic. Perhaps mood congruent judgment may increase and decrease with the amount of processing, depending on the informational basis. As suggested by Schwarz (in press), (mis-)attribution of the informational value of mood may be one possible way of disentangling the two processes. With regard to judgments based on a mood dependent recall, it is not exactly clear whether initially small differences between happy and sad individuals are necessarily accentuated when more elaborative processing is allocated. While more processing may sometimes lead to an accentuation (Tesser, 1978), this may strongly depend on the structure of the relevant material (Millar & Tesser, 1986; Judd & Lusk, 1984; Fiedler, 1997). Complicating things even more, it has been argued that the valence of individuals' mood may influence the amount of substantive processing, an issue that will be addressed in the next section.

(c) Third, it has been argued that relying on one's mood as a primarily judgmental basis does not necessarily imply mood congruent judgments. Under specific circumstances, feeling happy might entail negative judgments, and feeling sad might entail positive judgments (Martin, in press). For example, imagine recipients are informed that a particular movie was supposed to make the audience feel sad. In this situation recipients are more likely to report positive assessments of the judgmental target if it fulfilled its goal, that is when the movie made them feel sad, compared to a situation when the movie left them in a neutral mood. Martin and colleagues account for such findings with the mood-as-input-model (Martin, in press; Martin, Abend, Sedikides, & Green, 1997). This model also emphasizes that individuals' moods may serve as information. It is argued, however, that experiencing a happy (or sad) mood may not convey the same evaluative or motivational implication in every context. This implication may strongly depend on the configuration of the context. As a result, in some cases happy moods may entail more negative judgments, and vice versa. Schwarz (in press) has suggested that Martin, et al.'s (1997) findings could be reconciled with the "How-do-I-feel-about-it?" heuristic. His position holds that the effects are driven by changes in the criterion (a positive mood informs recipients that it was a happy movie, which in turn implies that the movie did not reach its goal, which in turn leads to more negative judgments) rather than by changes in the informational implications of recipients' affective state. Independent of this possibility, however, Martin's position rightly emphasizes the necessity of investigating more closely the question when and how the informational value of mood is entered into what specific judgments and with what precise implication.

Mood and Style of Information Processing

The research reported so far has addressed how mood may influence memory and evaluative judgments. In both cases, the primary focus has been on the congruency between the individual's mood state on the one hand, and the material retrieved from memory or the evaluative judgment on the other hand. The impact of mood may, however, extend far beyond this congruency aspect: the accumulated research findings suggest that mood may not only influence *what* information is processed, but also *how* information is processed. A broad spectrum of research focused on the style of information processing has consistently demonstrated that even rather subtle changes in affective states may influence performance in a wide variety of cognitive tasks.

The consequences of mood on the style of information processing have been investigated in very different domains. Given the scope of the present chapter it is not possible to address, however briefly, the various empirical contributions and theoretical discussions (for overviews see also Isen, 1987; Clore, Schwarz, & Conway, 1994; Forgas, 1995a, in press; Martin & Clore, in press; Schwarz & Clore, 1996). Instead, the remainder of this section focuses on what is perhaps the central issue: whether and how mood influences individuals' reliance on heuristic processing strategies. As a second issue, the impact of mood on individuals' cognitive flexibility and creativity will be briefly discussed.

The available research consistently suggests that happy moods are more strongly associated with heuristic processing strategies than sad moods. These processing differences have been observed across various different domains, and happy individuals' reliance on heuristics has emerged in different forms, such as the reliance on peripheral cues, stereotypes, scripts, or the availability heuristic. In what appear on the surface to be contradictory findings, another line of research suggests that happy moods increase the flexibility of cognitive processes and promote creative solutions to decision problems. In the remainder of this section the general findings from the domains most relevant for social psychology are summarized. This will be followed by a review of several models that trace happy individuals' reliance on heuristic processing strategies to the effect of happy moods decreasing processing motivation or processing capacity. Finally, these models are contrasted with accounts that do not imply mood dependent differences in processing motivation or capacity.

Mood and persuasion

Researchers interested in the interplay of affect and cognition have applied the dual process models of persuasion (Chaiken, 1980, 1987; Petty & Cacioppo, 1986; see also Eagly & Chaiken, 1993) and the related methodological paradigms to their domain. In a number of studies, different affective states were induced, and participants were subsequently exposed to persuasive messages that included either strong or weak arguments. In general, participants in sad moods reported more favorable attitudes toward the advocated position when they were exposed to strong arguments than when they were exposed to weak arguments. In contrast, participants in happy moods were less influenced by the message quality and were equally persuaded by strong and weak arguments. Equivalent findings were obtained for recipients' cognitive responses reflecting differences in message quality under sad and neutral, but not under happy, mood conditions. This general pattern of findings has been replicated in a number of studies using a range of different mood inductions and persuasive messages about a variety of attitudinal issues (for examples see Bless, Bohner, Schwarz, & Strack, 1990; Bless, Mackie, & Schwarz, 1992; Bohner, Crow, Erb, & Schwarz, 1992; Innes & Ahrens, 1991; Mackie & Worth, 1989; Sinclair, Mark, & Clore, 1994;

Wegener & Petty, 1994; Worth & Mackie, 1987). These findings have been complemented by the observation that attitudes of recipients in positive but not neutral moods reflect the presence of heuristic cues (Mackie & Worth, 1989; Worth & Mackie, 1987; see, however, Bohner, et al., 1992, which suggests an increased reliance on heuristic cues under sad moods). Based on the underlying dual process models of persuasion, the decreased effect of message quality and the increased impact of peripheral cues under happy mood conditions suggests that happy moods are associated with heuristic processing strategies, whereas sad moods are associated with a systematic elaboration of the information that is presented (for overviews see Bohner, Moskowitz, & Chaiken, 1995; Mackie, Asuncion, & Rosselli, 1992; Wegener & Petty, 1996; Schwarz, Bless, & Bohner, 1991).

Mood and person perception

Similar to attitude judgments, judgments about other persons may reflect two different processing strategies. On the one hand, judgments may involve a more heuristic processing strategy. In this case, they reflect the perceiver's general knowledge about the category to which the target is assigned, i.e. the implications of stereotype. On the other hand, judgments may be primarily based on available individuating information about a specific target person, thereby attenuating the impact of the stereotype (cf. Brewer, 1988; Fiske & Neuberg, 1990). A number of studies explored whether and how individuals' mood states influence the reliance on stereotypes in impression formation. For example, Bodenhausen, Kramer, & Süsser (1994; see also Bodenhausen, 1993) presented participants in different mood states with descriptions of an alleged student misconduct and asked them to determine the target's guilt. Happy participants judged the offender more guilty when he was identified as a member of a group that is stereotypically associated with the described offense than when this was not the case. This impact of the stereotype, however, was not observed for participants in sad mood states. A series study replicated this heightened impact of stereotypes on the processing by happy individuals. In addition, it revealed an increased impact of individuating information on judgments by sad rather than happy individuals (Bless, Schwarz, & Wieland, 1996). Edwards & Weary (1993) reported similarly converging evidence based on naturally depressed moods. Non-depressed participants were more likely to rely on category membership information than depressed participants, who were more strongly influenced by individuating information about the target. These findings are supplemented by the observation that impression formation judgments were more likely to reflect primacy effects when participants were in a happy rather than a sad mood (Sinclair & Mark, 1992).

   If we equate reliance on category membership information with reliance on peripheral cues, and reliance on individuating information with reliance on the presented arguments, these findings converge with those obtained in the persuasion domain. In combination, these findings suggest that individuals in a happy mood are more likely to rely on heuristics or stereotypes, while individuals in a sad mood are more likely to attend to the specific information provided.

Mood and other heuristics

The conclusion that happy individuals are more likely to rely on heuristic processing strategies is not restricted to domains of persuasion and person perception. For example, Isen and colleagues report that happy moods increase the likelihood that individuals rely on an availability heuristic (Tversky & Kahneman, 1973) when making frequency judgments (Isen, Means, Patrick, & Nowicki, 1982). In a related vein, happy moods have been found to increase the reliance on other forms of general knowledge structures. For example, when encoding a sequence of events that characterize typical activities, happy individuals are more likely than sad individuals to rely on pre-existing scripts. When confronted with a recognition test, happy individuals more readily recognize information consistent with script as previously presented, resulting in more hits for presented items and more intrusion errors for non-presented items (Bless, Clore, et al., 1996).

Another, often very heuristic, processing strategy for storing information in memory relies on an increased clustering of information. The discovery that happy moods seem to promote the use of this strategy (Isen, Daubman, & Gorgoglione, 1987; see also Bless, Hamilton, & Mackie, 1992, for related evidence) converges with other findings. This clustering is presumably associated with the use of broader categories under happy moods (Isen & Daubman, 1984) and with narrower categorizations under sad moods (see Sinclair, 1988). Forgas & Fiedler (1996), investigating categorization processes in the formation of intergroup judgments, report that happy individuals were more likely to discriminate against the outgroup, unless the situation implied a high relevance of the group membership information.

Mood and cognitive flexibility

At first glance it may seem at odds with the findings reported above that happy moods may not only promote the reliance on heuristics, but may also increase the flexibility of cognitive processes and creative solutions. For example, Isen and colleagues found an improved performance on Duncker's candle problem as well as in creativity tests when participancts were in a happy rather than a neutral mood (Isen, Daubman, & Nowicki, 1987; Isen, Johnson, Mertz, & Robinson, 1985).

The increased number of unusual associations may contribute in part to the observation that happy individuals can generate more similarities between objects (Murray, Sujan, Hirt, & Sujan, 1990) than individuals in a neutral mood. The ability to easily find similarities may promote the use of broader categories (see above). However, Murray and colleagues also reported that, when instructed, happy individuals can also create more differences between stimuli, which suggests a higher flexibility of cognitive processes under happy moods (for a similar conclusion see Hirt, McDonald, & Melton, 1996; Isen, 1987).

In sum, the available evidence suggests that individuals in a happy mood are more likely to rely on heuristics than individuals in a neutral or a sad mood, and that happy moods promote a more flexible style of processing in problem-solving and creativity tasks. Various explanations accounting for these findings are reviewed below. Most of this discussion has emphasized the heuristic rather than the flexibility aspect, although these two aspects may be highly intertwined (see Bless & Fiedler, 1995). This focus is presumably in part due to the more detailed specification of the processes that underlie persuasion and person perception as compared with creativity.

Theoretical accounts

Research in social cognition has consistently demonstrated that individuals' processing motivation and processing capacity have a pronounced impact on the use of heuristic processing strategies. Specifically, reduced processing motivation or capacity usually increases the reliance on heuristic processing strategies and decreases a systematic consideration of the specific information at hand (e.g. Chaiken, 1987; Fiske & Neuberg, 1990; Fiske & Taylor, 1991; Petty & Cacioppo, 1986). Given this background, it is not surprising that various accounts have proposed that the observed happy individuals' reliance on heuristics is mediated by happy moods decreasing the amount of processing, thus emphasizing either capacity deficits or motivational deficits as the likely cause (see also Schwarz & Clore, 1996, for a discussion of the various approaches).

Processing capacity   According to the associative network assumptions described above, being in a particular mood activates material that is associated with the respective mood. Working from the assumption that individuals have stored more positive than negative material (Matlin & Stang, 1979), researchers have argued that being in a happy mood limits processing capacity due to the activation of a large amount of interconnected positive material stored in memory (e.g. Isen, 1987; Mackie & Worth, 1989). Hence, individuals in a happy mood may have fewer cognitive resources than individuals in a neutral mood. These resources are, however, required by systematic processing strategies, and because they are absent happy individuals may default to less taxing heuristic strategies. The increased accessibility of a large amount of interconnected material may also explain the increased creativity under happy moods. As suggested by Isen (1987), individuals in a happy mood are more likely to come up with creative responses and problem solutions than individuals in a neutral mood because their happy mood activates a wider spectrum of material.

Cognitive tuning   Extending the mood-as-information hypothesis described above (Schwarz & Clore, 1983, 1988), Schwarz proposed that the affective state may inform the individual about the nature of the current situation (Schwarz, 1990; Schwarz & Clore, 1996; see also Frijda, 1988). It is assumed that individuals usually feel good in situations that are characterized by positive outcomes and/or in situations that do not threaten their current goals. In contrast, individuals usually feel bad in situations that threaten their current goals because of the presence of negative outcomes or the lack of positive outcomes. If different situations result in different affective states, individuals may consult their affect as a usually valid and quick indicator as to the nature of the current psychological situation. Specifically, positive affective states may inform the individual that the current situation poses no problem, while negative affective states may signal that the current situation is problematic. Based on the information provided by their affective state, individuals in a bad mood are more motivated to engage in detail-oriented systematic processing strategies, which is typically adaptive in handling problematic situations. In contrast, individuals in a good mood may see little reason to spontaneously engage in strenuous processing strategies, unless this is called for by other goals (see Schwarz, 1990; Schwarz & Clore, 1996, for more detailed discussions).

The reduced processing motivation under happy moods is only one implication of the cognitive tuning perspective. Additionally, it has been suggested that individuals' mood may influence the accessibility of procedural knowledge that is functional in situations typically associated with the respective mood state. In benign, non-threatening situations no specific action is usually required. Accordingly, positive affective states may not prime any particular procedure, resulting in a high variability of potentially activated procedural, semantic, and episodic knowledge. This in turn contributes to a high flexibility of cognitive processes and the creativity of problem solutions (Schwarz, 1990). On the other hand, individuals in a negative affective state are less likely to explore new, potentially risky solutions in situations that are already characterized as problematic. In combination, the motivational implications of individuals' mood state and the activation of different procedural knowledge may account for the differential reliance on heuristics on the one hand, and for the differences in cognitive flexibility on the other.

Rather direct evidence supporting the role of the informational value provided by individuals' mood is reported in a study by Sinclair, Mark, & Clore (1994). In this study, sad individuals differentiated between messages comprising either strong or weak arguments, while happy individuals did not, replicating the pattern of previous studies reported above. This differential pattern for happy versus sad recipients was eliminated, however, when recipients attributed their mood to the weather. Consistent with the implications of the mood-as-information hypothesis (Schwarz, 1990; Schwarz & Clore, 1996), this attribution discredited the informational value of recipients' mood, and in turn the effects on processing strategies.

Mood management   Different accounts implicitly or explicitly hold the assumption that individuals are motivated to maintain positive affective states and to enhance negative affective states (Isen, 1987; Wegener & Petty, 1994; Wegener, Petty, & Smith, 1995). Starting from the assumption that strenuous cognitive processes interfere with the goal of maintaining positive mood states, researchers argue that individuals in happy moods are less motivated to invest cognitive effort than sad individuals. As a consequence of this reduced motivation, happy individuals should be more likely to rely on a heuristic processing while sad individuals should be more likely to engage in a systematic processing. This effect may be overridden, however, if the task promises to maintain or even enhance individuals' positive mood (Wegener, Petty, & Smith, 1995). Investigating the mood management hypothesis in the persuasion domain, Wegener, et al. again found that attitudes of sad but not of happy recipients reflected the argument quality of a persuasive message. However, consistent with their hypothesis, the findings showed that happy recipients' attitudes reflected argument quality when recipients were informed that a careful processing of the arguments would make them feel happy. As pointed out by Schwarz & Clore (1996), it remains unclear from a mood management perspective why sad recipients seemed to have processed the message systematically even when they were rather blatantly informed that a careful processing would make them feel sad. Questioning the mood management hypothesis on a conceptual level, researchers have argued that individuals' motivation to improve their mood may be less pronounced than assumed. In many situations, individuals may pursue more long-term benefits at the costs of immediate mood management effects (for a discussion of the hedonic view and related evidence see Erber, 1996, in press; Erber, Wegner, & Therriault, 1996).

Processing capacity versus processing motivation   The general finding that happy individuals are more likely to rely on heuristic processing strategies than sad individuals is compatible with all three of the approaches described above. Happy individuals may rely on heuristic processing strategies because of their capacity deficits, because their affective state informs them the current situation is safe and benign and requires no careful analysis, or because this strategy allows them to avoid cognitive effort that would be incompatible with the maintenance of their mood state. Not surprisingly, various attempts have been made to test accounts that focus on processing motivation and accounts that focus on processing capacity against each other.

For example, Mackie & Worth (1989) reported empirical support for the reduced capacity assumption. In their studies, attitudes of happy participants again failed to reflect the quality of a persuasive message, whereas attitudes of participants in a neutral mood showed differential effects of exposure to strong or weak arguments. Happy participants did, however, differentiate between strong and weak arguments when they were encouraged to take as much time as they wanted to read the message. Mackie and Worth concluded that the extra processing time provided to participants eliminated the capacity deficits of happy participants, and this resulted in the observed differential impact of strong and weak arguments.

Addressing the assumption that happy moods reduce processing motivation, Bless, Bohner, Schwarz, & Strack (1990) observed that happy participants differentiated between strong and weak arguments when they were instructed to pay attention to argument quality. Taking a similar approach in the person perception domain, Bodenhausen, Kramer, & Süsser (1994) increased individuals' processing motivation with an accountability manipulation (Tetlock, 1983). This treatment reduced happy individuals' reliance on stereotype information and eliminated the differential impact under happy versus neutral mood conditions. Based on these findings, the researchers concluded that increased reliance on heuristics and stereotypes under happy moods is due to motivational deficits rather than pronounced reductions in processing capacity (Bless, Bohner, Schwarz, & Strack, 1990; Bodenhausen, Kramer, & Süsser, 1994). If happy moods had severely restricted individuals' processing capacity, simple instructions to pay attention to the argument provided should have been unlikely to overcome these constraints.

As Schwarz, Bless, & Bohner (1991) have already discussed, these studies are open to mutual reinterpretations. Whereas Mackie & Worth's (1989) instructions to take as much time as needed may also have affected subjects' processing motivation, Bless, Bohner, Schwarz, & Strack's (1990) instructions to attend to argument quality may also have reduced the capacity required for processing the persuasive message by providing a more focused task, which in turn reduced the necessary processing capacity.

Second thoughts about reduced processing under happy moods   The theoretical approaches discussed above share the notion that they trace happy individuals' reliance on heuristics to processing deficits, either in motivation or in capacity. It is interesting that, with very few exceptions, support for the various positions is mostly based on the demonstration that happy individuals' reliance on heuristics can be overridden by additional manipulations. For example, happy individuals' failure to differentiate in their attitude judgments between strong and weak arguments could be overcome by (a) informing people that processing the content would make them feel happy (Wegener, Petty, & Smith, 1995), (b) providing unlimited processing time (Mackie & Worth, 1989), or (c) instructing recipients to focus on the message content (Bless, Bohner, Schwarz, & Strack, 1990). However, the observation that the impact of manipulation "x" can override the impact of manipulation "y" is presumably rather indirect evidence that the effect of both manipulations is mediated by the same underlying mechanisms. Even leaving this aspect aside, overriding effects may often provide support of one particular position, but less frequently allow for testing different positions against one another.

Somewhat related, it almost appears that the accounts all but take for granted that the observed happy individuals' reliance on heuristics must result from motivational or processing capacity deficits. The underlying dual process models hold that a reduction in processing capacity and/or processing motivation increases the reliance on heuristics or stereotype information. In these models, processing deficits are treated as sufficient rather than necessary causes of heuristic processing (see, however, Chaiken, 1987). By inferring motivational or capacity deficits from a heuristic processing, one implicitly treats processing motivation and capacity as the only variables that may promote a reliance on heuristics (for a more detailed discussion of this aspect see Bless & Schwarz, in press). Interestingly, despite the pronounced interest in the reduced capacity and reduced motivation hypotheses, rather few attempts have been made to directly measure the amount of processing under different mood states.

The quality of the evidence supporting the notion that happy moods limit processing motivation or capacity becomes important as other accounts question the proposed link between mood and amount of processing. For example, working from the mood-as-input model (Martin, in press; Martin & Stoner, 1996; Martin, Ward, Achee, & Wyer, 1993), Martin argues that moods may increase or decrease cognitive effort. Martin proposes that the information about the individuals' current affective state may enter into different decisions about the given task, resulting in different implications for the allocated cognitive effort. This assumption is supported by the finding that happy participants invested more effort in a task than sad participants when instructed to continue as long as they enjoyed the task. However, when participants were instructed to continue until they were satisfied with their performance, happy participants invested less effort than sad participants (Martin, Ward, Achee, & Wyer, 1993). When satisfaction with their performance was made the criterion, happy participants were presumably more satisfied than sad participants, which in turn decreased the investment of additional effort. In contrast, when enjoyment was made the criterion, happy participants felt more enjoyment than sad participants, which in turn increased their motivation to continue the task.

Mood and general knowledge structures   The mood-and-general-knowledge assumption

(Bless, 1997; Bless, Schwarz, & Wieland, 1996) similarly questions the generality of mood effects on the amount of processing. Building on the lack of direct evidence for motivational or capacity deficits, it maintains that happy individuals' reliance on heuristics may not necessarily be mediated by the impact of mood on processing motivation or capacity. This approach shares the assumption that positive affective states may inform the individual that the current situation poses no problem, while negative affective states may signal that the current situation is problematic. In a departure from the position discussed above, it is argued, however, that the key effect of these different signals is not, or not only, motivational. Instead, the crucial difference may be related to individuals' reliance on pre-existing general knowledge structures (Bless, 1997; Bless, Clore, Schwarz, et al., 1996). Specifically, if being in a positive mood informs individuals that the present situation poses no particular problem, this "business as usual" signal may increase the likelihood that they rely on general knowledge structures, which usually serve them well. In contrast, if being in a negative mood signals a problematic situation, reliance on defaults and general knowledge structures may not be adaptive and individuals may be more likely to attend to the specifics of the information at hand. As a result, being in a positive mood would foster top-down processing, whereas being in a negative mood would foster bottom-up processing. These processing differences may often be associated with different amounts of processing. However, according to the mood-and-general-knowledge assumption, the reduced effort is the consequence rather than the cause of the reliance on heuristics (for a more detailed discussion see Bless & Schwarz, in press).

If we consider heuristic processing strategies as the application of general knowledge structures to specific information (Nisbett & Ross, 1980), the increased reliance on schemas, scripts, stereotypes, or global categories under happy moods is in line with the mood-and-general-knowledge assumption. In further support of this position, Bless, Schwarz, & Wieland (1996) have found that happy participants were more likely than sad participants to rely on their pre-existing knowledge in form of scripts when encoding new information, which again suggests increased heuristic processing under happy moods. However, when participants were provided with a secondary task during encoding, happy participants outperformed sad participants. This improved performance on the secondary task is hardly compatible with the assumption that motivational or capacity deficits caused the reliance on the script, in particular because the improvement was not observed under conditions when the "secondary" task was provided as the only task. In a related vein, it has been demonstrated that happy participants' increased reliance on stereotypes was accompanied by a particular impact of stereotype-inconsistent information on judgments (Bless, Schwarz, & Wieland, 1996), and by an improved recall for the stereotype-inconsistent information (Dovidio, 1998). Given that the elaboration on inconsistent information requires the allocation of additional resources (Stangor & McMillan, 1992), these findings render it unlikely that reduced resources caused happy individuals to rely initially on stereotypes.

In sum, the available evidence strongly suggests that different affective states are associated with different styles of information processing. The processing of individuals in positive affective states is characterized by a stronger reliance on heuristics and by an increased cognitive flexibility. In contrast, the processing of sad individuals often reflects careful consideration of the data at hand, and a reduced cognitive flexibility. While this differential reliance on heuristics is widely accepted, the exact underlying mechanisms are still debated. While most approaches implicitly or explicitly share the notion that individuals use their affective state as a source of information, they differ on what information is implied by a particular affective state, and what implications can be derived from this information (for an interesting integration of the different accounts see Schwarz & Clore, 1996). From this perspective more evidence is needed that directly addresses the question under which conditions affective states inform the individual about what and with what implication.

Conclusions and Outlook

In sum, the available evidence documents that individuals' affective states may influence a wide spectrum of cognitive processes. Research in the last two decades has not only discovered many interesting phenomena, but has also provided conceptual frameworks that contribute to a much better understanding of how our moods influence our social thinking. Despite the indisputable progress, many questions remain open and new questions have emerged. Perhaps the most important of these questions pertain to (a) different types of affective states, (b) the integration of the various effects, and (c) the link to other subjective experiences.

First, most research has focused on positive versus negative affective states. In most of the studies, the role of happy and sad moods was investigated. However, affective states differ not only in the valence, but in many other respects. Not surprisingly, anger and sadness may have very different implications on cognitive processes, although both have a negative valence (see Bodenhausen, Sheppard, & Kramer, 1994). Presumably, these differential effects can be reconciled within the present models. However, an investigation of these effects requires, and contributes to, a more detailed specification of these models.

Second, and perhaps most importantly, an integration of the various potential effects of individuals' affective states on their cognitive processes is needed. Some very interesting attempts have been proposed (for example, Clore, Wyer, et al., in press; Forgas, 1995a; Schwarz, in press). However, at present it seems that while these integrative models are able to explain a large variety of effects, they more or less lack a detailed specification of when to expect what kind of effect. In this respect, it is presumably not enough to point out the multiple roles of affective states and assign obtained patterns to one of these roles.

Third, more integrative developments in the future will need to link the mechanism underlying the interplay of affect and cognition to other, non-emotional subjective experiences or feeling states (Clore, 1992), such as ease of retrieval, feelings of familiarity, etc. (for approaches in this direction see, for example, Schwarz, in press; Schwarz & Clore, 1996). Regardless of the exact answers to the current research questions, it seems clear that the fascinating phenomenon that individuals' affective states may influence basic cognitive processes of social judgment and behavior will continue to attract the interest and attention of researchers.

References

Anderson, J. R. & Bower, G. H. (1973). *Human associative memory*. Washington, DC: Winston.

Blaney, P. H. (1986). Affect and memory: A review. *Psychological Bulletin, 99*, 229–246.

Bless, H. (1997). *Stimmung und Denken: Ein Modell zum Einfluß von Stimmungen auf Denkprozesse* [Affect and cognition]. Bern: Huber.

Bless, H., & Fiedler, K. (1995). Affective states and the influence of activated general knowledge. *Personality and Social Psychology Bulletin, 21*, 766–778.

Bless, H., & Schwarz, N. (in press). Sufficient and necessary conditions in dual process models: The case of mood and information processing. In S. Chaiken & Y. Trope (Eds.), *Dual Process Theories in Social Psychology*. New York: Guilford Press.

Bless, H., Schwarz, N., & Wieland, R. (1996). Mood and stereotyping: The impact of category and individuating information. *European Journal of Social Psychology, 26*, 935–959.

Bless, H., Hamilton, D. L., & Mackie, D. M. (1992). Mood effects on the organization of person information. *European Journal of Social Psychology, 22*, 497–509.

Bless, H., Mackie, D. M., & Schwarz, N. (1992). Mood effects on encoding and judgmental processes in persuasion. *Journal of Personality and Social Psychology, 63*, 585–595.

Bless, H., Bohner, G., Schwarz, N., & Strack, F. (1990). Mood and persuasion: A cognitive response analysis. *Personality and Social Psychology Bulletin, 16*, 331–345.

Bless, H., Clore, G. L, Schwarz, N., Golisano, V., Rabe, C., & Wölk, M. (1996). Mood and the use of scripts: Does happy mood make people really mindless? *Journal of Personality and Social Psychology, 63*, 585–595.

Bodenhausen, G. V. (1993). Emotions, arousal, and stereotype-based discrimination: A heuristic model of affect and stereotyping. In D. M. Mackie & D. L. Hamilton (Eds.), *Affect, cognition, and stereotyping: Interactive processes in group perception* (pp. 13–35). San Diego, CA: Academic Press.

Bodenhausen, G. V., & Lichtenstein, M. (1987). Social stereotypes and information processing strategies: Testing process models for stereotype use. *Journal of Personality and Social Psychology, 52*, 871–880.

Bodenhausen, G. V., Kramer, G. P., & Süsser, K. (1994). Happiness and stereotypic thinking in social judgment. *Journal of Personality and Social Psychology, 66*, 621–632.

Bodenhausen, G. V., Sheppard, L. A., & Kramer, G. P. (1994). Negative affect and social judgment: The differential impact of anger and sadness. *European Journal of Social Psychology, 24*, 45–62.

Bohner, G., Moskowitz, G. B., & Chaiken, S. (1995). The interplay of heuristic and systematic processing of social information. In W. Stroebe & M. Hewstone (Eds.), *European Review of Social Psychology*, Vol. 6 (pp. 33–68). Chichester, UK: Wiley & Sons.

Bohner, G., Bless, H., Schwarz, N., & Strack, F. (1988). When do events trigger attributions? The impact of valence and subjective probability. *European Journal of Social Psychology, 18*, 335–345.

Bohner, G., Crow, K., Erb, H.-P., & Schwarz, N. (1992). Affect and persuasion: Mood effects on the processing of message content and context cues. *European Journal of Social Psychology, 22*, 511–530.

Bower, G. H. (1981). Mood and memory. *American Psychologist, 36*, 129–148.

Bower, G. H., & Mayer, J. D. (1985). Failure to replicate mood congruent retrieval. *Bulletin of the Psychonomic Society, 23*, 39–42.

Bower, G. H., Montiero, K. P., & Gilligan, S. G. (1978). Emotional mood as a context for learning and recall. *Journal of Verbal Learning and Verbal Behavior, 17*, 573–585.

Brewer, M. A. (1988). A dual model of impression formation. In T. K. Srull & R. S. Wyer (Eds.), *Advances in Social Cognition, 1* (pp. 1–35).

Chaiken, S. (1980). Heuristic versus systematic information and the use of source versus message cues in persuasion. *Journal of Personality and Social Psychology, 39*, 752–766.

Chaiken, S. (1987). The heuristic model of persuasion. In M. P. Zanna, J. M. Olson, & C. P.

Herman (Eds.), *Social influence: The Ontario Symposium*, Vol. 5 (pp. 3–39). Hillsdale, NJ: Erlbaum.

Clore, G. L. (1992). Cognitive phenomenology: Feelings and the construction of judgment. In L. L. Martin & A. Tesser (Eds.), *The construction of social judgment* (pp. 133–163). Hillsdale, NJ: Erlbaum.

Clore, G. L., Schwarz, N., & Conway, M. (1994). Cognitive causes and consequences of emotion. In R. S. Wyer & T. K. Srull (Eds.), *Handbook of social cognition*. 2nd. edn. Vol. 1 (pp. 323–417). Hillsdale, NJ: Erlbaum.

Clore, G. L., Wyer, R. S., Jr., Dienes, B., Gasper, K., Gohm, C., & Isbell, L. (in press). Affective feelings as feedback: Some cognitive consequences. In L. L. Martin & G. L. Clore (Eds.), *Mood and social cognition: Contrasting theories*. Mahwah, NJ: Lawrence Erlbaum Associates.

Descartes, R. (1649/1961). *Passions of the soul: Essential works of Descartes*. Trans. L. Blair. New York: Bantam Books.

Dovidio, J. F. (1998). Subjective experience and intergroup relations: The role of positive affect. Paper presented at the EAESP conference on subjective experiences, Grasellenbach, Germany.

Eagly, A. H., & Chaiken, S. (1993). *The psychology of attitudes*. Fort Worth, TX: Harcourt Brace Jovanovich.

Edwards, J. A., & Weary, G. (1993). Depression and the impression-formation continuum: Piecemeal processing despite the availability of category information. *Journal of Personality and Social Psychology, 64*, 636–645.

Eich, E., & Macaulay, D. (in press). Cognitive and clinical perspectives on mood dependent memory. In J. P. Forgas (Ed.), *Feeling and thinking: The role of affect in social cognition*. New York: Cambridge University Press.

Eich, E., & Metcalfe, J. (1989). Mood dependent memory for internal versus external events. *Journal of Experimental Psychology: Learning, Memory, and Cognition, 15*, 443–455.

Eich, J. E. (1980). The cue-dependent nature of state-dependent retrieval. *Memory and Cognition, 8*, 157–173.

Ellis, H. C. (1991). Focused attention and depressive deficits in memory. *Journal of Experimental Psychology: General, 120*, 310–312.

Ellis, H. C., & Ashbrook, P. W. (1988). Resource allocation model of the effects of depressed mood states on memory. In K. Fiedler & J. Forgas (Eds.), *Affect, cognition, and social behavior* (pp. 25–43). Toronto: Hogrefe International.

Erber, R. (1996). The self-regulation of moods. In L. L. Martin & A. Tesser (Eds.), *Striving and feeling: Interactions among goals, affect, and self-regulation* (pp. 251–275). Mahwah, NJ: Lawrence Erlbaum Associates.

Erber, R. (in press). Mood and processing: A view from a self-regulation perspective. In L. L. Martin & G. L. Clore (Eds.), *Mood and social cognition: Contrasting theories*. Mahwah, NJ: Lawrence Erlbaum Associates.

Erber, R., Wegner, D. M., & Therriault, N. (1996). On being cool and collected: Mood regulation in anticipation of social interaction. *Journal of Personality and Social Psychology, 70*, 757–766.

Fiedler, K. (1997). Explaining and simulating judgment biases as an aggregation phenomenon in probabilistic, multiple-cue environments. *Psychological Review, 103*, 193–214.

Fiedler, K. (1991). On the task, the measures and the mood in research on affect and cognition. In J. Forgas (Ed.), *Emotion and social judgments* (pp. 83–104). Oxford, UK: Pergamon Press.

Fiedler, K. (in press). Explaining major findings and their boundary conditions in terms of mood dependent assimilation and accommodation. In L. L. Martin & G. L. Clore (Eds.), *Mood and social cognition: Contrasting theories*. Mahwah, NJ: Lawrence Erlbaum Associates.

Fiedler, K., & Forgas, J. P. (Eds.) (1988). *Affect, cognition, and social behavior*. Toronto: Hogrefe International.

Fiedler, K., Pampe, H., & Scherf, U. (1986). Mood and memory for tightly organized social information. *European Journal of Social Psychology, 16*, 149–164.

Fiske, S. T., & Neuberg, S. L. (1990). A continuum of impression formation from category-based to individuating processing: Influences of information and motivation on attention and interpretation. In M. P. Zanna (Ed.), *Advances in experimental social psychology*, Vol. 23 (pp. 1–74). Orlando, FL: Academic Press.

Fiske, S., & Taylor, S. (1994). *Social cognition.* 2nd. edn. Reading, MA: Addison-Wesley.

Forgas, J. P. (Ed.) (1991). *Emotion and social judgments.* Oxford: Pergamon Press.

Forgas, J. P. (1992a). Affect in social judgments and decisions: A multi-process model. In M. P. Zanna (Ed.), *Advances in experimental social psychology,* Vol. 25 (pp. 227–275). San Diego, CA: Academic Press.

Forgas, J. P. (1992b). On mood and peculiar people: Affect and person typicality in impression formation. *Journal of Personality and Social Psychology, 62,* 863–875.

Forgas, J. P. (1995a). Mood and judgment: The affect infusion model (AIM). *Psychological Bulletin, 117* (1), 39–66.

Forgas, J. P. (1995b) Strange couples: Mood effects on judgments and memory about prototypical and atypical targets. *Personality and Social Psychology Bulletin, 21,* 747–765.

Forgas, J. P. (Ed.) (in press-a). *Feeling and thinking: The role of affect in social cognition.* New York: Cambridge University Press.

Forgas, J. P. (in press-b). Affect and information processing strategies: An interactive relationship. In J. P. Forgas (Ed.), *Feeling and thinking: The role of affect in social cognition.* New York: Cambridge University Press.

Forgas, J. P., & Bower, G. H. (1987). Mood effects on person-perception judgments. *Journal of Personality and Social Psychology, 53,* 53–60.

Forgas, J. P., & Fiedler, K. (1996). Us and them: Mood effects on intergroup discrimination. *Journal of Personality and Social Psychology, 70,* 28–40.

Freud, S. (1940–1968). *Gesammelte Werke.* Frankfurt: Fischer.

Frijda, N. H. (1988). The laws of emotion. *American Psychologist, 43,* 349–358.

Hasher, L., Rose, K. C., Zacks, R. T., Sanft, H., & Doren, B. (1985). Mood, recall, and selectivity in normal college students. *Journal of Experimental Psychology: General, 114,* 104–118.

Hastie, R., & Park, B. (1986). The relationship between memory and judgment depends on whether the judgment task is memory-based or on-line. *Psychological Review, 93,* 258–268.

Hertel, P. T., & Hardin, T. S. (1990). Remembering with and without awareness in a depressed mood: Evidence of deficits in initiative. *Journal of Experimental Psychology: General, 119,* 45–59.

Hilgard, E. R. (1980). A trilogy of mind: Cognition, affection, and conation. *Journal of the History of the Behavioral Sciences, 16,* 107–117.

Hirt, E. H., McDonald, H. E., & Melton, R. J. (1996). Processing goals and the affect–performance link: Mood as main effect or mood as input? In L. L. Martin & A. Tesser (Eds.), *Striving and feeling: Interactions among goals, affect, and self-regulation* (pp. 303–328). Mahwah, NJ: Lawrence Erlbaum Associates.

Hirt, E. R., Melton, R. J., McDonald, H. E., & Harackiewicz, J. M. (1996). Processing goals, task interest, and the mood–performance relationship: A mediational analysis. *Journal of Personality and Social Psychology, 71,* 245–261.

Ingram, R. E. (1990). Self-focused attention in clinical disorders: Review and a conceptual model. *Psychological Bulletin, 107,* 156–176.

Innes, J. M., & Ahrens, C. R. (1991). Positive mood, processing goals, and the effects of information on evaluative judgment. In J. Forgas (Ed.), *Emotion and social judgment* (pp. 221–239). Oxford: Pergamon Press.

Isen, A. M. (1984). Toward understanding the role of affect in cognition. In R. S. Wyer, Jr., & T. K. Srull (Eds.), *Handbook of social cognition,* Vol. 3 (pp. 179–236). Hillsdale, NJ: Erlbaum.

Isen, A. M. (1987). Positive affect, cognitive processes, and social behavior. In L. Berkowitz (Ed.), *Advances in experimental social psychology,* Vol. 20 (pp. 203–253). San Diego, CA: Academic Press.

Isen, A. M., & Daubman, K. A. (1984). The influence of affect on categorization. *Journal of Personality and Social Psychology, 47,* 1206–1217.

Isen, A. M., Daubman, K. A., & Gorgoglione, J. M. (1987). The influence of positive affect on cognitive organization. In R. Snow & M. Farr (Eds.), *Aptitude, learning and instruction: Affective and conative processes* Vol. 3. Hillsdale, NJ: Erlbaum.

Isen, A. M., Daubman, K. A., & Nowicki, G. P. (1987). Positive affect facilitates creative problem solving. *Journal of Personality and Social Psychology, 52,* 1122–1131.

Isen, A. M., Johnson, M. M. S., Mertz, E., & Robinson, G. (1985). The influence of positive affect on the unusualness of word association. *Journal of Personality and Social Psychology, 48,* 1413–1426.

Isen, A. M., Means, B., Patrick, R., & Nowicki, G. (1982). Some factors influencing decision making strategy and risk-taking. In M. S. Clark & S. T. Fiske (Eds.), *Affect and cognition: The 17th Annual Carnegie Mellon Symposium on Cognition* (pp. 241–261). Hillsdale, NJ: Erlbaum.

Isen, A. M., Shalker, T. E., Clark, M. S., & Karp, L. (1978). Affect, accessibility of material in memory, and behavior: A cognitive loop? *Journal of Personality and Social Psychology, 36,* 1–12.

Jacobsen, E. (1957). Normal and pathological moods: Their nature and function. In R. S. Eisler, A. F. Freud, H. Hartman, & E. Kris (Eds.), *The psychoanalytic study of the child* (pp. 73–113). New York: International University Press.

James, W. (1890). The principles of psychology. In R. M. Hutchins (Ed.), *The great book of the western world* (p. 348). Chicago: Encyclopaedia Brittanica, LIII.

Judd, C. M., & Lusk, C. M. (1984). Knowledge structures and evaluative judgments: Effects of structural variables on judgment extremity. *Journal of Personality & Social Psychology, 46,* 1193–1207.

Kihlstrom, J. F. (1989). On what does mood-dependent memory depend? *Journal of Social Behavior and Personality, 4,* 23–32.

Levine, S., Wyer, R. S., Jr., & Schwarz, N. (1994). Are you what you feel? The affective and cognitive determinants of self-esteem. *European Journal of Social Psychology, 24,* 64–77.

Lichtenstein, M., & Srull, T. K. (1987). Processing objectives as a determinant of the relation between recall and judgment. *Journal of Experimental Social Psychology, 23,* 93–118.

Mackie, D. M., & Worth, L. T. (1989). Cognitive deficits and the mediation of positive affect in persuasion. *Journal of Personality and Social Psychology, 57,* 27–40.

Mackie, D. M., Asuncion, A. G., & Rosselli, F. (1992). The impact of positive affect on persuasion processes. In M. S. Clark (Ed.), *Review of personality and social psychology,* Vol. 14 (pp. 247–270). Beverly Hills, CA: Sage.

Martin, L. L. (in press). Moods don't cause effects, people do: A mood as input look at mood effects. In L. L. Martin & G. L. Clore (Eds.), *Mood and social cognition: Contrasting theories.* Mahwah, NJ: Lawrence Erlbaum Associates.

Martin, L. L., & Achee, J. W. (1992) Beyond accessibility: The role of processing objectives in judgment. In L. L. Martin & A. Tesser (Eds.), *The construction of social judgment* (pp. 195–216). Hillsdale: Erlbaum.

Martin, L. L., & Clore, G. L. (Eds.) (in press). *Mood and social cognition: Contrasting theories.* Mahwah, NJ: Lawrence Erlbaum Associates.

Martin, L. L., & Stoner, P. (1996). Mood as input: What people think about how they feel moods determines how they think. In L. L. Martin & A. Tesser (Eds.), *Striving and feeling: Interactions between goals, affect, and self-regulation* (pp. 279–301). Hillsdale, NJ: Lawrence Erlbaum Associates.

Martin, L. L., Abend, T., Sedikides, C., & Greene, J. D. (1997). How would if feel if . . .? Mood as input to a role fulfillment evaluation process. *Journal of Personality and Social Psychology, 73,* 242–253.

Martin, L. M., Ward, D. W., Achee, J. W., & Wyer, R. S. (1993). Mood as input: People have to interpret the motivational implications of their moods. *Journal of Personality and Social Psychology, 64,* 317–326.

Matlin, M. W., & Stang, D. J. (1979). *The Pollyanna principle.* Cambridge, MA: Schenkman.

Millar, M. G., & Tesser, A. (1986). Thought-induced attitude change: The effects of schema structure and commitment. *Journal of Personality and Social Psychology, 51,* 259–269.

Morris, W. N. (1989). *Mood: The frame of mind.* New York: Springer.

Murray, N., Sujan, H., Hirt, E. R., & Sujan, M. (1990). The influence of mood on categorization: A cognitive flexibility interpretation. *Journal of Personality and Social Psychology, 59,* 411–425.

Nasby, W., & Yando, R. (1982). Selective encoding and retrieval of affectively valent information. *Journal of Personality and Social Psychology, 43,* 1244–1255.

Nisbett, R., & Ross, L. (1980). *Human inference: Strategies and shortcomings in social judgment.*

Englewood Cliffs, NJ: Prentice-Hall.

Nowlis, V. (1965). Research with the mood adjective checklist. In S. S. Tomkins & C. E. Izard (Eds.), *Affect, cognition, and personality*. New York: Springer.

Nowlis, V., & Nowlis, H. H. (1956). The description and analysis of mood. *Annals of the New York Academy of Sciences, 65*, 345–355.

Parrott, W. G. (1993). Beyond hedonism: Motives for inhibiting good moods and for maintaining bad moods. In D. M. Wegner & J. W. Pennebaker (Eds.), *Handbook of mental control* (pp. 278–305). Englewood Cliffs, NJ: Prentice-Hall.

Parrott, W. G., & Sabini, J. (1990). Mood and memory under natural conditions: Evidence for mood incongruent recall. *Journal of Personality and Social Psychology, 59*, 321–336.

Perrig, W. J., & Perrig, P. (1988). Mood and memory: Mood-congruity effects in absence of mood. *Memory & Cognition, 16*, 102–109.

Petty, R. E., & Cacioppo, J. T. (1986b). The elaboration likelihood model of persuasion. In L. Berkowitz (Ed.), *Advances in Experimental Social Psychology, 19*, 124–203. New York: Academic Press.

Pribram, H. H. (1970). Feelings as monitors. In M. Arnold (Ed.), *Feelings and emotions* (pp. 41–53). New York: Academic Press.

Schwarz, N. (1990). Feelings as information: Informational and motivational functions of affective states. In R. M. Sorrentino & E. T. Higgins (Eds.), *Handbook of motivation and cognition: Foundations of social behavior*, Vol. 2 (pp. 527–561). New York: Guilford Press.

Schwarz, N. (in press). Feelings as information: Implications for affective influences on information processing. In L. L. Martin & G. L. Clore (Eds.), *Mood and social cognition: Contrasting theories*. Mahwah, NJ: Lawrence Erlbaum Associates.

Schwarz, N., & Bless, H. (1992). Constructing reality and its alternatives: An inclusion/exclusion model of assimilation and contrast effects in social judgment. In L. L. Martin & A. Tesser (Eds.), *The construction of social judgment* (pp. 217–245). Hillsdale: Erlbaum.

Schwarz, N., & Clore, G. L. (1983). Mood, misattribution, and judgments of well-being: Informative and directive functions of affective states. *Journal of Personality and Social Psychology, 45*, 513–523.

Schwarz, N., & Clore, G. L. (1988). How do I feel about it? Informative functions of affective states. In K. Fiedler & J. Forgas (Eds.), *Affect, cognition, and social behavior* (pp. 44–62). Toronto: Hogrefe International.

Schwarz, N., & Clore, G. L. (1996). Feelings and phenomenal experiences. In E. T. Higgins & A. Kruglanski (Eds.), *Social psychology: A handbook of basic principles* (pp. 433–465). New York: Guilford Press.

Schwarz, N., Bless, H., & Bohner, G. (1991). Mood and persuasion: Affective states influence the processing of persuasive communications. In M. Zanna (Ed.), *Advances in experimental social psychology*, Vol. 24 (pp. 161–197). New York: Academic Press.

Schwarz, N., Strack, F., Kommer, D., & Wagner, D. (1988). Soccer, rooms, and the quality of your life: Mood effects on judgments of satisfaction with life in general and with specific domains. *European Journal of Social Psychology, 17*, 69–79.

Siemer, M., & Reisenzein, R. (in press). Emotion and cognition. Effects of mood on evaluative judgments: Influence of reduced processing capacity and mood salience. *Emotion and Cognition*.

Sinclair, R. C. (1988). Mood, categorization breadth, and performance appraisal: The effects of order of information acquisition and affective state on halo, accuracy, information retrieval, and evaluations. *Organizational Behavior and Human Decision Processes, 42*, 22–46.

Sinclair, R. C., & Mark, M. M. (1992). The influence of mood state on judgment and action: Effects on persuasion, categorization, social justice, person perception, and judgmental accuracy. In L. L. Martin & A. Tesser (Eds.), *The construction of social judgment* (pp. 165–193). Hillsdale, NJ: Erlbaum.

Sinclair, R. C., Mark, M. M., & Clore, G. L. (1994). Mood-related persuasion depends on misattributions. *Social Cognition, 12*, 309–326.

Stangor, C., & McMillan, D. (1992). Memory for expectancy-congruent and expectancy-incongruent information: A review of the social and social developmental literatures. *Psychological Bulletin*,

111, 42–61.

Teasdale, J. D. R., Taylor, R., & Fogarty, S. J. (1979). Effects of induced elation–depression on the accessibility of memories of happy and unhappy experiences. *Behavior Research and Therapy, 18,* 339–346.

Tesser, A. (1978). Self-generated attitude change. In L. Berkowitz (Ed.), *Advances in experimental social psychology,* Vol. 11 (pp. 289–338). New York: Academic Press.

Tetlock, P. E. (1983). Accountability and complexity of thought. *Journal of Personality and Social Psychology, 45,* 74–83.

Tomkins, S. S. (1981). The quest for primary motives: Biography and autobiography of an idea. *Journal of Personality and Social Psychology, 41,* 306–329.

Tversky, A., & Kahneman, D. (1973). Availability: A heuristic for judging frequency and probability. *Cognitive Psychology, 5,* 207–232.

Ucros, C. G. (1989). Mood state-dependent memory: A meta-analysis. *Cognition and Emotion, 3,* 139–167.

Wegener, D. T., & Petty, R. E. (1994). Mood management across affective states: The hedonic contingency hypothesis. *Journal of Personality and Social Psychology, 66,* 1034–1048.

Wegener, D. T., & Petty, R. E. (1996). Effects of mood on persuasion processes. In L. L. Martin & A. Tesser (Eds.), *Striving and feeling: Interactions among goals, affect, and self-regulation* (pp. 303–328). Mahwah, NJ: Lawrence Erlbaum Associates.

Wegener, D. T., Petty, R. E., & Smith, S. M. (1995). Positive mood can increase or decrease message scrutiny: The hedonic contingency view of mood and message processing. *Journal of Personality and Social Psychology, 69,* 5–15.

Worth, L. T., & Mackie, D. M. (1987). Cognitive mediation of positive affect in persuasion. *Social Cognition, 5,* 76–94.

Wyer, R. S., Jr., & Srull, T. K. (1989). *Memory and cognition in its social context.* Hillsdale, NJ: Erlbaum.

Zajonc, R. B. (1980). Feeling and thinking: Preferences need no inferences. *American Psychologist, 35,* 151–175.

Chapter Nineteen

Attitudes, Persuasion, and Behavior

Gerd Bohner and Norbert Schwarz

Social psychologists conceptualize attitudes as "a psychological tendency that is expressed by evaluating a particular entity with some degree of favor or disfavor" (Eagly & Chaiken, 1993, p. 1; see chapter 20, this volume, for a review of different definitions). Although most definitions characterize attitudes as *relatively enduring* mental states, attitudes change as people interact with their social environment. In fact, the bulk of attitude research has addressed the conditions and processes of attitude change. Understanding the dynamics of attitude change is as useful for basic researchers who try to explain social information processing as it is vital for practitioners in business, health, law, marketing, or politics who are interested in effective strategies of influencing attitudes and behavior. The present chapter provides a selective review of mainstream theorizing in two key areas of attitude research. We first address attitude change through persuasion and subsequently review research into the attitude–behavior relationship. Issues pertaining to the conceptualization of attitudes and the emergence of context effects in attitude measurement are discussed by Schwarz and Bohner (chapter 20, this volume).

Persuasion

Persuasion research addresses the formation and change of attitudes as a result of information processing, often in response to messages about the attitude object. As Petty & Cacioppo (1981) noted, theories of attitude change can be classified according to the amount of cognitive effort that is involved in the change processes they address. We first review key examples of attitude change processes that involve relatively low versus relatively high cognitive effort, which have been identified in separate and largely unrelated research programs. Subsequently, we address current "dual-process" models of persuasion, which provide conceptual frameworks for the interplay of these different processes and identify the conditions under which each one is likely to come to bear.

Persuasion processes that require little cognitive effort

Starting from the assumption that attitudes are learned dispositions (Allport, 1935; Doob, 1947), early theorists tried to explain attitude change as a result of classical or operant conditioning. In classical conditioning, an initially neutral stimulus is repeatedly paired with another stimulus that strongly evokes a certain response; learning is said to have occurred when the initially neutral stimulus alone suffices to evoke the response. In operant conditioning, learning occurs when responses increase in frequency because they have posi-tive consequences (a process called reinforcement), or decrease in frequency because they have negative consequences (a process called punishment).

Classical conditioning   Attitude researchers showed that covert positive or negative evalu-ations can be created in humans as conditioned responses if novel stimuli are repeatedly paired with unconditioned stimuli that already elicit positive or negative responses. Razran (1940), for example, repeatedly exposed participants to various slogans, under one of three conditions: (a) eating a free lunch, (b) inhaling unpleasant smells, (c) sitting in a neutral setting. Both before and after exposure, participants' agreement with each slogan was as-sessed. Although participants were unable to recall which slogan was paired with which environment, they showed increased agreement with slogans that were paired with the free lunch, decreased agreement with slogans paired with disagreeable odors, and did not change their evaluation of slogans paired with the neutral setting. Staats & Staats (1958) used spoken words (e.g. sour, beautiful) as unconditioned stimuli and names of nationalities (e.g. Dutch, Swedish), presented visually, as conditioned stimuli. They found that post-conditioning attitudes toward the nationalities, assessed with a semantic differential scale, reflected the valence of the adjectives the nationalities had been paired with.

It has been disputed whether these effects are indeed due to a conditioning process or reflect conscious inferences instead. For example, participants may conclude that the na-tionalities actually possess the attributes with which they are presented and may infer addi-tional, evaluatively consistent attributes. They may also infer that the researcher expects them to provide evaluations that are congruent with the nationality–adjective pairings. This explanation in terms of demand characteristics was advanced by Page (1969), who found that "conditioning" effects were in fact stronger for people who reported in post-experimental interviews that they were aware of the contingency. Staats and his colleagues, in turn, criticized the reactivity of Page's methodology: Page's extensive interviews may have created awareness of the contingency in hindsight, especially in those participants who had shown a strong conditioning effect (Staats, Minke, Martin, & Higa, 1972).

To address this issue, subsequent research separated the assessment of evaluative re-sponses from the conditioning trials, or presented the unconditioned stimuli outside of conscious awareness. For example, Berkowitz & Knurek (1969) used the Staats & Staats (1958) procedures to create negative and positive attitudes, respectively, towards the names "Ed" and "George." Later, in an ostensibly unrelated experiment, each of their participants met two confederates who introduced themselves as Ed and George. Participants' ratings of the confederates, as well as the confederates' ratings of the participants' behavior, showed an effect of the previous conditioning. More recently, Krosnick, Betz, Jussim, & Lynn

(1992) asked students to watch slides depicting a target person engaged in various ambiguous activities. Depending on experimental condition, these slides were immediately preceded by briefly flashed pictures of positive (e.g. a bridal couple) or negative primes (e.g. a werewolf). This variation influenced the students' attitudes toward the stimulus person, even though participants were unable to detect the affective connotations of the primes. In combination, findings of this type render a simple demand–effects explanation of attitude conditioning unlikely.

Operant conditioning   Inspired by Skinner's (1957) account of human verbal behavior in terms of operant conditioning, several studies applied principles of reinforcement to attitude statements. For example, Hildum & Brown (1956) interviewed Harvard students about their attitudes toward certain university policies. In one condition, every time a student responded favorably, the interviewer reinforced this response by saying either "good" or "mm-hmm"; in another condition, the reinforcement was applied to unfavorable responses. Students who were reinforced for unfavorable statements finally reported a less positive attitude than those who were reinforced for favorable statements.

As with classical conditioning accounts, participants' awareness of the contingency (here between behavior and reinforcement) and compliance with demand characteristics may provide alternative explanations (see Dulany, 1962). However, Insko (1965) showed that attitude change as a result of verbal conditioning could still be detected after one week and in a completely different context, rendering demand characteristics an unlikely explanation. Insko & Cialdini (1969) proposed a two-factor theory of verbal reinforcement. They assumed that the interviewer's "good" or "mm-hmm" responses have two functions: they (a) serve as a cue to the position the interviewer approves of and (b) establish "rapport" between interviewer and respondent. The former represents *informational influence*; the latter, by creating a social incentive to agree with the experimenter, *normative influence*. Several experiments confirmed that both processes contribute to the effect of verbal conditioning, although they may not be necessary mediators.

To summarize, it is possible to influence people's attitudes about objects by establishing a close connection in space and time between (a) these objects and positive or negative stimuli (classical conditioning), or (b) between evaluative responses to the attitude object and reinforcements (operant conditioning). In everyday experience, we indeed consistently encounter many attitude objects in positive or negative contexts, satisfying the requirements for classical conditioning. Similarly, many evaluative responses to objects are likely to be rewarded or punished, and the formation of attitudes that maximize rewards and minimize punishments would be highly functional (see Shavitt, 1989, for a review of the functions of attitudes).

Feelings and subjective experiences as sources of attitudes   Whereas conditioning studies try to induce enduring attitude change by pairing the attitude object with pleasant or unpleasant contexts or consequences, other research demonstrated that hedonic experiences may influence attitudes through other mechanisms. For example, one economic strategy of making an evaluative judgment is to rely on the *feelings* that are apparently elicited by the attitude object. After all, things we like tend to evoke positive feelings, and things we dislike evoke negative feelings, so why not use our affective responses as a shortcut to an evaluative judgment? Unfortunately, however, it is difficult to distinguish between feelings elicited by the attitude object and feelings one happens to experience at the time of judgment, but for irrelevant reasons. Hence, when we ask ourselves, "How do I feel about this?" we may misread our pre-existing feelings as a response to the attitude object. Consistent with this notion, numerous studies demonstrated that individuals report more positive attitudes towards a wide variety of objects when they are in a happy rather than sad mood, unless they are aware that their mood is due to a source unrelated to the attitude object (for reviews see Schwarz, 1990; Bless, chapter 18, this volume). Such influences, however, are likely to be temporary and vanish as the mood dissipates.

Another subjective experience that individuals may draw on in forming an attitude judgment is the ease or difficulty with which relevant information can be brought to mind. For example, arguments that are easy to generate or process are perceived as more valid, and elicit more attitude change, than arguments that are difficult to generate or process (e.g. Wänke, Bless, & Biller, 1996; Wänke, Bohner, & Jurkowitsch, 1997). Bless (chapter 18, this volume) discusses the role of feelings and subjective experiences in information processing.

Heuristic processing   Consulting one's feelings as a basis of attitude judgments ("How do I feel about this?"; Schwarz, 1990) can be conceptualized as an example of heuristic processing. While this heuristic makes use of internal cues, persuasion researchers have mostly focused on heuristics that pertain to external cues (see Eagly & Chaiken, 1993, for a review). Examples for such persuasion cues are *expertise, likability,* and *consensus.* Thus, people may use the heuristic rules "Experts' statements are valid," "I agree with people I like," or "The majority is usually right," which leads them to agree with experts, likable people, and majorities more than with nonexperts, dislikable people, and minorities. To do so, they must (a) perceive a relevant heuristic cue and (b) have an applicable heuristic accessible in memory. As with conditioning and the use of feelings as information, individuals need not necessarily be aware that they are applying a heuristic in arriving at an attitude judgment. Heuristics are especially influential in situations where an individual has little motivation or ability to engage in more extensive forms of processing. Their use is guided by the "principle of least cognitive effort" (Allport, 1954; see Bohner, Moskowitz, & Chaiken, 1995).

Persuasion through effortful processing

Note that none of the preceding processes involved any detailed attention to the persuasive message or the nature of the attitude object. In contrast, other lines of research have focused on recipients' thoughts about what is being said by whom and why.

Processing of message content and persuasion   The importance of effortful processing of message content was first emphasized by Hovland and his colleagues in their message-learning approach to persuasion (Hovland, Janis, & Kelley, 1953). This approach does not represent a unitary theory; rather, it can be understood as an eclectic set of working assumptions. Its proponents assumed that attitude change is mediated by the learning and recall of message content, which would be facilitated by incentives to adopt the position advocated. Their research focused on various elements of the persuasion setting that would affect message learning.

The classes of independent variables examined were the message source (e.g. its expertise or trustworthiness), the message (e.g. its length and structure), recipient characteristics (e.g. self-esteem, intelligence), and the channel of the communication (e.g. written versus spoken). Internal mediating processes that were studied include *attention* to the message, *comprehension* of its content, *rehearsal* of arguments, and *yielding* to the message position. The dependent variables assessed were changes in beliefs, attitudes, and behavior.

By structuring the persuasion process in such a way, and by examining a host of interesting phenomena, the message-learning approach had a profound impact on later generations of persuasion research (for an overview of findings, see Petty & Cacioppo, 1981, ch. 3). However, due to its lack of a unifying theory, this approach accumulated ad hoc explanations for a variety of effects, which were often contradictory and could not be meaningfully integrated.

A major tenet of the message-learning approach, which was formalized in sequential persuasion models by McGuire (1969, 1985), was that the *reception* (= attention and comprehension) of a message would mediate persuasion. As reception was assumed to be reflected in the recall of message content, high correlations of message recall and attitude change should be the rule. Empirically, however, memory for message content turned out to be a poor predictor of persuasion (see Eagly & Chaiken, 1993, for an overview). Accordingly, researchers' attention turned to other cognitive mediators of attitude change, which emphasized not the passive reception but the active transformation, elaboration, and generation of arguments.

Active thought   Research into the role of active thought includes the study of role-playing as a persuasion technique (e.g. King & Janis, 1956), McGuire's work on the effects of forewarning (McGuire & Papageorgis, 1962), and the study of "mere thought" (Tesser, 1978).

King & Janis (1956) showed that participants who actively improvised a speech based on arguments they had previously read showed greater attitude change than others who merely read externally generated arguments into a tape recorder or silently to themselves. McGuire & Papageorgis (1962) proposed that forewarning recipients of the persuasive intent of a message might help them resist persuasion by stimulating the generation of counterarguments. Various studies have supported this hypothesis. They have also shown that forewarning is only effective if there is a time delay between warning and message, which enables recipients to actively generate counterarguments (for a review see Eagly & Chaiken, 1993).

Finally, work by Tesser (1978) revealed that even in the absence of a persuasive message, *mere thought* about an attitude object can lead to more extreme attitudes. This occurs because people have "naive theories" or schemata which make some attributes of an object more salient and facilitate inferences regarding related attributes. As a result of these directive influences, mere thought about the object increases the extremity of initially moderate attitudes. For example, Sadler & Tesser (1973) introduced research participants to a likable or dislikable "partner" (in fact, a tape recording). Then some participants were asked to think about their partner, while others performed a distraction task. Subsequently, all participants rated their partner on various scales and wrote down their thoughts about him. Compared to distracted participants, nondistracted participants evaluated the likable partner more favorably and listed more positive thoughts about him, but rated the dislikable partner more negatively and listed more negative thoughts about him.

The cognitive response approach   The accumulating evidence for the importance of active thought processes in attitude formation and change led to the formulation of the cognitive response approach to persuasion (Greenwald, 1968; Petty, Ostrom, & Brock, 1981). Its assumptions may be summarized as follows:

1   Individuals who are exposed to a persuasive message actively relate the content of this message to their issue-relevant knowledge and pre-existing attitude toward the message topic, thereby generating new thoughts or *cognitive responses*.
2   Attitude change is mediated by these cognitive responses.
3   The extent and direction of attitude change are a function of the valence of the cognitive responses in relation to the message's content and position. In this sense, cognitive responses can be (a) favorable, (b) unfavorable, or (c) neutral.
4   The greater the proportion of favorable responses and the smaller the proportion of unfavorable responses evoked by a message, the greater the attitude change in the direction advocated by the message.

The cognitive response approach, then, focuses on effortful, systematic processing, guided by the "naive scientist" metaphor of human information processing. To assess the mediational role of cognitive responses in persuasion, a new methodology was introduced, the *thought-listing technique*. Research participants are asked to list, within a given time, any thoughts that have come to mind while they read or heard a persuasive message. These thoughts are later content-analyzed and categorized according to their favorability (or other criteria; see Petty & Cacioppo, 1986a, pp. 38–40). To predict a variable's impact on persuasion, it is crucial to know how this variable affects recipients' cognitive responses to the message. Any factor that increases the likelihood of counterarguing (e.g. forewarning) should decrease persuasion, whereas any factor that increases the likelihood of favorable responses should increase persuasion. Furthermore, if a person's dominant cognitive responses to a message can be expected to be favorable (e.g. a political party member listening to a speech of the party leader), then any factor reducing the overall amount of processing should decrease persuasion, and the opposite should hold if a person's responses can be expected to be unfavorable. These assumptions have been incorporated and further developed in contemporary dual-process models of persuasion, and we address relevant findings in the next section.

Dual-process models of persuasion

As our selective review indicates, attitude change may occur through a variety of different processes, raising the question which one is likely to come to bear under which conditions?

Dual-process models of persuasion attempt to answer this question and have dominated persuasion research since the early 1980s (see the contributions in Chaiken & Trope (1999) for examples and reviews). The two most influential models are the elaboration likelihood model (ELM) proposed by Petty & Cacioppo (1986a, 1986b) and the heuristic–systematic model (HSM) proposed by Chaiken and colleagues (e.g. Bohner, Moskowitz, & Chaiken, 1995; Chen & Chaiken, 1999; Eagly & Chaiken, 1993). Both models incorporate the assumptions of the cognitive response approach about active, effortful processing, but also include persuasion effects based on effortless processing. They distinguish two prototypical modes of persuasion that form the high and low ends of a continuum of processing effort.

The elaboration likelihood model   In the ELM, these modes are called the *central route*, in which persuasion is mediated by effortful scrutiny of message arguments and other relevant information, and the *peripheral route*, which features the influence of peripheral cues and includes a variety of less effortful mechanisms such as conditioning, social identification, or the use of heuristics. Although these two routes have been presented as antagonistic in their impact on persuasion outcomes in early renditions of the ELM (e.g. Petty & Cacioppo, 1986a, 1986b), more recent discussions stressed that the assumed tradeoff between central and peripheral processing does not preclude a co-occurrence of both types of processes (e.g. Petty & Wegener, 1998). Which set of processes comes to bear depends on a recipient's *motivation* and *ability* to process a given message, which determines the message's "elaboration likelihood." Because people have limited time and resources, they cannot elaborate the details of every persuasive message they encounter – thus, peripheral-route processes are typically considered the default. As motivation and ability increase, however, central route processing of the message arguments becomes more likely.

To explore the relative impact of these different processes, researchers vary the presence of peripheral cues (like the expertise or likableness of the source) and the strength of the message arguments. When motivation or ability are low, recipients are likely to rely on peripheral cues and are more persuaded by a source of high rather than low expertise, for example. When motivation or ability are high, however, recipients elaborate on the content of the message and are persuaded by messages that elicit agreeing thoughts (referred to as positive cognitive responses), but not by messages that elicit mostly disagreeing thoughts (see Petty & Cacioppo (1986a, 1986b) for a review of relevant studies).

The systematic variation of argument quality plays an important methodological role in persuasion research. Specifically, it allows researchers to infer the role of a variable in the persuasion process from the result pattern it produces (Petty & Cacioppo, 1986a, 1986b). Research using this methodology demonstrated that the same variable may influence persuasion in different ways under different conditions, as an example may illustrate.

Figure 1 shows different possible patterns that may result from a treatment variable and we illustrate the use of this pattern by drawing on research into the role of distraction in the persuasion process. Early studies in the tradition of consistency theories and the message learning approach had shown that distracting recipients while they are exposed to counterattitudinal messages *increased* persuasion, at least under certain conditions (for a review, see Petty & Brock, 1981). This effect would be in line with dissonance theory (Festinger, 1957): as the effort of listening to a message increases under distraction, recipients may justify this

(1) No effect

(a) Low elaboration

(b) High elaboration

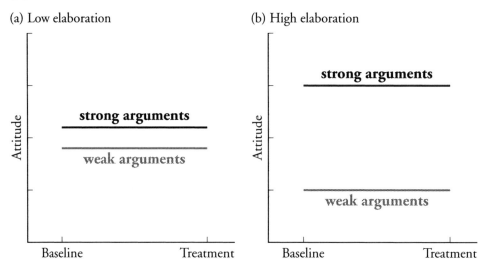

(2) Peripheral cue effect

(a) Positive

(b) Negative

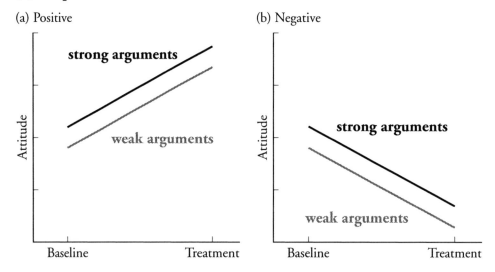

Figure 1 *(above and opposite)*   Possible effects of a treatment variable in the ELM (adapted from Petty & Cacioppo, 1986a, figure 2–3, p. 34).

(3) Objective elaboration

(a) Enhance

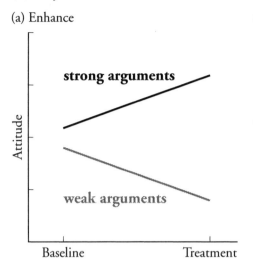

(b) Reduce

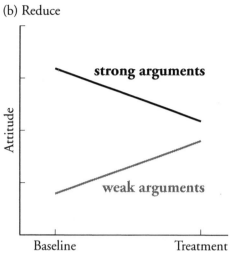

(4) Biased elaboration

(a) Positive

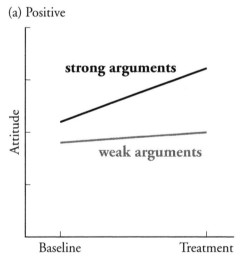

(b) Negative

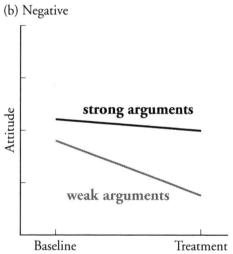

extra effort by changing their attitude in the direction advocated. The effect would also be in line with the cognitive-response approach: the dominant response to an attitude-discrepant message would be counterarguing, and if this process is disrupted, resistance to persuasion is weakened. To disentangle these competing mediational assumptions, Petty, Wells, & Brock (1976) independently varied the level of distraction and argument quality. They reasoned that strong messages would be difficult to counterargue to begin with and thus, according to the CRA, distraction should not enhance persuasion for these messages. The effort justification hypothesis would, however, still predict greater persuasion under high distraction (= high effort) than low distraction (= low effort).

The cognitive-response interpretation both accounted for existing findings and was ex-perimentally supported. Participants in the high-distraction condition agreed less with the message than those in the low-distraction condition when arguments were strong, but agreed more when arguments were weak; the favorability of their cognitive responses showed a parallel pattern (Petty, Wells, & Brock, 1976).

As this example illustrates, the ELM provides a useful framework for re-addressing top-ics in persuasion that had produced seemingly inconsistent findings. Similar interactions with argument quality have been observed for other variables that affect processing via either motivation or ability, such as message repetition, personal relevance, accountability, mood, and number of message sources (for an overview, see Petty & Wegener, 1998). An individual difference variable affecting the degree of elaboration, which was conceptual-ized and studied mainly in the context of the ELM, is the need for cognition (NFC; for a review see Cacioppo, Petty, Feinstein, & Jarvis, 1996). Individuals high in NFC enjoy and tend to engage in effortful thinking across situations and topics, whereas individuals low in NFC are generally unmotivated to expend much cognitive effort, unless forced to do so under situational pressure. Generally, high-NFC (as opposed to low-NFC) individuals have been found to show more central route processing of persuasive messages, but to be less susceptible to the impact of peripheral cues.

Variations in motivation and capacity may not only enhance or reduce the general amount of thinking (i.e. objective elaboration) as in the examples discussed; according to the ELM's biased elaboration postulate, variables may also introduce a positive or negative bias in central route processing. This has been shown for *prior knowledge*, which often enhances the ability to elaborate knowledge-consistent information, and for *forewarning*, which may motivate recipients to counterargue a message. In the absence of external biasing influ-ences, however, people may show a default bias toward favorable elaboration (see Petty & Wegener, 1998, for a review).

In sum, the ELM provides a comprehensive framework of persuasion processes that can accommodate the effects of a wide range of variables and their interactions. It has been criticized, however, for its lack of predictive power (e.g. Eagly & Chaiken, 1993). Specifi-cally, it is difficult to assess the level of elaboration likelihood independent of its effects (see figure 1), and it is often difficult to predict *a priori* in which of the multiple roles featured in the ELM a variable will serve. Furthermore, although Petty and his colleagues acknowl-edge that central and peripheral processes may co-occur (Petty & Wegener, 1998), they do not specify the mechanisms and conditions of their interplay. Both of these issues have been addressed more directly in the other current dual-processing framework of persua-sion, the heuristic-systematic model.

The heuristic-systematic model   The heuristic-systematic model (HSM) of persuasion also features two modes of processing: an effortless, top-down *heuristic* mode and an effortful, bottom-up *systematic* mode (Bohner, Moskowitz, & Chaiken, 1995; Chaiken, Liberman, & Eagly, 1989; Chen & Chaiken, 1999). According to the HSM, message recipients strike a balance between effort minimization and achieving confidence in their social judgments. The model emphasizes three broad motivational forces: *accuracy, defense,* and *impression* motivation. Heuristic and systematic processing can serve either of the three motives and are capable of co-occurring in an additive or interactive fashion under specified conditions.

The main similarities to the ELM lie in the HSM's concept of a processing continuum and the idea that processing effort is a function of motivation and cognitive capacity. *Systematic processing* is defined in a similar way as central route processing as a "comprehensive, analytic orientation in which perceivers access and scrutinize all informational input for its relevance and importance to their judgment task, and integrate all useful information in forming their judgments" (Chaiken, Liberman, & Eagly, 1989, p. 212). *Heuristic processing* is defined more narrowly and more specifically than the ELM's peripheral route. It entails the application of heuristics, simple rules of inference like "consensus implies correctness" or "experts' statements are valid." Although heuristic processing is thought to be a relatively effortless, default mode of processing, its occurrence does require the presence of a heuristic cue (e.g. a likable or expert source) which signals the applicability of a heuristic that is accessible in a recipient's memory.

Generally, systematic processing requires higher motivation and capacity than heuristic processing. However, the HSM's processing continuum features a restrictive and a less restrictive pole. Whereas heuristic processing predominates at low levels of this continuum, the use of more effortful strategies at higher levels does not preclude the continued operation of heuristics. At high levels of motivation and ability, both processing modes affect persuasion either independently or in an interactive fashion. The type and conditions of such interplay of processing modes are specified in four *co-occurrence hypotheses* (Bohner, Moskowitz, & Chaiken, 1995).

The *additivity hypothesis* states that heuristic and systematic processing may exert independent main effects on attitude judgments. This should mainly be the case when the outcomes of each process do not contradict each other, e.g. when an expert source presents cogent arguments. Various studies support this hypothesis (see Bohner, Moskowitz, & Chaiken, 1995, for a review). However, because systematic processing often provides the individual with more, and subjectively more relevant, information any additional effects of heuristic processing may be suppressed. This *attenuation hypothesis* also received ample support (e.g. Chaiken & Maheswaran, 1994; see Bohner, Moskowitz, & Chaiken, 1995).

A third form of interplay between the two processing modes is featured in the HSM's *bias hypothesis*. If message content is ambiguous or mixed (e.g. both strong and weak arguments), initial heuristic-based inferences may guide the interpretation of the message, leading to cognitive responses and attitudes that are assimilated to the valence of a heuristic cue. This has been demonstrated by Chaiken & Maheswaran (1994), who varied message ambiguity and source credibility. As expected, participants with high motivation and ability who received an ambiguous message assimilated cognitive responses and attitude judgments toward the credibility cue. This was not the case, however, when the message was unambiguously strong or weak, in which case only a main effect of argument strength emerged, consistent with the attenuation hypothesis.

Finally, the mirror image of assimilative bias is expressed in the HSM's *contrast hypothesis*. If initial heuristic-based expectancies about a message are blatantly violated, systematic evaluation of the arguments may lead to contrasting interpretations. Thus, positive expectancies that are violated lead to more negative cognitive responses and attitudes, whereas negative expectancies that are disconfirmed may induce a favorable processing bias. In line with this assumption, Bohner & Ruder (1998) observed that recipients expect that experts offer strong arguments, whereas nonexperts offer weak arguments. When message content obviously contradicted these expectations, a bias opposite in valence to the expectation was introduced. For example, a message ascribed to a renowned expert that contained weak arguments led to less positive cognitive responses and attitudes than the same message ascribed to a nonexpert – a contrast effect. In the case of ambiguous arguments, however, participants' expertise-based expectations led to biased assimilation of cognitive responses and attitude judgments.

More explicitly than the ELM, the HSM specifies external criteria of processing motivation. The model's *sufficiency principle* states that people strive for sufficient confidence in their attitude judgments. What is sufficient is determined by two constructs, the sufficiency threshold (ST) or desired confidence, and the actual confidence (AC). Both of these concepts vary between persons and situations. The ST may be raised under high task importance, personal relevance, accountability and so forth, whereas the AC may be decreased by a discrepancy in the valence of heuristic cues and content information (Maheswaran & Chaiken, 1991). The HSM assumes that whenever actual confidence is lower than the sufficiency threshold, the person will be motivated to process information, and that larger gaps are likely to require systematic processing, whereas smaller gaps may be closed by heuristic processing alone (see Eagly & Chaiken, 1993). Bohner, Rank, Reinhard, Einwiller, & Erb (1998) showed that a large ST–AC gap mediates effects of task importance on processing effort only if participants expect that they have the ability to close the gap by increased processing.

Finally, the HSM embraces the view of the social perceiver as a "motivated tactician" (see Fiske & Taylor, 1991) by emphasizing multiple motives that may guide information processing: *accuracy*, *defense*, and *impression* motivation. Thus, depending on both the situation and on individual differences, people may seek to hold attitudes that are a correct reflection of reality, but they may also strive to defend important values and self-defining beliefs, or try to adopt attitudes that are functional in making a good impression and "getting along" well with others. These qualitative differences in motivation are thought to be orthogonal to the more quantitative sufficiency principle. Thus, an individual may feel more or less confident with respect to any of the processing goals implied by the multiple-motive view.

Conclusions   To summarize, dual-process models have had a tremendous impact on the field of persuasion. The ELM provides the more comprehensive framework, incorporating effortful processing as well as a variety of low-effort processes, allowing distinctions between these processes and the various "roles" a persuasion variable may play on an empirical basis. The HSM is more confined in its conceptualization of low-effort processing, but at the same time includes more specific assumptions about motivational processes and the interplay of its two processing modes. Both models fared well in empirical tests and helped to spur renewed interest in persuasion processes.

Recently, however, dual-process approaches have been challenged by the proposal of a "unimodel" alternative (Kruglanski & Thompson, 1999). Kruglanski and Thompson argue that the dual-process distinction focuses too much on *types of content* (message arguments versus cues) rather than truly different *processes*, and that persuasion can be reduced to a single process of syllogistic reasoning about persuasive "evidence." Future research will have to show if this one-process alternative can replace the dual-process models and instigate new directions of persuasion research.

For many researchers, and all practitioners, persuasion research derives its interest value from the hope that changes in individuals' attitudes will translate into changes in actual behavior. Next, we consider this tricky issue.

Attitudes as Predictors of Behavior

Research into the attitude–behavior relationship is devoted to explaining the conditions under which attitudes predict behavior. As discussed in more detail by Schwarz & Bohner (chapter 20, this volume), attitude researchers initially assumed that individuals' attitudes guide their behavior toward the attitude object, resulting in a close relationship between these variables. Empirically, this hope has not been supported (see Wicker, 1969, for an early review) and by the early 1970s many researchers doubted that attitudes can be used to predict behavior. Subsequent research, however, suggests a more optimistic assessment and identified conditions under which a close relationship between attitudes and behavior can be observed.

Attitude–behavior correspondence

One reason for the failure to find strong attitude–behavior relations often lies in the lack of correspondence between the two measures. It is unlikely that one can predict with accuracy any *specific* behavior (e.g. "attending church next Sunday") from a *global* measure of attitude (e.g. general religious attitudes). But this is exactly the approach that was taken in most early studies. According to Ajzen & Fishbein (1977), a close relation between attitude and behavior can be expected only if both measures agree in their degree of specification (*correspondence principle*). Reviewing attitude–behavior studies, these authors found that the reported correlations between attitude and behavior were indeed larger for studies in which the specification of both measures was similar (see also Kraus, 1995).

This correspondence principle was demonstrated directly by Davidson & Jaccard (1979), who predicted a specific behavior – women's use of birth control pills over two years – from attitudinal measures that varied in specificity. Their results showed that the attitude–behavior correlation increased dramatically with increasing specificity of the attitude measure, from $r = .083$ when assessing attitudes toward "birth control" in general to $r = .572$ when assessing attitudes toward "using birth control pills during the next two years." Note, however, that increasing the prediction of specific behaviors involves a shift on the predictor side from attitudes toward *objects* to the more narrow concept of attitudes toward *behavior*.

As a complement to the strategy of maximizing specificity, Fishbein & Ajzen (1974) proposed that researchers should use *multiple acts* to optimize prediction from global measures of attitude. Just as specific measures of attitudes toward behavior predict specific behaviors, so do global measures of attitudes toward an object predict behaviors toward that object which are sampled and aggregated over a variety of contexts and points in time. Much as reliability increases with number of items in a scale, when aggregating across multiple behaviors any determinants of these behaviors other than the attitude in question tend to cancel each other out in the aggregate score. A compelling illustration of the aggregation principle was provided by Weigel & Newman (1976), who observed actual behavior in a field setting. These researchers assessed respondents' general attitudes toward the environment with a 16-item scale. Later, respondents were given the opportunity to engage in various pro-environmental behaviors over several weeks (e.g. signing a petition against offshore oil drilling; participating in a waste-recycling program), and their participation was unobtrusively recorded. As expected, the general attitude measure was a poor predictor of any of the specific behaviors, yet it correlated with an *aggregated* behavioral measure at an impressive $r = .62$.

Other researchers extended the discussion of the correspondence between attitudes and behaviors from measurement issues to the correspondence of the information on which attitude judgments and behavioral decisions are made. We address this issue in more detail in chapter 20, this volume, on attitude construction.

Moderators of the attitude–behavior relationship

In recent years, various indicators of *attitude strength* have been proposed as moderators of the attitude–behavior relationship (see Petty & Krosnick, 1995). One general hypothesis guiding this approach is that strong attitudes are better predictors of behavior than weak attitudes. Below we discuss strength in terms of intra-attitudinal consistency, accessibility, and cognitive effort in attitude formation.

Intra-attitudinal consistency   Attitudes have traditionally been considered to have a cognitive (beliefs), affective (feelings), and conative (behavior) component. From this perspective, the cognitive and affective components of a person's attitude can vary in their degree of consistency with the attitude as an overall evaluation. For instance, a person may believe that many actions of a government have harmful consequences, yet evaluate the government positively on the whole. Work by Rosenberg (1968) showed that high evaluative–cognitive consistency (ECC) of an attitude is related to its temporal stability and resistance against persuasion attempts. This suggested the hypothesis that high-ECC attitudes may also be better predictors of behavior. Norman (1975) found support for this hypothesis when comparing attitude–behavior correlations between groups of high versus low ECC participants.

Accessibility   Focusing on attitudes toward objects as predictors of behavior, Fazio (e.g. 1986, 1995) developed a theory that highlights the role of an attitude's *accessibility* as a moderator of attitude–behavior consistency. This development was originally inspired by work on the role of *direct experience* with the attitude object in predicting behavior. Regan & Fazio (1977) proposed that direct behavioral experience produces an attitude that is held with more clarity, confidence, and stability than an attitude formed through indirect information about the attitude object. These attributes should render experience based attitudes more accessible and should ultimately produce greater attitude–behavior consistency. These hypotheses were supported in numerous studies (for an overview see Fazio & Zanna, 1981). In a field study, for example, college students who had direct prior experience with a housing crisis showed greater attitude–behavior consistency in their attempts to alleviate the crisis than did students who held similar attitudes but had no direct experience (Regan & Fazio, 1977, Study 1).

The central process assumed to mediate this effect is the attitude's accessibility, operationally defined as the speed of attitude expression (Fazio, 1986). Conceptually, accessibility reflects the strength of association between the representation of the attitude object and an evaluation stored in memory. To guide behavior, this evaluation needs to be activated. Indeed, Fazio and colleagues have shown that attitudes based on behavioral experience are more accessible and that greater attitude accessibility goes along with greater attitude–behavior consistency. In addition to direct experience, *repeated expression* of an attitude has also been shown to increase its accessibility (see Fazio, 1986, 1995, for reviews).

Although it is plausible that attitude accessibility is an important mediator of attitudes' influence on behavior, it has been noted that both direct experience and repeated expression may bring about greater attitude–behavior consistency through other mediating processes (Eagly & Chaiken, 1998). Direct experience has been shown to increase the temporal stability of an attitude (Doll & Ajzen, 1992), and repeated expression of an attitude can increase both its extremity (Downing, Judd, & Brauer, 1992) and its importance (Roese & Olson, 1994). Further research is thus needed to disentangle the effects of accessibility from those of other aspects of attitude strength in mediating attitudes' impact on behavior.

Cognitive effort in attitude formation   As discussed above, the way in which attitudes are formed is at the core of dual-process models of persuasion. High motivation and ability lead to the formation of attitudes via effortful processing of relevant detailed information, whereas either low motivation or low ability leads to lower processing effort and reliance on simple judgmental rules. Especially within the ELM, the different routes to attitude formation have been linked to different degrees of attitude–behavior consistency. Petty & Cacioppo (1986a, 1986b) postulated that attitudes which were formed via the central route are more predictive of behavior than attitudes formed via the peripheral route. Various research findings are compatible with this hypothesis by showing that the attitudes of individuals who processed under high-relevance conditions were more predictive of behavior than those of people who processed under low-relevance conditions (see Petty & Wegener, 1998).

Individual differences   A number of personality variables have been linked to individual differences in attitude–behavior consistency. We can distinguish three broad mediating processes by which these traits seem to operate. They may affect (a) *attitude strength*; (b) the *relative importance of attitude* as opposed to other determinants of behavior; and (c) the *consistency of behavior*.

We already discussed the role of need for cognition in persuasion. As individuals high in NFC tend to engage in greater processing effort, they should form stronger attitudes, which are highly persistent, resistant to change, and predictive of behavior. Consistent with this view, Cacioppo, Petty, Kao, & Rodriguez (1986) found that the attitudes toward US presidential candidates of students high in NFC were better predictors of voting behavior than the attitudes of low-NFC students.

Two personality traits that affect the relative importance of attitudes (versus other factors) in guiding behavior are self-monitoring and self-awareness. People low in self-monitoring, whose social behavior is generally more reflective of their internal states (Snyder, 1974), show higher attitude–behavior correlations than people high in self-monitoring. High self-monitors' behavior, on the other hand, is guided more by situational demands and others' expectations. Part of this difference might be due to the fact that low self-monitors prefer and seek out situations in which attitudes can be openly expressed and enacted (Snyder & Kendzierski, 1982). A closer attitude–behavior relation has also been found for persons high (as opposed to low) in self-awareness (e.g. Carver, 1975). Highly self-aware individuals are chronically more likely than people low in self-awareness to focus attention on their internal states, including their attitudes; thus, at any given point in time, attitudes are more likely to be accessed and used as a basis for behavioral decisions.

Attitudes and behavior: summary and a note on causality   In sum, the correlation between attitude and behavior is strong to the extent that both measures correspond in specificity or aggregation, and that similar aspects, functions, and components of an attitude are salient at the time both attitude and behavior are measured. Furthermore, various indicators of attitude strength as well as personality variables have been identified as moderators of the attitude–behavior relation. It should be emphasized, however, that high correlations between attitude and behavior are not sufficient to infer that attitudes *cause* behavior. As discussed in more detail (chapter 20, this volume), one alternative is that behavior may influence attitudes, and another is that third variables, such as salient context-dependent beliefs, influence both attitude reports and behavior. To the extent that the context remains stable, this would result in higher attitude–behavior correlations without a direct causal link between the two constructs.

Expectancy-value models

In addressing the attitude–behavior relationship, it is important to keep in mind that attitudes are just one possible determinant of behavior. Recognizing the importance of other influential factors, a family of theories has been developed which placed attitudes in a network of predictor variables (e.g. Ajzen, 1991; Bentler & Speckart, 1979; Fishbein & Ajzen, 1975). These theories conceptualize attitudes as attitudes toward behavior; they are called *expectancy-value theories* because they define attitudes in terms of expectancy x value products.

The initial formulation, Fishbein & Ajzen's (1975) theory of reasoned action (TRA), and its extension, the theory of planned behavior (Ajzen, 1991), the model was extended by one additional predictor: perceived behavioral control (see figure 2). According to these models, the proximal cause of behavior is the *behavioral intention*, a conscious decision to engage in a certain behavior. Any influences on behavior that the theory accounts for are assumed to be mediated by this construct. The two major determinants of intention are *attitude* and *subjective norm*. Attitude toward the behavior is defined as a sum of expectancy x value products. Each of these products consists of the subjective probability (= expectancy) that the behavior has a certain consequence, multiplied by the value attached to this consequence. For example, a person may expect that by using the bus instead of driving she will certainly save money (a positive consequence with high likelihood) but may occasionally be late for work (a negative consequence with low likelihood). These two aspects combined would yield a moderately positive attitude toward using the bus.

The perceived social consequences of the behavior are treated separately, forming the construct of *subjective norm*. This second determinant of behavioral intention is also defined as a sum of products, each product consisting of the belief that a significant referent thinks one should perform the behavior, and the motivation to comply with this referent. For instance, a person may believe that his daughter thinks he should buy a sports car, but he may not be inclined to comply with his daughter; he may also believe that his wife would strongly disapprove of his buying the car, and he may be highly motivated to comply with his wife. If just these two referents are considered, the resulting subjective norm would be negative and would weaken the intention of buying the sports car.

Panel A

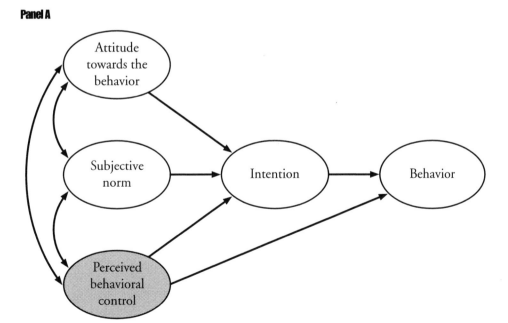

Figure 2   The theories of reasoned action (panel A adapted from Ajzen & Fishbein, 1980, figure 7.1, p. 84) and of planned behavior (panel B adapted from Ajzen, 1991).

Panel B

Behavior

Intention

Attitudes towards the behavior

Relative importance of attitudinal and normative components

Subjective norm

Beliefs that the behaviour leads to certain outcomes

Evaluation of the outcomes

Beliefs that specific referents think I should or should not perform the behavior

Motivation to comply with the specific referents

EXTERNAL VARIABLES

Demographic variables
Age, sex
Occupation
Socioeconomic status
Religion
Education

Attitudes towards targets
Attitudes towards people
Attitudes towards institutions

Personality traits
Introversion–extroversion
Neuroticism
Authoritarianism
Dominance

- - - → Possible explanations for observed relations between external variables and behavior

——→ Stable theoretical relations linking beliefs to behavior

In the TRA, any other, more distal variables were considered "external" to the theory (see figure 2, panel A). In the TPB (Ajzen, 1991), the model was extended by one additional predictor: *perceived behavioral control* (see figure 2, panel B). This extension was assumed to improve prediction especially for behaviors over which a person does not have complete voluntary control, and complex behaviors that require extensive planning (e.g. climbing a mountain). Perceived behavioral control was conceptualized as the expected ease of actually performing the intended behavior (cf. the concept of *self-efficacy*; Bandura, 1977); it was hypothesized to influence behavior either indirectly, via the behavioral intention, or directly. For example, a person who thinks it will not be easy to climb a certain mountain may be less likely to form a behavioral intention of doing so; she may also, however, be less likely to succeed once she has formed the intention to act. Consistent with Ajzen's reasoning, the inclusion of behavioral control provided better prediction of difficult behaviors (e.g. getting an "A" grade; Ajzen & Madden, 1986), but not of behaviors that can easily be performed (e.g. attending a meeting; Kelly & Breinlinger, 1995).

Other extensions of the TRA's list of predictor variables have been proposed (for an overview, see Eagly & Chaiken, 1993). Most notably, some theorists pointed out that behavior can be influenced by previous behavior or habit, and that these influences are not necessarily mediated by attitudes, subjective norms, or intentions (e.g. Bentler & Speckart, 1979). A meta-analysis (Ouellette & Wood, 1998) indicates that past behavior significantly contributes to the prediction of future behavior along either of two pathways: well-practiced behaviors in stable contexts (e.g. seatbelt use) recur because the processing that controls them becomes automatic; frequency of prior behavior then reflects habit strength and *directly* affects future behavior. Behaviors that are less well learned or occur in unstable contexts tend to remain under the control of conscious processing; under these circumstances, past behavior may influence future behavior *indirectly via intentions*.

These findings relate to the more general criticism that both the TRA and the TPB are limited in scope to conscious and deliberate behaviors, whereas they do not predict well behavior that is not consciously intended and not based on utilitarian deliberation (e.g. Fazio, 1986). Ajzen & Fishbein (1980) disputed this criticism by emphasizing that their model leaves room for the possibility that a behavioral intention has once been formed in the past, and that people may retrieve this previously formed intention rather than deliberating anew each time they engage in the behavior in question. Fazio (1990), however, delineated the conditions under which *attitudes toward targets* can activate behavior immediately and automatically. In his MODE model ("motivation and opportunity as determinants"), motivation and opportunity to deliberate moderate the processes through which behavior is controlled (cf. the dual-process models of persuasion discussed above). When an individual lacks motivation or opportunity to form a deliberate decision about performing a behavior, highly accessible attitudes about the target can automatically guide behavior by affecting the perception of the situation. Although the assumption that only highly accessible attitudes can be automatically activated is controversial (cf. Bargh, Chaiken, Govender, & Pratto, 1992), Fazio's position is generally consistent with accumulating evidence showing that social behavior may largely be subject to unconscious influences (e.g. Bargh, 1996).

In sum, expectancy-value theories have used a narrow definition of *attitude toward behavior* and have relegated the attitude concept to the background as one among many predictors of behavior. Through this increased specification they achieved considerable predictive power, especially in applied areas in which deliberate behaviors are studied (for reviews, see Ajzen, 1991; Eagly & Chaiken, 1993). Conversely, in Fazio's (1990) MODE model, the broad concept of *attitude toward a target* (in the sense of a summary evaluation) is back at center stage when it comes to predicting behavior under circumstances of low motivation or lack of opportunity to deliberate.

Concluding Remarks

As our selective review indicates, social psychologists have made considerable progress in understanding the dynamics of attitude change and the complexities of the attitude–behavior relationship. Moreover, the development of detailed process models has linked research in the attitude domain to broader issues of judgment and cognition, resulting in considerable cross-fertilization (see the contributions in Chaiken & Trope, 1999, for examples). One of the more controversial issues emerging from this development is whether we should think of attitudes as relatively enduring dispositions or as judgments that are constructed on the spot, based on whatever information happens to be accessible at that point in time. We address this issue in chapter 20, this volume.

References

Ajzen, I. (1991). The theory of planned behavior. *Organizational Behavior and Human Decision Processes, 50*, 179–211.

Ajzen, I., & Fishbein, M. (1977). Attitude–behavior relations: A theoretical analysis and review of empirical research. *Psychological Bulletin, 84*, 888–918.

Ajzen, I., & Fishbein, M. (1980). *Understanding attitudes and predicting social behavior.* Englewood Cliffs, NJ: Prentice-Hall.

Ajzen, I., & Madden, T. J. (1986). Prediction of goal-directed behavior: Attitudes, intentions, and perceived behavioral control. *Journal of Experimental Social Psychology, 22*, 453–474.

Allport, G. W. (1935). Attitudes. In C. Murchison (Ed.), *Handbook of social psychology*, Vol. 2 (pp. 798–844). Worcester, MA: Clark University Press.

Allport, G. W. (1954). *The nature of prejudice.* Cambridge, UK: Addison-Wesley.

Bandura, A. (1977). Self-efficacy: Toward a unifying theory of behavioral change. *Psychological Review, 84*, 191–215.

Bargh, J. A. (1996). Automaticity in social psychology. In E. T. Higgins & A. W. Kruglanski (Eds.), *Social psychology: Handbook of basic principles* (pp. 169–183). New York: Guilford Press.

Bargh, J. A., Chaiken, S., Govender, R., & Pratto, F. (1992). The generality of the automatic attitude activation effect. *Journal of Personality and Social Psychology, 62*, 893–912.

Bentler, P. M., & Speckart, G. (1979). Models of attitude–behavior relations. *Psychological Review, 86*, 452–464.

Berkowitz, L., & Knurek, D. A. (1969). Label-mediated hostility generalization. *Journal of Personality and Social Psychology, 13*, 200–206.

Bohner, G., & Ruder, M. (1998). When expertise fails: Contrast and correction processes in persuasion. Paper presented at the 1998 East–West Meeting of the European Association of Experimental Social Psychology, Gommern, Germany.

Bohner, G., Moskowitz, G., & Chaiken, S. (1995). The interplay of heuristic and systematic processing of social information. *European Review of Social Psychology, 6,* 33–68.

Bohner, G., Rank, S., Reinhard, M.-A., Einwiller, S., & Erb, H.-P. (1998). Motivational determinants of systematic processing: Expectancy moderates effects of desired confidence on processing effort. *European Journal of Social Psychology, 28,* 185–206.

Cacioppo, J. T., Petty, R. E., Feinstein, J. A., & Jarvis, W. B. G. (1996). Dispositional differences in cognitive motivation: The life and times of individuals varying in need for cognition. *Psychological Bulletin, 119,* 197–253.

Cacioppo, J. T., Petty, R. E., Kao, C. F., & Rodriguez, R. (1986). Central and peripheral routes to persuasion: An individual difference perspective. *Journal of Personality and Social Psychology, 51,* 1032–1043.

Carver, C. S. (1975). Physical aggression as a function of objective self-awareness and attitudes towards punishment. *Journal of Experimental Social Psychology, 11,* 510–519.

Chaiken, S., & Maheswaran, D. (1994). Heuristic processing can bias systematic processing: Effects of source credibility, argument ambiguity, and task importance on attitude judgment. *Journal of Personality and Social Psychology, 66,* 460–473.

Chaiken, S., & Trope, Y. (Eds.) (1999). *Dual-process theories in social psychology.* New York: Guilford Press.

Chaiken, S., Liberman, A., & Eagly, A. H. (1989). Heuristic and systematic information processing within and beyond the persuasion context. In J. S. Uleman & J. A. Bargh (Eds.), *Unintended thought* (pp. 212–252). New York: Guilford Press.

Chen, S., & Chaiken, S. (1999). The heuristic-systematic model in its broader context. In S. Chaiken & Y. Trope (Eds.), *Dual-process theories in social psychology.* New York: Guilford Press.

Davidson, A. R., & Jaccard, J. J. (1979). Variables that moderate the attitude–behavior relation: Results of a longitudinal survey. *Journal of Personality and Social Psychology, 37,* 1364–1376.

Doll, J., & Ajzen, I. (1992). Accessibility and stability of predictors in the theory of planned behavior. *Journal of Personality and Social Psychology, 63,* 754–765.

Doob, L. W. (1947). The behavior of attitudes. *Psychological Review, 54,* 135–156.

Downing, J. W., Judd, C. M., & Brauer, M. (1992). Effects of repeated expressions on attitude extremity. *Journal of Personality and Social Psychology, 63,* 17–29.

Dulany, D. E., Jr. (1962). The place of hypotheses and intentions: An analysis of verbal control in verbal conditioning. *Journal of Personality, 30,* 102–129.

Eagly, A. H., & Chaiken, S. (1993). *The psychology of attitudes.* Fort Worth, TX: Harcourt Brace Jovanovich.

Eagly, A. H., & Chaiken, S. (1998). Attitude structure and function. In D. Gilbert, S. T. Fiske, & G. Lindzey (Eds.), *Handbook of social psychology,* 4th. edn. (pp. 269–322). New York: McGraw-Hill.

Fazio, R. H. (1986). How do attitudes guide behavior? In R. M. Sorrentino & E. T. Higgins (Eds.), *Handbook of motivation and cognition* (pp. 204–243). New York: Guilford Press.

Fazio, R. H. (1990). Multiple processes by which attitudes guide behavior: The MODE model as an integrative framework. In M. P. Zanna (Ed.), *Advances in experimental social psychology,* Vol. 23 (pp. 75–109). New York: Academic Press.

Fazio, R. H. (1995). Attitudes as object–evaluation associations: Determinants, consequences, and correlates of attitude accessibility. In R. E. Petty & J. A. Krosnick (Eds.), *Attitude strength: Antecedents and consequences* (pp. 247–282). Mahwah, NJ: Erlbaum.

Fazio, R. H., & Zanna, M. P. (1981). Direct experience and attitude–behavior consistency. *Advances in Experimental Social Psychology, 14,* 161–202.

Festinger, L. (1957). *A theory of cognitive dissonance.* Stanford, CA: Stanford University Press.

Fishbein, M., & Ajzen, I. (1974). Attitudes toward objects as predictors of single and multiple behavioral criteria. *Psychological Review, 81,* 59–74.

Fishbein, M., & Ajzen, I. (1975). *Belief, attitude, intention, and behavior.* Reading, MA: Addison-Wesley.

Fiske, S., & Taylor, S. (1994). *Social cognition.* 2nd. edn. Reading, MA: Addison-Wesley.

Greenwald, A. G. (1968). Cognitive learning, cognitive response to persuasion, and attitude change. In A. Greenwald, T. Brock, & T. Ostrom (Eds.), *Psychological foundations of attitudes* (pp. 148–

170). New York: Academic Press.

Hildum, D. C., & Brown, R. W. (1956). Verbal reinforcement and interviewer bias. *Journal of Abnormal and Social Psychology, 53*, 108–111.

Hovland, C. I., Janis, I. L., & Kelley, J. J. (1953). *Communication and persuasion.* New Haven, CT: Yale University Press.

Insko, C. A. (1965). Verbal reinforcement of attitude. *Journal of Personality and Social Psychology, 2*, 621–623.

Insko, C. A., & Cialdini, R. B. (1969). A test of three interpretations of attitudinal reinforcement. *Journal of Personality and Social Psychology, 12*, 333–341.

Kelly, C., & Breinlinger, S. (1995). Attitudes, intentions, and behavior: A study of women's participation in collective action. *Journal of Applied Social Psychology, 25*, 1430–1445.

King, B. T., & Janis, I. L. (1956). Comparison of the effectiveness of improvised versus non-improvised role-playing in producing opinion change. *Human Relations, 9*, 177–186.

Kraus, S. (1995). Attitudes and the prediction of behavior: A meta-analysis of the empirical literature. *Personality and Social Psychology Bulletin, 21*, 58–75.

Krosnick, J. A., Betz, A. L., Jussim, L. J., & Lynn, A. R. (1992). Subliminal conditioning of attitudes. *Personality and Social Psychology Bulletin, 18*, 152–162.

Kruglanski, A. W., & Thompson, E. P. (1999). Persuasion by a single route: A view from the unimodel. *Psychological Inquiry, 10*, 83–109.

McGuire, W. J. (1969). The nature of attitudes and attitude change. In G. Lindzey & E. Aronson (Eds.), *The handbook of social psychology*, 2nd. edn. Vol. 3 (pp. 136–314). Reading, MA: Addison-Wesley.

McGuire, W. J. (1985). Attitudes and attitude change. In G. Lindzey & E. Aronson (Eds.), *The handbook of social psychology* 3rd edn. (pp. 233–346). Reading, MA: Addison-Wesley.

McGuire, W. J., & Papageorgis, D. (1962). Effectiveness of forewarning in developing resistance to persuasion. *Public Opinion Quarterly, 26*, 24–34.

Maheswaran, D., & Chaiken, S. (1991). Promoting systematic processing in low motivation settings: The effect of incongruent information on processing and judgment. *Journal of Personality and Social Psychology, 61*, 13–25.

Norman, R. (1975). Affective–cognitive consistency, attitudes, conformity, and behavior. *Journal of Personality and Social Psychology, 32*, 83–91.

Ouellette, J. A., & Wood, W. (1998). Habit and intention in everyday life: The multiple processes by which past behavior predicts future behavior. *Psychological Bulletin, 124*, 54–74.

Page, M. M. (1969). Social psychology of a classical conditioning of attitudes experiment. *Journal of Personality and Social Psychology, 11*, 177–186.

Petty, R. E., & Brock, T. C. (1981). Thought disruption and persuasion: Assessing the validity of attitude change experiments. In R. E. Petty, T. M. Ostrom, & T. C. Brock (Eds.), *Cognitive responses in persuasion* (pp. 55–79). Hillsdale, NJ: Erlbaum.

Petty, R. E., & Cacioppo, J. T. (1981). *Attitudes and persuasion: Classic and contemporary approaches.* Dubuque, Iowa: Brown.

Petty, R. E., & Cacioppo, J. T. (1986a). *Communication and persuasion: Central and peripheral routes to attitude change.* New York: Springer.

Petty, R. E., & Cacioppo, J. T. (1986b). The elaboration likelihood model of persuasion. *Advances in Experimental Social Psychology, 19*, 124–203.

Petty, R. E., & Krosnick, J. A. (Eds.) (1995). *Attitude strength*. Mahwah, NJ: Erlbaum.

Petty, R. E., & Wegener, D. T. (1998). Attitude change: Multiple roles for persuasion variables. In D. Gilbert, S. T. Fiske, & G. Lindzey (Eds.), *The handbook of social psychology*, Vol. 1 (pp. 323–389). New York: McGraw-Hill.

Petty, R. E., Ostrom, T. M., & Brock, T. (Eds.) (1981). *Cognitive responses in persuasion*. Hillsdale, NJ: Erlbaum.

Petty, R. E., Wells, G. L., & Brock, T. C. (1976). Distraction can enhance or reduce yielding to propaganda: Thought disruption versus effort justification. *Journal of Personality and Social Psychology, 34*, 874–884.

Razran, G. H. S. (1940). Conditioned response changes in rating and appraising sociopolitical slogans. *Psychological Bulletin, 37*, 481.

Regan, D. T., & Fazio, R. H. (1977). On the consistency between attitudes and behavior: Look to the method of attitude formation. *Journal of Experimental Social Psychology, 13*, 28–45.

Roese, N. J., & Olson, J. M. (1994). Attitude importance as a function of repeated attitude expression. *Journal of Experimental Social Psychology, 30*, 39–51.

Rosenberg, M. J. (1968). Hedonism, inauthenticity, and other goads toward expansion of a consistency theory. In R. P. Abelson, E. Aronson, W. J. McGuire, T. M. Newcomb, M. J. Rosenberg, & P. H. Tannenbaum (Eds.), *Theories of cognitive consistency: A sourcebook* (pp. 73–111). Chicago: Rand-McNally.

Sadler, O., & Tesser, A. (1973). Some effects of salience and time upon interpersonal hostility and attraction during social isolation. *Sociometry, 36*, 99–112.

Schwarz, N. (1990). Feelings as information: Informational and motivational functions of affective states. In E. T. Higgins & R. Sorrentino (Eds.), *Handbook of motivation and cognition: Foundations of social behavior*, Vol. 2 (pp. 527–561). New York: Guilford Press.

Shavitt, S. (1989). Operationalizing functional theories of attitude. In A. R. Pratkanis, S. J. Breckler, & A. G. Greenwald (Eds.), *Attitude structure and function* (pp. 311–337). Hillsdale, NJ: Erlbaum.

Skinner, B. F. (1957). *Verbal behavior*. New York: Appleton–Century–Crofts.

Snyder, M. (1974). Self-monitoring of expressive behavior. *Journal of Personality and Social Psychology, 30*, 526–537.

Snyder, M., & Kendzierski, D. (1982). Acting on one's attitudes: Procedures for linking attitude and behavior. *Journal of Experimental Social Psychology, 18*, 165–183.

Staats, A. W., & Staats, C. K. (1958). Attitudes established by classical conditioning. *Journal of Abnormal and Social Psychology, 57*, 37–40.

Staats, A. W., Minke, K. A., Martin, C. H., & Higa, W. R. (1972). Deprivation–satiation and strength of attitude conditioning: A test of attitude–reinforcer–discriminative theory. *Journal of Personality and Social Psychology, 24*, 178–185.

Tesser, A. (1978). Self-generated attitude change. In L. Berkowitz (Ed.), *Advances in experimental social psychology*, Vol. 11 (pp. 289–338). New York: Academic Press.

Wänke, M., Bless, H., & Biller, B. (1996). Subjective experience versus content of information in the construction of attitude judgments. *Personality and Social Psychology Bulletin, 22*, 1105–1113.

Wänke, M., Bohner, G., & Jurkowitsch, A. (1997). There are many reasons to drive a BMW: Does imagined ease of argument generation influence attitudes? *Journal of Consumer Research, 24*, 170–177.

Weigel, R. H., & Newman, L. S. (1976). Increasing attitude–behavior correspondence by broadening the scope of the behavioral measure. *Journal of Personality and Social Psychology, 33*, 793–802.

Wicker, A. W. (1969). Attitude versus action: The relationship of verbal and overt behavioral responses to attitude objects. *Journal of Social Issues, 25 (4)*, 41–78.

Chapter Twenty

The Construction of Attitudes

Norbert Schwarz and Gerd Bohner

Attitudes have long been considered a central concept of social psychology. In fact, early writers have defined social psychology as the scientific study of attitudes (e.g. Thomas & Znaniecki, 1918) and in 1954 Gordon Allport noted, "This concept is probably the most distinctive and indispensable concept in contemporary American social psychology" (Allport, 1954, p. 43). As one may expect of any concept that has received decades of attention, the concept of attitudes has changed over the years (see Allport, 1954, for an early review). The initial definitions were broad and encompassed cognitive, affective, motivational, and behavioral components. For example, Allport (1935) defined an attitude as "a mental and neural state of readiness, organized through experience, exerting a directive and dynamic influence upon the individual's response to all objects and situations with which it is related" (ibid., p. 810). A decade later, Krech & Crutchfield (1948) wrote, "An attitude can be defined as an enduring organization of motivational, emotional, perceptual, and cognitive processes with respect to some aspect of the individual's world" (ibid., p. 152). These definitions emphasized the enduring nature of attitudes and their close relationship to individuals' behavior. Some sociologists (e.g. Fuson, 1942) and psychologists (e.g. Campbell, 1950) even defined attitudes simply in terms of the probability that a person will show a specified behavior in a specified situation.

In subsequent decades, the attitude concept lost much of its breadth and was largely reduced to its evaluative component. In the succinct words of Daryl Bem, "Attitudes are likes and dislikes" (Bem, 1970, p. 14). Similarly, Eagly & Chaiken (1993), in a highly influential textbook, defined attitudes as "a psychological tendency that is expressed by evaluating a particular entity with some degree of favor or disfavor" (ibid., p. 1). Along the way, many functions that were initially ascribed to attitudes have been reassigned to other cognitive structures and the accumulating body of empirical findings drew many of the classic assumptions into question.

A growing body of literature suggests that attitudes may be much less enduring and stable than has traditionally been assumed. As we review below, self-reports of attitudes are highly context dependent and can be profoundly influenced by minor changes in question wording, question format, or question order. For some researchers, this malleability simply reflects measurement error (e.g. Schuman & Presser, 1981): people presumably hold stable attitudes, yet their assessment is subject to contextual influences. For other researchers, the same findings indicate that all we assess in attitude measurement are evaluative judgments that respondents construct at the time they are asked, based on whatever information happens to be accessible (e.g. Schwarz & Strack, 1991). From this perspective, the traditional attitude concept may not be particularly useful and we may learn more about human cognition and behavior from a detailed analysis of the underlying judgmental processes. Other researchers have taken intermediate positions in an attempt to maintain the traditional attitude concept. For example, Lord & Lepper (in press) and Tourangeau and his colleagues (e.g. Tourangeau, 1992) equate attitudes with relatively stable memory structures, but assume that individuals sample from these structures when they answer attitude questions. Hence, a stable attitude can result in variable attitude reports, depending on which aspect of the knowledge structure (attitude) is accessed. Others (e.g. Wilson, 1998) suggested that individuals may hold multiple attitudes about an object, accessing different ones at different points in time. As we illustrate below, it is surprisingly difficult to design conclusive empirical tests to evaluate the relative merit of these proposals and, with a few plausible assumptions, each is compatible with the available data. Yet, a scientific concept like "attitude" is to be evaluated on the basis of its explanatory power – and without taking judgmental processes into account, there is little that the attitude concept explains. In fact, the contemporary definition of attitudes as "likes and dislikes" (Bem, 1970, p. 14) equates attitudes with evaluative judgments. Hence, the first section of this chapter highlights judgmental processes and the second section applies these process assumptions to some findings that are typically considered evidence for the enduring nature of attitudes.

In response to the malleability of attitude reports, social psychologists have repeatedly tried to replace or supplement verbal self-report measures with other, presumably more direct, ways to assess individuals' evaluative responses to attitude objects. These attempts range from the "bogus pipeline" (Jones & Sigall, 1971) of the 1970s to the recent development of sophisticated "implicit" measures of attitudes (e.g. Dovidio & Fazio, 1992). Recent findings suggest that such measures may be just as context dependent as verbal reports, although the relevant contextual variables may differ. The third section addresses these developments, which are discussed in more detail by Banaji and colleagues (chapter 7, this volume) and Bassili (chapter 4, this volume).

Much as the enduring nature of attitudes has been called into question, another body of research suggested that attitudes may not be closely related to behavior either (see Wicker, 1969, for an influential early review). Instead, we may expect a close relationship between attitudes and behavior only under some specific, and relatively narrow, conditions (see chapter 19, this volume). These conditions can be fruitfully conceptualized within a judgment perspective, as we review in the final section.

Although we consider these topics central to current developments in attitude research, we are keenly aware that our coverage does not do justice to the broad range of topics that has been addressed under the attitude rubric. For treatments of topics not addressed in this chapter we refer readers to Eagly & Chaiken (1993, 1998), Petty & Wegener (1998), and Bohner & Schwarz (chapter 19, this volume).

Attitude Judgments: Lessons Learned from Context Effects

Attitudes are a hypothetical construct, invented by researchers to account for a body of phenomena. We cannot observe attitudes directly but infer them from individuals' self-reports and behavior. Accordingly, the processes underlying self-reports of attitudes are of central importance to our inferences about the nature of attitudes. Empirically, attitude measurement is highly context dependent and minor changes in question wording, format, or order can have a profound impact on the obtained reports (for reviews see Schuman & Presser, 1981; Schwarz & Sudman, 1992; Sudman, Bradburn, & Schwarz, 1996; Tourangeau & Rasinski, 1988). The underlying dynamics are increasingly well understood and reflect an intricate interplay of cognitive and communicative processes. Answering an attitude question entails several tasks (Strack & Martin, 1987; Tourangeau, 1984): respondents (a) need to interpret the question to determine the attitude object and evaluative dimension the researcher has in mind. Next, they (b) need to retrieve relevant information from memory. In most cases, a previously formed judgment that meets the specifics of the question will not be accessible and they have to draw on information that seems relevant to the question at hand. Relevant information includes features of the attitude object, the respondent's apparent affective response to the object, as well as information about the respondent's own behavior with regard to the object. Based on this information, respondents (c) need to compute a judgment. Having formed a judgment, they (d) can rarely report it in their own words but need to map it onto a set of response alternatives provided by the researcher. Finally, (e) respondents may want to edit their private judgment before they communicate it to the researcher for reasons of social desirability and self-presentation. Performance at each of these steps is context dependent, yet this context dependency has differential implications for the notion that people hold enduring attitudes.

Question comprehension

To answer a question, it is not sufficient to understand the words. For example, when asked, "What have you done today?" the words pose no particular problem, yet you still need to determine what the questioner is interested in. Should you report, for example, that you took a shower or not? To infer what the questioner has in mind (i.e. the *pragmatic* meaning of the question), respondents go beyond the words (i.e. the *literal* meaning of the question) and draw on contextual features, such as the content of preceding questions or the response alternatives provided by the researcher (see Sudman, Bradburn, & Schwarz, 1996, for a review). This context dependent interpretation of question meaning entails that the same literal question can acquire different pragmatic meanings in different contexts, resulting in what are essentially answers to substantively different questions. For example, Schwarz & Hippler (1995) asked respondents questions of the type, "How do you feel about Bill Clinton?" accompanied by an 11-point rating scale ranging from "don't think highly of him" to "think very highly of him." To answer this question, respondents have to determine if the researcher intends the wording "don't think highly of him" to refer to the presence of negative thoughts or merely to the absence of positive thoughts. To do so, they draw on contextual features, including such formal aspects as the numeric values of the rating scale. Specifically, respondents in this study inferred that "don't think highly of him" refers to the absence of positive thoughts when the numeric values ranged from 0 to 10, but to the presence of negative thoughts when they ranged from –5 to +5. Not surprisingly, this shift in the meaning of the verbal end anchor resulted in dramatic shifts in the obtained ratings and all politicians were evaluated more positively on the –5 to +5 scale.

Note that context effects at the question comprehension stage reflect differences in the understanding of the evaluative dimension or the identification of the attitude object, i.e. answers to substantively different questions. Hence, these effects do not bear on whether people hold enduring attitudes or construct an answer on the spot, but are compatible with both theoretical perspectives.

Recall and judgment

After respondents determine the intended meaning of the question, they need to form a judgment. To do so, they may engage in a systematic evaluation of features of the attitude object, draw on their own behavior towards the object, or use their apparent affective reaction or other phenomenal experiences as a basis of judgment. We address these options in turn.

Feature-based judgments: The construal of objects and standards

To arrive at a feature-based evaluation of the attitude object, respondents need to recall relevant information from memory to form a mental representation of the object and of a standard against which it can be evaluated (Schwarz & Bless, 1992a; see also chapters 11 and 12, this volume). In doing so, they are unlikely to recall all information that may potentially be relevant to the judgment, but truncate the search process as soon as enough information has come to mind to form a judgment with sufficient subjective certainty. Some of this information will be *chronically accessible* (Higgins, 1996) and will come to mind independent of contextual influences. Other information, however, will only come to mind because it has been used recently, e.g. to answer a preceding question. This *temporarily accessible* information results in context effects in attitude judgments, whereas chronically accessible information lends some context independent stability to these judgments.

The specific impact of chronically or temporarily accessible information depends on how it is *used*. Information that is included in the mental representation of the object results in *assimilation* effects, i.e. more positive (negative) judgments when positive (negative) information comes to mind. Suppose, for example, that respondents are asked of which party General Colin Powell has recently become a member (Stapel & Schwarz, 1998). This question not only brings the highly respected Colin Powell to mind, but the correct answer ("Republican Party") also invites his inclusion in the mental representation formed of that party. This representation now includes a positive element that may otherwise not have come to mind, resulting in more positive evaluations of the Republican Party than when no question about Powell was asked. Similarly, suppose that respondents are asked to evaluate the trustworthiness of American politicians and Richard Nixon happens to come to mind because he was addressed in a previous question. Richard Nixon can be included in the superordinate category "American politicians," resulting in judgments of lower trustworthiness than would otherwise be the case (Schwarz & Bless, 1992b). Nixon's negative impact, however, would be less pronounced the more other, trustworthy, members came to mind at the same time (Bless, Igou, Schwarz, & Wänke, in press). These assimilation effects simply reflect that the judgment is based on the features included in the mental representation of the object, i.e. the category "American politicians" or "Republican Party."

Next, suppose that the question about Powell asks which party offered him to run as its presidential candidate – an offer he declined. This question again brings Colin Powell to mind, but it invites his exclusion from the representation formed of the Republican Party. Nevertheless, Powell is highly accessible and may be used in constructing a very positive standard of comparison, relative to which the rest of the Republican Party looks less good. Empirically, this is the case and the party is evaluated more negatively than if no question about Powell were asked (Stapel & Schwarz, 1998). Similarly, suppose that Nixon is again brought to mind by a preceding question, yet the judgment does not pertain to the trustworthiness of the superordinate category "American politicians," but to the trustworthiness of a specific exemplar, say Newt Gingrich. Nixon would still be highly accessible, yet he cannot be included in the mental representation formed of the attitude object Newt Gingrich, reflecting that lateral categories are mutually exclusive. In this case, Nixon may be used in constructing a standard of comparison, relative to which Gingrich is evaluated as more trustworthy than would otherwise be the case. An experiment with German politicians as attitude objects confirmed these predictions (Schwarz & Bless, 1992b). Again, however, Nixon's influence on judgments of Gingrich would be attenuated the more other, more trustworthy, politicians are included in the construal of the standard, thus resulting in a less negative comparison point (Bless, Igou, Schwarz, & Wänke, in press). In more general terms, information that is used to construct a standard of comparison results in *contrast* effects. In this case, negative (positive) information results in a more negative (positive) standard, relative to which the attitude object is evaluated more positively (negatively).

As these examples illustrate, the *same* piece of accessible information can have *opposite* influences on attitude judgments, depending on how it is *used*. Information that is used in constructing a representation of the attitude object results in assimilation effects, whereas information used in constructing a standard results in contrast effects. Empirically, the influence of a given temporarily accessible piece of information can only be observed when its implications are more extreme than the implications of chronically accessible information used in forming the same representation. Moreover, the size of its influence decreases with the amount and extremity of other information used in forming the respective representation.

Numerous different variables influence how a given piece of information is used. These variables can be conceptualized in terms of three broad decisions (Schwarz & Bless, 1992a). First, why does this information come to mind? In general, individuals assume that what comes to mind does so in response to the topic they are thinking about, a pervasive assumption that Higgins (1998) termed the *aboutness principle*. Hence, accessible information is likely to be included in the representation formed of the object, unless subsequent decisions result in its exclusion. If respondents are aware, however, that the information may have come to mind for the "wrong" reason, e.g. because of a preceding question or priming task (e.g. Strack, et al., 1993), they exclude it from the representation of the attitude object (rendering the subsequent decisions irrelevant). Second, is the information representative of the attitude object? If yes, it is included in the representation formed, if not it is excluded and used in constructing a standard of comparison. Variables that influence this decision are the categorical relationship between the context information and the superordinate or lateral attitude object, as in the Nixon example reported above, the extremity of the context information, and similar determinants of perceived representativeness. Finally, conversational norms may prohibit the use of information that the listener may not be interested in, again resulting in the exclusion of this information from the temporary representation of the attitude object used in forming a judgment (e.g. Schwarz, Strack, & Mai, 1991). Whenever any of these decisions results in the exclusion of accessible information from the representation of the object, a contrast effect is likely to emerge; otherwise, assimilation effects are obtained.

Behavioral information

Alternatively, respondents may base their attitude judgments on information about their own behavior towards the attitude object. In doing so, they follow the same inference rules that an external observer would apply, as initially suggested by Bem's (1970, 1972) self-perception theory. For example, they may conclude that they like an activity when they seem to engage in it without external pressure or high rewards, yet that they don't like it when they seem to engage in it due to external pressures or high rewards. That is, they infer their attitudes from behavior under conditions that allow for correspondent inferences (Jones, 1979). Moreover, it is not individuals' actual behavior, but their perception of their behavior, that drives their attitude judgments. For example, Salancik & Conway (1975) presented participants with a list of religious behaviors, like "I go to church," and asked them to check all that apply. For some participants, the statements were paired with low frequency terms ("I sometimes go to church"), and for others with high frequency terms ("I frequently go to church"). Because most people are more likely to do all kinds of things "sometimes" rather than "frequently," participants endorsed more religious statements in the former than in the latter condition. Subsequently, these participants inferred that they held more religious attitudes, reflecting that they drew on the number of religious behaviors they seemed to engage in. Note that observers would, and do, arrive at the same conclusion in studies of this type, indicating that individuals do not have privileged access to their own attitudes, in contrast to what the traditional attitude concept would suggest.

Feelings and phenomenal experiences

As a final route to attitude judgments, respondents may draw on their feelings and phenomenal experiences. For example, they may use their apparent affective reaction to the attitude object as a basis of judgment, essentially asking themselves, "How do I feel about this?" (Schwarz & Clore, 1988). When the attitude object itself elicits a strong affective response, as when a spider phobic is exposed to a spider, this route may lead to relatively context independent judgments. Yet it is often difficult to determine the source of one's feelings and respondents may misread their pre-existing mood as a response to the attitude object, resulting in more positive evaluations when they are in a good rather than bad mood (see chapter 18, this volume).

Similarly, respondents may draw on their apparent physiological arousal or other bodily sensations as a source of information. They may conclude, for example, that they like a pin-up photograph more when false feedback suggests that it makes their heart beat faster than when it does not (Valins, 1966), or may be more likely to agree with a message when an unrelated task induces them to move their heads up and down (thus evoking the sensation of nodding one's head) rather than from side to side (thus evoking the sensation of shaking one's head; e.g. Wells & Petty, 1980).

Finally, they may infer from an experienced difficulty of retrieving positive (negative) information about the attitude object that there isn't much good (bad) to say about the object, and may base their judgment on this inference, consistent with Tversky & Kahneman's (1973) availability heuristic (see Schwarz, 1998, for a review).

Reliance on such experiential information often allows respondents to simplify the judgmental task. Hence, these sources of information are particularly likely to be used when the judgment task is complex and burdensome, when little other information is available, or when respondents' motivation is low, that is, under conditions that typically foster the use of heuristic strategies of judgment (Bohner, Moskowitz, & Chaiken, 1995; see chapters 11 and 18, this volume).

Summary

In sum, respondents can draw on a wide range of information and inference rules to arrive at an evaluative judgment and the outcome of these judgmental processes is highly context dependent. This context dependency calls into question that individuals hold enduring attitudes that they recall from memory to answer attitude questions. Instead, it suggests that attitude judgments are constructed on the spot, based on the information and inference rules that are most accessible at that point in time.

Formatting the answer

After having formed a judgment in their own minds, respondents need to map their judgments onto the response alternatives provided by the researcher. This process is again context dependent. For example, when a rating scale is presented, respondents need to determine the meaning of the scale points. To do so, they draw on the range of accessible related objects and anchor the endpoints of the scale with the most extreme objects that come to mind (e.g. Ostrom & Upshaw, 1968; Parducci, 1983). Hence, a given object will be rated as less extreme when presented in the context of a more extreme one, than when presented in the context of a less extreme one. In addition, if the number of to-be-rated objects is sufficiently large, respondents will attempt to use all categories of the rating scale about equally often to be maximally informative. Accordingly, the specific mappings depend on the range and frequency distribution of the to-be-evaluated objects.

As in the case of question comprehension effects, *response language* effects of this type do not bear on whether attitudes are enduring or constructed on the spot. They simply reflect that respondents draw on the context of the task to determine the meaning of the response alternatives (see Strack, 1994, for a review). Once a specific point on a rating scale has been checked, however, this answer may itself remain accessible for a limited time, serving as input into subsequent judgments and behavioral decisions (e.g. Sherman, Ahlm, Berman, & Lynn, 1979).

Editing the response

As a final step, respondents have to report their private judgments to the researcher. At this stage, they may want to edit their responses due to influences of social desirability or self-presentation. Although such effects have received considerable attention in public opinion research (for a review see DeMaio, 1984), their emergence is limited to topics that are highly personal and threatening in nature. Moreover, many of the more robust findings are theoretically ambiguous. For example, survey researchers observed that white Americans report more positive attitudes towards African-Americans when the interviewer is black rather than white (e.g. Hatchett & Schuman, 1976). From a social desirability perspective, the answers they give to the black interviewer presumably do not reflect their "true" attitude. Yet, the highly salient friendly, middle-class, and usually well-educated African-American interviewer may herself serve as input into the temporary representation formed of the superordinate category "African-Americans," resulting in more positive judgments for the reasons discussed above. In fact, simply presenting a well liked African-American on a larger list of individuals as part of an unrelated task (Bodenhausen, Schwarz, Bless, & Wänke, 1995) has been found to improve attitudes about the group under anonymous reporting conditions, which do not give rise to social desirability concerns. Hence, the extent to which interviewer effects reflect deliberate misreports of respondents' actual attitude judgments, or differential construals of the attitude object, often remains an open question.

Summary

As our selective review indicates, attitude reports are highly context dependent. Note, however, that only context effects at the judgment stage bear on whether individuals hold enduring attitudes or construct an attitude judgment when needed, based on the information accessible at that time. In contrast, context effects at the question comprehension and response formatting stage reflect influences on respondents' understanding of what the attitude object under consideration is, or how the response alternatives are to be interpreted and used. Finally, socially desirable responding presumably reflects a deliberate misrepresentation of one's enduring attitude or temporary judgment, again not bearing on whether individuals hold enduring attitudes. Next, we turn to the theoretical implications of these findings.

Context Effects and the Conceptualization of Attitudes

From a social judgment perspective, the observation that attitude reports are context dependent is not surprising. After all, human judgment is always context dependent, no matter if it pertains to simple psychophysical stimuli or complex social issues. The reviewed findings are difficult to reconcile, however, with the traditional assumption that people hold well-formed and enduring attitudes, which they can "look up" in memory – an assumption that is sometimes referred to as the "file-drawer" model of attitudes (e.g. Wilson & Hodges, 1992). To reconcile the file-drawer assumption with the emergence of context effects, some researchers suggested that people may only hold well-formed attitudes with regard to some objects, but not others (e.g. Converse, 1964). Well-formed, or *crystallized* attitudes can presumably be retrieved from memory, rendering context effects unlikely. Context effects are only expected when we assess *nonattitudes* (Converse, 1964), that is, opinions about objects for which respondents do not hold well-formed attitudes in the first place, and hence have to compute a judgment on the spot.

Of course, these distinctions are only useful to the extent that they generate different predictions for observable phenomena. Unfortunately, deriving diagnostic predictions is more difficult than one might expect. To make this point, we adopt a strong version of a construal model, assuming, for the sake of the argument, that respondents *always* need to compute a judgment from scratch and can't recall their previous evaluations. As anyone who remembers that a movie was "boring" – but can't recall any relevant details – realizes, this extreme assumption is unrealistic. Nevertheless, findings typically cited as support for the notion that individuals have enduring attitudes on some positions, although perhaps not on others, can be accommodated within such an extreme version of a judgment model, giving judgment models the advantage of accounting for findings that presumably challenge as well as support the traditional attitude concept.

The stability of attitude reports over time

First, consider the stability of attitude reports over time. From the perspective of file-drawer models, similar reports at different points in time suggest that respondents have a "crystallized" attitude towards the object that they can report with some accuracy. In its general form, this assumption is circular and contributes little to our understanding of the stability of attitude reports in the absence of independent evidence for the crystallization of attitudes. In contrast, construal models specify the conditions under which we are likely to obtain similar reports at different points in time, namely the conditions under which context effects will be small or absent. Specifically, repeating the judgment process at different points in time will result in similar judgments to the extent that respondents form similar mental representations of the attitude object and standard at each time, or draw on similar other sources of information. Several variables determine how likely this is to be the case.

Most obviously, no change is expected when the context of the attitude judgment remains the same, thus rendering the same information temporarily accessible at t1 and t2. Similarly, no change is expected when the judgment is solely based on chronically accessible information which comes to mind at both points in time, a situation that may arise when the context does not provide relevant information (e.g. Sia, Lord, Blessum, Ratcliff, & Lepper, 1997). Moreover, even under conditions where the mental representations formed at both times include a considerable amount of different information, these differences in representation will only result in different judgments when the information used at t1 and t2 has different evaluative implications. Simply replacing one piece of information with a different one of similar valence will not change the evaluative judgment (e.g. Sia, et al., 1997).

In addition, our previous discussion of the size of context effects bears directly on stability over time (see Schwarz & Bless, 1992a). As noted above, the size of assimilation effects decreases as the amount and evaluative consistency of other information included in the representation of the target increases (e.g. Bless, et al., in press). Hence, adding an additional piece of information at t2 to a representation of the object that is otherwise identical with the representation used at t1, will only result in change if the initial representation was (a) based on a small amount of information or was (b) evaluatively inconsistent, in which case that the new piece of information may tip the balance, or (c) the new information is more extreme than the average implications of the old information. Similar considerations apply to changes in the representation of the standard, again paralleling our previous discussion of the size of contrast effects.

In short, the variables that determine the size of context effects are also the variables that determine the stability of attitude judgments over time. As this selective discussion indicates, feature based construal models (e.g. Lord & Lepper, in press; Schwarz & Bless, 1992a) are compatible with the observation of change as well as stability in attitude reports – and specify the conditions under which such stability should be observed, rendering such models clearly testable. In contrast, the conclusion that individuals must have a well-formed attitude *because* their reports are stable over time is circular in the absence of other evidence. One such set of evidence pertains to measures of attitude strength.

Attitude strength

Several researchers suggested that attitudes vary in their degree of "strength," "centrality," or "crystallization" (see Krosnick & Abelson, 1992; Petty & Krosnick, 1995, for reviews). Empirically, these concepts have been difficult to operationalize and researchers have used a variety of indicators to assess attitude strength, including the intensity of respondents' feelings about the object, the certainty with which they report holding the attitude, or the importance they ascribe to it. Unfortunately, the various measures of attitude strength are only weakly related to one another (Krosnick & Abelson, 1992) and reports of attitude strength are themselves context dependent (e.g. Haddock, Rothman, Reber, & Schwarz, 1999). Moreover, the widely shared hypothesis that context effects in attitude measurement "are greater in the case of weaker attitudes has clearly been disconfirmed" (Krosnick & Abelson, 1992, p. 193). In the most comprehensive test of this hypothesis, based on more than a dozen experiments and different measures of attitude strength, Krosnick & Schuman (1988) found no support for it.

On the other hand, attitude strength has proved important in other domains of research. Most importantly, strongly held attitudes have been found to be more stable over time and less likely to change in response to persuasive messages. Moreover, they are better predictors of behavior than weak attitudes (see Krosnick & Abelson, 1992; chapter 19, this volume). Again, however, a construal approach allows for the same predictions. To the extent that we are likely to think more, and more often, about topics that are important to us, a larger amount of information would be chronically accessible. Increased chronic accessibility of a larger amount of information, in turn, would decrease the likelihood of arriving at a different judgment when a few new pieces of information are added to the representation in response to a persuasive message. Similarly, the individual would be likely to draw on a similar set of chronically accessible information when asked to report a judgment and when faced with a behavioral decision, resulting in greater consistency between the judgment and the behavior. Accordingly, a construal approach arrives at the same predictions if we make the plausible assumption that people think more about issues that are important to them. Therefore, the findings of the attitude strength literature do not *necessarily* reflect that the processes underlying reports of "strong" attitudes differ from the processes underlying reports of "weak" attitudes.

Attitude accessibility

In an impressive program of research, Fazio and his colleagues (for reviews see Fazio, 1995; chapter 4, this volume) suggested that some attitudes are more accessible than others, as reflected in respondents' reaction times. Presumably, a fast response to an attitude question indicates that a previously formed evaluation was accessible in memory, whereas a slow response indicates that an evaluation had to be computed on the spot, which takes time. Several studies have found that highly accessible attitudes, as inferred from fast answers, are more stable over time and are better predictors of behavior (see Fazio, 1995). Unfortunately, reaction time measures do not tell us which stage of the judgment process produces a fast or slow response. A fast response may reflect the retrieval of a highly accessible previous judgment as well as the high speed of a current computation. From a judgment perspective, fast computations would be expected under different conditions, only some of which map onto the attitude concept, yet all of which would result in the observed relationships between response time and stability over time or attitude-congruent behavior.

For example, an attitude object may elicit an affective response that may serve as a basis for a fast evaluative judgment. At first glance, the affective reaction is presumably what the attitude concept refers to, yet such reactions can be obtained in response to novel objects that have not previously been evaluated (Zajonc, 1980). Accordingly, fast evaluations do not necessarily reflect the accessibility of a previously formed attitude. Yet the affect-eliciting quality of the stimulus itself would result in consistent responses over time as well as affect-congruent behavior.

Fast computations would also be expected, for example, when all information that comes to mind is evaluatively consistent, whereas slow computations would be expected when the information is evaluatively inconsistent. Making this assumption, which is amenable to empirical testing, construal models would again arrive at the same predictions. When the knowledge bearing on an attitude object is evaluatively consistent, retrieving different pieces at different times would not result in different judgments. Moreover, retrieving different pieces when one makes a judgment and when one makes a behavioral decision would still result in a high consistency between the judgment and the behavior. It is only when different pieces of information have opposite implications that we should see low stability over time and low attitude–behavior consistency (Lord & Lepper, in press). Integrating the implications of these different pieces of information, however, would take time (as Bassili, 1998, observed for "ambivalent" attitudes), potentially resulting in the observed relationship between response time and stability or attitude–behavior consistency. Hence, the observed relationship does not *necessarily* reflect differences in the accessibility of existing attitudes, but may reflect differences in a mental construal process. Accordingly, the accessibility of a previously computed judgment in memory is a *sufficient* but not a *necessary* condition for fast evaluative responses, rendering the empirical findings less conclusive than often assumed.

Conclusions

Our conclusion from these conjectures is *not* that the literatures on attitude strength and attitude accessibility are necessarily mistaken. At present, we are not aware of data that bear on our conjectures in unequivocal ways. Rather, we simply note that the available findings are potentially compatible with judgment models if one makes some plausible additional assumptions. In our reading, this suggests that asking whether people "have" attitudes or not may be relatively futile for most practical purposes, despite the obvious theoretical interest value of the issue. Yet a judgment approach has important advantages over the traditional file-drawer assumption: it allows us to account for stability as well as change; predicts the conditions under which context effects are or are not likely to emerge; predicts their direction and size; and allows for the conceptualization of individual differences between respondents (e.g. expertise, attitude strength, and so on) as well as questionnaire variables within a single conceptual framework. For the time being, we consider such an approach more promising and parsimonious than attempts to distinguish "real" attitudes from supposedly less real ones.

Implicit Measures of Attitudes: A Solution to Context Dependency?

In response to the malleability of verbal reports, social psychologists have repeatedly attempted to develop measures that are less context dependent, presumably allowing researchers to assess respondents' "true" attitude. Early attempts were motivated by a desire
to reduce socially desirable responding. For example, Jones & Sigall's (1971) *bogus pipeline*
procedure was designed to convince respondents that a sophisticated machine would pick
up spontaneous muscle movements, thus informing the researcher about their "true" response, presumably making deliberate misrepresentations of their attitudes futile. As expected, Sigall & Page (1971) observed that white respondents reported more negative
attitudes towards African-Americans under these conditions. While this procedure may
discourage the deliberate misrepresentation of judgments of which the respondent is aware,
more recent developments try to assess evaluative reactions that may even escape the respondents' own awareness. To illustrate these approaches, we draw on two different uses of
priming procedures and reaction time measures. Both approaches assess the impact of
presenting an attitude object (prime) on the speed with which participants respond to a
subsequent target word. The first approach requires them to *evaluate* the target word,
whereas the second merely requires them to *identify* the target word, either by pronounc-
ing it as quickly as they can or by deciding whether it is a word or a nonword (see chapter
7, this volume, and chapter 4, this volume, for reviews).

Do facilitation effects reflect attitude strength?

As part of their research into attitude accessibility, Fazio and his colleagues (for reviews see
Dovidio & Fazio, 1992; Fazio, 1995) demonstrated that exposure to an attitude object
facilitates subsequent evaluative responses to unrelated targets that share the same valence.
In a typical experiment, participants are required to decide if an adjective (e.g. "disgusting") has a positive or a negative meaning. When the adjective is preceded by a valence-
congruent attitude object (e.g. "cockroach"), shown at exposure times that preclude
conscious awareness, participants are faster in responding that "disgusting" has a negative
meaning than when the adjective is preceded by a valence-incongruent attitude object (e.g.
"ice cream").

   Findings of this type are compatible with two different theoretical perspectives. On the
one hand, Fazio and his colleagues suggested that respondents have an evaluation of the
attitude object stored in memory, which is activated automatically upon exposure to the
object, facilitating subsequent valence-congruent responses. From this perspective, the facilitation pattern allows us to infer respondents' positive or negative attitudes towards the
primed object without ever asking them about it. Supporting the assumption that facilitation effects reflect respondents' stored attitudes, Fazio, Sanbonmatsu, Powell, & Kardes
(1986) only observed pronounced facilitation effects when respondents' evaluation of the
object was highly accessible in memory, as indicated by fast evaluative responses to the
attitude object itself. Yet subsequent studies by Bargh and colleagues (especially Bargh,
Chaiken, Raymond, & Hymes, 1996; Giner-Sorolla, Garcia, & Bargh, 1999) qualified

this conclusion. In Fazio's paradigm, respondents' evaluation of the attitude primes is assessed shortly before the priming procedure and evaluative judgments of the target words serve as the dependent variable, thus establishing evaluation as the key processing goal. To attenuate this processing goal, Bargh and colleagues separated the assessment of attitude strength from the experiment proper and used pronunciation tasks as the dependent variable. Under these conditions, they observed automatic facilitation effects even for weak attitude primes. Their results strongly suggest that facilitation effects reflect automatic, on-line evaluations: presumably, we automatically classify all stimuli as good or bad within split-seconds after exposure and valence-congruent primes facilitate this process without necessarily requiring the accessibility of a previously formed strong attitude (for different perspectives see Fazio, 1995; Bargh, 1997; Wegner & Bargh, 1998).

Do facilitation effects reflect attitudes or semantic knowledge?

Using lexical decision or pronunciation tasks as dependent variables, other researchers observed, for example, that racial primes (e.g. "black" or "white") facilitate the subsequent processing of target words (e.g. traits) that are consistent with racial stereotypes, but inhibit the processing of target words that are inconsistent with racial stereotypes (e.g. Wittenbrink, Judd, & Park, 1997). At present, the available literature suggests that facilitation effects observed on these semantic tasks are unrelated to explicit reports of racial attitudes, whereas facilitation effects observed on evaluative judgment tasks are related to explicit attitude measures (see Blair, in press; Wittenbrink, Judd, & Park, 1999). As Blair (in press) noted, some have concluded from this observation that the lexical decision and pronunciation tasks hold particular promise because they assess something that people are not willing to report explicitly or may not even be aware of. In contrast, others suggested that semantic facilitation effects may primarily reflect semantic knowledge about prominent attitude objects, knowledge that is widely shared within a society but not necessarily indicative of a given individual's attitude (e.g. Devine, 1989). Given the weak relationship of semantic facilitation measures with any variables that could serve as an independent validation (e.g. explicit reports or overt behavior), it remains unclear what exactly is being assessed. Moreover, the accumulating findings once again indicate that these measures are subject to context effects. Glaser & Banaji (1999), for example, observed that evaluatively extreme primes may inhibit rather than facilitate subsequent performance, thus reversing the usually obtained pattern.

Summary

As this selective review indicates, the hope that implicit measures can provide us with a context independent window on respondents' "true" attitudes may be overly optimistic. Instead, we conjecture that abundant context effects will emerge as research in this area progresses and we are hopeful that these context effects will illuminate the cognitive processes underlying implicit measures of attitudes. In our reading, investigations into the *interplay* of automatic and controlled processes in attitude judgment hold great promise and the temptation to equate one or the other set of measures with individuals' "true" attitudes may do more harm than good. Suppose, for example, that subliminal exposure to "cod liver oil" facilitates your identification of "disgusting" as a "bad" word, yet you know cod liver oil is good for you and you take it regularly. Which of these responses should we consider an unbiased indicator of your "true" attitude: your behavior (as Campbell, 1950, would have urged us), your verbal report ("Good for me, but I don't like the taste"), the speed with which you evaluate "disgusting" as a bad word, or the speed with which you can pronounce it? Chances are that we learn different things from each one, rendering the designation of one as the key phenomenon counterproductive.

Attitude Construal and the Attitude–Behavior Relationship

Theoretically, an observed relationship between an individual's attitude and his or her behavior may reflect (a) that the behavior serves as input into an attitude judgment, (b) that the attitude guides the individual's behavioral decisions, or (c) that the attitude judgment and the behavioral decision are based on the same input information. We have already addressed the first pathway in our discussion of attitude judgments and now turn to the latter two. Consistent with common sense notions, early attitude theorists assumed that "attitudes determine for each individual what he will do" (Allport, 1935, p. 806). Subsequent research failed to find compelling support for this assumption and by the early 1970s many researchers concluded that the influence of attitudes on behavior may be negligible (see Wicker, 1969). In the years since, social psychologists have made considerable progress in understanding the conditions under which substantial relationships between attitude reports and overt behavior can be observed (see chapter 19, this volume).

In our discussion of the consistency of attitude judgments over time we emphasized that similar judgments are to be expected when respondents form similar mental representations of the attitude object and a relevant standard at different points in time. The same logic holds for the relationship between attitude judgments and overt behaviors: attitude–behavior consistency is to be expected to the extent that the mental representation used in forming an attitude judgment has similar implications as the mental representation used in arriving at a behavioral decision. As Lord & Lepper (in press) noted, this *matching* assumption has a long tradition in social psychological theorizing, dating back to the seminal work of LaPiere (1934). In the 1930s, LaPiere traveled up and down the West Coast of the United States in the company of a Chinese student and his wife and the group received courteous service at numerous hotels and restaurants. But when later asked if they would accept "members of the Chinese race" as guests, over 90 percent of the establishments responded with a clear "no," consistent with the anti-Chinese prejudice of the time. Presumably, the proprietors' answers to LaPiere's question were based on a mental representation of "members of the Chinese race" that reflected the low social status and education of the majority of Chinese-Americans at that time. Yet in the actual behavioral situation they were confronted with a well-dressed couple in the company of a white professor, resulting in a pronounced mismatch between the information used to answer LaPiere's question and the information used for the crucial behavioral decision. This matching notion, which is at the heart of Lord & Lepper's (in press) attitude representation theory, provides a parsimonious theoretical rationale for the conditions under which we can observe attitude–behavior consistency and has important methodological implications.

When can we expect attitude–behavior consistency?

In general, attitude–behavior consistency will be higher when the attitude judgment and the behavioral decision are based on the same input information. This simple principle underlies many empirical regularities, although it may play out in complex ways under some conditions.

First, suppose that the attitude judgment is feature-based. In this case, attitude–behavior consistency is higher when the temporary representation formed of the attitude object at the time of judgment matches the temporary representation formed at the time of behavior. For example, Ramsey, Lord, Wallace, & Pugh (1994) observed that participants' attitudes towards former substance abusers were a better predictor of their behavior towards an exemplar when the description of the exemplar matched rather than mismatched participants' representation of the group, as assessed two weeks earlier. Because many exemplars (individuals or objects) provide a poor match with our general representation of the category to which they belong, it is difficult to predict behaviors towards exemplars from attitude judgments about the category. This notion further entails that attitude–behavior inconsistency should increase with the salience of the mismatch. Hence, it should be pronounced when the exemplar deviates from the category on easily observable features, but not when it deviates on less observable features.

Note, however, that behavioral decisions are not always based on specific information about the attitude object, e.g. on individuating information about the specific person we encounter. For example, being under cognitive load (e.g. Macrae, Milnae, & Bodenhausen, 1994) or being in a good mood (see chapter 18, this volume) increase reliance on preexisting knowledge structures at the expense of reliance on individuating information. Hence, we may expect that individuals' behavior towards an exemplar is more consistent with their attitude judgment about the category when they are in a good mood or under cognitive load because information about the exemplar is less likely to enter the decision process. Supporting this prediction, Blessum, Lord, & Sia (1998) observed a high consistency between participants' attitude judgments about gay men in general and their behavior towards a specific exemplar under these conditions, even when the specific exemplar did not match their representation of the category "gay men." Only in a neutral mood, and when given enough time, did the match between the category representation and the exemplar moderate participants' behavior.

Second, suppose that the attitude judgment is based on respondents' mood at the time of judgment (Schwarz & Clore, 1988). In this case, we may be hard put to detect any attitude–behavior consistency unless respondents happen to be in the same mood in the behavioral situation and the behavior is inconsequential, thus rendering one's apparent affective response sufficient for a decision. Moreover, any other difference in processing motivation at the time of judgment and behavior is similarly likely to decrease the attitude–behavior relationship. When asked in a consumer survey how much we like a Volvo, for example, we are likely to draw on fewer features of the attitude object than when pondering whether to actually buy a Volvo (see chapter 26, this volume), thus increasing the likelihood of mismatches between the two representations. In a similar vein, Wilson and his colleagues (for reviews see Wilson & Hodges, 1992; Wilson, Dunn, Kraft, & Lisle, 1989) observed that writing an essay that justifies one's attitude judgment can undermine the attitude–behavior relationship – in writing the essay, participants draw on many aspects they may not consider in the behavioral situation, thus reducing the match between the relevant representations.

Third, as Millar & Tesser (1992) noted, we engage in some behaviors for their instrumental value in reaching a goal and in other behaviors for the pleasures they provide. If so, attitude judgments should be a better predictor of instrumental behaviors when the judgment is based on a consideration of the behavior's instrumental implications rather than hedonic implications. But attitude judgments based on our hedonic assessments of the behavior should be an excellent predictor for consummatory behaviors, i.e. behaviors we engage in for enjoyment. An elegant series of studies confirmed this variant of the general matching hypothesis (e.g. Millar & Tesser, 1986).

Fourth, numerous studies have shown that attitude–behavior consistency is higher when the individual has direct behavioral experience with the attitude object (see Fazio & Zanna, 1981, for a review). For example, Regan & Fazio (1977) asked participants to rate how interesting they find different puzzles either after they worked on an example or after they examined a previously solved example. Participants' interest ratings were better predictors of how much time they spent on each puzzle in a subsequent free play period when their ratings were based on prior behavioral experience. Presumably, the prior experience resulted in a representation that provided a better match with participants' experiences during the free play period, than did the representation formed on the basis of examining an already solved example.

As a final example, attitude–behavior consistency is likely to be higher when individuals take the context in which the behavior is to be performed into account when they form an attitude judgment. In most cases, however, attitude judgments are assessed without mentally instantiating the context in which the attitude object may be encountered, resulting in low attitude–behavior consistency. Hence, attitudes assessed in a "cold" state, e.g. attitudes towards condom use assessed in a research setting, are poor predictors of actual behavior in a "hot" state, like an actual romantic encounter (for a review see Loewenstein & Schkade, 1999). A similar argument can be made for the role of subjective norms and perceptions of personal control, variables that figure prominently in Fishbein & Ajzen's (1975) theory of reasoned action and Ajzen's (1985) theory of planned behavior. As Lord & Lepper (in press) highlight, these variables are unlikely to enter the representation of the attitude object itself, but are prominent in the representation of the behavioral situation. Accordingly, taking these variables into account increases our ability to predict actual behavior over the predictive value of the attitude judgment alone.

In combination with our discussion of the temporal stability of attitude judgments, these examples highlight that consistency between attitude judgments at different points in time, or between attitude judgments and behavior, is likely to emerge when both responses are based on input information of similar valence. If so, however, we may hesitate to conclude that some pre-existing attitude plays a causal role in the behavioral decision.

Instead, the observed relationship may be rather *spurious*, reflecting that the attitude judgment and the behavioral decision are based on similar representations of the attitude object. Of course, this conclusion can be avoided when one equates the attitude with the knowledge representation on which the attitude judgment or the behavioral decision are based, as suggested by Lord & Lepper (in press) and Tourangeau (1992). However, this definitional move does not increase the explanatory power of the underlying process assumptions.

Methodological implications

The preceding discussion of matching and mismatching inputs also bears in straightforward ways on methodological issues. As Fishbein & Ajzen (1974) noted, we are more likely to observe attitude–behavior consistency when we use multiple behavioral criteria rather than a single criterion (see chapter 19, this volume). In terms of the preceding discussion, an aggregation across multiple behaviors or multiple situations increases the likelihood that some matches are included in the assessment. Moreover, attitude–behavior consistency increases the better the attitude question matches the behavioral criterion. For example, respondents' evaluation of "Donating money to the Democratic Party" is a better predictor of this particular behavior than their general evaluation of the Democratic Party *per se*. Such matches between the attitude question and the target behavior again increase the likelihood that both responses are based on similar representations.

Although multiple behavioral criteria and a close match between the attitude question and the act reliably improve predictions, it is quite obvious that this accomplishment falls short of the promise of early attitude theories. Instead of being able to predict a multitude of behaviors towards the attitude object across a broad range of situations, we now realize that we can only predict that the individual will do "something" that is consistent with his or her attitude judgment or need to ask a multitude of questions at a level of specificity that makes it more parsimonious to ask right away, "Do you intend to give money to the Democratic Party?" Unfortunately, an analysis of the cognitive processes underlying attitude–behavior consistency suggests that it is unlikely that we will ever be able to deliver on the sweeping promises of the classic attitude concept. In contrast, a detailed analysis of the underlying processes is likely to advance our understanding of the conditions under which our evaluations of an object and our behavior towards this object may, or may not, show consistency.

References

Ajzen, I. (1985). From intentions to actions: A theory of planned behavior. In J. Kuhl & J. Beckmann (Eds.), *Action control: From cognition to behavior* (pp. 11-39). New York: Springer Verlag.

Allport, G. W. (1935). Attitudes. In C. Murchison (Ed.), *Handbook of social psychology*. Worcester, MA: Clark University Press.

Allport, G.W. (1954). The historical background of modern social psychology. In G. Lindzey (Ed.), *Handbook of social psychology*, Vol. 1 (pp. 3–56). Cambridge, MA: Addison-Wesley.

Bargh, J. A. (1997). The automaticity of everyday life. In R. S. Wyer (Ed.), *The automaticity of everyday life: Advances in social cognition*, Vol. 10 (pp. 1–61). Mahwah, NJ: Erlbaum.

Bargh, J. A., Chaiken, S., Raymond, P., & Hymes, C. (1996). The automatic evaluation effect. *Journal of Experimental Social Psychology, 32,* 185–210.

Bassili, J. N. (1993). Response latency versus certainty as indexes of the strength of voting intentions in a CATI survey. *Public Opinion Quarterly, 57,* 54–61.

Bassili, J. N. (1996). The how and why of response latency measurement in telephone surveys. In N. Schwarz & S. Sudman (Eds.), *Answering questions: Methodology for determining cognitive and communicative processes in survey research* (pp. 319–346). San Francisco: Jossey Bass.

Bassili, J. N. (1998). Simultaneous accessibility: A prerequisite to heated intrapsychic conflict. Meetings of the International Society for Political Psychology, Montreal, Canada.

Bem, D. J. (1970). *Beliefs, attitudes, and human affairs.* Belmont, CA: Brooks/Cole.

Bem, D. J. (1972). Self-perception theory. In L. Berkowitz (Ed.), *Advances in experimental social psychology, 6,* 1–62. New York: Academic Press.

Blair, I. V. (in press). Implicit stereotypes and prejudice. In G. Moskowitz (Ed.), *Future directions in social cognition.* Mahwah, NJ: Erlbaum.

Bless, H., Igou, E. R., Schwarz, N., & Wänke, M. (in press). Reducing context effects by adding context information: The direction and size of context effects in political judgment. *Personality and Social Psychology Bulletin.*

Blessum, K. A., Lord, C. G., & Sia, T. L. (1998). Cognitive load and positive mood reduce typicality effects in attitude–behavior consistency. *Personality and Social Psychology Bulletin, 24,* 496–504.

Bodenhausen, G. V., Schwarz, N., Bless, H., & Wänke, M. (1995). Effects of atypical exemplars on racial beliefs: Enlightened racism or generalized appraisals? *Journal of Experimental Social Psychology, 31,* 48–63.

Bohner, G., Moskowitz, G., & Chaiken, S. (1995). The interplay of heuristic and systematic processing of social information. *European Review of Social Psychology, 6,* 33–68.

Campbell, D. T. (1950). The indirect assessment of social attitudes. *Psychological Bulletin, 47,* 15–38.

Converse, P. E. (1964). The nature of belief systems in the mass public. In D. E. Apter (Ed), *Ideology and discontent* (pp. 206–261). New York: Free Press.

DeMaio, T. J. (1984). Social desirability and survey measurement: A review. In C. F. Turner & E. Martin (Eds.), *Surveying subjective phenomena*, Vol. 2 (pp. 257–281). New York: Russell–Sage.

Devine, P. G. (1989). Stereotypes and prejudice: Their automatic and controlled components. *Journal of Personality and Social Psychology, 56,* 5–18.

Dovidio, J. F., & Fazio, R. H. (1992). New technologies for the direct and indirect assessment of attitudes. In J. Tanur (Ed.), *Questions about questions* (pp. 204–237). New York: Russell–Sage.

Eagly, A. H., & Chaiken, S. (1993). *The psychology of attitudes.* Fort Worth, TX: Harcourt Brace Jovanovich.

Eagly, A. H., & Chaiken, S. (1998). Attitude structure and function. In D. T. Gilbert, S. T. Fiske, & G. Lindzey (Eds.), *The handbook of social psychology*, Vol. 1 (pp. 269–322). New York: MacGraw-Hill.

Fazio, R. H. (1986). How do attitudes guide behavior? In R. M. Sorrentino & E. T. Higgins (Eds.), *Handbook of motivation and cognition: Foundations of social behavior*, Vol. 1 (pp. 204–243) New York: Guilford Press.

Fazio, R. H. (1995). Attitudes as object-evaluation associations: Determinants, consequences, and correlates of attitude accessibility. In R. E. Petty & J. A. Krosnick (Eds.), *Attitude strength* (pp. 247–282). Mahwah, NJ: Erlbaum.

Fazio, R. H., & Zanna, M. P. (1981). Direct experience and attitude–behavior consistency. *Advances in Experimental Social Psychology, 14,* pp. 161–202.

Fazio, R. H., Sanbonmatsu, D. M., Powell, M. C., & Kardes, F. R. (1986). On the automatic activation of attitudes. *Journal of Personality and Social Psychology, 50,* 229–238.

Fishbein, M., & Ajzen, I. (1974). Attitudes towards objects as predictors of single and multiple behavioral criteria. *Psychological Review, 81,* 59–74.

Fishbein, M., & Ajzen, I. (1975). *Belief, attitude, intention, and behavior: An introduction to theory and research.* Reading, MA: Addison-Wesley.

Fuson, W. M. (1942). Attitudes: A note on the concept and its research consequences. *American Sociological Review, 7,* 856–857.

Giner-Sorolla, R., Garcia, M. T., & Bargh, J. A. (1999). The automatic evaluation of pictures. *Social Cognition, 17,* 76–96.

Glaser, J., & Banaji, M. R. (1999). Assimilation and contrast in automatic evaluation. Unpublished manuscript, Yale University.

Haddock, G., Rothman, A. J., Reber, R., & Schwarz, N. (in press). Forming judgments of attitude certainty, importance, and intensity: The role of subjective experiences. *Personality and Social Psychology Bulletin.*

Hatchett, S., & Schuman, H. (1976). White respondents and race of interviewer effects. *Public Opinion Quarterly, 39,* 523–528.

Higgins, E. T. (1996). Knowledge activation: Accessibility, applicability, and salience. In E. T. Higgins & A. Kruglanski (Eds.), *Social psychology: Handbook of basic principles* (pp. 133–168). New York: Guilford Press.

Higgins, E. T. (1998). The aboutness principle: A pervasive influence on human inference. *Social Cognition, 16,* 173–198.

Jones, E. E. (1979). The rocky road from acts to dispositions. *American Psychologist, 34,* 107–117.

Jones, E. E., & Sigall, H. (1971). The bogus pipeline: A new paradigm for measuring affect and attitude. *Psychological Bulletin, 76,* 349–364.

Krech, D., & Crutchfield, R. S. (1948). *Theory and problems of social psychology.* New York: MacGraw-Hill.

Krosnick, J. A., & Abelson, R. P. (1992). The case for measuring attitude strength. In J. M. Tanur (Ed.), *Questions about questions* (pp. 177–203). New York: Russell–Sage.

Krosnick, J. A., & Schuman, H. (1988). Attitude intensity, importance, and certainty and susceptibility to response effects. *Journal of Personality and Social Psychology, 54,* 940–952.

LaPierre, R. (1934). Attitudes versus actions. *Social Forces, 13,* 230–237.

Loewenstein, G., & Schkade, D. (1999). Wouldn't it be nice?: Predicting future feelings. In D. Kahneman, E. Diener, & N. Schwarz (Eds.), *Well-being: The foundations of hedonic psychology* (pp. 85–105). New York: Russell–Sage.

Lord, C. G., & Lepper, M. R. (in press). Attitude representation theory. *Advances in Experimental Social Psychology, 31.*

Macrae, C. N., Milne, A. B., & Bodenhausen, G. V. (1994). Stereotypes as energy-saving devices: A peek inside the cognitive toolbox. *Journal of Personality and Social Psychology, 66,* 37–47.

Millar, M. G., & Tesser, A. (1986). Effects of affective and cognitive focus on the attitude–behavior relation. *Journal of Personality and Social Psychology, 51,* 270–276.

Millar, M. G., & Tesser, A. (1992). The role of beliefs and feelings in guiding behavior: The mismatch model. In L. L. Martin & A. Tesser (Eds.), *The construction of social judgments* (pp. 277–300). Mahwah, NJ: Erlbaum.

Ostrom, T. M., & Upshaw, H. S. (1968). Psychological perspective and attitude change. In A. C. Greenwald, T. C. Brock, & T. M. Ostrom (Eds.), *Psychological foundations of attitudes.* New York: Academic Press.

Parducci, A. (1965). Category judgments: A range–frequency model. *Psychological Review, 72,* 407–418.

Parducci, A. (1983). Category ratings and the relational character of judgment. In H. G. Geissler, H. F. J. M. Bulfart, E. L. H. Leeuwenberg, & V. Sarris (Eds.), *Modern issues in perception* (pp. 262–282). Berlin: VEB Deutscher Verlag der Wissenschaften.

Petty, R. E., & Krosnick, J. A. (Eds.) (1995). *Attitude strength.* Mahwah, NJ: Erlbaum.

Petty, R. E., & Wegener, D. T. (1998). Attitude change: Multiple roles for persuasion variables. In D. Gilbert, S. T. Fiske, & G. Lindzey (Eds.), *The handbook of social psychology,* Vol. 1 (pp. 323–389). New York: MacGraw-Hill.

Ramsey, S. L., Lord, C. G., Wallace, D. S., & Pugh, M. A. (1994). The role of subtypes in attitudes towards superordinate social categories. *British Journal of Social Psychology, 33,* 387–403.

Regan, D. T., & Fazio, R. H. (1977). On the consistency between attitudes and behaviors: Look to the method of attitude formation. *Journal of Experimental Social Psychology, 13*, 28–45.

Salancik, G. R., & Conway, M. (1975). Attitude inferences from salient and relevant cognitive content about behavior. *Journal of Personality and Social Psychology, 32*, 829–840.

Schuman, H., & Presser, S. (1981). *Questions and answers in attitude surveys.* New York: Academic Press.

Schwarz, N. (1996). *Cognition and communication: Judgmental biases, research methods, and the logic of conversation.* Hillsdale, NJ: Erlbaum.

Schwarz, N. (1998). Accessible content and accessibility experiences: The interplay of declarative and experiential information in judgment. *Personality and Social Psychology Review, 2*, 87–99.

Schwarz, N., & Bless, H. (1992a). Constructing reality and its alternatives: Assimilation and contrast effects in social judgment. In L. L. Martin & A. Tesser (Eds.), *The construction of social judgments* (pp. 217–245). Hillsdale, NJ: Erlbaum.

Schwarz, N., & Bless, H. (1992b). Scandals and the public's trust in politicians: Assimilation and contrast effects. *Personality and Social Psychology Bulletin, 18*, 574–579.

Schwarz, N., & Clore, G. L. (1988). How do I feel about it? Informative functions of affective states. In K. Fiedler & J. Forgas (Eds.), *Affect, cognition, and social behavior* (pp. 44–62). Toronto: Hogrefe International.

Schwarz, N., & Hippler, H. J. (1995). The numeric values of rating scales: A comparison of their impact in mail surveys and telephone interviews. *International Journal of Public Opinion Research, 7*, 72–74.

Schwarz, N., & Strack, F. (1991). Context effects in attitude surveys: Applying cognitive theory to social research. In W. Stroebe & M. Hewstone (Eds.), *European Review of Social Psycholoy*, Vol. 2 (pp. 31–50). Chichester, UK: Wiley.

Schwarz, N., & Sudman, S. (Eds.) (1992). *Context effects in social and psychological research.* New York: Springer Verlag.

Schwarz, N., Strack, F., & Mai, H. P. (1991). Assimilation and contrast effects in part–whole question sequences: A conversational logic analysis. *Public Opinion Quarterly, 55*, 3–23.

Sherman, S. J., Ahlm, K., Berman, L., & Lynn, S. (1979). Contrast effects and the relationship to subsequent behavior. *Journal of Experimental Social Psychology, 14*, 340–350.

Sia, T. L., Lord, C. G., Blessum, K., Ratcliff, C. D., & Lepper, M. R. (1997). Is a rose always a rose? The role of social category exemplar-change in attitude stability and attitude–behavior consistency. *Journal of Personality and Social Psychology, 72*, 501–514.

Sigall, H., & Page, R. (1971). Current stereotypes: A little fadin, a little faking. *Journal of Personality and Social Psychology, 18*, 247–255.

Stapel, D. A., & Schwarz, N. (1998). The Republican who did not want to become President: An inclusion/exclusion analysis of Colin Powell's impact on evaluations of the Republican Party and Bob Dole. *Personality and Social Psychology Bulletin, 24*, 690–698.

Strack, F. (1992). The different routes to social judgments: Experiential versus informational strategies. In L. L. Martin & A. Tesser (Eds.), *The construction of social judgments* (pp. 249–276). Hillsdale, NJ: Erlbaum.

Strack, F. (1994). Response processes in social judgment. In R. S. Wyer & T. K. Srull (Eds.), *Handbook of social cognition*, 2nd edn. Vol. 1 (pp. 287–322). Hillsdale, NJ: Erlbaum.

Strack, F., & Martin, L. (1987). Thinking, judging, and communicating: A process account of context effects in attitude surveys. In H. J. Hippler, N. Schwarz, & S. Sudman (Eds.), *Social information processing and survey methodology* (pp. 123–148). New York: Springer Verlag.

Strack, F., Schwarz, N., Bless, H., Kübler, A., & Wänke, M. (1993). Awareness of the influence as a determinant of assimilation versus contrast. *European Journal of Social Psychology, 23*, 53–62.

Sudman, S., Bradburn, N. M., & Schwarz, N. (1996). *Thinking about answers: The application of cognitive processes to survey methodology.* San Francisco: Jossey-Bass.

Thomas, W. I., & Znaniecki, F. (1918). *The Polish peasant in Europe and America.* Vol. 1. Boston, MA: Badger.

Tourangeau, R. (1984). Cognitive science and survey methods: A cognitive perspective. In T. Jabine, M. Straf, J. Tanur, & R. Tourangeau (Eds.), *Cognitive aspects of survey methodology: Building a bridge between disciplines* (pp. 73–100). Washington, DC: National Academy Press.

Tourangeau, R. (1992). Attitudes as memory structures: belief sampling and context effects. In N. Schwarz & S. Sudman (Eds.), *Context effects in social and psychological research* (pp. 35–47). New York: Springer Verlag.

Tourangeau, R., & Rasinski, K. A. (1988). Cognitive processes underlying context effects in attitude measurement. *Psychological Bulletin, 103,* 299–314.

Tversky, A., & Kahneman, D. (1973). Availability: A heuristic for judging frequency and probability. *Cognitive Psychology, 5,* 207–232.

Valins, S. (1966). Cognitive effects of false heart-rate feedback. *Journal of Personality and Social Psychology, 4,* 400–408.

Wegner, D. M., & Bargh, J. A. (1998). Control and automaticity in social life. In D. Gilbert, S. T. Fiske, & G. Lindzey (Eds.), *The handbook of social psychology*, Vol. 1 (pp. 446–496). New York: MacGraw-Hill.

Wells, G., & Petty, R. E. (1980). The effects of overt headmovements on persuasion: Compatibility and incompatibility of responses. *Basic and Applied Social Psychology, 1,* 219–230.

Wicker, A. W. (1969). Attitudes versus actions: The relationship of verbal and overt behavioral responses to attitude objects. *Journal of Social Issues, 25,* 41–78.

Wilson, T. D. (1998). Multiple attitudes. Unpublished manuscript, University of Virginia.

Wilson, T. D., & Hodges, S. D. (1992). Attitudes as temporary constructions. In L. L. Martin & A. Tesser (Eds.), *The construction of social judgments* (pp. 37–65). Hillsdale, NJ: Erlbaum.

Wilson, T. D., Dunn, D. S., Kraft, D., & Lisle, D. J. (1989). Introspection, attitude change, and attitude–behavior consistency. *Advances in Experimental Social Psychology, 22,* 287–338.

Wittenbrink, B., Judd, C. M., & Park, B. (1997). Evidence for racial prejudice at the implicit level and its relationship with questionnaire measures. *Journal of Personality and Social Psychology, 72,* 262–274.

Wittenbrink, B., Judd, C. M., & Park, B. (1999). Spontaneous prejudice in context: Evaluative versus conceptual judgments in automatic attitude activation. Unpublished manuscript, University of Colorado, Boulder, CO.

Zajonc, R. B. (1980). Feeling and thinking. Preferences need no inferences. *American Psychologist, 35,* 151–175.

Chapter Twenty-One

Values and Ideologies

Meg J. Rohan and Mark P. Zanna

Introductory social psychology textbooks often have no reference to the huge amounts of theorizing and research that concerns values and ideologies. However, textbook summaries may be almost impossible because there are many different definitions of values and ideologies and many different approaches to the constructs. For the same reason, our task of providing an overview of the two areas will be a challenge. However, because we believe that the constructs of values and ideologies are critically important to social psychologists, we will take the task out of the "too hard" basket and provide information about past and present theory and research that we think is fundamental to understanding the two constructs within a coherent framework.

A coherent framework requires resolution of one very basic difficulty. Both values and ideologies have been used to describe the causes of attitudinal and behavioral responses. The wisdom of Gordon Allport can provide direction for resolution of this problem. Allport once berated psychologists for failing to take account of the fact that people's values influence their perception of reality (Allport, 1955, p. 89). He suggested that values were the "dominating force in life" because they directed all of a person's activity towards the realization of his or her values (Allport, 1961, p. 543). Allport (1954) also discussed the construct of ideologies in the context of describing "rationalization." So, then, values can be understood as underlying causes for attitudinal and behavioral decisions, and ideologies can be understood in terms of conscious deliberation of values-driven decisions. Put another way, whereas values are the underlying or implicit causes of attitudinal and behavioral decisions, ideologies are the value based, explicit constructions used in consciously thinking or talking about decisions. Critical to this solution is that the term "values" should be reserved for what might be viewed as "abstract attitudes," and the term "attitude" should

Preparation of this chapter was supported in part by an Australian Research Council Small Grant to the first author and a Social Sciences and Humanities Research Council of Canada grant to the second author. We thank Syd Lovibond and Shalom Schwartz for their comments on earlier drafts.

be reserved for specific evaluations. Allport, as well as others (e.g. Eagly & Chaiken, 1993) have used the word "attitude" to describe both abstract as well as specific evaluations.

Also important to a coherent framework is the distinction between personal and what can be labeled social value systems. Theorists and researchers rarely, if ever, make this distinction. However, people not only have a set of personal value priorities, they also have perceptions of others' value priorities (e.g. those of friends, employers, fellow group members). Thus, both personal and social value systems are located within the individual. Although there is a great deal of work in which, for example, institutional, societal, or cultural value priorities are described, the focus of this chapter is on value systems located within the individual. Keeping in mind Allport's wisdom that values are the "dominating force" in people's lives, people's personal value systems then may be viewed in terms of their personal identity, and their social value systems in terms of their social identity.

We will organize our presentation of past and current theorizing and research by discussing three dominant approaches taken in the field of values and ideologies. All three approaches have the same endpoint: values and ideologies are critical to understanding and predicting people's attitudinal and behavioral decisions. We will conclude by highlighting three of the big unanswered questions.

The Personality Approach

The assumption underlying work classifiable as having a "personality" theme seems to be this: to the extent that people can be comprehensively described, their responses can be understood and predicted. Tied to this assumption is that the values or dominant ideologies embraced are systems in which endorsement of one value or ideology has implications for endorsement of other values and ideologies. Little or no attention is paid to the influence of the environment.

Values-focused work

Early theorists such as Alexander Shand (e.g. 1914) used the concept of "sentiments" – a concept somewhat consistent with the values construct – to describe people's "characters" comprehensively. Eduard Spranger (e.g. 1928) also was focused on comprehensively describing character, and suggested that people's characters contained an organization of six "attitudes" in which one "attitude" was more dominant than the others. For example, an "intellectualist" (ibid., p. 111) would be dominated by the "theoretic" attitude, whereas the "practical type" (ibid., p. 133) would be dominated by the "economic" attitude. The once very popular "Study of Values" instrument (Allport, Vernon, & Lindzey, 1960) was first developed in 1931 to assess the relative importance people placed on Spranger's six "attitudes."

Gordon Allport (e.g. 1955) discussed personal values in terms of people's "style," "philosophy of life," and their "stamp of individuality." He also highlighted the distinction between personal and social value systems, and suggested that reconciling the "personal" with the "tribal" was a lifelong process. If this reconciliation is viewed in terms of the potential conflicts between personal and social value priorities, it may be an important area of focus as a process common to all people. For example, it may be important to what has been discussed as interattitudinal consistency (e.g. Lavine, Thomsen, & Gonzales, 1997) and to investigations of "value fit" (e.g. Feather, 1975).

When researchers investigate the link between values and attitudes, often they may make the assumption that particular kinds of people have particular kinds of attitudes. If they do, they can be viewed as taking a personality approach. For example, Katz & Hass (1988) may have made this assumption in their investigation between values and racial attitudes. They found, for example, that Humanitarianism–Egalitarianism values were associated with positive attitudes towards Black Americans, whereas less positive attitudes were associated with Protestant work ethic values.

Ideology-focused work

Adorno, Frenkel-Brunswick, Levinson, & Sanford (1950) used the word "ideology" in a way that is more consistent with the values construct as we have described it than with the ideology construct. However, Adorno, et al. inspired a great deal of research into the relation between "personality" and "political ideology." For example, the "rigidity of the right" hypothesis was used to explain the origins of authoritarianism (that was understood in terms of a personality based construct): extremely conservative political positions taken by the highly authoritarian are a means to cope with deep-rooted psychodynamic conflicts. The "ideologue" hypothesis also located the origins of authoritarianism in personality: ideologues, whether they subscribed to authoritarian or permissive views, would do so in a dogmatic way because they view the world in terms of absolutes.

The personality–ideology link most often has been investigated at the level of groups, institutions, or cultures rather than at the level of the individual. For example, Rokeach (1973) suggested that political parties could be described in terms of the importance they placed on the values Equality and Freedom. This model has been comprehensively tested and extended. For example, Braithwaite (e.g. 1994) built upon Rokeach's ideas and suggested that two "value orientation dimensions" structure political ideologies. These "value orientations" are "International Harmony and Equality" and "National Strength and Order." However, Heaven, Stones, Nel, Huysamen, & Louw (1994) suggested that the National Strength and Order dimension may require revision for understanding political ideologies where there is political conflict or change. Note also that Sidanius (1990) has shown that the relation between values and political ideologies differed for "novices" (students) and "experts" (professionals in the political area): for novices, a "Salvation" value was the most important determinant of political ideology, whereas for experts it was "Equality."

The important lesson to be learned from theorists and researchers whose work reflects a "personality" theme is that values and ideologies are central to who a person is "as a person," both as an individual and as a group member.

The Representation Approach

The "representation" approach builds on the "personality" approach, and person based differences still are the focus. However, rather than assume a direct causal path from person based differences to attitudinal and behavioral decisions, a less direct path is implied. People's values and ideologies are assumed to cause a view of the world, and then this worldview causes attitudinal and behavioral decisions. Note, then, that a new construct – worldview – has been introduced. In the "representation" approach, the focus seems to be on the way that values and ideologies influence how people perceive the positivity and negativity of entities in their environments.

Values-focused work

Solomon Asch (1952) suggested that because "we act and choose on the basis of what we see, feel, and believe; meanings and values are part and parcel of our actions . . . to understand human action it is therefore essential to understand the conscious mode in which things appear to us" (ibid., pp. 64–65). Similarly, Sherif & Sherif (1956) discussed the notion of "psychological selectivity" and suggested that an observer's "desire, attitude, passion, interest, preoccupation, and the like" (ibid., p. 85) – terms that seem synonymous with "values" – will direct his or her attention towards some "perceivable objects" as being "figure" and others as "background." Kurt Lewin (1944/1952) gave the same message. He expressed the importance of values in people's psychological environment by suggesting that values determined "which types of activity have a positive and which have a negative valence for an individual in a given situation" (ibid., p. 41). More recently, Feather (1995) supported the assumption that values induce valences on potential actions and outcomes. He found that participants' choice of action alternative in response to a hypothetical scenario was related to their ratings of the attractiveness of the alternatives presented and to their value priorities primed by the scenario.

One of the earliest empirical demonstrations that personal value priorities influence the way people perceive entities in their environments was provided by Postman, Bruner, & McGinnies (1948). These researchers investigated the relation between people's personal "value orientation" (measured using the Allport–Vernon Study of Values) and "perceptual selectivity." There seems reason to suspect that if *social* value priorities were salient, they might also influence perceptions. The famous Hastorf & Cantril (1954) study in which Dartmouth and Princeton football fans' perceptions of a game were compared might be viewed in terms of the influence of social value priorities on perceptions (see chapter 11, this volume). The finding (Vallone, Ross, & Lepper, 1985) that Pro-Arab and Pro-Israeli television viewers saw different things in the same programs also might be understood from the perspective of the influence of social value priorities on perceptions.

The perception psychologist James Gibson (e.g. 1950) endorsed the notion that people's value priorities influence their perceptions of entities in their environments. He suggested that "outline and form are modified by meaning" (ibid., p. 209), gave the example that a nonsense form could be interpreted by one person as a woman's torso, by another as a dumbbell, and by a third as a violin, and commented that "it might be guessed that the three observers had somewhat different interests in life" (ibid., p. 210). Nevertheless, Gibson also pointed out that perception was not always or necessarily distorted by needs or affected by purposes, and admonished social psychologists for their overemphasis on the role of perception in the link between values and behavior. He reminded psychologists that "all human beings, everywhere, probably see the ground and the sky the same way" (ibid., p. 212).

Ideology-focused work

Mention the word "ideology" and discussion of Karl Marx often follows. One important topic in Marxist writings is the way those in power impose ways of thinking about entities in the environment on the less powerful. Karl Mannheim also is often discussed when the word "ideology" is mentioned. Mannheim labeled the type of ideology discussed in Marxist writings the "particular" ideology – the "more or less conscious disguises of the real nature of the situation" (Mannheim, 1936/1972, p. 49). He also contrasted this "particular" ideology with the "total" ideology that concerned "a subject's whole mode of conceiving things" and suggested that the "total" ideology be referred to as a "perspective" rather than as an ideology (ibid., p. 239). We think that "total" ideology is consistent with the construct "worldview." Others have also made distinctions that are somewhat similar to Mannheim's "particular" versus "total" distinction (e.g. Lane, 1962, p. 16).

Work in which the concept of ideology is used to describe the way people consciously frame the value relevance of their attitudinal and behavioral decisions can be classified as having a "representation" theme. For example, Ball-Rokeach and Loges (1996) suggested that "proponents on each side of an issue construct value choice frames to legitimate to themselves and communicate to others why their choice is more moral or competent than their opponents'" (ibid., p. 279). Kristiansen & Zanna's (e.g. 1994) value justification hypothesis also highlights people's desire and ability to use values to explain their decisions.

The ideological framing of issues may be at the heart of the classic example discussed by Seligman & Katz (1996). They asked how it was, in light of the idea that both issues involved killing, that Liberals could be blind to the inconsistency between opposition to the ending of convicted murderers' lives and support for the ending of the lives of fetuses, and Conservatives blind to the reverse. The answer may be that the ideology used in developing a position on one issue was irrelevant to the other, and therefore the inconsistency is not highlighted. For example, an "eye for an eye, a tooth for a tooth" ideology, or one that concerns the necessity of punishment for the maintenance of order, are specific to the capital punishment issue and irrelevant to the abortion issue. However, if an ideology that was relevant to both issues was used, then there would be awareness of the inconsistency in Conservative and Liberal positions. For example, relevant to both issues is an ideology in which the theme is "God, not humans, makes life and death decisions."

Differences in the ideological framing of issues also may explain why Kinder & Sears (1985) found that although party identification (e.g. Republican, Democrat) was a good predictor of voting behavior, it was not a good predictor of American public opinion on specific issues. Whereas the values–party identification–voting behavior link may be relatively uncomplicated, the link between values and the issues that are the focus of public opinion is far more complex. People's ideological framing of the issues may mean that they do not make the same attitudinal and behavioral decisions as the party with which they are identified.

Values may be used in unexpected ways when people use ideologies to establish a connection between values and attitudinal and behavioral decisions. For example, Tetlock, Armor, & Peterson (1994) found that some Southern slaveholders used the values "freedom" and "equality" in their ideological framing of a slave-related issue. Because Northerners were allowed to take their property across state lines, the slaveholders argued that restrictions on their freedom to take slaves – their "property" – outside the South violated equality principles. Rather than conclude that "values are remarkably slippery social constructions that take on different meanings over time and across political cultures" (Tetlock, Peterson, & Lerner, 1996, p. 34), "slipperiness" can be associated with ideologies.

Investigations into the ideology-related thinking processes also reflect a "representation" theme. For example, Tetlock and his colleagues have investigated the "integratively complex" thinking associated with ideologies, and developed the revised Value Pluralism Model for understanding "ideological reasoning" when decisions might satisfy one important value but fail to satisfy another (see Tetlock, Peterson, & Lerner, 1996; chapter 13, this volume). Integratively complex thinking, however, seems relatively rare and people "do their damnedest to avoid acknowledging – to themselves as well as to others – that important values conflict" (Tetlock, in press). This comment suggests caution in interpreting what people *say* are the values motivating their decisions, and suggests that the value-related reasons people give for their attitudinal and behavioral decisions should be understood primarily in terms of ideologies.

One important lesson to be learned from theorists and researchers whose work reflects a "representation" approach is that values and ideologies exert an inescapable influence on the way people see the world. Thus, in discussing the relation between values, ideologies, and decisions, attention to the construct "worldview" seems necessary. In addition, it seems necessary to separate investigations into the value-underpinnings of worldviews from investigations of value-related deliberations, explanations, justifications, or promotions of attitudinal and behavioral decisions.

The "Motivation" Approach

The "motivation" approach to values and ideologies seems to build on both the "personality" and the "representation" approaches. To the extent that basic motivations are considered integral to the way a person views the world and responds to it, then the concepts of basic motivations and personality may be understood as synonymous. How people represent entities in their environments – a focus in the "representation" approach – then can be investigated from the perspective of their basic motivations. In this approach, people's attitudinal and behavioral decisions are understood as value-driven responses to their environments.

Values-focused work

In general, researchers whose work reflects a motivation approach have focused on the way value priorities motivate a wide variety of attitudinal and behavioral decisions. For example, value priorities were found to be predictive of such things as juvenile delinquency, choice of friends, and frequency of religious participation (e.g. Rokeach, 1973). Jones & Gerard (1967) explicitly stated how people's value priorities motivate their attitudinal and behavioral decisions: "Values animate a person, they move him around his environment because they define its attractive and repelling sectors. This is true whether the individual values manure (for his garden) or diamonds (for his true love)" (ibid., p. 158).

However, there may be (at least) two ways in which people's value priorities motivate attitudinal or behavioral decisions. People may be motivated to avoid what they do not value, or may be motivated to obtain or achieve what they do value. Higgins (e.g. 1997) can be viewed as investigating these differing motivations. He suggested that although the "pleasure principle" has dominated the understanding of people's motivations, people either may be motivated primarily by a desire to gain pleasure (a "Promotion" regulatory focus) or may be motivated primarily by a desire to avoid pain (a "Prevention" focus).

Building on the work of important theorists such as Clyde Kluckhohn (e.g. 1951), Milton Rokeach developed a values theory and a measurement tool. Rokeach has been accorded the major credit for providing an impetus for values research since the late 1960s, and was an important inspiration for the values theory that we will now discuss. Detail is included because we think it represents "state of the art" in values theory.

Shalom Schwartz (e.g. 1992) refined a theory about the structure of human values, and provided evidence (using the measurement tool he developed) for the universality of this structure. Consistent with Rokeach, Schwartz focused on values as a means to satisfy "universal human requirements" and to "cope with reality" (Schwartz & Bilsky, 1987, p. 551). In a revision of the original theory, Schwartz formally defined values as "desirable, transsituational goals, varying in importance, that serve as guiding principles in people's lives" (Schwartz, 1996, p. 2). Values, according to Schwartz, are responses to "three universal requirements of human existence: biological needs, requisites for coordinated social interaction, and demands of group survival and functioning" (ibid.).

According to Schwartz, the (personal) value system is structured by two motivational dimensions. The Self-Transcendence/Self-Enhancement dimension reflects "a conflict between acceptance of others as equals and concern for their welfare versus pursuit of one's own relative success and dominance over others", and the Openness to Change/Conservation dimension reflects "a conflict between emphases on own independent thought and action and favoring change versus submissive self-restriction, preservation of traditional practices, and protection of stability" (ibid., p. 5). Ten universally relevant value types can be located along the two motivational dimensions (see figure 1).

These ten value types are considered a "nearly comprehensive" list (Schwartz, 1996, p. 2) and are Power, Achievement, Hedonism, Stimulation, Self-direction, Universalism, Benevolence, Tradition, Conformity, and Security. Values can be distinguished from one another in terms of the underlying motivational concern each value expresses. For example, the value type Power has a goal of "social status and prestige, control or dominance

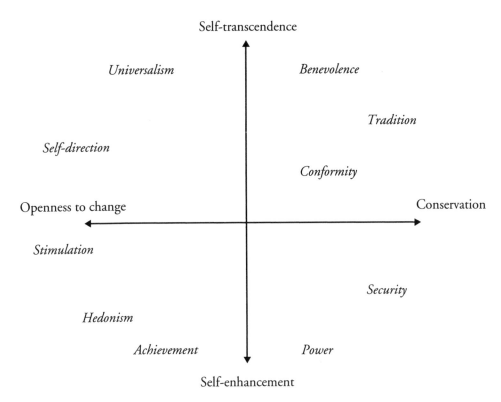

Figure 1   Location of ten value types along two "motivational" dimensions (after Schwartz, 1992).

over people and resources," whereas Universalism has a goal of "understanding, apprecia-tion, tolerance and protection for the welfare of all people and for nature" (ibid., p. 3). Values with similar underlying motivational concerns will be compatible, and those with different concerns will be in conflict. Thus, relations among each of the values in the system can be specified. Further, the relation between any "outside variable" (e.g. interper-sonal cooperation; see Schwartz, 1996) and value priorities should decrease in both direc-tions around the circular structure of the value system from the most positively associated value type to the least positively associated value type.

Recently, Oishi, Schimmack, Diener, & Suh (1998) provided an alternative way of measuring priorities on the personal values identified in the Schwartz value theory. In addition, Schwartz and his colleagues are currently testing a values inventory in which the reliance on abstract thought is reduced (and therefore even young adolescents can respond). Respondents are asked to compare themselves with people who display particular attitudes and behaviors, and the attitudes and behaviors included are theoretically linked to the underlying values. For example, to measure priorities related to the value type "tradition," male respondents are asked to rate their similarity to a person who is described the follow-ing way: "It is important to him to be polite to other people all the time. He believes he should always show respect to his parents and to older people."

Ideology-focused work

The motivation theme in the field of ideology can be viewed in terms of a focus on persuasion – either self-persuasion or persuasion of others – that decisions are "right." "Right" in this context can be viewed as meaning "satisfies desires or requirements." Being "right" allows people to maintain positive self-perceptions, and many have suggested that maintaining positive self-perceptions is a fundamental human motive (e.g. Steele, 1988; chapter 22, this volume). To persuade themselves (as individuals or as social group members) of the "rightness" of their attitudinal and behavioral decisions, people may use value based constructions. These constructions can be labeled "ideologies."

Decision-making according to values also is likely to be perceived as "good" and "moral." This suggestion is indirectly supported by what seems like a universal prohibition against hypocrisy. For example, consider work in which a "hypocrisy paradigm" works to bring professed attitudes in line with behavioral decisions (e.g. Aronson, Fried, & Stone, 1991). If values provide a structure through which to interpret reality, then decision-making according to values also may allow people to feel that "reality" has some consistency (see Cantril, 1950, p. 91). These "fundamental motives" for positive self-perceptions and consistency also may motivate people to use ideologies – which make value links explicit – as individuals or as members of social groups (or societies, or cultures) in making, explaining, justifying or promoting individual and group decisions (e.g. see Pratto, in press).

Research (e.g. Katz, 1960) in which people's "ego-defensive" use of attitudes has been investigated also might be considered from the perspective of ideologies. If ideologies serve to persuade people of their moral and adaptive competence, then to the extent that attitudinal decisions are explicitly made on the basis of an ideology that links them to values, then they may be correctly classified as "ego-defensive" attitudes. The importance of "ego-involvement" (Sherif & Cantril, 1947) or "value-relevant involvement" (Ostrom & Brock, 1969) in persuasion has been demonstrated convincingly (e.g. Johnson & Eagly, 1990). Eagly & Chaiken (1993) also have discussed the importance of this kind of involvement on the type of processing people use when faced with persuasive messages. In general, the more value-relevant the issue, the more systematic the processing.

Ideologies may be most useful when a tradeoff between important values is required. However, Tetlock and his colleagues (e.g. Fiske & Tetlock, 1997) have found that there are some value tradeoffs that people may not want to think or talk about. For example, in a laboratory simulation of Food and Drug Administration decisions, Tetlock & Boettger (1994) found that people used "buckpassing" and procrastination strategies when faced with a decision about a drug that would have benefits for some and fatal side-effects for others. In this research, a "taboo tradeoff" is defined as an explicit mental comparison or social transaction that violates deeply held normative intuitions about the integrity of certain forms of relationship and of the moral–political values that derive from those relationships. People often find questions or decisions about such comparisons morally offensive (e.g. being asked to estimate the monetary value of one's children, or of acts of friendship).

Tetlock and his colleagues (see Tetlock, in press) also are examining the consequences of ideologies in terms of the values to which their users make reference. Focus has been on political ideologies, and they have found, for example, that to the extent that a politician acknowledges value conflict (i.e. engages in more complex tradeoff reasoning), she or he is trusted and respected less (the "traitor effect"). If people are viewed as "intuitive politicians" who are "coping with the fundamental features of everyday decision environments" (Tetlock, 1992, p. 336), investigation of politicians' use of ideologies is likely to provide useful insight into people's less public use of ideologies.

In an investigation of what they labeled "persuasive rhetoric," but which might be labeled "ideology," Garst & Bodenhausen (1996) found that "kin markers" (phrases such as "brothers and sisters" or "for the sake of our children") were important in understanding the impact of the persuasive rhetoric. Specifically, they suggested that the difference in how much Democrats and Republicans scrutinized persuasive rhetoric depended upon whether it contained kin terms. For Republicans, the presence of kin terms cued important values and discouraged further message scrutiny. Garst and Bodenhausen concluded that the investigation of other kinds of "value markers" in persuasive rhetoric was an important area for future research. Such research seems directly relevant to investigations into the value associations contained in ideologies.

One lesson learned from work that reflects the "motivation" approach is the same as the one learned from work reflecting a "representation" approach: the ideology construct is fundamentally different from the values construct. However, more support for the fundamental difference has been provided. Thus, whereas values may be viewed as implicit structures, ideologies may be viewed as explicit, verbalizable constructions.

The "motivation" approach to the study of values and ideologies seems to be the dominant approach in the field at the moment. Because both "personality" and "representation" issues are addressed when the "motivation" approach is taken, it can be viewed as the approach that may remain the most conducive for the synthesis and extension of past work.

Unanswered Questions

Although there are many questions still to be addressed, three stand out as being fundamental to the advancement of the field. First, the process by which value systems and ideologies influence attitudinal and behavioral decisions must be clarified. Second, the notion that values are central to the self needs to be developed. Third, how change in value systems can occur needs to be described.

1   The process by which value systems and ideologies influence decisions

In figure 2, one way of thinking about the process by which value systems – both personal and social – and ideologies influence attitudinal and behavioral decisions is shown (see Rohan, 1998a, for further details).

This framework is based on the following set of definitions.

Values are defined as implicit organizers of judgments about the capacity of things, people, actions, and activities to satisfy requirements and desires, and value systems are

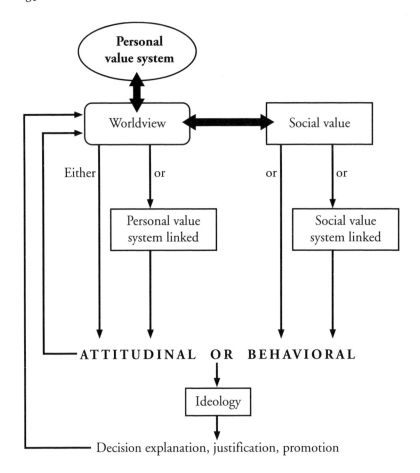

Figure 2   Proposed process by which values and ideologies influence attitudinal and behavioral decisions.

integrated structures within which there are stable and predictable relations among values. Personal value system structures exist as a result of a universal desire to live the best way possible; social value system structures exist because living well requires that people understand their social environments. Although people will have only one personal value system, they are likely to have more than one social value system. So, for example, people might have a "work group" social value system, a "family" social value system, and a "neighborhood" value system. Rules of parsimony underlie the assumption that social value system structure is the same as personal value system structure.

Worldviews are defined as people's fundamental beliefs that constitute their version of actual and potential realities, that is, about how things are or should be in their worlds. Whereas value systems are cognitive structures, people's worldviews evidence the effect of those structures. There is already some research in which the relation between people's personal value systems and their worldviews is investigated. For example, we (e.g. Rohan & Zanna, 1996) found strong correlations between high priorities on values relevant to tradition and conformity and right-wing authoritarian worldviews.

An *ideology* is defined as the rhetorical association or set of associations between things, people, actions, or activities and satisfaction of requirements and desires. Because values structure judgments about the capacity of things, people, actions, and activities to satisfy requirements and desires, ideologies will contain either implicit or explicit reference to values. Much of the work by Tetlock and his colleagues is directly relevant to this definition.

In this framework, although personal value priorities are viewed as causing attitudinal and behavioral decisions, their influence is not direct. Rather, the influence of personal and social value systems on people's worldviews is taken into account, and focus is on people's use of ideologies when they consciously consider the value links relevant to attitudinal and behavioral decisions. Because different ideologies may lead to different attitudinal and behavioral decisions, in one sense, ideologies might be conceptualized as "interfering" with the direct expression of value priorities. This may help to explain findings such as those described by Maio & Olson (1998), who found that when people analyze the reasons for their value priorities, their reported value priorities are likely to change.

A framework that specifies values–ideology–decision links may allow synthesis of past theory and research in the values and ideologies areas. The development of a comprehensive theory of self- and social-regulation then may be possible because values and ideologies have a critical role in such regulation. The first step towards synthesis is the interpretation of past research. For example, Ybarra & Trafimow (1998) examined how priming the "private self" and the "collective self" influenced whether people put more weight on their "attitudes" or perceived "subjective norms." Their results may be viewed in terms of how priming personal value systems ("the private self") or social value systems ("the collective self") leads to different attitudinal decisions.

The work by Prislin and her colleagues (e.g. Prislin & Ouellette, 1996) concerning "attitude embeddedness" also might be viewed in terms of the relevance of ideologies to attitudinal and behavioral decisions. Attitude embeddedness (measured in terms of the number of associations spontaneously generated by an issue) might be viewed as individual differences in the accessibility of relevant ideologies and the complexity of those ideologies.

Demonstrating again the need for definitional clarity and consensus, de St. Aubin (1996) defined a "personal ideology" as a worldview that was an individual's unique philosophy about how life should be lived and what forces influence human living. In this work, a point not discussed explicitly in the Schwartz value theory is highlighted: people's views about human nature. The importance of people's views about human nature was discussed by Kluckhohn & Strodtbeck (e.g. 1961), and people's "solution" to the problem of whether humans were viewed as evil or good was considered as a facet of their "value orientations" (that might understood as "worldviews"). The importance of people's views about human nature for attitudinal and behavioral decisions has been discussed at length by Wrightsman (e.g. 1991). It may be that people's priorities on Self-Transcendence or Self-Enhancement values are a result of their views of human nature. For example, people who have high priorities on Self-Transcendence values may have those priorities because of their views that people are essentially good. In support of this suggestion, de St. Aubin found that people who were highly humanistic were more likely to have high priorities on values that Schwartz (e.g. 1992) would classify as relating to the Self-Transcendence dimension (e.g.

Broadmindedness, World of Beauty). Perhaps, too, the other "problems" highlighted by Kluckhohn and Strodtbeck that have not been included in later work (human-nature orientation, activity orientation) need to be considered.

The link between values and attitudinal and behavioral decisions is one that has had intuitive and theoretical support for as long as psychologists and others have considered the causes of people's attitudes and behavior. Specification of the process by which value systems influence people's attitudinal and behavioral decisions, and clear definitions of the relevant constructs, is critical to systematic investigation.

2   Values and "the self"

Although values are viewed as being central to the self, the nature of this centrality is unclear. However, researchers have discussed the issue at length. For example, Bilsky & Schwartz (1994) examined the structural links between personality and personal value systems; Markus & Kitayama (1991) discussed cultural differences in self-construals that are linked to values; and Mirels & Darland (1990) investigated and discussed the relation between endorsement of a "Protestant Ethic ideology" and self-characterization.

One way to understand (and therefore investigate) the centrality of values is to view personal value systems as structuring self-knowledge, social value systems as structuring social knowledge, and self-esteem as being the result of a global assessment of success and prospects of success in satisfying personal requirements and desires (see Rohan, 1998a, 1999). Thus, because personal values structure judgments about the capacity of entities to satisfy these requirements and desires, personal values can be viewed as the basis for this assessment. Because people must negotiate their way through their social environment to satisfy their personal requirements and desires, the social value system construct also is needed to understand fully the assessment.

Important issues   At least six important issues relating to the centrality of values in the self can be raised. First, how clearly do people understand the nature of their personal and social value systems? Because value systems are implicit structures, people are likely to differ in the extent to which they have conscious access to them. Work in which "self-concept clarity" (e.g. Campbell, 1990) has been investigated might be relevant to this issue. In addition, this issue is critical to the measurement of people's value priorities. Accurate measurement using standard inventories in which people are asked explicitly about their value priorities surely depends on people's ability to think consciously about them.

Second, what are the consequences of a lack of understanding or confusion? Without clear understanding, for example, people's value systems cannot serve as stable standards against which they can evaluate their progress in satisfying their own requirements and desires or those of their group. Stable standards may be crucial to people's strivings for consistency, predictability, and positive self-evaluations that have been discussed at length in dissonance theory and other self-related theories (e.g. Aronson, 1992). Lack of understanding of personal value systems may have different consequences than a lack of understanding of social value systems. For example, a lack of understanding of personal value systems might lead to problematic self-esteem (because there is no basis for making the relevant global assessment), or what has been labeled "identity crisis" (e.g. Marcia, 1980), or a dependence on social value systems. In contrast, a lack of understanding of social value systems might lead to social anxiety because the "rules" for behavior will be unknown and lead to an inability to control a public image (see Leary & Kowalski, 1995). Lack of understanding also might be relevant to what Fazio and his colleagues have investigated as "attitude accessibility," and to research (Fazio & Powell, 1997) in which it was found that attitude accessibility moderated the relation between stress and health in college students. "Attitude" in this research referred to an association between a particular entity (e.g. a thing, person, social issue) and an evaluation. To the extent that people have easy access to their personal and social value systems, they are likely to have made clear associations between entities in their environments and their value priorities, and they may be more aware of how things, people, actions, and activities will serve to satisfy their own and group requirements and desires.

Third, how different or similar are people's personal and social value systems? For example, is it possible that there is greater similarity between the two systems for people who have high priorities on Conservation values (e.g. Tradition, Conformity) than for people who have high priorities on Openness to Change values (e.g. Self-Direction, Stimulation)? The findings that people who are prejudiced seem to be similar to each other (Adorno, et al., 1950) and high scores on scales measuring prejudice are often associated with high priorities on Conservation values (e.g. Rohan & Zanna, 1996) indicate that this may be the case. It seems likely that personal value priorities will dictate the extent to which personal and social value systems are similar.

Fourth, what are the consequences of differences between personal and social value systems? Research and theory focused on the differences and similarities between the "public self" and the "private self" may be relevant to this question (e.g. Tesser & Moore, 1986). The notion of *perceived* versus *actual* differences also may be important here, and may be related to the clarity associated with people's value systems. Further, differences and similarities between personal and social values systems may be important in understanding whether (and when) personal or social values are more or less accessible. The accessibility of values may be important for understanding the more direct causal paths (see figure 2) from personal value systems (through worldviews) to attitudinal and behavioral decisions and from social value systems to attitudinal and behavioral decisions. The degree to which "attitudes" (that often are conceptualized as including the more abstract attitudes that can be labeled "values") predict behavior has been discussed at length (e.g. Fazio, 1989).

Fifth, how do people reconcile what Allport labeled "the personal" (i.e. personal value systems) with "the tribal" (i.e. people's social value systems)? Research on moral reasoning might be relevant. For example, the "morality of self-interest" described by Kohlberg (e.g. 1981) might be viewed in terms of reconciliation in favor of the personal value system. In contrast, morality based solely on laws and social rules might be viewed in terms of reconciliation in favor of social value systems. The consequences of reconciling the "personal" and the "tribal" in favor of either may be an important topic. For example, intuition suggests that it may be more important for their self-esteem for people to feel they are responding according to their personal value priorities (see Lydon & Zanna, 1990). The way people think about their decisions also may be influenced by whether the decisions were based on personal or social value priorities. For example, Kristiansen & Matheson (1990) have discussed the possibility that although people may form their attitudes from the relative importance of various values, they subsequently may develop self-serving biases that affect the complexity of their thinking about an issue as well as the values they see as relevant to their decisions. The experimental paradigm designed by Murray, Haddock, & Zanna (1996) to manipulate whether people view themselves as having attitudes that serve a "value expressive" or "social adjustive" function may be useful, not only in understanding these self-serving biases, but also in understanding the self-evaluative consequences of responding according to personal or social value systems.

Sixth and final, what are the implications for therapeutic interventions to "raise" self-esteem or to "improve self-concept"? In light of the likely importance of people's clear understanding of their personal value systems for self-esteem, interventions might assist people to articulate their personal and social value priorities, and to identify similarities and differences in personal and social value priorities. People then may be directed towards endeavors they will find fulfilling because the endeavors can be designed to satisfy goals implied by personal value priorities. The importance of endeavors that satisfy (personal) goals was highlighted recently by Carver and Baird. Carver & Baird (1998) re-examined the hypothesis that value priorities related to goals of financial success and community involvement had different effects on "self-actualization." It was found, extending earlier research (e.g. Kasser & Ryan, 1993), that it was *why* people pursued these goals, as well as the goals themselves, that was important. Attention to the difference between personal and social value priorities also may enable understanding of self-satisfaction that is at some cost to others and self-satisfaction that is not.

Understanding the centrality of values in the self is likely to enable even more sophisticated and comprehensive investigations into the process by which value systems influence attitudinal and behavioral decisions.

3   Values and change

The lack of resolution to questions about the process by which value priorities influence attitudinal and behavioral decisions and of the centrality of values to the self perhaps explains why work in the area of value change, though promising, generally has been disappointing.

Rokeach (e.g. 1973) began a program of research he labeled "value self-confrontation" as a method of assisting people to change their attitudes or value priorities – and therefore their behavior. In a value self-confrontation paradigm, people are provided with feedback and interpretations concerning their own and others' value priorities, attitudes, and behaviors. This is intended to make them aware of inconsistencies that mean that either their professed attitudes or behavior do not meet their expectations of competence or morality prescribed by their important values. In general, long-term changes in attitudes or behavior are disappointingly rare (e.g. Kristiansen & Hotte, 1996). Is it possible that in this paradigm, people learn that their *ideologies* are not successfully allowing them to view their attitudes and behavior as being consistent with their important values? In response to this predicament, they simply may change the ideology used to persuade themselves or others of the "rightness" of their attitudinal or behavioral decisions. For example, consider people who are shown the contradiction between their pro-capital punishment attitude for which they used an "eye for an eye" ideology and their "pro-life" attitude for which they used a "life and death decisions are in God's hands" ideology. These people might be able to keep the same attitudes by using a "deservingness" ideology: "babies haven't done anything to deserve death"; "criminals deserve to die" (see Feather, in press, for a detailed discussion of values, justice and deservingness).

Schwartz (e.g. 1992) proposed that value priorities reflect underlying motivations, and that these motivations were associated with people's perceptions of the requirements of their existence. Thus, real change in people's personal value priorities is only likely to occur if there are changes in their own requirements or desires, and change in their social value priorities is only likely if there are changes in group requirements or desires (see Rohan, 1998b). If people perceive that their own or their groups' requirements or desires have changed, they will be motivated differently, and these motivational differences are likely to be reflected in the way they view the world and in their value priorities. For example, consider the finding that people become more conservative when they have children (e.g. Altemeyer, 1988). It is likely that when they became parents, the importance of consistency and stability is likely to have been increased – and thus priorities on values motivated by Conservation will have been raised.

The double arrows in figure 2 indicate how personal and social value systems might be modified. Changes in value systems are likely to be a result of changes in people's perceptions of their own and group requirements and desires, and will be reflected in their worldviews. Changes in perceptions of requirements and desires may be influenced, not only by changes in the environment, but also by people's attitudinal and behavioral decisions and their efforts to explain, justify, and promote those decisions (hence the arrows from these elements back to worldview).

In earlier times, "moral texts" were used in changing or teaching values. Essentially, these texts provided clear instructions about the "correct" values to hold in high esteem and how "moral" people think and behave, and were mainly directed at the adults involved in children's education. "Moral teaching" also was an important part of children's books. However, DeCharms & Moeller (1962) found that moral teaching in children's readers had practically disappeared by 1950, the last year analysis was conducted.

The relatively recent trend for people in institutions (including universities) and businesses to devise "mission statements" in which their "core values" are stated might be viewed as a resurgence of interest in providing instructions about the correct way to think and behave. It is unclear whether these "mission statements" reflect ideal social value systems, are ideological "rules" for behavior, or are a form of propaganda designed to change people's social value systems. For example, Collins & Porras (1996) suggested that companies needed to articulate their "core ideology" that should contain "core values" and "core purpose." These "core values" may be viewed as "mini-ideologies." For example, Walt Disney's "core values" are quoted as being "no cynicism"; "nurturing and promulgation of 'wholesome American values'"; "creativity, dreams, and imagination"; "fanatical attention to consistency and detail"; and "preservation and control of the Disney magic" (ibid., p. 68). However, "core purposes," such as "to make people happy" (Walt Disney) seem more like a description of institutions' most important or relevant values (e.g. Hedonism for Walt Disney).

Many social psychologists' attention on increasing understanding of what causes people's attitudinal and behavioral decisions is in the service of providing solutions to social problems that block harmonious social living. Thus, the importance of answering the big question of how value systems change – and can be influenced to change – seems obvious.

Summary and Implications

There is a huge amount of theoretical and research effort associated with the constructs of values and ideologies. The omission from social psychology textbooks of discussion concerning the knowledge accumulated about these constructs might lead people to believe that values and ideology-related theory and research is at the fringe of social psychology. However, we think that the two constructs are central to the field because they can be used to understand and predict people's attitudinal and behavioral decisions.

We have discussed some of the theory and research, and we have highlighted several important unanswered questions: the process by which values and ideologies influence attitudinal and behavioral decisions; how values are central to the self; and how change can occur in value systems. An important part of this discussion was presenting a way that the process by which values and ideologies influence decisions can be understood – and therefore investigated in a systematic way. The framework not only allows further understanding of the issues of value centrality and change, but also provides perspective for interpretation of past theory and research. Further, this framework has implications for investigating the development of values (a popular topic; see Grusec & Kuczynski, 1997, for a summary of current research and theory). It implies that researchers need to specify whether focus is on children's personal or social value systems, or whether focus is on children's learning of the ideologies that are available to them in their social environments.

The "take-home" message of this chapter is this: the constructs of values and ideologies should figure highly in social psychologists' attention. We hope that social psychologists renew their interest in the field, and realize that using the constructs of values and ideologies in understanding and predicting people's attitudinal and behavioral decisions is, after all, a tractable task.

References

Adorno, T. W., Frenkel-Brunswick, E., Levinson, D. J., & Sanford, R. N. (1950). *The authoritarian personality*. New York: Harper & Brothers.

Allport, G. W. (1954). The historical background of modern social psychology. In G. Lindzey (Ed.), *The handbook of social psychology*, Vol. 1 (pp. 1–46). Cambridge, MA: Addison-Wesley.

Allport, G. W. (1955). *Becoming: Basic considerations for a psychology of personality*. New Haven, CT: Yale University Press.

Allport, G. W. (1961). *Pattern and growth in personality*. New York: Holt, Rinehart, & Winston.

Allport, Vernon, & Lindzey, G. (1960). *Study of values. Manual and test booklet*. 3rd. edn. Boston, MA: Houghton Mifflin.

Altemeyer, B. (1988). *Enemies of freedom: Understanding right-wing authoritarianism.* San Francisco: Jossey-Bass.

Aronson, E. (1992). The return of the repressed: Dissonance theory makes a comeback. *Psychological Inquiry, 3,* 303–311.

Aronson, E., Fried, C., & Stone, J. (1991). Overcoming denial and increasing the intention to use condoms through the induction of hypocrisy. *American Journal of Public Health, 81,* 1636–1638.

Asch, S. E. (1952). *Social psychology.* Englewood Cliffs, NJ: Prentice-Hall.

Ball-Rokeach, S. J., & Loges, W. E. (1996). Making choices: Media roles in the construction of value-choices. In C. Seligman, J. M. Olson, and M. P. Zanna (Eds.), *The Ontario Symposium: The psychology of values,* Vol. 8 (pp. 277–298). Hillsdale, NJ: Erlbaum.

Bilsky, W., & Schwartz, S. H. (1994). Values and personality. *European Journal of Personality, 8,* 163–181.

Braithwaite, V. (1994). Beyond Rokeach's Equality–Freedom model: Two-dimensional values in a one-dimensional world. *Journal of Social Issues, 50,* 67–94.

Campbell, J. D. (1990). Self-esteem and clarity of the self-concept. *Journal of Personality and Social Psychology, 59,* 538–549.

Cantril, H. (1950). *The "why" of man's experience.* New York: Macmillan.

Carver, C. S., & Baird, E. (1998). The American dream revisited: Is it *what* you want or *why* you want it that matters? *Psychological Science, 9,* 289–292.

Collins, J. C., & Porras, J. I. (1996). Building your company's vision. *Harvard Business Review, 74,* 65–77.

de St. Aubin, E. (1996). Personal ideology polarity: Its emotional foundation and its manifestation in individual value systems, religiosity, political orientation, and assumptions concerning human nature. *Journal of Personality and Social Psychology, 71,* 152–165.

DeCharms, R., & Moeller, G. H. (1962). Values expressed in American children's readers: 1800–1950. *Journal of Abnormal and Social Psychology, 64,* 136–142.

Eagly, A. H., & Chaiken, S. (1993). *The psychology of attitudes.* Fort Worth, TX: Harcourt Brace Jovanovich.

Fazio, R. H. (1989). On the power and functionality of attitudes: The role of attitude accessibility. In A. R. Pratkanis, S. J. Breckler, & A. G. Greenwald (Eds.), *Attitude structure and function* (pp. 153–179). Hillsdale, NJ: Lawrence Erlbaum Associates.

Fazio, R. H., & Powell, M. C. (1997). On the value of knowing one's likes and dislikes: Attitude accessibility, stress, and health in college. *Psychological Science, 8,* 430–436.

Feather, N. T. (1975). *Values in education and society.* New York: Free Press.

Feather, N. T. (1995). Values, valences, and choice: The influence of values on the perceived attractiveness and choice of alternatives. *Journal of Personality and Social Psychology, 68,* 1135–1151.

Feather, N. T. (in press). *Values, achievement, and justice: Studies in the psychology of deservingness.* New York: Plenum Press.

Fiske, A. P., & Tetlock, P. E. (1997). Taboo trade-offs: Reactions to transactions that transgress the spheres of justice. *Political Psychology, 18,* 255–297.

Garst, J., & Bodenhausen, G. V. (1996). "Family values" and political persuasion: Impact of kin-related rhetoric on reactions to political campaigns. *Journal of Applied Social Psychology, 26,* 1119–1137.

Gibson, J. J. (1950). *The perception of the visual world.* Boston, MA: Houghton Mifflin.

Grusec, J. E., & Kuczynski, L. (Eds.) (1997). *Parenting and children's internalization of values: A handbook of contemporary theory.* New York: John Wiley and Sons.

Hastorf, A., & Cantril, H. (1954). They saw a game: A case study. *Journal of Abnormal and Social Psychology, 49,* 129–134.

Heaven, P., Stones, C., Nel, E., Huysamen, G., & Louw, J. (1994). Human values and voting intention in South Africa. *British Journal of Social Psychology, 33,* 223–231.

Higgins, E. T. (1997). Beyond pleasure and pain. *American Psychologist, 52,* 1280–1300.

Johnson, B. T., & Eagly, A. H. (1990). Involvement and persuasion: Types, traditions, and evidence. *Psychological Bulletin, 107,* 375–384.

Jones, E. E., & Gerard, H. B. (1967). *The foundations of social psychology.* New York: John Wiley &

Sons.

Kasser, T., & Ryan, R. M. (1993). A dark side of the American dream: Correlates of financial success as a central life aspiration. *Journal of Personality and Social Psychology, 65*, 410–422.

Katz, D. (1960). The functional approach to the study of attitudes. *Public Opinion Quarterly, 24*, 163–204.

Katz, I., & Hass, R. G. (1988). Racial ambivalence and American value conflict: Correlational and priming studies of dual cognitive structures. *Journal of Personality and Social Psychology, 55*, 893–905.

Kinder, D. R., & Sears, D. O. (1985). Public opinion and political action. In G. Lindzey & E. Aronson (Eds.), *Handbook of social psychology.* 3rd. edn. Vol. 2 (pp. 659–741). New York: Random House.

Kluckhohn, C. K. M. (1951). Values and value orientations in the theory of action. In T. Parsons & E. Sils (Eds.), *Toward a general theory of action* (pp. 388–433). Cambridge, MA: Harvard University Press.

Kluckhohn, F. R., & Strodtbeck, F. (1961). *Variations in value orientations.* Evanston, IL: Row, Peterson.

Kohlberg, L. (1981). *The philosophy of moral development: Essays on moral development.* Vol. 1. San Francisco: Harper & Row.

Kristiansen, C. M., & Hotte, A. M. (1996). Morality and the self: Implications for the when and how of value–attitude–behavior relations. In C. Seligman, J. M. Olson, and M. P. Zanna (Eds.), *The Ontario Symposium: The psychology of values,* Vol. 8 (pp. 77–105). Hillsdale, NJ: Erlbaum.

Kristiansen, C. M., & Matheson, K. (1990). Value conflict, value justification, and attitudes towards nuclear weapons. *Journal of Social Psychology, 130*, 665–675.

Kristiansen, C. M., & Zanna, M. P. (1994). The rhetorical use of values to justify social and intergroup attitudes. *Journal of Social Issues, 50*, 47–65.

Lane, R. E. (1962). *Political ideology: Why the American common man believes what he does.* New York: Free Press of Glencoe.

Lavine, H., Thomsen, C. J., & Gonzales, M. H. (1997). The development of interattitudinal consistency: The shared-consequences model. *Journal of Personality and Social Psychology, 72*, 735–749.

Leary, M. R., & Kowalski, R. (1995). *Social anxiety.* New York: Guilford Press.

Lewin, K. (1944/1952). Field theory in social science: Selected theoretical papers. London: Tavistock Publications.

Lydon, J. E., & Zanna, M. P. (1990). Commitment in the face of adversity: A value-affirmation approach. *Journal of Personality and Social Psychology, 58*, 1040–1047.

Maio, G. R., & Olson, J. M. (1998). Values as truisms: Evidence and implications. *Journal of Personality and Social Psychology, 74*, 294–311.

Mannheim, K. (1936/1972). *Ideology and utopia: An introduction to the sociology of knowledge.* London: Routledge & Kegan Paul.

Marcia, J. E. (1980). Identity in adolescence. In J. Adelson (Ed.), *Handbook of adolescent psychology* (pp. 159–187). New York: Wiley & Sons.

Markus, H. R., & Kitayama, S. (1991). Culture and the self: Implications for cognition, emotion, and motivation. *Psychological Review, 98*, 224–253.

Mirels, H. L., & Darland, D. M. (1990). The Protestant Ethic and self-characterization. *Personality and Individual Differences, 11*, 895–898.

Murray, S. L., Haddock, G., & Zanna, M. P. (1996). On creating value-expressive attitudes: An experimental approach. In C. Seligman, J. M. Olson, and M. P. Zanna (Eds.), *The Ontario Symposium: the psychology of values,* Vol. 8 (pp. 107–133). Hillsdale, NJ: Erlbaum.

Oishi, S., Schimmack, U., Diener, E., & Suh, E. M. (1998). The measurement of values and individualism–collectivism. *Personality and Social Psychology Bulletin, 24*, 1177–1189.

Ostrom, T. M., & Brock, T. C. (1969). Cognitive bonding to central values and resistance to a communication advocating change in policy orientation. *Journal of Experimental Research in Personality, 4*, 42–50.

Postman, L., Bruner, J. S., & McGinnies, E. (1948). Personal values as selective factors in perception. *Journal of Abnormal and Social Psychology, 43*, 142–154.

Pratto (in press). The puzzle of continuing group inequality: Piecing together psychological, social, and cultural forces in social dominance theory. In M. P. Zanna (Ed.), *Advances in experimental social psychology*, Vol. 31. San Diego, CA: Academic Press.

Prislin, R., & Ouellette, J. (1996). When it is embedded, it is potent: Effects of general attitude embeddedness on formation of specific attitudes and behavioral intentions. *Personality and Social Psychology Bulletin, 22*, 845–861.

Rohan, M. J. (1998a). A rose by any name?: Values, worldviews, and ideologies from an integrated perspective. Manuscript submitted for review.

Rohan, M. J. (1998b). Value priorities, value systems, and the value fingerprint: Reflections on development. Paper presented at the International Research Workshop on Values: Psychological Structure, Behavioral Outcomes, and Intergenerational Transmission. Maale-Hachamisha, Israel.

Rohan, M. J. (1999). Describing self-esteem: The achievement–integrity framework. Manuscript submitted for review.

Rohan, M. J., & Zanna, M. P. (1996). Value transmission in families. In C. Seligman, J. M. Olson, and M. P. Zanna (Eds.), *The Ontario Symposium: The psychology of values*, Vol. 8 (pp. 253–276). Mahwah, NJ: Erlbaum.

Rokeach, M. (1973). *The nature of human values*. New York: Free Press.

Rokeach, M. (1980). Some unresolved issues in theories of beliefs, attitudes, and values. *Nebraska Symposium on Motivation, 27*, 261–304.

Schwartz, S. H. (1992). Universals in the content and structure of values: Theoretical advances and empirical tests in 20 countries. In M. P. Zanna (Ed.), *Advances in experimental social psychology*, Vol. 24 (pp. 1–65). San Diego, CA: Academic Press.

Schwartz, S. H. (1996). Value priorities and behavior: Applying a theory of integrated value systems. In C. Seligman, J. M. Olson, & M. P. Zanna (Eds.), *The Ontario Symposium: The psychology of values*, Vol. 8 (pp. 1–24). Mahwah, NJ: Erlbaum.

Schwartz, S. H., & Bilsky, W. (1987). Toward a psychological structure of human values. *Journal of Personality and Social Psychology, 53*, 550–562.

Seligman, C., & Katz, A. N. (1996). The dynamics of value systems. In C. Seligman, J. M. Olson, and M. P. Zanna (Eds.), *The Ontario Symposium: The psychology of values*, Vol. 8 (pp. 53–75). Hillsdale, NJ: Erlbaum.

Shand, A. F. (1914). *The foundations of character: Being a study of the tendencies of the emotions and sentiments*. London: Macmillan.

Sherif, A. F., & Cantril, H. (1947). *The psychology of ego-involvements: Social attitudes and identifications*. New York: John Wiley & Sons.

Sherif, M., & Sherif, C. W. (1956). *An outline of social psychology*. Revd. edn. New York: Harper & Row.

Sidanius, J. (1990). Basic values and sociopolitical ideology: A comparison of political experts and political novices. *Perceptual and Motor Skills, 71*, 447–450.

Spranger, E. (1928). *Types of men: The psychology and ethics of personality*. Trans. P. J. W. Pigors. Halle, Germany: Max Niemeyer Verlag.

Steele, C. M. (1988). The psychology of self-affirmation: Sustaining the integrity of the self. In L. Berkowitz (Ed.), *Advances in experimental social psychology*, Vol. 21 (pp. 261–302). New York: Academic Press.

Tesser, A., & Moore, J. (1986). On the convergence of public and private aspects of self. In R. F. Baumeister (Ed.), *Public self and private self* (pp. 99–116). New York: Springer Verlag.

Tetlock, P. E. (1992). The impact of accountability on judgment and choice: Toward a social contingency model. In M. P. Zanna (Ed.), *Advances in experimental social psychology*, Vol. 25 (pp. 331–376). San Diego, CA: Academic Press.

Tetlock, P. E. (in press). Coping with trade-offs: Psychological constraints and political implications. In S. Lupia, M. McCubbins, and S. Popkin (Eds.), *Political reasoning and choice*. Berkeley: University of California Press.

Tetlock, P. E., & Boettger, R. (1994). Accountability amplifies the status quo effect when change creates victims. *Journal of Behavioral Decision Making, 7,* 1–23.

Tetlock, P. E., Armor, D., & Peterson, R. S. (1994). The slavery debate in Antebellum America: Cognitive style, value conflict, and the limits of compromise. *Journal of Personality and Social Psychology, 66,* 115–126.

Tetlock, P. E., Peterson, R. S., & Lerner, J. S. (1996). Revising the value pluralism model: Incorporating social content and context postulates. In C. Seligman, J. M. Olson, and M. P. Zanna (Eds.), *The Ontario Symposium: The psychology of values,* Vol. 8 (pp. 25–51). Hillsdale, NJ: Erlbaum.

Vallone, R. P., Ross, L., & Lepper, M. R. (1985). The hostile media phenomenon: Biased perception and perceptions of media bias in coverage of the "Beirut Massacre." *Journal of Personality and Social Psychology, 58,* 582–592.

Wrightsman, L. S. (1991). Interpersonal trust and attitudes toward human nature. In J. P. Robinson, P. R. Shaver, & L. S. Wrightsman (Eds.), *Measures of personality and social psychological attitudes* (pp. 373–412). New York: Academic Press.

Ybarra, O., & Trafimow, D. (1998). How priming the private self or collective self affects the relative weights of attitudes and subjective norms. *Personality and Social Psychology Bulletin, 24,* 362–370.

Chapter Twenty-Two

Self-Esteem

Abraham Tesser

One of the most basic responses to any object is evaluation (Tesser & Martin, 1996). Evaluative judgments reflect the extent to which we respond to things as good or bad, likable or dislikable, positive or negative, etc. Such judgments are extremely important in distinguishing objects, persons, ideas, things, or places. They account for most of the variance in mapping semantic meaning (Osgood, Suci, & Tannenbaum, 1957). This is true in the United States as well as other cultures (Osgood, 1974). Evaluation appears to be automatic: it is made faster than other kinds of judgments (Zajonc, 1980) and, often, without a conscious goal to make such judgments (Bargh, Chaiken, Govender, & Pratto, 1992; Fazio, Sanbonmatsu, Powell, & Kardes; 1986; but see Klinger, Burton, & Pitts, in press). When evaluative responses are associated with one's self they are known as self-esteem.

Arguably, the most important thing in one's life is the self. Given the importance of evaluative responding, it is no wonder then that the evaluation of self, or self-esteem, is a topic that has occupied social psychologists almost from the beginning of the discipline in its present form (e.g. James, 1890). Not only is there a long tradition of concern with this topic, but the amount of work associated with it is prodigious (Wylie, 1974, 1979). Indeed, in a recent review of the literature, Banaji & Prentice (1994) counted over 5,000 publications on this topic.

Self-esteem is a topic of non-scientific discussion and self-help books as well. Even the state of California has recognized the importance of self-esteem in everyday functioning (California Task Force, 1990). In short, the topic is an important one from a scientific and from a non-technical point of view. It is multifaceted and the literature is extensive. Thus, given the limitations of the present format, I must be selective. I touch only on aspects of this research that I find particularly important or interesting. (Reviews of additional aspects of this topic can be found in chapters 12, 16, and 23 of this volume).

Support for completing this chapter was generously provided by NIMH (K05 MH01233).

Self-esteem and Affect

I have defined self-esteem as an evaluative response toward the self. An evaluative response involves judgments of good–bad. Such judgments can be primarily cognitive, i.e. cool knowledge that I am either good or bad; or affective, i.e. hot positive or negative feelings about the self. Emotion seems to be a ubiquitous participant when the valuation of self is at issue, but what is its precise role?

Brown (1993) argues that self-esteem is primarily an affective response. "Brown (1994) compared self-esteem to a parent's esteem for his or her child: the affective response seems to appear strongly and immediately, without waiting for detailed cognitive appraisals" (cited in Baumeister, 1998, p. 695). Leary & Downs (1995) also argue that affect is part and parcel with self-esteem: "Precisely speaking, people do not suffer negative emotions because their self-esteem is damaged. Rather, decreased self-esteem and negative affect are co-effects of the [same] system" (ibid., p. 134).

Measures of self-esteem often correlate with affective variables. Self-esteem shows a positive association with life satisfaction (Myers & Diener, 1995), positive affect (Brockner, 1984), and a negative association with anxiety (Brockner, 1984), hopelessness (Crocker, Luhtanen, Blaine, & Broadnax, 1994), and depression (Tennen & Hertzberger, 1987). Nevertheless, Crocker & Wolfe (1998) caution us about *equating* self-esteem with affect. They remind us that correlations reveal little about the nature of an association. The correlations could indicate that self-esteem and affect are facets of the same underlying construct. However, the correlations might reflect a state of affairs in which affect causes self-esteem or in which changes in self-esteem cause changes in affect. Further, Crocker and Wolfe point out that self-esteem and affective variables like mood are conceptually distinct (Heatherton & Polivy, 1991). One's mood can change with circumstances even while one's evaluation of self remains consistent.

Affect is clearly associated with self-evaluation. However, that association could reflect affect as a source, affect as a consequence, or affect as simply a facet or outcropping of self-evaluation. We still do not understand the precise role(s) of affect in self-evaluation and self-evaluative processes. My own best guess is that affect is both a mediator (cause) and a consequence of *change* in self-esteem. Changes in self-esteem appear to be inevitably associated with affect and emotion (Tesser & Collins, 1988). Moreover, as we will see below, these affective changes may be crucial in instigating esteem-protective behaviors (Leary & Downs, 1995; Tesser, Martin, & Cornell, 1996). Thus, while self-esteem and emotion are not identical, emotion tends to play a crucial role in the phenomenological experience of self-esteem as well as the regulation of self-esteem.

Am I Good, Am I Bad: Self-esteem as a Trait

Sometimes self-esteem is treated as a trait. Self-esteem is seen to be an enduring, characteristic level of self-evaluation. Individuals differ with respect to their chronic level of self-esteem and these individual differences among levels are crucial to understanding behavior.

Indeed, most measures of self-esteem are of the individual difference variety. One of the most popular of these measures was developed by Morris Rosenberg (1965). Respondents are asked to indicate the extent to which they agree or disagree with ten relatively straight-forward statements such as: "I feel that I am a person of worth, at least on an equal basis with others." If self-esteem is an enduring trait, it should reveal high test–retest reliabilities. A review by McFarlin & Blascovich (1981) indicates that the Rosenberg scale and other instruments like it do show considerable stability over time.

If self-esteem is an important trait it should be related to other consequential feelings and behaviors. As noted above, trait self-esteem is related to a variety of affective states such as life satisfaction and depression (negative relationship). Reviews by Wylie (1974, 1979) indicate that it is also related to desire for control, achievement motivation, self-determi-nation, and need for approval. Balance theory (Heider, 1958) asserts that people tend to see the world in a simple, evaluatively balanced way, i.e. good things go with good things and bad things go with bad things. Until recently, a simplified summary of the theorizing regarding trait self-esteem was like a derivation from balance theory: Self-esteem, a good trait, is positively associated with other good things and negatively associated with bad things. The empirical world, however, is not that simple.

Recent work on aggression makes the point extremely well. Although there have been a number of suggestions that violent behavior is associated with low self-esteem, Baumeister, Smart, & Boden's (1996) interdisciplinary review of the evidence is not consistent with this expectation. Rather, they find that violence becomes more likely when another person or situation contradicts a person's highly favorable view of the self. An individual whose positive self-view is accurate is less likely to be confronted with inflammatory contradic-tory information than an individual whose positive self-view is inflated. Baumeister, Smart, & Boden (1996) suggest that murder, assault, rape, and domestic violence are often asso-ciated with threats to honor and threats to feelings of male superiority.

Some complications

Clearly, our understanding of trait self-esteem is becoming more complex and elaborated. Our hypotheses are less predictable from the simple perspective of balance theory. Even our view of trait self-esteem as an enduring characteristic is being questioned. Kernis and his associates (see Kernis & Waschull, 1995; Greenier, Kernis, & Waschull, 1995, for reviews) have found that individuals differ not only with respect to level of self-esteem but they also differ with respect to stability in the level of their self-esteem. (Stability of self-esteem is indexed by the standard deviation in an individual's level of self-esteem measured repeatedly over time.)[1] Stability of self-esteem seems to interact in important ways with level of self-esteem to predict behavior. For example, consistent with the Baumeister, Smart, & Boden (1996) thesis, persons with unstable high self-esteem are more aggressive than others (Kernis, Grannemann, & Barclay, 1989).

Why do some individuals appear to be more stable in their self-esteem than others? One answer recognizes that self-esteem may be subject to environmental events, at least to some extent. Thus, differences in stability of self-esteem may simply reflect differences in envi-ronmental variability across persons rather than fundamental individual differences. Other answers, more consistent with the spirit of self-esteem as a trait, are beginning to emerge. The notions of self-concept clarity (Campbell, 1990; Campbell, Trapnell, Heine, Katz, Lavallee, & Lehman, 1996) and contingencies of self-esteem (Crocker & Wolfe, 1998) are examples of such answers.

Self-esteem is related to self-concept. If I think of myself as kind, moral, smart, etc. I will tend to have high self-esteem. If I think of myself as unkind or not very smart, I will tend to have low self-esteem. However, what if I am uncertain about myself? Uncertainty appears to be related to low self-esteem. Campbell (1990) compared persons high and low in self-esteem and found that persons high in self-esteem show (1) greater confidence and extremity in their beliefs about the self; (2) greater stability in their self-beliefs over time; (3) greater consistency between their general self-beliefs and situation specific self-beliefs; and (4) greater internal consistency in the way they report their self-beliefs.

Campbell's work shows that the tenuousness with which we hold self-beliefs is related to self-esteem. She did not specifically correlate uncertainty with stability of global self-esteem. It seems quite plausible, however, that self-concept clarity and stability of self-esteem are related. Indeed, one of the components of self-concept clarity is belief stability.

Crocker & Wolfe (1998) more specifically address the question of self-esteem stability in their theory of "contingencies of worth." Crocker and Wolfe suggest that individuals can be rank ordered along a continuum on which one end is non-contingent self-esteem and the other end is contingent self-esteem. Persons with non-contingent self-esteem are certain about who they are. Although they may be disappointed when things do not go as they hope or delighted when things do go well, their evaluation of self does not fluctuate. That is, even persons with non-contingent self-esteem will experience affective shifts in response to self-relevant feedback, but they will not change their evaluation of self. From Carl Rogers' (1961) point of view, these people grew up in an unconditionally accepting environment and their feelings of worth do not depend on any particular success or failure. They are also reminiscent of Deci & Ryan's (1995) notion of the autonomous or self-determined self. Note, however, that Roger's and Deci and Ryan's analogs to the non-contingent self have positive self-esteem. Crocker and Wolfe suggest that there are also persons with non-contingent low self-esteem. Persons with non-contingent self-esteem should look very much like Kernis's stable self-esteem individuals.

Persons at the contingent end of this continuum have self-esteem that fluctuates. For them, self-esteem is contingent "on the belief that they have valued attributes or competencies, on approval and regard from others, being virtuous, or the exercise of power, and some people derive a sense of self worth from their collective identities" (Crocker & Wolfe, 1998, p. 19). Thus, self-esteem will fluctuate for non-contingents depending on their own behavior or feedback. Indeed, others have measured self-esteem by assessing respondents' evaluation of self in a variety of areas (e.g. Harter, 1993, Piers & Harris, 1969) and then summing across those areas. This is not satisfactory from Crocker and Wolfe's perspective because, they argue, different people have different contingencies of self-worth that they must satisfy. Fluctuations in self-esteem must be matched to fluctuations in the individual's own area of contingency.

Crocker and Wolfe identify nine contingencies of self that are frequently encountered, at least in college students. These are others' approval, appearance, God's love, friends and family, power, self-reliance, social identity, school competence and virtue. The following contingencies of self-esteem are more important for females than for males: others' approval, appearance, God's love, and competency. Black and white respondents differ on all contingencies except power and virtue. God's love is a more important contingency of self-esteem for Blacks than for Whites; the remaining contingencies (on which there are differences) are more important for Whites than for Blacks.

From a theoretical point of view, the Crocker and Wolfe perspective is quite integrative. Trait theorists in general have gone from simple expectations that a particular trait will reveal itself consistently across situations to more sophisticated views which find consistencies by taking the individual's subjective, idiosyncratic interpretation of situations into account (Mischel & Shoda, 1998). The Crocker and Wolfe formulation has that spirit. It helps us to understand why self-esteem may fluctuate (because at least for some people self-esteem is contingent) and it identifies many of the contingencies around which self-esteem fluctuates. This perspective, however, is still in its infancy and only future research will reveal its real potential.

Trait self-esteem: How shall we know it?

All of the research on trait self-esteem that I have reviewed so far depends on conscious, deliberate self-report to assess level of self-esteem. Such measures, if they are to be taken at face value, have two crucial assumptions that we know are questionable. One assumption is that persons will accurately report their self-esteem. Here one must be concerned with a variety of issues that psychometricians deal with perennially. Do different subjects use the scale with the same calibration? We treat scale scores as if all respondents use the categories in the same way but they may not. We generally give individual scores meaning by comparing them to other people on the same dimension, i.e. nomothetically, when, indeed, the subject may be formulating his or her response by looking within him or herself and comparing dimensions, idiographically. There are potential problems with response sets such as the tendency to agree (Cronbach, 1946) and, particularly in the case of self-esteem, to try to appear socially desirable (Crowne & Marlowe, 1964)

The second issue is even more fundamental than the first. Do individuals even know how positively they evaluate the self? Are there aspects of self-esteem that are consequential but not available to conscious awareness? Recent work on implicit memory (e.g. Tulving & Schacter, 1990) and automaticity in stereotypes (e.g. Devine, 1989) and attitudes (Bargh, et. al., 1992; Fazio, et. al., 1986) suggests that there are important, implicit, i.e. non-conscious, elements in a variety of psychological systems. The notion that there may be automatic, non-conscious elements connected with self-esteem seems plausible.

Greenwald & Banaji (1995, p. 11) define implicit self-esteem as "the introspectively unidentified (or inaccurately identified) effect of the self attitude on evaluation of self-associated and self-dissociated objects." They see evidence for implicit self-esteem in a variety of well established phenomena: the "mere ownership effect," i.e. objects become more positively evaluated by simply belonging to the self (Feys, 1991; Beggan, 1992); the "minimal group effect," i.e. regardless of how arbitrary the grouping, members of one's own group are treated more favorably than members of other groups (e.g. Tajfel & Turner, 1986); and the "initial letter effect," where individuals tend to like the letters in their own names, particularly the first letters of their names, more than other alphabet letters (Nuttin, 1985).

No "standard measure" of implicit self-esteem has yet surfaced. However, researchers are exploring a variety of possibilities. Following Fazio (e.g. Fazio, Powell, & Herr, 1983), Cline (e.g. Cline, in progress; Cline & Tesser, 1998) is measuring "implicit attitude toward the self." She primes subjects with symbols of the self (e.g. their name), and measures individual differences in the extent to which such primes speed up or slow down the evaluation of words with clear evaluative meaning, e.g. rose, Hitler. A positive evaluation of the self should speed up the identification of positive words and slow down the identification of negative words. The technique shows some promise, at least among women. Other possibilities for measuring individual differences in implicit response systems are being developed rapidly (Greenwald, McGhee, & Schwartz, 1998: see also chapter 4, this volume).

Am I Doing Better or Worse? Self-esteem as a State Variable

Concern with self-esteem as an enduring individual difference variable or trait is one approach to understanding. There is also an important, growing, and vibrant literature that focuses on the situations that lead to transient changes in self-evaluation. The component of self-esteem that fluctuates relatively rapidly, changing with circumstance, is known as state self-esteem. The regulation of state self-esteem has been the subject of thousands of studies (Banaji & Prentice, 1994).

The self-motives[2]

Underlying most of the studies of state self-esteem is the assumption that persons are motivated to achieve, maintain, or enhance a self-evaluation. Self-evaluation is a potential concern whenever there is new information or feedback about the self or some aspect of the self. If our only motive was to maintain a positive self-evaluation we would avoid or distort (potentially) negative feedback and approach or magnify the importance of (potentially) positive feedback. However, feedback may prompt other motives as well. (See chapters 12 and 16, this volume, for more detailed reviews of the motives related to self.)

Persons may be motivated to verify their current view of self. For persons with a positive evaluation of self, the motive to enhance and the motive to self-verify lead to the same prediction, i.e. approach positive information and avoid negative information. However, for persons with a negative self-view the enhancement and verification perspectives make different predictions. According to self-verification theory, persons with a negative self-view should seek out negative feedback. Swann (e.g. 1987) and his students and associates (e.g. Swann, Stein-Seroussi, & Geisler, 1992) have provided ample evidence for the existence of a self-verification motive. However, this motive is limited in the kinds of responses it prompts and the resources necessary for it to manifest itself. We can distinguish cognitive responses to feedback (I believe it, I don't believe it) from affective responses (I enjoy it; I hate it). Self-verification seems limited to cognitive responses (Shrauger, 1975). We can distinguish automatic behavior (quick, effortless) from controlled behavior (deliberate, effortful). Self-verification seems limited to non-spontaneous occasions (Swann, Hixon, Stein-Seroussi, & Gilbert, 1990). (See chapter 16, this volume, for a more complete review of self-verification.)

Feedback about the self may trigger a third motive: accuracy. According to Trope and his colleagues (Trope, 1986) it is important that all of us have an accurate view of our strengths and our weaknesses. Distortions and selective biases can take us only so far in a world with real outcomes. An accurate self-appraisal should allow us to avoid potential failures and seek out potential success. Thus, according to this framework, we should not seek out flattering feedback nor should we seek out feedback that verifies what we think of ourselves. We should seek out feedback that is most diagnostic of our skill, abilities, and other attributes. Indeed, under certain circumstances, individuals prefer diagnostic feedback to flattering feedback (e.g. Trope, 1980). Here too, however, exposure to negative information about the self is conditional. For example, individuals are willing to expose themselves to negative information when they are uncertain about themselves and the negative feedback is diagnostic (Trope, 1982). (Note that self-verification and accuracy motives seem to conflict in their predictions about self-certainty. The greater one's self-certainty, the *lower* the accuracy motivation but the greater the motive to self-verify.) Positive mood appears to be a useful personal resource for coping with stress (Aspinwall, 1998; chapter 27, this volume). Trope & Neter (1994) find that prior success and good mood are important precursors to exposure to diagnostic negative information.

Sedikides (1993), a psychologist who is not strongly identified with any of these positions, conducted a study to compare the "general" power of the three motives we have discussed: self-enhancement, self-verification, and accuracy. He asked people what information they would want if they were thinking about themselves. Questions that the subjects designed themselves revealed evidence for each of the motives. However, the most important motive for explaining his data was the motive to maintain self-esteem, followed by self-verification, and accuracy. My own point of view coincides with Sedikides's data. Clearly, on occasion people self-verify or seek out accurate information *regardless* of the implications for self-evaluation. However, the more general tendency is for people to defend or enhance self-evaluation. We turn now to a discussion of how we maintain a positive self-evaluation.

The arenas of self-esteem maintenance

How the self is defended or enhanced is, perhaps, the area that has attracted the most research attention. This research attempts to elaborate the squiggles in the signature of the motive to maintain a positive self-evaluation. Indeed, by now there is evidence for so many qualitatively different psychological defense mechanisms that I previously have referred to the collection as the "self-zoo" (Tesser, Martin, & Cornell, 1996).

Since comprehensive reviews of the self-esteem maintenance literature already exist (e.g. Banaji & Prentice, 1994; Baumeister, 1998; Hoyle, Kernis, Leary, & Baldwin, 1998), I will focus only on a sample of these mechanisms. Elsewhere (Tesser, Crepaz, Collins, Cornell,

& Beach, 1998), I have argued that three global approaches subsume much of the self-defense research. These approaches are social comparison, inconsistency reduction, and value expression. The approaches differ in that what they suggest constitutes a potential threat or enhancement to self-esteem and what behaviors or strategies an individual may adopt to defend or enhance the self.

Social comparison theory

A number of models suggest that the outcomes of others have consequences for one's own self-esteem (see chapter 12, this volume, for an elegant review of this literature). The particular approach to social comparison with which I am most familiar is the Self-Evaluation Maintenance (SEM) model (e.g. Tesser, 1988), so I will use it as an illustration. This model suggests that being outperformed by another can lower self-evaluation by inviting unflattering self-comparison, or it can raise self-evaluation – a kind of basking in reflected glory (e.g. Cialdini, Borden, Thorne, Walker, Freeman, & Sloan, 1976). These effects are enhanced with a psychologically close other. Another is psychologically close to the extent that the other shares salient features with the self, is in physical proximity with the self, etc., i.e. what Heider (1958) calls "unit relatedness" or, more recently, what group perception researchers (e.g. Hamilton, Sherman, & Lickel, 1998) call "entitativity." The relevance of the performance domain determines the relative importance of these opposing processes. Suppose the performance domain is unimportant to one's self-definition (low relevance). Then, the reflection process will be dominant and one's self-evaluation will be augmented by a close other's better performance. Suppose the performance domain is important to one's self-definition (high relevance). Then, the comparison process will be dominant and one's self-evaluation will be threatened by a close other's better performance. Thus, interacting combinations of three variables, performance, closeness, and relevance, are the antecedents to self-esteem threat or enhancement.

What might one do to enhance self-esteem or to reduce threats to self-esteem? One can change the relevance of the performance domain. This changes the relative importance of the comparison and reflection process (e.g. Tesser & Campbell, 1980; Tesser & Paulhus, 1983); or, one can increase or decrease closeness to the other and thereby amplify enhancing outcomes or dampen threatening outcomes (e.g. Pleban & Tesser 1981); or, one can increase or decrease the performance gap between self and other (Tesser & Smith, 1980).

I will continue to use the SEM model as an exemplar. However, it is important to note some recent developments that are illustrating the other side of the social comparison coin. We usually think of comparison with others affecting one's view of self. Recent research has turned this on its head and shown that one's view of self can affect the view of comparison others. For example, the poorer an individual performs in some domain, say athletics, the more charitable that individual is in evaluating the athletic performance of others – if I do poorly then people who do poorly are OK; if I do well then people who do poorly are rated down (Dunning & Cohen, 1992). Alicke, LoSciavo, Zerbst, & Zhang (1997) have shown that, under some conditions, when we are outperformed by another we don't downgrade our view of self, we upgrade the other's performance. It is less threatening to be outperformed by a "genius" than a person of normal ability.

The effect of threat to self on our view of others carries over to the group/stereotype literature. In 1950, Adorno, Frenkel-Brunswik, Levinson, and Sanford suggested that prejudice is functional: it sometimes operates to cover up our own inadequacies. Fein & Spencer (e.g. 1997; Spencer, Fein, Wolfe, Fong, & Dunn, 1998) have shown this experimentally. They have found that individuals who have experienced a threat to self-esteem show greater signs of derogating outgroups than those who are not threatened.

Cognitive consistency theory

The number of variations within this approach to self-evaluation regulation are also quite large (Abelson, Aronson, McGuire, Newcomb, Rosenberg, & Tannenbaum, 1968; chapter 16, this volume; Tesser & Martin, 1996). The exemplar with which we will be concerned is cognitive dissonance theory (Festinger, 1957). As originally formulated, dissonance theory was not a theory of self-esteem. Over the years, however, at least some investigators (e.g. Aronson, 1969; Greenwald & Ronis, 1978) have come to interpret dissonance in terms of threat to self-esteem.

According to dissonance theory, self-esteem is threatened by inconsistency. Holding beliefs/cognitions that are logically or psychologically inconsistent, i.e. dissonant, with one another is uncomfortable. For example, a student's cognition that she is opposed to a tuition increase is dissonant with the cognition that she freely chose to write an essay in favor of a tuition increase and such a choice will be threatening. How might the student reduce the threatening inconsistency? She can change her attitude toward a tuition increase or she can revoke her choice to write the essay, whichever is easier. If we assume that her choice was associated with a public commitment to an experimenter, for example, then changing her attitude toward the tuition increase is likely to be easier.

Social comparison mechanisms and consistency reduction mechanisms seem to have little in common. Threat from dissonance rarely has anything to do with the performance of another, i.e. social comparison. By the same token, inconsistency is generally irrelevant to an SEM threat, whereas others' performance is crucial. Attitude change is the usual mode of dissonance threat reduction; on the other hand, changes in closeness, performance, or relevance are the SEM modes.

Value expression theory

The notion that expressing one's most cherished values can affect self-esteem also has a productive history in social psychology (e.g. Smith, Bruner, & White, 1956; Katz, 1960, Rokeach, 1985). Simply expressing who we are, stating our important attitudes and values seems to have a positive effect on self-evaluation. The specific variation of value expression theory that I deal with here is self-affirmation theory (e.g. Steele, 1988).

According to Steele, self-evaluation has at its root a concern with a sense of global self-integrity. The concept of integrity is very broad. For example, Steele interprets the active ingredient of learned helplessness (e.g. Liu & Steele, 1986) and of many dissonant situations (e.g. Steele & Liu, 1983) to be a threat to self-integrity rather than a threat due to the experience of inconsistency. Self-integrity refers to holding self-conceptions and images that one is "adaptively and morally adequate, that is, as competent, good, coherent, unitary, stable, and capable of free choice, capable of controlling important outcomes, and so on" (Steele, 1988, p. 262).

If the locus of the threat to self-esteem is self-integrity then the behavior to reduce that threat is self-affirmation or a declaration of the significance of an important self-value. Since self-integrity is presumed to be general, the content of the affirmed self-value and the content of the threat to self-esteem may be totally independent. Although "self-integrity" is rather general, Steele has relied heavily on value expression to boost self-esteem. Note that the behavior of reaffirming a cherished value is qualitatively different from the SEM behaviors of changing closeness, relevance, or performance, or the dissonance behavior of attitude change.

Is self-esteem regulation one arena or many arenas?

If the antecedent circumstances and the resulting behaviors of different mechanisms are distinct, one may very well question whether there is a single self-esteem or three independent types of self-esteem. Each type identifies a qualitatively different variable to which self-evaluation is sensitive, i.e. social comparison, inconsistency, and value expression, and each has a qualitatively different behavioral strategy for regulating self-esteem.

Lewin (1935) and his students, particularly Ovsiankina (1928), have identified at least one way of addressing this question (see Tesser, Martin, & Cornell, 1996, for a discussion). Think of maintaining self-esteem as a goal. Goals have the property of equifinality (Heider, 1958), i.e. the path to the goal is irrelevant; one instrumentality is substitutable for another. If each of the self-esteem mechanisms is describing different ways of regulating a singular self-esteem, then one mechanism should be substitutable for another. A threat to self-esteem due to inconsistency may be reduced by basking in the reflected glory of a close other; a boost to the self via value expression may buffer the threat due to negative comparison, etc. On the other hand, there may be separate ego needs, e.g. a concern with ambiguity/inconsistency (e.g. Cialdini, Trost, & Newsom, 1995), or a concern with competence (e.g. White, 1959), for example. In this case, a threat due to dissonance would not be reduced by basking.

Evidence for substitutability

In a substitutability design an individual's self-esteem is altered via one mechanism and then the individual engages in a second mechanism. If the second mechanism "satisfies" the goal, the individual will not resume behavior connected with the first mechanism. Claude Steele's work on substitutability of self-evaluation mechanisms is perhaps the most elegant. Steele & Liu (1983) demonstrated that the self-affirmation mechanism could substitute for cognitive dissonance reduction. Participants were given high or low choice to write a counter-attitudinal essay (dissonance manipulation). Some participants then filled out a questionnaire concerning a very important value and others were given a questionnaire irrelevant to their values (self-affirmation manipulation). A measure of dissonance reducing attitude change was then administered. The typical dissonance finding was obtained for those participants who were given a questionnaire covering an unimportant value but not for participants that affirmed an important value. Self-affirmation appeared to eliminate the threat produced by dissonance, i.e. self-affirmation can substitute for or "turn off" dissonance reduction.

There is also evidence that self-affirmation affects the comparison and reflection processes associated with the SEM model. Tesser & Cornell (1991) allowed participants to affirm or not affirm an important aspect of the self and then gave subjects an SEM threat. Results indicated that when participants affirmed an important aspect of their self, the SEM threat pattern was completely eliminated. These results indicate that self-affirmation substitutes for SEM processes. The ability to affect other self-esteem maintaining processes is not limited to self-affirmation. Tesser & Cornell (1991, Study 2 and 3) observed that certain SEM situations could substitute for dissonance reduction. More recent work (Tesser, et al., 1998) rounds out the picture by showing that cognitive dissonance (Study 2) and SEM mechanisms (Study 1) substitute for self-affirmation and that dissonance substitutes for SEM (Study 3).

The confluence model

I have described the work above to give the reader a feel for the kind of research connected with the maintenance and regulation of self-evaluation. There are a couple of noteworthy aspects of this work. First, there is a dramatic diversity of approaches. In spite of different antecedents and consequences associated with each, under certain conditions, they substitute for one another in regulating self-esteem.[3] The metaphor I find apt is that of the confluence of a river. The streams entering the river may be separate but once they converge with the river the waters are indistinguishable. Regardless of the source of the water the river may be channeled in many different directions.

Evolution and Self-esteem

Given its importance it may be surprising to learn that empirical, experimental research on the origins of self-esteem are relatively recent. We are only beginning to address questions about the origins of self-esteem. (Our discussion of these issues draws heavily on the work of Leary & Downs, 1995, and Beach & Tesser, in press.)

A number of answers have been suggested to the question as to why there is a need for a positive view of self. Earlier I briefly discussed the relationship between self-esteem and emotion. I noted that changes in self-esteem tend to be associated with changes in affect (Tesser & Collins, 1988; Tesser, Millar, & Moore, 1988). Increased self-esteem is associated with positive affect and decreased self-esteem is associated with negative affect. Trait self-esteem tends to be related to affective traits such as depression and anxiety (Taylor & Brown, 1988). This suggests that the motive for positive self-esteem derives from preferences for positive affective states. One problem with this explanation is that it does not tell us why positive emotions tend to be associated with positive evaluations of the self.

Another suggestion is that people prefer high self-esteem because it helps them toward goal achievement. Indeed, self-esteem is associated with achievement. People high in self-confidence, e.g. self-efficacy (Bandura, 1977), tend to perform better and persist longer at various tasks. However, high self-esteem can also have negative consequences for achievement. Persons high in self-esteem may take on unrealistically difficult tasks. Indeed, persons high in self-esteem tend to persist longer even at impossible tasks (McFarlin, Baumeister, & Blascovich, 1984).

Some explanations have a decidedly evolutionary cast. Barkow's (1980) notion that self-esteem is an indicator of dominance in a group comes from evolutionary psychology. Prehomonid groups had dominance hierarchies. Individuals higher in the dominance hierarchy had greater access to mates, food, and all the other amenities of social life. With the development of cognitive abilities, came the ability to keep track of one's place in the hierarchy and the motivational mechanism, self-esteem, for moving toward dominance. Indeed, status within an organization affects self-esteem and may even be more important than resource favorability in shaping feelings of connectedness to organizations (Kramer & Neale, 1998).

Perhaps the most thoroughly researched explanation for the origin of self-esteem is provided by terror management theory. Pyszczynski, Greenberg, & Solomon (1997) suggest that with the evolutionary emergence of self-consciousness comes the awareness of death. The notion of the finality of death produces terror. Being a part of one's culture reduces that terror because the culture lives on or because it promises an afterlife. Thus, as long as the individual remains part of a viable culture he may achieve a kind of immortality. Self-esteem may have evolved as an affective indicator of the extent to which the individual is meeting cultural standards. As such, self-esteem is a buffer against the terror of death.

There have been many successful tests of terror management theory. Since the terror of death is central, it follows that concerns with cultural standards will be particularly pronounced when death is made salient. A number of studies using a variety of measures have confirmed this prediction. For example, people induced to think about death evaluate cultural heroes more positively, and cultural transgressors more negatively than people not thinking about death (Greenberg, Pyszczynski, Solomon, Rosenblatt, Veeder, Kirkland, & Lyon, 1990). People who focus on death also show greater attraction to persons who share their religious beliefs than people not focused on death (Greenberg, Simon, Pyszczynski, Solomon, & Chatel, 1992). The body of evidence for this theory is impressive. However, the theory is not comprehensive. There appear to be changes in self-esteem even when death is not salient and even when social norms are not at stake. For example, it is difficult to see how social comparison information makes one's death more or less salient and which social norms are being violated when another outperforms the self.

From the point of view of terror management theory, self-esteem derives from upholding cultural standards. Perhaps upholding cultural standards is related to self-esteem, at least to some extent, because upholding cultural standards makes us more attractive to the persons around us. Thus, another explanation for the origin of self-esteem is that it evolved as a sociometer (Leary & Downs, 1995). In a very broad-ranging review, Baumeister & Leary (1995) have shown the importance of social belonging and described the pain of being excluded from important groups. Indeed, as *homo sapiens* were emerging in the late Pleistocene, group life was crucial to survival. Maintenance of social bonds was clearly important for mating, defense, the acquisition of food, shelter, etc. One might suppose that only those who were able to maintain relationships and not be excluded from social groups survived. Given the importance of maintaining group membership, some mechanism should have evolved to avoid social exclusion (but see Maryanski & Turner, 1992). According to Leary & Downs (1995) self-esteem is such a mechanism. It functions "as a sociometer that (1) monitors the social environment for cues indicating disapproval, rejection, or exclusion and (2) alerts the individual via negative affective reactions when such cues are detected" (Leary & Downs, 1995, p. 129).

It is impossible to test directly a specific evolutionary path, and difficult to test the "innateness" of the need to belong. However, a review of the literature (Baumeister & Leary, 1995) and several new studies are consistent with the sociometer idea. For example, Leary, Tandor, Terdal, & Downs (1995) presented subjects with different behaviors (Study 1) and asked them to rate the extent to which others would reject them if they engaged in the behavior. Later, subjects rated the extent to which they would experience esteem-deflating emotions, e.g. shame, dejection, worthlessness, if they engaged in the behavior. They found a substantial positive correlation between these two sets of ratings. In a second study, subjects reported on personal events that had a positive or negative impact on their self-feelings. They then rated their self-feelings and the extent to which each of the situations involved social exclusion. Again, the correlation between these variables was significant. In a third and fourth study, subjects were randomly assigned to be either accepted or rejected by a group or another person. Rejected subjects showed greater negative self-feelings. These studies clearly suggest that behaviors or situations associated with exclusion are also associated with decrements in self-esteem.

The Leary and Downs hypothesis is plausible but I (Beach & Tesser, in press) believe that it does not go far enough. Leary and Downs suggest that self-esteem is rooted in concerns with being excluded by others. Certainly, however, we are not equally concerned with being excluded by all people and all groups. The SEM model (described above) captures that intuition. It suggests that the social consequences to self-esteem are amplified in the context of psychologically close others rather than distant others. Thus, self-esteem may be a more sensitive sociometer to exclusion among close than among distant others. This seems to make good sense from an evolutionary perspective. Certainly, there is an adaptive advantage to being concerned with those who are close, e.g. one's own group, than with members of other groups.

Leary and Downs (along with William James, 1890) recognize that the self-esteem of different people is sensitive to feedback in different domains. "People can follow many routes to social acceptance. Only when people have staked their connections to others on certain aspects of themselves should their self-esteem be affected by events that reflect on those aspects" (Leary & Downs, 1995, p. 137). However, Leary and Downs do not specify how certain aspects of the self become important to connections with others. The SEM model also recognizes the idea of different domains of self-esteem. The SEM construct of relevance refers to the extent to which doing well in some particular domain is important to the self.

Again, an evolutionary account of the SEM prediction is not very difficult to construct.

Clearly, there is a selective advantage in avoiding conflict and feeling good about members of one's own group. The tendency for conflict within groups would be reduced if individuals specialize in what they do. For example, if A is hunting while B is mending there is less reason and opportunity for conflict than if both hunted and mended. This would be particularly true if A was better at hunting and B was better at mending.[4] Indeed, A could be attracted to B because her mending produces something valuable to the group but does not threaten his own contribution and value to the group. The SEM model describes just such an adaptation. It predicts that one is unlikely to adopt a self-definition (role) involving an area in which a close other outperforms self. The consequence of this prediction is movement toward role specialization within the group and positive affect associated with other group members' achievements (the reflection process). This adaptation is quite specific but has important and relatively general consequences.

In sum, the current intellectual zeitgeist sees self-esteem as an adaptation to social rather than individual demands. For the most part, the accounts we reviewed here suggest that self-esteem is conditioned on our acceptability to others. Leary makes this point directly; Barkow in terms of social status; and terror management theory in terms of upholding cultural standards. The SEM model augments these accounts by predicting which persons and which self-aspects are likely to have the greatest impact on self-esteem.

A Coda on Culture

Thinking about evolution inevitably brings to mind questions about culture. Perhaps the work that most strongly captured the imagination and energies of self researchers in the 1990s was Markus & Kitayama's (1991) distinction between the independent self (e.g. distinct, autonomous, unique self) and the interdependent self (e.g. relational, connected, sociocentric self). This work suggests that our emphasis on striving for independence and realization of our own, unique personal potential may be a result of immersion in Western culture. In contrast, Southern European and Asian cultures put an emphasis on conformity, a self that "fits in" with important others. Triandis (1989) worked with a more articulated view of the self: private self (own view of states, traits, personal behavior); public self (generalized other's view of self), and collective self (specific group's view of self, e.g. family's view of self). More importantly, he studied cultural variables that are likely to be associated with an emphasis on one or the other aspects of self. For example, cultures that are more complex are associated with accentuation of public and private aspects of self. Individualistic cultures are associated with an emphasis on the private self and a de-emphasis of the collective self. Collectivism, external threat, and competition with outgroups increase the emphasis on the collective aspects of self.

Research addressing cultural influences on self is enjoying a new popularity. Moreover, the cultural view holds great promise for understanding the self. I present only a cursory view here because of space constraints and because the cultural position is thoroughly explored in chapters 2 and 23 of this volume.

Summary

We defined self-esteem as an evaluation of the self and suggested that changes in self-esteem are associated with affect. Self-esteem is sometimes treated as a trait. Classic research indicates that trait measures of self-esteem show good reliability and relate to a variety of other "good" attributes. More recent work suggests that self-esteem may be unstable or contingent, at least for some people, and that high levels of self-esteem sometimes may be related to "bad" attributes such as aggression. A second research tradition treats self-esteem as a state variable. Work in this tradition sometimes pits the motive to maintain a positive self-evaluation against other motives such as desires for accuracy or self-verification. There is evidence for all three of these motives, although the need to maintain a positive evaluation seems to be the most pervasive. There are many strategies for maintaining self-esteem, including the use of social comparison, cognitive consistency, and value expression. The observation that these strategies are qualitatively different from one another raises the question of whether there is one or several arenas of self-evaluation maintenance. Patterns of substitutability in these strategies suggest that self-esteem is a unitary motive. Finally, a review of conjecture regarding the evolutionary antecedents of self-esteem revealed a variety of approaches suggesting that self-esteem evolved to solve social problems.

Notes

1   The standard deviation is sensitive to systematic changes such as increases and decreases in self-esteem as well as random fluctuations. Research attempting to distinguish and understand such patterns is needed.
2   In the interest of brevity, the discussion of state self-esteem ignores chronic individual differences in self-esteem. It should be noted that differences in trait self-esteem are clearly related to self-enhancing behaviors (e.g. Blaine & Crocker, 1993) and may be related to the other motives as well.
3   Substitutability is not always observed. For example, Stone, Weigand, Cooper, & Aronson (1997) have shown that if people have a direct means of dealing with a threat to self-esteem they prefer the direct route to substituting a different mechanism.
4   The activities chosen for illustration are sex linked. Indeed, the earliest signs of specialization and role differentiation in evolutionary history center on gender and age distinctions.

References

Abelson, R. P., Aronson, E., McGuire, W. J., Newcomb, T. M., Rosenberg, M. J., & Tannenbaum, P. H. (Eds.) (1968). *Theories of cognitive consistency: A source book.* Chicago: Rand McNally.

Adorno, T. W., Frenkel-Brunswik, E., Levinson, D. J., & Sanford, R. N. (1950). *The authoritarian personality.* New York: Harper & Row.

Alicke, M. D., LoSchiavo, F. M., Zerbst, J., & Zhang, S. (1997). The person who outperforms me is a genius: Maintaining perceived competence in upward social comparison. *Journal of Personality and Social Psychology, 73,* 781–789.

Aronson, E. (1969). The theory of cognitive dissonance: A current perspective. In L. Berkowitz (Ed.), *Advances in experimental social psychology*, Vol. 4 (pp. 2–32). New York: Academic Press.

Aspinwall, L. G. (1998). Rethinking the role of positive affect in self regulation. *Motivation and Emotion, 22*, 1–32.

Banaji, M. R. & Prentice, D. A. (1994). The self in social contexts. *Annual Review of Psychology, 45*, 297–332.

Bandura, A. (1977). Self-efficacy: Toward a unifying theory of behavioral change. *Psychological Review, 84*, 191–215.

Bargh, J. A. (1992). Why subliminality might not matter to social psychology: Awareness of the stimulus vs awareness of its influence. In R. F. Bornstein & T. S. Pittman (Eds.) *Perception without awareness* (pp. 236–255). New York: Guilford Press.

Bargh, J. A., Chaiken, S., Govender, R., & Pratto, F. (1992). The generality of the automatic attitude activation effect. *Journal of Personality and Social Psychology, 62*, 893–912.

Barkow, J. (1980). Prestige and self-esteem: A biosocial interpretation. In D. R. Omark, F. F. Strayer, & D. G. Freedman (Eds.), *Dominance relations* (pp.319–332). New York: Garland.

Baumeister, R. F. (1998). The self. In D. T. Gilbert, S. T. Fiske, & G. Lindzey (Eds.), *Handbook of social psychology*, 4th. edn. (pp 680–740). New York: McGraw-Hill.

Baumeister, R. F., & Leary, M. R. (1995). The need to belong: Desire for interpersonal attachments as a fundamental human motivation. *Psychological Bulletin, 117*, 497–529.

Baumeister, R. F., Smart, L., & Boden, J. M. (1996). Relation of threatened egotism to violence and aggression: The dark side of high self-esteem. *Psychological Review, 103*, 5–33.

Beach, S. R. H., & Tesser, A. (in press). Self-evaluation maintenance and evolution: Some speculative notes. In J. Sulls & L. Wheeler (Eds.), *Handbook of Social Comparison*. Mahwah, NJ: Lawrence Erlbaum.

Beggan, J. K. (1992). On the social nature of nonsocial perception: The mere ownership effect. *Journal of Personality and Social Psychology, 62*, 229–237.

Blaine, B., & Crocker, J. (1993). Self-esteem and self-serving biases in reactions to positive and negative events. In R. Baumeister (Ed.), *Self-esteem: The puzzle of low self-regard* (pp. 55–85). New York: Plenum.

Brockner, J. (1984). Low self-esteem and behavioral plasticity: Some implications for personality and social psychology. In L. Wheeler (Ed.), *Review of personality and social psychology*, Vol. 4 (pp 237–271).

Brown, J. D. (1993). Self-esteem and self-evaluation: Feeling is believing. In J. Suls (Ed.), *Psychological perspectives on the self*, Vol. 4 (pp. 27–58). Hillsdale, NJ: Erlbaum.

Brown, J. D. (1994). Self-esteem: It's not what you think. Paper presented at the Society for Experimental Social Psychology, Lake Tahoe, NY.

California Task Force to Promote Self-Esteem and Personal and Social Responsibility (1990). *Toward a state of self-esteem*. Sacramento, CA: California State Department of Education.

Campbell, J. D. (1990). Self-esteem and clarity of the self-concept. *Journal of Personality and Social Psychology, 99*, 538–549.

Campbell, J. D., Trapnell, P. D., Heine, S. J., Katz, I. M., Lavallee, L. F., & Lehmen, D. R. (1996). Self-concept clarity: Measurement, personality correlates, and cultural boundaries. *Journal of Personality and Social Psychology, 70*, 141–156.

Cialdini, R. B., Trost, M. R., & Newsom, J. T. (1995). Preference for consistency: The development of a valid measure and the discovery of surprising behavioral implications. *Journal of Personality and Social Psychology, 69*, 318–328.

Cialdini, R. B., Borden, R. J., Thorne, A., Walker, M. R., Freeman, S., & Sloan, L. R. (1976). Basking in reflected glory: Three (football) field studies. *Journal of Personality and Social Psychology, 34*, 366–375.

Cline, J. (in progress). Development of an unobtrusive measure of the automatically activated affect associated with adult attachment representations. Dissertation, University of Georgia, Athens, GA.

Cline, J., & Tesser, A. (1998). Toward an unobtrusive measure of affect associated with attachment representations. Poster, American Psychological Association. San Francisco: American Psychological Association.

Crocker, J., & Wolfe, C. (1998). Contingencies of worth. Unpublished manuscript. Ann Arbor: University of Michigan.

Crocker, J., Luhtanen, R. K., Blaine, B., & Broadnax, S. (1994). Collective self-esteem and psychological well-being among Black, White, and Asian college students. *Personality and Social Psychology Bulletin, 20*, 503–513.

Cronbach, L. J. (1946). Response sets and test validity. *Educational and Psychological Measurement, 6*, 475–494.

Crowne, D., & Marlowe, D. (1964). *The approval motive.* New York: Wiley.

Deci, E. L., & Ryan, R. M. (1995). Human anatomy: The basis for the true self-esteem. In M. H. Kernis (Ed.), *Efficacy, agency, and self-esteem* (pp. 31–49). New York: Plenum.

Devine, P. G. (1989). Stereotypes and prejudice: Their automatic and controlled components. *Journal of Personality and Social Psychology, 56*, 5–18.

Dunning, D., & Cohen, G. L. (1992). Egocentric definitions of traits and abilities in social judgment. *Journal of Personality and Social Psychology, 63*, 341–355.

Fazio, R. H., Powell, M. C., & Herr, P. M. (1983). Toward a process model of the attitude–behavior relation: Accessing one's attitude upon mere observation of the attitude object. *Journal of Personality and Social Psychology, 44*, 723–735.

Fazio, R. H., Sanbonmatsu, D. M., Powell, M. C., & Kardes, F. R. (1986). On the automatic activation of attitudes. *Journal of Personality and Social Psychology, 50*, 229–238.

Fein, S., & Spencer, S. J. (1997). Prejudice as self-image maintenance: Altering the self through negative evaluation of others. *Journal of Personality and Social Psychology, 73*, 31–44.

Festinger, L. (1957). *A theory of cognitive dissonance.* Stanford: Stanford University Press.

Feys, J. (1991). Briefly induced belongingness to self and preference. *European Journal of Social Psychology, 21*, 547–552.

Greenberg, J., Simon, L., Pyszczynski, T., Solomon, S., & Chatel, D. (1992). Terror management and tolerance: Does mortality salience always intensify negative reactions to others who threaten one's world view? *Journal of Personality and Social Psychology, 63*, 212–220.

Greenberg, J., Pyszczynski, T., Solomon, S., Rosenblatt, A., Veeder, M., Kirkland, S., & Lyon, S. (1990). Evidence for terror management theory II: The effects of mortality salience on reactions to those who threaten or bolster the cultural worldview. *Journal of Personality and Social Psychology, 58*, 308–318.

Greenberg, J., Solomon, S., Pyszczynski, T., Rosenblatt, A., Burling, J., Lyon, D., Simon, L., & Pinel, E. (1992). Why do people need self-esteem? Converging evidence that self-esteem serves an anxiety buffering function. *Journal of Personality and Social Psychology, 63*, 913–922.

Greenier, K. D., Kernis, M. H., & Waschull, S. B. (1995). Not all high (or low) self-esteem people are the same: Theory and research on stability of self-esteem. In M. H. Kernis (Ed.), *Efficacy, agency and self-esteem* (pp. 51–72). New York: Plenum.

Greenwald, A. G., & Banaji, M. (1995). Implicit social cognition: Attitudes, self-esteem and stereotypes. *Psychological Review, 102*, 4–27.

Greenwald, A. G., & Ronis, D. L. (1978). Twenty years of cognitive dissonance: Case study of the evolution of a theory. *Psychological Review, 85*, 53–57.

Greenwald, A. G., McGhee, D. E., & Schwartz, J. L. K. (1998). Measuring individual differences in implicit cognition: The implicit association test. *Journal of Personality and Social Psychology, 74*, 1464–1480.

Hamilton, D. L., Sherman, S. J., & Lickel, B. (1998). Perceiving social groups: The importance of the entitativity continuum. In C. Sedikides & J. Schopler (Eds.), *Intergroup cognition and intergroup behavior* (pp. 47–74). Mahwah, NJ: Lawrence Erlbaum Associates.

Harter, S. (1993). Causes and consequences of low self-esteem in children and adolescents. In R. G. Baumeister (Ed.), *Self-esteem: The puzzle of low self-regard* (pp. 87–116). New York: Plenum.

Heatherton, T. F., & Polivy, J. (1991). Development and validation of a scale of measuring state self-esteem. *Journal of Personality and Social Psychology, 60*, 895–910.

Heider, F. (1958). *The psychology of interpersonal relations.* New York: Wiley.

Hoyle, R., Kernis, M. H., Leary, M. R., & Baldwin, M. W. (1998). *Identity, esteem, regulation.*

Boulder, CO: Westview Press.

James, W. (1890). *The principles of psychology.* Vol. 1. New York: Dover.

Johnson, M. M. S. (1986). The initial letter effect: Egoaattachment or mere exposure? Unpublished doctoral dissertation, Ohio State University.

Katz, D. (1960). The functional approach to the study of attitudes. *Public Opinion Quarterly, 24,* 163–204.

Kernis, M. H., & Waschull, S. B. (1995). The interactive roles of stability and level of self-esteem: Research and theory. In M. Zanna (Ed.), *Advances in Experimental Social Psychology, 27,* 93–141.

Kernis, M. H., Granneman, B. D., & Barclay, L. C. (1989). Stability and level of self-esteem as predictors of anger arousal and hostility. *Journal of Personality and Social Psychology, 56,* 1013–1022.

Klinger, M. R., Burton, P. C., & Pitts, G. S. (in press). Mechanisms of unconscious priming I: Response competition not spreading activation. *Journal of Experimental Psychology: Learning, Memory & Cognition.*

Kramer, R. M., & Neale, M. A. (Eds.) (1988). *Power and influence in organizations.* Thousand Oaks, CA: Sage.

Leary, M. R., & Downs, D. L. (1995) Interpersonal functions of the self-esteem motive: The self-esteem system as a sociometer. In M. Kernis (Ed.), *Efficacy, agency, and self-esteem* (pp. 123–144.) New York: Plenum.

Leary, M. R., Tandor, E. S., Terdal, S. K., & Downs, D. L. (1995). Self-esteem as an interpersonal monitor: The sociometer hypothesis. *Journal of Personality and Social Psychology, 68,* 518–530.

Lewin, K. (1935). *A dynamic theory of personality: Selected papers.* Trans. D. E. Adams and K. E. Zener. New York: McGraw-Hill.

Liu, T. J., & Steele, C. M. (1986). Attributional analysis as self-affirmation. *Journal of Personality and Social Psychology, 51,* 531–540.

McFarlin, D. B., & Blascovich, J. (1981). Effects of self-esteem and performance on future affective preferences and cognitive expectations. *Journal of Personality and Social Psychology, 40,* 521–531.

McFarlin, D. B., Baumeister, R. F., & Blascovich, J. (1984). On knowing when to quit: Task failure, self-esteem, advice and non–productive persistence. *Journal of Personality, 52,* 138–155.

Markus, H., & Kitayama, S. (1991). Culture and the self: Implications for cognition, emotion, and motivation. *Psychological Review, 98,* 224–253.

Maryanski, A., & Turner, J. H. (1992). *The social cage: Human nature and the evolution of society.* Stanford: Stanford University Press.

Mischel, W., & Shoda, Y. (1998). Reconciling processing dynamics and personality dispositions. *Annual Review of Psychology, 49,* 229–258.

Myers, D. G., & Diener, E. (1995). Who is happy? *Psychological Science, 6,* 10–19.

Nuttin, J. M. (1985). Narcissism beyond Gestalt and awareness: The name letter effect. *European Journal of Social Psychology, 15,* 353–361.

Osgood, C. E. (1974). Probing subjective culture: I. Cross-linguistic tool-making. *Journal of Communication, 24,* 21–35.

Osgood, C. E., Suci, G. J., & Tannenbaum, P. H. (1957). *The measurement of meaning.* Urbana: University of Illinois Press.

Ovsiankina, M. (1928). Die Wiederaufnahme unterbrochener Handlugen. *Pyschologische Forschung, 11,* 302–379.

Piers, E., & Harris, D. (1969). *Piers–Harris children's self-concept scale.* Los Angeles: Western Psychological Services.

Pleban, R., & Tesser, A. (1981). The effects of relevance and quality of another's performance on interpersonal closeness. *Social Psychology Quarterly, 44,* 278–285.

Pyszczynski, T., Greenberg, J., & Solomon, S. (1997). Why do we need what we need? A terror management perspective on the roots of human motivation. *Psychological Inquiry, 8,* 1–20.

Rogers, C. R. (1961). *On becoming a person.* Boston: Houghton Mifflin.

Rokeach, M. (1985). Inducing change and stability in belief systems and personality structures. *Journal of Social Issues, 41,* 153–171.

Rosenberg, M. (1965). *Society and the adolescent self-image.* Princeton, NJ: Princeton University

Press.

Sedikides, C. (1993). Assessment, enhancement, and verification determinants of the self-evaluation process. *Journal of Personality and Social Psychology, 65*, 317–338.

Shrauger, J. S. (1975). Responses to evaluation as a function of initial self-perceptions. *Psychological
Bulletin, 82*, 581–596.

Smith, M. B., Bruner, J. S., & White, R. W. (1956). *Opinions and personality*. New York: Wiley.

Spencer, S. J., Fein, S., Wolfe, C. T., Fong, C., & Dunn, M. A. (1998). Automatic activation of
stereotypes: The role of self-image threat. *Personality and Social Psychology Bulletin, 24*, 1139–
1152.

Steele, C. M. (1988). The psychology of self-affirmation: Sustaining the integrity of the self. In L.
Berkowitz (Ed.), *Advances in experimental social psychology*, Vol. 21 (pp. 261–302). New York:
Academic Press.

Steele, C. M., & Liu, T. J. (1983). Dissonance processes as self-affirmation. *Journal of Personality
and Social Psychology, 45*, 5–19.

Stone, J., Wiegand, A. W., Cooper, J., & Aronson, E. (1997). When exemplification fails: Hypocrisy and the motive for self-integrity. *Journal of Personality and Social Psychology, 72*, 1, 54–65.

Swann, W. B. (1987). Identity negotiation: Where two roads meet. *Journal of Personality and Social
Psychology, 53*, 1038–1051.

Swann, W. B., Stein-Seroussi, A., & Geisler, R. B. (1992). Why people self-verify. *Journal of Personality and Social Psychology, 62*, 392–401.

Swann, W. B., Hixon, J. G., Stein-Seroussi, A., & Gilbert, D. T. (1990). The fleeting gleam of
praise: Cognitive processes underlying behavioral reactions to self-relevant feedback. *Journal of
Personality and Social Psychology, 59*, 17–26.

Tajfel, H., & Turner, J. C. (1986). The social identity theory of intergroup behavior. In S. Worchel
& W. G. Austin (Eds.), *Psychology of intergroup relations* (pp. 7–24). Chicago: Nelson-Hall.

Taylor, S. E., & Brown, J. D. (1988). Illusion and well-being: A social psychological perspective on
mental health. *Psychological Bulletin, 103*, 193–355.

Tennen, H., & Herzberger, S. (1987) Depression, self-esteem, and the absence of self-protective
attributional biases. *Journal of Personality and Social Psychology, 52*, 72–80.

Tesser, A. (1988). Toward a self-evaluation maintenance model of social behavior. In L. Berkowitz
(Ed.), *Advances in experimental social psychology*, Vol. 21 (pp. 181–227). New York: Academic
Press.

Tesser, A., & Campbell, J. (1980). Self-definition: The impact of the relative performance and
similarity of others. *Social Psychology Quarterly, 43*, 341–347.

Tesser, A., & Collins, J. (1988). Emotion in social reflection and comparison situations: Intuitive,
systematic, and exploratory approaches. *Journal of Personality and Social Psychology, 55*, 695–709.

Tesser, A., & Cornell, D. P. (1991). On the confluence of self-processes. *Journal of Experimental
Social Psychology, 27*, 501–526.

Tesser, A., & Martin, L. (1996). The psychology of evaluation. In E. T. Higgins & A. W. Kruglanski
(Eds.), *Social psychology: Handbook of basic principles* (pp. 400–432). New York: Guilford Press.

Tesser, A., & Paulhus, D. (1983). The definition of self: Private and public self-evaluation maintenance strategies. *Journal of Personality and Social Psychology, 44*, 672–682.

Tesser, A., & Smith, J. (1980). Some effects of friendship and task relevance on helping: You don't
always help the one you like. *Journal of Experimental Social Psychology, 16*, 582–590.

Tesser, A., Martin, L., & Cornell, D. (1996). On the substitutability of self-protective mechanisms.
In P. M. Gollwitzer & J. A. Bargh (Eds.), *The psychology of action: Linking motivation and cognition to behavior* (pp. 48–67). New York: Guilford Press.

Tesser, A., Millar, M., & Moore, J. (1988). Some affective consequences of social comparison and
reflection processes: The pain and pleasure of being close. *Journal of Personality and Social Psychology, 54*, 49–61.

Tesser, A., Crepaz, N., Collins, J., Cornell, D., & Beach, S. R. H. (1998). Confluence of self-
defense mechanisms: On integrating the self zoo. Manuscript under review.

Triandis, H. C. (1989). The self and social behavior in differing cultural contexts. *Psychological
Review, 96*, 506–520.

Trope, Y. (1980). Self-assessment, self-enhancement and task preference. *Journal of Experimental Social Psychology, 16,* 116–129.

Trope, Y. (1982). Self-assessment and task performance. *Journal of Experimental Social Psychology, 18,* 201–215.

Trope, Y. (1986). Self-enhancement and self-assessment in achievement behavior. In R. M Sorrentino & E. T. Higgins (Eds.), *Handbook of motivation and cognition: Foundations of social behavior,* Vol. 2 (pp 350–378). New York: Guilford Press.

Trope, Y., & Neter, E. (1994). Reconciling competing motives in self-evaluation: The role of self-control in feedback seeking. *Journal of Personality and Social Psychology, 66,* 646–657.

Tulving, E., & Schacter, D. (1990) Priming and human memory systems. *Science, 267,* 301–306.

White, R. W. (1959). Motivation reconsidered: The concept of competence. *Psychological Review, 66,* 296–333.

Wylie, R. C. (1974). *The self-concept.* Revd. edn. Vol. 1. Lincoln: University of Nebraska Press.

Wylie, R. C. (1979). *The self-concept.* Revd. edn. Vol. 2. Lincoln: University of Nebraska Press.

Zajonc, R. B. (1980). Feeling and thinking: Preferences need no inferences. *American Psychologist, 35,* 151–175.

Chapter Twenty-Three

Self-Concept and Identity

Daphna Oyserman

> In its widest possible sense . . . a man's Self is the sum total of all that he can call his, not only his body and his psychic powers, but his clothes and his house, his wife and children, his ancestors and friends, his reputation and works. . . . If they wax and prosper, he feels triumphant, if they dwindle and die away, he feels cast down.
>
> James, 1890/1950, pp. 291–292

Self-concept and *identity* provide answers to the basic questions "Who am I?", "Where do I belong?", and "How do I fit (or fit in)?" In our society, each self-concept is assumed to be unique, different from any other self, and private – fully knowable only to the self (Fiske, Kitayama, Markus, & Nisbett, 1998). Improving oneself, knowing oneself, discovering oneself, creating oneself anew, expressing oneself, taking charge of one's self, being happy with oneself, being ashamed of oneself, are all essential self-projects, central to our understanding of what self-concept and identity *are* and how they *work*. Our images of the self we might be, expect to be, are afraid we might be, motivate current behavior and color understanding. *Self-concept* and *identity* are what come to mind when we think of ourselves (Neisser, 1993), including both personal and social identities (Stryker, 1980; Tajfel, 1981). They are our theory of our personality (Markus & Cross, 1990), what we know or can know about ourselves.

Being human means being conscious of having a self and the nature of the self is central to what it means to be human (Lewis, 1990). The self has been correlated with an array of life situations and life outcomes and is considered a psychological resource – self-concepts differ not only in content but also in their effectiveness (for reviews of assessment and context issues see Byrne, 1996; Harris, 1995; Wylie, 1989). Self-concepts differ in complexity (Linville, 1987), organization of positive and negative self-relevant information

Partial funding for this chapter comes from a W. T. Grant Faculty Scholar Award.

(Showers, Abramson, & Hogan, 1998), and the extent that they promote persistent striving versus disengagement, sense of general contentment or incipient despair. Variously conceptualized as a dependent, independent, mediator, and moderator construct, the self-concept has emerged as one of the most studied areas of psychology. *Psychological Abstracts* shows 23,943 publications from applied and basic science journals (including almost 150 from this year's *Journal of Personality and Social Psychology* alone) with the key word "self-concept" and standard textbooks on social psychology almost invariably contain chapters on self-concept and related concepts such as self-esteem. Recent reviews of self-concept and identity from a social psychological perspective include Banaji & Prentice (1994), Baumeister (1998), Brown (1998), Kihlstrom & Klein (1994), and Markus & Wurf (1987), and in the present volume the related constructs of self-esteem (chapter 22) and self-regulation (chapter 14) are reviewed. The focus of this chapter will be to integrate the main themes highlighted in self-concept research within a broader cultural and contextual perspective. In order to do so, I will briefly highlight themes in the social development of self-concept – its content, structure, and organization – and then turn to the ways that a sociocultural frame illuminates new issues and guides hypotheses testing.

Defining the Self-concept

The self-system is both an array of self-relevant knowledge, the tool we use to make sense of our experiences, and the processes that construct, defend, and maintain this knowledge (Epstein, 1973; Higgins, 1996; Markus, 1977). The self-concept functions as a repository of autobiographical memories, as an organizer of experience, and as an emotional buffer and motivational resource (Markus & Wurf, 1987). The notion that each of us has a self-concept, an idea or set of ideas of who we are, and that this conceptualization is relatively constant over time, is intuitively appealing. Not surprisingly, some aspect of the self-concept has been studied within all branches of psychology. Yet what is actually meant by self-concept seems variable across disciplines and research methodologies, as does the self's assumed and documented stability versus malleability. Most dramatically, clinical field trials suggest that it is hard to change one's self-concept, while experimental researchers routinely document that the self is extremely variable and easily changed by even minor experimental manipulations (Markus & Kunda, 1986).

   While clearly there is a self-concept that provides an answer to the "Who am I?" question quite simply by anchoring reality and providing the response "*I am me,*" what is meant by the self-concept in research and theorizing is often quite ambiguous. The best summary of what is normally meant in experimental research is likely to be the working self-concept – the part of the self-concept that is relevant or made salient in a particular situation (Markus & Kunda, 1986). Even here there is some ambiguity as to whether what is meant is the content that is temporarily accessible or the self-relevant cognitive processing mechanisms that are made temporarily salient. For example, a number of lines of research suggest that observing an other's successes or failures influences both the content of one's on-line or working self-concept and also the cognitive process that is salient – particularly the extent that one focuses on self-enhancement (selectively processing in a self-enhancing manner). Conversely, in quasi-experimental and correlational research, what is meant by the self-concept are the chronically salient aspects of the self-concept, most likely to be repeatedly brought to mind given the everyday contexts in which the individual is embedded.

That the self is both stable and mutable is in fact necessary to our theories of change and self-improvement. The self is seen as an active agent, seeking competence, resolution of life phase conflicts, and mastery in real world terms (see Brown, 1998), yet it is also viewed as importantly molded and shaped by early experiences and relationships (e.g. Aber, Allen, Carlson, & Cicchetti, 1989; Mikulincer, 1998; Rogers, 1954). What the self-concept does is mutually constructed by developmental shifts in cognitive abilities and the requirements of particular life tasks embedded in particular times and spaces (e.g. Maddux, 1991; Moretti, Higgins, & Simon, 1990). Yet in a particular situation, the self-concept is a centrally important cognitive concept and memory structure (Andersen, Glassman, & Gold, 1998). Relevance to the self is basic to such cognitive processes as similarity judgments (Catrambone, Beike, & Niedenthal, 1996) and increases processing speed and facilitates inferences (Catrambone & Markus, 1987; Markus, 1977; see Kihlstrom & Klein, 1994, for a review). What we remember, how we remember it, and the sense we make of our experience are each importantly shaped by our self-concepts.

Assessing the Self-concept

In spite of or perhaps because of its centrality for cognition and memory, assessing the content of self-concept continues to be an elusive goal. First, the self-concept contains a dizzying array of content, such a rich array of episodic, experiential, and abstracted information about the self that not all of it can be salient at any given point in time. Therefore, when asked to report on the self, individuals can only report on that subset of all the self-relevant information that is salient and therefore seems important or central at that point in time. Importantly, saliency-eliciting cues are likely to go unnoticed by the research participant. For example, a researcher interested in shyness is likely to find that average ratings of shyness are higher when instructions request a specific instance of shyness (easily brought to mind) and lower when instructions request a specific instance of extroversion (also easily brought to mind) (Fazio, Effrein, & Falender, 1981). This influence of accessible content, however, is influenced by the ease with which it comes to mind. Information that comes to mind easily is assumed to be more self-defining, more "true" of the self, than are self-descriptions that require effortful search in memory, so that in response to questions about the self-concept, we rely on what comes to mind easily to report on the self. Yet using this "ease of retrieval" heuristic in deciding what is true about the self-concept means that all self-concept measures are open to a variety of confounds (Schwarz, 1998; Schwarz, Bless, Strack, Klumpp, Rittenauer-Schatka, & Simons, 1991). Following the same example, researchers obtaining a longer list of instances of shyness (or extroversion) are likely to find lower ratings of these social characteristics because difficulty of bringing to mind the requested number of examples is used as a judgment cue in the research context. This means that paradoxically, bringing to mind twenty examples of shyness may convince the respondent that he is less shy than bringing to mind three or four examples.

Second, subtle contextual cues including features of the interview schedule can make salient particular aspects of the self, for example personal or social characteristics of the self (Trafimow & Smith, 1998). Because these contextual influences go unnoticed, the instrument and immediate setting may well create the context. For example Norenzayan, Schwarz, & Rothman (1996) found that the letterhead on which the questionnaire was printed influenced content of self-concept in open-ended descriptions. Participants used more social roles in describing themselves when the questionnaire was printed on a letterhead from the department of political science and more personal traits to describe themselves if they thought the study was taking place in a psychology department. Though the self-concepts of these participants could hardly be said to change as a result of the letterhead, what they reported about themselves did. It seems unlikely that this was a conscious act, therefore leading to the conclusion that the self-concept, though vital in guiding motivation, behavior, and understanding, is highly susceptible to social and situational structuring.

Operating a Self-concept: The Self-concept in Action

In spite of these difficulties in assessment, it seems clear that the self-concept is a social force: it influences what is perceived, felt, and reacted to and the behavior, perceptions, and reactions of others (Harris, 1995; Kihlstrom & Klein, 1994). It can be thought of as an information processor, functioning to reconfigure social contexts, diffuse otherwise negative circumstances, and promote positive outcomes for the self. The self-concept is inferred to be at work when making one's self momentarily salient results in behavioral change: when seeing oneself in the mirror (for a review, see Banaji & Prentice, 1994), bringing to mind one's group membership (Steele, 1997), or even when wearing a bathing suit (Fredrickson, et al., 1998). More directly, the self-concept is inferred to be at work when it moderates outcomes – among youth, positive racial–ethnic minority identity mediates risk of declining academic performance (Oyserman & Harrison, 1997), while positive self-views reduce risk of bullying (Egan & Perry, 1998). Self-relevant thinking, emotion regulation, and motivation (Banaji & Prentice, 1994; Greenwald & Pratkanis, 1984; Kihlstrom & Cantor, 1984; Markus & Wurf, 1987) are all examples of the self-in-action. For example, controlling for ability, persistence on a math task drops when minority status is made salient, but not for youth who self-define as both members of their minority group and also members of larger society (Oyserman, Kemmelmeier, & Brosh, 1999). For these dual identity youth, the self-concept responses to the "Who am I?", "Where do I belong?", and "How do I fit (in)?" questions bolster motivation and facilitate persistence as opposed to the stereotype threat experienced by their peers (Steele, 1997).

Because the self-concept frames experience and motivates action, the self-concept has been described as a "theory" about oneself that represents and organizes current self-knowledge and guides how new self-knowledge is perceived (Epstein, 1973). As a theory, the self-concept is made of the current state of knowledge about the self and is assumed to be veridical enough to help organize experience, focus motivation, regulate emotion, and guide social interaction. It is not assumed to reflect some absolute truth about one's skills, abilities, competencies, or worth. More than simply a theory about the self, some researchers have posited that the self-concept is the seat of basic effectance and competency drives, reflecting an innate need to become effective, more competent over time (Maslow, 1954), and a desire to improve the self. Models based in this premise, termed *self-assessment, learning, efficacy,* and *self-improvement* models (Maddux, 1991; Trope, 1986; see chapter 22, this volume, for a review), have received some support. These models suggest that individuals are motivated to seek out accurate information about the self in order to be able to improve the self (Wurf & Markus, 1991). Two other basic functions of the self-concept have been outlined (see chapter 22, this volume, for a review): the promotion of positive self-views, termed *self-evaluation maintenance* (chapter 22, this volume) or *self-affirmation* (Steele, 1988), and the provision of a consistent anchor for information processing, termed *self-consistency* or *self-verification* (Swann, 1997).

Since the early writings of James (1890/1950), feeling good about oneself, evaluating oneself positively, feeling that one is a person of worth, have been described as a basic goal of the self-concept, a basic human need, akin with the pleasure principle. Numerous studies have shown a robust tendency to maintain and enhance a positive image of the self (Greenwald, 1980). The notion that positive self-esteem is a fundamental human need is the basis for an array of self-concept theories, including group-based theories such as social identity theories (Haslam, Oakes, Turner, & McGarty, 1996; Tajfel, 1981; Turner, Hogg, Oakes, Reicher, & Wetherell, 1987) and collective self-esteem theory (Crocker, Luhtanen, Blaine, & Broadnax, 1994). According to self-esteem maintenance assumptions, all else being equal, individuals prefer to feel good about themselves and so will self-define in such a way as to maintain positive self-feelings. In this view, the self is a positivity-seeking information processor. It seeks out domains in which positive self-definitions are possible (e.g. Steele, 1988), disengages from domains in which positive self-definitions are not possible (James, 1890/1950), and compares the self to others in ways that reflect favorably on the self (e.g. Beauregard & Dunning, 1998). While tending toward somewhat rosy self-descriptions (Taylor & Brown, 1988), individuals differ in the extent that they bias their self-evaluations upward. The upward trend is most pronounced when evaluating the self on a dimension that is clearly valenced (Asendorpf & Ostendorf, 1998) and high self-esteem individuals may be better able to shift self-definitional focus to create a positive identity in the face of setback (Murray, Holmes, MacDonald, & Ellsworth, 1998).

In addition to its self-promotive functions, the self-concept also provides and maintains a cognitive anchor, a consistent yardstick, or way of making sense of who one is and therefore what to expect of the self and others. According to Swann's self-verification theory, individuals are motivated to preserve self-definitions and will do so by creating a social reality that conforms to their self-view (see Banaji & Prentice, 1994; Baumeister, 1998; Swann, 1997, for reviews of this perspective). The assumption is that we prefer a consistent sense of self in order to be able to use the self-concept to make predictions about the world (Greenwald, 1980), and to maintain relationships with those others with whom these self-definitions were created (see Higgins, 1996). This means that the self-concept is a conservative information processor. Important self-relevant information, even if negative, is maintained in the face of contradictory information if it is in a domain central to one's self-definition and one is given a chance to process it.

Building a Self-concept: The Self-concept as Structure

Clearly, the self-concept requires memory and in some basic way it is all of those things that we can remember about ourselves. However, it is not simply a collection of autobiographical memories, it is also a cognitive structure. We remember information better if it is linked to the self-concept (Kihlstrom & Klein, 1994) and currently salient self-concept content influences ongoing information processing, meaning-making and behavioral, motivational, and affective responses (Kemmelmeier & Oyserman, in press; Trafimow & Smith, 1998). A common conceptualization of the self-concept is that it is a multifaceted set of self-relevant schemas containing self-knowledge, guiding and directing action and providing future-oriented goals (Carver & Scheier, 1981; Epstein, 1973; Fiske & Taylor, 1994; Greenwald, 1982; Holland & Quinn, 1987; Markus, 1977). As a cognitive concept, self-concept is based in experience and as a cognitive structure, it shapes experience by guiding both what we pay attention to and the meaning we make of it.

By conceptualizing the self-concept as a set of self-schemas, researchers imply that the self-concept is not necessarily hierarchically organized. In fact, different models have been suggested (for a review, see Kihlstrom & Klein, 1994). First, abstract traits may cue specific exemplars, which are stored as situated memories, or specific exemplars. For example, thinking of one's self as shy may bring to mind the times one was too tongue-tied to volunteer one's opinion in a classroom debate. Second, specific exemplars may cue trait descriptors. For example, remembering a time one was tongue-tied may make salient the feeling that one is shy. Third, exemplars and trait descriptors may be independently stored in memory. In this case, bringing to mind a memory of one's self as shy would cue other such memories and these would be separate from memories of the self as tongue-tied and so on. Although the first model is often assumed to be correct, this assumption is not well supported (Marsh & Yeung, 1998) and current evidence suggests most support for the latter model type, termed *independent storage models.* These models do not assume that specific exemplars and abstracted traits are hierarchically arranged. Rather, when context or other cues make abstract trait information salient, specific examples are not elicited and similarly, when specific examples are elicited, this does not reliably cue general trait information. It is this independence that makes possible the ease of retrieval errors described above.

Developing a Self-concept: The Self-concept as Cognitive Product

How does this cognitive construct and memory structure, so central to our understanding of personhood, emerge? Developmental research suggests that the self-concept is both a *basic tool* of cognitive and social development and an important *consequence* of this development (see excellent reviews by Bretherton, 1992; Damon & Hart, 1988; Lewis, 1990). Sense of self initially involves simply sensing that one's body is separate from others, so that identity begins with a physical sense of the boundaries of one's body and where it is in space (Lewis, 1990). Yet because infants cannot engage their environment directly, this insight must occur within the context of interactions with others. Thus, the infant's emerging relationality scaffolds and supports its emerging identity. Adult caregivers frame and carry the interaction in the social space between infant and adult so that in some basic way, infants learn who they are through the sense their caretaker provides of who they are. These initial interactions, termed synchronized exchanges, involve caretaker and infant in linked interactions that take into account the responses of the other. Caretaker–infant synchrony develops rapidly in the first few months of life (Tronick & Gianino, 1986). The quality of this synchrony has been related to later child self-characteristics such as self-control (Feldman, Greenbaum, & Yirmiya, 1999) and affect regulation (Weinberg, Tronick, & Cohn, 1999). It is posited that these interchanges are the basis of attachment style or working model of relationality (Bretherton, 1992), that sets up a basic sense of worth, esteem, and efficacy (for a review, see Hammen, 1991).

Basic sense of efficacy in turn provides an impetus to explore the world, stimulating cognitive and language development – highlighting the influence of self-concept development on cognitive development. As the capacity for memory develops in the first year of life, infants begin to develop a more nuanced sense of identity because they can engage in and store differential interaction with different others. At two years of age, self-consciousness begins to emerge, solidifying by the end of the fourth year of life. Early self-consciousness involves being able to distinguish unexpected changes in the self. By age two, but not reliably before, toddlers touch their forehead when they look in the mirror and see a red paint smear (Lewis & Brooks-Gunn, 1979). A temporal sense of self follows by age four; at this age, toddlers reliably touch their forehead when viewing their paint-smeared forehead on a video monitor only when it is a "live tape" and not an image from a previously videotaped play session (Povinelli & Simon, 1998). This emerging self-concept is linked to self-conscious emotions such as embarrassment at recognizing the self, fear when the mother leaves, and pride in the self's accomplishments (for a review, see Hammen, 1991).

In the years from two to eight, as language develops, children begin to make self-descriptive statements, with content shifting from age two to eight from physical to psychological terms (Damon & Hart, 1988). In early adolescence, both past and future orientation to the self evolves and youth begin to use more abstract descriptions, shifting from descriptions of what they usually do to comparative assessments, to interpersonal concerns, to systematic beliefs and plans. Utilizing James's basic framework of dimensions of the self, Damon & Hart (1988) suggest a developmental progression from material, to social, to psychological perspectives on the self, with each new level integrating and transforming the previous one. As the psychological self evolves, youth grapple to integrate various perspectives on the self – how they present themselves to the world, who they aspire to become, who they were, and who they are now (Harter, 1990; Harter, Marold, Whitesell, & Cobbs, 1996; Ruble, Eisenberg, & Higgins, 1994). Development of a sense of the adult one will become has been viewed as a main task of adolescence, yet who one is and where one belongs continues to be central across adulthood (Erikson, 1968).

Constructing the Self: The Self-concept as Social Product

This multifaceted self-concept that takes on and grapples with the life phase-appropriate versions of the basic questions "Who am I?", "Where do I belong?", and "How do I fit (in)?" is clearly social in nature (see Higgins, 1996; Lewis, 1990; Markus & Cross, 1990). From the beginning, theorists have conceptualized the self-concept as a *social product* that develops through relationships with others and what they see in one's self. In this way, social reality can be more potent than behavioral or observed reality. For example, while related to their actual school performance, middle schoolers' academic self-concepts are more influenced by their parents' perceptions of their abilities than by their actual school grades (Frome & Eccles, 1998). William James (1890/1950) described this as the social aspect of the self-concept and *social selves* were described as the unique version of the self reflected in each human interaction. Other early conceptualizations of the self-concept also highlighted the ways others' views of us, or at least our perceptions of these appraisals, influence how we conceive of ourselves (Cooley, 1902). Others were seen as vital to the production and experience of being a self: "the self can exist for the individual only if he assumes the roles of the others" (Mead, 1921–1925/1964, p. 284). The self is thus experienced "indirectly, from the particular standpoints of other individual members of the same social group, or from the generalized standpoint of the social group"(Mead, 1934/1964, p. 138).

Selves are created within contexts and take into account the values, norms, and mores of the others likely to participate in that context. By adolescence, individuals are able to distinguish between the selves they would like to be and become and the selves others want them to be (Moretti, Higgins, & Simon, 1990). Students given a say in their social contexts are more likely to report expressing their "true" selves, the selves they want to be, rather than feeling compelled to present situation-appropriate "false" selves, the selves they know others want them to be (Harter, Waters, Whitesell, & Kastelic, 1998). Others are clearly present in the self-concept, they are standards of comparison – we feel good when we outperform others (see chapter 12, this volume), bask in the success of close others if there is little chance we will be compared negatively to them (see chapter 22, this volume). We feel less likely to succeed if similar others fail (Kemmelmeier & Oyserman, in press). In this way, the accomplishments and failures of close others help define the self. By 11 years of age if not sooner, children see the actions of close others as self-relevant, feeling pride in a close other's accomplishments and shame in their failings (Bennett, Yuill, Banerjee, & Thomson, 1998). More generally, others are arbitrators of personal worth and self-esteem drops in the face of public devaluation such as bullying or teasing (Egan & Perry, 1998; Graham & Juvonen, 1998), and is strengthened by peer acceptance (Roffey, Majors, & Tarrant, 1997).

But the influence of social contexts is not limited to self-relevant information gleaned from interactions with particular others. Who one *is* in a particular situation is importantly framed by the social context. Being a "solo," the only one of one's gender, racial–ethnic or other social category in a particular context makes these categories salient in self-definition (e.g. McGuire & Padawer-Singer, 1976). Moreover, solo status can intensify negative effects of stereotypes about members of one's social group on self-regard (e.g. Frable, Platt,

& Hoey, 1998). At the same time, we are loath to be too similar to others in our social groups, striving instead for an optimal level of both uniqueness and similarity (Brewer, 1991). In this way, self-concepts emerge through interactions, making one's most basic identities part and parcel of and specific to the particular groups within which one is embedded (Raeff, 1997).

By taking into account the influence of social statuses more generally, social psychological research has begun to explore more systematically areas previously left to fields such as cultural, race–ethnicity, and gender studies. Building on these earlier insights, the current generation of social psychological theorizing about the self is taking a new look at what constitutes a social context and the implications of social context for self-concept development, content, and structure, and the behavioral, motivational, and affective consequences of self-concept. For example, Croizet & Claire (1998) show that making one's working-class status salient impairs academic performance, while Shih, Pittinsky, & Ambady (1999) show that making one's Asian-ness salient improves or impedes performance depending on the content of the local social stereotype about being Asian.

These examples make clear that social contexts enable, elicit, and scaffold certain selves while dis-enabling, suppressing, and dismantling others even in the face of what might appear to be objective evidence of these self-dimensions. It is also becoming increasingly clear that the social construction of the self depends not only on particular relationships or immediate situations but also on larger sociocultural and historical factors. Being Serb or Albanian in Kosovor matters and is likely to establish ways of being in the world, open certain possible selves, and close off others. Feeling Serbian or Albanian in Kosovor sets up patterns of action, ways of making sense of the world in ways that are quite different from feeling Serbian or Albanian in the United States or Switzerland. The way that this matters for self-concept is not rooted in the influence of a particular other's view of the self but rather in a more global, societal stance as to whether the self can be fundamentally separate from group memberships.

Having and Being a Self: The Self-concept in Sociocultural Context

Societies and cultures differ in the way that they make sense of what it means to be an individual, the aspects of human experience that are centralized, and the resolutions to basic human dilemmas that they endorse or value (Hofstede, 1980). These basic dilemmas include how to deal with human inequality, the premium placed on reducing or avoiding uncertainty about the future, the nature of the valued or normative relationship between individuals and groups, and the value assigned to enhancing versus attenuating differences between the sexes (Hofstede, 1980). It seems reasonable to suppose that the self-concepts created in differing cultural milieux will take on these culture-specific ways of being (e.g. Weigert, Teige, & Teige, 1990). Yet, perhaps because it is so broadly encompassing as to be transparent, unnoticed, culture has not typically informed social psychological research on the self-concept (Bond & Smith, 1997; Oyserman & Markus, 1993, 1998; Oyserman, Coon, & Kemmelmeier, 1999). While the self-concept has long been viewed as a social product and the implications of contextual salience are mainstream research foci, the field is just beginning to explore the ways larger social structures such as culture may set up the nature of both the social interactions and immediate contexts. At issue for self-concept theorizing and research is whether self-concept development and processes studied in one cultural context can be generalized to others.

The bulk of the research described in this chapter focuses on North American participants and assumes a North American cultural context, so it is particularly important to understand how this cultural frame may influence how the self has been conceptualized and studied. Broadly speaking, North American and Western European cultures have been described as individualistic. That is, they socialize members to believe in individual rights and personal freedoms, the centrality of personal pleasure and autonomy, and the personal, private, and unique self. These cultures are viewed as not highly accepting of human difference, preferring models of equality to one's assuming hierarchy. Yet, though highly accessible and part of popular representations in these countries, this democratic, individualistic frame is also transparent, that which goes without saying so that its influence on the way the self is studied, the research questions asked, and the theories developed, is only recently being questioned.

Thus, current theories about personality (DeNeve & Cooper, 1998) and well-being (Ryff & Keyes, 1995) imply a bounded, autonomous goal-oriented self focused on attainment of personal happiness-making goals, able to make friends and develop helpful social networks with relative strangers – all characteristics of democratic individualism. Given the relative size of North American publication impact (Bond & Smith, 1997), it seems reasonable to propose that North American individualism is the standard prism through which psychological phenomena are construed, whether or not culture is an explicit unit of analysis (Fiske, Kitayama, Markus, & Nisbett, 1998; Oyserman & Markus, 1993). Yet by not making explicit a cultural frame, researchers have limited their opportunity to investigate the way culture may influence all aspects of the self-concept – its definition and assessment, its structure and functions. Having and being a self may not be a fully generalizable experience. In the remaining portion of this chapter, I review what we currently know about the generalizability of the North American and Western European self-concept presented until now (see chapter 2, this volume, for a review of the cultural psychology literature).

Societies that emphasize individualism are said to value individual rights, not duties or obligations, to emphasize personal autonomy and self-fulfillment, and believe that the self is created through personal achievements and accomplishments, not group memberships (Kim, 1994; Triandis, 1995). Within this cultural frame, the self is viewed as bounded, distinct, and stable, with attitudes and behavior ensuing derived from this stable self rather than being a social and situational product (Bellah, Madsen, Sullivan, Swidler, & Tipton, 1985; Kagitcibasi, 1999; Markus & Kitayama, 1991; Sampson, 1977; Triandis, 1989). Within this worldview, creating and maintaining a positive sense of self is assumed to be a basic human endeavor. Feeling good about oneself and having many unique or distinctive personal attitudes and opinions is valued (Oyserman & Markus, 1993; Markus, 1998; Triandis, 1995), as is positive self-esteem (Kitayama, Markus, Matsumoto, & Norasakkunkit, 1997). Concerns about the possibility that individualism is not a universal socialization goal are echoed in gender studies and racial–ethnic studies research as well (Frable, 1997).

Although societies differ in many ways, most commonly societies that emphasize individualism have been contrasted with societies that emphasize collectivism, summarized as a focus on the group membership or social aspects of the self (Schwartz, 1990). These societies emphasize somewhat different resolutions to basic human dilemmas. Rather than placing emphasis on the individual and his or her unique attributes, emphasis is on the individual's place within a group and the group's unique attributes (Triandis, 1995). In this way, the interdependence between the individual and ingroup is emphasized; because individuals are parts, not stand alone wholes, others are represented within the self-concept (Hofstede, 1980; Kim, 1994). Moreover, rather than striving to become valued due to unique individual abilities and independence, individuals strive to become valued due to their ability to maintain relationships and interpersonal harmony (Markus & Kitayama, 1991). The social, not the personal self is emphasized through cultural practices such as dropping use of personal pronouns, co-producing sentences (Kashima & Kashima, 1997), and using enigmatic similes in which the speaker provides half the simile so that meaning becomes clear only upon joint completion (Rohsenow, 1991).

Empirical support is accruing for the notion that when collectivism is salient ingroup membership is seen as a fixed, meaningful part of identity (Kim, 1994), personal goals and group needs are viewed as congruent (Oyserman, Sakamoto, & Lauffer, 1998), even when the group is faring poorly (Chen, Brockner, & Katz, 1998). Similarly, individuals who rate themselves as focused on collectivist values are lower in personal need for uniqueness, higher in self–other affiliation, and are also more sensitive to the other's rejection (Yamaguchi, Kuhlman, & Sugimori, 1995). Also, students from those societies which emphasized individualism more, viewed personal success as a particularly important basis of self-esteem, while participants from countries that emphasized individualism less viewed family life as a particularly important basis of self-esteem (Watkins, et al., 1998).

Cross-cultural research suggests the cultures place differential emphases on abstract versus episodic, experiential aspects of the self-concept, self-esteem maintenance versus self-improvement, and active versus quiescent self-related emotions. Rather than the self-enhancement or self-esteem maintenance goal central in cultures emphasizing individualism, cultures that emphasize collectivism make central self-goals such as fitting in and being a good group member, becoming more competent, and avoiding embarrassing oneself or others (for a review, see Oyserman, Coon, & Kemmelmeier, 1999). For example, preliminary support for the notion that societies differ in the extent that they emphasize self-esteem maintenance comes from research comparing Japanese and North American students. After receiving failure feedback, North American students are more likely to attempt to compensate or buffer self-feelings by working on easier problems or choosing another task, while Japanese students are more likely to choose the self-improvement strategy of working more on the failed task (Kitayama, Markus, Matsumoto, & Norasakkunkit, 1997).

To the extent that the self-concept is defined, studied, and theorized about within individualistic assumptions, self-concept research is likely to focus on the domains valued by individualism as a cultural frame. This appears to be the case. For example, since knowing and positively evaluating the self – self-concept and self-esteem – are intimately linked in Western tradition and common language, they are used interchangeably in much of the literature (Blascovich & Tomaka, 1991). Since being happy, outgoing, and sociable are valued characteristics within an individualistic cultural frame it is likely that these characteristics will be seen as normative. In fact, the ability to "bounce back" and focus on the positive rather than dwelling on the negative after failure is both culturally valued and – in North America – a characteristic of high rather than low self-esteem individuals (Dodgson & Wood, 1998). Further, the high cultural value placed on positive self-evaluation has resulted in a shift in the meaning of self-esteem from the notion that self-esteem means defining oneself as an adequate person, of equal value as others, toward implicitly assuming that positive self-regard means extremely positive identity (Baumeister, 1998).

In the West, particularly the US, source of much psychological theorizing on the self-concept (Bond & Smith, 1997), it is clear that people tend to have positive views of themselves, at least as assessed by our measures of self-esteem. While a focus on self-esteem seems less useful if researchers are to understand other functions of the self-concept, self-esteem is often used as a key individual difference variable and fluctuations in self-esteem are used to show the influence of social situations on the self. Yet in contexts other than the US, feeling good may be less of a cultural imperative.

Individualistic contexts highlight the importance of a positive self-view and focus attention on the self-concept as an array of traits. North American and European student based research evidence supports these assumptions about the nature of the self: individuals attempt to set up interactions in ways that protect positive self-views, and anticipating negative social feedback is disturbing (Leary, Haupt, Strausser, & Chokel, 1998). American children as young as kindergarteners learn to assess themselves and others in terms of stable and fixed traits (Heyman & Gelman, 1998). North Americans believe that self-interest is a prime motivating factor (Miller & Ratner, 1998) and view relationships with ambivalence, correctly assuming that close others may inhibit self-enhancing tendencies (Sedikides, Campbell, Reeder, & Elliot, 1998).

Yet we may be finding individualistically oriented selves and self-processes because our models focus on these and utilize mostly research participants from countries where individualism is likely to be chronically salient. Within a country, though individualism and collectivism could be separately primed to study the generalizability of findings about self-concept processes, this is typically not done. Further, self-concept and self-esteem are typically assessed, manipulated, or made salient in psychological research paradigms focusing on interactions with strangers, achievement situations, or situations in which attainment of personal goals is centralized, the very situations likely to make an individualistic worldview most prominent (Oyserman, Coon, & Kemmelmeier, 1999). North American and Western European research paradigms rarely study situations likely to evoke a collectivist worldview such as interactions with family members or situations where a sense of common fate with ingroup members has been elicited. Thus, they are unlikely to find evidence of these collective self-processes. Thus, the situations and participants that form the bulk of mainstream social psychological research on the self-concept are heavily weighted toward finding evidence of individualistic self-concept content and processes. This is not to say that evidence for collectivist processes and content would not be found if these were the focus of research attention.

Clearly, however, even within the US, not all contexts promote individualism; behaving individualistically may require power and resources not available across gender and ethnic boundaries (e.g. Kerber, 1991). American collective structures and created spaces afford and sustain the individual focus of American society, particularly the middle class white niche of that society that forms the bulk of our researchers and research participants. These contexts afford and bolster the centralization of the individual in construing cause and effect, and make personal choice, free will, and personal happiness plausible constructs. Clearly, one's place within the social structure influences whether and how individualism is expressed. Broadening the frame of self-concept research will facilitate research dealing with these context-bound aspects of the self. Thus, studying self-concept more broadly, by taking into account both the situations likely to be experienced and the goals likely to be pursued in contexts that make collectivism salient, would do much to deepen understanding of what the self-concept is and how it functions.

Cultural psychological theorizing has made the omission of culture as the broader context in standard self-concept research more obvious and has highlighted the congruence between theories of self-esteem maintenance and individualistic values. Only by broadening the focus of our research attention can we begin to learn the extent to which other goals – such as intimacy and relational goals – motivate the self. In addition, while people often focus on positive aspects of the self, it is also the case that people are interested in seeking accurate information about themselves and in preserving a sense of consistency, even if the consistent information reflects badly on one's self. By taking a broader perspective on the self-concept, the workings of these other self-goals can be more successfully pursued. Using a cultural perspective also highlights the potential for mismatches between the goals assumed by the larger culture and personal goals. For example, an individual may be focused on relationality or self-improvement in contexts that reward autonomy and self-enhancement.

Some research has taken into account issues emerging in this new look at the self. In particular, European literature on social identities (e.g. Tajfel, 1981; Tajfel & Turner, 1986; Turner, Hogg, Oakes, Reicher, & Wetherell, 1987) posits that group membership is an important component of one's identity and that individuals are motivated to view their groups as positive, distinct from other groups. In addition, a new look at social contexts is emerging from a convergence of evidence that contexts matter not only because they influence the situational content elicited by self-concept probes, but importantly because they influence the structure and function of self-concept. These converging lines of research include efforts to explore the effects of social stigma on self-esteem (Crocker, Luhtanen, Blaine, & Broadnax, 1994), the effects of race and racial identity on self-concept (Oyserman & Harrison, 1998), and the effects of gender on self-schemas (Cross & Madson, 1997; Markus & Oyserman, 1989). Together, these perspectives suggest ways that insights about the self-concept gained from studies of primarily white middle-class European American undergraduates are in fact culture-bound and could vary systematically by cultural frame. These insights, combined with the work on racial and ethnic aspects of identity and social identity more generally, provide insight into new directions in self-concept research.

While there is preliminary evidence suggesting that Euro-Americans and Western Europeans generally may be more likely to have the kinds of selves assumed by self-concept researchers, evidence is as yet preliminary and is often based on correlational methodologies (Oyserman, Coon, & Kemmelmeier, 1999). The strength of cultural perspectives lies in their challenge to the assumed universality of psychological theories of self-concept, but the perspective is hampered by a reliance on cross-national studies that assume that participants hold mutually exclusive, stable, and uniform individualistic or collectivistic views. By bringing cultural constructs to the study of self-concept, this paradigm has made clear that there are multiple self-goals – to be part of and connect with others and to be unique from and distinct from others. While cultural psychologists have not emphasized group boundaries *per se*, social identity theories highlight the need to take into account not only group membership but also the way that the group is constituted in relation to other groups. This research has utilized laboratory settings to manipulate group size, salience, permeability of boundaries, and other potentially relevant cues, showing that individuals who are committed to an identity respond differently to threats to this identity than noncommitted individuals (Jetten, Spears, & Manstead, 1998; Spears, Oakes, Ellemers, & Haslam, 1998). Cultural research, exploring cultural context, specific goals, constructs and contexts, including the influences of migration and other acculturation processes (for a review, see chapter 2, this volume), is likely to provide rich material for future research on the generalizability of self-processes.

References

Aber, J., Allen, J., Carlson, V., & Cicchetti, D. (1989). The effects of maltreatment on development during early childhood: Recent studies and their theoretical, clinical, and policy implications. In D. Cicchetti (Ed.), *Child maltreatment: Theory and research on the causes and consequences of child abuse and neglect* (pp. 579–619). New York: Cambridge University Press.

Andersen, S., Glassman, N., & Gold, D. (1998). Mental representations of the self, significant others, and nonsignificant others: Structure and processing of private and public aspects. *Journal of Personality and Social Psychology, 75*, 845–861.

Asendorpf, J., & Ostendorf, F. (1998). Is self-enhancement healthy? Conceptual, psychometric, and empirical analysis. *Journal of Personality and Social Psychology, 74*, 955–966.

Banaji, M., & Prentice, D. (1994). The self in social contexts. *Annual Review of Psychology, 45*, 297–332.

Baumeister, R. (1998). The self. In D. Gilbert, S. Fiske, & G. Lindzey (Eds.), *Handbook of social psychology* (pp. 680–740). New York: Oxford University Press.

Beauregard, K. S., & Dunning, D. (1998). Turning up the contrast: Self-enhancement motives prompt egocentric contrast effects in social judgments. *Journal of Personality and Social Psychology, 74*, 606–621.

Bellah, R., Madsen, R., Sullivan, W., Swidler, A., & Tipton, S. (1985). *Habits of the heart: Individualism and commitment in American life*. Berkeley: University of California Press.

Bennett, M., Lyons, E., Sani, F., & Barrett, M. (1998). Children's subjective identification with the group and in-group favoritism. *Developmental Psychology, 34*, 902–909.

Bennett, M., Yuill, N., Banerjee, R., & Thomson, S. (1998). Children's understanding of extended identity. *Developmental Psychology, 34*, 322–331.

Blascovich, J., & Tomaka, J. (1991). Measures of self-esteem. In J. Robinson, P. Shaver, & L. Wrightsman (Eds.), *Measures of personality and social psychological attitudes* (pp. 115–160). New York: Academic Press.

Bond, M., & Smith, P. (1997). Cross-cultural social and organizational psychology. *Annual Review of Psychology, 47*, 205–235.

Bretherton, I. (1992). Attachment and bonding. In V. Van Hasselt & M. Hersen (Eds.), *Handbook of social development* (pp. 133–155). New York: Plenum Press.

Brewer, M. (1991). The social self: On being the same and different at the same time. *Personality and Social Psychology Bulletin, 17*, 475–82.

Bronfenbrenner, U. (1995). The bioecological model from a life course perspective: Reflections of a participant observer. In P. Moen, H. Elder, Jr., & K. Luscher (Eds.), *Examining lives in context: Perspectives on the ecology of human development* (pp. 599–618). Washington, DC: American Psychological Association.

Brown, J. (1998). *The self.* Boston, MA: McGraw-Hill.

Byrne, B. (1996). *Measuring self-concept across the life span.* Washington, DC: APA Press.

Carver, C., & Scheier, M. (1981). *Attention and self-regulation: A control theory approach to human behavior.* New York: Springer-Verlag.

Catrambone, R., & Markus, H. (1987). The role of self-schemas in going beyond the information given. *Social Cognition, 5,* 349–368.

Catrambone, R., Beike, D., & Niedenthal, P. (1996). Is the self-concept a habitual referent in judgments of similarity? *Psychological Science, 7,* 158–163.

Chen, Y., Brockner, J., & Katz, T. (1998). Toward an explanation of cultural differences in in-group favoritism: The role of individual versus collective primacy. *Journal of Personality and Social Psychology, 75,* 1490–1502.

Cooley, D. (1902). *Human nature and the social order.* New York: Scribners.

Cooper, C., & Denner, J. (1998). Theories linking culture and psychology: Universal and community-specific processes. *Annual Review of Psychology, 49,* 559–584.

Crocker, J., Luhtanen, R., Blaine, B., & Broadnax, S. (1994). Collective self-esteem and psychological well-being among white, black, and Asian college students. *Personality and Social Psychology Bulletin, 20,* 503–13.

Croizet, J., & Claire, T. (1998). Extending the concept of stereotype threat to social class: The intellectual underperformance of students from low socioeconomic backgrounds. *Personality and Social Psychology Bulletin, 24,* 588–594.

Cross, S. E., & Madson, L. (1997). Models of the self: Self-construals and gender. *Psychological Bulletin, 122,* 5–37.

Crystal, D., Watanabe, H., Weinfurt, K., & Wu, C. (1998). Concepts of human differences: A comparison of American, Japanese, and Chinese children and adolescents. *Developmental Psychology, 34,* 714–722.

Damon, W., & Hart, D. (1988). *Self-understanding in childhood and adolescence.* New York: Cambridge University Press.

DeNeve, K. M., & Cooper, H. (1998). The happy personality: A meta-analysis of 137 personality traits and subjective well-being. *Psychological Bulletin, 124,* 197–229.

Dodgson, P., & Wood, J. (1998). Self-esteem and the cognitive accessibility of strengths and weaknesses after failure. *Journal of Personality and Social Psychology, 75,* 78–197.

Egan, S. K., & Perry, D. G. (1998). Does low self-regard invite victimization? *Developmental Psychology, 34,* 299–309.

Epstein, S. (1973). The self-concept revisited or a theory of a theory. *American Psychologist, 28,* 405–416.

Erikson, E. (1968). *Identity: Youth and crisis.* New York: Norton.

Exline, J., & Lobel, M. (1999). The perils of outperformance sensitivity about being the target of a threatening upward comparison. *Psychological Bulletin, 125,* 307–337.

Fazio, R., Effrein, E., & Falender, V. (1981). Self-perceptions following social interactions. *Journal of Personality and Social Psychology, 41,* 232–242.

Feldman, R., Greenbaum, C., & Yirmiya, N. (1999). Mother–infant affect synchrony as an antecedent of the emergence of self-control. *Developmental Psychology, 35,* 223–231.

Fiske, S., & Taylor, S. (1994). *Social cognition.* 2nd. edn. Reading, MA: Addison-Wessley.

Fiske, A., Kitayama, S., Markus, H., & Nisbett, R. (1998). The cultural matrix of social psychology. In D. Gilbert, S. Fiske, & G. Lindzey (Eds.), *Handbook of social psychology.* New York: McGraw-Hill.

Frable, D. (1997). Gender, racial, ethnic, sexual, and class identities. *Annual Review of Psychology, 48,* 139–162.

Frable, D., Platt, L., & Hoey, S. (1998). Concealable stigmas and positive self-perceptions: Feeling better around similar others. *Journal of Personality and Social Psychology, 74,* 909–922.

Frederickson, B. L., Roberts, T.-A., Noll, S. M., Quinn, D. M., & Twenge, J. M. (1998). That swimsuit becomes you. Sex differences in self-objectification, restrained eating, and math performance. *Journal of Personality and Social Psychology, 75,* 269–284.

Frome, P., & Eccles, J. (1998). Parents' influence on children's achievement-related perceptions. *Journal of Personality and Social Psychology, 74,* 435–452.

Graham, S., & Juvonen, J. (1998). Self-blame and peer victimization in middle school: An attributional analysis. *Developmental Psychology, 34,* 587–599.

Greenwald, A. (1980). The totalitarian ego: Fabrication and revision of personal history. *American Psychologist, 35,* 603–618.

Greenwald, A. (1982). Ego task analysis: An integration of research on ego-involvement and self-awareness. In A. Hastorf and A. Isen (Eds.), *Cognitive social psychology* (pp. 109–148). New York: Elsevier.

Greenwald, A., & Pratkanis, A. (1984). The self. In K. S. Wyer & T. Srull (Eds.), *Handbook of social cognition,* Vol. 3 (pp. 129–178). Hillsdale, NJ: Erlbaum.

Hammen, C. (1991). *Depression runs in families: The social context of risk and resilience in children of depressed mothers.* New York: Springer-Verlag.

Harris, J. (1995). Where is the child's environment? *Psychological Review, 102,* 458–489.

Harter, S. (1990). Adolescent self and identity. In S. S. Feldman & G. Elliot (Eds.), *At the threshold: The developing adolescent* (pp. 352–387). Cambridge, MA: Harvard University Press.

Harter, S., Marold, D., Whitesell, N., & Cobbs, G. (1996). A model of the effects of parent and peer support on adolescent false self behavior. *Child Development, 67,* 160–174.

Harter, S., Waters, P., Whitesell, N., & Kastelic, D. (1998). Level of voice among female and male high school students: Relational context, support, and gender orientation. *Developmental Psychology, 34,* 892–901.

Haslam, S. A., Oakes, P., Turner, J. C., & McGarty, C. (1996). Social identity, self-categorization, and the perceived homogeneity of ingroups and outgroups: The interaction between social motivation and cognition. In R. Sorrentino & E. T. Higgins (Eds.), *Handbook of motivation and cognition: The interpersonal context* (pp. 182–222). New York: Guilford Press.

Heyman, G. D., & Gelman, S. A. (1998). Young children use motive information to make trait inferences. *Developmental Psychology, 34,* 310–321.

Higgins, E. T. (1989). Continuities and discontinuities in self-regulatory and self-evaluative processes: A developmental theory relating self and affect. *Journal of Personality: Special Issue: Long-term stability and change in personality, 57,* 407–444.

Higgins, E. T. (1996). Shared reality in the self-system: The social nature of self-regulation. In W. Stroebe & M. Hewstone (Eds.), *European review of social psychology,* Vol. 7 (pp. 1–30). Chichester, UK: Wiley.

Hofstede, G. (1980). *Culture's consequences.* Beverly Hills, CA: Sage.

Holland, D., & Quinn, N. (1987). *Cultural models in language and thought.* Cambridge, UK: Cambridge University Press.

James, W. (1890/1950). *The principles of psychology.* New York: Dover.

Jetten, J., Spears, R., & Manstead, A. (1998). Defining dimensions of distinctiveness: Group variability makes a difference to differentiation. *Journal of Personality and Social Psychology, 74,* 1481–1492.

Kagitcibasi, C. (1996). *Family and human development across cultures.* Mahwah, NJ: Erlbaum.

Kashima, E., & Kashima, Y. (1997). Practice of self in conversations: Pronoun drop, sentence co-production and contextualization of the self. In K. Leung, U. Kim, S. Yamaguchi, & Y. Kashima (Eds.), *Progress in Asian social psychology* (pp. 164–179). Singapore: John Wiley & Sons.

Kemmelmeier, M., & Oyserman, D. (in press). When similar others fail: The gendered impact of downward social comparisons. *Journal of Social Issues,* forthcoming special issue, *Stigma: An Insider's View.*

Kerber, L. (1991). Can a woman be an individual? The discourse of self-reliance. In R. W. Curry and L. B. Goodheart (Eds.), *American chameleon: Individualism in trans-national context.* Kent, Ohio: Kent State University Press.

Kihlstrom, J., & Cantor, N. (1984). Mental representations of the self. *Advances in Experimental*

Social Psychology, 17, 1–47.

Kihlstrom, J., & Klein, S. (1994). The self as a knowledge structure. In R. Wyer, Jr., & T. Srull (Eds.), *Handbook of social cognition, Vol. 1: Basic processes* (pp. 153–208). Hillsdale, NJ: Lawrence Erlbaum Associates.

Kim, U. (1994). Individualism and collectivism: Conceptual clarification and elaboration. In U. Kim, H. C. Triandis, C. Kagitcibasi, S. Choi, & G. Yoon (Eds.), *Individualism and collectivism: Theory, method, and applications* (pp. 000–000). Thousand Oaks, CA: Sage.

Kitayama, S., Markus, H. R., Matsumoto, H., & Norasakkunkit, V. (1997). Individual and collective process in the construction of the self: Self-enhancement in the United States and self-criticism in Japan. *Journal of Personality and Social Psychology, 72*, 1245–1267.

Klaczynski, P., & Narasimham, G. (1998). Development of scientific reasoning biases: Cognitive versus ego-protective explanations. *Developmental Psychology, 34*, 175–187.

Leary, M., Haupt, A., Strausser, K., & Chokel, J. (1998). Calibrating the sociometer: The relationship between interpersonal appraisals and state self-esteem. *Journal of Personality and Social Psychology, 74*, 1290–1299.

Lewis, M. (1990). Self-knowledge and social development in early life. In L. Pervin (Ed.), *Handbook of personality: Theory and research* (pp. 277–300). New York: Guilford Press.

Lewis, M., & Brooks-Gunn, J. (1979). *Social cognition and the acquisition of self.* New York: Plenum Press.

Linville, P. (1987). Self-complexity as a cognitive buffer against stress-related illness and depression. *Journal of Personality and Social Psychology, 52*, 663–676.

McGuire, W., & Padawer-Singer, A. (1976). Trait salience in the spontaneous self-concept. *Journal of Personality and Social Psychology, 33*, 743–754.

Maddux, J. (1991). Self-efficacy. In C. R. Snyder (Ed.), *Handbook of social and clinical psychology: The health perspective* (pp. 57–78). Pergamon general psychology series, Vol. 162. New York: Pergamon Press.

Marcia, J. (1980). Identity in adolescence. In J. Adelson (Ed.), *Handbook of adolescent psychology* (pp. 159–187). New York: Wiley.

Markus, H. (1977). Self-schemata and processing information about the self. *Journal of Personality & Social Psychology, 35*, 63–78.

Markus, H., & Cross, S. (1990). The interpersonal self. In L. Pervin (Ed.), *Handbook of personality: Theory and research* (pp. 576–608). New York: Guilford Press.

Markus, H., & Kitayama, S. (1991). Culture and the self: Implications for cognition, emotion, and motivation. *Psychological Review, 20*, 568–579.

Markus, H., & Kunda, Z. (1986). Stability and malleability of the self-concept. *Journal of Personality and Social Psychology, 51*, 858–866.

Markus, H., & Oyserman, D. (1989). Gender and thought. The role of the self-concept. In M. Crawford & M. Gentry (Eds.), *Gender and Thought: Psychological perspectives* (pp. 1000–127)

Markus, H., & Wurf, E. (1987). The dynamic self-concept. *Annual Review of Psychology, 38*, 299–337.

Marsh, H., & Yeung, A. (1998). Top-down, bottom-up, and horizontal models: The direction of causality in multidimensional, hierarchical self-concept models. *Journal of Personality and Social Psychology, 75*, 509–527.

Maslow, A. (1954). *Motivation and personality.* New York: Harper.

Mead, H. (1921–1925/1964). *The genesis of the self and social control.* Indianapolis, In: Bobbs-Merrill.

Mead, H. (1934/1964). *Mind, self, and society: From the standpoint of a social behaviorist.* Chicago: University of Chicago Press.

Mikulincer, M. (1998). Adult attachment style and affect regulation: Strategic variations in self-appraisals. *Journal of Personality and Social Psychology, 75*, 420–435.

Miller, D., & Ratner, R. (1998). The disparity between the actual and assumed power of self-interest. *Journal of Personality and Social Psychology, 74*, 53–62.

Moretti, M., Higgins, E. T., & Simon, F. (1990). The development of self-system vulnerabilities: Social and cognitive factors in developmental psychopathology. In R. Sternberg (Ed.), *Competence considered* (pp. 286–314). New Haven, CT: Yale University Press.

Murray, S., Holmes, J., MacDonald, G., & Ellsworth, P. (1998). Through the looking glass darkly? When self-doubts turn into relationship insecurities. *Journal of Personality and Social Psychology, 75*, 1459–1480.

Neisser, U. (1988). Five kinds of self-knowledge. *Philosophical Psychology, 1*, 35–59.

Neisser, U. (1993). *The perceived self: Ecological and interpersonal sources of self-knowledge.* New York: Cambridge University Press.

Neisser, U. (1995). Criteria for an ecological self. In P. Rochat (Ed.), *The self in infancy: Theory and research* (pp. 17–34). Amsterdam, Netherlands: North-Holland/Elsevier Science Publishers.

Norenzayan, A., Schwarz, N., & Rothman, A. (1996). Conversational relevance in the presentation of the self. *International Journal of Psychology, 31*, 184–194.

Oyserman, D. (1993). The lens of personhood: Viewing the self and others in a multicultural society. *Journal of Personality and Social Psychology, 125*, 307–337.

Oyserman, D., & Harrison, K. (1998). Implications of ethnic identity: African American identity and possible selves. In J. K. Swim & C. Stangor (Eds.), *Prejudice: The target's perspective* (pp. 281–300). San Diego: Academic Press.

Oyserman, D., & Markus, H. (1990). Possible selves and delinquency. *Journal of Personality and Social Psychology, 59*, 111–125.

Oyserman, D., & Markus, H. (1993). The sociocultural self. In J. Suls (Ed.), *Psychological perspectives on the self*, Vol. 4 (pp. 187–220). Hillsdale, NJ: Erlbaum.

Oyserman, D., & Markus, H. (1998). Self as social representation. In U. Flick (Ed.), *The psychology of the social* (pp. 107–125). New York: Cambridge University Press.

Oyserman, D., Coon, H., & Kemmelmeier, M. (1999). How American is individualism? Lessons from cultural and cross-cultural research. Under revision, *Psychological Bulletin.* Ann Arbor: University of Michigan.

Oyserman, D., Kemmelmeier, M., & Brosh, H. (1999). Racial–ethnic minority identity schemas. Manuscript submitted for publication. Ann Arbor: University of Michigan.

Oyserman, D., Sakamoto, I., & Lauffer, A. (1998). Cultural accommodation: Hybridity and the framing of social obligation. *Journal of Personality and Social Psychology, 74*, 1606–1618.

Povinelli, D. J., & Simon, B. B. (1988). Young children's understanding of briefly versus extremely delayed images of the self: Emergence of the autobiographical stance. *Developmental Psychology, 34*, 188–194.

Raeff, C. (1997). Individuals in relationships: Cultural values, children's social interactions, and the development of an American individualistic self. *Developmental Review, 17*, 204–238.

Roffey, S., Majors, K., & Tarrant, T. (1997). Friends – who needs them? What do we know and what can we do? *Educational and Child Psychology, 14*, 51–56.

Rogers, C. (1954). *Becoming a person.* Oberlin, Ohio: Oberlin College.

Rohsenow, J. (1991). *A Chinese–English dictionary of enigmatic folk similes.* Tucson: University of Arizona Press.

Ruble, D., Eisenberg, R., & Higgins, E. T. (1994). Developmental changes in achievement evaluation: Motivational implications of self–other differences. *Child Development, 65*, 1095–1110.

Ryff, C., & Keyes, C. (1995). The structure of psychological well-being revisited. *Journal of Personality and Social Psychology, 69*, 719–727.

Sampson, E. E. (1977). Psychology and the American ideal. *Journal of Personality and Social Psychology, 35*, 767–782.

Schwarz, N. (1998). Accessible content and accessibility experiences: The interplay of declarative and experiential information in judgment. *Personality and Social Psychology Review, 2*, 87–99.

Schwarz, N., Bless, H., Strack, F., Klumpp, G., Rittenauer-Schatka, H., & Simons, A. (1991). Ease of retrieval as information: Another look at the availability heuristic. *Journal of Personality and Social Psychology, 61*, 195–202.

Schwartz, S. H. (1990). Individualism–collectivism: Critique and proposed refinements. *Journal of Cross-Cultural Psychology, 21*, 139–157.

Sedikides, C., Campbell, W., Reeder, G., & Elliot, A. (1998). The self-serving bias in relational context. *Journal of Personality and Social Psychology, 74*, 378–386.

Shih, M., Pittinsky, T., & Ambady, N. (1999). Stereotype susceptibility: Identity salience and shifts in quantitative performance. *Psychological Science, 10,* 80–83.

Showers, C., Abramson, L., & Hogan, M. (1998). The dynamic self: How the content and structure of the self-concept change with mood. *Journal of Personality and Social Psychology, 75,* 478–493.

Shweder, R. (1990). Cultural psychology: What is it? In J. Stigler, R. Shweder, & G. Herdt (Eds.), *Cultural psychology: Essays in comparative human development* (pp. 1–46). New York: Cambridge University Press.

Spears, R., Oakes, P., Ellemers, N., & Haslam, S. (Eds.) (1998). *The social psychology of stereotyping and group life.* Cambridge, Mass.: Blackwell.

Steele, C. M. (1988). The psychology of self-affirmation: Sustaining integrity of the self. In L. Berkowitz (Ed.), *Advances in experimental social psychology,* Vol. 21 (pp. 261–302). New York: Academic Press.

Steele, C. M. (1997). A threat in the air: How stereotypes shape intellectual identity and perform-ance. *American Psychologist, 52,* 613–629.

Stryker, S. (1980). *Symbolic interactionism: A social structural version.* Palo Alto, CA: Benjamin/Cummings.

Stryker, S. (1987). Identity theory: Developments and extensions. In K. Yardley & T. Honess (Eds.), *Self and identity: Psychosocial perspectives* (pp. 83–103). New York: Wiley.

Swann, W. (1997). The trouble with change: Self-verification and allegiance to the self. *Psychologi-cal Science, 8,* 177–180.

Tajfel, H. (1981). *Human groups and social categories: Studies in social psychology.* Cambridge, UK: Cambridge University Press.

Tajfel, H., & Turner, J. (1986). The social identity theory of intergroup behavior. In S. Worchel & W. Austin (Eds.), *Psychology of intergroup relations,* 2nd. edn. (pp. 7–24). Chicago: Nelson-Hall.

Taylor, S., & Brown, J. (1988). Illusion and well-being: A social psychological perspective on men-tal health. *Psychological Bulletin, 103,* 193–210.

Trafimow, D., & Smith, M. (1998). An extension of the "two-baskets" theory to Native Americans. *European Journal of Social Psychology, 28,* 1015–1019.

Triandis, H. C. (1989). The self and social behavior in differing cultural context. *Psychological Re-view, 93* (3), 506–520.

Triandis, H. C. (1995). *Individualism and collectivism.* Boulder, CO: Westview Press.

Tronick, E. Z., & Gianino, A. (1986). Interactive mismatch and repair: Challenges to the coping infant. *Zero to Three, 6,* 1–6.

Trope, Y. (1986). Self-enhancement and self-assessment in achievement behavior. In R. Sorrentino (Ed.), *Handbook of motivation and cognition: Foundations of social behavior* (pp. 350–378). New York: Guilford Press.

Turner, J. C., Hogg, M. A., Oakes, P. J., Reicher, S. D., & Wetherell, S. M. (1987). *Rediscovering the social group: A self-categorization theory.* Oxford: Blackwell Publishers.

Watkins, D., Akande, A., Fleming, J., Ismail, M., Lefner, K., Regmi, M., Watson, S., Yu, J., Adair, J., Cheng, C., Gerong, A., McInerney, D., Mpofu, E., Singh-Sengupta, S., & Wondimu, H. (1998). Cultural dimensions, gender, and the nature of self-concept: A fourteen-country study. *International Journal of Psychology, 33,* 17–31.

Weigert, A., Teige, J., & Teige, D. (1990). *Society and identity: Toward a sociological psychology.* Cambridge, UK: Cambridge University Press.

Weinberg, M., Tronick, E., & Cohn, J. (1999). Gender differences in emotional expressivity and self-regulation during early infancy. *Developmental Psychology, 35,* 175–188.

Wurf, E., & Markus, H. (1991). Possible selves and the psychology of personal growth. In D. Ozer (Ed.), *Perspectives in personality,* Vol. 3 (pp. 39–62). London: Jessica Kingsley Publishers.

Wylie, R. (1989). *Measures of self-concept.* Lincoln: University of Nebraska Press.

Yamaguchi, S., Kuhlman, D., & Sugimori, S. (1995). Personality correlates of allocentric tenden-cies in individualist and collectivist cultures. *Journal of Cross-Cultural Psychology, 26,* 658–672.

Chapter Twenty-Four

Identity Through Time: Constructing Personal Pasts and Futures

Michael Ross and Roger Buehler

People's sense of identity often includes a perception of who they were, who they are, and who they will be. While thinking about her sociability, a woman may remember being shyer as a teenager and anticipate becoming more outgoing as she ages. While evaluating her job performance, she may remember her previous positions and envision future promotions. In this chapter, we describe and contrast people's thoughts about their personal pasts and futures. We begin by discussing reasons that social psychologists should be concerned with these topics. Why not leave the study of autobiographical memory to cognitive psychologists and the study of the future to prophets or economists?

The Social Psychological Importance of Personal Pasts and Futures

The past matters

Social psychologists are interested in memory because it plays a key role in many of the phenomena of concern to them. Individuals or social groups in conflict often dispute their shared histories (Rouhana & Bar-Tal, 1998). They argue about who did what to whom, and when and why. Such quarrels can serve to maintain and exacerbate conflict, whether it be between nations or spouses. When a feud is longstanding, as in the Middle East, clashing views of events that transpired hundreds, even thousands of years ago, can arouse outrage today. These arguments about ancient history represent more than intellectual debates; the acceptance of some assertions over others can have important consequences. A group's claim to land and property is legitimized, legally and morally, by its accounts of the past. A major function of religious and national groups is to perpetuate their preferred versions of history. From an early age, children are taught history from the perspective of their group and to disregard opposing views. Along the same lines, contestants in a divorce base their claims to property and custody of children on their competing memories of the history of their marriage. Spouses are also likely to convey their own versions of the marriage to their friends and children.

People's personal histories are important to them, even in the absence of disputes. Individuals' assessments of their abilities, personalities, and self-worth are grounded in their memories of their pasts (e.g. Singer & Salovey, 1993). People form summary judgments of themselves such as: I am good at chess, poor at singing, and shy in groups of strangers but boisterous with close friends. These evaluations reflect individuals' recollections of their past experiences in the different domains. People who lose their autobiographical memories following a head injury lose their sense of self as well (Schacter, 1996).

People's memories also influence their current well-being and behavior. When individuals recall happy episodes their mood tends to improve and when they remember distressing episodes it tends to worsen. Researchers studying negative or positive emotions often temporarily create these feelings by prompting participants in experiments to recall unpleasant or pleasant personal experiences (e.g. Martin, 1990; Salovey, 1992). In everyday life, distressful events sometimes produce repetitive and intrusive memories that influence people's behavior and well-being (Davis, Lehman, Wortman, Silver, & Thompson, 1995; Holman & Cohen-Silver, 1998; Loftus, 1993; Pennebaker, 1990). For example, Nolen-Hoeksema & Morrow (1991) reported that frequency of rumination about an earthquake ten days after its occurrence predicted depression and symptoms of post-traumatic stress disorder seven weeks after the quake.

As authors of their own histories, people sometimes reinterpret past experiences and change their emotional impact (McFarland, Ross, & Giltrow, 1992; Strack, Schwarz, & Gschneidinger, 1985; Watson & McFarland, 1995). Remembering events that were initially unpleasant actually improves mood when people focus on beneficial, longer-term consequences of the episodes, such as personal growth and change (Watson & McFarland, 1995). There is other evidence for the therapeutic value of reinterpreting unpleasant experiences. Psychoanalysts often encourage patients to adopt explanations for past events that enhance their views of themselves (Spence, 1982). Likewise, social psychologists use attributional retraining techniques to influence people's beliefs about their experiences (e.g. Wilson & Linville, 1982). When successful, these attributional procedures shift people's explanations of previous failures from stable, uncontrollable causes (I am terrible at mathematics) to more unstable, controllable causes (I haven't tried hard enough). If people perceive failure as stable and uncontrollable, they are inclined to give up. If individuals perceive the cause of failure as controllable, then they are more likely to persist. They hope and expect to bring about success through their own efforts (Dweck, 1975, 1990). The trick is to distinguish outcomes that are possibly affected by one's own actions from outcomes that are not, and to adjust one's behavior accordingly.

The future matters

People's conceptions of the future often include their goals (e.g. marriage or job advancement) and their plans for attaining them. Such scenarios of the future influence people's current decisions and behavior; people act in ways that they believe will help them to obtain their objectives (Karniol & Ross, 1996). In addition to forming scenarios of how the future might unfold, people sometimes create images of possible selves, representations of how they might behave, look, or feel in the future (Cantor, Markus, Niedenthal, & Nurius, 1986; Markus & Nurius, 1986; Markus & Ruvolo, 1989). People imagine selves that they would like to achieve as well as those that they would prefer to avoid, and these images can motivate behavior. For example, a thin person who fears becoming obese may choose to nibble crackers instead of cheesecake.

People's thoughts about the future influence how they process information. Individuals pay increased attention to aspects of themselves and their surroundings that promote attainment of their objectives (Baumeister & Newman, 1994; Dweck, 1990; Gollwitzer, 1996; Kruglanski, 1989; Kunda, 1990). Gollwitzer's analysis of the different phases of goal pursuit illustrates how people's thoughts become attuned to the information that is most relevant for their present purposes. While deciding whether to pursue a goal, people impartially evaluate information related to the feasibility and desirability of various alternatives. After deciding on a particular goal, however, people ignore information about its desirability and focus instead on their plans for achieving it (Gollwitzer, Heckhausen, & Steller, 1990).

People also exaggerate the goal relevance of ambiguous behavior in their eagerness to obtain information about their likelihood of attaining their objectives (Vorauer & Ross, 1993, 1996). For instance, a friend of the authors was anxiously awaiting a response from a journal editor regarding whether he had accepted her manuscript for publication. Meanwhile, she exchanged several email messages with this editor. In his first two notes, the editor simply launched into his message without any salutation. In a third message, the editor greeted her by her first name (Dear –), closed with his own first name, and promised that he would make a decision soon. Our friend took his friendlier style as a good omen.[1] People are often reduced to the equivalent of reading tea leaves when they are desperate for information about how the future will unfold.

People's images of the future also influence their reactions to current circumstances (Frijda, 1986; Karniol & Ross, 1996; Markus & Nurius, 1986; Showers, 1992). Goals provide a basis for evaluating self-relevant events. A student who aspires to be a professional athlete is likely to be more devastated by failing to make the varsity team, than a student who lacks such ambitions. Individuals are sometimes willing to tolerate inferior outcomes in the present (e.g. work at demeaning jobs, maintain calorie-reduced diets) in order to achieve long-term goals. At times, people will refuse immediate rewards, if they believe doing so will help them to avoid trouble or to attain superior results in the future (Mischel, 1974, 1996).

We don't want to exaggerate the power of the future, however. All too often, people give into temptation and suffer the long-term consequences of their desire for immediate gratification (Platt, 1973), as numerous dieters and some US presidents are painfully aware. Many self-help books describe procedures that supposedly help individuals to pursue long-term objectives (e.g. wonder diets). As evidence of the difficulty of achieving this end, each year welcomes a new series of self-help books that attack exactly the same problems as the previous year's tomes.

Generating Memories and Forecasts

We have argued that the future and past matter because they influence people's present emotions, decisions, and behavior. We next consider how people create their pasts and imaginary futures. Both memories and forecasts occur in the present and typically in response to people's ongoing concerns. If people think about earlier relationship failures or future shopping trips, it is usually because some present event or idea leads them to consider these things. The means by which people generate memories or forecasts are quite similar. Autobiographical memories and forecasts are creative constructions of the human mind. The suggestion that memory is a creative act may seem surprising. Words such as remembering, recalling, recollecting, and reminiscing all imply thinking of something again, bringing forth earlier thoughts from memory into current consciousness. From this perspective, remembering is more similar to reproduction than to invention. Many psychologists and philosophers have suggested, however, that the past is often partly constructed or inferred, rather than simply retrieved from memory (e.g. Bartlett, 1932; Greenwald, 1980; McAdams, 1993; Mead, 1934, 1964; Neisser, 1967; Ross, 1989; Schacter, 1996). Neisser argues that only fragments of an episode are stored in memory. He suggests that people reconstruct an event from these bits of memory, just as a paleontologist reconstructs a dinosaur from a few bones.

Constructing memories

To examine the role of construction and inference, we consider a simplified depiction of the recollection process that includes three main components: an external event, an internal representation of that event in long-term memory, and a current recollection of the event. How are these components related to each other?

Although the internal representation resembles the external event, it is typically not a precise copy for several reasons:

1   People are unlikely to notice all of the aspects of a situation. In most everyday contexts, there is simply too much going on for a person to take it all in. Also, what perceivers detect depends, in part, on their vantage point, current concerns, and emotional and physical states (a sleepy person is likely to notice less than an alert individual).
2   People's current knowledge affects their perception and interpretation of events (Bransford & Franks, 1971; Bruner & Goodman, 1947; Mead, 1964; Spiro, 1977). Consider, for example, how a game of ice hockey or cricket would appear to an expert, as opposed to a person who views it for the first time.

3 People do not transfer everything that they observe from working memory to longer-term memory. Information that is not transferred cannot be recalled later.

Just as internal representations are not exact copies of external events, recollections are not necessarily precise reproductions of the original, internal representations stored in long-term memory. Both encoding and retrieval processes contribute to differences between recollections and initial representations. People's original representations of events vary in strength and quality (depending, for example, on the importance and distinctiveness of the event), with the result that individuals forget some episodes more rapidly than others (Brewer, 1988; Johnson, Hashtroudi & Lindsay, 1993). Also, repeated experiences of similar events may become confused with each other and combined into a generic memory (Carlston & Smith, 1996; Neisser, 1981). The details of specific events are difficult to extract from these general memories (Brewer, 1988; Linton, 1982).

During memory retrieval, people's current knowledge and beliefs influence their recollections. Memories consistent with people's present knowledge are often more accessible than memories containing contradictory information; as well, people tend to interpret ambiguous memories as congruent with their current knowledge (Anderson & Pichert, 1978; Bahrick, Hall, & Berger, 1996; Bartlett, 1932; Hastie, 1981; Hirt, 1990; Markus, 1977; Ross, 1989; Taylor & Crocker, 1981). Furthermore, when remembering an episode individuals often explain or justify their own and other people's behavior. These explanations may be inferred or revised while the episode is being reconstructed and may not have been part of the rememberer's original encoding of the event.

Ross (1989) examined the impact of a particular type of current knowledge on people's autobiographical recall. He proposed that when individuals try to recall what they were like in the past on some characteristic or trait (e.g. their attitude toward abortion five years ago or how shy they used to be) they construct the answer using two sources of information. The first is their present standing on the attribute (e.g. how shy they are now); the second is an implicit theory of how the trait is likely to have changed with time. Implicit theories incorporate specific beliefs regarding the inherent stability of an attribute, as well as general principles concerning the conditions likely to promote change. A theory of this sort is implicit in that people typically do not learn it through formal education and they may rarely discuss it.

People's implicit theories may often be quite accurate and yield recollections that correspond well with their original views. At other times, people's theories may lead them astray. Ross (1989) reported numerous examples of biases in recall that he attributed to misleading assumptions of personal stability. For example, several researchers demonstrated that people who had changed their attitudes exaggerated the consistency between their earlier and new opinions. In one of these studies, participants described how they had recalled their earlier attitudes. Many individuals reported that they assumed that their beliefs were stable over time and that they inferred their previous opinions from their current attitudes.

More recently, Levine (1997) asked supporters of Ross Perot to report their emotional reactions to his abrupt withdrawal from the US presidential race in July of 1992. Perot re-entered the race during the following October and eventually received nearly a fifth of the popular vote. After the elections in November, Levine asked supporters to recall their earlier emotional reactions to Perot's withdrawal and to describe their current feelings toward Perot. People's memories of their earlier emotions were biased in the direction of their current appraisals of Perot. McFarland & Ross (1987) found a similar effect for people's recollections of their earlier evaluations of their dating partners. People who fell more in love after their initial evaluations exaggerated, and those who fell less in love underestimated, the degree to which they had previously reported caring for their partner. The findings from these two studies suggest that people suppose that their emotional reactions to individuals are fairly stable over time and that they use their current assessments as a basis for inferring their earlier feelings.

Feldman Barrett (1997) studied the relation of people's enduring self-concepts to their recollections of their emotional reactions. Respondents kept diary ratings of their emotional experiences and subsequently recalled the emotions they had reported. Those who scored high on a neuroticism scale remembered experiencing more negative emotion than they had reported; conversely, respondents who scored high on extroversion remembered feeling more positive emotion than they had reported earlier.

Just as individuals sometimes exaggerate their stability, they may also overestimate the degree to which they have changed. Retrospective overestimation of change is likely when people experience a circumstance that they expect to produce change, but that in reality has minimal impact. Self-help programs are a context in which people's expectancies and hopes of change are likely to be disappointed. Although such programs often have considerable face validity, they tend to be remarkably unsuccessful (Ross & Conway, 1986). Conway & Ross (1984) studied the relation between memory and expectations for change in the context of a study skills program. They asked university students to evaluate their study skills and then randomly assigned half of them to a study skills program that lasted several weeks and the remaining half to a control condition. Although participants in the treatment program expected to improve their grades, their program, like most other study skills courses, was ineffective. At the conclusion of the course, participants in the treatment and control conditions were asked to recall their original ratings of their study skills. They were reminded that the researcher had their initial ratings and would assess the accuracy of their recall. Participants who took the course remembered their pre-program ratings as being worse than they had initially reported. In contrast, control participants, who had not received the program, exhibited no systematic bias in recall. The biased recollections of participants in the study skills course would support their theory that the program had improved their skills. More generally, a tendency to revise the past in order to claim personal improvement may explain why many individuals report that they benefit from ineffective pop therapies and self-improvement programs (Conway & Ross, 1984).

The research on autobiographical recall does not indicate that biased recollections are more common than accurate recollections, or that people's implicit theories of personal change or stability are generally false. Indeed, some researchers have reported impressive degrees of accuracy, as well as evidence of biased recall (e.g. Bahrick, Hall, & Berger, 1996; Feldman Barrett, 1997; Levine, 1997). Also, research conducted on autobiographical memory in other contexts has revealed that people's recollections can be fairly accurate, at least for the gist of past experiences (e.g. Neisser, 1981). The studies we have described do suggest, however, that individuals' self-concepts, beliefs, and implicit theories influence their memories.

Now, let's return to the scheme of the recollection process and subtract a couple of elements. Suppose that there was no external event, and therefore no internal representation of that event in long-term memory. Imagine, however, that people think about an event and discuss it with others. They may subsequently mistake the source of their recollection, believing that the thoughts stem from an external event that occurred to them (Johnson, Hashtroudi, & Lindsay, 1993; Johnson & Raye, 1981). Indeed the more often they think or talk about it, the more likely they are to believe that it is a genuine memory (Schacter, 1996). Researchers have also shown that leading questions and misleading information can cause people to confess to crimes they apparently didn't commit (Ofshe, 1992) and to report experiencing events that they only imagined (Ceci, Ross, & Toglia, 1987; Hyman & Pentland, 1996; Loftus, 1993).

People remember what they want to

There is another reason that people's recollections may differ from their original encoding of an episode. Recall is selective and goal driven. People don't necessarily retrieve everything they have stored; they recover details that suit their current purposes (e.g Anderson & Pichert, 1978; Ross & Buehler, 1994). To demonstrate the impact of motivation on reconstructive memory, researchers have altered people's beliefs about the desirability of specific behaviors and then assessed people's memories of their past actions (e.g. Klein & Kunda, 1993; McDonald & Hirt, 1997; Murray & Holmes, 1993; Ross, McFarland, & Fletcher, 1981; Sanitioso, Kunda, & Fong, 1990). Murray and Holmes asked undergraduates in dating relationships to report the amount of conflict they had with their partner while deciding on joint activities. Participants in the experimental condition then read a bogus psychological article that argued that the development of intimacy in a relationship depended on people's willingness to express disagreement. Thus, experimental participants who had earlier reported that they and their partner experienced little conflict now found out, much to their surprise, that this was actually bad news for their relationship. A control condition contained participants who had also reported low conflict with their partners, but who did not read the bogus article.

How did experimental participants cope with their new understanding that conflict was desirable? One thing they did was alter their views of their partner's past behaviors. When asked to assess their relationships on a number of dimensions, experimental participants were more likely than controls to endorse items such as "My partner clearly expresses his/her needs even when he/she knows that these needs conflict with my needs." In short, they "discovered" that their relationship was appropriately conflict-ridden. The precise mechanism underlying this finding is unclear. It seems likely, however, that participants selectively recalled and interpreted behaviors in accordance with their preferences.

There is a small research literature on memory for conflicts that provides intriguing evidence of the impact of motivation on recall. Baumeister and his colleagues (Baumeister, Stillwell, & Wotman, 1990; Baumeister, Wotman, & Stillwell, 1993; Stillwell & Baumeister, 1997) have studied how people who anger someone else (perpetrators) remember a dispute as compared to individuals who are provoked (victims). Provoking behavior is generally seen as less harmful and more justifiable by perpetrators than by victims. Along the same lines, young children recall disputes with their siblings in a manner that tends to absolve themselves of blame. They remember more harmful actions by their siblings than by themselves, as well as portray their own actions as justifiable, and their siblings' behavior as arbitrary and incomprehensible (Ross, Ross, Wilson, & Smith, in press). People seem to be more willing to accept responsibility for harmful actions in conflicts that happened a long time ago than in recent disputes (Wilson, Celnar, & Ross, 1997).

Recent studies of mood regulation provide further evidence of motivated remembering. Several theorists have suggested that individuals who are feeling blue may attempt to improve their moods by selectively retrieving pleasant memories (Clark & Isen, 1982; Isen, 1987; Singer & Salovey, 1988). In the first demonstration of this effect, Parrott & Sabini (1990) found that participants experiencing negative moods were more likely to recall pleasant events from their lives than were participants experiencing positive moods. Subsequent researchers suggested that certain personality traits may predispose individuals to alleviate negative affect by engaging in mood-incongruent recall (Boden & Baumeister, 1997; McFarland & Buehler, 1997; Smith & Petty, 1995). For example, McFarland and Buehler found that only individuals who are especially inclined to focus on their feelings recruited more pleasant memories after a negative mood induction than after a neutral mood induction.

In addition, the precise manner in which people focus on their moods moderates the impact of moods on memory (McFarland & Buehler, in press). When people adopt a reflective orientation to their moods (characterized by a willingness to attend openly to their feelings and an inclination to improve their feelings), they respond to negative moods by recalling pleasant past experiences. In contrast, when people assume a ruminative orientation to their moods (characterized by a sense that their feelings are threatening, confusing, and inescapable), they react to negative moods by remembering unpleasant past experiences.

When memories don't fit people's needs

The claim that recall is selective implies that people can retrieve memories that satisfy their current concerns. Sometimes, however, there is a mismatch between the information the person requires and the past that is represented in his or her memory. As a result, rememberers must reconstruct the past to suit their needs. One of us was recently invited to complete a survey on diet, life style, and health. The questions asked middle-aged respondents how many hours per week, on average, they spent on various activities in the past year (e.g. sitting, standing, or walking in the home), how frequently, on average, they consumed various beverages and foods (per day, per week, per month), and how often each year they engaged in recreational pursuits at different points in their life (e.g. swam at an outdoor pool, sunbathed, hiked, played baseball, soccer and football, or climbed a glacier between the ages 0–9, 10–19, 20–29, 30–39, 40–49, 50–59, 60+). Respondents were also asked to describe themselves now and in the past on specific dimensions (e.g. current weight and weight at 20 years of age).

One difficulty with many of these questions is that they cannot be answered simply by accessing relevant recollections. Few people have noted and stored in memory how many hours per week they sit at home, or how frequently they sunbathed per year between the ages of 20–29. Answers to such questions have to be constructed from memories (e.g. how many hours people remember sitting at home yesterday), arithmetic calculations (to derive averages), and people's intuitions about how they have changed or remained the same over time (e.g. how much weight have I gained since the age of 20?). Not surprisingly, perhaps, people's answers to such questions sometimes shift dramatically in response to changes in the framing of the items or response scales (Schwarz, Groves, & Schuman, 1998). When individuals make up answers on the spot, they tend to use whatever cues are available in a rather frantic attempt to respond to difficult queries.

We don't present this example as an indictment of surveys. Instead, we suggest that a disparity between current needs and stored information is a ubiquitous feature of everyday recall. Information is often not stored in a format that matches exactly what people need at the time of recall, as students writing examinations know only too well. Moreover the disparity may exist even when people pose questions to themselves. When individuals attempt to evaluate their friendliness or honesty, they may discover pertinent episodes stored in memory, but they will need to weigh, integrate, and interpret the information in a manner that allows them to answer the question at hand. How friendly am I if I am outgoing with my friends but shy and awkward with strangers? How honest am I if I return a wallet I find on the street to its rightful owner, but I cheat on my income tax? People's current goals and beliefs are likely to have a strong impact on the integration and interpretation process.

It has probably not escaped the reader's notice that there is a circularity to our description of the relation between recall and present beliefs. Just as people's current views are influenced by their memories, so too their prevailing beliefs affect their recollections. The process doesn't end here, however. When people revise the past on the basis of their current knowledge, their recollections can then serve the function of justifying and thereby strengthening their present beliefs. In a demonstration of the reciprocal relation between beliefs and recall, researchers first changed participants' attitudes using a persuasive communication (Ross, McFarland, Conway, & Zanna, 1983). Next, they prompted participants to recall behavior that was relevant or irrelevant to their new attitudes. Participants in the relevant-recall condition selectively recalled acting in a manner that was consistent with their new beliefs. Importantly, the recall of relevant behavior then served to bolster the new attitudes. Participants in the relevant-recall condition were more resistant to attacks on their new attitudes and more likely to state an intention to act on their new beliefs. These studies indicate that attitudes affect recall of past actions which, in turn, influences people's commitment to their attitudes.

Finally, note that people seem to underestimate the malleability of their own recollections and, as a result, have too much faith in the accuracy of their memories (e.g. Neisser & Harsch, 1992; Ross, 1997; Trope, 1978). Even when confronted with evidence that their own memory conflicts with someone else's, individuals tend to believe their own recollections (Ross, Buehler, & Karr, 1998). People appear to view themselves as relatively immune to the biases and errors in recall that afflict other individuals.

Constructing forecasts

In contrast to remembering, forecasting is obviously a creative act. People infer the future – it doesn't exist in the present. Forecasts are constructions based partly on imagination and partly on other relevant sources of information. For example, our expectations for how long it would take us to write this chapter reflected our beliefs about how busy we would be with work and family in the coming months, our memories of our earlier collaborative efforts, and our knowledge of the deadline for its submission.

That the future is clearly a construction does not mean that forecasters simply give their imagination free reign. Except in rare flights of runaway fantasy, people imagine futures that are consistent with their self-knowledge and theories about how the world works (Armor & Taylor, 1998; Johnson & Sherman, 1990). Having settled long ago into academic positions, the authors of this chapter are as unlikely to predict becoming starting pitchers for the New York Yankees as they are to recall having assumed this role in the past. Just as people construct pasts that are plausible to them in light of their current beliefs and theories, so too they imagine futures on the basis of their present knowledge (Johnson & Sherman, 1990; Loewenstein & Schkade, in press; Mead, 1934, 1964). As Loewenstein and Schkade observed, if beliefs and theories are important to remembering when people have past experiences to retrieve, then beliefs and theories likely play an even more important role in forecasting, especially of novel experiences.

People's depictions of the future often take the form of scenarios (Buehler, Griffin, & Ross, 1994; Dawes, 1988; Johnson & Sherman, 1990; Kahneman & Tversky, 1982a; Rehm & Gadenne, 1990; Zukier, 1986). Based on their beliefs about themselves and the circumstances they are likely to confront, people develop scenarios that describe, in a narrative representation, the progression of the present to the future. These scenarios frequently consist of concrete, causally linked sequences of events (e.g. I'll get to my office by nine a.m., work exclusively on the Gleber contract, and have it ready for signing by 12 noon). When people base predictions on such imagined scenarios do they appreciate the tentativeness of their forecasts, recognizing that the future could actually unfold in a variety of ways? Apparently not. People tend to construct a single, or very small number of scenarios, for any given judgment situation, and to assume the validity of their scenario representation (Griffin, Dunning, & Ross, 1990).

Memory researchers have shown that when people repeatedly imagine a past experience that did not occur, they become increasingly confident that it actually happened (Schacter, 1996). Along the same lines, when individuals imagine the occurrence of a future event, they become more convinced that it will come to pass (Johnson & Sherman, 1990; Koehler, 1991; Olson , Roese, & Zanna, 1996). Individuals instructed to imagine particular outcomes for events ranging from football games to presidential elections subsequently estimate those results as more likely (Carroll, 1978). People who are asked to explain why they might excel on upcoming tasks predict that they will perform better than do individuals who are asked to describe why they might fail (Campbell & Fairey, 1985; Sherman, Skov, Hervitz, & Stock, 1981). Apparently the construction of a scenario for a particular outcome focuses people's attention on that sequence of events and interferes with their ability to generate scenarios that would yield alternative outcomes (Hoch, 1984; Koehler, 1991).

As a result of this differential focus, the hypothesized scenario and outcome seem more probable.

Unfortunately, the hypothesized scenario is less likely to occur than people typically think (Kahneman & Tversky 1979, 1982b; Kahneman & Lovallo, 1993). Even when a particular scenario is relatively probable, the likelihood that a somewhat different sequence of events will occur is often greater. Consider a woman who plans to finish many complex projects on the weekend. Her careful detailed scenario for completing the projects may be more probable, in advance, than any other single scenario. Nevertheless, the chances of some event occurring that would prevent her from completing all of the projects may be greater, simply because of the vast number of potential impediments (power failures, illness, unexpected visits from friends, computer crashes, writing block, and so forth). Although each of these obstacles may have a relatively low likelihood of occurrence, the probabilities are additive; the likelihood that *some* unexpected event will arise is high.

In addition to promoting overconfidence, the scenario approach to prediction results in the neglect of other kinds of information that could help people to form more accurate forecasts. In discussing plan based predictions, Kahneman & Tversky (1979, 1982b) distinguished between two modes of judgment, which they labeled the inside and the outside views. The inside view corresponds to the focus on plan based scenarios that we have described: people derive their predictions from specific scenarios and impressions of the particular case at hand. The outside view treats the current case as an instance of a broader set of similar cases. For instance, people might base their forecasts of how long they will take to finish an upcoming project on a set of their own past experiences (personal base rates) or others' experiences (population base rates) with a set of similar projects. People could often make more realistic predictions if they adopted an outside view and considered relevant base rates (Dunning & Story, 1991; Osberg & Shrauger, 1986; Shrauger, Mariano, & Walter, 1998; Vallone, Griffin, Lin, & Ross, 1990).

The scenario approach to prediction tends to yield overly optimistic, as well as overly confident predictions. Theoretically, people could be too confident about either pessimistic or optimistic predictions, and scenario based thinking should not always produce optimistic forecasts. However, there is reason to suppose that people will typically construct scenarios that depict pleasant outcomes. When thinking about the future, people often focus on their goals (Karniol & Ross, 1996). They consider how events will transpire so as to produce their preferred outcomes. They often neglect to think about the possibility of setbacks or failures and how they might deal with such difficulties. As Armor & Taylor (1998) have noted, people rarely plan to fail. Thus scenario thinking is a cognitive mechanism that can help us to understand why people's forecasts often look suspiciously similar to their desires.

Finally, note that people do not always generate scenarios when contemplating their futures. The emphasis on scenarios may reflect the nature of events and plans that researchers have typically examined. Investigators have focused on the prediction and planning of single events that are relatively specific and discrete. In everyday life, people may sometimes contemplate their futures at a more general level. Rawls (1971) proposed that people develop an overarching life scheme that provides a framework for more specific and immediate plans. When people engage in life planning, they contemplate the possible purpose, content, and general course of their lives. Relative to everyday plans, life plans have a longer time frame, and involve goals that are more complex, abstract, vague, and open-ended (Smith, 1996). Whereas everyday plans are likely to include a scenario depicting a concrete sequence of decisions and actions, life plans are more likely to be at the level of a vague intention.

Predictions as wish fulfillment

Scenario thinking provides a cognitive explanation of optimistic forecasts. Motivation also plays an important role, in part by guiding the types of scenarios people generate. Across many domains, individuals' predictions of what will happen appear to reflect what they would like to see happen (Armor & Taylor, 1998; Kunda, 1990; Taylor & Brown, 1988). Lehman & Taylor (1988) studied California students who were assigned, on the basis of a lottery, to live in dormitories rated either seismically sound or unsound. When asked to predict the likelihood and severity of a future earthquake, students who were living in the unsafe dorms tended to downplay the threat.

People's rosy view of the future extends beyond their personal lives. Granberg & Brent (1983) examined data from national surveys conducted prior to eight US presidential elections and found that people tended to expect their preferred candidate to win by a ratio of about 4 : 1. Although very robust, this "preference–expectation link" was strongest in years in which the outcome was relatively unclear in advance, and among respondents who were highly involved but poorly informed. Analyses of panel data indicated that people's preferences were more stable than their expectations; they were more likely to bend their expectations to match their preferences than vice versa.

A more recent study examined the interplay between motivation and cognition in producing overly optimistic task completion estimates (Buehler, Griffin, & MacDonald, 1997). Individuals with incentives to finish tasks early showed more unrealistic optimism than those without such incentives. Canadians who expected an income tax refund predicted they would file their tax returns much earlier than those who did not expect a refund. In actual fact, the two groups mailed their forms at about the same time and later than either group predicted. A subsequent study identified mediating cognitive mechanisms by examining participants' thoughts as they generated task predictions. Monetary incentives for early completion led people to focus on plan based scenarios for the future and to ignore relevant past experiences. In other words, the motivation to finish early appeared to prompt the very pattern of cognitive processes that produces unrealistic optimism.

Imagined futures can be self-fulfilling

An additional consequence of scenario based predictions should tend to counteract unrealistic optimism: people's thoughts and forecasts sometimes influence what actually transpires. Asking people to imagine or predict specific future actions increases the likelihood of occurrence of the predicted actions (e.g. Greenwald, Carnot, Beach, & Young, 1987; Gregory, Cialdini, & Carpenter, 1982; Sherman, 1980; Sherman & Anderson, 1987). In an early demonstration of the self-fulfilling nature of predictions, Sherman (1980) asked one group of people whether they would agree to collect donations for the American Cancer Society if they were asked to do so; 48 percent said they would. By comparison, only 4 percent of a control group of respondents, who had not made predictions, agreed to help collect donations when asked to do so. As a result of making their predictions, however, the first group was much more helpful than controls: 31 percent of these participants agreed to collect donations when contacted several days later, thus bringing their behavior more in line with their forecasts.

Even in the absence of explicit predictions, the act of imagining future events may help to bring them about. Taylor & Schneider (1989) proposed that "mental simulations" of future episodes can facilitate goal achievement by increasing people's expectations of success, increasing their motivation, and suggesting concrete plans. Recent research suggests that mental simulations focused on precisely *how* the individual will attain the desired outcome, rather than on the outcome itself, can be particularly effective (Pham & Taylor, in press; Taylor, Pham, Rivkin, & Armor, 1998). For example, students who were instructed to simulate the process of studying for a midterm exam subsequently studied longer and received higher grades than students who did not mentally rehearse their exam preparation.

Similarly, Gollwitzer (1993, 1996) has argued that the process of forming clear, specific, future plans helps individuals to achieve their objectives. Gollwitzer notes that plans assist people to overcome problems with initiating and successfully executing goal-directed actions. Plans serve to connect an anticipated situational context (opportunity) with a specific, goal-directed behavior (action). Thus a man might plan: "As soon as my child falls asleep, I will go downstairs to my office, turn on the computer, and begin working on that Gleber contract." As a result of planning, people become more likely to detect the opportunities for achieving their goals (child is asleep) and to seize those opportunities when they arise (head straight to the office).

Mental simulations may be most effective if they lead people to vividly imagine the future. Memory researchers have shown that when people are asked to visualize past events that never happened, they are more likely to believe afterward that the episodes actually occurred (Hyman & Pentland, 1996; Johnson, Raye, Wang, & Taylor, 1979). For example, people who are asked to visualize childhood events that didn't occur are later more likely to report that these events transpired (Hyman & Pentland, 1996). By the same token, vividly imagining future events may increase people's belief in the occurrence of these episodes. Such increases in confidence may, in turn, prompt people to behave in ways that will cause the events to materialize.

The evidence that mental simulation and concrete planning can spur desired behavior might seem inconsistent with the finding that detailed, plan based future scenarios produce overly confident and optimistic forecasts. The answer is that scenario thinking and planning have dual effects, rendering predictions more optimistic and actions more likely to occur. Whether these mental processes produce overly optimistic forecasts depends on their relative impact on prediction and behavior. We suspect that mental simulations will often exert a stronger impact on people's predictions than on their behavior. Whether people's plans are self-fulfilling likely depends on such factors as the length of time between the plan and its execution (which may be associated with the probability that people's priorities will change) and the extent to which its implementation is affected by factors outside the control of the individual (e.g. Buehler & Griffin, 1996; Hoch, 1985; Wilson

& LaFleur, 1995). All too often, external events conspire to prevent even the best-intentioned and most committed individuals from fully accomplishing their objectives.

Improving predictions

Attempting to counteract overconfidence and unrealistic optimism, researchers have explored a number of possible interventions. One general approach, evident in the research just described, involves prompting people to bring their behavior in line with their forecasts. Where possible (such as when the events are relatively immediate and controllable) this may be the preferable approach (Armor & Taylor, 1998; Taylor, Pham, Rivkin, & Armor, 1998). An alternative tactic is to try to bring forecasts in line with likely behavior. In this regard, techniques based on prompting people to generate scenarios that differ from their initial scenario would appear promising (Dougherty, Gettys, & Thomas, 1997; Griffin, Dunning, & Ross, 1990; Hirt & Markman, 1995; Hoch, 1985). Such techniques directly target people's natural inclination to become committed to a single scenario for the future. Forecasters are not allowed to dwell exclusively on the scenarios they prefer or can readily generate.

In many business and organizational contexts, where uncertain and uncontrollable events present serious difficulties for long-term planning, techniques involving multiple scenarios have become popular forecasting tools (Bunn & Salo, 1993; Kuhn & Sniezek, 1996; Schnaars & Topol, 1987; Schoemaker, 1993). By the 1980s, more than half of the "Fortune 500" industrial companies were using such "scenario-analysis" techniques (Linneman & Klein, 1983). Despite the growing popularity of this approach in business contexts, the few relevant studies that evaluate its effects yield conflicting results.

Advocates of multiple scenario analysis claim that the approach prompts people to appreciate the unpredictability of the future, thus countering overconfidence in any one specific prediction and promoting contingency planning. Several studies indicate that asking people to contemplate more than one possible future outcome does serve to lower their confidence in the predictions they subsequently generate (Dougherty, Gettys, & Thomas, 1997; Griffin, Dunning, & Ross, 1990; Hoch, 1985; Schoemaker, 1993). Other researchers have found that considering alternative scenarios can actually increase people's confidence in an initially favored forecast (Kuhn & Sniezek, 1996; Schnaars & Topol, 1987). Rather than instilling a sense of cautious uncertainty, then, the alternative scenarios seemed to embolden forecasters. Researchers who found that alternative scenarios increase people's confidence in their forecasts presented scenarios to participants. In contrast, researchers who demonstrated a reduction of confidence required participants to generate their own scenarios. To be effective, alternative scenarios must seem credible to forecasters (Hirt & Markman, 1995; Kahneman & Tversky, 1982a). Conceivably, people find alternative scenarios that they generate themselves to be more plausible and relevant to their individual concerns than those provided by a researcher.

There is even less research assessing the impact of multiple scenario generation on accuracy than there is on confidence. Hoch (1985) reported that the generation of multiple scenarios increased the accuracy of predictions. In contrast, Wilson & LaFleur (1995) found that thinking about the reasons favoring and opposing one's predictions reduced the accuracy of forecasts. Finally, Schoemaker (1993) found no impact of multiple scenario generation on accuracy. At this point, there is little evidence that multiple scenario generation increases the accuracy of predictions.

Finally, people sometimes try to increase the accuracy of their forecasts by seeking advice from others, including experts and friends. Over the centuries, humans have consulted such "experts" as oracles, psychics, and, in more recent times, economists and financial consultants. In ancient Greece, the temple of Delphi was operated as a forecasting service (Makridakis, 1990). The oracles tended to offer equivocal predictions that were difficult to invalidate. In his history of the Ancient World recorded in the fifth century BC, Herodotus (1996) presented the tale of Croesus who asked the Delphi oracles whether he should attack the Persians. The oracles replied that if Croesus attacked the Persians, "he would destroy a mighty empire" (ibid., p. 23). So Croesus attacked the Persians and did destroy a great empire – his own. The Delphi oracles stayed in business for more than 500 years and became the wealthiest institution in Greece, even though the predictive power of their prophecies was low (Makridakis, 1990).

It is not clear that professionals in the forecasting business tend to perform much better today (Makridakis, 1990; Yates, 1990). For example, Makridakis reports that forecasts offered by financial experts are of little or no value. Statistical analyses reveal that, because changes in stock market prices are essentially random, forecasting future prices (either as a whole or for any individual stock) cannot be done any better by experts than by using "today's" closing price as the forecast. If stock market experts could forecast accurately, then professionally managed portfolios and mutual funds would outperform the market average. There is no strong indication that this is true. Although by chance some experts might outperform the market average for a certain period of time, there is little evidence that they can do so consistently.

In everyday life, people often consult family members or friends when pondering their personal futures. MacDonald & Ross (in press) compared students' predictions about the longevity of their own dating relationships, to predictions reported by their parents and roommates. The young lovers focused predominantly on the positive aspects of their relationships while generating their predictions and were too optimistic. Interestingly, the roommates and parents offered both less optimistic and more accurate predictions.

Observers are often less motivated than concerned individuals to focus on a biased subset of the available information. Thus, a knowledgeable, detached observer may be able to offer more realistic appraisals of your chances of sticking to a new diet or having your home renovations completed according to schedule. In contrast, observers who share your desires, may also share your overly optimistic views of the future. Buehler & Griffin (1998) found that when offered a cash incentive based on another person's achievements, observers' predictions for the performers were as optimistically biased as those of the performers themselves.

Optimism and temporal proximity of future events

People's pervasive optimism about the future declines as an event gets closer in time. For example, students anticipate a stronger performance on a midterm exam when asked on the first day of class than on the day of the examination itself (Gilovich, Kerr, & Medvec, 1993). One explanation of such effects is that different information becomes salient as the event approaches (for alternative interpretations see Gilovich, Kerr, & Medvec, 1993 and Savitsky, Medvec, Charlton, & Gilovich, 1998). Well before an exam, students may have exaggerated expectations about the amount of studying they will do. On the day of the examination, they know all too well how much they have studied. Along the same lines, Liberman & Trope (1998) noted that people's thoughts about events change as the events approach. They suggested that distant future events are assessed in terms of their desirability, whereas more immediate events are evaluated in terms of their feasibility. For example, when we contemplate a vacation six months from now, we think of "rest and relaxation"; when the same vacation is about to happen we focus on last-minute work arrangements, packing suitcases, and crowded airports. In their research, Liberman and Trope found that desirable events often appear better from a distant vantage point.

Sheppard, Ouellette, & Fernandez (1996) studied the impact of temporal proximity on people's expectations about test results. Students who were initially optimistic about their scores on an examination became overly pessimistic (relative to their actual performance) just before receiving their grades. Likewise, people undergoing tests for serious medical conditions, who are optimistic about their results weeks before they are known, abandon their optimistic outlook moments before learning the results (Taylor & Sheppard, 1998). Sheppard and his colleagues suggested that this shift from optimism to pessimism as feedback approaches is motivated, in part, by a desire to avoid feelings of disappointment. People lower their hopes to "brace themselves" for bad news.

This research on temporal proximity appears to indicate that people readily entertain quite different scenarios about the future. One day they anticipate glorious futures in which they achieve their desired goals; sometime later they are more pessimistic. These shifts reflect the changing information that is salient to people as they make their predictions and their shifting motivational concerns. We don't mean to imply, however, that people are quite willing to alter their predictions. As noted earlier, at any given point in time, individuals seem to be wedded to their current scenario of the future and assume that alternative scenarios are implausible.

Assessing the Accuracy of Forecasts

If people's long-term predictions tend to be as misguided as we imply, why do individuals continue to exhibit high confidence in their forecasting ability? One answer is that people process outcomes that confirm forecasts differently than those that disconfirm predictions. For example, even when an outcome is unambiguously different from the one they predicted, people may minimize the degree of their error. In one line of research (Gilovich, 1983; Gilovich & Douglas, 1986), gamblers who forecasted, and bet on, professional football games were later asked to think aloud about the outcomes of their bets. Individuals who made incorrect forecasts tended to convince themselves that they were almost right (and hence that their prediction was not really in error), whereas those who were correct were not inclined to consider that they were almost wrong. Tetlock (1998) obtained similar results in the realm of political prediction.

A second problem is that people do not precisely specify the evidence that will count as support for their predictions, and thus can end up "detecting" too much support (Gilovich, 1991). People's vaguely stated predictions can often be confirmed by various outcomes after the fact, many of which would not have been deemed acceptable criteria *a priori* (remember the Delphi oracles). This problem is exacerbated when the target of the prediction is inherently fuzzy or hard to define. Consider a worker who predicts that her newly appointed supervisor will create havoc. What exactly is havoc and how is it to be assessed? Because of the vagueness of the target outcome, this person may be overly impressed by any number of events with only tenuous connections to the prediction.

A third explanation for people's confidence in the accuracy of their predictions is that they misremember their forecasts. Once people know an outcome, they often claim to have predicted that very result, even though they didn't (Fischhoff, 1975; Fischhoff & Beyth, 1975). This hindsight bias may occur because individuals integrate the outcome information with their other relevant knowledge, creating a scenario in which the known outcome is the most plausible result (Fischhoff & Beyth, 1975). When a man's proposal of marriage is rejected, he may conclude: "Of course she'd say no. Why would a beautiful woman want to marry a loser like me?" When asked to retrieve an earlier prediction individuals are influenced by their current belief that the known outcome is highly likely. Having concluded that rejection was almost certain, our swain is likely to recall being more pessimistic than he actually was before he popped the question.

There may be another reason that this hindsight bias occurs. As noted earlier, individuals may generate not just one prediction, but a series of different predictions as an event approaches. Some days a lover might imagine that his proposal of marriage will be accepted and other days (probably closer in time to the proposal) that it will be rejected. The outcome that eventually occurs may then bring to mind whichever prediction matches it. When the lover then claims that he "knew" that he would be rejected, he is right – sort of. However, he also "knew" that the opposite outcome would happen.

Forecasting Future Feelings

Recently, researchers have begun to examine people's predictions of their future feelings. This area of research has important practical implications because people often base their decisions on how they think they will feel about different outcomes (Kahneman, 1994; Kahneman & Snell, 1992).

At a gross level, people are quite accurate in making such predictions. For example, most people probably think correctly that they would prefer a massage to an electric shock. People's predictions about the magnitude and duration of their emotional reactions to events are often wrong, however. In summarizing the rapidly growing literature on affective forecasting, Loewenstein & Schkade (in press) identified three separate, but interrelated, mechanisms that may produce errors in predicting feelings: people may hold incorrect implicit theories about the determinants of their feelings, they may focus on different considerations when predicting their reactions to events than when actually experiencing those events, and when in a "cold" state (e.g. when calm) they may have difficulty predicting how they will feel or behave in a "hot" state (e.g. when angry or sexually aroused).

First consider the problem of inaccurate intuitive theories. Gilbert, Pinel, Wilson, Blumberg, & Wheatley (1998) proposed that people underestimate their ability to cope with unpleasant events. In several studies, participants predicted they would be more devastated by such outcomes as a relationship break-up, a failed election bid by their favored candidate, negative test feedback, and the failure to obtain a job, than they in fact were. An anecdotal example may resonate with the reader. Think of someone who has endured a personal tragedy that you have not suffered yourself (e.g. loss of a spouse or a serious illness), and consider how well that person has coped with the problem. You may find yourself thinking that the person has managed surprisingly well, far better than you would under similar circumstances. We suggest that such feelings of surprise reflect the erroneous theories people have about human resilience. Individuals are able to transform, invent, and ignore information in ways that enable them to mitigate the impact of unpleasant events.

Lowenstein and Schkade discussed an additional obstacle to accurate affective forecasting. People may exaggerate the emotional impact of a future event because they focus on that event alone and fail to consider the effects of the many other factors that influence their well-being at any given time. Wilson (1997) termed this the "focalism" problem and described a study in which college students overestimated the emotional impact of an upcoming event, such as a win or loss by their school football team, unless they were prompted to consider the other events in their lives that would occur at that time.

A third source of prediction errors involves the "empathy gap" that exists between different hedonic states (Loewenstein, 1996; Loewenstein & Schkade, in press). People often have difficulty imagining how they will feel or behave when they encounter temptation, high arousal, or duress. Christensen-Szalanski (1984) found that a majority of expectant women who anticipated that they would not want to use anesthesia during childbirth, reversed their decision when they went into labor. Similarly, people with a full stomach may underestimate the difficulty of dieting when hungry; people who are not sexually aroused may underestimate their likelihood of failing to use condoms during intercourse; and people who are not in shopping malls may misjudge their urge to spend money when they get there.

Collective Remembering and Forecasting

Although we have portrayed remembering and forecasting as solitary acts, pasts and futures are shared as well as individual constructions. People's memories of their personal histories are affected by what others tell them about themselves. Thus, researchers studying people's earliest recollections cannot be certain whether individuals recall their own experiences or whether they inadvertently include information that other people have provided about an event (Ross, 1997; Usher & Neisser, 1993). Similarly, individuals' expectations for the future reflect information they obtain from their social environments.

Memories and futures are shared in other ways. People who work or live together often distribute information to be remembered among each other so that another person's mind can serve as an external memory repository (Hollingshead, 1998; Moreland, Argote, & Krishman, 1996; Wegner, 1987; Wegner, Erber, & Raymond, 1991). A married couple might distribute memory tasks as follows: "You remember the phone numbers of your family and I'll remember those of mine; you remember our doctor's appointments and I'll remember when the car needs an oil change; you remember the dates of our children's birthdays and I'll remember which baseball teams won the World Series over the last decade." Of course, memory tasks are typically not assigned as explicitly as these examples imply. The allocation often occurs naturally over time as a result of people's differing experiences, interests, and expertise. Dixon & Gould (1996) have proposed that cognitive collaboration increases with age, and may help older adults to compensate for age-related declines in individual memories.

Even more than remembering, planning for the future is likely to be a social rather than personal activity (Smith, 1996). In a social relationship, the plans and goals of one individual will greatly influence the plans and goals of others. Something as mundane as preparing a family meal often involves harmonization of the schedules and preferences of several people. Individuals may alter or delay their goals to satisfy those of significant others in their lives. In addition, individuals sometimes construct plans for others. For instance, parents and teachers design children's futures, and spouses choose meals or entertainment for each other. Often planning for another person involves trying to predict his or her likes and dislikes (e.g. regarding gifts, meals, and entertainment), a social form of affective forecasting that might be fraught with error.

Thus individuals can serve as external planners just as they serve as external memory reservoirs. Although psychologists have shown great interest in investigating people's forecasts, they have paid little attention to the social-interactive aspects of goal selection and planning, and to the fact that individuals typically synchronize their goals with the desires and plans of others. Such accommodations are likely to involve negotiation and compromise, to evoke happiness, disappointment, or anger, and to have long-term implications for individuals as well as their relationships. The study of the social aspects of goal setting would appear to be fertile ground for investigation.

Conclusions

Describing her vigil over her critically ill daughter, the novelist Isabel Allende (1995) wrote, "I am trampled by memories, all happening in one instant, as if my entire life were a single, unfathomable image. The child and girl I was, the woman I am, the old woman I shall be, are all water in the same rushing torrent. My memory is like a Mexican mural in which all times are simultaneous" (ibid., p. 23). The mind can serve as time machine (Tulving, 1983) that indeed renders all times simultaneous. However, the mind is an imperfect time machine. It transports people to the past, but individuals are unable to recapture completely their original experiences. It also transports individuals to the future, but the future that finally arrives may bear little resemblance to people's imaginings.

While traveling to the past, people sometimes rewrite history, altering details of previous episodes. Consequently, individuals need to be cautious about the judgments they form about themselves, other individuals, and social groups on the basis of evidence culled solely from memory. Mental time travel to the future has its own problems. Evolution has provided us with a brain that allows us to anticipate possible futures and thus to act to control our life course. That's the good news. The bad news is that people are often too optimistic and confident about their futures and fail to plan sufficiently for alternative possibilities. The bad news is tempered by the finding that predictions are sometimes self-fulfilling. When this is true, people are in a position to shape their own destinies. In every-day life, individuals sometimes specify the scope of their possibilities, as when they state that they can't imagine committing adultery or that they can imagine taking parachute lessons. Conceivably, a want of imagination can prevent people from striving for attainable objectives, but it might also keep them out of trouble. An implication of the research on the self-fulfilling nature of predictions is that people should be careful about what they wish for.

Like any voyage, mental time travel has both its risks and rewards. We have stressed the risks, in part because people are inclined to overlook them. Individuals tend to be too confident about the validity of both their memories and their forecasts. People need to remind themselves more often of two simple psychological principles. Memory is more malleable and the future is more uncertain than they typically imagine.

Note

1   The editor eventually rejected the manuscript.

References

Allende, I. (1995). *Paula*. New York: HarperCollins.

Anderson, R. C., & Pichert, J. W. (1978). Recall of previously unrecallable information following a shift in perspective. *Journal of Verbal Learning and Verbal Behavior, 17*, 1–12.

Armor, D. A., & Taylor, S. E. (1998). Situated optimism: Specific outcome expectancies and self-regulation. In M. P. Zanna (Ed.), *Advances in experimental social psychology*, Vol. 30 (pp. 309–379). New York: Academic Press.

Bahrick, H. P., Hall, L. K., & Berger, S. A. (1996). Accuracy and distortion in memory for high school grades. *Psychological Science, 7*, 265–271.

Bartlett, F. C. (1932). *Remembering: A study in experimental and social psychology.* Cambridge, UK: Cambridge University Press.

Baumeister, R. F., & Newman, L. S. (1994). How stories make sense of personal experiences: Motives that shape autobiographical narratives. *Personality and Social Psychology Bulletin, 20*, (6), 676–690.

Baumeister, R. F., Stillwell, A. M., & Wotman, S. R. (1990). Victim and perpetrator accounts of interpersonal conflict: Autobiographical narratives about anger. *Journal of Personality and Social Psychology, 59*, 994–1005.

Baumeister, R. F., Wotman, S. R., & Stillwell, A. M. (1993). Unrequited love: On heartbreak, anger, guilt, scriptlessness and humiliation. *Journal of Personality and Social Psychology, 64*, 377–394.

Boden, J. M., & Baumeister, R. F. (1997). Repressive coping: Distraction using pleasant thoughts and memories. *Journal of Personality and Social Psychology, 73*, 45–62.

Bransford, J. D., & Franks, J. J. (1971). The abstraction of linguistic ideas. *Cognitive Psychology, 2*, 331–350.

Brewer. W. F. (1988). Memory for randomly sampled autobiographical events. In U. Neisser & E. Winograd (Eds.), *Remembering reconsidered: Ecological and traditional approaches to the study of memory* (pp. 21–90). New York: Cambridge University Press.

Bruner, J. S., & Goodman, C. C. (1947). Value and need as organizing factors in perception. *Journal of Abnormal and Social Psychology, 42*, 33–44.

Buehler, R., & Griffin, D. (1996). Getting things done: The impact of predictions on task completion. Paper presented at the annual meeting of the American Psychological Association, Toronto, Canada.

Buehler, R., & Griffin, D. (1998). Motivated prediction for self and others. Unpublished manuscript, Wilfrid Laurier University.

Buehler, R., Griffin, D., & MacDonald, H. (1997). The role of motivated reasoning in optimistic time predictions. *Personality and Social Psychology Bulletin, 23*, 238–247.

Buehler, R., Griffin, D., & Ross, M. (1994). Exploring the "planning fallacy:" Why people underestimate their task completion times. *Journal of Personality and Social Psychology, 67*, 366–381.

Bunn, D. W., & Salo, A. A. (1993). Forecasting with scenarios. *European Journal of Operational Research, 68*, 291–303.

Campbell, J. D., & Fairey, P. J. (1985). Effects of self-esteem, hypothetical explanations, and verbalization of expectancies on future performance. *Journal of Personality and Social Psychology, 48*, 1097–1111.

Cantor, N., Markus, H. R., Niedenthal, P., & Nurius, P. (1986). On motivation and the self concept. In R. M. Sorrentino & E. T. Higgins (Eds.), *Handbook of motivation and cognition: Foundations of social behavior* (pp. 96–121). New York: Guilford Press.

Carlston, D. E., & Smith, E. R. (1996). Principles of mental representation. In E. T. Higgins & A. Kruglanski (Eds.), *Social psychology: Handbook of basic principles* (pp. 184–210). New York: Guilford Press.

Carroll, J. S. (1978). The effect of imagining an event on expectations for the event: An interpretation in terms of the availability heuristic. *Journal of Experimental Social Psychology, 14*, 88–96.

Ceci, S. J., Ross, D. F., & Toglia, M. P. (1987). Suggestibility of children's memory: Psycholegal implications. *Journal of Experimental Psychology: General, 116*, 38–49.

Christensen-Szalanski, J. J. (1984). Discount functions and the measurement of patients' values: Women's decisions during childbirth. *Medical Decision Making, 4*, 47–58.

Clark, M. S., & Isen, A. M. (1982). Toward understanding the relationship between feeling states and social behavior. In A. H. Hastorf & A. M. Isen (Eds.), *Cognitive social psychology* (pp. 73–108). New York: Elsevier/North Holland.

Conway, M., & Ross, M. (1984). Getting what you want by revising what you had. *Journal of Personality and Social Psychology, 47*, 738–748.

Davis, C. G., Lehman, D. R., Wortman, C. B., Silver, R. C., & Thompson, S. C. (1995). The undoing of traumatic life events. *Personality and Social Psychology Bulletin, 21*, 109–124.

Dawes, R. M. (1988). *Rational choice in an uncertain world.* Orlando, FL: Harcourt Brace Jovanovich.

Dixon, R. A., & Gould, O. N. (1996). Adults telling and retelling stories collaboratively. In P. B. Baltes & U. M. Staudinger (Eds.), *Interactive minds: Life-span perspectives on the social foundation of cognition* (pp. 221–241). New York: Cambridge University Press.

Dougherty, M. R. P., Gettys, C. F., & Thomas, R. P. (1997). The role of mental simulation in judgments of likelihood. *Organizational Behavior and Human Decision Processes, 70*, 135–148.

Dunning, D., & Story, A. L. (1991). Depression, realism, and the overconfidence effect: Are the sadder wiser when predicting future action and events? *Journal of Personality and Social Psychology, 61*, 521–532.

Dweck, C. S. (1975). The role of expectations and attributions in the alleviation of learned helplessness. *Journal of Personality and Social Psychology, 31*, 674–685.

Dweck, C. S. (1990). Self-theories and goals: Their role in motivation, personality, and development. In R. A. Dienstbier (Ed.), *Nebraska Symposium on Motivation: Perspectives on motivation,*

Vol. 38 (pp. 199–235). Lincoln: University of Nebraska Press.

Feldman Barrett, L. (1997). The relationship among momentary emotional experiences, personality descriptions, and retrospective ratings of emotion. *Personality and Social Psychology Bulletin, 23*, 1100–1110.

Fischhoff, B. (1975). Hindsight is not equal to foresight: The effects of outcome knowledge on judgment under uncertainty. *Journal of Experimental Psychology: Human Perception and Performance, 1*, 288–299.

Fischhoff, B., & Beyth, R. (1975). "I knew it would happen:" Remembered probabilities of once-future things. *Organizational Behavior and Human Performance, 13*, 1–16.

Frijda, N. H. (1986). *The emotions.* Cambridge: Cambridge University Press.

Gilbert, D. T., Pinel, E. J., Wilson, T. D., Blumberg, S. J., & Wheatley, T. A. (1998). Immune neglect: A source of durability bias in affective forecasting. *Journal of Personality and Social Psychology, 75*, 617–638.

Gilovich, T. (1983). Biased evaluation and persistence in gambling. *Journal of Personality and Social Psychology, 44*, 1110–1126.

Gilovich, T. (1991). *How we know what isn't so: The fallibility of reason in everyday life.* New York: Free Press.

Gilovich, T., & Douglas, C. (1986). Biased evaluations of randomly determined gambling outcomes. *Journal of Experimental Social Psychology, 22*, 228–241.

Gilovich, T., Kerr, M., & Medvec, V. H. (1993). Effect of temporal perspective on subjective confidence. *Journal of Personality and Social Psychology, 64*, 552–560.

Gollwitzer, P. M. (1993). Goal achievement: The role of intentions. In W. Stroebe & M. Hewstone (Eds.), *European review of psychology*, Vol. 4 (pp. 141–185). Chichester UK: Wiley.

Gollwitzer, P. M. (1996). The volitional benefits of planning. In P. M. Gollwitzer & J. A. Bargh (Eds.), *The psychology of action: Linking cognition and motivation to behavior* (pp. 287–312). New York: Guilford Press.

Gollwitzer, P. M., Heckhausen, H., & Steller, B. (1990). Deliberative and implemental mind-sets: Cognitive tuning toward congruous thoughts and information. *Journal of Personality and Social Psychology, 59*, 1119–1127.

Granberg, D., & Brent, E. (1983). When prophecy bends: The preference–expectation link in US presidential elections, 1952–1980. *Journal of Personality and Social Psychology, 45* (3), 477–491.

Greenwald, A. G. (1980). The totalitarian ego: Fabrication and revision of personal history. *American Psychologist, 35*, 603–618.

Greenwald, A. G., Carnot, C. G., Beach, R., & Young, B. (1987). Increasing voting behavior by asking people if they expect to vote. *Journal of Applied Psychology, 72*, 315–318.

Gregory, W. L., Cialdini, R. B., & Carpenter, K. M. (1982). Self-relevant scenarios as mediators of likelihood estimates and compliance: Does imagining make it so? *Journal of Personality and Social Psychology, 43*, 89–99.

Griffin, D. W., Dunning, D., & Ross, L. (1990). The role of construal processes in overconfident predictions about the self and others. *Journal of Personality and Social Psychology, 59*, 1128–1139.

Hastie, R. (1981). Schematic principles in human memory. In E. T. Higgins, C. P. Herman, & M. P. Zanna (Eds.), *Social cognition: The Ontario symposium*, Vol. 1 (pp. 39–88). Hillsdale, NJ: Erlbaum.

Herodotus (1996). *Histories.* Ware, UK: Wordsworth.

Hirt, E. R. (1990). Do I see only what I expect? Evidence for an expectancy-guided retrieval model. *Journal of Personality and Social Psychology, 58*, 937–951.

Hirt, E. R., & Markman, K. D. (1995). Multiple explanation: A consider-an-alternative strategy for debiasing judgments. *Journal of Personality and Social Psychology, 69*, 1069–1086.

Hoch, S. J. (1984). Availability and interference in predictive judgment. *Journal of Experimental Psychology: Learning, Memory, and Cognition, 10*, 649–662.

Hoch, S. J. (1985). Counterfactual reasoning and accuracy in predicting personal events. *Journal of Experimental Psychology: Learning, Memory, and Cognition, 11*, 719–731.

Hollingshead, A. B. (1998). Retrieval processes in transactive memory systems. *Journal of Personality and Social Psychology, 74*, 659–671.

Holman, E. A., & Cohen-Silver, R. (1998). Getting "stuck" in the past: Temporal orientation and coping with trauma. *Journal of Personality and Social Psychology, 74*, 1146–1163.

Hyman, I. E., Jr., & Pentland, J. (1996). The role of mental imagery in the creation of false childhood memories. *Journal of Memory and Language, 35*, 101–117.

Isen, A. M. (1987). Affect, cognition, and social behavior. In L. Berkowitz (Ed.), *Advances in experimental social psychology*, Vol. 20 (pp. 203–253). San Diego,CA: Academic Press.

Johnson, M. K., & Raye, C. L. (1981). Reality monitoring. *Psychological Review, 88*, 67–85.

Johnson, M. K., & Sherman, S. J. (1990). Constructing and reconstructing the past and the future in the present. In E. T. Higgins & R. M. Sorrentino (Eds.), *Handbook of motivation and social cognition: Foundations of social behavior*, Vol. 2 (pp.482–526). New York: Guilford Press.

Johnson, M. K., Hashtroudi, S., & Lindsay, D. S. (1993). Source monitoring. *Psychological Bulletin, 114*, 3–28.

Johnson, M. K., Raye, C. L., Wang, A. Y., & Taylor, T. H. (1979). Fact and fantasy: The roles of accuracy and variability in confusing imaginations with perceptual experiences. *Journal of Experimental Psychology: Human Learning and Memory, 5*, 229–240.

Kahneman, D. (1994). New challenges to the rationality assumption. *Journal of Institutional and Theoretical Economics, 150*, 18–36.

Kahneman, D., & Lovallo, D. (1993). Timid choices and bold forecasts: A cognitive perspective on risk taking. *Management Science, 39*, 17–31.

Kahneman, D., & Snell, J. (1992). Predicting a changing taste: Do people know what they will like? *Journal of Behavioral Decision Making, 5*, 187–200.

Kahneman, D., & Tversky, A. (1979). Intuitive prediction: Biases and corrective procedures. *TIMS Studies in Management Science, 12*, 313–327.

Kahneman, D., & Tversky, A. (1982a). The simulation heuristic. In D. Kahneman, P. Slovic, & A. Tversky (Eds.), *Judgment under uncertainty: Heuristics and biases* (pp. 201–208). Cambridge, UK: Cambridge University Press.

Kahneman, D., & Tversky, A. (1982b). Variants of uncertainty. *Cognition, 11*, 143–157.

Karniol, R., & Ross, M. (1996). The motivational impact of temporal focus: Thinking about the future and the past. *Annual Review of Psychology, 47*, 593–620.

Klein, W. M., & Kunda, Z. (1993). Maintaining self-serving social comparisons: Biased reconstruction of one's past behaviors. *Personality and Social Psychology Bulletin, 19*, 732–739.

Koehler, D. J. (1991). Explanation, imagination, and confidence in judgment. *Psychological Bulletin, 110*, 499–519.

Kruglanski, A. (1989). *Lay epistemics and human knowledge: Cognitive and motivational biases.* New York: Plenum.

Kuhn, K. M., & Sniezek, J. A. (1996). Confidence and uncertainty in judgmental forecasting: Differential effects of scenario presentation. *Journal of Behavioral Decision Making, 9*, 231–247.

Kunda, Z. (1990). The case for motivated reasoning. *Psychological Bulletin, 108*, 480–490.

Lehman, D. R., & Taylor, S. E. (1988). Date with an earthquake: Coping with a probable, unpredictable disaster. *Personality and Social Psychology Bulletin, 13*, 546–555.

Levi, A. S., & Pryor, J. B. (1987). Use of the availability heuristic in probability estimates of future events: The effects of imagining outcomes versus imagining reasons. *Organizational Behavior and Human Decision Processes, 40*, 219–234.

Levine, L. J. (1997). Reconstructing memory for emotion. *Journal of Experimental Psychology: General, 126*, 165–177.

Liberman, N., & Trope, Y. (1998). The role of feasibility and desirability considerations in near and distant future decisions: A test of temporal construal theory. *Journal of Personality and Social Psychology, 75*, 5–18.

Linneman, R. E., & Klein, H. E. (1983). The use of multiple scenarios by US industrial companies: A comparison study, 1977–1981. *Long Range Planning, 16*, 94–101.

Linton, M. (1982). Transformations of memory in everyday life. In U. Neisser (Ed.), *Memory observed* (pp. 77–91). San Francisco: Freeman.

Loewenstein, G. (1996). Out of control: Visceral influences on behavior. *Organizational Behavior and Human Decision Processes, 65*, 272–292.

Loewenstein, G., & Schkade, D. (in press). Wouldn't it be nice? Predicting future feelings. In E. Diener, N. Schwarz, & D. Kahneman (Eds.), *Foundations of hedonic psychology: Scientific perspectives on enjoyment and suffering.* New York: Russell Sage Foundation Press.

Loftus, E. F. (1993). The reality of repressed memories. *American Psychologist, 48,* 518–537.

Lyubomirsky, S., Caldwell, N. D., & Nolen-Hoeksema, S. (1998). Effects of ruminative and distracting responses to depressed mood on retrieval of autobiographical memories. *Journal of Personality and Social Psychology, 75,* 166–177.

McAdams, D. P. (1993). *The stories we live by: Personal myths and the making of the self.* New York: Morrow.

MacDonald, T. K., & Ross, M. (in press). Assessing the accuracy of prediction about dating relationship: How and why do lovers' predictions differ from those made by observers? *Journal of Personality and Social Psychology.*

McDonald, H. E., & Hirt, E. R. (1997). When expectancy meets desire: Motivational effects in reconstructive memory. *Journal of Personality and Social Psychology, 72,* 5–23.

McFarland, C., & Buehler, R. (1997). Negative affective states and the motivated retrieval of positive life events: The role of affect acknowledgment. *Journal of Personality and Social Psychology, 73,* 200–214.

McFarland, C., & Buehler, R. (in press). The impact of negative affect on autobiographical memory: The role of self-focused attention to moods. *Journal of Personality and Social Psychology.*

McFarland, C., & Ross, M. (1987). The relation between current impressions and memories of self and dating partners. *Personality and Social Psychology Bulletin, 13,* 228–238.

McFarland, C., Ross, M., & Giltrow, M. (1992). Biased recollections in older adults: The role of implicit theories of aging. *Journal of Personality and Social Psychology, 62,* 837–850.

Makridakis, S. G. (1990). *Forecasting, planning, and strategy for the 21st century.* New York: Free Press.

Markus, H. (1977). Self-schemata and processing information about the self. *Journal of Personality and Social Psychology, 35,* 63–78.

Markus, H., & Nurius, P. (1986). Possible selves. *American Psychologist, 41,* 954–969.

Markus, H., & Ruvolo, A. (1989). Possible selves: Personalized representations of goals. In L. A. Pervin (Ed.), *Goal concepts in personality and social psychology* (pp. 211–241). Hillsdale, NJ: Erlbaum.

Martin, M. (1990). On the induction of mood. *Clinical Psychology Review, 10,* 669–697.

Mead, G. H. (1934). *Mind, self and society.* Chicago: University of Chicago Press.

Mead, G. H. (1964). *Selected writings.* Ed. A. J. Reck. Chicago: University of Chicago Press.

Mischel, W. (1974). Processes in delay of gratification. In L. Berkowitz (Ed.), *Advances in experimental social psychology,* Vol. 7 (pp. 249–292). New York: Academic Press.

Mischel, W. (1996). Principles of self-regulation: The nature of willpower and self-control. In E. T. Higgins & A. Kruglanski (Eds.), *Social psychology: Handbook of basic principles* (pp. 329–360). New York: Guilford Press.

Moreland, R. L., Argote, L., & Krishman, R. (1996). Socially shared cognition at work: Transactive and group performance. In J. L. Nye & A. M. Brower (Eds.), *What's social about social cognition? Research on socially shared cognition in small groups* (pp. 57–84). London: Sage.

Murray, S. L., & Holmes, J. G. (1993). Seeing virtues in faults: Negativity and the transformation of interpersonal narrative in close relationships. *Journal of Personality and Social Psychology, 65,* 707–722.

Neisser, U. (1967). *Cognitive psychology.* New York: Appleton–Century–Crofts.

Neisser, U. (1981). John Dean's memory: A case study. *Cognition, 9,* 1–22.

Neisser, U., & Harsch, N. (1992). Phantom flashbulbs: False recollections of hearing the news about Challenger. In E. Winograd & U. Neisser (Eds.), *Affect and accuracy in recall: Studies of "flashbulb" memories* (pp. 9–31). New York: Cambridge University Press.

Nolen-Hoeksema, S., & Morrow, J. (1991). A prospective study of depression and posttraumatic stress symptoms after a natural disaster: The 1989 Loma Prieta earthquake. *Journal of Personality and Social Psychology, 61,* 115–121.

Ofshe, R. J. (1992). Inadvertent hypnosis during interrogation: False confession due to dissociative state; misidentified multiple personality, and the satanic cult hypothesis. *International Journal of*

Clinical and Experimental Hypnosis, 40, 125–156.

Olson, J. M., Roese, N. J., & Zanna, M. P. (1996). Expectancies. In E. T. Higgins & A. Kruglanski (Eds.), *Social psychology: Handbook of basic principles* (pp. 211–238). New York: Guilford Press.

Osberg, T. M., & Shrauger, J. S. (1986). Self-prediction: Exploring the parameters of accuracy. *Journal of Personality and Social Psychology, 51,* 1044–1057.

Parrott, W. G., & Sabini, J. (1990). Mood and memory under natural conditions: Evidence for mood incongruent recall. *Journal of Personality and Social Psychology, 59,* 321–336.

Pennebaker, J. W. (1990). *Opening up: The healing power of confiding in others.* New York: William Morrow.

Pham, L. B., & Taylor, S. E. (in press). From thought to action: Effects of process- versus outcome-based mental simulations on performance. *Personality and Social Psychology Bulletin.*

Platt, J. (1973). Social traps. *American Psychologist, 28,* 641–651.

Rawls, J. (1971). *A theory of justice.* Cambridge, UK: Cambridge University Press.

Rehm, J. T., & Gadenne, V. (1990). *Intuitive predictions and professional forecasts: Cognitive processes and social consequences.* Oxford, UK: Pergamon Press.

Ross, H., Ross, M., Wilson, A., & Smith, M. (in press). The dandelion war. In S. R. Goldman, A. C. Graesser, and P. Van den Broek (Eds.), *The Tom Trabasso Festschrift Volume.* Hillsdale, NJ: Erlbaum.

Ross, M. (1989). The relation of implicit theories to the construction of personal histories. *Psychological Review, 96,* 341–357.

Ross, M. (1997). Validating memories. In N. L. Stein, P. A. Ornstein, B. Tversky, & C. Brainerd (Eds.), *Memory for everyday and emotional events* (pp. 49–82). Hillsdale, NJ: Erlbaum.

Ross, M., & Buehler, R. (1994). Creative remembering. In U. Neisser & R. Fivush (Eds.), *The remembering self* (pp. 205–235). New York: Cambridge University Press.

Ross, M., & Conway, M. (1986). Remembering one's own past: The construction of personal histories. In R. M. Sorrentino & E. T. Higgins (Eds.), *Handbook of motivation and cognition: Foundations of social behavior,* Vol. 1 (pp. 122–144). New York: Guilford Press.

Ross, M., Buehler, R., & Karr, J. W. (1998). Assessing the accuracy of conflicting autobiographical memories. *Memory and Cognition, 26,* 1233–1244.

Ross, M., McFarland, C., & Fletcher, G. J. O. (1981). The effect of attitude on the recall of personal histories. *Journal of Personality and Social Psychology, 40,* 627–634.

Ross, M., McFarland, C., Conway, M., & Zanna, M. P. (1983). Reciprocal relation between attitudes and behavior recall: Committing people to newly formed attitudes. *Journal of Personality and Social Psychology, 45,* 257–267.

Rouhana, N. N., & Bar-Tal, D. (1998). Psychological dynamics of intractable ethnonational conflicts. *American Psychologist, 53,* 761–770.

Salovey, P. (1992). Mood-induced self-focused attention. *Journal of Personality and Social Psychology, 62,* 699–707.

Sanitioso, R., Kunda, Z., & Fong, G. T. (1990). Motivated recruitment of autobiographical memories. *Journal of Personality and Social Psychology, 59,* 229–241.

Savitsky, K., Medvec, V. H., Charlton, A. E., & Gilovich, T. (1998). "What, me worry?": Arousal, misattribution, and the effect of temporal distance on confidence. *Personality and Social Psychology Bulletin, 24,* 529–536.

Schacter, D. L. (1996). *Searching for memory.* New York: Basic Books.

Schnaars, S. P., & Topol, M. T. (1987). The use of multiple scenarios in sales forecasting: An empirical test. *International Journal of Forecasting, 3,* 405–419.

Schoemaker, P. J. H. (1993). Multiple scenario development: Its conceptual and behavioral foundation. *Strategic Management Journal, 14,* 193–213.

Schwarz, N., Groves, R. M., & Schuman, H. (1998). Survey methods. In D. T. Gilbert, S. T. Fiske, & G. Lindzey (Eds.), *The handbook of social psychology.* 4th. edn. Boston: McGraw-Hill.

Sedikides, C. (1992). Changes in the valence of the self as a function of mood. In M. S. Clark (Ed.), *Review of personality and social psychology,* Vol. 14 (pp. 271–311). Newbury Park, CA: Sage.

Shepperd, J. A., Ouellette, J. A., & Fernandez, J. K. (1996). Abandoning unrealistic optimism: Performance estimates and the temporal proximity of self-relevant feedback. *Journal of Personal-*

ity and Social Psychology, 70, 844–855.

Sherman, R. T., & Anderson, C. A. (1987). Decreasing premature termination from psychotherapy. *Journal of Social and Clinical Psychology, 5*, 298–312.

Sherman, S. J. (1980). On the self-erasing nature of errors of prediction. *Journal of Personality and Social Psychology, 39*, 211–221.

Sherman, S. J., Skov, R. B., Hervitz, E. F., & Stock, C. B. (1981). The effects of explaining hypothetical future events: From possibility to actuality and beyond. *Journal of Experimental Social Psychology, 17*, 142–158.

Showers, C. (1992). The motivational and emotional consequences of considering positive or negative possibilities for an upcoming event. *Journal of Personality and Social Psychology, 63*, 474–484.

Shrauger, J. S., Mariano, E., & Walter, T. J. (1998). Depressive symptoms and accuracy in the prediction of future events. *Personality and Social Psychology Bulletin, 24*, 880–892.

Singer, J. L., & Salovey, P. (1988). Mood and memory: Evaluating the network theory of affect. *Clinical Psychology Review, 8*, 211–251.

Singer, J. L., & Salovey, P. (1993). *The remembered self: Emotion and memory in personality.* New York: Free Press.

Smith, J. (1996). Planning about life: Toward a social-interactive perspective. In P. B. Baltes & U. M. Staudinger (Eds.), *Interactive minds: Life-span perspectives on the social foundation of cognition* (pp. 242–275). New York: Cambridge University Press.

Smith, S. M., & Petty, R. E. (1995). Personality moderators of mood congruency effects on cognition. *Journal of Personality and Social Psychology, 68*, 1092–1107.

Spence, D. P. (1982). *Narrative truth and historical truth: Meaning and interpretation in psychoanalysis.* New York: Norton.

Spiro, R. J. (1977). Remembering information from text: Theoretical and empirical issues concerning the "state of schema" reconstruction hypothesis. In R. C. Anderson, R. J. Spiro, & W. E. Montague (Eds.), *Schooling and the acquisition of knowledge* (pp. 137–165). Hillsdale, NJ: Erlbaum.

Stillwell, A. M., & Baumeister, R. F. (1997). The construction of victim and perpetrator memories: Accuracy and distortion in role-based accounts. *Personality and Social Psychology Bulletin, 23*, 1157–1172.

Strack, F., Schwarz, N., & Gschneidinger, E. (1985). Happiness and reminiscing: The role of time perspective, affect, and mode of thinking. *Journal of Personality and Social Psychology, 49*, 1460–1469.

Taylor, K. M., & Sheppard, J. A. (1998). Bracing for the worst: Severity, testing, and feedback timing as moderators of the optimistic bias. *Personality and Social Psychology Bulletin, 24*, 915–926.

Taylor, S. E., & Brown, J. D. (1988). Illusion and well-being: A social psychological perspective on mental health. *Psychological Bulletin, 103*, 193–210.

Taylor, S. E., & Crocker, J. (1981). Schematic biases of social information processing. In E. T. Higgins, C. P. Herman, & M. P. Zanna (Eds.), *Social cognition: The Ontario symposium*, Vol. 1 (pp. 89–134). Hillsdale, NJ: Erlbaum.

Taylor, S. E., & Schneider, S. K. (1989). Coping and the simulation of events. *Social Cognition, 7*, 174–194.

Taylor, S. E., Pham, L. B., Rivkin, I. D., & Armor, D. A. (1998). Harnessing the imagination: Mental simulation, self-regulation, and coping. *American Psychologist, 53*, 429–439.

Tetlock, P. E. (1998). Close-call counterfactuals and belief system defenses: I was not almost wrong but I was almost right. *Journal of Personality and Social Psychology, 75*, 639–652.

Trope, Y. (1978). Inferences of personal characteristics on the basis of information retrieved from one's memory. *Journal of Personality and Social Psychology, 36*, 93–106.

Tulving, E. (1983). *Elements of episodic memory.* Oxford, UK: Clarendon Press.

Usher, J. A., & Neisser, U. (1993). Childhood amnesia and the beginnings of memory for four early life events. *Journal of Experimental Psychology: General, 122*, 155–165.

Vallone, R., Griffin, D. W., Lin, S., & Ross, L. (1990). Overconfident prediction of future actions and outcomes by self and others. *Journal of Personality and Social Psychology, 58*, 582–592.

Vorauer, J., & Ross, M. (1993). Making mountains out of molehills: A diagnosticity bias in social perception. *Personality and Social Psychology Bulletin, 19*, 620–632.

Vorauer, J., & Ross, M. (1996). The pursuit of knowledge within close relationships: An informational goals analysis. In G. Fletcher and J. Fitness (Eds.), *Knowledge structures in close relationships: A social psychological approach* (pp. 369–398). Hillsdale, NJ: Erlbaum.

Watson, J., & McFarland, C. (1995). *The impact of recalling life events on mood: The role of current interpretation.* Paper presented at the meeting of the Canadian Psychological Association, Charlottetown, Prince Edward Island.

Wegner, D. M. (1987). Transactive memory: A contemporary analysis of the group mind. In B. Mullen & G. R. Goethals (Eds.), *Theories of group behavior* (pp. 185–208). New York: Springer-Verlag.

Wegner, D. M., Erber, R., & Raymond, P. (1991). Transactive memory in close relationships. *Journal of Personality and Social Psychology, 61*, 923–929.

Wilson, A. E., Celnar, C., & Ross, M. (1997). Siblings' self and other perceptions of past and present conflict. Poster presented at the annual meeting of the American Psychological Association, Chicago.

Wilson, T. D. (1997). Affective forecasting and the durability bias: The problem of focalism. In D. T. Gilbert (Chair), *Affective forecasting.* Symposium conducted at the annual meeting of the Society of Experimental Social Psychology, Toronto, Ontario, Canada.

Wilson, T. D., & LaFleur, S. J. (1995). Knowing what you'll do: Effects analyzing reasons on self-prediction. *Journal of Personality and Social Psychology, 68* (1), 21–35.

Wilson, T. D., & Linville, P. W. (1982). Improving the academic performance of college freshmen: Attribution theory revisited. *Journal of Personality and Social Psychology, 42*, 367–376.

Yates, J. F. (1990). *Judgment and decision making.* Englewood Cliffs, NJ: Prentice-Hall.

Zukier, H. (1986). The paradigmatic and narrative modes in goal-guided inference. In R. M. Sorrentino & E. T. Higgins (Eds.), *Handbook of motivation and cognition: Foundations of social behavior*, Vol. 1 (pp. 465–502). New York: Guilford Press.

PART IV

Applications

Chapter Twenty-Five

Psychology and Law

Günter Köhnken, Maria Fiedler, and Charlotte Möhlenbeck

Psychological research in legal contexts involves applying psychology's methodologies and knowledge to studying jurisprudence, substantive law, legal processes, and law breaking (Farrington, Hawkins, & Lloyd-Bostock, 1979). It is an area of applied research which refers to various fields of basic psychological research such as cognitive, developmental, personality, and social psychology. Furthermore, considerable overlaps exist to psychological assessment, clinical and organizational psychology.

The application of psychology to law has been differentiated into three areas (Kapardis, 1997): (1) psychology *in* law, (2) psychology *and* law, and (3) psychology *of* law. According to Blackburn (1996), "psychology in law" refers to specific applications of psychology within law (e.g. police psychology, psychology of eyewitness testimony). "Psychology and law" refers to psycholegal research into offenders, lawyers, judges, and jurors (e.g. jury decision making, offender treatment). "Psychology of law" covers areas of research like, for example, why people obey/disobey laws, the effects of laws, and the application of laws on people's behavior (e.g. therapeutic jurisprudence). The traditional term "forensic psychology" denotes the application of psychology in the courts.

Psycholegal research has a long tradition with an initial flourishing period at the beginning of the twentieth century (see, for example, Marbe, 1913; Münsterberg, 1908; Stern, 1903). Following a less active period, psycholegal research has grown enormously during the last three decades. Evidence for this revival is found in the publication of more and more books on various aspects of psychology and law (e.g. Bull & Carson, 1995; Kapardis, 1997; Kaplan, 1986; Ross, Read, & Toglia, 1994; Sporer, Malpass, & Köhnken, 1996), the establishment of journals (e.g. *Law and Human Behavior*; *Behavioral Sciences and the Law*; *Law and Psychology Review*; *Legal and Criminological Psychology, Public Policy, Psychology, and Law*), the constitution of national and international professional organizations, the growing number of national and international conferences and symposia, and the strong increase in empirical publications during the past twenty years.

The results of psychological research are applied to legal practice in various ways and at a number of levels within the criminal and civil justice system. For example, in the investigation of crime the police may use techniques of offender profiling to draw conclusions about the life style, criminal history, and residential location of a person who has committed a number of crimes (e.g. Canter, 1994; Jackson & Bekerian, 1997). Witnesses are interviewed using interview techniques which are based on research on memory and communication (Fisher & Geiselman, 1992). Lineup identifications are constructed according to guidelines which are derived from psychological research (e.g. Sporer, et al., 1995). At trial, attorneys may rely on advice and empirical analysis of social scientists when selecting juries (Ellsworth & Reifman, in press; Hans & Vidmar, 1982). Courts employ psychologists as expert witnesses to assist in evaluating witness statements. Finally, if a defendant is convicted he or she may be subject to correctional treatment that is derived from research on behavior modification and psychotherapy (McGuire, 1995).

It would be impossible to cover all areas of psycholegal research in this chapter. The discussion will therefore focus on psychological research in the area of criminal law. The vast majority of research has focused on various levels of the criminal justice system, whereas civil proceedings have received considerably less attention. This chapter will address topics from each of the three areas of psycholegal research as mentioned above: police psychology, including eyewitness identification and interviewing witnesses as an example of "psychology in law," jury decision making as an example of "psychology and law," and therapeutic jurisprudence as an example of "psychology of law."

Psychology and Policing

Psychology and policing has become a remarkably diverse field of applied psychology and covers almost all major areas of psychology (e.g. organizational psychology, personnel selection, clinical psychology and counseling, psychological assessment, social and personality psychology). Most of these topics are discussed in other chapters of this handbook and are therefore not covered here.

Direct operational assistance

Apart from an indirect impact of psychology on the police mission by optimizing personal skills and situational variables, psychology can directly support criminal investigations by providing empirically based guidelines for such things as conducting interviews or preparing eyewitness identification procedures.

Interviewing witnesses   Kebbell & Milne (1998) report that police officers are of the opinion that witnesses usually provide the central leads in criminal investigations. A report by the Rand Corporation (1975) also noted that a major factor that determines whether or not a crime is solved is the completeness and accuracy of the witness account. Indeed law enforcement personnel were found to spend as much as 85 percent of their total working time talking to people. Thus, a critical component of effective law enforcement is the ability of police officers to obtain accurate and detailed information from witnesses. However, police officers have also reported that witnesses rarely provided as much information as the officers required for an investigation (Kebbell & Milne, 1998).

One approach to increase the information a witness provides is forensic hypnosis. However, the empirical evidence for the memory enhancing potential of hypnosis is equivocal. Whereas some anecdotal reports claim that hypnosis may enhance memory in criminal cases (Reiser, 1980), controlled laboratory studies have produced mixed results (Smith, 1983; Wagstaff, 1984).

A less controversial technique for improving memory retrieval is the Cognitive Interview which was developed by Geiselman and Fisher (Geiselman, Fisher, Firstenberg, Hutton, Avetissian, & Prosk, 1984). In its original form it comprises four basic retrieval aids or mnemonic strategies together with some ways of helping witnesses to recall specific bits of information. First, interviewees are instructed to mentally reconstruct the context of the witnessed event, to form an image or an impression of the environmental aspects of the scene, and to remember their emotional feelings and thoughts. The second strategy is to encourage witnesses to report everything they remember, even if they think the details are not important. The third component is to ask witnesses to recall the event in a variety of temporal orders or to make retrieval attempts from different starting points, for example, from the most memorable element. Finally, witnesses are encouraged to recall the event from different physical locations, just as if they were viewing it with another person's eyes.

Fisher and Geiselman later refined the technique considerably, particularly by addressing the social dynamics and communication between the interviewer and the eyewitness (e.g. interview structure, rapport building, using non-verbal responses, witness-compatible questioning), and called this refined version the Enhanced Cognitive Interview (Fisher, Geiselman, Raymond, Jurkevich, & Warhaftig, 1987; for recent overviews see Fisher & Geiselman, 1992; Fisher, McCauley, & Geiselman, 1994).

During recent years the effectiveness of the Cognitive Interview has been evaluated in more than fifty experiments. In a series of experiments conducted by Geiselman and Fisher, the original version of the cognitive interview generated about 25–30 percent more correct information without increasing the number of false details. The cognitive interview enhanced memory in written reports as well as in oral interviews. Furthermore, the effect has been demonstrated with a variety of interviewees, including, for example, adults, children, and people with learning disabilities. It has also been shown that the cognitive interview may decrease the effect of misleading post-event information (Milne, Bull, Köhnken, & Memon, 1995).

A recent meta-analysis (Köhnken, Milne, Memon, & Bull, 1999) including 55 experiments with nearly 2,500 participants obtained a significant overall effect size $d = 0.87$ for the difference in correct information between cognitive and conventional or standard interviews. The overall difference for the amount of incorrect information, although considerably smaller, was also significant ($d = 0.28$). However, the average accuracy rate (i.e. the proportion of correct details relative to the total number of recalled details) was similar in both types of interview (85 percent for the cognitive interview compared to 82 percent for the standard interview). Thus, the Cognitive Interview generates more information than a standard police interview and this larger amount of information is no less accurate.

Eyewitness identification   Whereas courts and juries often view the identification of a defendant by an eyewitness as a particularly convincing piece of evidence, analyses of proven wrongful convictions have consistently shown that mistaken eyewitness identification is responsible for more miscarriages of justice than all other potential causes combined (Rattner, 1988). In a survey of 205 cases of wrongful convictions mistaken identification was found to be involved in 52 percent (Rattner, 1988). The most disturbing evidence for wrongful identifications as a major cause of miscarriages of justice comes from the use of DNA analysis. The re-evaluation of cases where people had been convicted and where DNA material had been preserved revealed 40 cases of wrongful convictions. Of these 40 cases, 36 (or 90 percent) involved eyewitness identification evidence in which one or more witnesses falsely identified the defendant (Wells, Small, Penrod, Malpass, Fulero, & Brimacombe, 1998).

Why do false identifications occur? On the one hand, witnesses may have had a poor view of the criminal; a long delay between the encounter and the recognition test may have weakened the memory representation of the culprit, or post-event information (e.g. a photo of an innocent suspect) may have contaminated the witnesses' memory. These and similar factors have in common that their likely effects on identification accuracy in a given case can only be post-dicted or estimated. Wells (1978) has labeled these variables *estimator variables*. On the other hand, the police may conduct the recognition test in a way that is biased towards the suspect (e.g. because he is the only blond person among a group of dark haired foils) or the witness may have observed the suspect being escorted by police officers. These factors are called *system variables* because they are under the control of the criminal justice system.

Estimator variables   Shapiro & Penrod (1986) conducted a meta-analysis in order to assess the effects of various estimator variables on identification accuracy. This meta-analysis included 128 experiments with 960 experimental conditions, almost 17,000 subjects, and more than 700,000 separate recognition judgments.

The results of the meta-analysis suggest that stable characteristics of eyewitnesses such as intelligence, gender, and personality traits (e.g. self-monitoring) are only weakly, if at all, related to identification accuracy. In particular, self-reported facial recognition skill is not reliably associated with actual performance. In a series of studies, Malpass, Parada, Corey, Chavez, Bowles, & McQuiston (1999) found very little consistency across two recognition tests. Shapiro & Penrod (1986) report that children and the elderly tend to perform more poorly in face recognition tasks than other adults. However, a more recent meta-analysis conducted by Pozzulo & Lindsay (1999) found that correct identification rates for children over the age of five were comparable to the performance level of adults. Four-year-old preschoolers, however, were less likely than adults and older children to make a correct identification when presented with a target-present lineup. In contrast, the adult rate of correct rejections in target-absent lineups was not reached by even the eldest children included in the analysis (aged 12–13 years).

The most important variable of the stable target characteristics seems to be facial distinctiveness. Faces that are highly attractive or highly unattractive are substantially better recognized than nondistinct faces. Whereas neither the race of the perpetrator nor the race of the witness alone are strongly associated with recognition performance these variables interact such that cross-race identifications are less accurate than own-race identifications (Chance & Goldstein, 1996). Malleable target characteristics are important predictors of identification accuracy. In particular, if the perpetrator wore a disguise or changed facial appearance between initial exposure and recognition test the identification accuracy is significantly reduced.

The majority of experiments on estimator variables has looked at the effects of environmental conditions at the time of the crime. In general, these situational factors were found to be important predictors of identification accuracy. For example, recognition performance is reduced for less salient targets, if the exposure duration is short, if the crime is less serious, if a weapon was present during the crime, and if the witness was intoxicated. The effects of stress and arousal are less clear due to ethical restrictions in the manipulation of high levels of arousal. However, there appears to be a tendency for extreme stress to reduce identification accuracy.

With regard to post-event factors Shapiro & Penrod (1986) found that face recognition accuracy shows a linear decline with retention interval. Interestingly, time delay has a smaller impact on the number of false identifications than it has on the proportion of correct recognitions.

System variables   Factors that are under the control of the criminal justice system are called system variables (Wells, 1978). With regard to recognition tests (lineups or photo arrays) false identifications can have two causes. First, random error can occur. In this case, the witness chooses the suspect purely by chance. Any other member of the lineup was just as likely to be selected as the alleged offender. Second, a false identification may result from systematic error. A systematic error occurs when certain properties of the lineup procedure or the composition of the lineup leads the witness to choose the suspect even if he or she is not the criminal.

Random errors   Witnesses may want to present themselves as "good" and constructive persons who can help the police catch the offender and thereby solve the crime. Further, witnesses tend to see the whole lineup procedure as a technique to convict an already sufficiently well-known criminal (e.g. Malpass & Devine, 1984). In the erroneous belief that the police are best served by a positive identification of one of the individuals in the lineup, they may choose the individual who most resembles the fuzzy picture of the offender in their memory. As long as no systematic errors are made that would direct the witnesses' choice to a specific individual the selection is likely to be more or less random. Under these circumstances the likelihood that an innocent suspect is selected is inversely related to the number of foils in the lineup or the photo array (Köhnken, Malpass, & Wogalter, 1996; Wells & Turtle, 1986). Consequently, the larger the pool of foils from which the suspect is chosen the more informative is the identification.

Systematic errors   A lineup is conducted in order to test the hypotheses that (a) the suspect is the guilty party, and (b) the suspect is not the criminal (null hypothesis). The lineup recognition test thus resembles an experiment and the general methodological principles for experimental research and hypothesis testing apply (Wells & Luus, 1990). From this point of view two types of systematic errors can be distinguished (Köhnken, Malpass, &

Wogalter, 1996; Malpass & Devine, 1983): (1) The composition of the lineup or the arrangement of the photographs can lead to the suspect standing out from the other individuals. Malpass & Devine (1983) referred to this as a *structural error*. (2) Errors can occur during the procedure of the recognition test that would lead the witness to select the suspect. This type of error is referred to as a *procedural error*.

Structural errors   Several experiments have demonstrated that unfair lineups where the suspects stands out from the foils can dramatically increase the risk of false identifications. For example, Lindsay & Wells (1980) found that an uninvolved person who was noticeably different from the other foils in a photo array was incorrectly identified by 70 percent of the subjects. It is therefore essential to select foils who are sufficiently similar to the suspect. This can be achieved by using a combination of "objective" and "subjective" selection procedures (Köhnken, Malpass, & Wogalter, 1996). In the objective selection procedure, selection of alternatives is determined by the presence of a few objectively important personal characteristics (e.g. size, weight, age, facial hair, race). However, the selection of alternatives on the basis of objective physical characteristics does not always ensure the formation of a fair group for the lineup. Often, when comparing his or her memory of the culprit to the individuals in the lineup, the witness is guided by highly subjective impressions. These non-objective impressions noted by the witness should also be taken into account in selecting the foils (Luus & Wells, 1991).

Procedural errors   Procedural errors are present when peculiarities during the preparation and execution of a lineup cause the witnesses to draw their attention to the police suspect. Such errors may, for example, result from repeated recognition tests. Sometimes the police request a witness to do a mug shot search. If a person is recognized on one of the mug shots he or she is arrested and a lineup identification may be staged by the police. However, several experiments have shown that witnesses tend to repeat their first decision in later lineups even if they are false (Brigham & Cairns, 1988).

Whereas these and some other potential sources of procedural errors are fairly obvious, false identifications may also result from more subtle, maybe even unintended manipulations like systematic changes in the nonverbal behavior of a police officer (e.g. Smith, Pleban, & Shaffer, 1982). In order to avoid such biases it has been suggested that a recognition test be conducted by a police officer who was not involved in the investigation and who has no knowledge as to who the suspect is (Köhnken, Malpass, & Wogalter, 1996; Wells, et al., 1998).

Evaluating Witness Statements: Assessment and Attribution of Credibility

Witness statements, whether they be descriptions of events or person identifications, can rarely be taken at face value. Numerous factors have been found to be able to cause discrepancies between statements and the actual facts. These factors can be separated into two different classes. On the one hand, witnesses, although trying to give a correct and complete report of an event or an accurate description of a person, may be subject to unintended errors and distortions, caused for example by forgetting, suboptimal perception conditions, misleading post-event information, etc. The term *accuracy* describes the extent to which statements are free from this kind of unintended error. On the other hand, a statement may deviate from reality because the witness deliberately tries to deceive the police or the court. Intentional deceptions or lies affect the truthfulness or credibility of a statement. Thus, in forensic psychology the term *credibility* describes the witness's motivation to give a truthful account of his or her experiences.

Deception is a communication phenomenon that involves at least two individuals: a communicator (or witness in the present context) and a recipient (e.g. a detective, a judge, or a juror). Consequently, research can focus on each of the two participants of an interaction. With regard to the communicator (or witness) it can be examined whether or not there are any behaviors that are systematically associated with the deceptiveness of a statement. Such behaviors have been called *correlates of deception* (Zuckerman, DePaulo, & Rosenthal, 1981), *authentic cues of deception* (Fiedler & Walka, 1993), or *objective indicators of deception* (Vrij, 1998). From a different point of view, a set of content characteristics has been proposed as being indicative for the truthfulness of a statement. These are called *reality criteria* (Steller & Köhnken, 1989).

Assessment of credibility

Objective indicators of truth and deception have been examined in four behavioral areas: (1) the content of the statement (e.g. amount and type of detail, logical consistency; see Steller & Köhnken, 1989); (2) the way the statement is verbally presented, i.e. speech behavior (e.g. speech rate, speech disturbances) and stylostatistic characteristics (e.g. word frequency statistics; see Morton & Farrindgon, 1992; Köhnken, 1985); (3) the accompanying nonverbal behavior of the witness (e.g. arm movements, facial expression; see Zuckerman, DePaulo, & Rosenthal, 1981); and (4) psychophysiological phenomena (e.g. electrodermal responses, heart rate, blood pressure; see Raskin, 1989).

Research on nonverbal and speech behavior suggests that some observable behaviors are indeed associated with deception. Several meta-analyses (Zuckerman, DePaulo, & Rosenthal, 1981; DePaulo, Stone, & Lassiter, 1985) have shown that of 24 different verbal, nonverbal, and speech behaviors, 14 are significantly related to deception. There appears to be a tendency for highly motivated compared to less motivated liars to decrease the frequency of a number of nonverbal behaviors (Vrij, 1998). In the area of speech behavior liars engage in more and/or longer speech hesitations, produce more speech errors (e.g. stutter, repetition) and grammatical errors, and show longer response latencies. However, the association of these behaviors with deception, although statistically significant, is rather weak.

Burgoon & Buller (1994) have proposed an "Interpersonal Deception Theory." They are critical of most investigations of deception for having used a unidirectional view, such that a liar actively transmits signals which a receiver passively absorbs. However, this paradigm lacks the process of interpersonal communication that involves feedback and mutual influence. In an ongoing conversation the character of deceit may change when deceivers continually monitor their own performance while adapting to the receiver's feedback. As a consequence, behavioral patterns evidenced at the outset of an exchange may differ radically from those manifested later (Buller & Aune, 1987). According to this position, averaging behavior frequencies across a lengthy interaction may produce weak effects, although clues to deception may indeed exist.

A very different approach to the assessment of the credibility of a statement has been developed in literature research and in psycholinguistics. In order to assign pieces of literature of unknown authorship to a certain author, the style of the disputed document was analyzed according to various statistical parameters (hence the term "stylostatistics") which are then compared with the respective data derived from an undisputed text. Such parameters are, for example, the number of words per sentence, the number of different words relative to the total number of words in a text body, the average word length, the proportion of verbs to adjectives, and the proportion of grammar (like prepositions, articles, etc.) as an indicator of the grammatical complexity of a sentence. Köhnken (1985) found that some of these stylostatistic parameters did reliably discriminate between truthful and fabricated statements.

An alternative way to assess the truthfulness of a statement was developed in German forensic psychology by Undeutsch (1967) and Arntzen (1983). Based on their work, Steller & Köhnken (1989) have compiled a list of criteria and described a procedure for evaluating the veracity of a statement which led to the development of Statement Validity Assessment (SVA) as a comprehensive method for evaluating witness statements. In contrast to research on nonverbal detection of deception, this approach focuses on the content of a statement rather than on the witness's nonverbal and speech behavior. Furthermore, SVA is not a "verbal lie detector." Instead of searching for "lie symptoms" it focuses on specific content characteristics which, if present in a statement, support the hypothesis that the account is based on genuine personal experience.

SVA consists of three major components. The first component is an open-ended investigative interview. The second component of SVA is a criteria-based content analysis (CBCA). In this phase the transcript of the statement is analyzed with regard to certain content characteristics (the reality criteria) like, for example, quantity of detail or the description of unexpected complications during the incident (Steller & Köhnken, 1989). Third, all obtained case information including the witness's cognitive and verbal abilities and information about the origin of the statement is integrated into a final judgment as to whether or not the statement is likely to be an account of what actually happened.

CBCA is based on the hypothesis – originally stated by Undeutsch (1967) – that truthful and fabricated statements differ in content and quality. This basic hypothesis comprises two components, one cognitive and the other motivational. The latter can be related to impression management theory (Tedeschi & Norman, 1985). The cognitive part of the hypothesis states that, given a certain level of cognitive and verbal abilities, only a person who has actually experienced an event will be able to produce a statement with the characteristics that are described in the CBCA criteria. The impression management component relates to motivation and social behavior. It is assumed that lying is a goal directed behavior and that a person who deliberately invents a story wants to be perceived as honest in order to achieve his or her goals. Therefore, the person is likely to avoid behaviors which, in his or her view, may be interpreted as clues to deception. For instance, if a liar believes that admitting lack of memory will undermine his or her perceived credibility, he or she will try to avoid such behavior. This impression management approach assumes that people have a common stereotype about the typical behavior accompanying a lie. Provided that a particular behavior can be sufficiently controlled it is expected that a liar, in order to conceal his or her lie, attempts to avoid such behavior.

Several studies have demonstrated that SVA can be a useful tool in distinguishing truthful from fabricated accounts. Using children of various age groups or adolescents, Esplin, Boychuk, & Raskin (1988), Joffe & Yuille (1992), Köhnken & Wegener (1982), Steller, Wellershaus, & Wolf (1992), and Yuille (1988) found significant differences either in at least some of the CBCA criteria or hit rates that were significantly better than chance level if the decisions had been based on CBCA. Other studies have also demonstrated that CBCA may reliably discriminate between truthful and fabricated adults' accounts (Köhnken, Schimossek, Aschermann, & Höfer, 1995; Porter & Yuille, 1996).

Alonso-Quecuty (1992), Höfer, Akehurst, & Metzger (1996), Sporer (1996), and Porter & Yuille (1995) have suggested supplementing the CBCA criteria with reality monitoring criteria (Johnson & Raye, 1981). Two studies that have combined these approaches have produced mixed results. Whereas Sporer (1996) reports beneficial effects of the additional reality monitoring criteria, Höfer, Akehurst, & Metzger (1996) found no differences.

Surprisingly little controlled research has been published regarding the inter-rater agreement in coding of the CBCA criteria, although reliability of coding is an essential requirement. Some studies report rather low agreement among raters (Anson, Golding, & Gully, 1993; Ruby & Brigham, 1997). However, a recently reported series of experiments (Köhnken & Höfer, 1998) suggests that these results may be due to insufficient training of the coders. These studies show that after a three week training program inter-rater agreement as well as re-test reliabilities are in a range which is deemed sufficient for personality questionnaires.

Attribution of credibility

Research on the attribution of credibility has examined how successful people are in discriminating truthful and deceptive statements, which behavioral cues they utilize for their judgments, and how access to different communication channels influences their attributions.

The results of several meta-analyses of more than fifty experimental studies provide a rather disillusioning picture. In these experiments the hit rates (i.e. the proportion of correct judgments) generally falls into a range between 45 percent and 60 percent, where 50 percent correct decisions can be expected by chance alone. The mean detection accuracy across all studies is only slightly (although significantly) better than the 50 percent chance level (DePaulo, Stone, & Lassiter, 1985; Zuckerman, DePaulo, & Rosenthal, 1981).

Interestingly, people with experience in credibility judgments (e.g. police and customs officers) achieve no better results than inexperienced subjects (DePaulo & Pfeifer, 1986; Vrij & Winkel, 1994). Experienced subjects are, however, more confident in the correctness of their judgments than lay people. Apparently the mere frequency of credibility judgments does not help to improve judgment accuracy because subjects don't receive any detailed feedback (DePaulo & Pfeifer, 1986; Fiedler & Walka, 1993; Vrij, 1994).

Legal Decision Making

Psychological research on courtroom proceedings differs from the other areas of research outlined in this chapter in one important respect. Whereas, for example, psychological aspects of eyewitness testimony or correctional treatment are relevant regardless of the specifics of national law, courtroom proceedings differ in various countries. Within the *adversarial system* of justice, which is by and large characteristic of English-speaking countries, the proceedings are structured as a dispute between two sides (Damaska, 1973). The role of the judge is kept to a minimum and can best be described as that of a referee. The evidence is presented by the prosecution and the defense. Although the jury trial is not an essential element of adversarial procedure, it is found most regularly within Anglo-Saxon countries (McEwan, 1995). An adversary process is marked by a clear distinction between matters of fact and matters of law. Matters of fact are for the lay-persons (the jury), whereas matters of law are for the judge (Sealy, 1989). In contrast, in *inquisitorial systems,* which are roughly descriptive for continental Europe, judges have a considerably more active role. They play a major part in the preparation of evidence before the trial and in the questioning of the defendant and the witnesses. Witnesses (including expert witnesses) are called by the court rather than testifying for one of the opposing sides. Most important, the judge or the panel of judges decides on guilt or innocence of the defendant, whereas in the adversarial system this decision is for the jury.

The first substantial contribution by psychologists to an understanding of jury functioning was presented by Kalven & Zeisel (1966), a survey of trial judges' opinions concerning jury verdicts, the determinants of jury verdicts, and the judges' evaluations of the quality of those verdicts. Another major landmark was the research program conducted by Thibaut and his associates (e.g. Thibaut & Walker, 1975), which had a significant impact on social psychology and its application to law. The jury has now become, beside the witness, the most popular research object in the entire area of psychology and law, especially in the criminal trial (Davis, 1989). Psychologists have, for example, examined the impact of jury size, decision rules, jury composition, instructions to the jury from the trial judge, and the evaluation of evidence by juries.

Jury size

Most countries with the adversarial system have opted for twelve-member juries, although proposals have been made in the USA to reduce the jury to a minimum of six members. It has been argued that larger juries have a better chance to be representative of the various social groups in a community and that the margin of error would diminish, compared to a small jury. Different twelve-member juries would therefore be more likely to reach the same decision than different six-member juries (Hans & Vidmar, 1982). Numerous experiments have been carried out to examine the effects of jury size on decisions (usually verdicts). As Vollrath & Davies (1980) conclude in their review, the surprising outcome from this now rather large body of data is that no significant size-attributable differences in verdicts have been found.

Jury selection

Since the seminal work of Kalven & Zeisel (1966) the possibility that jurors could be subject to judgment biases has received much attention in the literature. In search of factors that could cause such biases, the impact of personality variables, gender, demographic factors, and experimental influences on group performance in general has been examined in a number of studies. The basic idea underlying these efforts was that identification of variables that could cause biases would enable scientifically based procedures for the selection of jurors and thus reduce decision biases. However, the results of this line of research are mixed. For example, some studies found that men's verdicts differed in some cases from those of women (Efran, 1974), other studies did not find any differences related to gender (Griffitt & Jackson, 1973). Research on the effects of race has been equally inconsistent and the same is true for various personality variables. Thus, efforts for "scientific jury selection" (Kairys, Schulman, & Harring, 1975) seem to lack conclusive empirical support (Hans & Vidmar, 1982).

Moreover, the question is whether or not jury selection procedures, however sophisticated they may be, can indeed offer a solution to the problems. As Ellsworth & Reifman (in press) have emphasized, the characteristics of the person are far less important in determining who conforms, who obeys, and who turns away from a call for help than are the characteristics of the situation. Consequently, social psychologists have focused on situational factors as potential causes for deficiencies in jury performance (e.g. the disorganized presentation of evidence, the prohibition against asking for clarification or even taking notes, the oral recitation of lengthy instructions in an unfamiliar language; see Ellsworth & Reifman, in press). Reforms of the jury system that have been proposed by social scientists, therefore, focus on aspects of the jurors' tasks rather than on the jurors' qualifications. From this point of view it has been suggested, for example, that jurors be given an orientation session before trial (Heuer & Penrod, 1994), that the judge instruct jurors on law, both at the beginning and at the end of a trial (Liebermann & Sales, 1997), that the judge explain the reasons behind particular rules (Kassin & Sommers, 1997), and that jurors be provided with notebooks containing a list of witnesses and a glossary of technical terms (Munstermann, Hannaford, & Whitehead, 1997). Most of these reform proposals are based on theory and research from cognitive and social psychology.

Evaluation of evidence and decision making

How individual jurors and juries as groups evaluate the evidence and finally reach a decision has been investigated from two different perspectives. Psychologists have examined the cognitive processes in individual juror decision making. The other major research interest concerns the social dynamics of group decision making.

With regard to individual jurors' decision processes, up until the early 1980s research was dominated by the application of algebraic or stochastic models, mostly derived from Bayesian probability models (reviewed by Pennington & Hastie, 1981). The typical research paradigm was a laboratory experiment using undergraduate psychology students as mock jurors who read brief 10- to 20-sentence summaries of imaginary evidence. Usually, little attempt was made to mimic the conditions, procedures, and instructions of a typical jury trial (Pennington & Hastie, 1990). Furthermore, it has been argued that these models are too mechanical and much too elemental to provide a satisfactory account for what people actually do when making difficult decisions about complex events (Ellsworth & Mauro, 1998). A shift in perspective was initiated by Pennington & Hastie (1993), who criticized the artificiality of laboratory research on juror decision making. In contrast to previous research methods, these authors attempted to create conditions and stimulus events that were comparable to those at an actual trial. The participants were sampled from courthouse jury pools rather than from undergraduate psychology students and the analyses of evaluation and decision processes were based on think-aloud protocols.

From this research Pennington and Hastie concluded that the traditional mathematical models were inadequate and proposed an alternative model to explain evidence evaluation and decisions that is embedded in cognitive psychology (e.g. Kintsch & Van Dijk, 1978; Schank & Abelson, 1977): the *story* or *explanation model*. This model is supposed to provide a framework for explaining how jurors comprehend, recall, and use the evidence in criminal trials in terms of verdict categories. The idea is that jurors attempt to make sense of the entirety of evidence by imposing a summary structure on it that they feel captures what was true about the events referred to in the testimony. Furthermore, it is assumed that jurors engage in a deliberate effort to match the explanatory story that they had constructed with the verdict categories, seeking a "best fit" between one of the verdict categories and their story (Pennington & Hastie, 1990). In other words, it is hypothesized that the "story" mediates between the evidence presented and the final judgment or decision.

The story approach introduces some clarification regarding the mixed results on the effects of psychosocial variables on verdicts by suggesting that these variables are not related to verdicts directly. Instead, they are linked to stories, which in turn are related to verdicts. For example, Pennington & Hastie (1990) report that in some of their studies the social class of the juror was related to the harshness of verdicts. They found that jurors from poorer neighborhoods did not find the possession of a weapon particularly surprising, whereas jurors from a wealthier suburb did find this fact remarkable. As a consequence, these jurors inferred that the defendant had a special purpose in mind for the knife: namely to injure or kill the victim. This example shows that social class is related to particular life experiences which influence the way the jury members construct a story for this particular case but perhaps not for different cases.

Jury deliberation and group decision making

Two of the central assumptions underlying trial by jury are that (1) the deliberation will act as a counter-measure against individual biases and (2) that group decisions are superior to individual decisions. In particular, information seeking and processing is assumed to be more efficient in groups as compared to individuals. However, in contrast to these assumptions research by Janis (1972, 1982) has shown that under certain conditions (especially homogeneity, isolation, structural faults, lack of decision procedures) groups may be affected by the phenomenon of "groupthink." Under these circumstances groups tend to develop an illusion of invulnerability, a belief in a shared morality, closed-mindedness, and exhibit pressure on individual group members to conform with the majority opinion (e.g. Park, 1990; Tetlock, Peterson, McGuire, Chang, & Feld, 1992). One important consequence of these processes for the evaluation of evidence and the construction of a "story" is the tendency towards a biased search for and evaluation of information. This would then result in a strong confirmation bias (Snyder, 1984).

A series of studies by Schulz-Hardt and colleagues (Schulz-Hardt, Frey, Lüthgens, & Moscovici, 1999) has demonstrated that groups do indeed show a greater confirmation bias than individuals: they were more confident about the correctness of their decision as well as more selective when seeking information. This was particularly the case in homogeneous groups (i.e. when group members share the same initial opinion). Furthermore, the more certain the group members are, and the more they deem themselves to be unanimous, the more they look for consistent information (Frey, 1995).

Acre, Sobral, & Fariña (1992) have examined the impact of group homogeneity on jury decision making by forming ideologically homogeneous juries (only conservatives or progressives) and attributionally homogeneous juries (subjects preferring either internal or external attribution). They found that in some criminal cases these juries differed in post- but not in pre-deliberation verdicts, indicating that the bias derived from the deliberation of homogeneous groups. Pennington & Hastie (1986) found that evidence that is incongruent with the verdict is not equally considered. Acre (1995) concludes from these data that the appreciation of evidence during the deliberation is selective, that homogeneous juries either avoid using certain information that is not congruent with their bias or that they interpret it according to their bias. Hence, contrary to the assumptions underlying the trial by jury idea, individual bias may be magnified rather than reduced in the deliberation under homogeneous conditions.

Criminal Behavior: Explanation and Prediction

How criminal behavior is explained and predicted has enormous influence on all levels of the criminal justice system. Theoretical models of criminal behavior will more or less determine how a society deals with the phenomenon of crime. Such models can, for example, be used to assist the investigation of crime; crime prevention programs are influenced by theories of criminal behavior and this is even more so with regard to the treatment of offenders.

There appears to be some consistency about criminal behavior which calls for psychological explanation. Cross-sectional as well as longitudinal epidemiological research on criminal behavior has repeatedly shown that the prevalence of offending (officially recorded as well as self-reported) increases with age to reach a peak in the teenage years and from then on decreases through the twenties and thirties (e.g. Farrington, 1990; Gottfredson

& Hirschi, 1988; Stephenson, 1992). There is also a remarkable continuity of offending over time. In other words, the best predictor of offending at one age is offending at a preceding age. In a prospective longitudinal study, Farrington & West (1990) found that of those convicted as juveniles (age 10–16) almost 75 percent were reconvicted between the ages of 17 and 24, and nearly half of the juvenile offenders were reconvicted between ages 25 and 32. Furthermore, those convicted early tend to become the most persistent offenders, in committing large numbers of offences at high rates over long time periods.

From a psychological point of view, offending is a certain type of behavior, similar in many respects to other types of antisocial or deviant behaviors. Offending has indeed been found to be part of a more general anti-social behavior syndrome that arises in childhood and persists into adulthood (Robins, 1979). Farrington & West (1990) report that the most serious offenders at each age were deviant in a number of other aspects. Among other things, at age 18 offenders drank, smoked, and gambled more, used more drugs, admitted to drinking and driving, and fought more than did their non-convicted peers. Of 110 18-year-old males diagnosed as anti-social on non-criminal criteria, 70 percent were convicted up to the age of 20 and this anti-social tendency persists into adulthood.

Offending and anti-social behavior in general seem to be linked to a configuration of personality factors variously termed "hyperactivity–impulsivity–attention deficit." For example, Farrington, Loeber, & Van Kammen (1990) found that diagnosis of this syndrome at age 8–10 predicted juvenile convictions independently of conduct disorders at that age. Delinquency has also been related to certain patterns of thinking. In particular, criminal activities are associated with a strong tendency to justify and excuse criminal behavior. For example, Farrington, Biron, & LeBlanc (1982) have reported that offenders tend to blame the world for their problems and believe that they had a lot of bad luck. Mitchell & Dodder (1983) found that delinquents attempt to neutralize their guilt feelings by finding excuses and justifications for their behavior. They deny their responsibility as well as the injury of the victim. Over time, the justification employed to explain past delinquency may subsequently be used in an anticipatory way to justify future, intended deviation (Stephenson, 1992).

There also seems to be a considerable familial similarity in criminal behavior. In the Cambridge Study of Delinquent Development (West & Farrington, 1975), the percentage of boys convicted up to age 20 rose linearly from no convicted parents (18 percent) to one convicted parent (42 percent) and two convicted parents (61 percent). Of the boys with criminal brothers, 50 percent were convicted versus 19 percent of the boys with non-criminal brothers. Crime concentrates in families: 11 percent of families accounted for half of all convicted persons (Rowe & Farrington, 1997).

Does this pattern of results indicate that offending is a stable personality characteristic, a trait, or that the possession of certain personality characteristics facilitates criminality? Eysenck (1977) and Eysenck & Eysenck (1978) have put forward a theory that suggests just that. These authors hypothesize that extroverts are less well conditioned than introverts and therefore more difficult to socialize. They are said to be more sensation seeking and less likely to feel anxious when contemplating or performing a criminal act. This theory links criminal behavior to genetics in that extroversion–introversion is assumed to have a biological basis and that this is to a considerable degree rooted in genetics. Eysenck's theory on criminal behavior has been strongly criticized (e.g. Sarbin, 1979). Moreover, the empirical data do not seem to support this position. For example, Hollin (1989) concluded from a literature review that studies on the relation of extroversion and offending have had inconsistent results. Some did find the predicted relationship, others found no difference, while still others reported lower extroversion scores in offender groups. Furthermore, Raine & Venables (1981) failed to confirm the notion that poorly socialized people are less conditionable than better socialized individuals. West & Farrington (1973) reported that convicted juveniles did not differ in extroversion and neuroticism from their non-convicted peers.

Based on prospective longitudinal study and on literature reviews, Farrington (1992; Farrington & West, 1990) has suggested that a combination of factors eventually leads to delinquency. West & Farrington (1973) and Loeber & Stouthamer-Loeber (1986) reported that poor parental supervision and monitoring, erratic or harsh parental discipline, cruel, passive, or negligent parental attitude, and parental conflicts and separation were all important predictors of offending. Criminal, anti-social, and alcoholic parents tend to have criminal sons (Robins, 1979). These results suggest that offending occurs when the normal social learning process is disrupted by erratic discipline, poor supervision, and unsuitable parental models. These children tend to have a below-average intelligence (Wilson & Herrnstein, 1985; West & Farrington, 1973). Farrington (1992) hypothesizes that, because of their poor ability to manipulate abstract concepts, they have problems foreseeing the consequences of their offending and appreciating the feelings of victims. He further assumes that children with low intelligence are likely to fail in school and later to have erratic employment careers. As a consequence, they are less able to satisfy their desires for material goods, excitement, and social status by legal or socially approved methods and so tend to choose illegal or socially disapproved methods (Farrington, 1986).

Apparently, no definitive answer can be given yet as to the ultimate causes of criminal behavior. Empirical research in this area is extremely difficult due to the impossibility of experimental control. As a consequence, the available data are sometimes vague and inconclusive and subject to highly controversial debates.

Therapeutic Jurisprudence

The concept of therapeutic jurisprudence is a rather recent development in the field of psychology and law which has become increasingly popular during the last decade. The idea behind the concept of therapeutic jurisprudence is that legal rules and procedures and the roles of legal practitioners are social forces which produce therapeutic and anti-therapeutic consequences with regard to psychological well-being and behavior modification. It holds that scholars and practitioners must recognize this and modify behavior and systems to account for it, without violating legal norms (Hora & Schma, 1998).

Therapeutic jurisprudence was originally offered as a new perspective on mental health law. During the past ten years, however, it has developed into a therapeutic perspective on the law in general (Wexler, 1997). Scholars and practitioners have recognized that therapeutic jurisprudence has many applications, including in the areas of sentencing and correctional law, criminal law and procedure, family and juvenile law, disability law, workers' compensation law, personal injury and tort law, labor arbitration law, and contract law. Within the conceptual framework of therapeutic jurisprudence, for example, it has been discussed how the criminal justice system might traumatize victims of sexual battery, how workers' compensation laws might create the moral hazard of prolonging work-related injury, how a fault based (rather than a no-fault) tort compensation scheme might enhance recovery from personal injury, and how the current law of contracts might operate to reinforce the low self-esteem of disadvantaged contracting parties (see Wexler, 1999).

It has been emphasized that therapeutic jurisprudence does not intend to touch basic constitutional, moral, and normative values. Rather, it concentrates on how existing law, whatever its nature, can be therapeutically applied (Hora, Schma, & Rosenthal, 1999), although law reform still is an option. This approach requires an analysis of the effects of existing legal rules, and the way they are applied, on the psychological well-being and behavior of a particular sector of the population. If this analysis shows that the law or the way it is applied has negative (side-) effects, the first step within a therapeutic jurisprudence approach would be to look for procedures that could help to reduce these negative effects without altering the law itself or the way it is applied. If these procedures are insufficient the focus is shifted to the modification of the application of the law. If this, too, does not effectively reduce the observed negative effects, a reform of the law itself may be required.

An illustrative example of this approach is the treatment of those child witnesses who are presumed to be victims of sexual abuse. A number of studies have consistently shown that the criminal investigation as well as the trial process may have severe negative effects on the children (e.g. Goodman, Taub, Jones, England, Port, Rudy, & Prado, 1992; Spencer & Flin, 1990; Wolf, 1997; Dannenberg, Mantwill, Stahlmann-Liebelt, & Köhnken, 1997). These negative effects are by no means restricted to a potential traumatization of child witnesses. Emotional stress usually impairs information processing and, as a consequence, the evidence given by the child may be incomplete and/or incorrect (e.g. Yuille & Daylen, 1998). Furthermore, parents who anticipate severe negative effects for their children may be reluctant to report sexual abuse to the authorities in order to protect their children from additional stress.

In an attempt to reduce stress and potential traumatization of child witnesses without changing the law, court preparation programs have been introduced in various countries (e.g. Dezwirek-Sas, 1992; Keeney, Amacher, & Kastanakis, 1992; Köhnken, 1999). In addition to a court preparation program the British government has published a Memorandum of Good Practice for Interviewing Child Witnesses which has become the de facto standard for interviewing child witnesses by the police. The introduction of the Memorandum of Good Practice did not change the law but the way the existing procedural law is applied. Furthermore, several states of the US as well as the UK and Germany have introduced modifications of procedural law which allow child witnesses to give evidence without having to appear in a courtroom by using closed-circuit TV and the use of earlier video recorded interviews as evidence.

The explicit therapeutic perspective seems to have raised some interesting questions and generated some interesting research and writing that might otherwise not have occurred, and it brings together under a single conceptual umbrella a number of areas that otherwise might not seem to be particularly related.

References

Acre, R. (1995). Evidence evaluation in jury decision-making. In R. Bull & D. Carson (Eds.), *Handbook of psychology in legal contexts* (pp. 565–580). Chichester, UK: Wiley.

Acre, R., Sobral, J., & Fariña, F. (1992). Verdicts of psychosocially biased juries. In F. Lösel, D. Bender, & T. Bliesener (Eds.), *Psychology and law: International perspectives* (435–439). Berlin: De Gruyter.

Alonso-Quecuty, M. L. (1992). Deception detection and reality monitoring: A new answer to an old question? In F. Lösel, D. Bender, & T. Bliesener (Eds.), *Psychology and law: International perspectives* (pp. 328–332). Berlin: De Gruyter.

Anson, D. A., Golding, S. L., & Gully, K. J. (1993). Child sexual abuse allegations: Reliability of criteria-based content analysis. *Law and Human Behavior, 17*, 331–341.

Arntzen, F. (1983). *Psychologie der Zeugenaussage*. Munich: Beck.

Blackburn, R. (1996). What is forensic psychology? *Legal and Criminological Psychology, 1*, 3–16.

Brigham, J. C., & Cairns, D. L. (1988). The effect of mugshot inspections on eyewitness identification accuracy. *Journal of Applied Social Psychology, 18*, 1394–1410.

Bull, R. & Carson, D. (Eds.) (1995). *Handbook of psychology in legal contexts*. Chichester: Wiley.

Buller, D. B., & Aune, R. K. (1987). Nonverbal cues to deception among intimates, friends, and strangers. *Journal of Nonverbal Behavior, 11*, 269–290.

Burgoon, J. K., & Buller, D. B. (1994). Interpersonal deception III: Effects of deceit on perceived communication and nonverbal behavior dynamics. *Journal of Nonverbal Behavior, 18*, 155–185.

Canter, D. (1994). *Criminal shadows*. London: HarperCollins.

Chance, J. E., & Goldstein, A. G. (1996). The other-race effect and eyewitness identification. In S. L. Sporer, R. M. Malpass, & G. Köhnken (Eds.), *Psychological issues in eyewitness identification* (pp. 153–176). Mahwah, NJ: Erlbaum.

Damaska, M. (1973). Evidentiary barriers to conviction and two models of criminal procedure: A comparative study. *University of Pennsylvania Law Review, 506*.

Dannenberg, U., Mantwill, M., Stahlmann-Liebelt, U., & Köhnken, G. (1997). Reduzierung von Informationsdefiziten und Ängsten kindlicher Zeugen. In L. Greuel, T. Fabian, & M. Stadler (Eds.), *Psychologie der Zeugenaussage* (pp. 237–245). Weinheim: Beltz.

Davies, A. (1997). Specific profile analysis: A data-based approach to offender profiling. In J. L. Jackson & D. A. Bekerian (Eds.), *Offender profiling: Theory, research, and practice* (pp. 191–207). New York: Wiley.

Davis, J. H. (1989). Psychology and law: The last 15 years. *Journal of Applied Social Psychology, 19*, 199–230.

DePaulo, B. M., & Pfeifer, R. L. (1986). On-the-job experience and skill at detecting deception. *Journal of Applied Social Psychology, 16*, 249–267.

DePaulo, B. M., Stone, J. L., & Lassiter, G. D. (1985). Deceiving and detecting deceit. In B. R. Schenker (Ed.), *The self and social life* (pp. 323–370). New York: McGraw-Hill.

Dezwirek-Sas, L. (1992). Empowering child witnesses for sexual abuse prosecution. In H. Dent & R. Flin (Eds.), *Children as witnesses* (pp. 181–199). Chichester, UK: Wiley.

Efran, M. G. (1974). The effect of physical appearance on the judgment of guilt, interpersonal attraction and severity of recommended punishment on a simulated jury task. *Journal of Research in Personality, 85*, 395–461.

Ellsworth, P. C., & Mauro, R. (1998). Psychology and law. In D. T. Gilbert, S. T. Fiske, & G. Lindzey (Eds.), *The handbook of social psychology*, Vol. 2 (pp. 684–732). Boston: McGraw-Hill.

Ellsworth, P. C., & Reifman, A. (in press). Juror comprehension and public policy: Perceived problems and proposed solutions. *Psychology, Public Policy, and Law*.

Esplin, P., Boychuk, T., and Raskin, D. (1988). Application of statement validity analysis. Paper presented at the NATO Advanced Study Institute on Credibility Assessment, Maratea, Italy.

Eysenck, H. J. (1977). *Crime and personality*, 2nd. edn. London: Routledge & Kegan Paul.

Eysenck, H. J., & Eysenck, S. B. G. (1978). Psychopathy, personality and genetics. In R. D. Hare &

D. Schalling (Eds.), *Psychopathic behaviour* (pp. 197–223). Chichester, UK: Wiley.

Farrington, D. P. (1986). Stepping stones to adult criminal careers. In D. Olweus, J. Block, & M. R. Yarrow (Eds.), *Development of anti-social and pro-social behavior: Research, theories and issues.* New York: Academic Press.

Farrington, D. P. (1990). Age, period, cohort, and offending. In D. M. Gottfredson & R. V. Clarke (Eds.), *Policy and theory in criminal justice: Contributions in honor of Leslie T. Wilkins.* Aldershot, UK: Gower.

Farrington, D. P. (1992). Psychological contributions to the explanation, prevention and treatment of offending. In F. Lösel, D. Bender, & T. Bliesener (Eds.), *Psychology and law: International perspectives* (pp. 35–51). Berlin: De Gruyter.

Farrington, D. P., & West, D. J. (1990). The Cambridge study in delinquent development: A long-term follow-up of 411 London males. In H. J. Kerner & G. Kaiser (Eds.), *Criminality: Personality, behavior, and life history* (pp. 115–138). Berlin: Springer.

Farrington, D. P., Biron, L., & LeBlanc, M. (1982). Personality and delinquency in London and Montreal. In J. Gunn & D. P. Farrington (Eds.), *Abnormal offenders, delinquency and the criminal justice system* (pp. 153–201). Chichester, UK: Wiley.

Farrington, D. P., Hawkins, K., & Lloyd-Bostock, S. M. (1979). Introduction: Doing psycholegal research. In D. P. Farrington, K. Hawkins, & S. M. Lloyd-Bostock (Eds.), *Psychology, law and legal processes.* London: Macmillan.

Farrington, D. P., Loeber, R., & Van Kammen, W. B. (1990). Long-term criminal outcomes of hyperactivity–impulsivity–attention deficit and conduct problems in childhood. In L. N. Robins & M. Rutter (Eds.), *Straight and devious pathways from childhood to adulthood* (pp. 62–81). Cambridge, UK: Cambridge University Press.

Fiedler, K., & Walka, I. (1993). Training lie detectors to use nonverbal cues instead of global heuristics. *Human Communication Research, 20,* 199–223.

Fisher, R. P., and Geiselman, R. E. (1992). *Memory-enhancing techniques for investigative interviewing.* Springfield, IL: Charles C. Thomas.

Fisher, R. P, McCauley, M. R., and Geiselman, R. E. (1994). Improving eyewitness testimony with the cognitive interview. In D. Ross, J. D. Read, & M. Toglia (Eds.), *Adult eyewitness testimony: Current trends and developments.* Cambridge, UK: Cambridge University Press.

Fisher, R. P., Geiselman, R. E., Raymond, D. S., Jurkevich, L. M., and Warhaftig, M. L. (1987). Enhancing enhanced eyewitness memory: Refining the Cognitive Interview. *Journal of Police Science and Administration, 15,* 291–297.

Frey, D. (1995). Information seeking among individuals and groups and possible consequences for decision-making in business and politics. In E. Witte & J. Davis (eds.). *Understanding group behavior, Vol. II: Small group processes and interpersonal relations.* Hillsdale, NJ: Lawrence Erlbaum.

Geiselman, R. E., Fisher, R. P., Firstenberg, I., Hutton, L. A., Avetissian, I., & Prosk, A. (1984). Enhancement of eyewitness memory: An empirical evaluation of the cognitive interview. *Journal of Police Science and Administration, 12,* 74–80.

Goodman, G., Taub, E. P., Jones, D., England, P., Port, L., Rudy, L., & Prado, L. (1992). Testifying in criminal court: Emotional effects on child sexual assault victims. *Monographs of the Society for Research in Child Development, 57* (5), Serial No. 229.

Gottfredson, M., & Hirschi, T. (1988). Science, public policy and the career paradigm. *Criminology, 26,* 37–56.

Gottschalk, R., Davidson II, W. S., Gensheimer, L. K., & Mayer, J. P. (1987). Community-based interventions. In H. C. Quay (Ed.), *Handbook of juvenile delinquency* (pp. 266–289). New York: Wiley.

Griffitt, W., & Jackson, T. (1973). Simulated jury decisions: The influence of jury defendant attitude similarity–dissimilarity. *Social Behavior and Personality, 1,* 73–93.

Hans, V. P., & Vidmar, N. (1982). Jury selection. In N. L. Kerr & R. M. Bray (Eds.), *The psychology of the courtroom* (pp. 39–82). London: Academic Press.

Herdan, G. (1964). *Quantitative linguistics.* London: Butterworths.

Heuer, L., & Penrod, S. D. (1994). Trial complexity: A field investigation of its meaning and its effects. *Law and Human Behavior, 18,* 29–51.

Höfer, E., Akehurst, L., & Metzger, G. (1996). *Reality monitoring: A chance for further development of CBCA?* Paper presented at the Conference of the European Association on Psychology and Law, Siena, Italy.

Hollin, C. R. (1989). *Psychology and crime.* London: Routledge.

Hora, P. F., & Schma, W. G. (1998). Therapeutic jurisprudence. *Judicature, 82,* 8–12.

Hora, P. F., Schma, W. G., & Rosenthal, J. T. A. (1999). Therapeutic jurisprudence and the drug treatment court movement: Revolutionizing the criminal justice system's response to drug abuse and crime in America. *Notre Dame Law Review, 74,* 439–537.

Jackson, J. L., & Bekerian, D. A. (Eds.). *Offender profiling: Theory. research, and practice.* New York: John Wiley & Sons.

Janis, I. L. (1972). Victims of groupthink. Boston: Houghton Mifflin.

Janis, I. L. (1982). *Groupthink.* 2nd. revd. edn. Boston: Houghton Mifflin.

Joffe, R., and Yuille, J. (1992). Criteria-based content analysis: An experimental investigation. Paper presented at the meeting of the American Psychology–Law Society, San Diego.

Johnson, M. K., & Raye, C. L. (1981). Reality monitoring. *Psychological Reviews, 88,* 67–85.

Kalven, H., Jr., & Zeisel, H. (1966). *The American jury.* Boston: Little, Brown.

Kapardis, A. (1997). *Psychology and law.* Cambridge, UK: Cambridge University Press.

Kaplan, M. F. (Ed.) (1986). *The impact of social psychology on procedural justice.* Springfield, IL: Charles C. Thomas.

Kassin, S. M., & Sommers, S. R. (1997). Inadmissable testimony, instructions to disregard, and the jury: Substantive versus procedural considerations. *Personality and Social Psychology Bulletin, 23,* 1046–1054.

Kebbell, M., & Milne, R. (1998). Police officers' perceptions of eyewitness performance in forensic investigations. *Journal of Social Psychology, 138,* 323–330.

Keeney, K. S., Amacher, E., & Kastanakis, J. A. (1992). The court prep group: A vital part of the court process. In H. Dent & R. Flin (Eds.), *Children as witnesses* (pp. 201–209). Chichester, UK: Wiley.

Kintsch, W., & Van Dijk, T. A. (1978). Toward a model of text comprehension and production. *Psychological Review, 85,* 363–394.

Köhnken, G. (1985). Speech and deception of eyewitnesses: An information processing approach. In F. L. Denmark (Ed.), *Social/ecological psychology and the psychology of women* (pp. 141–163). Amsterdam: North-Holland.

Köhnken, G. (1999). Der Schutz kindlicher Zeugen vor Gericht. In G. Schütze, R. Lempp, & G. Köhnken (Eds.), *Forensische kinder- und jugendpsychiatrie und- psychologie.*

Köhnken, G., & Höfer, E. (1998). Assessing statement credibility. Paper presented at the International Congress of Applied Psychology, San Francisco.

Köhnken, G., & Wegener, H. (1982). Zur Glaubwürdigkeit von Zeugenaussagen. Experimentelle Überprüfung ausgewählter Glaubwürdigkeitskriterien [Credibility of witness statements: experimental examination of selected reality criteria]. *Zeitschrift für Experimentelle und Angewandte Psychologie, 29,* 92–111.

Köhnken, G., Malpass, R. S., & Wogalter, M. S. (1996). Forensic applications of lineup research. In S. L. Sporer, R. M. Malpass, & G. Köhnken (Eds.), *Psychological issues in eyewitness identification* (pp. 205–231). Hillsdale, NJ: Erlbaum.

Köhnken, G., Milne, R., Memon, A., & Bull, R. (1999). The cognitive interview: A meta-analysis. *Psychology, Crime and Law, 5,* 3–27.

Köhnken, G., Schimossek, E., Aschermann, E., & Höfer, E. (1995). The cognitive interview and the assessment of the credibility of adults' statements. *Journal of Applied Psychology, 80,* 671–684.

Liebermann, J. D., & Sales, B. D. (1997). What social science teaches us about the jury instruction process. *Psychology, Public Policy, and Law, 3,* 589–644.

Lindsay, R. C. L., & Wells, G. L. (1980). What price justice? Exploring the relationship of lineup fairness to identification accuracy. *Law and Human Behavior, 4,* 303–313.

Luus, C. A. E., & Wells, G. L. (1991). Eyewitness identification and the selection of distractors for lineups. *Law and Human Behavior, 14,* 43–57.

McCauley, M. R., & Fisher, R. P. (1995). Facilitating children's eyewitness recall with the revised cognitive interview. *Journal of Applied Psychology, 80,* 510–516.

McEwan, J. (1995). Adversarial and inquisitorial proceedings. In R. Bull & D. Carson (Eds.), *Handbook of psychology in legal contexts* (495–508). Chichester, UK: Wiley.

McGuire, J. (1995). *What works? Reducing reoffending.* Chichester, UK: Wiley.

Malpass, R. S., & Devine, P. G. (1983). Measuring the fairness of eyewitness identification lineups. In S. M. A. Lloyd-Bostock & R. B. Clifford (Eds.), *Evaluating witness evidence* (pp. 81–102). Chichester, UK: Wiley.

Malpass, R. S., & Devine, P. G. (1984). Research on suggestion in lineups and photospreads. In G. L. Wells & E. F. Loftus (Eds.), *Eyewitness testimony: Psychological perspectives* (pp. 64–91). New York: Cambridge University Press.

Malpass, R. S., Parada, M., Corey, D., Chavez, J., Bowles, S., & McQuiston, D. (1999). Reliability of face recognition. Manuscript submitted for publication.

Marbe, K. (1913). *Grundzüge der Forensischen Psychologie* [Elements of forensic psychology]. Munich: Beck.

Milne, R., Bull, R., Köhnken, G., & Memon, A. (1995). The cognitive interview and suggestibility. In G. M. Stephenson & N. K. Clark (Eds.), *Criminal behaviour: Perceptions, attributions and rationality* (pp. 21–27). Division of criminological and legal psychology occasional papers, 22. Leicester, UK: British Psychological Society.

Mitchell, J., & Dodder, R. A. (1983). Types of neutralization and types of delinquency. *Journal of Youth and Adolescence, 12,* 307–318.

Morton, A. Q., & Farringdon, M. G. (1992). Identifying utterance. *Expert Evidence, 1,* 84–92.

Münsterberg, H. (1908). *On the witness stand: Essays on psychology and crime.* New York: Clark, Boardman, Doubleday.

Munstermann, G. T., Hannaford, P. L., & Whitehead, G. M. (Eds.) (1997). *Jury trial innovations.* Williamsburg, VA: National Center for State Courts.

Park, W. W. (1990). A review of research on groupthink. *Journal of Behavioral Decision Making, 3,* 229–245.

Pennington, N., & Hastie, R. (1981). Juror decision making models: The generalization gap. *Psychological Bulletin, 89,* 246–287.

Pennington, N., & Hastie, R. (1986). Evidence evaluation in complex decision making. *Journal of Personality and Social Psychology, 51,* 242–258.

Pennington, N., & Hastie, R. (1990). Practical implications of psychological research on juror and jury decision making. *Personality and Social Psychology Bulletin, 16,* 90–105.

Pennington, N., & Hastie, R. (1993). The story model for juror decision making. In R. Hastie (Ed.), *Inside the juror: The psychology of juror decision making* (pp. 192–221). New York: Cambridge University Press.

Porter, S., & Yuille, J. C. (1996). The language of deceit: An investigation of the verbal clues to deception in an interrogation context. *Law and Human Behavior, 20,* 443–459.

Pozzulo, J. D., & Lindsay, R. C. L. (1999). Identification accuracy of children versus adults. Manuscript submitted for publication.

Raine, A., & Venables, P. H. (1981). Classical conditioning and socialization – a biosocial interaction. *Personality and Individual Differences, 2,* 273–283.

Rand Corporation (1975). The criminal investigation process, Vols. 1–3. Rand Corporation Technical Report R-1777-DOJ. Santa Monica.

Raskin, D. C. (1989). Polygraph techniques for the detection of deception. In D. C. Raskin (Ed.), *Psychological methods in criminal investigation and evidence* (247–296). New York: Springer.

Rattner, A. (1988). Convicted but innocent: Wrongful conviction and the criminal justice system. *Law and Human Behavior, 12,* 283–293.

Reiser, M. (1980). *Handbook of investigative hypnosis.* Los Angeles: Lehi.

Robins, L. N. (1979). Sturdy childhood predictors of adult outcomes: Replications from longitudinal studies. In J. E. Barrett, R. M. Rose, & G. L. Klerman (Eds.), *Stress and mental disorder.* New York: Raven Press.

Ross, D., Read, J. D., & Toglia, M. (Eds.) (1994). *Adult eyewitness testimony: Current trends and developments.* Cambridge, UK: Cambridge University Press.

Rowe, D. C., & Farrington, D. P. (1997). The familial transmission of criminal convictions. *Criminology, 35*, 177–201.

Ruby, C. L., & Brigham, J. C. (1997). The usefulness of the criteria-based content analysis technique in distinguishing between truthful and fabricated allegations: A critical review. *Psychology, Public Policy, and Law, 3/4*, 705–734.

Sarbin, T. R. (1979). The myth of the criminal type. In T. R. Sarbin (Ed.), *Challenges to the criminal justice system: The perspectives of community psychology*. New York: Human Science.

Saywitz, K. J., Geiselman, R. E., & Bornstein, G. K. (1992). Effects of cognitive interviewing and practice on children's recall performance. *Journal of Applied Psychology, 77*, 744–756.

Schank, R. C., & Abelson, R. P. (1977). *Scripts, plans, goals, and understanding*. Hillsdale, NJ: Lawrence Erlbaum Associates.

Schulz-Hardt, S., Frey, D., Lüthgens, C., & Moscovici, S. (1999). Biased information search in group decision making. Manuscript submitted for publication.

Sealy, A. P. (1989). Decision processes in the jury room. In H. Wegener, F. Lösel, & J. Haisch (Eds.), *Criminal behavior and the justice system: Psychological perspectives* (pp. 163–180). New York: Springer.

Shapiro, P., & Penrod, S. D. (1986). A meta-analysis of facial identification studies. *Psychological Bulletin, 100*, 139–156.

Smith, J. E., Pleban, R. J., & Shaffer, D. (1982). Effects of interrogator bias and a police trait questionnaire on the accuracy of eyewitness identification. *Journal of Social Psychology, 116*, 19–26.

Smith, M. (1983). Hypnotic memory enhancement of witnesses: Does it work? *Psychological Bulletin, 94*, 387–407.

Snyder, M. (1984). When belief creates reality. In L. Berkowitz (Ed.), *Advances in experimental social psychology*, Vol. 18 (pp. 247–305). New York: Academic Press.

Spencer, J. R., & Flin, R. (1990). *The evidence of children: The law and the psychology*. London: Sage.

Sporer, S. L. (1996). The less traveled road to truth: Verbal cues in deception detection in accounts of fabricated and self-experienced events. Paper presented at the meeting of the American Psychology–Law Society, Hilton Head.

Sporer, S. L., Malpass, R. M., & Köhnken, G. (Eds.) (1996). *The psychology of eyewitness identification: New evidence and practical guidelines*. Hillsdale, NJ: Erlbaum.

Sporer, S. J., Penrod, S. D., Read, J. D., & Cutler, B. L. (1995). Gaining confidence in confidence: A new meta-analysis on the confidence-accuracy relationship in eyewitness identification. *Psychological Bulletin*.

Steller, M., & Köhnken, G. (1989). Statement analysis: Credibility assessment of children's testimonies in sexual abuse cases. In D. C. Raskin (Ed.), *Psychological methods in criminal investigation and evidence* (pp. 217–245). New York: Springer.

Steller, M., Wellershaus, P., & Wolf, T. (1992). Realkennzeichen in Kinderaussagen: Empirische Grundlagen der Kriterienorientierten Aussageanalyse [Reality criteria in child witness statements: Empirical foundations of the criteria-based content analysis]. *Zeitschrift für Experimentelle und Angewandte Psychologie, 39*, 151–170.

Stephenson, G. M. (1992). *The psychology of criminal justice*. Oxford, UK: Blackwell Publishers.

Stern, W. (1903). *Beiträge zur Psychologie der Aussage, 1. Heft*. Leipzig: Barth.

Tedeschi, J. T., & Norman, N. (1985). Social power, self-presentation, and the self. In B. R. Schlenker (Ed.), *The self and social life* (pp. 293–322). New York: McGraw-Hill.

Tetlock, P. E., Peterson, R. S., McGuire, C., Chang, S., & Feld, P. (1992). Assessing political group dynamics: A test of the groupthink model. *Journal of Personality and Social Psychology, 63*, 403–425.

Thibaut, J., & Walker, L. (1975). *Procedural justice: A psychological analysis*. New York: Spectrum.

Undeutsch, U. (1967). Beurteilung der Glaubhaftigkeit von Aussagen [Evaluation of statement credibility]. In U. Undeutsch (Ed.), *Handbuch der Psychologie, Vol. 11: Forensische Psychologie* (pp. 26–181). Göttingen: Hogrefe.

Vollrath, D. A., & Davis, J. H. (1980). Jury size and decision rule. In R. J. Simon (Ed.), *The jury: Its role in American society*. Lexington: Lexington Books.

Vrij, A. (1994). The impact of information and setting on detection of deception by police detectives. *Journal of Nonverbal Behavior, 18*, 117–136.

Vrij, A. (1998). Nonverbal communication and credibility. In A. Memon, A. Vrij, & R. Bull (Eds.), *Psychology and Law: Truthfulness, accuracy and credibility* (pp. 32–58). Maidenhead, UK: McGraw-Hill.

Vrij, A., & Winkel, F. W. (1994). Objective and subjective indicators of deception. *Issues in Criminological and Legal Psychology, 20*, 51–57.

Wagstaff, G. F. (1984). The enhancement of witness testimony by "hypnosis:" A review and methodological critique of the experimental literature. *British Journal of Experimental and Clinical Hypnosis, 22*, 3–12.

Wells, G. L. (1978). Applied eyewitness research: System variables and estimator variables. *Journal of Personality and Social Psychology, 36*, 1546–1557.

Wells, G. L., & Luus, C. A. E. (1990). Police lineups as experiments: Social methodology as a framework for properly conducted lineups. *Personality and Social Psychology Bulletin, 16*, 106–117.

Wells, G. L., & Turtle, J. W. (1986). Eyewitness identification: The importance of lineup models. *Psychological Bulletin, 99*, 320–329.

Wells, G. L., Small, M., Penrod, S. D., Malpass, R. S., Fulero, S. M., & Brimacombe, C. A. E. (1998). Eyewitness identification procedures: Recommendations for lineups and photospreads. *Law and Human Behavior, 22*, 603–647.

West, D. J., & Farrington, D. P. (1973). *Who becomes delinquent?* London: Heinemann.

Wexler, D. B. (1997). The development of therapeutic jurisprudence: From theory to practice. Paper presented at the University of Virginia's Institute of Law, Psychiatry and Public Policy Practice conference.

Wexler, D. B. (1999). The Development of Therapeutic Jurisprudence: From Theory to Practice. 68 Revista Juridica, UPR 691 (1999).

Wilson, J. Q., & Herrnstein, R. J. (1985). *Crime and human nature.* New York: Simon & Schuster.

Wolf, P. (1997). *Was wissen Kinder und Jugendliche über Gerichtsverhandlungen?* Regensburg: Roederer.

Yuille, J. (1988). The systematic assessment of children's testimony. *Canadian Psychologist, 29*, 247–262.

Yuille, J. C., & Daylen, J. (1998). The impact of traumatic events on eyewitness memory. In C. P. Thompson, D. J. Herrmann, J. D. Read, D. Bruce, D. G. Payne, & M. P. Toglia (Eds.), *Eyewitness memory: Theoretical and applied perspectives* (pp. 155–178). Mahwah, NJ: Lawrence Erlbaum Associates.

Zuckerman, M., DePaulo, B. M., & Rosenthal, R. (1981). Verbal and nonverbal communication of deception. In L. Berkowitz (Ed.), *Advances in experimental social psychology*, Vol. 14 (pp. 1–57). New York: Academic Press.

Zuckerman, M., Koestner, R., & Colella, M. J. (1985). Learning to detect deception from three communication channels. *Journal of Nonverbal Behavior, 9*, 188–194.

Zuckerman, M., Koestner, R., & Driver, R. E. (1981). Beliefs about cues associated with deception. *Journal of Nonverbal Behavior, 6*, 105–114.

Chapter Twenty-Six

Consumer Behavior

Sharon Shavitt and Michaela Wänke

The Consumer Domain: An Introduction

The broad field of consumer behavior spans many of the topics of interest to social psychologists – from micro-level events (e.g. psychophysiological responding to advertisements) to macro-level processes (e.g. family decision making; organizational buying behavior). Indeed, the breadth and volume of work in consumer behavior easily fills an entire handbook (e.g. Robertson & Kassarjian, 1991). This chapter is not intended to cover that field comprehensively. Instead, we focus on highlighting selected principles of consumer information processing (CIP) relevant to intraindividual, social psychological theories. The articles cited are not intended to be comprehensive either, and for some topics we cite review papers or a small subset of research articles for the sake of brevity.

Consumer research has been greatly influenced by social psychology. A citation analysis of the field's leading journal, *Journal of Consumer Research*, revealed that, when comparing individual disciplines, social psychology has had a greater impact than even marketing or economics (Leong, 1989). With a growing interest in CIP, research in social cognition has become a primary source of influence. In the first section of this chapter we give a brief overview of the encoding, inference, and memory processes that relate to consumer judgments and decisions. It will become clear that, regarding the underlying cognitive processes, consumer judgment does not differ much from social judgment.

Naturally, however, research on consumer cognition has focused on some themes central to consumer behavior. Below, we select some of these topics to give more detailed insight. The selection of topics is meant to illustrate the relevance of social cognition to the consumer domain.

Having pointed out the many parallels between the consumer literature and the social cognition literature, in the second section we turn to the differences. In particular, we are concerned with what social cognition can learn from the consumer domain. We will point to some areas where consumer research could inspire a more complete understanding of human information processing and, thus, balance the overwhelmingly one-sided interdisciplinary exchange more equally.

1   How Consumers Make Product Judgments

Consumers are daily exposed to a host of product-relevant information. Depending on their involvement and cognitive resources they attend to it, encode it, make inferences from it, and may use the results of their processing for a product evaluation or even decision. Because product choices and judgments are at least partially memory based (Alba, Hutchinson, & Lynch, 1991) they are then dependent on which brands and which brand-beliefs and brand-related affective responses were stored and are retrieved from long-term memory at the time of judgment. Even when external information is available, memory may play a role. For example, when consumers are exposed to a range of brands and packaging claims in the supermarket, they may nevertheless recall past product experiences, TV commercials, or reviews from consumer organizations, or they may attend more to the brands that they recognize. Thus, consumer choices and judgments often depend to a large extent on the accessibility of relevant information (e.g. Baker & Lutz, 1988; Feldman & Lynch, 1988) and how the activated information is used. However, as distinct from social cognition research, CIP research tends to focus on trying to understand the effects of a specific marketing-relevant variable, for example advertising execution or brand familiarity, on the product judgment, rather than understanding the cognitive processes *per se*. The following overview reflects this orientation to some extent.

Encoding

Independent of whether the judgment is stimulus based or memory based, in order to be considered for a product decision the information must have been perceived. Moreover, the more processing capacity is devoted to a stimulus for comprehension and elaboration, the greater is its later accessibility. Consequently, much of traditional theorizing in advertising postulated that grabbing consumers' attention is the key to effective advertising (e.g. Lewis, 1898; Rossiter & Percy, 1987) and researchers often focused on factors that capture consumers' attention (see O'Guinn & Faber, 1991).

A few caveats should be noted, however. First, our review will show that, although selectivity and intensity of attention are often positively correlated, the opposite is also true. Whereas some factors of a stimulus may catch consumers' attention, they may be detrimental to more intense processing and elaboration. Ads using sexual stimuli are a good example (Severn, Belch, & Belch, 1990). Second, some attention-grabbing executions may create negative affect. Recent Bennetton campaigns, which have featured war casualties and AIDS victims, are an example. Indeed, a growing body of research suggests that consumers resent attention-grabbing advertising (e.g. Campbell, 1995; see also section 2, below). Third, and perhaps most importantly, focal attention may not be necessary for information to be perceived and be influential at a later time, as will be discussed later.

What elicits attention and elaboration?

Whether a brand, an ad, a package, or any product information catches consumers' attention depends on where (when) it is placed, the goals, involvement, and cognitive resources of the consumer, and the characteristics of the stimulus. Placement is one of the most basic factors, and consequently consumer researchers were interested early on in placement effects (for a review see Wilkie, 1994, ch. 8). In magazines the most prominent spot is the back cover, in TV it is the first commercial in the commercial break. In cultures that read from left to right and from top to bottom, information presented in the upper-left corner receives greatest attention compared to other positions. In supermarkets, brands have a better chance of being chosen when placed at eye-level than on a lower shelf, presumably because they attract more attention at eye-level.

This example, however, also illustrates that much depends on the search strategies of the consumer. A consumer highly motivated to find the least expensive brand may also search the less prominent shelves. Models of consumers' external information search have identified four main factors: motivation, ability, perceived costs, and perceived benefits (Moorthy, Ratchford, & Talukdar, 1997; Schmidt & Spreng, 1996). Consumers engage in more search processes when the costs of making a suboptimal decision are high and the benefits of extended search are high. For inexpensive, or repeatedly purchased products, or when the market is perceived as homogeneous so that more search will not detect decisively better alternatives, search is low. External search processes also depend on a consumer's product or market knowledge. Moderately knowledgeable consumers will engage most in external search processes. Consumers with low knowledge lack the necessary representations to make use of the acquired information. Consumers with high knowledge, on the other hand, tend to rely more on their stored knowledge. Finally, spontaneous attention is also influenced by the consumer's current goals. A hungry consumer will be more likely to notice a restaurant than a consumer not looking for a bite to eat.

Certainly, characteristics of the presented information play an important role in capturing attention, and this may be what many view as advertising's prime objective: creating eye-catching executions. Not surprisingly, vivid information is more likely to be noticed than pallid information, and indeed, in advertising, a picture may be worth a thousand words, at least in terms of creating attention, eliciting recall, triggering inferences, and influencing judgments (e.g. Childers & Houston, 1984; Mitchell, 1986; Smith, 1991). When it comes to drawing attention, salience may actually be more important than vividness. In general, ads that are unusual, surprising, novel, or incongruent with expectations will capture attention, but such effects of novelty wear off with repetition (e.g. Calder & Sternthal, 1980).

Whereas vivid and salient information certainly attracts more selective attention, some research suggests that the advantage of vivid and salient executions is due to the greater elaboration that they elicit (e.g. Unnava & Burnkrant, 1991; Goodstein, 1993). On the other hand, catching attention may also be at the cost of comprehension and elaboration. For example, Houston, Childers, & Heckler (1987) found better recall for ad information when the picture and verbal information were discrepant, but only when ad recipients had plenty of time to process the ad and not if presentation time was short. This example demonstrates that whether elaboration occurs, and thus how an advertisement's execution affects judgment, both depend on consumers' cognitive resources (e.g. Keller & Block, 1997) and, of course, personal involvement (Greenwald & Leavitt, 1984).

Retrieval

We mentioned above that product choices often do not occur at the time that brand-related information is presented. Thus, most choices rely on the information recalled at the time of judgment, which is why retrieval processes are of prime interest in consumer research (for a review see Mitchell, 1993). Note, however, that recent literature also attests to the influence of information that is not explicitly recalled, as will be discussed later.

When consumers form a judgment at the time of information encoding, they may later simply retrieve the stored judgment rather than construct it anew by retrieving product attributes (Srull, 1989). However, although consumers may be able to retrieve a previous judgment, they may conclude that it is not adequate for the present situation (e.g. their current goals or alternatives) and may try to retrieve or acquire information that allows for a new judgment or adjust the previous one (Lynch, Marmorstein, & Weigold, 1988). As with external search processes, the extent of internal (memory) search increases with involvement and with cognitive resources, as described earlier.

Certainly, a prime factor in information retrieval is the accessibility of the information. We have already mentioned some variables that affect the accessibility of product-related information by way of attention and elaboration. Accessibility of brand-related information also depends on how it is organized in memory. Biehal & Chakravarti (1983) distinguish between brand based structures, which facilitate brand comparisons, and attribute based structures, which facilitate attribute based comparisons. The manner in which information is stored in memory depends on the goals present at encoding. In addition, prototypical brands within a product category (e.g. Ward & Loken, 1986) and recently or frequently activated brands or brand information (attributes or judgments) also enjoy an accessibility advantage (e.g. Berger & Mitchell, 1989; Nedungadi, 1990). Frequent or recent activation of a brand in a particular usage situation increases the association of brand and usage situation, so that activation of the latter may activate the brand (Ratneshwar & Shocker, 1991). Recency and frequency are of particular relevance because both can be manipulated through amount of advertising.

But not all information accessible in the judgment situation is the result of marketing efforts. Consumers may also recall past experiences. In particular, they may be likely to recall negative product experiences (Schul & Schiff, 1993) given that such experiences are usually unexpected and may be more extreme.

In general, the theories and models popular in CIP postulate a positive relationship between the accessibility of diagnostic information and its impact on judgment (Baker & Lutz, 1988; Feldman & Lynch, 1988; Kisielus & Sternthal, 1984). If a piece of information comes to mind, its evaluative implications will affect the judgment in the respective direction. However, in line with social cognition findings that the retrieval of information does not necessarily predict how the information is used for the judgment (see chapter 11, this volume), recent research in the consumer domain also challenged this assumption. As we will illustrate below, accessible information may also elicit contrast effects in product evaluation (Meyers-Levy & Tybout, 1997; Wänke, Bless, & Schwarz, 1998, in press-a, in press-b). Moreover, the impact of information depends not only on whether it comes to mind but also how it comes to mind. Evaluations of brands, products, and services were more in line with the implications of retrieved information when consumers experienced the retrieval as easy compared to when the retrieval felt difficult (Wänke & Bless, in press; Wänke, Bless, & Biller, 1996; Wänke, Bohner, & Jurkowitsch, 1997). When retrieval is experienced or merely anticipated as difficult, the impact of the evaluative implications may even reverse.

Consumer interpretations and inferences

Consumers are active information processors in that they interpret information, categorize it, generate counterarguments and draw inferences from it (for a review, see Kardes, 1993). Whether and how consumers make inferences about missing information is a particularly well-researched topic (see Kardes, 1993). Not surprisingly, only rather knowledgeable consumers notice when relevant product information is missing, whereas less knowledgeable consumers do so only when prompted, for example when competitor brands carry the respective information. Once consumers detect that relevant information is missing, they may use the available information to make specific inferences, as described below. If, however, the available information does not lend itself to specific inferences or consumers are not able or willing to make those inferences, they may form cautious and moderate judgments that are held with low confidence.

Several strategies for how consumers may spontaneously or intentionally go beyond the information given have been investigated (see also Alba & Hutchinson, 1987). Most simply, consumers may assume that the brand possesses a particular attribute at the same (average) level as other brands, provided the variance among these other brands is low. Equally basic, consumers may infer an attribute level from the overall product evaluation, as a sort of halo effect. Subjective theories, for example that high price signals high quality, are another source of inferences. Consumers may also draw inferences from category membership. A large CIP literature, for example, has looked at how consumers' product evaluations are influenced by the fact that the product carries a brand name about which they already have well-formed expectations (see below).

Of course, consumers are not infallible when relying on heuristics or even systematic strategies when evaluating brands (for a review of potential biases see Kardes, 1993). One interesting and obviously misleading heuristic was documented by Carpenter, Glazer, & Nakamoto (1994). In their study, nondiagnostic but differentiating brand attributes increased brand evaluation, especially under high price. Apparently, consumers inferred that if an attribute is advertised it must be valuable.

If consumers can be prompted to generate inferences themselves, this can bring a number of benefits to the marketer. Consumer inferences may be more memorable (Moore, Reardon, & Durso, 1986) and less subject to counterarguing and reactance than explicitly stated information. Indeed, self-generated arguments and inferences are more persuasive and enduring (Sawyer & Howard, 1991; Shavitt & Brock, 1990), and attitudinal judgments based on self-generated inferences are more accessible than judgments involving less cognitive effort (for a review see Kardes, 1993). Accordingly, advertisements often leave claims open to inference.

However, relying on consumers' inferences is risky to the extent that consumers need sufficient knowledge, involvement, and cognitive resources to make spontaneous inferences (e.g. Johar, 1995; Sawyer & Howard, 1991). Moreover, the ease with which consumers make a particular inference may also play a role. Self-generated product benefits are only more persuasive than presented benefits when this generation is experienced or anticipated as easy (Wänke, Bless, & Biller, 1996; Wänke, Bohner, & Jurkowitsch, 1997), whereas difficult benefit generation backfires. Not surprisingly, prompting self-generated responses also backfires when those responses are unfavorable to the brand (Shavitt & Brock, 1986).

Choice

Consumer research is at least as interested in choice as in product judgment. This concerns not only how judgments affect actual behavior, but how information processing feeds into selections among multiple alternatives. One might assume that consumers form or retrieve a judgment about each alternative and subsequently choose the best brand. However, the range of alternatives may influence which attributes are attended to and how they are weighted. In addition, comparison processes introduce their own dynamics (e.g. Dhar & Simonson, 1992; Wänke, Schwarz, & Noelle-Neumann, 1995). Consequently a large literature in consumer research builds on research in behavioral decision making (for a review see Bettmann, Johnson, & Payne, 1991), which to a large extent is guided by exploring violations of presumably rational principles.

For example, although, logically, the relative choice between A and B should not be affected by adding C to the range of options, the likelihood of choosing product A increases versus product B when a product C is added that is (at least partly) inferior to A and makes A look good by comparison (Huber, Payne, & Puto, 1982; Tversky & Simonson, 1993). Choices also should not depend on how the alternatives are presented (framing effects), but they do. Consumers gladly accept a discount for paying cash instead of using their credit card (framing as a gain) but resent paying an extra fee for charging goods to their credit card (framing as a loss).

Recent research in consumer choice has begun to pay more attention to affective factors in decision making, in particular, research investigating predictions about future reactions and choices (e.g. Kahneman & Snell, 1992) and research involving hedonic choices (e.g. Dhar & Wertenbroch, 1997). One general finding is that people are surprisingly poor at predicting their own future hedonic reactions to products or experiences. Obviously, this deficit greatly affects the quality of consumer decisions as far as future outcomes are concerned, and it suggests that marketing strategies should be sensitive to the time lag between the purchase decision and actual consumption.

Highlighted Topics in Consumer Information Processing

Brand extensions

The overwhelming majority of new products are launched under an already-established brand name. This way marketers avoid the forbidding costs of creating a new brand image, exploiting instead an existing brand image in the hope that consumers will transfer existing brand beliefs to the new launch (for a review see Shocker, Srivastava, & Ruekert, 1994). In investigating the conditions for successful extensions, consumer research has built upon the assumption that consumers need to categorize the extension as a brand member in order to derive affect or beliefs from the brand membership. Consequently, research has focused on the antecedents of brand categorization.

Whether a new product is categorized as belonging to an existing brand was initially assumed to depend on the characteristics of product and brand, and how both contributed to category fit. This fit was assumed to facilitate the transfer of brand liking and/or the transfer of more specific brand beliefs. Most research looked at fit in terms of the product category (e.g. canned soup fits better as an extension of a food brand than a floor wax; Boush & Loken, 1991), the brand image (e.g. bracelets fit better with Rolex, which is associated with status products, than with Timex; Park, Milberg, & Lawson, 1991), or other kinds of relatedness (technology, manufacturing processes, etc.; Herr, Farquahar, & Fazio, 1996).

Other research showed that product categorization was not necessarily a function of the nature of the brand or product and inherent in their features but could also be manipulated by external factors, such as supplying consumers with specific category labels for grouping products together (Wänke, Bless, & Schwarz, in press-a). Moreover, whether a particular model was included or excluded from the brand representation could be influenced by marketing strategies (Wänke, Bless, & Schwarz, 1998).

Until recently, the focus on the antecedents of brand categorization came with a neglect of the consequences. The literature generally assumed that high fit resulted in high acceptance of the extension. But Broniarczyk & Alba (1994) demonstrated that even if brand beliefs are transferred to the extension, these attributes may not necessarily be desirable for the extension. Consumers may want different attributes in a compact car than in a sportscar. Other research challenged the previously held assumption that a failure to categorize the extension as a brand exemplar would merely decrease the transfer of brand beliefs. Wänke, Bless, & Schwarz (1998) found contrast effects; the brand extension was evaluated lower on brand beliefs when its inclusion in the brand was undermined as compared to when no information about its parent brand was given. It is argued that the brand and its previous models can serve as a standard of comparison against which the new model is measured. These results imply that an unsuccessful extension strategy may not only fail to exploit the brand image but may actually backfire. On the other hand, beliefs in opposition to the existing brand image may be useful for different positioning goals.

The reverse influence – how the brand extension affects perceptions of the parent brand – has mainly been studied from the perspective of diluting brand image (e.g. Loken & Roedder-John, 1993; Park, McCarthy, & Milberg, 1993). Again, the literature has focused on the category fit, and again one may assume that other influences may affect categorization processes. Moreover, categorization models suggest that including an extension into an existing brand category will result in assimilation of the parent brand to the evaluation of the extension, but exclusion from the existing brand category may result in contrast (e.g. Wänke, Bless, & Schwarz, in press-b).

Research on brand extensions parallels stereotype research in social psychology as far as the dynamics of categorization are concerned. In fact, market research often treats brands as personalities, rendering the parallels rather appealing. The parallels make brand extensions an excellent domain for the study of social psychological categorization models.

Mood effects on consumer judgments

Affect plays a role in many consumer topics, particularly in advertising, both as a dependent variable and an independent variable (for a review see Agres, Edell, & Dubitsky, 1990). A prime question in applied research is how affective states influence purchase behavior. Because purchase behavior is the complex end result of different factors, there is no clear answer to this question and it may depend very much on the product category.

For example, on the one hand the popular saying "when the going gets tough, the tough go shopping" suggests that bad mood states may increase purchase behavior overall. This belief is supported by studies that find increased consumption of what Gardner (1994) calls "mood-ameliorating" products, such as cigarettes and cookies, or at least more favorable attitudes towards such products (for a review see Gardner, 1994). On the other hand, the literature also suggests that consumers judge products more favorably when happy (Isen, Shalker, Clark, & Karp, 1978) and more negatively when sad (Axelrod, 1963). Products presented with stimuli inducing a happy mood are liked better than products associated with an unhappy mood, unless consumers are aware of the source of their mood (Gorn, Goldberg, & Basu, 1993). Moreover, happy mood may also induce less systematic processing of advertising (e.g. Batra & Stayman, 1990) and consequently a less critical product evaluation (for a general review of mood and information processing see chapter 18, this volume). In combination, this would suggest that the increased desire for some products following bad mood may be countered by the tendency toward more critical product attitudes.

One of the topics that has raised the most interest is the effect of moods induced by a TV program on the processing of commercials shown in the program. In other words, is advertising more effective when placed in a sitcom, a drama, or a documentary? A recent meta-analysis of relevant studies (Mattenklott, 1998) reveals ambiguous results for the effect of program induced mood on ad recall. Happy and funny programs seemed to be superior to extremely sad and depressing programs (e.g. about the Nuremberg trials) but inferior to neutral programs. It is argued that sad material is more involving than happy material and consequently distracts more from processing the ads that interrupt it. The programs that are affectively more neutral may increase the degree to which the commercials stand out, and thus the commercials are better recalled later (if one can assume that viewers stay tuned to the program – see below). As this illustrates, mood effects as elicited by TV programs are hard to distinguish from effects of arousal elicited by these programs. A study that separated arousal from valence (Pavelchak, Antil, & Munch, 1988) measured recall for ads shown during the Superbowl in the winning, losing, and a neutral city and found that recall remained unaffected by the valence of the emotion but was negatively related to the intensity of the emotion (i.e. arousal and extremity of emotion).

With regard to program effects on judgment, sad mood seems to decrease the liking for an advertised product (Axelrod, 1963; Yi, 1990). Interestingly, one study (Kamins, Marks, & Skinner, 1991) also looked at the affective tone of the commercial and found that the positive effect of happy programming only emerged for a happy commercial. A sad commercial, an appeal to drug abusers to seek professional help, was liked better when placed in a sad than in a happy program. In line with findings by Martin, Abend, Sedikides, & Green (1997), one may argue that consumers found the appeal more moving when in a sad rather than happy mood and consequently evaluated it more favorably.

Cross-cultural differences in advertising

As new global markets emerge, and existing markets become increasingly segmented along ethnic or subcultural lines, the need to communicate effectively with consumers who have different cultural values has never been more acute. Thus, it is no surprise that cultural differences are gaining increased attention in consumer research, as they are in social psychology.

Comparisons between individualistic cultures (e.g. North American and Western European countries) and collectivistic cultures (e.g. Asian, Latin American, and African countries; see chapter 2, this volume, for a general discussion of these concepts) have yielded sharp distinctions between these cultural types in the advertising appeals that tend to be used, as well as in the processing and persuasiveness of those appeals. For instance, American advertisers are often exhorted to focus on the brand's attributes and advantages (e.g. Ogilvy, 1985), based on the assumption that consumer learning about the brand precedes liking and buying the brand (e.g. Lavidge & Steiner, 1961).

In contrast, as Miracle (1987) has suggested, the typical goal of advertisements in Japan appears very different. There, ads tend to focus on "making friends" with the audience and showing that the company understands their feelings. The assumption is that consumers will buy once they feel familiar with and trust the company. Because Japan and other Pacific Rim countries are "high context" cultures that tend toward implicit and indirect communication practices (Hall, 1976), Miracle suggested that the mood and tone of commercials in these countries will be particularly important in establishing trust. Indeed, studies have shown that ads in Japan rely more on symbolism, mood, and aesthetics and less on direct brand comparisons than do ads in the US (e.g. Hong, Muderrisoglu, & Zinkhan, 1987).

This is not to suggest that advertisements in collectivist societies use a "soft sell" approach in contrast to a "hard sell," information-driven approach in the West. Information content in the ads of collectivist cultures can be very high, sometimes higher than in the US (for a review see Taylor, Miracle, & Wilson, 1997). It is more an issue of the type of appeal that the information is supporting.

For instance, a content analysis revealed that in Korea, compared to the US, magazine ads are more focused on family well-being, interdependence, and harmony, and are less focused on self-improvement, independence, and individuality (Han & Shavitt, 1994). However, as one might expect, the nature of the advertised product moderates these effects. Cultural differences emerge strongly for products that tend to be purchased and used with other persons (e.g. groceries, cars). Products that do not tend to be shared (e.g. health and beauty aids, clothing) are promoted more in terms of personal, individualistic benefits in both countries.

The persuasiveness of appeals appears to mirror cultural differences in their prevalence. An experiment by Han & Shavitt (1994) showed that appeals to individualistic values (e.g. "Solo cleans with a softness that you will love") are more persuasive in the US and appeals to collectivistic values (e.g. "Solo cleans with a softness that your family will love") are more persuasive in Korea. Again, however, this effect was much more evident for products that are shared (laundry detergent, clothes iron) than for those that are not (chewing gum, running shoes). Zhang & Gelb (1996) in an experiment in the US and China found a similar pattern in the persuasiveness of individualistic versus collectivistic appeals. Moreover, this effect was moderated by whether the advertised product is socially visible (camera) versus privately used (toothbrush).

As to the role of culture in the processing of ad information, research is in its infancy. What is known suggests that general models of cognitive processing and cognitive responding are useful frameworks across cultures (e.g. Aaker & Maheswaran, 1997; Shavitt, Nelson, & Yuan, 1997). However, cultural differences emerge in the diagnosticity of certain types of information. For instance, Aaker & Maheswaran (1997) showed that consensus information regarding other consumers' opinions is not treated as a heuristic cue by Hong Kong Chinese (as it is in the US; Maheswaran & Chaiken, 1991), but is instead perceived and processed as diagnostic information. Thus, collectivists resolve inconsistency in favor of consensus information, not brand attributes. This would be expected in a culture that stresses conformity and responsiveness to others' views. Yet cues whose (low) diagnosticity does not vary cross-culturally (e.g. number of attributes presented) elicit similar heuristic processing in the US and Hong Kong.

2   What Distinguishes the Consumer Domain from Other Social Domains?

In this section, we discuss some of the important and often unrecognized differences between the consumer domain and other social domains, and why those unique aspects may invite some expansion of social cognitive theories.

Distinction 1: Marketing Messages Have Important Implicit Effects

Marketing communications often influence consumers via mechanisms that are implicit and unconscious. In psychology, interest in implicit social cognition is rapidly increasing (see chapter 7, this volume). Nevertheless, although there are exceptions, most studies of communication and persuasion focus on conscious and explicit processes of message evaluation. Explicit processes are relevant in cases where focal attention is directed to the message. Indeed, in laboratory persuasion experiments, participants often have little choice but to so direct their attention. However, in the real world, hundreds of messages compete daily for our attention. Most of them are hardly noticed, yet they may well influence later judgments. Interest in implicit processes in the consumer domain predated much of the social cognition research on the topic. In a classic paper, Herbert Krugman (1965) hypothesized that consumer judgments and purchase decisions may often be influenced by incidental learning of advertising information (see also Greenwald & Leavitt, 1984). Moreover, a repetitive TV ad campaign may not only effect the "overlearning" of unattended product information, it may also change the *structure* of product perceptions. Thus, repeated exposure to an ad for, say, a soft drink may gradually shift the attributes that are salient in evaluating the beverage from "refreshing taste" to "youthful" or "modern." These shifts may not be detected by standard attitude measures. Indeed, they may not even be noticeable prior to a behavioral decision. As Krugman suggested, "the purchase situation is the catalyst that reassembles or brings out all the potentials for shifts in salience that have accumulated up to that point. The product or package is then suddenly seen in a new, "'somehow different' light although nothing verbalizable may have changed *up to that point.*" To assess such effects, "one might look for gradual shifts in perceptual structure, aided by repetition, activated by behavioral-choice situations, and *followed* at some time by attitude change" (Krugman, 1965, pp. 354–355; italics in original).

Recent research has yielded robust evidence that incidental exposure to information may affect consumer judgments and that it is not necessary that the consumer recollect the initial exposure or material (e.g. Janiszewski, 1993; Shapiro, MacInnis, & Heckler, 1997). In a typical study, consumers are exposed to advertisements, brand names, or packaging stimuli while their focal attention is directed elsewhere. In line with prior research on mere exposure effects (see Bornstein, 1989), these preattentive exposures elicit greater subsequent liking for the ad or brand, and even an increased likelihood of including the advertised product in a consideration set for a hypothetical purchase (Shapiro, MacInnis, & Heckler, 1997). Moreover, although behavioral effects of unattended ad exposure have not yet been demonstrated, recent findings in social cognition have shown that direct behavioral effects of incidentally encountered stimuli are possible when those stimuli prime existing stereotypes (e.g. Bargh, Chen, & Burrows, 1996). Thus, it seems likely that preattentively processed marketing messages could elicit behavioral effects when they activate existing product-user stereotypes or usage-related concepts in memory.

At a somewhat higher level of processing involvement, in which focal attention is directed at comprehending but not evaluating brand claims, simple repetition of ad claims heightens their perceived validity (e.g. Hawkins & Hoch, 1992; see also Hasher, Goldstein, & Toppino, 1977). Thus, existing research provides substantial support for Krugman's (1965) theorizing, at least in terms of the repetition-induced "overlearning" of information that receives little or no focal processing. The evidence is all the more impressive given that these studies typically rely upon explicit attitudinal measures.

Because a large proportion of the consumer information to which we are exposed is not elaborated or even perceived consciously, the consumer domain provides a prime field for further research on preattentive processes. In particular, studies are needed to examine the processes by which unattended messages can alter the structure of product or topic perceptions. Can repeated, preattentive exposures to an ad campaign influence not only whether a brand is liked but also whether the characteristics claimed in the ad (e.g. "youthful") become more salient and drive that evaluation? If the salience of advertised characteristics does indeed increase as a function of preattentive ad exposure, does it influence the basis on which one compares and selects (e.g. choosing the brand that is perceived to be "most youthful")? At what point, if ever, are these effects recognized by the consumer? In line with Krugman (1965), we suggest that research in this area will yield the strongest evidence to the extent that it relies on implicit measures of attribute salience, the behavioral choices that reflect relative salience, and other indirect measures.

Distinction 2: Marketing Messages Communicate via Non-verbal Channels

Social psychological research on message processing and persuasion has focused mainly on the processing of verbal information to the relative neglect of other modes of communication. But marketers use pictures, fonts, logos, colors, layouts, and other visual elements to draw attention, evoke associations, and convey meanings. The same is true for the use of music, jingles, sounds effects, and other auditory stimuli, as well as for fragrances and textures (e.g. "smooth as silk"; see Solomon, 1992). All of these non-verbal modalities may affect judgments directly. They may affect the processing of verbal information by distracting from, facilitating, or biasing it. They may serve as recall or recognition cues for brand information. But most importantly they may carry meaning in their own right.

Many CIP studies of non-verbal inputs have been inspired by psychological constructs and theories. For example, the role of attractive photographs or pleasing music in influencing brand attitudes via classical-conditioning or mood-eliciting processes has been explored (e.g. Gorn, Goldberg, & Basu, 1993; Stuart, Shimp, & Engle, 1987), as has the role of visual inputs as cues that can provide product information in simplified form (e.g. Mitchell & Olson, 1981; Petty, Cacioppo, & Schumann, 1983). Other work has paid greater attention to the unique qualities of these modalities and the ways in which they influence processing (e.g. Kellaris, Cox, & Cox, 1993; MacInnis & Park, 1991), as well as convey meaning (Phillips, 1997; Scott, 1990, 1994). It is on these latter effects of non-verbal inputs that we focus. We review a sampling of this large literature below, focusing primarily on the role of visual elements.

Visual elements are critical in virtually all forms of marketing communications and influence consumer perceptions in multiple ways. For instance, the colors used on packaging and in ads can directly influence product perceptions through their symbolic meanings and cultural associations. Gold lettering on a wine bottle conveys wealth and elegance, whereas yellow packaging for snack food connotes "fun" (for a review see Solomon, 1992).

CIP researchers have also shown that the effects of visuals on judgment and recall depend on the match between the degree or nature of the visual presentation and several other factors, such as the consumer's decision-making style (Meyers-Levy & Peracchio, 1996) and the level of visual imagery associated with the product information (Unnava &

Burnkrant, 1991). The effects of ad visuals also depend on the congruity or consistency between the verbal and visual elements in the ad (e.g. Smith, 1991; see Kellaris, Cox, & Cox, 1993, for similar conclusions regarding the congruity of verbal and musical elements). The function of the product attitude may also influence the way certain visual depictions are processed. Shavitt, Swan, Lowrey, and Wänke (1994) showed that pictures of spokes-persons convey social-image information that may be centrally processed when the product evaluation serves a social-identity function.

In a number of studies, researchers have investigated the effects of visual elements such as the camera angle of ad photos, the use of color in ads, and ad layout characteristics (e.g. Meyers-Levy & Peracchio, 1995, 1996). Under low motivation to process the ad, consistent with dual process models of persuasion, the general finding is that visual elements can act as peripheral cues. However, under higher motivation to process, the effects are more complex because visual elements can either enhance or impede attempts to evaluate the product. For instance, full color ads may outperform black-and-white ads when processed peripherally, but may swamp the available cognitive resources needed to scrutinize ad claims when processing more elaborately (see MacInnis & Park, 1991, for similar conclusions regarding the effects of musical elements on information processing).

Clearly, then, visuals are more than mere affect or simple cues that are easily processed. Researchers who analyze the meaning that pictures convey from a rhetorical standpoint have offered a distinct viewpoint on the processing and interpretation of visuals. For instance, Scott (1994) suggests that some psychological research on the effects of visuals has tended to view visuals as simple reflections of reality that require little interpretive activity. However, as she points out, viewers actively interpret visual material based on extensive past experience with pictorial stimuli. These experiences render visuals a shared symbol system, like language, that communicates not through resemblance to reality but through pictorial *conventions*. Viewers' interpretations are sensitive to context and to stylistic mannerisms in the visual depiction. Thus, for instance, a picture of a fluffy, black kitten paired with a package of toilet paper would elicit a metaphorical interpretation ("soft as a kitten"; Mitchell & Olson, 1981), but paired with an allergy medicine would elicit very different inferences, and rendered in Halloween style would trigger still other associations (see Scott, 1990, for similar conclusions regarding the rhetorical role of music in advertising).

We suggest that psychological understanding of information processing and persuasion would be enhanced by a greater focus on non-verbal elements, particularly by taking into account the rhetorical richness of those elements.

Distinction 3: Product Evaluation is Not the Only Goal of Consumers

Social psychological research on information processing focuses principally on the goal of forming valid attitudes or judgments toward objects or message topics. The result is that the knowledge derived from this voluminous literature consists largely of principles about how messages influence recipients' attitudes toward advocated positions. This is a very important body of knowledge, and earlier we discussed the profound influence it has had upon consumer research in general.

However, the assumption that the goal of topic-attitude validity drives message processing implies that people typically approach marketing communications with the goal of extracting brand information. Actually, their goals may be much broader, including the hedonic motives served by ad exposure. The notion that people can enjoy ad exposure may seem odd to psychologists, who typically study and view ads as (often unwelcome) carriers of product information. However, in a recent national survey, most respondents reported that they like to look at the advertisements to which they are exposed (Shavitt, Lowrey, & Haefner, 1998). Indeed, data on the structure of advertising attitudes have repeatedly shown that the hedonic experience associated with ad exposure contributes greatly to driving public attitudes toward advertising, sometimes more so than do perceptions of the usefulness or trustworthiness of ad information (see Shavitt, Lowrey, & Haefner, 1998).

Recognizing that enjoyment is a primary basis for evaluating advertising can draw attention to other CIP facets than those that assume argument based discourse. As Wells (1988) points out, many ads are not lectures but dramas. Ads with dramatic elements appear to be processed differently than argument based ads, eliciting persuasion via empathy rather than argument evaluation (Deighton, Romer, & McQueen, 1989). Dramatic appeals are effective to the extent that they generate feeling responses and a sense of verisimilitude to their stories.

The use of storytelling and entertainment as persuasive strategies is neither new nor limited to commercial appeals. Further social psychological research on these processes would illuminate our understanding of the persuasive effects of narratives in editorials, political speeches, charity appeals, as well as ads.

Distinction 4: The Message Itself is a Target of Judgment

As already noted, consumer researchers have recognized that consumers have other goals pertaining to persuasion events besides the formation of valid topic attitudes. Among these goals are the evaluation of the message itself and those responsible for it. Therefore, consumer research has emphasized recipients' reactions to the *enterprise* of advertising persuasion – focusing upon advertisements and the practice of advertising as attitude objects.

Attitude toward the ad

In a recent commercial for Kellogg's Special K cereal, a series of middle-aged men appear on screen, each bemoaning some aspect of his physical build. The ad gently parodies women's obsession with their weight by having the men speak in feminine clichés (e.g. "I have my mother's thighs. I just have to accept that."). The intended audience, health- and weight-conscious women, is likely to find the ad hilarious, if somewhat mocking. Yet, although the emphasis on weight-control is consistent with Special K's established positioning strategy in the highly competitive breakfast-cereal market, virtually no information about the cereal itself is presented in the commercial. How, then, can we conceptualize the likely persuasive impact of this campaign?

One might view the effects of this campaign as illustrating simple affect transfer or classical conditioning. One might consider the humorous nature of the ad as constituting a peripheral cue to product evaluation, although what would be cued by the humor is not clear. Or one might consider that ad viewers are processing this ad more thoughtfully, drawing inferences about the company based on the rhetorical strategy it has chosen. All of these inferences, perceptions, affective reactions, and the resultant *attitudes toward the ad* may ultimately influence perceptions of the advertised brand in a variety of ways.

The attitude-toward-the-ad construct (A_{ad}) has been extensively researched in CIP. A_{ad} has been conceptualized in ways that parallel other attitude definitions (for a review see Cohen & Areni, 1991). Thus, A_{ad} can be formed either via the central or the peripheral route and can be based on affective or cognitive factors. The key assumption is that the consumer's A_{ad} is distinct from her attitude toward the brand (A_{brand}), and that A_{ad} mediates the effect of an ad on A_{brand} under certain conditions (Mitchell & Olson, 1981). A number of mediational models have been proposed, and research has yielded evidence for different mechanisms by which A_{ad} might mediate advertising effects on A_{brand} (see Cohen & Areni, 1991).

A variety of factors are thought to influence A_{ad}. Pictures, music, and other non-verbal elements influence $A_{ad,}$ and some of the studies of non-verbal elements cited earlier have conceptualized these elements as influencing A_{brand} via their impact on A_{ad} (e.g. MacInnis & Park, 1991; Mitchell & Olson, 1981). In addition to executional factors, Lutz (1985) hypothesized a variety of other antecedents of A_{ad}, including the ad's credibility, attitude toward the advertiser and toward advertising, and the recipient's mood state. Recent evidence has supported the impact of some of these factors on A_{ad} (e.g. Obermiller & Spangenberg, 1998).

Ad skepticism

Research on ad skepticism has included studies of public opinion toward ad trustworthiness and believability of ads as well as research on the factors that elicit skeptical responses. Public opinion toward advertising has long been a focus of survey research (for a review see Calfee & Ringold, 1994). Many of these surveys point to widespread and enduring skepticism about advertising, coexisting with a belief in the utility of advertising information. Indeed, when focused upon their own experiences and personally relevant decisions, survey respondents view advertising as more reliable and express greater confidence in it than when rating the trustworthiness of advertising in general terms (Shavitt, Lowrey, & Haefner, 1998).

A number of factors affect the skepticism with which a message is received. For instance, certain attention-getting tactics in advertisements (e.g. the delayed identification of the product being advertised) may tend to invite consumer skepticism (Campbell, 1995). The effects of these tactics on persuasion appear to be mediated by inferences that the ad is attempting to manipulate, or unfairly persuade, the recipient. Once those inferences are triggered by structural features of the ad, resistance to persuasion may result.

Also, some people are more likely than others to respond skeptically to advertisements. Obermiller & Spangenberg (1998) showed that reliable individual differences in ad skepticism exist, and that one's degree of ad skepticism predicts the degree to which one responds unfavorably to ads. Ad skepticism is not unrelated to the more general social psychological construct of influenceability (see Rhodes & Wood, 1992). Indeed, as with individual differences in influenceability, individuals higher in ad skepticism tend to be higher in self-esteem. However, Obermiller and Spangenberg showed that ad skepticism does not reflect a general tendency to disbelieve communications. It appears instead to be associated with consumers' implicit theories about the marketplace.

Persuasion knowledge

The above research examples demonstrate the value of considering that advertising is a shared sociocultural experience with which consumers have extensive experience and about which consumers develop extensive folk knowledge (Friestad & Wright, 1994). They recognize that advertisements are designed to persuade, and that the visuals, music, and copy all are crafted with particular rhetorical intentions.

Thus, consumers likely approach advertisements with the goal of "sizing up" the qualities of the message and the agent behind it. Indeed, drawing such inferences can be important to making effective marketplace decisions. The Persuasion Knowledge Model (PKM: Friestad & Wright, 1994) focuses on these processes. According to the PKM, consumers over time develop personal knowledge about the tactics that persuasion practitioners use. In any persuasion episode, the consumer deploys her available knowledge about the topic, the agents, and about persuasive tactics in general in order to evaluate the situation and guide her responses to it. The model has some relevance to the social psychological literature on forewarning of persuasive intent (e.g. Haas & Grady, 1975) and on attribution-theory accounts of persuasion (e.g. Eagly, Wood, & Chaiken, 1978), but focuses in greater detail on lay knowledge about persuasion processes in general, as well as on the accumulation and impact of that knowledge.

Friestad and Wright theorize that persuasion knowledge may interact with and qualify the effects of other variables on persuasion. For instance, individual differences in persuasion knowledge may moderate the effectiveness of particular persuasive tactics. Also, the awareness or labeling of an agent's action as a "persuasion tactic" may prompt changes in the processing and effectiveness of the message, as well as in a consumer's construal of persuasion attempts in general. A number of studies have yielded data congenial to the PKM. For instance, extensive research has indicated that consumers draw specific, predictable conclusions about marketers and their products from particular ad campaign elements (conclusions that are unstated and possibly unintended by the advertiser). Kirmani (1997) demonstrated that the number of times an ad is repeated serves as a signal to the quality of an unfamiliar brand. However, at very high levels of repetition, consumers perceive the expenditure as excessive and infer that "something must be wrong" with the brand. This relationship between repetition and quality perceptions is mediated not by irritation and boredom (as implied by information-processing views of repetition; e.g. Batra & Ray, 1986; Cacioppo & Petty, 1979) but by perceptions about the manufacturer's confidence in the brand.

These findings point to the importance of recognizing that the consumer's task in responding to an ad campaign is much more complex than the evaluation of specific message arguments. The consumer responds to a broader set of message factors whose implications for judgment are often inferred through the use of extensive folk knowledge about the persuasion enterprise.

Conclusion

Clearly, social-cognition principles have translated very well into the consumer domain. Above, we have reviewed the substantial evidence for some of these principles in the consumer context. However, despite overlap in these domains, it should be stressed that consumer research is not simply social psychology applied to products instead of persons. Each field focuses on questions specific to its domain. That is, social-cognitive models have generally been designed to illuminate processes in the perception of persons, social groups, or social/political issues. CIP models have attempted to address issues that are salient in the marketplace of products and messages.

So far, the interdisciplinary exchange has been rather one-sided, but above we have pointed out a number of arenas where opportunities exist for more balanced exchange. Being cognizant of the unique features of the consumer domain will serve both to enhance knowledge about consumer behavior and to stimulate expansion of basic social-cognitive models.

References

Aaker, J. L., & Maheswaran, D. (1997). The effect of cultural orientation on persuasion. *Journal of Consumer Research, 24* (3), 315–328.

Agres, S. J., Edell, J. A., & Dubitsky, T. M. (1990). *Emotion in advertising: Theoretical and practical explorations.* New York: Quorum Books.

Alba, J. W., & Hutchinson, J. W. (1987). Dimensions of consumer expertise. *Journal of Consumer Research, 13,* 411–454.

Alba, J. W., Hutchinson, J. W., & Lynch, J. G. (1991). Memory and decision making. In T. S. Robertson & H. H. Kassarjian (Eds.), *Handbook of consumer behavior* (pp. 1–49). Englewood Cliffs, NJ: Prentice-Hall.

Axelrod, J. (1963). Induced moods and attitudes toward products. *Journal of Advertising Research, 3,* 19–24.

Baker, W. E., & Lutz, R. J. (1988). The relevance-accessibility model of advertising effectiveness. In S. Hecker & D. M. Stewart (Eds.), *Nonverbal communications in advertising* (pp. 59–84). Lexington, MA: Lexington.

Bargh, J. A., Chen, M., & Burrows, L. (1996). Automaticity of social behavior: Direct effects of trait construct and stereotype activation on action. *Journal of Personality and Social Psychology, 71* (2), 230–244.

Batra, R., & Ray, M. L. (1986). Situational effects of advertising repetition: The moderating influence of motivation, ability, and opportunity to respond. *Journal of Consumer Research, 12* (March), 432–445.

Batra, R., & Stayman, D. M. (1990). The role of mood in advertising effectiveness. *Journal of Consumer Research, 17,* 203–214.

Berger, I. E., & Mitchell, A. A. (1989). The effect of advertising on attitude accessibility, attitude confidence, and the attitude-behavior relationship. *Journal of Consumer Research, 16*, 269–279.

Bettmann, J. R., Johnson, E. J., & Payne, J. W. (1991). Consumer decision making. In T. S. Robertson & H. H. Kassarjian (Eds.), *Handbook of consumer behavior* (pp. 50–84). Englewood Cliffs, NJ: Prentice-Hall.

Biehal, G. J., & Chakravarti, D. (1983). Information accessibility as a moderator of consumer choice. *Journal of Consumer Research, 10*, 1–14.

Bornstein, R. F. (1989). Exposure and affect: Overview and meta-analysis of research, 1968–1987. *Psychological Bulletin, 106* (September), 265–289.

Boush, D., & Loken, B. (1991). A process tracing study of brand extension evaluations. *Journal of Marketing Research, 19*, 16–28.

Broniarczyk, S. M., & Alba, J. W. (1994). The importance of the brand in brand extension. *Journal of Marketing Research, 31*, 214–228.

Cacioppo, J. T., & Petty, R. E. (1979): Effects of message repetition and position on cognitive response, recall, and persuasion. *Journal of Personality and Social Psychology, 37* (January), 97–109.

Calder, B. J., & Sternthal, B. (1980). Television commercial wearout: An information processing view. *Journal of Marketing Research, 17*, 173–186.

Calfee, J. E., & Ringold, D. J. (1994). The seventy-percent majority: Enduring consumer beliefs about advertising. *Journal of Public Policy and Marketing, 13*, 228–238.

Campbell, M. (1995). When attention-getting advertising tactics elicit consumer inferences of manipulative intent: The importance of balancing benefits and investments. *Journal of Consumer Psychology, 4*, 225–254.

Carpenter, G. S., Glazer, R., & Nakamoto, K. (1994). Meaningful brands from meaningless differentiation: The dependence on irrelevant attributes. *Journal of Marketing Research, 31*, 339–350.

Childers, T. L., & Houston, M. J. (1984). Conditions for a picture-superiority effect on consumer theory. *Journal of Consumer Research, 15*, 643–654.

Cohen, J.B., & Areni, C. S. (1991). Affect and consumer behavior. In T. S. Robertson & H. H. Kassarjian (Eds.), *Handbook of consumer behavior* (pp. 188–240). Englewood Cliffs, NJ: Prentice-Hall.

Deighton, J., Romer, D., & McQueen, J. (1989). Using drama to persuade. *Journal of Consumer Research, 16* (3), 335–343.

Dhar, R., & Simonson, I. (1992). The effects of the focus of comparison on consumer preferences. *Journal of Marketing Research, 29*, 430–440.

Dhar, R., & Wertenbroch, K. (1997). Consumer choice between hedonic and utilitarian goods. Unpublished manuscript. New Haven, CT: Yale University.

Eagly, A. H., Wood, W., & Chaiken, S. (1978). Causal inferences about communicators and their effect on opinion change. *Journal of Personality and Social Psychology, 36*, 424–435.

Feldman, J. M., & Lynch, J. G. (1988). Self-generated validity and other effects of measurement on belief, attitude, intention, and behavior. *Journal of Applied Psychology, 73*, 421–435.

Friestad, M., & Wright, P. (1994). The persuasion knowledge model: How people cope with persuasion attempts. *Journal of Consumer Research, 21* (1), 1–31.

Gardner, M. P. (1994). Responses to emotional and informational appeals: The moderating role of context-induced mood states. In E. M. Clark & T. C. Brock (Eds.), *Attention, attitude, and affect in response to advertising* (pp. 207–221). Hillsdale, NJ: Lawrence Erlbaum Associates.

Goodstein, R. C. (1993). Category-based applications and extensions in advertising: Motivating more extensive ad processing. *Journal of Consumer Research, 20*, 87–99.

Gorn, G. J., Goldberg, M. E., & Basu, K. (1993). Mood, awareness, and product evaluation. *Journal of Consumer Research, 2*, 237–256.

Greenwald, A. G., & Leavitt, C. (1984). Audience involvement in advertising: Four levels. *Journal of Consumer Research, 11* (June), 581–592.

Haas, R. G., & Grady, K. (1975). Temporal delay, type of forewarning, and resistance to influence. *Journal of Experimental Social Psychology, 11* (September), 459–469.

Hall, E. T. (1976). *Beyond culture*. Garden City, NJ: Anchor Press/Doubleday.

Han, S., & Shavitt, S. (1994). Persuasion and culture: Advertising appeals in individualistic and collectivistic societies. *Journal of Experimental Social Psychology, 30*, 326–350.

Hasher, L., Goldstein, D., & Toppino, T. (1977). Frequency and the conference of referential validity. *Journal of Verbal Learning and Verbal Behavior, 16* (1), 107–112.

Hawkins, S. A., & Hoch, S. J. (1992). Low-involvement learning: Memory without evaluation. *Journal of Consumer Research, 19* (2), 212–225.

Herr, P. M., Farquahar, P. H., & Fazio, R. H. (1996). Impact of dominance and relatedness on brand extensions. *Journal of Consumer Psychology*, 135–160.

Hong, J. W., Muderrisoglu, A., & Zinkhan, G. M. (1987). Cultural differences in advertising expression: A comparative content analysis of Japanese and US magazine advertising. *Journal of Advertising, 16* (1), 55–62.

Houston, M. J., Childers, T. L., & Heckler, S. E. (1987). Picture-word consistency and the elaborative processing of advertisements. *Journal of Marketing Research, 24*, 359–370.

Huber, J., Payne, J. W., & Puto, C. (1982). Adding asymmetrically dominated alternatives: Violations of regularity and the similarity heuristic. *Journal of Consumer Research, 9*, 90–98.

Isen, A. M., Shalker, T. E., Clark, M., & Karp, L. (1978). Affect, accessibility of material in memory, and behavior: A cognitive loop? *Journal of Personality and Social Psychology, 36*, 1–12.

Janiszewski, C. (1993). Preattentive mere exposure effects. *Journal of Consumer Research, 20* (3), 376–392.

Johar, G. V. (1995). Consumer involvement and deception from implied advertising claims. *Journal of Marketing Research, 32*, 267–279.

Kahneman, D., & Snell, J. S. (1992). Predicting a changing taste: Do people know what they will like? *Journal of Behavioral Decision Making, 5*, 187–200.

Kamins, M. A., Marks, L. J., & Skinner, D. (1991). Television commercial evaluation in the context of program induced mood: Congruency versus consistency effects. *Journal of Advertising, 20*, 1–14.

Kardes, F. R. (1993). Consumer inference: Determinants, consequences, and implications for advertising. In A. A. Mitchell (Ed.), *Advertising exposure, memory and choice* (pp. 163–191). Hillsdale, NJ: Lawrence Erlbaum Associates.

Kellaris, J. J., Cox, A. D., & Cox, D. (1993). The effect of background music on ad processing: A contingency explanation. *Journal of Marketing, 57* (4), 114–125.

Keller, P. A., & Block, L. (1997). Vividness effects: A resource-matching perspective. *Journal of Consumer Research, 24*, 295–304.

Kirmani, A. (1997). Advertising repetition as a signal of quality: If it's advertised so much, something must be wrong. *Journal of Advertising, 26* (3), 77–86.

Kisielius, J., & Sternthal, B. (1984). Detecting and explaining vividness effects in attitudinal judgments. *Journal of Marketing Research, 21*, 54–64.

Krugman, H. E. (1965). The impact of television advertising: Learning without involvement. *Public Opinion Quarterly, 29* (3), 349–356.

Lavidge, R. C., & Steiner, G. A. (1961). A model for predictive measurements of advertising effectiveness. *Journal of Marketing, 25* (4), 59–62.

Leong, S. M. (1989). A citation analysis of the Journal of Consumer Research. *Journal of Consumer Research, 15*, 492–497.

Lewis, E. S. E. 1898: Die AIDA-Regel. Cited from H. Jacobi (1963). *Werbepsychologie*. Wiesbaden: Gabler.

Loken, B., & Roedder-John, D. (1993). Diluting brand beliefs: When do brand extensions have a negative impact? *Journal of Marketing, 57*, 71–84.

Lutz, R. J. (1985). Affective and cognitive antecedents of attitude toward the ad: A conceptual framework. In L. F. Alwitt & A. A. Mitchell (Eds.), *Psychological processes and advertising effects: Theory, research and applications* (pp. 45–63). Hillsdale, NJ: Erlbaum.

Lynch, J. G., Marmorstein, H., & Weigold, M. F. (1988). Choices from sets including remembered brands: Use of recalled attributes and prior overall evaluations. *Journal of Consumer Research, 15* (2), 169–184.

MacInnis, D. J., & Park, C. W. (1991). The differential role of characteristics of music on high- and low-involvement consumers' processing of ads. *Journal of Consumer Research, 18* (2), 161–173.

Maheswaran, D., & Chaiken, S. (1991). Promoting systematic processing in low-motivation settings: Effect of incongruent information on processing and judgment. *Journal of Personality and Social Psychology 61* (July), 13–25.

Martin, L. L., Abend, T., Sedikides, C., & Green, J. D. (1997). How would it feel if . . . ? Mood as input to a role fulfillment evaluation process. *Journal of Personality and Social Psychology, 73,* 242–253.

Mattenklott, A. (1998). Werbewirkung im Umfeld von Fernsehprogrammen: Programmvermittelte Aktivierung und Stimmung. *Zeitschrift für Sozialpsychologie, 29,* 175–193.

Meyers-Levy, J., & Peracchio, L. A. (1995). Understanding the effects of color: How the correspondence between available and required resources affects attitudes. *Journal of Consumer Research, 22,* 121–138.

Meyers-Levy, J., & Peracchio, L. A. (1996). Moderators of the impact of self-reference or persuasion. *Journal of Consumer Research, 22,* 408–423.

Meyers-Levy, J., & Tybout, A. M. (1997). Context effects at encoding and judgment in consumption settings: The role of cognitive resources. *Journal of Consumer Research, 24* (1), 1–14.

Miracle, G. E. (1987). Feel-do-learn: An alternative sequence underlying Japanese consumer response to television commercials. In F. G. Feasley (Ed.), *The proceedings of the 1987 conference of the American Academy of Advertising* (pp. R73–R78). Columbia, SC: University of South Carolina.

Mitchell, A. A. (1986). The effects of verbal and visual components of advertisements on brand attitudes and attitude toward the advertisement. *Journal of Consumer Research, 13,* 12–24.

Mitchell, A. A. (Ed.) (1993). *Advertising exposure, memory, and choice.* Hillsdale, NJ: Lawrence Erlbaum Associates.

Mitchell, A. A., & Olson, J. C. (1981). Are product attribute beliefs the only mediator of advertising effects on brand attitude? *Journal of Marketing Research, 18,* 318–332.

Moore, D. J., Reardon, R., & Durso, F. T. (1986). The generation effect in advertising appeals. *Advances in Consumer Research, 13,* 117–120.

Moorthy, S., Ratchford, B. T., & Talukdar, D. (1997). Consumer information search revisited: Theory and empirical analysis. *Journal of Consumer Research, 23,* 263–277.

Nedungadi, P. (1990). Recall and consumer consideration sets: Influencing choice without altering brand evaluations. *Journal of Consumer Research, 17,* 263–276.

Obermiller, C., & Spangenberg, E. R. (1998). Development of a scale to measure consumer skepticism toward advertising. *Journal of Consumer Psychology, 7* (2), 159–186.

Ogilvy, D. (1985). *Ogilvy on advertising.* New York: Vintage Books.

O'Guinn, T. C., & Faber, R. J. (1991). Mass communication and consumer behavior. In T. S. Robertson & H. H. Kassarjian (Eds.), *Handbook of consumer behavior* (pp. 349–400). Englewood Cliffs, NJ: Prentice-Hall.

Park, C. W., McCarthy, M. S., & Milberg, S. J. (1993). The effects associated with direct and associative brand extension strategies on consumer response to brand extensions. *Advances in Consumer Research, 20,* 28–33.

Park, C. W., Milberg, S., & Lawson, R. (1991). Evaluation of brand extensions: The role of product feature similarity and brand concept consistency. *Journal of Consumer Research, 18,* 185–193.

Pavelchak, M. A., Antil, J. H., & Munch, J. M. (1988). The Super Bowl: An investigation into the relationship among program context, emotional experience, and ad recall. *Journal of Consumer Research, 15,* 360–367.

Petty, R. E., Cacioppo, J. T., & Schumann, D. (1983). Central and peripheral routes to advertising effectiveness: The moderating role of involvement. *Journal of Consumer Research, 10* (2), 135–146.

Phillips, B. J. (1997). Thinking into it: Consumer interpretation of complex advertising images. *Journal of Advertising, 26* (2) 77–87

Ratneshwar, S., & Shocker, A. D. (1991). Substitution in use and the role of usage context in product category structures. *Journal of Marketing Research, 28,* 281–295.

Rhodes, N., & Wood, W. (1992). Self-esteem and intelligence affect influenceability: The mediation role of message reception. *Psychological Bulletin, 111,* 156–171.

Robertson, T. S., & Kassarjian, H. H. (Eds.), (1991). *Handbook of consumer behavior.* Englewood Cliffs, NJ: Prentice-Hall.

Rossiter, J. R., & Percy, L. (1987). *Advertising and promotion management.* New York: McGraw-Hill.

Sawyer; A. G., & Howard, D. J. (1991). Effects of omitting conclusions in advertisements to involved and uninvolved audiences. *Journal of Marketing Research, 28,* 467–474.

Schmidt, J. B., & Spreng, R. A. (1996). A proposed model of external consumer information search. *Journal of the Academy of Marketing Science, 24,* 246–256.

Schul, Y., & Schiff, M. (1993). Measuring satisfaction with organizations. *Public Opinion Quarterly, 57,* 536–551.

Scott, L. M. (1990). Understanding jingles and needledrop: A rhetorical approach to music in advertising. *Journal of Consumer Research, 17* (September), 223–237.

Scott, L. M. (1994). Images in advertising: The need for a theory of visual rhetoric. *Journal of Consumer Research, 21* (2), 252–273.

Severn, J., Belch, G. E., & Belch, M. A. (1990). The effects of sexual and non-sexual advertising appeals and information level on cognitive processing and communication effectiveness. *Journal of Advertising, 19,* 14–22.

Shapiro, S., MacInnis, D. J., & Heckler, S. E. (1997). The effects of incidental ad exposure on the formation of consideration sets. *Journal of Consumer Research, 24* (1), 94–104.

Shavitt, S., & Brock, T. C. (1986). Self-relevant responses in commercial persuasion: Field and experimental tests. In J. Olson & K. Sentis (Eds.), *Advertising and consumer psychology,* Vol. 3 (pp. 149–171). New York: Praeger Publishers.

Shavitt, S., & Brock, T. C. (1990). Delayed recall of copytest responses: The temporal stability of listed thoughts. *Journal of Advertising, 19* (4), 6–17.

Shavitt, S., Lowrey, P., & Haefner, J. (1998). Public attitudes toward advertising: More favorable than you might think. *Journal of Advertising Research, 38* (4), 7–22.

Shavitt, S., Nelson, M. R., & Yuan, R. M. L. (1997). Exploring cross-cultural differences in cognitive responding to ads. In M. Brucks & D. J. MacInnis (Eds.), *Advances in consumer research,* Vol. 24 (pp. 245–250). Provo, UT: Association for Consumer Research.

Shavitt, S., Swan, S., Lowrey, T. M., & Wänke, M. (1994). The interaction of endorser attractiveness and involvement in persuasion depends on the goal that guides message processing. *Journal of Consumer Psychology, 3* (2), 137–162.

Shocker, A. D., Srivastava, R. K., & Ruekert, R. W. (1994). Challenges and opportunities facing brand management: An introduction to the special issue. *Journal of Marketing Research, 31,* 149–158.

Smith, R. A. (1991). The effects of visual and verbal advertising information on consumers' inferences. *Journal of Advertising, 20,* 13–23.

Solomon, M. R. (1992). *Consumer behavior: Buying, having, and being.* Needham Heights, MA: Allyn and Bacon.

Srull, T. K. (1989). Advertising and product evaluation: The relation between consumer memory and judgment. In P. Cafferata & A. M. Tybout (Eds.), *Cognitive and affective responses to advertising* (pp. 121–134). Lexington, MA: Lexington Books/D. C. Heath.

Stuart, E. W., Shimp, T. A., & Engle, R. W. (1987). Classical conditioning of consumer attitudes: Four experiments in an advertising context. *Journal of Consumer Research, 14,* 334–349.

Sujan, M. (1985). Consumer knowledge: Effects on evaluation strategies mediating consumer judgments. *Journal of Consumer Research, 12,* 31–46.

Taylor, C. R., Miracle, G. E., & Wilson, R. D. (1997). The impact of information level on the effectiveness of US & Korean television commercials. *Journal of Advertising, 26* (1), 1–18.

Tversky, A., & Simonson, I. (1993). Context dependent preferences. *Management Science, 39,* 1179–1189.

Unnava, H. R., & Burnkrant, R. E. (1991). An imagery-processing view of the role of pictures in print advertisements. *Journal of Marketing Research, 28,* 226–231.

Wänke, M., & Bless, H. (in press). Possible mediators of ease of retrieval effects in attitudinal judgments. In H. Bless & J. Forgas (Eds.), *The role of subjective states in social cognition and behavior*. Psychology Press.

Wänke, M., & Bless, H. (in press). The effects of subjective ease of retrieval on attitudinal judgments: The moderating role of processing motivation. In H. Bless & J. P. Forgas (Eds.), *The message within: The role of subjective experience in social cognition and behavior*. Philadelphia: Psychology Press.

Wänke, M., Bless, H., & Biller, B. (1996). Subjective experience versus content of information in the construction of attitude judgments. *Personality and Social Psychology Bulletin, 22*, 1105–1113.

Wänke, M., Bless, H., & Schwarz, N. (1998). Context effects in product line extensions: Context is not destiny. *Journal of Consumer Psychology, 7*, 299–322.

Wänke, M., Bless, H., & Schwarz, N. (in press-a). Lobster, wine, and cigarettes: Ad hoc categorizations and the emergence of context effects. *Marketing Bulletin*.

Wänke, M., Bless, H., & Schwarz, N. (in press-b). Assimilation and contrast in brand and product evaluations: Implications for marketing. *Advances in Consumer Research*.

Wänke, M., Bohner, G., & Jurkowitsch, A. (1997). There are many reasons to drive a BMW: Does imagined ease of argument generation influence attitudes? *Journal of Consumer Research, 24* (2), 170–177.

Wänke, M., Schwarz, N., & Noelle-Neumann, E. (1995). Question wording in comparative judgments: Understanding and manipulating the dynamics of the direction of comparison. *Public Opinion Quarterly, 59*, 347–372.

Ward, J., & Loken, B. (1986). The quintessential snack food: Measurement of product prototypes. In R. J. Lutz (Ed.), *Advances in consumer research*, Vol. 13 (pp. 126–131). Provo, UT: Association for Consumer Research.

Wells, W. D. (1988). Lectures and dramas. In P. Cafferata & A. M. Tybout (Eds.), *Cognitive and affective responses to advertising*. Lexington, MA: Lexington Books/D. C. Heath.

Wilkie, W. L. (1994). *Consumer behavior*. New York: Wiley.

Yi, Y. (1990). The effects of contextual priming in print advertisements. *Journal of Consumer Research, 17* (2), 215–222.

Zhang, Y. & Gelb, B. D. (1996). Matching advertising appeals to culture: The influence of products' use conditions. *Journal of Advertising, 25* (3) 29–46.

Chapter Twenty-Seven

Dealing with Adversity: Self-Regulation, Coping, Adaptation, and Health

Lisa G. Aspinwall

How do people cope with chronic or life-threatening illness and other negative life events, such as bereavement, disability, and long-term unemployment? The study of adversity – of serious, protracted, and often uncontrollable negative experiences – has provided a great deal of information about how personal, social, and other resources are related to psychological well-being and physical health as people manage negative events and information.

In this chapter, I will review what is known about how people cope with adversity and how such efforts are related to psychological adaptation and physical health.[1] In doing so, I will draw on two large research literatures that have yet to be integrated: coping and self-regulation. *Coping* consists of activities undertaken to master, reduce, or tolerate environmental or intrapsychic demands perceived as representing potential threat, existing harm, or loss (Lazarus & Folkman, 1984). *Self-regulation* is defined as the process through which people control, direct, and correct their own actions as they move toward or away from various goals (chapter 14, this volume; Carver & Scheier, 1998). Although these literatures have developed largely in isolation, they share a fundamental concern with the relation of personal, social, and situational factors to people's emotions, thoughts, and behaviors as they anticipate or encounter adversity (Aspinwall & Taylor, 1997; Carver & Scheier, 1999; Skinner, in press).

One task of this review is to examine the unique contributions of each literature to understanding how people deal with adversity. I will examine potential contributions in five areas: (1) the conceptualization and measurement of stress and coping; (2) individual differences in coping and outcomes; (3) adaptational processes and outcomes; (4) social processes, such as social comparison and social support; and (5) emotions. In each area, I

I am grateful to Chuck Carver, Ron Duran, Doug Hill, JongHan Kim, Carolyn Morf, Len Pearlin, J. T. Ptacek, Shelley Taylor, and Camille Wortman for helpful comments on an earlier version of this chapter. Preparation of this chapter was facilitated by NSF grant SBR-9709677 awarded to Lisa G. Aspinwall.

will highlight a few examples to illustrate the potential for integration across these two active research areas.

What the Study of Self-regulation Has to Offer the Study of Coping

The first goal of this review is to consider several issues at the forefront of research in self-regulation that might profitably be exported to the study of stress and coping. I will first review some common problems in the conceptualization and measurement of stress, coping, and outcomes, and then suggest two ways in which concepts from self-regulation might afford greater precision in understanding what stressors are, what people are doing to manage them, and how specific ways of coping are related to psychosocial and health outcomes over time.

Problems in the conceptualization and measurement of stress, coping, and outcomes

In general, in its focus on identifying different ways of coping and relating them to psychosocial and health outcomes, the coping literature has spent relatively little time characterizing the stressor. As early as 1984, this lack of attention lead Susan Folkman to plead for greater conceptual clarity by asking researchers studying personal control and coping to specify, "Control over what?" Even today, "Coping with what?" would be a reasonable question to ask of most studies, including my own, with no easy answer.

Much of this problem stems from the nearly exclusive use of checklists to assess coping (for detailed critiques, see Coyne & Gottlieb, 1996; Stone, Greenberg, Kennedy-Moore, & Newman, 1991). Respondents are asked to select the most stressful aspect of their situation (e.g. entering college, cancer surgery, relocation) within a given time period (e.g. the past six months), and to rate their use of 50–60 different coping strategies ("made a plan of action and followed it," "tried to forget the whole thing," "let my feelings out somehow"; Folkman & Lazarus, 1980). This method can create substantial variation in what people are responding to when they complete inventories, because there may be many different stressors for each "stressful situation," and it is not known exactly what people are responding to as they complete the inventory. To make matters worse, these checklists also provide limited and inconsistent information about what people are doing to manage the stressor. For example, there is enormous variation, both within and between respondents, in what people are reporting on when they rate their use of various strategies (e.g. their frequency or their effectiveness; Stone, Greenberg, Kennedy-Moore, & Newman, 1991). There are also substantial biases in retrospective recall for coping strategies compared to same-day ratings, especially among people reporting high levels of stress (Smith, Leffingwell, & Ptacek, 1999). Finally, reports of coping may be at least somewhat confounded with psychological distress and/or physical symptoms. Frustration with these limitations has sparked the development of careful process-oriented approaches to *daily coping*, in which daily diary records – for example, of pain, social interaction, and coping – are collected, often in conjunction with physiological measures and objective assessments of demand (e.g. see Affleck & Tennen, 1996; Repetti, 1989; Stone & Neale, 1984).

In addition to these measurement problems, most approaches to coping fail to capture the complexity of the process. The predominant conceptual model in the study of stress and coping – Lazarus & Folkman's (1984) transactional model – is based on the idea that coping is a complex, ongoing process in which relations among appraisals of the event and one's resources to manage it, coping efforts, and outcomes are recursive (Lazarus, 1990). Current approaches simply do not capture these aspects of the transactional model. For example, coping checklists provide little information about the social or environmental context of a stressful event (Aldwin & Stokols, 1988; Coyne & Gottlieb, 1996; Revenson, 1990) or its meaning to the person. They also neglect the temporal ordering and functional interrelation among different coping strategies as people manage ongoing stressors and acquire information about them (Aspinwall & Taylor, 1997). For these reasons, it is difficult to determine what made the event stressful, what people did to manage it and why, and how specific ways of coping were related to psychosocial and health outcomes months later. In the following sections, I will examine two ways of conceptualizing stress and coping that may elucidate these issues.

The potential value of goals in understanding stress and coping

One useful starting point in understanding what the stressor is, what it means to people, and how they think about it would be to identify how negative events and information affect people's pursuit of their goals. That is, what specific goals are affected by the experience of adversity? A large literature on self-regulation and goal-striving has identified several properties of goals and the way we represent them that may be useful in clarifying the nature of stress and people's efforts to manage it (for reviews, see Austin & Vancouver, 1996; Gollwitzer & Bargh, 1996). In this section, I will present a few of these approaches and discuss their potential value in understanding responses to adversity.

Idiographic approaches to goal-striving

Idiographic approaches, whether they are called personal projects (Little, 1983), personal strivings (Emmons & King, 1988), life tasks (Cantor, 1990), or possible selves (Markus & Nurius, 1986), examine self-regulation with respect to important personally defined goals. Respondents are asked to list their goals (both hoped for and feared), rate such aspects as importance or centrality to the self-concept, indicate whether they are in conflict, and so forth, in ways that provide a rich picture of people managing multiple goals and self-conceptions.

These approaches offer several advantages over current methods. First, allowing respondents to identify and describe their goals makes it clear what people are responding to when they describe their coping efforts. As King (1996) has noted, behavior that appears counterproductive with respect to one goal may actually have been undertaken in the service of a completely different goal. For example, the student adjusting to college who reports drinking may be doing so to make new friends, not to avoid thinking about his chemistry course.

Second, this approach allows people to list multiple goals and to describe how they are related. People rarely work toward one goal or experience a stressor in isolation. Instead, the experience of a setback in one area is likely to create changes, for better or for worse, in efforts to meet other goals. Some researchers have hypothesized that individual differences in coping outcomes may actually be due to the differential impact of a focal stressor on other areas of life (Pearlin, Aneshensel, & LeBlanc, 1997). That is, the experience of adversity in one life domain, such as adopting a caregiving role, may have most of its impact on outcomes like depression by creating problems in other domains, such as work and social activities.

Third, these approaches provide one way to incorporate the study of the self into the study of stress and coping. Many studies have used constructs such as self-esteem or self-confidence to predict coping and outcomes, but relatively few studies have assessed the effects of adversity and ways of coping with it on the self-concept (see Kling, Ryff, & Essex, 1997, for an exception). The experience of serious illness and other life events is sure to create a multitude of changes in goals, the self-concept, and their interrelation that are just beginning to be examined (Emmons, Colby, & Kaiser, 1998). Further embedding the study of stress in the context of developmental tasks and larger life goals may provide additional insight into how people understand and respond to particular kinds of adversity.

Beliefs about the threatened goal

Beliefs about the nature and future course of a threatened goal are highly important influences on self-regulation. Consider a college freshman who receives a "D" on her first chemistry exam. The meaning of this event may critically depend on her beliefs about whether students typically mature and "hit their stride" as sophomores, or whether initial difficulties are a signal that one will encounter future difficulties (Aspinwall, 1997). Additionally, her beliefs about whether academic performance is a stable entity (you have it or you don't) or an incremental one that can be developed through effort will play a large role in how she prepares for the next exam (Dweck, 1996). Such beliefs may stem from many sources, for example, from a more general attributional style (Peterson & Seligman, 1984), from socially prescribed beliefs about the time course of adjustment to particular kinds of adversity (e.g. bereavement; Wortman & Silver, 1987), or from expectations about developmental phenomena, such as maturation and aging (Aspinwall, 1997).

Ways of framing goals

A third area that has yet to be fully mined for its value in understanding stress, coping, adaptation, and health is a rich literature on how people represent goals (approach vs. avoidance goals: Elliott, Sheldon, & Church, 1996; promotion vs. prevention regulatory focus: Higgins, 1996). These properties of goal-pursuit – whether one is coping to attain something or to avoid something – have profound implications for the strategies and criteria that people use to see if they have met their goal. For example, a person striving for an approach goal (being independent) will look for confirming instances of independence, whereas a person with an avoidance goal in the same domain (not being dependent) will monitor his behavior for instances of dependence. The former gets to experience moments of success, while the latter attends mostly to instances of failure (Coats, Janoff-Bulman, & Alpert, 1996). Such differences are likely to have profound implications for emotional experience, persistence, and self-confidence in the threatened domain and for psychological well-being over time (Coats, Janoff-Bulman, & Alpert, 1996; Elliot, Sheldon, & Church, 1996).

Summary

People's beliefs about how adversity affects multiple, personally defined goals, their beliefs about themselves, and their likely future outcomes are essential to understanding how people respond to negative events and information. Some of these concepts are just beginning to be incorporated in the study of stress and coping with good success. A broader and more systematic integration of these goal constructs with the study of stress and coping has even greater promise.

Understanding How Individual Differences are Related to Psychosocial and Health Outcomes

A second major way in which theories and concepts from self-regulation could advance the coping literature is in elucidating the processes through which individual differences are reciprocally related to psychosocial and health outcomes. A reliable cast of "heroes" and "villains" has emerged from two decades of studies of individual differences in coping. The heroes – optimism, control beliefs (e.g. self-mastery, self-efficacy), hardiness, and perhaps high self-esteem – are prospectively linked to constructive ways of coping, good psychosocial outcomes, and good health. In contrast, the villains – neuroticism, depression, anxiety, and pessimistic explanatory style – have been prospectively linked to ineffective and often destructive ways of coping, poor psychosocial outcomes, and an alarming array of poor health outcomes, including earlier mortality (see Taylor & Aspinwall, 1996, for a review).

Despite the consistency of these findings, relatively little is known about how these individual differences "work"; that is, how do the "good guys" help people achieve or maintain psychological well-being and physical health during times of stress, and how do the "bad guys" compromise such outcomes?

There are many potential mediators of such effects, including the effects of mood and chronic stress on immune function, stress reactivity, and health behaviors (Cohen & Rodriguez, 1995); however, the most-studied link between individual differences and adaptational outcomes is reported ways of coping with stress. In the following section, I present a model that may elucidate how specific individual differences are related to coping and outcomes as people respond to negative events and information.

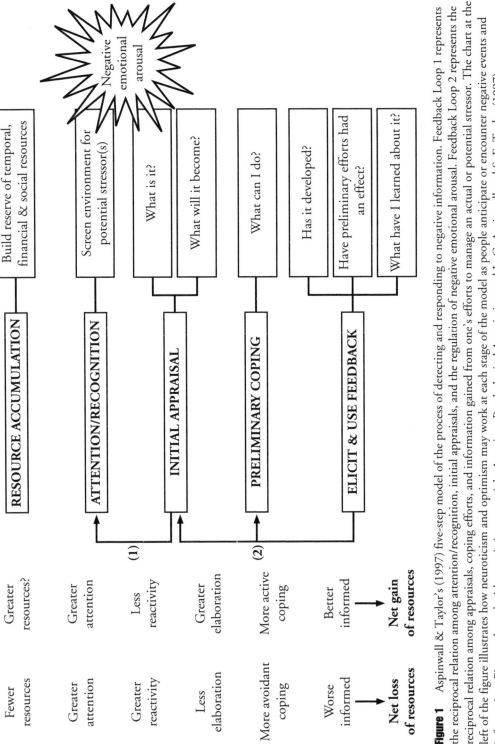

Figure 1 Aspinwall & Taylor's (1997) five-step model of the process of detecting and responding to negative information. Feedback Loop 1 represents the reciprocal relation among attention/recognition, initial appraisals, and the regulation of negative emotional arousal. Feedback Loop 2 represents the reciprocal relation among appraisals, coping efforts, and information gained from one's efforts to manage an actual or potential stressor. The chart at the left of the figure illustrates how neuroticism and optimism may work at each stage of the model as people anticipate or encounter negative events and information. Figure adapted with permission, copyright American Psychological Association and L. G. Aspinwall and S. E. Taylor (1997).

A process-oriented framework for understanding how psychological resources and vulnerabilities may "work" as people anticipate or encounter adversity

Figure 1 presents a five-part model of the process of detecting and responding to negative events and information (Aspinwall & Taylor, 1997). The first stage of the model is *resource accumulation*. Resources are the first step of our model for three reasons. According to Hobfoll's (1989) conservation of resources theory, people are motivated to retain, protect, and build resources. Hobfoll defines stress as the loss of resources, the potential loss of resources, or the failure to gain resources in proportion to one's investment in a task. These resources can be objects, personal characteristics (mastery, self-esteem), conditions (employment, marriage), or energies (time, money, knowledge) that have either symbolic or instrumental value to the individual. The presence of resources, therefore, plays a large role in determining the kinds of events and information that may be stressful to a given person. Second, most of the critical tasks of coping and self-regulation, such as attention to negative information, coping, and the use of feedback, require personal, social, and other kinds of resources. Third, increasing evidence suggests that such resources may be depleted over time as a function of the ways people deal with adversity (Bolger, Foster, Vinokur, & Ng, 1996; Smith & Wallston, 1992).

The next step of the model is *attention/recognition*. In this step, one screens the environment for potential stressors. If one is detected, a process of *initial appraisal* begins. In this step, people are trying to figure out what a potential or actual stressor is and what it is likely to mean for them. An important part of the model is that the detection of stressors often creates *negative emotional arousal* that may not only prompt efforts to regulate these emotions, but may also interfere with subsequent processing of information. Initial appraisals give rise to *preliminary coping efforts*, such as efforts to solve the problem, to gain more information about it, or to enlist the aid of others. A final and critical part of the model is the *elicitation and use of feedback* about the success of one's coping efforts and the information such efforts have yielded about the stressor and one's resources to manage it.

The model is recursive in three important ways that will be illustrated in greater detail in subsequent sections. First, as illustrated by Feedback Loop 1, attention, appraisal, and the regulation of emotion are interrelated as people maintain attention to actual or potential stressors. Second, as illustrated by Feedback Loop 2, appraisals may be revised in light of information obtained in the course of trying to manage the stressor. Finally, the entire sequence of events is recursive, as the component activities of the model – attention, appraisal, coping, and use of feedback – are related over time to the conservation, development, or depletion of resources. Such a process may account for intriguing patterns of resource depletion and gain that have been identified in a number of stressed populations.

In the following sections, I use this model to examine the role that psychological resources, like optimism, and psychological vulnerabilities, like neuroticism, may play at each stage in the model, starting with baseline resources and finishing with resource gain or depletion as a result of exposure to adversity. It is important to note that similar findings have been obtained for other potential resources (such as self-mastery, hardiness, and other control-related constructs) and vulnerabilities (such as anxiety, depression, and pessimism; see Aspinwall & Taylor, 1997, and Taylor & Aspinwall, 1996, for reviews). I have chosen optimism and neuroticism to highlight the possibility that psychological resources and vulnerabilities may have distinct effects. That is, the presence of positive beliefs or emotions may have unique effects on coping, adaptation, and health that cannot be explained by simply the absence of negative beliefs or emotions, and vice versa. A full discussion of the conceptual status of these two constructs, however, is beyond the scope of this chapter.

Understanding neuroticism as a psychological vulnerability

Neuroticism or negative affectivity is the propensity to experience negative emotions, such as anxiety, depression, and hostility (Watson & Clark, 1984). Often overlooked in the study of stress and coping is the possibility that certain individual differences are associated with greater exposure to stressful events in the first place and with differences in the baseline availability of social support. From the outset, people high in N have more stress to manage, and at every stage in the coping process, this individual difference appears to compromise effective appraisal and action. As I will describe, the net result may be cumulative loss of resources with each successive exposure to adversity.

Stress-generation and baseline resources   Large-scale panel studies of exposure to stressful life events find that people high in N experience more negative life events (Headey & Wearing, 1989), possibly through a process of interpersonal stress-generation. People high in N also report greater reactivity to negative events (Bolger & Schilling, 1991). Both greater exposure and greater reactivity to negative events increase cumulative load and deplete resources. Therefore, the person high in N who encounters a new negative event starts with fewer resources.

Attentional processes   Neuroticism has been found not only to increase attention to negative information, but also to make it difficult to turn away from it (Derryberry & Reed, 1994). Such amplifications in attention to threatening information are likely to affect coping in several ways. First, one might see potential threat or danger in most situations. Second, hypervigilance to negative information may deplete resources, because it takes energy to stay on the lookout for and respond to several different potential sources of stress. Third, the ability to regulate one's attention flexibly and appropriately is essential. A person devoting resources to monitoring several potential threats simultaneously may be unable to discriminate those that require immediate attention from those that do not.

Appraisal processes   Neuroticism is linked to greater appraisals of threat or loss, especially in ongoing situations, and to less favorable appraisals of problem-solving ability. This combination of high appraisals of threat and low appraisals of resources to manage it is, by definition, what creates stress in Lazarus & Folkman's (1984) model. It is also the pattern of appraisals that predicts physiological threat responses and poor performance on demanding mental tasks (Blascovich & Tomaka, 1996). As a result, as shown in Feedback Loop 1, even though people high in N may be devoting a great deal of attention to negative information, their appraisals of it may not correspond well to the nature of the stressor because of their greater reactivity to it.

Preliminary coping efforts The perception of low problem-solving resources may lead to the failure to engage in active coping. *N* has been linked to many forms of avoidant coping, such as wishing the problem would go away, avoiding thinking about the problem, and substance use, that are themselves linked to poor outcomes over time (Bolger, 1990; Holahan & Moos, 1986; McCrae & Costa, 1986; Watson & Hubbard, 1996). When people high in *N* do try coping actively, the poor quality of their appraisals may lead to coping efforts that do not match the problem.

Elicitation and use of feedback In addition to creating new problems, avoidant strategies carry another serious liability: they are less likely than active ones to elicit information about the problem. Avoidance coping is unlikely to elicit useful information about the particular problem or about coping in general and thus does not contribute to the acquisition and refinement of procedural knowledge about coping. Further, as distress increases, people's ability to generate alternatives and to use multiple criteria in their decisions has been shown to decrease, further compromising appraisals and coping efforts, especially if the problem is ongoing and changing (Aspinwall & Taylor, 1997). The increasing divergence between the coping strategies used and the nature of the problem illustrated in Feedback Loop 2 may further exacerbate the problem, because resources are being wasted while the problem is going unchecked.

Depletion of social resources Finally, although it is not shown as a separate step in the model, neuroticism and avoidant coping have both been prospectively linked to the depletion of social resources in ways that have implications for coping efforts and subsequent well-being. First, the use of social withdrawal as a coping strategy prospectively predicts declines in social support (Evans & Lepore, 1993; Smith & Wallston, 1992). Avoiding others during times of stress also prevents one from receiving appraisal support that might be useful in understanding the problem, from receiving informational and instrumental support that might aid in its solution, and from receiving emotional or esteem support that might offset feelings of failure and decreasing confidence.

A second pathway through which social resources are depleted begins when people make frequent, exaggerated efforts to obtain social support, often through excessive reassurance seeking (Coates & Wortman, 1980; Joiner, Metalsky, Katz, & Beach, in press). Intense displays of negative affect and poor coping have been shown to cut short social interaction, to create increasing distance between the sufferer and those who might help (Silver, Wortman, & Crofton, 1990), and to erode social support over time (Bolger, Foster, Vinokur, & Ng, 1996). Finally, these two patterns may be interrelated if people first make exaggerated attempts to obtain support, then withdraw when they find it lacking. The net result of either pathway is the depletion of valuable social resources for coping.

Summary: a downward spiral of ineffective coping and resource loss In sum, people high in *N* and related characteristics, such as depression and anxiety, appear to generate more stress and to respond to negative events and information in ways that deplete resources through hypervigilance, reactivity, ineffective coping efforts, social isolation or alienation, and diminished opportunities for learning about different ways of coping with problems. Additionally, once people are distressed, they may simply be less likely to perceive their resources favorably even when they do exist (Evans & Lepore, 1993). Working in concert, these factors may create a downward spiral of resource loss with exposure to adversity that increases one's vulnerability to psychological distress, social isolation, and poor health.

Understanding optimism as a psychological resource

A vastly different sequence of events characterizes the psychological resources in our list. I will use research on dispositional optimism, the generalized expectation of good future outcomes (Scheier, Carver, & Bridges, 1994), to illustrate how each step of the model may contribute to a net resource gain or to lower levels of resource loss following adversity among people with such resources.

Attention, appraisal, and the regulation of arousal   Increasing evidence suggests that optimism is related to the ability to attend to negative information that is self-relevant or otherwise useful. Aspinwall & Brunhart (1996) demonstrated that optimists differentially attend to and recall information about the risks of their own health behaviors, compared to benefit or neutral information, and compared to risk information about behaviors they do not practice. The exact mechanism underlying such effects has yet to be fully understood, but related experimental work supports the idea that induced positive states increase people's interest in and veridical processing of negative information about themselves (see Aspinwall, 1998, for review).

The ability to maintain attention to self-relevant negative information is likely to confer many advantages in appraising potential stressors. Additionally, optimism and related constructs, such as constructive thinking, have been linked to more favorable appraisals of problem-solving resources and to lower levels of threat-related physiological responding to demanding mental tasks (Katz & Epstein, 1991). As a result, as illustrated in Feedback Loop 1, optimists may be more likely to sustain attention to negative information and may therefore make more accurate and well-elaborated appraisals of it than pessimists.

Preliminary coping efforts   Optimism has been linked to greater reports of active coping in several studies. For example, in a prospective study of entering freshmen, Aspinwall & Taylor (1992) found that optimists were more likely to report active ways of coping (such as problem solving) and less likely to report avoidant ways of coping (such as avoiding thoughts about the problem). More active coping and less avoidant coping, in turn, predicted better adjustment to college three months later. These results provide a clear account of how resources like optimism may "work:" because optimists expect good outcomes, they actively work toward them when they encounter adversity.

There is, however, an interesting exception to these findings that may prove to be at least equally important in understanding optimists' responses to adversity. In some studies, optimism is not linked to greater active coping, but instead to greater acceptance of situations beyond one's control. For example, Carver and his colleagues (1993) found that optimistic women with breast cancer were more likely than pessimists to indicate that they had accepted the reality of the fact that they had surgery for breast cancer. This acceptance was related to lower psychological distress at various points in the year following the surgery. It may seem paradoxical that the same psychological "resource" can be linked to both active coping and to acceptance. That is, if the active ingredient in optimism is continued persistence in goal-directed behavior, why do optimists report greater acceptance of problems beyond their control? In the following section, I examine how the final step of the model may account for some of these effects.

Elicitation and use of feedback   As illustrated by Feedback Loop 2, active coping is more likely than avoidant coping to elicit information about a problem. Optimists not only tend to cope more actively, but seem also, as discussed earlier, to be better able to attend to negative information. As a result, they may be better able to benefit from feedback about the success or failure of their coping efforts. In this way, optimists may become well-informed about how and when to cope actively, even when their initial attempts are unsuccessful (Aspinwall & Taylor, 1997; see also Armor & Taylor, 1998; Aspinwall, Richter, & Hoffman, in press; Skinner, in press). Such knowledge may be useful in determining whether a problem is amenable to one's efforts or must simply be accepted.

Summary: an upward spiral of efficient coping and resource gain   Through the mechanisms outlined in this section, optimists may conserve resources by detecting and managing problems early in their course. Through their active preliminary coping efforts, they may also acquire procedural knowledge about different kinds of problems and ways of coping with them. Such knowledge may be useful in identifying which efforts are most likely to work for certain kinds of problems, leading to more efficient use of coping resources. In sum, optimism seems to lead people to act in ways that may preserve and even build resources, even under conditions of adversity.

   This analysis is consistent with others suggesting that positive emotions and experiences serve to build personal and social resources and to broaden action repertoires (Ashby, Isen, & Turken, 1999; Fredrickson, 1998; Isen, 1993). Extending coping research to examine how optimism and other psychological resources are related to the mobilization and preservation of social resources may also provide additional information about how different ways of managing stress are related to subsequent social resources and well-being. Working in concert, such processes may create an upward spiral of increasing resources, skills, and knowledge that may increase people's ability to anticipate and prevent stress and to cope more effectively when it does occur.

Summary

In the preceding sections, I examined two ways in which concepts and methods from the study of self-regulation might provide insight into the coping process. Reconceptualizing stressors in terms of their effects on goals and examining how personal resources and vulnerabilities may influence people's responses to negative events and information may provide insight into what is stressful to people, how people cope with adversity, and how such efforts are related to subsequent outcomes and resources.

What the Study of Coping Has to Offer the Study of Self-regulation

The second major goal of this review is to examine the ways in which studying the beliefs, behaviors, and emotions of people dealing with adversity provides a window on crucial self-regulatory processes that the study of ordinary activities and tasks cannot. In many ways, the study of coping with adversity is the study of personality under stress (Bolger, 1990; Bolger & Zuckerman, 1995). Serious illness and other negative life events threaten cherished goals, challenge long-held beliefs about the self and the world, and deplete personal and social resources over time. In addition, such events create the conditions of high distress and uncertainty that make the experiences, assistance, and reactions of others especially important in understanding what we are facing and how to manage it. As a result, the coping literature may be uniquely informative in three areas: (1) how people adapt to such challenges, (2) how social processes, such as social comparison and social support, affect coping, adaptation, and health, and (3) how negative and positive emotions affect ways of dealing with adversity. I will provide a brief review of each of these areas.

Adaptation to serious illness and other negative life events

People who have experienced some kinds of negative life events not only manage to survive, but also report profound changes in their lives, often to the point of rating their current situation as superior to their life before the event (Affleck & Tennen, 1996; Updegraff & Taylor, in press; see Davis, Lehman, & Wortman, 1999, for important exceptions). People often report having learned valuable information – both positive and negative – from their experience. The following section examines some of these changes and discusses their implications for understanding self-regulatory processes.

Cognitive adaptation to negative life events

How is it that people who have encountered severe adversity experience positive changes in their lives and maintain hope for the future? In her seminal paper on cognitive adaptation, Taylor (1983) suggested that these changes arise in response to three tasks that people undertake following a negative life event: *searching for meaning* (why did the event happen?, what is its impact?), *regaining mastery* (how can I keep the event from happening again?, how can I manage it now?), and *enhancing self-esteem*. Consider the following comments from Taylor's (ibid., p. 1,163) interviews of women with breast cancer:

> I have much more enjoyment of each day, each moment. I am not so worried about what is and what isn't or what I wish I had. All those things you get entangled with don't seem to be part of my life right now.
>
> I was very happy to find out I am a very strong person. I have no time for game-playing any more. I want to get on with life. And I have become more introspective and also let others

fend for their own responsibilities. And now almost five years later, I have become a very different person.

These comments illustrate a number of key elements of psychological adaptation to serious illness: the increased enjoyment of everyday activities, changes in control efforts, and changes in views of the self as stronger and more focused. I will consider each of these elements in more detail.

Finding meaning   Finding meaning in a negative event turns out to be a common (but by no means universal) response to serious illness (for reviews, see Davis, Lehman, & Wortman, 1999; Emmons, Colby, & Kaiser, 1998; Updegraff & Taylor, in press). In Taylor's (1983) interviews with women with breast cancer, 95 percent of the patients had generated some explanation for why their cancer occurred. No specific causal explanation was linked to better psychological adjustment, but the large number of patients who found some sort of explanation suggests that the process of finding some meaning is important.

Although there are many ways to find meaning, one frequently reported way involves finding benefit in adversity. In Affleck & Tennen's (1996) extensive program of research on adjustment to chronic illness, the vast majority of patients reported gains in the strength of their relationships with family and friends, perceptions of positive personality changes, such as greater patience, tolerance, empathy, and courage, and valued changes in life priorities and personal goals (see also Tedeschi & Calhoun, 1996). Interestingly, the perception of benefits from adversity and active attempts to remind oneself of such benefits are linked to other outcomes, such as lower mood disturbance and better health outcomes. For example, people who found meaning in their first heart attack were less likely to suffer a second one (Affleck & Tennen, 1996). Finding meaning in adversity has also been prospectively linked to improved immune function and decreased mortality among HIV-seropositive gay men dealing with the death of their partner (Bower, Kemeny, Taylor, & Fahey, 1998).

Restoring mastery   The coping literature provides many striking examples of people's attempts to restore feelings of control and mastery following adversity. Control may take many forms, such as seeing oneself as responsible for the event (Janoff-Bulman, 1989), or it may involve finding new outlets for achieving mastery. For example, people with serious illnesses seem to transfer their control efforts away from the stressor itself (the illness or their prognosis) and toward more manageable aspects of it (the management of symptoms and daily experience). Such selective control attempts – exercising control where one reasonably can and relinquishing control where it is not possible – are linked to superior psychological adjustment, especially as one's condition progresses (Heckhausen, 1997; Thompson, Sobolew-Shubin, Galbraith, Schwankovsky, & Cruzen, 1993).

Patterns of benefit-finding also seem to show this selective pattern. In a study of life changes following a diagnosis of cancer, Collins, Taylor, & Skokan (1990) found that respondents reported both positive and negative changes in five major domains (views of themselves, relations with others, priorities and daily activities, views of the future, and views of the world). Of particular interest, the two life domains that had the greatest ratio of positive to negative changes were those that were most directly controllable by the patients themselves – personal relationships and priorities and daily activities.

Restoring self-esteem   In Taylor's (1983) interviews, almost all of the respondents thought they were better off than other women with breast cancer. Self-enhancement through *downward comparisons* to others who are worse off has been found to be a common response to adversity (Buunk & Gibbons, 1997; Wills, 1981). Taylor, Wood, & Lichtman (1983) coined the term *selective evaluation* to describe not only the process of making downward comparisons, but of selecting dimensions that would allow one to achieve such favorable comparisons. The following excerpts illustrate this process (Taylor, 1983, p. 1,166):

> An older woman: "The people I really feel sorry for are these young gals. To lose a breast when you're so young must be awful. I'm 73; what do I need a breast for?"

> A younger woman: "If I hadn't been married, I think this thing would have really gotten to me. I can't imagine dating or whatever knowing you have this thing and not knowing how to tell the man about it."

By viewing their situations in ways that emphasized their relative advantage, the vast majority of respondents thought they were adjusting better than other women with breast cancer.

Downward comparisons are not the only way in which social comparison information is used by those coping with adversity. *Upward comparisons* to people doing better than the self play an important role in sustaining hope among people with serious illness (Taylor & Lobel, 1989). Interestingly, as was the case with the selective exercise of control efforts, people seem to be highly skilled in managing their exposure to comparison information to ensure that upward comparisons are encouraging, rather than discouraging. For example, people may avoid upward comparisons on dimensions they cannot change (such as the severity of the illness), but seek them on dimensions they can change (such as ways of coping with the illness; see Aspinwall, 1997, for review).

Learning from adversity: Taking *the good* and *the bad*

A second, related area of research on adjustment to adversity examines what people learn from negative life events. Most research on this topic has been conducted from the perspective of Janoff-Bulman's work on *assumptive worlds*. Janoff-Bulman (1989; Janoff-Bulman & Frieze, 1983) argued that we hold favorable beliefs about ourselves, about other people, and about the fairness and meaningfulness of events in the world that remain unquestioned until something negative happens to us. Negative life events challenge and may even shatter such beliefs. In a study of college students, those who had experienced negative life events, such as death of a parent or sibling, incest, rape, a fire that destroyed their home, or a disabling accident, scored lower on beliefs about the benevolence of the world and saw themselves as lower in self-worth than those who had not experienced such events (Janoff-Bulman, 1989).

These findings suggest that adversity has effects that go beyond the event itself to affect core beliefs about the self and the world. How do people cope with such challenges? Janoff-Bulman (1989) argued that one can (1) change one's beliefs, or (2) reinterpret the negative experience to fit one's existing beliefs. There is some evidence that people act in order to restore their worldview. For example, in order to avoid seeing the world as a random place in which bad things happen to good people, people may see themselves as having caused the negative event. To believe that one controlled one's fate means that one can do better next time or take additional precautions. This strategy to restore mastery seems to work, as long as people don't blame less mutable aspects of themselves, such as their character, for the negative event. In cases in which the event cannot be reinterpreted to match one's beliefs, people may experience persisting distress (Davis, Lehman, & Wortman, 1999).

As suggested earlier, people frequently report both positive and negative changes in response to adversity. However, many authors have questioned the nature and adaptiveness of self-reports of finding benefits in adversity. Do such reports, for example, reflect denial of negative experience or social pressure to report benefit in adversity? These are difficult questions to answer. With respect to the first question, perceptions of benefits seem to be largely uncorrelated with perceptions of the negative impacts of illness (Affleck & Tennen, 1996), a finding that suggests that finding benefit in adversity is not accomplished through denial of its negative aspects. Similarly, in the Collins, Taylor, & Skokan (1990) study, positive and negative changes were reported with nearly equal frequency in three major life domains. A recent experiment by King & Miner (in press) suggests that there are some relatively objective gains from finding benefit in adversity. In a variation of the Pennebaker (1993) disclosure paradigm, college students randomly assigned to write about the benefits they perceived from their experience of traumatic events experienced the same reduction in health center visits relative to controls over the next three months as those assigned to write about negative aspects of such events.

Individual differences and adaptation following adversity

Thus far, I have considered multiple aspects of psychological adaptation and suggested that the process of dealing with adversity involves learning both good and bad things about the self, the world, and other people, and learning that some things are more amenable to control than others. There is increasing interest in the implications of these aspects of adaptation for personality change and growth (Affleck & Tennen, 1996; Carver, 1998; Ickovics & Park, 1998; Tedeschi, Park, & Calhoun, 1998). Interestingly, there seem to be several reciprocal relations between individual differences and the adaptational processes reviewed here. First, certain individual differences, such as optimism, extroversion, and openness to experience, have been linked to finding positive changes in adversity (Affleck & Tennen, 1996; Tedeschi & Calhoun, 1996). In turn, self-reported personal growth from negative events has been linked to subsequent increases in optimism and positive affectivity (Park, Cohen, & Murch, 1996). Second, optimism and self-mastery have been linked to selective control attempts whereby people disengage from active attempts to control uncontrollable problems and report greater acceptance of such problems. It is likely that these two strategies – finding benefits and applying control efforts selectively – serve to preserve the favorable beliefs and expectations that promote them by helping people profit from adversity and by protecting people from repeated failures to exercise control (Aspinwall, Richter, & Hoffman, in press).

Implications of research on adaptation for the study of self-regulation

There are several implications of these findings for understanding self-regulation. The first is that people not only withstand, but may also learn from adversity. They may also make profound changes in their daily activities, personal priorities, and comparison standards. Thus, the experience of a major negative life event can create changes in the values and priorities that may fundamentally affect the goals people strive to obtain, as well as the standards people use to evaluate their progress (see chapter 12, this volume).

Understanding the causes and consequences of people's efforts to find meaning, restore mastery, and bolster self-esteem may lead to new insights into ways that people learn from adversity and into the kinds of events that make such efforts more difficult. Research to date suggests that the process of adaptation is considerably more complex than seeing all aspects of one's situation favorably or unfavorably following adversity. Additionally, accumulating evidence about the domains in which people with serious illness report finding benefit and meaning suggests a number of promising domains in which to study self-regulation with respect to important goals. Specifically, expanding the study of self-regulation beyond achievement-oriented tasks to consider such goals as positive relations with others, environmental mastery, meaning in life, and personal growth may give us new information about self-regulation with respect to larger life goals and developmental tasks (Emmons, Colby, & Kaiser, 1998; Ryff, 1989).

The role of social processes in coping, adaptation, and health

If coping is the study of personality under stress, it is just as surely the study of social processes under stress. Research on stress and coping has identified several ways in which the experience of adversity and different ways of coping with it not only alter people's social environments, but also change the ways they use information and assistance from other people. In this section, I will provide a brief overview of research relating social processes to coping, adaptation, and health and discuss the implications of this research for self-regulation more generally.

Social comparison and coping with adversity

Starting with Schachter's (1959) classic studies of fear and affiliation and continuing with present-day research on people facing highly threatening and uncertain situations, social comparisons have been found to play a central role in our attempts to understand what we are facing, how we should feel about it, and what we should do about it (Buunk & Gibbons, 1997). This information is so important to how we understand and manage adversity that simple exposure to someone who has undergone what we are about to face has dramatic health effects. In several field experiments, Kulik & Mahler (1997) found that male cardiac patients awaiting surgery who were randomly assigned to a postsurgical roommate (even one who had had surgery for a different condition) were less anxious and were released sooner from the hospital than patients assigned to a presurgical roommate. In this situation, social comparisons seem to aid people in two critical coping tasks: problem solving and the regulation of emotion. Seeing someone who has experienced surgery may benefit patients by providing information about the sensations and procedures they might experience after surgery (information useful in problem solving) and by providing living evidence that people do weather surgery (information useful in regulating emotions, such as anxiety).

Such findings have several implications for the study of self-regulation. With few exceptions, the study of self-regulation has been conceptualized as an individual process. In most approaches to goal-directed behavior, social comparisons enter the picture only or primarily when they affect the standards used to judge progress toward a goal. However, it is increasingly clear that social comparison information affects goal-directed behavior far earlier in the chain, starting with decisions about whether to adopt a specific goal (Ruble & Frey, 1991), and continuing with appraisals of tasks and their demands (Aspinwall, Frazier, & Cooper, 1999), perceptions of self-efficacy during the course of task engagement (Bandura & Jourden, 1991), the selection of specific coping methods, and decisions about disengagement (see Aspinwall, 1997, for a review).

Social support and coping with adversity

Social support has been linked through multiple pathways to more active coping efforts, better psychological outcomes, and better health outcomes among people confronting adversity (Cohen & Wills, 1985; Cohen, 1988; Holahan, Moos, Holahan, & Brennan, 1997; Taylor & Aspinwall, 1996). In her classic paper, Peggy Thoits (1986) defined social support as the participation of other people in an individual's coping efforts, including both problem-focused and emotion-focused coping. She outlined four functions of social support: *instrumental* (help with problem-solving efforts, such as rides to the doctor, loans, or other tangible assistance); *information* (also useful in problem solving); *appraisal* (help figuring out what the stressful event is and what it means); and *esteem support* (helping the person feel loved and valued, despite the adverse event). It may be worth noting that these well-documented functions of social support map nicely on to the three major tasks of cognitive adaptation identified by Taylor (1983), namely regaining mastery, finding meaning, and restoring self-esteem.

An important part of this large literature has examined how social support can go awry; that is, how the experience of adversity can lead members of one's social network to avoid the affected person or to interact in awkward and unhelpful ways (e.g. see Dunkel-Schetter & Wortman, 1982; Lehman, Ellard, & Wortman, 1986). As I reviewed earlier, how people cope with adversity, especially how they manage emotional distress and their needs for information and reassurance, also affects the amount and kind of social support they receive (Colby & Emmons, 1997). Such findings highlight the fact that social support is not a static resource, but one that is influenced by coping and also by potential helpers' own fears and beliefs about what would be helpful (Wortman & Silver, 1987). In turn, people who perceive that others are not meeting their needs often react in ways that further the divide between them and their social networks. A final level of complexity is added by emerging evidence that social support may not be a purely external resource. That is, the temperament and personality of the person seeking support seem to be related to both perceived and actual availability and use of social support (Taylor & Aspinwall, 1996). In sum, social support can play an important role in coping with adversity, but people dealing with adversity do not always receive or perceive the support they desire.

Summary

In this brief review of the role of social processes in coping with adversity, I have tried to highlight ways in which social comparisons and social support influence coping, adaptation, and health. In addition to their use as standards for self-evaluation, people use information and assistance from others to inform their coping efforts and to understand and regulate their emotions. Such information is also used to establish goals and priorities among them. In turn, the ways in which people cope with adversity seem to have reliable effects on the availability of social resources. Considering these social aspects of self-regulation may yield a more comprehensive portrait of social influences on goal-directed behavior.

The role of emotions in coping and self-regulation

A final area that is ripe for greater attention in both literatures is the effects of emotions on efforts to deal with adversity. In the coping literature, emotions are typically conceptualized as things that must be managed (as in emotion-focused coping), rather than as major influences on other parts of the coping process. In theories of self-regulation, affect is thought to arise from (Carver & Scheier, 1990) or to inform one's perceived rate of progress toward goals (Martin & Tesser, 1996). However, the effects of positive and negative affect, once elicited, on other aspects of self-regulation are not generally considered.

In the case of chronic illness and other stressors, it will be critical to understand how negative states such as fatigue, depression, uncertainty, anxiety, and pain influence self-regulatory processes. These states may have profound (and likely detrimental) influences on attention to and appraisals of potential problems, selection of coping strategies, and evaluation and integration of new information about problems and the success of one's efforts to manage them. However, there may be ways of expressing and managing negative emotions that have beneficial effects on mental and physical health (Pennebaker, 1993; Stanton, Danoff-Burg, Cameron, & Ellis, 1994). Understanding and cultivating these more adaptive ways may lead to the development of interventions to help people cope with adversity and to prevent the deterioration in social resources that may accompany the display of negative emotions.

Finally, the role of positive emotions in sustaining attention to negative information, fueling goal-pursuit, and generating multiple, creative solutions to one's problems remains understudied. These emotions may be linked to processes such as benefit-finding and re-minding, the selective exercise of control, and different kinds of social support in ways that are just beginning to be explored.

Summary and Conclusion

Chronic illness, negative life events, and other stressors represent an important set of circumstances in which to study personal and social factors in self-regulation, as resources are taxed over long periods of time; as valued goals, self-beliefs, and worldviews may be disconfirmed, reaffirmed, or changed; as social ties may be strengthened or weakened; and as negative and positive emotions may influence appraisals, coping efforts, and social behavior. Importantly, all of these things are going on at once, most often in life domains that are highly important to people.

What can be gained by considering potential interrelations between the stress and coping and self-regulation literatures? Some of the suggestions I've made here might broaden scope of inquiry of both literatures, but at the same time provide increased precision. First, reconceptualizing coping as goal-directed behavior might provide insight into the nature of stress, the kinds of coping strategies employed, and their effects on both the problem and the person. Second, a focus on how psychological and social resources "work" may extend the study of individual differences beyond the question of *which* factors are linked to psychosocial and health outcomes to ask *how* such relations are obtained. Greater attention to conceptual models of self-regulation, including research on psychological resources, attention to negative information, emotional regulation, problem solving, and procedural knowledge, would likely elucidate why certain individual differences are so reliably related to good or poor outcomes over time. Such models may also provide insight into the processes through which personality is maintained over the lifespan.

Third, research on self-regulation might profit from greater attention to both the processes and outcomes of psychological adaptation to stressful life events. People who experience adversity change their comparison standards, value different life domains than before, and often gain valuable knowledge about themselves, others, and the world as a result of the illness. They may change their goals, change the meaning or importance they accord to different goals, or make more nuanced distinctions between controllable and uncontrollable aspects of goals. These creative, adaptive changes to find meaning, exercise mastery, and restore self-worth have documented links to psychological well-being and, increasingly, to physical health that merit increased research attention. Importantly, these changes do not take place in a social vacuum, nor are they independent of the nature of the stressor. It will continue to be important to examine different kinds of life events and social responses to them that make it more or less difficult to find meaning, to exercise mastery, or to restore self-worth.

Fourth, greater attention to social processes, such as social comparison and social support, may provide insight not only into how people manage adversity, but also how people select, pursue, and disengage from different goals. Increased attention to the social interactions of people managing adversity may shed light on the processes that maintain, build, or deplete social resources, as well as those that generate conflictual interactions that are themselves potent sources of stress. Finally, greater attention to the role of both positive and negative emotions in the process of detecting and managing negative events and information may increase our understanding of emotions in such critical areas as problem solving, goal pursuit, and the maintenance or depletion of personal and social resources.

In conclusion, integrating the study of coping with adversity with the study of self-regulation may increase our understanding of what people are trying to do in their lives, what is stressful to people, why particular coping strategies are enacted, and how ways of dealing with adversity affect all areas of life.

Note

1   This review will necessarily be selective, rather than comprehensive. For reviews of major topics in stress, coping, adaptation and health, see Aspinwall & Taylor (1997); Basic Behavioral Science Task Force (1996); Buunk & Gibbons (1997); Cohen (1988); Friedman (1990); Kaplan (1996); Lazarus (1990); Pennebaker (1993); Revenson (1994); Suls & Harvey (1996); Taylor & Aspinwall (1990, 1996); Taylor, Repetti, & Seeman (1997); Tedeschi, Park, & Calhoun (1998); and Wortman & Silver (1987).

References

Affleck, G., & Tennen, H. (1996). Construing benefits from adversity: Adaptational significance and dispositional underpinnings. *Journal of Personality, 64*, 899–922.

Aldwin, C., & Stokols, D. (1988). The effects of environmental change on individuals and groups: Some neglected issues in stress research. *Journal of Environmental Psychology, 8*, 57–75.

Armor, D. A., & Taylor, S. E. (1998). Situated optimism: Specific outcome expectancies and self-regulation. In M. P. Zanna (Ed.), *Advances in experimental social psychology*, Vol. 30 (pp. 309–379). New York: Academic Press.

Ashby, F. G., Isen, A. M., & Turken, A. U. (1999). A neurological theory of positive affect and its influence on cognition. *Psychological Review, 106*, 529–550.

Aspinwall, L. G. (1997). Future-oriented aspects of social comparisons: A framework for studying health-related comparison activity. In B. P. Buunk & F. X. Gibbons (Eds.), *Health, coping, and well-being: Perspectives from social comparison theory* (pp. 125–165). Mahwah, NJ: Erlbaum.

Aspinwall, L. G. (1998). Rethinking the role of positive affect in self-regulation. *Motivation and Emotion, 22*, 1–32.

Aspinwall, L. G., & Brunhart, S. M. (1996). Distinguishing optimism from denial: Optimistic beliefs predict attention to health threats. *Personality and Social Psychology Bulletin, 22*, 993–1003.

Aspinwall, L. G., & Taylor, S. E. (1992). Modeling cognitive adaptation: A longitudinal investigation of the impact of individual differences and coping on college adjustment and performance. *Journal of Personality and Social Psychology, 63*, 989–1003.

Aspinwall, L. G., & Taylor, S. E. (1997). A stitch in time: Self-regulation and proactive coping. *Psychological Bulletin, 121*, 417–436.

Aspinwall, L. G., Frazier, L. E., & Cooper, D. A. (1999). Being shown up vs. being shown how: When upward comparisons foster superior performance. Manuscript in preparation.

Aspinwall, L. G., Richter, L., & Hoffman, R. R. (in press). Understanding how optimism "works:" Mediators and moderators. In E. C. Chang (Ed.), *Optimism and pessimism: Theory, research, and practice*. Washington: American Psychological Association.

Austin, J. T., & Vancouver, J. B. (1996). Goal constructs in psychology: Structure, process, and content. *Psychological Bulletin, 120*, 338–375.

Bandura, A., & Jourden, F. J. (1991). Self-regulatory mechanisms governing the impact of social comparison on complex decision-making. *Journal of Personality and Social Psychology, 60*, 941–951.

Basic Behavioral Science Task Force of the National Advisory Mental Health Council (1996). Vulnerability and resilience. *American Psychologist, 51*, 22–28.

Blascovich, J., & Tomaka, J. (1996). The biopsychosocial model of arousal regulation. In M. Zanna (Ed.), *Advances in experimental social psychology*, Vol. 28 (pp. 1–51). New York: Academic Press.

Bolger, N. (1990). Coping as a personality process: A prospective study. *Journal of Personality and Social Psychology, 59*, 525–537.

Bolger, N., & Schilling, E. A. (1991). Personality and the problems of everyday life: The role of neuroticism in exposure and reactivity to daily stressors. *Journal of Personality and Social Psychology, 59*, 355–386.

Bolger, N., & Zuckerman, A. (1995). A framework for studying personality in the stress process. *Journal of Personality and Social Psychology, 69*, 890–902.

Bolger, N., Foster, M., Vinokur, A. D., & Ng, R. (1996). Close relationships and adjustment to a life crisis: The case of breast cancer. *Journal of Personality and Social Psychology, 70*, 283–294.

Bower, J. E., Kemeny, M. E., Taylor, S. E., & Fahey, J. L. (1998). Cognitive processing, discovery of meaning, CD4 decline, and AIDS-related mortality among bereaved HIV-seropositive men. *Journal of Consulting and Clinical Psychology, 66*, 979–986.

Buunk, B. P., & Gibbons, F. X. (Eds.) (1997). *Health, coping, and well-being: Perspectives from social comparison theory*. Mahwah, NJ: Erlbaum.

Cantor, N. (1990). From thought to behavior: "Having" and "doing" in the study of personality and cognition. *American Psychologist, 45*, 735–750.

Carver, C. S. (1998). Resilience and thriving: Issues, models, and linkages. *Journal of Social Issues, 54* (2), 245–266.

Carver, C. S., & Scheier, M. F. (1990). Principles of self-regulation: Action and emotion. In E. T. Higgins & R. M. Sorrentino (Eds.), *Handbook of motivation and cognition*, Vol. 2 (pp. 3–52). New York: Guilford Press.

Carver, C. S., & Scheier, M. F. (1998). *On the self-regulation of behavior*. New York: Cambridge University Press.

Carver, C. S., & Scheier, M. F. (1999c). Stress, coping, and self-regulatory processes. In L. A. Pervin & O. P. John (Eds.), *Handbook of Personality*. 2nd. edn. (pp. 553–575). New York: Guilford Press.

Carver, C. S., Scheier, M. F., & Weintraub, J. K. (1989). Assessing coping strategies: A theoretically based approach. *Journal of Personality and Social Psychology, 56*, 267–283.

Carver, C. S., Pozo, C., Harris, S. D., Noriega, V., Scheier, M. F., Robinson, D. S., Ketcham, A. S., Moffat, F. L., Jr., & Clark, K. C. (1993). How coping mediates the effect of optimism on distress: A study of women with early stage breast cancer. *Journal of Personality and Social Psychology, 65*, 375–390.

Coates, D., & Wortman, C. B. (1980). Depression maintenance and interpersonal control. In A. E. Baum & J. E. Singer (Eds.), *Advances in environmental psychology: Applications of personal control*, Vol. 2 (pp. 149–182). Hillsdale, NJ: Erlbaum.

Coats, E. J., Janoff-Bulman, R., & Alpert, N. (1996). Approach versus avoidance goals: Differences in self-evaluation and well-being. *Personality and Social Psychology Bulletin, 22*, 1057–1067.

Cohen, S. (1988). Psychosocial models of the role of social support in the etiology of physical disease. *Health Psychology, 7*, 269–297.

Cohen, S., & Rodriguez, M. S. (1995). Pathways linking affective disturbances and physical disorders. *Health Psychology, 14*, 374–380.

Cohen, S., & Wills, T. A. (1985). Stress, social support, and the buffering hypothesis. *Psychological Bulletin, 98*, 310–357.

Colby, P. M., & Emmons, R. A. (1997). Openness to emotion as predictor of perceived, requested, and observer reports of social support. In G. R. Pierce, B. Lakey, I. G. Sarason, & B. R. Sarason (Eds.), *Sourcebook of social support and personality* (pp. 445–472). New York: Plenum Press.

Collins, R. L., Taylor, S. E., & Skokan, L. A. (1990). A better world or a shattered vision? Changes in perspective following victimization. *Social Cognition, 8*, 263–285.

Coyne, J. C., & Gottlieb, B. H. (1996). The mismeasure of coping by checklist. *Journal of Personality, 64*, 959–991.

Davis, C., Lehman, D. R., & Wortman, C. B. (1999). Searching for meaning following a life crisis:

Making sense of the literature. Manuscript submitted for publication.

Derryberry, D., & Reed, M. A. (1994). Temperament and attention: Orienting toward and away from positive and negative signals. *Journal of Personality and Social Psychology, 66,* 1128–1139.

Dunkel-Schetter, C., & Wortman, C. B. (1982). The interpersonal dynamics of cancer: Problems in social relationships and their impact on the patient. In H. S. Friedman & M. R. DiMatteo (Eds.), *Interpersonal issues in health care* (pp. 69–100). New York: Academic Press.

Dweck, C. S. (1996). Implicit theories as organizers of goals and behavior. In P. M. Gollwitzer & J. A. Bargh (Eds.), *The psychology of action: Linking cognition and motivation to behavior* (pp. 69–90). New York: Guilford Press.

Elliot, A. J., Sheldon, K. M., & Church, M. A. (1996). Avoidance, personal goals and subjective well-being. *Personality and Social Psychology Bulletin, 23,* 915–927.

Emmons, R. A., & King, L. A. (1988). Conflict among personal strivings: Immediate and long-term implications for psychological and physical well-being. *Journal of Personality and Social Psychology, 54,* 1040–1048.

Emmons, R. A., Colby, P. M., & Kaiser, H. A. (1998). When losses lead to gains: Personal goals and the recovery of meaning. In P. T. P. Wong & P. S. Fry (Eds.), *The human quest for meaning: A handbook of psychological research and clinical applications* (pp. 163–178). Mahwah, NJ: Lawrence Erlbaum Associates.

Evans, G. W., & Lepore, S. J. (1993). Household crowding and social support: A quasiexperimental analysis. *Journal of Personality and Social Psychology, 65,* 308–316.

Folkman, S. (1984). Personal control and stress and coping processes: A theoretical analysis. *Journal of Personality and Social Psychology, 46,* 839–852.

Folkman, S., & Lazarus, R. L. (1980). An analysis of coping in a middle-aged community sample. *Journal of Health and Social Behavior, 21,* 219–239.

Fredrickson, B. L. (1998). What good are positive emotions? *Review of General Psychology, 2,* 300–319.

Friedman, H. S. (1990). (Ed.) *Personality and disease.* New York: John Wiley & Sons.

Gollwitzer, P. M., & Bargh, J. A. (Eds.) (1996). *The psychology of action: Linking cognition and motivation to behavior.* New York: Guilford Press.

Headey, B., & Wearing, A. (1989). Personality, life events, and subjective well-being: Toward a dynamic equilibrium model. *Journal of Personality and Social Psychology, 57,* 731–739.

Heckhausen, J. (1997). Developmental regulation across adulthood: Primary and secondary control of age-related challenges. *Developmental Psychology, 33,* 176–187.

Higgins, E. T. (1996). Ideals, oughts, and regulatory focus: Affect and motivation from distinct pains and pleasures. In P. M. Gollwitzer & J. A. Bargh (Eds), *The psychology of action: Linking cognition and motivation to behavior* (pp. 91–114). New York: Guilford Press.

Hobfoll, S. E. (1989). Conservation of resources: A new attempt at conceptualizing stress. *American Psychologist, 44,* 513–524.

Holahan, C. J., & Moos, R. H. (1986). Personality, coping, and family resources in stress resistance: A longitudinal analysis. *Journal of Personality and Social Psychology, 51,* 389–395.

Holahan, C. J., Moos, R. H., Holahan, C. K., & Brennan, P. L. (1997). Social context, coping strategies, and depressive symptoms: An expanded model with cardiac patients. *Journal of Personality and Social Psychology, 72,* 918–928.

Ickovics, J. R., & Park, C. L. (1998). Paradigm shift: Why a focus on health is important. *Journal of Social Issues, 54* (2), 237–244.

Isen, A. M. (1993). Positive affect and decision making. In M. Lewis & J. M. Haviland (Eds.), *Handbook of emotions* (pp. 261–277). New York: Guilford Press.

Janoff-Bulman, R. (1989). Assumptive worlds and the stress of traumatic events: Applications of the schema construct. *Social Cognition, 7,* 113–136.

Janoff-Bulman, R., & Frieze, I. H. (1983). A theoretical perspective for understanding reactions to victimization. *Journal of Social Issues, 39* (2), 1–17.

Joiner, T. E., Metalsky, G. I., Katz, J., & Beach, S. R. H. (in press). Depression and excessive reassurance-seeking. *Psychological Inquiry.*

Kaplan, H. B. (Ed.) (1996). *Psychosocial stress: Perspectives on structure, theory, life-course, and meth-*

ods. San Diego, CA: Academic Press.

Katz, L., & Epstein, E. (1991). Constructive thinking and coping with laboratory-induced stress. *Journal of Personality and Social Psychology, 61*, 789–800.

King, L. (1996). Who is regulating what and why? The motivational context of self-regulation. *Psychological Inquiry, 7*, 57–60.

King, L. A., & Miner, K. N. (in press). Writing about the perceived benefits of traumatic events: Implications for physical health. *Personality and Social Psychology Bulletin.*

Kling, K. C., Ryff, C. D., & Essex, M. J. (1997). Adaptive changes in self-concept during a life transition. *Personality and Social Psychology Bulletin, 23*, 981–990.

Kulik, J. A., & Mahler, H. I. M. (1997). Social comparison, affiliation, and coping with acute medical threats. In B. P. Buunk & F. X. Gibbons (Eds.), *Health, coping, and well-being: Perspectives from social comparison theory* (pp. 227–261). Mahwah, NJ: Erlbaum.

Lazarus, R. L. (1990). Theory-based stress measurement. *Psychological Inquiry, 1*, 3–13.

Lazarus, R. L., & Folkman, S. (1984). *Stress, appraisal, and coping.* New York: Springer.

Lehman, D. R., Ellard, J. H., & Wortman, C. B. (1986). Social support for the bereaved: Recipients' and providers' perspectives on what is helpful. *Journal of Consulting and Clinical Psychology, 54*, 438–446.

Little, B. R. (1983). Personal projects: A rationale and method for investigation. *Environment and Behavior, 15*, 273–309.

McCrae, R. R., & Costa, P. T., Jr. (1986). Personality, coping, and coping effectiveness in an adult sample. *Journal of Personality and Social Psychology, 54*, 385–405.

Markus, H., & Nurius, P. (1986). Possible selves. *American Psychologist, 41*, 954–969.

Martin, L. L., & Tesser, A. (1996). *Striving and feeling: Interactions between goals, affect, and self-regulation.* Hillsdale, NJ: Erlbaum.

Park, C. L., Cohen, L. H., & Murch, R. L. (1996). Assessment and prediction of stress-related growth. *Journal of Personality, 64*, 71–105.

Pearlin, L. I., Aneshensel, C. S., & LeBlanc, A. J. (1997). The forms and mechanisms of stress proliferation: The case of AIDS caregivers. *Journal of Health and Social Behavior, 38*, 223–236.

Pennebaker, J. W. (1993). Putting stress into words: Health, linguistic, and therapeutic implications. *Behaviour Research and Therapy, 31*, 539–548.

Peterson, C., & Seligman, M. E. P. (1984). Causal explanations as a risk factor for depression: Theory and evidence. *Psychological Review, 91*, 347–374.

Repetti, R. L. (1989). Effects of daily workload on subsequent behavior during marital interaction: The roles of social withdrawal and spouse support. *Journal of Personality and Social Psychology, 57*, 651–659.

Revenson, T. A. (1990). All other things are not equal: An ecological approach to personality and disease. In H. S. Friedman (Ed.), *Personality and disease* (pp. 65–94). New York: John Wiley & Sons.

Revenson, T. A. (1994). Social support and marital coping with chronic illness. *Annals of Behavioral Medicine, 16*, 122–130.

Ruble, D. N., & Frey, K. S. (1991). Changing patterns of comparative behavior as skills are acquired: A functional model of self-evaluation. In J. Suls & T. A. Wills (Eds.), *Social comparison: Contemporary theory and research* (pp. 79–113). Hillsdale, NJ: Erlbaum.

Ryff, C. D. (1989). Happiness is everything, or is it? Explorations on the meaning of psychological well-being. *Journal of Personality and Social Psychology, 57*, 1069–1081.

Schachter, S. (1959). *The psychology of affiliation.* Stanford, CA: Stanford University Press.

Scheier, M. F., Carver, C. S., & Bridges, M. W. (1994). Distinguishing optimism from neuroticism (and trait anxiety, self-mastery, and self-esteem): A re-evaluation of the Life Orientation Test. *Journal of Personality and Social Psychology, 67*, 1063–1078.

Silver, R. C., Wortman, C. B., & Crofton, C. (1990). The role of coping in support provision: The self-presentational dilemma of victims of life crises. In B. R. Sarason & I. G. Sarason (Eds.), *Social support: An interactional view* (pp. 397–426). New York: John Wiley & Sons.

Skinner, E. A. (in press). Action regulation, coping, and development. In J. Brandtstädter & R. M. Lerner (Eds.), *Action and self-development: Theory and research through the life-span.* Thousand

Oaks, CA: Sage.

Smith, C. A., & Wallston, K. A. (1992). Adaptation in patients with chronic rheumatoid arthritis: Application of a general model. *Health Psychology, 11,* 151–162.

Smith, R. E., Leffingwell, T. R., & Ptacek, J. T. (1999). Can people remember how they coped?: Factors associated with discordance between same-day and retrospective reports. *Journal of Personality and Social Psychology, 76,* 1050–1061.

Stanton, A. L., Danoff-Burg, S., Cameron, C. L., & Ellis, A. P. (1994). Coping through emotional approach: Problems of conceptualization and confounding. *Journal of Personality and Social Psychology, 66,* 350–362.

Stone, A. A., & Neale, J. M. (1984). Effects of severe daily events on mood. *Journal of Personality and Social Psychology, 46,* 137–144.

Stone, A. A., Greenberg, M. A., Kennedy-Moore, E., & Newman, M. G. (1991). Self-report, situation-specific coping questionnaires: What are they measuring? *Journal of Personality and Social Psychology, 61,* 648–658.

Suls, J., & Harvey, J. H. (Eds.) (1996). Personality and coping: Special issue. *Journal of Personality, 64.*

Taylor, S. E. (1983). Adjustment to threatening events: A theory of cognitive adaptation. *American Psychologist, 38,* 1163–1173.

Taylor, S. E., & Aspinwall, L. G. (1990). Psychosocial aspects of chronic illness. In P. T. Costa, Jr., & G. R. VandenBos (Eds.), *Psychological aspects of serious illness: Chronic conditions, fatal disease, and clinical care* (pp. 3–60). Washington, DC: American Psychological Association.

Taylor, S. E., & Aspinwall, L. G. (1996). Mediating and moderating processes in psychosocial stress: Appraisal, coping, resistance and vulnerability. In H. B. Kaplan (Ed.), *Psychosocial stress: Perspectives on structure, theory, life-course, and methods* (pp. 71–110). San Diego, CA: Academic Press.

Taylor, S. E., & Lobel, M. (1989). Social comparison activity under threat: Downward evaluation and upward contacts. *Psychological Review, 96,* 569–575.

Taylor, S. E., Repetti, R. L., & Seeman, T. (1997). Health psychology: What is an unhealthy environment and how does it get under the skin? *Annual Review of Psychology, 48,* 411–447.

Taylor, S. E., Wood, J. V., & Lichtman, R. R. (1983). It could be worse: Selective evaluation as a response to victimization. *Journal of Social Issues, 39* (2), 19–40.

Tedeschi, R. G., & Calhoun, L. G. (1996). The Posttraumatic Growth Inventory: Measuring the positive legacy of trauma. *Journal of Traumatic Stress, 9,* 455–471.

Tedeschi, R. G., Park, C. L., & Calhoun, L. G. (Eds.) (1998). *Posttraumatic growth: Positive changes in the aftermath of crisis.* Mahwah, NJ: Erlbaum.

Thoits, P. A. (1986). Social support as coping assistance. *Journal of Consulting and Clinical Psychology, 54,* 416–423.

Thompson, S. C., Sobolew-Shubin, A., Galbraith, M. E., Schwankovsky, L., & Cruzen, D. (1993). Maintaining perceptions of control: Finding perceived control in low-control circumstances. *Journal of Personality and Social Psychology, 64,* 293–304.

Updegraff, J. A., & Taylor, S. E. (in press). From vulnerability to growth: The positive and negative effects of stressful life events. In J. Harvey & E. Miller (Eds.), *Handbook of loss and trauma.* Philadelphia, PA: Taylor & Francis.

Watson, D., & Clark, L. A. (1984). Negative affectivity: The disposition to experience aversive emotional states. *Psychological Bulletin, 96,* 465–490.

Watson, D., & Hubbard, B. (1996). Adaptational style and dispositional structure: Coping in the context of the five-factor model. *Journal of Personality, 64,* 737–774.

Wills, T. A. (1981). Downward comparison principles in social psychology. *Psychological Bulletin, 90,* 245–271.

Wortman, C. B., & Silver, R. L. (1987). Coping with irrevocable loss. In G. R. VandenBos & B. K. Bryant (Eds.), *Cataclysms, crises, and catastrophes: Psychology in action* (pp. 189–235). Washington, DC: American Psychological Association.

Chapter Twenty-Eight

The Psychological Determinants of Political Judgment

Victor C. Ottati

One might view political psychology simply as an application of psychological theory and research to the study of political behavior. Yet this characterization is misleading in at least two respects. First, it suggests that political psychology merely consists of conceptual replications of basic psychological research. In fact, examination of psychological functioning in a political context often requires that researchers develop new and more realistic models of psychological processing. Second, this conceptualization inaccurately portrays psychology as the source discipline and political science as the receptor discipline. To the contrary, political psychology involves a balanced dialogue between these two parent disciplines characterized by reciprocal intellectual exchange (Iyengar & Ottati, 1994).

This chapter focuses on recent research regarding the psychological determinants of two types of political judgment. The first is referred to as a "candidate evaluation judgment," here defined as an individual's summary evaluation of a political candidate along a bipolar, like-versus-dislike dimension. Because candidate evaluation figures prominently in determining the vote decision, it occupies a central role in the study of political behavior. The second category of judgment reflects the voter's specific position on a political issue (e.g. welfare). Because issue positions constitute the fundamental elements of public opinion, and because issue positions influence a variety of political decisions, an examination of this second type of judgment is equally fundamental to an understanding of political behavior.

The Psychological Determinants of Candidate Evaluation

Traditional models of candidate evaluation and voter decision making emphasized the sociological, attitudinal, and rational determinants of the voting choice (see Iyengar &

Ottati, 1994, for a review). Yet none of these approaches provided a realistic or precise description of the cognitive process mechanisms that underlie candidate evaluation and the voting decision. The present section reviews more recent advances in candidate evaluation research that have been inspired by developments in the social cognition and attitude literature. These approaches place greater emphasis upon mediating psychological process mechanisms.

In reviewing this work, a variety of factors that determine candidate evaluation are considered. The first two factors are of long-standing interest to political researchers. These are the candidate's specific issue positions and party affiliation. This is followed by a discussion of factors that occupy a central position in the social cognition and attitude literature, and more recent emphasis in the candidate evaluation literature. These are trait assessments of a political candidate, visual cues of a political candidate (physical attractiveness, facial expression), and the affective state of the voter. Lastly, because the voting choice involves a comparison between competing alternatives, research regarding the impact of comparative standards is discussed. Before discussing these determinants, however, it is important to distinguish different "procedural styles" that characterize the process whereby voters arrive at candidate evaluation judgments.

Processing style en route to candidate evaluation

Process models of candidate evaluation can be distinguished along two dimensions: (a) systematic versus heuristic processing (see Chaiken, Liberman, & Eagly, 1989), and (b) on-line versus memory based processing (see Hastie & Park, 1986). Systematic processing occurs when voters deliberatively consider a candidate's specific, individuating attributes to arrive at an overall candidate evaluation. This mode of processing requires that the voter possess adequate cognitive resources and motivation to carefully scrutinize information pertaining to the candidate. It is most commonly manifested as voter preference for a candidate who possesses specific issue positions that are shared by the voter (Ottati, 1990). Heuristic processing requires less capacity and effort. In this case, the voter relies on a simple heuristic cue (e.g. physical attractiveness, party membership) to evaluate the candidate (Ottati, 1990).

The distinction between on-line and memory based processing is of critical importance in the candidate evaluation literature. Survey researchers have implicitly embraced a memory based model by assuming candidate judgments are based on specific pieces of information retrieved from memory. If this is true, the net valence of recalled information should correlate strongly with global evaluation of the candidate. In contrast, the on-line model posits that the individual evaluates each piece of candidate information as it is encountered, and immediately integrates these valences into a running tally as each piece of information is acquired. This summary tally is stored in long-term memory. When a judgment is later required, this on-line tally is retrieved from memory rather than the specific pieces of information that contributed to it (Lodge, Steenbergen, & Brau, 1995; McGraw, Lodge, & Stroh, 1990). This on-line model predicts that the correlation between summary evaluation and the net valence of specific information recalled can be very low. Research confirms that this is often the case (e.g. Lodge, Steenbergen, & Brau, 1995). Lodge, Steenbergen,

& Brau (1995) recently examined the candidate evaluation process over a sizable time frame. Consistent with the on-line model, they found that memory for specific candidate information fades quickly, whereas memory for the summary evaluation remains relatively stable across time. Their findings also suggest that specific information recalled serves primarily to justify (not determine) the summary evaluation (see Krosnick, 1988; Ottati, Fishbein, & Middlestadt, 1988, for related evidence).

It is important to note, however, that on-line processing is not necessarily universal. Although on-line processing is prevalent among political experts, memory based processing often occurs among political novices (McGraw, Lodge, & Stroh, 1990). Political novices are especially likely to engage in memory based processing when candidate information is presented in a complex format (Rahn, Aldrich, & Borgida, 1994). Also, some people may compute a new judgment of a candidate based upon specific information recalled, even when they already possess a summary evaluation stored in memory.

Issues and candidate evaluation

According to classic democratic theory, voters should evaluate a candidate on the basis of the issues. Yet many researchers argue that citizens rarely possess the motivation or ability to systematically evaluate candidates in terms of such issue calculations. This characterization of the voter may be overly pessimistic, however. For one thing, the on-line model posits that candidate evaluation can be responsive to a candidate's specific issue positions even if voters are unable to recall these issue stances (Lodge, Steenbergen, & Brau, 1995). Second, if one abandons the assumption that issues are equally weighted when determining candidate evaluation, calculations of issue agreement often figure prominently in determining these judgments (Krosnick, Berent, & Boninger, 1994).

A variety of factors can affect the weight ascribed to a given issue. These include the subjective importance of the issue, personal relevance of the issue, the voter's subjective certainty that the candidate holds the issue position, the serial position in which the issue was originally encountered, the valence of the issue position, and media priming of the issue. Three of these determinants of issue weighting have been given the most extensive coverage in the candidate evaluation literature. These are subjective importance, valence (i.e. negativity effects), and media priming.

Subjective importance   Krosnick and his associates (e.g. Krosnick, Berent, & Boninger, 1994) have provided a comprehensive account of issue importance effects. They define issue importance as a subjective perception of importance that is specific to a given issue and that is relatively stable across time. Issues that are relevant to self-interest, ingroup interests, or core values are often high in subjective importance. Moreover, subjectively important issues are cognitively represented in a more organized fashion than unimportant issues (Berent & Krosnick, 1993). Subjectively important issues are given greater weight than unimportant issues when individuals evaluate a candidate. This effect is probably mediated by a variety of factors. These include increased accessibility of important issues and greater awareness of candidate differences on important issues (Krosnick, Berent, & Boninger, 1994).

Negativity effects   Negativity effects are present when individuals give greater weight to negative information relative to equally extreme and equally likely positive information (Lau, 1985). This effect is not limited to issue information. Negativity effects can occur for a candidate's trait characteristics, with negative traits carrying more weight than positive traits when predicting candidate evaluation (Klein, 1991).

Lau (1985) offers two explanations for negativity effects in political behavior. According to the "figure–ground hypothesis," individuals generally expect that others will possess positive characteristics. Negative information, due to its infrequency or novelty, stands out against this positive background and is given greater weight in determining judgments. From this perspective, negativity effects should be moderated by individual differences in the degree to which "background" expectations are indeed positive. Namely, individuals who generally trust politicians should be more likely to exhibit negativity effects than those who generally distrust politicians. Lau's second hypothesis, labeled the "cost orientation hypothesis," begins with the assumption that people are more motivated to avoid costs than approach gains. From this perspective, negativity effects should be most prevalent when individuals believe the election outcome will produce notable costs and benefits. Lau's (1985) findings support both predictions, suggesting both mechanisms elicit negativity effects.

Recent work on negativity effects raises questions about these interpretations. According to Skowronski & Carlston (1989), negative information is given considerable weight when it serves as a diagnostic cue that discriminates between a given trait inference (e.g. honest) and its alternative (e.g. dishonest). Factors such as novelty or infrequency may contribute to diagnosticity. However, this need not always be the case. For example, infrequent negative behaviors are often highly diagnostic when making honesty judgments, but not when making ability judgments (Skowronski & Carlston, 1989). Lau's (1989) finding that negativity effects are moderated by general expectations regarding the honesty of politicians is consistent with this formulation.

One might predict that negative political campaigning is an especially potent determinant of candidate evaluation due to negativity effects. In fact, the effects of negative campaigning (i.e. attacking the opponent) are quite complex. Effects of negative campaigning differ depending on whether the attack centers on the opponent's issue stances, character, or both, and also depending on whether the source of the attack falls within the voter's ideological ingroup or outgroup (Budesheim, Houston, & DePaolo, 1996). For example, candidates can energize their supporters by making strong character attacks that are justified with issue attacks (which the supporters will agree with). Yet this effect does not emerge for voters ideologically opposed to the source (Budesheim, Houston, & DePaolo, 1996). As this example illustrates, negative campaigning not only influences evaluations of the attack target, but also the source (see Houston, Doan, & Roskos-Ewoldson, 1998, for further evidence).

Media induced priming effects   Issues accessible in the voter's mind carry considerable weight when voters evaluate a candidate. Prominent and frequent media coverage of an issue serves to prime that issue, thereby increasing the accessibility and weight ascribed to that issue when voters evaluate a candidate. Effects of this nature have been demonstrated in both experimental (e.g. Iyengar & Kinder, 1987) and survey (e.g. Krosnick & Kinder, 1990) studies. This effect is magnified when coverage of an issue suggests that political officials are responsible for national conditions related to the issue (Iyengar & Kinder, 1987). Other moderators of this effect include relevance and political involvement. Not surprisingly, priming effects are more prominent when predicting judgments about the candidate that are relevant to the primed issue than when predicting judgments that are less directly relevant to the primed issue (Iyengar & Kinder, 1987). Evidence regarding the moderating role of political involvement (exposure, interest, knowledge) is somewhat mixed. Some studies indicate that media induced priming effects are more likely to emerge among political novices than experts. However, Krosnick & Brannon (1993) note that this research has failed to disentangle the effects of exposure, interest, and knowledge. When examining the unique contribution of these factors, Krosnick and Brannon find that political interest reduces priming effects whereas political expertise increases priming effects. Further research is needed to identify the psychological mechanism responsible for this effect.

Partisanship and candidate evaluation

Political researchers have long noted that partisanship is an important determinant of candidate evaluation. Partisanship plays a critical role in many traditional models of voting behavior, including the "Michigan School" model of voting preference (Campbell, Converse, Miller, & Stokes, 1960). In addition, many models of media influence suggest that, when campaigns do influence voter preferences, voters move in the direction of their prior partisan predispositions (Iyengar & Petrocik, 1998).

While early research concerning partisanship failed to focus on mediating process mechanisms, recent research has more directly assessed this question. This work suggests that the effect of party on candidate evaluation is mediated by a variety of process mechanisms that occur at distinct stages of information processing (see Iyengar & Ottati, 1994; Ottati & Wyer, 1992). These include selective exposure to information consistent with the voter's party orientation, biased encoding or interpretation of a candidate's policy positions, inferring that the candidate's specific policy positions coincide with the party stereotype, biased retrieval of a candidate's issue positions, and biased weighting of a candidate's issue positions (Iyengar & Ottati, 1994; Wyer & Ottati, 1993). Lodge & Hamill (1986) have explicitly considered the psychological mediators of the effect of party on candidate evaluation. They found that, relative to "party aschematics," "party schematics" were more likely to accurately categorize policy statements in terms of party. In addition, "party schematics" were more likely to exhibit a party consistency bias when using recognition measures of memory for a candidate's issue positions.

While the research described above suggests that the effect of party on candidate evaluation is mediated by biased processing of specific issue information, other work indicates party labels can function as heuristic cues that elicit category based evaluation of a political candidate (e.g. Fiske, 1986; Ottati, 1990). From this perspective, voters categorize the candidate in terms of party and simply evaluate the candidate on the basis of their evaluation of their party stereotype. This heuristic mode of party based candidate evaluation occurs when voters possess little or no individuating information pertaining to a candidate, or alternatively, when voters lack the ability or motivation to engage in more systematic, issue based processing (e.g. Fiske, 1986; Ottati, 1990). Consistent with this view, Ottati (1990) obtained party based evaluation effects in a comparative judgment task, but not in a singular judgment task (which presumably requires less cognitive capacity or ability). Individual differences in ability to process political information (i.e. political expertise) also moderate reliance upon the party stereotype. Rahn & Cramer (1996) report that political experts are less likely than novices to "apply" (i.e. give weight to) the party stereotype when evaluating a political candidate.

Factors that moderate party based candidate evaluation serve an analogous role as moderators of other heuristic cues. Ottati, Terkildsen, & Hubbard (1997) demonstrate that a candidate's ideology can function as a heuristic cue that determines candidate preference under conditions of low motivation. Miller & Krosnick (1998) demonstrate that the order in which names appear on the ballot determines voting preference when voters possess little information regarding the competing candidates.

Trait based candidate evaluation

Recent research emphasizes that candidate evaluation is not solely determined by political criteria (e.g. issues, partisanship). Many factors that influence evaluations of non-political actors also influence candidate evaluation. These include trait characteristics, the candidate's visual image, and the affective state of the voter. The role of trait perceptions is emphasized by models that describe the representation of candidate information. McGraw, Pinney, & Neumann (1991) argue that representations of a candidate contain two information clusters. One contains the candidate's issues positions, whereas the other contains traits. Other research questions this conclusion, arguing that trait inferences are partially based on reactions to a candidate's issue stands (Forgas, Kagan, & Frey, 1977; Miller, Wattenberg, & Malanchuk, 1986; Rahn, Aldrich, Borgida, & Sullivan, 1990). Many researchers propose that voters organize trait information in terms of a limited number of broad trait categories that remain relatively constant across elections (Kinder, 1986; Miller, Wattenberg, & Malanchuk, 1986). Examples of these trait categories include leadership/ competence and integrity/empathy (Kinder, 1986), as well as task oriented and socioemotional traits (Rahn, Aldrich, Borgida, & Sullivan, 1990).

Do traits and issues function as independent determinants of candidate evaluation? Kinder (1986) emphasizes that trait ratings exert an effect on candidate evaluation that is independent of issue considerations. However, Rahn, Aldrich, Borgida, & Sullivan (1990) suggest that the effect of political criteria (e.g. issues, ideology, partisanship) on voting preference is mediated by trait assessments of the candidate – suggesting considerable redundancy among these two classes of predictors.

If traits play a role in determining candidate evaluation, what is the relative weight ascribed to the various dimensions? Funk (1997) argues that, based on normative considerations, task oriented traits (i.e. competence) should be given greater weight than socioemotional traits (i.e. warmth). Consistent with this assumption, political experts were more likely than novices to give greater weight to the competence dimension (Funk, 1977). Because experts possess an extensive and complex knowledge base, they are presumably better able to discriminate important traits from traits of lesser importance.

Effects of visual cues on candidate evaluation

Research regarding the effects of visual cues on candidate evaluation has focused primarily on the effects of candidate physical attractiveness and facial expression.

Physical attractiveness Consistent with social psychological research on the physical attractiveness stereotype, several studies indicate that people evaluate physically attractive candidates more positively than physically unattractive candidates (e.g. Budesheim & DePaola, 1994; Ottati, 1990). This effect is clearly present when individuals possess no other relevant information pertaining to the candidate (Ottati, 1990). Yet physical attractiveness also influences candidate evaluation when accompanied by more substantive candidate information (e.g. issue stances, party). In this latter case, effects associated with physical attractiveness are more complex (Ottati, 1990; Riggle, Ottati, Wyer, Kuklinski, & Schwarz, 1992). Ottati (1990) finds that physical attractiveness is more likely to influence candidate evaluation in a comparative judgment task than in a more simple, singular judgment task. Even within the comparative judgment task, Ottati (1990) reports that physical attractiveness influences candidate evaluation only when the voter perceives that the candidate's party and issue stances are of opposite valence. However, Budesheim & DePaola (1994) failed to replicate this later finding and report that physical attractiveness influences candidate evaluation regardless of the valence ascribed to party and issue information.

Facial expression A number of studies demonstrate that a candidate's nonverbal cues (e.g. facial display) influence voters' evaluations of a candidate (e.g. Masters, Sullivan, Lanzetta, McHugo, & Englis, 1986; Ottati, Terkildsen, & Hubbard, 1997). An interesting question concerns how voters combine nonverbal with verbal candidate information to arrive at a summary evaluation. Many political researchers regard a candidate's facial expression as a stimulus cue that elicits positive or negative reactions to a candidate, with this effect being unique and distinct from the impact of a candidate's verbal remarks (e.g. Masters, Sullivan, Lanzetta, McHugo, & Englis, 1986). This account of facial display effects accounts for a variety of candidate image effects occurring throughout history. For example, in the Kennedy–Nixon debate, Nixon's facial expressions conveyed a sense of insecurity whereas Kennedy's facial expressions projected an image of confidence. Most political analysts believe that televised presentation of this debate negatively influenced evaluations of Nixon and positively influenced evaluations of Kennedy.

A second category of research focuses on facial displays that convey information that is discrepant from the implication of verbally acquired information. In this case, facial expressions might constitute a form of "nonverbal leakage" that betrays a person's true emotional state when that person's verbal statements are designed to deny or disguise an underlying emotion. Under such conditions, perceivers may give greater weight to the nonverbal channel (Mehrabian & Ferris, 1967). In the political arena, nonverbal leakage might undermine a candidate's denial of suspicious, inappropriate, or illegal behavior. Alternatively, nonverbal leakage might convey anger or irritation when a candidate's verbal remarks attempt to project a veneer of civility. Facial expressions that contradict a person's verbal remarks may also convey sarcasm or humor (Bugental, Kaswan, & Love, 1979). For example, if a disgusted expression accompanies the remark "Clinton's health care proposal is obviously completely flawless," it is clear that the speaker's intended meaning is precisely opposite to the literal meaning of the verbal utterance.

A third perspective emphasizes that a candidate's nonverbal cues moderate the voter's tendency to engage in systematic versus heuristic processing of verbally acquired information (Ottati, Terkildsen, & Hubbard, 1997; see also Wyer, et al., 1991). Ottati, Terkildsen, & Hubbard (1997) argue that neutral or more somber facial expressions signal that a candidate's verbal remarks address serious concerns that require systematic scrutiny. In contrast, happy displays signal that a candidate's verbal remarks address benign or "light" issues that do not require systematic scrutiny. Consistent with these assumptions, perceivers were more likely to engage in systematic, issue based candidate evaluation when the candidate's verbal remarks were accompanied by a neutral facial expression than when these remarks were accompanied by a happy facial expression. Conversely, the tendency to rely on candidate ideology as a heuristic basis for candidate evaluation was more pronounced in the happy display condition than in the neutral display condition (Ottati, Terkildsen, & Hubbard, 1997).

Episodic affect and candidate evaluation

Social psychological research concerning the effect of affect on social judgment is quite extensive. Under appropriate conditions, positive affective states elicit more positive social judgments than negative affective states. This effect may be mediated by mood congruent encoding, interpretation, or elaboration of information pertaining to the object judged (e.g. Forgas, 1995). Alternatively, this effect may occur when individuals (correctly or incorrectly) attribute their episodic affective state to the object judged (Schwarz & Clore, 1983). Episodic affect may also influence processing style en route to judgment (e.g. chapter 18, this volume; Schwarz, 1990; Martin, Ward, Achee, & Wyer, 1993).

In the candidate evaluation literature, many researchers report that beliefs about a candidate and emotional reactions to a candidate function as unique predictors of global candidate evaluation (Abelson, Kinder, Peters, & Fiske, 1982; Ottati, Steenbergen, & Riggle, 1992). However, this finding does not generalize across all conditions or methods of measurement. For example, beliefs fully account for the predictive role of emotions when using an open-ended measure of "emotionally relevant" beliefs (Ottati, 1997). Moreover, affective–cognitive ambivalence moderates these effects. The unique role of affect is prominent among individuals possessing oppositely valenced affective and cognitive reactions to a candidate. However, this unique effect is less pronounced among individuals possessing similarly valenced affective and cognitive reactions to a candidate (Lavine, Thomsen, Zanna, & Borgida, 1998).

Campaign strategists employ a variety of tactics designed to place voters in a good mood when they are exposed to a political candidate. The use of this strategy rests upon the assumption that positive reactions to contextual stimuli (e.g. the flag, music, hoopla) will translate into positive reactions to a political leader. Experimental attempts to investigate this phenomenon have often used non-political contextual cues (e.g. movie footage, success or failure at an irrelevant task) to place individuals in a positive or negative mood. Immediately following this "mood induction procedure," participants perform an ostensibly unrelated task in which they read about a political candidate. After some period of delay (e.g. two weeks), they report their evaluation of the candidate.

Using this procedure, Ottati & Isbell (1996) have demonstrated that the effect of mood on candidate evaluation is moderated by political expertise of the voter. Among political novices, mood produced an assimilation effect with positive mood eliciting more positive evaluations than negative mood. However, among political experts mood produced a contrast effect with positive mood eliciting more negative evaluations than negative mood. Thus, mood produced an assimilation effect among perceivers who processed the candidate information in an inefficient manner (novices), whereas mood produced a contrast effect among perceivers who processed this information in an efficient manner (experts). Supplementary analyses suggested that these effects were not mediated by biased recall of candidate information.

Ottati & Isbell (1996) postulate that mood during exposure to the candidate information is misattributed to the candidate, influencing on-line evaluation of the candidate. This summary evaluation is stored in memory and later retrieved to report a judgment – producing a mood assimilation effect among low efficiency perceivers (novices). Perceivers who process the candidate information in an efficient manner (experts) are assumed to possess the capacity or ability to correct for this judgmental bias. However, because they overestimate the initial biasing influence of mood, they over-correct for this influence. Among experts, this produces a contrast effect in which positive mood elicits a more negative candidate evaluation than negative mood.

Using a nearly identical procedure, Isbell & Wyer (1998) report that motivation to evaluate a political candidate moderates the impact of mood on candidate evaluation. Namely, mood produced an assimilation effect when participants possessed low motivation, whereas mood produced a contrast effect when participants possessed high motivation. Taken together, these studies suggest that individuals will attempt to correct for the biasing influence of mood when they possess the ability or motivation to do so (see also Petty & Wegener, 1993). As such, campaign tactics designed to elicit a positive mood in the voter may not always produce their intended effect.

Inspired by basic research on mood effects (Schwarz, Bless, & Bohner, 1991), a third line of research emphasizes that affective states influence motivation to carefully attend to a political communication. For example, Marcus & Mackuen (1993) demonstrate that anxiety stimulates attention toward political issues and discourages reliance upon habitual (e.g. heuristic) cues for voting. Nadeau, Niemi, & Amato (1995) argue that this effect is mediated by issue importance, and that this effect only occurs when voters expect that careful attention to an issue stands a realistic chance of influencing tangible outcomes. Clore & Isbell (in press) propose that, in addition to anxiety, sadness might produce more deliberative and systematic processing of political information (see Schwarz, Bless, & Bohner, 1991, for evidence in a non-political context).

In sum, the effect of affect on candidate evaluation is a multifaceted and complex phenomenon. Attempts to provide a comprehensive description of these effects must therefore include a variety of psychological mechanisms that operate under varying conditions (Glaser & Salovey, 1998; Ottati & Wyer, 1992).

Comparative standards and candidate evaluation

Politicians are often evaluated relative to some internally generated standard or relative to other political actors. Sullivan, Aldrich, Borgida, & Rahn (1990) hypothesize that voters might rely on either of two internally generated standards. The "superman model" predicts that voters will evince the greatest support for politicians who approach perfection – politicians who possess the highest possible altruism, willpower, and trustworthiness. The "everyman model" predicts that voters will show the greatest support for politicians who best typify the average person. From this second perspective, candidates who present themselves as too superior may be perceived as self-righteous, pretentious, or out of touch with the common person. Sullivan, Aldrich, Borgida, & Rahn (1990) obtain strong support for the "superman model," but also a modicum of support for the "everyman model." It is conceivable that voters value ideal qualities along certain dimensions while preferring that candidates remain average along other dimensions.

Other research focuses on the effects of externally presented standards. One such line of research emphasizes that voters are often presented with two competing candidates who serve as standards of comparison for each other in the general election. This approach is best exemplified by Houston & Roskos-Ewoldsen's (in press) "cancellation and focus" model (see also Tversky, 1977). According to this model, comparison involves starting from one candidate (the "subject") and mapping this candidate's features on to the opposing candidate (the "referent"). Shared features are canceled and thereby fail to influence preference judgments. Because individuals use the subject as a starting point, unique features of the subject carry considerable weight, whereas unique features of the referent are ignored when evaluating the candidates. Predictions generated by this model are strongly supported. If two competing candidates share positive features but possess unique negative features, voters prefer the referent over the subject. A reverse preference ordering occurs when the two candidates share negative features but possess unique positive features.

Other research considers the effects of externally presented standards contained within a public opinion survey. For example, Staper & Schwarz (1998) demonstrate that an item which makes respondents think about Colin Powell reduces their subsequent evaluation of Bob Dole. In this particular case, Powell serves as a positive standard against which Dole is contrasted. Contrast effects of this nature are discussed in more detail in chapter 20, this volume.

Summary of the candidate evaluation literature

The past two decades of political psychology research are marked by a tremendous interest in the psychological mediators of candidate evaluation judgments. This has led political psychologists to reconsider the influence of issues and partisanship by examining their effects within the context of more precise and realistic models of information processing. In addition, this has led political researchers to consider a variety of factors that have traditionally fallen within the purview of social cognition and attitude research (e.g. trait assessments, visual cues, episodic affect). Moreover, work regarding the psychological underpinnings of comparative judgment has been fruitfully applied to examine the process whereby comparative standards influence candidate evaluation judgments. Omitted from this section is a discussion of the effects of race, gender, economic performance, and other determinants of candidate evaluation. To gain a more comprehensive understanding of the candidate evaluation process, the reader is encouraged to explore additional sources (e.g. Lodge & McGraw, 1995).

The Psychological Determinants of Issue Opinion

What are the psychological determinants of an individual's position on a specific issue? For example, what psychological factors lead an individual to favor or oppose affirmative action? In addressing this question, this section considers several determinants of political issue judgments. The first factor, liberal versus conservative ideological orientation, has been explored since the very beginning of public opinion research. Research on a second set of factors, abstract values such as individualism and isolationism, can be viewed as outgrowth and reaction to this earlier, exclusive emphasis upon ideology. Third, this section reviews research that suggests specific issue positions are derived from underlying racist attitudes and motivations. The last portion of this section shifts attention toward more transient and situational determinants of public opinion by exploring the effects of context on political issue judgments. Before addressing these concerns, however, it is useful to highlight some important aspects of information processing that occur en route to political issue judgment.

Information processing en route to political issue judgment

Between the moment an individual is exposed to issue-relevant information and the moment an individual reports an issue judgment, many stages of information processing unfold. These include comprehension, encoding and interpretation, representation, retrieval, integration, and the report of an overt judgment. A comprehensive discussion of these stages as they apply to issue judgment is presented elsewhere (Iyengar & Ottati, 1994; Wyer & Ottati, 1993). For present purposes, it is useful to briefly highlight some important findings regarding the representation, retrieval, and use of political information when individuals formulate a specific issue judgment.

When representing issue information in memory, the individual may try to construct a temporally or causally related scenario of the policy event that includes its antecedents and consequences. Evidence suggests that positive and negative consequences associated with an issue are represented in separate clusters, and that this tendency is most pronounced among political experts (McGraw & Pinney, 1990). The particular set of consequences included in this representation may reflect the set of consequences primed by a communication, consequences that are chronically accessible in the message recipient, or both (Lau, Smith, & Fiske, 1991). Chronically accessible consequences associated with various issues interpretations often reflect the individual's priorities with regard to more abstract values.

Thus, specific policy positions may be organized around superordinate core values that are chronically accessible in the voter (e.g. free market conservatism, the Protestant work ethic).

When asked to report an issue judgment, individuals often engage in a limited search for issue-relevant information. In such cases, individuals might rely on heuristics or a previously computed judgment when reporting their issue opinion (Burnstein, Abboushi, & Kitayama, 1993). When more motivated, individuals will perform a more exhaustive or systematic search for case information relevant to the issue judgment. In this case, the individual must combine the implications of numerous criteria to arrive at an issue judgment. Evidence suggests that a limited search produces retrieval of unqualified and unidirectional information, resulting in more extreme issue judgments. Conversely, an exhaustive search often yields more qualified and mixed considerations, resulting in more moderate judgments (Burnstein, Abboushi, & Kitayama, 1993).

Having highlighted important aspects of information processing that occur en route to issue judgment, I now focus on the substantive content of information that determines these judgments. These include ideology, abstract values, and racism.

Ideology and political issue judgment

The central role ascribed to ideology in political thinking seems incontrovertible. Self-reported ideology (liberal versus conservative) is associated with a variety of individual difference dimensions. These include authoritarianism (Adorno, et al., 1950), resistance to stereotype disconfirmation (Karasawa, 1998), and integrative complexity (Tetlock, 1986). Yet despite the assumed centrality of ideology, early work suggested ideology plays only a weak role in determining specific issue positions. Converse (1964) noted that individuals lack "issue constraint." That is, knowing an individual holds a conservative position on one issue (e.g. defense) does not necessarily imply that the individual will adopt a conservative position on another issue (e.g. affirmative action). This finding contradicts the notion that specific issue positions are derived from a single, liberal versus conservative orientation. More recent work suggests that a liberal versus conservative ideological dimension may indeed underlie specific issue beliefs (e.g. Jacoby, 1995). However, ideology appears to determine specific issue positions only under certain conditions (Skitka & Tetlock, 1992, 1993).

Skitka & Tetlock (1992, 1993) consider the impact of ideology on issue positions related to the allocation of public assistance. Their "contingency model of distributive justice" emphasizes that endorsement of public assistance programs is contingent upon both scarcity and attribution. Scarcity exists when available resources are insufficient to help all individuals in need. Attribution involves the degree to which social problems (e.g. poverty) are attributed to internal-controllable causes (e.g. laziness) versus other factors (e.g. unfair social conditions). When need for public assistance is urgent and public assistance is likely to be effective, Skitka and Tetlock obtain the following results. Under scarcity conditions, both liberals and conservatives deny assistance to personally responsible (internal-controllable) claimants. In the absence of scarcity, liberals allocate assistance to all claimants (regardless of personal responsibility), whereas conservatives continue to deny assistance to personally responsible claimants. These results suggest ideology is indeed associated with opinions regarding public assistance. However, this effect is moderated by scarcity, attribution, need for assistance, and the perceived effectiveness of assistance. Analyses that ignore these contingencies may fail to uncover the relation between ideology and specific issue positions.

Values and political issue judgment

Many researchers question the assumption that individuals organize specific issue opinions along a single, bipolar liberal versus conservative ideological dimension (e.g. Conover & Feldman, 1984; Hurwitz & Peffley, 1987). From this perspective, specific issue beliefs may be derived from multiple crowning postures or values. While Converse's (1964) operationalization of issue constraint focused on the absence of horizontal inter-issue linkages, this more recent work focuses on vertical linkages that exist between more abstract values and specific issue beliefs. For example, Hurwitz & Peffley found considerable evidence of vertical linkages between "core values" (e.g. ethnocentrism), "general postures" (e.g. isolationism), and "specific issue positions" (e.g. Soviet policy, international trade). Individuals also differ in the degree to which they are "schematic" for a given value (Conover & Feldman, 1984). Schwartz, Bardi, & Bianchi (1998) have recently argued that political values reflect adaptation to objective political conditions. For example, their evidence suggests communist rule engenders a hierarchical perspective that emphasizes power distance as a means to ensure socially responsible behavior. More generally, they propose that objective political conditions afford or magnify the importance of certain values, which in turn form the basis of specific issue beliefs.

Tetlock's (Tetlock, Bernzweig, & Gallant, 1985; Tetlock, 1986) value pluralism model of ideological reasoning suggests that liberal and conservative ideologies are embedded in and related to a variety of value orientations that influence specific issue opinions. In addition, this model proposes that thinking about specific issues is often characterized by fundamental conflicts of value. For example, efforts to control crime may conflict with constitutional guarantees regarding the right to privacy. Integrative complexity with regard to a given issue is characterized by the conjunction of conceptual differentiation and integration. Conceptual differentiation is high when an individual recognizes that a policy possesses many facets or consequences that are relevant to multiple values. Because these values are often in conflict, a policy position will commonly be perceived as possessing both positive and negative consequences. Integration involves developing conceptual connections among differentiated components of a policy position, recognition of inherent tradeoffs, and resolution toward a reasonable opinion (Tetlock, 1986; Tetlock, Bernzweig, & Gallant, 1985). Low integrative complexity reflects reliance on a rigid and simplistic interpretation of a policy event that is based on either a single or minimal number of value dimensions.

Tetlock has demonstrated that integrative complexity is associated with ideology among members of the electorate (Tetlock, 1986) and among members of the Supreme Court (Tetlock, Bernzweig, & Gallant, 1985). His findings generally indicate that liberals possess higher integrative complexity than conservatives, and that integrative complexity reaches its peak among moderate liberals. Low integrative complexity among conservatives is assumed to arise from a rigid, dichotomous style of interpretation that develops as a means of restoring order to a chaotic and threatening world (Adorno, et al., 1950).

Gruenfeld (1995) has challenged Tetlock's conclusion, arguing that ideology is confounded with majority versus minority status in many of Tetlock's studies. Gruenfeld independently varied ideology and majority versus minority status in a content analysis of Supreme Court opinions. Her results support a "status contingency model" which predicts higher levels of complexity among majority members than minority members (Gruenfeld, 1995). Further questions are raised by Judd & Krosnick's (1989) model of representation. They argue that political expertise engenders greater consistency among political values and specific issue positions. This appears to contradict the notion that sophisticated thinkers are more likely to recognize conflict and inconsistency between multiple values related to a single issue position.

Racism and political issue judgment

It has long been suggested that racism plays a role in determining specific issue opinions. For example, opposition to affirmative action might reflect simple prejudice against blacks or other minorities. White racism toward blacks has been defined and measured in many ways. "Old-fashioned racism" is typically assessed in terms of agreement with survey items that explicitly ascribe negative trait characteristics to blacks. These derogatory items about blacks often focus on purported deficiencies in their innate ability or intelligence (Sidanius, Pratto, & Bobo, 1996; Virtanen & Huddy, 1998). Old-fashioned racism has declined since the 1950s (Sniderman & Piazza, 1993). However, many claim that racism continues to exist, albeit in a more subtle form. Survey measures of this more subtle, new form of racism often emphasize deficiencies in black motivation (Virtanen & Huddy, 1998). Kinder & Sears (1981) define "symbolic racism" as "resistance to change in the racial status quo based on moral feelings that blacks violate traditional American values of individualism, self-reliance, the work ethic, obedience, and discipline" (ibid., p. 416). Items composing this scale often emphasize that blacks are "lazy" and should "try" harder (see also Sidanius, Pratto, & Bobo, 1996).

Another modern approach views racism as an initial (perhaps even unconscious) negative reaction to blacks that is subsequently "adjusted" or "corrected for" on the basis of more conscious or deliberative thought processes (e.g. Fazio, Jackson, Dunton, & Williams, 1995; Devine, 1989). For example, Fazio, et al. (1995) presented subjects with a black versus white relevant prime immediately followed by a positive (e.g. ocean) or negative (e.g. poison) target word. Categorization of the target word as "good" or "bad" was facilitated when black primes were followed by negative words or white primes were followed by positive words. Interference occurred when black primes were followed by positive words or white primes were followed by negative words. The degree to which responses conform to this pattern serves as an implicit, unobtrusive measure of racism prior to "adjustment" or "correction."

A variety of studies suggest prejudice and racism can figure prominently in determining policy positions. Whites are more opposed to racially targeted policies than similar policies targeted toward poor people in general (Bobo & Kluegel, 1993). Indeed, individual differences in racism are associated with a number of issue positions. These include busing, affirmative action, and welfare. These effects occur even when controlling for a myriad of non-racial factors (Sears, Van Laar, Carillo, & Kosterman, 1997), including the effects of ideology, authoritarianism, and realistic self/group interest (Sears, 1997; Huddy & Sears, 1995). Moreover, the effect of new racism (e.g. symbolic racism) on these issue stances is distinct from the effect of old-fashioned racism. Sears, et al. (1997) report that symbolic racism predicts specific policy preferences even when controlling for old-fashioned racism. Virtanen & Huddy (1988) demonstrate that, while old-fashioned racism is associated with opposition to virtually all minority assistance programs, symbolic racism is associated with opinions regarding a more circumscribed set of assistance programs that reward individual initiative and effort.

Effects of context on reported issue position

Many theorists question the assumption that individuals possess stable, enduring political opinions. From this perspective, individuals "construct" a political opinion when they are asked to report a judgment. As a consequence, the immediate context of judgment can have a powerful impact on expressed opinions (Ottati, et al., 1989). According to the "inclusion/exclusion model" (Schwarz & Bless, 1992), an individual will retrieve a representation of the issue stimulus and a representation of some standard of comparison when asked to report an issue opinion. The information used to construct these two representations is influenced by both chronic accessibility (context independent factors) and temporary accessibility (context dependent factors). In survey research, the context of a particular issue judgment is defined by the survey items that precede that judgment. These contextual items temporarily prime information that is used to construct the representation of either the target issue or standard of comparison.

Assimilation effects emerge when information primed by a preceding item is included in the target issue representation. For example, Ottati, Fishbein, & Middlestadt (1988) asked respondents to judge whether "Citizens should have the right to speak freely in public." In one condition, this general item was preceded by a specific item pertaining to a favorable group (e.g. "The Parent–Teacher Association should have the right . . . "). In another condition, this general item was preceded by a specific item pertaining to a negative group (e.g. "The Ku Klux Klan should have the right . . . "). As expected, respondents expressed a more favorable attitude toward the general statement in the first condition than in the second condition. This assimilation effect emerged, however, only when the items were separated by eight filler items.

Contrast effects emerge when information primed by a preceding item is excluded from the target representation. This might occur if the primed item serves as an accessible standard of comparison, respondents consciously attempt to correct for the biasing influence of the priming episode, or conversational norms lead respondents to exclude the primed material (e.g. "KKK") from the target representation (e.g. "Citizens") to avoid redundancy of communication. These later two possibilities are most likely to occur when respondents are consciously aware that the former item bears upon their response to the subsequent item. Consistent with this conceptualization, Ottati, Fishbein, & Middlestadt (1988) obtained contrast effects when the two items were presented immediately adjacent to one another.

Summary of issue opinion literature

Research regarding the psychological determinants of political issue opinions has abandoned its original, exclusive focus on the role of ideology. By exploring the role that multiple values play in determining specific issue opinions, political psychologists have gained a more differentiated and realistic view of the determinants of public opinion. Moreover, research regarding the role of racism demonstrates that abstract ideology and value offer only a partial understanding of the etiology of public opinion. Lastly, research on context effects demonstrates that what was previously regarded as "measurement error" often reflects the systematic effect of situational context on political issue judgments. Omitted in the present section is a discussion of many other determinants of political issue opinions. These include the role of media, emotion, and cultural background. The reader is encouraged to explore related coverage of these issues (e.g. Delli-Carpini, Huddy, & Shapiro, 1997).

Conclusion

The field of political psychology has now grown into an extensive and detailed literature. This chapter has focused primarily on the most recent era of political psychology research, an era characterized by increased attention to the psychological mediators of political judgment and decision making. Two major conclusions can be derived from the research summarized in this chapter. One is theoretical while the other is methodological. First, political psychologists have become increasingly aware that political judgment is a highly complex and subtle phenomenon. Awareness of mediating process mechanisms has produced heightened sensitivity to the conditions that moderate the influence of a given factor on political judgment. Thus, for example, the question is no longer "Does the episodic affective state of the voter determine candidate evaluation?" This question has been replaced by two more sophisticated questions: (1) "What psychological process mediates the effect of episodic affect on candidate evaluation?" (2) "Under what conditions does the affective state of the voter determine candidate evaluation?" These theoretically driven questions give rise to related methodological issues. Namely, to obtain a clear understanding of moderating conditions, it is often useful to experimentally manipulate these moderating conditions. Thus, political psychologists are increasingly embracing an eclectic methodological approach that includes both survey and experimental methods of investigation. Disciplinary and methodological provincialism can only serve to impede progress within the field of political psychology. The most exciting developments in this field occur when psychologists and political scientists engage in a bona fide, reciprocal intellectual exchange.

References

Abelson, R. P., Kinder, D. R., Peters, M. D., & Fiske, S. T. (1982). Affective and semantic components in political person perception. *Journal of Personality and Social Psychology, 42*, 619–630.

Adorno, T., Frenkel-Brunswick, E., Levinson, D., & Sanford (1950). *The authoritarian personality.* New York: Harper & Row.

Berent, M. K., & Krosnick, J. A. (1993). Attitude importance and the organization of attitude-relevant knowledge in memory. Unpublished manuscript.

Bobo, L., & Kluegel, J. R. (1993). Opposition to race-targeting: Self-interest, stratification, ideology, or racial attitudes? *American Sociological Review, 58*, 443–464.

Budesheim, T. L., & DePaola, S. J. (1994). Beauty or the beast? The effects of appearance, personality, and issue information on evaluations of political candidates. *Personality and Social Psychology Bulletin, 20*, 339–348.

Budesheim, T. L., Houston, D., & DePaolo, S. J. (1996). Persuasiveness of in-group and out-group political messages: The case of negative political campaigning. *Journal of Personality and Social Psychology, 70*, 523–534.

Bugental, D. E., Kaswan, J. W., & Love, L. R. (1970). Perception of contradictory meanings conveyed by verbal and nonverbal channels. *Journal of Personality and Social Psychology, 16*, 647–655.

Burnstein, E., Abboushi, M., & Kitayama, S. (1993). How the mind preserves the image of the enemy: The mnemonics of Soviet–American relations. In W. Zimmerman & H. Jacobson (Eds.), *Behavior, culture, and conflict in world politics.* Ann Arbor: University of Michigan Press.

Chaiken, S., Liberman, A., & Eagly, A. (1998). Heuristic and systematic information processing within and beyond the persuasion context. In J. S. Uleman & J. A. Bargh (Eds.), *Unintended thought* (pp. 212–252). New York: Guilford Press.

Clore, G. L., & Isbell, L. M. (in press). Emotion as virtue and vice. In J. Kuklinski (Ed.), *Political psychology in practice.*

Conover, P., & Feldman, S. (1984). How people organize the political world: A schematic model. *American Journal of Political Science, 28*, 95–126.

Converse, P. E. (1964). The nature of belief systems in mass publics. In D. Apter (Ed.), *Ideology and discontent* (pp. 206–261). New York: Free Press.

Delli-Carpini, M. X., Huddy, L., & Shapiro, R. Y. (1997). *Research in micropolitics: Rethinking rationality*, Vol. 5. Greenwich, CT: JAI Press.

Devine, P. G. (1989). Stereotypes and prejudice: Their automatic and controlled components. *Journal of Personality and Social Psychology, 56*, 5–18.

Fazio, R. H., Jackson, J. R., Dunton, B. C., & Williams, C. J. (1995). Variability in automatic activation as an unobtrusive measure of racial attitudes: A bona fide pipeline? *Journal of Personality and Social Psychology, 69*, 1013–1027.

Fiske, S. T. (1986). Schema based versus piecemeal politics: A patchwork quilt, but not a blanket of evidence. In R. R. Lau & D. O. Sears (Eds.), *Political cognition: The 19th annual Carnegie symposium on cognition.* Hillsdale, NJ: Erlbaum.

Forgas, J. P. (1995). Mood and judgment: The affect infusion model (AIM). *Psychological Review, 117*, 39–66.

Forgas, J. P., Kagan, C., & Frey, D. (1977). The cognitive representation of political personalities. A cross-cultural comparison. *International Journal of Psychology, 12*, 19–30.

Funk, C. L. (1997). Implications of political expertise in candidate trait evaluations. *Political Research Quarterly, 50*, 675–697.

Glaser, J., & Salovey, P. (in press). Affect in electoral politics. *Personality and Social Psychology Review.*

Gruenfeld, D. H. (1995). Status, ideology, and integrative complexity on the US Supreme Court: Rethinking the politics of political decision making. *Journal of Personality and Social Psychology, 68*, 5–20.

Hastie, R., & Park, B. (1986). The relationship between memory and judgments depends on whether the task is memory based or on-line. *Psychological Review, 93,* 258–268.

Houston, D. A., & Roskos-Ewoldsen, D. (in press). The cancellation-and-focus model of choice and preferences for political candidates. *Basic and Applied Social Psychology.*

Houston, D. A., Doan, K., & Roskos-Ewoldsen, D. (in press). Negative political advertising and choice conflict. *Journal of Experimental Psychology: Applied.*

Huddy, L., & Sears, D. O. (1995). Opposition to bilingual education: Prejudice or the defense of realistic interests? *Social Psychology Quarterly, 58,* 133–143.

Hurwitz, J., & Peffley, M. A. (1987). How are foreign policy attitudes structured? A hierarchical model. *American Political Science Review, 81,* 1099–1120.

Isbell, L. M., & Wyer, R. S. (in press). Correcting for mood-induced bias in the evaluation of political candidates: The roles of intrinsic and extrinsic motivation. *Personality and Social Psychology Bulletin.*

Iyengar, S., & Kinder, D. R. (1987). *News that matters: Television and American opinion.* Chicago: University of Chicago Press.

Iyengar, S., & Ottati, V. (1994). Cognitive perspective in political psychology. In R. S. Wyer & T. K. Srull (Eds.), *Handbook of social cognition, Vol. 2: Applications* (pp. 143–187). Hillsdale, NJ: Erlbaum.

Iyengar, S., & Petrocik, J. R. (1998). "Basic rule" voting: The impact of campaigns on party and approval based voting. Paper presented at the Conference on Political Advertising in Election Campaigns, American University, Washington, DC.

Jacoby, W. G. (1995). The structure of ideological thinking in the American electorate. *American Journal of Political Science, 39,* 314–335.

Judd, C. M., & Krosnick, J. A. (1989). The structural bases of consistency among political attitudes: Effects of political expertise and attitude importance. In A. R. Pratkanis, S. J. Breckler, & A. G. Greenwald (Eds.), *Attitude structure and function* (pp. 99–128). Hillsdale, NJ: Erlbaum.

Karasawa, M. (1998). Eliminating national stereotypes: Direct versus indirect disconfirmation of beliefs in covariation. *Japanese Psychological Review, 40,* 61–73.

Kinder, D. R. (1986). Presidential character revisited. In R. R. Lau & D. O. Sears (Eds.), *Political cognition: The 19th annual Carnegie symposium on cognition* (pp. 233–255). Hillsdale, NJ: Erlbaum.

Kinder, D. R., & Sears, D. O. (1981). Prejudice and politics: Symbolic racism versus racial threats to the good life. *Journal of Personality and Social Psychology, 40,* 414–431.

Klein, J. G. (1991). Negativity effects in impression formation: A test in the political arena. *Personality and Social Psychology Bulletin, 17,* 412–418.

Krosnick, J. (1988). Psychological perspectives on political candidate perception: A review of the projection hypothesis. Paper presented at the 1988 annual meeting of the Midwest Political Science Association.

Krosnick, J. A., & Brannon, L. A. (1993). The media and the foundations of presidential support: George Bush and the Persian Gulf conflict. *Journal of Social Issues, 49,* 167–182.

Krosnick, J. A., & Kinder, D. R. (1990). Altering the foundations of popular support for the president through priming. *American Political Science Review, 84,* 497–512.

Krosnick, J. A., Berent, M. K., & Boninger, D. S. (1994). Pockets of responsibility in the American electorate: Findings of a research program on attitude importance. *Political Communication, 11,* 391–411.

Kuklinski, J. H., Riggle, E., Ottati, V., Schwarz, N., & Wyer, R. S. (1991). The cognitive and affective bases of political tolerance judgments. *American Journal of Political Science, 35,* 1–27.

Lau, R. R. (1985). Two explanations for negativity effects in political behavior. *American Journal of Political Science, 29,* 119–138.

Lau, R. R., Smith, R. A., & Fiske, S. T. (1991). Political beliefs, policy interpretations, and political persuasion. *Journal of Politics, 58,* 644–675.

Lavine, H., Thomsen, C. J., Zanna, M. P., & Borgida, E. (1998). On the primacy of affect in the determination of attitudes and behavior: The moderating role of affective–cognitive ambivalence. Unpublished manuscript.

Lodge, M., & Hamill, R. (1986). A partisan schema for political information processing. *American Political Science Review, 80,* 505–519.

Lodge, M., & McGraw, K. (1995). *Political judgment: Structure and process.* Ann Arbor: University of Michigan Press.

Lodge, M., Steenbergen, M. R., & Brau, S. (1995). The responsive voter: Campaign information and the dynamics of candidate evaluation. *American Political Science Review, 89,* 309–326.

McGraw, K., & Pinney, N. (1990). The effects of general and domain-specific expertise on political memory and judgment. *Social Cognition, 8,* 9–30.

McGraw, K., Lodge, M., & Stroh, P. (1990). Order effects in the evaluation of political candidates. *Political Behavior, 12,* 41–58.

McGraw, K., Pinney, N., & Neumann, D. (1991). Memory for political actors: Contrasting the use of semantic and evaluative organizational strategies. *Political Behavior, 13,* 165–189.

Marcus, G. E., & Mackuen, M. B. (1993). Anxiety, enthusiasm, and the vote: The emotional underpinnings of learning and involvement during presidential campaigns. *American Political Science Review, 87,* 672–685.

Martin, L. L., Ward, D. W., Achee, J. W., & Wyer, R. S. (1993). Mood as input: People have to interpret the motivational implications of their moods. *Journal of Personality and Social Psychology, 64,* 317–326.

Masters, R. D., Sullivan, D. G., Lanzetta, J. T., McHugo, G. J., & Englis, B. G. (1986). *Journal of Social Biological Structure, 9,* 319–343.

Mehrabian, A., & Ferris, S. R. (1967). Inference of attitudes from nonverbal communication. *Journal of Consulting Psychology, 31,* 248–252.

Miller, A. H., Wattenberg, M. P., & Malanchuk, O. (1986). Schematic assessments of presidential candidates. *American Political Science Review, 80,* 521–540.

Miller, J. M., & Krosnick, J. A. (in press). The impact of candidate name order on election outcomes. *Political Opinion Quarterly.*

Nadeau, R., Niemi, R. G., & Amato, T. (1995). Emotions, issue importance, and political learning. *American Journal of Political Science, 39,* 558–574.

Ottati, V. (1990). Determinants of political judgments: The joint influence of normative and heuristic rules of inference. *Political Behavior, 12,* 159–179.

Ottati, V. (1997). When the survey question directs retrieval: Implications for assessing the cognitive and affective predictors of global evaluation. *European Journal of Social Psychology, 26,* 1–21.

Ottati, V., & Isbell, L. M. (1996). Effects of mood during exposure to target information on subsequently reported judgments: An on-line model of misattribution and correction. *Journal of Personality and Social Psychology, 71,* 39–53.

Ottati, V., & Wyer, R. S. (1992). Affect and political judgment. In S. Iyengar & W. J. McGuire (Eds.), *Explorations in political psychology* (pp. 296–320). Durham, NC: Duke University Press.

Ottati, V., Fishbein, M., & Middlestadt, S. (1988). Determinants of voters' beliefs about the candidates' stands on the issues: The role of evaluative bias heuristics and the candidates' expressed message. *Journal of Personality and Social Psychology, 55,* 517–529.

Ottati, V., Steenbergen, M., & Riggle, E. (1992). The cognitive and affective components of political attitudes: Measuring the determinants of candidate evaluation. *Political Behavior, 14,* 423–442.

Ottati, V., Terkildsen, N., & Hubbard, C. (1997). Happy faces elicit heuristic processing in a televised impression formation task: A cognitive tuning account. *Personality and Social Psychology Bulletin, 23,* 1144–1157.

Ottati, V., Riggle, E. J., Wyer, R. S., Schwarz, N., & Kuklinski, J. (1989). The cognitive and affective bases of opinion survey responses. *Journal of Personality and Social Psychology, 57,* 405–415.

Petty, R. E., & Wegener, D. T. (1993). Flexible correction processes in social judgment: Correcting for context-induced contrast. *Journal of Experimental Social Psychology, 29,* 137–165.

Rahn, W. M., & Cramer, K. J. (1996). Activation and application of political party stereotypes: The role of television. *Political Communication, 13,* 195–212.

Rahn, W. M., Aldrich, J. H., & Borgida, E. (1994). Individual and contextual variations in political candidate appraisal. *American Political Science Review, 88,* 193–199.

Rahn, W. M., Aldrich, J. H., Borgida, E., & Sullivan, J. L. (1990). A social–cognitive model of candidate appraisal. In J. Ferejohn & J. Kuklinski (Eds.), *Information and democratic process* (pp. 136–159). Urbana: University of Illinois Press.

Riggle, E., Ottati, V., Wyer, R. S., Kuklinski, J., & Schwarz, N. (1992). Bases of political judgments: The role of stereotypic and nonstereotypic information. *Political Behavior, 14*, 67–87.

Schwartz, S. H., Bardi, A., & Bianchi, G. (1998). Value adaptation to the imposition and collapse of Communist regimes in Eastern Europe. Unpublished manuscript.

Schwarz, N. (1990). Happy but mindless: Mood effects on problem-solving and persuasion. In R. M. Sorrentino & E. T. Higgins (Eds.), *Handbook of motivation and cognition*, Vol. 2 (pp. 527–561). New York: Guilford Press.

Schwarz, N., & Bless, H. (1992). Constructing reality and its alternatives: An inclusion/exclusion model of assimilation and contrast effects in social judgment. In L. Martin & A. Tesser (Ed.), *The construction of social judgment* (pp. 217–245). Hillsdale, NJ: Erlbaum.

Schwarz, N., & Clore, G. L. (1983). Mood, misattribution, and judgments of well-being: Informative functions of affective states. *Journal of Personality and Social Psychology, 45*, 513–523.

Schwarz, N., Bless, H., & Bohner, G. (1991). Mood and persuasion: Affective states influence the processing of persuasive communications. In M. Zanna (Ed.), *Advances in experimental social psychology*, Vol. 24 (pp. 161–199). San Diego, CA: Academic Press.

Sears, D. O. (1997). The impact of self-interest on attitudes: A symbolic politics perspective on differences between survey and experimental findings: Comment of Crano (1997). *Journal of Personality and Social Psychology, 72*, 492–496.

Sears, D. O., Van Laar, C., Carillo, M., & Kosterman, R. (1997). Is it really racism? The origins of white Americans' opposition to race targeted policies. *Public Opinion Quarterly, 61*, 16–53.

Sidanius, J., Pratto, F., & Bobo, L. (1996). Racism, conservatism, affirmative action, and intellectual sophistication: A matter of principled conservatism or group dominance? *Journal of Personality and Social Psychology, 70*, 476–490.

Skitka, L. J., & Tetlock, P. E. (1992). Allocating scarce resources: A contingency model of distributive justice. *Journal of Experimental Social Psychology, 28*, 491–522.

Skitka, L. J., & Tetlock, P. E. (1993). Of ants and grasshoppers: The political psychology of allocating public assistance. In B. Mellers & J. Baron (Eds.), *Psychological perspectives on justice*. Cambridge, UK: Cambridge University Press.

Skowronski, J. J., & Carlston, D. E. (1989). Negativity and extremity biases in impression formation: A review of explanations. *Psychological Bulletin, 105*, 131–142.

Sniderman, P. M., & Piazza, T. (1993). *The scar of race*. Cambridge, MA: Harvard University Press.

Stapel, D. A., & Schwarz, N. (1998). The republican who did not want to become president: Colin Powell's impact on evaluations of the Republican Party and Bob Dole. Unpublished manuscript.

Sullivan, J. L., Aldrich, J. H., Borgida, E., & Rahn, W. (1990). Candidate appraisal and human nature: Man and Superman in the 1984 election. *Political Psychology, 11*, 459–484.

Tetlock, P. E. (1986). A value pluralism model of ideological reasoning. *Journal of Personality and Social Psychology, 50*, 819–827.

Tetlock, P. E., Bernzweig, J., & Gallant, J. L. (1985). Supreme Court decision making: Cognitive style as a predictor of ideological consistency of voting. *Journal of Personality and Social Psychology, 48*, 1127–1239.

Tversky, A. (1977). Features of similarity. *Psychological Review, 84*, 327–352.

Virtanen, S., & Huddy, L. (1998). Old-fashioned racism and new forms of racial prejudice. *Journal of Politics, 60*.

Wyer, R. S., & Ottati, V. (1993). Political information processing. In S. Iyengar & J. McGuire (Eds.), *Explorations in political psychology* (pp. 264–295). Durham, NC: Duke University Press.

Wyer, R. S., Budesheim, T. L., Shavitt, S., Riggle, E. D., Melton, R. J., & Kuklinski, J. H. (1991). Image, issues, and ideology: The processing of information about political candidates. *Journal of Personality and Social Psychology, 61*, 533–545.

Author Index

Subject Index

ability, incremental theory of 332
abnormal conditions focus (ACF), in causal
    attribution 194–5, 196, 197–8
aboutness principle 441
abstraction-concreteness 171, 172, 173
acceptance of situations beyond one's
    control 600–1, 605
accessibility
  or applicability 239–41, 246
  attitude 76–7, 427, 439–41, 446–7, 471
  category 238–41
  chronic or temporary political opinion 629
  in information retrieval 572
  of mental representations 119–20, 127,
    128
  passive 241–7
  role of 238–9
  of values 471
accidie 380, 388
accountability 352–3, 403
  and the activation of conversational
    norms 188–9
  and complexity 294
  effects on judgment 199–200, 227–8
accuracy motivation 248–9, 423–4, 485
achievement 35, 490
act identification theory 332
action
  and affect 321–2
  vs state orientation 341
  see also Rubicon model of action phases
action control theory (Kuhl) 341

action verbs 167–8, 170, 172–3, 176
activation 113, 114, 314
  see also spreading activation
ad skepticism 583–4
adaptation 4, 7, 18, 29, 50
  in adversity 591–610
  and cognitive styles 290, 294–6, 299–300
  role of social processes in 606–8
  and self-esteem 491–2
  to objective political conditions 627
additivity hypothesis 423
adjectives 170
adjusted-ratio-of-clustering (ARC) index
    70–1
adolescence 505, 506
adult cognition 57–8
adulthood, attachment in 49–51
adversarial system of justice 556
adversity
  confronting 316–19
  dealing with 591–610
  finding benefit in 603–4, 605, 608
  see also illness; negative life events
advertising
  attitudes 582–3
  cross-cultural differences in 577–8
  effective 570
  goals of 571–2
  mediational models 583
  and mood effects 576–7
  non-verbal information in 580–1, 583
  subliminal 84–5